Nineteenth-Century Literature Criticism

Guide to Gale Literary Criticism Series

When you need to review criticism of literary works, these are the Gale series to use:

If the author's death date is: **You should turn to:**

After Dec. 31, 1959
(or author is still living)

CONTEMPORARY LITERARY CRITICISM

for example: Jorge Luis Borges, Anthony Burgess,
William Faulkner, Mary Gordon,
Ernest Hemingway, Iris Murdoch

1900 through 1959

TWENTIETH-CENTURY LITERARY CRITICISM

for example: Willa Cather, F. Scott Fitzgerald,
Henry James, Mark Twain, Virginia Woolf

1800 through 1899

NINETEENTH-CENTURY LITERATURE CRITICISM

for example: Fedor Dostoevski, George Sand,
Gerard Manley Hopkins, Emily Dickinson

1400 through 1799

LITERATURE CRITICISM FROM 1400 TO 1800
(excluding Shakespeare)

for example: Anne Bradstreet, Pierre Corneille,
Daniel Defoe, Alexander Pope,
Jonathan Swift, Phillis Wheatley

SHAKESPEAREAN CRITICISM

Shakespeare's plays and poetry

Gale also publishes related criticism series:

CONTEMPORARY ISSUES CRITICISM

Presents criticism on contemporary authors writing
on current issues. Topics covered include the social
sciences, philosophy, economics, natural science, law,
and related areas.

CHILDREN'S LITERATURE REVIEW

Covers authors of all eras. Presents criticism on
authors and author/illustrators who write for the
preschool to junior-high audience.

ISSN 0732-1864

Volume 9

Nineteenth-Century Literature Criticism

Excerpts from Criticism of the
Works of Novelists, Poets, Playwrights,
Short Story Writers, and Other Creative Writers
Who Died between 1800 and 1900,
from the First Published Critical
Appraisals to Current Evaluations

Laurie Lanzen Harris
Emily B. Tennyson
Editors

Cherie D. Abbey
Associate Editor

 **Gale Research Inc.** · *DETROIT* · *LONDON*

STAFF

Laurie Lanzen Harris, Emily B. Tennyson, *Editors*

Cherie D. Abbey, *Associate Editor*

Jelena Obradovic Kronick, Janet S. Mullane, *Senior Assistant Editors*

Jeanne M. Lesinski, Patricia Askie Mackmiller, Gail Ann Schulte, Robert Thomas Wilson, *Assistant Editors*

Phyllis Carmel Mendelson, Anna C. Wallbillich, *Contributing Editors*

Lizbeth A. Purdy, *Production Supervisor*
Denise Michlewicz Broderick, *Production Coordinator*
Eric Berger, *Assistant Production Coordinator*
Robin Du Blanc, Kelly King Howes, *Editorial Assistants*

Victoria B. Cariappa, *Research Coordinator*
Jeannine Schiffman Davidson, *Assistant Research Coordinator*
Kevin John Campbell, Rebecca Nicholaides, Leslie Kyle Schell,
Filomena Sgambati, Valerie J. Webster, *Research Assistants*

Linda Marcella Pugliese, *Manuscript Coordinator*
Donna D. Craft, *Assistant Manuscript Coordinator*
Colleen M. Crane, Maureen A. Puhl, Rosetta Irene Simms, *Manuscript Assistants*

Jeanne A. Gough, *Permissions Supervisor*
Janice M. Mach, *Permissions Coordinator*
Susan D. Nobles, *Assistant Permissions Coordinator*
Patricia A. Seefelt, *Assistant Permissions Coordinator, Illustrations*
Margaret A. Chamberlain, Sandra C. Davis, Mary M. Matuz, *Senior Permissions Assistants*
Kathy Grell, Josephine M. Keene, *Permissions Assistants*
H. Diane Cooper, Dorothy J. Fowler, Yolanda Parker, Mabel C. Schoening, *Permissions Clerks*
Margaret Mary Missar, *Photo Research*

The paper used in this publication meets the minimum requirements
of American National Standard for Information Sciences—Permanence
Paper for Printed Library Materials, ANSI Z39.48-1984. ∞™

Frederick G. Ruffner, *Publisher*
James M. Ethridge, *Executive Vice-President/Editorial*
Dedria Bryfonski, *Editorial Director*
Christine Nasso, *Director, Literature Division*
Laurie Lanzen Harris, *Senior Editor, Literary Criticism Series*

Library of Congress Catalog Card Number 81-6943
ISBN 0-8103-5809-3
ISSN 0732-1864

Printed in the United States of America.
Published simultaneously in the United Kingdom
by Gale Research International Limited
(An affiliated company of Gale Research Inc.)

Contents

Preface

The nineteenth century was a time of tremendous growth in human endeavor: in science, in social history, and particularly in literature. The era saw the development of the novel, witnessed radical changes from classicism to romanticism to realism, and contained intellectual and artistic ideas that continue to inspire authors of our own century. The importance of the writers of the nineteenth century is twofold, for they provide insight into their own time as well as into the universal nature of human experience.

The literary criticism of an era can also give us insight into the moral and intellectual atmosphere of the past, for the criteria by which a work of art is judged reflect current philosophical and social attitudes. Literary criticism takes many forms: the traditional essay, the book or play review, even the parodic poem. Criticism can also be of several types: normative, descriptive, interpretive, textual, appreciative, generic. Collectively, the range of critical response helps us to understand a work of art, an author, an era.

The Scope of the Work

The success of two of Gale's current literary series, *Contemporary Literary Criticism (CLC)* and *Twentieth-Century Literary Criticism (TCLC),* which excerpt criticism of creative writing from the twentieth century, suggested an equivalent need among students and teachers of literature of the nineteenth century. Moreover, since the critical analysis of this literature spans almost two hundred years, a vast amount of critical material confronts the student.

Nineteenth-Century Literature Criticism (NCLC) presents significant passages from published criticism on authors who died between 1800 and 1900. The author list for each volume of *NCLC* is carefully compiled to represent a variety of genres and nationalities and to cover authors who are currently regarded as the most important writers of this era as well as those whose contribution to literature and literary history is significant. The truly great writers are rare, and in the intervals between them lesser but genuine artists, as well as writers who enjoyed immense popularity in their own time and in their own countries, are important to the study of nineteenth-century literature. The length of each author's entry is intended to reflect the amount of critical attention the author has received from critics writing in English and from foreign critics in translation. Articles and books that have not been translated into English are excluded. However, since many of the major foreign critical studies have been translated into English and are excerpted in *NCLC,* author entries reflect the critical viewpoints of many nationalities. Each author entry represents a historical overview of the critical response to the author's work: early criticism is presented to indicate initial responses, later selections represent any rise or decline in the author's literary reputation. We have also attempted to identify and include excerpts from the seminal essays on each author, and to include recent critical comment providing modern perspectives on the writer. Thus, *NCLC* is designed to serve as an introduction for the student of nineteenth-century literature to the authors of that period and to the most significant commentators on these authors.

NCLC entries are intended to be definitive overviews. In order to devote more attention to each writer, approximately fifteen authors are included in each 600-page volume compared with about sixty authors in a *CLC* volume of similar size. Because of the great quantity of critical material available on many authors, and because of the resurgence of criticism generated by events such as an author's centennial or anniversary celebration, the republication of an author's works, or publication of a newly translated work or volume of letters, an author may appear more than once. One or two author entries in each volume of *NCLC* are devoted to single works by major authors who have appeared previously in the series. Only those individual works that have been the subject of extensive criticism and are widely studied in literature courses will be selected for this in-depth treatment.

The Organization of the Book

An author section consists of the following elements: author heading, biographical and critical introduction, principal works, excerpts of criticism (each followed by a bibliographical citation), and an additional bibliography for further reading.

- The *author heading* consists of the author's full name, followed by birth and death dates. The unbracketed portion of the name denotes the form under which the author most commonly wrote. If an author wrote consistently under a pseudonym, the pseudonym will be listed in the author heading and the real name given in parentheses on the first line of the biographical and critical introduction. Also located at the beginning of the biographical and critical introduction are any name variations under which an author wrote, including transliterated forms for authors whose languages use nonroman alphabets. Uncertainty as to a birth or death date is indicated by a question mark.

- A *portrait* of the author is included when available. Many entries also feature illustrations of materials pertinent to an author's life, including manuscript pages, letters, book illustrations, and representations of important people, places, and events in an author's life.

- The *biographical and critical introduction* contains background information that elucidates the author's creative output. When applicable, biographical and critical introductions are followed by references to additional entries on the author in past volumes of *NCLC* and in other literary reference series published by Gale Research Company. These include *Dictionary of Literary Biography, Children's Literature Review,* and *Something about the Author.*

- The list of *principal works* is chronological by date of first book publication and identifies genres. In those instances where the first publication was in other than the English language, the title and date of the first English-language edition are given in brackets. Unless otherwise indicated, dramas are dated by the first performance, rather than first publication.

- *Criticism* is arranged chronologically in each author section to provide a perspective on any changes in critical evaluation over the years. In the text of each author entry, titles by the author are printed in boldface type. This allows the reader to ascertain without difficulty the works being discussed. For purposes of easier identification, the critic's name and the publication date of the essay are given at the beginning of each piece of criticism. Unsigned criticism is preceded by the title of the journal in which it appeared. For an anonymous essay later attributed to a critic, the critic's name appears in brackets at the beginning of the excerpt and in the bibliographical citation.

- Important critical essays are prefaced with *explanatory notes* as an additional aid to students using *NCLC*. The explanatory notes provide several types of useful information, including: the reputation of the critic, the importance of a work of criticism, the specific approach of the critic (biographical, psychoanalytic, structuralist, etc.), and the growth of critical controversy or changes in critical trends regarding an author's work. In many cases, these notes include cross-references to related criticism in the author's entry or in the additional bibliography.

- A complete *bibliographical citation* designed to facilitate the location of the original essay or book follows each piece of criticism. An asterisk (*) at the end of the citation indicates that the essay is on more than one author.

- The *additional bibliography* appearing at the end of each author section suggests further reading on the author. In some cases it includes essays for which the editors could not obtain reprint rights. An asterisk (*) at the end of a citation indicates that the essay is on more than one author.

An appendix lists the sources from which material in the volume is reprinted. It does not, however, list every book or periodical consulted for the volume.

Cumulative Indexes

Each volume of *NCLC* includes a cumulative index to authors listing all the authors who have appeared in *Contemporary Literary Criticism, Twentieth-Century Literary Criticism, Nineteenth-Century Literature Criticism,* and *Literary Criticism from 1400 to 1800,* along with cross-references to the Gale series *Children's Literature Review, Authors in the News, Contemporary Authors, Contemporary Authors Autobiography Series, Dictionary of Literary Biography, Something about the Author,* and *Yesterday's Authors of Books for Children.* Users will welcome this cumulated author index as a useful tool for locating an author within the various series. The index, which lists birth and death dates when available, will be particularly valuable for those authors who are identified with a certain period but whose death date causes them to be placed in another, or for those authors whose careers span two periods. For example, Fedor Dostoevski is found in *NCLC,* yet Leo Tolstoy, another major nineteenth-century Russian novelist, is found in *TCLC.*

NCLC also includes a cumulative nationality index to authors. Authors are listed alphabetically by nationality, followed by the volume numbers in which they appear.

A cumulative index to critics is another useful feature of *NCLC*. Under each critic's name are listed the authors on whom the critic has written and the volume and page where the criticism appears.

Acknowledgments

No work of this scope can be accomplished without the cooperation of many people. The editors especially wish to thank the copyright holders of the excerpts included in this volume, the permissions managers of the book and magazine publishing companies for assisting us in securing reprint rights, and the staffs of the Detroit Public Library, University of Michigan Library, and Wayne State University Library for making their resources available to us. We are also grateful to Jeri Yaryan and Anthony Bogucki for their assistance with copyright research.

Suggestions Are Welcome

The editors welcome the comments and suggestions of readers to expand the coverage and enhance the usefulness of the series.

Authors to Appear in Future Volumes

About, Edmond Francois 1828-1885
Aguilo I. Fuster, Maria 1825-1897
Ainsworth, William Harrison 1805-1882
Aksakov, Konstantin 1817-1860
Aleardi, Aleadro 1812-1878
Alecsandri, Vasile 1821-1890
Alencar, Jose 1829-1877
Alfieri, Vittorio 1749-1803
Allingham, William 1824-1889
Almquist, Carl Jonas Love 1793-1866
Alorne, Leonor de Almeida 1750-1839
Alsop, Richard 1761-1815
Altimirano, Ignacio Manuel 1834-1893
Alvarenga, Manuel Inacio da Silva
    1749-1814
Alvares de Azevedo, Manuel Antonio
    1831-1852
Anzengruber, Ludwig 1839-1889
Arany, Janos 1817-1882
Arene, Paul 1843-1893
Aribau, Bonaventura Carlos 1798-1862
Arjona de Cubas, Manuel Maria de
    1771-1820
Arnault, Antoine Vincent 1766-1834
Arneth, Alfred von 1819-1897
Arnim, Bettina von 1785-1859
Arnold, Thomas 1795-1842
Arriaza y Superviela, Juan Bautista
    1770-1837
Asbjornsen, Peter Christian 1812-1885
Ascasubi, Hilario 1807-1875
Atterbom, Per Daniel Amadeus
    1790-1855
Aubanel, Theodore 1829-1886
Auerbach, Berthold 1812-1882
Augier, Guillaume V.E. 1820-1889
Azeglio, Massimo D' 1798-1866
Azevedo, Guilherme de 1839-1882
Bagehot, Walter 1826-1877
Bakin (pseud. of Takizawa Okikani)
    1767-1848
Bakunin, Mikhail Aleksandrovich
    1814-1876
Baratynski, Jewgenij Abramovich
    1800-1844
Barnes, William 1801-1886
Batyushkov, Konstantin 1778-1855
Beattie, James 1735-1803
Beckford, William 1760-1844
Becquer, Gustavo Adolfo 1836-1870
Bentham, Jeremy 1748-1832
Beranger, Jean-Pierre de 1780-1857
Berchet, Giovanni 1783-1851
Berzsenyi, Daniel 1776-1836
Black, William 1841-1898
Blair, Hugh 1718-1800
Blake, William 1757-1827
Blicher, Steen Steensen 1782-1848

Bocage, Manuel Maria Barbosa du
    1765-1805
Boratynsky, Yevgeny 1800-1844
Borel, Petrus 1809-1859
Boreman, Yokutiel 1825-1890
Borne, Ludwig 1786-1837
Botev, Hristo 1778-1842
Bremer, Fredrika 1801-1865
Brinckman, John 1814-1870
Bronte, Emily 1812-1848
Brown, Charles Brockden 1777-1810
Browning, Robert 1812-1889
Buchner, Georg 1813-1837
Burney, Fanney 1752-1840
Campbell, James Edwin 1867-1895
Campbell, Thomas 1777-1844
Carlyle, Thomas 1795-1881
Castelo Branco, Camilo 1825-1890
Castro Alves, Antonio de 1847-1871
Channing, William Ellery 1780-1842
Chatterje, Bankin Chanda 1838-1894
Chivers, Thomas Holly 1807?-1858
Claudius, Matthais 1740-1815
Clough, Arthur Hugh 1819-1861
Cobbett, William 1762-1835
Colenso, John William 1814-1883
Coleridge, Hartley 1796-1849
Collett, Camilla 1813-1895
Comte, Auguste 1798-1857
Conrad, Robert T. 1810-1858
Conscience, Hendrik 1812-1883
Cooke, Philip Pendleton 1816-1850
Corbiere, Edouard 1845-1875
Crabbe, George 1754-1832
Crawford, Isabella Valancy 1850-1886
Cruz E Sousa, Joao da 1861-1898
Desbordes-Valmore, Marceline
    1786-1859
Deschamps, Emile 1791-1871
Deus, Joao de 1830-1896
Dickinson, Emily 1830-1886
Dinis, Julio 1839-1871
Dinsmoor, Robert 1757-1836
Dumas, Alexandre (pere) 1802-1870
Du Maurier, George 1834-1896
Dwight, Timothy 1752-1817
Echeverria, Esteban 1805-1851
Eden, Emily 1797-1869
Eminescy, Mihai 1850-1889
Engels, Friedrich 1820-1895
Espronceda, Jose 1808-1842
Ettinger, Solomon 1799-1855
Euchel, Issac 1756-1804
Ferguson, Samuel 1810-1886
Fernandez de Lizardi, Jose Joaquin
    1776-1827
Fernandez de Moratin, Leandro
    1760-1828

Fet, Afanasy 1820-1892
Feuillet, Octave 1821-1890
Fontane, Theodor 1819-1898
Forster, John 1812-1876
Frederic, Harold 1856-1898
Freiligrath, Hermann Ferdinand
    1810-1876
Freytag, Gustav 1816-1895
Gaboriau, Emile 1835-1873
Ganivet, Angel 1865-1898
Garrett, Almeida 1799-1854
Garshin, Vsevolod Mikhaylovich
    1855-1888
Gezelle, Guido 1830-1899
Ghalib, Asadullah Khan 1797-1869
Godwin, William 1756-1836
Goldschmidt, Meir Aron 1819-1887
Goncalves Dias, Antonio 1823-1864
Griboyedov, Aleksander Sergeyevich
    1795-1829
Grigor'yev, Appolon Aleksandrovich
    1822-1864
Groth, Klaus 1819-1899
Grun, Anastasius (pseud. of Anton
    Alexander Graf von Auersperg)
    1806-1876
Guerrazzi, Francesco Domenico
    1804-1873
Gutierrez Najera, Manuel 1859-1895
Gutzkow, Karl Ferdinand 1811-1878
Ha-Kohen, Shalom 1772-1845
Halleck, Fitz-Greene 1790-1867
Harris, George Washington 1814-1869
Hayne, Paul Hamilton 1830-1886
Hazlitt, William 1778-1830
Hebbel, Christian Friedrich 1813-1863
Hebel, Johann Peter 1760-1826
Hegel, Georg Wilhelm Friedrich
    1770-1831
Heiberg, Johann Ludvig 1813-1863
Herculano, Alexandre 1810-1866
Hernandez, Jose 1834-1886
Hertz, Henrik 1798-1870
Herwegh, Georg 1817-1875
Herzen, Alexander Ivanovich 1812-1870
Hoffman, Charles Fenno 1806-1884
Holderlin, Friedrich 1770-1843
Holmes, Oliver Wendell 1809-1894
Hood, Thomas 1799-1845
Hooper, Johnson Jones 1815-1863
Hopkins, Gerard Manley 1844-1889
Horton, George Moses 1798-1880
Howitt, William 1792-1879
Hughes, Thomas 1822-1896
Imlay, Gilbert 1754?-1828?
Irwin, Thomas Caulfield 1823-1892
Issacs, Jorge 1837-1895
Jacobsen, Jens Peter 1847-1885

Jippensha, Ikku 1765-1831
Kant, Immanuel 1724-1804
Karr, Jean Baptiste Alphonse 1808-1890
Keble, John 1792-1866
Khomyakov, Alexey S. 1804-1860
Kierkegaard, Soren 1813-1855
Kinglake, Alexander W. 1809-1891
Kingsley, Charles 1819-1875
Kivi, Alexis 1834-1872
Klopstock, Friedrich Gottlieb 1724-1803
Koltsov, Alexey Vasilyevich 1809-1842
Kotzebue, August von 1761-1819
Kraszewski, Josef Ignacy 1812-1887
Kreutzwald, Friedrich Reinhold
    1803-1882
Krochmal, Nahman 1785-1840
Krudener, Valeria Barbara Julia de
    Wietinghoff 1766-1824
Lamartine, Alphonse 1790-1869
Lamb, Charles 1775-1834
Lampman, Archibald 1861-1899
Landon, Letitia Elizabeth 1802-1838
Landor, Walter Savage 1775-1864
Larra y Sanchez de Castro, Mariano
    1809-1837
Lautreamont (pseud. of Isodore Ducasse)
    1846-1870
Lebensohn, Micah Joseph 1828-1852
Leconte de Lisle, Charles-Marie-Rene
    1818-1894
Lenau, Nikolaus 1802-1850
Leontyev, Konstantin 1831-1891
Leopardi, Giacoma 1798-1837
Leskov, Nikolai 1831-1895
Lever, Charles James 1806-1872
Levisohn, Solomon 1789-1822
Lewes, George Henry 1817-1878
Lewis, Matthew Gregory 1775-1817
Leyden, John 1775-1811
Lobensohn, Micah Gregory 1775-1810
Longstreet, Augustus Baldwin 1790-1870
Lopez de Ayola y Herrera, Adelardo
    1819-1871
Lover, Samuel 1797-1868
Luzzato, Samuel David 1800-1865
Macedo, Joaquim Manuel de 1820-1882
Macha, Karel Hynek 1810-1836
Mackenzie, Henry 1745-1831
Malmon, Solomon 1754-1800
Mangan, James Clarence 1803-1849
Manzoni, Alessandro 1785-1873
Mapu, Abraham 1808-1868
Marii, Jose 1853-1895
Markovic, Svetozar 1846-1875
Martinez de La Rosa, Francisco
    1787-1862
Mathews, Cornelius 1817-1889
McCulloch, Thomas 1776-1843
Merriman, Brian 1747-1805

Meyer, Conrad Ferdinand 1825-1898
Montgomery, James 1771-1854
Moodie, Susanna 1803-1885
Morike, Eduard 1804-1875
Morton, Sarah Wentworth 1759-1846
Muller, Friedrich 1749-1825
Murger, Henri 1822-1861
Nekrasov, Nikolai 1821-1877
Neruda, Jan 1834-1891
Nestroy, Johann 1801-1862
Newman, John Henry 1801-1890
Niccolini, Giambattista 1782-1861
Nievo, Ippolito 1831-1861
Nodier, Charles 1780-1844
Novalis (pseud. of Friedrich von
    Hardenberg) 1772-1801
Obradovic, Dositej 1742-1811
Oehlenschlager, Adam 1779-1850
Oliphant, Margaret 1828-1897
O'Neddy, Philothee (pseud. of
    Theophile Dondey) 1811-1875
O'Shaughnessy, Arthur William
    Edgar 1844-1881
Ostrovsky, Alexander 1823-1886
Paine, Thomas 1737-1809
Parkman, Francis 1823-1893
Peacock, Thomas Love 1785-1866
Perk, Jacques 1859-1881
Pisemsky, Alexey F. 1820-1881
Pompeia, Raul D'Avila 1863-1895
Popovic, Jovan Sterija 1806-1856
Praed, Winthrop Mackworth 1802-1839
Prati, Giovanni 1814-1884
Preseren, France 1800-1849
Pringle, Thomas 1789-1834
Procter, Adelaide Ann 1825-1864
Procter, Bryan Waller 1787-1874
Pye, Henry James 1745-1813
Quental, Antero Tarquinio de 1842-1891
Quinet, Edgar 1803-1875
Quintana, Manuel Jose 1772-1857
Radishchev, Aleksander 1749-1802
Raftery, Anthony 1784-1835
Raimund, Ferdinand 1790-1836
Reid, Mayne 1818-1883
Renan, Ernest 1823-1892
Reuter, Fritz 1810-1874
Rogers, Samuel 1763-1855
Ruckert, Friedrich 1788-1866
Runeberg, Johan 1804-1877
Rydberg, Viktor 1828-1895
Saavedra y Ramirez de Boquedano,
    Angel de 1791-1865
Sacher-Mosoch, Leopold von 1836-1895
Saltykov-Shchedrin, Mikhail 1826-1892
Satanov, Isaac 1732-1805
Schiller, Johann Friedrich von
    1759-1805

Schlegel, August 1767-1845
Schlegel, Karl 1772-1829
Scott, Sir Walter 1771-1832
Scribe, Augustin Eugene 1791-1861
Sedgwick, Catherine Maria 1789-1867
Senoa, August 1838-1881
Shelley, Mary W. 1797-1851
Shelley, Percy Bysshe 1792-1822
Shulman, Kalman 1819-1899
Sigourney, Lydia Howard Huntley
    1791-1856
Silva, Jose Asuncion 1865-1896
Slaveykov, Petko 1828-1895
Slowacki, Juliusz 1809-1848
Smith, Richard Penn 1799-1854
Smolenskin, Peretz 1842-1885
Stagnelius, Erik Johan 1793-1823
Staring, Antonie Christiaan
    Wynand 1767-1840
Stendhal (pseud. of Henri Beyle)
    1783-1842
Stifter, Adalbert 1805-1868
Stone, John Augustus 1801-1834
Taine, Hippolyte 1828-1893
Taunay, Alfredo d'Ecragnole 1843-1899
Taylor, Bayard 1825-1878
Tennyson, Alfred, Lord 1809-1892
Terry, Lucy (Lucy Terry Prince)
    1730-1821
Thompson, Daniel Pierce 1795-1868
Thompson, Samuel 1766-1816
Thomson, James 1834-1882
Tiedge, Christoph August 1752-1841
Timrod, Henry 1828-1867
Tommaseo, Nicolo 1802-1874
Tompa, Mihaly 1817-1888
Topelius, Zachris 1818-1898
Turgenev, Ivan 1818-1883
Tyutchev, Fedor I. 1803-1873
Uhland, Ludvig 1787-1862
Valaoritis, Aristotelis 1824-1879
Valles, Jules 1832-1885
Verde, Cesario 1855-1886
Villaverde, Cirilio 1812-1894
Vinje, Aasmund Olavsson 1818-1870
Vorosmarty, Mihaly 1800-1855
Warren, Mercy Otis 1728-1814
Weisse, Christian Felix 1726-1804
Welhaven, Johan S. 1807-1873
Werner, Zacharius 1768-1823
Wescott, Edward Noyes 1846-1898
Wessely, Nattali Herz 1725-1805
Whitman, Sarah Helen 1803-1878
Wieland, Christoph Martin 1733-1813
Woolson, Constance Fenimore
    1840-1894
Wordsworth, William 1770-1850
Zhukovsky, Vasily 1783-1852

Théodore (Faullain) de Banville

1832-1891

(Also wrote under pseudonym of Bracquemond) French poet, dramatist, essayist, short story writer, novelist, and critic.

Banville was an influential member of the Parnassian movement in nineteenth-century French literature. His poetry reflects the precepts of this movement, whose members adopted Théophile Gautier's concept of art for art's sake in an attempt to create objective, technically masterful verse that would rival the plastic arts in its emphasis on form. In many of his works, including *Trente-six ballades joyeuses* (*The Ballads*) and *Rondels,* Banville demonstrated his use of strictly prescribed verse forms, and in his treatise *Petit traité de poésie française,* he detailed his poetic theories.

After spending an idyllic childhood in Moulins, France, Banville was educated at the Pension Sabatier in Paris, where he was influenced by the works of medieval and Romantic French poets and began to compose poetry. Upon graduating in 1839, Banville enrolled in a Parisian law school, but left in 1842 to publish a collection of short poems entitled *Les cariatides.* This volume, which contains works in a variety of poetic forms and treats such diverse subjects as Greek mythology and nostalgia for childhood, reflects the influence of the Romantic poets Alfred de Musset and Victor Hugo, among others. A number of established nineteenth-century writers, including Gautier, Charles Baudelaire, and Alfred de Vigny received the work favorably, and Vigny, in particular, encouraged the young poet.

In his second volume of poetry, *Les stalactites,* Banville treated the themes of love and beauty as well as mythological subjects. Scholars agree that this transitional work demonstrates Banville's increasing lyricism and mastery of rhyme and meter. In 1857, Banville composed what commentators consider his most original work, *Odes funambulesques.* In these parodies of the traditional ode, Banville satirized the philistinism of the French bourgeoisie. Colloquial language, verbal virtuosity, and circus imagery characterize the *ode funambulesque,* which literally means the tightrope walker's ode. Commentators acclaimed Banville's innovative use of language in this work and coined the adjective *banvillesque* to describe his use of short lines, varied meter, unusual rhymes, and subjects of local and popular interest. Although Banville satirized the degeneration of music, the exploitation of children, and prostitution, the humorous tone and carnival atmosphere of the *Odes funambulesques* established his reputation as a verbal acrobat rather than as a social critic.

Another hallmark of Banville's verse is his use of fixed-form genres that originated in France during the Middle Ages. Among these are the *chant royal, pantoum, rondeau,* and *triolet,* as well as the *ballade* and *rondel.* Several of his works clearly demonstrate the stylistic influence of the medieval poets François Villon and Charles d'Orléans. Although critics uniformly praise this verse for its virtuosic technique, they often find its subject matter frivolous. There is, however, universal admiration for his revival of archaic French literary forms.

Although Banville is known primarily as a poet, he wrote prolifically and published eighteen volumes of poetry, sixteen

dramas, a novel, and seven volumes of newspaper articles. Among his numerous contributions to periodicals are the poems that appeared in the short-lived but significant Parisian journal *Le parnasse contemporain,* for which the Parnassian poets are named. Though Banville's impact on the main currents of French literature was limited, he affected several major French poets and a number of minor ones. He influenced Paul Verlaine's use of imagery and briefly encouraged Arthur Rimbaud, who sent him poetry and sought his advice. In addition, Banville was a friend of Baudelaire's and became the executor of his literary estate and editor of a posthumous edition of his works.

Of Banville's considerable prose productions, only his essay *Petit traité* and his drama *Gringoire* have elicited sustained critical response. In *Petit traité,* Banville explained his poetic theories, treating such subjects as the definition and purpose of poetry, the rules of versification, and the creative process. He emphasized rhyme as the most important element in verse and urged a return to the Renaissance and medieval verse forms in which rhyme determines the structure of the poem. Though several scholars consider *Petit traité* the codification of Parnassian poetics and an inspiring and practical guide to French versification, others suggest that its importance lies mainly in what it reveals about Banville's artistic development. In *Gringoire,* Banville recounts the adventures of the poet Pierre Gringoire, who is believed to be a fictional composite of the medieval French poets Villon and Pierre Gringore. Critics often praise this work for its lyric prose, graceful humor, and well-delineated characters. Although it was regularly performed in the nineteenth century by the Comédie-Française, the French national theater, it is seldom staged today.

After Banville's death, his popularity steadily waned. Most critics attribute this decline to his concentration on contemporary subjects, which has rendered his work largely inaccessible to twentieth-century readers. Yet many literary historians assert that Banville substantially influenced his French contemporaries as well as the English poets Charles Algernon Swinburne, Austin Dobson, and Andrew Lang, who introduced the French poet's works to the English public and emulated his fixed-form poems. Banville's revival of medieval poetic genres, in addition to his contributions to the Parnassian movements in France and England, has secured his reputation as an influential though little-known nineteenth-century French poet.

PRINCIPAL WORKS

Les cariatides (poetry) 1842
Les stalactites (poetry) 1846
Odelettes (poetry) 1856
Odes funambulesques [as Bracquemond] (poetry) 1857
Gringoire [first publication] (drama) 1866
   [*Gringoire* published in *Gringoire. The Deputy of Bombignac*, 1881]
Les exilés (poetry) 1867
Idylles prussiennes (poetry) 1871
Petit traité de poésie française (essay) 1872
Trente-six ballades joyeuses (ballads) 1873
   [*The Ballads*, 1913]
Rondels (poetry) 1875
Poésies complètes. 6 vols. (poetry) 1878-1907
Mes souvenirs (memoirs) 1882
Oeuvres de Théodore de Banville (poetry, dramas, and essay) 1972

CHARLES BAUDELAIRE (essay date 1861)

[A French poet and critic, Baudelaire is best known for his collection of poems Les fleurs du mal *(The Flowers of Evil), which is ranked among the most influential works of French poetry. In* The Flowers of Evil *Baudelaire analyzes, often in shocking terms, his urban surroundings, erotic love, and conflicts within his own soul. Underlying these topics is Baudelaire's belief that the individual, if left to his own devices, is inherently evil and will be damned. Only that which is artificial can be construed as absolutely good. Poetry, according to Baudelaire, should in turn serve only to inspire and express beauty. This doctrine forms the basis of both his poetry and his criticism. A close friend and admirer of Banville throughout his life, Baudelaire praised his colleague's literary style in the following review "Théodore de Banville" which originally appeared in the French periodical* Revue fantaisiste *on August 1, 1861.]*

The qualities [of *Les Cariatides*] most apparent to the eye were brilliance and wealth of expression; but the numerous and unconscious imitations, the very variety of tone, according as the young poet underwent the influence of this or that predecessor, contributed in no small way to distract the reader's mind from the principal merit of the author, from that which was later to

be his great originality, his claim to glory, his trademark. I am referring to sureness in lyric expression. I do not deny, mind you, that *Les Cariatides* contains some admirable pieces which the poet could be proud to sign even today. I wish only to point out that the ensemble of the work, with its brilliance and variety, did not reveal at the outset the special nature of the author, whether that nature was not fully *developed*, or whether the poet was still under the fascinating charm of all the poets of the great era.

But in *Les Stalactites* . . . the thought seems clearer and better defined; the object of the quest can be better surmised. The color, less lavish, shines nevertheless more brightly, and the form of each object stands out in a sharper silhouette. *Les Stalactites* represents, in the growth of the poet, a particular phase where it could be said that he tried to react against his original tendency toward an effusiveness that was too prodigal, too undisciplined. Several of the best pieces in this volume are very short and suggest the restrained elegance of ancient pottery. Yet it is only later, after reveling in a thousand difficulties, in a thousand gymnastic exercises, which only true lovers of the Muse can appreciate at their true value, that the poet, combining in perfect harmony the exuberance of his original nature and the experience of his maturity, was to produce, one serving the other, poems of consummate skill and of a *sui generis* charm, such as **"La Malédiction de Vénus," "L'Ange Mélancolique,"** and above all certain sublime stanzas which have no title, but which will be found in the sixth volume of his complete poems—stanzas worthy of Ronsard in their boldness, their elasticity, and their breadth, and whose opening lines, full of grandiloquence, presage superhuman transports of pride and joy. (pp. 260-61)

But what is this mysterious charm which the poet himself knew he possessed and which he intensified until he made of it an enduring virtue? If we cannot define it exactly, perhaps we shall find some words to describe it, perhaps we shall be able to discover in part the sources from which it derives.

I once said, I no longer remember where: "The poetry of Banville represents the beautiful hours of life, those hours when one feels happy to think and to be alive."

I read a statement by a critic: "To divine the heart of a poet, or at least his chief preoccupation, let us seek in his works the word or words that appear there with the greatest frequency. The word will explain the obsession."

If my feelings did not deceive me (as will soon become obvious) when I said: "Banville's talent represents the beautiful hours of life," and if I find in his works a word which, by its frequent repetition, seems to indicate a natural propensity and a fixed purpose, I shall have the right to conclude that this word can serve, better than any other, to characterize the nature of his talent as well as the sensations contained *in the hours of life when one feels most alive*.

This word is the word *lyre*, which for the author evidently possesses a prodigiously comprehensive meaning. *Lyre* expresses that almost supernatural state, that intensity of life when the heart *sings*, when it is *constrained to sing*, like the tree, the bird, and the sea. By a reasoning which perhaps errs in recalling mathematical methods, I come to the conclusion that the poetry of Banville, by suggesting first of all the idea of *beautiful hours*, then by constantly presenting to the eye the word *lyre* (*lyre* being expressly used to convey the *beautiful hours*, the ardent spiritual vitality, the hyperbolical man, in a word), the talent of Banville is essentially, decidedly, and deliberately lyric. (pp. 261-62)

Théodore de Banville must be considered an original poet of the highest type. Indeed, if one glances over contemporary poetry and its best representatives, it is easy to see that it has reached a mixed state of a very complex nature; plastic genius, philosophical ideas, lyric enthusiasm, satiric wit, are combined and intermingled in infinitely varied amounts. Modern poetry is related at one and the same time to painting, music, sculpture, decorative art, satiric philosophy, and to the analytic spirit; and, however happily and skillfully blended it may be, it emerges with obvious indications of a subtlety borrowed from various arts. Some could perhaps see in this symptoms of depravity of taste. But that is a question which I do not wish to discuss here. Banville alone, as I have already said, is purely, naturally, and intentionally lyric. He has returned to the means of poetic expression used by earlier writers, finding them no doubt entirely adequate and perfectly adapted to his purpose. (p. 265)

Théodore de Banville refuses to be drawn [to decadent art]. . . . His art, like that of the ancients, expresses only what is beautiful, joyous, noble, great, rhythmic. Consequently, in his works you do not hear the dissonant, discordant music of the witches' sabbath, any more than the yelping of irony, that vengeance of the conquered. In his verse everything has a festive, innocent air, even sensual pleasure. His poetry is not only regret and nostalgia for the Paradisiac state, but even a very deliberate return to it. From this point of view we can then consider him an original writer of the bravest type. In a completely satanic or Romantic atmosphere, in the midst of a chorus of imprecations, he has the audacity to sing the goodness of the gods and to be a perfect *classicist*. I intend this word to be understood in its most noble meaning, in the truly historic sense. (p. 266)

> *Charles Baudelaire, "Reflections of Some of My Contemporaries: Théodore de Banville," in his* Baudelaire As a Literary Critic *edited and translated by Lois Boe Hyslop and Francis E. Hyslop, Jr., The Pennsylvania State University Press, University Park, 1964, pp. 258-66.*

STÉPHANE MALLARMÉ   (essay date 1865)

[*A renowned French poet and essayist, Mallarmé formulated the theories of the French Symbolist movement and composed musical, evocative poems of innovative syntax and complex metaphor. In the following excerpt from his panegyric essay "Symphonie littéraire," which was originally published in the February 1, 1865 issue of* L'artist, *Mallarmé considers his friend Banville an incarnation of the eternal poet.*]

It is because in our time [Banville] represents the poet, the eternal and classical poet, faithful to the goddess and living amid the forgotten glory of heroes and gods. His word is an endless song of enthusiasm from which spring music and the cry of the soul drunk with all glory. The sinister winds that speak in the terror of the night, the picturesque abysses of nature—these he neither wants to hear nor must he see them: he walks like a king through the Edenic enchantment of the golden age, celebrating for all time the nobility of the rays and the redness of the roses, the swans and the doves, and the dazzling whiteness of the young lily,—the happy earth! This is how *he* must have been who first received the lyre from the gods and spoke the blinded ode ["l'ode éblouie"] before our ancestor Orpheus. Thus Apollo himself.

> *Stéphane Mallarmé, in an extract from the conclusion to* Théodore de Banville *by Alvin Harms, Twayne Publishers, 1983, p. 164.*

ARTHUR RIMBAUD   (poem date 1871)

[*The following excerpt is drawn from a poem written by Rimbaud to Banville. While Rimbaud had previously emulated Banville and sought his advice, here he demonstrates his rejection of Parnassian poetics by satirizing Banville's poetry, particularly his use of nature imagery. The poem, "What Is Said to the Poet Concerning Flowers," originally appeared in French in 1871 as "Ce qu'on dit au poète à propos de fleurs."*]

Thus, always, toward the black azure,
Where shimmers the sea of topazes,
The Lilies, clysters of ecstasy,
Will function in your evening!

In our age of sago,
When Plants work hard,
The Lily will drink the blue feelings of disgust
From your religious Prose!

—Monsieur de Kerdrel's lily,
The Sonnet of 1830,
The Lily you give to the Poet
With the pink and the amaranth!

Lilies! Lilies! We can't see any!
And in your Verse, like the sleeves
Of Sinful Women who walk softly,
Those white flowers always tremble!

Always, dear one, when you bathe,
Your shirt with yellow armpits
Swells in the morning breeze
Above the dirty forget-me-nots!

Love lets through at your customs
Only Lilacs—O seesaws!
And Wood Violets,
Sugary spit of black nymphs! . . .

O Poets, if you had
Roses, blown Roses,
Red on laurel stems,
And swollen with a thousand octaves!

If BANVILLE made some snow down,
Blood-spotted, whirling,
Blacking the wild eye of the stranger
With his ill-disposed readings!

Concerning your forests and meadows,
O very peaceful photographers,
The Flora is as diverse
As stoppers on decanters!

Always the French vegetables,
Cross, phthisical, ridiculous,
Where the bellies of basset dogs
Navigate peacefully in the twilight;

Always, after frightful drawings
Of blue Lotuses or Sunflowers,
Rose prints, holy subjects
For young girls making their communion!

The Asoke Ode jibes with the
Loretto window stanza;
And heavy brilliant butterflies
Dung on the Daisy.

Old greenery, old stripes!
O vegetable crackers!
Fancy flowers of old Parlors!
—For beetles, not rattlesnakes,

Those crying vegetable dolls
That Grandville would have put in leading-strings,
And those wicked stars with eyeshades
Nursed with colors!

Yes! Your droolings from shepherds' pipes
Make precious glucoses!
—Pile of fried eggs in old hats,
Lilies, Asokas, Lilacs and Roses! . . .

(pp. 105-09)

Arthur Rimbaud, "What Is Said to the Poet Concerning Flowers," in his Complete Works, Selected Letters, *edited and translated by Wallace Fowlie, The University of Chicago Press, 1966, pp. 105-14.*

GEORGE SAINTSBURY   (essay date 1873)

[*Saintsbury was an English literary historian and critic of the late nineteenth and early twentieth centuries. A prolific writer, Saintsbury composed a number of histories of English and European literature as well as several critical works on individual authors, styles, and periods. His essay on Banville, excerpted below, is the earliest substantial notice accorded in England to Banville's poetry. In it Saintsbury favorably assesses* Idylles prussiennes *and* Odes funambulesques.]

[Declamation] is by no means M. de Banville's forte. In this he differs strikingly from another great contemporary poet, Leconte de Lisle, from whose works specimens of almost perfect declamation . . . can be produced in profusion. But our author has neither miscalculated his powers nor attempted an unsuitable task [in *Idylles Prussiennes*]; on the contrary, he has given yet another example of the reticence and self-control for which he has already been praised. Avoiding the common and fatal error of pitching the voice in the popular key, he has by skilful depression and transposition obtained a suitable style—the style of meditative and almost humorous satire, of which he is a master. The result, making allowance for the enormous difficulties of subject and treatment, is certainly a success; perhaps it is not unsuccessful even if such allowance be not made. It is not to be denied that the wit is sometimes forced, and the mirth not unfrequently a mere *rire jaune* [forced laugh], but on the whole Théodore de Banville may be safely pronounced to have achieved more thoroughly than any other French poet the perilous and ungrateful adventure which he has undertaken. There are, of course, many pieces in the volume which are not entitled to any share of this praise. Some are trivial; a few, such as **"Cauchemar"** and **"Le Mourant,"** are not free from the immoderate invective and the theatrical patriotism which disfigured **"L'Année Terrible."** **"Le Turco,"** whatever it may be to French taste, is to English critical eyes simply vulgar. But there are others which show none of these faults. **"La Bonne Nourrice"** gives a fine picture of Death, helmeted and purple clad, lulling her beloved Bismarck to sleep. **"L'Ane"** and **"Les Rats"** are two decidedly good satirical pieces, suggested by the omnivorous habits of the besieged Parisians. (pp. 241-42)

"Marguerite Schneider" is a really fine address to the young damsel whose fondness for earrings gave her so evil a notoriety. The poet proposes as the most appropriate pendants two drops of blood, ruby-like and ever ready to fall. But the gem of the book is without doubt **"L'Épée."** . . .

Of the whole volume it may be said that the form is incomparably superior to the matter, and this fact, which is not likely to render it popular with the average reader, must always give it a special interest in the eyes of the instructed and critical lover of poetry.

Still dearer to such a critic should be the *Odes Funambulesques*, and for the same reason. It is probable indeed that this wonderful book has not found many English readers, not merely because of its multitude of minute Parisian details and personalities, but still more, it is to be feared, because comparatively few Englishmen have the patience or the inclination to observe the artistic exellence of its grotesque extravagances. An English critic once held it up as a sort of scarecrow, an instance of the inevitable tendencies of the romantic school. If it be so, so much the better for the school which can "inevitably" produce such poems as **"La Belle Véronique,"** **"Variations Lyriques,"** **"La Ville Enchantée,"** and above all the epilogue, and so to speak moral, of the book, **"Le Saut du Tremplin."** . . . In *Idylles Prussiennes* we have the poet struggling with, and in a great degree mastering an unpromising, uncongenial, but inevitable subject; in *Odes Funambulesques* we see him voluntarily assuming the motley that he may prove the omnipotence and omnipresence of his art, and its fitness at all times and in all places for making the common as if it were not common. But to relieve this view of Art Militant, now with helmet and sword, now with cap and bauble, it is only fair to give a glimpse of the poet's Art Triumphant, in her peculiar sphere and treating congenial subjects. . . . For this purpose Théodore de Banville's contributions to the *Parnasse Contemporain* (November, 1869) are especially suited, being his last production before the disturbing events of 1870. They consist of one poem of some length, **"La Cithare,"** admirable in style and language, and recalling by its semi-classical manner the earlier works of the poet, and of ten ballads composed "à la manière de François Villon." These latter are all good, especially that **"Des Belles Chalonnaises,"** and **"De la Bonne Doctrine;"** but there is one of [supereminent beauty]. . . . It is entitled **"Ballade de Banville aux Enfants Perdus."** (p. 242)

George Saintsbury, in a review of "Idylles Prussiennes," in The Academy, *Vol. IV, No. 75, July 1, 1873, pp. 241-43.*

THÉOPHILE GAUTIER   (essay date 1874)

[*Gautier holds an important place in French letters as a transitional figure in the movement from Romanticism to Realism and as the originator of the concept of art for art's sake, which formed the basis of Parnassian aesthetics. Gautier discusses the style of Banville's poetry in this excerpt from his lengthy essay, "The Progress of French Poetry since MDCCCXXX," which was orginally published in French in 1874 as "Le progrès de la poésie française depuis 1830."*]

After the great outburst of [Romantic] poetry, to which the Renaissance alone is comparable, there was an abundant aftermath. Every youth turned out his volume of verse stamped with the imitation of the master he preferred, and occasionally betraying imitation of more than one. Out of this Milky Way, that spanned the sky with its whiteness formed of innumerable and not very distinct nebulae, the first one to emerge with a bright and particular scintillation was Théodore de Banville, whose first volume, . . . "The Caryatids," made a sensation. Although the Romanticist school had accustomed the public to precocious talent, amazement was felt at the union of such rare merit in so young a man. Théodore de Banville was scarcely twenty-one, and could lay claim to the title of minor. . . . It certainly was possible, in a collection of poems so diverse in tone and mode, to note here and there the influence of Victor Hugo, Alfred de Musset, and Ronsard, whose fervent admirer the poet has rightly continued to be, but it is also easy to discern in it the man's own individuality. Théodore de Banville is exclusively a poet; prose does not seem to exist, so far as he is concerned. . . . He possessed as a birthright that wondrous tongue which the world hears without understanding it, and in poetry he was the master of that rarest, loftiest, and winged form, lyricism. He is indeed lyrical, invincibly lyrical, at all times and in all subjects, and almost whether he will or no, so to speak. Like Euphorion, the symbolical offspring of Faust and Helen, he flutters above the flower of the mead, borne aloft by breezes that swell his draperies with their changing prismatic colours. Incapable of restraining his flight, he no sooner touches the earth than he forthwith springs skywards and loses himself in the golden dust of a luminous beam.

This tendency is still more marked in the "Stalactites," in which the poet yields fully to his lyrical intoxication. He floats amid splendour and sound, and the blue and rosy lights of apotheosis flame behind his stanzas as a natural background to them; at times also there is a great burst of fire, as at the end of an opera. Banville feels the beauty of words; he loves to have them brilliant, rich, and rare, and he sets them in gold round his thought as it might be a bracelet round a woman's arm. This is one of the charms of his verse; the greatest charm perhaps. Joubert's clever remarks may be applied to him: "The words light up when the poet's finger communciates its phosphorus to them; the words of poets retain a meaning even when detached from other words, and satisfy one in their isolation as do fine sounds; they seem to be luminous speech, gold, pearls, diamonds, and flowers."

The new school had made scant use of mythology. Its members preferred "breeze" to "zephyr;" they called the sea "sea," and not Neptune. When Théodore de Banville, following Goethe's example, introduced the white-limbed Tyndarides into the sombre, feudal manor of the Middle Ages, he brought back into the Romanticist stronghold the company of ancient deities. . . . He dared to speak of Venus, of Apollo, and the Nymphs; these lovely names attracted him and delighted him as though they had been agate and onyx cameos. At first he saw antiquity much as Rubens did. The chaste pallor and calm outlines of the marble statues were not enough for him as a colourist, so his goddesses exhibited amid the waves or the clouds pearly bodies, veined with azure, flushed with rose, ruddy hair with topaz and amber tones, and rounded forms of an opulence that would have been avoided by Greek art. Roses, lilies, azure, gold, purple, hyacinth abound in Banville's work; he casts over everything he sees a veil woven of sunbeams, and his ideas, like princesses in fairy tales, move through emerald green meadows, wearing dresses the colour of moonshine, sunshine, and the passing hour.

Of late years Banville, who rarely dropped the lyre to take up the pen, published "The Exiles," in which he has a broader manner and appears to have attained his final form of expression, if one may so say of a poet who is still young, very much

alive, and capable of producing many works yet. Mythology plays a great part in this volume, in which Banville shows himself more Greek than in any other, although his gods and goddesses occasionally have a Florentine air that recalls Primaticcio, and seem to be descending from the ceilings or imposts of Fontainebleau, wearing silverlaced azure cothurns. This proud and gallant Renaissance port appropriately imparts animation to the somewhat cold correctness of pure antiquity.

"The Amethysts" is the title of a small volume marked by typographical elegance and coquetry, in which the author, inspired by Ronsard, has attempted to revive rhythms abandoned since the crossing of masculine and feminine rimes became obligatory. From this mingling of rimes, now prohibited, he has drawn exquisitely harmonious effects. The stanzas in feminine rimes have a softness, a suavity, a gentle melancholy. . . . The crossed masculine rimes have astonishing fulness and sonority. It is impossible to speak too highly of the exquisite skill with which the author handles rhythms which Ronsard, Remy Belleau, Antoine Baïf, Du Bellay, Jean Daurat, and the poets of the Pleiades made so much of. Like the lesser odes of the Vendômois poet [Ronsard], these small pieces have for subjects love, gallantry, or anacreontic philosophy.

I have so far shown but one side of Banville's talent, the serious side. But his Muse wears two masks, the one grave, the other laughing, for this lyric poet of ours is also a jester at times. The "Odes funambulesques" (Odes of the Tight-rope) dance upon the tight-rope with a balance-pole or without, showing the narrow sole of their shoes rubbed with chalk, and performing above the crowd amazing feats with a flashing of spangles and embroidery, and sometimes they take such extraordinary leaps that they lose themselves in the stars.

The sentences twist like contortionists; the rimes jangle like Chinese bells, and the clown describes the crude daubs of signs with mock gravity as he points to each with his long wand. It is something like a mountebank's clap-trap, like a studio joke, like parody and caricature. Taking the pattern of a famous ode, the poet laughingly cuts out the costume of a dwarf as deformed as those painted by Velasquez and Paolo Veronese, and he makes the parrots sing the nightingale's song. Never did fancy squander riches more recklessly. (pp. 241-47)

> *Théophile Gautier, "The Progress of French Poetry Since MDCCCXXX," in his* The Works of Théophile Gautier: A History of Romanticism, the Progress of French Poetry Since MDCCCXXX, *Vol. 16, edited and translated by F. C. de Sumichrast, The Jenson Society, 1906, pp. 231-360.**

[WILLIAM ERNEST HENLEY]   (essay date 1883)

[Henley was a minor English poet, dramatist, critic, and editor. In this review of Mes souvenirs, *he discusses Banville as "the poet of artifice" and provides an appreciative assessment of Banville's major works.]*

M. de Banville is the poet of artifice and the artificial. For him the stage is the only world; there is no nature so natural as that depicted on the boards; there is no humanity so human as that which the actor puts on with his wig. For him the flowers grow plucked and bound into nosegays; passion has no existence outside the Porte-Saint-Martin; the universe is a place of rhymes and rhythms, and the human heart a supplement to the dictionary. He delights in babbling of green fields, and Homer, and Shakspeare, and the Eumenides. . . . But it is shrewdly suspected that he loves these things rather as words than as facts, and that in his heart of hearts he is better pleased with Pierrot and Columbine than with Rosalind and Othello, with the studio Greece of Gautier than with the living Hellas of Sophocles. Heroic objects are all very well in their way, of course. They produce superb effects in verse, and they are of incomparable merit considered as colours and jewels for well-turned sentences in prose. But they have no real existence as ideas; their function is purely verbal; they are the raw material of the outward form of poesy, and they come into being for no other end than to glorify a climax, to adorn a refrain, to sparkle and sound in odelets and rondels and triolets, to shine and tinkle and chime all over the eight-and-twenty members of a fair ballade! That this is not by any means an exaggeration of M. de Banville's attitude towards man and nature there are half a dozen volumes—**'Les Cariatides,' 'Le Sang de la Coupe,' 'Rimes Dorées,' 'Trente-Six Ballades Joyeuses'**—of brilliant workmanship to prove. And the odd thing is that to a theory of art and life that can be thus whimsically described we are indebted for some of the best writing of modern times. M. de Banville has very little sympathy with fact, whether heroic or the reverse, whether essential or accidental; but he is an artist in words and cadences, and an artist of the rarest type. He writes of [Pierrot, Columbine, and Léandre], . . . and all the marionettes of that pleasant puppet show which he mistakes for the world, with the rhetorical elegance and distinction, the verbal force and glow, the rhythmic beauty and propriety, of a great poet; he models a group of flowers in wax as passionately and cunningly, and with as perfect an interest in the process and as lofty and august a faith in the result, as if he were carving the Venus of Melos.· . . . He is profoundly artificial, but he is naïve and simple and even innocent in his artifice; so that not only is he seldom or never offensive, but he is often interesting and even affecting. He knows so well what should be done, and so well how to turn his knowledge to account, that he not seldom succeeds in achieving something that is really and truly a work of art—something, that is to say, in which there is substance as well as form, in which the matter is equal with the manner, in which the imagination is human as well as aesthetic, and the invention not merely verbal, but emotional and romantic also. The dramatic and poetic value of such achievements in style as **'Florise'** and **'Diane au Bois'** is open to question; but there can be no doubt that **'Gringoire'** is one of the best plays of its epoch. There is an abundance of "epical ennui" in **'Le Sang de la Coupe'** and **'Les Stalactites'**; but such admirable work as the **"Nous n'irons plus au bois,"** and as the charming epigram in which the poet paints a processional frieze of Hellenic virgins, are in their way high-water marks of French verse. Face to face with verse and prose of this sort it is difficult indeed to refrain from concluding that M. de Banville is, with all his faults, almost a great writer. . . .

M. de Banville is by habit and tradition a lyric poet, and [in **'Mes Souvenirs'**] he writes of facts with the vagueness and the enthusiasm peculiar to his kind. For the past, too—or rather for that fraction of it in which he is peculiarly interested—he has nothing but worship. He is naturally the most amiable of critics, unless, of course, he is criticizing the rhymes of Voltaire and the cadences of Boileau; and for the men he has known and admired all his life he has only the criticism of adoration. He looks back at them in a rapture of contemplation that finds expression in the noblest adjectives in the dictionary, in the most august comparisons in literature and art. To him M. Hugo is "le Maître" [the Master], with a capital M; poor Albert Glatigny suggests no less a genius than François Villon; Baudelaire shows as a kind of aesthetic Monte-Cristo. . . . It is obvious that a volume written at this pitch throughout can hardly have much value as a contribution to literary and artistic history; and, in fact, the worth of **'Mes Souvenirs,'** considered under this aspect, is not great. It is, however, uncommonly pleasant reading, and it contains a great deal of good feeling and a great many graceful stories and amiable descriptions, with not a little excellent writing and not a few delightful sentences and expressions of the art of form. (p. 116)

> *[William Ernest Henley], in a review of "Mes souvenirs," in* The Athenaeum, *No. 2883, January 27, 1883, pp. 116-17.*

EDMUND GOSSE   (poem date 1891)

[*A distinguished English literary historian, critic, and biographer, Gosse wrote extensively on seventeenth- and eighteenth-century English literature. His commentary in* Seventeenth-Century Studies *(1883),* A History of Eighteenth Century Literature *(1889),* Questions at Issue *(1893), and other works is generally regarded as sound and suggestive. The following poetic eulogy appeared several weeks after Banville's death. For additional criticism by Gosse, see excerpt below, 1923.*]

One ballade more before we say goodnight,
  O dying Muse, one mournful ballade more;
Then let the new men fall to their delight,
  The Impressionist, the Decadent, a score
  Of other fresh fanatics, who adore
Quaint demons, and disdain thy golden shrine;
Ah! faded goddess, thou wert held divine
  When we were young! But now each laurelled head
Has fallen, and fallen the ancient glorious line;
  The last is gone, since Banville too is dead.

Peace, peace a moment, dolorous Ibsenite!
  Pale Tolstoist, moaning from the Euxine shore!
Heredity, to dreamland take thy flight!
  And, fell Psychology, forbear to pour
  Drop after drop thy dose of hellebore,
For we look back to-night to ruddier wine
And gayer singing than these moans of thine!
  Our skies were azure once, our roses red,
Our poets once were crowned with eglantine;
  The last is gone, since Banville too is dead.

With flutes and lyres and many a lovely rite
  Through the mad woodland of our youth they bore
Verse, like an ichor in a chrysolite,
  Secret yet splendid, and the world forswore,
  One breathing-space, the mocking mask it wore.
Then failed, and then fell those children of the vine,—
Sons of the sun,—and sank in slow decline;
  Pulse after pulse their radiant lives were shed;
To silence we their crystal names consign;
  The last is gone, since Banville too is dead.

Prince-Jeweller, whose facet-rhymes combine
All hues that glow, all rays that shift and shine,
  Farewell! thy song is sung, thy splendour fled!
No bards to Aganippe's wave incline;
  The last is gone, since Banville too is dead.

> *Edmund Gosse, "Ballade; for the Funeral of the Last of the Joyous Poets," in* The Athenaeum, *No. 3309, March 28, 1891, p. 407.*

ARTHUR SYMONS (essay date 1891)

[An English critic, poet, dramatist, short story writer, and editor, Symons initially gained notoriety as an English decadent in the 1890s, and he eventually established himself as one of the most important critics of the modern era. His sensitive translations from the works of Paul Verlaine and Stéphane Mallarmé offered English poets an introduction to the poetry of the French Symbolists. Though he was a gifted translator and linguist, it was as a critic that Symons made his most important contribution to literature. His The Symbolist Movement in Literature *provided his English contemporaries with an appropriate vocabulary with which to define their new aesthetic—one that communicated their concern with dreamlike states, imagination, and a reality that exists beyond the boundaries of the senses. Symons also discerned that the concept of the symbol as a vehicle by which a "hitherto unknown reality was suddenly revealed" could become the basis for an entire modern aesthetic, and he therefore laid the foundation for much of modern poetic theory. The following is a positive overview of Banville's dramatic, poetic, and critical writings.]*

In Théodore de Banville France has lost one of its most distinguished men of letters—an exquisite lyric poet and a writer of the most delightful lyrical prose.... Banville, whether he wrote in verse or in prose, was a poet and nothing but a poet. Never was a man more entirely absorbed in the art to which he was devoted. He lived all his life in a state of poetic exaltation, not so much indifferent to external events as unconscious of them—I mean what are called important events, for he was Parisian of the Parisians, and delighted in the little incidents of the hour which could be put into verse. But, though he loved nature and man, he loved art more than either—more than anything in the world, which was nevertheless so bright and satisfying to him. More than any poet of the day, he realised the joy of life.... Among a great company of pessimistic poets Théodore de Banville remained true to the old faith ... that the poet should be a messenger of joy, a singer of the beautiful. (p. 56)

[He] had no theory of life to propound, except that spring is joyous, spring is fleeting, therefore gather the rosebuds while ye may.... His philosophy is a frank, instinctive Epicureanism, a delicious acceptance of all that is charming in the moments as they pass, the utmost joy in them, and the least possible remembrance—if to remember is to regret—when they have gone for ever. It never occurred to him to question whether life was worth living, or whether this was other than the best of all possible worlds. With so ingenuous a faith in things as they are, he laid himself open to the charge of being superficial; and indeed if it is the poet's duty to deal with what are called great questions—the questions that disturb the mind of the modern curate—then Banville failed in his duty. But if Ronsard—if Herrick—had any conception of the proper province of poetry, then Banville too, in his different, but not radically different way, was a poet. (pp. 56-7)

Les Cariatides, his first volume, was a marvellous achievement for a poet of nineteen. The influence of Hugo—whom Banville never ceased to worship as the poet of poets—was naturally evident. It is quite in the early romantic manner, with stanzas full of proper names, poems addressed to the Venus of Milo, poems about sultanas. But there is also, and already, the soaring lyric flight, and even a certain power of sustaining the flight. The boy has a vocabulary, and if he has not a style, he knows very well, at all events, how to say what he wants to say. And there are *dixains* in the manner of Clément Marot, *rondeaux, rondeaux rédoublés, triolets*—the old forms that Banville has done so much to bring into use again. *Les Stalactites,* as the author tells us, from the standpoint of twenty-three, are decidedly more mature than *Les Cariatides.* That fundamental characteristic of Banville, lyric joy, had indeed been evident from the first, but here it breaks forth more spontaneously, more effectually. "An immense appetite for happiness and hope lies at the root of our souls. To reconquer the lost joy, to remount with intrepid foot the azure stairway leading to the skies"—such, Banville tells us in his preface, is the incessant aspiration of modern man—his own aspiration, he should have said. In 1852 appeared a characteristic little play, *Le Feuilleton d'Aristophane,* the first, and perhaps the most famous, of Banville's lyric dramas. It is ... done with immense spirit and gaiety, and with a wealth of real poetry instead of a meagre measure of doggerel. It is full of wit and a fantastic, essentially modern kind of poetry, which is yet entirely individual. It was followed by some charming books of prose (*Les Pauvres Saltimbanques, La Vie d'une Comédienne*), and then came a little volume of *Odelettes* ..., a book of spring verses, dedicated by Banville to his friends. Next year appeared anonymously, in a quaint green-covered pamphlet—the book was scarcely more than a pamphlet—the *Odes Funambulesques.*

"The *Odes Funambulesques* have not been signed," said the preface, "because they were not worth the trouble." "Here are fantasies assuredly more than frivolous; they will do nothing to change the constitution of society, and they have not even, like some poems of our time, the excuse of genius. Worse, the ideal boundary which marks the limits of good taste is overstepped at every moment." ... So the author introduces his rope-dancing verses. Their allusiveness renders them difficult reading for us to-day, yet they have the qualities that remain. To be familiar, to be jocular, to burlesque the respectabilities, to overflow into parody, to exhibit every kind of rhythmical agility—to dance on the tight-rope of verse—and yet to be always poetical, always the lyric poet, is a feat which few have ever accomplished, a feat which Banville has never accomplished so deftly as in these wittily-named *Odes Funambulesques.* There is a series of *Occidentales,* parodies of Hugo's *Orientales;* there are satires in the stately manner, and satires which explode into sparks like fireworks.... Banville has spread a feast of light-hearted gaiety which has even now a certain savour. (pp. 57-8)

In the same year with the *Odes Funambulesques* a collection of some of Banville's most serious and lofty work was printed under the name of *Le Sang de la Coupe,* and in 1866 (after more plays and more books of prose) appeared his finest volume of serious poems, *Les Exilés,* and his finest play, *Gringoire,* well known to English playgoers under the name of *The Ballad-Monger.*

In the preface to *Les Exilés* Banville says: "This book is perhaps the one into which I have put the most of myself and my soul, and if one book of mine is to last, I would desire that it should be this one." This book, into which he tells us he has put the most of himself, is entirely impersonal, and it is characteristic of Banville that this should be so. What was deepest in him was a passion for art, for poetry, which to him was literally, and not figuratively, something inspired. "Like the art of antiquity, his art," said Gautier, "expresses only what is beautiful, joyous, noble, grand, rhythmical." The poems in *Les Exilés* are mainly on classic themes; they have always a measure of classic charm—a large, clear outline, a purity of line, a suave colour. There is fire in them as well as grace; some of them are painted with hot flesh-tints, as **"Une Femme de Rubens."** But the classical note predominates.... (p. 58)

[Banville's *Petit Traité de Poésie Française* is] the most poetically written of all textbooks to poetry, the most dogmatic, by no means the least practical, and altogether the most inspiring. The volume called *Mes Souvenirs*—sketches and anecdotes of most of the Romantics, known and unknown—is simply the most charming book of literary *souvenirs* in the world. In 1884 came another volume of effervescent verse, *Nous Tous*, and only last year a new collection, *Sonnailles et Clochettes*—poems published in newspapers, really journalistic verse, which is really poetry. It is a new art, which it amused Banville to invent and practise; for how amusing it is, said he, "to offer people pebbles of Eldorado, pearls and diamonds, saying gaily, Only a penny a-piece!"

For many years Banville was the dramatic critic of *Le National*, where he used to write, every Sunday, a *causerie* full of excellent sense and delicious nonsense. One scarcely knows whether to say that his prose writing was like his conversation, or that his conversation was just the same as his prose. Literature was an art which he had mastered so perfectly that it had become a second nature to him. He talked with the same sparkling ease, the same exquisite surety and harmony of phrase, with which he wrote. Those dramatic criticisms of *Le National*—too ephemeral in subject to be ever reprinted—are still delightful reading if one turns to them; and it is curious to compare the witty good sense, the silvery paradoxes of Banville with the heavy dogma, the persistent seriousness of the dramatic criticisms which M. Zola, during a part of the same period, was contributing to *Le Voltaire*. . . . M. Zola's dramatic criticism was a campaign; Banville was content to let poor plays be the excuse for good literature. Not that he was without his convictions, far less without his preferences. His primary conviction was, that nothing in the world is so precious as good poetry, and it followed from this conviction that he cared chiefly in plays for what was poetical. In a number of charming little plays—*Le Beau Léandre, Diane au Bois, Les Fourberies de Nérine, Le Baiser*—he has shown us what he himself conceived as the poetic drama. It is a return to fairyland, the first home of poetry—a way of escape from realism and the newspapers, into a land of mere impossible romance, the land of Pierrot, of Riquet with the Tuft, of the Sleeping Beauty. This was the real world to Banville, and it needed but a word to set his brain travelling into the country of dreams. (pp. 58-9)

Banville's poetry astonishes one, first of all, by its virtuosity. He is the greatest master of rhyme who has ever used the French language . . . , one of the greatest masters of rhythm and poetical technique, a very Swinburne. But he is not merely great by reason of his form. It is true that he has no passion and little that can be called intellectual substance. His verse is nothing but verse, but it is that; it is sheer poetry, with no other excuse for its existence than this very sufficing reason, its own beauty. Banville sometimes deals with splendid themes, as in the **"Malédiction de Cypris,"** but he never sought very carefully for subjects; confident of his singing-voice, he sang. And he sang of the eternal commonplaces, eternally poetical—of the nightingale, the night, and the stars, of April and the flowers, of wine and of song, of loves as light and charming as their classic names. . . . What he wrote was mostly "occasional verse," but he carried it to the verge of sublimity. That has been done before—by Catullus, by Herrick, for example—but whenever it is done it is an achievement, and Banville, alone among modern poets, has won this difficult success. (pp. 59-60)

> *Arthur Symons, "Théodore de Banville," in Macmillan's Magazine, Vol. LXIV, May, 1891, pp. 56-60.*

ALGERNON CHARLES SWINBURNE   (poem date 1891)

[*Swinburne was an English poet, dramatist, and critic. He was renowned during his lifetime for his lyric poetry, and he is remembered today for his rejection of Victorian mores. His explicitly sensual themes shocked his contemporaries; although they demanded that poetry reflect and uphold current moral standards, Swinburne's only goal, implicit in his poetry and explicit in his critical writings, was to express beauty. He was also instrumental in introducing French literature to English readers. In addition to translating the ballads of François Villon, Swinburne composed verse in the medieval French fixed-form genres. This panegyric ballad was written shortly after Banville's death.*]

Death, a light outshining life, bids heaven resume
    Star by star the souls whose light made earth divine.
Death, a night outshining day, sees burn and bloom
    Flower by flower, and sun by sun, the fames that
        shine
    Deathless, higher than life beheld their sovereign
        sign.
Dead Simonides of Ceos, late restored,
Given again of God, again by man deplored,
    Shone but yestereve, a glory frail as breath.
Frail? But fame's breath quickens, kindles, keeps in
        ward,
    Life so sweet as this that dies and casts off death.

Mother's love, and rapture of the sea, whose womb
    Breeds eternal life of joy that stings like brine,
Pride of song, and joy to dare the singer's doom,
    Sorrow soft as sleep and laughter bright as wine,
    Flushed and filled with fragrant fire his lyric line.
As the sea-shell utters, like a stricken chord,
Music uttering all the sea's within it stored,
    Poet well-beloved, whose praise our sorrow saith,
So thy songs retain thy soul, and so record
    Life so sweet as this that dies and casts off death.

Side by side we mourned at Gautier's golden tomb:
    Here in spirit now I stand and mourn at thine.
Yet no breath of death strikes thence, no shadow of
        gloom,
    Only light more bright than gold of the inmost mine,
    Only stream of incense warm from love's own
        shrine.
Not the darkling stream, the sundering Stygian ford,
Not the harm that smiles and severs as a sword,
    Not the night subduing light that perisheth,
Smite, subdue, divide from us by doom abhorred,
    Life so sweet as this that dies and casts off death.

Prince of song more sweet than honey, lyric lord,
Not thy France here only mourns a light adored,
    One whose love-lit fame the world inheriteth.
Strangers too, now brethren, hail with heart's accord
    Life so sweet as this that dies and casts off death.

> *Algernon Charles Swinburne, "The Ballad of Melicertes; in Memory of Théodore de Banville," in The Athenaeum, No. 3322, June 27, 1891, p. 828.*

R. E. PROTHERO   (essay date 1891)

[*Prothero provides an overview of Banville's writing and enumerates its merits and faults. Despite praise for* Gringoire *and* Petit traité de poésie française, *Prothero asserts that Banville will be remembered as a poet: "His name will be inseparably associated with those of Victor Hugo and Théophile Gautier as one of three*

Caricature of Banville by André Gill that appeared on the cover of Les hommes d'aujourd'hui. *Mary Evans Picture Library.*

poets who have most powerfully influenced the French poetry of the past half-century.'']

Banville's kindly nature delighted in holding out a helping hand to his brethren. Consequently the greater part of his literary and dramatic criticism is too extravagantly eulogistic to be valuable. His *Petit Traité de Poésie Française* is, however, an epoch-making work, which is regarded by French poets of today with the same respect that versifiers of 1830 paid to Victor Hugo's Preface to *Cromwell*. With this remarkable exception, Banville's critical writings are marred by exaggerations which do more credit to his heart than his head. The same characteristics appear in the *Souvenirs* and the long series of sketches of Paris life. Just as the peasant of the Bourbonnais abhors figures, eschews definite statements, avoids decisive answers, so Banville has no sympathies with facts, and writes of his friends, or of Paris, with the vagueness and enthusiasm of a lyric poet. The world which he describes is the world of the stage, and the men and women are all acting parts assumed for the occasion. . . . *La Lanterne Magique* deserves notice as an illustration of the accuracy with which Banville gauged the temper of his day. It is a collection of stories to be read in the two minutes which people of fashion could spare for reading— stories which Madame could read whilst her maid was putting on her stockings, or which Monsieur could devour when, hat on head and cane in hand, he waits till Madame has buttoned the last button of her gloves. (pp. 278-79)

As a prose-writer Banville's style is warm, brilliant, and brightly coloured. It is the style of a poet. . . . Voluminous author though he was, it is only by *Gringoire* and the *Petit Traité de la Poésie Française* that his name will live in prose literature. As criticism, as social history, or as biographical material, his work, in spite of its literary excellence, is of little value. But as a poet he has filled seven considerable volumes with verse which in form is almost perfect; and he occupies so peculiar a position in the poetic development of the century, that, in spite of his artificiality and comparative unpopularity, his name will be inseparably associated with those of Victor Hugo and Théophile Gautier as one of three poets who have most powerfully influenced the French poetry of the past half-century. (p. 279)

Against the maudlin tenderness, and against the slatternly appearance, of French poetry in 1842, Banville made a lifelong protest, which in form was partly original, partly derived from his predecessors, and which not only gave to verse a fresh impulse, but opened to it a new line of development. (p. 280)

Banville possesses almost unrivalled skill in the form and manner of poetry. In words and cadences he is a consummate artist. He distinguishes, with almost unerring instinct, among a number of words expressing the same order of ideas, the one which most definitely sums up the desired impression, or which conveys the exact shade of meaning with the perfect fit of a kid glove. He loves words for their own sake, for their grace of movement, their enchantment of colour, the charm of their syllables; and he groups them in such a way as to produce the richest possible effects. With the same artistic instinct, he chooses the rhyme which forms the most perfect symphony in sound with the vision he desires to evoke. In his skilful hands metre is adapted to sense, not as though she were a slave bound to obedience, but as if she was the divine mistress at whose voice ideas and words fall into harmonious order. Rhyme is linked to thought, and transformed in sympathy with the subject, till it becomes anything, from an Amazon in corslet of steel to a nymph babbling to the brook, and even to a dancer balancing on the tight rope. One thing only rhyme could not, in Banville's opinion, become—a citizeness loaded with jewelry.

If Banville's matter had been equal to his manner, he would have been beyond all question a great poet. But his substance is so inferior to his form that he is rarely anything else than a great writer. The faults which mar the value of his prose works reappear in his poetry. There is the same artificiality, the same disregard for facts, the same exaggeration. He has verbal enthusiasms, aesthetic passions, artistic emotions; but human sympathy is wanting. He sees in the world nothing but beauties and glories. If things are obtrusively mean or ugly, he identifies them with the most divine forms of which they are the degraded manifestations. He removes the inequalities which constitute the misery and the perplexity of life by raising every deteriorated variety to the primary perfection from which it is derived. He looks at life through ruby-coloured spectacles. As all his aspirants to poetic fame are Homers, or as all his friends are Saladins, so he recognises no differences in conditions, no shades of colour. White is to him the whiteness of the lily or the swan; blue is the azure depth of heaven, green the brilliant clearness of the emerald. His world is a puppet-show, and even the classic or heroic past is to him little more than poetic furniture. He is lavish of romantic allusions, because they give colour and richness to the external form of his verse, and not because he values the delicacy of feudal honour that shines through the coarseness of feudal manners. As literary stock-in-trade, he delights in the company of the gods and goddesses of Olympus. Sometimes indeed he writes of classic subjects with classic restraint and statuesque simplicity. . . . (pp. 281-82)

But more generally his treatment is pictorial rather than statuesque, and he prizes the creations of pagan mythology as words or colours, not as ideas or symbolisms. (p. 282)

The distinctive note of Banville's lyric verse is gaiety. Even the metrical flow of his lines suggests happiness by the gliding ease of its movements. He sings with inexhaustible delight the rapture of existence to an age that was weary of life. He dwells in an enchanted palace of which his fancy was the architect, a stranger to the disquietude, discontent, and despair of the century. By nature he was designed for the Italian Renaissance; but his belated birth threw him into the midst of a positive and melancholy era. He was not the contemporary of his generation, and the anachronism explains his relative unpopularity as a poet. A man who can transport his fellows out of their black thoughts into a fairyland of the imagination is endowed with a priceless gift and a sacred mission. But the power is only wielded by those who have themselves felt and suffered. It is in this respect that Banville is so inferior to Victor Hugo. Both poets are optimists. Hugo knows that the problem of evil exists, and that he is surrounded by grim realities. And it is the effort which he makes that gives his finest flights their force, and redeems even his noisy rhetoric. Banville's optimism is part of his nature. His self-deceptions are involuntary, his illusions unstudied, his hallucinations natural. They cost him no effort, and therefore offer no relief or consolation to those whose temperaments are differently constituted.

Banville, then, is intensely artificial and irrepressibly gay. He has but little human sympathy. But his passion for art is so sincere, his aesthetic conscience so sensitive, his knowledge so complete, his resources so abundant, that he has produced works in which form and substance are simultaneously raised into artistic masterpieces. (pp. 282-83)

> *R. E. Prothero, "Théodore de Banville," in* The Nineteenth Century, *Vol. XXX, No. CLXXIV, August, 1891, pp. 275-84.*

ANDREW LANG   (essay date 1891)

[*Lang was an influential Scottish poet, translator, and critic. He advanced the cause of French letters in England by translating many of Banville's ballads in addition to the works of the medieval French poets François Villon, Pierre de Ronsard, and Joachim du Bellay. The following is a largely positive critical survey of Banville's dramas.*]

It is in his drama of *Gringoire* . . . that M. De Banville's prose shows to the best advantage. (pp. 66-7)

Gringoire is a play very different from M. De Banville's other dramas. . . . [The poet has often declared] that "comedy is the child of the ode," and that a drama without the "lyric" element is scarcely a drama at all. While comedy retains either the choral ode in its strict form, or its representative in the shape of lyric enthusiasm (*le lyrisme*), comedy is complete and living. *Gringoire*, to our mind, has plenty of lyric enthusiasm; but M. De Banville seems to be of a different opinion. His republished *Comédies* are more remote from experience than *Gringoire*, his characters are ideal creatures, familiar types of the stage, like Scapin and "le beau Léandre," or ethereal persons, or figures of old mythology, like Diana in *Diane au Bois*, and Deidamia in the piece which shows Achilles among women [*Déidamie*]. M. De Banville's dramas have scarcely prose enough in them

to suit the modern taste. They are masques for the delicate diversion of an hour, and it is not in the nature of things that they should rival the success of blatant buffooneries. (pp. 68-9)

[*Le Beau Léandre* is] a piece with scarcely more substance than the French scenes in the old Franco-Italian drama possess. We are taken into an impossible world of gay non-morality, where a wicked old bourgeois, Orgon, his daughter Colombine, a pretty flirt, and her lover Léandre, a light-hearted scamp, bustle through their little hour. . . . The strength of the piece is the brisk action in the scene when Léandre protests that he can't rob Orgon of his only daughter, and Orgon insists that he can refuse nothing except his ducats to so charming a son-in-law. (pp. 69-70)

[The] sombre thread in [*Déidamie*] is lent by the certainty of Achilles' early death, the fate which drives him from Déidamie's arms, and from the sea king's isle to the leagues under the fatal walls of Ilion. Of comic effect there is plenty, for the sisters of Déidamie imitate all the acts by which Achilles is likely to betray himself—grasp the sword among the insidious presents of Odysseus, when he seizes the spear, and drink each one of them a huge beaker of wine to the confusion of the Trojans. On a Parisian audience the imitations of the tone of the *Odyssey* must have been thrown away. . . . With the accustomed pedantry, M. De Banville, in the scene of the banquet, makes the cup-bearer go round dealing out a little wine, with which libation is made, and then the feast goes on in proper Homeric fashion. These overwrought details are forgotten in the parting scenes, where Déidamie takes what she knows to be her last farewell of Achilles, and girds him with his sword. . . . (pp. 70-1)

Let it be noted that each of M. De Banville's more serious plays ends with the same scene, with slight differences. In *Florise* . . . the wandering actress of Hardy's troupe leaves her lover, the young noble, and the shelter of his castle, to follow where art and her genius beckon her. In *Diane au Bois* the goddess "that leads the precise life" turns her back on Eros, who has subdued even her, and passes from the scene as she waves her hand in sign of a farewell ineffably mournful. Nearer tragedy than this M. De Banville does not care to go; and if there is any deeper tragedy in scenes of blood and in stages strewn with corpses, from that he abstains. His *Florise* is perhaps too long, perhaps too learned. . . . (p. 71)

[The character Florise] is somewhat too allegorical and haughty a creature; while Colombine and Nérine [of *Les Fouberies de Nérine*] are rather tricksy imps than women of flesh and blood. M. De Banville's stage, on the whole, is one of glitter and fantasy. . . . (p. 72)

> *Andrew Lang, "Théodore de Banville," in his Essays in Little, Charles Scribner's Sons, 1891, pp. 51-76.*

ANATOLE FRANCE   (essay date 1892)

[*France was a French novelist and critic of the late nineteenth and early twentieth centuries. According to contemporary literary historians, France's best work is characterized by clarity, control, perceptive judgment of world affairs, and the Enlightenment traits of tolerance and justice. In the following excerpt from* On Life & Letters, *originally published in French in 1892 as* La vie littéraire, *France comments on the style and subject matter of Banville's verse.*]

Théodore de Banville is perhaps of all poets he who has pondered least over the nature of things and the condition of human beings. Consisting of an absolute ignorance of universal laws, his optimism was immovable and perfect. Never for a moment did the bitter taste of life and death rise to the lips of this charming assembler of words.

It is true that he loved, sought and found the beautiful. But for him beauty did not result from the intimate structure of things or persons, and from the harmony of ideas; it was, to his thinking, an ingeniously wrought veil to be thrown over the reality, a coverlet, a glittering cloth to cover Cybele's couch and table. His charming infirmity was always to tint the world with many colours, with the hues of mother-of-pearl, to regard Nature with a wonder-working gaze that flooded all things with azure and tender rose. We must suppose that one day long ago, in a park dear to lovers, a little Cupid, hidden beneath a myrtle in which doves were making love, brushed with the tip of his wing the glasses which Providence was about to place on M. de Banville's nose; for otherwise M. de Banville could not have seen only pleasing things in this world; certain spectacles must have given him an idea of evil and suffering, of which he always remained ignorant; without these glasses M. de Banville could not have seen the tremendous six days' work under the gracious aspect which it has always revealed to him; he could not have seen it bright and airy as Armida's ballet. If, in his Biblical heaven, the ancient Javeh ever conceives the whim of reading M. de Banville's descriptive verses, he will never recognize, under so many ornaments, his rude creation, nourished with blood and tears. He will close the book at the tenth page, and cry: "By Lucifer! I did not make the earth as pleasant as that! This poet, who sings better than my seraphim, visibly exaggerates the elegance of my work." (pp. 221-22)

In this world of ours, through which so many vulgar or lamentable forms are passing, M. Théodore de Banville saw principally gods and goddesses. The Venuses whom he saw had tresses "with fine golden gleams, and their beautiful pointed breasts revealed veins of a pale azure."

They are not Greeks. The Venus of the Hellenes is too pale. And she has committed the crime of being a geometrician and a metaphysician. Thought revolves within her lovely head with the exactitude of a planet traversing the Zodiac. She meditates upon the force that creates the worlds and maintains harmony in them. M. de Banville's Venuses are Venetian. They do not know a word of mythology. They are akin to those figures of which the painters say that they *plafonnent;* that is, they are flat, they do not stand out from the wall or ceiling.

The poet's Olympus is an Olympus of banqueting-halls and ballrooms. Clad in heroic carnival costume, the knights and ladies go by two by two, gracefully dancing under the painted dome to the sound of soft music. This is the poetic world of M. Théodore de Banville.

There is nothing in it to speak to the heart, nothing to perturb the soul. No bitterness corrupts the sweetness which one drinks in with one's eyes and ears. Sometimes the *festa* is held in Watteau's "Cythera," sometimes in a lilac-scented garden, and tight-rope walkers and rope-dancers take part in it; sometimes even it is held in booths of the fair. There, after a thousand wonderful tricks:

> Enfin, de son vil échafaud
> Le clown sauta si haut, si haut
> Qu'il creva le plafond de toile,

Au son du cor et du tambour,
Et le coeur dévoré d'amour
Alla rouler dans les étoiles.

[At length, from his low stage
The clown leaped so high, so high
That he burst the cloth of the ceiling,
To the sound of the horn and the drum
And his heart, devoured by love,
Went to roll among the stars.]

Théodore de Banville, who thus set a clown in heaven like a new constellation, beside Perseus and Andromeda, valued in these virtuosi of dislocation the qualities of suppleness and imagination which he himself possessed in the highest degree, as a rope-dancing poet. For this lyric poet was, in his poetry, when he pleased, an unequalled clown. Our old Scarron is but a clog-dancer beside him. That Théodore de Banville has invented a comic species of rhythm and a comic manner of rhyming individual to himself has been denied, no doubt correctly. For that matter, no one ever invents anything. But that this rare poet has most happily and abundantly practised this art of lyric buffoonery cannot be denied. The truth is that this forgotten manner which in our ancient literature is known as burlesque has been renewed, transformed and embellished by our poet; he has made it his own in all its branches; so much so that one may say that he has created a manner of his own. The *Odes funambulesques* and *Les Occidentales* are perhaps the most original things that Théodore de Banville has written. What man of letters is there who is unacquainted with, who does not still try to relish that innocent, amiable, smiling satire, which lends grace to caricature and style to frivolity, that folly which still retains, after twenty and thirty years, an air of youth. . . . (pp. 223-25)

When Théodore de Banville is not the rope-dancing poet he is the poet's poet, the supreme virtuoso. It has justly been said that he was the last of the romantics and the first of the Parnassians. He took Hugo's verse, made it supple, broke it asunder, drew it out to excess and lit it up with resplendent rhymes.

During the second portion of his life and work M. de Banville applied himself to restoring the old rigid poetical forms: rondeau, ballade, chant royal, lay and virelay. He displayed in these reproductions a dexterity by no means common and all the technical skill of a poetic Viollet-le-Duc. One might philosophize at length upon attempts of this kind. They are, it may be, only an amusement; but we cannot deny that it is a graceful amusement.

He has expounded his poetical theories in a little manual of poetry [*Petit traité de poésie française*] which one reads with pleasure, but which does not give evidence of very much knowledge or reflection. It is the work of a nightingale turned metaphysician. After all, the theory of French verse is difficult and obscure, and it is not perhaps the poets' business to construct it. (pp. 225-26)

> *Anatole France, "Théodore de Banville," in his* On Life & Letters, *fourth series, edited by Frederic Chapman, translated by Bernard Miall, Dodd, Mead & Company, Inc., 1924, pp. 219-27.*

AARON SCHAFFER (essay date 1921)

[*The following is a concise appreciation of Banville's drama* Gringoire. *For additional commentary by Schaffer, see excerpt below, 1929, and Additional Bibliography.*]

Banville's *Gringoire,* though written in verse, is truly a lyric drama. Nothing could be more fascinatingly unreal than the theme of the play—the union of a tattered poet, liable to the death-penalty for the composition of a treasonable poem, with the beautiful daughter of a wealthy merchant, herself more angel than human being, the whole consummated by the very king who is the target of the poet's verses. The language of the play is throughout highly poetical, the utterances of the poet-hero, Gringoire, abounding in striking figures of speech and mythological allusions; moreover, by the use of a few archaisms drawn from the vocabulary of the fifteenth century, Banville very skilfully succeeds in carrying us back in imagination to the romantic Middle Ages. The dialogue is spirited and not without its frequent touches of graceful humor. And, finally, the six characters are all sharply, the central figure, at least, masterfully, delineated. The play is easily one of Banville's most finished productions, and one of those that will operate most potently towards handing the name of the poet down to posterity. (p. xxii)

> *Aaron Schaffer, "The Year 1469 in French History,"
> in* Gringoire *by Théodore de Banville and* Le Luthier
> de Crémone *by Francois Coppée, edited by Aaron
> Schaffer, Henry Holt and Company, 1921, pp. xi-
> xxii.**

ARNOLD WHITRIDGE   (essay date 1923)

[*Whitridge explores Banville's poetic theories and his use of humor and satire in the* Odes funambulesques *and* Idylles prussiennes. *This essay was originally published in the* North American Review *in December, 1923.*]

We are apt . . . to think of Banville too much as a mere master of technique. Certainly he carried to perfection the art of the ballade, the triolet, and the rondeau, but he was not styled the legislator of the new Parnassians on the strength of these accomplishments. His *Petit Traité de Poésie Française* is the codification of the Parnassian theories of poetry. Anatole France [see excerpt above, 1892] dismissed it summarily as expressing a nightingale's metaphysics, and no doubt Banville's conception of poetry is curiously unintellectual. He staked everything on what he called "richesse implacable de la rime" [the implacable richness of rhyme]. By richness he meant repetition not only of the vowel but of the supporting consonant. "Breeze" and "freeze," for instance, would be a respectably affluent rhyme, whereas "breeze" and "squeeze" is obviously a poor, poverty-stricken thing. The poet's inspiration must find its vent in such rhymes, and the reader must seek enjoyment in his perception of the ingenuity displayed. Banville also insisted on the importance of utilizing the musical resources of the language by recognizing the sonority of certain words and calculating their aesthetic effect. It is easy to see how Mallarmé, following in his footsteps, arrived at the conclusion that the value of poetry lay more in the sound of words than in their sense. (pp. 105-06)

Banville's poetic theories might well be ignored if they did not happen to go hand in hand with his sense of humor. We have mentioned his connection with the Parnassians. As a young man he wrote a vast amount of statuesque poetry, but in the mythical desert island library which all of us are forever envisaging Banville will be represented by his one volume of *Odes Funambulesques.* In this collection of parody and lyric satire rhyme again plays the leading part. We have nothing in English that quite compares with it. Bergson's philosophic treatise on laughter explains humor as a sudden jerk to the imagination. This definition would seem to fit the average parody, which relies on the constant juxtaposition of the trivial and the sublime. But parody for the most part confines itself to ridiculing an idea, whereas Banville always strives for the double jerk of sense plus sound. He never forgets that he is primarily a lyric poet, and his satire consequently exhibits his own dexterity more than the absurdities of his victim. (pp. 107-08)

Banville never labors anything. He dances around the bourgeois, his favorite object of satire, darting in occasionally to tweak his nose without ever tumbling into didacticism on one side or bitterness on the other. He belonged to the generation that made a fetich of despising the commonplace. The bourgeois epitomized normalcy, and Banville . . . always regarded normalcy as the unpardonable sin. Throughout all his satire runs the unexpected vein of good humor. No one resented his sallies. He could describe the bourgeois at the theatre, his ill-fitting clothes and his inept criticism, without apparently arousing the slightest antipathy. His shafts are barbed, but they are never poisoned. English poetry has no tight-rope artist to match against Théodore de Banville. (pp. 109-10)

Now, to tip the balance, we must admit the obvious limitations of the *Odes Funambulesques.* Even when he would be most serious Banville can never throw off his air of trifling. This growing incapacity to speak from the heart is still more evident in the *Idylles Prussiennes,* where for the first time the outer world ruthlessly thrusts itself upon his attentions. His raw material consisted of beauty, love, and poetry, out of which he wove exquisite fabrics. Humor was merely incidental. Instead of being, as it usually is, a measure of intellectual depth, Banville's humor was rather a blind to distract attention from the shallowness of his thought. Not understanding realism, either on the stage or in life, he instinctively fought it with the only weapons at his command.

The *Idylles Prussiennes* represent the gallant attempt to laugh in the midst of disaster. While France was plunging from incomprehensible optimism to unplumbed depths of despair Banville's rivulet of satire made its way through the daily papers. The only weapon left to the conquered is irony, and for a workman of his happy nature sustained irony is an unsatisfactory tool. One must be something of a misanthrope, which he never was, to be a great satirist. Try as he will, the fires of contempt do not burn with a hard, gem-like flame. The tragic intensity of a Raemaekers is never even approached in these rather toothless satires. Like the *Odes Funambulesques,* they are essentially lyrical, and lyric poetry is a bad medium for transmitting hatred. Bismarck and Moltke are substituted for the complacent bourgeois, whom Banville had so often rallied, but now, when he would exchange persiflage for downright castigation, something is lacking. A Voltaire or a Pope can always "without sneering teach the rest to sneer." Banville is too ingenuous; the limpid flow of his stanzas leaves the Prussians singularly unscathed.

One of the most typical of the *Idylles Prussiennes* is *L'Épée,* a poem in which he laments that swordsmanship no longer plays a part in modern warfare. . . . It is not surprising that these innocuous war poems made little impression upon the public. Banville had nothing to say that could possibly arrest the national imagination at such a moment. (pp. 110-12)

We should perhaps consider the *Idylles* as a form of military service rather than as a contribution to literature. Banville's continual ill-health prevented any active participation in the war, so he goaded the enemy as best he could with the lash of lyric satire. (pp. 113-14)

Arnold Whitridge, "Théodore de Banville," in his Critical Ventures in Modern French Literature, *Charles Scribner's Sons, 1924, pp. 102-18.*

SIR EDMUND GOSSE (essay date 1923)

[*In this positive assessment written in 1923, Gosse discusses the reactions of Banville's contemporaries to his poetry and his influence on other nineteenth-century writers. For additional commentary by Gosse, see excerpt above, 1891.*]

[Banville's] influence on the *technique* of verse, when I was young, would alone justify a particular attention to his merits to-day. His theories and practice bore fruit in the writings of English poets as diverse as Swinburne, Austin Dobson, and Andrew Lang.... [The **"Petit Traité de Poésie Française"**] was a revelation to the men who were then young, and whose part in the evolution of English poetry, though greatly undervalued to-day, will inevitably recover its honourable prestige. When the next revulsion to beauty and melody arrives, Théodore de Banville will be read once more, for diamonds are sure to be retrieved, even though for a generation they are lost in the mire. (p. 347)

Anatole France has said that the soul of Banville was like a garden full of flowers, and we may add that in that garden was an imp pretending to make melodies on a violin that was a toy. His whole life was spent in playing imaginary music, but when he was older the instrument grew to be a real one; it grew to be a lyre, not the majestic *phorminx* of Milton and Hugo, but a little *chelys* of tortoiseshell, held tight against the heart while Banville twanged it.

This became part of the poet, became, indeed, himself; "la lyre, c'est vous" [you are the lyre], his admirers used to assure him. No other French poet has lived who has showed so prodigious a skill in versifying; he was "le roi des rimes" [the king of rhyme], and to understand the magic which he exercised we have to go back to the frenzy created here by Swinburne's "Dolores" and "Faustine" in 1866. The new Georgians do not understand it, nor do their brethren in France. The **"Odes Funambulesques,"** with their flamboyant and excessive dexterity, produced a species of delirium. Even Victor Hugo felt the intoxication, and reeled along the shore of his island. Nor was it only the melody of the sparkling odes which set folk dancing. Banville, extremely unlike the author of "Atalanta" in other respects, had Swinburne's faculty for recalling to poetic diction worn and superannuated words, and endowing them with new life. This is a gift which presently meets with ingratitude, since these words, once recovered soon cease to give the pleasure of surprise. No one, I suppose, under the age of sixty can realise what we felt when we first read

> Leaves pallid and sombre and ruddy,
>   Dead fruit of the fugitive years,
> Some stained as with wine and made bloody,
>   And some as with tears,

nor reproduce the impression of **"Le Saut du Tremplin."**

The typical word to describe Banville is "funambulesque," and he so named the most characteristic of his poems. A *funambule* is a rope-dancer, and no versifier has ever lived who achieved more marvellous feats on the lyrical trapeze than he. He even did himself an injustice by his extreme agility, since the public is volatile, and soon grows tired of an exhibition of mere nimbleness. An incredible performance in the air may become wearisome through its own apparent lack of effort, and a reaction comes in favour of walking slowly on flat ground, even with the aid of a stick.

It was a fault in Banville that he carried his mastery of form to such an extreme perfection that an ungrateful audience turned away from him at last as from a clown that attempts too many somersaults. This was doing a wonderful talent great injustice, but it may be admitted that the artist himself was partly to blame. He combated the popular error with dignity. He says: "I do not regard Rhyme, as fools pretend to think I do, as a thing uniformly dazzling and sumptuous, but as being varied, diverse, amorously wedded to thought, transfigured by close attention to the nature of the subject, and uniform only in its faithful and constant concordance with harmonic propriety." This was true; but a satiated public would persist in seeing nothing in Banville but a clown in spangled tights.

For so gentle and inoffensive a bard, Banville suffered much at the hands of detraction. Somebody has always to be the last, and it was Banville's fate to close the great Cénacle, so that he inherited some of the abuse of the Philistines. His earliest volume of poems, "Les Cariatides," was published in 1842, when he was a law-student just nineteen; it long preceded the earliest issues of Leconte de Lisle, who was his senior by five years and has therefore been inaccurately supposed to have influenced Banville. "Les Cariatides," on the contrary, is of the long-haired, crimson-waistcoated order, voluptuous and capricious, carrying on the early enthusiasm of Gautier in the full-blooded tradition of the Cénacle. The little book was fiercely attacked, and the young bard was told that his poems "smelt of tobacco and rum, and reflected the ill-regulated passions and sensuous appetites of a society without law and without manners." But the noble Alfred de Vigny, out of the "ivory tower" of his retirement, sent him a letter of warm approval, and from the first Banville was accepted by his fellows, whatever the harsh reviewers might say.

It is odd, or would be if we did not recognise the instinctive hatred of any new kind of beauty which animates the ordinary man—it is odd that anyone, in the first instance, should have failed to respond to Banville's appeal, since his freshness of spirit was untouched by the despair and darkness which are the cankers of an old society. He came ... at the close of the Romantic movement, but he bore none of the stigmata of decay. The central emotion in his poetry is joy. Baudelaire, whose temperament was the antithesis of his, was fascinated by a happiness he could not share, and could hardly comprehend [see excerpt above, 1861]. He said of Banville that he was the symbol of all the happy hours in life. It was a strange phenomenon, this apparition, in the autumn of the deep Romantic sadness, of a spirit in whom the sap of April seemed to leap. In the **"Odes Funambulesques,"** the little flower-like comedies, most of all perhaps in the masterly **"Trente-Six Ballades Joyeuses,"** ... were peals of laughter, heard out of the provoking shelter of the boskage.

Anatole France has said that the Muse of Théodore de Banville is a "Venetian Venus" [see excerpt above, 1892]. This phrase happily sums up the curious mixture of the rigidly antique and the frivolously modern which we meet with in his writings. He had much of Watteau in his nature, and something of Aristophanes. In his plays, which are as artificial and as exquisite as old Dresden china, Aphrodite seems to be playing the part of Columbine, and flirting outrageously with an Indian Bacchus, who is disguised as Harlequin. The odes of Banville may be called Pindaro-comic; they treat of the varnished slipper of Madame Panache in language and metre worthy of the most high gods of Hellas. This is an attitude which provokes the rage of the implacable enemies of a joyous lyrical inspiration, for whom nothing ought to be written which does not expand the American maxim that "Life is real, Life is earnest." Théodore de Banville is the extreme type of those outcasts of the higher seriousness who determine to be poets before everything, and to be nothing but poets. . . . Unhappily, the very magnificence of the effort is its own destruction; the audience grows tired, and turns away at last from so extravagant an apotheosis. (pp. 348-51)

Sir Edmund Gosse, "Théodore de Banville," in his
Silhouettes, *Charles Scribner's Sons, 1925, pp. 347-52.*

AARON SCHAFFER   (essay date 1929)

[*Focusing on Banville's increasing mastery of technique, Schaffer traces the poet's artistic development and discusses his contribution to French lyric poetry. For additional commentary by Schaffer, see excerpt above, 1921, and Additional Bibliography.*]

Banville was primarily the poet of the sheer joy of living. To be sure, he soon learned full well that life grants with all too sparing a hand its moments of joy, and the note of disillusioned sadness is never long absent from his verses. But the point to be remembered is that he wanted passionately to experience the joy of living and to reproduce it in his poetry. Artistic to the very roots of his being, he found himself entirely out of tune with the money-grubbing materialism of his epoch and, like the Romanticists of whom he might be called a belated survivor, he sought to escape the time in which he lived and to find happiness in a world of his own creating. Now, for Banville, the happiest era in the history of mankind was that of the pre-Aristotelian gods and heroes, of painters and sculptors, of . . . the man who was "beautiful and good," that is, beautiful therefore good. And so, turning his back upon the uninspired prose of a Scribe and what to him seemed the soulless pseudo-classicism of seventeenth and eighteenth century France, he bathed himself in the radiance of classical antiquity and its reflection that was the Renaissance. Banville, like Louis Ménard, was a true Hellene, a pagan in the best sense of the word, and, unlike Ménard, he concentrated his attention upon the attainment of the Hellenic ideal in art. That he always achieved this ideal even the most enthusiastic of his sympathizers would perforce deny, but to overlook his ambition and to pass him scornfully by as a "delightful acrobat" is to do him a grave injustice. And whatever he may have failed to accomplish, one achievement must stand to his everlasting merit—his resuscitation of the verse-forms employed by the poets of pre-classical France, Charles d'Orléans, Villon, and Ronsard. . . . (pp. 131-32)

[Though Banville] frequently, and not unsuccessfully, essayed poetry of serious subject-matter, he was more at home in the sprightly or fanciful vein. This is manifest even in *les Cariatides*, where the lengthy Hugonian compositions are far less striking than the much shorter, gayer poems in imitation of the late mediaeval types. For it is highly significant that, at his very *début*, Banville was already concerned with Villon, Marot, Ronsard, and du Bellay, as may be seen from the frequency with which they are mentioned, and that he employs such verse-forms as the triolet, the rondeau, the double rondeau, and the

madrigal, which were later to attain to such technical perfection in his hands. . . . [Many of the poems in this volume] celebrate the love of life, the contempt for the *bourgeois* characteristic of Gautier and the Jeunes-France, and reveal the predilection for the subject-matter of Greek poesy and for the manner of Villon, Marot, the Pléiade, and the Romanticists which remain throughout life the unchanging elements of the Banvillean poetics. Though *les Cariatides* reflects the gropings of a young versifier not yet escaped from the larva of imitation, it is clearly prophetic of what was to come, and without it the later Banville would scarcely be comprehensible.

In the preface to his second volume of verse, *les Stalactites*, Banville calls attention to what he believes a poetic advance on his part: he has shed most of the stiltedness, of the stiff technical correctness of *les Cariatides*. . . . What the poet here has in mind is the abandonment of the sacerdotal heaviness of the adolescent prone to take himself too seriously, and the determination to give free rein to the joy of living and singing which were the very breath of his life. For it was as natural for Banville to carol in rhyme as it is for the mockingbird to burst into song; the music of poetry expressed for him the music of the macrocosm. Little did it matter what he sang; in *les Stalactites* . . . the poems are all concerned with the conventional themes: love, wine, roses. But the handling begins to show greater mastery of the medium; the metrical, rhythmic, and stanzaic patterns are more varied and are marked by greater abandon. . . . It is especially in the use of the short verse that Banville excelled, and we find him employing it from the very outset of his career.

With the publication of *les Odelettes* . . . , Banville took his place among the master-technicians in verse; and it was upon the appearance of this same volume that the poet was definitely branded as perpetrating "de la poésie sans idées" [poetry without subject]. . . . [As] its name would imply, the *odelette* is the ode in a playful humor; it is to the ode what the crayon sketch is to the finished painting in oils. Banville justifies his use of this *genre* by showing that greater than he had employed it before him: Anacreon, Horace, and the members of the Pléiade. For sheer bedazzzlement of metre and rhyme and for variety of rhyme-scheme, *les Odelettes* had hardly any equal outside the work of Banville himself. Profound poetry this certainly is not; and the reflections of Anacreon and of Ronsard, whom Banville calls "mon maître" [my master], are so abounding as to rob the volume of any real claim to originality of content; but sparkling, laughing poetry it most certainly is, and, as such, can not be frowned out of court in scorn. . . . The *Odelettes* testify to Banville's mastery of the short line, the short stanza, the short poem, which must be characterized by a sure choice of words and an unerring sense of rhyme to become effective. . . . Most of the *Odelettes* are addressed, by way of title, to one or another of the poet's friends; thus, we have poems **"A Sainte-Beuve," "A Henri Murger," "A Arsène Houssaye," "A Edmond et Jules de Goncourt," "A Philoxène Boyer,"** and two **"A Théophile Gautier."** The little volume puts one in mind of nothing so much as a string of glittering beads that dances, carefree, on the neck of its mistress; and the poems are, for the most part, as empty of thought as are those beads or the head above them.

In the *odelette*, Banville was merely resuscitating, according to his own avowal, a poetic *genre* that had been a favorite in earlier literary epochs. His indulgence in this lighter vein of poetry was the result of his conviction that the lyric Muse had fallen on evil days, that men were interested only in the accumulation of wealth and the enjoyment of such pleasures as can be bought with money. This feeling seems to have taken on constantly increasing force during the decade from 1846 to 1856, until the poet arrived at the conclusion that the only means of retaining the public's interest in art was the assumption of the role of Aristophanic clown. The serious "ode," *à la* Hugo, now patently moribund, Banville set about inventing a new type which should stand in the same relation to the ode as does caricature to genuine painting. This type he gave the name of *ode funambulesque* ("funambule" being the French word for "tight-rope-walker"), and in 1857 he published a volume of these acrobatic odes. In the *Odes funambulesques,* as he explains in the poem, **"la Corde roide,"** Banville had exchanged the aureole of the prophet for the flour-mask of the clown in order to hold the attention of the stupid *bourgeoisie* by belaboring it vigorously. . . . And, from the height of his tight-rope, Banville, in a series of poems that are little short of astounding for audacity of rhyme and metre, proceeds to thwack, in no uncertain manner, the smug *bourgeoisie* with its even more smug leaders, statesmen, journalists, and literary favorites. The targets of the *Odes funambulesques* are, for the most part, individuals whose names would have long since completely disappeared but for these poems, which are, therefore, almost incomprehensible without a commentary; for subject-matter, thus, the volume is practically worthless. And yet, *les Odes funambulesques* has not only survived, but it has survived as one of the important phenomena in nineteenth-century French poetry, as perhaps the supreme illustration of what can be done with mere words. It is a poetic *tour de force,* a feat of technical legerdemain that has few peers. There is a profusion of rhyme-schemes that dazzles eye as well as ear; besides the forms regularly practiced at the time, such sixteenth-century types as the ballade, the chant royal, the triolet, and the virelai are deliciously rejuvenated. Especially in the triolet has Banville attained the extreme limits of the *funambulesque.* . . . (pp. 136-42)

One of Banville's chief services to French lyric poetry . . . was his revivification of the highly artistic verse-forms which had been so skillfully practiced in the fifteenth and sixteenth centuries and then had been allowed to lapse into complete oblivion. Several of Banville's collections of verse are devoted, in their entirety, to one or another of the older forms. . . . It would not be too much to say that, in the hands of Banville, French lyric poetry underwent a thorough renewal, which restored much of the graceful charm that it had lacked for two and a half centuries. Though he added little to the sum total of ideas, he not inconsiderably enriched the prosody of his people. For it can not be too often repeated that Banville was a poet as the nightingale is a songbird, innately and almost unconsciously. Indeed, . . . Banville's strongest claim to the approbation of posterity lies in the fact that he applied the theory of "art for art's sake" more strictly than did any other poet, not excluding even the originator of the theory, Thèophile Gautier, whom he always held in high reverence.

Thus far, Banville has appeared to us principally in the guise of apostle of a sort of pagan pantheism, Anacreontic rather than Platonic. Between the years 1857 and 1867, however, though he knew the joys of unquestioned success, he suffered the bitterness concomitant upon the loss of cherished friends and illusions, and in the latter year he published what is perhaps, after *les Odes funambulesques,* his most important contribution to French lyric poetry, *les Exilés.* Here, for the most part, the poet is in an elegiac mood; he is bewailing the "exiled," the Greek gods who have been banished from modern life and

the spirit of joyous beauty which they personified. This note is especially sounded in **"l'Exil des Dieux,"** and **"le Festin des Dieux."** . . . This collection of verse is a speaking refutation of the charge that Banville is a mere "clown in poetry"; if he thought about nothing else, he was certainly gravely perturbed over the disappearance of art from the concerns of men and he fought, virtually until he drew his dying breath, the battle of the truth that is beauty. (pp. 142-44)

[Whatever] and however flagrant his shortcomings might be, he deserved well of France for having held high the banner of poesy in an age when poesy had begun its disappearance from a prosaic world of machinery, novels, and science. Add to this the fact that his door was always open to welcome the struggling poet who would rather starve than compromise his ideals, and that he was indubitably supreme in at least the "funambulesque" *genre* he had invented, and it is not difficult to understand the fascination which he exercised over the younger Parnassians, a fascination exceeded only slightly by that of Leconte de Lisle. Banville was the very incarnation of the music of verse; with the lover of musical French poetry he will always be a favorite. (pp. 145-46)

> *Aaron Schaffer, "Théodore de Banville and His Disciples," in his* Parnassus in France: Currents and Cross-Currents in Nineteenth-Century French Lyric Poetry, *University of Texas, 1929, pp. 130-46.*

ROBERT T. DENOMMÉ (essay date 1972)

[Denommé discusses Banville's importance to the Parnassian movement in light of the poet's strong admiration for the major French Romantic writers. He also considers Banville's technical mastery and conception of perfect beauty.]

The fact that so many critics and literary historians continue to identify Théodore de Banville as the author of the "official" exposition of Parnassian doctrine constitutes one of the most singular ironies that has sprung from the history of the movement. When *Le Petit Traité de poésie française* first appeared as serialized chapters in the *Echo de la Sorbonne* in 1870, it provoked the immediate displeasure of Leconte de Lisle and the more prominent practitioners of Parnassianism.

For all of its obvious concern with rhyme and rhythm and the technical intricacies of French versification, Banville's treatise conveyed a disturbingly cavalier approach to the problem of poetic expression which only served to irritate his more serious and staid congeners. The very desultoriness of his half-serious, half-ironic remarks on form and inspiration invested his essay with precisely the kind of debonair attitude that appeared to undermine the seriousness of the problem at hand. The fact of the matter was that *Le Petit Traité de poésie française,* as a Parnassian statement on the art of versification, rested upon a most ironic if not altogether grotesque paradox.

Banville interspersed his commentary with such frequent reference to the genius of Hugo that *Le Petit Traité* reads, at various intervals, as an eloquent homage to the illustrious poet of the French Romantic movement. Moreover, the generous acknowledgment made to Hugo, Tennint, and Sainte-Beuve in the sections on rhyme, meter and rhythm virtually endowed the treatise with a distinctly partisan Romantic ingredient. With the exception of Glatigny, the Parnassian poets dismissed Banville's attempt to formalize the rules of poetic expression as an inept if not unfortunate pleasantry. Banville's curious admiration for Hugo's lyricism, as a practicing Parnassian, sprang from the contradictory impulses he felt within himself as a poet. His ostensible adherence to Parnassian doctrine from 1866 to 1886 was motivated principally by his determination to dominate his inspiration so that it might be enclosed in forms that would best ensure its survival in art. The Parnassian conception of artistic permanence, suggested through the hard and plastic texture of carefully contrived forms and imagery, appealed to him sufficiently to make of him a champion of Art for Art's Sake despite his professional esteem for the poetry of Victor Hugo.

In actual fact, *Le Petit Traité de poésie française* lacks the kind of scholarly and scientific rigor that would have enlisted the enthusiasm and approbation of Leconte de Lisle and Heredia. The treatise's real value lies in that which it reveals about Banville's poetic philosophy. It has been convincingly illustrated that his intransigent theoretical stand on rhyme and meter and his categorical rejection of enjambment and inversion, for example, are repeatedly and somewhat shamelessly contradicted in his own poetic practice. What *Le Petit Traité* unveils is the poet's enervated attempt to camouflage personal poetic inspiration with the kind of external formal accouterment that would impart his verse with a greater sense of objectivity and impassibility. It is precisely the detectable unfolding of Banville's quest for formal perfection in order to conceal his essentially Romantic temperament that infuses his verse, from time to time, with a decipherable lyrical quiver.

Banville's psychological attachment to the spirit of Romanticism asserted itself with startling effrontery in the 1871 edition of Lemerre's *Parnasse contemporain*. The **"Ballade de ses regrets pour l'an 1830"** [Ballad on his nostalgia for the year 1830], composed in 1869, underscored the poet's obvious preference for the expansive lyricism associated with Hugo and Musset. Banville's nostalgic recollection of the opening of the July Monarchy contrasts the more hopefully expectant mood of the era with the overriding disillusionment and pessimism that characterized Parnassian expression during the 1860s. The **"Ballade de ses regrets"** identified Banville spiritually with the bygone Romanticism of the 1830s in the official publication of the Parnassian poets:

> O Poésie, ô ma mère mourante,
> Comme tes fils t'aimaient d'un grand amour,
> Dans ce Paris, en l'an mil huit cent trente.
> Enfant divin, plus beau que Richelieu,
> Musset chantait; Hugo tenait la lyre,
> Jeune, superbe, écouté comme un dieu.
> Mais à présent, c'est bien fini de rire.

> [Oh Poetry! my dying mother, know how your sons loved you in Paris during the year 1830! Musset, the enchanting child, much more handsome than Richelieu, sang your hymn. The young and splendid Hugo played on his lyre, and the people listened to him as if he were a god. But now, the time is gone for hope and laughter.]

Le Petit Traité de poésie française, to a degree, corroborated Banville's sense of nostalgia for the past. His insistent recommendation that poets return to the use of such poetic forms as the rondeau, the triolet and the ballad, so popular during the Middle Ages and the Renaissance, was motivated principally by the desire to disassociate himself from the bleakness of the 1860s and 1870s. The rondeau, the triolet, and the ballad evoked the kind of grace, wit, and gaiety which Banville ur-

gently sought to restore to his own verse and to that of his contemporaries.

To achieve the sense of remoteness from the present and to suggest the carefree fantasy which he associated with the poetic forms of the Middle Ages and the Renaissance, Banville urged that painstaking care be given to the elaboration of a pleasing rhyme scheme in poetry. Indeed, the aphorism on the importance of rhyme in *Le Petit Traité* constituted the central point around which all other considerations converged: "Rhyme emerges as the only harmony achieved in verse, and rhyme makes up the entire verse." Banville's conception of the rhyme can hardly be considered as original; Sainte-Beuve enunciated the same principle earlier in his *Tableau historique et critique de la poésie française et du théâtre français au XVIe siècle* [Historical and critical survey of French poetry and theatre in the sixteenth century].

For Banville, harmony was the springboard that permitted the poet-clown to turn somersaults into the gayety and grace of the Middle Ages and the Renaissance. If he chose to render both ideas and inspiration subservient to rhyme, it was in order to achieve the type of harmony which he identified with art and poetry. In a sense, his advocacy of harmony in poetry pointed more in the direction of Symbolism than of Parnassianism. Moreover, his virtual obsession to obtain it stemmed from a Romantic urge to escape from his own predicament. His ostensible allegiance to Parnassianism was predicated upon the need to externalize the substance of his poetic inspiration into a workable mold and formula. Most of his verse translates such a visible preoccupation with rhyme and rhythm.

Three of Banville's best-known poetry collections, [*Les Cariatides, Les Stalactites,* and *Améthystes*] carry in their train strong intimations of durable substances and sharply defined contours in a manner reminiscent of Gautier's *Emaux et camées*. Indeed, it might be argued that each title indicated conveys a sense of remoteness and noninvolvement; like the jewels, enamels and semiprecious hangings, the individual poems are meant to appeal to the reader's visual imagination through the precision of their expression and the beauty of their imagery. The suggested alliance between poetry and sculpture, alluded to in Gautier's celebrated manifesto poem of 1857, "L'Art," was, to a certain degree, advanced by Banville a year earlier in the ode, **"A Théophile Gautier."** *Les Stalactites* of 1846, however, contained still another poem by Banville on the topic of plasticity and poetry.

This earlier poem is of interest to us because it reveals so well the frame of reference in which Banville approached the tenets of Art for Art's Sake and Parnassianism.

> Sculpteur, cherche avec soin, en attendant l'extase,
> Un marbre sans défaut pour en faire un beau vase;
> Cherche longtemps sa forme et n'y retrace pas
> D'amours mystérieux ni de divins combats;
>
> • • • • •
>
> Qu'autour du vase pur, trop beau pour la Bacchante,
> La verveine mêlée à des feuilles d'acanthe
> Fleurisse, et que plus bas des vierges lentement
> S'avancent deux à deux, d'un pas sûr et charmant,
> Les bras pendant le long de leurs tuniques droites
> Et les cheveux tressés sur leurs têtes étroites.

> [Sculptor, while waiting for the ecstasy of inspiration, look carefully for a piece of flawless marble from which to make a beautiful vase.

Think carefully before you decide on the shape you wish to give it, and do not try to portray on it the mysterious loves and the divine battles of mythology. . . . May the elegant contours of your perfect vase emerge too beautiful for the gaze of Bacchus's priestess, and let the ornamental verbenas, intertwined with the leaves of the acanthus, appear in full bloom. A little lower, show the slowly cadenced but charming procession of the virgins walking two by two, with their long slender arms gracefully drooping beside their straight tunics and with their hair braided on their narrow heads.]

Within the idealized context of Greek antiquity, Banville sought to define his conception of perfect, lasting beauty. The lines do not concern themselves with any actual fact or reality, but more precisely with a project involving the collaboration of two creative artists. What the poet conceives, the sculptor will attempt to render in a visibly durable work of art. What the poem reveals is Banville's rejection of any principle associated with violence or disorder. For all of its mosaic structure, the first part of the poem (only one line has been quoted in the excerpt) relates precisely what the artist should exclude from Greek mythology. The second part of this program poem appears in sharp antithesis to the first: the titanic battles of the demigods make way for the harmony and grace suggested in the images of the verbenas, the acanthus and the slow procession of the elegant virgins. The quasi-sculptural description of the virgins is endowed with a religious and distant purity which, in this instance, conforms perfectly to the Parnassian conception of objectivity and impassibility.

The technical dexterity, so prominently noticeable in this program piece, points to the development of Banville's remarkable talent for dealing with intricate rhymes and rhythms. The poem's directness proceeds from the conspicuous absence of any distracting type of inversion, and whatever enjambments may be detected serve to enhance and prolong the illusion of movement suggested by the mosaic tableaus and the sculptural portraits placed on the richly ornamented Greek vase. In a radical departure from sixteenth-century French versification, Banville arranges his *rimes riches* in alternating groups of two masculine rhymes and two feminine rhymes. The somewhat rapid pace of the beginning of the poem slows down progressively in the second part by a frequent recourse to words possessing more complicated rhythms and fuller sonorities: *lentement* and *charmant*, for example.

In short, the rhyme scheme employed conveys a detectable musical charm and reveals the conscious effort of the poet to obtain definite desired effects. This program poem, like the majority of those included in *Les Stalactites,* aims at the illustration of a simple and harmonious beauty rather than at the expression of any obvious sentiment or emotion. The ecstasy referred to in the opening line is that achieved through the quiet contemplation of a work of art. Such an ecstacy was expressly calculated to remove both the creative artist and the reader or the beholder from the immediate contingencies of a limited reality in order to transport them to an idealized world containing perfect forms and harmonies. (pp. 64-70)

Robert T. Denommé, "Théodore de Banville and the Obsession with Formal Perfection," in his The French Parnassian Poets, *Southern Illinois University Press, 1972, pp. 64-75.*

ALVIN HARMS   (essay date 1983)

[*The following excerpt is drawn from Harms's study* Théodore de Banville *which includes information on many works not ordinarily treated by critics, including Banville's novel* Marcelle Rabe. *Here Harms analyzes the themes and style of Banville's lesser known collections of poetry,* Roses de Noël *and* Sonailles et clochettes, *as well as his many volumes of short stories.*]

One of the striking features of Banville's poetry is its protean changeability. He moves with ease from the cynical but witty conversational monologue of a Musset to Hugolian hyperbole; he passes effortlessly from the rhythms of Villon to those of Charles d'Orléans, Clément Marot, or Ronsard; he captures accents of André Chénier or of Baudelaire; and at other times his sculptured miniatures make us think of Gautier or Heredia. In *Roses de Noël* we find yet another dimension, the poetry of memories and the family. (pp. 93-4)

Banville's purpose in *Roses de Noël* might be summed up partly by a passage in **"Exil,"** in which he says that he is sending his mother his kiss, his tender caress, his soul, and his voice, as expressions of his love. But he also had his eye on *le vert laurier* ("the green laurel"), with which he was concerned all his life. Possibly with the example of Ronsard in the back of his mind, he had the conscious ambition of immortalizing his mother (and perhaps himself). . . . (p. 95)

It is clear that Madame Banville's role in her son's life was of immense importance. She was many things to him. **"Toute mon âme"** recalls how she loved him and nursed him. She was an inspiration not only to him but also to his sister, instilling in them love of beauty and disdain for vulgarity. Banville acknowledges his debt to her for having opened the world of poetry for him (**"Ta Voix," "Le Ruisseau"**). He remembers her especially as a comforter and recalls scenes from childhood when he and his sister would run to their mother's lap to receive her kisses, which would banish all their pain.

She is something more to the man-poet. She assumes symbolic dimensions, becoming part of the stream of eternal time in which she lives on through her son. ''Et c'est toi que tu sens en moi lutter, poursuivre / Le but. . .'' (It is you whom you feel struggling in me, pursuing the goal), he says in **"Le Ruisseau,"** the opening poem, adding this unusual image: ''Telle, aux humides prés, la Naïade ravie, / Dont le sort incertain est celui du ruisseau, / Rêveuse, en flots d'argent voit s'écouler sa vie'' . . . (Thus, in watered meadows, the delighted Naiad whose fate is that of the stream, dreamy, sees her life flowing away in a silvery stream). This mythological element may seem out of place in such personal poetry, but the concept of a mythological figure partaking of the essence of nature and at the same time being distinct from it embodies exactly the relationship Banville wishes to express; namely, that in her son's life she sees her own, at the same time standing back from it and viewing it as in a mirror. (pp. 95-6)

The handful of poems scattered here and there in other collections and devoted to Banville's sister, wife, stepson, mother, father, and his native village all reflect the happiness and affection he knew in the family where he grew up and in the one he founded himself. *Roses de Noël* is the most complete poetic document relating to [marital bliss in the Banville family], and although all its poems are addressed to his mother they have biographical value to the extent that they show Banville's perception of his family and of his own life. (p. 96)

But by far the most complete evocation of his childhood is to be found in **"Pourquoi seuls?"** As memory is piled upon memory the poet's emotion is heightened and he feels an urgency to lose himself in this sea of the past. He invites his mother to share these memories, which have the power to illuminate the darkness of life, an idea to which he returns several times in the collection.

After the happy childhood comes separation:

> Entre nous, ô tourment!
> Sont les villes sans nombre et leur
>   bourdonnement,
> Le temps, les nuits, les jours, le silence,
>   l'espace,
> Les collines, les bois, les cieux, le vent
>   qui passe. . . .

> (Between us, oh torment, are cities without
> number and their buzzing, time, nights, days,
> silence, space, hills, woods, skies, the passing
> wind.)

He has drunk disgust and bitterness and learned that other kisses betray (**"Douces Larmes"**). He has found that in his "arid days" all is vanity and lies, that nothing lasts, and that hope and dreams are like roses whose petals are carried off by the night wind. Only his mother's love has remained as a talisman for him (**"Feuilles mortes"**). (p. 98)

It seems natural to refer to Banville as the poet of the *Odes Funambulesques* or even of *Les Exilés,* but who would think of calling him the poet of *Roses de Noël*? And yet this collection deserves a better fate. The fact that the poems in it are unpretentious and sometimes have about them an air of improvisation makes their art seem unobtrusive, but we should be skeptical of Banville's statement that they are not art. Few poets have held their vocation in higher esteem than Banville, and it is difficult to imagine him writing any verse without art. But in its personal lyricism the collection is unique in Banville's work. In its celebration of memory and the past it is the most Romantic of his collections and deserves more recognition than it has had as poetry of the family. It is not easy to think of another poet who, in the intensity of his joy in living, clings more avidly to every moment, unwilling to let any pass into oblivion, for the past contains the dawn of tomorrow. . . . (p. 100)

Nous Tous with ninety-six poems, *Sonnailles et Clochettes* with sixty-two, and *Dans la Fournaise* with seventy-seven, are among the largest of his collections but unfortunately not among his best. In them he was trying to realize his dream of "marrying poetry with the newspaper." He celebrates what he calls "le journalisme poétique," stating his conviction that there is a place in the newspaper for "that poetry of a very French vein, lively, ironic, precise, and lyrical," a legacy of Villon. . . . His aim was to reach a large number of readers. "Isn't it attractive to rhyme from day to day for the readers of the newspaper; that is to say, for every one?" he asks in the foreword of *Sonnailles et Clochettes*. He calls these poems *caprices légers* ("light caprices") or "petits poèmes." In a sense he was doing what he had done in the *Idylles Prussiennes,* except that his subject was not history but everyday life. Indeed, nowhere else in his poetry is the element of realism, understood as a reflection of everyday prosaic life with emphasis on its uglier aspects, as pronounced as in these last three collections.

While it cannot be contested that Banville perceived daily life with unusual intensity, his taste can occasionally be regarded as questionable. . . . He treats the most banal subjects: the weather, styles, smoking, restaurant food, hats, umbrellas, and ladies' garments. These are all part of the reality of modern life as he observes it in Paris. His love of Paris is evident. . . . [It] represents "la Vie / Moderne, frémissante, avide, inassouvie, / Belle de douleur calme et de sévérité" (modern life, pulsating, eager, unsated, beautiful in its calm sorrow and severity); and its sights, activities, and occupations are endlessly rich (**"Aimer Paris,"** *Dans la Fournaise*).

There is a seamy side to its life as well. Violence, crime, passions, prostitution, and the cult of matter are part of it. It is a kind of jungle, "Toute entière livrée à la matière vile / Et d'où le chaste azur s'efface et disparaît" (entirely given up to vile matter and where the chaste azure is erased and disappears), and men are like panting, ferocious beasts (**"La Forêt,"** *Dans la Fournaise*). **"La Nuit"** (*Sonnailles et Clochettes*) is the best of several poems evoking the night life of the city. Also comparing Paris to a dark forest inhabited by wild animals, it conveys the spirit of the city's night life through the image of the prostitute: the Seine in its bed sobs and stretches like a courtesan, while the poet kisses the burning fire on the two lips of Rhyme. Meanwhile, publishers count their money, prostitutes practice their profession, and criminals are out on the street. But Banville can never long remain earthbound; fantasy is as real as matter, and the miraculous is normal rather than exceptional. At the end of the poem we find a larger vision reminding us that life is not only the degradation of the streets:

> Et dans l'immensité des cieux
> On voit au-dessus de nos fanges
> Comme un long choeur silencieux
> Errer les figures des Anges.

> (And in the immensity of the skies can be seen
> roaming above our mire, like a long and silent
> choir, the figures of Angels.)

It is worth noting what a modern and even prophetic ring Banville's perceptions of everyday reality have. The life he presents is so often close to the problems of the twentieth century. Crime, prostitution, and poverty are of course not only modern social problems, but his ability to place them in the context of a large city makes them appear modern. (pp. 102-03)

In some instances Banville's perception of social problems might even apply to our own time. In **"Carnaval"** (*Sonnailles et Clochettes*) a man is asked why he is not dressed in a carnival costume. His reply might well remind us of the way some contemplative cults of our day are sometimes viewed: he says he is disguised as a young man analyzing himself and looking at his navel. In another poem, **"Les Grâces"** (*Dans la Fournaise),* Banville identifies three great social ills by stating that the three Graces of Greek mythology have been replaced in modern times by "Absinthe, Névrose et Morphine." Our age might call them alcoholism, mental illness, and drug abuse. Great concern is felt nowadays in much of the world about a shortage of energy resources. But we are not the first to know such fears. The speaker in a poem dated December 23, 1890, laments that soon the earth's resources will be exhausted. Wild animals will be extinct, vegetable life will disappear, the fire of the bowels of the earth will be replaced by snow, coal and other minerals will be exhausted, and hunger and disease will prevail (**"Fleur,"** *Dans la Fournaise*).

Contemporary issues often lead back to what is more permanent in the human condition. Even as the speaker reflects on the depletion of the earth's resources, a lovely girl passes by and he is reminded that, while the earth may well be old, "Comme la jeune fille est jeune!" (How young the young girl is!). Love and beauty are not exhaustible like mineral resources. But the other side of the coin, equally a part of the human condition, is the corruption of the flesh, a state powerfully suggested in an image in **"Triomphe"** *(Dans la Fournaise):* an attractive and seductive woman is presented, for whom the men will die or go mad. But when the wind lifts her dress one can see a wound festering, with edges yellow and green, infested with crawling worms, a sight that can hardly be contemplated without a shudder of disgust and revulsion.

Apart from their emphasis on the more prosaic aspects of reality, these last three collections offer little that is new, and as poetry they are not among Banville's best. Their sheer volume contributes to their repetitiveness and eventually their monotony. But when placed in the context of his total poetic output they help to form a unified whole of it in that they are a kind of recapitulation of what has preceded. We can see in them the same technical mastery, themes, attitudes, and moods. In them Banville is still preoccupied by the theme of the poet's mission and place in life, presenting him as an exile and sufferer. As in *Les Exilés* the poet is a preserver of the gods. "Car les Dieux ne seront pas morts / Tant qu'il restera des poètes" (For the gods will not be dead as long as there are poets), he concludes in **"Pessimisme"** *(Sonnailles et Clochettes).* In **"Soleil couchant"** *(Dans la Fournaise)* the sunset symbolizes a kind of *Götterdämmerung,* a twilight of the gods on the point of death. But one among them stands out, white and luminous, radiating gentleness and love. Here we see again a reflection of Banville's faith in Christ. (pp. 104-05)

Many of the aspects associated with his funambulist poetry are also present in Banville's last collections. The mixture of incongruous elements is one of them. Sometimes the effect is almost surrealistic. In **"Scientifique"** *(Sonnailles et Clochettes),* for example, nymphs appear in a Romantic moonlight setting to tell the poet that the music of the zephyrs is really the voice of spring speaking through phonographs. Familiar style, occasional use of English words, verbal surprises, and rich rhymes often forming puns are some other features we have encountered before. His enjambements are, if anything, even more daring.... Buffoonery and wit are also present. (p. 106)

[Banville's] prose fiction fills eight volumes. The last of these is a novel entitled **Marcelle Rabe,** while the other seven contain nearly three hundred short stories grouped under the following titles: *Contes pour les femmes, Contes féeriques, Contes héroïques, Contes bourgeois, Dames et Demoiselles, Les Belles Poupées,* and **Madame Robert.** *Contes pour les femmes, Dames et Demoiselles,* and **Madame Robert** are devoted largely to the theme of love. As we might expect, tales of fantasy are to be found in *Contes féeriques,* the original title of which was *Contes fantastiques.* Stories of violence predominate in *Contes héroïques,* presenting extraordinary characters and exaggerated accomplishments. *Contes bourgeois* provides an unflattering image of bourgeois life dominated by self-interest, folly, unhappiness in marriage, hypocrisy, and incomprehension of the artist. (pp. 132-33)

In a sense Banville's "Avant-Propos" to *Contes pour les femmes* may be regarded as a foreword to his short stories as a whole. It is here that he indicates what he was hoping to achieve and why he chose the short story form. He begins by remarking that whereas life styles and settings are constantly being renewed, literary forms are limited in number and for that reason

they have to be preserved and rehabilitated if they fall into disuse, as he has done for certain verse forms. He proposes to do the same for the old French *conte:*

> Today, no longer alone this time, but at the same time as other writers with a passionate interest in our origins, I am trying to restore the old French *conte,* to give an honorable place to it in our literature. It has seemed to me that with its lively and precise pace, it could marvelously well serve to represent modern life, so dense, so complicated and diverse, that it is impossible to apprehend it in large masses and that it can really only be grasped in its episodes, as in short rhapsodies, in which the innumerable skirmishes of that *Iliad* are seen and fixed on the run.

Banville's reference to the *Iliad* suggests that he is thinking of life as an epic, and in the episodic approach he envisages he is very much a man of the nineteenth century. But contrary to many of his contemporaries who wrote epics consisting of numerous individual poems, Banville proposes to write in prose and to depict modern life rather than the past. However, an outstanding and monumental model for such an undertaking already existed: Balzac's *Comédie humaine.* Indeed Banville evokes largely the same world as Balzac, attempts to situate his *milieux* with precision, and peoples his stories with characters from a variety of social strata and occupations. His ambition seems to be to produce an epic of modern Parisian life in all its complexity. (pp. 133-34)

Although many of Banville's characters are unusual, they are not epic heroes. Banville makes little distinction between fiction and reality, or fiction and fantasy. One blends into the other. Madame Récamier, Baudelaire, Buloz, Vieuxtemps, Sara Bernhardt, Gounod, and Gavarni move in the same world as fictitious characters and interact with them. Characters from mythology, legend, and history—Hercules, Roland, Proteus, for example—inhabit the same world and at the same time. But that is not all: fairies intermingle with people, Satan comes to sit for Gavarni, and the Demon of Perversity confronts Baudelaire, as if these events were part of everyday life. In this way Banville introduces too many characters from reality to create an autonomous fictional world, and too many elements of fantasy to produce the illusion of everyday life.

His world is almost never ordinary. Even when he tries to present everyday reality there is about it a certain "air de décor féerique" (atmosphere of a fairylike setting).... [The] reader encounters the supernatural and the uncommon at every turn: a naked statue appears and disappears, an American newspaper editor knows events before they occur, a swan sings.... (pp. 134-35)

At a first reading, Banville's stories may give the feeling of richness and variety of characters and events, corresponding to what he regards as the complexity and density of modern life. The impression of diversity is reinforced at times by the introduction of relatively trivial matters. For example, the first few stories in **Contes pour les femmes** are not fiction at all, but rather essays on, or discussions of, such topics as how to escort a lady, how to receive her, or how to understand her. In reality the characters are not so numerous after all. Names may change but many of the characters remain basically the same from one story to another. The poet or other artist, the prostitute, the virtuous woman—these remain essentially unchanged regardless of name. Action and events, for all their apparent diversity, in the end serve mostly to illustrate ideas or visions, very nearly the same ones as in Banville's lyric poetry and in his theater, but perhaps somewhat more somber.

In his prose fiction, if anywhere, Banville occasionally touches the boundaries of a domain dear to the Naturalists, in which social problems such as poverty, prostitution, and alcoholism are central, but he never fully enters it. As elsewhere in his writings, he is keenly aware of the imperfections of life, not only as they relate to the nature of man, but also as he sees them in his own age. (p. 135)

[The] subject of love and women is a major one in Banville's prose. Themes relating to it range from the more superficial question of etiquette, dress, and decorum to the most fundamental nature of woman and the relationship between the sexes. Discussions concerning the subtleties of love abound, not without some echoes of similar discussions in more distant periods of French literature. One dominant idea is the impossibility of perfect love on earth. (p. 136)

[Another subject is the growth of technology.] Like banality, technology erodes the autonomy of the individual and is the enemy of the creative spirit. In several of his stories he tries to imagine where a continuation of material progress may eventually lead, sometimes anticipating very nearly twentieth-century experiences. The most imaginative of these stories are **"Mademoiselle Agathe"** and **"Voleur de feu,"** both from *Contes féeriques.* . . .

"Voleur de feu" looks one hundred and fifty years into the future to the year 2030. In a sense anticipating the likes of George Orwell, it forsees interstellar and interplanetary travel, and governments dispensing light, water, heat, and even air for breathing. People have by this time become so accustomed to the loss of their individuality that, by a curious twist of Banvillean irony, one of the main concerns of 2030 is that individualism is threatening to replace "collective common sense." (p. 138)

The most important characters in Banville's stories are artists, especially poets. More frequently than any other persons they appear as observers, narrators, or protagonists, and they constitute a valuable source of information about the nature of poetry or art in a wider sense and the place of the artist in the world. The poet Etienne Saignol in **"Intermède"** *(Contes féeriques)* makes us think of Banville's art. Gifted "with an extraordinary genius for comedy and an ability in the art of making French rhymes produce somersaults and tours de force which can bring joy to jaded minds, he willingly yields to a certain taste for farce which he has drawn from the old storytellers, and in the work of this charmer with words and phrases, admirer of Aristophanes, there is a bit of the caricaturist." . . . Perhaps this characterization of Saignol's talent also explains further why Banville was attracted to the old French *conte.* As we have seen over and over, there is also "a bit of the caricaturist" in Banville and much of the verbal acrobat with a taste for comic effects.

What is striking here is that this approach "can bring joy to jaded minds." Was the comic perspective a way of reaching a wider public? It is clear that reaching a wider public was not synonymous for Banville with being a popular writer. His conception of art as noble and lofty precludes any idea of easy success through compromise. . . . It is more likely that in speaking of jaded minds Banville was thinking of the mentality that accepts the commonplace at every turn. His desire to awaken

such spirits was closely linked to what he regarded as the aim of poetry, perhaps nowhere better stated than by Saignol on the occasion of a poetry contest in the French Academy: "Poetry can have no other aim than itself, and if it can improve man it is by awakening in him the noble instinct of the beautiful, and not at all by any kind of demonstration . . .". (pp. 139-40)

What of the qualities of Banville's prose? (p. 144)

On the whole, his narrative technique is rather uniform. He usually begins with a conversation enunciating some hypothesis or idea, and then one of the speakers relates a story to illustrate it. To lend credibility to his tales, Banville sees to it that the narrator is a character who has actually experienced what is being related or has observed it. Banville takes the reader into his confidence and often gives an air of reality to the tale by making it seem that the starting point or other aspect of an event is common knowledge. For this purpose he finds the expression *comme on le sait* ("as everyone knows") particularly useful. (p. 145)

As for Banville's style generally in his short stories, the characteristics that many readers may find most striking, along with its ease and lightness, are its conciseness and economy. He has the ability to suggest a physical portrait by means of a carefully chosen detail or comparison. Consider, for example, this impression of Madame Schone in **"Le Rat qui s'est retiré du monde"** *(Fables choisies mises en prose* in *Dames et Demoiselles):* Her "little turned-up nose seemed to be trying to fly away like a bird." . . . Similarly a few brush strokes can suggest a character, as we see in **"La Fin de la fin"** *(Contes pour les femmes),* where the shrewd maid Virginie is presented in this manner: "She was Parisian, deeply corrupted, having in her heart the seven capital sins and others as well, a skillful milliner, a grinder, a talented hairdresser, learned like a book, having perfect notions of good and evil, in order always to do evil, and on special occasions if necessary knowing how to cook in order to make people eat who ordinarily never eat." . . . Such conciseness gives his narrative a rapidity sometimes recalling that of Voltaire's prose. (pp. 146-47)

Banville's conciseness sometimes manifests itself in single-sentence portraits combining physical and moral attributes. These one-sentence formulae are not limited to portraits. Maxim-like pronouncements, proverbs, pastiches, and paradoxical statements are liberally sprinkled throughout his prose. A proverb, "Là où la chèvre est attachée, il faut qu'elle broute" (the goat has to graze where she is tied up), sums up the poet's acceptance of his lot in life (**"Rue de l'Eperon,"** *Contes féeriques* . . .). (p. 147)

Banville's style is never dull. His characters, though they may lack psychological depth, are alive. His narrative techniques are sound. But in spite of the rewards that readers can surely find in Banville's prose, they are likely to come away with the feeling that he is not primarily a storyteller. Paradoxically, the man so often accused of lacking ideas appears in his prose fiction to be more interested in the ideas illustrated by the stories than in the stories themselves. Readers may also be disconcerted by a sense of disorientation in Banville's world, which makes no distinction between an autonomous realm of fiction with its own realities and the world in which we live. (p. 148)

Alvin Harms, in his Théodore de Banville, *Twayne Publishers, 1983, 184 p.*

ADDITIONAL BIBLIOGRAPHY

Grant, Elliott M. "Theodore de Banville As a Poet of Revolt." *Philological Quarterly* IV, No. 4 (October 1925): 373-80.
    Discusses Banville's poetry in relation to the social and economic developments in France during the Second Empire. Grant contends that Banville's works constitute a "vigorous and all-embracing protest against a materialistic civilization."

Jones, Louisa E. "The Literary Legend II." In her *Sad Clowns and Pale Pierrots: Literature and the Popular Comic Arts in 19th-Century France,* pp. 174-231. Lexington, Ky.: French Forum, Publishers, 1984.*
    Includes a detailed analysis of pantomime and circus iconography in Banville's poetry.

King, Russell S. "The Poet As Clown: Variations on a Theme in Nineteenth-Century French Poetry." *Orbis Literarum* 33, No. 3 (1978): 238-52.*
    A comparative study of the poet as clown in the works of Banville, Charles Baudelaire, Alfred de Musset, Paul Verlaine, Stéphane Mallarmé, and Jules Laforgue. King maintains that in *Odes funambulesques,* Banville was the "first major poet to represent the clown as a symbolic analogue of the poet."

Schaffer, Aaron. "The Sources of Théodore de Banville's *Gringoire.*" *Modern Language Notes* XXXVI, No. 4 (April 1921): 225-29.
    Discusses the historical context and sources of the drama *Gringoire.*

———. "The *Trente-six ballades joyeuses* of Theodore de Banville." *Modern Language Notes* XXXVII, No. 6 (June 1922): 328-33.*
    A poem-by-poem comparison of Banville's ballads to those of François Villon, whose style and themes Banville imitated.

———. "Anacreontic Poetry and the Funambulesque Genre (Banville, Soulary, Albert Glatigny)." In his *The Genres of Parnassian Poetry: A Study of the Parnassian Minors,* pp. 233-46. The Johns Hopkins Studies in Romance Literatures and Languages, vol. xx. Baltimore: Johns Hopkins Press; London: Humphrey Milford, 1944.
    Highlights the untranslated French critical appraisals of Banville's poetry by Maurice Souriau, Francis Vincent, and Max Fuchs.

George (Henry) Borrow

1803-1881

English novelist, linguist, essayist, translator, and travel writer.

Borrow is regarded as an imaginative and entertaining though minor English prose writer. Many of his writings were inspired by his extensive travels and his observation of human nature. He was particularly interested in the culture of the Gypsies with whom he lived, studying their language and customs. His life has proved fascinating to many commentators, including Paul Elmer More, who described him as "one of the most enigmatical and tantalizing personalities of English literature." He wrote a great deal, in many genres, and although much of his writing has been poorly received, some of it is considered a noteworthy contribution to English literature. Many of his experiences are recounted in his travel books, *The Bible in Spain; or, The Journeys, Adventures, and Imprisonments of an Englishman, in an Attempt to Circulate the Scriptures in the Peninsula* and *Wild Wales: Its People, Language, and Scenery* and in his autobiographical novels *Lavengro; The Scholar—The Gypsy—The Priest* and *The Romany Rye; A Sequel to "Lavengro."* Borrow's uniting of autobiographical fact with fiction in these and other works has stirred intense critical controversy: it has been alternately described as his greatest achievement and his most serious fault.

Borrow was born in East Dereham in Norfolk, England. Because his father was a professional soldier in a regiment that traveled extensively throughout the British Isles, Borrow's education was erratic until the family settled in Norwich, where he attended grammar school. After an apprenticeship with a solicitor from 1819 through 1824, he left for London to become a writer. He began his career by writing hackwork for the publisher Sir Richard Phillips and by contributing articles to the *Universal Review* and the *New Monthly Magazine*. Little is known about Borrow's movements during the years 1826 through 1832, to which biographers refer as his "veiled period." It is known, however, that he traveled throughout Great Britain and Europe and demonstrated his aptitude for languages by publishing his first translations, including *Faustus: His Life, Death, and Descent into Hell* by Friedrich Maximilian von Klinger and the collection *Romantic Ballads, Translated from the Danish, and Miscellaneous Pieces*.

In 1833, Borrow joined the British and Foreign Bible Society and was sent to Saint Petersburg (now Leningrad) to develop a Manchu translation of the New Testament. Two years later he returned briefly to London before departing for Portugal and Spain, where he distributed the Bible. After leaving the Bible Society in 1840, Borrow and his wife, Mary Clarke, returned to England where they settled on her estate in Oulton. There, Borrow led a reclusive existence; he demonstrated little interest in English society or contemporary literary figures, preferring instead the company of Gypsies, whom he invited to camp on his estate. Borrow soon began writing *The Zincali; or, An Account of the Gypsies of Spain* and *The Bible in Spain*, which are based on his experiences. *The Zincali* contains vivid descriptions of Spanish life, accounts of Borrow's dealings with the Gypsies, excerpts and translations from their poetry, and a glossary of their language. Although *The Zincali* was Borrow's first work to achieve critical acclaim, *The Bible in Spain*

was both a popular and critical success. The work is composed primarily of letters that Borrow wrote to the Bible Society detailing his experiences while distributing the Bible to the Spanish people. Although *The Bible in Spain* appealed to Borrow's contemporaries because of its religious themes, it can also be read as a travel book. Because of the title, many readers initially expected a straightforward and uplifting account of missionary work; instead, they were captivated by Borrow's lively and picturesque descriptions of the Spanish countryside and the customs and manners of the Spanish people.

After *The Bible in Spain* was published, many critics called on Borrow to write a history of his life. Eight years passed before he published his next work, and during this hiatus his previously appreciative audience grew impatient and eventually indifferent. Several publisher's notices of Borrow's upcoming work appeared in periodicals. The title of this much-anticipated work kept changing—from *Lavengro, A Biography*, to *Lavengro—A Dramatic History*, to *Life, a Drama*, to *Lavengro, an Autobiography*, to its final form, *Lavengro; The Scholar—The Gypsy—The Priest*—and many readers understandably looked forward to an autobiography. The work that eventually appeared confounded all expectations. Ostensibly an account of the youthful adventures of its hero, *Lavengro* is, according to the preface, "a dream, partly of study, partly of adventure," a description that sparked the continuing critical debate about whether the work's account of its youthful hero's adventures is fact or fiction. The genre perplexed both readers and critics, and *Lavengro* was unsuccessful. Six years later, Borrow published *The Romany Rye*, which recounts the narrator's further experiences with Gypsies and other outcasts. The appendix, in which he included a vitriolic attack on Catholics and on his critics, further alienated readers.

Although Borrow continued to publish original works and translations, he never again succeeded in capturing public interest. In *Wild Wales,* he chronicled his family's 1854 walking tour through Wales. The work includes descriptions of scenery, straightforward travel information, and translations and criticism of Welsh poetry. Although it marks a return to the travel narrative genre that Borrow had successfully used in the *The Bible in Spain, Wild Wales* did not share in its predecessor's success. Borrow's last work, *Romano Lavo-Lil: Word Book of the Romany; or, English Gypsy Language,* which contains a history and vocabulary of the Gypsy language, speculations on its origins, and examples of Gypsy proverbs, was equally unpopular, and he died in obscurity.

Borrow's works are difficult to classify because most contain elements of several different genres. His translations of poetry from over thirty languages, including German, Danish, Persian, Russian, Welsh, and Romany, the Gypsy tongue, are rarely discussed by critics, although some praise his ease with language while faulting his awkward versification. He devoted particular attention to Romany, and critics credit his early work, including *The Zincali* and *The Bible in Spain,* with generating public interest in the Gypsies. Yet much progress had been made in the field of comparative philology and in the study of the Gypsy language during the thirty years between the publication of *The Bible in Spain* and *Romano Lavo-Lil,* and later critics have reproached Borrow for his inferior and inaccurate scholarship in the latter work.

Borrow's prose works, including the travel books *The Bible in Spain* and *Wild Wales* and the autobiographical novels *Lavengro* and *The Romany Rye,* exhibit the qualities for which he is remembered today. Critics consistently note their loose, episodic structure and compare Borrow favorably with such picaresque writers as Daniel Defoe and Alain René Le Sage. Many have praised the "open-air" quality evident in his descriptions of life on the road. His characterizations, too, are commended for their sensitive portrayal of the Gypsies, who were new to English readers and thus provided original and intriguing subject matter.

The profound connection between Borrow's life and work has received much critical attention. More than most writers, he depended heavily upon the events of his life for his subject matter and completely disregarded the distinction between fiction and autobiography. Borrow's representation of his own personality in his works has also received consistent attention from critics fascinated by his arrogant self-confidence, humor, virulent anti-Catholicism, and romantic descriptions of life on the road among the Gypsies. While some term this trait egotistic, most consider the personal quality of his work its greatest charm and praise in particular the evolution of his narrative persona. Yet because Borrow relied so heavily on his own experiences, critics have debated whether his gift was for simple observation or imaginative creation, which many consider the distinction of an artist. This controversy is most evident in the discussion of *Lavengro* and *The Romany Rye.* Since their first publication, critics have debated whether these works should be interpreted as novels or autobiographies. According to Ian

R. Maxwell, the absence of a straightforward plot prevented Borrow's contemporaries from viewing the works as novels; they believed that the events were primarily true and only credited Borrow with the arrangement of the material. In his respected biography of Borrow, William I. Knapp treated *Lavengro* and *The Romany Rye* as autobiography, an interpretation that influenced many subsequent critics who argued that the works' formlessness and episodic nature proved Borrow's lack of artistic ability. While modern commentators agree that he relied heavily on his own experiences, many see evidence of conscious artistry in *Lavengro* and *The Romany Rye.* In the 1940s, John E. Tilford contended that early critics overlooked the works' artistry by concentrating on the authenticity of events rather than on form. Tilford and subsequent critics have examined such elements of Borrow's literary technique as his use of first person narration, the gradual unfolding of the narrator's personality, reappearing characters and themes, structure, and dialogue, and they conclude that *Lavengro* and *The Romany Rye* possess a unified form.

Borrow's popularity has declined considerably since its apogee immediately following the appearance of *The Bible in Spain.* Yet even then he was known as an author of popular works rather than as a great artist. In 1899, Knapp's appreciative biography helped to refocus attention on Borrow. A small cult of "Borrovians," ardent admirers who were as fascinated by Borrow's personality as by his work, emerged at that time, but interest again faded between the World Wars. Although his works continue to appeal to a small group, most modern readers are unacquainted with Borrow, the flamboyant wanderer and friend of the Gypsies.

PRINCIPAL WORKS

Faustus: His Life, Death, and Descent into Hell [translator; from *Fausts Leben, Thaten, und Hollenfahrt* by Friedrich Maximilian von Klinger] (novel) 1825

Romantic Ballads, Translated from the Danish, and Miscellaneous Pieces [translator] (poetry) 1826

The Zincali; or, An Account of the Gypsies of Spain (essay, dictionary, and translations) 1841

The Bible in Spain; or, The Journeys, Adventures, and Imprisonments of an Englishman, in an Attempt to Circulate the Scriptures in the Peninsula (travel narrative) 1842

Lavengro; The Scholar—The Gypsy—The Priest (autobiographical novel) 1851

The Romany Rye; A Sequel to "Lavengro" (autobiographical novel) 1857

Wild Wales: Its People, Language, and Scenery (travel narrative) 1862

Romano Lavo-Lil: Word Book of the Romany; or, English Gypsy Language (essay, dictionary, and translations) 1874

Letters of George Borrow to the British and Foreign Bible Society (letters) 1911

The Works of George Borrow. 16 vols. (travel narratives, autobiographical novels, dictionaries, essays, and translations) 1923-24

*Celtic Bards, Chiefs, and Kings (essay) 1928

*This work is believed to have been written between 1857 and 1860.

GEORGE BORROW   (essay date 1841)

[*In his preface to* The Zincali, *first published in 1841, Borrow outlines his intention in the work: to describe the Spanish Gypsies without romance, exaggeration, or malice.*]

It is with some diffidence that the author ventures to offer [*The Zincali; or, An Account of the Gypsies of Spain*] to the public.

The greater part of it has been written under very peculiar circumstances, such as are not in general deemed at all favourable for literary composition;—at considerable intervals, during a period of nearly five years passed in Spain,—in moments snatched from more important pursuits—chiefly in ventas and posádas [markets and roadside inns], whilst wandering through the country in the arduous and unthankful task of distributing the Gospel among its children.

Owing to the causes above stated, he is aware that his work must not unfrequently appear somewhat disjointed and unconnected, and the style rude and unpolished: he has, nevertheless, permitted the tree to remain where he felled it. . . . (p. xi)

At the same time he flatters himself that the work is not destitute of certain qualifications to entitle it to approbation. The author's acquaintance with the Gypsy race in general dates from a very early period of his life. . . . Whatever he has asserted, is less the result of reading than of close observation, he having long since come to the conclusion that the Gypsies are not a people to be studied in books, or at least in such books as he believes have hitherto been written concerning them.

Throughout he has dealt more in facts than in theories, of which he is in general no friend. (p. xii)

But if he has avoided as much as possible touching upon subjects which must always, to a certain extent, remain shrouded in obscurity; for example, the original state and condition of the Gypsies, and the causes which first brought them into Europe, he has stated what they are at the present day, what he knows them to be from a close scrutiny of their ways and habits, for which, perhaps, no one ever enjoyed better opportunities; and he has, moreover, given—not a few words culled expressly for the purpose of supporting a theory, but one entire dialect of their language. . . . (pp. xii-xiii)

With respect to the Gypsy rhymes in the second volume, he wishes to make one observation which cannot be too frequently repeated, and which he entreats the reader to bear in mind; they are *Gypsy compositions,* and have little merit save so far as they throw light on the manner of thinking and speaking of the Gypsy people, or rather a portion of them, and as to what they are capable of effecting in the way of poetry. It will, doubtless, be said that the rhymes are *trash*—even were it so, they are original, and on that account, in a philosophic point of view, are more valuable than the most brilliant compositions pretending to describe Gypsy life, but written by persons who are not of the Gypsy sect. Such compositions, however replete with fiery sentiments, and allusions to freedom and independence, are certain to be tainted with affectation. Now in the Gypsy rhymes there is no affectation, and on that very account they are different in every respect from the poetry of those interesting personages who figure, under the names of Gypsies, Gitános, Bohemians, &c., in novels and on the boards of the theatre.

It will, perhaps, be objected to the present work, that it contains little that is edifying in a moral or Christian point of view: to such an objection the author would reply, that the Gypsies are not a Christian people, and that their morality is of a peculiar kind, not calculated to afford much edification to what is generally termed the respectable portion of society. Should it be urged that certain individuals have found them very different from what they are represented in these volumes, he would frankly say that he yields no credit to the presumed fact, and at the same time he would refer to the vocabulary contained in the second volume, whence it will appear that the words *hoax* and *hocus* have been immediately derived from the language of the Gypsies, who, there is good reason to believe, first introduced the system into Europe, to which those words belong. (pp. xiii-xiv)

The author is anxious to direct the attention of the public towards the Gypsies, but he hopes to be able to do so without any romantic appeals in their behalf, by concealing the truth, or by warping the truth until it becomes falsehood. In the following pages he has depicted the Gypsies as he has found them, neither aggravating their crimes nor gilding them with imaginary virtues. He has not expatiated on "their gratitude towards good people, who treat them kindly and take an interest in their welfare;" for he believes that of all beings in the world they are the least susceptible of such a feeling. Nor has he ever done them injustice by attributing to them licentious habits, from which they are, perhaps, more free than any race in the creation. (pp. xv-xvi)

> *George Borrow, in a preface to his* The Zincali; or,
> An Account of the Gypsies of Spain, *Vol. I, second
> edition, John Murray, 1843, pp. xi-xvi.*

[HERMAN MERIVALE]   (essay date 1841)

[*The Zincali; or, An Account of the Gypsies of Spain*] is a strange book, of which the greatest part, as the author tells us, was written under very peculiar circumstances [see excerpt above, 1841]. . . . [We] must say that Mr. Borrow exhibits a very happy taste for making the most of his privileges and character as a cosmopolite—a knack of irritating the reader's curiosity by imparting half glimpses of the unaccountable things he has seen—the romantic corners of the earth which he has visited—the ways and learning of mysterious races of mankind with which he has become acquainted. Who does not feel a strong attraction to [such] an author . . . ? (pp. 45-6)

'In Andalusia,' says our author, 'the Gitano, or gypsy language, has been cultivated to a great degree by individuals who have sought the society of the Gitanos from a seat for their habits, their manners, and their songs; and such individuals have belonged to all classes—amongst them, noblemen and members of the priestly order.' Such as are addicted to the Gitanos and their language, are called, in Andalusia, *los del' afición,* or 'those of the predilection.' Mr. Borrow is very plainly 'one of the predilection.' His imagination seems to have been captivated, in early youth, with the romance attached to the unknown origin of his singular people, as well as the wild freedom of their habits. . . . [By virtue of his knowledge of the gypsy language,] Mr. Borrow succeeded every where in captivating their hearts, wrapt up in impenetrable hatred and distrust of strangers. They took him for one of themselves; and in that confidence they gave him a full insight into their policy, their manner of life, their savage principles of independence. (p. 47)

[Antiquarians] perhaps may consider [the second volume to be the] more valuable of the two. It contains a glossary of the Spanish dialect of the gypsies. . . . It contains also plenty of gypsy couplets, with Mr. Borrow's translations, which it seems to require a very strong dose of the 'afición' to digest at all;—resembling, but at an humble distance, those ditties in which the street minstrels of Britain inveigh against the workhouse and the new police. The only remarkable thing about them is, that the connected sense is seldom carried beyond one stanza; a curious exemplification of the unfitness of the gypsy mind for continued attention. (p. 67)

[*Herman Merivale*], *"The Gypsies of Spain," in* The Edinburgh Review, *Vol. LXXIV, No. CXLIX, October, 1841, pp. 45-67.*

[RALPH WALDO EMERSON] (essay date 1842)

[*Emerson was one of the most influential figures of the nineteenth century. An American essayist and poet, he founded the Transcendental movement and shaped a distinctly American philosophy which embraced optimism, individuality, and mysticism. His philosophy stresses the presence of ongoing creation and revelation by a god apparent in everything and everyone, as well as the essential unity of all thoughts, persons, and things in the divine whole. The following is a review of* The Zincali; *for his comments on* The Bible in Spain, *see excerpt below, 1843.*]

[*The Zincali*] is equally sure of being read here as in England, and is a most acceptable gift to the lovers of the wild and wonderful. There are twenty or thirty pages in it of fascinating romantic attraction, and the whole book, though somewhat rudely and miscellaneously put together, is animated, and tells us what we wish to know. Mr. Borrow visited the Gypsies in Spain and elsewhere . . . and seems to have been commended to this employment by the rare accomplishment of a good acquaintance with the language of this singular people. How he acquired his knowledge of their speech, which seems to have opened their hearts to him, he does not inform us; and he appears to have prospered very indifferently in the religious objects of his mission; but to have really had that in his nature of education which gave him access to the gypsy gang, so that he has seen them, talked confidentially with them, and brought away something distinct enough from them.

He has given us sketches of their past and present manner of life and employments, in the different European states, collected a strange little magazine of their poetry, and added a vocabulary of their language. He has interspersed some anecdotes of life and manners, which are told with great spirit.

This book is very entertaining, and yet, out of mere love and respect to human nature, we must add that this account of the Gypsy race must be imperfect and very partial, and that the author never sees his object quite near enough. For, on the whole, the impression made by the book is dismal; the poverty, the employments, conversations, mutual behavior of the Gypsies, are dismal; the poetry is dismal. Men do not love to be dismal, and always have their own reliefs. If we take Mr. Borrow's story as final, here is a great people subsisting for centuries unmixed with the surrounding population, like a bare and blasted heath in the midst of smiling plenty, yet cherishing their wretchedness, by rigorous usage and tradition, as if they loved it. It is an aristocracy of rags, and suffering, and vice, yet as exclusive as the patricians of wealth and power. We infer that the picture is false; that resources and compensations exist, which are not shown us. . . . The condition of the Gypsy may be bad enough, tried by the scale of English comfort, and yet appear tolerable and pleasant to the Gypsy, who finds attractions in his out-door way of living, his freedom, and

sociability, which the Agent of the Bible Society does not reckon. And we think that a traveller of another way of thinking would not find the Gypsy so void of conscience as Mr. Borrow paints him, as the differences in that particular are universally exaggerated in daily conversation. And lastly, we suspect the walls of separation between the Gypsy and the surrounding population are less firm than we are here given to understand. (pp. 127-28)

[*Ralph Waldo Emerson*], *in a review of "The Zincali; or, An Account of the Gypsies of Spain," in* The Dial, *Vol. III, No. I, July, 1842, pp. 127-28.*

RICHARD FORD (letter dates 1842)

[*Ford was a contemporary admirer of Borrow. Critics believe that his comments on* The Zincali *in the following letters to Borrow, dated June 7, September 3, and September 12, 1842, in addition to his review of that work (see excerpt below, 1842), greatly influenced Borrow while he was writing* The Bible in Spain. *Here, Ford exhorts Borrow to concentrate in his next work on his own experiences and observations rather than on the artistic aspects of his writings. For Ford's review of* The Bible in Spain, *see excerpt below, 1843.*]

How I wish you had given us more about yourself [in *The Zincali*], instead of the extracts from those blunder-headed old Spaniards, who knew nothing about Gypsies! I shall give you a *rap* on that, and a hint to publish your whole adventures for the last twenty years.

I am glad to see that you are accustomed to a little bantering on the company you have kept and the small spiritual success. I have been much entertained with your book and hope to make a review like it—that is, entertaining and instructive. (pp. 353-54)

⋆ ⋆ ⋆ ⋆ ⋆

My advice again and again is to avoid all fine writing, all descriptions of mere scenery and trivial events. What the world wants are racy, real, genuine scenes, and the more out of the way the better. Poetry is utterly to be avoided. If Apollo were to come down from heaven, John Murray would not take his best manuscript as a gift. Stick to yourself, to what you have been, and the people you have mixed with. The more you give us of odd Jewish people the better. . . . Avoid *words*, stick to *deeds*. Never think of how you express yourself; for good matter *must* tell, and no fine writing will make bad matter good. Don't be afraid that what *you* may not think good will not be thought so by others. It often happens just the reverse. . . . New facts seen in new and strange countries will please everybody; but old scenery, even Cintra, will not. We know all about that, and want something that we do not know. . . . The grand thing is to be bold and to avoid the common track of the silver paper, silver fork, blue-stocking. Give us adventure, wild adventure, journals, thirty language book, sorcery, Jews, Gentiles, rambles, and the *interior* of Spanish prisons—the way you got in, and the way you got out. No author has yet given us a Spanish prison. Enter into the iniquities, the fees, the slang, etc. It will be a little *à la Thurtell*, but you see the people like to have it so. Avoid rant and cant. Dialogues always tell; they are dramatic and give an air of reality.

⋆ ⋆ ⋆ ⋆ ⋆

I hear from Murray that you have a ***Bible in Spain*** on hand. Enrich it with personal scenes and adventures. Give us a peep into Spanish prisons. Sprinkle it with anecdotes of your own rambles in out of the way lands.

Avoid more descriptions—*palabras* [words]. Stick to facts—your own biography, languages—how you learnt them, what you know, where you have been. Everything about prisons *must* take. People like to know about things which *excite,* and which they never have seen themselves and never would wish to see. Throw the Spanish treatises overboard. They are always twaddlers, did not dare write the truth, wrote for an ignorant prejudiced people who only wanted to have their own mistaken notions confirmed. (pp. 361-62)

> *Richard Ford, from four letters to George Borrow from June 7, 1842 to September 12, 1842, in* Life, Writings and Correspondence of George Borrow (1803-1881), *Vol. I, edited by William I. Knapp, G. P. Putnam's Sons, 1899, pp. 353-54, 361-62.*

[JOHN GIBSON LOCKHART] (essay date 1842)

[*Although Lockhart wrote several novels, his fame rests on his biography of Sir Walter Scott and his critical contributions to* Blackwood's Edinburgh Magazine *and the* Quarterly Review. *From 1817 to 1825, he was a principal contributor to* Blackwood's, *a Tory periodical that was founded to counter the influential Whig journal* The Edinburgh Review. *His trenchant wit contributed to the early success of the magazine and earned him the nickname of "The Scorpion." Later, as editor of the* Quarterly, *he was a less acerbic critic. He is regarded as a versatile, if somewhat severe, critic whose opinions of his contemporaries, though lacking depth, are generally considered accurate when not distorted by political animosities. In the following excerpt, Lockhart reviews* The Zincali *and* The Bible in Spain.]

[The literary merits of **'The Zincali'**] were considerable—but balanced by equal demerits. Nothing more vivid and picturesque than many of its descriptions of scenery and sketches of adventure: nothing more weak and confused than every attempt either at a chain of reasoning, or even a consecutive narrative of events that it included. It was evidently the work of a man of uncommon and highly interesting character and endowments; but as clearly he was quite raw as an original author. The glimpses of a most curious and novel subject that he opened were, however, so very striking, that, on the whole, that book deserved well to make a powerful impression, and could not but excite great hopes that his more practised pen would hereafter produce many things of higher consequence. [**'The Bible in Spain'**] will, we apprehend, go far to justify such anticipations. In point of composition, generally, Mr. Borrow has made a signal advance; but the grand point is, that he seems to have considered and studied himself in the interval; wisely resolved on steadily avoiding in future the species of efforts in which he had been felt to fail; and on sedulously cultivating and improving the peculiar talents which were as universally acknowledged to be brilliantly displayed in numerous detached passages of his **'Gipsies.'** (pp. 169-70)

[We congratulate Mr. Borrow sincerely on **'The Bible in Spain',**] a work which must vastly increase and extend his reputation—which bespeaks everywhere a noble and generous heart—a large and vigorous nature, capable of sympathising with everything but what is bad—religious feelings deep and intense, but neither gloomy nor narrow—a true eye for the picturesque, and a fund of real racy humour. (p. 197)

> [*John Gibson Lockhart*], "*Borrow's 'Bible in Spain'*," *in* The Quarterly Review, *Vol. LXXI, No. CXLI, December, 1842, pp. 169-97.*

THE EXAMINER (essay date 1842)

[*The Bible in Spain*] is a most remarkable book. Highly as we praised the *Gypsies of Spain,* much as we had reason to expect from any subsequent effort of the writer, we were certainly not prepared for anything so striking as this. Apart from its adventurous interest, its literary merit is extraordinary. Never was book more legibly impressed with the unmistakeable mark of genius. . . .

[We] say of the *Bible in Spain* that notwithstanding its sober, grave, and truthful pretensions, it has of nothing reminded us so much as of dear delightful *Gil Blas* [a novel by Alain Réné Le Sage]. It has surprising vigour, raciness, and originality of style; the combination, in its narrative of extraordinary minuteness, vivacity, and local truth; it has wonderful variety of grades of character, and an unceasingly animated interest of adventure; notwithstanding some peculiar and strongly-marked opinions of the writer, it has a wide tolerance and an untiring sympathy; notwithstanding the gravity of its purpose, its tone is gay, good-humoured, witty and light-hearted: in a word, it is a captivating book. Perhaps no man ever made so good a hero to himself as Mr Borrow. He is of heroic stuff. Without a pretence or an affectation, he is constantly before us: never compromising a single opinion, he never forfeits a single sympathy. He is so evidently a pure-minded, sincere, and honest man. He believes, loves, endures—or he disbelieves, hates, contests—with almost childish singleness and truth of heart. It is as impossible to doubt his creed in religion as to question his charity in social practice. You may think the one as narrow and sectarian as you please, but you cannot deny the universality and gentleness of the other. . . .

These qualities, we say, make a hero of Mr Borrow. . . . (p. 804)

> *A review of "The Bible in Spain," in* The Examiner, *No. 1820, December 17, 1842, pp. 804-05.*

[RICHARD FORD] (essay date 1842)

[*Ford's lengthy review of* The Zincali *closely recounts Borrow's experiences in Spain and praises the author's first-hand knowledge of the Spanish Gypsies, the subject of that work. In the excerpt below, Ford praises Borrow's vigorous and racy style yet faults him for the lack of organization which he feels renders the work fragmentary and repetitious. Ford's remarks here and in his letters to Borrow (see excerpt above, 1842) are believed to have profoundly influenced Borrow in the composition of* The Bible in Spain. *For Ford's comments on that work, see excerpt below, 1843.*]

Mr. Borrow, in spite of his name and subject, is a very original author, which is something nowadays, when men, women and children all write, and all very much like one another. He is the legitimate father of his own book [*The Zincali*]; he has neither kidnapped nor disfigured the offspring of other people's brains; the smell of the field and tent is on his pages, not that of a folio-garnished laboratory, where new books are manufactured out of old materials. He has never been initiated into that mystery; his works, like those of all clever but self-taught artists, whether handling pen or pencil, show that he has never had a regular master; the rough gipsey-colt has never been in the hands of Dr. Dionysius Lardner.

Mr. Borrow suits his style to his theme. His desultory chapters stroll from subject to subject, defying the critic as his vagrant heroes do the constable; there is no mistake in their costume or complexion; they are tanned with the brownest dye of the

Sierra Morena; they tell the tale of their birth, parentage and education, picked up, just as they came to his hand, on the highways and byways. Mr. Borrow, finding his capacious pockets were getting too full and too heavy for his locomotive propensities, has turned out the heterogeneous items without giving himself the trouble to arrange them; he has jumped into type just as an otter does into a pond, from an instinctive feeling that it would be a comfort. We have here the cream of his mind, the first run of the grapes before the screw of the press has been applied, or the process of rectification or adulteration commenced.

He pleads, in defence of sins of omission and commission, "a want of leisure to amend his rude, unpolished and unconnected pages," etc.; "he has suffered the tree to remain where he felled it" [see excerpt above, 1841]. This excuse will not do. No defendant can be permitted to take advantage of his own *lâches* [carelessness]. If he comes into court a claimant for the honours and profits of literature, he must observe the rules of the tribunal. There are indeed plenty of cubic feet of sound timber in his tree, but he must saw it up himself; the public customer looks for scantlings, not for logs. Mr. Borrow is too full of curious stuff to be allowed to bolt out of the course at his first start for want of breaking.

We do not quarrel hypercritically with mere style; rough notes, dotted down on the spot with the coarsest lead-pencil, are worth, as Gray said, a cartload of recollections refurbished in the closet. The sayings and doings of gipsies can scarcely be written down

> upon gilt-edged paper,
> With a neat crow-quill slight and new.

There is a certain fitness in a bold, broad touch, which gives to sketches made from real nature a force and identity. . . . It is precisely when Mr. Borrow takes the most pains that he fails; he cannot conceal the art, the study which he has bestowed; his high-wrought passages, as might be expected from his acquaintance with Spanish literature, are apt to be somewhat stilty and overdone. His own natural style, although irregular, is racy, graphic and vigorous: he only wants to be put in the right way, for we fully acquit him of writing negligently on purpose; his whole book shows that the quality of his mind is honest, practical and straightforward, and that he hates pretension and affectation. Our objections lie to the plan, to the framework of his book; there is no well-defined object steadily begun, continued and worked out: like a petted spaniel he plays with his food, and never picks the bone clean after the fashion of a hungry terrier. His portfolio contains sparkling and detached bits of scenery and costume, but no panoramic view, which, taken from a commanding eminence, brings the whole subject before the mind's eye, and fixes a defined impression on the memory. It is too fragmentary, too much a thing of shreds and patches; it may be compared to the several tunes of an itinerant organ, which, however pleasing in themselves, are anything but a sonata, and, what is worse, the same airs come over and over again. Thus we have frequent repetitions in these pages, and the amount of information which, if brought together, would have been considerable, is weakened by being scattered. (pp. 367-69)

> [*Richard Ford*], *"Borrow's 'Account of the Gipsies of Spain',"* in *The British and Foreign Review, Vol. XIII, No. XXVI, 1842, pp. 367-415.*

[RICHARD FORD]   (essay date 1843)

[*Although Ford had earlier faulted* The Zincali *for its lack of organization (see excerpt above, 1842), in this laudatory review of* The Bible in Spain *he only complains about the fact that Borrow has not revealed enough about himself. Ford's essay also contains a lengthy discussion of Spanish history and religion that condemns Spanish Catholics, describing them as intolerant bigots and fanatics.*]

Mr Borrow does not profess to be a 'tourist or writer of books of travel;' his is the record of a missionary adventure in a benighted land from whence many Xaviers have sallied forth, but where few have entered. **'The Bible in Spain'** and its first appearance—this juxtaposition of things having no apparent connexion, brings the serious, solemn, and sublime in constant contact with the ridiculous, the lowly, and the wicked. The book is a spiritual 'Don Quixote,' a 'Gil Blas,' a 'Pilgrim's Progress' into a land of contradiction; where exception is the rule, where the virtues and civilization of Christian Europe clash with the vices and barbarism of the heathen East. Its author, if at times serious even unto sadness, is never churlish or ascetic—never morose or misanthropic; the milk of human-kindness flows in his veins; his disposition is cheerful, such as becomes the bearer of tidings of peace—solemn as becomes their vital import. His every feeling is an inlet of joy; his pages, true exponents of the man, are studded with heartfelt admiration for the beauties of nature; and the rare feasts spread every where as for a banquet in this 'valley of the shadow of death.'

The **'Gypsies of Spain'** [also known as **'The Zincali'**], Mr Borrow's former work, was a Spanish olla—a hotch-potch of the jockey tramper, philologist, and missionary. It was a thing of shreds and patches—a true book of Spain; the chapters, like her bundle of unamalgamating provinces, were just held together, and no more, by the common tie of religion; yet it was strange, and richly flavoured with genuine *borracha*. It was the first work of a diffident, unexperienced man, who, mistrusting his own powers, hoped to conciliate critics by leaning on Spanish historians and gypsy poets. These corks, if such a term can be applied to the ponderous levities by which he was swamped, are now cast aside; he dashes boldly into the tide, and swims gallantly over the breakers. (p. 105)

[Although, in Borrow's words,] the 'descriptions of scenery and sketches of character have been supplied from memory,' they are fresh and entire. It is the identity of the *camera lucida;* the country is drawn with the daylight of a sketch made out of doors, and on the spot; the figures in the foreground, as if they had sat for their portraits. Mr Borrow's memory must be prodigious; doubtless his facility of acquiring language is connected with this natural faculty. A constant reference to a serious soul-absorbing end, concentrated attention; long and solitary rides in lonely Spain, throw a man on himself, and engender a reflective communing habit; facts and things are fixed, and associated with each other; the slight and single threads by which each particular is tied, are drawn up one after another, until thickening into a rope, they raise a whole existence from the deep wells of memory; a trifle of no apparent importance furnishes the key wherewith is unlocked a cabinet of things rare and strange, which are docketed and put away; the match is applied to a train of dormant recollections, which light up into bright joys, or may be into the wormwood of bitterness; a rude touch shakes down from the cypress branch the rain-drops long suspended, which start into a shower of tears.

How much has Mr Borrow yet to remember, yet to tell! let him not delay. His has been a life, one day of which is more crowded than is the fourscore-year vegetation of a squire or alderman. Hitherto not even the rapid succession of events which usually obliterate each other, has dimmed the vivid recollections of our author; every thing seems sealed on a memory, wax to receive and marble to retain. He is not subjective. He has the new fault of not talking about self. We vainly wish to know what sort of a person must be the pilgrim in whose wanderings we have been interested: That he has left to other pens. (pp. 135-36)

> [*Richard Ford*], *in a review of "The Bible in Spain; or, The Journeys, Adventures, and Imprisonments of an Englishman, in an Attempt to Circulate the Scriptures in the Peninsula," in* The Edinburgh Review, *Vol. LXXVII, No. CLV, February, 1843, pp. 105-38.*

[RALPH WALDO EMERSON]   (essay date 1843)

[*The Bible in Spain*] is a charming book, full of free breezes, and mountain torrents, and pictures of romantic interest. Mr. Borrow is a self-sufficing man of free nature, his mind is always in the fresh air; he is not unworthy to climb the sierras and rest beneath the cork trees where we have so often enjoyed the company of [Miguel de Cervantes's] Don Quixote. And he has the merit, almost miraculous to-day, of leaving us almost always to draw our own inferences from what he gives us. We can wander on in peace, secure against being forced back upon ourselves, or forced sideways to himself. It is as good to read through this book of pictures, as to stay in a house hung with Gobelin tapestry. The Gipsies are introduced here with even more spirit than in his other book [*The Zincali*]. He sketches men and nature with the same bold and clear, though careless touch. (pp. 534-35)

> [*Ralph Waldo Emerson*], *in a review of "The Bible in Spain; or, The Journeys, Adventures, and Imprisonments of an Englishman in an Attempt to Circulate the Scriptures in the Peninsula," in* The Dial, *Vol. III, No. IV, April, 1843, pp. 534-35.*

[P. A. MURRAY]   (essay date 1843)

[*The* Dublin Review, *from which the following excerpt was taken, was considered the central voice of Catholicism in Great Britain during the nineteenth century. Murray condemns the anti-Catholic bias of* The Bible in Spain *and of Richard Ford's review of that work in the* Edinburgh Review *(see excerpt above, 1843).*]

Truly these are magnificent eulogiums [in Richard Ford's essay in the *Edinburgh Review*] and scattered with no sparing hand; such as might befit some shadowy being of the poet's dream, some being who wanted but "the adornment of bright wings," to look like an inhabitant of a higher sphere—an angel of peace, whose feet are beautiful on the mountains, whose glance is sunshine, whose voice is music. Well, we read the extracts from Mr. Borrow's book in the *Edinburgh Review,* and then we sent for the book itself, and read it attentively. Alas! what a change came over the lovely vision of human perfection which the reviewer had conjured up before our too easy imagination. This serious, and sweet, and cheerful creature, with the "inlets of joy," and the "studded pages," this new evangelist, this wingless cherub stood revealed before us, in his own reality—a gloomy bigot, and furious fanatic; petulant, frivolous, cynical, vulgar, pedantic; tasteless, arrogant, abusive. We speak of him only as he has pictured himself in his own book, as he exists there: who George Borrow is, or rather what he is, we know not, except as far as his book and his reviewer tell us. His book is a clumsy, ill-written, disgusting libel upon Catholicity; and, but for the virulent anti-Catholic phrenzy that pervades it, we can hardly conceive it possible

that it would have found a dozen readers, or a single panegyrist. Frantic antipathy to the Pope, and to every thing Catholic, not only forms the burden of these three (for there are *three*) volumes, but it is the whole, their alpha and omega, their body and spirit: take this away, and you do not leave even a gibbering skeleton behind. In reading them through, we felt as one in a night-mare, with all the goblins dancing on him; as one in pitchy darkness with a troop of devils yelling in his ears. (pp. 448-49)

[We] could give but the faintest and poorest idea of the stuff which forms his work. Such may be, for aught we know, the sort of fare most suited to the taste of those who read the ordinary books of travels: but of the Bible in Spain we read very little; and of that little, we believe very little. The history of his direct labours in the circulation of the Scriptures, might be comprised in about one-twentieth the bulk of the entire narrative: and the account of his success might be expressed in a single word—nothing. No, we need not look for a Gypsey or a Turkish phrase, to tell what he has effected, in his efforts to illuminate the gentiles of Spain: a common English term expresses all—nothing, absolutely nothing. (pp. 452-53)

> [*P. A. Murray*], *in a review of "The Bible in Spain; or, The Journeys, Adventures, and Imprisonments of an Englishman, in an Attempt to Circulate the Scriptures in the Peninsula," in* Dublin Review, *Vol. XIV, No. XXVIII, May, 1843, pp. 443-80.*

GEORGE BORROW   (essay date 1851)

[*The following excerpt is from Borrow's often-quoted preface to* Lavengro. *His description of the work as "a dream, partly of study, partly of adventure" has sparked the ongoing critical debate on the precise nature of the work and the success of Borrow's mixture of fact and fiction. In addition to the portion excerpted below, the preface includes a diatribe against Catholicism, or "Popery."*]

[In *Lavengro: The Scholar—The Gypsy—The Priest,*] I have endeavoured to describe a dream, partly of study, partly of adventure, in which will be found copious notices of books, and many descriptions of life and manners, some in a very unusual form.

The scenes of action lie in the British Islands;—pray be not displeased, gentle reader, if perchance thou hast imagined that I was about to conduct thee to distant lands, and didst promise thyself much instruction and entertainment from what I might tell thee of them. I do assure thee that thou hast no reason to be displeased, inasmuch as there are no countries in the world less known by the British than these selfsame British Islands, or where more strange things are every day occurring, whether in road or street, house or dingle.

The time embraces nearly the first quarter of the present century: this information again may, perhaps, be anything but agreeable to thee; it is a long time to revert to, but fret not thyself, many matters which at present much occupy the public mind originated in some degree towards the latter end of that period, and some of them will be treated of.

The principal actors in this dream, or drama, are, as you will have gathered from the title-page, a Scholar, a Gypsy, and a Priest. Should you imagine that these three form one, permit me to assure you that you are very much mistaken. Should there be something of the Gypsy manifest in the Scholar, there is certainly nothing of the Priest. With respect to the Gypsy—

decidedly the most entertaining character of the three—there is certainly nothing of the Scholar or the Priest in him; and as for the Priest, though there may be something in him both of scholarship and gypsyism, neither the Scholar nor the Gypsy would feel at all flattered by being confounded with him.

Many characters which may be called subordinate will be found, and it is probable that some of these characters will afford much more interest to the reader than those styled the principal. The favourites with the writer are a brave old soldier and his helpmate, an ancient gentlewoman who sold apples, and a strange kind of wandering man and his wife.

Amongst the many things attempted in this book is the encouragement of charity, and free and genial manners, and the exposure of humbug, of which there are various kinds, but of which the most perfidious, the most debasing, and the most cruel, is the humbug of the Priest. (pp. 1-2)

> *George Borrow, in a preface to his* Lavengro: The Scholar—The Gypsy—The Priest, *1851. Reprint by E. P. Dutton & Co., 1906, pp. 1-4.*

[WILLIAM BODHAM DONNE]   (essay date 1851)

> [*Donne views* Lavengro *as a narrative through which Borrow simultaneously recounted his adventures and speculated on the meaning of life. He praises the work's mixture of imagination with fact, a characteristic that many other early critics found confusing.*]

[In his preface to "**Lavengro**" (see excerpt above, 1851)] Mr. Borrow designates his present work as "a dream of study and adventure;" and the word *dream,* admitting of wide interpretation, and not having been, as we think, in this instance, rightly interpreted, has induced many persons to believe the narrative to be wholly imaginative, or that, at least, it deals indiscriminately with fact and fiction. Indeed, more than one of Mr. Borrow's recent critics have complained that now he has pitched his gipsies' tent upon debateable ground, and that the facts, if facts they be, are disguised by embellishment, while the fiction is incumbered by some lingering shackles of reality. We believe, however, these objections to rest upon a misconception of the author's meaning in his employment of the word "dream." Mr. Borrow weighs his words well, and has, in our opinion, used the term advisedly. In fact, with the purpose he had in view, we do not see that he could have chosen a more exact or expressive word.

For "**Lavengro**" begins from the beginning, from the place of birth and the parish-register. It traces from earliest infancy the awakening and the growth of the author's mind, as well as the accidents which determined or modified his singular career. Circumstances are accordingly mentioned in its pages, conversations recorded, scenes described, and characters analysed, of which, from their date, the author himself can have retained only a most dim recollection, even when he has not derived his information wholly from the reports of others. Such reminiscences, however imbibed, float on the farthest horizon of the past, are disconnected from contemporary acts and emotions; and thus resemble the scenery of dreams, in which the separate links of reality are connected and coloured by imaginative accessories. To the man, indeed, childhood is little more than a dream. He exaggerates its happiness; he imperfectly remembers its infelicities; he recalls its days rather than its seasons; and when he attempts to re-unite its intervals and fragments, his fancy rather than his memory aids him in the process of re-construction. In every record of a man's life the introductory chapters are more or less dreamlike.

We are far, however, from distrusting the memory of manhood, when it reverts to the scenes and sources of its first impressions. The virgin-tablets of the mind are the most susceptible, capacious and retentive. Facts are imbedded, feelings stamped indelibly, and words, even casual words are traced upon the brain of childhood in characters of fire. . . .

We do not, therefore, ascribe to the word "dream," in Mr. Borrow's preface, any meaning incompatible with a certain reality in the adventures or with the essential veracity of "**Lavengro.**" But it is neither, strictly speaking, an autobiography nor a book of travels. It partakes of the nature of both, but it aims at something higher and more comprehensive than either. In the first place it describes the formative causes and the progressive stages of its author's mind; and in the next it traces some of those by-currents of life which rather accompany than aggrandise the main social stream. Mr. Borrow has studied man and acquired the speech of man in unusual scenes and in rarely-frequented schools, at the bridge-foot and on the moorland, beside great waters and in wooded dingles, in the hubbub of the market and in the silence of plains. His pictures are symbolic daguerreotypes. They represent living scenes; but they also suggest much more than they represent. His gipsies, his Armenians, his Jews, his Methodists, his tinkers, his landlords, and his bruisers are representative men. Their language suggests to him philological speculations; their habits furnish him with ethnological and physiological hints; their virtues and their vices equally point to many unrecorded social phenomena. "**Lavengro**" is, in short, a species of poetic drama, which combines the veracity of Hogarth with the visions of Bunyan. (p. 271)

"**The Scholar, the Gipsy, and the Priest**" is a poem—wanting, indeed, the accompaniment of verse, but possessing all the other attributes of an imaginative work of a high order. Fact and fancy, indeed, interpenetrate one another like the hues of shot-silk. Where actual scenes and persons are described, Lavengro adheres to his original with scrupulous veracity. He is giving evidence upon strange yet serious matters, and he permits himself no license of invention. When, on the other hand, the purposes of his work demand a normal, rather than a special exposition of races, principles, or social phenomena, his imagination knows no other law than the law of harmony and probability—the law which regulates the "Œdipus" of Sophocles, the Vision of Dante, the Weird Sisters and the fairy people of "Macbeth" and the "Midsummer Night's Dream," and the Witch Sabbath in "Faust." To discredit the reality of "**Lavengro**" because of its imaginative accessories, to overlook the imaginative accessories because of their marriage with fact, is a kind of criticism which would reject Shakspeare's historical plays because they contain some passages from Hall's Chronicle, or [Dante's] "Divina Comedia" because it alludes to events and depicts characters familiar to every Florentine of the fourteenth century. (p. 273)

> [*William Bodham Donne*], *in a review of "Lavengro," in* Tait's Edinburgh Magazine, *Vol. 18, January, 1851, pp. 270-76.*

THE LITERARY WORLD   (essay date 1851)

An extraordinary book by an extraordinary man, will be the sentence which will escape the lips of most readers upon laying down, in a state of excited, breathless suspense, this volume of *Lavengro.* It is the autobiography, shadowed forth more or less vaguely or directly, of George Borrow, the Gipsy adventurer, the distributor of the Sacred Scriptures, the vivid narrator, and, withal, the most irrefragable Englishman of the— *Bible in Spain.* It is a curious record of a life, certainly remarkable in incident, but, perhaps, equally as remarkable for the direct, intense perception of ordinary things which may happen to many men, but to few of whom is given an unsealed vision to perceive, or the miraculous art—seemingly a simple one—of presenting them in the unrefracting medium of a clear, manly, forthright style. To George Borrow the whole world is vital. Everyday events come from him with the air of romance. The streets through which you walk in his pages have a firmer outline than in other men's books, and a clearer perspective; as for the men you meet with, you see them in intense life and individuality—yet the portraits are painted by a few strokes of the pencil. It is a word and a blow throughout. (p. 148)

* * * * *

Mr. Borrow, in his preface, tells us that his book contains "many descriptions of life and manners, some in a very unusual form" [see excerpt above, 1851]. The reader will be tempted to exclaim, very unusual! as he is startled by the novelty of a heroine in an old apple woman on old London bridge, the hustling of an Armenian by a pickpocket, the exchange of a Bible for a copy of *Moll Flanders,* a poisoning by an old gipsy woman, a gentleman of education with white hands tooling a donkey cart about England to mend holes in old brass kettles and the like of that: a dog-fight in dirty Westminster, alternating with a prayer-meeting in Wales; an encounter with a bully on the road, the "Flaming Tinman''—but with all this he will find a good sound substratum of humanity—a probability in the improbability of the apple woman, healthy, hearty animalism in the "stand up" with the tinman. (p. 168)

> *A review of "Lavengro," in* The Literary World, *Vol. VIII, Nos. 212 and 213, February 22 and March 1, 1851, pp. 148-50; 168-70.*

[WILLIAM STIRLING] (essay date 1851)

[*Like many contemporary and subsequent critics of* Lavengro, *Stirling faults its mixture of fact and fiction and contends that "the whole tone of the narrative inspires a profound distrust."*]

After the publication of *The Zincali,* and the still more successful *Bible in Spain,* George Borrow became an object of much curiosity. And if we read him aright, this is what he likes best in the world. Others desire to have their names sounded by the loud blast of fame; Mr. Borrow would choose that men should hold their breath at the mention of him. . . . In *The Zincali* he displays immense knowledge of gypsies, thieves, and the outcasts of society—displays it prodigally and ostentatiously, but never hints at the mode of its acquisition. So also in *The Bible in Spain,* though he details minutely all his proceedings there, he is silent as to his antecedents and— relatives. The book opens off Cape Finisterre, and closes at Tangier. He knows all languages; he dives into all secrets. He mystifies everybody, but nobody mystifies him. The Jews take him for a Jew; the gypsies for a gypsy. He makes revelations concerning the things of Spain which would astound the Minister of the Interior or the Prefect of Police. Circumstances are his creatures. His universe seems to divide itself into two parts, George Borrow, active; the universe, *minus* George Borrow, passive. No wonder that so many simple people thought him uncanny. . . . At the very least, if he be a mere mortal, his life

has not run in the humdrum routine to which most of us are condemned, and must be well worth the reading, provided always that George Borrow would have the goodness to write it.

Whether [*Lavengro*] is an autobiography, whether it is even *meant* to be an autobiography, we are as much at a loss to pronounce after reading the three volumes, as we were after reading the title-page. The author commences his Preface by stating that he has endeavoured to describe 'a dream, partly of study, partly of adventure' [see excerpt above, 1851]. Does he mean by this phrase to re-assert a doctrine which, we are told, was a favourite thesis with him in his youth; viz. that *life* is a dream—that the things of sense *are* not, but only *seem?* 'By this ye may perceive that life's a dream.' 'We are such stuff as dreams are made of,' &c. &c. A hundred commonplaces from the poets might be quoted in confirmation of a theory which Berkeley has supported, and which may, perhaps, be inferred from Plato; but a doubting world is not to be converted by a parenthesis of Mr. Borrow. He ought surely to have vouchsafed us some explanation. Philosophy apart, is this a history of his life, or a romance of which he is the hero? If we assume it to be the latter, while it is really the former, we may give mortal offence by questioning the possibility of this or that incident. And it is our earnest wish to keep on good terms with the man who fought and thrashed the Flaming Tinman—unless, indeed, he dreamed it. (pp. 272-73)

The story of *Lavengro* will content no one. It is for ever hovering between Romance and Reality, and the whole tone of the narrative inspires a profound distrust. Nay, more, it will make us disbelieve the tales in *The Zincali* and *The Bible in Spain.*

We have more than once been struck by a resemblance between George Borrow and Hermann Melville. People were inclined to believe in *Typee* and *Omoo,* till their author, grown bold by impunity, ventured on *Mardi.* Both authors are utterly destitute of the dramatic, or, to speak pedantically, the mimetic faculty. In Borrow's former books this want was less apparent. In the case of Spanish gypsies and Barbary Jews, classes with which one's acquaintance is slight, one was inclined to suppose that they *might* habitually talk *à la Borrow;* but when we find the same language put into the mouths of our own countrymen and countrywomen, we then see that it is George Borrow himself who is spokesman for all. In one respect, and one only, this book is an improvement on his last; it is free from that threadbare cant which jarred so incongruously with the jockeyism.

While galloping over the *dehesas* [pastures] and *despoblados* [wilderness] of Spain, he was wont (as we all remember) to shoe his horse with a text and break his fast with a pious ejaculation, producing them, bagman-like, as specimens of the article he had for sale; and if ever a rencontre with his congenial gypsies tempted him away from the main subject, he used to make up for it by inflicting a sermon on his readers. Now all is changed; he writes as if he were little better than one of the wicked. There was a time when he denounced pugilism as 'brutalizing and degrading,' now he laments its decline, and prognosticates, therefore, national defeat. In these, and other respects, *Lavengro* is the very antithesis of *The Bible in Spain.* (p. 282)

On the other hand, the egotism of the writer is as conspicuous and as offensive as ever—all the more offensive, perhaps, because it consists rather in what he assumes and implies than what he says. Everybody marvels at his wisdom, everybody is influenced by his will. He treats the round world as if it were a foot-ball made for his sport. 'His education,' he tells us, 'is perfect.' 'No mean judge has pronounced him to be Lavengro,' the master of words, *the* philologist and scholar, *par excellence*. We very much question whether his knowledge of languages be higher in kind than that of a polyglott courier. A philologist is one who studies, not languages, but language. Mr. Borrow is perpetually displaying his acquaintance with words, words, words! whether he knows anything of the respective structures and mutual relations of this and that language, we have yet to learn. For all that appears, he is no more a philologist than a stone-mason is an architect. (pp. 282-83)

We trust that the apparent pedantry and egotism of *Lavengro* have not provoked us into any expressions which might seem to exceed the fair license of the reviewer. Indeed, we should not have devoted so much space to the analysis of the book did we not suppose the author to be capable of better things. With his really extensive knowledge of books, men, and life, he could well afford to divest himself of assumption and conceit. Leaving self out of view, he might write a capital *picaresque* novel; or, if he must keep to his favourite subject, let him give us the Life of George Borrow in a plain unvarnished way. As it is, he has attempted to combine *dichtung* [fiction] and *wahrheit* [truth], and has produced something which is neither the one nor the other; and under the name of *Lavengro* has presented us with a creature 'neither fish nor flesh' (to use the beautiful words of Taliesin), but an impossible medley of [Ariosto's] *Orlando Furioso* and [Tobias Smollett's] *Peregrine Pickle*. (p. 283)

> [William Stirling], "Lavengro—'The Master of Words'," in Fraser's Magazine, Vol. XLIII, No. CCLV, March, 1851, pp. 272-83.

GEORGE BORROW (essay date 1857)

[In his appendix to The Romany Rye, *from which the following is excerpted, Borrow responds at length to criticism of* Lavengro. *He describes that work, explains and defends its didactic purpose, and attacks his critics in a vituperative manner. In addition, Borrow specifically denies that* Lavengro *is an autobiography.*]

Lavengro is the history up to a certain period of one of rather a peculiar mind and system of nerves, with an exterior shy and cold, under which lurk much curiosity, especially with regard to what is wild and extraordinary, a considerable quantity of energy and industry, and an unconquerable love of independence.

Those who read this book with attention—and the author begs to observe that it would be of little utility to read it hurriedly—may derive much information with respect to matters of philology and literature; it will be found treating of most of the principal languages from Ireland to China, and of the literature which they contain; and it is particularly minute with regard to the ways, manners, and speech of the English section of the most extraordinary and mysterious clan or tribe of people to be found in the whole world—the children of Roma. But it contains matters of much more importance than anything in connection with philology, and the literature and manners of nations. Perhaps no work was ever offered to the public in which the kindness and providence of God have been set forth by more striking examples, or the machinations of priestcraft been more truly and lucidly exposed, or the dangers which result to a nation when it abandons itself to effeminacy, and

a rage for what is novel and fashionable, than the present. (pp. 311-12)

A certain set of individuals calling themselves critics have attacked *Lavengro* with much virulence and malice. If what they call criticism had been founded on truth, the author would have had nothing to say. The book contains plenty of blemishes, some of them, by the bye, wilful ones, as the writer will presently show; not one of these, however, has been detected and pointed out; but the best passages in the book, indeed whatever was calculated to make the book valuable, have been assailed with abuse and misrepresentation. The duty of the true critic is to play the part of a leech, and not of a viper. Upon true and upon malignant criticism there is an excellent fable by the Spaniard Iriarte. The viper says to the leech, "Why do people invite your bite, and flee from mine?" "Because," says the leech, "people receive health from my bite, and poison from yours." "There is as much difference," says the clever Spaniard, "between true and malignant criticism, as between poison and medicine." Certainly a great many meritorious writers have allowed themselves to be poisoned by malignant criticism; the writer, however, is not one of those who allow themselves to be poisoned by pseudo-critics; no! no! he will rather hold them up by their tails, and show the creatures wriggling, blood and foam streaming from their broken jaws. First of all, however, he will notice one of their objections. "The book isn't true," say they. Now one of the principal reasons with those that have attacked *Lavengro* for their abuse of it is, that it is particularly true in one instance, namely, that it exposes their own nonsense, their love of humbug, their slavishness, their dressings, their goings out, their scraping and bowing to great people; it is the showing up of "gentility-nonsense" in *Lavengro* that has been one principal reason for raising the above cry; for in *Lavengro* is denounced the besetting folly of the English people, a folly which those who call themselves guardians of the public taste are far from being above. "We can't abide anything that isn't true!" they exclaim. Can't they? Then why are they so enraptured with any fiction that is adapted to purposes of humbug, which tends to make them satisfied with their own proceedings, with their own nonsense, which does not tell them to reform, to become more alive to their own failings, and less sensitive about the tyrannical goings on of the masters, and the degraded condition, the sufferings, and the trials of the serfs in the star Jupiter? Had *Lavengro* instead of being the work of an independent mind, been written in order to further any of the thousand and one cants, and species of nonsense prevalent in England, the author would have heard much less about its not being true, both from public detractors and private censurers.

"But *Lavengro* pretends to be an autobiography," say the critics; and here the writer begs leave to observe, that it would be well for people who profess to have a regard for truth, not to exhibit in every assertion which they make a most profligate disregard of it; this assertion of theirs is a falsehood, and they know it to be a falsehood. In the preface Lavengro is stated to be a dream; and the writer takes this opportunity of stating that he never said it was an autobiography; never authorized any person to say that it was one; and that he has in innumerable instances declared in public and private, both before and after the work was published, that it was not what is generally termed an autobiography: but a set of people who pretend to write criticisms . . . attack his book with abuse and calumny. He is, perhaps, condescending too much when he takes any notice of such people; as, however, the English public is wonderfully led by cries and shouts, and generally ready to take part against any person who is either unwilling or unable to defend himself, he deems it advisable not to be altogether quiet with those who assail him. The best way to deal with vipers is to tear out their teeth; and the best way to deal with pseudo-critics is to deprive them of their poison-bag, which is easily done by exposing their ignorance. The writer knew perfectly well the description of people with whom he would have to do, he therefore very quietly prepared a stratagem, by means of which he could at any time exhibit them, powerless and helpless, in his hand. Critics, when they review books, ought to have a competent knowledge of the subjects which those books discuss.

Lavengro is a philological book, a poem if you choose to call it so. Now, what a fine triumph it would have been for those who wished to vilify the book and its author, provided they could have detected the latter tripping in his philology—they might have instantly said that he was an ignorant pretender to philology—they laughed at the idea of his taking up a viper by its tail, a trick which hundreds of country urchins do every September, but they were silent about the really wonderful part of the book, the philological matter—they thought philology was his stronghold, and that it would be useless to attack him there; they of course would give him no credit as a philologist, for anything like fair treatment towards him was not to be expected at their hands, but they were afraid to attack his philology—yet that was the point, and the only point in which they might have attacked him successfully; he was vulnerable there. How was this? Why, in order to have an opportunity of holding up pseudo-critics by the tails, he wilfully spelt various foreign words wrong—Welsh words, and even Italian words— did they detect these mis-spellings? not one of them, even as he knew they would not, and he now taunts them with ignorance; and the power of taunting them with ignorance is the punishment which he designed for them—a power which they might but for their ignorance have used against him. (pp. 366-68)

The writer wishes to ask here, what do you think of all this, Messieurs les Critiques? Were ye ever served so before? But don't you richly deserve it? Haven't you been for years past bullying and insulting everybody whom you deemed weak, and currying favour with everybody whom you thought strong? "*We* approve of this. We disapprove of that. Oh, this will never do. These are fine lines!" The lines perhaps some horrid sycophantic rubbish addressed to Wellington, or Lord So-and-so. To have your ignorance thus exposed, to be shown up in this manner, and by whom? A gypsy! Ay, a gypsy was the very right person to do it. But is it not galling, after all?

"Ah, but *we* don't understand Armenian, it cannot be expected that *we* should understand Armenian, or Welsh, or—Hey, what's this? The mighty *we* not understand Armenian or Welsh, or— Then why does the mighty *we* pretend to review a book like *Lavengro*? From the arrogance with which it continually delivers itself, one would think that the mighty *we* is omniscient; that it understands every language; is versed in every literature; yet the mighty *we* does not even know the word for bread in Armenian. . . . [The] truth is, that the mighty *we*, with all its pretension, is in general a very sorry creature, who, instead of saying nous disons, should rather say nous dis. . . . Lavengro, who is anything but profane, would suggest that critics, especially magazine and Sunday newspaper critics, should commence with nous dis, as the first word would be significant of the conceit and assumption of the critic, and the second of the extent of the critic's information. The *we* says its say, but when fawning sycophancy or vulgar abuse are taken from that say, what remains? Why a blank, a void. . . . (pp. 369-70)

[*Lavengro*] is a book written for the express purpose of inculcating virtue, love of country, learning, manly pursuits, and genuine religion, for example, that of the Church of England, and for awakening a contempt for nonsense of every kind, and a hatred for priestcraft, more especially that of Rome. (p. 391)

> *George Borrow, in an appendix to his* The Romany Rye, *1857, pp. 311-92. Reprint by E. P. Dutton & Co., 1906, 392 p.*

[WHITWELL ELWIN]   (essay date 1857)

[*In his largely favorable review of* Lavengro *and* The Romany Rye, *Elwin begins by reproaching Borrow for his attack on* Lavengro's *critics in the Appendix to* The Romany Rye *(see excerpt above, 1857). Although Elwin finds Borrow's combination of autobiographical fact and fiction confusing, he praises the descriptions and characterizations in these works.*]

Mr. Borrow is very angry with his critics. They have attacked 'Lavengro' with 'much virulence and malice.' . . . Mr. Borrow proceeds upon the assumption that the author of a work is the best judge of its merits and defects, which, if it be true, authors ought always to be their own reviewers. Can he seriously imagine that the world would then receive a juster account of books than at present, and is he prepared to admit that all the manufacturers of last year's epics were Miltons, and all the dramatists Shakespeares? . . . What a man fancies to be his strength is often his weakness. If a work is neglected, he maintains it to be his masterpiece; if he is praised for his humour, he vaunts his pathos; if his prose alone finds favour, he rests his hope of immortality upon his verse.

Mr. Borrow seems to us to be no exception to the ordinary rule. He asserts that 'Lavengro' is a philological book, and that the philology was 'the really wonderful part of it.' It is, at least, a very insignificant part, for all the information it contains upon the subject might be written upon a visiting-card, and, when dispersed among three octavo volumes, attracts little more notice than a solitary thistle in a field of corn. Admitting that philology is Mr. Borrow's strength, he has been far too sparing of it in 'Lavengro' to derive much advantage from the plea. Nevertheless the blemishes to which he confesses are confined, by his own account, to this boasted philology: 'That was the point, and *the only point,* on which those who wished to vilify the author might have attacked him successfully—he was vulnerable there. How was this?' His answer is, that it was a trap. . . . He wilfully spelt some Welsh, Italian, and Armenian words wrong, and probably, without designing it, some English words also, and no reviewer thought proper to print for him a list of his errata. . . . This is exactly the kind of criticism which may be expected from a man when he sits in judgment on his own works. He can detect no other fault than a few misspellings, and these, without exception, wilful. (pp. 468-70)

Though we do not think that Mr. Borrow is a good counsel in his own cause, we are yet strongly of opinion that Time in his case has some wrongs to repair, and that 'Lavengro' has not obtained the fame which was its due. It contains passages which in their way are not surpassed by anything in English literature. The truth and vividness of the descriptions both of scenes and persons, coupled with the purity, force, and simplicity of the language, should confer immortality upon many of its pages. That they have not attracted more notice is partly we believe owing to the introduction into the narrative of numerous details which were hardly worthy to be recorded, and partly to the uncertainty which was felt as to whether the circumstances related were facts or fiction. Very much of their interest and value depends upon their being actual transcripts from life, and an occasional air of romance destroyed the confidence of the reader. Mr. Borrow has rather increased than removed the doubts which previously existed upon the point. 'The writer,' he states, speaking of **'Lavengro'** in [the Appendix to **'The Romany Rye'**], 'never said it was an autobiography, never authorised any person to say that it was one, and has in innumerable instances declared in public and private, both before and after the work was published, that it was not what is generally termed an autobiography.' Yet when he comments upon his work in his own person he treats the incidents as real, and speaks of Lavengro and the author as the same individual. . . . [Various] portions of the history are known to be a faithful narrative of Mr. Borrow's career, while we ourselves can testify, as to many other parts of his volumes, that nothing can excel the fidelity with which he has described both men and things. Far from his showing any tendency to exaggeration, such of his characters as we chance to have known, and they are not a few, are rather within the truth than beyond it. However picturesquely they may be drawn, the lines are invariably those of nature. Why under these circumstances he should envelop the question in mystery is more than we can divine. (pp. 472-73)

The author states in the Appendix that one of his favourite pursuits was 'to hunt after strange characters,' and it is as a series of sketches of English scenes and English people that, in our opinion, [the work's] great value consists. Every one acquainted with the lower orders of this country must pronounce the descriptions to be as accurate as they are picturesque. They abound in dramatic and delicate strokes of nature . . . and are painted with a force that bring men, events, and prospects before the eye with the vividness of reality. In this power of verbal delineation Mr. Borrow has never been outdone, but the merit unfortunately is accompanied with a defect. To the circumstances which give liveliness and distinctness to the picture he has too often superadded insignificant details which encumber his canvas. Nobody can produce an effect with fewer or simpler words; and with a little more discrimination of what was worthy to be recorded, he would never again have to complain of neglect. His descriptions of scenery have a peculiar sublimity and grace. The stamp of the Creator, which is upon the prospect itself, seems transferred to his page, and by the mere power of his expressive language the reader, without one word of direct moralizing, is led from nature up to nature's God. With such gifts as these Mr. Borrow may defy his critics if he will put the best part alone of his mind into print, and will cease to interleave passages which deserve to be immortal with more perishable stuff. (pp. 500-01)

[*Whitwell Elwin*], *"Roving Life in England," in* The Quarterly Review, *Vol. CI, No. CCI, April, 1857, pp. 468-501.**

THE SPECTATOR   (essay date 1862)

["**Wild Wales**"] is the first really clever book we remember to have seen in which an honest attempt is made to do justice to the Welsh character and Welsh literature. If Welshmen had any wish to propitiate the Saxons in their favour, they would undoubtedly feel considerably indebted to the experienced, shrewd, and discerning traveller who passed through a great portion of their country on foot a few years ago, and now

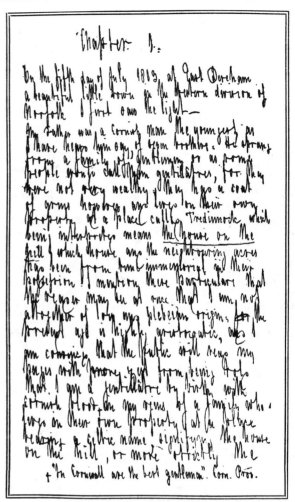

The first page of the manuscript of Lavengro.

presents the world with a most entertaining account of his adventures. . . .

In the course of Mr. Borrow's wanderings he caught very happily the salient points in the Welsh character, and he has depicted them with those light, free touches which none but George Borrow can hit off to such perfection. Many a man would have gone over the route taken by Mr. Borrow and come back with the report that all was barren. But "**Romany Rye**" goes about his work after a different method, and, with much of the freshness, humour, and geniality of his early days, he tells us of the folks he encountered, and the magnificent scenes he gazed upon during his lighthearted roviage. His knowledge of the Welsh language was a very great assistance for him, although more than once he came across a rugged "Cwinraeg," who refused to answer him or answered him in English—unwilling to acknowledge that a Saxon could speak Welsh. His knowledge of old Welsh literature is immeasurably greater than that which most educated Welshmen possess, and his admiration for the bards is something wonderful. Dsfydd av Gwilym he calls "the greatest poetical genius that has appeared in Europe since the revival of literature"—praise that we must venture to submit is absurdly exaggerated, and is certainly more than Welshmen claim for the bard. . . . He went some distance out of his way to visit the spot where Gronwy Owen was born, of whose "Cywydd y Farn" (Day of Judgment), he remarks:—
"'The Cywydd of Judgment' contains some of the finest things

ever written—that description of the toppling down of the top crag of Snowdon, at the Day of Judgment, beats anything in Homer.'' The figure in question is, no doubt, a grand and striking one; but we do not know where Mr. Borrow has found the ''description'' he prizes so much. Here are the words:—

> Ail i'r'ar ael Eryri,
> Cyfartal hoewal a hi,

which Mr. Borrow thus translates:—''The brow of Snowdon shall be levelled with the ground, and the eddying waters shall murmur round it.'' This does not totally eclipse Homer;—but it is better to find a clever man like Mr. Borrow having an undue partiality for the Welsh bards than devoting his powers, as so many before him have done, to turning them into derision. He has taken generally an enthusiastic view of the Welsh character, that a longer residence among the people would have corrected. (p. 1416)

[George Borrow] ought to have been a Welshman, for he is very fond of giving knock-down blows; he likes the country and its language, and he is very hearty in his likes and dislikes. As it is, he has written the best book about Wales ever published. It would be easy, perhaps, to pick out faults; but the time spent in the process would be entirely misapplied, and a fair idea would not be given of the work. We have preferred to judge it as a whole, not caring to boggle and wrangle over minor defects in what is intrinsically good. . . .

Let the tourist who writes his yearly volume of superficiality and twaddle read George Borrow and envy him! It is half a pity that such a man cannot go walking about for ever, for the benefit of people who are not gifted with legs so stout and eyes so discerning. May it be long before the ''Romany Rye'' lays by his satchel and his staff, and ceases to interest and instruct the world with his narratives of travel! (p. 1417)

> *''Mr. Borrow's 'Wild Wales','' in* The Spectator, *Vol. 35, No. 1799, December 20, 1862, pp. 1416-17.*

[GEORGE HENRY LEWES] (essay date 1863)

[*Lewes was one of the most versatile men of letters of the Victorian era. A prominent English journalist, he was the founder, with Leigh Hunt, of* The Leader, *a radical political journal which he also edited from 1851 to 1854. He served as the first editor of* The Fortnightly Review *from 1865 to 1866, a journal which he had also helped to establish. Critics often cite Lewes's influence on the novelist George Eliot, to whom he was companion and mentor, as his principal contribution to English letters, but they also credit him with critical acumen in his literary commentary, most notably in his dramatic criticism. In the following excerpt, Lewes comments on* Wild Wales.]

It is difficult to characterize the work just issued by Mr. George Borrow, without preface or explanation of any kind, under the title of **Wild Wales.** We are dubious whether it is simply a record of his walks through Wales, or whether he has mingled a quantity of very mild and not very amusing fiction with actual experiences. In any case the book is extremely defective, and contains an unpardonable proportion of triviality and self-glorification. Really it is too much to demand that we should read the record of every glass of ale which Mr. Borrow drank—usually with his criticism on its quality—or be patient under the fatiguing triviality of ''I paid my bill and departed,'' which occurs incessantly; the more so because, while he is careful to inform us that he paid the bill, he never once mentions the amount; the detail he records is superfluous, the detail he omits

would at least have been serviceable to future travellers. Snatches of commonplace conversation, and intensely prosaic translations of Welsh poems, swell out this book, and render it rather tiresome reading. Nevertheless, although its defects tax the patience of the reader, the work is not without its charm. In the first place it has the inalienable interest of *out-of-doorness*. A sweet breath of the country turns over its pages. In the next place there is a graphic picture of the Welsh people as seen from the outside by a genial pedestrian. Mr. Borrow appears to have been many years interested in Welsh literature and history, and this ramble furnishes him with an occasion of learning something of Welsh scenery and people. In one volume, instead of three, the work might have been an attractive guide-book for pedestrians. (pp. 137-38)

> *[George Henry Lewes], in a review of ''Wild Wales,'' in* The Cornhill Magazine, *Vol. VII, No. 37, January, 1863, pp. 137-38.*

THE ATHENAEUM (essay date 1874)

When it was known that the author of '**Lavengro**' and the '**Rommany Rye**' had in the press a dictionary of the English Gipsy Dialect all who took an interest in the ''Black-blooded folk,'' as they delight to call themselves, looked forward to the appearance of the volume with no small curiosity. The '**Romano Lavo-Lil,**' however, adds but little to our knowledge of the subject; the vocabulary consists of not more than 1,200 or 1,300 words; and even this number must be still further reduced, since many of the words are but variants of those already given.

The author seems to make the mistake of confounding the amount of Rommanis which he has collected in this book with the actual extent of the language itself. He tells us, for instance, that the Gipsies have no word for ''green,'' whereas they have an equivalent in the not at all rare word *selno;* it would, indeed, be strange if they had no name for the colour of the trees and hedges under which they camp, and of the grass upon which they sit, to say nothing of the green coat which was until recently the indispensable garment of a well-to-do son of Rom.

Mr. Borrow is quite right in assigning to the Gipsy language a Sanscrit, or, at least, an Indian origin, as he does in his Preface . . . ; and it would have been well had he confined himself merely to such general philological propositions. When, however, he proceeds to give the etymology of particular words, he exhibits an ignorance, not only of the Oriental languages which he cites, but even of the first principles of comparative philology, which is absolutely ludicrous.

It appears to be quite enough for him to find the faintest resemblance in sound between a word in Gipsy and in any other language; and the two are at once set down as identical, without regard to the family of languages to which they respectively belong, and in many instances without even a correspondence in sense. (p. 556)

These errors are the more unpardonable, as Mr. Borrow might have found a rational account of the derivation of nearly every Rommany word in the works of Potts, Miklosich, Paspati, or any other well-known Continental writer upon the subject. A slight acquaintance with any of these would have saved him from the elementary blunders into which his own want of knowledge of Oriental languages has betrayed him. . . .

We miss, too, in Mr. Borrow's glossary many words which are of common occurrence in Gipsy mouths, such as *shinger-*

bal, "a horn"; *shock,* "a branch"; *dordy,* "behold"; &c., while others are so disguised by eccentric spelling as to be scarcely recognizable. Who, for instance, would recognize the familiar *patsĕrus,* "trust," in Mr. Borrow's *pazhorrus,* or would know without the appended translation that *"Cotorres of mi-Dibbles lil"* represented *cutters of mi Duvels lil,* "bits of God's book"? . . .

One portion of the book is devoted to *Betie rokrapenes* and *Romano jinnypen*—"Little sayings" and "Gipsy philosophy" ("wisdom of the Egyptians," as Mr. Borrow renders it), consisting presumably of *verbatim* reports of speeches actually uttered by Gipsies. Pieces of this kind are, more than anything else, valuable to the philologist; for they are specimens of the language as it exists at the present time, and as such are, of course, more trustworthy than information elicited by direct questioning. But our confidence in the purity of the specimens here given is much shaken by the fact that we discover in many of them indisputable traces of the idiosyncrasy of the author himself, and indications that some of them at least have been, if not entirely composed by himself, at least filtered through his mind, and cast more or less into his own form of expression. We find, for instance, the word *bavolengro* used in no less than three places in the sense of "ghost," instead of *mullo,* the correct Gipsy equivalent. We have no hesitation in asserting that the word *bavolengro* would be almost unintelligible to a Gipsy, and would most certainly fail to convey to his mind any such idea as "ghost," "spirit," "soul," or the like. The word, indeed, does not exist in the language. . . .

We feel that in criticizing this work we are treading on delicate ground, for we shall be reminded that Mr. Borrow was one of the very first to give a clear account of the Gipsies in English, and that . . . not a few of the "Rommany Ryes," of those who have studied the Gipsies and their language, owe their first taste for the subject to the perusal of Mr. Borrow's books. But we cannot allow merely sentimental considerations to prevent us from telling the honest truth. The fact is, that the **'Romano Lavo-Lil'** is nothing more than a *réchauffé* [rehash] of the materials collected by Mr. Borrow at an early stage of his investigations, and nearly every word and every phrase may be found in one form or another in his earlier works. Whether or not Mr. Borrow *has* in the course of his long experience become the *deep* Gipsy which he has always been supposed to be, we cannot say; but it is certain that his present book contains little more than he gave to the public forty years ago, and does not by any means represent the present state of knowledge on the subject. But at the present day, when comparative philology has made such strides, and when want of accurate scholarship is as little tolerated in strange and remote languages as in classical literature, the **'Romano Lavo-Lil'** is, to speak mildly, an anachronism. (p. 557)

> *A review of, "Romano Lavo-Lil: Word-Book of the Romany; or, English Gipsy Language," in* The Athenaeum *No. 2426, April 25, 1874, pp. 556-57.*

GEORGE SAINTSBURY (essay date 1886)

[*Saintsbury was an English literary historian and critic of the late nineteenth and early twentieth centuries. A prolific writer, Saintsbury composed a number of histories of English and European literature as well as several critical works on individual authors, styles, and periods. Saintsbury's complimentary essay on Borrow is an overview of his career. After enumerating the general merits and defects of Borrow's work, Saintsbury discusses what he terms*

the author's greatest accomplishments: The Bible in Spain, Lavengro, The Romany Rye, *and* Wild Wales.]

There is this difficulty in writing about [Borrow], that the audience must necessarily consist of fervent devotees on the one hand, and of complete infidels, or at least complete know-nothings, on the other. To any one who, having the faculty to understand either, has read **'Lavengro'** or **'The Bible in Spain,'** or even **'Wild Wales,'** praise bestowed on Borrow is apt to seem impertinence. To anybody else (and unfortunately the anybody else is in a large majority) praise bestowed on Borrow is apt to look like that very dubious kind of praise which is bestowed on somebody of whom no one but the praiser has ever heard. I cannot think of any single writer (Peacock himself is not an exception) who is in quite parallel case. And, as usual, there is a certain excuse for the general public. Borrow kept himself during not the least exciting period of English history quite aloof from English politics, and from the life of great English cities. But he did more than this. He is the only really considerable writer of his time in any modern European nation who seems to have taken absolutely no interest in current events, literary and other. Putting a very few allusions aside, he might have belonged to almost any period. . . . He who lived through the whole period from Waterloo to Maiwand has not, as far as I remember, mentioned a single English writer later than Scott and Byron. He saw the rise, and, in some instances, the death, of Tennyson, Thackeray, Macaulay, Carlyle, Dickens. There is not a reference to any one of them in his works. He saw political changes such as no man for two centuries had seen, and (except the Corn Laws, to which he has some half-ironical allusions, and the Ecclesiastical Titles Bill, which stirred his one active sentiment), he has referred to never a one. He seems in some singular fashion to have stood outside of all these things. . . . Shakespeare, we know, was for all time, not of one age only; but I think we may say of Borrow, without too severely or conceitedly marking the difference, that he was not of or for any particular age or time at all. If the celebrated query in Longfellow's 'Hyperion,' "What is time?" had been addressed to him, his most appropriate answer, and one which he was quite capable of giving, would have been, "I really don't know."

To this singular historical vagueness has to be added a critical vagueness even greater. . . . [He] could not judge a work of literature as literature at all. If it expressed sentiments with which he agreed, or called up associations which were pleasant to him, good luck to it; if it expressed sentiments with which he did not agree, and called up no pleasant associations, bad luck. (pp. 170-71)

[The] curiously piecemeal, and the curiously arbitrary character of Borrow's literary studies in languages other than his own, is noteworthy in so great a linguist. The entire range of French literature, old as well as new, he seems to have ignored altogether—I should imagine out of pure John Bullishness. He has very few references to German, though he was a good German scholar. . . . Italian, though he certainly knew it well, is equally slighted. His education, if not his taste for languages, must have made him a tolerable (he never could have been an exact) classical scholar. But it is clear that insolent Greece and haughty Rome exerted no attraction upon him. I question whether even Spanish would not have been too common a toy to attract him much if it had not been for the accidental circumstances which connected him with Spain. (p. 172)

[Even Borrow's] defects have the attraction for the most part of a certain strangeness and oddity. If they had not been accompanied by great and peculiar merits he would not have emerged from the category of the merely bizarre, where he might have been left without further attention. But, as a matter of fact, all, or almost all, of his defects are not only counter-balanced by merits, but are themselves for the most part exaggerations or perversions of what is in itself meritorious. With less wilfulness, with more attention to the literature, the events, the personages of his own time, with a more critical and common-sense attitude towards his own crochets, Borrow could hardly have wrought out for himself (as he has to an extent hardly paralleled by any other prose writer who has not deliberately chosen supernatural or fantastic themes) the region of fantasy, neither too real nor too historical, which Joubert thought proper to the poet. Strong and vivid as Borrow's drawing of places and persons is, he always contrives to throw in touches which somehow give the whole the air of being rather a vision than a fact. Never was such a John-a-Dreams as this solid, pugilistic John Bull. Part of this literary effect of his is due to his quaint habit of avoiding, where he can, the mention of proper names. . . . A paraphrase, an innuendo, a word to the wise he delights in, but anything perfectly clear and precise he abhors. And by this means and others, which it might be tedious to trace out too closely, he succeeds in throwing the same cloudy vagueness over times as well as places and persons. A famous passage—perhaps the best known, and not far from the best he ever wrote—about Byron's funeral, fixes, of course, the date of the wondrous facts or fictions recorded in 'Lavengro' to a nicety. Yet who, as he reads it and its sequel (for the separation of 'Lavengro' and 'The Romany Rye' is merely arbitrary, though the second book is, as a whole, less interesting than the former), ever thinks of what was actually going on in the very positive and prosaic England of 1824-5? The later chapters of 'Lavengro' are the only modern 'Romance of Adventure' that I know. . . . Without any apparent art, certainly without the elaborate apparatus which most prose tellers of fantastic tales use, and generally fail in using, Borrow spirits his readers at once away from mere reality. If his events are frequently as odd as a dream, they are always as perfectly commonplace and real for the moment as the events of a dream are—a little fact which the above-mentioned tellers of the above-mentioned fantastic stories are too apt to forget. It is in this natural romantic gift that Borrow's greatest charm lies. But it is accompanied and nearly equalled both in quality and degree by a faculty for dialogue. Except Defoe and Dumas, I cannot think of any novelists who contrive to tell a story in dialogue and to keep up the ball of conversation so well as Borrow; while he is considerably the superior of both in pure style and in the literary quality of his talk. Borrow's humour, though it is of the general class of the older English—that is to say, the pre-Addisonian humorists—is a species quite by itself. It is rather narrow in range, a little garrulous, busied very often about curiously small matters, but wonderfully observant and true, and possessing a quaint dry savour as individual as that of some wines. A characteristic of this kind probably accompanies the romantic Ethos more commonly than superficial judges both of life and literature are apt to suppose; but the conjunction is nowhere seen better than in Borrow. . . . [Humour and satire] were not dissociated in Borrow. His purely satirical faculty was very strong indeed, and probably if he had lived a less retired life it would have found fuller exercise. At present the most remarkable instance of it which exists is the inimitable portrait-caricature of the learned Unitarian, generally known as "Taylor of Norwich." . . . I do not hesitate to call [this sketch] one of the most masterly things of the kind in literature. (pp. 173-74)

[It is] impossible to ascertain how much of the abundant character drawing in his four chief books ['The Bible in Spain,' 'Lavengro,' 'The Romany Rye,' and 'Wild Wales'] (all of which, be it remembered, are autobiographic and professedly historical) is fact and how much fancy. It is almost impossible to pen them anywhere without coming upon personal sketches, more or less elaborate, in which the satiric touch is rarely wanting. (pp. 174-75)

On these four books Borrow's literary fame rests. His other works are interesting because they were written by the author of these, or because of their subjects, or because of the effect they had on other men of letters, notably Longfellow and Mérimée, on the latter of whom Borrow had an especially remarkable influence. These four are interesting of themselves.

The earliest has, I believe been, and for reasons quite apart from its biblical subject perhaps deserves to be, the greatest general favourite, though its literary value is a good deal below that of 'Lavengro.' 'The Bible in Spain' records the journeys which, as an agent of the Bible Society, Borrow took through the Peninsula at a singularly interesting time, the disturbed years of the early reign of Isabel Segunda. . . . The book is so delightful that, except when duty calls, no one would willingly take any exception to any part or feature of it. The constant change of scene, the romantic episodes of adventure, the kaleidoscope of characters, the crisp dialogue, the quaint reflection and comment relieve each other without a break. I do not know whether it is really true to Spain and Spanish life, and, to tell the exact truth, I do not in the least care. If it is not Spanish it is remarkably human and remarkably literary, and those are the chief and principal things.

'Lavengro,' which followed, has all the merits of its predecessor and more. It is a little spoilt in its later chapters by the purpose, the anti-papal purpose, which appears still more fully in 'The Romany Rye.' But the strong and singular individuality of its flavour as a whole would have been more than sufficient to carry off a greater fault. There are, I should suppose, few books the successive pictures of which leave such an impression on the reader who is prepared to receive that impression. The word picture is here rightly used, for in all Borrow's books more or less, and in this particularly, the narrative is anything but continuous. It is a succession of dissolving views which grow clear and distinct for a time and then fade off into a vagueness before once more appearing distinctly; nor has this mode of dealing with a subject ever been more successfully applied than in 'Lavengro.' (pp. 176-77)

I believe that some of the small but fierce tribe of Borrovians are inclined to resent the putting of the last of this remarkable series, 'Wild Wales,' on a level with the other three. With such I can by no means agree. 'Wild Wales' has not, of course, the charm of unfamiliar scenery and the freshness of youthful impression which distinguish 'The Bible in Spain'; it does not attempt anything like the novel-interest of 'Lavengro' and 'The Romany Rye'; and though, as has been pointed out above, something of Borrow's secret and mysterious way of indicating places survives, it is a pretty distinct itinerary over a great part of the actual principality. I have followed most of its tracks on foot myself, and nobody who wants a Welsh guide-book can take a pleasanter one, though he might easily find one much less erratic. It may thus have, to superficial observers, a positive and prosaic flavour as compared with the romantic character of the other three. But this distinction is not real. The tones are a little subdued, as was likely to be the case with an elderly gentleman of fifty, travelling with his wife and step-daughter, and not publishing the record of his travels till he was nearly ten years older. The localities are traceable on the map and in Murray, instead of being the enchanted dingles and the half-mythical woods of 'Lavengro.' The personages of the former books return no more, though with one of his most excellent touches of art, the author has suggested the contrast of youth and age by a single gipsy interview in one of the later chapters. . . . [Some] readers may be repelled by the strong literary colour of the book, which is almost a Welsh anthology in parts. But those few who can boast themselves to find the whole of a book, not merely its parts, and to judge it when found, will, I think, be not least fond of 'Wild Wales.' If they have, as every reader of Borrow should have, the spirit of the roads upon them, and are never more happy than when journeying on "Shanks his mare," they will, of course, have in addition a private and personal love for it. It is, despite the interludes of literary history, as full of Borrow's peculiar conversational gift as any of its predecessors. . . . As to incident, one often, as before, suspects him of romancing, and it stands to reason that his dialogue, written long after the event, must be full of the "cocked-hat-and-sword" style of narrative. But his description, while it has all the vividness, has also all the faithfulness and sobriety of the best landscape-painting. See a place which Kingsley or Mr. Ruskin, or some other master of our decorative school, have described—much more one which has fallen into the hands of the small fry of their imitators—and you are almost sure to find that it has been overdone. This is never, or hardly ever, the case with Borrow, and it is so rare a merit, when it is found in a man who does not shirk description where necessary, that it deserves to be counted to him at no grudging rate.

But there is no doubt that the distinguished feature of the book is its survey of Welsh poetical literature. I have already confessed that I am not qualified to judge the accuracy of Borrow's translations, and by no means disposed to overvalue them. But any one who takes an interest in literature at all, must, I think, feel that interest not a little excited by the curious Old Mortality-like peregrinations which the author of 'Wild Wales' made to the birth place, or the burial-place as it might be, of bard after bard, and by the short but masterly accounts which he gives of the objects of his search. Of none of the numerous subjects of his linguistic rovings does Borrow seem to have been fonder, putting Romany aside, than of Welsh. . . . But it needs no knowledge of Welsh whatever to perceive the genuine enthusiasm, and the genuine range of his acquaintance with the language from the purely literary side. When he tells us that Ab Gwilym was a greater poet than Ovid or Chaucer I feel considerable doubts whether he was quite competent to understand Ovid and little or no doubt that he has done wrong to Chaucer. But when, leaving these idle comparisons, he luxuriates in details about Ab Gwilym himself, and his poems, and his lady loves, and so forth, I have no doubt about Borrow's appreciation (casual prejudices always excepted) of literature. Nor is the charm which he has added to Welsh scenery by this constant identification of it with the men, and the deeds, and the words of the past to be easily exaggerated.

Little has been said hitherto of Borrow's more purely, or if anybody prefers the words formally, literary characteristics. They are sufficiently interesting. He unites with a general plainness of speech and writing, not unworthy of Defoe or Cobbett, a very odd and complicated mannerism, which, as he had the wisdom to make it the seasoning and not the main substance of his literary fare, is never disgusting. The secret of this may be, no doubt, in part sought in his early familiarity with a great

many foreign languages, some of those idioms he transplanted into English, but his is by no means the whole of the receipt. Perhaps it is useless to examine analytically that receipt's details, or rather (for the analysis may be said to be compulsory on any one who calls himself a critic), useless to offer its results to the reader. One point which can escape no one who reads with his eyes open is the frequent, yet not too abundant repetition of the same or very similar words—a point wherein much of the style of persons so dissimilar as Carlyle, Borrow, and Thackeray consists. This is a well-known fact—so well-known indeed that when a person who desires to acquire style hears of it, he often goes and does likewise, with what result all reviewers know. The peculiarity of Borrow as far as I can mark it, is that, despite his strong mannerism, he never relies on it as too many others, great and small, are wont to do. His character sketches, of which, as I have said, he is so abundant a master, are always put in the plainest and simplest English. So are his flashes of ethical reflections which, though like all ethical reflections often one-sided, are of the first order of insight. (pp. 179-81)

[Borrow's] attraction is one neither mainly nor in any very great degree one of pure form. His early critics compared him, and the comparison is natural, to Le Sage. It was natural I say, but it was not extraordinarily critical. Both men wrote of vagabonds, and to some extent of picaroons; both neglected the conventionalities of their own language and literature; both had a singular knowledge of human nature. But Le Sage is one of the most impersonal of all great writers, and Borrow is one of the most personal. And it is undoubtedly in the revelation of his personality that [a] great part of his charm lies. It is, as has been fully acknowledged, a one-sided wrong-headed not always quite right-hearted personality. But it is intensely English, possessing at the same time a certain strain of romance which the other John Bulls of literature mostly lack. . . . (pp. 181-82)

Borrow has—what after all is the chief mark of a great writer—distinction. . . . [The great writers] succeed only in being themselves, and that is what Borrow does. His attraction is rather complex, and different parts of it may, and no doubt do, appeal with differing force to this and that reader. . . . He wants editing, for his allusive fashion of writing probably makes a great part of him nearly unintelligible to those who have not from their youth up devoted themselves to the acquisition of useless knowledge. . . . The great mass of his translations, published and unpublished, and the smaller mass of his early hackwork, no doubt deserves judicious excerption. . . . But all these things are only desirable embellishments and assistances. His real claims and his real attractions are comprised in four small volumes. . . . It is not a large literary baggage, and it does not attempt any very varied literary kinds. If not exactly a novelist in any one of his books, Borrow is a romancer in the true and not the ironic sense of the word in all of them. He has not been approached in merit by any romancer who has published books in our days, except Charles Kingsley; and his work, if less varied in range and charm than Kingsley's, has a much stronger and more concentrated flavour. Moreover, he is the one English writer of our time, and perhaps of times still farther back, who never seems to have tried to be anything but himself; who went his own way all his life long with complete indifference to what the public or the publishers liked, as well as to what canons of literary form and standards of literary perfection seemed to indicate as best worth aiming at. A most self-sufficient person was Borrow, in the good and ancient sense, as well as to some extent in the bad and modern sense.

And what is more, he was not only a self-sufficient person, but very sufficient also to the tastes of all those who love good English and good literature. (pp. 182-83)

George Saintsbury, "George Borrow," in *Macmillan's Magazine, Vol. LIII, No. 315, January, 1886, pp. 170-83*.

LESLIE STEPHEN (essay date 1892)

[*Stephen is considered one of the most important literary critics of the late Victorian and early Edwardian era. In his criticism, which was often moral in tone, Stephen argues that all literature is nothing more than an imaginative rendering, in concrete terms, of a writer's philosophy or beliefs. It is the role of criticism, he contends, to translate into intellectual terms what the writer has told the reader through character, symbol, and plot. Stephen's analyses often include biographical judgments of the writer as well as the work. As Stephen once observed: "The whole art of criticism consists in learning to know the human being who is partially revealed to us in his spoken or his written words." In the following excerpt, Stephen depicts Borrow as an idiosyncratic traveler whose writings evoke the flavor of country life in a way that captivates the reader.*]

Borrow is a "humourist" of the first water. He lives in a world of his own—a queer world with laws peculiar to itself, and yet one which has all manner of odd and unexpected points of contact with the prosaic world of daily experience. Borrow's Bohemianism is no revolt against the established order. He does not invoke nature or fly to the hedges because society is corrupt or the world unsatisfying, or because he has some kind of new patent theory of life to work out. He cares nothing for such fancies. On the contrary, he is a staunch conservative, full of good old-fashioned prejudices. He seems to be a case of the strange reappearance of an ancestral instinct under altered circumstances. Some of his forefathers must have been gipsies by temperament if not by race; and the impulses due to that strain have got themselves blended with the characteristics of the average Englishman. The result is a strange and yet, in a way, harmonious and original type which made the **"Bible in Spain"** a puzzle to the average reader. The name suggested a work of the edifying class. Here was a good respectable emissary of the Bible Society going to convert poor papists by a distribution of the Scriptures. He has returned to write a long tract setting forth the difficulties of his enterprise, and the stiff-neckedness of the Spanish people. The luckless reader who took up the book on that understanding was destined to a strange disappointment. True, Borrow appeared to take his enterprise quite seriously, indulges in the proper reflections, and gets into the regulation difficulty involving an appeal to the British minister. But it soon appears that his Protestant zeal is somehow mixed up with a passion for strange wanderings in the queerest of company. To him Spain is not the land of staunch Catholicism, or of Cervantes, or of Velasquez, and still less a country of historic or political interest. Its attraction is in the picturesque outcasts who find ample roaming-ground in its wilder regions. . . . [No] one not thoroughly at home with gipsy ways, gipsy modes of thought, to whom it comes quite naturally to put up in a den of cutthroats, or to enter the field of his missionary enterprise in company with a professional brigand travelling on business, could have given us so singular a glimpse of the most picturesque elements of a strange country. Your respectable compiler of handbooks might travel for years in the same districts all unconscious that passing vagabonds were so fertile in romance. The freemasonry which exists amongst the class lying outside the pale of respectability enables Borrow

to fall in with adventures full of mysterious fascination. . . . Men who live in strange company learn the advantage of not asking questions, or following out delicate inquiries; and these singular figures are the more attractive because they come and go, half-revealing themselves for a moment, and then vanishing into outside mystery; as the narrator himself sometimes merges into the regions of absolute commonplace, and then dives down below the surface into the remotest recesses of the social labyrinth. (pp. 186-89)

It is the old picturesque country life which fascinates Borrow, and he was fortunate enough to plunge into the heart of it before it had been frightened away by the railways. **"Lavengro"** is a strange medley, which is nevertheless charming by reason of the odd idiosyncrasy which fits the author to interpret this fast vanishing phase of life. It contains queer controversial irrelevance—conversations or stories which may or may not be more or less founded on fact, tending to illustrate the pernicious propagandism of Popery, the evil done by Sir Walter Scott's novels, and the melancholy results of the decline of pugilism. And then we have satire of a simple kind upon literary craftsmen, and excursions into philology which show at least an amusing dash of innocent vanity. But the oddity of these quaint utterances of a humourist who seeks to find the most congenial mental food in the Bible, the Newgate Calendar, and in old Welsh literature, is in thorough keeping with the situation. He is the genuine tramp whose experience is naturally made up of miscellaneous waifs and strays; who drifts into contact with the most eccentric beings, and parts company with them at a moment's notice, or catching hold of some stray bit of out-of-the-way knowledge follows it up as long as it amuses him. He is equally at home compounding narratives of the lives of eminent criminals for London booksellers, or making acquaintance with thimbleriggers, or pugilists, or Armenian merchants, or becoming a hermit in his remote dingle, making his own shoes and discussing theology with a postboy, a feminine tramp, and a Jesuit in disguise. The compound is too quaint for fiction, but is made interesting by the quaint vein of simplicity and the touch of genius which brings out the picturesque side of his roving existence, and yet leaves one in doubt how far the author appreciates his own singularity. (pp. 190-91)

Certainly it is a queer topsy-turvy world to which we are introduced in **"Lavengro."** It gives the reader the sensation of a strange dream in which all the miscellaneous population of caravans and wayside tents make their exits and entrances at random, mixed with such eccentrics as the distinguished author, who has a mysterious propensity for touching odd objects as a charm against evil. All one's ideas are dislocated when the centre of interest is no longer in the thick of the crowd, but in that curious limbo whither drift all the odd personages who live in the interstices without being caught by the meshes of the great network of ordinary convention. Perhaps the oddity repels many readers; but to me it always seems that Borrow's dingle represents a little oasis of genuine romance—a kind of half-visionary fragment of fairyland, which reveals itself like the enchanted castle in the vale of St. John, and then vanishes after tantalising and arousing one's curiosity. It will never be again discovered by any flesh-and-blood traveller; but, in my imaginary travels, I like to rusticate there for a time, and to feel as if the gipsy was the true possessor of the secret of life, and we who travel by rail and read newspapers and consider ourselves to be sensible men of business, were but vexatious intruders upon this sweet dream. There must, one supposes, be a history of England from the Petulengro point of view, in which the change of dynasties recognised by Hume and Mr.

Freeman, or the oscillations of power between Lord Beacons-field and Mr. Gladstone, appear in relative insignificance as more or less affecting certain police regulations and the inclo-sure of commons. It is pleasant for a time to feel as though the little rivulet were the main stream, and the social outcast the true centre of society. The pure flavour of the country life is only perceptible when one has annihilated all disturbing influences; and in that little dingle with its solitary forge be-neath the woods . . . , that desirable result may be achieved for a time, even in a London library. (pp. 191-92)

> *Leslie Stephen, "Country Books," in his* Hours in a Library, *Vol. III, revised edition, 1892. Reprint by John Murray, 1919, pp. 164-92.*

LIONEL JOHNSON (essay date 1899)

[*The following excerpt was originally published in* Outlook *on April 1, 1899.*]

You may prefer Popish priests to Protestant pugilists; you may loathe philology and ale; you may feel for the tragic house of Stuart; you may take no personal interest in East Anglia, Wales, or Spain, and but little in gypsies: yet, if by natural grace you have it in you to love Borrow's genius, you forgive him all. By natural grace, I say: for if you come fresh to Borrow, as to a writer whom you "ought to know," and find his charm hard of access, difficult of approach, you will never reach it; you will think him an over-praised eccentric. But they, to whom life, in the natural order, can give nothing better than to walk alone in "the wind on the heath," and to lie out on the hillside under the stars; to know that strange false dawn whereat all nature wakes, and turns to sleep again; to go on their rejoicing way at sunrise, loving their free solitariness:—these are the born Borrovians. The appeal is elemental, primaeval; to the savage in the blood, the ancestral nomad: wonderful as they are, not Borrow's dealings with men, not his trafficking with Spanish *posadas* and Welsh cottages and gypsy camps, not his converse with his kind in town or country, but his intercourse and converse with Nature at her untameable wildest, mark what is deepest in his heart, most leaping in his pulses. It is the voice of Jasper Petulengro, but the soul of George Borrow, which praises in a famous dialogue the simple majesties of the means of natural joy in living. " 'Life is sweet, brother.' 'Do you think so?' 'Think so!—there's night and day, brother, both sweet things; sun, moon, and stars, brother, all sweet things; there's likewise a wind on the heath. Life is very sweet, brother; who would wish to die?' . . . 'In sickness, Jasper?' 'There's the sun and stars, brother.' 'In blindness, Jasper?' 'There's the wind on the heath, brother.' . . ." Does not that send the blood glowing through the veins to read? And that is the finer spirit of the four masterpieces: *The Bible in Spain, Lavengro, The Romany Rye, Wild Wales;* to read which is to wash soul and body in the open air, to be purified from the stains of civili-zation, to meet and greet the Mighty Mother. O rare George Borrow! Yet readers new to Borrow might well say to him what Plato would have had his ideal citizens say to the poet: "You are a very wonderful, and accomplished, and extraor-dinary person; but we don't think we want any more of you." (pp. 200-01)

[Borrow] imagined nothing; but what he saw, did, said, or heard, that he embellished,—not by adding embroideries, but by curtailing superfluities, and leaving a clean, clear, and in-stantly arresting outline. And he took pains to avoid dulness; do he but ask his way of a tinker, or order his meal at an inn,

or set to upon learning Irish, he will take care that the event shall be emphatic, a matter of pointed interest. Uncongenial critics have cried out upon this, not understanding it; they have either failed to note the elasticity and terseness of the realism, or they have paid it an unconscious compliment. His **"Bible in Spain"** is the most marked example of his manner. His other masterpieces are frankly personal; but there he chronicles a public mission, and his title indicates it. Yet his readers observe (and some of them with a peculiar amusement), that the Bible is far less the book's theme than are Borrow and his night-rides, and his remarkable servants, and his food and his gyp-sies, and himself and his, in general and at large. George Borrow is always his own protagonist, be it the Borrow know-ing in beer and horseflesh, or the Borrow charging the Pope full tilt, or the Borrow helpless and agonising in the hold of the mysterious "Fear." . . . (pp. 202-03)

All his books are in great measure autobiographical; all, there-fore, records of wanderings, even from infancy; all are written in an English which attains its dramatic end with an amazing certainty and success. It is an unerring combination of the homely and the eloquent, the homespun and the high-wrought; the words are living creatures. Mr. Meredith, Mr. Pater, Mr. Stevenson grew into their styles, finding their way. Borrow seems to have come into the world with his proper gift of style, so indissolubly wedded to his nature, so inseparable from his themes. These goodly books are among the most wayward ever written. You cannot answer a curious friend who asks: "What is *Lavengro* about?" You can but say: "Gypsies, and obscure languages, and London publishers, and tinkers, and mad peo-ple, and an applewoman, and Salisbury Plain, and an Arme-nian, and a Welshman. . . ." Whereat dissatisfaction upon the part of your friend. But what the four books mean and are to their lovers is upon this sort. Written by a man of intense personality, irresistible in his hold upon your attention, they take you far afield from weary cares and business into the enamouring airs of the open world, and into days when the countryside was uncontaminated by the vulgar conventions which form the worst side of "civilized" life in cities. They give you the sense of emancipation, of manumission into the liberty of the winding road and fragrant forest, into the freshness of an ancient country-life, into a *milieu* where men are not copies of each other. And you fall in with strange scenes of adventure, great or small, of which a strange man is the centre as he is the scribe; and from a description of a lonely glen you are plunged into a dissertation upon difficult old tongues, and from dejection into laughter, and from gypsydom into journalism; and everything is equally delightful, and nothing that the strange man shows you can come amiss. And you will hardly make up your mind whether he is most Don Quixote, or Rousseau, or Luther, or Defoe; but you will always love these books. . . . (pp. 203-04)

> *Lionel Johnson, "O Rare George Borrow!" in his* Post Liminium: Essays and Critical Papers, *edited by Thomas Whittemore, Elkin Mathews, 1911, pp. 200-04.*

LAFCADIO HEARN (lecture date 1902?)

[*Considered one of modern America's leading impressionistic critics, Hearn produced a large body of work that testifies to his love of the exotic and the beautiful. His sketches, short stories, and novellas demonstrate a vision of evil and the supernatural reminiscent of Edgar Allan Poe and Charles Baudelaire. His lectures on American and European literature are exceptional for*

*their divergence from the conventions of Victorian criticism. Be-
cause Hearn made no written record of these presentations, his
lectures were reconstructed from students' notes. His comments
on Borrow were delivered in a lecture at the University of Tokyo
sometime between 1896 and 1902.]*

Into English literature, Borrow brought a new element, a new
quality of romantic narration. None of his books is, in the
strictest sense of the word, either a novel or a romance; they
are all romantic narrative of things really felt and seen. He did
not attempt any complete framework of story; there is no beginning and no end; there is no order; there is no sequence. I
do not know how to explain his method better than by telling
you that most of his works resemble note-books. Nevertheless,
these books have a charm and a quality absolutely original,
and still command a great deal of admiration and attention,
especially from the young. He perceived that the most ordinary
incident of everyday life could be made interesting, and the
most ordinary emotions and impressions obtained value by
proper literary treatment; and out of almost nothing he was
able to produce volumes, half fiction, half truth, such as had
never been produced before. It is somewhat of a puzzle to
determine where the true thing ends and where the fiction
begins; but the best critics are inclined to think that the fiction
lies chiefly in the combination of incidents, and the truth in
the incidents themselves. This theory allows us to feel a great
deal of respect for the author. It is not a case like Defoe's,
who wrote out of his imagination. Borrow wrote fact; but he
combined the facts of different years and different places in
such a manner as to give you an idea that they belong to a
particular, brief period of experience. He has had no imitators
worth mentioning, because the particular skill with which he
constructed his books depended upon a genius of the most
original kind. Perhaps no Englishman could successfully imitate him. But I observe that some of the finest modern French
work—sketches of travel in particular—is being constructed
upon lines remarkably similar to the method of Borrow. I do
not think this is an imitation; it is rather a spontaneous creation
of the same sort; and it is the work of men who, like Borrow,
have passed their lives in wandering about the world. (pp. 186-87)

> *Lafcadio Hearn, "George Borrow," in his* Life and
> Literature, *edited by John Erskine, William Heine-
> mann, 1922, pp. 181-87.*

CLEMENT SHORTER   (lecture date 1903)

*[In addition to the following lecture delivered on the occasion of
the Borrow Centenary in 1903, Shorter published a biography of
Borrow that has been highly praised (see Additional Bibliography).]*

Lavengro with its continuation **The Romany Rye,** is a great
work of imagination, of invention; it is in no sense a photograph, a memory picture, and it abounds in humour as it abounds
in many other great characteristics. What makes an author
supremely great? Surely a certain quality which we call genius,
as distinct from the mere intellectual power of some less brilliant writer:—

> True genius is the ray that flings
> A novel light o'er common things

and here it is that Borrow shines supreme. He has invested
with quite novel light a hundred commonplace aspects of life. . . .
To say that *Lavengro* merely indicates keen observation is absurd. Not the keenest observation will crowd so many adventures, adventures as fresh and as novel as those of [Le Sage's]

Gil Blas or [Defoe's] Robinson Crusoe, into a few months'
experience. "I felt some desire," says Lavengro, "to meet
with one of those adventures which upon the roads of England
are generally as plentiful as blackberries in autumn." I think
that most of us will wander along the roads of England for a
very long time before we meet an Isopel Berners, before we
have such an adventure as that of the blacksmith and his horse,
or of the apple woman whose favourite reading was *Moll Flanders*. These and a hundred other adventures, the fight with the
Flaming Tinman, the poisoning of Lavengro by the gypsy
woman, the discourse with Ursula under the hedge, when once
read are fixed upon the memory for ever. And yet you may
turn to them again and again, and with ever increasing zest.
The story of Isopel Berners is a piece of imaginative writing
that certainly has no superior in the literature of the last century.
It was assuredly no photographic experience. Isopel Berners
is herself a creation ranking among the fine creations of womanhood of the finest writers. I doubt not but that it was inspired
by some actual memory of Borrow. . . . [Whether] there were
ever a real Isopel we shall never know. We do know that
Borrow has presented his fictitious one with infinite poetry and
fine imaginative power. We do know, moreover, that it is not
right to describe Isopel Berners as a marvellous episode in a
narrative of other texture. *Lavengro* is full of marvellous episodes. Some one has ventured to comment upon Borrow's
style—to imply that it is not always on a high plane. What
does that matter? Style is not the quality that makes a book
live, but the novelty of the ideas. Stevenson was a splendid
stylist, and his admirers have deluded themselves into believing
that he was, therefore, among the immortals. But Stevenson
had nothing new to tell the world, and he was not, he is not,
therefore of the immortals. Borrow is of the immortals, not by
virtue of a style, but by virtue of having something new to
say. He is with Dickens and with Carlyle as one of the three
great British prose writers of the age we call Victorian, who
in quite different ways have presented a new note for their own
time and for long after. It is the distinction of Borrow that he
has invested the common life of the road, of the highway, the
path through the meadow, the gypsy encampment, the country
fair, the very apple stall and wayside inn with an air of romance
that can never leave those of us who have once come under
the magnificent spell of *Lavengro* and the *Romany Rye*. Perhaps
Borrow is pre-eminently the writer for those who sit in arm-
chairs and dream of adventures they will never undertake. . . .
Borrow stands with Carlyle and Dickens in *our* century, by
which I mean the nineteenth century; with Defoe and Goldsmith
in the eighteenth century, as one of the really great and imperishable masters of our tongue. (pp. 87-91)

> *Clement Shorter, "To the Immortal Memory of George
> Borrow," in his* Immortal Memories, *Hodder and
> Stoughton, 1907, pp. 61-93.*

ARTHUR CONAN DOYLE   (essay date 1907)

*[Doyle was a late nineteenth- and early twentieth-century English
novelist and short story writer who is best remembered as the
creator of Sherlock Holmes.]*

[Borrow] was a very strange man, bigoted, prejudiced, obstinate, inclined to be sulky, as wayward as a man could be. So
far his catalogue of qualities does not seem to pick him as a
winner. But he had one great and rare gift. He preserved through
all his days a sense of the great wonder and mystery of life—
the child sense which is so quickly dulled. Not only did he
retain it himself, but he was wordmaster enough to make other

Borrow's fight with the Flaming Tinman. Historical Pictures Service, Chicago.

people hark back to it also. As he writes you cannot help seeing through his eyes, and nothing which his eyes saw or his ear heard was ever dull or commonplace. It was all strange, mystic, with some deeper meaning struggling always to the light. If he chronicled his conversation with a washerwoman there was something arresting in the words he said, something singular in her reply. If he met a man in a public-house one felt, after reading his account, that one would wish to know more of that man. If he approached a town he saw and made you see—not a collection of commonplace houses or frowsy streets, but something very strange and wonderful, the winding river, the noble bridge, the old castle, the shadows of the dead. Every human being, every object, was not so much a thing in itself, as a symbol and reminder of the past. He looked through a man at that which the man represented. Was his name Welsh? Then in an instant the individual is forgotten and he is off, dragging you in his train, to ancient Britons, intrusive Saxons, unheard-of bards, Owen Glendower, mountain raiders and a thousand fascinating things. (pp. 97-8)

But, my word, what English the fellow could write! What an organ-roll he could get into his sentences! How nervous and vital and vivid it all is!

There is music in every line of it if you have been blessed with an ear for the music of prose. (p. 99)

Arthur Conan Doyle, in a chapter in his Through the Magic Door, *1907. Reprint by Doubleday, Page & Company, 1925, pp. 94-106.**

R.A.J. WALLING   (essay date 1909)

[*Walling's study of Borrow's life and career contains the following general discussion of* The Bible in Spain, Lavengro, The Romany Rye, Wild Wales, *and Borrow's verse translations. Walling focuses on Borrow's Celtic ancestry and background and its influence on his life and work.*]

[In] point of art, **"The Bible in Spain"** does not bear comparison with **"Lavengro."** For what it is worth, that is a deliberate judgment. But it should be said that no such comparison ought to be instituted. The two books are widely different in inspiration, in purpose, in execution. The record of the Spanish journeys has an interest of its own, and may stand on its own merits. As a descriptive and narrative writer Borrow had few superiors in his time. His style smacks of Defoe, smacks of the Bible, smacks of the archaic poets and romancers he loved so well. But it is his own style—at once a noble and spacious style and no style at all. There is no preciosity and there is little elegance in it; but there is naturalism, virility, grandeur. Only when he becomes didactic does his power decline. Then, in spite of his tremendous vigour of invective, he rarely rises above the level of the leader-writer, with his eye on the thing nearest to his fond prejudices, searching for the most offensive word that happens to be handy.

There is probably less sermonising in **"The Bible in Spain"** than in **"Lavengro"** and **"The Romany Rye."** Borrow is in love with Spain as Spain. He abounds in admiration of the country and its climate, the nobility of its people and their "stern, heroic virtue." He does not gloss over the savagery and crime to be found among them, but he observes that there is very little of low, vulgar vice in the great body of the Spanish nation. (pp. 296-97)

"The Bible in Spain" is a piece of Borrow. That provides its principal charm. It is not peppered with "dots and asterisks" in the same way as **"Lavengro,"** and does not depend for any great part of its effect on ellipsis. But it is still delightfully irresponsible and inconsequential, full of quaint snatches of character, of rough sketches of picturesque figures, of bits of adventure which lead nowhere, yet carry the reader on from incident to incident with a fascination as irresistible as the elusive attractions of [Sterne's] "Tristram Shandy." There are solid values as well. There are the rugged, unpremeditated eloquence of its descriptions, the vivid colouring of its persons in the piece, and the never-flagging gallop of its action. One would be hard pressed to name a book of its kind in which stir and progression are more constant.

On every page peep realistic portraits at which the reader has just time to glance before he is hurried on. (p. 299)

It is the essence of Spain that Borrow gives us in his inimitable, erratic way, its hot love and burning hate, its high chivalry and its profound roguery, the ineffable beauty of its women and the ugly rags of its mendicants, the solemn dignity of its people and their saline wit, contrasted with his own sententiousness and his peculiar, mordant humour. The vitality of the book, the continuing effect of its best scenes, and the never-failing interest of its adventures, are wonderful.

Yet there is hardly a Borrovian who does not prefer **"Lavengro"** and **"The Romany Rye,"** regarding them as one book, to anything else that Borrow ever did. It is incomparably the finest and most fragrant efflorescence of his genius. The fascination exercised by **"Lavengro"** over a considerable part of the human race is difficult to explain: its secret is as elusive as a great deal else in Borrow. But its existence cannot be questioned. It has hypnotised men of vastly different temperaments, causing this one to devote his life to the delightful, if unprofitable, pursuit of the mysteries concealed behind Borrow's "dots and asterisks" and the filling up of his ellipses, and that one to become a student of Romany and a "gypsiologist" who would otherwise have remained indifferent to the history and character of the chals and chis.

Many discussions have been held upon the nature of this secret. It still avoids capture; it cannot be precipitated into words. Some explanation of its effects may be offered, but even that can be but tentative. The book appeals to primal instincts. It quivers with life. It stirs the deepest emotions of those who have the sub-conscious love of Nature—the instinct for Nature which manifests itself not in petty eulogies of the fine things of the world, but in silent, ecstatic content with Earth. Gypsies have it strongly developed; indeed, it explains gypsyism. The book abounds in the unconventional strong man, in his joy of conflict, in his curiosity about human villainy, and his admiration of all heroic qualities. (pp. 302-03)

["Lavengro," in which I include "The Romany Rye,"] defies analysis or classification. It is "a thing of shreds and patches," a hotch-potch of odds and ends of learning and speculation, an uneven jumble of incidents; doubtless it is all the critics of 1851 said it was. Yet it is a great book, a treasured book, a book to read five times . . . , to dip into and be tempted on and on, chapter by chapter. It has all the faults that the purists allot to it—much tiresome iteration, many split infinitives, gross errors of taste, much fuliginous and turgid writing. Yet it is a great work of literature, compelling, overpowering in many ways. It often rises in eloquence to remarkable heights and glows with all the hues of poetry: mark the dialogue on death, the midnight vigil in the Dingle. The force of sheer description in the poison scene and in the fight with the Flaming Tinman can hardly be surpassed. . . . All Borrow's affectation of learning, all his word-chasing, all his preaching, are forgiven in the intense joy of such scenes as these. When Jack Slingsby said to him, "It's a fine thing to be a scholar," he retorted, "Not half so fine as to be a tinker." It is the hedgesmith in Lavengro that gives his book its ineffable charm. "There is something highly poetical about a forge," and Borrow has caught and transmitted its poetry to us. (pp. 309-10)

Borrow, in spite of his pose of Anglo-Saxonism, was a true Celt, a very wisp of the Celtic spirit itself. The fact explains everything about his tour in Wales, his intercourse with Welshmen, and his success in achieving a book ["Wild Wales"] which they are quite willing to confess is one of the best books ever written about their country. The spell was upon him, and he was content to let it work without attempting to divide it, chemically or mechanically, into its component elements. It worked through the scenery which he described with his peculiar skill, whether of massive mountain and lonely lake, or of sweet vale and tinkling cascade. It worked through the language, which he admired for its wonderful soft music concealed under apparently fortuitous concourses of crabbed consonants. It worked through the character of the people for whom he had so strong an affinity hidden behind all his affectation of downrightishness, John-Bullish egotism and pride. He was completely successful in his tribute to Wales—one of the finest in English literature. (p. 320)

[In "The Sleeping Bard," which Borrow translated from the Welsh author Elis Wyn, what] concerns us is the quality of Borrow's rendering. His style lent itself admirably to the interpretation of the ideas in the book, and whatever the excellences or defects of his work as a translator, the effect he produces, especially in the most lurid parts of the "Visions," is often superb. There is magnificent prose in the last section, the "Vision of Hell"—notably in the dialogues between Lucifer and his hosts. Lucifer's address to the "potentates of Hell! princes of the black abodes of Despair!" is a gigantic conception of the eternal warfare of Good and Evil, couched in language of extraordinary power. . . . While Borrow was engaged in transferring these scenes into English, contrasting the peaceful figure of the Bard asleep on the summit of Cader Idris with the appalling spectacles of his dreams, delighting in the process of heaping horror upon horror and crashing them against the "squeamish nonsense" of his age, he did not fail to be effective. It was when he took to verse that he failed: the metrical translations at the end of each section are the weakest things in the book. (pp. 325-27)

Borrow's purely poetical works remain to be considered. The ballad literature of many lands had overpowering fascination for him. This was a perfectly natural affinity. In the ballads, if anywhere, is to be found the "homely, plain writing" which Borrow admired. In them, too, were enshrined the histories of the characters he loved or the heroes he adored. If the public had afforded him more encouragement, we should have had a series of transcripts and translations spreading over many years. Fortunately, sheer force of circumstances pushed Borrow into another literary channel and gave us his prose books. Borrow's lyrical genius is hardly a matter for discussion; it simply does not exist. . . . Most of his verse is artificial, stilted, and in the most violent contrast with the vigorous naturalism of his prose. He seemed to have a lyrical sense, but no capacity for recording its impressions. The result is a mass of doggerel, here and there lightened and vivified by a stanza or two of real beauty, happening simply where a concourse of chances gave him subject, imaginative idea, and words which harmonised. These flashes of inspiration, however, are rare.

The "Romantic Ballads" which he translated in his youth from the old Danish and from Oehlenschlaeger are exceedingly interesting because of their matter: the legends include some of the great ones of the Northern world. But Borrow's verse would provide a deep disappointment for any reader who, having made acquaintance with his prose through "Lavengro," for example, had conceived high expectations of his poetry. (pp. 329-30)

["The Death Raven," his translation of a ballad by Oehlenschlaeger,] produces an eerie effect of magic forces acting in the natural world—the Death Raven as the spirit of Evil bargaining with its victim and wreaking hideous woe and bloody tragedy till it is finally overcome by the vengeance of a pure maiden who calls to her aid the supernal powers against the infernal. But Borrow is in literal difficulties all the time, and the story hitches and tears on the irregularities and ugly angles of his verse. . . . The best thing in the book is the ballad of "Swayne [or Svend] Vonved." . . . (pp. 333-34)

The "Ballads" have some interest, but, with the exception of "Svend Vonved," they have small merit, and it is not surprising that the public took so little notice of them that the second edition was never required. Borrow made much better play with his Danish legends and his heroes of the North in his later prose books, where they take their proper place as the material of soufflés or as flavouring in a tasty mélange. (p. 336)

R.A.J. Walling, in his George Borrow: The Man and His Work, *Cassell and Company, Ltd., 1909, 356 p.*

[W. D. HOWELLS] (essay date 1914)

[*Howells was the chief progenitor of American realism and an influential American literary critic during the late nineteenth and early twentieth centuries. Although he wrote nearly three dozen novels, few of them are read today. Despite his eclipse, however, he stands as one of the major literary figures of the late nineteenth century; having successfully weaned American literature from the sentimental romanticism of its infancy, he earned the popular sobriquet "the Dean of American Letters." In the following excerpt, Howells recounts his ambivalence toward the mixture of fact and fiction in Borrow's travel books and novels.*]

A pleasant sort of fiction greatly in favor twenty-five or thirty years ago, but now quite gone out of fashion, was the novel which took a pretended voyage or tour for its outline, and then filled in with real incidents of travel which were the supposed experiences of its imaginary characters. The author was free to deal with the facts as he would, but he must not rearrange landscapes, or make compositions of scenery; and upon the whole, he respected the integrity of his own scheme. But of course the species was always tending to become entirely fiction. . . .

The antithesis to this form was never so abundant in examples, and never so popular, because, perhaps, it never started so honestly with the reader. It took a real tour or voyage for its outline, and filled in with invented incidents which were the supposed experience of its veritable characters. Such a method must soon invite detection and bring the author under condemnation for outright fibbing, when he may have been meaning no worse than the indulgence of a lively invention, for the purpose of amusing as well as instructing. The master in this sort, so superlatively master as to seem sole in it after De Foe, was the author of *The Bible in Spain* and *Wild Wales,* books which impress one as scarcely less fictitious than *Robinson Crusoe* itself. . . . [Borrow] employed his own travels in the Peninsula and the Principality as the base of moving accidents, which move the reader less and less with belief in their verity as they delightfully follow one another. They may have really happened; but if you begin by thinking they all did happen, you possibly end by thinking that . . . none of them did. . . . Whether one wholly accepts this view, however, or rejects it, one is aware of having formed some such impression from the book itself, though one may have begun it with much the same faith in its veracity as the author himself probably had, or began by having.

On the surface [*The Bible in Spain*] commends itself as a pious record of Protestant observation in the most backward of Catholic countries, but as the plot thickens and the drama deepens, the religious interest is lost in the excitement of the personal adventure, which for one's pleasure one does not require to be veracious. (p. 958)

Borrow is in every way an anomaly. . . . He was by nature a poet of exuberant, not to say belligerent imagination, and in his life as in his literature he was at odds with whatever opinion people formed of him. You cannot read his books without feeling their contrary-minded charm, which does not permit you either to believe him altogether or to deny him entirely, and in his personal contacts it must have been much the same. Nobody can question his sincerity, and it would be difficult for anybody to affirm his honesty, or defend his proneness to say the thing which is not equally with the thing which is. Apparently he was perfectly willing to stick to the fact when it would serve his purpose; when it would not, not. It is in his simulated real narrative that he seems to survive rather more

than in his frankly posited fiction; that is, we fancy more people continue to read *The Bible in Spain* and *Wild Wales* than *Lavengro* and *The Romany Rye;* and yet there are fanatical adherents of the novels who will not let you think of them as less than great works of imagination. This we should certainly say they were not, while we should own that few authors have been more completely themselves in their work. Borrow's mannerisms recall a very little the poses of Sterne, yet the liberal air in which he moves and the variety of his scene difference him beyond any resemblance to the other master. Sterne is affected while Borrow is perverse; both are wilful. Upon the whole Sterne's little group of eccentrics who evolve the story of *Tristram Shandy* are more tiresome than Borrow's gipsies, whose genuine nature occasionally imparts a relief from their factitious character. One of the figures of his fiction which remains most distinctly with the reader is the impossible Isopel Berners, whose wilding personality has some such allure as that of Uncle Remus's "Mrs. Meadows and the gals," in their association with his rabbits and foxes and other four-footed *dramatis personae* on the terms of a common interest and equal intelligence. She is no more accounted for than they in her odd circumstance; we do not even understand that she is of gipsy blood; a piquant mystery lastingly involves her, and she is worth more to the imagination than all the horse-trading and kettle-mending tribe of undoubted gipsies. These, even in the fable which the author weaves about them, never quite convince one of their aesthetic importance; Borrow himself cannot establish for them any strong claim upon one's affection, much less one's respect. (p. 959)

In novels the author rightfully reports or invents at will, and cannot justly be accused of anything worse than romancing. It is in his books of travel, like *The Bible in Spain* and *Wild Wales,* that Borrow's romancing may be called by the harsher name of lying; but even there it cannot be quite justly called so. After some reflection, we think we should prefer to characterize it as that softer and more innocent form of falsehood which may be known by the children's euphemism of story-telling. Of course, it is falsehood, and so far so bad; but it is not malicious or injurious falsehood. (pp. 959-60)

[If Borrow should ultimately be classed with such careful narrators as] Marco Polo and De Tocqueville, we shall be the first to rejoice, and we should possibly never have had any complaint to make of him if he had plainly said at the beginning that his narrative was largely fanciful or must at least be taken with many grains of salt, or, at any rate, some. We do not yet see, however, how he could quite have done this; it might have prevented a reader, whose suspicions he had roused, from believing anything he said. We think, of course, that between George Washington and George Borrow, the instant veracity of George Washington was to be preferred, yet George Washington himself did not go about proclaiming that he had chopped the cherry-tree, or was going to chop it; he waited until he was asked who did chop it, and then he owned the truth. In law, which is said to be the perfection of reason, a man is not obliged to say anything to incriminate himself, and it is to be remembered that Borrow, in undoubtedly carrying *The Bible in Spain,* to people quite without it, was engaged in a work upon which he would not be justified in bringing discredit by a promise of inveracity. To warn the reader beforehand that he was going to play fast and loose with him would be a deed without a name, or at least without a precedent in the history of literature. (p. 961)

[*W. D. Howells*], *in a review of "The Bible in Spain," in* Harper's Monthly Magazine, *Vol. CXXVIII, No. DCCLXVIII, May, 1914, pp. 958-61.*

GEORGE MOORE and SIR EDMUND GOSSE (conversation
date 1919)

[*The following is a transcription of a conversation between the
novelist George Moore and the critic Sir Edmund Gosse. The
subject to which Moore refers in the first paragraph is Gosse's
contention "that literature written for money is worthless from
an aesthetic point of view." For additional commentary by Gosse,
see excerpt below, 1923.*]

[Moore. I was surprised to learn] that Borrow was a contemporary of Scott. A century at least should divide them, I said,
and I fell to thinking of one writing *The Bible in Spain,* his
eye always on the object, thinking only how he might discover
every voice and aspect of Spain in English prose, and the other
improvising novels to buy farms. Borrow is an integral part of
my subject, I said, for now I come to consider it, like Sterne,
he saved his talent by refraining from storytelling.

Gosse. But he did write stories: *Lavengro* and *The Romany
Rye.*

Moore. These admirable books have always been looked upon
as biographies into which Borrow introduced many imaginary
anecdotes; and it seems worth while to point out that the strange
mixture of fact and fiction which has caused so much wonderment among his admirers was imposed upon Borrow by the
very nature of his talent, too great to permit him to write a
literature of oiled ringlets and perfumery, and not great enough
to allow him to create outside of his own observation and
knowledge, in other words, to evoke human souls out of his
instinctive knowledge of how human life is made.

Gosse. We had an interesting talk on that subject not very
many days ago, you maintaining that Serge Aksakoff was not
the principal character, but Serge's father, whereas I looked
upon the narrator as the chief character. But I can see now that
I was wrong, for Serge does not attempt to narrate himself like
Rousseau; he is less in his narrative than Borrow is in *Lavengro.*

Moore. Much less than Borrow is in *Lavengro,* a mere mouthpiece. But Borrow is a masked man, whose identity we would
pierce and who excites our wonderment as he goes by, sum-
moning his world into being like Goya. A very Goya before
he saw Spain, in Ireland; for what is more like Goya than the
old woman whom he found groaning over a straw fire in a
ruined castle somewhere near Clonmel, and the man Borrow
met hunting hare with hound in the bog as he returns home?
I know no book that I would as soon read again as *The Bible
in Spain.* Landscape after landscape, and Goya and his people
everywhere. Is there not somewhere in the book a dwarf who
turns somersaults in front of Borrow's horse, or did I invent
it? (pp. 59-60)

[Moore. Unlike] Goya, he left us no portraits of women as
he should have done, for he was a bachelor till he was nearly
forty; and it is the bachelor who tells us the feminine soul
truthfully. The only exception to the rule that I can think of is
Borrow, whose books are stamped with an indifference to
women. Yes, Gosse, it is so; if there were no bachelors we
should know nothing of women. (p. 60)

[Moore.] In *Wild Wales* we are in a real country filled with
real people, and Borrow enchants us with his talks with the
wayfarers as he walks through the hills, having conveniently
left his wife and daughter behind. Numerous are his characters
as are the people that come and go through the pages of the
Bible.

Gosse. How he enjoys his beer, and how the quality of the
beer fixes a certain picturesque site in his memory. And of the
truth of this to nature I can vouch, having wandered into Wales
for the purpose of verifying the accuracy of Borrow's observation, for I too remember a certain town by the excellence of
the glass of beer I drank in its inn. (pp. 61-2)

[Gosse.] He was born in the eighteenth; I should say he was
a contemporary of Sir Walter Scott, as your friends told you,
and as your thesis, or a great part of it, is that literature written
for money is worthless from an aesthetic point of view, and
from every point of view in a few years, I think that Borrow
is the illustration you require. All his books, with one exception, were failures, commercial failures, with the exception of
The Bible in Spain, and it was not the literary merits of *The
Bible in Spain* that caused it to be read. It was read for the
sake of the propaganda; if it had been less well written it would
probably have been still more widely read. It was read for the
sake of the propaganda; if it had been less well written it would
probably have been still more widely read. And if you care to
emphasize your paradox that a man's name directs the course
of his life, you can say that George Borrow is a name that
would be approved by his admirers if his books had come to
us anonymously. You will be safe in saying as much, for the
name is plain, straightforward, without subterfuge or evasion,
in perfect agreement with the man's literary style and his wont.
I can hear you call it an honest English name. . . . (p. 62)

Moore. The name seems to me (like the books he wrote) to
represent one side of the man's character vividly enough, but
there must have been another side, and one that played a large
part in the comedy of his life, else he would not have troubled
to keep it out of sight so completely. (p. 63)

> *George Moore, in a conversation with Sir Edmund
> Gosse, in his* Avowals, *n.p., 1919, pp. 43-101.**

EDMUND GOSSE (essay date 1923)

[*A distinguished English literary historian, critic, and biographer,
Gosse wrote extensively on seventeenth- and eighteenth-century
English literature. His commentary in* Seventeenth-Century Studies *(1883),* A History of Eighteenth Century Literature, *(1889),*
Questions at Issue *(1893), and other works is generally regarded
as sound and suggestive. For additional commentary by Gosse,
see excerpt above, 1919.*]

During the life-time of that singular adventurer, George Borrow, no one would have dreamed of admitting him to a place
among the principal writers of his time, although his *Bible in
Spain* made him prominent for a moment. But since his death
the fame of Borrow has steadily increased, and is now firmly
grounded on his picturesque and original studies in romanti-
cised autobiography. Much spoiled by their irregularity, their
freakishness and their intellectual prejudices, excellent only in
parts as the best of his books must always be considered, the
really vivid chapters of *Lavengro* and the *Romany Rye* have a
masculine intelligence, a breadth and novelty of vision, which
make them unique. It is part of the fascination of Borrow that
in spite of his vanity in many things,—as pre-eminently in his
tiresome and presumptuous airs as a philologist,—when he is
really himself, his originality acts unconsciously, with a violence and ardour which carry the reader entirely away for the
time being, although they are sure presently to flag and fall.
(p. 270)

> *Edmund Gosse, "The Early Victorian Age—
> 1840-1870," in his* English Literature, an Illustrated

Record: From the Age of Johnson to the Age of Tennyson, Vol. IV, *revised edition, The Macmillan Company, 1923, pp. 200-302.**

HERBERT G. WRIGHT   (essay date 1928)

[*The following excerpt is from Wright's introduction to the first publication of* Celtic Bards, Chiefs and Kings, *Borrow's study of Welsh literature and history.*]

[**"Celtic Bards, Chiefs and Kings"**] is a remarkable contribution to the study of Welsh literature. . . . [Borrow's attempt] to give a connected account of Welsh poetry deserves high praise. Naturally his work has its limitations. Modern research would reject some of his material, and in details he sometimes goes wrong. It would, however, be unjust to ignore Borrow's merits. He wrote with knowledge, the result of some thirty years' reading. . . . [He] went to the originals and obtained his information at first hand. A careful investigation of the sources he used shows how much more at home Borrow was with his theme than his contemporary, Matthew Arnold. We miss the brilliant and unreliable generalisations, it is true; but we feel that the foundations of **"Celtic Bards, Chiefs and Kings"** are far more securely laid than those of "The Study of Celtic Literature."

Borrow brought a tremendous enthusiasm to bear on his task. Sometimes, it must be admitted, his zeal outruns his judgment, as when he claims for his favourite Dafydd ap Gwilym that he is Ovid, Horace, Tibullus, Martial, and Tyrtaeus all in one. Borrow himself anticipates objections, and explains that before ap Gwilym can ever be appreciated in English he must find a great translator, even as Homer found Pope. A lucky thing for Homer, thinks Borrow, that his name was not David Williams, and that he did not write in Welsh. One need not take this too seriously, for it was never Borrow's way to do or say things by halves, and he is almost equally lavish in his praise of others among his favourite Welsh poets. Occasionally, moreover, he turns his knowledge of foreign literature to better account than in discussing Dafydd ap Gwilym. Thus, in dealing with Ellis Wynn's "Sleeping Bard" he recalls the "Visions" of Quevedo, finding a similarity to which attention has recently again been drawn. . . . In the main, too, it must be admitted that Borrow's estimate of the relative importance of the Welsh poets is not out of proportion. True, there are some names we might hear less of or dispense with altogether, and others of whom we would fain hear more, but those writers to whom Borrow devotes most space and care are the great bards of Wales. Borrow was, therefore, by no means devoid of taste or judgment; he had at least some sense of discrimination. But he was not a great critic, and at bottom he was more interested in human nature than in aesthetic values. Literature appealed to him in the first place, as he repeatedly shows, as a revelation of the author's character.

Interwoven with Borrow's account of the bards is a good deal of history, that of the Celtic chieftains and kings. When Borrow included these in his book he had in mind Owen Glendower, Griffith ap Nicholas, Ryce ap Thomas, and the two Tudor sovereigns, Henry VII and Henry VIII. Incidentally he drew a striking picture of the intriguing nobles who defeated Richard III and placed Henry VII on the throne and also of Henry VIII's contemporaries, Ferdinand and Isabella, Maximilian, Francis, Wolsey, and the Popes. It need scarcely be said that Borrow is not a dispassionate historian. On the contrary, he is a keen partisan and paints his characters in the brightest or blackest colours, according to his leanings. (pp. 5-8)

If Borrow has his weaknesses as a writer on history, he has also his merits. He has visualised each of his personages as a man of flesh and blood, has formed a clear opinion of his character, and pats him approvingly on the back or administers to him a sound cudgelling, as if he were one of his own kith and kin. What a contrast between Borrow's Griffith ap Nicholas or Ryce ap Thomas and the pale chieftains of the dry-as-dust chronicle in the "Cambrian Register," where Borrow found them sleeping the sleep of many centuries! He enlivens his narrative by introducing imaginary conversations or correspondence. (pp. 11-12)

The use of the rhetorical question and his love of the dramatic are also marked features of Borrow's work. One sees here, too, that fondness for fighting which Borrow, the son of a soldier, always displayed, whether in his adventures in England and Spain or in his translations of Danish ballads. His pictures of the Battle of the Spurs, of Bosworth Field, and of the struggle at Mortimer's Cross are among the best things he has written. (p. 12)

[Though] in **"Celtic Bards, Chiefs and Kings"** Borrow, the lover of the open road, is less to the fore than in many of his other works, there are compensations. We have admirable illustrations of his powers as a writer, many passages being as graphic, vivid, and vigorous as the best of his writings; we see, perhaps more clearly than anywhere else, his erudition and his indefatigability in the quest of curious information, and, lastly, the work adds much to our knowledge of that singular agglomeration of imagination, sympathy, generous impulse, violent prejudice, and shrewd mother-wit—George Borrow. (pp. 25-6)

> *Herbert G. Wright, in an introduction to* Celtic Bards, Chiefs and Kings *by George Borrow, edited by Herbert G. Wright, John Murray, 1928, pp. 1-26.*

PAUL ELMER MORE   (essay date 1928)

[*More was an American critic who, along with Irving Babbitt, formulated the doctrines of New Humanism in early twentieth-century American thought. The New Humanists were strict moralists who adhered to traditional conservative values in reaction to an age of scientific and artistic self-expression. In regard to literature, they believed that the aesthetic qualities of a work of art should be subordinate to its moral and ethical purpose. More was particularly opposed to Naturalism, which he believed accentuated the animal nature of humans, and to any literature, such as Romanticism, that broke with established classical tradition. His importance as a critic derives from the rigid coherence of his ideology, which polarized American critics into hostile opponents (Van Wyck Brooks, Edmund Wilson. H. L. Mencken) or devoted supporters (Norman Foerster, Stuart Sherman, and, to a lesser degree, T. S. Eliot). He is especially esteemed for the philosophical and literary erudition of his multi-volumed Shelburne* Essays *(1904-21). In the following excerpt, More places Borrow firmly in the picaresque tradition.*]

The good Borrovian probably got his first initiation into the sect (for Borrow, like Peacock, is one of those originals who gather about them a peculiar people) through the sheer love of adventure. Certainly there is enough of that commodity in Borrow to allure the boy and still fascinate the man, despite the long stretches of dulness and the occasional effect of repetition that somehow seem almost inevitable to a *genre* which ought theoretically to be freest from them. But the Borrovian

A drawing of Mumper's Dingle from Lavengro, *where Borrow camped alongside Isopel (Belle) Berners. Courtesy of The Putnam Publishing Group.*

has another anchor to hold his interest. As from the mere entertainment of Borrow's works, which are little more than a continued autobiography, he is drawn on to study the writer, he finds himself looking at one of the most enigmatical and tantalizing personalities of English literature. . . . The outlines of the desired portrait are clear enough, but when I have thought to touch the heart of the man I have been curiously piqued and baffled. At times I have been ready to believe that the enigma really had no answer, and there was no possibility of seeing the face behind the masque simply because no such face existed and the masque was all. Which would be only another way of saying that Borrow escapes us by possessing the innocence and elusiveness of Nature herself.

Yet in a superficial way Borrow is one of the easiest of men to place. Both in his life and his writings he belongs clearly to the great picaresque tradition which begins as a conscious kind with the [anonymous novel] *Lazarillo de Tormes* and in England is continued by Nash and Defoe and Smollett, and was not forgotten by Thackeray when he created his magnificent Becky Sharp. (pp. 127-28)

The path of the picaresque writer is . . . in one sense narrow and sharply defined. His rôle is to set forth the underside of life with all its variety of incident and its hostility to prescription, but he must do all this with a kind of imperturbability of conscience which converts evil into innocence. The moment he displays a touch of moral indignation he passes from the

picaresque to the preacher or the satirist, and if he shows the least disposition to gloat over things evil as disgusting or revolting he falls into the mood of the modern realist. Now in that strait road Borrow walked with all the apparent carelessness of [Le Sage's] Gil Blas. . . . From childhood to old age his pleasure was to associate with vagabonds and thimble-riggers, horse-thieves and poisoners, prize-fighters and cutthroats, and these are the people of his books. (p. 136)

[If] Borrow's works follow the narrow tradition of the picaresque by escaping on one side all the qualms of conscience, they are equally true to the norm by avoiding on the other side the peculiar appeal of the heart which is the essence of most modern romanticism. Perhaps their most striking trait is just this unexpected absence of emotion in scenes where the follower of Wordsworth would revel in sentiment. (p. 138)

It might seem sufficient to say that to Borrow, as to the other masters of the picaresque style, the desolate and unusual scenes of nature were only a continuation, so to speak, of the spirit of adventure among strange human beings, and that the absence of sentimental personification was as necessary to the proper effect in the one case as the absence of moral concern was in the other. In a way that is true; but it is by no means the whole truth. Somehow, without a touch of that conscious blending of the human and the natural by which the romantic writer awakens our sentimental emotions, and with seldom a word to indicate that his own heart was moved, Borrow has succeeded in giving to Nature a magic power to charm or appall the soul which many an artificer in sentiment might envy. There are, for example, two or three pages in *The Bible in Spain* describing the nocturnal journey from Bembibre to Villafranca, which for terror and sublimity it would be hard to match in any other English book; yet only in a single brief sentence, so far as I remember, does any hint appear of deep feeling on the part of the writer himself.

The absence of direct human emotion in Borrow is even more surprising, not to say tantalizing, than his continence in the romantic sentiment of nature. It should seem at times as if he were utterly devoid of heart and the common passions of mankind. Think for a moment of the episode in Mumper's Dingle and all its emotional possibilities. It may not appear so extraordinary that he can go through the great fight with the Flaming Tinman as if his breast had never swelled with the feeling of rage or hatred or revenge, but where is the language to describe his relation to Isopel Berners? With minute detail he tells how she and he lived in their tents side by side in the remote and secret glen. We see the tall queen of the roads with all her blonde beauty and crown of yellow hair, a superb Amazon whose right hand was the flail of evil doers and puny tempters; night after night we see her by the solitary light of the camp-fire serving her companion in simple devotion, her pride humbled to pliant submission, yet, so far as any expression escapes the writer, you would not know that he possessed a body. When the woman in her threatens to break out, he crushes her with lessons in the Armenian verb, drilling her in these antic exercises as a master might train a dog; but it is a wise reader who can say whether he does this deliberately to avoid the perils of the equivocal situation or as a pure pedant with no pulse to leap at danger. The whole episode is cruel and in any other author would be sterile and unnatural. Yet withal, though there is no word of passion in these chapters, indeed scarcely a word of human feeling—save after Isopel has fled, and then the note of regret is feeble and false—they are able by some trick of composition, perhaps by the very absence of what is expected, to fix themselves in memory as one of the great love scenes of our literature. Was ever woman so coldly wooed before, we exclaim; but there exudes from that wooing, nevertheless, some thin, impalpable air of passion which he who breathes shall never forget. (pp. 139-40)

Borrow appears to me—as I seek the man himself within his books—essentially a picaresque character to whom life was an adventure in which the conscience and heart had no concern; yet he was still on the one side as clean himself as the wind on the heather and as fearless in missionary work as a Jesuit, and on the other side he can convey to the reader some of the subtlest emotions of romanticism. I state the contrasts sharply, knowing that they might perhaps be shaded away by exceptions and modifications; but they are there and they pique curiosity. (p. 142)

Paul Elmer More, ''George Borrow,'' in his The Demon of the Absolute, *Princeton University Press, 1928, pp. 127-42.*

EDD WINFIELD PARKS (essay date 1938)

[*Parks discusses the relation between self-revelation and conscious artistry in Borrow's fiction.*]

It is a fortunate fact that we cannot see ourselves as others see us; even more fortunate, perhaps, that others cannot see us as we see ourselves. In the history of literature only a few men have mirrored themselves for the world to gaze upon without first making certain that the glass was concave or convex. Montaigne and Pepys wrote in the most intimate manner about themselves; most authors have written with careful expurgations, with skeletons closely hidden in dark closets. . . .

George Borrow belongs to this second class. Almost everything he wrote was about himself: like Montaigne, he was most interested in himself. But Borrow also had a flair for dramatics; in him, as in Napoleon, there was a good bit of the poseur. Consciously or unconsciously changing the facts when it pleased him to do so, he told the story of his life not exactly as it happened, but as the creative artist in him felt it should have happened. Yet this picture Borrow presents of himself, touched up though it is by a master hand, is authentic and intrinsically honest. For a man reveals himself in everything he writes: if within himself there is validity and intellectual integrity, his work will have in turn worth and beauty. Something of these Borrow had, and something of them he caught in his books. But the true thing, the essence of the books, was Borrow himself—one of the strangest characters literature has ever known. (p. 313)

It is [his] restless personal quality, [his] intensity, which attracts readers. Borrow reveals himself—and the integrity behind this fiery intolerance, which sometimes alarms us in contemporaries, inevitably attracts us with magnetic force to writers of an earlier day, whose opinions can no longer do harm. Here is no structural art, no objectified form; it is not as an artist that Borrow must be judged. Although he dramatizes and heightens, he remains personal: fiction is employed only to buttress fact. A slow writer, a conscious artist, Borrow barely enters into the domain of art with a whole book. Whether fiction or fact, the dingle episode with Isopel Berners is properly objectified, for all its personal nature, and his unerring vignettes of character with their selectivity of detail reveal his strength. Even the dry craggy humor grows mainly out of idiosyncrasies of character, as in the episode of the man who can not for long be a good philosopher or a good German because he is not a good smoker.

But Borrow himself constantly obtrudes. And we would sacrifice something strange and fascinating if these parts, so imperfect and damaging to the structure of his work, were omitted. His opinions are out of line—a Tory in a land dominated by Liberals, hating or ignoring industrial progress; a frequenter of by-ways who attacked the straightness and direction of the main road; a man who saw but one side of a question, and frequently only one part of that—and violently expressed; they are the ideas of a narrow, sometimes crabbed, partisan mind. Yet a man's personality may compensate in an imperfect world for some artistic imperfections: the question becomes, eventually, not one of judgment by the critic but of acceptance by the reader.

Borrow's prose redeems in part his irregularities. It has the qualities of a clear mountain stream rushing cleanly and precipitously along, with jutting troublesome boulders in the shape of archaic phrasings and inordinate apostrophes to break the sweep and united strength of his writing. His models show the bent of his own mind: the Bible, the old Court trials, Bunyan, DeFoe, Swift, Cobbett, and Byron. Not subtlety but strength, not decoration but intrinsic richness, were the excellences in style he aimed at, and largely attained; but in a florid age his prose sounded hard and dry, so that one critic was misled into writing that he had no style. His work seemed, also, devoid of sentiment. Richness of style and sentiment there is, however, under the outer covering of spare dryness, for those to find who have an ear for words and sentences.

The highly personalized writer will always have a place, though rarely the highest place, in literature as long as men remain interested in vital personalities. Properly, work of this type is outside the scope of criticism, for it appeals directly to sympathies and prejudices and habits of thought. Although Borrow wrote no book which is strictly a novel, he made himself, virtually, the hero of autobiographical works that have the character of picaresque novels. That he succeeded in spite of his method may be the highest testimony to his style and to his validity as a person. (pp. 317-18)

> *Edd Winfield Parks, "Portrait of Lavengro: A Biographical Essay on George Borrow," in his* Segments of Southern Thought, *The University of Georgia Press, 1938, pp. 313-76.*

PETER QUENNELL (essay date 1941)

[*The essay from which the following was excerpted was originally published in the* New Statesman and Nation *on November 15, 1941.*]

George Borrow is Borrow's hero [in **Lavengro**]. He is an unusual hero, however—not always brave, far from resolute, in no career that he undertakes conspicuously successful, a moody, gloomy, pottering, reflective personage. All he asks is that we should regard him as a highly exceptional being, in the sense that, for good or ill, he is not as other men. Portents have attended him from early childhood. He has a strange power over poisonous snakes, a way with horses. In the nursery he is at first uncommonly dull and silent—but the Jewish pedlar notes at once that he is a gifted child—afterwards an extremely voracious reader. Instead of acquiring Greek, he learns Irish: when he is articled to the law, he engages in an intensive study of a mediaeval Welsh poet, the celebrated Ab Gwilym. Yet his studies (he is prepared to admit) are fragmentary and undisciplined: for the point he emphasises is not his genius but his personal separateness—the isolation that is the constant background of his thoughts and feelings. Lavengro is a lonely man with a thousand casual acquaintances—a man whose life is full of incidents and interests, but has little continuity. He drifts at large through the world, which flows cloudily past him. It is the panorama of a dream—inconsequent as are many dreams, but endowed with a visionary magnitude and a dreamlike vividness.

Borrow's sense of his own identity—and his self-portrait of a certain type of lonely, ineffective, thoughtful man—holds the narrative together from opening to closing chapters. We have all of us known such self-centred solitaries: but, whereas that type of egotism is usually dim and arid, Borrow turned his self-absorption to brilliant creative profit. Not many other modern writers have been able to give so pungent an air of individuality to the scenes or the personages that they describe: none can make more of a single unrelated incident. Borrow's finest passages are unforgettable: the impression they leave on the reader's imagination is never quite effaced. (pp. 147-48)

The extent of Borrow's indebtedness to Defoe is sufficiently clear: but equally obvious are the differences in their approach and outlook. Defoe's most impressive passages are built up of a painstaking accumulation of prosaic details—it is through the addition of one fact to another that, little by little, he achieves effects of surprising dignity: Borrow's grasp of an historical fact is subordinate to his appreciation of its emotional context. Borrow could not have completed a *Moll Flanders:* but then, Defoe could not have written the story of the man who believed in the magic touch or of the Welsh preacher who had committed the sin against the Holy Ghost—two absorbing studies of psychological malady. Borrow belonged to a revolutionary experimental age which, though it left the world an uglier, harsher, more confusing place, immensely enlarged the frontiers of the human consciousness. The limitations of the nineteenth-century mind, and the spiritual *malaise* and flashes of poetic insight by which it was often visited, receive illustration in the diversity and complexity of Borrow's dream-novel. (p. 151)

> *Peter Quennell, "George Borrow," in his* The Singular Preference: Portraits & Essays, *William Collins Sons & Co. Ltd., 1952, pp. 145-51.*

JOHN E. TILFORD, JR. (essay date 1949)

[*In the introduction to the essay excerpted below, Tilford examines earlier criticism that labeled* Lavengro *and* The Romany Rye *episodic and formless. Through his own analysis of their structure and themes, he finds that these works demonstrate an intentional artistic and unified form. He discusses the two novels as one work which he divides into three parts: Part I describes the hero's youth and includes Chapters I-XXVIII from* Lavengro; *Part II covers his year in London from Chapters XXIX-LVII of* Lavengro; *and Part III details his subsequent wanderings from the rest of* Lavengro, *Chapters LVIII-C, through the whole of* The Romany Rye, *Chapters I-XLVII (or, in Tilford's notation, Chapters CI-CXVII).*]

If **Lavengro-Romany Rye** is viewed as an autobiographical novel [rather than as a straightforward autobiography], ... one is more disposed to recognize the kind of artistry not associated with ingenuous autobiography. The story does have picaresque elements, both of form and content, and, like many long novels, is often episodic and rambling. But instead of being merely "a collection of incidents and dialogues," it has a persistent main action, the parts of which are related in a scheme predominantly logical and move toward an end—that is, it has structure. More comprehensively, it possesses form, which not only includes structure but embodies all thematic elements which lend it significance and help fulfill the author's purposes. It is the integration of all of these—action, structure, themes, purposes—that leads to artistic form. The intention of this study is to examine that integration in **Lavengro-Romany Rye** and to show that the resultant form, though by no means flawless, is far more artistic than has hitherto been supposed.

Like [Le Sage's] *Gil Blas* and [Dickens's] *David Copperfield,* **Lavengro-Romany Rye** possesses the basic unity deriving from the presence of a hero-narrator. Unlike *Gil Blas,* however, which is a series of loosely related episodes, Borrow's novel has a single main action which (with some qualifications) persists from beginning to end. And unlike *David Copperfield,* which consists of so many plot elements that David is often less a protagonist than a chronicler, **Lavengro-Romany Rye** is simple in plotting, and the hero Lavengro is almost always the center of attention.

The main action of the novel takes the hero from birth to early manhood in three stages, which are unified within themselves and integrated with one another. Part I (Chaps. I-XXVIII) depicts the childhood and youth of Lavengro, showing how his character develops and bringing him into contact with the major influences on his mind—the Gypsies, foreign languages, a "radical" scholar, and Protestantism. As his father, a soldier, is successively stationed in various parts of Great Britain, Part I is inevitably somewhat episodic, but it preserves a reasonable continuity. Some leaping and lingering, too, is natural to the autobiographical method of narration: the hero perforce recollects his early life not as a continuous story but as a series of events spread over many years—events ostensibly recalled because of their vividness and significance. Saintsbury aptly called *Lavengro* "a succession of dissolving views" [see excerpt above, 1886]; but he overlooked the progressive organization of these views, especially in Part I—almost every one is implicitly or explicitly meaningful in the hero's development.

Part II (Chaps. XXIX-LVII) takes Lavengro to London (after his father's death) and shows him seeking literary fame through his translations from Welsh, Danish, and German. It concentrates on this single action and covers only "somewhat more than a year"—hence its structure is much tighter than that of Part I. For the new life there is a new structure, and the story moves with a new cadence. The main action proceeds emphatically from the hopeful Lavengro's arrival to the point where, in desperation, he writes the potboiler "Joseph Sell" and leaves the city. It centers in his relations with the publisher, for whom he does hackwork after his translations are rejected. His literary ambitions are treated in scene after scene: when he reads a newspaper in an inn, when he views Byron's cortege, and when he converses with such characters as Taggart, an Armenian merchant, and the Gypsies. . . . Though many scenes in this part are calculated to acquaint him with the world of London and to add to the color and richness of the story, none strays for long from the central action and most are related to it.

In Part III (Chaps. LVIII-CXLVII) Lavengro wanders about the countryside trying to regain his health and spirits, to find an occupation, and to think out his philosophy of life. (pp. 370-71)

Part III, with ninety chapters, covers about four months. There are many casual episodes and seeming digressions that make it the most rambling portion of the novel, with the most leisurely cadence, and the one most deserving, apparently, to be called "picaresque." The digressions, in eighteenth-century tradition, include life-histories told by six characters. Yet, obscured as the main action often is, it nonetheless persists: Lavengro never forgets his search for a labor and a philosophy. Many times he takes counsel with himself: What is to be his work? What purpose has he in life? What is the meaning of life itself? . . . As the major episodes of Part III are motivated by his search for a labor and a purpose, or are related to it, the part is given a basic, though loose, structural plan. (p. 372)

Like all novelists Borrow seeks coherence in his story by relating characters and events to his hero and to each other. Sometimes, as in [Smollett's] *Roderick Random*, this method involves little more than having characters turn up with amazing and convenient fortuity; sometimes, as in [Dickens's] *Great Expectations,* causal relations are more intricately developed. Borrow utilizes both techniques; and he takes special pains with the personal histories of Part III. In earlier novels such yarns, though perhaps diverting, had little if any connection with the major plots. In his novel, however, Borrow forms an unusually vast network of associations not only between the histories and the action proper, but also among the histories themselves. . . . The piquant thing about these relations is that Borrow rarely if ever points them out to the reader, which somehow makes them seem less conspicuous than a bare summary indicates. Moreover, Lavengro himself often has some important effect on the history-tellers' affairs, and they on his.

Such devices may seem naïvely factitious today in serious fiction, however ingeniously employed. Yet when Edward Thomas says that Borrow uses "recognition and reappearances to satisfy a rather primitive taste in fiction" [see Additional Bibliography], he forgets that Borrow's taste is no more primitive than that of most of his contemporaries. The noteworthy fact is that Borrow thus helps his story hang together and makes its events seem significantly interdependent—in short, he creates a self-contained, imaginative world of his own.

But Borrow's structural technique often rises to a higher artistic level than that suggested by such typing of plot threads, as may be exemplified by the central episode of Part III. For Belle's entrance he makes careful preparations. Lavengro, lonely and discouraged, first hears of her in a casual remark by Slingsby the tinker; and in the chapters preceding her arrival Borrow emphasizes his hero's solitude and perplexity and skilfully arouses suspense. . . . By the time Belle has helped save Lavengro from the Flaming Tinman and has decided to stay with him, it is clear that she is the companion for his loneliness and perhaps a means of his finding a purpose in life. Chapter LXXXIX, wherein their association begins developing, clearly indicates Borrow's consciousness of structural techniques. Here almost every important element of the dingle episode is anticipated: Belle's falling in love with Lavengro; his self-conscious, teasing behavior toward her; his proposal that they go to America and her premonition that she will go alone; his teaching her Armenian; and even the man in black, who enters as the chapter ends. It hardly needs to be urged how significant a part of meaningful structure—and ultimately of form—such preparation and the ultimate fulfilment are. Though the pace is leisurely and there is some padding, Borrow prepares his reader for important turns, often by a series of hints of subtly cumulative impact, so that what happens seems probable. In the dingle episode, as in many another, the pattern becomes clearer as the action proceeds and the outcome is properly both anticipated and surprising. Even in such interludes as Lavengro's talks with the man in black and with the Gypsies, the romance is a continual undercurrent: always the implicit tension derives from Lavengro's relations with Belle. The careful preparation and development, Lavengro's gradual realization of Belle's importance to him, his hopeful expectancy after his proposal, his agonizing wait for her answer, and his "deep melancholy" following her refusal—all substantiate Borrow's careful attention to structural artistry.

The point is not that Borrow's methods here and elsewhere in the novel are particularly original. The point is that he is using the techniques of construction common to all novelists. Though there is some structural deterioration in the last division of Part III, from the beginning of the novel to the end of the dingle episode most events outside the personal histories are related to the progress of the narrative—with due allowance, of course, for the flexibility usual in long biographical stories.

Borrow's formal artistry may be best appreciated by studying the relations of the ideas and purposes of his novel to its structure. He did not intend his work to be simply a tale of unusual adventures—the general assumption—as he carefully explained in the Preface to *Lavengro* and the Appendix to *The Romany Rye* [see excerpts above, 1851 and 1857]. As a novel of adventures *Lavengro-Romany Rye* does move on the story level. But, concurrently, as a novel of ideas it moves on two complex thematic levels. The first of these concerns ideas pertinent to the development of the hero; the second concerns Borrow's didactic and satiric comment on society and religion. The themes of these two levels are intimately related to each other and to the action of the story. Those pertinent to the hero's development . . . I shall call motifs. The three most important are suggested in the sub-title of *Lavengro*, "The Scholar—The Gypsy—The Priest," as Borrow playfully hints in the Preface.

The Scholarly Motif (to follow this suggestion) is in part philological and literary, dealing with Lavengro's talent for tongues and his interest in literature, and in part philosophical, dealing with a rationalistic approach to being and morality. The Gypsy Motif derives from the ideas and characteristics of Lavengro's Romany pal, Jasper Petulengro: a shrewd materialism, fierce independence, love of outdoor activity, and a kind of skeptical hedonism. The Religious Motif ("Priestly Motif" would be too restrictive here) reflects the influence on Lavengro of Protestant Christianity. (pp. 372-75)

The three major motifs are introduced early in the novel and, separately and in conjunction, continue throughout, like the leitmotifs of a music-drama. (p. 375)

[The Religious Motif] is the least important of the three, though it continually weaves in and out of the story. . . .

The predominating Scholarly and Gypsy Motifs, if fully traced, would present a pervading, fugue-like development. The literary aspect of the Scholarly Motif permeates all: probably no other novel is so full of literary allusions as this one—whether to Homer, Goethe, Defoe, Scott, or, above all, the Welsh bards and Scandinavian ballad-makers—allusions which are an intimate, often indispensable part of the story. The Gypsy Motif, strong in Part I, yields in Part II to the Scholarly; but it is implicit in all of Part III, notably in Lavengro's itinerant life, his tinkering (a traditional Gypsy occupation), and his strong desire for independence. It predominates, of course, when the Gypsies themselves are present, and these chapters . . . are intrinsically interesting as well as significant in the development of the narrative. In them, by a series of skillful contrasts, Borrow suggests the basic antipathies between English and Romany character, morality, and ways of life; and Lavengro finally realizes that the Romany way is not for him and that he has really been avoiding the responsibilities of his talents and heritage. . . .

[These two motifs] cumulatively intertwine into a unifying thematic cable. The Gypsy Motif (represented by Lavengro's curiosity about the origin of the Romanies) and the Scholarly Motif (represented by his attempt to solve that mystery through philology) form a quest which persists from the first of the novel to the very last lines. Suggestive of the importance of this quest is Borrow's own estimate of his work as "a philological book, a poem if you choose to call it so" [see excerpt above, 1857]. (p. 378)

The conclusion offers the final clue to the quest which Lavengro has never forgot through all his tribulations and adventures; and it further suggests that he has found a use for his talents and learning, and, in a broader sense, a purpose for his life— the attempt to understand man through study of his languages, for, as he said, language is "a medium for becoming acquainted with the thoughts and feelings of the various sections into which the human race is divided." . . . [The] conclusion signifies a coalition between the two most important, and often conflicting, influences on his life. In London he pursued the Scholarly way, and failed; on the road and in the dingle he pursued the Gypsy way, and failed. Now he can pursue both together, in

a fashion, and presumably succeed, for he seems to go forth with hope.

Borrow's conclusion is altogether appropriate to a novel of curiosity and seeking: it should not really "end"; it should only pause, on the note of expectancy. And the conclusion of this novel sounds the dominant chords of the story, unites action and meaning, and enriches the form. (p. 380)

[Certain] of Borrow's techniques have probably caused critics to overlook his formal artistry. At a time when novelists were continually informing readers how to feel about their characters and how to interpret events—as a few pages of Thackeray, Eliot, or Trollope will demonstrate—Borrow, using methods more characteristic of later fiction, employed relatively few exegetical signposts. Occasionally he makes Lavengro plainly state how his character is developing, or suggest the implications of a scene, or point up the moral lesson; but most of the time the reader must do the interpreting himself. . . . And though Borrow's implicit social and religious comment is usually clear, he inclines to indicate his hero's inner experience rather symbolically than literally (as in the exquisite pastoral scene . . .). In short, Borrow did in his Appendix what his contemporaries were doing in the texts of their novels. (p. 383)

Lavengro-Romany Rye; contrary to prevalent opinion, is not merely "picaresque," or "episodic," or a planless "collection of incidents and dialogues." Rather, within its leisurely developed framework one can discern a structural design deriving from a meaningfully wrought story, and, despite serious faltering toward the end, an overall unity of form. The inescapable inference is that the entire work, as well as the individual parts, was consciously planned and executed to achieve certain effects and significances; otherwise there could not be the complex interrelations of action and idea, the continual preparation for things to come, or the progressive movement in the pattern of the story. Borrow was imperfect as planner and executioner. He wanted the final sure touch of restraint, he often failed to achieve economical fusion of content and form, and his didactic reach exceeded his artistic grasp. Nonetheless he was a literary artist of unusual capacities who attained in his novel a richness of form inadequately appreciated. (p. 384)

> John E. Tilford, Jr., "The Formal Artistry of 'Lavengro-Romany Rye'," in PMLA, 64, Vol. LXIV, No. 3, June, 1949, pp. 369-84.

MARTIN ARMSTRONG (essay date 1950)

[*In his* George Borrow, *Armstrong discusses Borrow's works in relation to his life, his experiences with publishers, and the reactions of critics and the public to his works. He presents a psychological portrait of the author that emphasizes his frequently precarious emotional state. The following excerpt focuses on Borrow's use of literary technique in* Lavengro *and* The Romany Rye.]

The reader who, having finished *Lavengro,* advances into *The Romany Rye* soon becomes aware of a curious change in the nature of the narrative. The speed has slowed down and each incident is treated at much greater length. *Lavengro* covers several years, *The Romany Rye* only a few weeks. There is no golden rule for the management of time in fiction. In *David Copperfield* we find Dickens taking a sudden pleat in his leisurely time-sequence and disposing of several years in a single chapter. . . . After a momentary shock I accept Dickens's device, but I am disconcerted by Borrow's sudden change of rhythm, which persists throughout the book. It seems to throw out the balance of the novel. But the novel, we must remember, was not completed. If it had been, possibly the balance would have been restored, and so it would not be fair criticism to insist on the book's apparent topheaviness.

As to method and form, these can hardly have entered into Borrow's calculations at the outset. Both were dictated by the fact that the book was primarily intended to be an autobiography. Therefore the method of narration is that of the first person singular. Borrow himself tells the whole story, and almost every page from beginning to end fairly bristles with ''I'' and ''I said.'' As to the form, it would necessarily be that simplest of all kinds, a succession of events held together by the mere fact that they are the experiences of the narrator. But when Borrow resolved to embellish, to abandon pure autobiography and indulge in invention, he seems to have become vaguely aware of the need for a more closely knit form. His method of achieving this is more ingenuous than ingenious: it consists in reintroducing at a later stage characters which have appeared or at least been mentioned before. In *Lavengro* we read how the hero, climbing down from the coach on his arrival in London, is accosted by a sinister creature who tries to extort money from him. Later, when Lavengro is trying to barter the apple-woman's *Moll Flanders* for a Bible, he finds that the book has been stolen from his pocket. Later again, he detects a pickpocket in the act of robbing an Armenian merchant, catches the thief, and restores the stolen pocket-book. Later again, at Greenwich Fair, he gets into conversation with a thimble-rigger who turns out to be not merely the pickpocket who stole *Moll Flanders* from him and the pocketbook from the Armenian, but also the sinister person who attempted to swindle him on his first arrival in London.

Now the only justification for coincidences in literature is that the writer shall get away with them. If Borrow can make us believe in this threefold coincidence, well and good. But he doesn't; and at least one of the reasons for his failure is that he has not given his miscreant any particular character or even visual identity. The man does not exist for us as a person; therefore his reappearance gives us no shock of recognition. For any effect he has on the story he might as well have been four different people.

Another example of Borrow's ingenuous use of this device is rather more successful. In the early part of *Lavengro* we meet Borrow's sixteen-year-old schoolfellow Murtagh at the school at Clonmel, to whom he gives a pack of cards in exchange for lessons in Irish. We do not hear of Murtagh again until he turns up near the end of *The Romany Rye* practising the art of thimble-rigging at Horncastle Fair and tells Borrow a fantastic and highly amusing story about how his pack of cards was confiscated in an Irish religious house in Italy and how he subsequently detected the Rector, the Sub-Rector, the Almoner, and His Holiness the Pope enjoying a game of cards with the confiscated pack. . . . Now Murtagh has the luck to be an Irishman; in other words, his speech is highly characterized (Borrow does this extremely well), and so, when he reappears at the end of *The Romany Rye,* we identify him, welcome him, and so accept the coincidence. (pp. 50-3)

Any reference to the use of coincidence in fiction inevitably calls up the name of Dickens. . . . Time and again Dickens drags a character into the middle of an episode with which, one would have supposed, it can have no conceivable connection and by sheer perseverance and ingenuity compels us to accept the imposition. Why do we accept it? Because, however unlikely the intrusion, the character, once it has been dragged

in, begins to function in the episode. In Borrow's coincidences, on the other hand, this does not happen. Each remains an isolated incident which performs no necessary function in the network of the story. Therefore, so far from compelling belief, it rouses our scepticism. Clearly, then, Borrow's ideas of construction are of a vague and rudimentary kind. (pp. 53-4)

Yet the problem of construction in autobiography is almost non-existent. The flow of events related by the person who experienced them provides ready-made all the construction the form demands. Borrow's difficulty, when still aiming at pure autobiography, must have been simply due to his haphazard method of composition. . . . He had no preconceived ideas, no conscious technique at his disposal: he worked as a child works on a jigsaw puzzle. No wonder the work filled him with exasperation and despair. (p. 54)

[*Lavengro* and *The Romany Rye*] are clogged with material that is not good enough or not good at all. They are clogged, too, by clumsy and verbose writing, for Borrow's style is unstable. It fluctuates disconcertingly between the excellent, the adequate, and the regrettable. He constantly uses the word *individual* when he means man, woman, or person, and the word *calculated* in phrases such as ''I had seen no object calculated to call them forth'' where ''no object to call them forth'' would have been enough, and the journalese reluctance to call a spade a spade appears throughout his work. A horse becomes a *quadruped;* horses, *the equine race;* beer, *the beverage;* blood, *the vital fluid;* fish, *the finny brood;* and birds, *the feathered tribe.* (pp. 57-8)

I have pointed out what I believe to be contributing causes of the [works'] failure—a style which fluctuates between vivid, muscular prose and drab verbosity; a lack of shape and structure; incomplete fusion between matters of fact and fiction, in other words, a lack of the faculty of imagination; and characters which perform no necessary function in the development of the story. But what of the characters themselves? To attribute their failure to co-operate in the building of the story to some shortcoming in themselves is to put the cart before the horse. The truth is that they do not so function because the novel has no plot, no development for them to function in. The proper relation of characters and plot is one of interdependence. One might say that characters are the medium through which the novelist expresses his plot, or equally that the plot is the medium through which he unfolds his characters. (pp. 62-3)

How does this apply to Borrow's characters? Let us consider the most important of them. Borrow, as we gather from *Lavengro*'s sub-title, *The Scholar, The Gypsy, The Priest,* considered them to be himself, Jasper Petulengro, and the Man in Black, but most readers will agree that the Man in Black must certainly give precedence to Isopel Berners.

Jasper Petulengro haunts the novel like a ghost. Like a ghost he turns up when least expected and does not linger long. He has little influence on the course of events. But although he contributes hardly anything to the novel's development and does not himself develop as a character, he does contribute an atmosphere and a good deal of highly characteristic talk. It is because he does little else that he never becomes a solid character: he remains a ghost, elusive, episodic. Perhaps this is an advantage in his case: his elusiveness invests him with mystery, and mystery has an attraction of its own. He represents the unconventional world of escape, of freedom, for which one half of Borrow's nature perpetually craves. Jasper's identity, then, is created not by his actions in the face of events but by what he says and how he says it. In the creation of character, lingo—the style of speech appropriate to a particular person—is an important element. It invests the character with a certain idiosyncrasy and acts like a brightly coloured label which enables the reader instantly to identify him at each reappearance. Now when a character has an obviously distinctive lingo—for example a Gypsy, an Irishman, or a Scotsman—Borrow reproduces it admirably, as in the case of Jasper, Murtagh the Irishman, and young David Haggart the Scot, but he fails notably in the subtler distinctions, such as those produced by class or age. When, in the early part of *Lavengro,* he describes in dramatic dialogue an encounter between himself as a child of six and a couple of Gypsies, his own talk has all the qualities of a grown man's and none whatever of that of a child. The effect of this is to give an air of falsity to the incident. Or take the case of Isopel Berners. She is a young hucksteress, born in a workhouse, but she is English and so she would have no distinction of speech beyond that which belongs to her class. Sometimes Borrow succeeds in putting into her mouth a kind of speech appropriate to her nature, but at other times he seems to forget this obligation with the result that, to our astonishment, Belle changes unexpectedly into a well-bred young lady of the mid-nineteenth century. In the following passage Lavengro and Belle are sitting outside their tents in Mumper's Dingle talking about the approaching thunderstorm.

> 'My dislike is not pretended,' said Belle, 'I hate the sound of it, but I love my tea and it was kind of you not to wish to cast a cloud over my little pleasures; the thunder came quite time enough to interrupt it without being anticipated—there is another peal. I will clear away and see that my tent is in a condition to resist the storm; and I think you had better bestir yourself.'

Now that is hardly the talk of a strapping young female pedlar, very handy with her fists and bred in a workhouse. Details such as this seriously detract from Belle's actuality. It is as if, just when the definition of her image is becoming sharp, she suddenly goes out of focus. Already she had begun to take on the lineaments of reality; we had seen her in action more than once, notably when she came to Lavengro's rescue in his fight with the Flaming Tinman, and so these relapses into conventional literature are the more upsetting. She fluctuates between the real and the unreal: we are attracted by her and yet we cannot wholly believe in her. In short, Borrow shows us in Belle Berners the makings of a charming and highly original character which he lacks the genius to complete. (pp. 63-5)

What of the other chief characters? The Man in Black, the Priest of the sub-title, is a greater talker than all the rest and his talk sharply conveys his personality; but he is totally static. He does not function; he merely talks, his role being to act as a mouthpiece for the monstrous, though often exceedingly amusing, misrepresentations by which Borrow seeks to discredit the Roman Catholic Church. We might similarly review all the characters in the novel, but we would search in vain for one that was alive and growing. They are drawn in the flat, not created in the round. This is not to say that they are for that reason unsuccessful. Borrow had a very sharp eye and, on occasion, considerable powers of description, and many of these sketch-portraits are vivid and attractive. They must be considered failures only when circumstances demand of them a fuller measure of life than they possess.

But there is still one character to be considered, that of the Scholar, George Borrow, alias Lavengro, alias the Romany Rye. It may be presumed that whatever judgment we may pass on all the others, we shall hardly stigmatize him, the creator of them all, as unreal. But we are dealing here not with historic fact but with literature, and it depends entirely on George Borrow's skill as a writer whether Lavengro is convincingly real or more shadowy than the most shadowy of his creations. Indeed he *is* his own creation as much as any of the others. That he is a strange, baffling, and rather uncomfortable character can hardly be denied.

Unless the reader is very simple-minded, he will become conscious, before he has got very far in *Lavengro,* that the narrator is not wholly preoccupied with telling his story. He is equally preoccupied with impressing his own importance on the reader: in fact, when the reader has got to the end of *The Romany Rye* he may be inclined to suspect that the chief motive of the whole work has been to exhibit the learning, physical prowess, and general impressiveness of the narrator.

In short, I do not think that Borrow has been more successful with Lavengro than with his other characters. While creating him he has had his eye on the reader more often than on himself: his object has been not to illuminate but to dazzle. Consequently Lavengro is the offspring of melodrama rather than a man of flesh and blood, and it is not until we have studied the character of Borrow that the character of Lavengro becomes enthralling. (pp. 65-6)

> *Martin Armstrong, in his* George Borrow, *Arthur Barker Ltd., 1950, 101 p.*

ROBERT R. MEYERS   (essay date 1966)

[*Meyers examines Borrow's various prose styles, including the colloquial, ornate, realistic, and romantic; in addition, he describes how Borrow altered his narrative and descriptive technique to suit his material in individual works.*]

It is possible to distinguish several prose styles in Borrow's books. He may move abruptly from a colloquial style in his vivid travel sections to a heavily ornate and artificial style which he seems to consider appropriate for his philosophical moods. Or he may turn suddenly from his usual restrained and realistic technique of description to momentary dalliance with Romanticism—meaning, in his case, excessive idealization of rural life, a strange use of fancy in some bits of description, and sentimental melancholy. (p. 70)

Borrow wisely chose to write colloquially when he related his adventures. The plainness of his style contrasts vividly with the lush prose of most of the adventure stories of his contemporaries. . . . Here is [an extract] from a travel narrative published three months before Borrow's story of his Spanish adventures:

> Crashing through bushes in their fall, and rebounding from rock to rock, the noble steeds struggled madly to dash their feet into the soil and stop their downward course—but all in vain. With nostrils wide distended, and blood pouring from every limb, they toiled and wrestled with their fate. The deep abyss swallowed them up; and the wild vulture, scenting his carrion from afar, floated madly downward from the topmost peak of the a mountain, from which he had been a spectator of their fate. His talons

were fixed in the still quivering flank of one of the horses, which turned its dying eyes in terror on its ruthless destroyer; but, with a hoarse croak, the vulture darted his beak into the maddened charger's side, and a moment of fearful agony put an end to its woes forever.

Every sentence is over-written. The writer is particularly enamored of "madly" and "maddened." Sentimentalism runs riot. Beside this hysterical rhetoric we may place the description of an exciting moment in Borrow's Spanish tour:

> Only a quarter of an hour previous I had passed three ghastly heads stuck on poles standing by the wayside; they were those of a captain of banditti and two of his accomplices, who had been seized and executed about two months before. Their principal haunt was the vicinity of the bridge, and it was their practice to cast the bodies of the murdered into the deep black water which runs rapidly beneath. Those three heads will always live in my remembrance, particularly that of the captain, which stood on a higher pole than the other two: the long hair was waving in the wind, and the blackened, distorted features were grinning in the sun. (*The Bible* . . .)

In this restrained telling, with precise location of the spot lending veri-similitude, Borrow permits himself only one emotional adjective, "ghastly"; and it proves, as one reads on, to be a rather restrained description of what any modern reader would think horrible. There is no hysteria or sentimentalism, although the episode could easily call for both. (pp. 72-3)

Such writing must have been an interesting novelty for many of Borrow's readers. It explains why critics invariably spoke of his naturalness, his forthrightness, his refusal to employ super-eloquence. (pp. 73-4)

[In comparison] with some other writers of the nineteenth century, Borrow's prose seems at times almost miraculously lucid and vital. As a travel writer, he surpassed most of his contemporaries and richly deserves the compliments they paid his prose. He excelled in three important areas of the travel story: narration, description, and dialogue. We shall take a closer look at each.

Borrow's *narrative* is chronological rather than causal, except for minor and unhappy exceptions. The method is that of the first person singular. Every page is studded with "I" and "I said." The succession of events is held together only by the fact that all of them represent experiences of the narrator. This is fortunate for Borrow, since he was attracted far more by simple action than by thought. Passages of meditation do not represent him at his best. "It is from action that his imaginative force derives," Augustus Ralli said accurately. This is why *The Bible in Spain* succeeded beyond his other books; it was filled with swift-moving action, free from those bogs of heavy moralizing which mar the pages of *Lavengro* and *The Romany Rye*.

Borrow did not long leave his readers in doubt as to his choice of the chronological method in the Spanish adventure story. The first sentence begins: "On the morning of the 10th of November . . ." The technique continues to the last paragraph of the book, which begins: "Thus had passed Friday, the sacred day of the Moslems. . . ." Plot exists in Borrow's books only

if one uses the term as broadly as René Wellek when he says, "One of the oldest and most universal plots is that of the Journey, by land or water." Borrow, who travels upon both, makes of his books only what happens in time sequence upon these journeys.

Although the chronological transitions sometimes become rather wooden, the reader is at least saved from dreary accounts of trips and episodes which have no excitement value. Borrow wisely omits his monotonous trips back to England; he treats the Spanish adventure much as if it were one long, unbroken journey. (pp. 75-6)

Some of the transitions are not so simply chronological, of course. Not a few of them are strangely abrupt, reminiscent of Sterne. . . . Borrow may break off a discussion in the middle, without explanation and without ever returning to it. Once, when his landlord is talking, the conversation ends in this manner:

> "Those were merry days, Don Jorge. By the by, I forgot to ask your worship of what opinion you are?"
>
> The next morning whilst I was dressing, the old Genoese entered my room. . . . (*The Bible* . . .)

The unanswered question is left to hang in the reader's memory, tantalizingly; Borrow is playing enigmatic author. But, despite occasional abrupt transitions, Borrow's technique is customarily smooth and chronological.

It is also episodic. Persons appear, are described in terms that suggest they are important, then drop from the story never to be mentioned again. The episodes often take the form of sharply cut vignettes, brief and memorable, free from much of the authorial intrusion which marred so many Victorian adventure stories. Some must rank among the best writing of the century.

The best illustration of this may be the account of Borrow's fight with the Flaming Tinman. (pp. 76-7)

Some of Borrow's liveliest writing sets the stage for the great battle. . . . [The fight] begins in earnest with short paragraphs suggesting the breathlessness and fury of it. Borrow does not digress to talk of the nobility of the art of self-defense, the joy of fighting for a young girl's honor, or any of the other philosophical themes which many other Victorian authors might have found implicit in the episode. (p. 77)

Narrative is Borrow's forte. Wherever one turns in his books there are vividly told stories, long and short. Informal, free from the heavy diction characteristic of so many writers of the time, straightforward in the telling, they remain impressive to the present. They move swiftly; Borrow does not intrude upon them with moralizing reflections. Had he busied himself more with narrative and less with preaching of one kind or another, his later books would probably have succeeded as did *The Bible in Spain*.

Borrow usually employs *description* to accomplish one of three objectives: the fixing of scene or setting as a backdrop for the adventure he narrates; the presentation of guide-book sketches of places, without concern for action, or even, frequently, for relevance to the principal themes of the book; and the characterization of some of the myriads of persons he meets in the course of his travels. In all of these instances he tends generally to preserve the informal manner of his narrative technique.

His fidelity to detail has been warmly praised. . . . The reportorial quality of [his] descriptions was of great value to Borrow in that it convinced his Victorian readers of his sobriety and truthfulness. And Borrow was even better in his descriptions of natural scenery, where his enthusiasm and photographic powers combined to create superb effects.

He is particularly skillful at picturing nature in her moments of violence and terror. Speaking of the sierras of Spain and Portugal [in *The Bible in Spain*], he describes them as "those singular mountains which rise in naked horridness, like the ribs of some mighty carcass from which the flesh has been torn." . . . (pp. 78-9)

In his portraits of storms on land and sea, Borrow reaches his peak. Almost at once in his tale of the Spanish adventures we are caught up in a storm. . . . Vividly, he narrates the violent action taking place until he is ready for some of the finest descriptive writing in the account:

> The lightning enveloped us as with a mantle, the thunders were louder than the roar of a million cannon, the dregs of the ocean seemed to be cast up, and in the midst of all this turmoil, the wind, without the slightest intimation, *veered right about,* and pushed us from the horrible coast faster than it had previously driven us towards it. . . .

The images are concrete and clear: "mantle," "cannon," "dregs"—all strike a reader as clearly expressive of what Borrow was trying to say in each case. Sound and motion come through vividly in the long triple parallelism, making the storm one of the most vivid in English literature.

Nature's more genial aspects find Borrow not, perhaps, less responsive, but certainly less original in his description. He hears the water rippling over the sand or murmuring softly; the birds sing melodiously; tears of rapture flow. . . . All that can be said for him is that he never over-writes as some of his contemporaries do. But on occasion he effectively throws over a natural scene the gauzy veil of wonder and romance. His description of the view from Elvir Hill is a high moment in *Lavengro*. . . . Visionary and fairy-like as it is, Borrow makes it minister to his principal interest, man. (pp. 79-80)

Borrow's guide-book sketches of localities have been mentioned. They often have no connection with any action or themes; Baedeker-like, they simply point out places of interest for the tourist. This is especially true of *The Bible in Spain, The Zincali,* and *Wild Wales,* of course, where Borrow seems to feel that he is writing, among other things, a travel guide which may be helpful for future visitors. (pp. 81-2)

Sometimes the guide-book description is more literary than this, however, and Borrow seems carried away by concern for elegance and poetic inversions ("grand are its mountains and no less grand are its plains"); carefully structured parallelisms ("here a deep ravine . . . yonder an eminence . . ." and "little that is blithesome and cheerful, but much that is melancholy"); and rhetorical questions ("And who are the travellers of these districts?"). But, at the other extreme, he becomes too prosaic, writing a guidebook sketch which is inserted into his narrative abruptly and awkwardly, as is his brief and almost grudging concession to the town of Rivadeo: "Rivadeo is one of the principal seaports of Galicia, and is admirably suited for commerce on a deep firth into which the river Mirando debouches.

It contains many magnificent buildings, and an extensive square or plaza, which is planted with trees" (*The Bible* . . .).

Here Borrow does not even bother to provide himself with a good transitional sentence which will carry his reader smoothly from the narrative into the set-piece of description. He seems to feel that, although Rivadeo must be briefly described for those who will read his book as a tourist's guide, it is unworthy of more than the dryest, most conventional observation. (pp. 82-3)

Borrow used another kind of description with great facility. Some of his finest characterizations are done through description. He characterizes little through dialogue, with a few brilliant exceptions. Generally, he expresses his view of personality by lingering upon physical details, using the appearance of the face, clothing, and bodily movements to produce the impression he desires. A good example is his characterization by description of the dwarfish, idiot guide who was to take him to Finisterre. . . . (p. 83)

Borrow makes dramatic improvement [in his use of dialogue] as he writes his way through *The Bible in Spain.* The speeches in *The Zincali* had been almost uniformly poor in quality. . . . Even in the account of the Spanish tours, Borrow begins slowly. The first chapter . . . has only two sentences of dialogue. Both are formal, one being spoken by a sailor and the other by a monk. There is no dialogue at all in the second chapter, and in the third only two brief conversations between Borrow and a man from Palmella.

Even when he finally gets going with longer passages of dialogue, Borrow is inept for a time. When he talks with the three principals of a college in Lisbon, for example, it is impossible to make any distinctions among their speeches, except that the college authorities say "*Blessed* Virgin," whereas Borrow stubbornly insists on saying simply, "Virgin." Otherwise, any one of the speeches could be put into the mouth of any other character without incongruity. All of the speakers are stiffly elegant in speech. Says one: "'It will afford us extreme satisfaction to show you over it; it is true that satisfaction is considerably diminished by the reflection that it possesses nothing worthy of the attention of a traveler'." . . . Even when allowances are made for the dignity of formal conversation among the Victorians, we find this passage appallingly heavy. (p. 88)

Even so, there are isolated instances of skillful dialogue in *The Bible in Spain,* giving promise of better things to come in the later books. (p. 89)

The fullest characterization by dialogue is managed in the case of the guide, Antonio. There are certain "tags" in Antonio's speeches, through several chapters of the narrative; and there is a definite quality of sharp positiveness in what he says. These distinguish him clearly from other characters who appear in the Spanish wanderings. Antonio uses the word "brother" constantly, giving his speech a tribal or religious flavor. He frequently barks his sentences explosively: "The swine have killed their brother; would that every Busno was served as yonder hog is. Come in, brother, and we will eat the heart of that hog." . . . (pp. 89-90)

After such lively speech, it is jarring to find passages in which Antonio sounds absurdly pompous. This man, who is said "to be acquainted with all the cut-throats in Galicia" and usually speaks their language, once talks like this:

I have acquired at various times a great many words amongst the Gallegan domestics in the kitchens where I have officiated as cook, but am quite unable to understand any long conversations. . . . The worst of this language is, that everybody on first hearing it thinks that nothing is more easy than to understand it, as words are continually occurring which he has heard before; but these merely serve to bewilder and puzzle him, causing him to misunderstand everything that is said. . . .

This language is obviously that of Borrow, not of Antonio; and the reader wonders about the inconsistency. It is less perplexing when Borrow puts such artificial speech into the mouth of an educated character. When he mentions his old Norwich philosopher friend, William Taylor, for example, he always heightens the style. He has him say such things as: ''Oh my respectable and cherished friend, where was it that I had last the felicity of seeing your well-remembered and most remarkable physiognomy?'' . . . The comment appears in the midst of plain prose. Borrow apparently feels that Taylor should always be characterized by the use of involved rhetoric.

Lavengro and *The Romany Rye* represent Borrow's fullest development in skillful use of dialogue. The mercurial exchanges between Borrow and Jasper Petulengro are unusual for the times. Unplagued by mechanical devices, often going for pages at a time without even a single ''he said,'' they are spiced with abrupt answers, gypsy dialect, and the sudden shifts in topic which are characteristic of real conversation. (pp. 90-1)

Moving back and forth between highly colloquial gypsy talk and highly literary, Borrow achieves some artistic distance between his readers and his characters. His gypsies at times sound real enough to be convincing, but the poetry put into their mouths at other times expresses the sentiments Borrow had about their exotic personalities. He liked creating for them a speech compounded of racy slang, Biblical allusions and rhythm, and here and there a dash of high rhetoric. . . .

But an impression should not be left that all of the inconsistencies in Borrow's dialogue can be so justified. Nothing is more painful than to hear the magnificent Isopel Berners, born in a workhouse and possessed of a vocabulary that reflects the fact, occasionally speaking in the hothouse diction of an aristocratic young gentlewoman. (p. 92)

The general impression from Borrow's books is that he makes steady progress in dialogue skill from the pages of his Spanish adventure story through brilliant conversations in *Lavengro* and *The Romany Rye*. Some of the characterizations he achieves through dialogue are among the finest triumphs in his books. He profited by the conviction Richard Ford once expressed to him [see excerpt above, 1842]: ''Dialogues always tell; they are dramatic and give an air of reality.'' (p. 93)

It has been pointed out that much of the credit for Borrow's literary successes must be given to the fact that his personality, revealed in his books, captivated thousands who might never have been drawn to him otherwise. Flamboyant, bizarre, unique—all of these adjectives have been applied to that personality. But since Borrow was a writer, it is through the styles he employs that the elements of his personality most fully reveal themselves. We have already seen that his style varies as he works with different motifs in his books; it is equally true that it varies as different aspects of his personality come to the fore. He was humorist, Romanticist, egoist—these and more—and

all the facets of his personality clearly shape his style at various times.

Few persons who have read Borrow's books have failed to see that he had a strange, quirky sense of humor. Critics spoke of his ''irrepressible love for humor,'' of ''his fund of real racy humor,'' and of his being a master of the drily comic. (p. 98)

Oddities, quaintness—Borrow's books are filled with them, and perhaps most of them come from his habit of exploiting whatever is strange in the personages he meets. Odd himself, he emphasizes the peculiarities which he finds in the characters who people his books. It may be only a touch, as in the portrait of the notary of Pontevedra, or it may be a more extended treatment, like that given to the poet Parkinson, a man who occasionally called at the law office where Borrow spent some five years of apprenticeship as a young man. He can, in spite of the seriousness with which he usually took himself, even laugh at his own person occasionally. (p. 99)

Borrow is never ludicrously comical; he never unbends that far. Unlike his contemporary Dickens, he is unable or unwilling to mix humor with pathos. Nor does he approach the genius of Thackeray that could conceal beneath a light exterior a depth of meaning and a world of thought which Borrow could not fathom. He is not playful, although once or twice he seems to try playfulness, but it comes off clumsily. Perhaps he is more like Bulwer-Lytton and Kingsley in that, like them, he makes his humor subservient to a higher purpose. His humor is generally that of the Christian gentleman who permits himself a wry smile at the absurdities of society as he presses on in his various callings—colporteur, linguist, enlightened wanderer.

Sometimes Borrow's personality expresses itself through Romantic prose, touching the scenes and events around him with an airy, gossamer quality. He uses archaic diction, rich allusiveness, and his interest in ancient languages and history to contrast with his usual plain style. He turns from the hardheaded and practical realist—who could fear God but knew how to take his own part, who knew how to use a strong right arm and to outwit the most cunning bandits—to the dreamer with a predilection for the mysterious, the remote, the strange, and the fantastic. It is probably the romance of exotic and half-forgotten languages which drew Borrow to them in the first place, since he never seems deeply concerned about scientific accuracy.

The whole Spanish adventure has been viewed as a Romantic adventure, with Borrow playing a role similar to Don Quixote's in its whimsy and in its futility. . . . The idea is an attractive one, especially when one remembers that Borrow really accomplished almost nothing in Spain so far as proselyting was concerned. Yet so romantic an affair did he make it at times that one is likely to forget his failures and to view the entire campaign as a gloriously successful battle between one brave man and the hosts of the enemy. (pp. 101-02)

The *locus classicus* for illustrating Borrow's romantic nature is the famed ''wind on the heath'' passage from *Lavengro*. . . . Few books or essays ever printed about Borrow have omitted this passage. It is prepared for when Borrow, wandering along the heath, ''came to a place where, beside a thick furze, sat a man, his eyes fixed intently on the red ball of the setting sun.'' The man was Borrow's friend Jasper, who told Borrow that since they last met his father and mother had died. Borrow then asks the gypsy for his opinion of death:

"When a man dies, he is cast into the earth, and his wife and child sorrow over him. If he has neither wife nor child, then his father and mother, I suppose; and if he is quite alone in the world, why, then, he is cast into the earth, and there is an end of the matter."

"And do you think that is the end of a man?"

"There's an end of him, brother, more's the pity."

"Why do you say so?"

"Life is sweet, brother."

"Do you think so?"

"Think so! There's night and day, brother, both sweet things; sun, moon, and stars, brother, all sweet things; there's likewise the wind on the heath. Life is very sweet, brother; who would wish to die?"

"I would wish to die—"

"You talk like a gorgio—which is the same as talking like a fool—were you a Romany chal you would talk wiser. Wish to die, indeed! A Romany chal would wish to live forever!"

"In sickness, Jasper?"

"There's the sun and stars, brother."

"In blindness, Jasper?"

"There's the wind on the heath, brother; if I could only feel that, I would gladly live forever."

Only the middle part of this, beginning "Life is sweet" and ending, "who would wish to die?" is usually anthologized. But a more accurate picture of Borrow's approach to and departure from this high moment of Romantic style is given by making the extract larger. The somber acceptance of human fate in the first few lines gives added power to the unquenchable and perphaps illogical *joie de vivre* which Jasper expresses. Sick or blind, one may still experience the great elemental forces of nature; the wind on the hearth blows cleanly; life is sweet and zestful. This is not Romanticism of the moonlight school, where fairies, goblins, and witches enchant. It is a sunlight variety, where bodies participate energetically in any dreams of the mind. It is a "racing" Romanticism, not a counterpane variety. This strangely quick responsiveness to the bizarre and the fabulous in his environment is another aspect of Borrow's many-sided personality, and he employs for it a special prose style quite different from his usual plainness. (pp. 104-06)

Robert R. Meyers, in his George Borrow, Twayne *Publishers, Inc., 1966, 156 p.*

MICHAEL COLLIE (essay date 1982)

[The following is excerpted from Collie's biographical and critical study of Borrow. Here he analyzes Borrow's pictorial technique in Lavengro *and* The Romany Rye *and describes how Borrow used the picturesque mode to provide an objective distance between the narrator, Lavengro, and the other characters, as well as between himself and his readers.]*

[There are many examples] in *Lavengro* of Borrow's delicate pictorial handling of the physical scene, of what we could call his composing habit, his habit of training the reader's eye to an arrangement or disposition of objects in nature which, while it conjures pleasing effects, also denies the reader knowledge of the artist's participation in the scene he portrays, since it is not possible to interrogate the picturesque: you take it or leave it as it is, enjoy or do not enjoy its conventional formulations. This technique, as utilised in *Lavengro,* whether by design or not, has two consequences—two at least. The first is that the English landscape is represented as uncluttered, serene, free of tension between person and person, free of tension between person and environment, and still accessible, meaningfully, to the foot-traveller. If Borrow had been trying to show what Britain was like in the late 1840s, what it was like socially and politically, he would have been open to the charge of deliberate falsification, but in fact his is not at all a documentary method but one limited to the particularities of fictional biography, in which the ego appears in a dream landscape, as Borrow accurately perceived when he changed his title. The second consequence of this technique of the picturesque is even more important. The scene observed is essentially a scene 'over there'. It is distant. The observer is not involved in what he sees. Even when the protagonist of *Lavengro*—its 'I'—is physically present in the scene being described, the author's habit of mind is such that any episode, for example an episode that is represented as really having occurred, is reformulated, reshaped, or reconstructed into a scene observed with a calm and scrupulous detachment. This absolved Borrow from the need to tell the truth about himself. The picturesque mode is anti-confessional in its effect and, although *Lavengro* is enlivened by a whole series of encounters between Borrow and people met on the road, this being a great part of its appeal, that such encounters are so immediate, varied and colourful and reconstructed in such vigorous dialogue, a common feature is that they never last. There are no permanent relations between people in *Lavengro,* relations that grow, develop and mature; and there are no instances of a serious challenge, as it were, to the fictional authority of the narrator. He decides what will and will not be revealed, the action never being so dramatised that a character might round upon the narrator and challenge his view of things. His view goes unchallenged, so it constitutes the totality of what the reader is given, which indeed is a lot. The point is, then, that not only does Borrow keep out of *Lavengro* anything like an honest account of his own adolescence, his own sexual experiences, his own personal disasters, his relations with his mother, father and brother, and not just his relations with them but also his knowledge of them, but that he chooses a style for the book, or hits upon it somehow in the process of writing, which constitutes an all-pervasive controlling device that allows him to protect his instinct for privacy while at the same time seeming to be open, bland, honest and sincerely, utterly involved. . . . [His] ironical comments on some of his own set-pieces indicate that he fully appreciated the convenience, to him personally, of an inherited and widely understood picturesque mode. He was essentially an artist not a reporter, an artist of the visible not of the invisible. (pp. 207-08)

[Borrow] successfully adopted that useful and well-established Victorian strategy of distinguishing sharply between the private and the public, so successfully, indeed, that some readers who wanted to know about his adventures did not believe he had ever in fact known anyone like Isopel Berners, who so dominates the end of *Lavengro* and the beginning of *The Romany Rye*. . . . [He] found it impossible to write an autobiography that was a report on a person who already existed, but possible, though difficult, to write an autobiography in which a person was imagined as existing who was acceptable to the sensibility of the author. In *Lavengro* and *The Romany Rye* he became the person who he wanted to be, refused to present himself as the person others had seen that he was, and by creating a character called Lavengro, a scholar gypsy, freed himself imaginatively from the constraint of being no more than the sum of his own actions. The two books are a celebration of this remarkable feat. (p. 228)

Michael Collie, in his George Borrow: Eccentric, *Cambridge University Press, 1982, 275 p.*

ADDITIONAL BIBLIOGRAPHY

Bigland, Eileen. *In the Steps of George Borrow.* London: Rich and Cowan, 1951, 355 p.
A readable and well-researched biography. Bigland recounts the story of Borrow's life in the framework of her own journey ''in the steps of George Borrow.''

Birrell, Augustine. ''George Borrow.'' In his *The Collected Essays & Addresses of the Rt. Hon. Augustine Birrell: 1880-1920, Vol. II,* pp. 92-105. New York: Charles Scribner's Sons, 1923.
An appreciative essay by a noted Borrovian. Birrell describes Borrow's effect upon readers as ''contagious.''

Doyle, A. Conan. ''Borrowed Scenes.'' In his *Danger! and Other Stories,* pp. 163-84. New York: George H. Doran Co., 1919.
A parody of Borrow's travel accounts.

Elam, Samuel Milton. *George Borrow.* New York: Alfred A. Knopf, 1929, 139 p.
A semi-fictional biography that extrapolates from the known facts of Borrow's life. Elam focuses on three aspects of Borrow's life, depicting him as a Gypsy, a philologist, and a Christian.

Fréchet, René. *George Borrow (1803-1881): Vagabond polyglotte, agent biblique, écrivain.* Paris: Didier, 1956, 378 p.
A comprehensive biographical and critical study, available only in French.

Herbert, Lucille. ''George Borrow and the Forms of Self-Reflection.'' *University of Toronto Quarterly* X, No. 2 (Winter 1971): 152-67.
Discusses *Lavengro* and *The Romany Rye* in relation to the tradition of subjective narrative that includes such other works as Thomas Carlyle's *Sartor Resartus,* George Moore's *Confessions of a Young Man,* and Søren Kierkegaard's *Either/Or.*

Knapp, William I. *Life, Writings and Correspondence of George Borrow (1803-1881).* 2 vols. New York: G. P. Putnam's Sons; London: John Murray, 1899.
An essential guide for the student of Borrow. Knapp's biography has been praised for its impartiality, accuracy, thoroughness, and enthusiasm.

Maxwell, Ian R. '''But the Fight! With Respect to the Fight, What Shall I Say?''' *AUMLA,* No. 37 (May 1972): 18-36.
A detailed study of the narrative form of *Lavengro* based on its opening chapters. Maxwell agrees with the majority of modern critics who note evidence of conscious artistry in *Lavengro* and categorize it as a novel; he sees the structure of the work as ''based very little on plot, rather on an elaborate pattern of impressions.''

Pritchett, V. S. ''George Borrow in Spain.'' *The Geographical Magazine* XV, No. 8 (December 1942): 376-81.

Discusses Borrow's account of his travels in Spain and praises its ''fidelity to the scene.''

Rickett, Arthur. ''George Borrow.'' In his *The Vagabond in Literature,* pp. 57-85. London: J. M. Dent & Co., 1906.
A biographical and character sketch that depicts Borrow as a vagabond.

Shorter, Clement K. *The Life of George Borrow.* New York: E. P. Dutton & Co., 1919, 284 p.
A biography by a dedicated Borrovian. Because it includes personal letters and papers that were unavailable to William I. Knapp (see annotation above), Shorter's work functions as a complement to the earlier biography. It is an expanded version of Shorter's *George Borrow and His Circle,* published in 1913.

Starkie, Walter. Introduction to *The Romany Rye,* by George Borrow, pp. vii-xxxii. London: Cresset Press, 1948.
A discussion of Gypsy lore in English scholarship and of Borrow's relations with the Gypsies.

Thomas, Gwendolyn M.L. ''Where Was Borrow's Dingle?'' *Discovery* XVIII, No. 215 (November 1937): 350-52.
Locates the site of Borrow's dingle, the glade depicted in *Lavengro* and *The Romany Rye* where Lavengro camped alongside Isopel Berners and fought the Flaming Tinman, as outside the town of Whitechurch, near the Wales border.

Tilford, J[ohn] E., Jr. ''Contemporary Criticism of *Lavengro*: A Reexamination.'' *Studies in Philology* XLI, No. 3 (July 1944): 442-56.
Reviews early criticism of *Lavengro* and *The Romany Rye* to counter the widely held view, proposed by Borrow himself and by his biographer William I. Knapp (see annotation above), that contemporary response to these works was negative. Tilford, a noted Borrow scholar, asserts instead that ''critics showed an uncommon appreciation and gave an intelligent appraisal of *Lavengro* and *The Romany Rye.*''

———. ''The Critical Approach to *Lavengro-Romany Rye.*'' *Studies in Philology* LXVI, No. 1 (January 1949): 79-96.
Discusses the critical confusion surrounding the genres of *Lavengro* and *The Romany Rye.* Tilford examines the genesis of *Lavengro* and Borrow's intention in that work to prove that both it and *The Romany Rye* are indeed novels.

———. ''A Note on Borrow's Bookish Dialogue.'' In *South Atlantic Studies for Sturgis E. Leavitt,* edited by Thomas B. Stroup and Sterling A. Stoudemire, pp. 199-205. Washington, D.C.: Scarecrow Press, 1953.
Examines the differences between the Gypsy and English dialogue in Borrow's works.

Vesey-FitzGerald, Brian. *Gypsy Borrow.* London: Dennis Dobson, 1953, 161 p.
A biography that examines Borrow's interrelations with the Gypsies and suggests that he was a member of that people.

Watts-Dunton, Theodore. ''George Borrow.'' In his *Old Familiar Faces,* pp. 25-68. London: Herbert Jenkins, 1916.
A character sketch by a friend of Borrow's that relies heavily on personal anecdotes.

Williams, David. *A World of His Own: The Double Life of George Borrow.* Oxford: Oxford University Press, 1982, 178 p.
A biography.

Wise, Thomas J. *A Bibliography of the Writings in Prose and Verse of George Henry Borrow.* 1914. Reprint. London: Dawsons of Pall Mall, 1966, 316 p.
A comprehensive bibliography of the first editions of Borrow's works published through 1914.

John Clare

1793-1864

English poet and prose writer.

For his vivid and exact descriptions of rural life and scenery, Clare is ranked with the foremost English nature poets. However, critics have been unable to reach a consensus as to which of Clare's works are his greatest. Attempts to place him within the context of the poetic climate of the first half of the nineteenth century reach widely divergent conclusions. Much of the history of Clare criticism is dominated by two varying approaches: while some commentators define his importance with reference to the tradition of eighteenth-century descriptive verse, others emphasize the Romantic qualities of his poetry. Recent studies illustrating the singularity of Clare's vision of nature by contrasting his poetry with that of the major Romantics have contributed to the diversity of critical opinion.

Clare was born and raised in the Northamptonshire village of Helpston, England, and its countryside provided the inspiration for most of his poetry. The only son of impoverished farm laborers, Clare worked during his childhood on the farm to help support his family. As a result, his formal education was limited to three months a year, first at a small school in his native village and later at a school in nearby Glinton. Clare's poetic gift was fostered by his parents' knowledge of folk ballads and his own reading of the works of the eighteenth-century descriptive poet James Thomson. Inspired by his *Seasons,* Clare begin to write verse during intervals of farm work. Clare's formal education ended at the age of fourteen, when financial demands forced him to obtain permanent employment. In 1809, while working at the Blue Bell Inn in Helpston, Clare fell in love with Mary Joyce, the daughter of a wealthy farmer. Although Mary's father quickly broke off the relationship because of her suitor's inferior social status, the memory of his first love never left Clare, and she became the subject of many of his poems.

During the years following his employment at the Blue Bell Inn, Clare tried various occupations before attempting in 1818 to publish a volume of poems by subscription. Although this scheme proved unsuccessful, the prospectus of the proposed volume attracted the attention of the influential London publisher John Taylor, who agreed to publish Clare's work. *Poems Descriptive of Rural Life and Scenery* is a nostalgic lament for the open fields and common meadow-lands of Clare's boyhood; this common land, which had been used for centuries by peasant farmers, was "enclosed," or fenced off, by an 1809 Act of Parliament and subsequently was available only to those who owned it. Taylor's introduction to *Poems,* which emphasized the poverty-stricken conditions under which most of the poems were written, largely determined the immediate critical response to the volume. Despite the work's enormous popular success, contemporary reaction to *Poems* was patronizing; while Clare's peasant background and minute descriptions of nature formed the basis for a number of comparisons of his poetry with that of Robert Burns and Robert Bloomfield, commentators also criticized his grammatical inaccuracies and provincial expressions. Some of the most enthusiastic reviews contained pleas for Clare's financial support, and he found himself the recipient of a small annuity, which enabled him to

marry Martha Turner, whom he met while working at a lime-kiln in Rutlandshire.

By the time Clare published his second volume of poetry, *The Village Minstrel, and Other Poems,* the vogue for rural verse that was responsible for the success of *Poems* had subsided, and the book sold poorly. While Clare was preparing his next work, *The Shepherd's Calendar; With Village Stories, and Other Poems,* Taylor advised him to "elevate his views" in accordance with the taste for imaginative, sentimental verse. However, Clare refused to comply, and *The Shepherd's Calendar,* which consists primarily of an account of village and farming life, met the same fate as *The Village Minstrel.*

During these years, Clare struggled to support his growing family on his annuity and sporadic income from gardening and field work. The isolation and spiritual loneliness he experienced in Helpston, as much as the poverty, was a source of growing concern, and he complained to Taylor that he lived "among the ignorant like a lost man." In 1832, through the auspices of a benevolent patron, Lord Fitzwilliam, Clare and his family moved from their small, crowded home to a larger cottage in nearby Northborough. Although Clare was grateful to Fitzwilliam, he was grieved by the departure from the countryside of Helpston, and he made this traumatic move the subject of two poems, "Decay" and "The Flitting." With the failure of

The Rural Muse in 1835, Clare's mental health collapsed. He began to experience delusions that he was the poet Lord Byron or the famous boxer Jack Randall, and that Mary Joyce was his first wife, while Martha Turner was his second. In 1837 Clare was confined to a private asylum in High Beech. He escaped four years later and returned to Northborough for five months, finishing two long poems with titles borrowed from Lord Byron, "Don Juan" and "Child Harold." His physical health improved, but the delusions persisted, and in 1841, he was taken to the Northampton General County Lunatic Asylum. There, Clare wrote incessantly, yet only a few of the asylum poems, which treat rural themes and subjects but are in general more reflective than his earlier verse, appeared in contemporary journals and newspapers. These, his last works, received little notice, and Clare died in obscurity at the Northampton asylum twenty-three years after his incarceration.

The history of Clare criticism is marked by controversy and contention, which Edmund Blunden aptly described as "a puzzling profusion of good and bad critiques." Several key issues dominate the commentary, including whether Clare's early or late work is his most distinguished, the influence of the Romantic poetic tradition on his work, and whether he was merely a descriptive poet or was capable of conveying ideas. Recent commentators frequently note that it was Arthur Symons, in his 1908 introduction to a selection of Clare's poems, who offered the first appraisal of his poetry free from the condescension that colored the early reviews. Like many later critics, Symons divided Clare's poetry into several periods of development. Attaching literal significance to Clare's statement in "Sighing for Retirement" that he "found the poems in the fields, / And only wrote them down," Symons argued that the early verse contained "more reality than poetry." Continuing the debate, J. W. Tibble, in his 1935 introduction to *The Poems of John Clare*, maintained that Clare's nature imagery was increasingly fused with emotions and ideas. John Speirs, on the other hand, declared that Clare was essentially a pictorial poet and contended that his verse displayed little development. In contrast to the majority of Clare's critics during the first half of the twentieth century, Speirs asserted that Clare's finest work was his pre-asylum verse, which is informed by the influences of such earlier descriptive poets as Thomson, William Cowper, and George Crabbe. Focusing on Clare's attitude toward landscape and the changes effected by enclosure, his ability to convey physical sensations, and his use of dialect, recent commentators have generally confirmed Elaine Feinstein's contention that Clare's "maturest means of expression came from his sense of the solidity of 'the real world'," as revealed in the early poetry. The current interest in Clare's language has prompted many critics to censure Taylor for his attempts to expunge the "low" and provincial from Clare's poetry. In a 1964 republication of *The Shepherd's Calendar* and in *Clare: Selected Poems and Prose,* which appeared two years later, editors Eric Robinson and Geoffrey Summerfield made an effort to print what Clare actually wrote rather than Taylor's edited version of the poems. Robinson and Summerfield, in their introduction to the later volume, cautioned against exaggerating the importance of the asylum lyrics because of the intensity of a few poems.

Many critics have endeavored to measure Clare's importance by comparing him to the major Romantic poets. In appreciative reviews of both *Poems Chiefly from Manuscript* and *Madrigals and Chronicles,* John Middleton Murry praised Clare's penetrating descriptions of nature, but noted that his poetry was devoid of the intellectual element that characterized the works of John Keats and William Wordsworth. Edmund Gosse, in a much harsher analysis, also emphasized the weakness of Clare's thought, arguing that his verse lacked the "organic sensibility" of Wordsworth's. Geoffrey Grigson challenged Murry's interpretation of Clare's achievement and contended that the ideas expressed concerning love, freedom, eternity, and artistic creativity in certain of the asylum lyrics raised him "far above the mere 'naturalist' of his common reputation." In a reassessment of Clare's poetry that centered on the asylum poems "A Vision" and "Invite to Eternity," Murry discussed Clare as a visionary poet comparable in certain respects to William Blake. Harold Bloom elaborated on Murry's comparison of Clare and Blake, examining the successive stages of Clare's poetic growth within the context of the Romantic dialectic between nature and imagination.

Scholars have achieved no consensus concerning the relative merits of the early and late poetry and the relationship between Clare's works and those of his predecessors and contemporaries. Nevertheless, his reputation as a leading nature poet is firmly established, and the steadily increasing amount of critical interest in his work attests to his importance. William Howard noted in 1981 that Clare's reputation continues to grow in a manner the poet himself approved; as Clare expressed it, "the quiet progress of a name gaining its ground by gentle degrees in the world's esteem is the best living shadow of fame to follow."

PRINCIPAL WORKS

Poems Descriptive of Rural Life and Scenery (poetry) 1820
The Village Minstrel, and Other Poems (poetry) 1821
The Shepherd's Calendar; With Village Stories, and Other Poems (poetry and short stories) 1827
The Rural Muse (poetry) 1835
Poems (poetry) 1908
John Clare: Poems Chiefly from Manuscript (poetry) 1920
Madrigals and Chronicles: Being Newly Found Poems Written by John Clare (poetry) 1924
Sketches in the Life of John Clare, Written by Himself (autobiography and sketches) 1931
The Poems of John Clare. 2 vols. (poetry) 1935
Poems of John Clare's Madness (poetry) 1949
The Letters of John Clare (letters) 1951
The Prose of John Clare (autobiography, journal, and essays) 1951
The Later Poems of John Clare (poetry) 1964
The Shepherd's Calendar (poetry) 1964
Clare: Selected Poems and Prose (poetry and sketches) 1966

JOHN CLARE   (essay date 1818)

[*In 1818, Clare attempted to publish a volume of poems by subscription but failed. However, its prospectus, from which the following excerpt is drawn, was brought to the attention of the prominent London publisher John Taylor, who subsequently published Clare's first three volumes of poetry. Here, Clare asks the public to make allowances for his poetry on the basis of his modest origins. Later, Clare revoked this plea (see excerpt below, 1827).*]

The public are requested to observe, that the Trifles humbly offered for their candid perusal can lay no claim to eloquence of composition, (whoever thinks so will be deceived,) the greater part of them being *Juvenile* productions; and those of a later date offsprings of those leisure intervals which the short remittance from hard and manual labour sparingly afforded to compose them. It is hoped that the humble situation which distinguishes their author will be some excuse in their favour, and serve to make an atonement for the many inaccuracies and imperfections that will be found in them. The least touch from the iron hand of *Criticism* is able to crush them to nothing, and sink them at once to utter oblivion. May they be allowed to live their little day, and give satisfaction to those who may choose to honour them with a perusal, they will gain the end for which they were designed, and their author's wishes will be gratified. Meeting with this encouragement, it will induce him to publish a similar collection, of which this is offered as a specimen.

> *John Clare, in an extract from* Clare: The Critical Heritage, *edited by Mark Storey, Routledge & Kegan Paul, 1973, p. 30.*

[JOHN TAYLOR]   (essay date 1820)

[*Taylor's introduction to* Poems *largely determined the immediate critical response to the volume. He emphasizes the poverty-stricken conditions under which most of the poems were written and provides biographical facts which invariably became linked to later critical commentary.*]

[The poems in *Poems Descriptive of Rural Life and Scenery*] will probably attract some notice by their intrinsic merit; but they are also entitled to attention from the circumstances under which they were written. They are the genuine productions of a young Peasant, a day-labourer in husbandry, who has had no advantages of education beyond others of his class; and though Poets in this country have seldom been fortunate men, yet he is, perhaps, the least favoured by circumstances, and the most destitute of friends, of any that ever existed. (p. i)

[At his own home, Clare] saw Poverty in all its most affecting shapes, and when he speaks of it, as in the **"Address to Plenty,"** . . . he utters "no idly-feign'd poetic pains:" it is a picture of what he has constantly witnessed and felt. One of our poets has gained great credit by his exterior delineations of what the poor man suffers; but in the reality of wretchedness, when "the iron enters into the soul," there is a tone which cannot be imitated. Clare has here an unhappy advantage over other poets. (pp. ii-iii)

In the **"Dawnings of Genius,"** Clare describes the condition of a man, whose education has been too contracted to allow him to utter the thoughts of which he is conscious. . . . There is, perhaps, no feeling so distressing to the individual, as that of Genius . . . struggling in vain for sounds to convey an idea of its almost intolerable sensations, . . . and that this would have been Clare's fate, unless he had been taught to write, cannot be doubted: a perusal of his Poems will convince any one, that something of this kind he still feels, from his inability to find these words which can fully declare his meaning. From the want of a due supply of these, and from his ignorance of grammar, he seems to labour under great disadvantages. On the other hand, his want forces him to an extraordinary exertion of his native powers, in order to supply the deficiency: he employs the language under his command with great effect, in those unusual and unprecedented combinations of words which

must be made, even by the learned, when they attempt to describe perfectly something which they have never seen or heard expressed before. And in this respect Clare's deficiencies are the cause of many beauties,—for though he must, of course, innovate, that he may succeed in his purpose, yet he does it according to that rational mode of procedure, by which all languages have been formed and perfected. Thus he frequently makes verbs of substantives, as in the lines,

> Dark and darker *glooms* the sky—
> To *pint* it just at my desire—

Or verbs of adjectives, as in the following,

> Spring's pencil *pinks* thee in thy flushy stain.

But in this he has done no more than the man who first employed *crimson* as a verb: and as we had no word that would in such brief compass supply so clearly the sense of this, he was justified no doubt in taking it. (pp. vii-ix)

Another peculiarity in Clare's writing, which may be the occasion of some misunderstanding in those who are critically nice in the construction of a sentence, is the indifference with which he regards words as governing each other; but this defect, which arises from his evident ignorance of grammar, is never so great as to give any real embarrassment to the reader. An example occurs [in **"A Reflection in Autumn"**]:—

> Just so 'twill fare with me in Autumn's Life,

instead of "the Autumn of Life;" but who can doubt the sense? And it may be worth while to mention here another line, which for the same reason may be objected to by some persons:—

> But still Hope's smiles unpoint the thorns of Care—

as if he had intended to say "Hope smiling;" yet as the passage now stands it has also great propriety, and the Poet's conception of the effect of those smiles may have been, that they could blunt the thorns of care. But Clare, as well as many other poets, does not regard language in the same way that a logician does. He considers it collectively rather than in detail, and paints up to his mind's original by mingling words, as a painter mixes his colours. And without this method, it would be impossible to convey to the understanding of the reader an adequate notion of some things, and especially of the effects of nature, seen under certain influences of time, circumstance, and colour. (pp. xi-xii)

Examples of the use of Colour may be seen in the Sonnets— [**"The Primrose," "The Gipsy's Evening Blaze," "A Scene,"**] . . . and in the following verse [from **"Summer Morning"**]:—

> First sunbeam, calling night away,
>   To see how sweet thy summons seems,
> Split by the willow's wavy grey,
>   And sweetly dancing on the streams. . . .

The whole of the Sonnet [**"The River Gwash"**] is an instance of it, down to the line

> And moss and ivy speckling on my eye.

A dry critic would call the former passages redundant in epithets; and the word *speckling* would excite, perhaps, his spleen in the latter: but ask the question, and you will probably find that this critic himself has no eye for colour,—that the light, and shade, and mezzotint of a landscape, have no charms for him,—that "his eye indeed is open, but its sense is shut;" and then, what dependance can be placed upon his judgment in these matters?

Clare, it is evident, is susceptible of extreme pleasure from the varied hues, forms, and combinations in nature, and what he most enjoys, he endeavours to pourtray for the gratification of others. He is most thoroughly the Poet as well as the Child of Nature; and, according to his opportunities, no poet has more completely devoted himself to her service, studied her more closely, or exhibited so many sketches of her under new and interesting appearances. There is some merit in all this, for Wordsworth asserts, "that, excepting a passage or two in the 'Windsor Forest' of Pope, and some delightful pictures in the Poems of Lady Winchelsea, the Poetry of the period intervening between the publication of [Milton's] *Paradise Lost,* and [Thomson's] *Seasons* [60 years], does not contain a single new image of external nature." But Clare has no idea of excelling others in doing this. He loves the fields, the flowers, "the common air, the sun, the skies;" and, therefore, he writes about them. He is happier in the presence of Nature than elsewhere. He looks as anxiously on her face as if she were a living friend, whom he might lose; and hence he has learnt to notice every change in her countenance, and to delineate all the delicate varieties of her character. (pp. xiii-xv)

It is now thirteen years since Clare composed his first poem: in all that time he has gone on secretly cultivating his taste and talent for poetry, without one word of encouragement, or the most distant prospect of reward. That passion must have been originally very strong and pure, which could sustain itself, for so many years, through want, and toil, and hopeless misery. His labour in the fields through all seasons, it might be thought, would have disgusted him with those objects which he so much admired at first; and his taste might have altered with his age: but the foundation of his regard was laid too deeply in truth to be shaken. On the contrary, he found delight in scenes which no other poet has thought of celebrating. "The swampy falls of pasture ground, and rushy spreading greens," "plashy streams," and "weed-beds wild and rank," give him as much real transport as common minds feel at what are called the most romantic prospects. And if there were any question as to the intensity or sincerity of his feeling for Poetry and Nature, the commendation of these simple, unthought of, and generally despised objects would decide it. (pp. xv-xvi)

The Author and his Poems are now before the public; and its decision will speedily fix the fate of the one, and, ultimately, that of the other: but whatever be the result to either, this will at least be granted, that no Poet of our country has shewn greater ability, under circumstances so hostile to its developement. And all this is found here without any of those distressing and revolting alloys, which too often debase the native worth of genius, and make him who was gifted with powers to command admiration, live to be the object of pity or contempt. The lower the condition of its possessor, the more unfavourable, generally, has been the effect of genius on his life. That this has not been the case with Clare may, perhaps, be imputed to the absolute depression of his fortune. It is certain that he has not had the opportunity hitherto of being injured by prosperity; and that he may escape in future, it is hoped that those persons who intend to shew him kindness, will not do it suddenly or partially, but so as it will yield him permanent benefit. Yet when we hear the consciousness of possessing talent, and the natural irritability of the poetic temperament, pleaded in extenuation of the follies and vices of men in high life, let it be accounted no mean praise to such a man as Clare, that, with all the excitements of *their* sensibility in *his* station, he has preserved a fair character, amid dangers which presumption did not create, and difficulties which discretion could not avoid.

In the real troubles of life, when they are not brought on by the misconduct of the individual, a strong mind acquires the power of righting itself after each attack, and this philosophy, not to call it by a better name, Clare possesses. If the expectations of "better life," which he cannot help indulging, should all be disappointed, by the coldness with which this volume may be received, he can [as he stated in **"Helpstone"**]

—put up with distress, and be content.
(pp. xxi-xxii)

[John Taylor], in an introduction to Poems Descriptive of Rural Life and Scenery *by John Clare, Taylor and Hessey, 1820, pp. i-xxiii.*

THE MONTHLY MAGAZINE   (essay date 1820)

To judge from the sketch given [in John Taylor's introduction to *Poems Descriptive of Rural Life and Scenery* (see excerpt above, 1820)] of the humble and laborious life of this obscure genius [John Clare], we are surprised to discover such a display of poetical talent and force of mind in circumstances so little favourable to the development of the human faculties. Considered as the productions of a common labourer, they are certainly remarkable, and deserving of encouragement and commendation; but, to maintain that they have the smallest pretensions to comparative excellence with the writings of others out of his own sphere, would be ridiculous and unjust, and would be trying them by a poetical law from which they ought to be exempt. We do not therefore require that they should possess the correctness and elegance of more classic bards. We must decide upon them by their own merits, and the positive degree of excellence they may possess.... Though Mr. C.'s poems are not devoid of merit, they will not stand the test of a trial by themselves....

We must, in justice to Mr. C. mention that ... one favourable feature of his poetry is, that it evidently improves. He has still, however, much to overcome.

A review of "Poems Descriptive of Rural Life and Scenery," in The Monthly Magazine, *London, Vol. XLIX, No. 337, March 1, 1820, p. 164.*

THE NEW MONTHLY MAGAZINE   (essay date 1820)

[Without the knowledge of Clare's life provided in John Taylor's introduction to *Poems Descriptive of Rural Life and Scenery* (see excerpt above, 1820)], any decision on the productions themselves would be premature; since, if they possess sufficient intrinsic merit to please, they will obtain some additional commendation from a consideration of the circumstances under which they were composed: whilst those circumstances may fairly be pleaded in extenuation of whatever defects they display, and may serve as an apology for the absence of that transcendent excellence which more favoured poets have attained. (p. 326)

Of the subjects of these poems, and the style in which they are composed, two things are chiefly to be remarked: first, that they contain true and minute delineations of external nature, drawn from *actual observation;* and secondly, that they abound with provincialisms, and are not unfrequently blemished by grammatical inaccuracies. Clare is strictly a descriptive poet; and his daily occupation in the fields has given him a manifest advantage over those minstrels whose pastoral strains are inspired by the contemplation of the furze and stinted herbage of Hampstead Heath, or the sooty verdure of a London square. In his descriptions we find no "sweet buds" and "wavy grass," and "leafy glories," twice and thrice and thirty times repeated. He revels in an unbounded luxuriance of epithets; in his minuteness of detail he seems at a loss where to stop; he paints every mode of colour and of form, and when his attention is attracted by objects which he cannot define by ordinary language, he invents new forms of expression, as singular as they are vigorous and appropriate. . . . He looks on plants, insects, and animals with the eye of a naturalist, and his accuracy, in this respect, shews that he has been a watchful observer of their habits. . . . If associations are only wanting to convey an image correctly to the mind, Theocritus or Virgil could bring forward none but what this untaught Northhamptonshire hind enumerates. Their works are to him, as they were to the Ayrshire peasant [Robert Burns], *"a fountain shut up, and a book sealed;"* but Clare is acquainted with a language less understood than Greek or Latin—the language of the human heart, and he reads in a book which requires no commentary— the book of nature. Of the figures of rhetoric he makes no display; but when he does employ them, he employs them with propriety. Thus, when he personifies the Storm, who, "tyrant-like,"

> Takes delight in doing harm,
> Down before him crushing all,
> Till his weapons useless fall;
> And as in oppression proud,
> Peal his howlings long and loud.
> While the clouds, with horrid sweep,
> Give (as suits a tyrant's trade)
> *The sun a minute's leave to peep,*
> *To smile upon the ruins made.*

Can there be a personification more just, or an image more beautiful, than that with which it concludes? He imagines himself protected from the injuries of this tyrant by Plenty, and he has recourse to a simile, which might inspire the most polished poet with emulation.

> Oh, how blest 'mid these alarms,
> I should bask in Fortune's arms,
> Who defying every frown,
> Hugs me on her downy breast,
> Bids my head lie easy down,
> And on Winter's ruins rest.
> *Emblematic simile,*
> *Birds are known to sit secure,*
> *While the billows roar and rave,*
> *Slumbering in their safety sure,*
> *Rock'd to sleep upon the wave.*

The poems which please us best are, **"Noon;"** lines **"To a Rosebud in humble Life;"** the **"Harvest Morning;"** lines **"On an Infant's Grave;"** those addressed **"To an April Daisy," "Summer Evening," "Summer Morning,"** the **"Dawnings of Genius,"** and the Sonnets. (pp. 328-29)

[Clare, as John Taylor admits,] is addicted to imitation, and we think he imitates Burns too frequently. This is imprudent. The similarity of their conditions will so often induce a comparison, that it would be more judicious in Clare to attempt an original career, than to cramp the vigour of his muse by adopting a manner. He is, like his predecessor, "Nature's never wean'd, though not her favour'd child;" and while he confines himself to the description of her charms, he needs not the aid of any mortal brother; but neither his songs and ballads, his

"Familiar Epistle to a Friend," nor his **"Dolly's Mistake,"** and **"My Mary,"** which last are by far the worst pieces in the volume, will bear to be brought in competition with the deep pathos, the rich and genuine humour displayed in similar productions of the unequalled Scottish minstrel. Yet Clare has succeeded admirably in **"The Meeting,"** which is imitated from Burns' "O were I on Parnassus Hill." . . . (p. 329)

To the poems is subjoined a glossary, that serves to explain the provincial expressions "many of which," as the writer of the introduction acutely observes, were once general, and "may be called part of the unwritten language of England." We readily subscribe to his opinion, that some of them are "as well sounding and significant as any that are sanctioned by the press." But, surely, such expressions as "bangs," "chaps," (for "young fellows,") "eggs on," "fex," (a petty oath,) "flops," "snifting and snufting," &c, are mere vulgarisms, and may as well be excluded from the poetical lexicon, as they have long since been banished from the dictionary of polite conversation: neither can we imagine, although we confess ourselves uninformed in this particular, that "to pint it," can be understood to signify, "in the midland counties," or elsewhere, "to drink a pint of ale," any more than to "steak it," or to "chop it" would imply to eat a beef steak or a mutton chop. (pp. 329-30)

> *"Clare's Poems," in* The New Monthly Magazine, *Vol. XIII, No. LXXIV, March, 1820, pp. 326-30.*

THE ECLECTIC REVIEW (essay date 1820)

If it be the characteristic privilege of genius, as distinguishable from mere talent, 'to carry on the feelings of childhood into the powers of the man,'—to combine the child's sense of wonder and novelty with the every day appearances of nature,

> With sun and moon and stars throughout the year,
> With man and woman,

and if there be any truth in the assertion, that, 'so to represent familiar objects as to awaken the minds of others to a like healthy freshness of sensation concerning them, is its most unequivocal mode of manifestation,'—there can be no hesitation in classing the Author of [*Poems Descriptive of Rural Life and Scenery*], to whatsoever rank in society he should prove to belong, among the most genuine possessors of this dangerous gift. . . . [A] genuine and powerful interest, that does more honour to its object, cannot fail to be excited by the perusal of these exquisitely vivid descriptions of rural scenery, in every lover of nature, who will feel a sort of affinity to the Author; and the recollection that the sensibility, the keenness of observation, and the imaginative enthusiasm which they display, have discovered themselves in an individual of the very humblest station in society, in a day-labourer, whose independence of spirit alone has sustained him above actual pauperism, will be attended by sensations similar to those with which he would recognise some member of his own family in a state of degradation. Talent is, we admit, cheap enough in the present day: the average stature of mind has been raised pretty extensively throughout society. But genius such as characterises these productions of John Clare, is not common in any rank. . . . (pp. 327-28)

For minute fidelity and tastefulness of description, we know scarcely any thing superior to the sketches of '**Noon,**' '**Summer Morning,**' and '**Summer Evening.**' It is evident from a line introduced between inverted commas in the first of these, that the Author had seen Cunningham's 'Day.' This, however, is the extent of his obligations. Clare's descriptions are as far superior in spirit, and picturesque beauty, and tasteful expression, to the namby pamby style of Cunningham's pastorals, as the scenes from which he derives his inspiration, are to Vauxhall gardens. It is, indeed, remarkable, that Clare's style should be so free from the vices of that school of poetry, to which his scanty reading appears to have been confined. Colloquialisms and provincialisms abound in his poems, and attest its substantial originality; but of the grosser vulgarity of affected expression, of all attempt at fine writing, he has steered most commendably clear. (p. 331)

We are not disposed under present circumstances, to find fault with any of the specimens which [the Editor of *Poems*] has presented to us, of Clare's genius; and it was quite proper that they should appear with all their inaccuracies and provincialisms, just as they proceeded from his pen. But as the permanent interest of the volume will depend on the intrinsic merits of the composition, we cannot imagine that a few corrections from the hand of Clare himself, at the suggestion of his Editor, would render a new edition less valuable. We by no means intend this remark to apply to the greater number of the words thrown into the glossary,—some of them needlessly enough; as, for instance, 'folds,' 'standard trees,' 'tools,' 'won't,' &c. Many of the provincial terms are forcibly expressive, and can scarcely fail to be understood. What we chiefly refer to, is, an occasional grammatical blemish, although both the diction and the construction of the periods, are, upon the whole, singularly chaste and correct. A more important improvement, however, would consist in a careful revision of the selection of pieces offered to the Public. Several in the present volume, we should be extremely glad to see displaced by subsequent productions; in particular, **'My Mary,' 'Dolly's Mistake,'** and **'The Country Girl.'** Clare does not succeed in humour: his poems display a playful fancy, but it is a playfulness quite distinct from the unbridled joyousness of dramatic humour, or the epigrammatic smartness of wit. Humour belongs to other scenes than the quiet landscape of human life. . . . What may be the effect of further cultivation and a more extended experience, on the mind of Clare, we will not venture to predict. It belongs to the nature of real genius, to convert all knowledge to its own nutriment, and to enrich itself with the spoils of time. . . . Clare is hardly likely to produce anything much more beautiful than some of the descriptive passages in the present volume. However this may be, he will not in future be able to yield with the same zest and simplicity of feeling, and in the same unsolicitous mood as formerly, to the tide of his own emotions; and though he may write better, he will scarcely enjoy in an equal degree the luxury of his solitary thoughts. (pp. 339-40)

> *A review of "Poems Descriptive of Rural Life and Scenery," in* The Eclectic Review, *Vol. XXXI, No. XIII, April, 1820, pp. 327-40.*

THE QUARTERLY REVIEW   (essay date 1820)

[*The following appreciative assessment of* Poems *emphasizes the spiritual quality of Clare's relationship with nature and is one of the most frequently quoted early appraisals of his works.*]

[*Poems, Descriptive of Rural Life and Scenery*] bears indubitable evidence of being composed altogether from the impulses of the writer's mind, as excited by external objects and internal sensations. Here are no tawdry and feeble paraphrases of former poets, no attempts at describing what the author *might*

have become acquainted with in his limited reading: the woods, the vales, the brooks—

> the crimson spots
> I' the bottom of a cowslip,—

or the loftier phenomena of the heavens, contemplated through the alternations of hope and despondency, are the principal sources whence the youth, whose adverse circumstances and resignation under them extort our sympathy, drew the faithful and vivid pictures before us. (p. 166)

Clare is rather the creature of feeling than of fancy. He looks abroad with the eye of a poet, and with the minuteness of a naturalist, but the intelligence which he gains is always referred to the heart; it is thus that the falling leaves become admonishers and friends, the idlest weed had its resemblance in his own lowly lot, and the opening primrose of spring suggests the promise that his own long winter of neglect and obscurity will yet be succeeded by a summer's sun of happier fortune. The volume, we believe, scarcely contains a poem in which this process is not adopted; nor one in which imagination is excited without some corresponding tone of tenderness, or morality. When the discouraging circumstances under which the bulk of it was composed are considered, it is really astonishing that so few examples should be found of querulousness and impatience, none of envy or despair.

The humble origin of Clare may suggest a comparison with Burns and Bloomfield, which a closer examination will scarcely warrant. (pp. 172-73)

To the pointed wit, the bitter sarcasm, the acute discrimination of character, and the powerful pathos of Burns, Clare cannot make pretension; but he has much of his tender feeling in his serious poetry, and an animation, a vivacity, and a delicacy in describing rural scenery, which the mountain bard has not often surpassed. . . . The poetical compositions of [Clare and Bloomfield] have few points of contact. [Bloomfield's] *Farmer's Boy* is the result of careful observations made on the occupations and habits, with few references to the passions of rural life. Clare writes frequently from the same suggestions; but his subject is always enlivened by picturesque and minute description of the landscape around him, and deepened, as we have said, with a powerful reference to emotions within. The one is descriptive, the other contemplative. (p. 173)

> *"Clare's 'Poems'," in* The Quarterly Review, *Vol. XXIII, No. XLV, May, 1820, pp. 166-74.*

[JOHN GIBSON LOCKHART]   (essay date 1820)

[*Although Lockhart wrote several novels, his fame rests on his biography of Sir Walter Scott and his critical contributions to* Blackwood's Edinburgh Magazine *and the* Quarterly Review. *From 1817 to 1825, he was a principal contributor to* Blackwood's, *a Tory periodical that was founded to counter the influential Whig journal the* Edinburgh Review. *His trenchant wit contributed to the early success of the magazine and earned him the nickname of "The Scorpion." Later, as editor of the* Quarterly, *he was a less acerbic critic. Nevertheless, he is notorious for his series of scathing articles in* Blackwood's *on the "Cockney School" of poetry, in which he assailed John Keats and Leigh Hunt on the basis of political differences and, indirectly, for their inferior education and upbringing. In contrast, Lockhart recognized the talents of William Wordsworth, Samuel Taylor Coleridge, and Percy Bysshe Shelley, despite his aversion to their political principles. He is regarded as a versatile, if somewhat severe, critic whose opinions of his contemporaries, though lacking depth, are generally considered accurate when not distorted by political animosities. Here, Lockhart objects to the "enormous puffing of the Northamptonshire peasant" and denies that Poems merits the approbation of Clare's patrons.*]

When one thinks of Hogg, and of the silent but sure progress of his fame—or of Allan Cunningham, and of the hold he has taken of the heart of Scotland almost without being aware of it himself—one cannot help feeling some qualms concerning the late enormous puffing of the Northamptonshire peasant, John Clare. I have never seen [*Poems Descriptive of Rural Life and Scenery*], but from all the extracts I have seen, and from all the private accounts I have heard, there can be no doubt Clare is a man of talents and a man of virtue; but as to poetical genius, in the higher and the only proper sense of that word, I fear it would be very difficult to shew that he deserves half the fuss that has been made. Smoothness of versification and simplicity of thought seem to be his chief merits; but alas! in these days these are not enough to command or to justify such a sounding of the trumpet. . . . Clare has exhibited powers that not only justify but demand attention and kindness—but his generous and enlightened patrons ought to pause ere they advise him to become any thing else than a peasant—for a respectable peasant is a much more comfortable man, and always will be so, than a mediocre poet. Let them pause and think of the fate of the far more highly-gifted Burns, and beware alike of the foolish zeal and the sinful neglect of *his* countrymen. (p. 322)

[*John Gibson Lockhart*], "*Extracts from Mr Wastle's Diary,*" *in* Blackwood's Edinburgh Magazine, *Vol. VII, No. XXXIX, June, 1820, pp. 317-23.*

THE LITERARY CHRONICLE AND WEEKLY REVIEW (essay date 1821)

[Numerous as are the pieces in *The Village Minstrel, and Other Poems*], there are scarcely any that we would have wished to be withheld. . . . The principal poem, the '**Village Minstrel**,' was . . . finished soon after [*Poems Descriptive of Rural Life and Scenery*] made its appearance. Clare is himself the hero of his poem, and paints, with glowing vigour, the misery in which he then was, and his anxiety for his future fate. It is a fine picture of rural life, and the author luxuriates in his love of natural objects and his description of rustic sports and village scenes, notwithstanding the melancholy reflections and forbodings with which they are accompanied. (p. 624)

[The '**Village Minstrel**'] would justify all the praise that has been bestowed on John Clare, who, in vivid descriptions of rural scenery, in originality of observation and strength of feeling, richness of style and delicacy of sentiment, may rank with the best of poets of the day, though a humble and untutored peasant.

Among the minor poems in these volumes, we have been much pleased with '**Autumn**,' '**Cowper Green**,' '**Song of Praise**,' and some of the pastorals, a style in which Clare would have been successful, had he not abandoned it early in his poetic career. The songs and sonnets are many of them very pretty, and some of them possess considerable merit. . . .

Though there is no species of poetry more common than the sonnet, yet there are few who succeed in it. Clare has indulged in it largely, and given us no less than sixty specimens of his talents in this species of composition, in which we think him very successful. . . .

With all our predilections for the first fruits of natural genius, we must admit that Clare has improved by cultivation; and though some of his earlier productions are striking from their neatness and simplicity, yet his more matured efforts, though not deficient in this respect, have a refinement of language and a correctness of style, which give them an increased value. Should these new volumes extend the public patronage sufficiently to relieve him from that oppressive anxiety which still bears him down, we may fairly expect the poet to take a loftier and more extensive range of subject, and to add new claims to those he already possesses as a man of genius; though stronger claims to public sympathy and public support no one can present, than the poor Northamptonshire peasant; and with all the warmth of admiration for his talents, and sympathy for his miseries, we recommend him and his works to the public. (p. 625)

A review of "The Village Minstrel, and Other Poems," in The Literary Chronicle and Weekly Review, *Vol. III, No. 125, October 6, 1821, pp. 623-25.*

THE MONTHLY MAGAZINE, LONDON (essay date 1821)

[*The author of this review of* The Village Minstrel *disapproves of Clare's stylistic innovations, particularly his use of the Northamptonshire dialect, and unfavorably compares the volume's title poem to James Beattie's* The Minstrel. *Despite admiration for Clare's sonnets, the critic concludes that* The Village Minstrel *is at best mediocre.*]

[*The Village Minstrel, and Other Poems*] contains much that is good, and even beautiful; and we are disposed not only to point out its merits with readiness, but to acknowledge them with pleasure. . . . But considering these poems with reference only to their literary excellence, the need of commendation to which some parts of them may be justly entitled, is altogether a distinct question from the necessity, or even the propriety of bringing them before the tribunal of the public. The latter is what Partridge would have termed a *non sequitur*. We are willing to give full credit to the motives of those, whose benevolence has prompted them to introduce the effusions of the Northamptonshire peasant to general notice, but we may reasonably doubt how far thay have been the means of enriching, in any great degree, our stores of national poetry, or are likely to bind a wreath more permanent than that woven by the caprice of fashion, or the prevailing appetite for novelty, round the brows of the object of their patronage. (pp. 321-22)

[The author of *The Village Minstrel*] is undeniably superior in correct observation, vigour of intellect, and native talent, to many others who have come before us with pretensions of a similar description. . . . [However, we] do not conceive that occasional sweetness of expression, or accurate delineations of mere exterior objects, can atone for a general deficiency of poetical language, or the indulging in a style devoid of uniformity and consistency. "The Village Minstrel" is the principal poem in the collection, and is evidently intended to afford a picture of the peculiar circumstances and early scenes of the author's life. To himself this topic is no doubt peculiarly interesting; and his descriptions may very probably be productive of amusement to those who are familiar with the originals. To us, however, the writer's mention of himself appears, in general, too egotistical and querulous, and the local subjects and rural amusements, whatever opinion may be entertained of the colours in which he has pourtrayed them, have not, we think, been very judiciously selected for the purpose of inspiring general interest. There is, besides, something more than homeliness, approximating to vulgarity, in many of his themes, and it must be admitted that these are described in most suitable language. What shall we say, for instance, of lines like the following?

But soldiers, *they're the boys to make a rout.*

The *bumptious* serjeant struts before his men.

His friends so poor and clothes *excessive dear.*

And *don't* despise your betters *'cause* they're old.

Up he'd *chuck sacks* as one would hurl a stone.
(p. 322)

If it be urged that such language is appropriate to the subjects treated of, we reply, that subjects to which such language is best adapted, are not those which a poet should have chosen; or, if selected for the exercise of his muse, he should have spoken of them in the dialect that "the muses love." . . .

Another disadvantage attending ["**The Village Minstrel,**"] is, the involuntary comparison which it forces on the mind with the exquisite poem [*The Minstrel* by Beattie]; a comparison that can hardly prove favourable to the Northamptonshire bard. We do not allude to the plan of the poem, for Mr. Clare's Minstrel appears to be without any, and is composed principally of detached descriptions, most of which might change places with one another, without the reader's being conscious of the alteration. But not only in the structure of the verse, but in many imitative passages, we seem to perceive an attempt to present us in Lubin [the title character of Clare's poem] with a species of travestie of our old acquaintance Edwin [the title character of Beattie's work], and we cannot approve of the experiment. Indeed the author of the present collection seems, on more than one occasion, to have lost sight of his ground, being previously occupied by those whom he could hardly expect to displace. We could have dispensed with his verses on "**Solitude,**" after Grainger's Ode on the same subject; his "**Sorrows for the Death of a favourite Tabby Cat,**" will hardly be sympathised in, by those who bear Gray's Selima in remembrance, and it is very unfortunate for his "**Song to a City Girl,**" that it cannot be read without recalling to our minds the inimitable old ballad, "Oh, come with me, and be my love." . . .

[In *The Village Minstrel,* the consequences of Clare's lack of education] are perpetually visible. The author seems always incapable of sustaining an equal flight; and hence, if we meet with a passage we are disposed to approve, it is frequently but an introduction to specimens of the bathos, which could not be exceeded by the citations of the learned Scriblerus himself. . . .

The following verses we have no hesitation in pronouncing beautiful; indeed it appears to us, that there are no others equal to them in the whole collection:

I cannot pass the very bramble, weeping
  Neath dewy tear-drops that its spears surround,
Like harlot's mock'ry, on the wan cheek creeping,
  Gilding the poison that is meant to wound.

But would any one imagine, that they are almost immediately preceded, in the same piece, by such a line as,

Winding the zig-zag lane, turning and turning?

Again, speaking of the lark, Clare says,

With day-break's beauties *I have much been taken,*
  As thy first anthem breath'd its melody.

Can there be a greater contrast, than that between the richness and force of the latter of these two lines, and the feeble vulgarity of that which precedes it?

We must likewise mark our strong disapprobation of the innovating style introduced in many parts of these volumes, by the employment of unauthorised contractions, and the use of words that have hitherto been strangers alike to our prose and poetry. Take, out of many, the subjoined specimens.

And then, for sake *of's* boys and wenches dear.

And's merry sport when harvest came again.

And *well's* he knows, with ceremony kind.

While I, as unconcern'd, went *soodling* on.

He heard the *tootling* robin sound her knell.

If *yah* set any store by one *yah* will.

How he to scape *shool'd* many a pace beyond.

We leave it to the sober judgment of our readers, to decide, whether these, though indisputable, are desirable additions to our language. We may perhaps be told, that a Glossary is annexed to the book; but this does not alter our view of the subject. If the example of Burns, Ramsay, Ferguson, or other Scottish poets be pleaded, we answer, that they employed a dialect in general use through an entire country, and not the mere *patois* of a small district. If the peculiar phraseology of the Northamptonshire rustics is to be licensed in poetry, we see no reason why that of Lancashire, Somersetshire, and other counties should not be allowed an equal currency; and thus our language would be surprisingly enriched, by the legitimization of all the varieties of speech in use among the *canaille* throughout the kingdom. (p. 323)

The annexed instances, as well as numerous others, of "vile alliteration," are likewise to us, who are no admirers of that figure of speech, a strong impeachment of the author's good taste.

While maidens fair, with *bosoms bare,*
Go *coolly* to their *cows.*

Now wenches *listen,* and *let lovers lie.*
Hay-makers hustlin from the rain to *hide.*

Keep off the bothering bustle of the wind.

We trust our readers will readily perceive that the above strictures have not been dictated by a spirit of fastidious or splenetic criticism; they have been prompted solely by a wish to rescue our literature from the inroads attempted to be made upon it by false taste or mistaken benevolence. It is with real pleasure that we turn from this unwelcome part of our task, to point out some favourable specimens of the native talent which we have already said the author possesses, and which would, we doubt not, in other circumstances than those in which he has been placed, have developed themselves to much greater advantage. (pp. 323-24)

[In our opinion] the writer of the present collection has excelled in his sonnets more than in any other species of composition that he has attempted. The second volume contains upwards of fifty of these short poems, many of which need not shrink from a comparison with the productions of loftier bards in the same department. (pp. 324-25)

Several passages in the [sonnets **"Hereafter," "Peace,"** and **"Autumn"**] are very pleasing, and in no small degree poetical; indeed, they must be confessed to be very superior to any thing that could have been anticipated from the limited resources and defective education of a man like Clare. So far, therefore, he is certainly entitled to praise. But we fear, when every allowance is made, that sober judges will hardly be disposed to assign these poems at the utmost, a place above mediocrity. . . . (p. 325)

> *A review of "The Village Minstrel, and Other Poems,"* in The Monthly Magazine, *London, Vol. LII, No. 360, November 1, 1821, pp. 321-25.*

CHARLES LAMB   (letter date 1822)

[*An English essayist, critic, and poet, Lamb is considered one of the leading figures of the Romantic movement. In the following letter to Clare, who became his friend and correspondent after the publication of* Poems, *Lamb advises him to avoid the use of rustic slang in his poetry.*]

The quantity of your observation [in *Poems Descriptive of Rural Life and Scenery* and *The Village Minstrel, and Other Poems*] has astonished me. What have most pleased me have been **"Recollections after a Ramble,"** and those . . . pieces in eight syllable lines, my favourite measure, such as **"Cowper Hill"** and **"Solitude."** In some of your story-telling Ballads the provincial phrases sometimes startle me. I think you are too profuse with them. In poetry *slang* of every kind is to be avoided. There is a rustick Cockneyism, as little pleasing as ours of London. Transplant Arcadia to Helpstone. The true rustic style, the Arcadian English, I think is to be found in Shenstone. Would his "Schoolmistress," the prettiest of poems, have been better, if he had used quite the Goody's own language? Now and then a home rusticism is fresh and startling, but where nothing is gained in expression, it is out of tenor. It may make folks smile and stare, but the ungenial coalition of barbarous with refined phrases will prevent you in the end from being so generally tasted, as you deserve to be. (p. 46)

> *Charles Lamb, in a letter to John Clare on August 31, 1822, in his* The Letters of Charles Lamb, *Vol. 2, revised edition, J. M. Dent & Sons Ltd., 1945, pp. 46-7.*

JOHN CLARE   (essay date 1827)

[*In the following excerpt from his preface to* The Shepherd's Calendar, *first published in 1827, Clare asks that the work be judged on its intrinsic merits rather than on criteria that emphasizes his peasant origins. The excerpt contrasts sharply with his prospectus, in which Clare requested that his poetry be judged in light of his humble circumstances (see excerpt above, 1818).*]

I leave the following Poems to speak for themselves,—my hopes of success are as warm as ever, and I feel that confidence in my readers' former kindness, to rest satisfied, that if the work is worthy the reward it is seeking, it will meet it; if not, it must share the fate of other broken ambitions, and fade away. I hope my low station in life will not be set off as a foil against my verses, and I am sure I do not wish to bring it forward as an excuse for any imperfections that may be found in them. (pp. 200-01)

> *John Clare, in an extract from* Clare: The Critical Heritage, *edited by Mark Storey, Routledge & Kegan Paul, 1973, pp. 200-01.*

[JOSIAH CONDER]   (essay date 1827)

[*Conder was editor of the* Eclectic Review *from 1814 to 1837 and a poet himself. In this commendatory assessment of* The Shepherd's Calendar, *he points to Clare's "progressive improvement" in asserting that his poems "may now challenge admiration on the ground of their intrinsic merit and interest." Of the reviews of* The Shepherd's Calendar, *Clare preferred Conder's; in a letter to John Taylor dated December 10, 1827, he stated, "I like the* Eclectic *much the best . . . there is a heartiness in the praise and that coming from a Poet pleases me much better."*]

John Clare, we confess, is a favourite with us; we hope he is with our readers, and for a similar reason; he is so true to nature, that his verse may be said to reflect the very images and colouring of the scenes he describes, rather than to be the tapestry-work of the fancy. His poetry seems to have no other business than simply, as it murmurs on, to image to the mind's eye the natural objects which the season and the place may present. There they are, softened by the reflection, but just as they breathe or bloom; and any poor wight, in cities pent, by means of this *camera lucida*, may see them as he sits with his book in his hand, by the side of his hanging garden of flower-pots, uttering his melancholy *O rus, quando te aspiciam* [O country home, when shall I see you]? We dare not vouch, however, that every one of his readers will have true pastoral taste enough fully to relish his poetry, or be able to appreciate the nice observation which it discovers. To those who would think the country dull, John Clare's poetry must needs be insipid. He is professedly but a landscape-painter, and not of Turner's school; he might rather be compared to Morland, only that, in sentiment and feeling, he rises so far above him. (pp. 509-10)

For nice observation, and fidelity, and native feeling, Clare . . . will stand a comparison with any of our descriptive poets. If we meet with few elevated sentiments or philosophic remarks, which in him could only be affectation, it is high praise, but well deserved, that he is always natural and in character, and never aims at a style above his compass. (p. 511)

[Among the miscellaneous poems in *The Shepherd's Calendar; with Village Stories and Other Poems*], it is with sincere satisfaction that we perceive an occasional thoughtful reference to such topics as death and eternity; the total avoidance of which in most of the poems, excites the fear, that the Poet has not yet learned to look upon the beauties of Nature as faint types at best of a far more exceeding and eternal glory,—has not yet drunk into that spirit which should enable him, amid the scenes of his rural wanderings, to

> lift to Heaven an unpresumptuous eye,
> And smiling say, My Father made them all.

We do not now speak as critics, for it were not fair to find fault with his poems for what they do not contain; nor would we wish the Poet to affect sentiments he does not feel, and to *hitch in* an awkward sentence or two of a religious complexion. There are 'tongues in trees' and 'sermons in stones;' and in this species of divinity, Clare's poetry is not deficient. It is for his own sake, as much as for that of his readers, that we could wish him oftener to

> reach the Bible down from off the shelf,
> To read the text, and look the psalms among;—

till, haply, he might imbibe from the sacred page a higher inspiration, and perceive, not only how "the heavens declare the glory of God," but that "the statutes of the Lord are right, rejoicing the heart, and his testimonies sure, making wise the simple." Then, should he live, as we hope he will, to produce a fourth volume, we should expect to find him reaching a higher strain.

[*The Shepherd's Calendar*], as compared with Clare's first efforts, exhibits very unequivocal signs of intellectual growth, an improved taste, and an enriched mind. This progressive improvement is one of the surest indications of a mind endowed with the vigorous stamina of genius. . . . In the preface to the present volume [see excerpt above, 1827], he expresses a just and manly confidence of success. 'I hope,' he says, 'my low station in life will not be set off as a foil against my verses; and I am sure I do not wish to bring it forward as an excuse for any imperfections that may be found in them.' We like this spirit. There is a sort of praise which, in its tone, differs little from contempt, and with which no poet would be satisfied. His compositions may now challenge admiration on the ground of their intrinsic merit and interest. (pp. 518-19)

> [*Josiah Conder*], "*Clare's 'Shepherd's Calendar',*"
> in The Eclectic Review, *n.s. Vol. XXVII, June, 1827,*
> *pp. 509-21.*

[JOHN WILSON]   (essay date 1835)

[*A Scottish critic, essayist, novelist, poet, and short story writer, Wilson is best known as Christopher North, the name he assumed when writing for Blackwood's Edinburgh Magazine, a Tory periodical to which he was a principal contributor for over twenty-five years. He is chiefly famous for his* Noctes Ambrosianae, *a series of witty dialogues originally published in* Blackwood's *between 1822 and 1835, in which contemporary issues and personalities are treated at once with levity, gravity, and pungent satire. Wilson is not recognized as a great critic. His criticism, which was frequently written in haste, is often deficient in sagacity, analysis, and finish. He could be severe and stinging, and he reserved his harshest words for gifted young writers whom he sincerely wanted to help by objectively analyzing their work. His other critical opinions are largely regarded as the projections of his varying moods; his conflicting assessments of William Wordsworth's poetry, for instance, are often cited as evidence of his subjectivity. Indiscriminate benevolence, on the other hand, led him to equate such authors as Joanna Baillie and William Shakespeare. Here, Wilson provides a mixed review of* The Rural Muse. *While emphasizing the originality of Clare's mind, Wilson notices a departure from the predominantly descriptive verse of his previous volumes and urges the poet to return to rural themes and subjects. This stricture angered John Taylor, who had advised Clare since the publication of* Poems *to introduce a metaphysical strain into his poetry. In a letter to Clare dated August 3, 1835, Taylor indignantly commented that Wilson "has no conception of the Imaginative Faculty in Poetry, in which your Genius excels, & which is the highest Faculty of the Poet. He therefore fails to estimate properly your character as a Poet, and advises you to imitate Bloomfield! This is sad Foolery."*]

It is with heartfelt pleasure that we take up [*The Rural Muse: Poems*] by John Clare, the Northamptonshire Peasant. . . . We rejoice to find that the Rural Muse has been with him during his long retirement—that his fine sensibilities have suffered no

abatement under the influence of time—and that, though he says [in his preface] "ill health has almost rendered me incapable of doing any thing," it has not in any degree weakened his mental powers or dulled his genius. Let us hope that . . . he may live to sing many such sweet songs as these—and in domestic peace and comfort long enjoy his fame. Yes—his fame. For England has singled out John Clare from among her humble sons . . . as the most conspicuous for poetical genius, next to Robert Bloomfield. That is a proud distinction—whatever critics may choose to say; and we cordially sympathize with the beautiful expression of his gratitude to the Rural Muse [in "**Address to the Rural Muse,**"] when he says—

> Like as the little lark from off its nest,
> Beside the mossy hill, awakes in glee,
> To seek the morning's throne, a merry guest—
> So do I seek thy shrine, if that may be,
> To win by new attempts another smile from thee.

The poems now before us are, we think, at least equal to the best of his former productions, and characterised by the same beauties—among which we may mention as the most delightful—rich and various imagery of nature. (p. 231)

The Northamptonshire Peasant always writes with sincerity and simplicity—like one to whom "dear is the shed to which his soul conforms." Indeed the great charm of his poetry is that it deals with what is nearest and dearest to him—and that much as he loves nature, that sweet and humble nature in midst of whose delights he lives—he never flies into any affected raptures—never seeks to intensify beyond the truth any emotion he owes to her—but confides in her inspiration with a grateful and a filial heart. And verily he has had his reward. For thus has he been privileged to converse with nature, who is well-pleased with her pious son—and makes revelations to him, at her own sweet will. . . . (p. 232)

John Clare often reminds us of James Grahame. They are two of our most artless poets. Their versification is mostly very sweet, though rather flowing forth according to a certain fine natural sense of melody, than constructed on any principles of music. So, too, with their imagery, which seems seldom selected with much care; so that, while it is always true to nature, and often possesses a charm from its appearing to rise up of itself, and with little or no effort on the poet's part to form a picture, it is not unfrequently chargeable with repetition—sometimes, perhaps, with a sameness which, but for the inherent interest in the objects themselves, might be felt a little wearisome—there is so much still life. (p. 234)

It is not to be thought, however, that the Northamptonshire Peasant does not often treat more directly of the common pleasures and pains, the cares and occupations of that condition of life in which he was born and has passed all his days. He knows them well, and has illustrated them well, though seldomer in this volume than in his earlier poems; and we cannot help thinking that he may greatly extend his popularity, which in England is considerable, by devoting his Rural Muse to subjects lying within his ken and of everlasting interest. Bloomfield's reputation rests on his "Farmer's Boy"—on some exquisite passages on "News from the Farm"—and on some of the tales and pictures in his "May-day." His smaller poems are very inferior to those of Clare—but the Northamptonshire Peasant has written nothing in which all honest English hearts must delight, at all comparable with those truly rural compositions of the Suffolk shoemaker. It is in his power to do so—would he but earnestly set himself to the work. He must be more familiar with all the ongoings of rural life than his com-peer could have been; nor need he fear to tread again the same ground, for it is as new as if it had never been touched, and will continue to be so till the end of time.... Nor need he fear being an imitator. His mind is an original one, and this volume proves it; for though he must have read much poetry since his earlier day—doubtless all our best modern poetry—he retains his own style, which, though it be not marked by any very strong characteristics, is yet sufficiently peculiar to show that it belongs to himself, and is a natural gift. Pastorals—eclogues—and idyls—in a hundred forms—remain to be writ-ten by such poets as he and his brethren; and there can be no doubt at all, that if he will scheme something of the kind, and begin upon it, without waiting to know fully or clearly what he may be intending, that before three winters, with their long nights, are gone, he will find himself in possession of more than mere materials for a volume of poems, that will meet with general acceptation, and give him a permanent place by the side of him he loves so well—Robert Bloomfield. (pp. 239-40)

[Perhaps] the pleasantest portion of the volume is that which consists of sonnets—no fewer than eighty-six—and almost all expressive of "moods of my own mind," when meditating either on his own lot or on that of his rural neighbors.... In the humble hands ... of John Clare, the sonnet discourses most excellent music. (p. 243)

> [*John Wilson*], *"Clare's 'Rural Muse'," in* Black-wood's Edinburgh Magazine, *Vol. XXXVIII, No. CCXXXVIII, August, 1835, pp. 231-47.*

THE NEW MONTHLY MAGAZINE (essay date 1835)

Mr. Clare's muse, at all times chaste and elegant, and fre-quently reaching a pathos and feeling uncommon enough in these days of superficial writing, has contributed some of his happiest productions to grace [*The Rural Muse*]. The reader will also be pleased to observe a far superior finish, and a much greater command over the resources of language and metre in the later compositions of this truly pastoral writer, who, pre-sented at first to the public notice by the genuine spirit of poetry displayed in his less experienced days, has gone on constantly improving, and enlarging his claim to popular ap-probation. The poem which opens his last work, an **"Address to the Rural Muse,"** will be found a very favourable illustration of what we have observed. It is a fine specimen of manly feeling, and of that quiet inspiration which, without any os-tentatious attempt at display, speaks directly and powerfully to the heart. **"Summer Images"** is another beautiful poem, and affords a pleasing example to show from what common materials a superior composition may be produced under the touch of a skilful hand. The pieces which follow are of various degrees of merit, but almost all of a character likely to add to Mr. Clare's fame. We would particularly specify **"The Eter-nity of Nature,"** Stanzas **"On seeing a Skull on Cowper Green,"** **"The Autumn Robin,"** and **"The Skylark."** Of the sonnets we are not inclined to think so highly. It is given but to few names in literature to overcome the difficulties attending the most common, and at the same time most wayward and per-plexing kind of composition. The simply pathetic and pleas-ing,—all the more gentle emotions, whether joyful or mel-ancholy,—which the contemplation of Nature in her most familiar garb is qualified to inspire, fall legitimately within the province of Mr. Clare's singularly felicitous power of song. As long as he keeps to these, there is no fear of his being accounted otherwise than as a poet who must be a general favourite with

all in whom a love of his art is inherent; to his name, we may add, the volume he has just published will add no trifling increase of reputation.

> *A review of "The Rural Muse," in* The New Monthly Magazine, *Vol. XLIV, No. CLXXVI, August, 1835, p. 510.*

THOMAS DE QUINCEY (essay date 1840)

[*An English critic and essayist, De Quincey used his own life as the subject of his best-known work,* Confessions of an English Opium Eater, *in which he chronicled his addiction to opium. In addition, De Quincey contributed reviews to a number of London journals and earned a reputation as an insightful if occasionally long-winded literary critic. At the time of De Quincey's death, his critical expertise was underestimated, though his prose talent had long been acknowledged. In the twentieth century, some crit-ics still disdain the digressive qualities of De Quincey's writing, yet others find that his essays display an acute psychological awareness. In the excerpt below, which originally appeared in* Tait's Edinburgh Magazine *in December, 1840, De Quincey main-tains that the botanical detail of Clare's poetry accounts for both its merits and defects. He notes that while his poems are valuable as a "calendar" of rural life, they are often devoid of "feeling." This argument recurs throughout early Clare criticism.*]

[Clare's] poems were not the mere reflexes of his reading. He had studied for himself in the fields, and in the woods, and by the side of brooks. I very much doubt if there could be found in his poems a single commonplace image, or a descrip-tion made up of hackneyed elements. In that respect, his poems are original, and have even a separate value, as a sort of cal-endar (in extent, of course, a very limited one) of many rural appearances, of incidents in the fields not elsewhere noticed, and of the loveliest flowers most felicitously described. The description is often true even to a botanical eye; and in that, perhaps, lies the chief defect; not properly in the scientific accuracy, but that, in searching after this too earnestly, the feeling is sometimes too much neglected. However, taken as a whole, his poems have a very novel quality of merit, though a quality too little, I fear, in the way of public notice.... As regarded his own poems, [Clare's admiration for William Wordsworth] seemed to have an unhappy effect of depressing his confidence in himself. It is unfortunate, indeed, to gaze too closely upon models of colossal excellence. Compared with those of his own class, I feel satisfied that Clare will always maintain an honourable place. (pp. 144-45)

> *Thomas De Quincey, "Thomas Noon Talfourd, 'The London Magazine', Mr. John Taylor and His Book on the Authorship of 'Junius', the Poet Clare, Allan Cunningham," in his* The Collected Writings of Thomas De Quincey, *Vol. III, edited by David Mas-son, A. & C. Black, 1897, pp. 126-59.**

CYRUS REDDING (essay date 1841)

[*Redding's sympathetic descripton of his visit with Clare at High Beech was the first substantial account to be published of the poet's life in the asylum. The essay, which originally appeared in the* English Journal *on May 15 and May 29, 1841, includes a plea for financial support for Clare and reprints several of the asylum poems.*]

The artless description of Nature's works in Clare is, in reality, the result of very close observation, and the recapitulation of that which is not only familiar, but to which the Poet is ardently attached, whether under delusion or in perfect possession of his mental faculties. Wherever he goes, Nature, in the general form obvious to all, is his theme, but he is versed in her minuter aspects. (p. 254)

True, there are repetitions in the verses of Clare, and much similarity of metaphor and subject. It would be wonderful if this were not the case with one who has been educated at the plough, and toiled in fields through the first years of existence, in place of passing his time in academic bowers. A few grammatical lapses and indefensible elisions may well be excused. Let those who can only see these things, albeit well grounded in grammar, write with equal excellence destitute of the genius which breaks through trammels genius alone could overcome. It is that mysterious power which leads to the productions of such writers as Clare, so seldom seen—productions, simple as they are, that hundreds and thousands who could write a volume without one repetition or one breach of Priscian, could no more rival than they could ride to the moon upon Lindley Murray's pedantic and lumbering 'Grammar.'

But they are not alone the trivial things of Nature that occupy the verse of Clare. The expansive landscape so varied and beautiful, the hill and stream, the humanities of life, are all equally subjects of his poetry. In Clare, too, there is a peculiar locality always prevalent, his themes belonging to that part of England frequented by the nightingale, which goes no further north than York, and enters not the mild climate of Devonshire and Cornwall. His subjects come out of the very heart of England, and many of the words he uses are unknown beyond the central part of the island. Another quality remarkable in Clare is his admiration of woman; a fond, respectful, 'true love' attachment to the sex distinguishes his writings.

Clare may be styled the illustrator of the rural scenery of his native land to a degree of fidelity, as well as minuteness, that has not been before approached; almost every flower, tree, and shrub that springs freely from the free soil of England has been noticed in his verses in its proper site, as it bourgeons and blows. Bloomfield generalises more; indeed, it may be questioned if he knew a tithe of what Clare knows of the minutiae of Nature, the result of position and his love of beautiful things.

It is to be lamented, perhaps, that he has not taken his rural muse sometimes a higher flight; but his leisure for a work of any considerable length must have been scanty, and his excellencies may, perhaps, be best exhibited as they are now written down before us. (pp. 255-56)

[In the poems written at the asylum in High Beech] we do not say that Clare has surpassed his preceding productions; moreover, they are printed rough and uncorrected, as they were first committed to paper. They have been composed under the shadow of insanity, in circumstances to which the Poet is well awake, and the irksomeness of which he feels. We ask, however, whether the inhabitant of an asylum for lunatics ever wrote, in assimilation to preceding works, so well before; and whether it be not a discredit to the age that such a man should be permitted to wear out his days under the depression of a cankering care for his future support, which outrages reason painfully, though not heavily? (p. 256)

> *Cyrus Redding, in an extract from* Clare: The Critical Heritage, *edited by Mark Storey, Routledge & Kegan Paul, 1973, pp. 247-56.*

EDWIN PAXTON HOOD (essay date 1851)

[*Hood's study, in which he integrates the facts of Clare's life into an overall appraisal of his career, was the most expansive to have appeared by the mid-nineteenth century. One of the few early critics to recognize the reflective quality of Clare's verse, Hood refuses to classify him as "merely a rustic Poet." Instead, Hood claims that Clare's vision of nature is one of "eternal youth and eternal mystery."*]

[Now, even in literary circles, Clare's poems] are unreferred to, if not entirely unknown. Their purity, their excessive modesty, their intense devotion to Nature in the woods and the fields, in an age when the woods and fields have been comparatively forsaken, these may be assigned as some of the reasons for the obscurity which has gathered round the name of one of the sweetest singers of the children of Labour. Clare is Bloomfield's successor, and he is very far his superior, dwelling among the ever-varying scenes of Nature, and abounding, as he unquestionably does, with homely images, he is yet not merely a rustic Poet, or a rural Bard. Such poets receive, but do not give; they take passing sensible impressions of the Georgic world, but they do not reflect themselves. From such writers we scarcely expect reflection; their Bucolics abound in prettiness and generalities, without the boldness of generalization; but Clare has more fully individualized his scenery than any poet of his class, always excepting Burns: it is the poetry of Rural Life and Taste—but it is Rural Life with the dignity of the man, not with the rudeness or mannerism of the clown. It is worth some inquiry what makes the evident distinction between the methods of Cowper, and Wordsworth, and Keats, and Tennyson; and between all these again and our humbler friend, of whom we are now speaking, all love the country, but few love it as Clare loves it. Yet, it seems indispensable to the proper appreciation of rural scenery, that we should not only take our walks there, but find our work there. Clare writes, as Gilbert White would have written, had he been a poet. He threads his way through all Nature's scenery with a quiet meditation and reflection, and frequently those reflections, if not the result of profound thought, yet bear the stamp of profound beauty. Clare's life is in the country. There are those who study the country, and read the volume of the town by its side; there are those who bring to the study of the country extensive readings and learning; there are those who make each scene of country life only the key to their own imaginations, and move, indeed, very far from the scenery of their original thought; but Clare takes the country literally as it is; he brings to it no learning, no historical suggestion; he seeks in the country none of the monuments of haughty human grandeur; he unfolds no political philosophy; he seeks no high idealization; he takes the lesson lying on the surface, and frequently it is so simple and natural that it affects us to tears. The fields of Nature are not so much a study to which he retires, or an observatory which he mounts; they are rather a book which he reads, and, as he reads, turns down the page. We should be prepared to expect after this, what we do actually find—an extreme homeliness of style and thought—we mean homeliness in its highest and best sense—not lowness, not vulgarity—the very reverse of all these. Clare walks through the whole world around him with the impression, that he cannot go where "universal love smiles not around." His whole soul is a fountain of love and sensibility, and it wells forth in loving verse for all, and to all creatures. The lessons of his verses may be described as coming, rather than being sought; for they grow up before him; he does not dig for them, and, therefore, his poems are rather fancies and feelings than imaginations. He throws his whole mind, with all its sensitiveness, into the country; yet, not so much does he hang over its human life as the life of Nature, the love and the loveliness of this beautiful world. Traditional tales he does not narrate. A bird's nest has far more attraction to his eyes than the old manorhouse, or the castle. The life of the cottage, too, is a holy life for him; his home is there, and every season brings, day by day, its treasures of enjoyment and of peace to him. In a new and noble sense all his poems are pastorals; he sings of rural loves and trystings, and hopes, and joys. He never, indeed, loses himself, as many of us do, in vague generalities, for he has seen all he mentions in his song; he has been a keen observer of the ways of Nature; he knows her face in all its moods, and to him the face is always cheerful. Other poets go out into the walks of Nature to spend a holiday; they love her, but to see her is an occasional pleasure, but to Clare it is an every-day existence. He has no holiday with Nature; he walks with her as friend with friend. Other poets select a river, or a mountain, and individualise it, but to Clare all are but parts of the same lovely Home, and as every part of the home is endeared—the chair, the shelf, the lattice, the wreathing flower, the fire-place, the table—so is every object in Nature a beloved object, because the whole is beloved. Other poets entertain, as they enter the avenues of Nature, a most solemn awe and dread: we have said that Clare never forgets himself in low coarseness, so neither does he ever shrink or shiver beneath the dread of an overaweing presence; he walks with Nature as an angel walks with goodness—naturally, cheerfully, fraternally.

Fancy, Feeling, and Philosophy or Reflection, these are the characteristics of [Clare's verse]. Most rural poets have indulged merely in the Feeling, but the Feeling has not been sufficiently sensitive or profound for Reflection, and the mind has not been active enough for Fancy—that is rich and ariel humour of our poet, in which he enters into the life of an insect. Insects, which to many are, have been, and will be, simply an annoyance, are to him fairies with coloured hood and burnished wings, disguised in a sort of splendid masquerade, rocked to sleep in the smooth velvet of the pale hedge rose, or slumbering like princes in the heath bell's purple hood, secure from rain, from dropping dews, in silken beds and painted hall; a jolly and a royal life this seems, this band of playfellows mocking the sunshine on their glittering wings, or drinking golden wine and metheglin from the cup of the honied flower. It is in a deeper mood that the ploughman reflects upon the eternity of Nature; to the simplest things in Nature, to his eye, there is entwined a spirit sublime and lasting: the daisy, trampled under foot strikes its root into the earth, and in the distant centuries of time, the child will clap its tiny hands with pleasure and cry "A Daisy!" its little golden bosom frilled with snow, will be the same, as bright as when Eve stooped to pluck it in Eden. Cowslips of golden bloom, will come and go as fresh two thousand years hence as now; brooks, bees, birds, from age to age, these will sing on when all the more ambitious things of earth shall have passed away; and not only the fact continues, but the fact in the same form; for Clare, like Audubon, is not content to be merely sentimental, he fixes his eye on the proprieties and ever recurring mysteries of Nature, all Nature's ways are mysteries, hence "the red thighs of the humble bee" travel wide and far, when he

> Breakfasts, dines, and most divinely sups
> With every flower, save golden buttercups,
> On whose proud bosoms he will never go,
> But passes by with scarcely 'How do 'e do?'
> Since in their snowy, shining, gaudy cells,
> Haply the Summer's honey never dwells.

Eternal youth and eternal mystery, the unfading beauty and the unfading sublimity of Nature—these are everywhere seen; seen as remarkably in the most insignificant as in the most majestic. The fancies and the freaks of Nature are a sort of pledge of unfailing truthfulness. (pp. 141-47)

[Clare's poems] reveal an intimacy and acquaintance with Nature; an eye perpetually on the watch to notice the colouring and the scenery of things, as well as the thing itself. We remember no Poet of any walk, who has lived so much with Nature; who has pressed so far within her visible portals; who has so reverently gathered the mosses and the wild flowers growing in the neighbourhood of her temple. . . . [It] is not from inability to penetrate so far, but from modesty and sensitiveness, that Clare has taken his chief delight in lingering over common things, and folding in fondness to his heart the least and most fragile of Nature's forms, and finding the things of beauty and the joy for ever where none but those who love Nature with a lover's passion ever look. (pp. 149-50)

[Clare] indulges in no extravaganzas; all his images are simple, natural, and affecting; he never selects images he has not seen: perhaps, the words *mountain* and *forest* do not occur throughout his poems. They are moulded from the long level wastes and fens, the vast moors of his own and the adjacent counties. Some have scouted the idea of poetry, and boldness of thought and variety of conception in the fen country; they have not been there, nor have they learned the philosophy of our poet when he says:—

> Be thy journey e'er so mean,
> Passing by a cot or tree,
> In the rout there's something seen,
> Which the curious love to see.
> In each ramble, Taste's warm souls,
> More of Wisdom's self can view,
> Than blind Ignorance beholds
> All life's seven stages through.

(p. 152)

At the risk of exciting a misunderstanding and a sneer, we may call Clare the Wordsworth of Labour. In saying this, the great distance both of attainment and position is borne in mind, and perhaps the immeasurable distance of original genius. Of this, however, it is well nigh impossible to speak. Clare's genius is one of that order depending greatly upon cultivation and communion with exalted minds; Wordsworth is a teacher, appearing once in the course of many ages, and combining in himself some exquisite sympathies never found, in the same degree, in any poet of any previous age. All that learning, travel, education in the most sublime scenery of Nature, leisure, solitude, association with the most gifted spirits, long life—all that these combined could do was lavished upon him. The reverse of all these forms the history of Clare; yet in him we notice the same intense affection for the simplest things in Nature—the same disposition to self-communion—the same power to reflect back a lesson, and to treat Nature in all her visible manifestations as an intimation and a prophecy; the same exuberant overflowing of tenderness and love—the same disposition to preserve the soul in "a wise quietness"—the same love of the sonnet and ease of utterance through that formal barrier of expression. (pp. 155-56)

When it is remembered how Clare received his education, how little opportunity he has had of cultivating acquaintance with books, and how few associations he can have had of a refining character, the affluence of his language, and its exquisite music and freedom from every jarring coarseness become truly astonishing. (pp. 156-57)

Edwin Paxton Hood, ''John Clare, the Peasant Poet,'' in his The Literature of Labour: Illustrious Instances of the Education of Poetry in Poverty, *Partridge & Oakey, 1851, pp. 128-64.*

to 1900: Chamber—Craigie, Vol. IV, *edited by Sir Leslie Stephen and Sir Sidney Lee, Oxford University Press, London, 1887, pp. 384-86.*

NONCONFORMIST   (essay date 1873)

[The following excerpt is drawn from a critique of J. L. Cherry's widely reviewed Life and Remains of John Clare, *a biography that contained over two hundred pages of asylum poetry and prose fragments, thereby exposing a broader audience to Clare's asylum verse. This essay first appeared in the* Nonconformist *on February 19, 1873.]*

[In Clare's asylum poetry, there] is all the unaffected simplicity, the quiet love of nature, and the quaint use of local phrases, which gave such a peculiar colour to his earlier works. There is a clearness, a sanity, and now and then a perfection of expression, which could never suggest aberration of any kind. Clare was always sweet, with a sustained lingering intensity of tone. His poems only needed a quantum of strength to have claimed the title of great. But this is never found in Clare. He is a sweet singer, but a singer of the second or of the third order only—lacking wholly the robustness, the dash, which we so admire, say, in Burns or Beranger. He is pensive, he is glad, he can be merry; but he is never boisterous in any mood, and he rather lacks strong humour, which above all gives richness and fulness of poetic character. In this, he is like Keats: he walked in a world of his own, and ''watered'' the impressions of other men, so far as he got hold of them, rather than dashed into the atmosphere which they coloured, identifying himself with wide variety of character and emotion. His harp was sweet, tenderly sweet, but it had few strings, and the ceaseless striking of them wore them through very soon; and thereafter they gave out only an echo amid disharmonies, and that at long intervals.

> *From a review of ''Life and Remains of John Clare,'' in* Clare: The Critical Heritage, *edited by Mark Storey, Routledge & Kegan Paul, 1973, p. 289.*

L. S. [LESLIE STEPHEN]   (essay date 1887)

[Stephen is considered one of the most important literary critics of the late Victorian and early Edwardian eras. His analyses often include biographical judgments of the writer as well as the work. As Stephen once observed: ''The whole art of criticism consists in learning to know the human being who is partially revealed to us in his spoken or his written words.'' Here, Stephen asserts that Clare's poetry is remarkable as the product of an uneducated peasant; however, he contends that one must know the circumstances under which the poems were written to appreciate them.]

Clare's poetry is modelled upon that of the cultivated classes, instead of expressing the sentiments of his own class. Lamb advised him to avoid his rustic 'slang,' and recommended Shenstone's 'Schoolmistress' in preference to 'Goody's own language' [see excerpt above, 1822]. Clare becomes less vernacular in his later poems, and the advice may have suited the man. The result is, however, that the want of culture is not compensated by vigour of local colouring. Though Clare shows fine natural taste, and has many exquisite descriptive touches, his poetry does not rise to a really high level; and, though extraordinary under the circumstances, requires for its appreciation that the circumstances should be remembered. (p. 386)

> *L. S. [Leslie Stephen], ''John Clare,'' in* The Dictionary of National Biography, from the Earliest Times

ARTHUR SYMONS   (essay date 1908)

[An English critic, poet, dramatist, short story writer, and editor, Symons initially gained notoriety as an English decadent in the 1890s, and he eventually established himself as one of the most important critics of the modern era. Though he was a gifted translator and linguist, it was as a critic that Symons made his most important contribution to literature. His The Symbolist Movement in Literature *provided his English contemporaries with an appropriate vocabulary with which to define their new aesthetic—one that communicated their concern with dreamlike states, imagination, and a reality that exists beyond the boundaries of the senses. Symons also discerned that the concept of the symbol as a vehicle by which a ''hitherto unknown reality was suddenly revealed'' could become the basis for an entire modern aesthetic, and he therefore laid the foundation for much of modern poetic theory. In his introduction to* Poems, *Symons traces the development of Clare's poetry. He argues that the exact descriptions of nature in Clare's first two volumes give way in* The Shepherd's Calendar *to a melodic and less enumerative type of verse. According to Symons, the poet's development climaxes in the works of the asylum period, when ''for the first time, Clare's lyrical faculty gets free.'' Symons's preference for the asylum poetry signals the beginning of a trend in Clare criticism that persisted through the late 1950s.]*

In Clare's early work, which is more definitely the work of the peasant than perhaps any other peasant poetry, there is more reality than poetry.

> I found the poems in the fields,
> And only wrote them down,

as he says with truth, and it was with an acute sense of the precise thing he was saying that Lamb complimented him in 1822 on the 'quantity' of his observation [see excerpt above]. It is difficult to know how much of these early poems were tinkered for publication by the too fastidious publisher Mr. Taylor, and what is most smooth and traditional in them is certainly not what is best. The ballads and love-songs have very little value, and there is often a helplessness in the language, which passes from the over-familiar to the over-elevated. Later on he would not have called the glow-worm 'tasteful illumination of the night', nor required so large a glossary of provincialisms. As it is, when he is not trying to write like Burns, or in any way not quite natural to him, he gives us, in a personal and unusual manner, a sense of the earth and living things, of the life of the fields and farmyards, with a Dutch closeness, showing us himself,

> Toiling in the naked fields,
> Where no bush a shelter yields,

in his hard poverty, and with his sensitiveness to weather, not only as it helps or hinders his labour. You see him looking up from it, looking and listening, and noting down everything he has observed, sometimes with this homely detail:

> Now buzzing, with unwelcome din,
> The heedless beetle bangs
> Against the cow-boy's dinner-tin
> That o'er his shoulder hangs.

No one before him had given such a sense of the village, for Bloomfield does not count, not being really a poet; and no one has done it so well again until a greater poet, Barnes, brought more poetry with him. Clare's poetry begins by having something clogging in it; substance, and poetical substance, is there, but the poetry has hardly worked its way out to freedom. (pp. 4-5)

It must not be assumed that because Clare is a peasant his poetry is in every sense typically peasant poetry. He was gifted for poetry by those very qualities which made him ineffectual as a peasant. The common error about him is repeated by Mr. Lucas in his *Life of Lamb*: 'He was to have been another Burns, but succeeded only in being a better Bloomfield'. The difference between Clare and Bloomfield is the difference between what is poetry and what is not, and neither is nearer to or farther from being a poet because he was also a peasant. The difference between Burns and Clare is the difference between two kinds and qualities of poetry. Burns was a great poet, filled with ideas, passions, and every sort of intoxication; but he had no such minute local lore as Clare, nor, indeed, so deep a love of the earth. He could create by naming, while Clare, who lived on the memory of his heart, had to enumerate, not leaving out one detail, because he loved every detail. Burns or Hogg, however, we can very well imagine at any period following the plough with skill or keeping cattle with care. But Clare was never a good labourer; he pottered in the fields feebly, he tried fruitless way after way of making his living. What was strangely sensitive in him might well have been hereditary if the wild and unproved story told by his biographer Martin [see Additional Bibliography]: that his father was the illegitimate son of a nameless wanderer, who came to the village with his fiddle, saying he was a Scotchman or an Irishman, and taught in the village school, and disappeared one day as suddenly as he had come. The story is at least symbolic, if not true. That wandering and strange instinct was in his blood, and it spoiled the peasant in him and made the poet. (pp. 15-16)

[Clare] kept his reason as long as he was left to starve and suffer in [the hut in Helpston], and when he was taken from it, though to a better dwelling, he lost all hold on himself. He was torn up by the roots, and the flower of his mind withered. What this transplanting did for him is enough to show how native to him was his own soil, and how his songs grew out of it. Yet the strange thing is that what killed him as a human mind exalted him as a poetic consciousness, and that the verse written in the asylum is of a rarer and finer quality than any of the verse written while he was at liberty and at home. (p. 17)

[It] cannot be said in Clare's very earliest work we have an utterance which literary influences have not modified. [But the] impulse and the subject-matter are alike his own, and are taken directly from what was about him. There is no closer attention to nature than in Clare's poems; but the observation begins by being literal; nature a part of his home, rather than his home a part of nature. The things about him are the whole of his material, he does not choose them by preference out of others equally available; all his poems are made out of the incidents and feelings of humble life and the actual fields and flowers of his particular part of England. He does not make pictures which would imply aloofness and selection; he enumerates, which means a friendly knowledge. It is enough for him, enough for his success in his own kind of poetry, to say them over, saying, 'Such they were, and I loved them because I had always seen them so'. He begins anywhere and stops anywhere. Some simple moralising, from the fall of leaves to the fading of man, rounds a landscape or a sensation of autumn. His words are chosen only to be exact, and he does not know when he is obvious or original in his epithets. When he begins

to count over aspects, one by one, as upon his fingers, saying them over because he loves them, not one more than another, setting them down by heart, with exactly their characteristics, his words have the real sound of what they render, and can be as oddly impressive as this:

> And the little chumbling mouse
> Gnarls the dead weed for her house;

or, in a poem on **'The Wild-flower Nosegay'**, can make so eager and crowded a grouping of names:

> Crimp-filled daisy, bright bronze buttercup,
>   Freckt cowslip peeps, gilt whins of morning's dew,
> And hooded arum early sprouting up
>   Ere the white thorn bud half unfolds to view,
> And wan-hued lady-smocks, that love to spring
>   'Side the swamp margin of some plashy pond;
> And all the blooms that early Aprils bring,
>   With eager joy each filled by playful hand.

His danger is to be too deliberate, unconscious that there can be choice in descriptive poetry, or that anything which runs naturally into the metre may not be the best material for a particular poem. Thus his longer poems, like *The Village Minstrel,* drop from poetry into realism, and might as well have been written in prose. He sets himself to write *Village Tales,* perhaps to show that it was possible to write of village life, not as he said Crabbe did, 'like a magistrate'. He fails equally when he sets himself (perhaps in competition with Byron's famous and overrated 'Dream') to elaborate an imaginary horror in the poem which he too calls **'The Dream';** or, setting himself too deliberately to secure in verse the emphasis of an actual storm, loses all that poetry which comes to him naturally when he is content not to search for it.

To Clare childhood was the only time of happiness, and his complaint is that 'Poesy hath its youth forgot'. His feeling towards things was always that of a child, and as he lived so he wrote, by recollection. When, in *The Shepherd's Calendar,* he writes the chronicle of the months, he writes best when he gives the child's mood rather than the grown-up person's, and always regrets that reason has come with years, because reason is disheartening. Yet still, as when he was a child, he is friends with all he sees, and he sometimes forgets that anything exists but birds, insects, and flowers. By this time he has a firmer hold on his material, and his lists turn now to pictures, as when he sees

> Bees stroke their little legs across their wings,
> And venture short flights where the snowdrop hings
> Its silver bell, and winter aconite
> Its buttercup-like flowers that shut at night;

or looks up to where,

> Far above, the solitary crane
> Wings lonely to unfrozen dykes again,
> Cranking a jarring, melancholy cry,
> Through the wild journey of the cheerless sky;

or, in May, sees in a quaint figure

> The stooping lilies of the valley,
> That love with shades and dews to dally,
> And bending droop on slender threads,
> With broad hood-leaves above their heads,
> Like white-robed maids, in summer hours,
> Beneath umbrellas shunning showers.

His epithets strengthen and sharpen; earlier he would not have thought of speaking of 'bright glib ice', or of the almanac's 'wisdom gossiped from the stars'. A new sense of appropriate melody has come into the verse, which has lost none of its definite substance, but which he now handles more delicately. One even realises that he has read Keats much more recently than Thomson.

Much of the verse contained in the last book published by Clare, *The Rural Muse,* . . . appeared in annuals of the time, and would seem to have been written for them. He repeats all his familiar notes, with a fluency which long practice and much reading have given him, and what he gains in ease he loses in personal directness. Others besides himself might have written his meditation on the nightingale and on the eternity of time, and when he questions the skull on Cowper's Green we remember with more pleasure the time when he could write of the same locality as he really knew it. Here and there, as in the coloured fragment on **'Insects'**, he is himself, and there are a few of the many sonnets which convey a sudden aspect of nature or comment aptly upon it. But it may be questioned whether the impression made on us by **The Rural Muse** is wholly the fault of Clare. . . . [The publisher's selection of material from Clare's original manuscripts] may have been well calculated for the public of the day, though, as the book failed, perhaps it was not. A number of long tales in verse, some of the more trivial comic pieces, the poems written in series, like the **'Pewit's**, the **'Pettichap's'**, the **'Yellow Wagtail's**, the **'Yellowhammer's'**, and yet other birds' nests, were left out with little or no loss; but some of the rollicking and some of the quieter poems are, though a little rough and unfinished, more personal than anything in the published book. (pp. 18-23)

With **The Rural Muse** of 1835 ends the control of Clare over his work, and all the subsequent work [from his years in the asylums] . . . will be found in Mr. J. L. Cherry's invaluable *Life and Remains of John Clare* [see Additional Bibliography]. . . . Mr. Cherry tells us that his selection has been made from the manuscripts of more than five hundred poems; and he adds: 'Of those which are printed, scarcely one was found in a state in which it could be submitted to the public without more or less of revision and correction'. I have tried in vain to find the original manuscripts, which I would have liked to have printed exactly as they were written, having convinced myself that for the most part what Clare actually wrote was better than what his editors made him write.

And I was the more anxious to get at the real text because it is more worth getting at than that of any other of Clare's earlier poems. Here, for the first time, Clare's lyrical faculty gets free. Strangely enough, a new joy comes into his verse, as if at last he is at rest. It is only rarely, in this new contentment, this solitude even from himself, that recollection returns. Then he remembers

> ——I am a sad lonely hind:
> Trees tell me so, day after day,
> As slowly they wave in the wind.

He seems to accept nature now more easily, because his mind is in a kind of oblivion of everything else; madness being, as it were, his security. He writes love songs that have an airy fancy, a liquid and thrilling note of song. They are mostly exultations of memory, which goes from Mary to Patty, and thence to a Gypsy girl and to vague Isabellas and Scotch maids. A new feeling for children comes in, sometimes in songs of childish humour, like **'Little Trotty Wagtail'** or **'Clock-a-Clay'**,

made out of bright, laughing sound; and once in a lovely poem, one of the most nearly perfect he ever wrote, called **'The Dying Child'**, which reminds one of beautiful things that have been done since, but of nothing done earlier. As we have them, and so subtle an essence could scarcely be extracted by any editor, there is no insanity; they have only dropped nearly all of the prose. A gentle hallucination comes in from time to time, and, no doubt, helps to make the poetry better. (pp. 23-4)

Arthur Symons, in an introduction to Poems *by John Clare, edited by Arthur Symons, Henry Frowde, 1908, pp. 3-24.*

ALAN PORTER (essay date 1920)

[*Porter was an admirer of Clare's who, with Edmund Blunden, edited* Poems Chiefly from Manuscript, *a work that in conjunction with* Madrigals and Chronicles *prompted a new appraisal of the poet. Porter's strident declaration that Clare is a "major poet, compeer with Keats, and Shelley, and Blake" became the major point of contention in the critical debate that developed during the 1920s. Porter's essay first appeared in the* Oxford Outlook *in May, 1920.*]

In his lifetime John Clare was forgotten, starved, and by his utter destitution driven mad: after his death a more complete oblivion obscured his name. In the four books he published there is a knowledge and love of rural life that makes our nature poets, Wordsworth, Hartley Coleridge, Crabbe, Thomson, Grahame, Tennyson, Bloomfield, seem paltering amateurs and jugglers with pretty sentiment; and it seems strange that the rich music and the clear imagination of his greatest poems are not everywhere familiar. (p. 320)

It is as hard, however, to convince the reactionary, old high Tory party of literature-dabblers that Clare is great as if he were still living. 'Tennyson we know, and Matthew Arnold; but never a great writer has followed these.' It is impossible that any precursor should be great and have escaped their omniscience. It follows, therefore, that Clare is a minor poet; enthusiasm for him is pardonable, and lack of proportion is natural, in the young, but with age and experience come sanity and balance. What need to hear a line of Clare? He must be a minor poet. Thus they are deliberately deaf, and if you read them a poem, 'It has much merit,' they will say. 'A ploughman, wasn't he? Did he ever write a poem to which a regiment of soldiers could march?' He did, he did; but, oh, one cannot argue with dunderheads like these.

And yes, ploughman he was; this circumstance has harmed his fame more than any other. Perpetually Clare asked that no allowance should be made for his poverty; and as persistently people counted a rung to heaven climbed when they pretended to patronship or spoke him well. In truth Clare needs no allowance, no compassion; merely a freedom from prejudice. To an open and sensitive mind his writing will prove him a major poet, compeer with Keats, and Shelley, and Blake. (pp. 320-21)

Clare's first book was unequivocally a bad book. It had been selected by a good-natured publisher from an already huge mass of material; he chose the most conventional, dull, and moral poems. Their author being a ploughman, his publisher ventured to improve them and regularise them. There are, nevertheless, disturbing flashes of poetry. On the whole, the book should be read only by preconceived lovers of Clare.

We have good reason to hate this bookseller. . . . He might have issued a thin volume of great poetry. I weigh the word and do not speak in hyperbole. He published instead a book which had an immediate and staggering popularity. Clare's reputation was made and ruined. The really discriminate readers of verse saw that his book did not deserve success, and paid no attention to his later works. The wider public soon forgot their three-month wonder, or, if at any time they saw another of Clare's books in Taylor and Hessey's, opening the covers they were discouraged to find a so vastly superior beauty and vigour. (p. 321)

> *Alan Porter, in an extract from* Clare: The Critical Heritage, *edited by Mark Storey, Routledge & Kegan Paul, 1973, pp. 320-21.*

H. J. MASSINGHAM   (essay date 1921)

[*In his review of* Poems Chiefly from Manuscript, *Massingham attempts to place Clare within the context of the poetic climate of the first half of the nineteenth century. Pointing to the singular blend of imagination and fact in his works, the critic asserts that Clare cannot be considered a minor poet. Massingham recognizes his development, from a poet who merely recorded his observations of nature to one who imaginatively recreated them, as the determining factor in assessing his achievement: to Massingham, the asylum poems are "unambiguously lived in the country of the imagination" and represent the culmination of Clare's poetic growth.*]

There are over 140 chosen poems in [*John Clare: Poems, Chiefly from Manuscript*], and the first question to be asked of so ample and orderly a landscape is its topography. How does Clare fit into the map of his own poetic period? It is perfectly clear that he is on a divergent tack of poetic evolution from the Romantic Revivalists, proper or improper. There are bits out of the Preface to [Wordsworth's] "Lyrical Ballads" which might be modelled into one for himself, but, granted a fragment or two, Clare and the Lake Poets part company. In the whole of this volume there are only four lines which suggest that Clare had ever read a line of Wordsworth's—from **"The Fallen Elm"**:

Thou owned a language by which hearts are stirred
Deeper than by a feeling clothed in word,
And speakest now what's known of every tongue,
Language of pity and the force of wrong.

In the same poem there is an angry reference to the enclosures, the only clear political impression (the sonnet to Buonaparte is a stiff and impersonal exercise) in the book. It cannot be too strongly stated that Clare is a poet of the spirit—a transparent spirit through which things filtered—and not of the mind; that his attitude to nature is less conscious, less formulated, less burdened (or elevated) by human or abstract preoccupations than any other poet's in the language. Clare's men and women and children are part of the landscape—they grow and shine like flowers—part whether of the actual or the imaginative landscape, none too easy to disentangle, and not, as they are in Wordsworth, Shelley, Coleridge, Byron and Keats (in the second draft of "Hyperion"), moralized beings in a purposed relationship with the universe. Clare does indeed moralize, and frequently, not in the manner of his contemporaries, nor of the eighteenth century, but, surprising as it sounds, of the seventeenth. There is very little positive imitation of any poet or period in Clare; but, dropping the metaphysics, there is more than a stray reminder of the lyrical quietism of Marvell and Bishop King, musing upon the vanishing shows of the world, extending even to turns of phrase.

It is needless to discuss the slander upon Clare as a "better Bloomfield." The only likeness between the two men is that neither of them was a "peasant poet," and for precisely opposite reasons. Whatever the facts of Bloomfield's career, he writes about nature as from a countrified coffee-house, and it was doubtless through his facility in generalization and personifying qualities, and in a towny diction which conveys not a single sharp image nor particular impression, that his rural Muse made such a good thing out of her borrowed clout. But Clare, whether wandering in fancy or rarefied fact, is fastidiously concrete and precise, never the eloquent professionalist, exploiting the object to the phrase. The objective, the ordinary, the plain speaking in Clare, which makes even his flattest diarizing so vivid and so individual, has been indulgently smiled upon by the wiseacres of nearly a hundred years. But it is one of his greatest virtues, and places him in the van of the romantic liberators who destroyed the professional tricks of eighteenth-century poetry. "Tasteful illumination of the night" (viz. the glowworm)—it is very rare indeed to find Clare cutting that kind of decorative figure. The one eighteenth-century poet with whom Clare is on any kind of poetic terms is Collins. . . . Both the long poems **"Autumn"** and **"Summer Images"** bear the Collins stamp, and beautiful phrases like "Here poor integrity can sit at ease" and the swallow "unsealing morning's eye" are Collins to a hair. The parallel must not be pressed too far, for Clare's experience of nature is richer, more intimate and varied than Collins's, while Collins stands more to pose; he is better balanced, and a greater master of his instrument, and his verse altogether more of a formal and symmetrical pattern. Yet Clare in his mood of elegiac repose joined to beguiling melody is the only nineteenth-century poet to take over the Collins tradition, reshape it, and bear it through all the distractions of a period abounding in poetic experiment and discovery. (p. 9)

It is a commonplace that Clare possessed a greater knowledge of earth and natural life than any other poet whose appeal is one of literature. Both as a man and a creator he was, I think, primarily a spiritual type, but he did not find the gift of the spirit inconsistent with a knowledge of its material works. Now a portion of his expression is quite patently nothing more than rhymed natural history, a quite literal picking of nature's pocket without, so to speak, any reinvesting of his gains in the poetic funds. But it has not been pointed out that this side of Clare is as much detached from his general poetic significance as Tennyson's bad biology is from his picture-writing.

The real question in an attempt at justly estimating an artist who cannot any longer be handled as a minor poet is whether the body of his work translated or transliterated its material; whether, in Coleridge's words, it trusted more to the memory than the imagination; whether it observes or creates, describes or sees; whether a radical defect in imaginative will confused truth to nature with truth to poetry. The great advantage of [*Poems, Chiefly from Manuscript*] is that it helps us to come to a decision by observing the continuous growth of the poet's mind—a growth not interrupted nor diverted into new channels of expression in the Asylum period, but strangely crowned. The majority of the poems in this period, with their quickened rhythm, airier music, finer sensibility and greater freedom not from but *in* nature, are unambiguously lived in the country of imagination. But it is wholly arbitrary to assume that madness was the mother of imagination. Clare lived all his life in verse: it was food, comfort, religion, happiness—his living—and the natural play of his spirit between nature and verse explains why the external odds against him so little affected his content and serenity. And the history, the internal conflict of a poetic achievement which bears so little outward sign of it was the accommodation he nearly always sought and often found between imagination and fact, and which, when found, leaves us with the conviction that he was not only a true but a unique poet. He was unique because he solved his own special problem in his own way, and he solved it partly because of his peculiar advantages in inheriting a racial tradition in pastoral poetry and in possessing a native genius in close relationship with the soil; partly because his approach to nature is not deliberate nor in any way philosophical; and partly because his own spiritual nature was endowed with a power of identifying himself with the dumb thought, the inner life of nature, not as a visionary, but simply as a lover. In this faculty Keats alone, I think, of all the Romantic poets, is kin with him. The best poems of the Middle Period are neither pure data nor pure imagination, but an individual blend of both which does express the music of his own soul and ''the inward stir of shadowed melody'' in nature in one. In the Asylum period he was to become more imaginative, and at the same time more closely drawn into the truth behind the forms of nature; and when he was removed from his own place and wrote the pathetic verses about it, he might have said that he was uprooted and (with Swift) would wither at the top. But if his mind failed him, his poetic spirit did not, and what he lost in the acute sense of a particular locality, he gained in a wider interpretation.

Where Clare fell short has already been partly indicated, and his over-facility is obvious; his most serious lack, however, is in the quality of the blend between fact and imagination. It is too diffused, too seldom fused into a concentrated flame. His gentlest of spirits is as innocent of passion and intensity as of prophetic vision and of that profound nostalgia which is only content with a seventh heaven reconciling the ultimate end of human thought and feeling with the principles of all things. Nevertheless the final value of Clare is that he does not imitate, but creates his own world. (pp. 9-10)

> *H. J. Massingham, ''John Clare,'' in* The Athenaeum, *No. 4732, January 7, 1921, pp. 9-10.*

JOHN MIDDLETON MURRY (essay date 1921)

[*Murry was a noted English essayist, magazine editor, and literary critic during the first half of the twentieth century. A longtime contributor of literary criticism to the* Times Literary Supplement, *he was the last editor of the distinguished review the* Athenaeum *before it was absorbed into the* Nation *and founding editor of the* Adelphi. *Considered a perceptive critic whose work reveals his ''honesty to the point of masochism,'' he has contributed important studies on the works of Katherine Mansfield, John Keats, Fedor Dostoevski, William Blake, and his intimate friend D. H. Lawrence. In his enthusiastic review of* Poems Chiefly from Manuscript, *which originally appeared in the* Times Literary Supplement *on January 13, 1921, Murry compares Clare's poetry to that of William Wordsworth and Keats in order to remind himself that Clare is not of the stature of his famous contemporaries. Murry accepts Clare's limitations—his prolixity, lack of technical control, and narrow imaginative scope—and pronounces him ''the love poet of nature.'' Murry's conviction, presented here and in a later essay (1924), that Clare's poetry is devoid of the intellectual element that characterizes the works of Keats and Wordsworth is echoed by Edmund Gosse (1924) and John Speirs (1935) and challenged by Eric Robinson and Geoffrey Summerfield (1966).*]

[The] eagerness with which we welcome [*John Clare: Poems Chiefly from M.S.*] is likely to be so genuine and so justified as to disturb our sense of proportion. Into a generation of poets who flirt with nature suddenly descends a true nature-poet, one whose intimate and self-forgetful knowledge of the ways of birds and beasts and flowers rises like the scent of a hay-field from every page. Surely the only danger is that the enthusiasm of our recognition may be excessive; the relief overpowering with which we greet a poet who not only professes, but proves by the very words of his profession, that his dream of delight is

> To note on hedgerow baulks, in moisture sprent,
>   The jetty snail creep from the mossy thorn,
> With earnest heed and tremulous intent,
>   Frail brother of the morn,
> That from the tiny bents and misted leaves
>   Withdraws his timid horn,
>   And fearful vision weaves.

We have indeed almost to be on our guard against the sweet, cool shock of such a verse; the emotional quality is so assured and individual, the language so simple and inevitable, the posture of mind so unassuming and winning, that one is tempted for a moment to believe that while Wordsworth was engaged in putting the poetry of nature wrong by linking it to a doubtful metaphysic, John Clare was engaged in putting it right.

And so in a sense it was. As a poet of nature Clare was truer, more thoroughly subdued to that in which he worked than Wordsworth. Wordsworth called upon the poet to keep his eye upon the object; but his eye was hardly so penetrating and keen as Clare's. Yet Wordsworth was a great poet, and Keats, with whom Clare's kinship was really closer, was a great poet, and Clare was not; and it is important in the case of a poet whose gifts and qualities are so enchanting as Clare's are to bear in mind from the outset the vital difference between them. Wordsworth belongs to another sphere than Clare in virtue of the range of his imaginative apprehension: Keats in virtue not only of his imagination, but also of his art. In one respect Clare was a finer artist than Wordsworth, he had a truer ear and a more exquisite instinct for the visualizing word; but he had nothing of the principle of inward growth which gives to Wordsworth's most careless work a place within the unity of a great scheme. Wordsworth's incessant effort to comprehend experience would itself have been incomprehensible to Clare; Keats's consuming passion to make his poetry adequate not merely in content but also in the very mechanism of expression to an emotional experience more overwhelming even than Wordsworth's would have seemed to him like a problem of metaphysics to a ploughboy.

Clare was indeed a singer born. His nature was strangely simple, and his capacity for intense emotion appears at first sight to have been almost completely restricted to a response to nature. The intensity with which he adored the country that he knew is without a parallel in English literature; of him it seems hardly a metaphor to say he was an actual part of his countryside. Away from it he pined; he became queer and irresponsible. With his plants and birds and bees and fields he was among his own people. The spiked thistle, the firetail, the hare, the white-nosed and the grand-father bee were his friends. Yet he hardly humanized them; he seems rather to have lived on the same level of existence as they, and to have known them as they know each other. We feel that it is only by an effort that he manages to make himself conscious of his emotion towards them or of his own motive in singing of it. In those rare moments he conceives of the voice of Nature as something eternal, outlasting all generations of men, whispering to them to sing also. Thus, while he sits under the huge old elm which is the shepherd's tree, listening to 'the laugh of summer leaves above',

> The wind of that eternal ditty sings,
> Humming of future things that burn the mind
> To leave some fragment of itself behind.

That is the most imaginative statement Clare ever made of his own poetic purpose. He, the poet, is one more of Nature's voices; and the same thought or the same instinct underlies the most exquisite of his earlier poems, *Song's Eternity* . . . :

> Mighty songs that miss decay,
> What are they?
> Crowds and cities pass away
> Like a day.
> Books are out and books are read;
> What are they?
> Years will lay them with the dead—
> Sigh, sigh;
> Trifles unto nothing wed,
> They die.
>
> Dreamers, mark the honey bee,
> Mark the tree
> Where the bluecap *tootle-tee*
> Sings a glee
> Sung to Adam and to Eve—
> Here they be.
> When floods covered every bough
> Noah's ark
> Heard that ballad singing now;
> Hark, hark,
>
> *Tootle tootle tootle tee.*
> Can it be
> Pride and fame must shadows be?
> Come and see—
> Every season owns her own;
> Bird and bee
> Sing creation's music on;
> Nature's glee
> Is in every mood and tone
> Eternity.

In many ways that is the most perfect of Clare's poems; it has a poetic unity of a kind that he attained but seldom, for in it are naturally combined the highest apprehension of which Clare was capable and the essential melody of his pre-eminent gift of song. It is at once an assertion and an emotional proof of the enduringness of the voice of Nature. Clare does not, like the modern poet who has chosen the same theme, adduce the times and the seasons and thereby challenge the evolutionary theory; his history is the history of myth. Not the Neanderthal man but Adam and Eve heard the bluecap's same immortal song; for it is not the fact, but the sense of song's eternity that the poet has to give us. Clare does it triumphantly. Moreover, in this poem, which we believe must henceforward take its place by right in every anthology of English poetry, Clare achieved that final perfection of form which was so often to elude him. The bird-note begins, rises, dies away: and the poem is finished.

Clare's music was a natural music; as with Shelley's skylark, his art was unpremeditated and his strains profuse. He was perhaps never to find a form which fitted his genius so intimately as that of *Song's Eternity*. His language was to become more coherent and more vivid; but the inward harmony that is essential to a great poem was too often to escape him. He was like a child so intoxicated with his wonderful gift for whistling and with his tune that he whistled it over and over again. The note is so pure, the tune so full of delight that we can never be tired; we listen to it as we listen to the drowsy enchantment of the monotony of sounds on a summer's afternoon, for it is as authentic and as sweet as they. The eternity of song was in Clare's blood. . . . (pp. 7-11)

Clare's difficulty as a poet, in fact, can and ought to be put baldly; he did not know when to stop. Why, indeed, should he stop? He was either a voice, one of the unending voices of Nature, or he was an eye, an unwearied eye watching the infinite process of Nature; perhaps never a poet consciously striving by means of art to arouse in men's minds an emotion like his own. All the art he had was that which he gained from his recollection of other poets' tunes; the structure of their harmony eluded him, he remembered only the melodies. Take, for instance, his extremely beautiful *Autumn*: the melody comes directly from Collins's famous [*Ode to Autumn*]; yet how greatly Clare enriches it, as though with a material golden stain of autumn! The last leaf seems to be falling at our feet, the last bee zooming in our ears.

> Heart-sickening for the silence that is thine,
> Not broken inharmoniously as now
> That lone and vagrant bee
> Booms faint with weary chime.
> Now filtering winds thin winnow through the woods
> In tremulous noise that bids at every breath
> Some sickly cankered leaf
> Let go its hold, and die.

Not only these, but any one of a dozen other stanzas in the poem have a richer mellowness, reveal a finer sensitiveness than any in Collins's lovely *Ode*. For all that the melody derives from Collins, we are borne away from him to the neighbourhood of Keats's great poem [*To Autumn*]. But Collins had a classical, almost Miltonic, sense of form; what he lacked in the richness of direct perception he supplied by his careful concentration of emotional effect: so that, despite the more splendid beauty of the elements of Clare's poems, we dare not say it is really as fine as Collins's *Ode*. Collins gathers up all his more exiguous perceptions into a single stimulus to emotion: Clare lets them fall one by one, careless of his amazing jewels. Set his *Autumn* against Keats's three strophes, where the imagination has come to crystallize perceptions not less rich in themselves than Clare's into a single symbol—the very spirit of Autumn.

> Who hath not seen thee oft amid thy store?
> Sometimes whoever seeks abroad may find
> Thee sitting careless on a granary floor
> Thy hair soft lifted by the winnowing wind;
> Or on a half-reaped furrow sound asleep
> Drowsed with the fume of poppies, while thy hook
> Spares the next swathe and all its twined flowers;
> And sometimes like a gleaner thou dost keep
> Steady thy laden head across a brook
> Or by a cyder-press, with patient look,
> Thou watchest the last oozings hours by hours.

Clare could not do that; for Keats had Collins's art and Clare's richness of perception, and he had also that incomparable imaginative power which alone can create the perfect symbol of an overwhelming and intricate emotion.

Yet we need to invoke Keats to explain Clare, and to understand fully why his wealth of perception was refined into so few perfect poems. Collins himself is not sufficient for the purpose; one cannot well invoke the success of a poorer to explain the failure of a richer nature. Keats, the great poetic artist, however, subsumes Clare. . . . [Where] in English poetry shall we find a power of poetic discipline greater than [Keats's], a more determined and inevitable compulsion of the whole of a poet's emotional experience into the single symbol, the one organic and inevitable form? In him were combined miraculously the humanity that can reject no element of true experience and the artistic integrity to which less than a complete mastery and transformation of experience is intolerable. When, therefore, we invoke Keats to explain Clare, when we feel the need to merge Clare into Keats in thought in order that we may discover his own poetic fulfilment, by completing the great pattern of which he is a fragment, we are passing a judgment upon the value and quality of Clare's own work of which the implications are unescapable. It is a fragment, but it is a fragment of the Parthenon pediment, of intrinsic value, unique, and beyond price.

Clare's qualities were authentic and without alloy. It was the power to refine and shape his metal that was denied him; his workshop is littered not with dross but with veritable gold—of melody, of an intensity of perception (truly, his 'mind was burned'), and, more rarely, of flashes of that passion of the pure imagination which is the mysterious source of the magic of poetry. Let our partial quotation of *Song's Eternity* suffice to prove the quality of his spontaneous melody. For the intensity of perception we may choose at random any page in [*Poems Chiefly from M.S.*]. Is not a picture such as this cast upon 'that inward eye'?

> Where squats the hare to terrors wide awake
> Like some brown clod the harrows failed to break.

Such things are scattered throughout Clare; they range from the quiet vision of the actual, focused by a single word, such as

> The old pond with its water-weed
> And danger-daring willow tree,
> Who leans, an ancient invalid,
> O'er spots where deepest waters be,

to the authentic fancy of

> Here morning in the ploughman's songs is met
> Ere yet one footstep shows in all the sky,
> And twilight in the East, a doubt as yet,
> Shows not her sleeve of gray to know her by.

How perfect is the image, as perfect to its context and emotion as the 'sovran eye' of Shakespeare's sun! And what of the intense compression of a phrase like 'ploughed lands thin travelled by half-hungry sheep', precise not merely to a fact, but to an emotion?

This unmistakable core of pure emotion lies close to the surface throughout Clare. His precision is the precision of a lover; he watches nature as a man might watch his mistress's eyes; his breath is bated, and we seem to hear the very thumping of his heart, and there are moments when the emotion seems to rise in a sudden fountain and change the thing he sees into a jewel. 'Frail brother of the morn' to a jetty snail is the tender cry of a passionate lover; there is a delicateness in the emotion expressed which not even Wordsworth could attain when he called upon the Lesser Celandine. It is love of this kind that gives true significance to the poetry of nature, for only by its alchemy can the thing seen become the symbol of the thing felt: washed by the magic tide of an overwhelming emotion, the object shines with a pure and lucid radiance, transformed from a cause to a symbol of delight, and thus no longer delighting the senses and the emotions alone, but the mind. This mysterious faculty is not indeed the highest kind of poetic imagination, in which the intellect plays a greater part in the creation of the symbol; this emotional creation leaps from particular to particular, it lacks that endorsement from a centre of disciplined experience which is the mark of the poetic imagination at its highest: but it is purely poetic and truly creative.

In this authentic kind Clare was all but a master, and it may even be suspected that his unique gift would have suffered if he had possessed that element of technical control which would have made him a master indeed. For when we come to define as narrowly as we can the distinctive, compelling quality of his emotion, we find that in addition to tenderness we need the word impulsive. Clare's most beautiful poetry is a gesture of impulsive tenderness. It has a curious suddenness, almost a catch in the voice.

> The very darkness smiles to wear
> The stars that show us God is there.

We find, too, a still more authentic mark of the tenderness of impulsive love in his way of seeing his birds and beasts as ever so little absurd. 'Absurd' has a peculiar and delightful meaning in the converse of lovers; Clare's firetail is 'absurd' in precisely the same sense.

> Of everything that stirs she dreameth wrong,
> And pipes her 'tweet-tut' fears the whole day long.

And so, too, are his bees—the 'grandfather bee', the wild bees who 'with their legs stroke slumber from their eyes', 'the little bees with coal-black faces, gathering sweets from little flowers like stars'; even the riddle of the quail appears to be rather a delicate and loveable waywardness in the bird than a mere ignorance in the man.

> Among the stranger birds they feed,
> Their summer flight is short and low:
> There's very few know where they breed
> And scarcely any where they go.

A tenderness of this exquisite and impulsive kind might have been damaged as much as strengthened by a firmer technical control; a shiver of constraint might have crept into the gesture itself and chilled it; and perhaps we may touch the essential nature of Clare's emotion most closely in the mysterious and haunting Asylum poem, . . . *Secret Love*. (pp. 11-15)

[In *Secret Love*] Clare is invoking the memory of Mary Joyce, the girl lover whom he did not marry, and who, though long since dead, lived for him as his true wife when he was immured in the asylum. But the fact of this strange passion is less remarkable than its precise quality; it is an intolerable tenderness, an unbearable surge of emotion eager to burst forth and lavish itself upon an object. Whether it was his passion for Mary Joyce which first awakened him to an awareness of the troublous depths of emotion within we cannot tell, for this poem is in itself no evidence of fact. But it bears witness unmistakable to the quality of the emotion which underlay all that is characteristic and unforgettable in his poetry.

When we have touched the unique emotional core which consists throughout the work of a true poet, we have come perhaps as near as we can to his secret. We stand as it were at the very source of his creation. In the great poetic artist we may follow out the intricacies and ramifications of the intellectual structure by which he makes the expression of his central emotion complete, and the emotion itself permanent. In Clare the work is unnecessary. The emotion is hardly mediated at all. The poetic creation is instinctive and impulsive; the love is poured out, and the bird, the beast, the flower is made glorious. It is the very process which Stendahl described as *la cristallisation de l'amour* [the crystallization of love].

We may therefore most truly describe Clare as the love poet of nature. . . . In eternity perhaps a woman, but in the actual Nature was Clare's mistress; her he served and cherished with a tenderness and faithful knowledge unique in the poetry of nature. Like a true lover he stammered in long speeches, but he spoke to her the divinest and most intimate things. Assuredly his lines were cast so that he had no need of woman even in eternity, and perhaps the truest words he ever wrote of himself are those of [**"I am"**], the poem by which he is most generally known:

> I long for scenes where man has never trod;
>   A place where woman never smiled nor wept;
> There to abide with my creator, God,
>   And sleep as I in childhood sweetly slept;
> Untroubling and untroubled where I lie;
>   The grass below—above the vaulted sky.

(pp. 16-18)

John Middleton Murry, "The Poetry of John Clare," in his John Clare and Other Studies, *Peter Nevill Limited, 1950, pp. 7-18.*

EDMUND GOSSE (essay date 1921)

[*A distinguished English literary historian, critic, and biographer, Gosse wrote extensively on seventeenth- and eighteenth-century English literature. His commentary in* Seventeenth-Century Studies *(1883),* A History of Eighteenth Century Literature *(1889),* Questions at Issue *(1893), and other works is generally regarded as sound and suggestive. Gosse's review of* Poems Chiefly from Manuscript *first appeared in the London* Sunday Times *on January 23, 1921. Gosse has little to say in Clare's favor: his verse is "repetitious," "monotonous," and "diluted," his talent "stunted and ineffective." According to Gosse, Clare's observation of nature is "prolonged beyond measure, and is relieved by no reflection." Gosse elaborated upon this point in a later review (1924) of* Madrigals and Chronicles, *judging the work in light of Edmund Blunden's and John Middleton Murry's assessments (see excerpts below, 1924).*]

The position of Clare in English literature is curiously undetermined, after more than a century. Criticism has never unanimously accepted him. . . . He had no gifts except his dreamy sweetness of character, his childlike simplicity, and his redundant flow of verses. Let us not blame Society for the 'national disgrace' of not helping Clare, since Clare could not be helped. In these our days, there are organizations which may be, and should be, appealed to. Yet, even now, if there be a man who drinks, and has a tendency to insanity, and can ply no useful trade, such a case is heart-breaking, and does not call for a burst of indignation against 'Society'.

Clare wrote verse with inexhaustible fluency. Even in the asylum, he scribbled off enormous quantities of it, and well may [the editors of *Poems, Chiefly from Manuscript*] speak of his 'incredible facility'. The great interest of the volume before us

lies in the fact that with a small but very judicious selection of his published work, it gives a majority of pieces hitherto unknown. There were still left of these, I believe, more than a thousand. . . . However, it is very improbable that these would add to our gratification, if they were printed. They would rather add to the sense of dispersion, of dilution, which the work of Clare already awakens. His range was extremely limited, and he repeated his effects over and over again. His poetry is like honey and water; the water is pure and the honey Hymettan, but the brew is desperately thin. There is not one startling felicity, one concentrated ray, in the whole body of his work. It is clean and delicate, but tiresomely monotonous, and, above all, the spirit in it is diluted.

Leslie Stephen justly said of Clare's poetry that it shows how 'want of culture is not compensated by vigour of local colouring' [see excerpt above, 1887]. There are certain men of untaught genius who have been independent of scholastic training. No one regrets its absence in Blake or Burns, nor would Shakespeare be improved by more Latin and much Greek. But Clare is not on the level of these great spirits, and the gifts of nature were starved in him by lack of intellectual nourishment; his own mental resources were insufficient for the development of his talent, and it remained stunted and ineffective. (pp. 344-45)

If ever there was born into the world a talent which demanded protection and indulgence, bodily comfort and intellectual sustenance, it was that of Clare, and to him all these things were permanently denied. Hence, the only mental accomplishment which he secured in any fullness was that which needed no cultivation but the activity of his own eyes.

He noted with extraordinary keenness and accuracy the animals and birds and plants which lived around him in Northamptonshire. Nothing escaped him in the fields, and he set everything down in verse: 'I dwell in trifles like a child', he said, but he gave these trifles a beautiful setting, especially in his sonnets, where the form obliged him to effect some condensation. '**Summer Images**' is an example of his less concentrated manner, where the attention finds itself gratified, but at last wearied by dwelling on 'the jetty snail' and 'the green-swathed grasshopper' through a poem of two hundred lines. The observation is exquisite, but it is prolonged beyond measure, and is relieved by no reflection.

The new poems [in *Poems, Chiefly from Manuscript*] exhibit the metrical skill of Clare in a fresh light. A long piece, called '**Song's Eternity**', is written in a charming stanza, of which this is an example:—

> Dreamers, mark the honey bee;
>   Mark the tree
> Where the bluecap, 'tootle tee',
>   Sings a glee
> Sung to Adam and to Eve—
>   Here they be.
> When floods covered every bough,
>   Noah's ark
> Heard that ballad singing now;
>   Hark, hark.

We seem to be walking along a Northamptonshire lane, and suddenly, through the silence, there comes to us the sound of someone who is playing the flute in a field behind the hedge. We pause in rapture; we smell the beans in blossom; 'dear brother robin', just above us, listens and emulates the song; the sky begins to assume a 'watchet hue'; and still the flute shrills on. "Tootle, tootle, tootle, tee!" in a softly-coloured

Fenland landscape—that is the sum of John Clare's poetry from boyhood to the grave. (pp. 345-46)

Edmund Gosse, in an extract from Clare: The Critical Heritage, *edited by Mark Storey, Routledge & Kegan Paul, 1973, pp. 343-46.*

EDMUND BLUNDEN (essay date 1924)

[*Blunden was associated with the Georgians, an early twentieth-century group of English poets who reacted against the prevalent contemporary mood of disillusionment and the rise of artistic modernism by seeking to return to the pastoral, nineteenth-century poetic traditions associated with William Wordsworth. In this regard, much of Blunden's poetry reflects his love of the sights, sounds, and ways of rural England. As a literary critic and essayist, he often wrote of the lesser-known figures of the Romantic era as well as the pleasures of English country life. Blunden's preface to* Madrigals and Chronicles, *in which he succinctly describes the distinguishing characteristics of Clare's poetry, is discussed by Edmund Gosse (1924).*]

The characteristics of Clare's Poetry are, an unparalleled intimacy with the English Countryside; a rare power of transfusing himself into the life of everything beneath the sky, save certain ardours and purposes of men; a natural ease of diction, well suited to hold the mirror up to Nature; a sense of the God in the Fly and the Cataract; a haunting—Mary Joyce the Symbol—of an Ethereal Love, Woman *in excelsis;* and, as the charm for his casual hearer, a delicate and elemental music.

Apart from his aloofness from many themes, there are defects in his Poetry which may easily be over-emphasized. His conception of an eternal singing leaves many of his individual Poems insufficiently wrought up. One must regret that no critical mind of strong instinct was ordinarily accessible to him, to school him into a closer walk with form, to require of him the final touches. For myself, I do not dismiss a Poem of obvious emotional and imaginative value, because of some rebellious rhyme or momentary flaw; and in the perplexing task of selecting from a great number the Pieces now first published I have sometimes preferred the one with the imperfections to its rivals of better shapeliness but slighter immanent impulse. (pp. xiii-xiv)

Edmund Blunden, in a preface to Madrigals & Chronicles: Being Newly Found Poems *by John Clare, edited by Edmund Blunden, The Beaumont Press, 1924, pp. vii-xiv.*

JOHN MIDDLETON MURRY (essay date 1924)

[*In his commendatory review of* Madrigals and Chronicles, *Murry discusses Clare as a pictorial or descriptive poet. He contends that "Clare's faculty of sheer vision is unique in English poetry; not only is it far purer than Wordsworth's, it is even purer than Shakespeare's." The paradox, Murry asserts, is that Clare's vision is "too perfect"; discussing his works in relation to William Wordsworth's and John Keats's prescriptions for good poetry, Murry argues that Clare's "seeing" arrested the development of those thoughts "necessary to . . . the writing of the finest poetry." Clare, Murry concludes, is "not a great poet, but assuredly not a little one." Murry's interpretation of the nature of Clare's achievement, which first appeared in the* Times Literary Supplement *on August 21, 1924, is disputed by Geoffrey Grigson (1950).*]

Not many poets justify and repay editorial picty more bountifully than John Clare. Though comparatively few of his poems achieve the beauty of form which is the evidence of completely mastered and related perceptions, scarce one of them is without a strange intrinsic beauty of the perception itself. Clare's sensibility was of the finest and most delicate, and his emotional response to nature almost inhumanly sweet and pure. His weakness lay in his power of poetic thought. Inevitably, in reading [**Madrigals and Chronicles: Being Newly Found Poems Written by John Clare**], we are reminded once more, as we were reminded at the time of [**Poems Chiefly from Manuscript**], of Wordsworth. Even more than then the comparison of Clare with Wordsworth seems necessary if we are to gain that precise sensation of Clare's individuality, without which it is scarcely possible to know a poet fully. And not only does Wordsworth appear necessary to a criticism of Clare, but Clare to a criticism of Wordsworth. The reference is reciprocal: it is also quite unavoidable. We doubt whether anyone could read, without thinking immediately of Wordsworth, Clare's beautiful poem in this volume on **The Primrose Bank:**

> With its little brimming eye
> And its crimp and curdled leaf
> Who can pass its beauties by?

For here evidently was someone to whom a primrose by the river's brim was in a sense, just a primrose: but it was wholly a primrose, not 'something more' indeed, but altogether itself. 'Its little brimming eye,' 'its crimp and curdled leaf,' are phrases which almost make us hold our breath in order not to disturb the exquisite perfection of their truth. And this truth is of such a kind that it is complete: there is nothing more to be said, and perhaps nothing more to be thought. At least it is hard to imagine that the poet to whose vision a primrose thus appeared, who could express what he saw with an ease and naturalness such that the expression strikes as part of the very act of seeing, in whose eyes (it is obvious) 'Solomon in all his glory was not arrayed like one of these,' should ever have thought, or ever have had the impulse to think, about what he saw. The particularity of the created universe was sufficient for him; he saw each several thing in itself as sovereign and beautiful. What more did he need, what more can we ask?

Clare's faculty of sheer vision is unique in English poetry; not only is it far purer than Wordsworth's, it is purer even than Shakespeare's. Or, it might be wiser to say, Shakespeare passed so quickly beyond this stage of pure vision that only traces of it remain. And yet we feel there is an intrinsic impossibility that vision of this kind, so effortless and unparading, should ever pass beyond itself; we feel it must demand so complete an engagement and submission of the whole man that it leaves no margin for other faculties. Clare's vision, we might say paradoxically, is too perfect. Shakespeare had as much of it as a man can have if he is to develop into a full maturity; Wordsworth had some of it. Wordsworth's vision came to him in flashes, therefore it seemed to him an abnormal and extraordinary visitation which needed to be related by thought and meditation to ordinary experience. We may put it in this way: if Wordsworth had seen a primrose as Clare saw it—and he did occasionally see things thus—he would have felt that he was seeing 'into the heart of things,' whereas Clare—who seems always to have seen in this way—felt that he was merely seeing things. It is dangerous to be made after so unusual a pattern, and Clare was locked up.

The penalty was monstrous, an indescribable refinement of torture for this child-man whose very life was seeing things. . . . Those thoughts, for which his seeing left no room to grow, are necessary to . . . the writing of the finest poetry. Words-

Clare's cottage at Helpston.

worth, in his preface to the second *Lyrical Ballads,* was essentially right.

> All good poetry is the spontaneous overflow of powerful feelings: and though this be true, poems to which any value can be attached were never produced on any variety of subjects but by a man who, being possessed of more than usual organic sensibility, has also thought long and deeply.

Never were the primary conditions of poetry, as Wordsworth defined them, more exactly satisfied than by Clare. He was possessed of infinitely more than 'usual organic sensibility,' and all his poetry is 'the spontaneous overflow of powerful feelings.' Wordsworth's general definition is a precise description of Clare's work: the epithets, 'organic' of his sensibility and 'spontaneous' of his emotion, fit Clare more happily than any other poet who comes to mind. And the reason is that the poetic natures of Clare and Wordsworth were closely allied. The difference between them is that Clare could not, while Wordsworth could, think long and deeply.

This inability of Clare's was a defect of his quality; and it was because Wordsworth's sensibility was not so pure or so uninterrupted as Clare's that he had the opportunity and the need for thought. . . . [We] are often aware of [Wordsworth's thought]

as an element that is not really fused with his perception, but super-imposed upon it, and Wordsworth's poetry then takes on that slightly didactic, slightly distasteful tone of which Keats (who belonged to the Shakespearian order) was so acutely conscious when he wrote about Wordsworth:

> We hate poetry that has a palpable design upon us, and if we do not agree, seems to put its hand into its breeches pocket. Poetry should be great and unobtrusive, a thing which enters into one's soul, and does not startle or amaze it with itself, but with its subject. How beautiful are the retired flowers! How they would lose their beauty were they to throng to the highway, crying out, 'Admire me, I am a violet! Dote upon me, I am a primrose!'

In this criticism of Wordsworth by a still finer poetic mind than his own, the ground is, as it were, once more cleared for a just approach to Clare. Again the very words are apt to him. His poetry is 'unobtrusive.' 'How beautiful are the retired flowers!' is true of him perhaps more than any other poet. His poetry has no 'palpable design upon us'; it has no design upon us at all.

The cause of Clare's so curiously fitting into these utterances of his great poetic contemporaries, is, first, that he was in the essential as authentic a poet as they and, secondly, that he was allied to Wordsworth by the nature of his 'organic sensibility' and to Keats by his wonderful spontaneity. Wordsworth would have denied poetic 'greatness' to Clare because of his lack of thought, but Keats would have denied poetic 'greatness' to much of Wordsworth's work because of its lack of spontaneity and unobtrusiveness. These criticisms, in their ascending order, are just and profound, and they establish the real precedence of these three true poets. Moreover, this conclusion follows: in order that Clare should have been as great a poet as he was a true one, the quality of his thought would have needed to be equal to the quality of his perception, equally spontaneous, equally organic. Then he would have been, in Keats's phrase, both 'great and unobtrusive,' and a very great poet indeed. As it is, he is unobtrusive and true, not a great poet, but assuredly not a little one—a child, on whom the rarest and most divine gift of vision had so abundantly descended that he could not become a man.

The quality in Clare which most enthrals us, the general quality of which the quintessence is manifest in the beauty of his seeing, is one which we can only describe as a kind of *naïveté*. If we use a similitude, we might say it was an abiding sense of a quite simple fraternity with all the creatures of the world save self-conscious man. Man, the thinker, the calculator, the schemer, falls outside this universe of simple comprehension, and is the inhabitant of an alien world. He will not enter. He has no wedding garment. And the reality of Clare's vision and its power over our hearts is such that there are moments when our conviction that this is a limitation of Clare's understanding suddenly abandons us and we have a secret fear that his may be the true and unattainable wisdom. 'Except ye become as little children. . . .' That fear does not remain with us; we know that the word is not thus literally to be understood. Our childhood must come to us as the achievement of our manhood. We cannot divest ourselves of our birthright. But Clare's *naïveté* reinforces the admonition of the word, that unless we can achieve, out of all our wisdom and despair, a comprehension as pure as was his vision, we shall have lost the day.

For in Clare's vision is indubitable truth, not comprehensive, not final, but because it strikes our hearts as truth, and is truth, it is prophetic of the final and comprehensive truth. It is melody, not harmony:

> Yes, night is happy night,
> The sky is full of stars,
> Like worlds in peace they lie
> Enjoying one delight.

But true melody, as this is, is separated from false harmony by a whole universe of error. If it has not been troubled by thought, it has also not been corrupted by the temptation to turn stones into bread. The spontaneous feeling of

> [He] felt that lovely mood
> As a birthright God had given
> To muse in the green wood
> And meet the smiles of heaven,

though it does not itself achieve it, would at least never be satisfied by thought that was not as spontaneous as itself; it would have no room for the speculations of mere intellectual pride. And Clare's nascent thoughts, as far as they go, are as true as his feelings; indeed they *are* feelings:

> I thought o'er all life's sweetest things
> Made dreary as a broken charm,
> Wood-ridings where the thrush still sings
> And love went leaning on my arm.

Experience, the organic knowledge from which organic thought is born, was for Clare the dreary breaking of a charm. The phrase is beautifully, agonisingly true. Up to the extreme verge of his capacity Clare never betrayed himself. On the one side his world of his vision, on the other side broken charms and mystery; he did not, he could not, try to reconcile them. When he was shut out by destiny and the hand of man from his own world, he lived within the memory of it. (pp. 19-23)

> *John Middleton Murry, "The Case of John Clare,"*
> *in his* John Clare and Other Studies, *Peter Nevill*
> *Limited, 1950, pp. 19-24.*

SIR EDMUND GOSSE   (essay date 1924)

[*In the following review of* Madrigals and Chronicles, *Gosse takes as his point of departure Edmund Blunden's and, to a lesser extent, John Middleton Murry's comments upon the work (see excerpts above, 1924). Gosse dismisses Murry's review of* Madrigals and Chronicles *as a "riot of hyperbole," but responds less censoriously to Blunden's preface to the volume. While he considers the preface "nearly true," he complains that Clare's poetry lacks the intellectual element that Blunden ascribes to it. According to Gosse, "Clare's is sheer descriptive poetry" and represents a limited accomplishment. Gosse's essay was first published in the London* Sunday Times *on October 24, 1924.*]

[The publication of **"Poems Chiefly from Manuscript"** and **"Madrigals"**] has greatly augmented the importance of Clare as a figure on our crowded Parnassus, and has made it certain that he can never again be overlooked, as he was between 1820 and 1920. He will take his place as one of the authentic English poets, and the only danger now to be apprehended is that he will be exalted unwisely. It is a natural weakness in those who have had the good fortune to find hidden treasure to exaggerate the value of what has so romantically been unearthed. The poetry of Clare is charming, his approach to Nature genuine and sincere, but when the claim is put forward that he was a great artist, for the sake of his own reputation we must be on our guard. When a responsible reviewer declares that Clare's faculty was "far purer than Wordsworth's," and "purer even than Shakespeare's" [see excerpt above by John Middleton Murry, 1924], it is time to weigh our standards of merit.

Although Clare is his discovery, Mr. Blunden is not betrayed into this riot of hyperbole [in his preface to **"Madrigals"** (see excerpt above, 1924).] He does not rank Clare above Wordsworth and Shakespeare as a poet of Nature. His definition of the theme is not injured by depreciation of other writers to the advantage of his Northamptonshire labourer, and yet it calls for a certain further discrimination. (pp. 104-05)

[His preface] is well said—although I am afraid I cannot follow the fling about God and the Fly and the Cataract—and I think that each clause is *nearly* true, calculated, that is, to prepare the reader for what he will find in Clare, without mentioning what he will not find. Let us now take an example from the poet himself, the very characteristic sonnet called **"The Foddering Boy,"** and see how far it justifies Mr. Blunden's definition. . . . (p. 105)

[In this poem], to a wonderful degree, we find the "unparalleled intimacy with the country-side," and an exactitude of observation which nowadays we call "photographic," but where is the "transfusion" which Mr. Blunden promised us? Every detail which photography can seize is precisely rendered, but all is exterior; there is not a phrase that shows the poet "transfusing" himself into the life of the Foddering Boy. Clare's is sheer descriptive poetry, painted with a wonderful delicacy and conscientiousness, but all from the outside. He concentrates his attention on the stray path rambling through the furze, on the patter of squirrels over the green moss, on the shaggy marten startling the great brown horned owl, and always has at his command the just phrase, the faultless vision, the economy and daring of epithet. His notes of birds and flowers are those of a naturalist, and it is, perhaps, ungracious to remark that this was a fashion of his time, as we may still see in such pieces as the botanical sonnets of Charlotte Smith. Clare does the pictorial and half-scientific business much better, of course, than Charlotte Smith did it, but surely we are far indeed in his water-colour drawings from the exaltation of [Wordsworth's] "Tintern Abbey." . . . (pp. 105-06)

In the generation which preceded Clare's, Canning had pointed out that observation without reflection is of secondary value in imaginative literature. This is a remark which is too often forgotten in the criticism of descriptive poetry. To bring vividly before us the "oval leaves" of waterweed in the deep dyke among the rushes, to note the "marble" clouds of spring, to paint the wet blackbird cowering down on the whitethorn bush, requires a rare and beautiful talent which the Northamptonshire labourer possessed in a very remarkable degree. No one must dream of denying or belittling so precious a gift. But to excel in such clear painting is to be William Hunt or de Wint, not Titian or Velasquez. It is to be a Little Master of high accomplishment, but not a Great Master in Poetry.

What is lacking is the intellectual element, the "organic sensibility" which Wordsworth demanded, and which he himself enjoyed in a superlative fullness. It is, to quote another Great Master, to be able to create out of the phenomena of Nature "forms more real than living man." This Clare could not do. He saw the tattered gold of the ragwort with perfect sincerity, and he makes us see it, but the sight suggests nothing to him beyond its own fresh beauty. It does not induce in him a train of thoughts, as the sight of the celandine did in Wordsworth. The admirers of Clare lay great stress on the stanza in which he describes the primrose [in **"The Primrose Bank"**]

> With its little brimming eye,
>   And its yellow rims so pale,
>   And its crimp and curdled leaf—
> Who can pass its beauties by?

The accuracy of the picture is wonderful, but it is too much like a coloured plate in a botanical treatise. Here is nothing that transcends unreflecting observation, nothing that speaks to the spirit of Man. Indeed, without carping, we are bound to admit that here one is speaking to whom a primrose on a river's bank was just a primrose, and "nothing more." But the highest poetry requires more. So, too, let any unprejudiced lover of verse compare Clare's ode to the Skylark ["**The Skylark Leaving Her Nest**"] . . . with either Shelley's or Wordsworth's, and he must confess that the Northamptonshire stanzas, charming as they are, belong to a lower order of inspiration.

It was the misfortune of Clare that, with unsurpassed exactitude of vision and delicate skill in stating fact, he was devoid of all reflective power. I am surprised that Mr. Blunden, whose introduction displays candour as well as sympathy, does not admit this defect. Clare had no thoughts. He wandered through the country, storing up images and sounds, but he wove his reproductions of these upon no intellectual basis. His was a camera, not a mind; and while we must admit that he showed a praiseworthy reserve in not pretending to find any philo-

sophical relation between his negatives and the human spirit, still, the fact cannot be ignored that the philosophy was absent.

Connected with the absence of thought is the imperfection of form, which Mr. Blunden acknowledges, but is a little too indulgently disposed to slur over. He attributes it, perhaps justly, to Clare's lack of primary education, yet it seems more likely, in one who had read all the best English verse, to have been an inherent defect. Clare had a bad ear; he was satisfied to rhyme "alone" with "return," "crow" with "haw," and "season" with "peas in." His metrical structure is often loose, and his grammar not above reproach. Yet on these technical trifles I would not insist.

Let it not be thought that though I hint a fault I hesitate dislike. On the contrary, the verses of Clare give me great pleasure, and those not least which are contained in this collection of **"Madrigals."** His poetry is English in the extreme; not a phrase, not an epithet takes us out of our country, and hardly out of Clare's own county. As the habits of local life become modified by time, his record of Northamptonshire ways and scenes will increase in value. His "word-painting," to use a Victorian phrase now much fallen into disfavour, will keep alive his simple lyrics, and will remind successive generations how

> The little violets blue and white,
> Refreshed with dews of sable night,
> Come shining in the morning-light
>   In thorn-enclosèd grounds;
>
> And whether winds be cold or chill,
> When their rich smells delight instil,
> The young lamb blaas beside the hill
>   And young spring happy sounds.
>
>   (pp. 106-09)

Sir Edmund Gosse, "Nature in Poetry," in his Silhouettes, *William Heinemann Ltd., 1925, pp. 101-09.**

EDMUND BLUNDEN   (essay date 1929)

[Blunden analyzes "Autumn" as an example of Clare's transference of his love for women to nature.]

[John Clare is] in some lights the best poet of Nature that this country and for all I know any other country ever produced. Clare was known in his time as the Northamptonshire Peasant Poet, and is, I am afraid, still looked upon as such by many of those who have heard of him. Simple as he may at a hasty reckoning appear, he is not so when he is known better: Clare is a rustic, but imaginative enough to see the meaning of that; he is an exact naturalist, but a poet of the mystical temper as well; he is not learned, but makes considerable excursions into learning, by which he is enabled not to stand still between naïvety and great art, and can be at home in both. There is extraordinary development in his poetry between the early clownish scrawl of alehouse ballads and the later work of which the Dantesque "I am! but what I am none cares or knows!" is the most generally reprinted. . . . [My] eyes are on the poem **"Autumn,"** written at the time of his maturest and least distracted powers, and certainly one of the most sustained and creative of his pieces. (p. 51)

Perhaps it will be reckoned fantastic to interpret Clare's **"Autumn"** in this almost psychic way, but a great part of his verse is a history of the transference of love in him from woman to Nature. He describes the poet as "a secret thing, a man in love none knoweth where"; he sums up his autobiography in lyrics of which the correct text has not been found ["**Secret Love,**"] but which even in their injured state reveal the thrilling enigma of his heart. "I hid my love when young"—and then, the companionship of woman became more beautiful and immutable in a wood-change:

> I met her in the greenest dells
> Where dewdrops pearl the wood bluebells;
> The lost breeze kissed her bright blue eye,
> The bee kissed, and went singing by.
> A sunbeam found a passage there,
> A gold chain round her neck so fair;
> As secret as the wild bee's song
> She lay there all the summer long.

Having this Grace, this Dryad always in hope and almost in ocular proof, Clare wrote his poems as if for her; not all of them, but the later kind, when his old friends in London had died or drifted from him. He did not fail at times to regard verse as an art for the use of mankind, and indeed accomplished such examples of his intellectual eagerness as a series of poems in the manner of Elizabethan writers; but more and more he conceived his chief singing to be an offering to that mystery whom he loved, a repetition of all her endowments, her lineaments, her devotions and delights. So hastening on and giving her "his posies, all cropt in a sunny hour" with childlike haste and ecstasy, he did not shape his compositions in the intense school of Collins and Keats. They lose, in the arbitration of our criticism, for that reason. . . . But we can, by a sympathy of the imagination, approach Clare's poem in the light of his wooing of the "fair Flora," the wind-spirit, the music-maker, the shepherdess, and accept his unpremeditated and disunited perfections so. No one has surpassed these perfections in themselves, these tokens of his secret love. They may be classed as "observation," but only true passion can observe in Clare's way,

> By overshadowed ponds, in woody nooks,
> With ramping sallows lined, and crowding sedge,
>   Which woo the winds to play,
>   And with them dance for joy;
>
> And meadow pools, torn wide by lawless floods,
> Where water-lilies spread their oily leaves,
>   On which, as wont, the fly
>   Oft battens in the sun;
>
> Where leans the mossy willow half way o'er,
> On which the shepherd crawls astride to throw
>   His angle clear of weeds
>   That crowd the water's brim;
>
> Or crispy hills, and hollows scant of sward,
> Where step by step the patient lonely boy
>   Hath cut rude flights of stairs
>   To climb their steepy sides;
>
> Then track along their feet, grown hoarse with noise,
> The crawling brook, that ekes its weary speed,
>   And struggles through the weeds
>   With faint and sudden brawl.

You cannot reply "Notebook, notebook" to this exactitude, this close inventory of little things, of which Clare's work presents an infinity; it is the eye of a lover that feasts on such glances, gestures, and adornings of his mistress. Through all, her life gives life, her wonder gives wonder. The fly on the lily-leaf might have little meaning, did not the "sorceress" set

him there, and what she does is to Clare touched with hieroglyphic eternity.

Hence, too, this happiness of animation, this familiar characterising of what are called "objects of landscape." All are equal here in the universal fancy of autumn. The sedge and the winds have their pastime apart like a group of children; the floods were common trespassers; the lonely boy and weary brook alike are patient in their labours of indolence. In the poem too there is another lonely boy, who exactly like the sedge "woos the winds" with his song. The lark springs up "to cheer the bankrupt pomp" of the time, and it is when the wind "bids" that the cankered leaf "lets go its hold"; in short, it is all one whether a ploughman passes or a bee. They bear the impress of the strange siren Autumn, and play their part without distinction of power and glory. I must not deaden this vitality of Clare's nature-vision with too much talking. He has commented on it himself in several poems, giving "every weed and blossom" an equality with whatever this world contains:

> All tenants of an ancient place
>   And heirs of noble heritage,
> Coeval they with Adam's race
>   And blest with more substantial age.
>
> For when the world first saw the sun
>   These little flowers beheld him too,
> And when his love for earth begun
>   They were the first his smiles to woo.

It is that last word, if one word can be, which is the keyword to John Clare's long life of unselfish uncopied nature-poetry. (pp. 55-9)

> *Edmund Blunden, "The Spirit Wooed: Collins, Keats, Clare," in his* Nature in English Literature, *Harcourt Brace Jovanovich, 1929, pp. 38-59.**

J. W. TIBBLE (essay date 1935)

[Tibble, with his wife, Anne, coauthored two biographies of Clare (see Additional Bibliography), which contributed to the continuing interest in his poetry in the twentieth century; they also coedited editions of his letters and prose. The following excerpt is drawn from the introduction to Tibble's edition of Clare's poems, the most comprehensive collection of his poetry to date. Tibble's study is a chronological reading of Clare's artistic development. According to the critic, Clare's earliest poems, written in the tradition of eighteenth-century descriptive poetry, were followed by the descriptive verse of The Shepherd's Calendar *period (1821-24), which is characterized by an implied emotional response to nature. The poems written between 1824 and 1834, Tibble asserts, are essentially lyrical compositions in which nature imagery is increasingly fused with Clare's explicit emotional response to enclosure. In the asylum poetry of the last phase of Clare's development, he purged nature imagery and emotion of their personal reference.]*

Clare's method seems to lie midway between the [methods of Keats and Wordsworth]. Like Wordsworth's his poems are usually the record of an experience already completely realized, but unlike Wordsworth he seldom allowed an interval to elapse between the experience and its recording. . . . Like Keats, he experienced the immediate excitement of composition; but the poem did not arise primarily out of that excitement. It was not the words that excited him, the actual making of the poem, so much as the power of the words to prolong and renew that rapture which he felt in the presence of nature.

Clare was not, we feel, interested in words as words; nor did he pay much attention to their formal grouping into sentences. The unit for him was the short phrase or clause—the verbal expression of the image upon which his attention was focused. As image succeeded image, phrase followed phrase; the image expressed in a subordinate clause would distract his attention and the subject of the main sentence be forgotten and left in the air. He used few punctuation marks, an occasional dash serving many purposes. We must, of course, remember the meagre nature of Clare's formal training in the art of writing at school; thereafter until 1820 his writing was all in verse; and while he composed in that medium with astonishing fluency, the orderly exposition of a theme in prose always gave him great difficulty. In descriptive and personal passages the gifts of exact observation and vivid imagery notable in his poetry were ample compensation; he had also a fine ear for verse rhythms; but in prose and verse he often left grammar and syntax to take care of themselves.

If the resulting blemishes are obvious enough, the finer qualities of Clare's poetry are in large measure due to this preoccupation with the immediate experience, the image seen or recollected and the emotion it evoked in him. (pp. viii-ix)

[Spontaneity], directness, simplicity, and vividness are present in all Clare's best work; it is only when he is generalizing, dealing in ideas at second hand, recording emotions not completely realized in an image, that his expression becomes commonplace or vague. Uncertainty creeps in when he is forced to seek deliberately and consciously for the word or phrase to convey what he feels. The manuscripts show clearly enough that he seldom worked over a poem; most of the poems appear in more than one manuscript, not a few in four or five, but the later versions are either simple copies of the earlier with minor alterations only, or else they are practically new poems, rewritten with a fresh inspiration. **'Summer Images,'** for example, was first written . . . in the unrhymed stanza of Collins's 'Ode to Evening' . . . ; it was then entirely rewritten in a longer rhyming stanza. . . . It is illuminating to compare the two versions and note where the re-reading has evoked in Clare a new and richer emotional experience, and where, occasionally, he is simply padding to make up the longer verse.

The earlier **'Summer Images'** belongs to the *Shepherd's Calendar* period, 1821-4, when Clare first clearly emerged from his apprenticeship to the eighteenth-century poets, and his own native mode was firmly established. We no longer find the 'woolly charge,' the 'feathered race,' the 'tasteful illumination of the night,' the echoes of Thomson, Goldsmith, and John Cunningham which mingle with the authentic Clare in the earlier poems. His technique at this period is well revealed in the [following lines from the first version of **'Summer Images'**]:

> Jet-black and shining, from the dripping hedge
> Slow peeps the fearful snail,
>   And from each tiny bent
>   Withdraws his timid horn.

The image could not be conveyed with more economy, directness, and clarity, and the poems of this period abound with such description. But it is true that something is not actually present which we are accustomed to look for in poetry—the particular emotion aroused in Clare by the image. It is implied; such sharp definition and clarity can be achieved only by a man of 'more than ordinary sensibilities'; and the above verse alone would put another man of similar sensibilities in full possession of the emotion felt by Clare but not explicitly expressed. Now when he rewrote the verse some years later, he made this emotion explicit, fusing it with the image:

> And note on hedgerow baulks, in moisture sprent,
>   The jetty snail creep from the mossy thorn,
> With earnest heed and tremulous intent,
>   Frail brother of the morn,
> That from the tiny bents and misted leaves
>   Withdraws his timid horn,
>   And fearful vision weaves.

The initial clarity is retained, but the verse is greatly enriched by the projection into the image of Clare's own emotions, in lines three, four, and seven. We cannot doubt that the emotions existed when Clare wrote the original verse. In fact, it was simply because they were so obviously there, because this kind of insight was so normal to him in the presence of nature, that he often took it for granted and left it unexpressed; if he could only fix the image in its immediate clarity, he knew that the simple description alone would re-evoke in him the accompanying emotion; and he seems to have assumed that all men were so constituted. (pp. ix-xi)

[We] have here the main clue to the further development of Clare's technique. We find the fusion of emotion and image described above more and more common in the poems written in the ten years following 1824. What was it that compelled Clare to do something which was, in a sense, unnatural to him? His own role, as he saw it, was to hold the mirror up to nature, to set down the immediate impression in its first clarity. Yet from the first there were circumstances which often prevented him from resting content with the immediate impression, which made him contrast what was with what had been, and thrust to the front the emotional and personal elements in the experience. The turning back to the Golden Age of childhood was not, with Clare, simply a consequence of growing old, enclosure by the shades of the prison house; it was due to enclosure of another kind which changed the face of his beloved countryside and degraded the village society and tradition into which he was born. The change was not in him but in nature itself; wherever he went the fields and woods he saw change—heaths enclosed, pastures ploughed up, trees destroyed. [**'Helpstone,'** the first poem printed in *The Poems of John Clare*,] is a regret for a Helpstone that was no more; but the full force of the change was not felt until later, when change in nature became linked with the loss of his first love, Mary Joyce, and the decline of his own fortunes which had seemed so bright in 1820. There was, indeed, always enough left to give him abundant delight; but the sense of loss and decay increased with the years; in the earlier poems it either appeared as an excuse for that mood of gentle melancholy which young poets often affect, or else issued in impersonal description of satire, as in **'The Parish.'** After 1824 we meet it more and more frequently in the form of a poignant emotion suffusing the imagery. After 1824 he wrote no more narrative and few long descriptive poems; his work became essentially lyrical. Mr. Blunden has charted this process in his *Nature in English Literature*, with special reference to the poem **'Autumn'** [see excerpt above, 1929]. . . . 'A great part of his verse is the history of the transference of love in him from woman to Nature.' His early inspiration, his rural muse, Nature, conventionally personified, becomes the 'Sweet Vision, with the wild dishevelled hair,' the 'wild sorceress' of **'Autumn,'** upon whose glances, gestures, and adornments he feasts with the eye of a lover; she assumes more and more clearly the lineaments of his lost love, Mary Joyce, whom he sometimes saw so vividly in dreams that he could no longer doubt her existence as his 'guardian genius.' . . . She was at once Mary Joyce, the spirit of love, the spirit of nature, his muse, and the guardian of his fame. And certainly Clare needed her guardianship in 1832 when the removal from Helpstone led him to take stock of his fortunes and review all the hopes that had fallen by the wayside. The result is seen when poems like **'The Flitting'** . . . and **'Remembrances'** are compared with earlier autobiographical poems such as **'The Village Minstrel.'** He has now found a direct and poignant expression for those sorrows and joys which in the earlier poems 'no words can utter and no tongue can tell.' Moreover, in **'Song's Eternity'** and other lyrics . . . , we have the first appearance of the mood and tone of the asylum lyrics; emotion, image, and idea, are purged of their personal reference without losing directness and intensity.

But Clare had not yet been forced to accept that sacrifice of the man to the poet which made this kind of vision normal to him; earth was not yet 'but a name.' And as the strain intensified in the years succeeding 1832, it resulted in a cleavage between the two elements which had been forced together against Clare's natural inclination. In 1835-6 we find him trying to escape from the emotional turmoil, deliberately and defiantly excluding it from his verse and turning to stark, objective description of natural scenes. . . . We feel in [the series of sonnets written at this time] what almost amounts to a contempt for artistic polish, and for all personal and emotional intrusions, and for man, except as part of the natural scene. When he does write personally it is in this mood:

> I hate the very noise of troublous man
> Who did and does me all the harm he can.
> Free from the world I would a prisoner be
> And my own shadow all my company.

But below the surface the emotional turmoil intensified, and after the breakdown of 1837 and when Clare was indeed a prisoner, it found its own expression in the verses taken from the High Beech note-books. . . . Here the personal takes charge; and under the half-delusion, half-pretence that he was Byron, he describes without restraint his mental Odyssey. The verses are overcharged with emotion; they are the raw material of poetry rather than poetry itself; but even in this troubled underworld of lost hopes, Clare's 'guardian' accompanied him, appearing in her different guises—Mary Joyce, now his 'first wife' as well as 'nature's self,' the spirit of love, which 'lives on in every kind of weather,' nature, freedom.

The addition of freedom to the list of Clare's 'esteems' is the clue to an understanding of the asylum poetry. The significance lies not in his longing for freedom—the asylum was always 'prison' to him—but in his achievement of that freedom in his verses. The price of freedom was a dissociation of the man and the poet; the man struggled on, unreconciled to prison, wrestling with delusions and melancholy; the poet escaped from 'earth and its delusions,' 'wrote till earth was but a name,' and kept his 'spirit with the free.' He had at last reached a plane of vision upon which emotion was no longer a disturbing factor but could be 'recollected in tranquillity,' its cause becoming its symbol. (pp. xi-xiii)

There are 'certain ardours and purposes of men' which are beyond Clare's range, but within the limits he set himself there is variety enough. This variety, like that of the country round Helpstone, the 'Clare country,' may not be obvious to the tourist in search of beauty spots. But it lies quietly in wait to delight the eye which has learned to look for the infinite rich-

ness of detail in Nature's underworld, and the ear which can discover the ceaseless variation of mood and tone within the repeated theme of days and seasons. Nor should his preoccupation with the 'diminutives of Nature,' and the delicacy of his etching, lead us to overlook the native vigour and robustness of his expression, a vigor fed by the tradition which gave him his store of dialect words and old ballads. We may be grateful too for Clare's chronicling of village life, customs, and occupations, as they existed in his childhood, and for his vivid picture in **'The Parish'** of the effect of enclosure on village life. The satirical mode was not natural to him, and his debt to the eighteenth-century satirists was openly acknowledged; yet his adaptation of his models to fit his local and particular theme is skilful and trenchant enough. Very different is the approach and mood of the **'Village Tales'**; again, Clare's natural gifts did not lie in the direction of narrative or dramatic verse; yet these bucolics have a quiet charm of their own if the reader can surrender himself to it. Clare's interest here is not so much in the story itself as in the undertones and undercurrents of emotion evoked in the characters, especially the effects of success and disappointment in love. Clare's imaginative projection is often as successful here as in his faithful delineation and interpretation of the world of nature. (pp. xiv-xv)

J. W. Tibble, in an introduction to The Poems of John Clare *by John Clare, edited by J. W. Tibble, E. P. Dutton & Co. Inc., 1935, pp. v-xvi.*

JOHN SPEIRS (essay date 1935)

[*In the following review of* The Poems of John Clare, *Speirs contends that the work emphasizes Clare's limitations, particularly his lack of development. He maintains that Clare's verse lacks the "inner purpose," or intellectual element, that distinguishes the poetry of John Keats and William Wordsworth, an argument advanced earlier by John Middleton Murry (1921 and 1924) and Edmund Gosse (1924). Unlike most commentators during the first half of the twentieth century, Speirs asserts that Clare's finest work is his early, descriptive verse written in the poetic tradition of the eighteenth century. His preference for the early poetry is shared by most of Clare's most recent critics.*]

[Whether **The Poems of John Clare**] will add anything actual to the reputation [**Poems Chiefly from Manuscript**] established is doubtful. It may well have the contrary effect of reinforcing the reader's sense of Clare's limitations. There is certainly here an overwhelming quantity of genuine stuff, but a stuff that is all of the same sort, so that the ultimate effect of it in such bulk is to emphasize its own sameness. . . . It seems to have been part of the purpose [of the editor] to represent different phases of Clare's development. Actually what is of value in Clare's work seems to develop singularly little, and this is a radically adverse criticism to make of any poet. Certain of the Asylum poems have been seen as something different, marking a final phase, and have even been regarded as Clare's finest work. There is in these an ecstatic note and occasionally a hint that Victorian influences have filtered through, but only the fact that they are nearer to what the nineteenth century had learnt to think poetry ought to be like could have blinded readers to their unsatisfactoriness in comparison with Clare's characteristic work, which remains essentially eighteenth century in quality.

What an edition of the collected poems does facilitate is a study of the particular influences which formed and later informed Clare's work. In his earlier work the influences of Thomson, Shenstone, Collins, Gray, Cowper and Crabbe separately are explicit, and the 'literary' eighteenth century remains implicit throughout his work. The following lines come comparatively late:

> From every nook the smile of plenty calls,
> And reasty flitches decorate the walls,
> Moore's Almanack where wonders never cease—
> All smeared with candle-snuff and bacon-grease.

It would be impossible to mistake these lines for Pope, but it is equally impossible not to recognize that but for Pope they would not have existed as what they are. This relationship between Clare's characteristic (which is also his valuable) work and the 'literary' eighteenth century is what distinguishes him from Burns, with whom, as a 'peasant poet,' he has often been compared, and whose work provoked him to one or two imitations. . . . [Clare] is notably free at his best from the Miltonic inversions and diction of his 'literary' masters, though there are traces in his work of the *L'Allegro* Milton as well as of the blank verse Milton who so tyrannized over the later eighteenth century. He even draws considerably upon the vocabulary of peasant speech. To this extent he has indeed a certain affinity with Burns. (pp. 84-6)

It is easier to see why Clare is a poet than why he is not a great poet. His poetry, and that considering his facility is a surprisingly large proportion of his work, is the product of an extraordinary intimacy with the nature that surrounded him, particularly with the *minutiae,* insects, blossoms, of the inexhaustible meadow-life. He is a nature-poet as Wordsworth is not, for Wordsworth is a psychologist interested fundamentally in the workings of his mind. What Clare's poetry evidences is a complete absorption with that other life, not felt as another life. It consists of perceptions crystallized richly and presented with a particularity and concreteness which are a warrant of their absolute authenticity. Yet it is a profusion that is spilt, almost one is tempted to say let run to waste. Clare has no hard core of individuality compelling his perceptions to serve an inner purpose. He has no inner purpose. He is scarcely even conscious of himself. . . . It is what distinguishes Clare . . . from the great poets Wordsworth and Keats . . . who begin from particular observation whereas Clare both begins and ends there. (p. 86)

> *John Speirs, in a review of "The Poems of John Clare," in* Scrutiny, *Vol. IV, No. 1, June, 1935, pp. 84-6.*

W. KENNETH RICHMOND   (essay date 1947)

[*In the following examination of Clare as a peasant poet writing in the tradition of English folk poetry, Richmond focuses on the poem "Pleasures of Spring."*]

[Clare's tragedy is so significant] that his case is worth examining in detail. As peasant-poet he had gifts, attitudes of which the Romantics were scarcely aware: and in its humble way the quality which he wished to contribute was something more enduring than any which they possessed. (p. 159)

As a folk-poet he was constitutionally unfitted to be a romantic, for romanticism implied individualism, idealism . . . therefore for him there was only one way out—cruellest idiocy. He could only have expressed himself fully through contacts with people like himself and with the earth by which he lived: only in them could he know himself more perfectly as a man and as a poet. Without this necessary environment his major instincts were denied. . . .

There are, then, two Clares: the Seeker and the Lost. The first is solid, real: the second, for all its eldritch, latter-day prophecy, is hollow, unreal. The poetry of the one is gloriously visual—the peasant's eye: the other is visionary, the same eye in an inward frenzy rolling. . . . [Though] his ultimate darkness was not entirely unrelieved, pierced here and there by squinting gleams, the light had been taken away from him. His best work, as his first reviewer was quick to point out, was "composed altogether from the impulses of the writer's mind, *as excited by external objects*" [see excerpt above from the *Quarterly Review,* May, 1820]. The peasant finds his meaning in the soil. Remove that and he is like a fish out of water. (p. 162)

[Without some appreciation of the continuity of the folk-poetry tradition in England], we shall not be able to account for Clare's uniqueness. It made him the peculiar blend of weakness and strength that he was—indigent and indigene. It explains his many faults of style, diffuseness, formlessness, repetitiveness, his carelessness of grammar or sense, the too-obviousness of his sentiment, his inability to state an argument: explains, too, his unpredictableness, the sudden glories, the concise, intermittent phrase that hits the ear and mind unawares, taking the winds of poetry with beauty. (p. 168)

In its maturity, Clare's genius was peculiarly descriptive: later still it turned contemplative; but from start to finish all he wrote was shaped by the loose ballad-pattern, every verse underlined by a vocal influence. Even in his last asylum drivellings it was the same:

> And then they closed the shutters up
> And then they closed the door.

One of his fellow inmates has recorded how the poet "*always sang with a repeat . . . with a degree of emphasis that seemed to be rather elevating and somewhat touching*". Precisely. (p. 169)

[The unpublished poem **"Pleasures of Spring,"** which was written in 1828,] contains the real Clare. Rambling, shapeless, gratuitous as it is, it is nevertheless more than worthy of being resurrected—and not merely for its occasional beauties, either. It reveals the peasant-poet in all his strength and weakness. It alternates between bathos and sublimity in most unaccountable fashion: irritates, disappoints, bores . . . and suddenly delights. As a whole it is very far from satisfactory and yet (paradoxically) on the whole it satisfies. (p. 175)

If the characteristic faults of the oral tradition in English verse are to be diffuse, to be un-self-critical, to lack art, then the **"Pleasures of Spring"** has them all in full measure.

> The blackthorn deepens in a darker stain
> And *brighter freckles* hazle shoots regain;
> The woodland rose in bright aray is seen
> Whose bark receives, like leaves, a vivid green;
> And *foulroyce twigs as red as stock doves' claws*
> Shines in the woods, to gain the bard's applause.

Gaucheness and felicity. One line reflects all the hackneyed abstractions and conventional diction of the worser kind of the eighteenth-century verse: the next comes up as fresh as a daisy. Was ever poetry quite so consistently, so aggravatingly uneven? Yet these are but minor undulations: as with Caedmon or Langland there is no effort to maintain more than a minimum-standard style, to achieve any *personal* success. The poet is content to wind about and in and out: there is plenty of time; and like the true Englishman he knows he will muddle through in the end. So the **"Pleasures"** pursues the even tenor of its way, aiming nowhere, getting nowhere . . . admiring trees and flowers by the wayside, noticing countrymen at work in the fields, pausing now to indulge in idle thoughts (all vague), telling now of children's games, geese on the green, village superstitions, now the celandine,

> Like a bright star Spring-tempted from the sky
> Reflecting on its leaves the sun's bright rays
> That sets its pointed glories in a blaze
> —So bright that children's fancys it decieves
> Who think that sunshine settles in its leaves. . . .

So Clare strays. His Milkmaid "loiters along": his Shepherd "guesses on": his Husbandman "muses in pleasure on his homeward way": his Boy "soodles on". So does the poem. It is written as a labourer might hoe a field of turnips, with no eye on the ending, no thought of what is to come next, but with a massive, unquestioning patience which sustains the work and makes it not ignoble. It has a heavy and leisurely dignity such as only the born landworker can achieve—dignity which is none the less real for being so little acknowledged.

Judged by usual standards of heroic-couplet criticism most of the **"Pleasures of Spring"** is pedestrian, a clumsy attempt to copy a style that Crabbe had already written far better, Goldsmith best of all. Compare it with [Goldsmith's] "The Deserted Village" and it is a thing of clay. Both grammar and spelling are atrocious, the rhymes almost invariably obvious, the sentiment commonplace: and when it comes to expressing even the most elementary thought Clare tends to be muddle-headed or, worse, loose-mouthed. The language is an unhappy mixture: one moment birds are "left mourning in their sad despair" (stuffed, no doubt)—the next a live Northamptonshire Lapwing comes "whewing" overhead, a Kite "swees" in the wind and a Partridge goes "nimbling" through the stubbles. There is much that might well be omitted. Clare was nothing if not prolific. As the scop had sung, so he wrote—for the sheer pleasure of "unlocking the word horde"—and when it came to erasure or revision he was too indolent or else too indifferent. Words came, he put them down and was content to leave them at that. Like the hoer in the field, it never occurred to him to consider—certainly not to reconsider—his work, nor did he deem it necessary to smooth off raw edges. Whatever other infinite capacities his genius possessed, that of taking pains was certainly not one: the poem remained a draft. (pp. 176-77)

From the critical point of view it would, no doubt, have been better otherwise, but there it is: the peasant-poet remains a poet *and* a peasant. We must take him for what he is, accept the rough with the smooth, remembering the disabilities which so offset the abilities. (pp. 177-78)

> *W. Kenneth Richmond, "The Peasants' Revolt," in his* Poetry and the People, *Routledge, 1947, pp. 150-80.**

GEOFFREY GRIGSON (essay date 1950)

[*In his introduction to* Selected Poems of John Clare, *Grigson disputes John Middleton Murry's contention that Clare was merely a pictorial poet (see excerpt above, 1924). Citing the development of Clare's response to nature, from vision to meditated vision and from feelings to ideas, Grigson asserts that Clare was "rather more than the lyric poet writing in answer to an intermittency of impulse." According to Grigson, the ideas expressed concerning nature, love, freedom, eternity, and artistic creativity in certain of Clare's asylum poems "raise him . . . far above the mere 'naturalist' of his common reputation."*]

No one, so great is the quantity of his manuscripts, will ever publish a complete edition of Clare. He versified rather than put down in prose what might have filled the note-books of another poet. Much of it is poetry humdrum and flat, though lit very often with precise and pure observation. Observation and description are not poetry, or at least cannot be poetry of the higher order; and no 'nature poet', if such an imagined phenomenon has ever appeared, can have been more than one of the lesser poets. But we have so long confused nature with art that we speak of Clare and even of Wordsworth as 'nature poets'. All appreciation of Clare, so far, has attended too much to Clare in this sense, to Clare's innocence of perception, that 'faculty of sheer vision', which the acutest of his critics, Mr. Middleton Murry, has maintained is not only 'far purer than Wordsworth's' but even purer than Shakespeare's [see excerpt above, 1924]. Clare's vision intensifies the selected reality of most things it describes:

> From dark green dumps among the dripping grain
>   The lark with sudden impulse starts and sings
> And mid the smoking rain
>   Quivers her russet wings . . .

The difference between Clare and Wordsworth [according to Mr. Murry] was that Wordsworth could think, while Clare could not. The one produced harmony, the other melody.

Elsewhere Mr. Murry argued that an object would evoke Clare's feelings, and that the feelings could only be passed on by describing the object, which is certainly true of many of Clare's poems, as it would be true of the sketches of his exact contemporary, John Constable. But the claims of the limitation of Clare's thought and the restriction of his poems to the transmission of innocent feeling and of his perpetual childishness, in a good sense, his perpetual immaturity, are too absolute; and so are the parallel claims that Clare learnt nothing of aesthetic economy and form. Clare thought more at length and more deeply than has been allowed. . . . As Constable thought of painting as an art by which he was able to pass on his feeling, so Clare, it is true, held that poetry was another name for feeling. He tells us so again and again. His 'feelings grew into song'. His own poetry grew from learning and loving the material of nature, from vision, into meditated vision. From feeling, he came to meditate upon feeling, upon himself and so upon man, and so at last he reached out into a poetry of ideas or at any rate of ideas limited. . . . An increasing series of deprivations threatened Clare's mind, indeed unbalanced him from the delicate thread of his life, but increased his self-knowledge and made him look more and more for meanings in that nature in which like Hölderlin and so many artists of his spiritual type he found a consolation which he did not discover, after the happiness of childhood, in the society of men. In the end, Clare's deeper perceptions had to race against his psychosis. With ups and downs the psychosis gained upon him. But before his mind lost its power completely, his ideas of nature, love, creative joy, freedom, and eternity had developed and had informed that small number of poems which raise him so far above the mere 'naturalist' of his common reputation. Moreover with this development there came, as chaotic notions cleared into certain ideas, an increased rhythmical subtlety combined with an improved economy of form. (pp. 11-14)

[Clare] had known the poems of Wordsworth and Coleridge for a good many years, . . . and he had found in them, no doubt in [Wordsworth's] 'Resolution and Independence' and certainly in Coleridge's 'Pains of Sleep', the last two lines of which remained so long in his mind, evidence of situations like his own. . . . He recorded in his diary of [Wordsworth's] 'White Roe of Rylstone' that it contained 'some of the sweetest poetry' he had ever met with, though it was 'full of his mysteries'. The mysteries gained on him. The notion of creative joy took hold of him, as he puzzled over Coleridge's 'Dejection', and over [Wordsworth's] 'Intimations' ode. Moved by these two poems as well as by [Wordsworth's] 'Tintern Abbey', he wrote not long after that curious extract of Wordsworth, Coleridge and Clare called **Pastoral Poesy,** to celebrate 'the dower of self-creating joy'. Many more of his poems on love, immortality, and the immortality of nature, and hope are obviously affined to the 'mysteries' of Wordsworth and Coleridge.

> To be beloved is all I need
> And whom I love, I love indeed——

Coleridge's two lines were, so to say, answered by Clare, if there was no one else to love and be loved in that fullness, through the creation of the ideal of Mary Joyce. Twice, with a length of time in between, he worked the lines into poems calling on Mary.

If Wordsworth and Coleridge helped him to meaning, relation and harmony, it was help received and not plagiarism committed. In many ways the cases of all three poets (and the case of John Constable) were much alike. All three and Constable were contemporaries caught up in the exaltations and the preordination of their peculiar time; only Clare, however much his limits closed him in, was blessed with that resilience by which he never lost the shaping power of his imagination. In **'The Progress of Rhyme'** in the twenties, Clare defined poetry as hope, love and joy. He wrote later of tramps who 'dally with the wind and laugh at hell'. He was another such tramp on the long roads, but one driven down them by thoughts desperately acquired; and when he came to **'A Vision'** in August 1844, for a while at least he was the victor and not the victim. Love and joy, of the earth and even of heaven, had been found out by him, or had left him. Hope he had surpassed and he proclaimed his penetration to eternity. . . . (pp. 15-17)

However much Blake might have visited upon Clare that reproof of allowing the natural man to rise up against the spiritual man which he applied to Wordsworth, he would have applauded **'A Vision'** as repentance, as an immortal moment reached after and attained. (p. 17)

The making of poems was part of [Clare], like laughing, feeling sad or feeling elated, like waking and sleeping. Indeed it was most of him. And this is worth saying, obvious as it may be, because so much poetry is always so diseased by being, not a willed product, but a willed product outside the nature of the poet.

If there is too little of will, too much of flow about Clare's writing, will can only be applied to refine what is given, and to create the circumstances by which more is given. Clare did labour, nevertheless, upon what he received, only the flow from him was enormously incessant through his life like the flow of a river breaking up through flowers out of limestone. It might have defied the labour of a poet far better equipped by the formalities of education. But he was rather more than the lyric poet writing in answer to an intermittency of impulse.

There are 'classic' poets who contrive something at least of shape either because they avoid, or because they are forced by the exigency of their nature very far into, the bubbling of life.

And there are classics forced into that bubbling and greater in themselves than the confusion, which they are able to subdue. Such a romantic as Clare is stationed between them. He goes further than the one class and as far as the other, but his power to cut and shape what is solid out of what is chaotic is certainly limited and was reached expensively and late; yet he makes and endures the right exploration. . . . [Beyond] the delight that comes of reading Clare selectively, even so romantic and fluent a writer has something to teach. Not only is he an exemplar of the pure life of the artist, a purity founded upon an unevasive appetite, but he is a poet who employs a language unsoiled in his strongest work, which he is able to shape into the most emotive of melodic rhythms. He was unique. His uniqueness and stature cannot be diminished by talk of his origins or his shortcomings, or by talk of the peculiarity of the romantic decadence in human affairs. There is a universal element even in the extreme romantic posture. The relationship between man and nature varies, but since man is conscious, it can never be an equilibrium. Clare is a poet who became homeless at home, naturally and tragically conscious of exclusion from nature. Wriggle as we may, that, many times worse, is still our own position. Clare's asylum foretells our need for an asylum, his deprivations foretell our own deprivation. Our modern selves have to eat (if we admit to any) our own sins. Clare, as he exclaimed in **'I Am'**, was the self-consumer of his woes. We could be pardoned, then, for seeing our own case in Clare's. Yet not quite our case, for in Clare there was no failure of nerve, no concealment of such failure under the rhetoric of a false heroism.

What then we have in Clare is a poet in defeat entirely undefeated. (pp. 18-20)

> *Geoffrey Grigson, in a introduction to* Selected Poems
> of John Clare *by John Clare, edited by Geoffrey
> Grigson, Routledge & Kegan Paul Ltd., 1950, pp.
> 1-20.*

THE TIMES LITERARY SUPPLEMENT   (essay date 1956)

[*Pointing out that imperfections occur in all writing, this anonymous reviewer accepts the defects of Clare's verse and entreats the literary world to adopt him into the canon of English poetry alongside John Keats, Samuel Taylor Coleridge, and William Wordsworth.*]

The canon of English poetry seemed until recent years fairly settled, fairly complete. There might be shifts of interest and concern, an occasional dethronement (likely to be followed by a quick restoration) might occur, a few minor figures might slip their way in; but it did seem . . . that we could be fairly sure who was who; who, at any rate, was in the lists, up to, let us say, Hardy and Kipling and Yeats. . . . .

But what are we to say of [an] intruder into the canon—John Clare? No one seems absolutely sure. . . .

Do we really allow [Clare's] place inside the canon in an unreluctantly granted relationship to Giant Keats, Giant Coleridge or Giant Wordsworth? . . .

Or shall we always argue and vacillate about Clare, always remember his "humble position in life," always group him with Crabbe, and a few more, among "doubtfuls" of literature, who should not really be doubted at all?

The last is the important question. Since unwilling duchesses have so long ago been forced to lick stamps, and since we have long been surrounded with poets proclaiming their humble origin, Clare's origin would hardly seem to matter or cause concern any more. When other poets (Hopkins, for one) wrote down for themselves Clare's wonderful and terrible poem "I am: yet what I am none cares or knows" (much as poets have so often written out for comfort Wordsworth's "Resolution and Independence"), they asked themselves no questions about Clare's education, Clare's syntax and grammar, Clare's single subjects and plural verbs or the other way round. They were moved instead by Clare's admission that he as well was forced to be the "self-consumer of his woes"; and no doubt they admired his refusal, even then, to admit wreck in shipwreck.

But is it Clare's destiny or Clare's poetry we find so touching, or both in one? That, too, is a question to answer. We all know, at last, how poignantly Clare lived, failed and triumphed. Would no genuine power be left, or would his poems be drained of an adventitious content, supposing that we knew nothing at all of Clare's history?

Long ago Professor Tibble suggested—a little too forwardly—that Clare "was not interested in words as words" [see excerpt above, 1935]: Clare focused himself upon an image, the image found its words, its phrasing, and so poems were built up. It is true that Clare hardly reshapes his language to a characteristic degree; he hardly produces a Clare language, as, for example, there is a Christopher Smart language, a very particular impression having been given to his words, as Smart said, "by punching, that when the reader casts his eye upon 'em, he takes up the image from the mould which I have made." Just as that punched impression can be good or bad (Hopkins or Dylan Thomas; Hardy or Francis Thompson), so a good or a bad poetry can exist in a language fined, simply, as a Spanish vintner fines his sherry with whites of egg, but not greatly transformed; in that way, Clare's language, for all his less perfect, less educated command of it, is not so different, after all, from Wordsworth's or Byron's or Blake's; and no more than faulty syntax or grammar does this imply that our knowledge of Clare's history is the mere liquid which is spilt into the poems to make them alive and active. We need know nothing of Clare's biography to accept melodious statements of the human predicament when Clare asks:

> Is love's bed always snow

or when he says that:

> Flowers shall hang upon the palls
> Brighter than patterns upon shawls.

Faced with Clare's imperfections, we still have to ask who is perfect. In fact, we should do well to remember Hopkins answering Bridges, when Bridges complained that the poetry of William Barnes, that "perfect artist," as Hopkins called him, lacked fire. It might be so: "but who is perfect all round?" said Hopkins. "If one defect is fatal what writer could we read?"

Is Clare also the arrested child of vision? When Mr. Middleton Murry said so in 1924 [see excerpt above], there were not poems enough, there was not an ordered enough history of Clare's poetry to show him wrong. We must not be too much misled by Clare's own statements. He certainly said that Nature would be his widow, that he found his poems in the fields and only wrote them down; and he did not feel with an especial subtlety or sophistication of mind. But to his own melodic exploration, his own experience of the human dilemma, he did apply thoughts about which his biographers [John W. Tibble and Anne Tibble (see Additional Bibliography, 1956)] should

have been more emphatic—thoughts he had borrowed from Coleridge, and also from Wordsworth. His notion of "self-creating joy," which he mentioned, for example, in **"Pastoral Poesy"** and which was one of the names of his Mary Joyce, was never forgotten, and was pondered, and developed, by Clare. Coleridge's "Dejection" and Wordsworth's "Intimations" ode, it seems quite obvious, enabled Clare to recognize "joy" in himself; and Clare was luckier than Coleridge (or Wordsworth), not losing so quickly or completely this joy he had to project and so receive.

Also one may search the [Tibbles'] new Life, or the old one, for a single, particular word, for the single image of the sun; in which the development of Clare's poetry—Clare's life indeed—can also be traced from beginning to end. The sun is the king-image of Clare's poetry, much as it is of Turner's painting. It is the red and roundy, red-complexioned sun of early poems and early experience, which rose over the fens as Clare went to work, winter or summer. It gives a glitter to cesspools (in **"The Mouse's Nest"**). It is, or it was—"A splendid sun hath set!"—Clare's *alter ego,* Lord Byron. The sun, indeed, is hope, nature, love ("sun of undying light"), eternity; proffering at last to Clare the "eternal ray" he snatched to write himself into freedom and immortality in his deepest and most clinching poem [**"I Lost the Love of Heaven"**].

So far in the exegesis of Clare, it is that sun-filled, nearly sun-worshipping sense of the whole of him, that pondered development, of joy and love and eternity and freedom, that metamorphosis from time into timelessness, which needs still to be comprehended, without little-lambish deflections. It needs to be shown—and is not shown starkly enough, unequivocally enough, by his biographers—that in a dozen or two dozen poems, in which imagination does its melodic and verbal shaping with unusual energy and completeness, Clare does became a momentous poet—momentous at least to those readers whose experiences have matured their sensibility, their power, and their need, to respond. If in one way Hopkins is a dangerous intruder into the canon, so in another way is Clare, since he strips away certain current pretensions about verse-reading as an intellectual exercise and not a central experience, and since he demands discernment, in a situation not already mapped out and signposted.

> *"King of the Forest,"* in The Times Literary Supplement, *No. 2826, April 27, 1956, p. 252.*

J. MIDDLETON MURRY (essay date 1956)

[In a revaluation of Clare, Murry delineates two deficiencies in his earlier assessments (1921 and 1924): his inattention to Clare's powers as a visionary poet, which he discusses in the portion of the essay excerpted below, and his insufficient recognition of the uniqueness of Clare's picture of the effects of enclosure. Here, Murry argues that Clare emerges as a "true" poet in a small number of visionary asylum poems, especially in "A Vision," which represents a spiritual and poetic triumph over the forces threatening to disintegrate Clare's personality. In emphasizing the similarities between "A Vision" and the work of William Blake, Murry is joined by Harold Bloom (see Additional Bibliography).]

[In my earlier appreciation of Clare,] I did insufficient justice to the power of Clare as a visionary poet—that is to say, a poet of experience outside the familiar range of our experience, and incommensurable with it. The group of his poems which fall within the category is a small one, and they were written during the early years of his madness. Most of them appear to have been written in or about 1844; one is dated 1847, after which Clare's sudden access of the power of intense concentration, emotional and intellectual seems to have left him. He wrote many charming things; but they became slighter and slighter; and very few of them reached the level of the copious best of his pre-asylum work. The wonderful freshness of perception disappears. What remains is his native facility in rhyming, ennobled by rare flashes of the old vividness.

Roughly speaking, what confronts us is the phenomenon of a poet of unique though limited achievement who, under the stress of the threatening disintegration of his personality, suddenly becomes the vehicle for the utterance of thoughts hitherto beyond the reaches of his soul, of terrors and triumphs which belong to the struggle to maintain the integrity of the human personality against the powers that would engulf it. Nothing in Clare's pre-asylum poetry has prepared us for quite this kind of intensity. He has passed into a new dimension of experience.

Certainly the most famous, and probably the finest, of these visionary poems is the one entitled *A Vision*. (pp. 56-7)

[It] stands, by the most rigorous judgment, equal with some of the finest of Blake. And it is almost equally mysterious. What is plain about it is that it is a song of spiritual triumph. It celebrates, in itself embodies and eternizes, a moment of victory: at once, spiritual and poetic. Clare, for this creative instant, has fought free of the powers of darkness, and is himself: a new self, deepened and purified by the struggle he has endured. And this new and deeper self is a self of pure poetry. For, almost from the beginning, Clare had experienced his own essence as poetry. The rapture of his heightened perceptions had uttered itself immediately in rhyme. This natural song, shaped upon whatever patterns he could find, had been the mode of his real, or most essential and personal existence: the speech of his own reality, of the love which was for him the mode of true being.

> Poets love nature, and themselves are love.

In this sense, it was inevitable that the achievement of a deeper, purer self, torn free from the powers of disintegration, and momentarily triumphant over them, should be the achievement of a poem of a new and higher order. *A Vision* is Clare's victory.

But, on a rather lower level, we may fairly ask: What does the poem mean? There is one important clue in Clare's earlier poetry: in the opening lines of *The Village Minstrel*. . . .

> While learned poets rush to bold extremes,
> And sunbeams snatch to light the muse's fires,
> An humble rustic hums his lowly dreams,
> Far in the swale where poverty retires,
> And sings what nature and what truth inspires.

In *A Vision* Clare himself has become 'a learned poet rushing to bold extremes', and more. But the humbler lines are a complete commentary on the pride and splendour of [these lines from *A Vision*].

> I snatch'd the sun's eternal ray
> And wrote till earth was but a name.

The writing he meant was the writing of that poem and no other; his former poetry of earth, in the writing of that poem, was dissolved away. And indeed it was. He had, and knew he had, fought his way to the pinnacle. He was there. He was himself, *dans sa vraie vérité*.

Then the hyperbole of the last verse [of *A Vision*], beginning: 'In every language upon earth . . .' It is not fanciful, nor pedestrian, to connect this with one of Clare's hallucinations. 'When . . . I courted your mother, I knew nine languages', he wrote to his son from the asylum, but, he explained, he kept them to himself, and only betrayed his knowledge in conversation with parsons and gentry. The knowledge of many languages belonged, for Clare, to the free-masonry of the learned, who as poets 'snatched sunbeams'. It had been part of his secret endowment; now, having climbed the pinnacle, he proclaims it. (pp. 58-9)

[The] last two lines [of *A Vision*]:

> I gave my name immortal birth
> And kept my spirit with the free.

What does the last line mean? Probably, more things than one. That he kept, in spite of his prison and the inward assaults upon his own identity, his essential liberty—the spiritual liberty of which the poem is the utterance. That he, having become, with loveliness, 'the bard of immortality', joined the free on the heights of eternal song. These meaning are there. But there is surely another. In one of his later songs he writes, of the raindrops:

> They come from heaven and there the Free
> Sends down his blessings upon me;

and in another he writes of flowers:

> Even in prison they can solace me
> For where they bloom God is, and I am free.

In the concluding lines of the impressive piece *Written in a Thunderstorm* . . . , he had besought the elements:

> Bid the earth and its delusions pass away
> But leave the mind, as its Creator, free.

And there is the lovely end of *The Dying Child*:

> His soul seemed with the free,
> He died so quietly.

To be with the free, evidently, also meant for Clare to be one with God, as he conceived God. A further link between these meanings is supplied by another of his visionary poems: usually entitled *John Clare*.

> I feel I am, I only know I am
>   And plod upon the earth as dull and void:
> Earth's prison chilled my body with its dram
>   Of dullness and my soaring thoughts destroyed.
> I fled to solitudes from passion's dream,
>   But strife pursued—I only know I am.
> I was a being created in the race
>   Of men, disdaining bounds of place and time,
> A spirit that could travel o'er the space
>   Of earth and heaven, like a thought sublime,
> Tracing creation—like my Maker, free,—
>   A soul unshackled—like eternity,
> Spurning earth's vain and soul-debasing thrall—
> But now I only know I am,—that's all.

It is possible, even probable, that this was written after *A Vision*, and represents a moment of awareness that he had fallen from the visionary pinnacle, yet one of sufficient control to enable him to express, at least in part, what he had won and lost. Anyway, I do not believe that the condition described in 'I was a being . . .' is the condition of his pre-asylum days, of the incessant composition of nature poetry. Or, at least, it is that condition transfigured by a subsequent flash of insight. Clare did not, in the earlier days, conceive or experience himself as like 'a thought sublime, tracing creation'. That fine phrase belongs to a different order of self-knowledge. The new thrilling and perilous dimension has broken in, wherein he is, or had been, one with God: consubstantial and co-eternal with his Creator. And that is the deepest meaning of the phrase: 'I kept my spirit with the free.'

It is not that the description of what he was is, in essence, false to what he had actually been. Clare's condition, as the maker of spontaneous and incessant poetry of nature, with its continual breath-taking revelation of simple things as they are, . . . recalls Keats's description of the soul of a child as it enters the world, which is the vale of soul-making.

> There may be intelligences or sparks of the divinity in millions—but they are not souls till they acquire identities, till each one is personally itself. Intelligences are atoms of perception—they know and they see and they are pure, in short they are God.

To apply this simple and profound terminology to the growth of his poetic nature, the pre-asylum Clare was an unconscious atom of God. His perilous triumph, won at the cost of an imminent disintegration of his personal identity, was the flash of the knowledge that he was one with God. There is nothing exorbitant in this. It is a familiar realization of the mystic experience. And Clare's sudden illumination transfigured his own poetic past, and revealed to him his own meaning as a poet, as it were in a lightning flash. (pp. 59-62)

[Clare's victory in *A Vision*] is in some sense a passing beyond the love of woman, which has failed him.

> I loved, but woman fell away,
> I hid me from her faded flame.

This connects with the lines from *I am:*

> I fled to solitudes from passion's dream
> But strife pursued.

In *A Vision* he is beyond that strife, which is a word he often uses in his 'mad' poems for the mental conflict which seethed in him between the past and the present, between darkness and illumination, between hope and despair, and above all between the knowledge that his love of Mary had been doomed long ago, and the hope of possessing her presence for ever. This mental tumult is described and transcended in the opening lines of *A Vision*—

> I lost the love of heaven above
> I spurned the lust of earth below
> I felt the joys of fancied love,
> And hell itself my only foe.—

where, it seems, the heavenly love lost is his childhood love of Mary, and the fancied love was his dream of being married to her, threatened by the terrors of his 'dark and fathomless' mind. He is where he longs to be in *I am:*

> I long for scenes, where man hath never trod,
> A place where woman never smiled or wept . . .

But in two beautiful poems of this group [*Invite to Eternity* and *It Is the Evening Hour*], Mary is the companion of his purified spirit. *Invite to Eternity* is an extraordinary achievement. It appears to have originated in a moment when he was able to

accept the disintegration of his personality and to see in that very condition an opening of the gate to eternity—a strange eternity where Mary may be his veiled companion. . . . It haunts the mind and will not be forgotten. The pathos of the condition of 'sad non-identity' has never received more perfect utterance. (pp. 63-6)

As it is—at any rate for me—impossible to say whether *A Vision* or *Invite to Eternity* is the finer poem, so it is impossible to say which of the two very different conditions of mind, or states of soul, which they express, is the higher. *A Vision* is excited, *Invite* is calm. 'Beyond woman' was a position hard for Clare to attain, and the tension of struggle is in *A Vision:* it bears the marks of scars. The sad lucidity of *Invite* is serene. They embody different, but equally astonishing victories of the poetic spirit over disaster. (p. 66)

> *J. Middleton Murry, "Clare Revisited," in his* Un-professional Essays, *Jonathan Cape, 1956, pp. 53-111.*

DONALD DAVIE (essay date 1964)

[*Davie favors* The Shepherd's Calendar *over Clare's asylum verse, arguing that the strength of his poetry derives from its straightforward, non-metaphoric language. According to Davie, Clare's early verse constitutes "not a naive or limited kind of minor poetry, but one kind of great poetry, sane, robust and astringent." Davie's essay marks a shift in Clare criticism toward a preference for the early verse.*]

[Anyone] who goes to poems for poetry and not another thing will prefer the sane Clare of *The Shepherd's Calendar* to the lunatic Clare. . . .

Not that the late poems aren't worth the trouble. Every so often they come up with

> I love to see the shaking twig
> Dance till shut of eve.

And even in a scrap like that one can isolate Clare's peculiar purity, in the prosaic word 'shaking', so honestly and unfussily Clare's name for what a twig does. It strikes against and qualifies and thereby validates the much less straightforward and yet more commonplace 'dance', which follows. 'Dance' for what a twig does is a word with a metaphor inside it, an analogy or many analogies; 'shaking' stays stubbornly close the thing it names, and won't let us look away or beyond to anything analogous.

And this is the virtue of earlier Clare also. It is the reason behind his use of dialect, which is not for him a valuable resource, an artful freaking of language. He says that robins 'tutle' because this is his and his neighbours' name for what robins do, not a *mot juste* sought for and triumphantly found; not the one exquisitely right word, just the one right one. It is not so far from what Pound applauded in Johnson's *Vanity of Human Wishes*, 'the merits of the lexicographer', for whom one thing has one name, and only one name.

This shows up in Clare in the conspicuous absence of 'elegant variation'. If things have fixed names, then the same words will and must recur as often as the same things are spoken of. And so in *The Shepherd's Calendar* 'crackling stubbles' is not embarrassed by the proximity of 'crackling stubs', 'sliving' does not mind being jostled by 'they slive', 'splashy fields' naturally provide 'splashing sports'; and in the later poems, the poems of madness,

> The rushbeds touched the boiling spring
> And dipped and bowed and dipped again
> The nodding flower would wabbling hing

becomes a few lines later

> The rush tufts touched the boiling sand
> Then wabbling nodded up anew. . . .

It's true that when Clare uses decasyllabic couplets, as he does in the best parts of [The Shepherd's Calendar] (though some of the octosyllabics are also fine), he escapes the characteristically Augustan or post-Popian cadences, as Bloomfield in his verse-tales doesn't. Nevertheless, Clare almost certainly regarded himself as writing in a tradition stemming from Thomson through Bloomfield, as competing therefore for the neoclassical laurels of 'English Theocritus', stakes that Wordsworth and Coleridge, Keats and Shelley, were not entered for. Accordingly Clare can use the personification, for instance, with Augustan aplomb and wit:

> The ploping guns sharp momentary shock
> Which eccho bustles from her cave to mock.

And when in his madness he identified himself with Byron, and tried to write a Childe Harold and a Don Juan, the manoeuvre was not altogether senseless: Byron's special and Augustan kind of Romanticism is the only kind that can be invoked to make Clare any sort of Romantic poet, and indeed the poet who exhorted the 'deep and dark blue Ocean' to 'roll' shared Clare's attitude to words as names—there are no metaphors hidden in Byron's 'deep' and 'dark' and 'blue', any more than in Clare's 'shaking' or his 'wabbling'. . . .

As for the feelings that got into [his] poems, one can see that from [a] Victorian-Romantic standpoint, which prized melodiousness and plasticity and subjectivity, Clare's [The Shepherd's Calendar] was disconcertingly too faithful to the various angularities of a social and physical world irreducibly outside the mind which registered it.

This is not the mistake which modern taste will make. But when we praise Clare for his 'observation', we do hardly any better. For as Walter De La Mare said, 'mere observation will detect the salient sharply enough' but, in Tennyson for instance, it often 'crystallises what should be free and fluent with a too precise, an overburdened epithet.' Clare never does this. His words are like the words of Edward Thomas, of which De La Mare said:

> They are there for their own sake, of course,
> but chiefly because the things they represent
> have been lived with and loved so long that
> their names are themselves.

This describes not a naive or limited kind of minor poetry, but one kind of great poetry, sane, robust and astringent.

> *Donald Davie, "John Clare," in New Statesman,*
> *Vol. LXVII, No. 1736, June 19, 1964, p. 964.*

ERIC ROBINSON AND GEOFFREY SUMMERFIELD (essay date 1966)

[*In their approbatory introduction to* Selected Poems and Prose of John Clare, *Robinson and Summerfield challenge John Middleton Murry's contention that Clare was essentially a pictorial poet (see excerpt above, 1921), citing the "conscious pattern"* of Edenic imagery in his poetry as evidence of his intellectual maturity. While noting the "unmistakable intensity and vibrance" of Clare's asylum verse, Robinson and Summerfield caution against attributing too much importance to the later poetry; they maintain that "Clare would still have been one of the finest poets of his century if he had died in 1837 before he had entered the asylum." In portions of the introduction not excerpted below, Robinson and Summerfield emphasize the historical value of Clare's picture of the social and economic effects of enclosure. In addition, they dispute the notion that Clare's poetry displays no development. According to these critics, the poems of Clare's maturity, written during the 1830s, are "less traditionally poetic" and more reflective than his earliest poetry. This essay was first published in 1966 in Clare: Selected Poems and Prose.*]

If the countryside about Helpstone was not only the map of Clare's boyhood but also part of a rural landscape cruelly altered by enclosure, it was something even more significant. Helpstone was Clare's Paradise, his Garden of Eden. This observation is no literary conceit but plain truth. There is a similarity here between Wordsworth's philosophy in the 'Ode on the Intimations of Immortality' and Clare's imaginative position; but Clare goes much further than Wordsworth in actually identifying the fields of his boyhood with Eden—even, he says, with something more than Eden:

> I sat beside the pasture stream
> When Beautys self was sitting by
> The fields did more than Eden seem
> Nor could I tell the reason why

In the landscape of Eden before the Fall, Clare's boyhood love, Mary Joyce, is present—she is the Eve to Clare's Adam. Unless we recognize that this is the conscious pattern of imagery in Clare's poetry, we are bound to miss a great deal of his point. Everything in his boyhood environment assumes a new character, a vividness far beyond accurate natural history, a deeper identity because it is part of what Clare calls 'Loves register'. In this 'register', not just trees but every single tree, not just grass but every single blade of grass is a special act of the Creator and participates in the freshness before the Fall. This is where Middleton Murry, one of the best critics of Clare, goes astray, when, writing of the differences between Clare and Wordsworth, he says that Clare in some ways was a truer poet than Wordsworth, because he had

> a truer ear and a more exquisite instinct for words; *but he had nothing of the principle of inward growth which gives to Wordsworth's most careless work a place within the unity of a great scheme.* Wordsworth's incessant effort to comprehend experience would itself have been incomprehensible to Clare.

Wordsworth's effort would not have been incomprehensible to Clare because he had made, himself, the same effort. This can best be seen by examining Clare's poetry extensively, but it can be illustrated, to a limited degree, in this selection also. Thus, in **'Shadows of Taste'**, he writes:

> Some in recordless rapture love to breath[e]
> Natures wild Eden wood and field and heath.
>
> (p. 112)

and in **'The Morning Wind'**:

> Theres more then music in this early wind
> Awaking like a bird refreshed from sleep
> And joy what Adam might in eden find
> When he with angels did communion keep.
>
> (p. 138)

The daisies, he tells us, in **'The Flitting'** (p. 176) are as old as Adam and were there when the earth first beheld the sun. Sometimes the allusions to this Eden are explicit, but quite often it is the sharpness of Clare's vision alone that serves to remind us of the 'great scheme' to which his experience belonged. (pp. xvi-xvii)

Though most of the poems written in his closing years are love songs or ballads, and though most of them, at least superficially, speak of enjoyments in nature, felt in the past or even in the present, a sombre note is occasionally struck. The consequence of free will in Adam's Paradise was the Fall and the introduction of sin into the world. Thus the time would come when there would be a terrible Day of Judgement. The sequence is followed in 'Spring' in Thomson's *Seasons*: first a picture of Eden, showing the contentment of rural society, enjoying cheerful labour and refreshed by song; then the Fall where all the harmony of Eden is destroyed; and then the Deluge and the Day of Judgement. In Clare's poetry, the theme of Judgement, which had always been there, grew stronger and gained fuller expression in his later years. In 1841 he wrote the apocalyptic poem:

> There is a day a dreadful day
> Still following the past
> When sun and moon are past away
> And mingle with the blast
>
> There is a vision in my eye
> A vacuum oer my mind
> Sometimes as on the sea I lye
> Mid roaring waves and wind

Imitations of the psalms often follow a similar trend, and thunder and shipwreck are frequent subjects. His early reading of Falconer's *Shipwreck* and similar works now provided him with an imagery of terror. 'An invite to Eternity' (p. 196) asks the maiden to go with the poet:

> Where the path hath lost its way
> Where the sun forgets the day

and

> Where stones will turn to flooding streams
> Where plains will rise like ocean waves
> Where life will fade like visioned dreams
> And mountains darken into caves

Even the poems which ostensibly deal with lighter matters like the poem about the ladybird or **'Clock a Clay'** (p. 199) may have a disturbing note of fear and insecurity about them, while the famous **'I am'** (p. 195) speaks of 'the living sea of waking dreams'. There is no question that Clare in his later years developed a very distinctive voice, an unmistakable intensity and vibrance, such as the later pictures by Van Gogh possess, but we must also guard against attributing too much importance to the poems of his madness because we live in an age fascinated by the problems of mental stress. It is salutary, after reading some of the last poems, to turn back to a poem like **'Sabbath Bells'** (p. 157) where the free response of Clare to Nature is untinged by despair and doubt or to the Augustan calm of **'Summer Images'** (p. 143) or **'The Nightingales Nest'** (p. 72). And when one does so, it is the continuity of Clare's life and ways of thought and feeling which claims one's attention, rather than the disruptions of insanity.

Finally it ought to be remembered that Clare would still have been one of the finest poets of his century if he had died in 1837 before he had entered an asylum. His published work at that time was already a considerable achievement even though it had been tampered with by Taylor. And even in 1837 there were many poems still in manuscript which had never been published and none of Clare's prose had been published at all. He was a most prolific and fertile writer, and could perhaps be called 'the green man of English poetry'. His work is still read a hundred years after his death and his fame will grow when his work is presented in a form which will make some overall estimate of it possible. Clare asked for no pretentious gravestone. He felt that if his work lived, then an imposing tombstone would be unnecessary; if his work did not live, then no tombstone, however elaborate, would save him from oblivion. There is no doubt that Clare will live. (pp. xxxi-xxxiii)

> *Eric Robinson and Geoffrey Summerfield, in an introduction to* Selected Poems and Prose of John Clare *by John Clare, edited by Eric Robinson and Geoffrey Summerfield, Oxford University Press, 1967, pp. xiii-xxxiii.*

ELAINE FEINSTEIN (essay date 1968)

[*Feinstein maintains that Clare's early descriptive and satirical verse is superior to that of his asylum period. She argues that such pre-asylum poems as "The Parish" and* The Shepherd's Calendar *derive their strength from Clare's "sense of the solidity of 'the real world'," a quality lacking in much of the asylum verse. While Feinstein concedes that Clare's asylum poems, particularly "Child Harold" and "Don Juan," are interesting experiments with sound, she concludes that they have "certainly won disproportionate praise."*]

Clare's intelligence was not political. He never brought his mind to bear on the complex machinery of power, and he had little respect for the men who had to manipulate it. What he saw honestly, he also saw simply. He condemned Enclosure and the Corn Laws because he saw and felt what misery they had brought, but he had no faith in any political remedy. The virtues of the old village life, the Eden of his childhood, could hardly be brought back by Act of Parliament. And if there were things that could be done by legislation, even by people whose motives were tainted, Clare had no hope of it.

So Clare was no Radical, though Lord Radstock, one of his earliest patrons, thought he detected signs of "radical and ungrateful sentiments" in Clare's first book of poems. Clare feared change as passionately as Lord Radstock, and with reason. In his generation, every change had been for the worse. Men in full work had been reduced to paupers on the edge of starvation.... [It] was one of the accidents of enclosure that the farming class grew richer as their labourers grew poorer.... The close contact of former days, when labourers might share a meal with farmers, had gone and as the distance between the classes grew the whole quality of their relationship altered. With this new distance, the labourer could be used and thrown aside without any regard for his dignity or even his need. It is this feeling which runs through poems like **"On a Lost Greyhound"** where Clare makes an analogy between a greyhound left to die when he can no longer catch hares, and the poor man thrown aside when the harvest is in. It is Clare's passionate resentment of this new attitude which Lord Radstock must have felt in **"Dawnings of Genius"**, a poem (on a theme made familiar by Gray) about stirrings of talent in the uneducated. Even though this is not a good poem, it has a shrewder sense of the horror than Gray gives us. Clare makes the wastage of mind directly the responsibility of the employer, who is only interested in getting the last ounce of physical labour out of a body.

Clare hated the desire for Gain, the acquisitive instinct which he could see becoming more and more powerfully the motive of action in society. And it is this, rather than a hatred of the ruling class, which lies behind the lines Lord Radstock had Taylor remove from the poem **"Helpstone"**.

> Accursed Wealth: O'er-bounding human laws,
> Of every evil thou remain'st the cause:
> Victims of want, those wretches such as me,
> Too truly lay their wretchedness to thee:
> Thou art the bar that keeps from being fed,
> And thine our loss of labour and of bread;
> Thou art the cause that levels every tree,
> And woods bow down to clear a way for thee.

Even in these early poems, such as **"Winter"** . . . , we find those physical details of the life of the poor which are Clare's greatest poetic strength in dealing with this material. As he gains confidence as a poet, his ability to record the conditions of the life he sees about him becomes as sharp and terse as Crabbe. (pp. 5-7)

Crabbe's *Parish Register,* published in 1807, is a much more polished and elegant a piece of work than Clare's **The Parish,** which was never brought to a sufficient finish for publication. But Clare's admirers have been unnecessarily apologetic for **The Parish,** for the coarseness is not entirely a demerit. In Crabbe's *Parish Register,* tone, syntax, and rhythm all assert that Crabbe has the horror of the situations he describes well under control; in Clare's **Parish** the bluntness, and trenchancy of rhythm and vocabulary suggest an angry man. (p. 7)

Clare's bitterness [in **The Parish**] is most strongly felt against the people who grew richer as the labouring class grew poorer, and in doing so lost their natural role in the village. Farmers' daughters who would in other days have helped to milk the cows now had to paint and pretend to know about poetry. He makes fun of the airs these new young ladies give themselves, and gloats a little over their difficulty in finding husbands. But his real hatred is reserved for the young men of the same class, who go about hunting or debauching young girls, in much the same spirit. And the vivacity of his hatred gives his language its quality. The characteristic short words, the preference for the many consonanted monosyllable, makes each sentence come out like a grunt or a splutter; you can hear the anger in a speaking voice.

> A dirty hog that on the puddles's brink
> Stirs up the mud and quarrels with the stink.

He put the farmers' new interest in politics in much the same class as their daughters' interest in the arts, as an affectation rather than a genuine concern, and mocks them for reading the accounts of parliamentary debates as though they were Members of Parliament themselves. As he sees it, it is just one more sign of their neglect of the proper role, one more hypocrisy; a hypocrisy very similar to the one practised in religion. They mouth liberal sentiments, as they mouth Christian sentiments. None of it prevents them from oppressing the poor.

> Who votes equality that all men share
> And stints the pauper of his parish fare.

Clare has very little trust or respect for the general process of democracy, describes elections in terms of dirty flags and ribbons, and the "hunting of votes" as a degrading pursuit. The local council he sees in the hands of the same people, serving the same interests: extortion of rates from the poor, and the punishment of dithering wretches who buy bread instead of paying them.

Of those who administer the law he has most respect for Justice Terror. Downright, severe, opinionated, his main virtue in Clare's eyes is his lack of fear of the farmers. However capricious his judgements may be, at least they are as likely to go against the farming class as the labourers. All for Church and State and no nonsense about reform—he might be a caricature of an idealised John Bull of any age up to the present. And yet it is possible to see what Clare means when he claims "The poor can name worse governors than him". Ferocity was preferable to the remote indifference of the new men. The judge's behaviour was the other side of the paternalism Clare praises so gratefully in the charity of the "good old vicar", of days gone by.

For the virtues admired by society of his own day Clare has no time. Thrift he exposes in the person of Farmer Thrifty, as a mixture of opportunism and ruthlessness; in the person of Old Saveall, as heartless avarice. He sees the old loyalties replaced by the servile willingness of creatures like Bumtagg to carry out the cruellest commands of their masters.

From such a torment of observation, Clare produced one of the fieriest political poems in the language. Perhaps more surprisingly, from 1823 onwards he also managed to produce his finest and most joyful poem of village life, **The Shepherd's Calendar.** Clare had to wait until 1827 before this poem appeared before the public; when it did it sold no more than 400 copies and attracted little praise. One reason why it did not is suggested by the review in *The Literary Gazette* where it is criticised for showing too much comfort in the life of the English peasantry. And the reviewer has noticed a quality which is remarkable. In **The Shepherd's Calendar** Clare shows us that exposure to extreme hardship brings certain joys with it. Not the implausible "content" of earlier pastoral poetry, but a well-documented, minutely particular account of moments of intense animal well-being. There may well have been readers who wanted something more picturesque and more straightforwardly pitiable. (pp. 9-11)

All through the poem Clare's peasants are alive to joy even in drudgery. In **"March"** an old woman stills her spinning wheel to go out in the lovely sunshine, pulling out a pair of scissors from her pocket to cut herself a bunch of flowers. In **"July"** the innocent sexual frolicking over lunch in the fields, gains immeasurably from the sense of exhaustion which makes rest and shade so delightful. Harvest time itself pushes every working creature to the limit of endurance. Small children have to be taken into the fields to work alongside their mothers. The sun burns

> Thro holes or openings that have lost a pin

but the mother is forced to keep the child at work by pointing out that those who are idle at harvest time go hungry the rest of the year. At last when he points to his scratched legs, and gives himself up completely to misery, she stops work long enough to comfort him with the promise of money to buy sweets on Saturday. In a situation miserably loaded with a sense of pressure, Clare makes us chiefly conscious of the tenderness between the mother and her child.

All the seasons in **The Shepherd's Calendar** have their traditional festivities, and even "Want" seems to be able to take part in them; at Christmas for instance, "Want" is able to procure a holly bough, and most children seem to have Christmas presents. All through the poem there is a simple directness of knowledge which makes Clare invaluable as a social observer. (pp. 11-12)

All Clare's critics have commented on the remarkable intensity of physical sensation in Clare's poetry, particularly in *The Shepherd's Calendar*. What is celebrated throughout the poem is in some sense animal pleasure or release, and everywhere it is the acuteness of the physical detail that we remember. When in "**February**" we read of a thaw it is the different quality of the *noises* in the warmer wetter air that we are made conscious of. The poem is full of an extraordinary exuberance which never fails to take into account the physical pressures of the life described. There can be few accounts of children's games which more vividly suggest the total absorption of childhood. Even into adolescence, there is the same possibility in the young driver of horse and cart, for instance, of being whipped to an extraordinary euphoria of the moment. . . . (pp. 17-18)

These pleasures are the more intense because they form part of a life seen on the whole as lived at the edge of total exposure. "**January**" . . . is a good example of this. Clare gives us our first sight of winter from the fireside where comfortable farmers sip ale and gossip over their papers. When he takes us outside into the world of the thresher and the hedger we feel the exposure as bitterly as stepping out of door into a cold wind. Equally, when the hedger "knocks from his shoes the caking snow" and steps into a room with a fire in it, we are made to feel the relief as physically as words can make us.

And it is not only the human beings of Clare's world who are given this kind of reality. All through *The Shepherd's Calendar* the animals are present to us with all the stench and pressure of their physical needs. Some of Clare's best lyrics describing the behaviour of animals comes from this period. And their ability to move us is never tainted with anthropomorphic sentiment. He gives them feelings, but animal feelings; they are not, in that, so different from his villagers. His observation in the second verse of "**The Hedgehog**" has the curiosity of a naturalist like Gilbert White of Selborne, whom we know he read with fascination. (But the detail of the hedgehog's tiny mouth is the observation of a poet.) The persecution of the badger is made horrible for us because the badger is cursed with terrible resources of strength and resilience which make him go on fighting. But they are animal resources. And the battering that he gets is made horribly clear to us by the noise of the poem itself. The short crude monosyllables that . . . [Clare preferred] in all the poems of this period attack us with their blunt thuds.

> Till kicked and torn and beaten out he lies
> And leaves his hold and cackles, groans and dies.

In the later poems of Clare's madness, natural description loses much of this crude immediacy. Nostalgically, poignantly, we receive our impressions at a remove. His simplest lines have an emotional tincture drawn from his own situation:

> How peaceable it seems for lonely men
> To see a crow fly in the thin blue sky.

The images he takes from Nature are given an odd, often distorting twist, which some of his critics have enjoyed far more than his earlier directness. In places, he seems to return to the simple pastoral expressions of his earliest poems. Whatever the excellence of Clare's mad poetry, the maturest ex-

pression of his descriptive talent is to be found in the years before he was removed from the ordinary circle of his village experience. (pp. 18-19)

[Clare's mental illness] was very different in character from the religious mania so marked in the madness of Cowper and Smart. Clare had never been markedly religious, though he often expresses sentiments of simple piety, and . . . he was not oppressed by a sense of guilt. Even in his madness he had no direct communication with God; indeed, in some moods he is far from certain of divine power. In "**Don Juan**" he complains that he is "sick of teazing God with prayers" and comes close to blaming God for his imprisonment in the madhouse he felt as hell on earth. The poems which speak of a calm acceptance of God's power are some of the most serene of Clare's later poems. (p. 20)

But madness opened no doors of supernatural perception to Clare. His was a bleak and lonely imprisonment, lit with flashes of rage at the world of "lying and grimace" outside the asylum. Perhaps his withdrawal from such a world was partly a relief— "a soothing silence o'er the noise of strife", but also a sort of paralysis which he talks of constantly as a "freezing", sometimes a "freezing to stone". And in this new state of being his poetry too suffers a remarkable change.

There are still poems packed with details, touches like the description of a "green woodpecker" looking for "rotten trees to clink" which might have come out of *The Shepherd's Calendar*. Others make use of metaphors which are new and often sinister, as though madness had woken in Clare a new pattern of making connections. In "**A Rhapsody**", for instance, coming night is described as

> All dark and absent as a corpse's eye.

These images are surprising, but often pleasing and appropriate. There are poems, however, which show a much more marked break with the kind of poetry Clare wrote while still at home. (p. 21)

[One] of the exciting qualities of Clare's mature descriptive poetry was the pursuit of a verbal equivalent for physical reality. In many of the lyrics of Clare's madness he abandons this aim completely. He seems more attracted to abstract and literary phrases, and even to be deliberately rejecting dialect expression, or indeed, any words gross in texture. At the same time he permits himself to write more coarsely than ever before in the satirical poem "**Don Juan**". This splitting of his vocabulary into two restricted ranges may well be connected with an unresolved split in his attitude towards sex, something which runs through all his mad writing. He has at one and the same time a violent hatred for the whole of the female sex, and an ethereal and spiritualised passion for his lost love Mary Joyce. Sometimes the two feelings appear in one letter. Perhaps because his narrow vocabulary in the lyrics to Mary reflects some such torment, the lyrics do not read conventionally, although they lack all the qualities we associate with Clare's mature poetry.

It is their music which is remarkable. Clare had always been interested in the Elizabethans, and had, earlier in his life, succeeded in passing off pastiches of Elizabethan writers as genuine. In these last lyrics he uses what he had learnt of their skill in the disposition of syllables to make subtle patterns of sound, which, far more than any content of the words, create a pleasing melancholy.

Some of his experiments with sound are extremely sophisticated. In the poem ["**Child Harold**"] he plays an intricate game with stress and expectancy. Reading the first verse we are conscious of points of strain occurring when the refrain comes back because it has a very definite rhythm, and that rhythm is different from the preceding line that it rhymes with. Short lines rhyming in the centre of each verse help to control the cadences very tightly; and in the second verse it is a real relief to have the refrain at the end of the verse falling on the expected notes.

These lyrics to his lost love are poems which the admirers of Clare's late period have found particularly ensnaring; and certainly they are a delight to read. To prefer them to the last products of his mature mind working as a whole, however, is another matter; critics should not allow themselves to be too romantically attached to the idea of Mary's visionary presence.

For Clare's satirical poetry of this period there has been less admiration; and this is on the whole just. "**Don Juan**" is not incomprehensible nor inconsistent; but it is also neither direct nor first-hand, like the satire we find in *The Parish*. (p. 22)

[The] main excitement of ["**Don Juan**"] derives from the element of pastiche. Clare catches at Byron's casual spontaneity with considerable grace. The reader is inclined to value the poem mainly as an exercise in tone, almost as a game. And in this Clare is certainly successful. He controls the sound of the verse admirably. Rather as in the lovely lyrics discussed earlier, Clare seems in his satirical mood also to be more interested in the control of sound than the sense.

We may come now to the position of Clare's mad poetry in the whole body of his work. It has certainly won disproportionate praise. Symons, for instance, says that: "Clare's poetry begins by having something clogging in it; substance and poetical substance is there, but the poetry has hardly worked its way out to freedom" [see excerpt above, 1908], and Grigson is so attracted to the evanescent vision of Mary, that he speaks of her affecting Clare as Hölderlin was affected by his Diotima. Generally, it is the "freedom" Clare's madness brought his poetry, which has won admiration. And there is a sense in which there is a new freedom, partly a new connective faculty of metaphor (though that is rarer in these poems than a reading of the critics might lead one to think), partly a new and real excitement in the use of sound.

But many of those who find greatness in these last poems of Clare do so because they are anxious to find in him a spirituality his earlier poetry is without. It is easy to make the mistake of Taylor, Clare's first editor, who blamed him for letting the description prevail over the sentiment. Clare's maturest means of expression came from his sense of the solidity of "the real world". And there is little of this quality in the bleak and alienated movements of his mad poetry. (pp. 24-5)

Elaine Feinstein, in an introduction to Selected Poems *by John Clare, University Tutorial Press Ltd., 1968, pp. 1-25.*

THOMAS R. FROSCH (essay date 1971)

[*Frosch analyzes the successive modifications in visual, auditory, and synesthetic imagery in Clare's poetry. According to Frosch, these stylistic variations are indicative of the dominant theme of Clare's verse—the mutability of both nature and his perception of it—and represent Clare's lifelong "attempt to come to terms with the problematical experience of change."*]

For Clare the landscape is never twice the same, and the poet's sensitivity to its alterations, and his own, is such that the description of a scene becomes an act of powerful confrontation with natural and human mutability. That both the describer and the described are constantly changing, along with the corollary that the quality and identity of each at a given moment is dependent upon the other, constitutes the overreaching theme of Clare's poetry, and he frequently treats it explicitly. In the Wordsworthian "**Swordy Well**," for example, the landscape has changed because the poet loves it in another way than he did as a child, not as the secure environment of play, but as the manifestation in all its minutiae of a wonder and a power that minimize man in a comforting way. And the landscape has changed in "**Cowper**," because it has, actually in itself, been transfigured by art:

> And every place the poet trod
> And every place the poet sung
> Are like the Holy Land of God,
> In every month, on every tongue.

My argument is that Clare is enacting the confrontation with such changes even when he seems to be giving us description for its own sake; that in his moments of apparently "pure" description his stylistic manners, his ways of describing, are the gestures of a dramatic situation; and that the large imaginative drama that unifies his career, the attempt to come to terms with the problematical experience of change, can be read in the modifications in his way of portraying natural objects. Indeed, such a reading suggests that the changes of style function as the poet's dialectical counterattack to the sense of loss that was apparently, to the man who died in Northampton Asylum, unendurably acute.

A comparison of two poems ["**The Lark's Nest**," from a sequence of pieces on birds and nests written between 1825 and 1835, and "**Birds' Nests**," the last poem Clare wrote, dated variously between 1860 and 1864] on one of Clare's favorite subjects will highlight these modifications. (p. 137)

Both poems are subtly expressive, developing images of secure repose and fresh life, but they proceed quite differently. "**The Lark's Nest**" exhibits a series of static pictures; the poet's eye focuses upon a succession of objects—bird, eggs, nest—set before him one by one, and he is concerned with graphic detail and completeness of description. Motion, when it does appear in the imagery, is modulated toward the stationary: the dripping of the rain from the wheat suggests a hypnotizing regularity; the lark's flight is a picture frozen in the past, brought in as a piece of information to enrich the current perception. The total scene is experienced as a display, and the crucial action in the poem is that of the observer's eye, as if moving through a page, turning from object to object in a clearly arranged visual field and finally coming upon the new egg.

The fixed quality of this piece and the centering of the description upon its topic are absent in "**Birds' Nests**." Here, the poet's attention is attracted by phenomena seemingly peripheral to his subject, the nests, which indeed make their appearance only by inference in the second line. Instead, Clare is interested in the back-and-forth flying of the bird, singing as it builds its nest; the wind blowing across the fen; the cow chewing her cud; the warm glowing of the south; and the warm shining of the sun. The scene is developed through the juxtaposition of apparently random details, and the style of transition . . . creates an effect of simultaneous activities surrounding the observer and competing for his attention. A greater

Clare's cottage at Northborough.

concentration of active verbs to carry the descriptive burden (6 in 7 lines, as opposed to 6 in 16 lines) reinforces the feeling of movement. The scene is captured as it flashes by, as it imposes itself upon the poet's senses.

The first poem, then, has the character of a studied set of observations. It is an exemplification of a phenomenon, relatively abstracted from time and process; and in presenting his scene Clare sets up his images rather like props on a stage. The second poem offers a direct, momentary perception, in which a sense of time is evoked not only in the structuring of the images, but also in the localization of the experience as an instant of early springtime. The poet appears in both poems as part of the total scene, but in the first he is the observer, the subject marking the details of the landscape, and he is also our knowledgeable guide; while in the second the world is no longer at rest, and its motion includes the poet: he is a piece of what he perceives, object of the bird's spell, implicitly the primary recipient of the effects of wind and sun. Both nests belong to a complex of figures of secret space, a spot within nature which still offers the intimacy and the renewal that, in the poet's memory, once characterized the entire landscape. Such a space is Clare's naturalistic version of Shelley's island in "Epipsychidion," the "wreck of Paradise." But the feeling of personal involvement in the scene in the second poem intimates that Clare is now conscious that looking at a nest is, what under the surface it always was for him, a matter of looking for it.

Clare's late poetry, in general, shows a marked tendency to regard fleeting rather than fixed objects, and a dominant attraction to glimmerings, shadows, motion, fluidity. The change is from a primarily spatial orientation, in which time is deliberately minimized, and phenomena are generalized and so endowed with timelessness, to a temporal scheme, in which things are perceived as happening and passing. Contrary to the persistent notion of Clare as a poet who moved away from the particulars of nature into a radically internalized poetic mode, this is a change from a landscape of mental abstraction to one of direct perception, in that an interest in the typical structure of an event is replaced by an interest in the experience of the event as something singular. The early urge toward a thoroughness of precise description would seem to be, among other things, an encyclopedic procedure that removes the object from immediate experience, giving us a version of it that will generally hold true (stressing, for example, the color of the lark's egg and the composition of its nest), and with the kind of organization and the degree of detail that are only available to study and calculation; this, in contrast to a version which is true only for a specific instant (stressing the bleak wind and the cow chewing her cud), and which tries to register the shock of confrontation.

The early desire for timelessness and abstraction is even more evident in a second strategy, one that, like the strategy of descriptive completeness and "objectivity," is instinctive, rather

than programmatic. The early landscape is an insistently moralized one, as Clare reads universal meanings in the countryside; nature is experienced as a text, and the Peasant Poet is
its sensitive interpreter. Thus, Clare tells us in **"The Voice of
Nature"** that natural objects are symbols, the alphabet of God's
language: "In nature's open book I read, and see / Beauty's
rich lesson in this seeming-pea. . . ." The landscape is the
common book in which "all may read and meet with joy
again," and nature is an intermediary between the poet's sensibility and an order and being beyond the perceptual. The
early poems, heavily influenced by Clare's readings in Thomson and other eighteenth-century landscape poets, may occasionally seem predictable in their diction and philosophy, but
Clare's distinctive power in the tradition of the *paysage moral-
isé* [moralized landscape] is rooted in his belief, fulfilled in
practice, that the meanings of nature are only to be found
through acute observation of the specifics of the landscape.
"Crowds see no magic in the trifling thing. . . ."

The response of reading universal meanings, to a great extent,
drops out in the late work. Now when Clare generalizes from
what he sees, he does so about its relationship to himself, its
personal significations, and the ways in which it is intertwined
with his consciousness. But, most often, he has moved from
a pictorial recording of the landscape to a direct, sensuous
encounter with it. There is a new urgency of observation; the
meeting of man and landscape is a confrontation of the poet's
senses and emotions with the immediate data of experience.
Coherence is now sought not in interpretation, but at the perceptual level. (pp. 138-40)

Clare's growing tendency away from the static and the typical
and toward the fluid and the accidental involves, at its roots,
a change in the sensory disposition of his images. Several
modes of visual imagery can be distinguished in his work. The
early poetry is primarily a verse of what we tend to consider
the normal eye, which sees objects firmly established within
the cone of pictorial perspective. In a second mode, that of
"Birds' Nests" and **"Beanfield,"** the poet focuses on the edges
of the perspectival field, the horizons and the vanishing points;
and the landscape is no longer solidly centered before him, but
glittering and elusive. Many of the poems in this style are about
vanishing itself, and in them Clare tries to catch objects in
their moments of departure, to actually look at the phenomenon
of disappearance.

A step beyond this is a third mode, in which one might say
that the poet's eye breaks through the vanishing point. The
conventional structure of perspectival sight, with its boundaries, its static pictorialism, and its clear spatial relations of
objects to each other and to the anchor of the observing self,
breaks down, and we are in a new world, which the poet
sometimes calls "eternity." But the onset of a visionary style
of imagery is not to be taken as a shift from material to spiritual,
or from observation to introspection; it is, rather, a sensory
reorganization, in which the visual phenomena earlier assigned
to the edges of sight have become centralized. The manifestations of motion and the elusive effects of light that are subordinated in the world of **"The Lark's Nest"** have become the
predominant, and often sole, appearances of a dimension which
is non-pictorial, flexible in its spatial relationships, a world
we would tend to describe in terms not of the solid and the
visual, but of the fluid and the auditory.

Clare was never satisfied with the normative landscape of the
perspectival eye. In his **"Essay on Landscape,"** he praises the
paintings of Peter De Wint because they are free from what
he calls the artificial tricks of perspectival composition. The
landscape cannot accurately be arranged within such containing
borders, because it has no real perceptual limits in itself and
is endlessly open to sensory exploration. In De Wint, "the eye
is led over the Landscape as far as a sunbeam can reach & the
sky & earth blends into a humanity of greetings & beautiful
harmony & symmetry of pleasant imaginings—There is no
harsh stoppage no bounds to space or any outline further then
there is in nature." But, contrary to Clare's suggestion, this
is not a type of seeing that we customarily experience. The
technical problem underlying the changes in his style is that
of English Romanticism in general: to reject the perspectival
eye and still keep within a world of direct perception. Clare
wanted greater accuracy in representing a world that is not
fixed but moves and changes, a landscape that appears to the
poetic, not the bodily eye.

Driven toward such new vision, the poet of *Child Harold*, like
Wordsworth, is attracted to moments in which the perspectival
outlines become blurred:

> Sweet comes the misty mornings in September
> Among the dewy paths how sweet to stray
> Greensward or stubbles as I well remember
> I once have done—the mist curls thick & gray
> As cottage smoke—like the net work on the spray
> Or seeded grass the cobweb draperies run
> Beaded with pearls of dew at early day
> & o'er the pleachy stubbles peeps the sun
> The lamp of day when that of night is done.

It is as if the breakdown of ordinary visual form, asserted
through the images of mist, smoke, network, and cobweb draperies, produces the benevolent dawn; and, read in the context
of Clare's overarching quest, the lines seem to describe not a
return from night to day, but a penetration through night, via
a midworld of blended sight and memory, to another landscape.

Increasingly a poet of mist and darkness, Clare reaches for a
dimension just beyond the vanishing point, and that new area
of awareness is associated with a feeling of eternity; for now
the distinctions and the limits of the eye are disintegrated into
a sense of boundlessness, the so-called oceanic consciousness.
But Clare's interest cannot be termed a *mysticism* of nature,
for, like Wordsworth, Shelley, and Keats, he tries to constitute
such consciousness in a form of direct bodily apprehension.
Like them also, he frequently achieves this through a shift from
the visual to the auditory or the synesthetic. Often [as in *Child
Harold*] it seems that sight is in the process of dissolving into
sound:

> This twilight seems a veil of gause & mist
> Trees seem dark hills between the earth & sky
> Winds sob awake & then a gusty hist
> Fanns through the wheat like serpents gliding bye. . . .

Such lines require a literal response, for, as **"Swordy Well"**
explains, the landscape exists as the poet perceives it. Here,
metaphor assumes the force of transformation, as the trees of
daylight perception are replaced by the hills of twilight perception. "Seems," however, implies that the poet is not sure;
indeed this is precisely a state in which no visual appearance
can be ascertained. Contrast the definitiveness with which the
auditory is developed, as the winds "sob awake" and assume,
in the figure of the serpents, the unequivocal presence of embodiment.

Auditory imagery increases in Clare as the world of the eye becomes consciously problematic, a dimension of loss, as Clare recognizes that appearances will not maintain themselves in the timeless structure of perspectivism. The ear provides consolation, and the poet, unable to see what he wishes, is soothed [in *Child Harold*] by "Sounds, soft as visions murmured oer in bed." He is "wrecked of all hopes" and wishes only for the hidden solitude of the forest where he can hear "the clapping gate / & voices calling to the rambling cows." . . . His poetry of despair is filled with such appeals to the ear. . . . (pp. 141-43)

But the ear can help provide, more than consolation, a complete perceptual and emotional renovation, as in the last stanza of **"Evening,"** in which the remaking of the scene through the unifying tone of the moonlight and the sound of the nightingale simultaneously remakes the poet from one who gazes at the scene to one who is involved, elatedly, in it. . . . [In **"Evening,"**] Clare's descriptions of apparently ordinary scenes are, at a deep level, stylistic battlegrounds, in which the poet is fighting free of the despair and isolation ultimately produced by a static perspective that detaches the viewer from his moving world.

In the preceding illustrations Clare has effected a poetic transformation either by replacement (sounds for sights) or through a natural mediating agent (mist, darkness, moonlight). But in the following lines [from *Child Harold*] he goes further by simply converting, without external mediation, a single figure, (the beloved) from visible ("painted") to auditory ("replies") and finally to visionary ("sun"):

> Can fancy read the feeling painted there
> —Those hills of snow that on her bosom lies—
> Or beauty speak for all those sweet replies
> That through love's visions like the sun is breaking. . . .

Love's visions, in the context of Clare's poetry, are prospects of loss; love's vocal replies are intimations of presence or return. Here, perceptual possibilities have become counters for the poet to play with as he builds a new, responsive landscape.

Thematically, *Child Harold* involves precisely this attempt to translate Mary Joyce, the lost love of Clare's youth, into the new landscape, thus to recover her permanently in the dimension of boundlessness. Now she is absent from his sight, and nothing in the visible world can bring back her appearance:

> I've sought her in the fields & flowers
> I've sought her in the forest groves
> In avenues & shaded bowers
> & every scene that Mary loves
> E'en round her home I seek her here
> But Mary's abscent everywhere. . . .

In a later poem ["**Stanza**"] he can no longer even remember what she looked like: "Black absence hides upon the past, / I quite forget thy face. . . ." But she still lives for him in the world of sound; and so, in . . . *Child Harold*, he sketches an explicitly paradisiacal landscape organized according to the sound of bells associated with her. . . . [In tone] this is a poetry traced with dejection and a sense of ultimate defeat. The poet is in one world, Mary in another; Clare in *Child Harold* characteristically writes about the world of sound as one yearning for it, but feeling that essentially he does not belong to it. The static, pictorial world of *The Shepherd's Calendar* has shattered for Clare, and in *Child Harold* he passes through a phase of intense, troubled concentration on the vanishing point, the lo-

cation of disappearance, in an effort to make that fled world "evergreen."

But the verse of the final Northampton period is one that, with a greater sense of imaginative poise, hovers at the vanishing point, sometimes breaking through it into a landscape wholly liberated from the poet's past. Now, even when he takes up the role of the lover and observer of nature, the landscape he cherishes is that of the ear. . . . (pp. 143-45)

Clare's late handling of two of his crucial topics, wind and autumn, strikingly illuminates his development. The wind usually appears in his landscape as a signal of loss; it is an emblem of the imminent destruction that almost always contextualizes his visions of happy scenes. Often, as in **"Birds' Nests,"** he counterposes it to an imagery of security and renovation. Accordingly, **"Winter Winds Cold and Blea"** is structured upon an opposition of the harsh winds and the warm, welcoming bosom of a lover waiting for the speaker indoors: "Free from the chilly air / I will meet thee." But in the late poem, **"The Wind Waves o'er the Meadows Green,"** the wind is no longer one element in the scene, but the entire scene itself. . . . (p. 145)

[Clare repeatedly wrote] of spring and autumn, portraying them as the exact instants of transformation, the entrance and departure of phenomena in his field of sight. But autumn, especially, is for him "the sweetest of any" season (**"The Dark Days of Autumn"**). As the vanishing point of the life of the landscape, it is the problem his senses and imagination must confront, and his handling of the theme provides the reader with a clear pathway into the expressive drama carried out in his descriptive style. Over and over he is drawn to watch and contemplate things in their departure, and the situation is treated with a powerful ambivalence, for as autumnal phenomena pass into a "black absence" of the eye, they potentially provide the poet's senses with a juncture to the landscape of sound. So, in **"The Dark Days of Autumn,"** Clare is able to celebrate the moment in which the prospect of fulfillment is lost, and there is "Scarce a wild blossom left to enliven the scene": "I love to see yellow leaves fall in my song." Observing how the winds sing around the dying leaves, he exults in the changes: "There's health i' the strife o't and joy i' the sound." Like dawn, mist, evening, and moonlight, the season blurs distinctions as its colors unify the landscape. Like the wind, it makes things over in the aspect of transformation: "Look where we may, the scene is strange and new, / And every object wears a changing hue" (**"An Autumn Morning"**).

"Autumn" ("I love the fitful gust") and **"The Autumn's Wind"** are composed entirely in an imagery of sound, motion, and blurred visibilia, as Clare attempts to capture the effects of the wind: smoke from cottages, falling acorns, the ruffled feathers of birds, the suddenly upturned gray undersides of poplar leaves. The objects before his eyes are literally being blown out of sight, and the experience is strangly comforting to him. . . . In these poems, Clare seems to derive consolation from confronting the source of his anguish and his loss. He is in the aftermath of the painful deprivations. Frequently there is something in the tone of his Northampton work that resembles the detachment of tragic knowledge, and this combines with an urgency about rendering things not as they are, but as he finds them in the moment, to give his late work its distinctive flavor.

Of the autumnal pieces, **"Autumn"** ("The thistledown's flying" . . .) has the most radical imagery and is a poem in which Clare explicitly breaks through observation of the vanishings into something new. The strangeness of the setting is established at once, as everything in the poem appears in furious motion even though there is no wind. The objects of this landscape are no longer fixed in their forms and qualities; they are violently changing identity before the eye, burning, glittering, metamorphosing. A spring boils and bubbles like liquid in a blazing pot; the parched ground is like overbaked bread; the fields glitter like water; "gossamers twitter, flung from weed unto weed." In the last stanza, the lyric, ostensibly a naturalistic account of an ordinary phenomenon, breaks loose into a vision of a new world created through conflagration:

> Hill-tops like hot iron glitter bright in the sun,
> And the rivers we're eying burn to gold as they run;
> Burning hot is the ground, liquid gold is the air;
> Whoever looks round sees Eternity there.

Thus Clare elaborates a simple comparison of the color of autumn and the color of flame. But the elaboration, depending upon the sudden possession of the visual field by the flickering effects of light and color, the things passing in the corners of the eyes, is one that would not have occurred to Clare in his early work. Compare [this to "**September**"] of *The Shepherd's Calendar,* in which the poet wanders

> Where autumn's shadows idly muse
> And tinge the trees in many hues:
> Amid whose scenes I'm fain to dwell,
> And sing of what I love so well. . . .

The early gesture of description has another purpose: the poet is trying to preserve the cycle of rural life, raising it to a timeless, stationary plane through the generalized documentations of a loving eye-witness. (pp. 146-48)

One notes, looking back through the pre-*Child Harold* verse, that Clare was always drawn to the auditory, the flowing, and the transitional, and, most of all, that he was always concerned with the signs of vanishing. But in his late work these attractions monopolize his perception, with the effect that he sees a totally different landscape. In the Northampton scenes of autumn, we are at the moment of passing beyond the limits of the world of *The Shepherd's Calendar,* a world we accept as the one we ordinarily experience. That landscape lies behind Clare in fragments, and he is forced, both by circumstances and his own desires, to try to see his way through to a new one. And he is a poet with no organization of ideas or beliefs external to his verse to aid him in this quest, nor anything, ultimately, with which to answer the changes of nature except the changes of his poetic style. (p. 149)

> *Thomas R. Frosch, "The Descriptive Style of John Clare," in* Studies in Romanticism, *Vol. 10, No. 1, Winter, 1971, pp. 137-49.*

JANET M. TODD   (essay date 1973)

[*Todd's expressed purpose in* In Adam's Garden: A Study of John Clare's Pre-Asylum Poetry, *from which the following excerpt is drawn, is to trace the central themes of Clare's poetry, "the eulogistic images of the golden age for society and of Eden for nature," and to illustrate "the essential distinction of Clare's mode from the dominant Romantic mode of the early nineteenth century." Here Todd contrasts Clare's evocation of the early golden age of society, written in the tradition of eighteenth-century descriptive poetry, with that of the Romantic pastoralists. In addition, she discusses Clare's conflicting attitudes toward pre-enclosure rural society as evidenced in the poems "Helpstone," "The Village Minstrel," "Rural Morning," "Autumn," and* The

Shepherd's Calendar. *For additional recent studies contrasting Clare's poetry with that of the major Romantics, see L. J. Swingle (1975) and W. J. Keith (1980).*]

Against the ever increasing poverty and bleakness of his life in the first half of the 1820s, Clare set the ideal of an earlier society, one which he felt he had known as a child and, as an adult, was seeing in its decline. This society had a harmony of elements, a sufficiency of means, and an essential equality of persons, all qualities that were slowly disappearing from his contemporary village. The society lived in harmony with external nature, neither plundering it nor completely controlling it, and it followed in its work and play the elemental fluctuations of time and season. In Clare's early poetry, this ideal, still partially realized by the society of his early maturity, is often referred to as golden. . . . It was in the tradition of Thomsonian descriptive poetry that Clare began to write seriously, and he was clearly influenced by the conception of the golden age he found in Thomson and in the other eighteenth-century poets whom he subsequently read. (p. 5)

By the time of Clare's second book of poems [*The Village Minstrel*] . . . , and more obviously by his third [*The Shepherd's Calendar*] . . . , the georgic descriptive poem was clearly past its heyday. The new dominant mode of describing rural matters developed from the Romantic pastoral, a combination of idealized English country descriptions and the poet-swain's responses. This was the mode of Wordsworth, in whose poetry nature became the vehicle of emotions and the spiritual companion of isolated men rather than a harmonious background to a rural community. The descriptive poem over which the new genre had triumphed thus came to seem anachronistic to the reading public; yet Clare, in spite of growing evidence of its critical defeat, continued in this mode. . . . (p. 9)

Clare in the early 1820s was writing in a genre that differed in its genesis and development from that adopted by most of his fashionable contemporaries. It is thus important to differentiate his golden age from that of the Romantic pastoralists like Wordsworth. Wordsworth's golden age country setting is derived from his belief that the most elemental passions are found most purely in the rustic situation, and it did not purport to be a realistic description of the externals of his society. However, since their subject was the social details themselves, the exponents of the descriptive poem tended to avoid idealization, aiming to present an actual picture of whatever society they knew. Clare's need for a model society . . . had to be served by the actual society he knew, although his use of his childhood and early adulthood provided the distance necessary to turn the real into an ideal. Clare's unique contribution to the georgic is that he located his ideal much closer in time to the moment of the poem than was usually the case. By doing so, he made the ideal as much a subject of his poetry as the world of reality which it was used to measure. But at the same time its temporal closeness to the present argues that Clare's ideal society at best is flawed; it is a perfection that yet must accommodate human imperfection.

"**Helpstone,**" the first poem of Clare's first volume, *Poems Descriptive of Rural Life and Scenery,* provides an early example of the imperfection of the social ideal. The poem is a traditional topographical one, a description of a place with the narrator as both poet and perceiver within the poem. The narrator contemplates the town, and the prospect calls to his mind his vanished childhood in this setting. In lines that echo Gray's evocation of childhood in an earlier topographical poem, "Ode on a Distant Prospect of Eton College,'' the adjective ''golden'' is used to evoke the golden society of Clare's youth:

> And, oh! those years of infancy the scene,
> Those dear delights, where once they all have been,
> Those golden days, long vanish'd from the plain,
> Those sports, those pastimes, now belov'd in vain;
> When happy youth in pleasure's circle ran,
> Nor thought what pains awaited future man. . . .

The poem is a nostalgic lament for past joys and for a land that has been destroyed by enclosures; the poet sorrows for both ''the vanish'd green'' and his own time of greenness: ''But now, alas! those scenes exist no more; / The pride of life with thee, like mine, is o'er.'' At the end the narrator relates his childhood and that of the land to a lost golden age in a combined apostrophe to Helpstone and his past: ''Oh, happy Eden of those golden years / Which memory cherishes, and use endears.'' Here, then, it seems that Clare has already a conception of a golden age, and is locating it in the immediate past of his childhood. Yet, even thus distanced, the ideal is modified, and the modification reveals how ambivalent Clare's attitude is to the pre-enclosure village. Helpstone is described on the one hand as a paradise and on the other as ''humble,'' ''mean,'' ''unletter'd,'' and a place of ''useless ignorance.'' The final section of the poem with its undiluted nostalgia for ''those charms of youth'' and for ''home'' seems more an ignoring of the facts he has stated than a resolving of them. (pp. 11-12)

[''**The Village Minstrel**''] is a long poem, written in Spenserian stanzas, a form perhaps suggested to Clare by Thomson's ''Castle of Indolence'' or James Beattie's ''Minstrel.'' In many ways an unsatisfactory work in its discursiveness, sentimentality, and ambivalence, it yet presents most clearly the view of himself, his life, his art, and his society that Clare held in his earliest poetic years. Of this view, sentimentality and ambivalence are integral parts. Sentimentality conveys, through the self-indulgence that allows it, the horror that Clare felt at his lonely situation. It also excuses to some extent the passivity of the response he made at this time to the forces destroying his society. The ambivalence comes, as in ''**Helpstone**,'' from the juxtaposition of idyllic and sordid aspects of rural society. Sometimes the latter are embedded in predominantly idyllic passages; sometimes they are isolated as the unique characteristics of a later age. This later, post-enclosure age is thus certainly unpleasant, but the pre-enclosure one is not entirely golden. Once again, then, the detailed description of the georgic mode, combined with the temporal closeness of the age he described, mitigated against Clare's presentation of a simple ideal for a complex reality.

In the first section of ''**The Village Minstrel**,'' the village is a society that lives in harmony with nature; it has left the wild places relatively untouched for the poet Lubin to wander in, and it marks the progress of the seasons with traditional festivities. It is a place of social harmony among the different classes, where man and master drink together and where workers toil in social freedom in the open fields. It is a place too of innocent rural love. At the same time, however, the village is a center of rowdiness and gossip, of ''parish-huts where want is shov'd to die,'' and of ''harden'd brutes,'' whose insensitive cruelty destroys women as it later destroys nature. . . . (pp. 12-13)

Likewise, the presentation of Lubin, the narrator-poet and an image of Clare, is complex. In the initial stanza of the poem,

he is a ''humble rustic,'' humming ''his lowly dreams,'' singing ''what nature and what truth inspires.'' The other side of his situation is made clear in the second stanza where he is a ''luckless clown,'' treated with ''black neglect,'' whose fancy is worn down by ''toil and slavery.'' A further modification of the picture of the rustic swain is effected by the third stanza, which describes his father as a ''hind born to the flail and plough, / To thump the corn out and to till the earth.'' The vocabulary here reinforces the contrast with the initial stanza, for the plainness is far from the poetic diction, the ''muse,'' ''charms,'' and ''pastures,'' of the opening of the poem.

In the second section of ''**The Village Minstrel**,'' Clare describes the coming of enclosure. After this event, the picture presented of the pre-enclosure world loses much of its complexity, and the idyllic, natural, harmonious side of the older village is emphasized almost to the exclusion of the cruel and insensitive elements that Clare had recorded earlier and that had, in a way, allowed the enclosure movement to proceed. Sitting with the shepherds to bewail the loss of the past, the poet finds he can remember only the golden characteristics of the old village life, its festivities, its freedom, and its harmonious relationship with nature. . . . (p. 14)

The effect of the social change on Lubin is similarly uncomplicating. Where his attitude had been ambivalent toward the society which he had at once revered and yet constantly escaped from into nature, after the coming of enclosure it is one of total sympathy with the dispossessed peasants. His alienation from the dominant men who have forced the enclosures on his village therefore needs no qualification. So, too, he finds himself at one with the land that has been despoiled, and he can take a simile for himself from the enclosed world. He is like a ''cornflower'' in a field of grain, the isolated natural being whose kind once covered the whole land before man-controlled grain was sown in usurpation. Lubin claims an identification with a society with which he was, before its destruction, only in partial accord, and he has given that society a natural rightness that it only partly possessed when it existed as a chronological actuality. (pp. 14-15)

In the poems that followed Clare's publication of his first volume of poetry, the contrast between the ideal and unpleasant aspects of village society was often made deliberately and effectively through juxtaposition, reinforced by a contrast between literary and colloquial diction. In ''**Rural Morning**'' . . . , for example, the idyllic aspects of the rural scene are juxtaposed to the brutish in the figures of the horseboy Hodge and the maiden. The former's gait is ''soodling,'' while the girl is as ''sweet as the thyme that blossoms where she kneels.''

An even more effective, deliberate use of the contiguity of details is found in ''**Autumn**.'' . . . The harmonious picture of rural folk, rustic boys, cowboys, and scrambling shepherds, all in a setting of red-berried trees under ''thin-spun clouds,'' is qualified by the presentation of the other side of rural society, the murdering gunner whose destructive act breaks this harmony, just as surely as winter destroys the pageant of autumn. In this poem, both the literary experience of the season, which is the contemplation by the poet of natural harmony, and the country folk's active experience of it are modified, the former by the cruelty of man, the latter by the cruelty of winter. Thus the poem presents a drama of winter overtaking summer:

> More coldly blows the autumn-breeze;
> Old winter grins a blast between;
> The north-winds rise and strip the trees,
> And desolation shuts the scene. . . .

But there is another drama, that of a poet trying to create an image of a golden society into which the other cruel reality he knows intrudes:

> But hide thee, muse, the woods among,
>   Nor stain thy artless, rural rhymes;
> Go leave the murderer's wiles unsung,
>   Nor mark the harden'd gunner's crimes. . . .
>   (pp. 16-17)

Most of the poems of Clare's early volumes deal with the pre-enclosure rustic society and himself within that society. Very rarely is the presentation simply of either an ideal society or a degenerate one. The contradictions and complexities of the world he portrays reflect Clare's attitude toward the society he had both revered and avoided as a child and youth, and reveal the difficulties inherent in the use of childhood as an ideal. As he studied more deeply his rustic neighbors, and considered the struggle and hardship of his own adulthood, the balance he had achieved and exploited, in such poems as **"Autumn,"** between the golden and tarnished aspects of reality was gradually destroyed. The tension created by the disturbance of such a balance and the straining of the poet to re-establish it give to Clare's depictions of the twilight of pre-enclosure England an emotional and dramatic interest that is not usually characteristic of georgic descriptive poetry. These qualities are pre-eminently seen in *The Shepherd's Calendar,* where the use of a contemporary setting exacerbates the problem of the intrusion of unpleasant aspects of reality into the ideal. (p. 17)

[*The Shepherd's Calendar* is] primarily a description of the qualified golden age of Clare's early maturity. He does not always differentiate the pre- and post-enclosure ages, but it seems that the time of the poem is Clare's present, in a partially enclosed society. Throughout the poem there are suggestions that the golden age is not at its height, effected primarily through the juxtaposition of idyllic scenes depicting the harmony of man with nature with those that clearly state his separation from it. The decadence is further implied in the poet's frequently expressed nostalgia for early childhood, seen as a better time than the present of the poem. There is, however, within *The Shepherd's Calendar,* demonstrated by **"August,"** a progression to something approaching the iron age, a progression that is not a linear development but a cumulative one. Each month has contrasting, juxtaposed aspects, but the later months have rather more of the iron age characteristics than the early ones.

Appropriate to a poem organized on the seasons and describing the iron age characteristics incrementally as the months pass, the new age is often associated with winter. Just as the year declines into winter from the harmony and joy of the spring months, in the same way the movement toward the iron age is a decline and can be expressed in terms of the annual fall into winter. In keeping with this parallel, the enclosure movement, the chief symbol for the new wintry age, has the same effect on nature as winter itself: in **"November"** a "dreary nakedness the field deforms," and in many enclosure poems, such as **"The Mores,"** a similar nakedness and deformity result from the winter man brings. November's wintry bareness is then prophetic of the coming bareness from enclosure, a bareness which is not, however, a prelude to a new spring. (pp. 20-1)

The Shepherd's Calendar is Clare's last long descriptive poem and his last sustained attempt to describe the pre-enclosure village society. After this, . . . he turned increasingly for his subjects to nature and his own sensibility, the prevailing topics

of the poetry in his age. *The Shepherd's Calendar* marks the end of a phase of Clare's poetic life. Yet, in spite of his progression from it and in spite of its unpopularity with post-Romantic readers, Clare's treatment of his society in his early poems does not represent an anachronistic dead end which he followed because of his isolation from Romantic theory and practice. Clare wrote in a genre that has not retained its popularity, but one which has qualities of visual precision and factual truthfulness lacking in more subjective genres. Because of these qualities, Clare's early poems present collectively a picture of rural society which is nowhere attempted by the major Romantic poets and which is rare in all English literature. (pp. 26-7)

Janet M. Todd, in her In Adam's Garden: A Study of John Clare's Pre-Asylum Poetry, *University of Florida Press, 1973, 83 p.*

PETER LEVI, S.J. (lecture date 1975)

[*In* John Clare and Thomas Hardy, *from which the following excerpt is drawn, Levi bases his comparison of the two authors on the similarities between the language of their writings. One of the few critics to provide a study of Clare's prose, Levi argues that it is "freer, wilder and more striking than his poetry."*]

If I say there is something uniquely genuine, a special greenness of the sap, in John Clare, I am not to deny there is something else genuine in Keats, in Shelley, in Dr Johnson both in prose and poetry, and in Gilbert White of Selborne. What was important in John Clare's genuineness was neither the extremity of his madness nor the sweetness and harshness of his rural youth. They do mark him and limit him and define him. But in his artistry his workshop was the English language, and what is genuine in him can be seen and felt as language. That is the only medium in which we know him. When Clare says of the judgement of the common people about Byron at his funeral that 'the breathings of eternity and the soul of time are indicated in that prophecy' and when Dr Johnson says that 'In lexicography, as in other arts, naked science is too delicate for the purposes of life', one is conscious of a community in the language even between utterly different writers. (p. 5)

John Clare presented himself as a deep witness to rural tradition in language and in life. He was, and he knew he was, a quiet, intense observer of a world that was dying. He was brought up in the traditional, rather organic world of English villages before the enclosures. He laments enclosures as the physical and spiritual annihilation of that world. It is hard today to believe things were so simple, not longer drawn out, but on the evidence of his own remarkable and detailed observations, he seems to be right. So many poets have lost so many paradises in the course of English history, but we should take John Clare seriously. There has never been another such poet. Some flush of romanticism does colour John Clare, more in his poetry than in his prose, but he ranges far and wide in the fields, he never exaggerates, there is something scientific about his preoccupation with the details of natural history, his eyes are as pure as stones. (pp. 5-6)

What an extraordinary instrument [Clare's] prose is, as subtle as the horns of a snail, and yet confident in its progression. There is a list of fragmentary jottings he wrote late in life, about 1847. It could have been the notes for a poem, but it reads better as it is: it has enough intensity, and an informality and a sharpness of detail, which preserve it alive. In some ways it recalls Christopher Smart, but both in rhythm and in substance there is a sturdiness and a common sense quality. Clare in his madness was not like Smart in his. The words are these:

> The rustling of leaves under the feet in woods and
>   under hedges
> The crumping of cat ice and snow down wood-rides,
>   narrow lanes and every street causeway
> Rustling thro a wood or rather rushing, while the wind
>   hallows in the oak tops like thunder;
> The rustle of birds' wings startled from their nests or
>   flying unseen into the bushes
> The whizzing of larger birds overhead in a wood, such
>   as crows, puddocks, buzzards, etc.,
> The trample of robins and woodlarks on the brown leaves,
>   and the patter of squirrels on the green moss;
> The fall of an acorn on the ground, the pattering of nuts
>   on the hazel branches as they fall from ripeness;
> The flirt of the ground-lark's wing from the stubbles—
>   how sweet such pictures on dewy mornings when the
>   dew flashes from its brown feathers! . . .

The accuracy is what is so good. The sensibility is strong, it has the sturdiness and usefulness of White of Selborne, and at the same time the intensity of Smart. John Clare is a camera with a glittering crystal lens, but he hears and feels and thinks and watches at once. The only let down is the phrase, 'how sweet such pictures on dewy mornings'. This phrase is at least truthful, but it has that formalised sentiment of the late eighteenth and early nineteenth century about it which sometimes invades his poems. Yet he could hardly be without that. It was inbuilt into the popular as well as the literary culture of John Clare's generation. (pp. 7-8)

[Clare] wrote in an essay on **'Popularity in Authorship'** in 1825 of those old children's favourites like *Cock Robin* and *Babes in the Wood* that 'leave impressions at the core and grow up with manhood and are beloved on'. But he says that 'Poets anxious after common fame imitate these things by affecting simplicity, and become unnatural.' The genuine vigour of John Clare's own writing belongs to another order. At the age of thirteen he fell in love with Thomson's *Seasons*. He is using the whole of the best eighteenth-century culture as far as it was available to him. His long poem **The Village Minstrel** is a remarkable piece of realism. It is a country equivalent of Gay's *Trivia*. Its humour and its social observation are as strong as its crystalline accuracy about the living world, and that accuracy itself is inseparable from force of language, skill as a poet; it is among other things a formidably skilful poem, it is hard at the edges, it uses its form. Its rhythm and its special breathing are intimate to it. It owes something to Gray's *Elegy* but Clare, with his own deeper roots in village life, goes far beyond the confined territory and the petrified viewpoint of that earlier masterpiece. **The Village Minstrel** is not a poem of short intense beauties, it is more like the drifting light of the sun between clouds, its big scale is an essential part of it. There are many startling lines and sharp observations, but there are possibly no two verses of such a cumulative intense accuracy as the prose fragments I have already quoted. Clare's prose is freer, wilder and more striking than his poetry. (pp. 8-9)

I would not like to judge that in Clare or in [Thomas] Hardy we are hearing something dead, something irrecoverable; my conception is that we are hearing something alive and vast, we are hearing some of the most living arteries in the huge growth of the English language. But we cannot distinguish the language in its vitality from the realities important to us that these two poets discuss. The better, the more vigorous and agile and

subtle the language is, the more real this desirable knowledge of reality seems to be. . . . The skills of these writers are not different in kind from those of others, though every poet has his special virtues, which are no doubt worth dwelling on. But both Clare and Hardy in different ways and different degrees seem to have a special inwardness with the language, or is it with some special areas of English reality? There is something reliable about their poetry, and it has a country handsomeness of language about it. (pp. 15-16)

[In comparison to Hardy,] John Clare is not so subtle or so brilliantly controlled in his breathing, in his rhythms, except perhaps in two or three very well-known poems of despair, but he is almost more accurate than Hardy in the pointing of a phrase, in the physical presence to the reader of any small observation. When he goes home with the harvest, listening to 'the threadbare ballad from each quavering tongue', his talent could be called that of a thwarted novelist, but when

> A solitaire through autumn's wan decay
> He heard the tootling robin sound her knell,

Clare was using his talent in the way that it most counted, and as we can most clearly sense it. There is no end to the looseness of his forms or the vivid accuracy of his observations. I like for example his

> ploughboys at their Sunday bath,
> When leisure left them at their wading free
> In some clear pit hemmed round wi' willow tree. . . .

The realism is pleasant and the looseness of the verse is appropriate. If you put these ploughboys into a tighter context you would have to transform them. As it is John Clare achieves what a landscape painter might achieve; the line 'In some clear pit hemmed round wi' willow tree' is rough and realistic and sufficiently sympathetic. The lines occur in a much longer poem in which a far bigger picture of life in the country is slowly built up. These lines contribute to it in several ways. One takes the notion of no leisure except on Sunday, at the same time the essential peace and pleasure of the ploughboys, the clear pit, the willows, and the fact, if one had forgotten it, that no one knew how to swim. Naturally, he remarks that 'bashful milkmaids couldn't help but see'. John Clare in **The Village Minstrel** builds up a context of life without informality but without any false notes. (pp. 16-17)

Perhaps I ought to return to the prose in which I believe an interesting deposit of the best of him is to be found. There are sentences that would hardly disgrace the most dense work of Dr Johnson in the *Rambler* essays. 'No man should suffer fame to eat up his excellence and lie fallow to listen to the music of her melody. When a man grows proud of his abilities and lies dormant, fame is his creditor to whom he becomes bankrupt.' Of course those are despairing and self-spurring sentences, but they may fairly be called professional, they show what Clare could do on common ground, not what he is in his own special talent. . . . John Clare was a serious talent, a considerable writer. His lack of success was a freak of chance, a reflection of early nineteenth-century society. (p. 17)

[His] is a voice we hear once only. We are hungry for more of it, but we are lucky to have it that once. . . . (p. 18)

However formal [Clare and Hardy] may become, they never cease to tell us something true about life, for instance to describe it, with moral implications that we must confront as we may. And that of course is an underlying question about John Clare and Thomas Hardy. What do they teach us and are we to believe them? That is a question that arises for individual readers of individual poems. If it never arose these would not be important authors. If it always arose they might be intolerable. There is a certain morality which I do have some suspicion they share, but it would be hard to spell it out. It is rough, tender and hopeless, and I find it moving in their language. If it is not altogether an illusion, it must be in the English language. It is hard to think of two writers one could better read, to understand those gruff and helpful moral qualities that attach to the countryside. They both talk habitually in real terms. (p. 19)

Peter Levi, S.J., in a lecture delivered before the University of London on January 16, 1975, in his John Clare and Thomas Hardy, *The Athlone Press, 1975, 19 p.**

L. J. SWINGLE (essay date 1975)

[*Swingle contrasts Clare's early, descriptive poetry with the works of Percy Bysshe Shelley, William Wordsworth, Samuel Taylor Coleridge, and John Keats in order to illustrate Clare's distinctiveness. Swingle's approach differs from those of such earlier twentieth-century commentators as John Middleton Murry (1921, 1924, and 1956), Edmund Gosse (1924), John Speirs (1935), and Harold Bloom (see Additional Bibliography), who examine the similarities between Clare's poetry and that of the major Romantics.*]

[We] best learn to appreciate the nature of Clare's poetic achievement by seeking to judge him according to his own axioms. Instead of searching for Blake or Wordsworth or Keats in Clare in order to affirm, "Clare also does this!", we need to search for Clare in Clare, so to affirm, "Clare distinctively does this!" To accomplish this, it is necessary to turn away from the apocalyptic fascinations of Clare's late, asylum poetry (which is, as Bloom rightly perceives, Blakean) [see excerpt above, 1959-60]. Instead, we must look closely at the earlier, largely descriptive poetry that Clare delighted to write, and stubbornly insisted upon writing, in his sanity. Of primary interest to us will be the poetry composed according to that curious formula which, as Mr. Reeves notes [see Additional Bibliography], appears so often in Clare: "I love to see" or "I love to hear," followed by long catalogues of phenomena seen and heard, all elements given equal weight, all seemingly granted equal significance. It is this kind of Clarean poem that proves hard to deal with, if one attempts to study Clare according to assumptions dictated by the kind of poetry his contemporaries write. Our attempt will be to study it by turning the coin of critical method over, setting Clare off against his contemporaries, thus developing a collision of contraries. In attempting this, I must lay claim to the same license Blake claims in his *Marriage of Heaven and Hell:* for the sake of emphasis, I will often allow Clare-Devil the choicer lines in the dramatic dialogue.

In his descriptive poetry, Clare resists the tendency of his famous contemporaries to project upon the appearances of the non-human world "out there" the products of the human mind's desires. "Bird thou never wert," cries Shelley to his skylark; and the world out there suddenly takes on the colorings of Romance. It appears as Other, no longer familiar, hence perhaps no longer subject to the ills that beset the nature of things as we ordinarily conceive it. Old terminology, therefore, no longer applies: that is no "bird" out there; rather it is a Shape, a Form, a World of Delight. This of course is the direction in which all the major Romantics move, or, more precisely, try

to move. . . . [For Shelley, Wordsworth, Coleridge, and Keats], the bird is first and foremost a manifestation of life profoundly different from human life as we ordinarily know it. Its song is a mystery not quite translatable, a language from a foreign country. (pp. 274-75)

But in Clare the bird does not transfigure into mystery. It remains stubbornly bird-like [as in **"February: A Thaw"** from *Shepherd's Calendar*]: "The wren a sunny side the stack / Wi short tail ever on the strunt / Cockd gadding up above his back / Again for dancing gnats will hunt." If anything, in fact, Clare's birds become more humanly comprehensible than we might ordinarily conceive a bird to be. They are afraid, angry, or ecstatic according to their situations, behaving like human beings who by chance have wings and feathers. . . . Clare will not grant what the major Romantics wish to posit: that the non-human world might be in fact a supra-human world, embodying a paradisical alternative to human uncertainties and suffering. Instead, for Clare, the human and the non-human worlds both participate in the same perilous existence. In Clare's vision, we enter a world of creatures, some human, some non-human— all of which share the same, anxious state of being. Birds may sing like angels, but they hunger and they fear like men.

Musing on the notion of pathetic fallacy, one might decide that Clare, therefore, is the one who allows the mind's dispositions to color description. But from Clare's perspective, it is the major Romantics who more love their minds' fancies than the actual appearances of things. They posit the mystery, the non-human Otherness, of the outer world not because that is how it in fact appears but because that is how they want it to appear. To so see the outer world creates for them a refuge, an open space they can fill with spiritual possibilities. In support of Clare's perspective, one might recall Keats's "Epistle to John Hamilton Reynolds." There Keats looks "Too far into the sea" of the outer world, and he spots "The gentle robin, like a pard or ounce, / Ravening a worm." His reaction to this vision is to retreat from a "too distinct" glimpse into "the core / Of an eternal fierce destruction" by determining to take "refuge" in "new romance." (pp. 275-76)

In contrast, Clare makes his poetic home in precisely that "too distinct" vision of things which Keats would dismiss from consciousness. "It is not commonly known," Clare remarks in his **"Natural History Letters,"** "that the robin is a very quarrelsome bird it is not only at frequent warfare with its own species but boldly attacks every other small bird that comes its way & is generally the conquerer." . . . Clare is intrigued rather than disturbed by this; and he is pleased to know this fact "not commonly known." This is where Clare thinks he discovers his edge on his fellow poets. They may have more formal education than he does, better access to books and learned conversation; they may be able to write familiarly of Truth, Beauty, and Dryads. But Clare has read hard at the Book of Creatures; and he will not retreat from writing of what he has seen there. Thus not only does he accept the vision of robin as ravener of worms, he goes a good deal further:

> In the barn hole sits the cat
> Watching within the thirsty rat
> Who oft at morn its dwelling leaves
> To drink the moisture from the eves
> The redbreast with his nimble eye
> Dare scarcely stop to catch the flye
> That tangled in the spiders snare
> Mourns in vain for freedom there.
> (*Shepherd's Calendar:* "September" . . .)

Clare's robin is not only an eater; it is also potentially one of the eaten. Involved in the complex dynamics of creaturely survival and destruction, it lives a life poised on the brink of both possibilities: perhaps it can steal the fly from the spider's web, and so gain at the expense of the spider; but perhaps to seize the fly will only render it victim to the cat, so saving by accident the endangered rat. Clare's creatures live in a labyrinth of dangerous, interconnected possibilities.

Much of Clare's poetry thus stands as unsettling ironic commentary upon the poetic fancies of the major Romantics. Turning from Shelley's "To a Skylark," for example, we encounter Clare's **"The Skylark."** As in Shelley, so in Clare's poem the skylark flies "with happy wings" high above the turmoil of earthly existence; but Clare keeps in mind the fact that what goes up comes down again. Clare's skylark has a "low nest" upon the ground, where "squats the hare, to terrors wide awake," where buttercups "Opening their golden caskets to the sun / . . . make schoolboys eager run, / To see who shall be first to pluck the prize." And it is these ravaging schoolboys startling the skylark from "her half-formed nest" which cause her to fly into the air. Once the boys pass by, the skylark "drops, and drops, till in her nest she lies, / Which they unheeded passed—not dreaming then / That birds which flew so high would drop agen / To nests upon the ground, which anything / May come at to destroy." Here, as in the verses on the robin above, the pervasive atmosphere is one of danger. The skylark has escaped, because the boys did not "then" dream it would drop again. But this "then" sounds a subtly ominous note: will the boys be so unknowing next time?

This ominous note is characteristic in Clare, and it gives his descriptive poetry a nervous, uneasy edge which some readers have not noticed. Hints of something similar can be traced in the descriptive tradition, extending back to Thomson's *Seasons*. . . . But Clare pursues this element much further, until it becomes the intriguingly distinctive feature in his vision of things. Clare's creatures scurry about through his descriptive poetry, sometimes destroying and being destroyed, but more often merely treading the brink of destruction and managing, for the moment, to escape. Violence can enter the poetry in raw, abrupt lines: "The boy that stands and kills the black-nosed bee" (**"The Stone-Pit"**). More often, it hovers in the background and creates tension. Words like "escape," "hide," and "safety" punctuate the verse, balancing themselves against such words as "fearful," "dread," "terror," and "startled." But the balance is never quite stable, because we are frequently reminded that an escape is only temporary. (pp. 277-78)

At first glance, Clare's vision seems a microcosmic anticipation of Tennyson's "Nature, red in tooth and claw." But the curious difference is that, while Tennyson (like Keats before him) finds the ravagings of nature cause for anguish, Clare on the whole does not. True, in some poems we encounter a passing lament for man's part in the drama, as at the conclusion of **"Summer Evening,"** where Clare muses sadly, "Thus nature's human link and endless thrall, / Proud man, still seems the enemy of all." And Clare can write indignantly sometimes about man's more violent attacks upon other creatures. . . . However, this strain in Clare's poetry is conventional: it is Clare treading carefully in the footsteps of Cowper, befriender of hares. We come closer to Clare's own poetic voice in such passages as this: "I love at early morn from new mown swath / To see the startled frog his rout pursue" (**"Summer Images"** . . .). Clare does not really feel much affection for creatures in themselves. It is not so much the frog that attracts him; what he loves is to see the "startled" frog.

Clare's "love" is less a matter of sympathy and good-will for the creatures he writes about than of a pure, almost scientific curiosity simply about seeing them. . . . And what especially stirs Clare's curiosity, what he continually returns to in his trains of imagery, are the dynamic relations of stress among creatures, patterns of aggression and fear, pursuit and retreat. It is popularly supposed that in such poems as the much anthologized **"Badger,"** for example, Clare writes out of deep sympathy for the pursued. But I think this notion is quite mistaken. . . . Clare is attracted to the dynamics of violence more out of curiosity than out of identification with the underdog. . . . Unlike his Romantic contemporaries and unlike Tennyson, Clare takes "Nature, red in tooth and claw" as the given condition of things. He reserves his astonishment for what seem to him the wondrous dynamics of teeth and claws at work.

Actually, "at work" is probably not quite the right phrase. What seems to have especially intrigued Clare is that creatures enjoy the activity of stalking other creatures. Clare's "chubby boy, / In self-delighted whims, will often throw / Pebbles to hit and splash" the sunny leaves of water-lilies (**"Water-lilies"**). And his herdboys "anxious after play / Find sports to pass the time away":

> pelting wi unerring eye
> The heedless swallows starting bye
> Oft breaking boughs from trees to kill
> The nest of whasps beside a hill
> Till one gets stung then they resort
> And follow to less dangerous sport
>
> • • • • •
>
> And scare the squirrels lively joys
> Wi stones and sticks and shouting noise. . . .
> (**"A Sunday with Shepherds and Herdboys"** . . .)

This catalogue of playful violences rambles cheerfully on. Clare is not indicting human perversity here, nor lamenting man's estrangement from the innocent calm of nature. To the contrary, . . . both man and "natural" creatures share the same impulses. Thus in **"The Meadow Lake,"** for example, it is the musing shepherd who is calm, while his dog enjoys the kind of sports the boys in the above poem indulge in: disturbing a placid scene, the dog plunges into the peaceful lake "with a gladsome heart / To hunt the water-rat and scared moor-hen." And in **"The Vixen,"** young fox cubs, themselves "from danger never free," are first pursued by a boy who pokes into their hole with a stick; but then, escaping, they become in turn pursuers, as they now gaily "start and snap at blackbirds bouncing by / To fight and catch the great white butterfly." The boy pursues the fox cubs, who pursue the blackbirds, who pursue the butterfly.

Such poetry involves us in a literary experience unlike what we ordinarily meet with in the work of the major Romantics. Clare's creatures, human and non-human, interact in complex patterns of pursuit and escape; and these interactions are highly charged with conflicting colorings of sport and earnest, pleasure and terror. A given moment of interaction arranges these colorings in some particular configuration; but in the next moment, the roles of aggressor and victim change, and the configuration changes accordingly. Our reader's temptation, of course, is to add a moral coloring of our own, painting the Saints and Sinners according to our sympathy with the oppressed. But the Saints become the Sinners; and the ultimate effect of the poetic experience is to lead us to abandon our own coloring efforts, and accept instead those non-judgmental colorings of the poetry's shifting surface. We are encouraged, finally, to embrace a sort of kaleidoscopic experience, in which we appreciate the aesthetics of interaction and shifting conflicts instead of identifying with one element or another, and so being drawn into the conflict as vicarious participants and suffering the anxieties the conflict produces. (pp. 281-82)

Wordsworth has been termed the spectator *ab extra.* But Clare lays a more valid claim to that title. Wordsworth is profoundly *ad hominem,* ultimately, as are all the major Romantics. . . . It is most significant that, while Wordsworth embraces both Man and Nature in his musings, his *tertium quid* is "*Human Life.*" Wordsworth's trains of imagery must be finally yoked firmly to the human viewpoint, directed by the overriding requirements imposed by purely human concerns. But Clare, in contrast, would have wanted to write for that *tertium quid* simply "Life." Clare wants to stand back from both man and nature ("*I love . . .*"), leaning neither toward the one pole nor toward the other. Instead he wants to establish his still point within the tension of their interactions, perhaps like God: "And he who studies natures volume through / And reads it with a pure unselfish mind / Will find Gods power all round in every view / As one bright vision of the almighty mind" ["**Child Harold**"]. Clare's attempt is to maintain a "pure unselfish mind," a mind which "loves" to see and hear without distorting the purity of perception through a predisposition toward judging or evaluating what is perceived. Such a mind can rise above the limitations of selfish, merely human concerns, and so embrace God's "power." This word "power" touches the very essence of Clare's pre-asylum poetry, underscoring Clare's infatuation with the dynamic tensions in life. Other, selfish minds worry about whether that "power" means "love" or "hate." Clare would have us transcend such cares, and attain his "one bright vision." (pp. 283-84)

> *L. J. Swingle, "Stalking the Essential John Clare: Clare in Relation to His Romantic Contemporaries," in* Studies in Romanticism, *Vol. 14, No. 3, Summer, 1975, pp. 273-84.*

W. J. KEITH (essay date 1980)

[*Keith contrasts Clare's perception of nature with that of William Wordsworth, focusing on their differing social viewpoints and attitudes toward technical experimentation. According to Keith, Wordsworth's vision of nature is broad and intellectualized while Clare's, though equally genuine, is "local to the core" and "unconnected with the paraphernalia of Romantic theorizing." Therefore, Keith asserts, Clare's poetry resists such abstract interpretations as that by Harold Bloom (see Additional Bibliography).*]

The most obvious and at the same time most crucial difference between [Clare and Wordsworth] was one of class. It is fashionable nowadays to profess to ignore the 'peasant-poet' aspect of Clare which so fascinated his contemporaries, but the matter is too central to pass over without comment. We have no right to gloat complacently over his disadvantages and wonder at the miracle of his appearance in 'polite letters'; at the same time, we should realize how Clare's position as an agricultural labourer enabled him to gain a knowledge of, and develop a viewpoint towards, the countryside that was totally different from Wordsworth's. This obviously has profound implications for the kind of poetry that he was to write. Although Wordsworth's poems are full of humbly born countrymen and countrywomen of all class-gradations . . . , they are presented from the outside—and generally from above. Wordsworth wrote about

these people and expressed a genuine concern for them, but despite his theoretical principles about 'low and rustic life,' he could never be as one of them. Clare, by contrast, was himself 'the Northamptonshire peasant'; he knew from first-hand experience the world of rustic labour that Wordsworth portrayed with sincere but none the less detached sympathy in *Lyrical Ballads.* Above all, he spoke—and wrote—the rustic dialect, and the country people and things that form the staple of his poetry are thus presented vividly and accurately in an appropriate language.

It would be impossible to over-emphasize the significance of these social differences upon the kinds of poetry that each was capable of producing. Because Clare was younger and came under the influence of earnest and often misguided well-wishers who tried to mould him into an educated poet, we can find a number of Wordsworthian echoes and imitations within his verse. But these should not be mistaken for any basic similarity. (pp. 40-1)

Although it is not difficult to point to characteristics which the two writers share—a liking for simplicity in subject and language, a fascination with the theme of childhood vision and its loss in adult life—these should not obscure the profound differences that extend even to the treatment and tone of poems written on comparable subjects. Clare's vision, as genuine as Wordsworth's, is unconnected with the paraphernalia of Romantic theorizing. When he is at his most characteristic, Clare is content with nature as it is. The mind of man is decidedly not his haunt and the main region of his song; his poems are 'filled with flowers' rather than with 'works of human kind.' Moreover, he makes no attempt to probe beyond experience towards a mystical or metaphysical superstructure. . . . It is absurd to speak, as Harold Bloom does, of 'Clare's dialectic' [see Additional Bibliography] . . . ; such terminology is inappropriate, not (one hastens to add) on account of any snobbish assumptions about the quality of Clare's education or the capacity of the rustic mind, but because his very real poetic intelligence is simply not conducive to any kind of abstract categorization. Clare has to be protected from those on the one hand who would see him as a primitive and untutored peasant and those on the other who would romanticize him into a natural philosopher. (pp. 41-2)

A less obvious, but no less important, difference between Wordsworth and Clare, ultimately determined by their differing angles of social viewpoint, is to be found in their attitudes to the local. Wordsworth . . . only occasionally wrote (as in 'Michael') as a local poet. Clare, by contrast, was local to the core. There can be no poetic tension between traveller and native in Clare's poems. . . . Wordsworth looked through the local or the immediate; Clare, by virtue of his comprehensive knowledge of a confined locality, saw much that Wordsworth could never see. Living in a less 'picturesque' countryside, Clare is rarely concerned with the larger scenic qualities of the landscape. Northamptonshire provided no opportunities for flirtation with the Sublime. Clare is never tempted into 'a comparison of scene with scene,' to quote Wordsworth's confession in *The Prelude* . . . ; as he notes in his sonnet to Wordsworth,

> I love to stoop and look among the weeds
> To find a flower I never knew before.

There may be a sly allusion here to Wordsworth's 'Small Celandine,' but the lines offer an image of Clare peering into the minutiae of nature and finding his own world in a grain of local sand that is profoundly characteristic.

If Wordsworth's poems about the effect of the natural landscape upon man are more varied and more profound than Clare's, Clare's poems about individual birds and flowers are decidedly superior to Wordsworth's. . . . [The difference between Clare's and Wordsworth's poetry] is fundamentally one of perception. If Wordsworth is a towering monument to the dignity to which nature poetry can attain, Clare, who once claimed that he kicked his poems out of the clods, presents not a humbler but a less intellectualized alternative: a nature poetry in which the emphasis remains on the natural object.

The difference can be seen most clearly if we turn to **'The Lamentations of Round Oak Waters'** . . . and **'The Lament of Swordy Well.'** . . . While neither poem shows Clare at his best, both bear eloquent witness to his close association with local landmarks. In the first he imagines that, while lamenting his own unhappy lot, he hears Round Oak Waters express a similar complaint 'in grievous murmurs':

> Unequall'd tho' thy sorrows seem—
>   And great indeed they are—
> Oh, hear my sorrows for my stream,
>   You'll find an equal there.

When they are articulated, we recognize these sorrows as one of Clare's recurring preoccupations (in **'Remembrances'** and elsewhere), his disgust at the changes brought upon the landscape by Enclosure:

> Oh, then what trees my banks did crown!
>   What willows flourished here!
> Hard as the axe that cuts them down
>   The senseless wretches were.

The complaint is direct and the tone bitter; significantly, the poem remained unpublished in Clare's lifetime. But the directness and bitterness shared by man and place create an effect outside Wordsworth's range. Clare is able—and this becomes even more evident in **'The Lament of Swordy Well'**—to subsume his own character into that of the locality. While it is easy to retort, with partial truth, that he merely imposes his own attitudes on to his subject, the fact remains that he varies the extent to which the man is comparable to the place. In the first poem the whole argument depends upon the balanced comparison: the forces threatening the labouring class are equally threatening to the landscape. In the second, Clare develops the possibilities of the idea and is able to reproduce Swordy Well's unique viewpoint:

> The muck that clouts the ploughman's shoe,
>   The moss that hides the stone,
> Now I've become the parish due
>   Is more than I can own.

The final pun may suggest Hood, but the muck is Clare's original, unromantic contribution, and it provides a context for the mossy stone that firmly distinguishes it from Wordsworth's in 'She Dwelt Among the Untrodden Ways.' The Clare who can project himself into Swordy Well looks forward . . . to the Clare who can view the world from the perspective of a ladybird in **'Clock-a-clay.'** But it is not yet an *imaginative* projection. Because Helpston is so intimate a reality for him, Clare can pass from his own folk-mind to the mind of the locality without any apparent sense of strain.

Because Clare's outlook was more rustic than Wordsworth's he showed little interest in the latter's technical experimentation. Suspicious of artifice, Clare mistrusted formal considerations as alien to his unbounded vision. The nature he loved was above 'Form'; he delighted in Thomson's 'rural confusion' (**'Summer'** . . .). The following passage from **'Cowper Green'** is relevant here:

> Some may praise the grass-plat whims,
> Which the gard'ner weekly trims,
> And cut hedge and lawn adore,
> Which his shears have smoothen'd o'er:
> But give me to ponder still
> Nature, when she blooms at will,
> In her kindred taste and joy,
> Wildness and variety. . . .

In these lines Clare not only explains his preferences in landscape (which go far towards explaining his aesthetic as distinct from socio-political objections to Enclosure) but also indicates his dislike of artificial moulding and structuring. Because he liked his nature unbounded, he preferred his poetry formless. 'Pleas'd I list the rural themes,' he announces in **'Summer Morning'** . . . , and so leads on to another natural catalogue. The frequently anthologized **'Summer Images,'** impressive as it is stanza by stanza, is a list rather than a poem; there is no logical reason why it should have sixteen stanzas or sixty. (pp. 42-5)

Similar reservations have to be made, I believe, even about a poem as fresh and appealing as **'The Shepherd's Calendar.'** Individual lines are superb, individual images unforgettable; as a whole, however, it exists only as a succession of keenly observed and precisely etched pictures. It lacks 'appropriate form,' and because we find in Clare comparatively little of the conscious technical experimentation so conspicuous in Wordsworth, we are tempted to formulate a distinction between artlessness in the former and the illusion of artlessness in the latter. But such categorizations are too neat to be just. After all, Wordsworth has his poetic disasters and these, though recognized and deplored, are not allowed to detract from his obvious creative achievements. It is true that Clare fails sufficiently often to raise doubts whether his successes are due to happy accident or to deliberate design; but there is no doubt that he also achieves artistic excellence sufficiently often to worthy of serious (and discriminating) critical attention. (p. 45)

W. J. Keith, "John Clare," in his The Poetry of Nature: Rural Perspectives in Poetry from Wordsworth to the Present, *University of Toronto Press, 1980, pp. 39-66.*

WILLIAM HOWARD (essay date 1981)

[*Howard's* John Clare *is a chronological study of Clare's poetic growth in which his literary career is divided into four distinct stages: two Helpston periods, the first from 1809 to 1824 and the second from 1824 to 1832; the Northborough period from 1832 to 1841; and the years from 1842 to 1864, which he spent in the Northampton asylum. Here, Howard analyzes the structure, imagery, and symbolism of poems dating from each of the four periods in relation to Clare's own statements concerning his method of poetic composition.*]

Clare deserves his reputation for striking and detailed descriptions of natural objects, but such description was not the end he strove for; he sought a means of communicating his special vision of the natural world. Although he maintained that his art consisted primarily of recording what he saw or felt in the presence of nature, he also noticed a difference between what he perceived and what was perceptible to those who lacked a poet's sensitivity. This attitude accounts for his apparently simple explanation of perception in **"Sighing for Retirement,"** where he contends:

> I found the poems in the fields,
> And only wrote them down. . . .

[A] poem is wrought, for Clare, by bringing the special powers of a poet's mind to bear on the raw material it finds in nature. This view considers the poet a collector and a recorder of perceptions, of artifacts which appear to him complete at the moment he finds them, rather than a creator who invents and arranges new images into works of art. Clare deplored much of the artifice he saw in the poetry around him because it interfered with the direct communication from the natural world, through the poet, to the reader. (p. 28)

One of his most persistent themes is artistic integrity, an integrity which he often gauged by a poet's fidelity to the natural image. He distrusted those who moved away from what was perceived in nature. . . . The poet's power arises from his ability to transfer a natural image from the material world into a verbal equivalent on the page. Clare's desire to achieve this faithful correspondence between the original landscape and the literary one became the touchstone for his critiques of other poets. He scorned those who allowed a consciousness of their audience to interfere with their vision of the natural world. . . . (p. 29)

Clare seldom drew his images from any source other than nature. Since images project more than verbal meaning, he felt that they, more than the words used to describe them, contained the essence of poetry: "True poesy is not in words / But images that thoughts express" [he stated in **"Pastoral Poesy."**] As the Tibbles have pointed out, Clare's poetry often relies on the image rather than the word, the picture rather than the syntactical formality of the discourse. "Clare was not," they feel, "interested in words as words; nor did he pay much attention to their formal grouping into sentences. The unit for him was the short phrase or clause—the verbal expression of the image upon which his attention was focused" [see excerpt above by J. W. Tibble, 1935]. This distinction is useful if we do not lose sight of Clare's intense interest in dialect and in the right word or phrase to capture his image. He was interested in words insofar as they were his only means of conveying what he saw, but the real art, for Clare, lay in the quality of perception which transcends mere verbal description, that could be conveyed only through thoughts requiring more than the individual word for their effect.

To transcribe natural images accurately required more than simply holding the mirror to nature. . . . Clare found that to "look on nature with a poetic eye magnifies the pleasure she herself being the very essence & soul of Poesy." A lens, rather than a mirror, intensified the joy Clare felt when perceiving natural images, giving to the image itself the aura of wonder which pervades most of his nature poetry. This alteration revealed to Clare's especially sensitive mind not simply a bird, but a hermit, not a snowdrop, but a "lovely woman"—in short, not an object but a corresponding image which transformed the original object into a source of greater joy.

This lens was the poet's mind. Like Wordsworth, Clare was aware that he perceived nature with a sensitivity not common to all men. In his attempts to explain the mental faculty that

enabled him to do so, he differed from Wordsworth in details—and especially in vocabulary—but he agreed that some men were better equipped to perceive objects in an aesthetic way. The distinguishing faculty he called "taste." . . . [Taste] for Clare was the capacity to perceive and appreciate the beauty inherent in natural objects. It enabled him to "look on nature with a poetic feeling." (pp. 30-1)

A second mental peculiarity of the poet that alters his perception of natural objects Clare called "genius." Although he often used that term to denote nothing more than superior intelligence, in several of his comments on poetic composition he reserves for it a more technical meaning. In **"Dawning of Genius,"** for example, he defines it as "a pleasing rapture of the mind / a kindling warmth to Learning unconfin'd." Whereas he considered taste to be a latent desire for the appreciation of beauty which selects images for the poet's consideration, he saw genius as a faculty which acts upon the perceived images in a state of mental excitement, or "rapture." Taste applies to the initial perception, genius to the ensuing mental reaction to it. . . . Genius is active: it kindles, glows, and flutters. It is identified with warmth, joy, sympathy, and fondness, indicating it is an attitude that reacts to the images "endeared" to it by taste. If it is not quite Coleridge's "colouring of the imagination," it is at least a force that transforms the ordinary into the valued through a process of mental excitement. And Clare's consistent use of the imagery of ignition—[**"Dawning of Genius"**]—itself reveals the burst of emotional insight he embodied in the term. (pp. 34-5)

Genius, then, is another attribute of the poetic mind which, independently of education or intellectual refinement, enables the poet to respond to the aesthetic elements of nature. . . . [Taste and genius] are responsible for the alteration of the natural image. One is by definition selective, therefore altering through exclusion of unwanted details; the other is highly emotional, therefore distorting by the subjectivity of its response. Combined, they provide the poet with a capacity to perceive nature poetically.

The prerequisite for initiating the mental activity that produced poetry, Clare felt, was an environment of complete isolation and relative silence in which a reciprocal communication with nature was possible. The reverence he held for solitude he summed up in his admission [in **"Universal Goodness"**] that "solitude and God are one." . . . [Solitude with nature] initiates an escalating process of response which culminates in the poet extracting, or gleaning, a new state of mind which, because he suggests it is habitual, has become a permanent part of his experience. In [**"On Visiting a Favourite Place"**] this gentle pleasure arising from solitude is replaced by a more forceful response: "A mind overflowing with excess / of joys that spring from solitude." Clare responded to silence; it was more to him than simple absence of sound. Thus his desire for solitude was based on the prospect, always a pleasant one for him, of silent communication. . . . (pp. 36-7)

Clare found that silent meditation awakened his mind to poetic activity by warming his heart into higher moods. His contemplation of nature was seldom relaxing because his mind responded to the stimuli of silence in much the same way Coleridge's does in "Frost at Midnight." His awakening was impulsive, beyond his own powers to arrest. . . . This awakening is the first mental act of Clare's poetic process. (p. 38)

Clare is much less specific about the second stage of this poetic process, the transfer of selected images to the mind. He does indicate that it is an automatic, inexplicable movement from the landscape to a meditative mind, when he acknowledges in **"Sunset Visions"** that, simply, "something cometh to the gazing mind." And in the context of his statement in **"Pastoral Poesy"** that true poetry consists "not in words, but images," his later comment in that poem that "an image to the mind is brought" implies a similar view of this transference. The movement is from external to internal, from concrete object to abstract thought. . . . (pp. 38-9)

While Clare believed that anyone with a poet's mind—not only writers, since illiterate shepherds and ploughmen are constantly looking on nature with a "poetic eye" in his verse—could experience this special insight, he also felt that their heightened perception depended on that mind being in a particularly receptive state. Because

> An image to the mind is brought
> Where happiness enjoys
> An easy thoughtlessness of thought
> And meets excess of joys.

[As these lines from **"Pastoral Poesy"** suggest,] the image is transferred to a mind that is engaged in an unselfconscious, or unself-analyzing, intellectual activity. It implies there must be thoughts, but that they must not be thoughts *of* thoughts. The mental activity must be directed out toward the external object rather than back into its own locus of mentation. Clare was saying the same thing when he stressed the unconscious aspects of the honest poet in his essay on **"Popularity in Authorship."** . . . And he reiterated it later in life in *Child Harold:*

> And he who studies natures volume through
> And reads it with a pure unselfish mind
> Will find Gods power all round in every view
> As one bright vision of the almighty mind.

Purity and unselfishness presuppose a receptive mind which does not attempt to manipulate what it sees. Such a mind produces revelations of what Wordsworth would call "the life of things." In Clare's scheme this lack of self-consciousness allows the operation of the "inward powers" of genius on images supplied by the selective element of taste.

The natural propensity of the mind in this state is to attempt to preserve the image presented to it. Thus when viewing a landscape in his sonnet **"Written in Autumn,"** Clare attempts to freeze the scene even though it appeals to him by its transitoriness. This paradox he expresses in his desire for autumn to "lastingly decline." [In **"A Sunset"**] he describes this attempt more fully:

> I gazd upon them wi' a wishing eye
> And longd but vainly for the painters power
> To give existance to the mingling dye
> And snatch a beauty from an evening hour.

Again the significant characteristic of the scene is its transitoriness, and again the poet wishes to make it static by giving it "existence" and by snatching its beauty out of the progression of change in which it is involved. In Clare's realization of the futility of such an attempt, coupled with his desire to continue it, lies the poignancy of this poetic experience. (pp. 39-40)

Clare recognized in the poetic process a natural tendency of mind to capture the fleeting image, and this tendency was revealed in the form his poetry took, not only in the sonnets and shorter lyrics, but also in the succession of individual scenes which constitute many of his longer poems. (p. 41)

[The] image he tries to preserve is not merely a tree or a stream, or even an interesting amalgam of natural objects. He does not consider the natural object perceived by the sensitive mind as simply a material, so much as a fusion of material and literary image—a metaphor or a symbol. In its ability to appreciate this fusion, the poetic mind is unique. (p. 42)

Clare never does make it clear at what point in the poetic process the object adopts the qualities of metaphor or symbol, but his statement [in **"Pastoral Poesy"**] that it occurs to one in "fitful glee" and "fancys many moods" would suggest that the transformation occurs in conjunction with the mental excitement of genius, a suggestion supported by his claim that "taste is a uniformity of excellence it modif[ies] expression and selects images it aranges and orders matters and thoughts but genius creates them." The creative function of genius distinguishes it from the rather mechanical proclivity of taste. Creation of thoughts suggests the active fusion of the real object and the imagined one into the concept of joy which invariably results. (p. 44)

The eventual result of this mental activity is what Clare calls [in **"Expression"**] the "throbbing utterance of the soul," the work of art. [He states in **"Spring Songs"** that his] exalted state of mind produces a desire to express the quality of his immediate experience:

> The very winds sing sonnets to the sky
> And sunshine bids them welcome—so that I
> Feel a new being as from healthier climes
> And shape my idle fancys into rhymes
> Of natures extacy in bursting flowers.

With characteristic humility Clare credits nature with the real creative power, but his apparently naïve comment is only a reiteration of his special concept of the poet as transcriber. . . . [The] poet's mind interacts with nature to produce both the ecstasy and the rhymes. The ideal product of this interaction is a work of art which has grown out of, and gained its character from, the original experience. . . . (p. 45)

When discussing Clare's concept of the poem, we must bear in mind that he believed thoughts, not words, were the proper medium for expression. The image is not merely concrete, and therefore definable by a single word, but involves an abstract element which can only be conveyed through a combination of words which add up to a whole greater than the sum of its parts. For example, the effect of Clare's well-known portrait of the badger is not only contained in the special qualities of language he employs, or in associations inherent in the word "badger," but in the thoughts which arise from his cumulative description of the badger's appearance and actions. The dramatic situation and the action described in the following portion of [**"The Badger"**] create a memorable picture of the embattled animal even though they are conveyed in simple, almost nonemotive diction and syntax:

> He falls as dead and kicked by boys and men
> Then starts and grins and drives the crowd agen
> Till kicked and torn and beaten out he lies
> And leaves his hold and cackles groans and dies.

The syntax here, with its double repetition in the first line and triple repetition in the second, third, and fourth, reinforces the action and is more evocative than in most of the poem, but of all the words only "cackles" draws any attention to itself. The poem depends primarily on the image it presents to the mind, on our "seeing" and responding to an overall picture.

This is not to suggest that Clare ignored the right choice of word, or failed to realize the value of his craft as a writer, but only that he saw diction and syntax as subservient to the recreation of a picture to which they contributed. His feelings were complex enough that he was constantly aware of the inadequacy of language to convey the full impact of his experience.... The real poem is what the poet uses words to convey, a mental phenomenon contained in thoughts and expressed only imperfectly through words. (pp. 45-7)

By thus directing the emphasis away from the verbal composition of the poem to the thoughts that emerge from it, Clare reaffirms his claim that grammatical rules are irrelevant to poetry. He felt that "whatever is intelligible to others is grammar & whatever is common sense is not far from carrectness," and in a more colorful mood he vowed "grammar in learning is like tyranny in government—confound the bitch I'll never be her slave." Since the formulation of proper syntactical structures was not necessary to convey his pictures of nature, he felt justified in condemning not only grammar, but poetic diction as well. Although he championed the cause of rustic language, notably in his debates with Charles Lamb, and was himself no mean verbal craftsman, he was more concerned with shifting the emphasis from the mode of expression to the object or scene or event being described and to the thought which arose from the contemplation of it. (p. 47)

The impression left by Clare's comments on his method of composition indicate he did not share Wordsworth's faith in the efficacy of "emotion recollected in tranquility." ... [He] made every effort to record the experience as soon after it occurred as he could. (pp. 50-1)

The immediacy of this method resulted in an acknowledged influence of the poet's environment and personal mood at the time of composition on the poem produced. We cannot, of course, be sure what his situation was while composing all of the poems, but most of them, like most Romantic poems, were descriptive of actual experiences. Consequently, these influences are often woven into the fabric of the poem. His nature poems are almost always situational and even many of the songs, excluding the traditional ballads which he refurbished, betray the situation of the poet at the time of composition. Even his narratives are frequently descriptive of personal experiences.... [Often] the meter of a piece was influenced by the "dancing measure" Clare had in his head at the time or the sound of his mother's spinning wheel near him as he wrote. (p. 52)

Although he was at times capable of composing to order—his letters contain several pleas for subject matter to try his talents—by far the bulk of his poetry, and that the most accomplished of it, was composed during either a direct poetic experience or an indirect simulation of the original. The result of these methods of composition is poetry that is highly metaphoric, since derived from a process of perception which "saw" natural objects as metaphors or symbols, and highly personal, since based almost exclusively on individual experiences of the poet in nature. (p. 56)

[The first period in Clare's literary life, from 1809 to 1824, was] marked by considerable experimentation with the use of an immediate experience as a structuring device for his poems. The title of his first poem, "**Morning Walk,**" suggests that his method came naturally to him.... [His] early poetry contains glimpses of what was later to develop into coherent and unified poems built on a framework of the poet's personal experiences. For the moment, however, his experimentation produced only a very clumsy and often embarrassingly naïve use of the experience. Seldom tracing the progress of his aesthetic response to nature, he was content to restrict himself to physical situations from which he viewed the landscape, or to rambling walks which would connect several scenes into the scope of a single experience. Any meditative passage in these poems is usually a short segment sharply distinct from the action described, though often related to something perceived during the walk.

Most of the weaknesses of his early work are evident in "**Lines Written in a Summer Evening.**" Although there is a suggestion of unity in the chronological sequence of the observer's description, the poem lacks the focus usually provided by the physical situation of the poet. It shifts from one scene to another with no sense of being viewed through the single window of his mind. We see characters and objects outdoors which are ostensibly related to his position by his distinguishing between "far and near," but we also see Dobson preparing for bed *inside* his cottage. Only in the final eight lines is the poet's location established:

> Now, as stretching o'er the bed,
> Soft I raise my drowsy head
> Listening to the ushering charms
> That shake the elm tree's mossy arms
> Till sweet slumbers stronger creep
> Deeper darkness stealing round
> Then as rock'd, I sink to sleep
> Mid the wild wind's lulling sound.

If the activity portrayed in the rest of the poem has been directly perceived by the poet, the concluding lines must involve a change of location—since he is now in bed—from one which has not even been established. Nor is his decription of the external scene limited to a reasonable selection of what one person is likely to see from a given position; it is crammed full with at least twenty-three varieties of birds and animals as well as ten human beings, and it begs for selectivity or artistic economy. Ironically, when the poet does enter the poem his presence is an unwelcome intrusion. His indignant outburst against mischievous boys and his burdensome moralizing on Providence, although they do arise out of the events described, do not give the impression of being provoked by his immediate experience, as the sentiment in "**The Flood**" does. They appear instead as abruptly inserted, made-to-order platitudes. This inability to fuse the objectivity of the observer and the subjectivity of the commentator is particularly evident in these early poems and is overcome in the later works by stressing the subjectivity resulting from the limited perceptions of a single observer. (pp. 58-60)

Clare's images in this period are often stereotyped, rising out of literary convention rather than his individual response to nature. Unlike "**The Flood,**" where the metaphor of a monster emerges from an accumulation of terms used to describe the stream, thus giving a coherent picture of physical and metaphysical destruction, his early poems abound in metaphors imposed upon them from without. In "**Summer Evening**" there is a conglomeration of individual metaphors which, when they are not simply idiomatic expressions, are used to illuminate isolated objects with no relation either to each other or to an overall plan. The poem includes the conventional personifications of Providence, ignorance, and sleep, but, with the exception of a fascinating picture of a bat "in hood and cowl," there is very little metaphor beyond the "murmuring" brook and "sleeping" flowers. A similar lack of pattern characterizes **"Recollections after an Evening Walk"** in which the individual metaphors are more colorful, but fail to convince us that the poetic process creates rather than imposes metaphors. **"To an Insignificant Flower"** attempts to form a pattern of metaphor by equating the flower with Emma, beauty, a swain, and the poet, but the result is a naïve and obviously contrived lyric. More evidence of experimenting with image patterns can be found in **"Recollections after a Ramble,"** where a series of references to the lark's "anthem," the wood's "song," birds' "songs," and nature's "anthem" suggests an underlying metaphoric structure. The references are too few for a poem of this length, however, and not clearly enough related to each other or to a central metaphor to be considered an effective pattern.

The first Helpston period, then, is notable for experimentation and limited achievement in the use of a personal experience to give form and substance to Clare's poetry. The reputation he established in his first two volumes of verse was founded more on minute observation of his natural environment and intimate knowledge of rustic life than on the technical competence of a poet mature in his craft. He had, by this time, formulated much of his evolving theory of poetry, however, and the years that followed saw him create his own style from his personal response to nature. (pp. 63-4)

The poetry he composed at Helpston [during the second period of his literary life,] between 1824 and 1832, reveals a more sophisticated use of the experience as a structural device and a more confident utilization of metaphor. Although many poems of this period have a tendency to ramble without a controlling structure, others indicate an increasing adherence on Clare's part to the truth of the experience, a tendency to dwell on mental activities rather than on physical ones, and a conscious attempt to demonstrate within the poem how it arose from the poet's actual perception. And although he often uses conventional metaphors expressed through archaic diction and syntax, he increasingly derives his imagery from the scene he is describing. This results not only in a much more natural mode of description, uniquely his own, but also in a unity and economy superior to the earlier works. (p. 65)

Although Clare demonstrates [in **"Autumn"**] and in several other poems of this period his ability to exploit the immediate experience for an artistic purpose, he does not do so consistently. For example, **"Walks in the Woods,"** though an obvious improvement over poems of the first Helpston period, displays only a casual connection between descriptive passages. On the other hand, we are now constantly reminded that the poem's scope is limited by the poet's physical range of perception, even though he breaks out of this limitation into digressions which undermine the structure. In addition, the experience described is a mental one, although there is only passing reference to, and partial development of, the poetic process. (p. 69)

The token gesture toward deriving metaphors out of the situation in **"Walks in the Woods"** is characteristic of Clare's experimentation in this period and is repeated continually in the poetry of these years. The following example from **"Pastoral Fancies"** by its very awkwardness illustrates both his desire to extract imagery from the immediate scene and his limited progress to date:

> My rod and line doth all neglected lye
> A higher joy mine former sport destroys
> Nature this day doth bait the hook and I
> The glad fish am thats to be caught there bye.

We can be forgiven if we are reminded, here, of metaphysical poetry. The conceit is artificial in its expression, but it does obviously spring to his mind from his personal situation at the time. Clare's attempt to be "literary" betrays his lack of confidence in his own ability to elicit images from nature.

The most successful poems of the period, however, overcome his diffidence. **"Snow Storm"** is the product of a confident poet who hints at a comprehensive symbol without the need to labor his point. . . . [It has been published] as two sonnets, but it is obvious from the second sonnet's reliance on the first for its intelligibility that Clare intended the two to constitute one twenty-eight-line, two-stanza poem. Considered as such, it reveals a physical experience which emerges into a imaginative one and in the process develops a metaphor out of the physical appearance of the scene. (pp. 70-1)

The Shepherd's Calendar shows Clare groping for a form that will sustain a long descriptive poem and producing several interesting advances over the other, shorter, poems of this period, but never unifying his vision into an organic whole.

The calendar scheme itself offers a logical means of interrelating Clare's multifarious observations, but it soon grows tedious when not supported by other, less mechanical, devices. Clare partially complements this method with recurring allusions to various rural occupations as they alter throughout the year. Ploughman, thresher, and hedger all appear in their appropriate season and are linked by the shepherd who is active in one form or another throughout the year. He fills center stage in June, his busiest month, requiring the shearing of his flock and providing him with the social pleasures of those who gather for that activity. In July he is simply accessory to the scene, his own activity dependent on completion of the haying which commands most of the attention in that month. Even during the harvest the shepherd is briefly remembered: "For shepherds are no more of ease possest / But share the harvests labours with the rest." This continuity of interest in the shepherd links each month with the others and maintains a sense of progression. Scrupulously adhered to, it could have provided the structure the poem needs, but the richness and variety of life Clare wanted to describe would hardly submit to such a restricting format. What was required was a dominant form which would develop out of the unique characteristics of each month, and a variety of individual sections which would prevent monotony. (pp. 73-4)

[A] poem requires form that emerges as effortlessly out of the material as Clare's imagery does. Too many of the "months" in this work lack that form. Storey has argued that *The Shepherd's Calendar* "is in many ways a test case for Clare's poetry. . . . For if his descriptive poetry is to be vindicated, it is in this work that we must seek that vindication" [see Additional Bibliography, 1974]. A more appropriate place to look for Clare's best description contained in intricately wrought poems is in the sonnets and descriptive lyrics. This poem was Clare's major achievement to date, but he did not cease to develop his powers in 1823. The years that followed saw major developments and improvements in his technique without any diminution of his powers of perception. (p. 82)

[The period in Clare's artistic life from 1832 to 1841] produced the majority of his masterpieces. . . . [Some of these poems] reveal a new dimension in his treatment of experience and metaphor. He continued writing nature poems which, like **"To the Nightingale,"** are rooted in a personal experience in the same way as those of the former period, and he began writing more and more songs which, though often traditional in both form and content, relied occasionally now and increasingly later on an inspirational experience similar to that which we have seen in his descriptive poems.

Like the poems of the previous period, but more polished in many respects, is **"On Visiting a Favourite Place."** It opens with the memory of former pleasures, embodied in the symbol of Eden, that Clare enjoyed in the spot he is revisiting, and proceeds to bask in a corresponding pleasure in the present moment:

> There is a breath—indeed there is
> Of eden left—I feel it now
> Of something more then earthly bliss
> That falls and cheers my sullen brow.

He combines both his past and his present responses to the scene by stressing the escalating emotion that accompanies both and inspires him to preserve the experience in song. . . . The effect of solitude on the tranquil receptivity of a poet's mind soon produces overflowing emotions and the impulse to create poetry (''verses dancing on my tongue''). Similar references to various stages of the poetic process are dispersed throughout the poem, although they are not contained within a chronological narrative of rising feeling. The poem and the process, however, culminate in the final lines where Clare recalls the transformation of the scene that occurred during his former musings there:

> I viewed the trees and bushes near
> And distance till it grew to grey
> A power divine seemed everywhere
> And joys own rapture where I lay
> The furze clumps in their golden flowers
> Made edens in these golden hours.

Only now do we see the significance of Clare's recognizing an edenic atmosphere when he first returns to the scene in the opening lines; the ''breath of eden'' was created out of a previous transformation of the landscape by his poetic eye and now unites the two otherwise distinct experiences. And his memory of the conversion of furze clumps into types of Eden sparks the writing of the poem; it is the remarkable aspect of the scene from which he proceeds.

The whole poem is governed by this symbol; the innocent joy associated with Eden permeates Clare's response to the details he describes. And all these details are subordinated to his position in the landscape, all exist in the poem because of their influence on his state of mind. The trees and mole hills bid him welcome and the ant resents his presence, but none of the creatures or plants mentioned are superfluous. Apart from the simple personification throughout the poem, Clare's figurative language also demonstrates his growing ability to create metaphors out of his immediate surroundings. (pp. 83-5)

This progress is clearly marked in **"What is There in the Distant Hills"** and **"Song's Eternity."** In both poems Clare focuses as intently as he is able on the physical objects that surround him, in order to elicit from them an understanding of his own position in the natural scheme of things. Each derives its unity from the interrelationship between Clare's experience at the time he initially composes the poem and other experiences foreign both in time and place. From a fixed, rather than a rambling, point of view he ponders two sets of natural phenomena, producing poems reduced in the scale of their physical perceptions, but intensified in their vision. In the for-

mer he concentrates on his immediate location to examine the universal power of ''the common things of everyday'' to excite pleasure; in the latter he hears the sound of a bird singing *now* as a type of nature's continuous impulse toward song. (p. 85)

During the last period of his life, spent in the asylum at Northampton, Clare writes less frequently of his individual response to nature. When he does it is either to mourn his loss of contact with it or to use it as an objective correlative to his other emotional experiences. The bulk of his work written between 1842 and his death in 1864 consists of songs, and most of his descriptions of nature are adapted to the requirements of that subgenre. Clare seems to have been unable, or unwilling, to sustain the experimentation with experience and metaphor which reached its zenith in his High Beech days, possibly because of his increasingly disturbed mind which was obviously capable of fine outbursts of song and poetry, but not of consistent development in his art. He left incomplete his two ambitious works of 1841, **"Child Harold"** and **"Don Juan,"** and confined himself to short poems for the rest of his life. But a more likely reason for his decline in experimentation with the kind of poem we have been discussing stems from his being allowed less frequent rambles outside the asylum walls, hence fewer poetic experiences upon which to base his poems. As a result, he wrote made-to-order love songs and several poems from former, remembered experiences. . . . The few poems in which he does employ personal experiences use them very simply, with none of the complexity or subtlety of his best previous ones. (p. 91)

Because Clare's theory of poetic composition stressed the value of symbols elicited from nature, we might expect to find a large number of them in his work. And since these symbols are the result of a single mind responding to its environment over half a century, we might be justified in looking for a unified pattern which would reflect the changing nature of these responses as the mind itself matured. In practice Clare's poetry returns again and again to the same group of metaphors and symbols; as a consequence, we can measure his growth, both personally and poetically, in the altering attitude to them. His recurring motifs include the ''book'' of nature and the bird as a symbol of poetic utterance, as well as the sun and wind which dominate so much of his verse. A more pervasive pattern of interrelated symbols which gives a sense of profound unity to the body of his work has been noted by Eric Robinson and Geoffrey Summerfield [see excerpt above, 1966]:

> In the landscape of Eden before the Fall, Clare's boyhood love, Mary Joyce, is present—she is the Eve to Clare's Adam. Unless we recognize that this is the conscious pattern of imagery in Clare's poetry, we are bound to miss a great deal of his point. . . .

In this scheme Eden symbolizes not only childhood innocence but a complex state of mind which, although primarily experienced in childhood, could also recur in select, but brief, periods throughout the rest of his life. The decreasing ability to maintain this state as he grew older, therefore, represented for him the loss of Eden, and the mental state that resulted from this loss he expressed in another symbol, the wasteland. (pp. 184-85)

During that part of his life which he compared to a wasteland, however, he never lost sight of the possibility of moments of edenic insight recurring. Even in his desert we get glimpses of paradise which make his life outside Eden tolerable and at times even enjoyable. He formulated no theory, either psychological or philosophical, to support his view, but [as **"Wreck of the Emelie"** reveals] he was constantly aware of the effect of these glimpses on his state of mind:

> The healthfull mind that muses and inhales
> The green eyed dews of morning finds his way
> To paradise Gods choice self planted vales. . . .

His conversion of the desert into an Eden produced brief periods of intense response to the beauties of nature which provided the germ for many of his mature poems. The existence of these glimpses was enough to sustain him in the wasteland of his later life. . . . As symbols, Eden and the desert provide additional structure to the body of Clare's work by marking a constant polarity between the moods of sensitivity, freedom, and love, and those of melancholy, anger, and despair. They also demonstrate development by tracing the gradual decline of edenic experiences into the predominantly barren landscape of his later years.

Clare's ability to conceive symbols larger than those of a single poem and to apply them more or less consistently throughout his life is another indication of his true stature as a poet. He is gradually gaining the recognition he deserves and the amount of his available writings is slowly increasing. . . . From the evidence it appears his reputation grows according to the formula he himself approved: "the quiet progress of a name gaining its ground by gentle degrees in the world's esteem is the best living shadow of fame to follow." (pp. 185-87)

William Howard, in his John Clare, *Twayne Publishers, 1981, 205 p.*

ADDITIONAL BIBLIOGRAPHY

Barrell, John. *The Idea of Landscape and the Sense of Place, 1730-1840: An Approach to the Poetry of John Clare,* Cambridge: Cambridge at the University Press, 1972, 244 p.

A highly regarded examination of Clare's pre-asylum poetry within the context of the enclosure of Helpston. Through a detailed analysis of the imagery, language, and syntax of the early poems, Barrell demonstrates how Clare's "sense of place"—his tendency to "localise" and "particularise" the effects of enclosure on the landscape of Helpston—contrasts with the generalized landscape descriptions of such eighteenth-century poets as James Thomson.

Bloom, Harold. "Beddoes, Clare, Darley, and Others: John Clare." In his *The Visionary Company: A Reading of English Romantic Poetry,* rev. ed., pp. 444-56. Ithaca, N.Y.: Cornell University Press, 1971.

Examines the successive stages of Clare's poetic growth within the context of the Romantic nature/imagination dialectic. Bloom focuses on the asylum poems "Secret Love," "An Invite to Eternity," "I Am," and "A Vision," which he favorably likens to William Blake's visionary poetry. This essay was written in 1959-60.

B[lunden], [Edmund]. "Biographical." In *John Clare: Poems Chiefly from Manuscript,* by John Clare, edited by Edmund Blunden and Alan Porter, pp. 9-45. London: Richard Cobden-Sanderson, 1920.

An attempt to dispel the misconceptions about Clare's life generated by his previous biographers.

———. *Keats's Publisher: A Memoir of John Taylor (1781-1864).* London: Jonathan Cape, 1936, 256 p.*

A detailed account of John Taylor's career. Blunden describes Clare's early association with the publisher and includes numerous references to their frequently tumultuous friendship.

Brownlow, Timothy. "A Molehill for Parnassus: John Clare and Prospect Poetry." *University of Toronto Quarterly* XLVIII, No. 1 (Fall 1978): 23-40.

Determines Clare's place within the tradition of topographical poetry, a genre of the seventeenth and eighteenth centuries that focuses on a particular landscape. Brownlow demonstrates how Clare developed a "unique" kaleidoscopic, microscopic, and kinetic vision of nature out of that tradition.

———. *John Clare and Picturesque Landscape.* Oxford: Clarendon Press, 1983, 158 p.

Examines Clare's early descriptive poetry within the context of the picturesque tradition. Brownlow focuses on Clare's knowledge of natural history and painting, his use of landscape, and his relationship to topographical poetry.

Cherry, J. L. *Life and Remains of John Clare.* London: Frederick Warne and Co., 1873, 349 p.

A biography of Clare chiefly notable for its two hundred pages of asylum poems and prose fragments.

Chilcott, Tim. "Taylor and Clare: 1819-37." In his *A Publisher and His Circle: The Life and Work of John Taylor, Keats's Publisher,* pp. 86-128. London: Routledge & Kegan Paul, 1972.

Examines Clare's relationship with John Taylor. Although Chilcott is primarily interested in pointing out Taylor's perceptiveness as a literary critic, the essay contains observations on the development of Clare's poetry, from his early, descriptive verse to his later, more reflective work.

Constantine, David. "Outside Eden: John Clare's Descriptive Poetry." In *An Infinite Complexity: Essays in Romanticism,* edited by J. R. Watson, pp. 181-201. University of Durham 150th Anniversary Series, vol. 1. Edinburgh: Edinburgh University Press, 1983.

Contends that Clare's "greatest gift and blessing, and his one true asylum" was his ability to discern beauty in nature despite the emotional loss he suffered by the enclosure of Helpston.

Crossan, Greg. *Romantic Reassessment: A Relish for Eternity, The Process of Divinization in the Poetry of John Clare.* Edited by James Hogg. Salzburg Studies in English Literature, edited by Erwin A. Stürzl, no. 53. Salzburg: Universität Salzburg, 1976, 276 p.

Notes a unifying thread in Clare's poetry in his "habit of investing all the preoccupations of his life with religious meaning" and examines Clare's attitudes toward nature, poetry, women, and the past. Crossan integrates a survey of Clare criticism into his discussion and provides a detailed bibliography listing editions of Clare's works published after his death, reviews and studies of his poetry, and reference volumes containing important background information.

Crowson, Daniel. *Rambles with John Clare.* Helpston, England: C. E. Cutforth, 1978, 63 p.

A pamphlet describing the countryside of Helpston by a native of the village. Crowson provides maps of Helpston and pictures of many of the places that inspired Clare's poetry.

Eagle, Solomon [pseudonym of John Collings Square]. "John Clare." In his *Books in General, third series,* pp. 129-34. London: Hodder & Stoughton, 1921.

A biographical and critical sketch. Eagle applauds Clare's accurate descriptions of nature and comments on the patronizing tone of John Taylor's introduction to *Poems* (see excerpt above, 1820).

Grainger, Margaret. *John Clare: Collector of Ballads.* Peterborough Museum Society Occasional Papers, no. 3. Peterborough, England: Museum, 1964, 23 p.

A consideration of Clare's interest in the music and poetry of folk ballads. Grainger argues that Clare belonged to no poetic school and that the ballad tradition was the most important influence on his poetry. She provides an appendix listing ballads that Clare collected, including those published in posthumous collections of his works.

Graves, Robert. "The Clark Lectures, 1954-1955: The Road to Rydal Mount." In his *The Crowning Privilege: The Clark Lectures, 1954-1955,* *also Various Essays on Poetry and Sixteen New Poems,* pp. 45-69. London: Cassell & Co., 1955.*

Contrasts the literary careers of Clare and William Wordsworth.

Gregory, Horace. "On John Clare, and the Sight of Nature in His Poetry." In his *The Shield of Achilles: Essays on Beliefs in Poetry,* pp. 21-32. New York: Harcourt, Brace and Co., 1944.

A general discussion of Clare's life and poetry. Gregory focuses on Clare's response, both as a man and as a poet, to his short-lived fame following the publication of *Poems.*

Grigson, Geoffrey. Introduction to *Poems of John Clare's Madness,* by John Clare, edited by Geoffrey Grigson, pp. 1-50. London: Routledge and Kegan Paul, 1949.

A biographical and critical study in which Grigson discusses Clare's asylum poetry in relation to his mental illness. As in his introduction to *Selected Poems of John Clare* (see excerpt above, 1950), Grigson cites the supremacy of Clare's asylum verse over his earlier poetry.

Hall, Spencer T. "Bloomfield and Clare." In his *Biographical Sketches of Remarkable People, Chiefly from Recollection, with Miscellaneous Papers and Poems,* pp. 155-73. London: Simpkin, Marshall and Co., 1873.*

A biographical portrait in which Hall denounces early critics of Clare's poetry for emphasizing his peasant origins. Hall also provides an account of his visits with Clare at the asylum in Northampton.

Hewlett, Maurice. "Peasant Poets." In his *Last Essays of Maurice Hewlett,* pp. 82-7. London: William Heinemann, 1925.*

Views Clare as the quintessential peasant poet. According to Hewlett, Clare's verse exhibits the characteristic qualities of peasant poetry: minute observation, stark simplicity, realism, and the "lyric cry," which the critic defines as the "pure and simple utterance in words of the passion in the heart."

Jack, Ian. "Clare and the Minor Poets." In his *English Literature: 1815-1832,* pp. 130-84. Oxford: Oxford at the Clarendon Press, 1963.*

An overview of Clare's works. Jack focuses on *The Shepherd's Calendar,* which he ranks with "all but the greatest" poetry in the English language.

Lewis, C. Day. "Country Lyrics." In his *The Lyric Impulse,* pp. 103-29. Cambridge: Harvard University Press, 1965.*

An appreciation of Clare as a lyric poet.

Lubbock, Percy. Review of *Madrigals and Chronicles,* by John Clare. *The Nation & The Athenaeum* 35, No. 23 (6 September 1924): 694.

Argues that Edmund Blunden exaggerated Clare's importance in his preface to *Madrigals and Chronicles* (see excerpt above, 1924).

[Lynd, Robert]. Review of *John Clare: Poems,* by John Clare. *The Nation* XXVIII, No. 17 (22 January 1921): 581-82.

Denies that Clare's works rank beside those of William Wordsworth, Percy Bysshe Shelley, John Keats, William Blake, Robert Burns, and William Collins. According to Lynd, Clare's place in literature is comparable to that of William Henry Hudson, a popular late nineteenth and early twentieth-century naturalist and writer.

Martin, Frederick. *The Life of John Clare.* 2d ed. London: Frank Cass & Co., 1964, 319 p.

The first full-length account of Clare's life. Martin's work, which was originally published in 1865, is considered the most romanticized biography of Clare. Nevertheless, it is valued by modern critics because of Martin's access to documents now lost.

Mitford, Mary Russell. "Peasant Poets: John Clare." In her *Recollections of a Literary Life; or, Books, Places, and People,* pp. 115-26. New York: Harper & Brothers, 1852.

A sympathetic description of Clare's life at the asylums in High Beech and Northampton.

Moult, Thomas. "The Poetry of the Green Man." *English Review* 32 (February 1921): 186-89.

Asserts that in his asylum poetry, Clare achieved an imaginative vision of nature comparable to those of William Wordsworth and John Keats.

Oswald, Robert. "John Clare." *Gentleman's Magazine* 292, No. 2056 (April 1902): 382-95.

A concise biographical portrait based on J. L. Cherry's *Life and Remains of John Clare* (see annotation above).

Palgrave, Francis T. "Landscape in Recent Poetry—Coleridge, Keats, Shelley." In his *Landscape in Poetry from Homer to Tennyson with Many Illustrative Examples,* pp. 196-230. London: Macmillan and Co., 1897.*

Praises Clare's asylum poetry for its pathos.

Peckham, Houston. "John Clare, a Forgotten Nineteenth-Century Poet." *South Atlantic Quarterly* XII, No. 1 (January 1913): 50-9.

Calls for greater recognition of Clare as a sonneteer, lyricist, and philosophical poet, but asserts that his fame will rest on his vivid and accurate descriptions of nature.

Reeves, James. Introduction to *Selected Poems of John Clare,* by John Clare, edited by James Reeves, pp. xi-xxix. Melbourne: William Heinemann, 1954.

A critical, biographical, and psychological study in which Reeves suggests that a knowledge of Clare's life is essential to an understanding of his poetry. Reeves examines Clare's poetry within the context of his "manic-depressive temperament" and asserts that his poems are the "expression of happiness" because "their composition is Clare's triumph over suffering." The critic cautions against a selective reading of Clare's work, arguing that his "natural taste, craftsmanship, and poetic integrity" are most discernible when his poetry is studied as a whole.

Robinson, Eric, and Summerfield, Geoffrey. "John Clare: An Interpretation of Certain Asylum Letters." *The Review of English Studies* XIII, No. 50 (1962): 135-46.

Deciphers and analyzes three previously unpublished asylum letters written in a code in which all vowels and the letter "y" are omitted.

Rothery, Agnes. "Four Poets and Four Gardens." In her *The Joyful Gardener,* pp. 151-66. New York: Dodd, Mead & Co., 1949.*

Emphasizes Clare's love of nature. According to Rothery, Clare, "more than any other [poet], spoke not so much as an observer of the growing world, but almost as if that world were speaking through him."

Squire, J. C. "John Clare." In his *Books Reviewed: Critical Essays on Books and Authors,* pp. 1-8. 1920. Reprint. Port Washington, N.Y.: Kennikat Press, 1968.

A brief appreciation of Clare as a descriptive poet. Squire considers Clare a poet of the second order.

Stoddard, Richard Henry. "John Clare." In his *Under the Evening Lamp,* pp. 120-34. New York: Charles Scribner's Sons, 1892.

Discounts the possibility of judging Clare's poetry. According to Stoddard, Clare's poetry is "not the kind . . . to criticize, for it is full of faults, but to be read generously and tenderly, remembering [his] lowly life."

Storey, Mark. *The Poetry of John Clare: A Critical Introduction.* New York: St. Martin's Press, 1974, 228 p.

An introductory study aimed primarily at students who are unfamiliar with Clare's poetry. Storey traces the development of Clare's poems, from the "earliest gropings and imitations to the later poetry of vision." As part of his attempt to establish the coherence of Clare's work as a whole, Storey demonstrates that the early periods of his poetic development were "important stages in the growth of a mind essentially visionary." While Storey makes no effort to place Clare within the context of the poetic climate of the first half of the nineteenth century, he extensively examines his debt to the poetic tradition of the late eighteenth century.

————, ed. *Clare: The Critical Heritage*. The Critical Heritage Series, edited by B. C. Southam. London: Routledge & Kegan Paul, 1973, 453 p.

> An anthology of Clare criticism drawn from books, magazines, newspapers, and letters from the earliest reviews through 1964. Also included are extracts from Clare's own letters in which he discusses critical and public reaction to his works. Annotations preface many of the critical pieces, and Storey's introduction is a helpful overview of Clare's fluctuating reputation.

Thomas, Edward. "Women, Nature, and Poetry." In his *Feminine Influence on the Poets,* pp. 65-90. New York: John Lane Co., 1911.*

> Discusses Clare's identification of nature with love in his asylum poetry.

————. "The East Coast and Midlands: John Clare." In his *A Literary Pilgrim in England,* pp. 224-35. New York: Dodd, Mead and Co., 1917.

> A biographical and critical study in which Thomas commends Clare for his detailed descriptions of natural scenery and rural life.

Tibble, J[ohn] W., and Tibble, Anne. Introduction to *The Letters of John Clare,* by John Clare, edited by J. W. Tibble and Anne Tibble, pp. 13-20. London: Routledge & Kegan Paul, 1951.

> Underscores the value of Clare's correspondence as a record of the progression of his mental illness.

————. *John Clare: His Life and Poetry.* Melbourne: William Heinemann, 1956, 216 p.

An abbreviated version of the Tibbles' 1932 *John Clare: A Life,* but with added critical commentary on Clare's poetry.

————. *John Clare: A Life.* Rev. ed. Totowa, N.J.: Rowman and Littlefield, 1972, 442 p.

> The standard biography. This work supersedes the Tibbles' earlier *John Clare: A Life,* which was published in 1932.

Todd, Janet M. "John Clare: A Bibliographical Essay." *British Studies Monitor* IV, No. 2 (Winter 1974): 3-18.

> Assesses twentieth-century critical commentary on Clare and discusses the merits and defects of the various Clare biographies. In addition, Todd delineates the reasons for Clare's fluctuating reputation, points out textual variations in the collected editions of his works, and lists magazine articles that contain previously unpublished poems and letters written by Clare.

Williams, Raymond. "The Green Language." In his *The Country and the City,* pp. 127-41. New York: Oxford University Press, 1973.*

> A consideration of Clare's poetry within the context of the rural and social changes effected by enclosure. Williams maintains that "Clare marks the end of pastoral poetry, in the very shock of its collision with actual country experience."

Wilson, June. *Green Shadows: The Life of John Clare.* London: Hodder & Stoughton, 1951, 271 p.

> A sympathetic biography. Wilson excerpts liberally from Clare's correspondence and autobiographical sketches.

Samuel Taylor Coleridge

1772-1834

English poet, critic, essayist, dramatist, and journalist.

Coleridge is considered one of the most significant poets and critics in the English language. As a major figure in the English Romantic movement, he is best known for three poems, "The Rime of the Ancient Mariner," "Kubla Khan," and "Christabel," and one volume of criticism, *Biographia Literaria; or, Biographical Sketches of My Literary Life and Opinions*. While "The Ancient Mariner," "Kubla Khan," and "Christabel" were poorly received during Coleridge's lifetime, they are now praised as classic examples of imaginative poetry, illuminated by Coleridge's poetic theories, of which he said in the *Biographia Literaria,* "My endeavours should be directed to persons and characters spiritual and supernatural, or at least romantic." Coleridge's other great contribution to literature lies in his critical writings. His criticism, which examines the nature of poetic creation and stresses the relationship between emotion and intellect, helped free literary thought from the Neoclassical strictures of eighteenth-century scholars. Coleridge's analyses, particularly those on William Shakespeare, channeled the concepts of the German Romantic philosophers into England and were instrumental in establishing the modern view of Shakespeare as a masterful depicter of human character. However, many of Coleridge's critical endeavours, like several of his poems, remain unfinished. Through the years, critics have faulted his lack of sustained concentration, contending that he misused his talents. Though the recent publication of his voluminous correspondence and notebooks challenges the notion of Coleridge as unproductive, the extensive editing required to compile such a work reinforces the argument that his disorganization contributed to years of critical neglect.

Born in Devon, Coleridge had a happy childhood until he was ten, when his father died. The boy was then sent away to school at Christ's Hospital in London. Later, Coleridge described his years there as desperately lonely; only the friendship of Charles Lamb, a fellow student, offered solace. From Christ's Hospital, Coleridge went to Jesus College, Cambridge, where he earned a reputation as a promising young writer and brilliant conversationalist. However, he accrued enormous gambling debts, and his financial difficulties, coupled with the pain of an unrequited romance, caused him to enlist in the army. Coleridge's brothers located him and paid his debts, and the next spring he returned to Cambridge. He was still plagued by personal problems, however, and left in 1794 without completing his degree. Coleridge then traveled to Oxford University, where he befriended Robert Southey. The two developed a plan for a "pantisocracy," or egalitarian agricultural society, to be founded in Kentucky. For a time, both were absorbed by their revolutionary concepts and together composed a number of works informed by their politically radical ideas, including a drama, *The Fall of Robespierre*. Their plan also required that each member be married so Coleridge, solely at Southey's urging, wed Sara Fricker, the sister of Southey's fiancée. Unfortunately, the match proved disastrous, and Coleridge's unhappy marriage was a source of grief to him throughout his life. To compound Coleridge's difficulties, Southey lost interest in the scheme, abandoning it in 1795.

Coleridge's fortunes changed when in 1796 he met the poet William Wordsworth, with whom he had corresponded casually for several years. Their rapport was instantaneous, and the next year Coleridge moved to Nether Stowey in the Lake District, the site of their literary collaboration. Influenced by Wordsworth, whom Coleridge considered the finest poet since John Milton, Coleridge composed the bulk of his most admired work. Because he had no regular income, he was reluctantly planning to become a Unitarian minister when, in 1798, the prosperous china manufacturers Josiah and Thomas Wedgwood offered him a lifetime pension so that he could devote himself to writing. Aided by this annuity, Coleridge entered a prolific period that lasted from 1798 to 1800, composing "The Ancient Mariner," "Christabel," "Frost at Midnight," and "Kubla Khan." In 1798, Coleridge also collaborated with Wordsworth on *Lyrical Ballads,* a volume of poetry which they published anonymously. Wordsworth composed the majority of the poems and also wrote the now-famous preface, which stated that these poems "were written chiefly with a view to ascertain how far the language of conversation in the middle and lower classes is adapted to the purposes of poetic pleasure." Coleridge's contributions included "The Ancient Mariner," published in its original, rather archaic form. Most critics found the poem incomprehensible, including Southey, who termed it "a Dutch attempt at German sublimity." The poem's unpopularity impeded the volume's success, and it was not until the twentieth century that *Lyrical Ballads* came to be recognized as the first literary document of English Romanticism.

Following the publication of *Lyrical Ballads*, Coleridge traveled to Germany where he developed an interest in the German philosophers Immanuel Kant, Friedrich von Schelling, and August Wilhelm and Friedrich von Schlegel; he later introduced German aesthetic theory in England through his critical writings. Upon his return in 1799, Coleridge settled in Keswick, near the Lake District, which now gained for him the title "Lake Poet," which he shared with Wordsworth and Southey. The title is generally believed to be misleading, however, for Coleridge only spent brief periods of his life in the area. The move to Keswick marked the beginning of an era of chronic illness and personal misery for Coleridge. When his health suffered because of the damp climate, he took opium as a remedy, but quickly became addicted. His marriage, too, was failing; Coleridge had fallen in love with Wordsworth's sister-in-law, Sara Hutchinson. He was separated from his wife, but because he did not condone divorce, he did not remarry. In an effort to improve his health and morale, Coleridge traveled to Italy, but returned to London more depressed than before. He began a series of lectures on poetry and Shakespeare which are now considered the basis of his reputation as a critic, yet they were not entirely successful at the time because of his disorganized methods and presentation. Coleridge's next undertaking, a periodical entitled *The Friend*, which offered essays on morality, taste, and religion, failed due to financial difficulties. He continued to visit the Wordsworths, yet was morose and anti-social. When a mutual friend confided Wordsworth's complaints about his behavior, an irate Coleridge immediately returned to London. His reaction was perhaps fueled in part by his jealousy of Wordsworth's productivity and prosperity. Although the two men were finally reconciled in 1812, they never again achieved their former intimacy.

Coleridge's last years were spent under the care of Dr. James Gilman, who helped him control his opium habit. Despite Coleridge's continuing melancholy, he was able to dictate the *Biographia Literaria* to his friend John Morgan. The *Biographia Literaria* contains what many critics consider Coleridge's greatest critical writings. In this work, he developed aesthetic theories which he had intended as the introduction to a great philosophical opus that was never completed. Coleridge published many other works during this period, including the two early fragments "Kubla Khan" and "Christabel," as well as a number of political and theological writings. This resurgence of productivity, coupled with his victory over his addiction, brought him renewed confidence. His newfound happiness, however, was marred by failing health; he died in 1834 of complications from his life-long dependence on opium. Upon learning that his old friend had passed away, Wordsworth remarked that Coleridge was the only "wonderful" man he had ever known.

Though critical estimation of Coleridge increased dramatically after his death, relatively little was written on him until the turn of the century. Opinions of his work vary widely, yet few today deny the talent evident in "The Ancient Mariner," "Kubla Khan," and "Christabel." "The Ancient Mariner," the only work which he completed, best incorporates Coleridge's imaginative versification and the intertwining of reality and fantasy. The tale of a seaman who kills an albatross, "The Ancient Mariner" presents a variety of religious and supernatural images to depict a moving spiritual journey of doubt, renewal, and eventual redemption. Many of the poem's symbols have

sparked radically different interpretations, and several commentators consider the poem an allegorical record of Coleridge's own spiritual pilgrimage. Critics also debate the nature of the Mariner's salvation and question whether the poem possesses a moral; Coleridge's own comment was that the poem's major fault consisted of "the obtrusion of the moral sentiment so openly on the reader.... It ought to have had no more moral than the *Arabian Nights'* tale of the merchant's sitting down to eat dates...."

Coleridge's concern with religious themes is also evidenced in "Kubla Khan," which was published with a note explaining the strange circumstances of its composition. Coleridge wrote that he fell asleep while reading an account of how the Chinese emperor Kubla Khan had ordered the building of a palace within a walled garden. Three hours later Coleridge woke and began to write down the several hundred lines which he claimed he had composed during his sleep. However, he found that the rest of the poem had disappeared from his mind. In a later note appended to the text, he added that he had taken opium and hence described his dream as "a sort of reverie." For many years, critics considered "Kubla Khan" merely a novelty or fragment of limited meaning, but John Livingston Lowes's 1927 study, *The Road to Xanadu: A Study in the Ways of the Imagination,* revealed the imaginative complexity of the work and explored the many literary sources which influenced the poem, including the works of Plato and Milton. Though Coleridge himself dismissed "Kubla Khan" as simply a "psychological experiment," the poem is now considered a forerunner of the work of the Symbolists and Surrealists in its presentation of the unconscious. In Coleridge's other poetic fragment, "Christabel," he combined exotic images with gothic romance to create an atmosphere of terror. Like "The Ancient Mariner," "Christabel" deals with the themes of evil and guilt in a setting pervaded by supernatural elements. Most critics now contend that Coleridge's inability to sustain the poem's eerie mood prevented him from completing "Christabel."

The *Biographia Literaria*, the best known of Coleridge's critical writings, was inspired by his disdain for the eighteenth-century empiricists who relied on observation and experimentation to formulate their aesthetic theories. In this work, he turned to such German philosophers as Kant and Schelling for a more all-encompassing interpretation of art. From Schelling, Coleridge drew his "exaltation of art to a metaphysical role," and his contention that art is analagous to nature is borrowed from Kant. A number of critics, in fact, have argued that he plagiarized their theories. While Coleridge acknowledged his debt to the Germans, he denied that he had stolen their concepts. Of the different sections in the *Biographia Literaria,* perhaps the best known is Coleridge's definition of the imagination. He describes two kinds of imagination, the primary and secondary: the primary is the agent of perception which relays the details of experience, while the secondary interprets these details and creates from them. The concept of a dual imagination forms a seminal part of Coleridge's theory of poetic unity, in which disparate elements are reconciled as a unified whole. According to Coleridge, the purpose of poetry was to provide pleasure "through the medium of beauty."

Coleridge's other great critical achievement is his work on Shakespeare. Ironically, Coleridge's Shakespearean criticism is among the most important in the English language, though it was never published in formal essays and instead comes down to posterity in the form of marginalia and transcribed reports from lectures. Informed by his admiration for and understanding of Shakespeare, Coleridge's critical theory allowed for more in-depth analysis of the plays than did the writings of his eighteenth-century predecessors. Coleridge's emphasis on individual psychology and characterization marked the inception of a new critical approach to Shakespeare which had a profound influence on later studies. In his roles as critic and poet, Coleridge displayed a concern for creativity as a guiding force both for the individual and for the universe. Literature, Coleridge concluded, required an intertwining of emotion and thought to be truly imaginative. His acknowledgement of the power of the imagination offered subsequent critics a new perspective for literary interpretation.

Studies in the twentieth century focus on various readings of Coleridge's poetry and criticism, and the controversies over their merit have long since abated. Today, his problems of disorganization are largely ignored, and most critics agree that his writings constitute a seminal contribution to literature. While a few commentators, most notably J. Middleton Murry and F. R. Leavis, have termed both Coleridge's criticism and stature overrated, the majority acknowledge his poetical talent and insight. Contemporary scholars now look to Coleridge as the intellectual center of the English Romantic movement.

PRINCIPAL WORKS

The Fall of Robespierre [with Robert Southey]   (drama)   1794
Poems on Various Subjects   (poetry)   1796; also published as *Poems* [revised edition], 1797
Ode on the Departing Year   (poetry)   1797
Osorio [first publication]   (drama)   1797; also published as *Remorse* [revised edition], 1813
Fears in Solitude   (poetry)   1798
*Lyrical Ballads [with William Wordsworth]   (poetry) 1798; also published as *Lyrical Ballads* [revised edition], 1800
Wallenstein [translator; from the dramas *Die Piccolomini* and *Wallensteins Tod* by Johann Christoph Friedrich von Schiller]   (drama)   1800
Poems   (poetry)   1803
Christabel. Kubla Khan: A Vision. The Pains of Sleep (poetry)   1816
The Statesman's Manual   (essay)   1816
Biographia Literaria; or, Biographical Sketches of My Literary Life and Opinions   (essays)   1817
Sibylline Leaves   (poetry)   1817
Zapolya: A Christmas Tale   (drama)   1817
The Poetical Works of Samuel Taylor Coleridge. 3 vols. (poetry, dramas, and translation)   1828
The Literary Remains of Samuel Taylor Coleridge. 4 vols. (poetry, essays, and drama)   1836-39
The Complete Works of Samuel Taylor Coleridge. 7 vols. (poetry, dramas, translation, and essays)   1853
Coleridge's Miscellaneous Criticism   (criticism)   1936
Collected Letters. 6 vols.   (letters)   1956-71
The Notebooks of Samuel Taylor Coleridge. 3 vols. (notebooks)   1957-73

*This work includes the poem "The Rime of the Ancient Mariner."

WILLIAM WORDSWORTH   (essay date 1798)

[*An English poet and critic, Wordsworth was central to English Romanticism. His literary criticism reflects his belief that neither the language nor the content of poetry should be stylized or elaborate and that the purpose of a poet was to feel and express the relation between man and nature. Wordsworth collaborated with Coleridge on the* Lyrical Ballads, *and though Wordsworth is traditionally considered a guiding force of Romanticism,* Lyrical Ballads *does not contain conventionally Romantic qualities. The following is the preface, or "advertisement," as it is often called, to the first edition of the* Lyrical Ballads *published in 1798. According to Wordsworth, these poems were experiments with conversational language, intended to depict "a natural delineation of human passions, human characters, and human incidents." He adds that the emotional intent of the poems, particularly "The Ancient Mariner," is meant to emulate such earlier poets as William Cowper and Alexander Pope.*]

It is the honourable characteristic of Poetry that its materials are to be found in every subject which can interest the human mind. The evidence of this fact is to be sought, not in the writings of Critics, but in those of Poets themselves.

The majority of the following poems [in *Lyrical Ballads*] are to be considered as experiments. They were written chiefly with a view to ascertain how far the language of conversation in the middle and lower classes of society is adapted to the purposes of poetic pleasure. Readers accustomed to the gaudiness and inane phraseology of many modern writers, if they persist in reading this book to its conclusion, will perhaps frequently have to struggle with feelings of strangeness and aukwardness: they will look round for poetry, and will be induced to enquire by what species of courtesy these attempts can be permitted to assume that title. It is desirable that such readers, for their own sakes, should not suffer the solitary word Poetry, a word of very disputed meaning, to stand in the way of their gratification; but that, while they are perusing this book, they should ask themselves if it contains a natural delineation of human passions, human characters, and human incidents; and if the answer be favourable to the author's wishes, that they should consent to be pleased in spite of that most dreadful enemy to our pleasures, our own pre-established codes of decision.

Readers of superior judgment may disapprove of the style in which many of these pieces are executed it must be expected that many lines and phrases will not exactly suit their taste. It will perhaps appear to them, that wishing to avoid the prevalent fault of the day, the author has sometimes descended too low, and that many of his expressions are too familiar, and not of sufficient dignity. It is apprehended, that the more conversant the reader is with our elder writers, and with those in modern times who have been the most successful in painting manners and passions, the fewer complaints of this kind will he have to make. (pp. 7-8)

"The Rime of the Ancyent Marinere" was professedly written in imitation of the *style,* as well as of the spirit of the elder poets; but with a few exceptions, the Author believes that the language adopted in it has been equally intelligible for these three last centuries. (p. 8)

William Wordsworth, in an advertisement in Lyrical Ballads *by William Wordsworth and Samuel Taylor Coleridge, edited by R. L. Brett and A. R. Jones, Methuen and Co. Ltd., 1963, pp. 7-8.*

[ROBERT SOUTHEY] (essay date 1798)

[Though often overlooked by modern scholars, Southey is recognized by historians as a significant member of the Lake School of poetry, a group which included Coleridge and William Wordsworth. In his own day, Southey was considered a prominent literary figure, and his writings received serious critical assessment from his contemporaries. While a student at Oxford University, Southey met Coleridge. They shared a distaste for the English government, which they sought to replace with a "pantisocracy," or egalitarian agricultural society. Though the two composed politically radical verse and a drama, their dreams of utopia faded as their lives became financially secure. Of the two, Southey became much more conservative and devoted his time to literary criticism. In his assessment of the Lyrical Ballads, *Southey claims that the "experiment" alluded to by Wordsworth (see excerpt above, 1798) is not successful. He concedes that although many of the verses of "The Ancient Mariner" are beautiful, "in connection they are absurd or unintelligible." Nonetheless, his assessment is mixed; he acknowledges the "genius" to be found in the poems and ranks their author "with the best of living poets." It should be noted that the first version of "The Ancient Mariner" was written in more archaic language and did not contain the explanatory notes which Coleridge later provided.]*

The majority of [the poems in *Lyrical Ballads*], we are informed in the advertisement, are to be considered as experiments.

> They were written chiefly with a view to ascertain how far the language of conversation in the middle and lower classes of society is adapted to the purposes of poetic pleasure.
>
> (pp. 197-98)

[The **"Rime of the Ancyent Marinere"** is] a ballad (says the advertisement) 'professedly written in imitation of the *style*, as well as of the spirit of the elder poets.' We are tolerably conversant with the early English poets; and can discover no resemblance whatever, except in antiquated spelling and a few obsolete words. This piece appears to us perfectly original in style as well as in story. Many of the stanzas are laboriously beautiful; but in connection they are absurd or unintelligible. (p. 200)

We do not sufficiently understand the story to analyse it. It is a Dutch attempt at German sublimity. Genius has here been employed in producing a poem of little merit.

With pleasure we turn to the serious pieces, the better part of the volume. **"The Foster-mother's Tale"** is in the best style of dramatic narrative. **"The Dungeon"** and **"The Lines upon the Yew-tree Seat"** are beautiful. (p. 201)

The 'experiment,' we think, has failed, not because the language of conversation is little adapted to 'the purposes of poetic pleasure,' but because it has been tried upon uninteresting subjects. Yet every piece discovers genius; and, ill as the author has frequently employed his talents, they certainly rank him with the best of living poets. (p. 204)

> *[Robert Southey], in a review of "Lyrical Ballads, with a Few Other Poems," in* The Critical Review, *Vol. XXIV, October, 1798, pp. 197-204.*

[CHARLES BURNEY] (essay date 1799)

Though we have been extremely entertained with the fancy, the facility, and (in general) the sentiments, of [the pieces contained in *Lyrical Ballads*], we cannot regard them as *poetry*, of a class to be cultivated at the expence of a higher species

of versification, unknown in our language at the time when our elder writers, whom this author condescends to imitate, wrote their ballads.—Would it not be degrading poetry, as well as the English language, to go back to the barbarous and uncouth numbers of Chaucer? (pp. 202-03)

We have had pleasure in reading the *reliques of antient poetry*, because it was antient; and because we were surprised to find so many beautiful thoughts in the rude numbers of barbarous times. These reasons will not apply to *imitations* of antique versification.—We will not, however, dispute any longer about names; the author shall style his rustic delineations of lowlife *poetry*, if he pleases, on the same principle on which Butler is called a poet, and Teniers a painter: but are the doggrel verses of the one equal to the sublime numbers of a Milton, or are the Dutch boors of the other to be compared with the angels of Raphael or Guido?—When we confess that our author has had the art of pleasing and interesting in common way by his natural delneation of human passions, human characters, and human incidents, we must add that these effects were not produced by the *poetry:*—we have been as much affected by pictures of misery and unmerited distress, in *prose*. The elevation of soul, when it is lifted into the higher regions of imagination, affords us a delight of a different kind from the sensation which is produced by the detail of common incidents. (p. 203)

The author's first piece, the **Rime of the ancyent marinere,** in imitation of the *style* as well as of the spirit of the elder poets, is the strangest story of a cock and a bull that we ever saw on paper: yet, though it seems a rhapsody of unintelligible wildness and incoherence, (of which we do not perceive the drift, unless the joke lies in depriving the wedding guest of his share of the feast,) there are in it poetical touches of an exquisite kind. . . .

The Nightingale sings a strain of true and beautiful poetry;—Miltonic, yet original; reflective, and interesting, in an uncommon degree. (p. 204)

The Dungeon. Here candour and tenderness for criminals seem pushed to excess. Have not jails been built on the humane Mr. Howard's plan, which have almost ruined some counties, and which look more like palaces than habitations for the perpetrators of crimes? Yet, have fewer crimes been committed in consequence of the erection of those magnificent structures, at an expence which would have maintained many in innocence and comfort out of a jail, if they have been driven to theft by want?

The mad Mother; admirable painting! in Michael Angelo's bold and masterly manner. (p. 207)

Each ballad is a tale of woe. The style and versification are those of our antient ditties: but much polished, and more constantly excellent. (p. 209)

So much genius and originality are discovered in this publication, that we wish to see another from the same hand, written on more elevated subjects and in a more cheerful disposition. (p. 210)

> *[Charles Burney], in a review of "Lyrical Ballads, with a Few Other Poems," in* The Monthly Review, *London, n.s. Vol. XXIX, June, 1799, pp. 202-10.*

THE BRITISH CRITIC (essay date 1799)

The attempt made in [*Lyrical Ballads*] is one that meets our cordial approbation; and it is an attempt by no means unsuccessful. The endeavour of the author is to recall our poetry, from the fantastical excess of refinement, to simplicity and nature. (p. 364)

We fully agree with the author, that the true notion of poetry must be sought among the poets, rather than the critics [see excerpt above, 1798]; and we will add that, unless a critic is a poet also, he will generally make but indifferent work in judging of the effusions of Genius. In the collection of poems . . ., we do not often find expressions that we esteem too familiar, or deficient in dignity; on the contrary, we think that in general the author has succeeded in attaining that judicious degree of simplicity, which accommodates itself with ease even to the sublime. It is not by pomp of words, but by energy of thought, that sublimity is most successfully achieved; and we infinitely prefer the simplicity, even of the most unadorned tale in this volume, to all the meretricious frippery of the *Darwinian* tattle.

The Poem of **"the Ancyent Marinere,"** with which the collection opens, has many excellencies, and many faults; the beginning and the end are striking and well-conducted; but the intermediate part is too long, and has, in some places, a kind of confusion of images, which loses all effect, from not being quite intelligible. The author, who is confidently said to be Mr. Coleridge, is not correctly versed in the old language, which he undertakes to employ. . . . The opening of the Poem is admirably calculated to arrest the reader's attention, by the well-imagined idea of the Wedding Guest, who is held to hear the tale, in spite of his efforts to escape. The beginning of the second canto, or fit, has much merit, if we except the very unwarrantable comparison of the Sun to that which no man can conceive:—"like God's own head,"a simile which makes a reader shudder; not with poetic feeling, but with religious disapprobation. (p. 365)

Whether the remaining poems of the volume are by Mr. Coleridge, we have not been informed; but they seem to proceed from the same mind; and in the Advertisement, the writer speaks of himself as of a single person accountable for the whole. It is therefore reasonable to conclude, that this is the fact. They all have merit, and many among them a very high rank of merit, which our feelings respecting some parts of the supposed author's character do not authorize or incline us to deny. The **"Poem on the Nightingale,"** which is there styled *a conversational Poem,* is very good; but we do not perceive it to be more conversational than Cowper's Task, which is the best poem in that style that our language possesses. (p. 366)

A review of "Lyrical Ballads, with a Few Other Poems," in The British Critic, *Vol. XIV, October, 1799, pp. 364-69.*

LORD BYRON   (poem date 1809)

[*An English poet and dramatist, Byron is considered one of the most important poets of the nineteenth century. Because of the satiric nature of much of his work, Byron is difficult to place within the Romantic movement. His most notable contribution to Romanticism is the Byronic hero, a melancholy man, often with a dark past, who eschews societal and religious strictures to seek truth and happiness in an apparently meaningless universe. The following excerpt from his satire,* English Bards and Scotch Reviewers, *first published in 1809, derides Coleridge's choice of subject matter in his poem "Lines to a Young Ass."*]

Shall gentle Coleridge pass unnoticed here,
To turgid ode, and tumid stanza dear?
Though themes of innocence amuse him best,
Yet still obscurity's a welcome guest.

If Inspiration should her aid refuse
To him who takes a Pixy for a muse,
Yet none in lofty numbers can surpass
The bard who soars to elegize an ass.
How well the subject suits his noble mind!
"A fellow-feeling makes us wond'rous kind."

(p. 12)

Lord Byron, "English Bards and Scotch Reviewers," in The British Satirist: Comprising the Best Satires of the Most Celebrated Poets, from Pope to Byron, *Richard Griffin & Co., 1826, pp. 1-46.**

HENRY CRABB ROBINSON   (letter date 1811)

[*A nineteenth-century English journalist, Robinson is remembered today for his voluminous correspondence and diaries, which chronicled London's social and intellectual history. He acted as "reporter" for several of Coleridge's lectures on Shakespeare and here stresses the unevenness of the critic's treatment of his subject. While Robinson contended that Coleridge's lectures were not instructive, though possessing moments of brilliance, modern critics place Coleridge as one of Shakespeare's preeminent commentators. Coleridge's remarks on Shakespeare come down to posterity largely as fragmentary notes, marginalia, and reports by auditors such as Robinson, rather than in formal essays.*]

You will I dare say be curious to know my opinion of Coleridge's lectures. . . . [In a word], Coleridge's lectures do high honour to him as a man of genius, but are discreditable to him (perhaps I might use with[ou]t injustice a stronger word) as a man who has a duty to discharge; for either he wants judgement to know what he ought to introduce in his lectures, or is overpowered by very culpable indolence & will not qualify himself to do justice to his subject, his hearers, or himself. His pretended lectures are unmethodical rhapsodies, moral, metaphysical & literary; abounding in brilliant thoughts, fine flashes of rhetoric, ingenious paradoxes, occasionally profound & salutary truths but they are not a scientific or constructive course of reading on any one subject a man can wish to fix his attention on. He is to lecture on Shakespear[e], Milton & the modern poets. We have in fact had one lecture on the minor poems of Shakespear[e], & have been *three nights* alone employed on *Romeo & Juliet,* which we are promised the conclusion of. The course is to consist of 15 lectures & 8 are over!!!

As a specimen, I will give you a syllabus of his sixth lecture advertised to be on *Romeo & Juliet* & Shakespear[e]'s female characters—viz: A defence of the old singing mode of reading; An attack upon Lancaster especially his modes of punishment; a defence of school-flogging. Then by a mighty spring (tho' I could not see where he fixed his foot to leap from) a beautiful statement of the opposite character of the ages of Elizabeth & Ch. I.; a commonplace dissertation on the distinct character of the European languages; an abuse of poetic diction à la Wordsworth & a long attempt to vindicate Shakespeare from the charge of impurity—However his following lecture was most excellent: he discussed the minor characters of *Romeo & Juliet* & delivered an eloquent declamation on the nature of Love which he promised in the next lecture to apply to the lovers. Alas! the next & last lecture was worse if possible than the sixth. He began unhappily with an analogy he resolved to draw between Religion & Love; no very great undertaking for a man of such powers of combination: But then he proceeded to the nature of brotherly & sisterly love & gave us a dissertation on incest. I could not attend to the rest; I know only that we are for the 4th time to hear *Romeo & Juliet* tonight. The fact is that C. cannot be induced to read Shakespear[e]; and finding himself unprepared with paritcular and appropriate observations: he has recourse to his old common-place books out of which he reads whatever chances to catch his eye. In which he certainly finds very beautiful things which only offend me from their being thus impertinently and irrelevantly brought forward. (pp. 126-27)

> *Henry Crabb Robinson, in a letter to Thomas Robinson on December 14, 1811, in his* Blake, Coleridge, Wordsworth, Lamb, &c., *edited by Edith J. Morley, 1922. Reprint by Manchester University Press, 1932, pp. 126-28.*

THE CRITICAL REVIEW (essay date 1816)

"**Christabel**" is a romantic fragment; the first part, as the author informs us, having been written in 1797, and the second in 1800, during which interval Mr. Coleridge visited Germany, still retaining the fabric of the complete story in his mind "with the wholeness no less than with the liveliness of a vision," and as the vivid impression continues to the present day, he undertakes "to embody in verse the three parts yet to come, in the course of the present year." We sincerely hope that this promise will be realized, but we fear that the task will be at least wearisome to a man of the listless habits of Mr. Coleridge. For ourselves we confess, that when we read the story in M.S. two or three years ago, it appeared to be one of those dreamlike productions whose charm partly consisted in the undefined obscurity of the conclusion—what that conclusion may be, no person who reads the commencement will be at all able to anticipate. The reader, before he opens the poem, must be prepared to allow for the stuperstitions of necromancy and sorcery, and to expect something of the glorious and unbounded range which the belief in those mysteries permits; the absurd trammels of mere physical possibility are here thrown aside, like the absurd swaddling clothes of infants, which formerly obstructed the growth of the fair symmetry of nature. (p. 505)

["**Christabel**"] is enriched with more beautiful passages than have ever before been included in so small a compass. Nothing can be better contrasted than Christabel and Geraldine—both exquisite, but both different—the first all innocence, mildness, and grace; the last all dignity, grandeur, and majesty: the one with all those innate virtues, that working internally, mould the external shape to corresponding perfectness—the other possessing merely the charm of superficial excellence: the one the gentle soul-delighting Una—the other the seeming fair, but infamous Duessa. (p. 509)

> *A review of ''Christabel. Kubla Khan, a Vision. and The Pains of Sleep,'' in* The Critical Review, *n.s. Vol. III, No. V, May, 1816, pp. 504-10.*

[JOSIAH CONDER] (essay date 1816)

[The effect of **Christabel. Kubla Khan, a Vision. The Pains of Sleep**] upon readers in general, will be that of disappointment. It may be compared to a mutilated statue, the beauty of which can only be appreciated by those who have knowledge or imagination sufficient to complete the idea of the whole composition. The reader is obliged to guess at the half-developed meaning of the mysterious incidents, and is at last at the end of the second canto, left in the dark, in the most abrupt and unceremonious manner imaginable. Yet we are much mistaken if this fragment, such as it is, will not be found to take faster

hold of the mind than many a poem six cantos long. Its merit, in point of originality, will be lost on most readers, in consequence of the prior appearance of so great a quantity of verse in the same style and measure. But the kind of interest which the tale is calculated to awaken, is quite different from that of the description of poems alluded to. Horror is the prevailing sentiment excited by **Christabel:** not that mixture of terror and disgust with which we listen to details of crime and bloodshed, but the purely imaginative feeling, the breathless thrill of indefinite emotion of which we are conscious when in the supposed presence of an unknown being, or acted upon by some influence mysteriously transcending the notice of the senses— that passion which Collins has so beautifully apostrophized under the name of Fear, in the Ode beginning

> Thou to whom the world unknown
> With all its shadowy shapes is shewn;
> Who seest appall'd the unreal scene,
> When Fancy lifts the veil between.
>
> (p. 566)

As to **Kubla Khan,** and the **Pains of Sleep,** we can only regret the publication of them, as affording a proof that the Author over-rates the importance of his name. With regard to the former, which is professedly published as a psychological curiosity, it having been composed during sleep, there appears to us nothing in the quality of the lines to render this circumstance extraordinary. We could have informed Mr. Coleridge of a reverend friend of ours, who actually wrote down two sermons on a passage in the Apocalypse, from the recollection of the spontaneous exercise of his faculties in sleep. To persons who are in the habit of poetical composition, a similar phenomenon would not be a stranger occurrence, than the spirited dialogues in prose which take place in the dreams of persons of duller invention than our poet, and which not unfrequently leave behind a very vivid impression.

We closed the present publication with sentiments of melancholy and regret, not unmixed with pity. In what an humbling attitude does such a man as Coleridge present himself to the public, in laying before them these specimens of the rich promise of excellence, with which sixteen years ago he raised the expectations of his friends,—pledges of future greatness which after sixteen years he has failed to redeem! He is now once more loudly called upon to break off his desultory and luxurious habits, and to brace his mind to intellectual exertion. Samson could never have despaired of recovering his strength, till the baldness of age should fall upon him. We cherish a hope that the principle of strength, though dormant, is still unimpaired in our poet's mind, and that he will yet awake in his strength. (pp. 571-72)

> *[Josiah Conder],''Christabel. Kubla Khan, a Vison. The Pains of Sleep,'' in* The Eclectic Review, *n.s. Vol. V, June, 1816, pp. 565-72.*

[THOMAS MOORE] (essay date 1816)

> [*A nineteenth-century Irish poet, Moore is best known for his exotic epic poem* Lalla Rookh. *Moore also wrote biographies and, occasionally, criticism. This review is indicative of the generally negative reception afforded Coleridge at this time, as evidenced in reviews by Josiah Conder (see excerpt above, 1816), William Hazlitt, and Christopher North (see excerpts below, 1816 and 1817). Coleridge was an especially vulnerable target because of his preference for German philosophy. Moore's essay, which commences with a general attack on the Lake School of poetry and closes by ridiculing Coleridge's political beliefs, is considered*

an outstanding example of the invective typifying these reviews, but of negligible critical value.]

The advertisement by which [*Christabel. Kubla Khan, a Vision. The Pains of Sleep*] was announced to the publick, carried in its front a recommendation from Lord Byron,—who, it seems, has somewhere praised *Christabel* as 'a wild and singularly original and beautiful poem.' Great as the noble bard's merits undoubtedly are in poetry, some of his latest *publications* dispose us to distrust his authority, where the question is what ought to meet the public eye; and the works before us afford an additional proof, that his judgment on such matters is not absolutely to be relied on. Moreover, we are a little inclined to doubt the value of the praise which one poet lends another. It seems now-a-days to be the practice of that once irritable race to laud each other without bounds; and one can hardly avoid suspecting, that what is thus lavishly advanced may be laid out with a view to being repaid with interest. Mr Coleridge, however, must be judged by his own merits.

It is remarked, by the writers upon the Bathos, that the true *profound* is surely known by one quality—its being wholly bottomless; insomuch, that when you think you have attained its utmost depth in the work of some of its great masters, another, or peradventure the same, astonishes you, immediately after, by a plunge so much more vigorous, as to outdo all his former out-doings. So it seems to be with the new school [of Lake poets], or, as they may be termed, the wild or lawless poets. After we had been admiring their extravagance for many years, and marvelling at the case and rapidity with which one exceeded another in the unmeaning or infantine, until not an idea was left in the rhyme—or in the insane, until we had reached something that seemed the untamed effusion of an author whose thoughts were rather more free than his actions—forth steps Mr Coleridge, like a giant refreshed with sleep. . . . (pp. 58-9)

One word as to the metre of *Christabel,* or, as Mr Coleridge terms it, '*the Christabel*'—happily enough; for indeed we doubt if the peculiar force of the definite article was ever more strongly exemplified. He says, that though the reader may fancy there prevails a great *irregularity* in the metre, some lines being of four, others of twelve syllables, yet in reality it is quite regular; only that it is 'founded on a new principle, namely, that of counting in each line the accents, not the syllables.' We say nothing of the monstrous assurance of any man coming forward coolly at this time of day, and telling the readers of English poetry, whose ear has been tuned to the lays of Spenser, Milton, Dryden, and Pope, that he makes his metre 'on a new principle!' but we utterly deny the truth of the assertion, and defy him to show us *any* principle upon which his lines can be conceived to tally. We give two or three specimens, to confound at once this miserable piece of coxcombry and shuffling. Let our 'wild, and singularly original and beautiful' author, show us how these lines agree either in number of accents or of feet.

> Ah wel-a-day!—
> For this is alone in—
And didst bring her home with thee in love and in charity—
> I pray you drink this cordial wine—
> Sir Leoline—
> And found a bright lady surpassingly fair—
> Tu—whit!—Tu—whoo!

Kubla Khan is given to the public, it seems, 'at the request of a poet of great and deserved celebrity;'—but whether Lord Byron the praiser of 'the *Christabel,*' or the Laureate, the praiser of Princes, we are not informed. As far as Mr Coleridge's 'own opinions are concerned,' it is published, 'not upon the ground of any *poetic* merits,' but 'as a PSYCHOLOGICAL CURIOSITY!' In these opinions of the candid author, we entirely concur; but for this reason we hardly think it was necessary to give the minute detail which the Preface contains, of the circumstances attending its composition. . . . It was in the year 1797, and in the summer season, Mr Coleridge was in bad health;—the particular disease is not given; but the careful reader will form his own conjectures. He had retired very prudently to a lonely farm-house; and whoever would see the place which gave birth to the 'psychological curiosity,' may find his way thither without a guide; for it is situated on the confines of Somerset and Devonshire, and on the Exmoor part of the boundary; and it is, moreover, between Porlock and Linton. In that farm-house, he had a slight indisposition, and had taken an anodyne, which threw him into a deep sleep in his chair, (whether after dinner or not he omits to state), 'at the moment that he was reading a sentence in Purchas's Pilgrims,' relative to a palace of Kubla Khan. The effects of the anodyne, and the sentence together, were prodigious: They produced the 'curiosity' now before us; for, during his three-hours sleep, Mr Coleridge 'has the most vivid confidence that he could not have composed less than from two to three hundred lines.' On awaking, he 'instantly and eagerly' wrote down the verses here published; when he was (he says, '*unfortunately*') called out by a 'person on business from Porlock, and detained by him above an hour;' and when he returned, the vision was gone. The lines here given smell strongly, it must be owned, of the anodyne; and, but that an under dose of a sedative produces contrary effects, we should inevitably have been lulled by them into forgetfulness of all things. (pp. 64-5)

Persons in this poet's unhappy condition, generally feel the want of sleep as the worst of their evils; but there are instances, too, in the history of the disease, of sleep being attended with new agony, as if the waking thoughts, how wild and turbulent soever, had still been under some slight restraint, which sleep instantly removed. Mr Coleridge appears to have experienced this symptom, if we may judge from the title of his third poem, *The Pains of Sleep;* and, in truth, from its composition—which is mere raving, without any thing more affecting than a number of incoherent words, expressive of extravagance and incongruity.—We need give no specimen of it.

Upon the whole, we look upon this publication as one of the most notable pieces of impertinence of which the press has lately been guilty; and one of the boldest experiments that has yet been made on the patience or understanding of the public. It is impossible, however, to dismiss it, without a remark or two. The other productions of the Lake School have generally exhibited talents thrown away upon subjects so mean, that no power of genius could ennoble them; or perverted and rendered useless by a false theory of poetical composition. But even in the worst of them, . . . there were always some gleams of feeling or of fancy. But the thing now before us, is utterly destitute of value. It exhibits from beginning to end not a ray of genius; and we defy any man to point out a passage of poetical merit in any of the three pieces which it contains, except, perhaps, the following lines [from *Christabel*], and even these are not very brilliant; nor is the leading thought original—

> Alas! they had been friends in youth;
> But whispering tongues can poison truth;
> And constancy lives in realms above;
> And life is thorny; and youth is vain;

And to be wroth with one we love,
Doth work like madness in the brain.

With this one exception, there is literally not one couplet in the publication before us which would be reckoned poetry, or even sense, were it found in the corner of a newspaper or upon the window of an inn. Must we then be doomed to hear such a mixture of raving and driv'ling, extolled as the work of a *'wild and original'* genius, simply because Mr Coleridge has now and then written fine verses, and a brother poet chooses, in his milder mood, to laud him from courtesy or from interest? (p. 66)

> [Thomas Moore], *"Christabel. Kubla Khan, a Vision. The Pains of Sleep," in* The Edinburgh Review, *Vol. XXVII, No. LIII, September, 1816, pp. 58-67.*

[WILLIAM HAZLITT]   (essay date 1816)

[One of the most important commentators of the Romantic age, Hazlitt was an English critic and journalist. He is best known for his descriptive criticism in which he stressed that no motives beyond judgment and analysis are necessary on the part of the critic. A critic must start with a strong opinion, Hazlitt asserted, but he must also bear in mind that evaluation is the starting point—not the object—of criticism. Hazlitt's often recalcitrant refusal to engage in close studies, however, led other critics to wonder whether he was capable of sustained analysis. His hostility toward Coleridge was well known, and this review of The Statesman's Manual, *a discussion of theological politics, was to have a lasting effect on Coleridge's reputation. Hazlitt indicates his scorn for Coleridge's apparent lack of philosophical conviction and disorganization. However, despite the contempt Hazlitt expresses, most commentators believe that it is Hazlitt's perception of Coleridge's changed values that inspired his wrath. Hazlitt objected strongly to Coleridge's intolerance of political and philosophical beliefs that he had formerly supported, as well as to his new adherence to German aesthetic theory. Though Hazlitt conceded in a later essay that Coleridge was "the only person from whom I ever learnt anything," he also wrote that Coleridge had composed nothing of value with the exception of "The Ancient Mariner" (see excerpts below, 1818 and 1825).]*

[In *The Statesman's Manual*] we meet with an abundance of 'fancies and good-nights,' odd ends of verse, and sayings of philosophers; with the ricketty contents of his commonplace book, piled up and balancing one another in helpless confusion; but with not one word to the purpose, or on the subject. An attentive perusal of this Discourse is like watching the sails of a windmill: his thoughts and theories rise and disappear in the same manner. Clouds do not shift their places more rapidly, dreams do not drive one another out more unaccountably, than Mr Coleridge's reasonings try in vain to 'chase his fancy's rolling speed.' His intended conclusions have always the start of his premises,—and they keep it: while he himself plods anxiously between the two, something like a man travelling a long, tiresome road, between two stage coaches, the one of which is gone out of sight before, and the other never comes up with him; for Mr Coleridge himself takes care of this; and if he finds himself in danger of being overtaken, and carried to his journey's end in a common vehicle, he immediately steps aside into some friendly covert, with the Metaphysical Muse, to prevent so unwelcome a catastrophe. In his weary quest of truth, he reminds us of the mendicant pilgrims that travellers meet in the Desert, with their faces always turned towards Mecca, but who contrive never to reach the shrine of the Prophet: and he treats his opinions, and his reasons for them, as lawyers do their clients, and will never suffer them to come together lest they should join issue, and so put an end to his business. It is impossible, in short, we find, to describe this strange rhapsody, without falling a little into the style of it. (pp. 444-45)

Our Lay-preacher, in order to qualify himself for the office of a guide to the blind, has not, of course, once thought of looking about for matters of fact, but very wisely draws a metaphysical bandage over his eyes, sits quietly down where he was, takes his nap, and talks in his sleep—but we really cannot say very wisely. He winks and mutters all unintelligible, and all impertinent things. Instead of inquiring into the distresses of the manufacturing or agricultural districts, he ascends to the orbits of the fixed stars, or else enters into the statistics of the garden plot under his window, and, like Falstaff, 'babbles of green fields:' instead of the balance of the three estates, King, Lords, and Commons, he gives us a theory of the balance of the powers of the human mind, the Will, the Reason, and—the Understanding: instead of referring to the tythes or taxes, he quotes the Talmud; and illustrates the whole question of peace and war, by observing, that 'the ideal republic of Plato was, if he judges rightly, to "the history of the town of Man-Soul" what Plato was to John Bunyan:'—a most safe and politic conclusion!

Mr Coleridge is not one of those whom he calls 'alarmists by trade,' but rather, we imagine, what Spenser calls 'a gentle Husher, Vanity by name.' If he does not excite apprehension, by pointing out danger and difficulties where they do not exist, neither does he inspire confidence, by pointing out the means to prevent them where they do. We never indeed saw a work that could do less good or less harm; for it relates to no one object, that any one person can have in view. It tends to produce a complete *interregnum* of all opinions; an *abeyance* of the understanding; a suspension both of theory and practice; and is indeed a collection of doubts and moot-points—all hindrances and no helps. An uncharitable critic might insinuate, that there was more quackery than folly in all this;—and it is certain, that our learned author talks as magnificently of his *nostrums,* as any advertizing impostor of them all—and professes to be in possession of all sorts of morals, religions, and political panaceas, which he keeps to himself, and expects you to pay for the secret. He is always promising great things, in short, and performs nothing. . . . [We suspect] that our author has not made up his own mind on any of the subjects of which he professes to treat, and on which he warns his readers against coming to any conclusion, without his especial assistance; by means of which, they may at last attain to 'that imperative and oracular form of the understanding,' of which he speaks as 'the form of reason itself in all things purely rational and moral.' In this state of voluntary self-delusion, into which he has thrown himself, he mistakes hallucinations for truths, though he still has his misgivings, and dares not communicate them to others, except in distant hints, lest the spell should be broken, and the vision disappear. Plain sense and plain speaking would put an end to those 'thick-coming fancies,' that lull him to repose. It is in this sort of waking dream, this giddy maze of opinions, started, and left, and resumed—this momentary pursuit of truths, as if they were butterflies—that Mr Coleridge's pleasure, and, we believe, his chief faculty, lies. He has a thousand shadowy thoughts that rise before him, and hold each a glass, in which they point to others yet more dim and distant. He has a thousand self-created fancies that glitter and burst like bubbles. In the world of shadows, in the succession of bubbles, there is no preference but of the most shadowy, no attachment but to the shortest-lived. Mr Coleridge accordingly has no principle but that of being governed entirely by his own caprice, indolence, or vanity; no opinion that any body else holds, or even he himself, for two moments together. His fancy is stronger than his reason; his apprehension greater than his comprehension. He perceives every thing, but the relations of things to one another. His ideas are as finely shaded as the rainbow of the moon upon the clouds, as evanescent, and as soon dissolved. . . . [The] general character of Mr Coleridge's intellect is a restless and yet listless dissipation, that yields to every impulse, and is stopped by every obstacle; an indifference to the greatest trifles, or the most important truths; or rather, a preference of the vapid to the solid, of the possible to the actual, of the impossible to both; of theory to practice, of contradiction to reason, and of absurdity to common sense. Perhaps it is well that he is so impracticable as he is: for whenever, by any accident, he comes to practice, he is dangerous in the extreme. Though his opinions are neutralized in the extreme levity of his understanding, we are sometimes tempted to suspect that they may be subjected to a more ignoble bias; for though he does not ply his oars very strenuously in following the tide of corruption, or set up his sails to catch the tainted breeze of popularity, he suffers his boat to drift along with the stream. We do not pretend to understand the philosophical principles of that anomalous production, 'the Friend;' but we remember that the practical measures which he there attempted to defend, were the expedition to Copenhagen, the expedition to Walcheren, and the assassination of Buonaparte, which, at the time Mr Coleridge was getting that work into circulation, was a common topic of conversation, and a sort of *forlorn hope* in certain circles. A man who exercises an unlimited philosophical scepticism on questions of abstract right or wrong, may be of service to the progress of truth; but a writer who exercises this privilege, with a regular leaning to the side of power, is a very questionable sort of person. There is not much of this kind in the present Essay. It has no leaning any way. (pp. 445-47)

[*William Hazlitt*], "*Coleridge's 'Lay-Sermon'*," in
The Edinburgh Review, *Vol. XXVII, No. LIV, December, 1816, pp. 444-59.*

SAMUEL TAYLOR COLERIDGE   (essay date 1817)

[*The following, taken from Coleridge's 1817 publication of the* Biographia Literaria, *is his famous definition of imagination and fancy.*]

The imagination then I consider either as primary, or secondary. The primary imagination I hold to be the living power and prime agent of all human perception, and as a repetition in the finite mind of the eternal act of creation in the infinite I AM. The secondary I consider as an echo of the former, co-existing with the conscious will, yet still as identical with the primary in the kind of its agency, and differing only in degree, and in the mode of its operation. It dissolves, diffuses, dissipates, in order to re-create; or where this process is rendered impossible, yet still, at all events, it struggles to idealize and to unify. It is essentially *vital,* even as all objects (as objects) are essentially fixed and dead.

Fancy, on the contrary, has no other counters to play with but fixities and definites. The fancy is indeed no other than a mode of memory emancipated from the order of time and space; and blended with, and modified by that empirical phaenomenon of the will which we express by the word *choice.* But equally with the ordinary memory it must receive all its materials ready made from the law of association. (p. 167)

Samuel Taylor Coleridge, "On the Imagination, or Esemplastic Power," in his Biographia Literaria; or, Biographical Sketches of My Literary Life and Opinions, *edited by George Watson, 1817. Reprint by Dutton, 1960, pp. 161-67.*

[CHRISTOPHER NORTH (PSEUDONYM OF JOHN WILSON)]
(essay date 1817)

[*A Scottish critic, Wilson is best known as Christopher North, the name he assumed when writing for* Blackwood's Edinburgh Magazine, *a Tory periodical to which he was a principal contributor for over twenty-five years. Wilson is not recognized as a great critic. His criticism, which was frequently written in haste, is often deficient in judgment, analysis, and finish. He often reserved his harshest words for gifted young writers whom he sincerely wanted to help by objectively analyzing their work. His other critical opinions are largely regarded as the projections of his varying moods. The* Biographia Literaria *inspired the attack excerpted below. Though Coleridge had intended the book as a serious commentary on the methods of criticism, Wilson interpreted the work as Coleridge's revenge on his reviewers. Wilson charges Coleridge with obscurity, inconsistency, and political hypocrisy, an assessment that prompted the poet to contemplate a libel suit.*]

[Coleridge's *Biographia Literaria*] does not contain an account of his opinions and literary exploits alone, but lays open, not unfrequently, the character of the Man as well as of the Author; and we are compelled to think, that while it strengthens every argument against the composition of such Memoirs, it does,

The cottage at Nether Stowey which Coleridge occupied from 1797 to 1800.

without benefitting the cause either of virtue, knowledge, or religion, exhibit many mournful sacrifices of personal dignity, after which it seems impossible that Mr Coleridge can be greatly respected either by the Public or himself.

Considered merely in a literary point of view the work is most execrable. He rambles from one subject to another in the most wayward and capricious manner; either from indolence, or ignorance, or weakness, he has never in one single instance finished a discussion; and while he darkens what was dark before into tenfold obscurity, he so treats the most ordinary common-places as to give them the air of mysteries, till we no longer know the faces of our old acquaintances beneath their cowl and hood, but witness plain flesh and blood matters of fact miraculously converted into a troop of phantoms. That he is a man of genius is certain; but he is not a man of a strong intellect nor of powerful talents. He has a great deal of fancy and imagination, but little or no real feeling, and certainly no judgment. He cannot form to himself any harmonious land-scape such as it exists in nature, but beautified by the serene light of the imagination. He cannot conceive simple and majes-tic groupes of human figures and characters acting on the the-atre of real existence. But his pictures of nature are fine only as imaging the dreaminess, and obscurity, and confusion of distempered sleep; while all his agents pass before our eyes like shadows, and only impress and affect us with a phantas-magorial splendour.

It is impossible to read many pages of this work without think-ing that Mr Coleridge conceives himself to be a far greater man than the Public is likely to admit; and we wish to waken him from what seems to us a most ludicrous delusion. He seems to believe that every tongue is wagging in his praise,—that every ear is open to imbibe the oracular breathings of his inspiration. Even when he would fain convince us that his soul is wholly occupied with some other illustrious character, he breaks out into laudatory exclamations concerning himself; no sound is so sweet to him as that of his own voice: the ground is hallowed on which his footsteps tread; and there seems to him something more than human in his very shadow. He will read no books that other people read; his scorn is as misplaced and extravagant as his admiration; opinions that seem to tally with his own wild ravings are holy and inspired; and, unless agreeable to his creed, the wisdom of ages is folly; and wits, whom the world worship, dwarfed when they approach his venerable side. His admiration of nature or of man,—we had almost said his religious feelings towards his God,—are all narrowed, weakened, and corrupted and poisoned by inveterate and diseased egotism; and instead of his mind reflecting the beauty and glory of nature, he seems to consider the mighty universe itself as nothing better than a mirror, in which, with a grinning and idiot self-complacency, he may contemplate the Physiognomy of Samuel Taylor Coleridge. Though he has yet done nothing in any one department of human knowledge, yet he speaks of his theories, and plans, and views, and discov-eries, as if he had produced some memorable revolution in Science. He at all times connects his own name in Poetry with Shakspeare, and Spenser, and Milton; in politics with Burke, and Fox, and Pitt; in metaphysics with Locke, and Hartley, and Berkeley, and Kant;—feeling himself not only to be the worthy compeer of those illustrious Spirits, but to unite, in his own mighty intellect, all the glorious powers and faculties by which they were separately distinguished, as if his soul were endowed with all human power, and was the depository of the aggregate, or rather the essence, of all human knowledge. (pp. 5-6)

The truth is, that Mr Coleridge is but an obscure name in English literature. In London he is well known in literary so-ciety, and justly admired for his extraordinary loquacity: he has his own little circle of devoted worshippers, and he mis-takes their foolish babbling for the voice of the world. . . . In Scotland few know or care any thing about him; and perhaps no man who has spoken and written so much, and occasionally with so much genius and ability, ever made so little impression on the public mind. . . . Yet, insignificant as he assuredly is, he cannot put pen to paper without a feeling that millions of eyes are fixed upon him; and he scatters his *Sibylline Leaves* around him, with as majestical an air as if a crowd of enthu-siastic admirers were rushing forward to grasp the divine pro-mulgations, instead of their being, as in fact they are, coldly received by the accidental passenger, like a lying lottery puff or a quack advertisement.

This most miserable arrogance seems, in the present age, con-fined almost exclusively to the original members of the Lake School, and is, we think, worthy of especial notice, as one of the leading features of their character. It would be difficult to defend it either in Southey or Wordsworth; but in Coleridge it is altogether ridiculous. (p. 6)

Of the latter days of his literary life Mr Coleridge gives us no satisfactory account. The whole of the second volume [of *Bio-graphia Literaria*] is interspersed with mysterious innuendos. He complains of the loss of all his friends, not by death, but estrangement. He tries to account for the enmity of the world to him, a harmless and humane man, who wishes well to all created things, and "of his wondering finds no end." He up-braids himself with indolence, procrastination, neglect of his worldly concerns, and all other bad habits,—and then, with incredible inconsistency, vaunts loudly of his successful efforts in the cause of Literature, Philosophy, Morality, and Religion. Above all, he weeps and wails over the malignity of Reviewers, who have persecuted him almost from his very cradle, and seem resolved to bark him into the grave. He is haunted by the Image of a Reviewer wherever he goes. They "push him from his stool," and by his bedside they cry, "Sleep no more." They may abuse whomsoever they think fit, save himself and Mr Wordsworth. All others are fair game—and he chuckles to see them brought down. But his sacred person must be in-violate; and rudely to touch it is not high treason, it is impiety. Yet his "ever-honoured friend, the laurel-honouring-Laure-ate," is a Reviewer—his friend Mr Thomas Moore is a Re-viewer—his friend Dr Middleton, Bishop of Calcutta, was the Editor of a Review—almost every friend he ever had is a Reviewer;—and to crown all, he himself is a Reviewer. (p. 14)

It has not been in our power to enter into any discussion with Mr Coleridge on the various subjects of Poetry and Philosophy, which he has, we think, vainly endeavoured to elucidate. But we shall, on a future occasion, meet him on his own favourite ground. No less than 182 pages of the second volume are dedicated to the poetry of Mr Wordsworth. He has endeavoured to define poetry—to explain the philosophy of metre—to settle the boundaries of poetic diction—and to shew, finally, "what it is probable Mr Wordsworth meant to say in his dissertation prefixed to his *Lyrical Ballads*. As Mr Coleridge has not only studied the laws of poetical composition, but is a Poet of con-siderable powers, there are, in this part of his Book, many acute, ingenious, and even sensible observations and remarks; but he never knows when to have done,—explains what re-quires no explanation,—often leaves untouched the very dif-ficulty he starts,—and when he has poured before us a glimpse of light upon the shapeless form of some dark conception, he seems to take a wilful pleasure in its immediate extinction, and leads "us floundering on, and quite astray," through the deepening shadows of interminable night.

One instance there is of magnificent promise, and laughable non-performance, unequalled in the annals of literary History. Mr Coleridge informs us, that he and Mr Wordsworth (he is not certain which is entitled to the glory of the first discovery) have found out the difference between Fancy and Imagination [see excerpt above, 1817]. This discovery, it is prophesied, will have an incalculable influence on the progress of all the Fine Arts. He has written a long chapter purposely to prepare our minds for the great discussion. The audience is assembled—the curtain is drawn up—and there, in his gown, cap, and wig, is sitting Professor Coleridge. In comes a servant with a letter; the Professor gets up, and, with a solemn voice, reads it to the audience.—It is from an enlightened Friend; and its object is to shew, in no very courteous terms either to the Professor or his Spectators, that he may lecture, but that nobody will understand him. He accordingly makes his bow, and the curtain falls; but the worst of the joke is, that the Professor pockets the admittance-money,—for what reason, his outwitted audience are left, the best way they can, to "fancy or imagine."

But the greatest piece of Quackery in the Book, is his pretended account of the Metaphysical System of Kant, of which he knows less than nothing. (pp. 16-17)

We cannot take leave of Mr Coleridge, without expressing our indignation at the gross injustice, and, we fear, envious persecution, of his Criticism on Mr Maturin's "Bertram." He has thought it worth his while to analyse and criticise that Tragedy in a diatribe of fifty pages. He contends evidently against his own conviction, that it is utterly destitute of poetical and dramatic merit, and disgraceful, not to Mr Maturin alone, but to the audiences who admired it when acted, and the reading Public, who admired it no less when printed. There is more malignity, and envy, and jealousy, and misrepresentation, and bad wit, in this Critical Essay, than in all the Reviews now existing, from the *Edinburgh* down to the *Lady's Magazine.* Mr Coleridge ought to have behaved otherwise to an ingenious man like Mr Maturin, struggling into reputation, and against narrow circumstances.... [If] Mr Coleridge saw faults and defects in "Bertram," he should have exposed them in a dignified manner, giving all due praise, at the same time, to the vigour, and even originality, of that celebrated Drama. Mr Coleridge knows that "Bertram" has become a stock play at the London Theatres, while his own **"Remorse"** is for ever withdrawn. Has this stung him? Far be it from us to impute mean motives to any man. But there is a bitterness—an anger—a scorn—we had almost said, a savage and revengeful fierceness—in the tone of Mr Coleridge, when speaking of Mr Maturin, which it is, we confess, impossible to explain, and which, we fear, proceeds (perhaps unknown to his metaphysical self) from private pique and hostility, occasioned by superior merit and greater success. (p. 17)

We have felt it our duty to speak with severity of this book and its author,—and we have given our readers ample opportunities to judge of the justice of our strictures. We have not been speaking in the cause of Literature only, but, we conceive, in the cause of Morality and Religion. For it is not fitting that He should be held up as an example to the rising generation (but, on the contrary, it is most fitting that he should be exposed as a most dangerous model), who has alternately embraced, defended, and thrown aside all systems of Philosophy, and all

creeds of Religion;—who seems to have no power of retaining an opinion,—no trust in the principles which he defends,—but who fluctuates from theory to theory, according as he is impelled by vanity, envy, or diseased desire of change,—and who, while he would subvert and scatter into dust those structures of knowledge, reared by the wise men of this and other generations, has nothing to erect in their room but the baseless and air-built fabrics of a dreaming imagination. (p. 18)

> *[Christopher North (pseudonym of John Wilson)], "Observations on Coleridge's 'Biographia Literaria',"* in Blackwood's Edinburgh Magazine, *Vol. II, No. VII, October, 1817, pp. 3-18.*

WILLIAM HAZLITT   (essay date 1818)

[In the following, which first appeared in his 1818 publication English Poets, *Hazlitt abandoned the vitriol of his earlier writing on Coleridge (see excerpt above, 1816). Though Hazlitt disparages Coleridge's dramas, he concedes that Coleridge, more than any other person, possessed the gift of conversation as an art form. Another scathing review by Hazlitt appears below (1825).]*

I should say a few words of Mr. Coleridge; and there is no one who has a better right to say what he thinks of him than I have. "Is there here any dear friend of Caesar? To him I say, that Brutus' love to Caesar was no less than his." But no matter. His ***Ancient Mariner*** is his most remarkable performance, and the only one that I could point out to any one as giving an adequate idea of his great natural powers. It is high German, however, and in it he seems to "conceive of poetry but as a drunken dream, reckless, careless, and heedless of past, present, and to come." His tragedies (for he has written two) are not answerable to it; they are, except a few poetical passages, drawling sentiment and metaphysical jargon. He has no genuine dramatic talent. There is one fine passage in his ***Christabel***, that which contains the description of the quarrel between Sir Leoline and Sir Roland de Vaux of Tryermaine.... But I may say of him here, that he is the only person I ever knew who answered to the idea of a man of genius. He is the only person from whom I ever learnt anything. There is only one thing he could learn from me in return, but *that* he has not. He was the first poet I ever knew. His genius at that time [1798] had angelic wings, and fed on manna. He talked on for ever; and you wished him to talk on for ever. His thoughts did not seem to come with labour and effort, but as if borne on the gusts of genius, and as if the wings of his imagination lifted him from off his feet. His voice rolled on the ear like the pealing organ, and its sound alone was the music of thought. His mind was clothed with wings; and raised on them, he lifted philosophy to heaven. In his descriptions, you then saw the progress of human happiness and liberty in bright and never-ending succession, like the steps of Jacob's Ladder, with airy shapes ascending and descending, and with the voice of God at the top of the ladder. (pp. 220-22)

> *William Hazlitt, "On Coleridge," in his* Lectures on the English Poets and the English Comic Writers, *edited by William Carew Hazlitt, George Bell and Sons, 1894, pp. 190-222.*

[JOHN GIBSON LOCKHART]   (essay date 1819)

[A Scottish critic, Lockhart wrote several novels, but his fame rests on his biography of Sir Walter Scott and his critical contributions to Blackwood's Edinburgh Magazine *and the* Quarterly Review. *From 1817 to 1825 he was a principal contributor to*

Blackwood's, a Tory periodical which was founded to counter the influential Whig journal, the Edinburgh Review. *He is regarded as a versatile if somewhat severe critic whose opinions of his contemporaries, though lacking depth, are generally considered accurate when not distorted by political animosities. After the earlier harsh reviews, the following essay exemplifies the positive reception subsequently accorded Coleridge's work. Lockhart discusses Coleridge's characteristics as a poet and stresses his originality. The critic's emphasis on the musicality and mysterious qualities of Coleridge's verse provided the focus of numerous later studies in the nineteenth century. Because of the tone of the essay, numerous scholars believe that Lockhart wrote the review as a conciliatory gesture to compensate for Christopher North's earlier attack (see excerpt above, 1817), which also appeared in* Blackwood's. *While Lockhart genuinely admired Coleridge, commentators have also suggested that he wrote this in part to persuade Coleridge to become a contributor to the magazine.*]

The longest poem in the collection of the *Sibylline Leaves,* is the "**Rime of the Ancient Mariner**"—and to our feeling, it is by far the most wonderful also—the most original—and the most touching of all the productions of its author. From it alone, we are inclined to think an idea of the whole poetical genius of Mr. Coleridge might be gathered, such as could scarcely receive any very important addition either of extent or of distinctness, from a perusal of the whole of his other works. To speak of it at all is extremely difficult; above all the poems with which we are acquainted in any language—it is a poem to be felt—cherished—mused upon—not to be talked about—not capable of being described—analyzed—or criticised. It is the wildest of all the creations of genius—it is not like a thing of the living, listening, moving world—the very music of its words is like the melancholy mysterious breath of something sung to the sleeping ear—its images have the beauty—the grandeur—the incoherence of some mighty vision. The loveliness and the terror glide before us in turns—with, at one moment, the awful shadowy dimness—at another, the yet more awful distinctness of a majestic dream.

Dim and shadowy, and incoherent, however, though it be—how blind, how wilfully, or how foolishly blind must they have been who refused to see any meaning or purpose in the Tale of the Mariner! The imagery, indeed, may be said to be heaped up to superfluity—and so it is—the language to be redundant—and the narrative confused. But surely those who cavilled at these things, did not consider into whose mouth the poet has put this ghastly story. . . . We have no difficulty in confessing, that the ideas on which the intent of this poem hinges, and which to us seem to possess all beauty and pathos, may, after all, have been neglected by the poet with a too great neglect of the ordinary sympathies. But if any one will submit himself to the magic that is around him, and suffer his senses and his imagination to be blended together, and exalted by the melody of the charmed words, and the splendour of the unnatural apparitions with which the mysterious scene is opened, surely he will experience no revulsion towards the centre and spirit of this lovely dream. (pp. 5-6)

The effect of the wild wandering magnificence of imagination in the details of the dream-like story is a thing that cannot be forgotten. It is as if we had seen real spectres, and were for ever to be haunted. The unconnected and fantastic variety of the images that have been piled up before us works upon the fancy, as an evening sky made up of half lurid castelled clouds—half of clear unpolluted azure—would upon the eye. . . .

The conclusion has always appeared to us to be happy and graceful to the utmost degree. The natural surface-life of the world is brought close into contact with the life of sentiment—the soul that is so much alive, and enjoys, and suffers as much in dreams and visions of the night as by daylight. One feels with what a heavy eye the Ancient Mariner must look and listen to the pomps and merry-makings—even to the innocent enjoyments—of those whose experience has only been of things tangible. One feels that to him another world—we do not mean a supernatural, but a more exquisitely and deeply natural world—has been revealed—and that the repose of his spirit can only be in the contemplation of things that are not to pass away. (p. 7)

Of all the author's productions, the one which seems most akin to the "**Ancient Mariner,**" is "**Christabel,**" a wonderful piece of poetry, which has been far less understood, and is as yet far less known than the other. This performance does not make its appearance in the *Sibylline Leaves*—but we hope Mr. Coleridge will never omit it in any future collection. (pp. 7-8)

"**Christabel,**" as our readers are aware, is only a fragment, and had been in existence for many years antecedent to the time of its publication. Neither has the author assigned any reason either for the long delay of its appearance, or for the imperfect state in which he has at last suffered it to appear. In all probability he had waited long in the hope of being able to finish it to his satisfaction; but finding that he was never revisited by a mood sufficiently genial—he determined to let the piece be printed as it was. It is not in the history of "**Christabel**" alone that we have seen reason to suspect Mr. Coleridge of being by far too passive in his notions concerning the mode in which a poet ought to deal with his muse. It is very true, that the best conceptions and designs are frequently those which occur to a man of fine talents, without having been painfully sought after: but the exertion of the Will is always necessary in the worthy execution of them. It behoves a poet, like any other artist, after he has fairly conceived the idea of his piece, to set about realising it in good earnest, and to use his most persevering attention in considering how all its parts are to be adapted and conjoined. It does not appear that even the language of a poem can arise spontaneously throughout like a strain of music, any more than the colours of the painter will go and arrange themselves on his canvass, while he is musing on the subject in another room. Language is a material which it requires no little labour to reduce into beautiful forms,—a truth of which the ancients were, above all others, well and continually aware. For although vivid ideas naturally suggest happy expressions, yet the latter are, as it were, only insulated traits or features, which require much management in the joining, and the art of the composer is seen in the symmetry of the whole structure. Now, in many respects Mr. Coleridge seems too anxious to enjoy the advantages of an inspired writer, and to produce his poetry at once in its perfect form—like the palaces which spring out of the desert in complete splendour at a single rubbing of the lamp in the Arabian Tale. But carefulness above all is necessary to a poet in these latter days, when the ordinary medium through which things are viewed is so very far from being poetical—and when the natural strain of scarcely any man's associations can be expected to be of that sort which is most akin to high and poetical feeling. There is no question there are many, very many passages in the poetry of this writer, which shew what excellent things may be done under the impulse of a happy moment—passages in which the language—above all things—has such aerial graces and would have been utterly beyond the reach of any person who might have attempted to produce the like, without being able to lift his spirit into the same ecstatic mood. It is not to be denied, however, that among the whole of his poems there are only a few in the composition of which he seems to have been blessed all throughout with the same sustaining energy of afflatus. The "Mariner"—we need not say—is one of these. The poem "Love" is another—and were "Christabel" completed as it has been begun, we doubt not it would be allowed by all who are capable of tasting the merits of such poetry, to be a third— and, perhaps, the most splendid of the three.

It is impossible to gather from the part which has been published any conception of what is the meditated conclusion of the story of "Christabel." Incidents can never be fairly judged of till we know what they lead to. Of those which occur in the first and second cantos of this poem, there is no doubt many appear at present very strange and disagreeable, and the sooner the remainder comes forth to explain them, the better. One thing is evident, that no man need sit down to read "Christabel" with any prospect of gratification, whose mind has not rejoiced habitually in the luxury of visionary and superstitious reveries. He that is determined to try every thing by the standard of what is called common sense, and who has an aversion to admit, even in poetry, of the existence of things more than are dreamt of in philosophy, had better not open this production, which is only proper for a solitary couch and a midnight taper. Mr. Coleridge is the prince of superstitious poets; and he that does not read "Christabel" with a strange and harrowing feeling of mysterious dread, may be assured that his soul is made of impenetrable stuff. (pp. 8-9)

[In the "**Rime of the Ancient Mariner**" and "**Christabel**,"] the poetical faculties of Coleridge are abundantly exhibited in the whole power and charm of their native beauty. That such exercise of these faculties may have been so far injudicious as not calculated to awaken much of the ordinary sympathies of mankind—but rather addressing every thing to feelings of which in their full strength and sway only a few are capable—all this is a reproach easy to be made; and in a great measure perhaps it may be a well-founded reproach. But nothing surely can be more unfair, than to overlook or deny the existence of such beauty and such strength on any grounds of real or pretended misapplication. That the author of these productions is a poet of a most noble class—a poet most original in his conceptions— most masterly in his execution—above all things a most in- imitable master of the language of poetry—it is impossible to deny. His powers indeed—to judge from what of them has been put forth and exhibited—may not be of the widest—or even of the very highest kind. So far as they go, surely, they are the most exquisite of powers. In his mixture of the awful and all the gentle graces of conception—in his sway of wild— solitary—dreamy phantasies—in his music of words—and magic of numbers—we think he stands absolutely alone among all the poets of the most poetical age. (p. 11)

> [*John Gibson Lockhart*], "*Essays on the Lake School of Poetry, No. III—Coleridge,*" in Blackwood's Edinburgh Magazine, *Vol. VI, No. XXI, October, 1819, pp. 3-12.*

LEIGH HUNT (essay date 1821)

[*An English poet and essayist, Hunt is remembered as a literary critic who encouraged and influenced several young Romantic poets, especially John Keats and Percy Bysshe Shelley. Hunt produced volumes of poetry and critical essays and, with his brother John, established the* Examiner, *a weekly liberal newspaper. In his criticism, Hunt articulated the principles of Romanticism, emphasizing imaginative freedom and the expression of a personal emotional or spiritual state. In the following excerpt, first published in the* Examiner *on October 21, 1821, Hunt suggests that Coleridge's poetry derives from his love of scholarly pursuits, a theory that was developed in the twentieth century by John Livingston Lowes (see excerpt below, 1927). To Hunt, the tendency to love and revere knowledge is reflected in Coleridge's work. Hunt especially praises "Christabel," "Kubla Khan," and "The Ancient Mariner" and proposes that the latter work serves as a lesson "to those who see nothing in the world but their own unfeeling commonplaces." Hunt's comments on Coleridge's imagination are later reiterated by many critics.*]

Mr. Coleridge speaks very modestly of his poetry—not affectedly so, but out of a high notion of the art in his predecessors. He delighted the late Mr. Keats, in the course of conversation, with adding, after he had alluded to it, "if there is any thing I have written which may be *called poetry*": and the writer of the present article heard him speak of verses as the common tribute which a young mind on its entrance into the world of letters pays to the love of intellectual beauty. His poetry however has an "image and superscription" very different from this current coin. We do not, it is true, think that it evinces the poetical habit of mind. . . . But it is full of imagination and of a sense of the beautiful, as suggested by a great acquaintance with books and thoughts, acting upon a benevolent mind. It is to the scholar of old books and metaphysics what Milton's was to the Greek and Italian scholar. It is the essence of the impression made upon him by that habit of thinking and reading which is his second nature. Mr. Coleridge began with metaphysics when at school; and what the boy begins with, the man will end with, come what will between. He does not turn metaphysical upon the strength of his poetry, like Spenser and Tasso; but poet upon the strength of his metaphysics. Thus in the greater part of his minor poems he only touches upon the popular creeds, or wilful creations of their own, which would occupy other poets, and then falls musing upon the nature of things, and analysing his feelings. In his voyage to Germany, he sees a solitary wildfowl upon "the objectless desert of waters," and says how interesting it was. It was most probably from a train of reflection on the value of this link between land and the ship that he produced his beautiful wild poem of the "**Ancient Mariner**," which he precedes with a critico-philosophical extract from Burnet's *Archaeologia*. We do not object to this as belonging to his genius. We only instance it as shewing the nature of it. In the same spirit he interrupts his "**Christabel**" with an explanation of the wish sometimes felt to give pain to the innocent; and instead of being content to have written finely under the influence of laudanum, recommends "**Kubla-Khan**" to his readers, not as a poem, but as "a psychological curiosity." All this however is extremely interesting of its kind, and peculiar. It is another striking instance of what we have often remarked—the tendency of all great knowledge and deep delight in it, of whatever kind, to extend itself into poetry, which lies like a heaven in the centre of the intellectual world for those to go to and be refreshed with, more or less, who are not bound to the physical world like slaves to the soil. Every lover of books, scholar or not, who knows what it is to have his quarto open against a loaf at his tea, to carry his duodecimo about in his pocket, to read along country roads or even streets, and to scrawl his favourite authors with notes (as "S.T.C." is liberally sanctioned to do those of others by a writer in the *London Magazine*), ought to be in possession of Mr. Coleridge's poems, if it is only for "**Christabel**," "**Kubla Khan**," and the "**Ancient Mariner**." The first comprises all that is ancient and courteous in old rhythm, and will also make any studious gentleman, who is not sufficiently imaginative, turn himself round divers times in his chair, as he ought to do, to see if there is not "something in the room." **"Kubla Khan"** is a voice and a vision, an everlasting tune in our mouths, a dream fit for Cambuscan and all his poets, a dance of pictures such as Giotto or Cimabue, revived and re-inspired, would have made for a Storie of Old Tartarie, a piece of the invisible world made visible by a sun at midnight and sliding before our eyes. (pp. 170-72)

[The tale of the **"Ancient Mariner"**] is a lesson to those who see nothing in the world but their own unfeeling commonplaces, and are afterwards visited with a dreary sense of their insufficiency. Not to have sympathy for all, is not to have the instinct that suffices instead of imagination. Not to have imagination, to supply the want of the instinct, is to be left destitute and forlorn when brute pleasure is gone, and to be *dead-in-life*. This poem would bear out a long marginal illustration in the style of the old Italian critics, who squeeze a sonnet of Petrarch's into the middle of the page with a crowd of fond annotations. Be the source of its inspiration what it may, it is a poem that may serve as a test to any one who wishes to know whether he has a real taste for poetry or not. And be Mr. Coleridge what he may, whether an author inspired by authors or from himself, whether a metaphysical poet or a poetical metaphysician, whether a politician baulked and rendered despairing like many others by the French Revolution, or lastly, and totally, a subtle and good-natured casuist fitted for nothing but contemplation, and rewarded by it with a sense of the beautiful and wonderful *above* his casuistry, we can only be grateful for the knowledge and delight he affords us by his genius, and recognise in him an instance of that departure from ordinary talent, which we are far from being bound to condemn because it does not fall in with our own humours. (p. 176)

> *Leigh Hunt, "Sketches of the Living Poets: No. 4, Mr. Coleridge," in his* Literary Criticism, *edited by Lawrence Huston Houtchens and Carolyn Washburn Houtchens, Columbia University Press, 1956, pp. 166-76.*

WILLIAM HAZLITT (essay date 1825)

[*The following is taken from the essay which is considered the culmination of Hazlitt's commentary on Coleridge. The critic derides Coleridge's intellectual aspirations and concludes that he abused the talent he possessed.*]

Mr. Coleridge has 'a mind reflecting ages past': his voice is like the echo of the congregated roar of the 'dark rearward and abyss' of thought. He who has seen a mouldering tower by the side of a crystal lake, hid by the mist, but glittering in the wave below, may conceive the dim, gleaming, uncertain intelligence of his eye: he who has marked the evening clouds uprolled (a world of vapours) has seen the picture of his mind, unearthly, unsubstantial, with gorgeous tints and ever-varying forms—

> That which was now a horse, even with a thought
> The rack dislimns, and makes it indistinct
> As water is in water.

Our author's mind is (as he himself might express it) *tangential*. There is no subject on which he has not touched, none on which he has rested. With an understanding fertile, subtle, expansive, 'quick, forgetive, apprehensive,' beyond all living precedent, few traces of it perhaps remain. He lends himself to all impressions alike; he gives up his mind and liberty of

thought to none. He is a general lover of art and science, and wedded to no one in particular. He pursues knowledge as a mistress, with outstretched hands and winged speed; but as he is about to embrace her, his Daphne turns—alas! not to a laurel! Hardly a speculation has been left on record from the earliest time, but it is loosely folded up in Mr. Coleridge's memory, like a rich, but somewhat tattered piece of tapestry: we might add (with more seeming than real extravagance) that scarce a thought can pass through the mind of man, but its sound has at some time or other passed over his head with rustling pinions.

On whatever question or author you speak, he is prepared to take up the theme with advantage—from Peter Abelard down to Thomas Moore, from the subtlest metaphysics to the politics of the *Courier*. There is no man of genius, in whose praise he descants, but the critic seems to stand above the author, and 'what in him is weak, to strengthen, what is low, to raise and support': nor is there any work of genius that does not come out of his hands like an illuminated Missal, sparkling even in its defects. If Mr. Coleridge had not been the most impressive talker of his age, he would probably have been the finest writer; but he lays down his pen to make sure of an auditor, and mortgages the admiration of posterity for the stare of an idler. If he had not been a poet, he would have been a powerful logician; if he had not dipped his wing in the Unitarian controversy, he might have soared to the very summit of fancy. But, in writing verse, he is trying to subject the Muse to *transcendental* theories: in his abstract reasoning, he misses his way by strewing it with flowers.

All that he has done of moment, he had done twenty years ago: since then, he may be said to have lived on the sound of his own voice. (pp. 35-7)

A scholar (so to speak) is a more disinterested and abstracted character than a mere author. The first looks at the numberless volumes of a library, and says, 'All these are mine': the other points to a single volume (perhaps it may be an immortal one) and says, 'My name is written on the back of it.' This is a puny and grovelling ambition, beneath the lofty amplitude of Mr. Coleridge's mind. No, he revolves in his wayward soul, or utters to the passing wind, or discourses to his own shadow, things mightier and more various!—Let us draw the curtain, and unlock the shrine. (p. 38)

One of the finest and rarest parts of Mr. Coleridge's conversation is, when he expatiates on the Greek tragedians (not that he is not well acquainted, when he pleases, with the epic poets, or the philosophers, or orators, or historians of antiquity) . . . , his thoughts being let loose as his body is chained on his solitary rock, and his afflicted will (the emblem of mortality)

> Struggling in vain with ruthless destiny.

As the impassioned critic speaks and rises in his theme, you would think you heard the voice of the Man hated by the Gods, contending with the wild winds as they roar; and his eye glitters with the spirit of Antiquity! (p. 39)

It was not to be supposed that Mr. Coleridge could keep on at the rate he set off. He could not realize all he knew or thought, and less could not fix his desultory ambition. Other stimulants supplied the place, and kept up the intoxicating dream, the fever and the madness of his early impressions. Liberty (the philosopher's and the poet's bride) had fallen a victim, meanwhile, to the murderous practices of the hag Legitimacy. . . . Such is the fate of genius in an age when, in the unequal contest with sovereign wrong, every man is ground to powder who is not either a born slave, or who does not willingly and at once offer up the yearnings of humanity and the dictates of reason as a welcome sacrifice to besotted prejudice and loathsome power.

Of all Mr. Coleridge's productions, the **Ancient Mariner** is the only one that we could with confidence put into any person's hands, on whom we wished to impress a favourable idea of his extraordinary powers. Let whatever other objections be made to it, it is unquestionably a work of genius—of wild, irregular, overwhelming imagination, and has that rich, varied movement in the verse, which gives a distant idea of the lofty or changeful tones of Mr. Coleridge's voice. In the **Christabel**, there is one splendid passage on divided friendship. The Translation of Schiller's *Wallenstein* is also a masterly production in its kind, faithful and spirited. Among his smaller pieces there are occasional bursts of pathos and fancy, equal to what we might expect from him; but these form the exception, and not the rule. (pp. 42-3)

His Tragedy, entitled **Remorse,** is full of beautiful and striking passages; but it does not place the author in the first rank of dramatic writers. But if Mr. Coleridge's works do not place him in that rank, they injure instead of conveying a just idea of the man; for he himself is certainly in the first class of general intellect.

If our author's poetry is inferior to his conversation, his prose is utterly abortive. Hardly a gleam is to be found in it of the brilliancy and richness of those stores of thought and language that he pours out incessantly, when they are lost like drops of water in the ground. (p. 44)

[Mr. Coleridge] delights in nothing but episodes and digressions, neglects whatever he undertakes to perform, and can act only on spontaneous impulses without object or method. . . . While he should be occupied with a given pursuit, he is thinking of a thousand other things: a thousand tastes, a thousand objects tempt him, and distract his mind, which keeps open house, and entertains all comers; and after being fatigued and amused with morning calls from idle visitors [he] finds the day consumed and its business unconcluded. (p. 45)

Mr. Coleridge, in writing an harmonious stanza, would stop to consider whether there was not more grace and beauty in a *Pas de trois,* and would not proceed till he had resolved this question by a chain of metaphysical reasoning without end. (pp. 45-6)

> William Hazlitt, *"Mr. Coleridge,"* in his The Spirit of the Age; or, Contemporary Portraits, *1825. Reprint by Oxford University Press, London, 1947, pp. 35-47.*

SAMUEL TAYLOR COLERIDGE   (conversation date 1830)

[Coleridge's famed response to Mrs. Barbauld, taken from his The Table Talk and Omniana of Samuel Taylor Coleridge, *defines his intent in "The Ancient Mariner." His admission that the poem possessed "too much" of a moral has been the subject of various interpretations by later critics.]*

Mrs. Barbauld once told me that she admired **The Ancient Mariner** very much, but that there were two faults in it—it was improbable, and had no moral. As for the probability, I owned that that might admit some question; but as to the want of a moral, I told her that in my own judgement the poem had too much; and that the only, or chief fault, if I might say so, was the obtrusion of the moral sentiment so openly on the

reader as a principle or cause of action in a work of such pure imagination. It ought to have had no more moral than the *Arabian Nights'* tale of the merchant's sitting down to eat dates by the side of a well, and throwing the shells aside, and lo! a genie starts up, and says he *must* kill the aforesaid merchant, *because* one of the date shells had, it seems, put out the eye of the genie's son.

> *Samuel Taylor Coleridge, in a conversation with Henry Nelson Coleridge on May 31, 1830, in his* The Table Talk and Omniana of Samuel Taylor Coleridge, *Oxford University Press, 1917, p. 106.*

[HENRY NELSON COLERIDGE]   (essay date 1834)

[Henry Nelson Coleridge, the nephew of the author, was married to Coleridge's beloved daughter, Sara, and also edited his collected works. This essay is considered the first serious consideration of Coleridge's poems, particularly "Kubla Khan" and "Christabel." He praises Coleridge's technical skill and emphasizes the connection between Coleridge's metaphysical pursuits and his poems.]

[The best poems in **The Poetical Works of S. T. Coleridge**] are distinguished in a remarkable degree by the perfection of their rhythm and metrical arrangement. The labour bestowed upon this point must have been very great; the tone and quantity of words seem weighed in scales of gold. It will, no doubt, be considered ridiculous by the Fannii and Fanniae of our day to talk of varying the trochee with the iambus, or of resolving either into the tribrach. Yet it is evident to us that these, and even minuter points of accentual scansion, have been regarded by Mr. Coleridge as worthy of study and observation. We do not, of course, mean that rules of this kind were always in his mind while composing, any more than that an expert disputant is always thinking of the distinctions of mood and figure, whilst arguing; but we certainly believe that Mr. Coleridge has almost from the commencement of his poetic life looked upon versification as constituting in and by itself a much more important branch of the art poetic than most of his eminent contemporaries appear to have done. And this more careful study shows itself in him in no technical peculiarities or fantastic whims, against which the genius of our language revolts; but in a more exact adaptation of the movement to the feeling, and in a finer selection of particular words with reference to their local fitness for sense and sound. Some of his poems are complete models of versification, exquisitely easy to all appearance, and subservient to the meaning, and yet so subtle in the links and transitions of the parts as to make it impossible to produce the same effect merely by imitating the syllabic metre as it stands on the surface. The secret of the sweetness lies within, and is involved in the feeling. It is this remarkable power of making his verse musical that gives a peculiar character to Mr. Coleridge's lyric poems. In some of the smaller pieces, as the conclusion of the **'Kubla Khan,'** for example, not only the lines by themselves are musical, but the whole passage sounds all at once as an outburst or crash of harps in the still air of autumn. The verses seem as if *played* to the ear upon some unseen instrument. And the poet's manner of reciting verse is similar. It is not rhetorical, but musical: so very near recitative, that for any one else to attempt it would be ridiculous; and yet it is perfectly miraculous with what exquisite searching he elicits and makes sensible every particle of the meaning, not leaving a shadow of a shade of the feeling, the mood, the degree, untouched. . . . Mr. Coleridge has no *ear* for music, as it is technically called. Master as he is of the intellectual recitative, he could not *sing* an air to save his life. But his delight in music is intense and unweariable, and he can detect good from bad with unerring discrimination. (pp. 7-8)

There are some lines entitled '**Hendecasyllables,**' . . . which struck us a good deal by the skill with which an equivalent for the well-known Catullian measure has been introduced into our language. We think the metrical construction of these few verses very ingenious, and do not remember at this moment anything in English exactly like it. . . .

The minute study of the laws and properties of metre is observable in almost every piece in these volumes. Every kind of lyric measure, rhymed and unrhymed, is attempted with success; and we doubt whether, upon the whole, there are many specimens of the heroic couplet or blank verse superior in construction to what Mr. Coleridge has given us. (p. 9)

[Whether] in verse, or prose, or conversation, Mr. Coleridge's mind may be fitly characterized as an energetic mind—a mind always at work, always in a course of reasoning. He cares little for anything, merely because it was or is; it must be referred, or be capable of being referred, to some law or principle, in order to attract his attention. This is not from ignorance of the facts of natural history or science. His written and published works alone sufficiently show how constantly and accurately he has been in the habit of noting all the phenomena of the material world around us; and the great philosophical system now at length in preparation for the press demonstrates, we are told, his masterly acquaintance with almost all the sciences, and with not a few of the higher and more genial of the arts. Yet his vast acquirements of this sort are never put forward by or for themselves; it is in his apt and novel illustrations, his indications of analogies, his explanation of anomalies, that he enables the hearer or reader to get a glimpse of the extent of his practical knowledge. He is always reasoning out from an inner point, and it is the inner point, the principle, the law which he labours to bring forward into light. (pp. 12-13)

All this, whether for praise or for blame, is perceptible enough in Mr. Coleridge's verse, but perceptible, of course, in such degree and mode as the law of poetry in general, and the nature of the specific poem in particular, may require. But the main result from this frame and habit of his mind is very distinctly traceable in the uniform subjectivity of almost all his works. He does not belong to that grand division of poetry and poets which corresponds with paintings and painters; of which Pindar and Dante are the chief;—those masters of the picturesque, who, by a felicity inborn, view and present everything in the completeness of actual objectivity—and who have a class derived from and congenial with them, presenting few pictures indeed, but always full of picturesque matter; of which secondary class Spenser and Southey may be mentioned as eminent instances. To neither of these does Mr. Coleridge belong; in his '**Christabel,**' there certainly are several *distinct pictures* of great beauty; but he, as a poet, clearly comes within the other division which answers to music and the musician, in which you have a magnificent mirage of words with the subjective associations of the poet curling, and twisting, and creeping round, and through, and above every part of it. . . . [When] we point out the intense personal feeling, the self-projection, as it were, which characterizes Mr. Coleridge's poems, we mean that such feeling is the soul and spirit, not the whole body and form, of his poetry. For surely no one has ever more earnestly and constantly borne in mind the maxim of Milton, that poetry ought to be *simple, sensuous, and impassioned.* . . .

The poetry before us is distinct and clear, and accurate in its imagery; but the imagery is rarely or never exhibited for description's sake alone; it is rarely or never exclusively objective; that is to say, put forward as a spectacle, a picture on which the mind's eye is to rest and terminate. You may if your sight is short, or your imagination cold, regard the imagery in itself and go no farther; but the poet's intention is that you should feel and imagine a great deal more than you see. His aim is to awaken in the reader the same mood of mind, the same cast of imagination and fancy whence issued the associations which animate and enlighten his pictures. You must think with him, must sympathize with him, must suffer yourself to be lifted out of your own school of opinion or faith, and fall back upon your own consciousness, an unsophisticated man. . . . From his earliest youth to this day, Mr. Coleridge's poetry has been a faithful mirror reflecting the images of his mind. (pp. 13-14)

No writer has ever expressed the great truth that man makes his world, or that it is the imagination which shapes and colours all things—more vividly than Coleridge. Indeed, he is the first who, in the age in which we live, brought forward that position into light and action. (p. 14)

The '**Remorse**' and '**Zapolya**' strikingly illustrate the predominance of the meditative, pausing habit of Mr. Coleridge's mind. (p. 23)

'**Zapolya**' is professedly an imitation of [William Shakespeare's] 'The Winter's Tale,' and was not composed with any view to scenic representation. Yet it has some situations of dramatic interest in no respect inferior to the most striking in the '**Remorse;**' the incidents are new and surprising, and the dialogue is throughout distinguished by liveliness and force. The predominant character of the whole is, like that of the '**Remorse,**' a mixture of the pastoral and the romantic, but much more apparent and exclusive than in the latter. . . . '**Zapolya**' has never been appreciated as it deserves. It is, in our opinion, the most *elegant* of Mr. Coleridge's poetical works; there is a softness of tone, and a delicacy of colouring about it, which have a peculiar charm of their own, and amply make amends for some deficiency of strength in the drawing. (pp. 26-7)

Mr. Coleridge's dramatic talent is of a very high and original kind. His chief excellence lies in the dialogue itself,—his main defect in the conception, or at least in the conduct, of the plot. We can hardly say too much for the one, or too little for the other. (p. 28)

[The] '**Ancient Mariner**' is, and will ever be, one of the most perfect pieces of imaginative poetry, not only in our language, but in the literature of all Europe. We have, certainly, sometimes doubted whether the miraculous destruction of the vessel in the presence of the pilot and hermit, was not an error, in respect of its bringing the purely preternatural into too close contact with the actual framework of the poem. The only link between those scenes of out-of-the-world wonders, and the wedding guest, should, we rather suspect, have been the blasted, unknown being himself who described them. There should have been no other witnesses of the truth of any part of the tale, but the 'Ancient Mariner' himself. This by the way: but take the work altogether, there is nothing else like it; it is a poem by itself; between it and other compositions, . . . there is a chasm which you cannot overpass; the sensitive reader feels himself insulated, and a sea of wonder and mystery flows round him as round the spell-stricken ship itself. . . . The '**Ancient Mariner**' displays Mr. Coleridge's peculiar mastery over the wild and preternatural in a brillant manner; but in his next poem, **'Christabel,'** the exercise of his power in this line is still more skilful and singular. The thing attempted in **'Christabel'** is the most difficult of execution in the whole field of romance— witchery by daylight; and the success is complete. (pp. 28-9)

We are not amongst those who wish to have **'Christabel'** finished. It cannot be finished. The poet has spun all he could without snapping. The theme is too fine and subtle to bear much extension. It is better as it is, imperfect as a story, but complete as an exquisite production of the imagination, differing in form and colour from the **'Ancient Mariner,'** yet differing in effect from it only so as the same powerful faculty is directed to the feudal or the mundane phases of the preternatural.

From these remarkable works we turn to the love poems scattered through the volumes before us. There is something very peculiar in Mr. Coleridge's exhibition of the most lovely of the passions. His love is not gloomy as Byron's, nor gay as Moore's, nor intellectual as Wordsworth's. It is a clear unclouded passion, made up of an exquisite respect and gentleness, a knightly tenderness and courtesy,—pure yet ardent, impatient yet contemplative. (p. 30)

We know no writer of modern times whom it would not be easier to characterize in one page than Coleridge in two. The volumes before us contain so many integral efforts of imagination, that a distinct notice of each is indispensable, if we would form a just conclusion upon the total powers of the man. Wordsworth, Scott, Moore, Byron, Southey, are incomparably more uniform in the direction of their poetic mind. But if you look over these volumes for indications of their author's poetic powers, you find him appearing in at least half a dozen shapes, so different from each other, that it is in vain to attempt to mass them together. It cannot indeed be said, that he has ever composed what is popularly termed a *great* poem; but he is great in several lines, and the union of such powers is an essential term in a fair estimate of his genius. . . . It is the *predominance* of this power, which, in our judgment, constitutes the essential difference between Coleridge and any other of his great contemporaries. He is the most imaginative of the English poets since Milton. Whatever he writes, be it on the most trivial subject, be it in the most simple strain, his imagination, *in spite of himself,* affects it. (pp. 33-4)

We speak of Coleridge . . . as the poet of imagination; and we add, that he is likewise the poet of thought and verbal harmony. That his thoughts are sometimes hard and sometimes even obscure, we think must be admitted; it is an obscurity of which all very subtle thinkers are occasionally guilty, either by attempting to express evanescent feelings for which human language is an inadequate vehicle, or by expressing, however adequately, thoughts and distinctions to which the common reader is unused. (p. 34)

[*Henry Nelson Coleridge*], *"Coleridge's 'Poetical Works',"* in The Quarterly Review, *Vol. LII, No. CIII, August, 1834, pp. 1-38.*

[R. C. WATERSTON]   (essay date 1834)

[*Waterston provides one of the first American assessments of Coleridge's work and calls for a reappraisal; thus far, he argues, the writings have not been "justly estimated." He praises the poetry for its versatility, diction, condensation, and originality and contends that the source of these attributes is religious strength. According to Waterston, the poetry of Coleridge forms a body of*

Christian thought: "The root of all his greatness (is) Christian love and Christian benevolence—and it is the only atmosphere in which true poetry can exist."]

Probably no writings of the present day have been more variously estimated, than those of Coleridge. They have been ridiculed by some, and cherished with the warmest admiration by others. But, whether good or bad, they should be looked upon with peculiar interest, coming as they do from the pen of one, who has long been distinguished in many of the highest branches of literature.

We believe that, in this sphere, he is not yet justly estimated; for, while some have been extravagant in their applause, others have poured upon him the most unmerited abuse. Against the criticisms of Coleridge's detractors, we confidently refer our readers to the works themselves. They prove their own beauty and power, far more eloquently than we could do. The indescribable impress of genius is stamped on all he has written. At all times there is a melody in his language, and an ethereality in his aspirations, which throw a spell upon the mind, and win it to admiration. His works are full of ideal and moral beauty; of pure, deep, and elevating sentiment; now conveyed to us by the soft and silvery music of sweet song, and now swelling in organ-peals from his more elaborate and lofty productions.

One of the first distinguishing traits of Coleridge, is his versatility. True, there is one mind visible through all, yet few have written so much with so little sameness. There is the **'Hymn to Mont Blanc,'** with its unrivalled grandeur, and **'Genevieve'** with its ravishing beauty, the energetic wildness of the **'Ancient Mariner,'** and the supernatural witchery of **'Christabel,'** all distinct in their character, yet all perfect in their kind. The style is always in exact accordance with the subject, and the subject is ever varied. Now we gaze upon the aërial forms of spirits, now are bewildered by magnificent scenery, and now look quietly upon his little child. Now his thoughts are conveyed in the simplest form, and now in the antique stateliness of the olden time.

His next distinguishing attribute is his inimitable mastery of language, his exquisite and liquid melody of diction. We know of no writer, since the age of Elizabeth, who owes so much to this single element of power. He stands here absolutely alone. While we read, we seem to be accompanied by a quiet and dreamy music. We might quote passages of exceeding sweetness from almost every page, to show how nearly akin to music mere words may be made to flow. Whatever he touches, seems to breathe forth with the same magical power. We might recommend, then, the study of Coleridge to all who would know the true value of language, and the perfect mellowness of versification, with which a gifted mind may pour forth its conceptions.

Another marked feature of his poetry is condensation. He always implies more than he expresses. His writings throughout have a sinewy strength of expression. He gathers up vast treasures of thought, and melts them all down to a single line. With one tone he electrifies the soul. His sentences are pictures. His very words live and breathe, and send forth, now low murmurs of joy, and now the piercing wail of grief. He never dwells long on one thought. He strikes the key-note, and leaves the echo of its melody to swell on in the mind of the reader. Thus, through the whole flow of his poetry, there is a deep under-current of thought. And while the careless reader may amuse himself with the rainbow-painted bubbles that float upon the surface, the reflecting mind will behold bright and beautiful conceptions, flashing upward from below. He will feel as the

Greta Hall, Coleridge's home in the Lake District. Coleridge briefly shared this house with Robert Southey.

mariner would feel, if the waters of the unfathomable ocean should become transparent like pure ether, and he could gaze down upon its groves of coral, and its amber-fretted caves.

Still another attribute of Coleridge, and not the least distinguishing, is his originality. Here, if we mistake not, is one reason, why his works have not been more appreciated. Originality is like new coin; people hardly know its real worth. It bears not the usual image and superscription; and though the metal may be of triple value, they hesitate to receive it. Thus the very thing, which should gain a crown for its possessor, too often hangs like a millstone about his neck. Coleridge has gone into the secret chambers of his own mind, both for his style, and for his thoughts. He is an enthusiastic admirer of his friend Wordsworth, yet he feels the fallacy of much of his poetic theory, and has not followed its principles. He has also no small portion of the German spirit, yet nothing that looks like plagiarism, or even imitation. (pp. 438-39)

Other striking characteristics of Coleridge, are his picturesqueness, his graphic delineation, his distinct and vivid description. They may not be found in equal degree in all his poetry, but still they give a freshness and life to all his productions. While we read, real scenes are made visible to us. We see distinct and definite pictures, without any effort of the mind, and they stand out like a present reality. We can actually look upon the dark rocks, and see the yellow leaves of the ash quivering in the wind, or into the distant and quiet valley, where the silver stream flows silently along, over its soft bed of verdure. (p. 440)

Yet his pictures are never *mere* pictures. He does not so much notice the outward form, as the in-dwelling life. His most graphic descriptions, though clear and distinct, have no external glitter. There is no hard crystallization of fancy, encrusting them over. All is natural and mellow;—all has life and feeling. With a true Promethean spirit, he gives a living soul to inanimate things, and makes external objects the types and emblems of inward gifts and emotions.

In these preliminary remarks, we cannot but allude to the habitual spirit of love that pervades his writings. The words, which he has put into the mouth of his Ancient Mariner, beautifully express the feeling which he ever delights to cherish;

> He prayeth best, who loveth best
>   All things, both great and small;
> For the dear God who loveth us,
>   He made and loveth all.

Thus his whole heart is filled with universal benevolence. The vast creation is to him crowded with beauty, and life. He feels a sympathy, while he listens to the whispering leaves, or the glad murmur of the distant brook as it leaps onward to the ocean. (p. 441)

[His] writings exhibit throughout a deep religious spirit. His heart has been kindled by fire from the heavenly altar. He feels that Christian faith is the perfection of human reason, and that without it the fountains of the heart would be sealed, and its hopes forever blighted. This is in fact the root of all his greatness; Christian love, and Christian benevolence;—and it is the only atmosphere in which true poetry can exist. (p. 442)

['**Juvenile Poems**'] do not show in so high a degree that richness of versification, powerful thought, and vivid picturing, which distinguish his subsequent writing. Yet they evidently contain the elements of the same poetic power. They are peculiarly valuable, as a standard, to show the progressive development of his faculties. They prove, that his mind was strengthened and elevated by continued study and reflection. (p. 443)

['**Sibylline Leaves**'] combines tenderness and pathos; simplicity of language, with sublimity of thought. It has delicious descriptions of nature, beautiful expressions of domestic affection, and grand and lofty views of Christian character. The poem entitled '**Fears in Solitude**' . . . is full of beauty and power. Its imagery is distinct, its versification exquisite, its sentiment profound. (pp. 445-46)

The next poem in the '**Sibylline Leaves**' is the famous war-eclogue, entitled '**Fire, Famine, and Slaughter**.' This, for vigor and wildness, might rival the chants of the Furies of old. It is full of electric fire. . . . (p. 446)

In Coleridge's '**Love Poems**,' there often seems to be something wanting. They have too little of the feelings common to humanity. They are too ideal. Human tenderness melt into spiritual admiration. True devotion fades into a kind of Platonic sympathy. The intense and passionate love, which breathes out in the simple language of nature, is too often lost in metaphysical abstractions. There are however striking exceptions to this; and the most remarkable one is his '**Genevieve**.' This is, in truth, one of the most sweet and touching poems in our language. We should rejoice to trace out the beautiful arrangement and combination of this sweet ballad. It has not the voluptuous passion of Byron, or the intellectual calmness of Wordsworth; but a deep fervor, mingled with a softness of melancholy peculiarly his own. It is quiet, yet intense; simple, yet accurate in its metaphysical analysis; spiritual, yet warm with the glow of delicate feeling.

To these succeed the '**Meditative Poems**,' any one of which might have established his fame. Here we can see that he not only looks *at* things, but *into* them. Here we behold in a marvellous degree his keen perception of the beautiful, and his supreme love for the good. Here, too, we feel that the seen and the present exist not more truly to his mind, than the ideal and the eternal. No portion of his writings displays the height and the depth of his genius, in a more striking light than this. These poems are well called 'Meditative;' for they not only show us the moral grandeur of the author's musings, but infuse into the mind of the reader a portion of the same spirit. He lifts us into higher and holier worlds, and gathers about us on every side scenes of touching and solemn beauty. And yet he changes not the outer world, so much as the mind. He gives our hearts a new sense. (p. 447)

['**The Ancient Mariner**'] shows the power of conscience, and that power working through superstition;—and this comes with great truth, and natural simplicity, from the lips of an old seafaring man. Upon the ocean, where the operations of nature are so wild and vast, the ignorant mind instinctively becomes superstitious, reaches into the misty and obscure, and conjures up a thousand shadowy phantoms. (p. 451)

This beautiful poem embodies one of the great laws of our internal being,—that it makes its own world. The first peculiar attribute of the mind is to conceive,—to form images,—to create. Now its imaginings and creations must necessarily take the hue and color of itself,—be it good or evil. The next great law is association. Every object upon which we look, and every event of which we think, must be covered by the subtle web of past associations. The mind is, what the past has made it; and when it looks abroad on Nature, it cannot strip itself of these countless recollections. Thus the mind fuses and moulds every thing into its own likeness,—till wherever it looks it gazes upon—*itself*. Thus, with the Ancient Mariner, his mind has become disjointed, and every thing partakes of its own deformity. It has become diseased, and every thing has been tinged by its own blighted vision, till the actual world is peopled by phantoms, and the very face of beauty becomes ghost-like. There may be others who will think the effect too great for the cause,—and when we look at the ordinary sympathies of mankind, this appears to be true. The mere shooting of a sea-bird would hardly seem to merit the fearful judgments that follow, but we must think less of the deed itself, and more of the spirit that led to it. We shall then see that he had lost that Love, which is the harmony of all things, and that his heart must necessarily moulder within him, till again purified and kindled by holy affection. We should remember, that he had violated the law of human sympathy, and in that way struck a blow at the Creator of all.

Love is the central, sun-like principle of the moral universe. God is love. Every work in the wide creation is a symbol of that love. This is the great harmony of the whole. The mind of man is a portion of God's universe. It is the living link between it, and Him;—and as it parts with this heavenly principle, it wrenches itself away, by its own unworthiness, from the great whole. It becomes in discord with the spiritual world, as well as the natural; and thus dissevers itself from both. It crushes its best affections, and tears out the very nerve of its inner life. It sins against itself, and the divine law; and must be purified by its own fire. This is the key to the Ancient Mariner. (p. 452)

['**Christabel**'] is a singularly wild and remarkable production. . . . It belonged to that peculiar class of poetry, which never has, and never will awaken sympathy in the universal heart. It wants clearness; it is too ideal; and there are many, who cannot pierce its thick and shadowy mysticisms. It is not wholly founded either upon the intellect, or the passions,—and thus strikes a chord, which in all minds has not a corresponding key. Yet let not those, who cannot perceive its beauties, censure the judgment of those who can. (p. 453)

[In '**Remorse**'] he has discovered a deep insight into the most hidden springs of the mind, and has made them visible to us with wonderful distinctness, both in the calm of quiet thought, and the dizzy whirl of passion.

As the title of the play denotes, one of its great purposes is to show the workings of Remorse upon a base and guilty mind. (p. 454)

In this drama we have the unfolding of some of the most delicate, and some of the most awful workings of the soul. It gives passions, and the struggle of passions. It shows us those bright and beautiful hopes, that cluster around the heart of woman, even amid trial and desolation, and lays bare to our sight the horrible convulsions of that mind, on which guilt gnaws like a fanged monster. (pp. 454-55)

[We] can only say, concerning the true power and living spirit of Coleridge's writings, 'seek, and ye shall find.' His works are solid with meaning. They suggest truths, and leave them to be drawn out by the reader. Goethe has said, that 'a work which leaves nothing to divine, can be no true, consummate work; its highest destination must be to excite reflection: and no one can truly love a work till he has been compelled to follow it out, and complete it in his own mind.'

It has been said that Coleridge's works are fragments;—that they have no unity. We think it is not so. His works, taken singly, are fragments; put together, they make a whole. His poetry is a part of his philosophy. It is the golden clasp, that connects the chain. It is his philosophy, after he has breathed into it a living soul. In his **'Aids to Reflection,'** he says, 'religion is not a theory, but a *life;'* so it is with his philosophy: and in his poetry he shows this. He shows how it changes the whole man, and opens the inward perceptions. In fact, throughout his whole poetry his Christian philosophy flows, like the sap, into every branch, and leaf, and blossom. Those who would study the one, then, should study the other. They are the productions of one mind. They unfold the same principles,—and explain and support each other. . . .

[In] his poetry we find perfect truth. Nature is represented as it really is; not dry and dead, but full of meaning. It not only has form, but life. He never veils Nature, but unveils it, that we may see the light from within. Matter is to him full of spirit. It is an instrument in God's hand to develope the soul. . . . It is this, which gives such value to the writings of Coleridge. It is this, which makes him, not merely a moral writer, but strictly a religious writer. Not that he always writes upon religious subjects, but that he writes upon all subjects in a religious way. He has the religious spirit; the heavenly spirit; the spirit of love. Thus his writings are good; they purify, they elevate, they quicken, they impart himself.

The works of such a writer are of no country; they are the world's. They belong to no age,—but to all men of all ages. They contain truth,—and truth is eternal. They are written with reference to the life to come, and have therefore a spiritual power. For the character of such a writer, we can hardly feel too great a reverence. He has brought out the inner man. He has made the senses do homage to the spirit. He has drunk in from Nature and Revelation, till they have expanded and beautified his soul. (pp. 457-58)

[R. C. Waterston], *"Coleridge's Poems," in* The North American Review, *Vol. XXXIX, No. LXXXV, October, 1834, pp. 437-58.*

CHARLES LAMB   (essay date 1834)

[*An essayist, critic, and poet, Lamb is credited with initiating the revival of interest in Elizabethan and Restoration drama in nineteenth-century England. His critical comments on the plays of John Webster, Jeremy Taylor, Thomas Haywood, and John Ford, recorded in the form of notes to his anthology,* Specimens of the English Dramatic Poets Who Lived About the Time of Shakespeare, *demonstrate a literary taste and refinement new in his time. Unlike some of his contemporaries, Lamb never tried to construct an all-embracing, systematic critical theory. Instead, his method was to point out fine passages in particular works and convey his enthusiasm to his readers. Lamb is chiefly remembered, however, for his* Essays of Elia, *a series of familiar essays which are admired for their breadth, quaint style, and intimate tone. The following was written on November 21, 1834, in the album of a friend of Lamb's and later published in a memorial notice following Lamb's death.*]

When I heard of the death of Coleridge, it was without grief. It seemed to me that he long had been on the confines of the next world,—that he had a hunger for eternity. I grieved then that I could not grieve. But since, I feel how great a part he was of me. His great and dear spirit haunts me. I cannot think a thought, I cannot make a criticism on men or books, without an ineffectual turning and reference to him. He was the proof and touchstone of all my cogitations. He was a Grecian (or in the first form) at Christ's Hospital, where I was deputy Grecian; and the same subordination and deference to him I have preserved through a life-long acquaintance. Great in his writings, he was greatest in his conversation. In him was disproved that old maxim, that we should allow every one his share of talk. He would talk from morn to dewy eve, nor cease till far midnight, yet who ever would interrupt him,—who would obstruct that continuous flow of converse, fetched from Helicon or Zion? He had the tact of making the unintelligible seem plain. Many who read the abstruser parts of his 'Friend' would complain that his works did not answer to his spoken wisdom. They were identical. But he had a tone in oral delivery, which seemed to convey sense to those who were otherwise imperfect recipients. He was my fifty years old friend without a dissension. Never saw I his likeness, nor probably the world can see again.

Charles Lamb, "The Death of Coleridge," in his The Works of Charles Lamb, *edited by Thomas Hutchinson, Oxford University Press, London, 1940, p. 454.*

M. F. [SARAH MARGARET FULLER]   (essay date 1836)

[*A distinguished critic and early feminist, Fuller played an important role in the developing cultural life of the United States during the first half of the nineteenth century. As a founding member of the Transcendentalist journal,* The Dial, *and later as a contributor to Horace Greeley's* New York Tribune, *she was influential in introducing European art and literature to the United States. She wrote social, art, and music criticism, but she is most acclaimed as a literary critic; many rank her with Edgar Allan Poe as the finest in her era. Towards the end of Coleridge's life, his writings were championed by the Transcendentalists. Though Fuller does·not offer a general assessment of Coleridge's work, she acknowledges his intellectual and "suggestive power." These qualities, to Fuller, insure his place in literary history.*]

Of Coleridge I shall say little. Few minds are capable of fathoming his by their own sympathies, and he has left us no adequate manifestation of himself as a poet by which to judge him. For his dramas, I consider them complete failures, and more like visions than dramas. For a metaphysical mind like his to attempt that walk, was scarcely more judicious than it would be for a blind man to essay painting the bay of Naples. Many of his smaller pieces are perfect in their way, indeed no writer could excel him in depicting a single mood of mind, as **"Dejection,"** for instance. . . . Give Coleridge a canvass, and he will paint a single mood as if his colors were made of the mind's own atoms. . . . There is nothing of the spectator about Coleridge; he is all life; not impassioned, not vehement, but searching, intellectual life, which seems "listening through the frame" to its own pulses.

I have little more to say at present except to express a great, though not fanatical veneration for Coleridge, and a conviction that the benefits conferred by him on this and future ages are as yet incalculable. Every mind will praise him for what it can best receive from him. He can suggest to an infinite degree; he can *in*form, but he cannot *re*form and renovate. To the unprepared he is nothing, to the prepared, every thing. Of him may be said what he said of Nature,

> We receive but what we give,
> In kind though not in measure.

I was once requested, by a very sensible and excellent personage, to explain what is meant by **"Christabel"** and **"The Ancient Mariner."** I declined the task. I had not then seen Coleridge's answer to a question of similar tenor from Mrs. Barbauld [see excerpt above, 1830], or I should have referred to that as an expression, not altogether unintelligible, of the discrepancy which must ever exist between those minds which are commonly styled *rational,* (as the received definition of *common* sense is insensibility to *uncommon* sense,) and that of Coleridge. As to myself, if I understood nothing beyond the execution of those "singularly wild and original poems," I could not tell my gratitude for the degree of refinement which Taste has received from them. To those who cannot understand the voice of Nature or Poetry, unless it speak in Apothegms, and tag each story with a moral, I have nothing to say. . . . It is for his suggestive power that I thank him. (pp. 325-26)

> *M. F. [Sarah Margaret Fuller], "Modern British Poets," in* The American Monthly Magazine, *Vol. VIII, October, 1836, pp. 320-33.**

JOHN RUSKIN   (letter date 1843)

[*Ruskin, one of the leading English theorists and critics of the nineteenth century, had three major areas of accomplishment, contributing analyses of art, politics, and literature. He was a renowned art critic, and near the end of his life he devoted himself to political and economic issues. He also wrote literary criticism which is informed by these concerns as well as by his broad knowledge of the Bible and Classical and contemporary literature. In the following letter, Ruskin acknowledges Coleridge's skill as a poet but disparages his lack of discipline and "moral influence."*]

I love Coleridge, and I believe I know nearly every line of both the **Ancient Mariner** and **Christabel**—not to speak of the **Three Graves** and the **Hymn in Chamouni,** and the **Dejection**. . . . But after all Coleridge is nothing more than an intellectual opium-eater—a man of many crude though lovely thoughts—of confused though brilliant imagination, liable to much error—error even of the heart, very sensual in many of his ideas of pleasure—indolent to a degree, and evidently and always thinking without discipline; letting the fine brains which God gave him work themselves irregularly and without end or object—and carry him whither they will. . . . I believe Coleridge has very little moral influence in the world; his writings are those of a benevolent man in a fever.

> *John Ruskin, in a letter to Rev. Walter Brown in 1843, in his* The Literary Criticism of John Ruskin, *edited by Harold Bloom, Anchor Books, 1965, p. 1.**

[THOMAS DE QUINCEY]   (essay date 1845)

[*An English critic and essayist of the Romantic era, De Quincey used his own life as the subject of his best-known work,* Confessions of an English Opium Eater, *in which he chronicled his addiction to opium. In addition, De Quincey contributed reviews to a number of London journals and earned a reputation as an insightful if occasionally prolix literary critic. While a student at Oxford, De Quincey visited Coleridge, whom he had long admired; ironically, Coleridge warned him of the dangers of opium.*

Here, De Quincey expresses his deep admiration for Coleridge's vast literary and intellectual achievements.]

Weigh him the critic must in the golden balance of philosophy the most abstruse—a balance which even itself requires weighing previously, or he will have done nothing that can be received for an estimate of the composite Coleridge. This astonishing man . . . besides being an exquisite poet, a profound political speculator, a philosophic student of literature through all its chambers and recesses, was also a circumnavigator on the most pathless waters of scholasticism and metaphysics. He has sounded, without guiding charts, the secret deeps of Proclus and Plotinus; he had laid down buoys on the twilight, or moonlight, ocean. . . ; he had cruised over the broad Atlantic of Kant and Schelling, of Fichte and Okén. Where is the man who shall be equal to these things? (p. 118)

> [*Thomas De Quincey], "Coleridge and Opium-Eating," in* Blackwood's Edinburgh Magazine, *Vol. LVII, No. CCCLI, January, 1845, pp. 117-32.*

ALGERNON CHARLES SWINBURNE   (essay date 1875)

[*Swinburne was an English poet, dramatist, and critic. He was renowned during his lifetime for his lyric poetry, and he is remembered today for his rejection of Victorian mores. His explicitly sensual themes shocked his contemporaries. Swinburne's only goal, implicit in his poetry and explicit in his critical writings, was to express beauty. In the following, Swinburne praises Coleridge as a great literary figure, but concedes that, though some of his poems are among the finest ever written, much of his work is poor. To Swinburne, "Christabel" and "Kubla Khan" are the best of Coleridge's verse, because "it is more conceivable that another man should be born capable of writing the 'Ancient Mariner' than one capable of writing these." Although Swinburne judges Coleridge's blank verse a failure, he concludes that Coleridge will be remembered as a great imaginative, rather than passionate, poet.*]

[Coleridge] seems to me a figure more utterly companionless, more incomparable with others, than any of his kind. Receptive at once and communicative of many influences, he has received from none and to none did he communicate any of those which mark him as a man memorable to all students of men. What he learnt and what he taught are not the precious things in him. He has founded no school of poetry, as Wordsworth has, or Byron, or Tennyson; happy in this, that he has escaped the plague of pupils and parodists. Has he founded a school of philosophy? He has helped men to think; he has touched their thought with passing colours of his own thought; but has he moved and moulded it into new and durable shapes? Others may judge better of this than I, but to me, set beside the deep direct work of those thinkers who have actual power to break down and build up thought, to construct faith or destroy it, his work seems not as theirs is. And yet how very few are even the great names we could not better afford to spare, would not gladlier miss from the roll of "famous men and our fathers that were before us." Of his best verses I venture to affirm that the world has nothing like them, and can never have: that they are of the highest kind, and of their own. They are jewels of the diamond's price, flowers of the rose's rank, but unlike any rose or diamond known. . . . Judged by the justice of other men, he is assailable and condemnable on several sides; his good work is the scantiest in quantity ever done by a man so famous in so long a life; and much of his work is bad. His genius is fluctuant and moonstruck as the sea is, and yet his mind is not, what he described Shakespeare's to be, "an oceanic mind." (pp. 259-60)

For from the very first the two sides of his mind are visible and palpable. Among all verses of boys who were to grow up great, I remember none so perfect, so sweet and deep in sense and sound, as those which he is said to have written at school, headed **"Time, Real and Imaginary."** And following hard on these come a score or two of "poems" each more feeble and more flatulent than the last. Over these and the like I shall pass with all due speed, being undesirous to trouble myself or any possible reader with the question whether **"Religious Musings"** be more damnable than **"Lines to a Young Ass,"** or less damnable. Even when clear of these brambles, his genius walked for some time over much waste ground with irregular and unsure steps. Some poems, touched with exquisite grace, with clear and pure harmony, are tainted with somewhat of feeble and sickly which impairs our relish; **"Lewti"** for instance, an early sample of his admirable melody, of tender colour and dim grace as of clouds, but effeminate in build, loose-hung, weak of eye and foot. Yet nothing of more precious and rare sweetness exists in verse than that stanza of the swans disturbed. His style indeed was a plant of strangely slow growth, but perfect and wonderful in its final flower. Even in the famous verses called **"Love"** he has not attained to that strength and solidity of beauty which was his special gift at last. For melody rather than for harmony it is perfect; but in this oenomel there is as yet more of honey than of wine.

Coleridge was the reverse of Antaeus; the contact of earth took all strength out of him. He could not handle to much purpose any practical creed; his political verse is most often weak of foot and hoarse of accent. (pp. 261-62)

Of his flight and his song when in the fit element, it is hard to speak at all, hopeless to speak adequately. It is natural that there should be nothing like them discoverable in any human work; natural that his poetry at its highest should be, as it is, beyond all praise and all words of men. He who can define it could "unweave a rainbow;" he who could praise it aright would be such another as the poet. The **"Christabel,"** the **"Kubla Khan,"** with one or two more, are outside all law and jurisdiction of ours. When it has been said that such melodies were never heard, such dreams never dreamed, such speech never spoken, the chief thing remains unsaid, and unspeakable. There is a charm upon these poems which can only be felt in silent submission of wonder. (pp. 262-63)

More amenable to our judgment, and susceptible of a more definite admiration, the **"Ancient Mariner,"** and the few other poems cast in something of a ballad type which we may rank around or below it, belong to another class. The chief of these is so well known that it needs no fresh comment. Only I will say that to some it may seem as though this great sea-piece might have had more in it of the air and savour of the sea. Perhaps it is none the worse; and indeed any one speaking of so great and famous a poem must feel and know that it cannot but be right, although he or another may think it would be better if this were retrenched or that appended. And this poem is beyond question one of the supreme triumphs of poetry. (p. 263)

The **"Ancient Mariner"** has doubtless more of breadth and space, more of material force and motion, than anything else of the poet's. And the tenderness of sentiment which touches with significant colour the pure white imagination is here no longer morbid or languid, as in the earlier poems of feeling

and emotion. It is soft and piteous enough, but womanly rather than effeminate; and thus serves indeed to set off the strange splendours and boundless beauties of the story. For the execution, I presume no human eye is too dull to see how perfect it is, and how high in kind of perfection. Here is not the speckless and elaborate finish which shows everywhere the fresh rasp of file or chisel on its smooth and spruce excellence; this is faultless after the fashion of a flower or a tree. Thus it has grown: not thus has it been carved.

Nevertheless, were we compelled to the choice, I for one would rather preserve **"Kubla Khan"** and **"Christabel"** than any other of Coleridge's poems. It is more conceivable that another man should be born capable of writing the **"Ancient Mariner"** than one capable of writing these. The former is perhaps the most wonderful of all poems. In reading it we seem rapt into that paradise revealed to Swedenborg, where music and colour and perfume were one, where you could hear the hues and see the harmonies of heaven. For absolute melody and splendour it were hardly rash to call it the first poem in the language. . . . All the elements that compose the perfect form of English metre, as limbs and veins and features a beautiful body of man, were more familiar, more subject as it were, to this great poet than to any other. (pp. 264-65)

All these least details and delicacies of work are worth notice when the result of them is so transcendent. (p. 265)

Of all Coleridge's poems the loveliest is assuredly **"Christabel."** It is not so vast in scope and reach of imagination as the **"Ancient Mariner;"** it is not so miraculous as **"Kubla Khan;"** but for simple charm of inner and outer sweetness it is unequalled by either. The very terror and mystery of magical evil is imbued with this sweetness; the witch has no less of it than the maiden; their contact has in it nothing dissonant or disfiguring, nothing to jar or to deface the beauty and harmony of the whole imagination. (p. 266)

The finest of Coleridge's odes is beyond all doubt the **"Ode to France."** . . . There is in it a noble and loyal love of freedom. . . . The prelude is magnificent in music, and in sentiment and emotion far above any other of his poems; nor are the last notes inadequate to this majestic overture. Equal in force and sweetness of style, the **"Ode on Dejection"** ranks next in my mind to this one. . . . (p. 268)

It is noticeable that only his supreme gift of lyrical power could sustain Coleridge on political ground. His attempts of the kind in blank verse are poor indeed:—

>   Untimely breathings, sick and short assays.

Compare the nerveless and hysterical verses headed **"Fears in Solitude"** (exquisite as is the overture, faultless in tone and colour, and worthy of a better sequel) with the majestic and masculine sonnet of Wordsworth, written at the same time on the same subject: the lesser poet—for, great as he is, I at least cannot hold Wordsworth, though so much the stronger and more admirable man, equal to Coleridge as mere poet—speaks with a calm force of thought and resolution; Coleridge wails, appeals, deprecates, objurgates in a flaccid and querulous fashion without heart or spirit. . . . Blank verse Coleridge could never handle with the security of conscious skill and a trained strength; it grows in his hands too facile and feeble to carry the due weight or accomplish the due work. I have not found any of his poems in this metre retouched and reinvigorated as a few have been among his others. One such alteration is memorable to all students of his art; the excision from the

"**Ancient Mariner**" of a stanza (eleventh of the Third Part) which described the Death-mate of the Spectre-Woman, his bones foul with leprous scurf and green corruption of the grave, in contrast to the red lips and yellow locks of the fearfuller Nightmare Life-in-Death.... [His studies in blank verse] remain mostly in a hybrid or an embryonic state, with birthmarks on them of debility or malformation. Two of these indeed have a charm of their own, not shallow or transient: the "**Nightingale**" and "**Frost at Midnight.**" In colour they are perfect, and not (as usual) too effusive and ebullient in style. Others, especially some of the domestic or religious sort, are offensive and grievous to the human sense on that score. Coleridge had doubtless a sincere belief in his own sincerity of belief, a true feeling of his own truth of feeling; but he leaves with us too often an unpleasant sense or taste—as it were a tepid dilution of sentiment, a rancid unction of piety. (pp. 268-71)

Our study and our estimate of Coleridge cannot now be discoloured or misguided by the attraction or repulsion to which all contemporary students or judges of a great man's work cannot but be more or less liable. Few men, I suppose, ever inspired more of either feeling than he in his time did. To us his moral or social qualities, his opinion on this matter and his action in that, are nothing except in so far as they affect the work done, the inheritance bequeathed us. With all fit admiration and gratitude for the splendid fragments so bequeathed of a critical and philosophic sort, I doubt his being remembered, except by a small body of his elect, as other than a poet. His genius was so great, and in its greatness so many-sided, that for some studious disciples of the rarer kind he will doubtless, seen from any possible point of view, have always something about him of the old magnetism and magic. The ardour, delicacy, energy of his intellect, his resolute desire to get at the roots of things and deeper yet, if deeper might be, will always enchant and attract all spirits of like mould and temper. But as a poet his place is indisputable. It is high among the highest of all time. An age that should forget or neglect him might neglect or forget any poet that ever lived. At least, any poet whom it did remember such an age would remember as something other than a poet; it would prize and praise in him, not the absolute and distinctive quality, but something empirical or accidental. That may be said of this one which can hardly be said of any but the greatest among men; that come what may to the world in course of time, it will never see his place filled. Other and stronger men, with fuller control and concentration of genius, may do more service, may bear more fruit; but such as his was they will not have in them to give. The highest lyric work is either passionate or imaginative; of passion Coleridge's has nothing; but for height and perfection of imaginative quality he is the greatest of lyric poets. This was his special power, and this is his special praise. (pp. 274-75)

Algernon Charles Swinburne, "Coleridge," in his Essays and Studies, *Chatto & Windus, 1875, pp. 259-75.*

GEORG BRANDES   (essay date 1875)

[*Brandes, a Danish literary critic and biographer, was the principal leader of the intellectual movement which helped to bring an end to Scandinavian cultural isolation. His major critical work,* Hovedstrominger i det aarhundredes litteratur (Main Currents in Nineteenth Century Literature), *won him admiration for his ability to view literary movements within the broader context of all of European literature. The following excerpt was originally published in 1875 in* Naturalismen i England (Naturalism in England), *Volume IV of* Main Currents. *Here, Brandes discusses Coleridge's*

place in literary history and terms "Christabel" "the first English poem which is permeated by the genuine Romantic spirit." However, Brandes considers the poem overrated; its chief merit is its depiction of the demonic element. He also points out stylistic flaws in "The Ancient Mariner," but praises its realistic imagery; like the rest of Coleridge's poetry, he claims, the poem does not reflect Coleridge's personal emotions.]

Christabel was planned as the first of a series of poetical romances, the remainder of which never came into being. It is, without doubt, the first English poem which is permeated by the genuine Romantic spirit; and the new cadences, the new theme, the new style of versification, the novelty generally, made a powerful impression on contemporary poets. The irregular and yet melodious metre appealed so strongly to Scott that he employed it in his first Romantic poem, *The Lay of the Last Minstrel.* He frankly confesses how much he owed to the beautiful and tantalising fragment, *Christabel,* which he, like the other poets of the period, made acquaintance with in manuscript; for Coleridge read it aloud in social gatherings for twenty years before it saw the light as public property. Byron, too, heard it first on one of these occasions. Before hearing it he had, in one of his longer poems (*The Siege of Corinth* ...), written some lines which were not unlike some in *Christabel.* To these lines he, on a future occasion, appended a note in which he praises Coleridge's "wild and singularly original and beautiful poem.".... Danish critics, thoroughly initiated into the mysteries of this style by Tieck and the brothers Schlegel, and by their own poet Ingemann, cannot possibly attach so much importance to this fragment. Its excessive naïveté and simplicity, the intentional childishness in style and tone, are to us what buns are to bakers' children. The chief merit of the poem, apart from its full-toned, sweet melody, lies in the peculiar power with which the nature of the wicked fairy is presented to us, the *daemonic* element, which had never been present in such force in English literature before. We must, however, remember that, though the first part of the poem was written in 1797, the second was written and the first revised in 1800—that is to say, *after* Coleridge had travelled with Wordsworth in Germany, and there made acquaintance with contemporary German poetry, its medieval ground-work, and its latest tendency.

Coleridge's one other poem of any length, *The Ancient Mariner,* which is even more artificially naïve in style than *Christabel,* and is provided, in the manner of the medieval ballads retailed in the little shops in back streets, with a prose index of contents on the margin of the pages, is now the most popular of all his poems, although it was fiercely attacked on its first appearance. (pp. 76-7)

[Though] *The Ancient Mariner* may not take a high place when compared with poetry which has extricated itself from Romantic swaddling-bands, it stands high above most of the kindred productions of German Romanticism. In spite of all its Romantic fictitiousness, it breathes of the sea, the real, natural sea, whose changing moods and whose terrifying, menacing immensity it describes. The fresh breeze, the seething foam, the horrible fog, and the hot, copper-coloured evening sky with its blood-red sun—all these elements are nature's own; and the misery of the men tossing helplessly on the ocean, the starvation, the burning thirst that drives them to suck the blood from their own arms, the pallid countenances, the terrible death-rattle, the horrible putrefaction—all these elements are realities, represented with English realistic force. (p. 79)

And it is a very English trait that Coleridge himself should have been thoroughly capable of seeing the weak points of such a poem as his own famous ballad. The national quality of humour assisted him to this independence of judgment. We have the following anecdote from his own pen. "An amateur performer in verse expressed a strong desire to be introduced to me, but hesitated in accepting my friend's immediate offer, on the score that he was, he must acknowledge, the author of a confounded severe epigram on my *Ancient Mariner,* which had given me great pain. I assured my friend that if the epigram was a good one, it would only increase my desire to become acquainted with the author, and begged to hear it recited, when, to my no less surprise than amusement, it proved to be one which I had myself inserted in the *Morning Post.*" When Coleridge tells us, too, that he himself wrote three sonnets expressly for the purpose of exciting a good-natured laugh at the artificial simplicity and doleful egotism of the new poetical tendency, and that he took the elaborate and swelling language and imagery of these sonnets from his own poems, we cannot deny that his endeavours to keep free from the entanglement in theories which was the weak point in German Romanticism, bespeak rare intellectual superiority. (p. 80)

The few poems which [Coleridge] wrote in the course of a comparatively long life are distinguished by the exquisite melodiousness of their language; their harmonies are not only delicate and insinuating like Shelley's, but contrapuntally constructed and rich; they have a peculiar, ponderous sweetness; each line has the taste and weight of a drop of honey. In poems such as *Love* and *Lewti,* which are the two sweetest, and in an Oriental fantasy like *Kubla Khan,* which was inspired by a dream, we hear Coleridge flute and pipe and sing with all the changing cadences of the most exquisite nightingale voice. . . .

But Coleridge's poetry is as unplastic as it is melodious, and as unimpassioned as it is mellifluous. It is of the fantastic Romantic order; that is to say, it neither expresses strong, personally experienced emotions, nor reproduces what the author has observed in the surrounding world. (p. 82)

> Georg Brandes, "Naturalistic Romanticism," in his Naturalism in Nineteenth Century English Literature, *Russell & Russell, 1957, pp. 72-84.**

DANTE GABRIEL ROSSETTI   (poem date 1881)

[*Equally renowned as a painter and poet, Rossetti was the leader of the Pre-Raphaelite Brotherhood, a group of artists and writers who sought to emulate the purity and simplicity of the Italian Proto-Renaissance School of art. The following poem expresses Rossetti's admiration for Coleridge.*]

His Soul fared forth (as from the deep home-grove
  The father-songster plies the hour-long quest,)
  To feed his soul-brood hungering in the nest;
But his warm Heart, the mother-bird, above
Their callow fledgling progeny still hove
  With tented roof of wings and fostering breast
  Till the Soul fed the soul-brood. Richly blest
From Heaven their growth, whose food was Human
    Love.

Yet ah! Like desert pools that show the stars
  Once in long leagues,—even such the scarce-snatched
    hours
  Which deepening pain left to his lordliest powers:—
Heaven lost through spider-trammelled prison-bars.
  Six years, from sixty saved! Yet kindling skies
  Own them, a beacon to our centuries.

> *Dante Gabriel Rossetti, "Five English Poets—Samuel Taylor Coleridge," in his* Ballads and Sonnets, *Ellis and White, 1881, p. 315.*

LESLIE STEPHEN   (lecture date 1888)

[*Stephen is considered one of the most important literary critics of his age. In his criticism, Stephen argues that all literature is nothing more than an imaginative rendering, in concrete terms, of a writer's philosophy or beliefs. It is the role of criticism, he contends, to translate into intellectual terms what the writer has told the reader through character, symbol, and plot. Stephen's analyses often include biographical judgments of the writer as well as the work. In the following, taken from a lecture given at the Royal Institute of Great Britain on March 9, 1888, Stephen discusses the way in which Coleridge's life is reflected in his writings. Stephen maintains that Coleridge's poetry and criticism*]

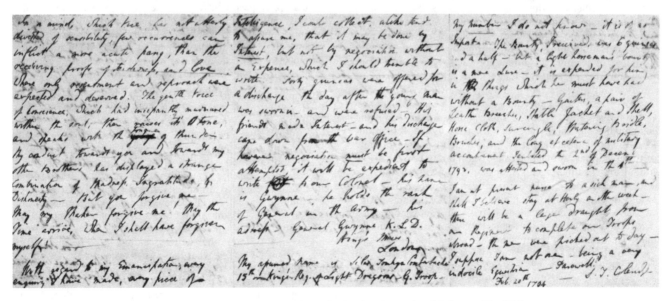

Facsimile of a letter from Coleridge to his brother James dated February 20, 1794.

evidence a rejection of earlier artistic principles, primarily those of seventeenth- and eighteenth-century poets who infused their writing with moral and religious messages. Stephen argues that Coleridge's importance as a critic lies in his ability to interpret poetry as the communication of pleasure; however, he also believes that Coleridge wasted his critical talent through his inherent laxity.]

My excuse for venturing to say something of Coleridge—certainly one of the most fascinating and most perplexing figures in our literary history—is simply this: I have been forced to investigate with some care the details of his career; and I ought to be able not to answer the question, but to provide a little "vehiculatory gear" towards answering it. Coleridge's philosophy must of course be judged by considerations extraneous to his personal history. Yet I think, as a professional biographer is in duty bound to think, that philosophy is, more often than philosophers admit, the outcome of personal experience; and Coleridge's singular history may throw some light upon his teaching. Here we meet the hagiologist and the iconoclast, the twin plagues of the humble biographer. The hagiologist burns incense before his idol till it is difficult to distinguish any fixed outline through the clouds of gorgeously tinted vapour. Coleridge thought himself to have certain failings. His relations fully agreed with him. His worshippers regard these meek confessions as mere illustrations of the good man's humility, and even manage to endow the poet and philosopher with all the homely virtues of the respectable and the solvent. To put forward such claims is to challenge the iconoclast. He, a person endowed by nature with a fine stock of virtuous indignation, has very little trouble in picturing the poet-philosopher as a shambling, unreliable, indolent voluptuary, to whom an action became impossible so soon as it presented itself as a duty, and who, even as a man of genius, must be condemned as unfaithful to his high calling. And so we raise the usual edifying discussion as to the privileges of genius. Do they include superiority to the Ten Commandments? Can you expect a poet to confine himself to one wife? May a man neglect his children because he has written *The Ancient Mariner* and *Christabel*? (pp. 329-31)

For my purpose it is enough to ascertain the facts. I have not to decide whether Coleridge should receive excommunication or canonisation; whether he deserved to go straight to heaven or to pass a period—and, if so, how long a period—in purgatory. It is difficult to settle such questions satisfactorily. I desiderate an accurate diagnosis, not a judicial sentence. Coleridge sinned and repented. I take note of sin and of repentance as indications of character. I do not pretend to say whether in the eye of Heaven the repentance would be an adequate set-off for the sin. But I premise one apology for anything that may sound iconoclastic, and which I think is worth the consideration of the amiable persons who undertake to rehabilitate soiled reputations. A man's weakness can rarely be overlooked without underestimating his strength. If Coleridge's intellect were, as De Quincey said in his magniloquent way, "the greatest and most spacious, the subtlest and most comprehensive, that has yet existed among men" (what a philosopher one must be to pronounce such a judgment!) why were the results so small? Because the ethereal soul was chained to a fleshy carcase. To deny this is to force us to assume that what he did was all that he could do. You must either exaggerate his actual achievements beyond all possible limits, or save your belief in his potential achievements by admitting that his intellect never had fair play. (pp. 331-32)

[The *Biographia Literaria*] has a special biographical value though its statements, coloured by the illusions to which he was then specially subject, have passed muster too easily with his biographers. Its aim is chiefly to protest against the neglect of the public and the dispensers of patronage. Such complaints generally remind me of a rifleman complaining that the target persists in keeping out of the line of fire. But if we must pardon something to a man so grievously tried for endeavouring to shift a part of the responsibility upon other shoulders than his own, we must be upon our guard against accepting censures which involve injustice to others. Nothing but Coleridge's strange illusions could be an apology, for example, for his complaints that the Ministry had not rewarded a writer whose greatest successes had been scornful denunciations of their great leader, Pitt. The book, of course, is put together with a pitchfork. It is without form or proportion. . . . (pp. 349-50)

Now it is remarkable that even at this time, when his demoralisation had gone furthest, he could still pour out many pages of criticism, quite irrelevant to the professed purpose of the book, and yet such as was beyond and above the range of any living contemporary. Coleridge at his worst lost the power of finishing and concentrating—of which he had never had very much—but not the power of discursive reflection. He must be compared not to a tree which has lost its vital fibre, but to a vine deprived of its props, which, though most of its fruit is crushed and wasted, can yet produce grapes with the full bloom of what might have been a superlative vintage. But there is one fact of the *Biographia* for which the apology of illusion is more requisite even than for his misstatements of fact. Coleridge has often been accused of plagiarism. I do not believe that he stole his Shakespeare criticism from Schlegel, and, partly at least, for the reason which would induce me to acquit a supposed thief of having stolen a pair of breeches from a wild Highlandman. But it is undeniable that Coleridge was guilty of a serious theft of metaphysical wares. The only excuse suggested is that the theft was too certain of exposure to be perpetrated. But as it certainly was perpetrated, this can only be an apology for the motive. The simple fact is that part of his scheme was to establish his claims to be a great metaphysician. But it takes much trouble and some thought to put together what looks like a chain of *a priori* demonstration of abstract principles. Coleridge, therefore, persuaded himself that he had really anticipated Schelling's thoughts and might justifiably appropriate Schelling's words. He threw out a few phrases about "genial coincidence"—perhaps the happiest circumlocution ever devised for what Pistol called "conveying"—and adopted Schelling in the lump. (pp. 350-51)

And now I come to the very difficult task of indicating, as briefly as I can, the bearing of these remarks upon Coleridge's multifarious activity. It is not possible to sum up in a few phrases the characteristics of a man who wrote upon metaphysics, theology, morals, politics, and literary criticism; who made a deep impression in all the departments of thought; whose utterances are scattered up and down in fragmentary treatises, in complex arguments which generally break off in the middle, and in miscellaneous jottings upon the margins of books; whose opinions have been differently interpreted by different disciples, and have in great part to be inferred from his comments upon other writers, and can only be intelligible when we have settled what those writers meant, and what he took them to mean; who frequently changed his mind, and who certainly apprears, to thinkers of a different order, to add obscurity even to subjects which are necessarily obscure. Nor is the difficulty diminished when, as in my case, the commentator belongs to what must be called the antagonistic school, and is even most properly to be described as a thorough Philistine who is dull enough to glory in his Philistinism. (pp. 351-52)

The brilliant Coleridge of Nether Stowey, the buoyant young poet-philosopher who had not been to Germany, was still a curious compound of imperfectly fused elements. His Liberalism had led him to the Unitarianism of Priestley and the associative philosophy of Hartley. But he had also dipped into Plotinus and into some of the mystical writers who represent the very opposite pole of speculation. The first doctrine was imposed upon him from without, the other was that which was really congenial to his temperament. For Coleridge was, above all, essentially and intrinsically a poet. The first genuine manifestations of his genius are the poems which he wrote before he was twenty-six. The germ of all Coleridge's utterances may be found—by a little ingenuity—in *The Ancient Mariner*. For what is the secret of the strange charm of that unique achievement? I do not speak of what may be called its purely literary merits—the melody of versification, the command of language, the vividness of the descriptive passages, and so forth—I leave such points to critics of finer perception and a greater command of superlatives. But part, at least, of the secret is the ease with which Coleridge moves in a world of which the machinery (as the old critics called it) is supplied by the mystic philosopher. (pp. 352-53)

[The world of *The Ancient Mariner*] is a world in which both animated things, and stones, and brooks, and clouds, and plants are moved by spiritual agency; in which, as he would put it, the veil of the senses is nothing but a symbolism everywhere telling of unseen and supernatural forces. What we call the solid and the substantial becomes a dream; and the dream is the true underlying reality. The difference between such poetry and the poetry of Pope, or even of Gray, or Goldsmith, or Cowper—poetry which is the direct utterance of a string of moral, political, or religious reflections—implies a literary revolution. Coleridge, even more distinctly than Wordsworth, represented a deliberate rejection of the canons of the preceding school; for, if Wordsworth's philosophy differed from that of Pope, he still taught by direct exposition instead of the presentation of sensuous symbolism. The distinction might be illustrated by the ingenious criticism of Mrs. Barbauld, who told Coleridge that *The Ancient Mariner* had two faults—it was improbable and had no moral. Coleridge owned the improbability, but replied to the other stricture that it had too much moral, for that it ought to have had no more than a story in the *Arabian Nights* [see excerpt above, 1830]. Indeed, the moral, which would apparently be that people who sympathise with a man who shoots an albatross will die in prolonged torture of thirst, is open to obvious objections. (pp. 354-55)

In saying that Coleridge was primarily a poet, I did not mean to intimate that he was not also a subtle dialectician. There is no real incompatibility between the two faculties. A poetic literature which includes Shakespeare in the past and Browning in the present is of itself a sufficient proof that the keenest and most active logical faculty may be combined with the truest poetical imagination. Coleridge's peculiar service to English criticism consisted, indeed, in a great measure, in a clear appreciation of the true relation between the faculties, a relation, I think, which he never quite managed to express clearly. Poetry, as he says, is properly opposed not to prose but to science. Its aim, he infers, is not to establish truth but to communicate pleasure. The poet presents us with the concrete symbol; the man of science endeavours to analyse and abstract the laws embodied. (pp. 356-57)

Coleridge, having practised, proceeded to preach. That a poet should also be a good critic is no more surprising than that any man should speak well on the art of which he is master. . . . Coleridge's specific merit was not, as I think, that he laid down any scientific theory. I don't believe that any such theory has as yet any existence except in embryo. He was something almost unique in this as in his poetry, first because his criticism (so far as it was really excellent) was the criticism of love, the criticism of a man who combined the first simple impulse of admiration with the power of explaining why he admired; and secondly, and as a result, because he placed himself at the right point of view; because, to put it briefly, he was the first great writer who criticised poetry as poetry, and not as science. The preceding generation had asked, as Mrs. Barbauld asked: "What is the moral?" [see excerpt above, 1830]. Has [Shakespeare's] *Othello* a moral catastrophe? What does [Milton's] *Paradise Lost* prove? Are the principles of Pope's *Essay on Man* philosophical? or is Goldsmith's *Deserted Village* a sound piece of political economy? The reply embodied in Coleridge's admirable criticisms, especially Shakespeare, was that this implied a total misconception of the relations of poetry to philosophy. The "moral" of a poem is not this or that proposition tagged to it or deducible from it, moral or otherwise; but the total effect of the stimulus to the imagination and affections, or what Coleridge would call its dynamic effect. That will, no doubt, depend partly upon the philosophy assumed in it; but has no common ground with the merits of a demonstration in Euclid or Spinoza. It is this adoption of a really new method which makes us feel, when we compare Coleridge, not only with the critics of a past generation, but even with very able and acute writers such as Jeffrey or Hazlitt, who were his contemporaries, that we are in a freer and larger atmosphere, and are in contact with deeper principles. It raises another question, for it leads to Coleridge's most conscious aim. Nothing is easier than to put the proper label on a poet—to call him "romantic," or "classical," and so forth; and then, if he has a predecessor of like principles, to explain him by the likeness, and if he represents a change of principles, to make the change explain itself by calling it a reaction. The method is delightfully simple, and I can use the words as easily as my neighbours. The only thing I find difficult is to look wise when I use them, or to fancy that I give an explanation because I have adopted a classification. Coleridge, both in poetry and philosophy, conceived himself to be one of the leaders of such a reaction. He proposed to abolish the wicked, mechanical, infidel, prosaic eighteenth century and go back to the seventeenth. (pp. 357-59)

[Coleridge] was fond of saying that all men were born Aristotelians or Platonists: Platonists, if, in his favourite distinction, the reason and the imagination dominated in them, and Aristotelians, if they had only the understanding, the almost vulpine cunning, which was shared even by the lower animals, which meant prudence in morality, reliance upon mere external evidence in theology, and pure expediency in politics. How the Aristotelians had come to rule the world ever since the opening of the eighteenth century is a question which, so far as I know, he never answered. . . . It was as much in his character of poet as of philosopher that Coleridge hated political economy, the favourite science of the Benthamites; for, according to him, it was an illustration of their destructive method. The economist deals with mere barren abstractions, and then misapplies them to the concrete organism, the life of which, according to him, has been destroyed by his dissecting knife. Coleridge goes too far in speaking as if analysis were in itself a mischievous instead of an important process, much as Wordsworth thought that every man of science was ready to botanise on his mother's grave. But, on the other hand, the clear conviction that a society could only be explained as an organic and continuous whole enables him to point out very distinctly the limits of the opposite school. One indication of this contrast may be found in Coleridge's theory of Church and State. (pp. 361-62)

He regards society as an organism, a something which has grown through long centuries, and therefore to be studied in its vital principle, not to be analysed into a mere mechanism for distributing certain lumps of happiness. . . . Coleridge feels the necessity of connecting his organic principles with some genuine philosophical principle. . . . He tried to put together his views at a time when his mind had been hopelessly enervated; when he could guess and beat about a principle, but could never get it fairly stated or see its full bearings. He is struggling for utterance, still clinging to the belief that he can elaborate a system, but never getting beyond prolegomena and fruitful hints. He says that to study politics with benefit we must try to elaborate the "idea" of Church and State, and the "idea," as he explains, is identical with what scientific people call a law. But how the law or laws of an organism are to be determined by some transcendental principle overruling and independent of experiences, is just the point which remains inexplicable. He seems to appreciate what we now call the historic method. He uses the sacred phrase "evolution," which is simply the general formula of which the historic method is a special application. But we find that by evolution he means some strange process suggestive of his old mystical employment. . . . To state the theory of evolution in verifiable and scientific terms was reserved for Darwin; when we meet it in Coleridge we seem to be going back to Pythagoras; and yet it is the same thought which is struggling for an utterance in singular and bewildering terms. . . . (pp. 363-65)

But, to come to a conclusion: though I cannot think that Coleridge ever worked with his mind clear, or was, indeed, capable of the necessary concentration and steadiness of thought by which alone philosophical achievements are possible; though I hold, again, that if he had succeeded he would have found that he was not so much refuting his opponents as supplying a necessary complement to their teaching, I can still believe that he saw more clearly than any of his contemporaries what were the vital issues; that in his detached and desultory and inconsistent fashion he was stirring the thoughts which were to occupy his successors; and that a detailed examination would show in how many directions a certain Coleridgian leaven is working in later fermentations. (p. 365)

Coleridge never constructed a system. If a philosophy, or its creator, is to be judged by the systematic characters, Coleridge must take a very low place. But when we think what philosophical systems have so far been; what flimsy and air-built bubbles in the eyes of the next generation; how often we desire, even in the case of the greatest men, that the one vital idea (there is seldom so much as one!) could be preserved, and the pretentious structure in which it is involved permitted once for all to burst; we may think that another criterion is admissible; that a man's work may be judged by the stimulus given to reflection, even if given in so intricate a muddle and such fragmentary utterances that its disciples themselves are hopelessly unable to present it in an orderly form. Upon that ground, Coleridge's rank will be a very high one, although, when all is said, the history, both of the man and the thinker, will always be a sad one—the saddest in some sense that we can read, for it is the history of early promise blighted and vast powers all but running hopelessly to waste. (pp. 366-67)

Leslie Stephen, "Coleridge," in his Hours in a Library, *Vol. IV, revised edition, G. P. Putnam's Sons, 1904, pp. 327-67.*

WALTER PATER (essay date 1889)

[*Pater is one of the most famous proponents of aestheticism in English literature. Distinguished as the first major English writer to formulate an explicitly aesthetic philosophy of life, he advocated the "love of art for art's sake" as life's greatest offering. Exalting art and the artist, Pater's writings have appealed to and influenced many authors. Pater's essay on Coleridge reflects Pater's growing discontent with the Church of England and Christian doctrine. He argues that Coleridge's desire to "apprehend the absolute" and his "excess of seriousness" weakened his poetic talent, though Pater also praises "The Ancient Mariner" for its unity and perfect intertwining of Romantic and supernatural elements. Ultimately, he contends that Coleridge's attempt to affix stringent principles to every aspect of art instead of adhering to a more flexible philosophy interfered with Coleridge's intellectual development.*]

[The] literary life of Coleridge was a disinterested struggle against the relative spirit. With a strong native bent towards the tracking of all questions, critical or practical, to first principles, he is ever restlessly scheming to "apprehend the absolute," to affirm it effectively, to get it acknowledged. It was an effort, surely, an effort of sickly thought, that saddened his mind, and limited the operation of his unique poetic gift.

So what the reader of our own generation will least find in Coleridge's prose writings is the excitement of the literary sense. And yet, in those grey volumes, we have the larger part of the production of one who made way ever by a charm, the charm of voice, of aspect, of language, above all by the intellectual charm of new, moving, luminous ideas. Perhaps the chief offence in Coleridge is an excess of seriousness, a seriousness arising not from any moral principle, but from a misconception of the perfect manner. There is a certain shade of unconcern, the perfect manner of the eighteenth century, which may be thought to mark complete culture in the handling of abstract questions. . . . [On] Coleridge lies the whole weight of the sad reflection that has since come into the world, with which for us the air is full, which the "children in the market-place" repeat to each other. His very language is forced and broken lest some saving formula should be lost—*distinctities, enucleation, pentad of operative Christianity;* he has a whole armoury of these terms, and expects to turn the tide of human thought by fixing the sense of such expressions as "reason," "understanding," "idea." Again, he lacks the jealousy of a true artist in excluding all associations that have no colour, or charm, or gladness in them; and everywhere allows the impress of a somewhat inferior theological literature. (pp. 68-70)

He had an odd, attractive gift of conversation, or rather of monologue, as Madame de Staël observed of him, full of *bizarreries,* with the rapid alternations of a dream, and here or there an unexpected summons into a world strange to the hearer, abounding in images drawn from a sort of divided imperfect life, the consciousness of the opium-eater, as of one to whom the external world penetrated only in part, and, blent with all this, passages of deep obscurity, precious, if at all, only for their musical cadence, echoes in Coleridge of the eloquence of those older English writers of whom he was so ardent a lover. And all through this brilliant early manhood we may discern the power of the "Asiatic" temperament, of that voluptuousness, which is connected perhaps with his appreciation of the intimacy, the almost mystical communion of touch, between nature and man. (pp. 70-1)

The *Aids to Reflection, The Friend, The Biographia Literaria:* those books came from one whose vocation was in the world of the imagination, the theory and practice of poetry. And yet, perhaps, of all books that have been influential in modern times, they are furthest from artistic form—bundles of notes; the original matter inseparably mixed up with that borrowed from others; the whole, just that mere preparation for an artistic effect which the finished literary artist would be careful one day to destroy. Here, again, we have a trait profoundly characteristic of Coleridge. He sometimes attempts to reduce a phase of thought, subtle and exquisite, to conditions too rough for it. He uses a purely speculative gift for direct moral edification. Scientific truth is a thing fugitive, relative, full of fine gradations: he tries to fix it in absolute formulas. The *Aids to Reflection, The Friend,* are efforts to propagate the volatile spirit of conversation into the less ethereal fabric of a written book; and it is only here or there that the poorer matter becomes vibrant, is really lifted by the spirit. (pp. 72-3)

Coleridge's prose writings on philosophy, politics, religion, and criticism, were, in truth, but one element in a whole lifetime of endeavours to present the then recent metaphysics of Germany to English readers, as a legitimate expansion of the older, classical and native masters of what has been variously called the *a priori,* or absolute, or spiritual, or Platonic, view of things. His criticism, his challenge for recognition in the concrete, visible, finite work of art, of the dim, unseen, comparatively infinite, soul or power of the artist, may well be remembered as part of the long pleading of German culture for the things "behind the veil." To introduce that spiritual philosophy, as represented by the more transcendental parts of Kant, and by Schelling, into all subjects, as a system of reason in them, one and ever identical with itself, however various the matter through which it was diffused, became with him the motive of an unflagging enthusiasm, which seems to have been the one thread of continuity in a life otherwise singularly wanting in unity of purpose, and in which he was certainly far from uniformly at his best. Fragmentary and obscure, but often eloquent, and always at once earnest and ingenious, those writings, supplementing his remarkable gift of conversation, were directly and indirectly influential, even on some the furthest removed from Coleridge's own masters; on John Stuart Mill, for instance, and some of the earlier writers of the "high-church" school. Like his verse, they display him also in two other characters—as a student of words, and as a psychologist, that is, as a more minute observer or student than other men of the phenomena of mind. . . . [His] morbid languor of nature, connected both with his fitfulness of purpose and his rich delicate dreaminess, qualifies Coleridge's poetic composition even more than his prose; his verse, with the exception of his avowedly political poems, being, unlike that of the "Lake School," to which in some respects he belongs, singularly unaffected by any moral, or professional, or personal effort or ambition,— "written," as he says, "after the more violent emotions of sorrow, to give him pleasure, when perhaps nothing else could;" but coming thus, indeed, very close to his own most intimately personal characteristics, and having a certain languidly soothing grace or cadence, for its most fixed quality, from first to last. After some Platonic soliloquy on a flower opening on a fine day in February, he goes on—

> Dim similitudes
> Weaving in mortal strains, I've stolen one hour
> From anxious self, life's cruel taskmaster!

> And the warm wooings of this sunny day
> Tremble along my frame and harmonise
> The attempered organ, that even saddest thoughts
> Mix with some sweet sensations, like harsh tunes
> Played deftly on a sweet-toned instrument.

The expression of two opposed, yet allied, elements of sensibility in these lines, is very true to Coleridge:—the grievous agitation, the grievous listlessness, almost never entirely relieved, together with a certain physical voluptuousness. He has spoken several times of the scent of the bean-field in the air:— the tropical touches in a chilly climate; his is a nature that will make the most of these, which finds a sort of caress in such things. *Kubla Khan,* the fragment of a poem actually composed in some certainly not quite healthy sleep, is perhaps chiefly of interest as showing, by the mode of its composition, how physical, how much of a diseased or valetudinarian temperament, in its moments of relief, Coleridge's happiest gift really was; and side by side with *Kubla Khan* should be read, as Coleridge placed it, the *Pains of Sleep,* to illustrate that retarding physical burden in his temperament, that "unimpassioned grief," the source of which lay so near the source of those pleasures. (pp. 81-4)

What shapes itself for criticism as the main phenomenon of Coleridge's poetic life, is not, as with most true poets, the gradual development of a poetic gift, determined, enriched, retarded, by the actual circumstances of the poet's life, but the sudden blossoming, through one short season, of such a gift already perfect in its kind, which thereafter deteriorates as suddenly, with something like premature old age. Connecting this phenomenon with the leading motive of his prose writings, we might note it as the deterioration of a productive or creative power into one merely metaphysical or discursive. In his unambitious conception of his function as a poet, and in the very limited quantity of his poetical performance . . . he was a contrast to his friend Wordsworth. That friendship with Wordsworth, the chief "developing" circumstance of his poetic life, comprehended a very close intellectual sympathy; and in such association chiefly, lies whatever truth there may be in the popular classification of Coleridge as a member of what is called the "Lake School." Coleridge's philosophical speculations do really turn on the ideas which underlay Wordsworth's poetical practice. His prose works are one long explanation of all that is involved in that famous distinction between the Fancy and the Imagination. (pp. 87-8)

It is in a highly sensitive apprehension of the aspects of external nature that Coleridge identifies himself most closely with one of the main tendencies of the "Lake School"; a tendency instinctive, and no mere matter of theory, in him as in Wordsworth. . . . He has a like imaginative apprehension of the silent and unseen processes of nature, its "ministries" of dew and frost, for instance; as when he writes, in April—

> A balmy night! and though the stars be dim,
> Yet let us think upon the vernal showers
> That gladden the green earth, and we shall find
> A pleasure in the dimness of the stars.

(pp. 90-2)

In his changes of political sentiment, Coleridge was associated with the "Lake School"; and there is yet one other very different sort of sentiment in which he is one with that school, yet all himself, his sympathy, namely, with the animal world. That was a sentiment connected at once with the love of outward nature in himself and in the "Lake School," and its assertion of the natural affections in their simplicity; with the homeliness and pity, consequent upon that assertion. (pp. 94-5)

[*Christabel* and *The Rhyme of the Ancient Mariner*] belong to the great year of Coleridge's poetic production, his twenty-fifth year. In poetic quality, above all in that most poetic of all qualities, a keen sense of, and delight in beauty, the infection of which lays hold upon the reader, they are quite out of proportion to all his other compositions. The form in both is that of the ballad, with some of its terminology, and some also of its quaint conceits. (p. 95)

The Ancient Mariner, as also, in its measure, *Christabel,* is a "romantic" poem, impressing us by bold invention, and appealing to that taste for the supernatural, that longing for *le frisson,* a shudder, to which the "romantic" school in Germany, and its derivations in England and France, directly ministered. In Coleridge, personally, this taste had been encouraged by his odd and out-of-the-way reading in the old-fashioned literature of the marvellous. . . . Fancies of the strange things which may very well happen, even in broad daylight, to men shut up alone in ships far off on the sea, seem to have occurred to the human mind in all ages with a peculiar readiness, and often have about them, from the story of the stealing of Dionysus downwards, the fascination of a certain dreamy grace, which distinguishes them from other kinds of marvellous inventions. This sort of fascination *The Ancient Mariner* brings to its highest degree: it is the delicacy, the dreamy grace, in his presentation of the marvellous, which makes Coleridge's work so remarkable. The too palpable intruders from a spiritual world in almost all ghost literature, in Scott and Shakespeare even, have a kind of crudity or coarseness. Coleridge's power is in the very fineness with which, as by some really ghostly finger, he brings home to our inmost sense his inventions, daring as they are—the skeleton ship, the polar spirit, the inspiriting of the dead corpses of the ship's crew. *The Rhyme of the Ancient Mariner* has the plausibility, the perfect adaptation to reason and the general aspect of life, which belongs to the marvellous, when actually presented as part of a credible experience in our dreams. Doubtless, the mere experience of the opium-eater, the habit he must almost necessarily fall into of noting the more elusive phenomena of dreams, had something to do with that: in its essence, however, it is connected with a more purely intellectual circumstance in the development of Coleridge's poetic gift. (pp. 96-7)

[It is a fine,] delicately marvellous supernaturalism, fruit of his more delicate psychology, that Coleridge infuses into romantic adventure, itself also then a new or revived thing in English literature; and with a fineness of weird effect in *The Ancient Mariner,* unknown in those older, more simple, romantic legends and ballads. It is a flower of medieval or later German romance, growing up in the peculiarly compounded atmosphere of modern psychological speculation, and putting forth in it wholly new qualities. The quaint prose commentary, which runs side by side with the verse of *The Ancient Mariner,* illustrates this—a composition of quite a different shade of beauty and merit from that of the verse which it accompanies, connecting this, the chief poem of Coleridge, with his philosophy, and emphasising therein [a] psychological interest . . . , its curious soul-lore.

Completeness, the perfectly rounded wholeness and unity of the impression it leaves on the mind of a reader who fairly gives himself to it—that, too, is one of the characteristics of a really excellent work, in the poetic as in every other kind of art; and by this completeness, *The Ancient Mariner* certainly

gains upon *Christabel*—a completeness, entire as that of Wordsworth's *Leech-gatherer,* or Keats's *Saint Agnes' Eve,* each typical in its way of such wholeness or entirety of effect on a careful reader. It is Coleridge's one great complete work, the one really finished thing, in a life of many beginnings. *Christabel* remained a fragment. In *The Ancient Mariner* this unity is secured in part by the skill with which the incidents of the marriage-feast are made to break in dreamily from time to time upon the main story. And then, how pleasantly, how reassuringly, the whole nightmare story itself is made to end, among the clear fresh sounds and lights of the bay, where it began, with

> The moon-light steeped in silentness,
> The steady weather-cock.

So different from *The Rhyme of the Ancient Mariner* in regard to this completeness of effect, *Christabel* illustrates the same complexion of motives, a like intellectual situation. Here, too, the work is of a kind peculiar to one who touches the characteristic motives of the old romantic ballad, with a spirit made subtle and fine by modern reflection. . . . (pp. 98-100)

A warm poetic joy in everything beautiful, whether it be a moral sentiment, like the friendship of Roland and Leoline, or only the flakes of falling light from the water-snakes—this joy, visiting him, now and again, after sickly dreams, in sleep or waking, as a relief not to be forgotten, and with such a power of felicitous expression that the infection of it passes irresistibly to the reader—such is the predominant element in the matter of his poetry, as cadence is the predominant quality of its form. "We bless thee for our creation!" he might have said, in his later period of definite religious assent, "because the world is so beautiful: the world of ideas—living spirits, detached from the divine nature itself to inform and lift the heavy mass of material things; the world of man, above all in his melodious and intelligible speech; the world of living creatures and natural scenery; the world of dreams." (pp. 101-02)

The student of empirical science asks, Are absolute principles attainable? What are the limits of knowledge? The answer he receives from science itself is not ambiguous. What the moralist asks is, Shall we gain or lose by surrendering human life to the relative spirit? Experience answers that the dominant tendency of life is to turn ascertained truth into a dead letter, to make us all the phlegmatic servants of routine. The relative spirit, by its constant dwelling on the more fugitive conditions or circumstances of things, breaking through a thousand rough and brutal classifications, and giving elasticity to inflexible principles, begets an intellectual *finesse* of which the ethical result is a delicate and tender justice in the criticism of human life. Who would gain more than Coleridge by criticism in such a spirit? We know how his life has appeared when judged by absolute standards. We see him trying to "apprehend the absolute," to stereotype forms of faith and philosophy, to attain, as he says, "fixed principles" in politics, morals, and religion, to fix one mode of life as the essence of life, refusing to see the parts as parts only; and all the time his own pathetic history pleads for a more elastic moral philosophy than his, and cries out against every formula less living and flexible than life itself.

"From his childhood he hungered for eternity." There, after all, is the incontestable claim of Coleridge. . . . Coleridge, with his passion for the absolute, for something fixed where all is moving, his faintness, his broken memory, his intellectual disquiet, may still be ranked among the interpreters of one of the constituent elements of our life. (pp. 103-04)

Walter Pater, "Coleridge," in his Appreciations:
With an Essay on Style, *1889. Reprint by Johnson
Reprint Corporation, 1967, pp. 65-104.*

ARTHUR SYMONS (essay date 1904)

[*An English critic, Symons initially gained notoriety as an English
decadent of the 1890s and eventually established himself as one
of the most important critics of the modern era. His* The Symbolist
Movement in Literature *provided his English contemporaries with
an appropriate vocabulary with which to define their aesthetic—
one that communicated their concern with dreamlike states, imagination, and a reality that exists beyond the boundaries of the
senses. Symons contends that Coleridge lacked Christian faith
and sought the absolute because he needed an anchor for his
fluctuating beliefs. Although this pursuit was fruitless, his search
for perfection enabled him to become both a poet and philosopher.
According to Symons, Coleridge is "the one philosophical critic
who is also a poet," and he praises Coleridge's analyses of
Shakespeare's dramas. Symons considers Coleridge a master of
imaginative narrative whose poetry reveals skill and sensitivity
to color and sound. Symons concludes that the "perfection of
Coleridge's style in poetry comes from an equal balance of the
clear, somewhat matter-of-fact qualities of the eighteenth century
with the remote, imaginative qualities of the nineteenth century."*]

What Coleridge lacked was what theologians call a "saving
belief" in Christianity, or else a strenuous intellectual immorality. He imagined himself to believe in Christianity, but
his belief never realized itself in effective action, either in the
mind or in conduct, while it frequently clogged his energies
by weak scruples and restrictions which were but so many
internal irritations. He calls upon the religion which he has
never firmly apprehended to support him under some misfortune of his own making; it does not support him, but he finds
excuses for his weakness in what seem to him its promises of
help. Coleridge was not strong enough to be a Christian, and
he was not strong enough to rely on the impulses of his own
nature, and to turn his failings into a very actual kind of
success. . . .

To Coleridge there was as much difficulty in belief as in action,
for belief is itself an action of the mind. He was always anxious
to believe anything that would carry him beyond the limits of
time and space, but it was not often that he could give more
than a speculative assent to even the most improbable of creeds.
Always seeking fixity, his mind was too fluid for any anchor
to hold in it. He drifted from speculation to speculation, often
seeming to forget his aim by the way, in almost the collector's
delight over the curiosities he had found in passing. . . . To
Coleridge all systems were of importance, because in every
system there was its own measure of truth. He was always
setting his mind to think about itself, and felt that he worked
both hard and well if he had gained a clearer glimpse into that
dark cavern. (p. 319)

Coleridge's search, throughout his life, was after the absolute,
an absolute not only in thought but in all human relations, in
love, friendship, faith in man, faith in God, faith in beauty;
and while it was this profound dissatisfaction with less than
the perfect form of every art, passion, thought, or circumstance, that set him adrift in life, making him seem untrue to
duty, conviction, and himself, it was this also that formed in
him the double existence of the poet and the philosopher, each
supplementing and interpenetrating the other. (p. 321)

"The ultimate end of criticism," said Coleridge, "is much
more to establish the principles of writing than to furnish rules
how to pass judgment on what has been written by others."
And for this task he had an incomparable foundation—imagination, insight, logic, learning, almost every critical quality
united in one; and he was a poet who allowed himself to be a
critic. Those pages of the **"Biographia Literaria"** in which he
defines and distinguishes between imagination and fancy [see
excerpt above, 1817], the researches into the abstract entities
of poetry in the course of an examination of Wordsworth's
theories and of the popular objections to them, all that we have
of the lectures on Shakespeare, into which he put an illuminating idolatry, together with notes and jottings preserved in
the **"Table-Talk,"** **"Anima Poetae,"** the **"Literary Remains,"** and on the margins of countless books, contain the
most fundamental criticism of literature that has ever been
attempted, fragmentary as the attempt remains. "There is not
a man in England," said Coleridge with truth, "whose thoughts,
images, words, and erudition have been published in larger
quantities than *mine;* though I must admit, not *by,* nor *for,*
myself." He claimed, and rightly, as his invention, a "science
of reasoning and judging concerning the productions of literature, the characters and measures of public men, and the
events of nations, by a systematic subsumption of them, under
principles deduced from the nature of man," which, as he
says, was unknown before the year 1795. He is the one philosophical critic who is also a poet, and thus he is the one critic
who instinctively knows his way through all the intricacies of
the creative mind.

Most of his best criticism circles around Shakespeare; and he
took Shakespeare almost frankly in the place of Nature, or of
poetry. He affirms, "Shakespeare knew the human mind, and
its most minute and intimate workings, and he never introduces
a word, or a thought, in vain or out of place." This granted—
and to Coleridge it is essential that it should be granted, for
in less than the infinite he cannot find space in which to use
his wings freely—he has only to choose and define, to discover
and to illuminate. In the "myriad-minded man," in his "oceanic
mind," he finds all the material that he needs for the making
of a complete aesthetics. Nothing with Coleridge ever came to
completion; but we have only to turn over the pages about
Shakespeare, to come upon fragments worth more than anyone
else's finished work. I find the whole secret of Shakespeare's
way of writing in these sentences: "Shakespeare's intellectual
action is wholly unlike that of Ben Jonson or Beaumont and
Fletcher. The latter see the totality of a sentence or passage,
and then project it entire. Shakespeare goes on creating, and
evolving B out of A, and C out of B, and so on, just as a
serpent moves, which makes a fulcrum of its own body, and
seems forever twisting and untwisting its own strength."
(pp. 324-25)

Unlike most creative critics, or most critics who were creative
artists in another medium, Coleridge, when he was writing
criticism, wrote it wholly for its own sake, almost as if it were
a science. His prose is rarely of the finest quality as prose
writing. Here and there he can strike out a phrase at red-heat,
as when he christens Shakespeare "the one Proteus of the fire
and flood"; or he can elaborate subtly, as when he notes the
judgment of Shakespeare, observable in every scene of the
"Tempest," "still preparing, still inviting, and still gratifying,
like a finished piece of music"; or he can strike us with the
wit or the pure intellect, as when he condemns certain work
for being "as trivial in thought and yet enigmatic in expression,
as if Echo and the Sphinx had laid their heads together to
construct it." But for the most part it is a kind of thinking
aloud, and the form is wholly lost in the pursuit of ideas. With

his love for the absolute, why is it that he does not seek after an absolute in words considered as style, as well as in words considered as the expression of thought? In his finest verse Coleridge has the finest style perhaps in English; but his prose is never quite reduced to order from its tumultuous amplitude or its snake-like involution. Is it that he values it only as a medium, not as an art? His art is verse, and this he dreads, because of its too mortal closeness to his heart; the prose is a means to an end, not an end in itself.

The poetry of Coleridge, though it is closely interwoven with the circumstances of his life, is rarely made directly out of those circumstances. To some extent this is no doubt explained by a fact to which he often refers in his letters, and which, in his own opinion, hindered him not only from writing about himself in verse, but from writing verse at all.... With only a few exceptions, the wholly personal poems, those actually written under a shock of emotion, are vague, generalized, turned into a kind of literature. The success of such a poem as the almost distressingly personal **"Ode on Dejection"** comes from the fact that Coleridge has been able to project his personal feeling into an outward image, which becomes to him the type of dejection; he can look at it as at one of his dreams which become things; he can sympathize with it as he could never sympathize with his own undeserving self. And thus one stanza, perhaps the finest as poetry, becomes the biography of his soul,

> There was a time when, though my path was rough,
>   This joy within me dallied with distress,
> And all misfortunes were but as the stuff,
>   Whence Fancy made me dreams of happiness:
> For hope grew round me, like the twining vine,
> And fruits, and foliage, not my own, seemed mine.
> But now afflictions bow me down to earth:
> Nor care I though they rob me of my mirth;
>   But oh! each visitation
> Suspends what nature gave me at my birth,
>   My shaping spirit of Imagination.
> For not to think of what I needs must feel,
>   But to be still and patient all I can,
> And haply by abstruse research to steal
>   From my own nature all the natural man—
>   This was my sole resource, my only plan:
> Till that which suits a part infects the whole,
> And now is almost grown the habit of my soul.

Elsewhere, in personal poems like **"Frost at Midnight,"** and **"Fears in Solitude,"** all the value of the poem comes from the delicate sensations of natural things which mean so much more to us, whether or not they did to him, than the strictly personal part of the matter. You feel that there he is only using the quite awake part of himself, which is not the essential one. He requires, first of all, to be disinterested, or at least not overcome by emotion; to be without passion but that of abstract beauty, in Nature, or in idea; and then to sink into a quite lucid sleep, in which his genius came to him like some attendant spirit.

In the life and art of Coleridge, the hours of sleep seem to have been almost more important than the waking hours.... To Coleridge, with the help of opium, hardly required, indeed, there was no conscious division between day and night, between his dreams and intuitions, but dreams and pure reason. And we find him, in almost all his great poems, frankly taking not only his substance but his manner from dreams, as he dramatizes them after a logic and a passion of their own. His technique is the transposition into his waking hours of the unconscious technique of dreams. It is a kind of verified in-

spiration, something which came and went, and was as little to be relied upon as the inspiration itself. On one side it was an exact science, but on the other a heavenly visitation. Count and balance syllables, work out an addition of the feet in the verse by the foot-rule, and you will seem to have traced every miracle back to its root in a natural product. Only, something, that is, everything will have escaped you. As well dissect a corpse to find out the principles of life. That elusive something, that spirit, will be what distinguishes Coleridge's finest verse from the verse of, well, perhaps of every conscious artist in our language. For it is not, as in Blake, literally unconscious, and wavering on every breath of that unseen wind on which it floats to us; it is faultless; it is itself the wind which directs it, it steers its way on the wind, like a seagull poised between sky and sea, and turning on its wings as upon shifted sails. (pp. 325-28)

"Lewti" is a sort of preliminary study for **"Kubla Khan"**; it, too, has all the imagery of a dream, with a breathlessness and awed hush, as of one not yet accustomed to be at home in dreams.

"Kubla Khan," which was literally composed in sleep, comes nearer than any other existing poem to that ideal of lyric poetry which has only lately been systematized by theorists like Mallarmé. It has just enough meaning to give it bodily existence; otherwise it would be disembodied music. It seems to hover in the air, like one of the island enchantments of Prospero. It is music not made with hands, and the words seem, as they literally were, remembered. It has outlasted the century, and may still be used as a touchstone; it will determine the poetic value of any lyric poem which you place beside it. Take as many poems as you please, and let them have all the merits you please, their ultimate merit as poetry will lie in the degree of their approach to the exact, unconscious, inevitable balance of qualities in the poetic art of **"Kubla Khan."**

In **"The Ancient Mariner,"** which it seems probable was composed before, and not after **"Kubla Khan,"** as Coleridge's date would have us suppose, a new supernaturalism comes into poetry, which, for the first time, accepted the whole responsibility of dreams. The impossible, frankly accepted, with its own strict, inverted logic; the creation of a new atmosphere, outside the known world, which becomes as real as the air about us, and yet never loses its strangeness; the shiver that comes to us, as it came to the wedding-guest, from the simple good faith of the teller; here is a whole new creation, in subject, mood, and technique. Here, as in **"Kubla Khan,"** Coleridge saw the images ''as *things*''; only a mind so overshadowed by dreams, and so easily able to carry on his sleep awake, could have done so; and, with such a mind, ''that willing suspension of disbelief for a moment, which constitutes poetic faith,'' was literally forced upon him.... To Coleridge, whatever appealed vitally to his imagination *was* real; and he defended his belief philosophically, disbelieving from conviction in that sharp marking off from imaginary of the real as that which is part of the ordinary attitude of man in the presence of mystery.

It must not be forgotten that Coleridge is never fantastic. The fantastic is a playing with the imagination, and Coleridge respects it. His intellect goes always easily as far as his imagination will carry it, and does not stop by the way to play tricks upon its bearer. Hence the conviction which he brings with him when he tells us the impossible. And then his style, in its ardent and luminous simplicity, flexible to every bend of the spirit which it clothes with flesh, helps him in the idiomatic translation of dreams.

"The Ancient Mariner" is the most sustained piece of imagination in the whole of English poetry; and it has almost every definable merit of imaginative narrative. It is the only poem I know which is all point and yet all poetry; because, I suppose, the point is really a point of mystery. It is full of simple, daily emotion, transported by an awful power of sight, to which the limits of reality are no barrier, into an unknown sea and air; it is realized throughout the whole of its ghastly and marvelous happenings; and there is in the narrative an ease, a buoyancy almost, which I can only compare with the music of Mozart, extracting its sweetness from the stuff of tragedy; it presents to us the utmost physical and spiritual horror, not only without disgust, but with an alluring beauty. But in "Christabel," in the first part especially, we find a quality which goes almost beyond these definable merits. There is in it a literal spell, not acting along any logical lines, not attacking the nerves, not terrifying, not intoxicating, but like a slow, enveloping mist, which blots out the real world, and leaves us unchilled by any "airs from heaven or blasts from hell," but in the native air of some middle region. In these two or three brief hours of his power out of a lifetime, Coleridge is literally a wizard. . . . "Christabel," as it stands, is a piece of pure witchcraft, needing no further explanation than the fact of its existence.

Rossetti called Coleridge the Turner of poets, and indeed there is in Coleridge an aërial glitter which we find in no other poet, and in Turner only among painters. With him color is always melted in atmosphere, which it shines through like fire within a crystal. It is liquid color, the dew on flowers, or a mist of rain in bright sunshine. His images are for the most part derived from water, sky, the changes of weather, shadows of things rather than things themselves, and usually mental reflections of them. (pp. 328-30)

"The Ancient Mariner" is full of images of light and luminous color in sky and sea; Glycine's song in "Zapolya" is the most glittering poem in our language, with a soft glitter like that of light seen through water. And he is continually endeavoring, as later poets have done on a more deliberate theory, to suffuse sound with color or make colors literally a form of music. . . . (p. 331)

Side by side with this sensitiveness to color, or interfused with it, we find a similar, or perhaps a greater, sensitiveness to sound. Coleridge shows a greater sensitiveness to music than any English poet except Milton. . . . "Christabel," more than anything of Coleridge, is composed like music; you might set at the side of each section, especially of the opening, *largo, vivacissimo,* and, as the general expression signature, *tempo rubato.* I know no other verse in which the effects of music are so precisely copied in metre. Shelley, you feel, sings like a bird; Blake, like a child or an angel; but Coleridge certainly writes music. (p. 332)

[The] perfection of Coleridge's style in poetry comes from an equal balance of the clear, somewhat matter-of-fact qualities of the eighteenth century with the remote, imaginative qualities of the nineteenth century. "To please me," said Coleridge in "Table-Talk," "a poem must be either music or sense." The eighteenth-century manner, with its sense only just coupled with a kind of tame and wingless music, may be seen quite by itself in the early song from "Robespierre":

> Tell me, on what holy ground
> May domestic peace be found.

Here there is both matter and manner, of a kind; in "The Kiss" of the same year, with its one exquisite line,

The gentle violence of joy.

there is only the liquid glitter of manner. We get the ultimate union of eighteenth and nineteenth century qualities in "Work without Hope," and in "Youth and Age," which took nine years to bring into its faultless ultimate form. There is always a tendency in Coleridge to fall back on the eighteenth-century manner, with its scrupulous exterior neatness, and its comfortable sense of something definite said definitely, whenever the double inspiration flags, and matter and manner do not come together. . . . In "Youth and Age," think how much is actually said, and with a brevity impossible in prose; things, too, far from easy for poetry to say gracefully, such as the image of the steamer, or the frank reference to "this altered size"; and then see with what an art, as of the very breathing of syllables, it passes into the most flowing of lyric forms. Besides these few miracles of his later years, there are many poems, such as . . . "Love, Hope, and Patience supporting Education," in which we get all that can be poetic in the epigram softened by imagination, all that can be given by an ecstatic plain thinking. The rarest magic has gone, and he knows it; philosophy remains, and out of that resisting material he is able, now and again, to weave, in his deftest manner, a few garlands. (pp. 333-34)

Arthur Symons, "Coleridge," in The International Quarterly, *Vol. IX, No. II, June-September, 1904, pp. 317-34.*

J. SHAWCROSS (essay date 1907)

[*Shawcross, who edited the 1907 edition of the* Biographia Literaria, *is known for his important interpretation of Coleridge's critical theory of fancy and imagination (see excerpt above, 1817). The critic also discusses Coleridge's theoretical debt to the German philosophers Friedrich von Schelling and Immanuel Kant.*]

The variety of motives which gave rise to the *Biographia Literaria* reveals itself in the miscellaneous character of the work. Intended in the first instance as a preface to the *Sibylline Leaves,* it grew into a literary autobiography which itself came to demand a preface. This preface itself outgrew its purposed limits, and was incorporated in the whole work, which was finally issued in two parts—the autobiography (two vols.) and the poems. Originally, no doubt, Coleridge's motive in writing the preface was to explain and justify his own style and practice in poetry. To this end it was necessary that he should state clearly the points on which he took exception to Wordsworth's [poetic] theory. All this, however, seemed to involve an examination of the nature of poetry and the poetic faculty: and this in its turn suggested, if it did not demand, a radical inquiry into the preconditions of knowledge in general. To Coleridge . . . the distinction of fancy and imagination was a distinction of equal import for philosophy and for poetry. But having thus been led to a consideration of fundamental problems, there was danger that he would pursue them for their own sake; especially when the occasion was afforded him of attacking his old bugbear, the mechanical philosophy. (p. lv)

In the opening page of the work itself, Coleridge anticipates the charge of a personal motive in writing. 'The narration' (he writes) 'has been used chiefly for the purpose of giving continuity to the work, in part for the reflections suggested to me by the particular events: but still more as introductory to a statement of my principles in Politics, Religion, and Philosophy, and the application of the rules, deduced from philosophical principles, to poetry and criticism.' But it cannot be

Pencil sketch of Coleridge in 1833.

said that the narrative portion of the book, detached and fragmentary as it is, really fulfils this introductory purpose, or relieves the student from the task of reconstructing, from this and other sources, the gradual development of Coleridge's opinions to the point which they had now attained. Indeed, as Coleridge admits, the very narrative itself was made to serve three distinct ends, each of which was an obstacle to the fulfilment of the other two.

But enough has been said of the miscellaneous character of the **Biographia Literaria**. It remains to consider what definite contribution to Coleridge's theory of the imagination it actually contains. (p. lvi)

In tracing the origin of the theory in Coleridge's mind, . . . his early doubts as to the validity of the mechanical explanation of knowledge, if they did not originate in, were yet confirmed by, the testimony of the imagination in its poetic function. Its power to reveal a new aspect of things, and compel our faith in its revelation, naturally suggested a new attitude to the problem of knowledge. For although on the one hand the mind in its poetic interpretation of outward forms is limited and determined by the nature of those forms, yet it is equally free and creative in respect of them, in so far as it invests them with a being and a life which as mere objects of the senses they do not possess. Moreover, the basis of this activity being the desire for self-expression (not of the individual merely, but of the universal self), the fitness of the external world to be the vehicle of such expression pointed to its participation in a common reality with the self which it reflected. But the fact that the imagination is a restricted gift rendered it impossible to regard it as universally active in the process of knowledge.

At this point Coleridge became acquainted with Kant's works and found in his account of the mind a definite place assigned to the imagination as an indispensable factor in the attainment of knowledge. For since the understanding, as a purely intellectual faculty, was incapable of reaching the manifold of sense, it was necessary to call in the services of the imagination, which in virtue of its twofold nature presents that manifold in a form suitable for its subsumption under the categories. The imagination as thus operative is not a mere faculty of images: still less is it the faculty of poetic invention: its peculiar characteristic lies in the power of figurative synthesis, or of delineating the forms of things in general. Moreover, in performing this function it is subject to the laws of the understanding: its procedure, therefore, contributes nothing to our knowledge of the origin of phenomena. But for this very reason of its conformity to the understanding, its deliverances are objective, that is, valid for all thinking beings: and are in this respect to be distinguished from the creations of its reproductive activity, which as subject to empirical conditions (the laws of association) have merely individual and contingent validity. Finally, in the aesthetic judgement, the imagination, though still receiving its law from the understanding, is yet so far free, that its activity is determined not by the necessity of a particular cognition, but by its own character as an organ of knowledge in general.

Kant thus distinguishes three functions or activities of the imagination: as reproductive, in which it is subject to empirical conditions; as productive, in which it acts spontaneously and determines phenomena instead of being determined by them, but yet in accordance with a law of the understanding; and as aesthetic, when it attains its highest degree of freedom in respect of the object, which it regards as material for a possible, not an actual and impending, act of cognition.

For the first and last of these functions Coleridge had already found a name and a description. To Kant's reproductive imagination corresponds the fancy. To the imagination as poetic Coleridge assigns . . . a far greater dignity and significance than Kant could possibly allow it. For in Kant's view even the highest activity of the imagination (its symbolical interpretation of beauty) has no warranty in the supersensuous ground of things. Meanwhile the second of these three functions, to Kant by far the most important (as a universal factor in knowledge), presented Coleridge with fresh matter for reflection. Here, too, it was impossible for him to stop short with Kant. That insight into reality which characterized the imagination in its highest potency must also adhere to it in its universal use. The fact that the poet, in impressing his conscious self upon the world of objects, seemed to penetrate to the core of their being, might at least suggest the explanation of all knowledge as founded on a similar self-recognition of the subject in the object, and indicate the imagination as the organ of this recognition.

From Kant, however, Coleridge received no justification for such an hypothesis, though a suggestion might have been furnished in the unity of apperception as the basic principle of all acts of knowledge. On passing to the study of Fichte, he found a development of Kantean doctrine for which he had only a qualified approval. 'By commencing with an act, instead of a thing or substance . . . , Fichte supplied the idea of a system truly metaphysical, and of a metaphysique truly systematic (i.e. having its spring and principle within itself). But this fundamental idea he overlaid with a heavy mass of mere notions. . . . Thus his theory degenerates into a crude egoismus, a boastful and hyperstoic hostility to Nature, as lifeless, godless, and altogether unholy.' It is not difficult to understand how little such a conception of nature would be welcome to Coleridge. Nor could the account of the imagination in Fichte's system commend itself to him. For having no external foundation for its activity, this faculty is consumed in the perpetual endeavour to outstrip the limits of self, in a restless self-torture which issues in unsubstantial mockeries of creation. Such a conclusion, however much it might appeal to certain moods in Coleridge as in us all, was certainly inimical to the faith which never wholly deserted him—the belief in a Spirit which spoke directly to the soul of man, but also revealed itself mediately through the forms of nature.

How far Coleridge's endeavours to find a philosophical expression for this faith had brought him when first his study of Schelling began, is a matter which cannot be accurately determined; nor what those 'genial coincidences' may have been, to which he alludes in the *Biographia Literaria.* The large verbal borrowings from Schelling in the course of the 'deduction of the imagination' suggest that when he began to write he had accepted Schelling's account of the faculty, or at least found his own conclusions happily expressed therein. (pp. lvii-lx)

Now to the imagination Schelling daringly assigns a function of high, indeed of the highest, dignity and importance. It is proclaimed as the organ of truth, and of truth not as the artist only, but as the philosopher apprehends it. And the quality, which makes it thus their common instrument, is the power of reconciling opposites in virtue of their inner unity; of discovering the ground of harmony between apparent contradictories. Such a reconciliation is demanded by transcendental philosophy. For the task of this philosophy is to discover *in consciousness itself* an explanation of the apparent contradiction involved in the fact, that the self or subject is conceived as both active and passive as regards the object, as both determining it and determined by it. Such a solution can take only one form: the recognition, namely, that these apparently opposed and unrelated activities are really but a twofold aspect of the same activity, that the power which determines is also the power which is determined. As the transcendental philosopher starts from the fact of consciousness, it is in consciousness itself that he must discover the original and prototype of this activity. And this he finds in the act of pure self-consciousness, in which the subject becomes its own object, and subject and object are therefore identical. Now from its very nature the apprehension of this pure self-consciousness, or pure activity returning upon itself, cannot be other than immediate and intuitive. Moreover, as reflecting the ultimate ground of all knowledge, it is productive and an act of the same power, whereby that ultimate principle is reflected objectively in the work of art. In either case the reflective or productive power is the imagination.

But the imagination, in this its highest potency, is itself identical in kind, though not in degree, with that very activity which it contemplates and reflects. For the original act whereby pure intelligence (the Absolute or Urselbst, as Schelling calls it) objectifies and limits itself in order to contemplate itself in its limitation, is an act of imagination, and indeed the primary act, an act which is subsequently repeated in the experience of every individual mind, in becoming conscious of an external world. This degree of imagination is common to all thinking beings. But as we rise in the scale of self-knowledge, the faculty reaches a higher intensity and is confined proportionately in extent, till in its highest power it pertains only to a chosen few. (pp. lx-lxi)

In attributing to the imagination the function in consciousness of reconciling opposites and so underlying all acts of knowledge, Schelling is but developing the conception of Kant, according to which the faculty mediates between the understanding and the senses. But to Kant this reconciling power implied no community of nature between the self and its object; the knowledge to which it contributed was valid only for the self from which it drew its unifying principle. When, however, the imagination is conceived as recognizing the inherent interdependence of subject and object (as complementary aspects of a single reality), its dignity is immeasurably raised. . . . Coleridge rightly apprehended the agreement of Schelling's conception, in its cardinal features, with his own; to unify and so to create is, in the view of both writers, the characteristic function of the imagination. And of this unification the principle is found in the self, conceived not abstractly but as the whole nature of man, or all that is essential to that nature. Thought and feeling, in their original identity, demand expression through an organ which itself partakes of both.

To Schelling's conception it has been objected, that in constituting the imagination the peculiar organ of philosophy, he countenances the claim of every visionary to a respectful hearing, be his system never so wild and fantastic. But this is to misinterpret his meaning, and to fall into the common error of confounding fancy with imagination. If the faculty of imagination be not equally active in all men, its activity is none the less independent of the idiosyncrasies of the individual, its witness is none the less a witness of universal validity. By calling it the organ of philosophy, Schelling means that philosophy must start from a fundamental experience, and that it is the imagination which renders this fundamental experience possible. And to Schelling this ultimate fact of experience appeared to be given, inwardly, in what he called the intellectual intuition, and outwardly, in the products of art. (pp. lxii-lxiii)

But at the same time Schelling acknowledged that of these facts one at least (the object of intellectual intuition) could not be made universally conscious. He therefore started from a datum which it was not in the power of all men to realize. No appeal to a universal spiritual faculty was here possible. All that lay open to him was to point to the creations of art, as the guarantee and evidence (evidence made visible to all) of that ultimate ground of all knowledge and being which the philosopher alone could directly contemplate.

Now, that poetry and philosophy, if their message be true, must be founded on the same spiritual experience, Coleridge would have readily acknowledged; indeed, it was the truth for which he had been contending throughout his life. To this truth, moreover, his own mental history bore witness; for he was conscious that the same impulse lay at the root of his poetic and speculative creation, the impulse to give again that which he had felt and known. By his own confession in later years, it was the same 'spirit of power' which had stirred him throughout—

> A matron now, of sober mien,
> Yet radiant still and with no earthly sheen,
> Whom as a faery child my childhood woo'd
> Even in my dawn of youth—Philosophy;
> Tho' then, unconscious of herself, pardie,
> She bore no other name than Poesy.

And his description of his poetic manner, given in that 'down of youth' which he here recalls, shows that he was conscious of his inclination to confuse these kindred modes of communicating truth. It was the conviction that in either case the whole self must be active in the apprehension of reality, which in the first instance opened his eyes to the error of the empiricists in their one-sided interpretation of a partial aspect of things. And it was to a poet (to *the* poet of the age) that he looked for a final confutation of this false philosophy. In Wordsworth's *Excursion* he had anticipated 'the first genuine philosophic poem', which in its conclusion was to have emphasized the message of which the age stood most in need. (pp. lxiv-lxv)

This task, however, Wordsworth had shown no inclination to undertake; and the sense that it was still waiting to be accomplished was present with Coleridge, when he was composing his literary life. And here the 'genial coincidence' of his opinions with those of Schelling stood him in good stead. For at this time at least he seems to have believed that in the transcendental philosophy was exemplified this process of 'true idealism perfecting itself in realism, and realism refining itself into idealism', and this through intuitions as 'alone adequate to the majesty of truth'. Hence it was that he incorporated into his book so much of Schelling's doctrines as suited his immediate purpose, without perhaps reflecting on their ultimate implications. (p. lxv)

After introducing, in chapter iv, the distinction of imagination and fancy, Coleridge proceeds to investigate it psychologically. He begins with an historical discussion of the theory of association, and compares Aristotle's theory with that of Hartley; the inadequacy of the 'mechanical theory' is then exposed, and the true nature of association explained. Having thus cleared the ground, Coleridge next purposed to show 'by what influences of the choice and judgement the associative power becomes either memory or fancy, and to appropriate the remaining offices of the mind to the reason and the imagination'. But this promise of a psychological treatment of the distinction is not fulfilled: indeed we hear little more of the fancy until, in the final summing up, it is defined side by side, or rather in contrast, with the imagination. After some intervening chapters of general or biographical interest, Coleridge advances to the statement of his system, from which he proposes 'to deduce the memory with all the other functions of intelligence', but which, as a matter of fact, he views in connexion with one faculty only—the imagination. In a series of theses he discovers the final principle of knowledge as 'the identity of subject and object' in 'the Sum, or I Am', which 'is a subject which becomes a subject by the act of constructing itself objectively to itself; but which never is an object except for itself, and only so far as by the same act it becomes a subject'. Originally, however, it is not an object, but 'an absolute subject for which all, itself included, may become an object'. It must, therefore, be an act. Thus it follows that consciousness in its various phases is but a self-development of absolute spirit or intelligence. This process of self-development Coleridge asks us to conceive 'under the idea of an indestructible power with two counteracting forces, which by a metaphor borrowed from astronomy, we may call the centrifugal and centripetal forces'. Such a power he 'assumes for his present purpose, in order to deduce from it a faculty the generation, agency, and application of which form the contents of the ensuing chapter'.

This faculty is the imagination or esemplastic power. (pp. lxvi-lxvii)

The distinction [drawn by Coleridge between the primary and secondary imagination] is evidently between the imagination as universally active in consciousness (creative in that it externalizes the world of objects by opposing it to the self) and the same faculty in a heightened power as creative in a poetic sense. In the first case our exercise of the power is unconscious: in the second the will directs, though it does not determine, the activity of the imagination. The imagination of the ordinary man is capable only of detaching the world of experience from the self and contemplating it in its detachment; but the philosopher penetrates to the underlying harmony and gives it concrete expression. The ordinary consciousness, with no principle of unification, sees the universe as a mass of particulars: only the poet can depict this whole as reflected in the individual parts. It is in this sense (as Coleridge had written many years before) that to the poet 'each thing has a life of its own, and yet they have all our life'. And a similar contrast is present to Schelling when he writes that 'through the objective world as a whole, but never through a single object in it, an Infinite is represented: whereas every single work of art represents Infinity'.

With the definition of fancy which now follows we are already familiar. / 'Fancy has no other counters to play with but fixities and definites. The fancy is indeed no other than a mode of memory emancipated from the order of time and space; and blended with and modified by that empirical phenomenon of the will which we express by the word choice. But equally with the ordinary memory it must receive its materials all ready-made from the laws of association.' ... As connected by the fancy, objects are viewed in their limitations and particularity; they are 'fixed and dead' in the sense that their connexion is mechanical and not organic. The law, indeed, which governs it is derived from the mind itself, but the links are supplied by the individual properties of the objects. Fancy is, in fact, the faculty of mere images or impressions, as imagination is the faculty of intuitions. It is in this sense that Coleridge sees in their opposition an emblem of the wider contrast between the mechanical philosophy and the dynamic, the false and the true.

But with all this we have nothing of the promised 'deduction' of the imagination, still less that of the memory and other 'functions of intelligence'. The definition of fancy is founded, apparently, on the psychological discussion of the earlier chapters, not on the theory of knowledge propounded later on. As to the imagination, it seems at first sight, from the close coincidence of Coleridge's statement with that of Schelling, that he had accepted Schelling's system wholesale and with it his account of that faculty. But the sudden termination of the argument, and the unsatisfactory vagueness of the final summary, in which he does not really commit himself to Schelling's position, suggest that that position was not in fact his own. And this suggestion is confirmed by other evidence.

That Coleridge's attitude from the first to Schelling's philosophy was by no means one of unqualified approval, we have already seen. But in the *Transcendental Idealism* which he studied at a time when he was deeply engaged on aesthetic problems, he found a peculiar attraction. Here for the first time the significance of 'the vision and the faculty divine' seemed to be adequately realized. At first it appeared to Coleridge that he had met with a systematized statement of his own convictions, the metaphysic of poetry of which he was in search. But he was soon to find that the supposed concurrence did not exist—that the Transcendentalism of Schelling in fact elevated the imagination at the expense of other and more important factors in our spiritual consciousness.

No doubt the feature most unsatisfactory to Coleridge in the *Transcendental Idealism* and in Schelling's philosophy in general was its vague conception of the ultimate ground of reality. For Schelling's absolute, which is prior to and behind self-consciousness, from which self-consciousness originates, is conceived as mere self-less identity or total indifference, of which all that can be said is that it is neither subject nor object, but the mere negation of both. From such an abstract principle, it is evident, no living bond of union can be derived to hold together the complementary elements in self-consciousness when it is mysteriously generated: hence subject and object, intelligence and nature, appear as parallel lines of co-ordinate value, connected by a merely logical necessity. In such a system there was clearly no place for the God of Coleridge's faith, as a Spirit to whom self-consciousness is essential, a Being 'in whom supreme reason and a most holy will are one with an infinite power'. Thus it is that in his own account in the *Biographia Literaria* Coleridge is all the time striving to identify Schelling's 'intellectual intuition' of subject and object in their absolute identity with the religious intuition, the direct consciousness of God.

But this, of course, involves him in contradictions. For the power of intellectual intuition, the philosophic imagination is, as Schelling conceived, a gift confined to a favoured few, not a state of being in which all can, by moral effort, raise themselves: his philosophy cannot therefore take the form of a moral appeal. And here Coleridge, so long as his thoughts are concerned primarily with the imagination and its deduction, is inclined to follow him. The solution of the problem is to discover 'for whom and to whom the philosophical intuition is possible'. For 'there is a philosophic no less than a poetic genius, which is differenced from the highest perfection of talent, not by degree, but by kind'. If, however, this intuition of the supersensuous is none other than the consciousness of God, it must evidently be regarded as a spiritual condition accessible to all: and in that case its organ must be in a faculty essential to the spiritual constitution of man. (pp. lxviii-lxxi)

> *J. Shawcross, in an introduction to* Biographia Literaria, *Vol. I by S. T. Coleridge, edited by J. Shawcross, 1907. Reprint by Oxford University Press, London, 1958, pp. xi-lxxxix.*

J. MIDDLETON MURRY (essay date 1920)

[*Murry was an influential literary critic and noted magazine editor during the first half of the twentieth century. A longtime contributor of literary criticism to the* Times Literary Supplement, *he was the last editor of the distinguished review the* Athenaeum *before it was absorbed into the* Nation *and founding editor of the* Adelphi. *Considered a perceptive critic whose work reveals his "honesty to the point of masochism," he has contributed important studies on the works of John Keats, Fedor Dostoevski, and William Blake. In the following, Murry examines Coleridge's criticism of Wordsworth's poetic principles in the* Biographia Literaria. *While Coleridge's arguments are valid, Murry contends, they are often convoluted. Murry particularly admires the criticism of William Shakespeare's* Venus and Adonis, *but nonetheless asserts that Coleridge is often praised blindly and indiscriminately. According to Murry, Coleridge's greatest talent as a critic rests in his interpretative, rather than theoretical, ability.*]

It is probably true that *Biographia Literaria* is the best book of criticism in the English language; nevertheless, it is rash to assume that it is a book of criticism of the highest excellence.... Its garrulity, its digressions, its verbiage, the marks which even the finest portions show of submersion in the tepid

transcendentalism that wrought such havoc upon Coleridge's mind—these are its familiar disfigurements. They are not easily removed; for they enter fairly deeply even in the texture of those portions of the book in which Coleridge devotes himself, as severely as he can, to the proper business of literary criticism.

It may be that the prolixity which with he discusses and refutes the poetical principles expounded by Wordsworth in the preface of *Lyrical Ballads* [see excerpt above, 1798] was due to the tenderness of his consideration for Wordsworth's feelings.... That is honourable to Coleridge as a man; but it cannot exculpate him as a critic. For the points he had to make for and against Wordsworth were few and simple. First, he had to show that the theory of a poetic diction drawn exclusively from the language of 'real life' was based upon an equivocation, and therefore was useless. This Coleridge had to show to clear himself of the common condemnation in which he had been involved, as one wrongly assumed to endorse Wordworth's theory. He had an equally important point to make for Wordsworth. He wished to prove to him that the finest part of his poetic achievement was based upon a complete neglect of this theory, and that the weakest portions of his work were those in which he most closely followed it. In this demonstration he was moved by the desire to set his friend on the road that would lead to the most triumphant exercise of his own powers.

There is no doubt that Coleridge made both his points; but he made them, in particular the former, at exceeding length, and at the cost of a good deal of internal contradiction. He sets out, in the former case, to maintain that the language of poetry is essentially different from the language of prose. This he professes to deduce from a number of principles. His axiom—and it is possibly a sound one—is that metre originated in a spontaneous effort of the mind to hold in check the workings of emotion. From this, he argues, it follows that to justify the existence of metre, the language of a poem must show evidence of emotion, by being different from the language of prose. Further, he says, metre in itself stimulates the emotions, and for this condition of emotional excitement 'correspondent food' must be provided. Thirdly, the emotion of poetical composition itself demands this same 'correspondent food.' The final argument, if we omit one drawn from an obscure theory of imitation very characteristic of Coleridge, is the incontrovertible appeal to the authority of the poets.

Unfortunately, the elaborate exposition of the first three arguments is not only unnecessary but confusing, for Coleridge goes on to distinguish, interestingly enough, between a language proper to poetry, a language proper to prose, and a neutral language which may be used indifferently in prose and poetry, and later still he quotes a beautiful passage from Chaucer's *Troilus and Cressida* as an example of this neutral language, forgetting that, if his principles are correct, Chaucer was guilty of a sin against art in writing *Troilus and Cressida* in metre. The truth, of course, is that the paraphernalia of principles goes by the board. In order to refute the Wordsworthian theory of a language of real life supremely fitted for poetry you have only to point to the great poets, and to judge the fitness of the language of poetry you can only examine the particular poem. Wordsworth was wrong and self-contradictory without doubt; but Coleridge was equally wrong and self-contradictory in arguing that metre *necessitated* a language essentially different from that of prose.

So it is that the philosophic part of the specifically literary criticism of the *Biographia* takes us nowhere in particular. The valuable part is contained in his critical appreciation of Wordsworth's poetry and that amazing chapter—a little forlorn, as most of Coleridge's fine chapters are—on 'the specific symptoms of poetic power elucidated in a critical analysis of Shakespeare's *Venus and Adonis*.' In these few pages Coleridge is at the summit of his powers as a critic. So long as his attention could be fixed on a particular object, so long as he was engaged in deducing his general principles immediately from particular instances of the highest kind of poetic excellence, he was a critic indeed. (pp. 184-87)

The object of this examination has been to show, not that the *Biographia Literaria* is undeserving of the high praise which has been bestowed upon it, but that the praise has been to some extent undiscriminating. It has now become almost a tradition to hold up to our admiration Coleridge's chapter on poetic diction. . . . As a matter of fact, what Coleridge has to say on poetic diction is prolix and perilously near commonplace. Instead of making to Wordsworth the wholly sufficient answer that much poetry of the highest kind employs a language that by no perversion can be called essentially the same as the language of prose, he allows himself to be led by his German metaphysic into considering poetry as a *Ding an sich* and deducting therefrom the proposition that poetry *must* employ a language different from that of prose. That proposition is false, as Coleridge himself quite adequately shows from his remarks upon what he called the 'neutral' language of Chaucer and Herbert. But instead of following up the clue and beginning to inquire whether or not narrative poetry by nature demands a language approximating to that of prose, and whether Wordsworth, in so far as he aimed at being a narrative poet, was not working on a correct but exaggerated principle, he leaves the bald contradiction and swerves off to the analysis of the defects and excellences of Wordsworth's actual achievement. . . . What is worth while learning from Coleridge is . . . not his behaviour with 'a principle,' but his conduct when confronted with poetry in the concrete, his magisterial ordonnance (to use his own word) and explication of his own aesthetic intuitions, and his manner of employing in this, the essential task of poetic criticism, the results of his own deep study of all the great poetry that he knew. (pp. 192-93)

> J. Middleton Murry, ''Coleridge's Criticism,'' in his Aspects of Literature, W. Collins Sons & Co. Ltd., 1920, pp. 184-93.

JOHN LIVINGSTON LOWES   (essay date 1927)

[*An American critic, Lowes propounded the thesis that great literature is produced by the unconscious fusion of the author's literary influences, personal experiences, and imagination. Of his* The Road to Xanadu, *Lowes states that he had two aspirations: to analyze the workings of Coleridge's imagination and to display ''how, in two great poems [''Kubla Khan'' and ''The Ancient Mariner''], out of chaos the imagination frames a thing of beauty.''* The Road to Xanadu *is considered both the beginning and the foundation of the serious modern study of Coleridge's poetry and has also established the sources for the primary images and locales in both poems. In the following, Lowes confirms Coleridge's own assessment (1830) of ''The Ancient Mariner'' as ''a work of pure imagination.'' Lowes regards the moral of that poem not as an intentional, didactic message, but as one element in a work unified by Coleridge's ''constructive imagination.'' Lowes's interpretation of Coleridge's imagination and rejection of the moral's relevance is later disputed by Robert Penn Warren (1946).*]

'The Rime of the Ancient Mariner' is 'a work of pure imagination,' and Coleridge himself has so referred to it [see excerpt above, 1830]. And this study, far from undermining that declaration, is lending it confirmation at every turn. For a work of pure imagination is not something fabricated by a *tour de force* from nothing, and suspended, without anchorage in fact, in the impalpable ether of a visionary world. No conception could run more sharply counter to the truth. And I question, in the light of all that is now before us, whether any other poem in English is so closely compacted out of fact, or so steeped in the thought and instinct with the action which characterized its time. Keats, in 'La belle Dame sans Merci,' distilled into a single poem the quintessence of mediaeval romance and balladry. And what 'La belle Dame sans Merci' is to the gramarye of the Middle Ages, **'The Rime of the Ancient Mariner'** is to the voyaging, Neoplatonizing, naively scientific spirit of the closing eighteenth century. It has swept within its assimilating influence a bewildering diversity of facts in which contemporary interest was active. The facts are forgotten, and the poem stays. But the power that wrought the facts into the fabric of a vision outlasts both. And if we are rifling the urns where the dead bones of fact have long quietly rested, it is because the unquenchable spirit which gives beauty for ashes is there not wholly past finding out. (pp. 240-41)

When Coleridge set to work on **'The Rime of the Ancient Mariner,'** its plot, not unlike the budding morrow in midnight, lay, . . . beneath a queer jumble of fortuitous suggestions: an old seaman, a skeleton ship with figures in it, a shot bird, a 'spectral persecution,' a ship sailed by dead men, a crew of angelic spirits. The formative design of the voyage, surpassingly adapted as it was to the incorporation of masses of associated impressions, possessed in itself a large simplicity of outline. The supernatural machinery (at the outset a thing of shreds and patches) presented, on the other hand, a problem complex to the last degree. . . . [In] the moulding of the separate fragments that underlie the plot, subliminal associations and conscious imaginative control have again worked hand in hand. And when at last the poem was completed, the plot which Coleridge had wrought from his intractable and heterogeneous elements was a consistent and homogeneous whole.

For the action has a beginning, and a middle, and an end. In the first half of the poem the agency of an avenging daemon is in the ascendent; in the second, the prevailing power of an angel band. It is an overt act of the Mariner which precipitates the daemonic vengeance; it is an inner impulse counter to the act which brings to pass the angelic intervention; and in the end it is 'the penance of life' which falls upon the rescued wanderer, a fated wanderer still. Exciting force, rising action, climax, falling action, catastrophe—all are there. And through the transfer to the Mariner of the legendary associations of the Wandering Jew, undying among the dead, Cruikshank's dream—its figures metamorphosed into Death and Life-in-Death—is built into the basic structure of the plot. And under the influence of another ship, sailed by an angelic crew, the suggestion of the navigation of the Mariner's vessel by the bodies of the dead is so transformed as to provide that cardinal antithesis of angelic and daemonic agencies on which the action of the poem turns. And finally, by a stroke of consummate art, ship and poem alike are brought back in the end to the secure, familiar, happy world from which they had set out. The supernatural machinery is a masterpiece of constructive skill. But only, I think, in the light of the genesis of its component parts can the triumph of the faculty which shaped them into unity be fully understood. (pp. 293-94)

'During the first year that Mr. Wordsworth and I were neighbours,' the famous fourteenth chapter of the *Biographia Lit-*

eraria begins, 'our conversations turned frequently on the two cardinal points of poetry, the power of exciting the sympathy of the reader by a faithful adherence to the truth of nature, and the power of giving the interest of novelty by the modifying colors of imagination. *The sudden charm, which accidents of light and shade, which moon-light or sun-set diffused over a known and familiar landscape,* appeared to represent the practicability of combining both. . . . In this idea originated the plan of the **"Lyrical Ballads"**; in which it was agreed, that my endeavours should be directed to persons and characters supernatural, or at least romantic; *yet so as to transfer from our inward nature a human interest and a semblance of truth* sufficient to procure for these shadows of imagination that willing suspension of disbelief for the moment which constitutes poetic faith. . . . With this view I wrote the **"Ancient Mariner."**'

The far-reaching significance of the paragraphs from which I have just quoted has met with universal recognition. It is, however, their vital bearing on the interpretation of a single basic element of **'The Ancient Mariner'** which concerns us now. For if Coleridge's words mean anything, they mean that some interest deeply human, anchored in the familiar frame of things, was fundamental to his plan. What, in a word, *is* the 'known and familiar landscape' which, in the poem, persists unchangeable beneath the accidents of light and shade? Are there truths of 'our inward nature' which do, in fact, uphold and cherish, as we read, our sense of actuality in a phantom universe, peopled with the shadows of a dream?

Every mortal who finds himself enmeshed in the inexplicable or the fantastic reaches out instinctively to something rooted deep, in order to retain a steadying hold upon reality. That is the predicament of the reader of **'The Ancient Mariner.'** There before him, to be sure, are the tangible facts of a charted course beneath the enduring skies. But the broad bright sun peers through skeleton ribs, and the moon glitters in the stony eyes of the reanimated dead, and the dance of the wan stars is a strange sight in the element. The most ancient heavens themselves have suffered, with the sea, the touch of goblin hands. But Coleridge's sure instinct was not, for all that, at fault. For through the spectral *mise en scène* of **'The Ancient Mariner,'** side by side with the lengthening orbit of the voyage, there runs, like the everlasting hills beneath the shifting play of eerie light, another moving principle, this time profoundly human: one of the immemorial, traditional convictions of the race. And it constitutes the most conspicuous formal element of the poem.

The last stanza of each of the first six parts of **'The Ancient Mariner'** marks a step in the evolution of the action. Let us isolate their salient phrases for a moment from their context.

> Part I: . . . with my cross-bow
> *I shot the* Albatross.

There is the initial act.

> Part II: Instead of the cross, *the Albatross*
> *About my neck was hung.*

And the consequences first attach themselves to the transgressor.

> Part III: Four times fifty living men . . .
> They dropped down one by one . . .
> *And every soul, it passed me by,*
> *Like the whizz of my cross-bow!*

The consequences pass beyond the doer of the deed, and fall upon his shipmates. And now 'Life-in-Death begins her work on the Ancient Mariner,' till at last the turning-point of the action comes:

> O happy living things! no tongue
> Their beauty might declare:
> A spring of love gushed from my heart,
> And I blessed them unaware:
> Sure my kind saint took pity on me,
> And I blessed them unaware.

And then:

> Part IV: The self-same moment I could pray;
> And from my neck so free
> *The Albatross fell off, and sank*
> *Like lead into the sea.*

And so the burden of the transgression falls. But its results march on relentlessly.

> Part V: The other was a softer voice,
> As soft as honey-dew:
> Quoth he, 'The man hath penance done,
> *And penance more will do.'*

But the voyage, at least, has a destined end, and with the Hermit's entrance, a new note is heard.

> Part VI: He'll shrieve my soul, *he'll wash away*
> *The Albatross's blood.*

But even absolution leaves the doer, now as before, 'the deed's creature.'

> Part VII: Since then, at an uncertain hour,
> That agony returns:
> And till my ghastly tale is told,
> This heart within me burns.
>
> *I pass, like night, from land to land;*
> *I have strange power of speech;*
> *That moment that his face I see,*
> *I know the man that must hear me:*
> *To him my tale I teach.*

The train of cause and consequence knows no end. The Mariner has reached his haven, and his soul is shrieved, and now (in the brief comment of the gloss) *'the penance of life* falls on him.' And with that the action of the poem, though not the poem, ends.

There, thrown into strong relief by the strategic disposition of the stanzas which disclose it, is the ground-plan of **'The Ancient Mariner,'** as a master-architect has drawn and executed it. Through it runs the grand structural line of the voyage; and with its movement keep even pace—like those Intellectual Spirits that walk with the comets in their orbits—the daemons, and spectral shapes, and angels which are also agents in the action. Each of the three shaping principles has its own independent evolution, and each is interlocked with the unfolding of the other two. The interpenetration and coherence of the fundamental unifying elements of the poem is an achievement of constructive imagination, seconded by finished craftsmanship, such as only the supreme artists have attained. 'I learnt from him,' said Coleridge of his old master, Boyer, 'that Poetry, even that of the loftiest and, seemingly, that of the wildest odes, had a logic of its own, as severe as that of science; and more difficult, because more subtle, more complex, and dependent on more, and more fugitive causes.' And that describes the logic of **'The Ancient Mariner.'** (pp. 295-98)

The sequence . . . which follows from the Mariner's initial act accomplishes two ends: it unifies and (again to borrow Coleridge's coinage) it 'credibilizes' the poem. Has it still another end, to wit, edification? I am well aware of Coleridge's homiletical propensity. Nevertheless, to interpret the drift of **'The Ancient Mariner'** as didactic in its intention is to stultify both Coleridge and one's self. . . . Coleridge is not intent on teaching (profoundly as he believed the truth) that what a man soweth, that shall he also reap; he is giving coherence and inner congruity to the dream-like fabric of an imagined world. *Given that world*—and were it not given, there would be no poem, and were it otherwise given, this poem would not be—given that world, its inviolate keeping with itself becomes the sole condition of our acceptance, 'for the moment,' of its validity. And that requirement Coleridge, with surpassing skill, has met.

But the fulfilment of the indispensable condition carries with it an equally inevitable corollary. For that inner consistency which creates the illusion of reality is attained at the expense of the integrity of the elements which enter into it. They too, no less than the poet's own nature, are 'subdued to what they work in, like the dyer's hand.' And once wrought into keeping with each other and with the whole, by as far as they have taken on the colours of their visionary world, by so far have they ceased to be, thus coloured, independent entities, with a status of their own. Even poetry cannot transform reality and have it, untransmuted, too. And through the very completeness of their incorporation with the texture of **'The Ancient Mariner,'** the truths of experience which run in sequence through it have lost, so far as any inculcation of a moral through the poem is concerned, all didactic value.

For the 'moral' of the poem, *outside the poem,* will not hold water. It is valid only within that magic circle. The great loop of the voyage from Equator to Equator around the Cape runs true to the chart. But daemons, and spectres, and angels, and *revenants* haunt its course, and the Mariner's voyage, magnificent metamorphosis of fact though it be, can scarcely be regarded as a profitable guide to the fauna of equatorial and arctic seas. The relentless line of cause and consequence runs likewise, unswerving as the voyage, through the poem. But consequence and cause, *in terms of the world of reality,* are ridiculously incommensurable. The shooting of a sea-bird carries in its train the vengeance of an aquatic daemon, acting in cojunction with a spectre-bark; and an impulse of love for other living creatures of the deep summons a troop of angels to navigate an unmanned ship. Moreover, because the Mariner has shot a bird, four times fifty sailors drop down dead, and the slayer himself is doomed to an endless life. The punishment, measured by the standards of a world of balanced penalties, palpably does not fit the crime. But the sphere of balanced penalties is not the given world in which the poem moves. Within *that* world, where birds have tutelary daemons and ships are driven by spectral and angelic powers, consequence and antecedent are in keeping—if for the poet's moment we accept the poet's premises. and the function of the ethical background of **'The Ancient Mariner,'** as Coleridge employs it, is to give the illusion of inevitable sequence to that superb inconsequence. The imaginative use of familiar moral values, like the imaginative use of the familiar outline of a voyage, is leagues away from the promulgation of edifying doctrine through the vehicle of a fairy-tale.

It would be a work of supererogation thus to labour a point which Coleridge himself might be thought to have rendered fairly obvious, were it not that this rudimentary principle of the poem has been persistently misinterpreted. A distinguished modern critic, for example, after drawing from certain verses of Browning the inference that, in Browning's view, 'to go out and mix one's self up with the landscape is the same as doing one's duty,' proceeds as follows: 'As a method of salvation this is even easier and more aesthetic than that of the Ancient Mariner, who, it will be remembered, is relieved of the burden of his transgression by admiring the color of water-snakes!' Occurring as it does in a justly severe arraignment of pantheistic revery as 'a painless substitute for genuine spiritual effort,' this statement, despite its touch of piquant raillery, must be taken seriously as an interpretation of what Coleridge is supposed to teach. It is immaterial that the Mariner's admiration of water-snakes is not the means of salvation . . . which the plain words of the poem state. The value of the criticism lies in its exposition of what happens when one disregards the fundamental premises of a work of art, and interprets it as if it were solely a document in ethics. Carried to its logical conclusion, such an interpretation makes Coleridge precisely to the same degree the serious exponent of the moral fitness of the 'ruthless slaying of the crew because the Mariner had killed a bird'—and that is the *reductio ad absurdum* of everything. Coleridge, in some of those all too frequent moments when he was not a poet, may well have betrayed an addiction to 'pantheistic revery.' But when he wrote **'The Ancient Mariner,'** he was constructing on definite principles, with the clearest possible consciousness of what he was about, a work of pure imagination. (pp. 299-301)

There is no mistaking the point of [Coleridge's commentary in 1830 concerning *The Ancient Mariner*]. Coleridge may (he felt) have carried his premises too far for safety in a world of Mrs. Barbaulds who yearn for a moral with their poetry, as they hanker after bread and butter with their tea. With the moral sentiment so patent in the poem they would be bound to put in their thumb and exultantly pull out their plum—as indeed they have. '*The obtrusion of the moral sentiment so openly on the reader* as a principle or cause of action in a poem of such pure imagination'—that was what gave Coleridge pause. 'The only, or chief fault' of the poem, as he saw it, was a fault of technique. Instead of procuring a momentary suspension of disbelief, he ran the risk of implanting firmly a belief! Of the historic Mrs. Barbauld he need on that score have had no fear. For her, even in the Mariner's valedictory piety, which does, I fear, warrant Coleridge's (and our own) regret, the moral sentiment was not obtruded openly enough. Had the mariner shot a shipmate instead of an albatross, she would have understood—and there would have been no **'Ancient Mariner.'**

For the very triviality of the act which precipitates its astounding train of consequences is the *sine qua non* of the impression which the poem was intended to convey. The discrepancy is essential to the design. And I really know no better short-cut to the comprehension of the poem's unique art than to imagine (as I lightly suggested a moment ago) the substitution of a human being, as the victim, for a bird. A tale the inalienable charm of which (as Coleridge himself perceived) lies in its kinship with the immortal fictions of the *Arabian Nights,* becomes, so motivated, a grotesque and unintelligible caricature of tragedy. Springing from the fall of a feather, it becomes a dome in air, built with music, yet with the shadows of supporting arch and pillar floating midway in the wave. For its world is, in essence, the world of a dream. Its inconsequence is the dream's irrelevance, and by a miracle of art we are possessed, as we read, with that sense of an intimate logic, consecutive and irresistible and more real than reality, which is the dream's supreme illusion. . . . The events in a dream do not produce each other, but they *seem* to. And that is the sole requirement of the action of the poem. (pp. 302-03)

Is a poem like **'The Ancient Mariner'** merely the upshot of the subliminal stirrings and convergences of countless dormant images? Or is it solely the product of an unremittingly deliberate constructive energy, recollecting of its own volition whatever is necessary to its ends, consciously willing every subtle blending of its myriad remembered images? Or is the seeming discord susceptible of resolution?

Behind **'The Rime of the Ancient Mariner'** lie crowding masses of impressions, incredible in their richness and variety. That admits no doubt. But the poem is not the sum of the impressions, as a heap of diamond dust is the sum of its shining particles; nor is the poet merely a sensitized medium for their reception and transmission. Beneath the poem lie also innumerable blendings and fusings of impressions, brought about below the level of conscious mental processes. That too is no longer open to question. But the poem is not the confluence of unconsciously merging images, as a pool of water forms from the coalescence of scattered drops; nor is the poet a somnambulist in a subliminal world. Neither the conscious impressions nor their unconscious interpenetrations constitute the poem. They are inseparable from it, but it is an entity which they do not create. On the contrary, every impression, every new creature rising from the potent waters of the Well, is what it now is through its participation in a *whole*, foreseen as a whole in each integral part—a whole which is the working out of a controlling imaginative design. The incommunicable, unique essence of the poem is its *form*.

And that form is the handiwork of choice, and a directing intelligence, and the sweat of a forging brain. The design of **'The Ancient Mariner'** did not lie, like a landscape in a crystal, pellucid and complete in Coleridge's mind from the beginning. It was there potentially, together with a hundred hovering alternatives, in a *mélange* of disparate and fortuitous suggestions. To drive through that farrago, 'straightforward as a Roman road,' the structural lines of the charted voyage, and the balanced opposition of daemonic and angelic agencies, and the unfolding consequences of the initial act—that involves more than the spontaneous welling up of images from secret depths. Beyond a doubt, that ceaseless play of swift associations which flashed, like flying shuttles, through Coleridge's shaping brain, was present and coöperating from the first. I am not suggesting that Coleridge, on or about the 13th of November, 1797, withdrew from the rest of himself into the dry light of a 'cool cranium' to excogitate his plan, and then and only then threw open the doors to his other faculties, and summoned the sleeping images from their slumber. All his powers, conscious and unconscious, at the inception of the poem no less than while it 'grew and grew,' moved together when they moved at all. And there are few pages of this study which have not disclosed, directly or indirectly, traces of creative forces operating without reference to the bidding of the will. The last thing I have in mind is to minimize that obscure but powerful influence. But the energy which made the poem a poem, rather than an assemblage of radiant images, was the capacity of the human brain to think through chaos, and by sheer force of the driving will behind it to impose upon confusion the clarity of an ordered whole. And over the throng of luminous impressions and their

subliminal confluences 'broods like the Day, a Master o'er a Slave,' the compelling power of the design. Whatever their origin, the component images have been wrought into conformity with a setting determined by the conception which constructs the poem. Through that amazing confluence of associations out of which sprang the shining creatures of the calm, strikes the huge shadow of the ship, lending the picture the symmetry which is the secret of its balanced beauty, and at the same time locking it into the basic structure of the poem. The breathless moment when the sun's rim dips, and the stars rush out, and the dark comes at one stride—that magnificent cluster-point in the chaos of elements has its *raison d'être*, not in itself, but in the incredible swiftness which the downward leap of night imparts to the disappearance of the spectre-bark. The bloody sun stands right up above the mast in a hot and copper sky, not for its own sake as a lucidly exact delineation of a galaxy of images, but as a great sea-mark in the controlling outline of the voyage. The images which sow the poem as with stars owe their meaning and their beauty to a form which is theirs by virtue of the evolution of a plan. (pp. 304-06)

But Coleridge, it will be pointed out, has put himself on record against himself. For when the poem reappeared, revised, in 1800, he appended a sub-title: **'A Poet's Reverie.'** (p. 306)

[If] there is anything on earth which **'The Ancient Mariner'** is *not*, it is a reverie. (p. 307)

> *John Livingston Lowes, in his* The Road to Xanadu: A Study in the Ways of the Imagination, *Houghton Mifflin Company, 1927, 639 p.*

MAUD BODKIN   (essay date 1934)

[*Bodkin's literary principles are derived from the theories of the Swiss psychologist Carl Jung. Jung posited that inherited ideas or modes of thought are derived from the collective history, or "collective unconscious," of humankind and are present in the unconscious of each individual. Evidence for this theory is supplied by recurring motifs, termed "archetypes," in the recorded traditions of diverse cultures throughout human history. Jung and his followers also explored archetypal patterns in modern literature. Here, Bodkin discusses the archetypal patterns found in a stanza of "The Ancient Mariner."*]

I will now attempt, focusing upon [this stanza]:

> Her beams bemocked the sultry main,
> Like April hoar-frost spread;
> But where the ship's huge shadow lay,
> The charmed water burnt alway
> *A still and awful red.*

with its contrast of white moonlight and red shadow, to give something of what I find to be the experience communicated.

In following the description of the Mariner's vigil upon the stagnant sea, it is not till I come to this stanza that I recognize an image detaching itself spontaneously and strongly from the synthetic grasp of the poem's meaning. I live in the Mariner's anguish of repulsion—from the rotting deck where lay the dead, and rotting sea and slimy creatures—with no discernible image at all, other than the voice speaking with inflexions of despair, and the faint organic changes that go with such inflexions—unless, of course, I demand an image. When I did that on one occasion, there appeared an image of a crowd of people struggling for a bus at a particular London street corner. For a moment I thought the numerical suggestion in the 'thousand thousand slimy things' had broken right away from its context;

A cartoon by the English caricaturist Max Beerbohm which satirizes Coleridge's allegedly long-winded conversation.

but then, catching the atmosphere of my street-corner image, I recognized the mood of shrinking disgust that had operated in calling up the picture.

With the transition from the Mariner's utter despair to his yearning vision of the moon in its soft journeying through the sky, there comes a stirring of images which, however, do not emerge spontaneously from out the magic of the charged verse; but when I come to the lines that lead from the white moonlight to the 'huge shadow' of the ship where the water burns red, the emotional stress upon that colour-word has become so intense that an image breaks out from it of a red that burns downward through shadow, as into an abyss. . . . The word 'red' has a soul of terror that has come to it through the history of the race. . . . [It] is as though the Mariner, his deliverance just begun through the power of the moon's beauty, for the moment falls again to Hell in the red shadow of the ship. (pp. 43-5)

Let us pass now to the storm—the roaring wind and streaming rain and lightning, by which the stagnant calm and drought is broken, when the Mariner's impulse of love has undone the curse that held both him and Nature transfixed.

> The upper air burst into life!
> And a hundred fire-flags sheen,
> To and fro they were hurried about!
> And to and fro, and in and out,
> The wan stars danced between.

> And the coming wind did roar more loud
> And the sails did sigh like sedge;
> And the rain poured down from one black cloud;
> The Moon was at its edge.

> The thick black cloud was cleft, and still
> The Moon was at its side:
> Like waters shot from some high crag,
> The lightning fell with never a jag,
> A river steep and wide.

(p. 46)

In my own mind the streaming rain and lightning of the poem is interrelated with storms felt and seen in dreams. Fading impressions of such rain and lightning recalled on waking have clothed themselves in the flowing words of the poem and become fused with these.

Is it . . . the racial mind or inheritance, active within the individual sensibility, whether of Coleridge or of his reader, that both assimilates the descriptions of tropical storms, and sees in a heightened pattern those storms of our own country that 'startle', and overpower, and 'send the soul abroad'? . . .

The thought of the storm image, and the place it has held in the mind, not of Europe only but of a wider, older culture, takes us back to [an] order of conception . . . wherein the two aspects we now distinguish, of outer sense impression and inly felt process, appear undifferentiated. (p. 47)

The storm which for the experiencing mind appears not as differentiated physical object but as a phase of its own life, is naturally thought of as let loose by prayer, when prayer transforms the whole current and atmosphere of the inner life. In Coleridge's poem the relief of rain follows the relaxing of the inner tension by the act of love and prayer, as naturally and inevitably as do sleep and healing dreams.

> The silly buckets on the deck,
> That had so long remained,
> I dreamt that they were filled with dew;
> And when I awoke, it rained.
>
> My lips were wet, my throat was cold,
> My garments all were dank;
> Sure I had drunken in my dreams,
> And still my body drank.

We accept the sequence with such feeling as that with which we accept the narration in terms of recognized metaphor, of a psychical sequence of emotional energy-tension and release. . . . (p. 48)

> *Maud Bodkin, "A Study of 'The Ancient Mariner' and of the Rebirth Archetype," in her* Archetypal Patterns in Poetry: Psychological Studies of Imagination, *1934. Reprint by Oxford University Press, London, 1963, pp. 26-89.**

I. A. RICHARDS (essay date 1934)

[*Richards is considered a forerunner of New Criticism, a critical movement which emphasizes close reading and explication of a text rather than a study informed by the biographical, historical, or moral vision of the artist. Richards's studies often stress the nature of symbolic language.* Coleridge on Imagination, *from which the following excerpt is drawn, is thought to be Richards's repudiation of his earlier positivist view of poetry as a "pseudo-statement." From this point onward in his career, Richards interpreted poetry as a form of truth and knowledge. In the following, Richards assesses Coleridge's definition of fancy and imagination in the* Biographia Literaria *(see excerpt above, 1817).*]

Coleridge's best-known formulation of the difference between Imagination and Fancy comes at the end of the first volume of *Biographia* in those astonishing paragraphs . . . in which he contents himself for the present with stating the main result of a chapter that was never to be written. And although many readers have gathered from them that the distinction is in some way 'metaphysical'; that the Primary Imagination is a finite repetition of creation; that the Secondary Imagination is an echo of the primary; that it dissolves to recreate or, at least, 'to idealize and to unify'; and that it is vital, as opposed to Fancy which 'has no other counters to play with but fixities and definites' and is 'a mode of memory emancipated from the order of space and time'; neither Coleridge's grounds for the distinction nor his applications of it have as yet entered our general intellectual tradition. When they do, the order of our universes will have been changed. Here is a representative application:

> One of the most noticeable and fruitful facts in psychology is the modification of the same feeling by difference of form. The Heaven lifts up my soul, the sight of the ocean seems to widen it. We feel the same force at work, but the difference, whether in mind or body that we should feel in actual travelling, horizontally or in direct ascent, *that* we feel in Fancy.

For what are our feelings of this kind but a motion Imagined, with the feelings that would accompany that motion, less distinguished, more blended, more rapid, more confused, and, thereby, co-adunated? Just as white is the very emblem of one in being the confusion of all. . . .

This note is perhaps more a test of an understanding of Coleridge's theory than an exposition of it. Yet, when the theory has become a clearly defined speculative instrument, it would be hard to find a better example of its use. Before examining the example, however . . . , the theory must be given as explicit a formulation as I can contrive.

Coleridge begins in *Biographia* . . . , after the opposition: "Milton had a highly *imaginative,* Cowley a very *fanciful* mind," by comparing the relation between fancy and imagination to that between delirium and mania. The ground of the comparison is made clear elsewhere:

> You may conceive the difference in kind between the Fancy and the Imagination in this way, that if the check of the senses and the reason were withdrawn, the first would become delirium, and the last mania. . . .

But . . . these results of the removal of the check do not imply an approximation of imagination to mania. . . . (pp. 72-4)

Under these checks of the senses and reason, of the activity of thought and the vivacity of the accumulative memory, the mind in its normal state uses *both* Fancy and Imagination. Coleridge often insisted—and would have insisted still more often had he been a better judge of this readers' capacity for misunderstanding—that Fancy and Imagination are not exclusive of or inimical to one another. (p. 75)

[He] could have reversed the *dictum,* for the counters, the 'fixities and definites' that fancy plays with, are only counters at all, only exist to be played with, through earlier acts of perception. They have come into being, been formed, by earlier acts of Imagination; but, so far as *Fancy only* is now at work, they are not being *re*formed, they are not being integrated, co-adunated into a new perception.

We are on the verge here of a very difficult inquiry into the senses of the words, *unity, integration,* and *one;* or into the problem of the types of unity that mental processes may have. And we can avoid this vast philosophic quagmire only by remembering that here too 'our puny boundaries' are not things that we perceive but that we make. In drawing, with Coleridge, a line between Imagination as a bringing into one—an esemplastic power—and Fancy as an assembling, aggregating power, we must bear in mind the purpose for which we draw it. The importance and the persistence of the purpose, and the utility of the distinction, establish the line, and it has no other establishment. If we were to say, for example, that the division was laid down in Nature, that would be here no more than a grandiose way of referring to the same or other purposes and utilities.

The problem to attack then is not the abstract one: What is unity in itself? (which, apart from concrete examples, is a pseudo-question) nor: What ought we to mean by 'unity'? (interesting though this might be on another occasion) but: What hypothesis can we invent which will be useful to us in describing and reflecting upon a difference we notice between certain examples which, we shall agree, are different.

Let us begin with the examples which Coleridge treats in most detail—the two opposed passages from [William Shakespeare's] *Venus and Adonis*. . . . As Fancy we have:

> Full gently now she takes him by the hand,
> A lily prison'd in a gaol of snow,
> Or ivory in an alabaster band;
> So white a friend engirts so white a foe. . . .

Of Fancy, Coleridge says:

(1) That it is 'the faculty of bringing together images dissimilar in the main by some one point or more of likeness distinguished'. . . .

(2) That these images are 'fixities and definites' . . . , they remain when put together the same as when apart.

(3) That the images 'have no connexion natural or moral, but are yoked together by the poet by means of some accidental coincidence'. . . .

(4) The activity putting them together is that of choice, which is 'an empirical phenomenon of the will'—that is, *not* the will as a principle of the mind's being, striving to realize itself in knowing itself, *but* an exercise of selection from among objects already supplied by association, a selection made for purposes which are not then and therein being shaped but have been already fixed.

Fancy, indeed, is the mind's activity in so far as Hartley's associationism seems to apply to it.

Now let us examine the lines in detail and test these descriptions upon them. The two middle lines are those which show Fancy most clearly.

Adonis' hand: Venus' hand: :lily: gaol of snow

Adonis' hand and a lily are both fair; both white; both, perhaps, pure (but this comparison is more complex, since the lily is an *emblem* of the purity which, in turn, by a second metaphor is lent to the hand). But there the links stop. These additions to the hand *via* the lily in no way change the hand (or, incidentally, the lily). They in no way work upon our perception of Adonis or his hand. It would be difficult for them to do so in view of other things in the poem:

> With this she seizeth on his sweating palm. . . .

and the only whiteness he has shown so far is that of anger,

> Twixt crimson shame, and anger ashy pale. . . .

The same absence of interaction between the parts of the comparison is shown equally with *prison'd* and *gaol of snow*. In contrast to the implied efforts or will to escape of the *prison'd* hand, a lily would be the most patient of captives. And anything *less* resembling a gaol of snow than Venus' hand could hardly be chosen—except in *two* uncombined 'points of likeness distinguished', *two* accidental coincidences, namely that the gaol and the hand are both enclosures and both white.

But Venus' hand is not a static enclosure, and the whitenesses will seem less compatible the more we consider them. In another kind of poetry, we might take the imcompatibility of our feelings about flesh and snow as a positive part of the interaction. A Goddess' hand might well be inhuman; but not here. (pp. 75-9)

It is clear—and becomes clearer on closer inspection—that, unless we give the lines a strained reading which the context

does not invite, there is no relevant interaction, no interinanimation, between these units of meaning.

I have taken them here (following Coleridge) as *images; that is, as units that might be seen 'in the mind's eye', or otherwise *imaged;* but the same would be true whatever the distinguishable units we introduced were, whether these were notions, feelings, desires or attitudes. However we take them we shall find that *the links* between them are accidental, contribute nothing to the action; though *the absence* of relevant links does. Pondering the links does not enrich the poem. (p. 79)

Another way of describing this would be to say that Shakespeare is not here realizing—or attempting to realize—the contact of the hands in words: either as felt by Adonis, or by Venus, or as seen by himself or by us as possible witnesses. He is doing something quite different. If we say that he is *describing* their hands in these lines we should recognize what different activities can be put behind this word. . . . Shakespeare is not making a bad description of a kind in which any modern novelist could beat him; he is doing something else. He is making pleasing collocations that are *almost* wholly unconnected with what he is writing about.

Why he is doing this (and what this is) are large questions. The answer would be partly historical; it would show that the purposes that poets may pursue are much more various than we ordinarily suppose. It would be partly psychological; it would show that the structure or *constitution* of poetic meanings may vary from extreme federalism, as here, to the strictest centrality. . . . (pp. 80-1)

If we like to say here, with Coleridge, that knowing the perilous nature of his subject in *Venus and Adonis*—how easily cloying—Shakespeare is deliberately practising 'alienation and aloofness' in his own and his readers' feelings, 'dissipating the reader's notice', the speculation can at least serve to indicate the effect. The commonest characteristic effect of Fancy is the coolness and disengagement with which we are invited to attend to what is taking place. (pp. 81-2)

We can turn now to Coleridge's instance of Imagination: Adonis' flight.

> Look! how a bright star shooteth from the sky
> So glides he in the night from Venus' eye.
>
> How many images and feelings are here brought
> together without effort and without discord—
> the beauty of Adonis—the rapidity of his flight—
> the yearning yet helplessness of the enamoured
> gazer—and a shadowy ideal character thrown
> over the whole. . . .
> (From Thomas Raysor, *Shakespearean Criticism*)

Here, in contrast to the other case, the more the image is followed up, the more links of relevance between the units are discovered. As Adonis to Venus, so these lines to the reader seem to linger in the eye like the after-images that make the trail of the meteor. Here Shakespeare is realizing, and making the reader realize—not by any intensity of effort, but by the fulness and self-completing growth of the response—Adonis' flight as it was to Venus, and the sense of loss, of increased darkness, that invades her. The separable meanings of each word, *Look!* (our surprise at the meteor, hers at his flight), *star* (a light-giver, an influence, a remote and uncontrollable thing) *shooteth* (the sudden, irremediable, portentous fall or death of what had been a guide, a destiny), *the sky* (the source of light and now of ruin), *glides* (not rapidity only, but fatal ease too), *in the night* (the darkness of the scene and of Venus' world now)—all these separable meanings are here brought into one. And as they come together, as the reader's mind finds cross-connexion after cross-connexion between them, he seems, in becoming more aware of them, to be discovering not only Shakespeare's meaning, but something which he, the reader, is himself making. His understanding of Shakespeare is sanctioned by his own activity in it. As Coleridge says: "You feel him to be a poet, inasmuch as for a time he has made you one—an active creative being."

This, then, is an *observable* difference from which we set out, though it is unhappily not true that all can observe it equally or equally clearly. But that is a general difficulty afflicting all studies of mental processes since the conditions of the observations vary with the skill and prepossessions of the reader. The account we please to give of the difference, our preference for one account of it rather than another, is another matter. Whether we observe the difference, and how, depends upon our habits in reading. Whether—having observed it—we choose to *describe* it in one way or another, depends upon the ideas and the methods we find most convenient *in general* in discussing our mental affairs; which, in turn, depend upon the purposes of the discussion.

Anyone who is well acquainted with Coleridge's ways of discussing Fancy and Imagination will notice that I have, at several places above, translated them in terms which might sometimes have been repugnant, as suggesting mechanical treatment, to Coleridge himself. In place of 'the power by which one image or feeling is made to modify many others and by a sort of *fusion to force many into one,*' I have used phrases which suggest that it is the number of connexions between the many, and the relations between these connexions, that give the unity—in brief, that the co-adunation is the inter-relationship of the parts. If we are careful to separate the *description* of a process or experience from the experience itself, this should not mislead. The terms in which we describe the experience will vary with the purposes we need the description for. Admitting this, we shall not suppose that units corresponding to these terms actually occur in the experience. . . . But a perfect description, if such a description introduced or omitted nothing, would just be the experience itself over again. We should be left by it where we were, and be not a jot advanced towards our purpose in making a description, which is to gain a systematic method of comparison between experiences.

Our descriptions must apply. Whatever the machinery of distinctions they employ and thereby impose upon the experiences, they must record differences in the experiences which they do not impose, which are prior to and independent of the imposed distinctions. It is the merit of Coleridge's Fancy and Imagination as descriptive devices that they note such actual differences in the experiences they apply to. With this, a first step towards systematic comparisons between the structures of the meanings of poetry has been made. And, still more important, with it the way towards a further technique of comparison has been opened. But to explore it successfully we must assume that our descriptions are products of our technique, not simple copies of the experiences we are describing; and that we may change them within limits *without* thereby changing our view of the point of difference between the experiences we are comparing with their aid.

Under this charter of technological liberty let me attempt another description of the difference between Fancy and Imagination—a re-formulation which may be of assistance in the next chapter, where I consider Coleridge's remark that 'the sense of musical delight, with the power of producing it, is a gift of the imagination', and his doctrines of the relation of metre to poetry.

> In Imagination the parts of the meaning—both as regards the ways in which they are apprehended and the modes of combination of their effects in the mind—mutually modify one another.

> In Fancy, the parts of the meaning are apprehended as though independent of their fellow-members (as they would be if they belonged to quite other wholes) and although, of course, the parts together have a joint effect which is not what it would be if the assemblage were different, the effects of the parts remain for an interval separate and collide or combine *later,* in so far as they do so at all.

The points which most pressingly need elucidation in these formulations, concern:

(1) The parts of a meaning; in what sense, here, have meanings parts?

(2) Apprehension; how, if at all, is the apprehension of a meaning to be separated from its effects?

(3) Mutual modification; what is this?

(4) How are we to separate such joint effects as all collocations must have—merely through the normal relativity (or inherent unity) of mental process—from the special modes of combination of effects on which the distinction, largely, turns?

In attempting to answer these questions, we are face to face with the chief difficulty of all such work, and can escape it only by holding firmly to this guiding principle: that we are not trying, in our descriptions, to say *what happens*, but framing a speculative apparatus to assist us in observing a difference.

(1) Meanings my be said to have any parts which, for our purposes, we find useful as instruments in comparing them. Here some of the most useful parts seem to be:

*Awareness of the words as *words:* as sensory presentations (shapes on the paper, movements of the organs of speech, sounds associated with them), with whatever else, and there may be much, that must be included in an account of what words, as opposed to their meanings, are.

Sense: i.e. thoughts of things, of states of affairs, that arise with perception of the words; their plain prose meaning, as we sometimes say; together with such imagery as may, in certain types of minds, accompany these thoughts and be a medium or support to them.

Feeling: i.e. reverberations or emotional or practical attitudes towards the things, or states of affairs, thought of in the sense.

Tone: i.e. attitudes of the reader to the writer (or of writer to reader) implicitly assumed or explicitly controlled at every point in all writing.

Under each of these headings will appear (as we use higher and higher powers of the speculative analytic instrument) myriads of distinguishable 'units', whose connexions with one another, and with 'units' under other headings are an inexhaustible field for enquiry.

(2) The apprehension of the meaning of a set of words is, for a *reader,* a selection from their effects upon him. (For a *writer,* this *may* be reversed, the finding of the words be an effect of an apprehension.) I take *apprehension,* in the formulations above, arbitrarily: as the more immediate part of our response to the words. It is separated, on the hither side, from our mere recognition of the words as *these* not *those* words; and, on the farther side, from later ramifications and reverberations of effects due to our simultaneous and successive apprehensions—this first-order 'superficial' response to them. But apprehension is not to be equated simply with Sense as above described. Feeling and tone factors come into the first stages of the interpretation of words in poetry.... The patterns of our thoughts *represent,* in various ways, the world we live in. The patterns of our feelings represent only a few special forms of our commerce with it.

(3) With parts of a total meaning so conceived, their 'mutual modification' becomes a way of describing the development of the response which is this meaning. After apprehending how *a bright star shooteth from the sky* we respond to Adonis' gliding otherwise. And reciprocally the development of Feeling (and Tone) from *bright star shooteth* is modified by our knowledge, for example, that Adonis is going to his death. Latent possibilities in it are called out. In comparison, latent possibilities in *lilies* and *gaols* of *snow* are not called out by the co-presence in the response of Adonis' and Venus' hands. Our apprehension of them stays at the sketchy stage it reached with our first bare understanding of the words.

(4) Yet, of course, the line

A lily prison'd in a gaol of snow

as a comparison for their hands, does have a joint effect. There is a resultant unity of meaning—the unity which any utterance has no matter what the internal relations of its parts. It has a meaning, that is to say.... What we have to consider are differences in the mode of formation of a joint effect.

The example (any such example) is puzzling—which, here, is instructive—in a number of respects. Being without syntax, we are free to combine the parts as we please. As separate apprehensions of meanings for the separate words, they are not set in any fixed relations to one another to begin with. And this mere freedom gives these parts an opportunity, *if we avail ourselves of it,* to modify one another from the start which would be lost if we gave the words a definite syntax and formed a sentence.

This mutual modification, did it occur—most readings will exercise only Fancy—would be Imagination, a lowly and elementary example of it; and of no literary importance because, being contextless, the mutual modification is at the mercy of the freaks of the reader's interpretation, and thus any valuable result would be the reader's private poem. The fact, however, that an absence of syntax is a favourable condition for Imagination is important. It explains why languages whose syntax we do not understand sometimes seem inherently poetical, *e.g.* literal, word for word translations from 'primitive' tongues or from Chinese; why ambiguous syntax is so frequent in Shakespeare; and why, in much of the modern verse which derives from Mr Ezra Pound, it is easy to mistake a mere freedom to interpret as we will for controlling unity of sane purpose—that is, purpose integrated with and relevant to our lives as wholes.

The danger of such a remark as this, however, is that it may lead us to conceive Imagination in terms of value, to say that

it is mutual modification *to a good end.* This was undoubtedly most often Coleridge's view. But Imagination, as I have described it, can be shown in trivial examples. And Fancy can be shown in important matters, though the range of powers, from good to bad, of Imagination seems, as we should expect, to be greater than that of Fancy. In Imagination, as I have taken it, the joint effect (worthless or not) ensues only through and after a reciprocal stressing, one by another, of the parts as they develop together, so that, in the ideal case, all the possible characters of any part are elicited and a place found for them, consentaneous with the rest, in the whole response. In Fancy, on the other hand, only a limited nd fixed selection of the possible characters (and thus possible effects) of the parts are admitted into the process. The stressing is done by the final effect, which ruthlessly excludes all but a limited number of interactions between the parts, setting strict frontiers of relevance about them. Doubtless the ideal case of Imagination is rare; if enough of the possibilities of the part-meanings come in we overlook any that must stay out. With Fancy, we either 'overlook' them in quite another sense, we voluntarily and expressly ignore them; or we let an awareness of their *irrelevance* in to gain a mixed effect, of burlesque for instance.... (pp. 82-92)

For convenience I have taken, as examples of Fancy and Imagination, short passages of a few lines only. But the contrast might be illustrated equally with whole works. Thus, in prose fiction, the detective novel is a type of Fancy, but any presentation of an integral view of life will take the structure of Imagination. The units imaginatively disposed may themselves be products of fancy; and, conversely, a series of imaginative passages may be arranged (as beads on a string) in the mode of Fancy.... (p. 95)

Imagination, as Coleridge uses it, is, of course, very often a term implying higher values than *Fancy* (critics who point this out with an air of discovery or complaint should re-read him). The conception was devised as a means of describing the wider and deeper powers of some poetry. It is a descriptive psychological term in the sense that it points to facts which explain certain values.... [The] exercise of the Imagination is, for Coleridge, more valuable than the operations of Fancy. We can, if we wish, relax these conditions, and make the terms purely descriptive. We shall then have instances of Imagination which are valuable and instances which are not, and we must then go on to contrive a further theory, a theory of values which will explain (so far as we are able to do so at present) these differences of values.... Coleridge does not so separate his psychology from his theory of value. His theory of Imagination is a combination of the two, and there is much to be said in favour of this more difficult order of procedure. It does more justice to the unity of mental process, and, if such an exposition is understood, there is less risk of suggesting that the value aspects of our activities are independent of, or supernumerary to, their nature—less risk of our taking the same question twice as though it were two questions, not one.

Coleridge's treatment pins itself to a factual difference between some events in our mind and others. It is a difference which cannot be adequately described by taking account only of the events in isolation. We must take account of their place and function in the whole activity of the mind—and of this not only as an individual life but as a representative of what he calls the '*all in each* of human nature'.... A description which must reach so far becomes, I think, inevitably valuative. But in saying this I am taking sides in an old and still far from concluded debate—the question, simplified, being: whether a *complete* factual account of a life would leave anything to be discussed, under a separate irreducible head, as its value? It may well be, though, that this description of the question (and perhaps any description) is ambiguous. Our descriptions are verbal machines exposed to the danger that we ourselves misuse them after we have made them. The facts they try to render would soon be lost to us if we had to rely upon these descriptions.

Fortunately we have a more direct and surer method of identifying the work of the Imagination: namely, through the Imagination itself. In spite of all aberrations there is a persistent tradition—as constant as any theory of human nature and its conditions would allow us to expect—which recognizes acts of Imagination. Literally they are *recognized:* the *all in each* finds again in them the same enlargement. Arnold said that great poetry interests the permanent passions; but this, as so often happens, splits what is one into two. For the passions are *in* the poetry and the poetry is only the way this interest and these passions go in it. No description of imagination is of any use to those who do not otherwise sometimes know this way—as poets; or know when they are in it, as readers; yet it is the way—however often fashion, miscomprehension, obstructive pre-possessions, or dullness may hide it from us. (pp. 96-8)

I. A. Richards, in his Coleridge on Imagination, *1934. Reprint by Indiana University Press, 1960, 236 p.*

F. R. LEAVIS (essay date 1940)

[*Leavis was an influential contemporary English critic. His critical methodology combines close textual criticism with predominantly moral and social concerns; however, Leavis is not interested in the individual writer per se, but rather with the usefulness of his or her art in the scheme of civilization. Leavis believes that Coleridge's mind was "rarely gifted," and he also maintains that Coleridge's achievements were negligible, that his philosophy of art is not useful to students of literature, and that only Chapter XV of* Biographia Literaria, *on William Shakespeare's* Venus and Adonis, *reveals Coleridge's critical abilities. A survey of his criticism "is impressive evidence of what he might have done," Leavis concludes. This essay first appeared in* Scrutiny *in June, 1940.*]

That Coleridge was a rarely gifted mind is a commonplace. It is perhaps equally a commonplace that what he actually accomplished with his gifts, the producible achievement, appears, when we come to stocktaking, disappointingly incommensurate. That 'perhaps' registers a hesitation: judges qualified in the religious and inellectual history of the past century might, I think, reply that actually Coleridge was a great power, exercising influence in ways that must be credited to him for very notable achievement, and that we cannot judge him merely by reading what is extant of him in print. My concern, however, is with the field of literary criticism. That his performance there justifies some disappointment is, I believe, generally recognized. But I believe too that this recognition stresses, in intention, rather the superlativeness of the gifts than shortcoming in the performance. The full disparity, in fact, doesn't get clear recognition very readily; there are peculiar difficulties in the way—at least, these are the conclusions to which, after reconsidering the body of Coleridge's work in criticism, I find myself brought. (p. 41)

Coleridge's philosophy of art is Coleridge's philosophy, and though no doubt he has an important place in the history of English thought, not even the student of philosophy, I imagine, is commonly sent to Coleridge for initiations into key-problems, or for classical examples of distinguished thinking. And the literary student who goes to Coleridge in the expectation of bringing away an improved capacity and equipment for dealing critically with works of literature will, if he spends much time on the 'philosophy of art', have been sadly misled.

It is by way of defining the spirit of my approach that I assert this proposition, the truth of which seems to me evident. Actually, of course, its evidence gets substantial recognition in established academic practice: the student usually starts his reading—or at least his serious reading—of *Biographia Literaria* at chapter XIV. Nevertheless, since the appropriate distinction is not formulated and no sharp separation can be made in the text, the common effect of the perusal can hardly be clarity—or clear profit. It is certain, on the other hand, that Coleridge's prestige owes a great deal to the transcendental aura; his acceptance as a master of 'theoretical criticism' is largely an awed vagueness about the philosophy—a matter of confused response to such things as

> The primary IMAGINATION then, I consider, to be the living power and prime agent of all human Perception, and as a repetition in the finite mind of the eternal act of creation in the infinite I AM [see excerpt above, 1817].

The essential distinction ought to be plain enough to us, but that Coleridge himself should not have made it sharply and have held firmly to it cannot, given the nature of his genius, surprise us; on the contrary, even if he had been a much more orderly and disciplined worker than he was we still couldn't have expected in his work a clear separation between what properly claims the attention of the literary critic and what does not. 'Metaphysics, poetry and facts of mind,' he wrote, 'are my darling studies.' The collocation of the last two heads suggests the sense in which Shelley's phrase for him, 'a subtle-souled psychologist', must often, when he impresses us favourably in the literary-critical field, seem to us an apt one, and, on the other hand, it is difficult not to think of the first head as a nuisance. Yet we can hardly suppose that we could have had the psychologist without the metaphysician; that the gift of subtle analysis could have been developed, at that date, by a mind that shouldn't also have exhibited something like the Coleridgean philosophic bent. But that makes it not less, but more necessary to be firm about the distinction that concerns us here.

I had better at this point indicate more fully the specific equipment that might seem to have qualified Coleridge for great achievements in literary criticism—to be, indeed, its modern instaurator. The 'subtle-souled psychologist', it seems not superfluous to emphasize, was intensely interested in literature. He was, of course, a poet, and the suggestion seems to be taken very seriously that he indulged the habit of analytic introspection to the extent of damaging the creative gift he turned it upon. However that may be, it is reasonable to suppose that the critic, at any rate, profited. (pp. 42-3)

Asked to point to a place that could be regarded as at the centre of Coleridge's achievement and indicative of its nature, most admirers would probably point to the famous passage on imagination at the end of chapter XIV of *Biographia Literaria*. . . . (p. 45)

It is an impressive passage—perhaps too impressive; for it has more often, perhaps, caused an excited sense of enlightenment than it has led to improved critical practice or understanding. The value we set on it must depend on the development and illustration the account of imagination gets in such context as we can find for it elsewhere in Coleridge and especially in his own critical practice. The appropriate commentary according to general acceptance would, I suppose, bear on the substitution by Coleridge of an understanding of literature in terms of organism, an understanding operating through an inward critical analysis, for the external mechanical approach of the neo-classic eighteenth century. That Coleridge has a place in literary history to be indicated in some such terms is no doubt true. And yet we ought hardly to acquiesce happily in any suggestion that the subsequent century exhibits a general improvement in criticism. What in fact this view—the academically accepted one, I believe—of Coleridge amounts to is that, of the decisive change in taste and literary tradition that resulted from the Romantic movement, Coleridge is to be regarded as the supreme critical representative.

And it has to be recognized that, in effect, his 'imagination' does seem to have amounted to the Romantic 'creative imagination'. (pp. 45-6)

My concern is with the intrinsic interest of his extant critical work—with his achievement in that sense. A critic may have an important place in history and yet not be very interesting in his writings. . . . Coleridge, on the other hand, may be more interesting than the claims made for him as an influence suggest. What credit we give him for the interesting possibilities of that passage on imagination depends, as has been said, on the way the account is developed and illustrated.

The Fancy-Imagination contrast hardly takes us any further. Coleridge does little with it beyond the brief exemplification that cannot be said to justify the stress he lays on the two faculties he distinguishes. . . . The best that can be said for Coleridge is that, though he was undoubtedly serious in positing the two faculties, actually the distinction as he illustrates it is a way of calling attention to the organic complexities of verbal life, metaphorical and other, in which Imagination manifests itself locally: Fancy is merely an ancillary concept. And Coleridge certainly gives evidence of a gift for critical analysis. . . . (pp. 46-7)

But 'capacity'—again it is evidence of qualifications we are adducing. What corresponding achievement is there to point to? The work on Shakespeare constitutes the nearest thing to an impressive body of criticism, and everyone who has tried to read it through knows how disappointing it is. . . . [When] we take stock of what there is to be said in favour of the Shakespeare criticism, we . . . find ourselves considering, not achievement, but evidence of a critical endowment that *ought* to have achieved something remarkable. Even those who rate it more highly would, I imagine, never think of proposing the work on Shakespeare to the student as a classical body of criticism calculated to make much difference to his powers of appreciation or understanding.

What is, I suppose, a classical document is the group of chapters on Wordsworth in *Biographia Literaria*. But if they are that it is at least partly for reasons of historical interest, because Coleridge on Wordsworth is Coleridge on Wordsworth, and not because of achieved criticism of a high order contained in them. The treatment of the poetry, however interesting, hardly amounts to a profound or very illuminating critique. The discussion of poetic diction provides, of course, more evidence of Coleridge's peculiar gifts, especially in the argument about metre in chapter XVIII. That Coleridge perceives certain essential truths about poetic rhythm and metre—truths that are not commonplaces, at any rate in academic literary study—is plain. But anything approaching the satisfactory treatment of them that he seems preeminently qualified to have written he certainly doesn't provide. (pp. 47-8)

Coleridge's unsatisfactoriness isn't merely what stares at us in the synopsis of *Biographia Literaria*—the disorderliness, the lack of all organization or sustained development: locally too, even in the best places, he fails to bring his thought to a sharp edge and seems too content with easy expression. Expression came, in fact, too easily to him; for a man of his deep constitutional disinclination to brace himself to sustained work at any given undertaking, his articulateness was fatal. He could go down to the lecture-hall at the last minute with a marked copy of Shakespeare and talk—talk much as he talked anywhere and at any time. And what we read as Coleridge's writings comes from that inveterate talker, even when the text that we have is something he actually wrote, and not reported discourse. (pp. 48-9)

[Chapter XV of *Biographia Literaria*] seems to me to show Coleridge at his best. It is headed, 'The specific symptoms of poetic power elucidated in a critical analysis of Shakespeare's Venus and Adonis and Lucrece', and this heading is significant: it suggests with some felicity the nature of Coleridge's peculiar distinction, or what should have been his peculiar distinction, as a critic. He speaks in his first sentence, referring no doubt mainly to the passage on imagination, of 'the application of these principles to purposes of practical criticism'. Actually, principle as we are aware of it here appears to emerge from practice; we are made to realize that the 'master of theoretical criticism' who matters is the completion of a practical critic. The theory of which he is master (in so far as he is) doesn't lead us to discuss his debt to Kant or any other philosopher; it comes too evidently from the English critic who has devoted his finest powers of sensibility and intelligence to the poetry of his own language. (pp. 49-50)

Though the other heads of the chapter contain nothing as striking, we tend to give full credit to what is best in them. In the first and third, for instance, Coleridge makes it plain (as he has already done in practical criticism) that the 'imagery' that matters cannot be dealt with in terms of 'images' conceived as standing to the verse as plums to cake; but that its analysis is the analysis of complex verbal organization:

> It has therefore been observed that images, however beautiful, though faithfully copied from nature, and as accurately represented in words, do not of themselves characterize the poet. They become proofs of original genius only as far as they are modified by a predominant passion; or by associated thoughts or images awakened by that passion; or when they have the effect of reducing multitude to unity, or succession to an instant; or lastly, when a human and intellectual life is transferred to them from the poet's own spirit.

But there would be little point in further quotations of this kind. Such imperfectly formulated things hardly deserve to be remembered as classical statements, and nothing more is to be adduced by way of justifying achievement than the preceding long quotation. And there is nowhere in Coleridge anything more impressive to be found than that. We are left, then, with the conclusion that what we bring from the re-survey of his critical work is impressive evidence of what he might have done. (p. 51)

Coleridge's prestige is very understandable, but his currency as an academic classic is something of a scandal. Where he is prescribed and recommended it should be with far more by way of reservation and caveat (I have come tardily to realize) than most students can report to have received along with him. He was very much more brilliantly gifted than Arnold, but nothing of his deserves the classical status of Arnold's best work. (p. 52)

> *F. R. Leavis, "Coleridge in Criticism," in his* The Critic As Anti-Philosopher: Essays & Papers, *edited by G. Singh, The University of Georgia Press, 1983, pp. 41-52.*

MARIUS BEWLEY (essay date 1940)

[*Bewley discusses the conflict in "The Ancient Mariner" between the poem's dramatic elements and moral motives. This conflict, Bewley proposes, results in a thematic ambiguity which clouds the poem's meaning. Bewley's essay first appeared in* Scrutiny *in 1940.*]

One need not cavil at applying the term moralist to Coleridge. He was concerned with philosophy and religion and politics in a way that the merely frivolous can never be concerned with them, and particularly in establishing a vital relationship between them and the world. It would be remarkable if behind the explicit motive of *The Ancient Mariner* it were not possible to catch glimpses of an ulterior and possibly more real impulse at work. Coleridge's poetry may be rated on too high a level,

An unfinished portrait of Coleridge in 1806 by his close friend, the American painter Washington Allston.

but to assume that he approached it as a pedestrian task not essentially different from ledger work would be to do him an injustice. For good or ill Coleridge could not help drawing in some measure from his full sensibility. The *raconteur* of supernatural tales is, in *The Ancient Mariner*, not quite free from the moralist. The moral element is forgotten, if indeed it was ever recognized as present; it is changed, choked out by theatrical fripperies. All else is put aside in the fuller attention that is given to the merely dramatic motive. But although the moral motive is scotched, ineffectual fragments are still to be seen in odd corners of the poem as indications of that ambiguity which in the beginning was not absent from Coleridge's mind and which still tends to make one slightly puzzled in reading *The Ancient Mariner.*

I have suggested that this ambiguity is, then, a dispute between the dramatic and the moral motives in composition, and that from the beginning Coleridge exerted his full force on behalf of the first; that he succeeded in what he wished, but was only not sufficiently neat in disposing of the remains of the latter. The ineffective moral motive of *The Ancient Mariner* is a Christian one. It stresses the necessity of supernatural love as the order in creation. It is degraded and like an appendage when at last it comes to a head in the last stanza but two of the poem:

> He prayeth best, who loveth best
> All things both great and small;
> For the dear God who loveth us,
> He made and loveth all.

But disguised and unsatisfactory as its expression is, it is still the central idea of the whole poem, the core around which the action is developed, and without which the sequence of events would be meaningless. In tracing the play of this stunted moral motive, so much thrust into the background, against the length of the poem, a certain roughness of handling is necessitated. But if the interpretation seems arbitrary it is not meant to mark the boundaries of the motive with any precision, but only to point to its existence in the poem.

The transgression of the Ancient Mariner in killing the Albatross is a violation of that supernatural charity which should rule throughout creation. The sanctions which are imposed for the death of the Albatross do not seem remarkable when one reflects that the extraordinariness of the bird does not exist in its own right. . . . [The Albatross] has been deliberately placed by the Ancient Mariner on the same plane of creation which he himself occupies, and the full play of the will to which this deliberation gives scope brings to the Ancient Mariner's act of violence a special guilt.

The punishment which the Ancient Mariner undergoes begins to abate when he is able to generate stirrings of love in the soul once again for created things. . . . It is at the beginning of Part V that [the moral motive] becomes operative in the positive sense. Up to this point the Ancient Mariner has been the active agent, but his will has not worked in harmony with the divine goodness, which now, through the operation of a supernatural mechanism, begins the work of regeneration in his soul. There follows quickly that passage in which the seraph band enters the bodies of the crew. It is one of the most dramatic passages in the poem. Bearing with its reminiscences of the Incarnation and the Resurrection, it is but a further insistence on the controlling principle of love which springs from God.

This interpretation, though it is obvious enough, is not the one most immediate and apparent. Indeed, it lies far back in the poem. We are likely to overlook it entirely, despite the kind of obviousness which it can claim, and it would make little difference but for the moral overtone which it strikes, and which reaches our ears like a faint echo suggesting a more considerable substance than search is likely to verify. The reader more probably assumes, for example, that the Albatross is a bird of sinister significance whose death liberates inexplicable threads of mystery to wave in the atmosphere. The sequence of action is, as a result, microscoped to a moral inconsequentiality from this point onwards. It was what Coleridge wanted. He even assists the reader to the interpretation by his marginal note referring to the bird of good omen. As the poem stands it is indeed the interpretation that should be made; but the moral motive which was sketched in above, ignored and distorted, hovers in the background and implies a moral integrity which does not exist.

The dramatic purpose of the poem is realized by means of the supernatural mechanism. But as this mechanism is a means to the dramatic fulfilment of the poem, it works also towards the failure of the moral motive. Still, the function which the machinery performs it performs well, and it is one which necessitated a mechanism of this order. The peculiar quality of the supernatural machinery consists in its being localized; one might almost say, *essentially* localized. If the supernatural is to be treated at all it is inevitable that it should be given extension, and to do this is to tie it down to a particular place. Yet it is not impossible that these necessary materializations should appeal to the reader only as inevitable symbols of states of being that cannot otherwise be expressed. Dante achieved this. But Coleridge places his supernatural beings against the geography of an unknown world in such a manner that their respective mysteries enforce each other. This means that while the mystery of the world is increased, that of the supernatural not only decreases but changes in character. . . . The achievement of Coleridge is that he succeeds in re-creating an amosphere of mystery that a long line of explorers from Vasco da Gama to Byrd have been at some effort to take from us.

This air of mystery is created by direct statement and by playing the supernatural against a terrestrial background. It is stated directly, for example, in lines such as,

> We were the first that ever burst
> Into that silent sea.

Coleridge's process of building up this air of mystery, inasmuch as it concerns itself with descriptions of "ice as green as emerald," the relative position of the sun, the rather weird effect of personifying and capitalizing "the STORM-BLAST," the suitably dramatic choice of the South Pole and then the Line as the course of the ship's voyage, and particularly the skeleton ship with its crew, Death and Life-in-Death, is sometimes theatrical, but it is innocent always. It is indeed this innocence that keeps the whole machinery at times from creaking. By innocence here I mean that accomplished lack of sophistication which is sometimes so characteristic of Coleridge. By felicitous touches Coleridge tapped forgotten emotional connotations. He is able to suggest fabulous mediaeval sea-monsters with some subtlety:

> Yea, slimy things did crawl with legs
> Upon the slimy sea.

But this direct statement of the geographical mystery is intensified by the familiar movements of the demons of the middle air through their element, by the skeleton ship, which, with its plunging and tacking and veering, gives the impression of being a constant inhabitant of the Pacific, by the Polar Spirit—

in short, by that sense of supernatural population which seems to be a part of the background against which it moves. The atmosphere of *The Ancient Mariner* is heavily charged. The earth is a mysterious place, but its mystery is not, strictly speaking, the mystery of rocks and stones and trees. It is in good part the mystery of the spiritual beings who reside in them and whose identities are, for the poem's purposes, not clearly distinct.

To have succeeded in re-creating this air of mystery, or, more correctly, in creating this new air of mystery, is not after all a major achievement. It is comparatively trivial. Yet if we search for a more substantial value in *The Ancient Mariner* the search will not be fruitful. The moral value of the poem is sacrificed to the attainment of a somewhat frivolous distinction. The texture of the poetry itself is never adequate to its purpose, but it is not, for the most part, interesting. It is inflexible because it is manufactured to compass a certain preconceived effect, and one that, from Coleridge's own words, which were quoted above, is scarcely closed to suspicion. It is not likely that words of such impersonal calculation should have led on to poetic attempts whose roots were buried deep in the essential impulses of the man. The chief objection must be, I think, that *The Ancient Mariner* brings into play a machinery that is by its nature moral, but caricatures and deflects that machinery from its true purpose, that a smaller satisfaction may be realized. (pp. 169-74)

> *Marius Bewley, "Coleridge: The Poetry of Coleridge," in* The Importance of Scrutiny: Selections from "Scrutiny, a Quarterly Review," 1932-1948, *edited by Eric Bentley, New York University Press, 1964, pp. 169-74.*

D. W. HARDING   (essay date 1941)

[*Harding emphasizes the personal emotion of isolation in "The Ancient Mariner," contending that the Mariner's overwhelming loneliness is his punishment for killing the Albatross, the symbol of love. Though Coleridge also depicts the Mariner's emotional recovery, Harding argues that the recovery is "incomplete." He states that "the Mariner is obviously not represented as having advanced through his suffering to a fuller life; and he no more achieves a full rebirth than Coleridge ever could."*]

The human experience around which Coleridge centres [*The Ancient Mariner*] is surely the depression and the sense of isolation and unworthiness which the Mariner describes in Part IV. The suffering he describes is of a kind which is perhaps not found except in slightly pathological conditions, but which, pathological or not, has been felt by a great many people. He feels isolated to a degree that baffles expression and reduces him to the impotent, repetitive emphasis which becomes doggerel in schoolroom reading:

> Alone, alone, all, all alone,
> Alone on a wide wide sea!

At the same time he is not just physically isolated but is socially abandoned, even by those with the greatest obligations:

> And never a saint took pity on
> My soul in agony.

With this desertion the beauty of the ordinary world has been taken away:

> The many men so beautiful!
> And they all dead did lie. . . .

All that is left, and especially, centrally, oneself, is disgustingly worthless:

> And a thousand thousand slimy things
> Lived on; and so did I.

With the sense of worthlessness there is also guilt. When he tried to pray

> A wicked whisper came and made
> My heart as dry as dust.

And enveloping the whole experience is the sense of sapped energy, oppressive weariness:

> For the sky and the sea, and the sea and the sky
> Lay like a load on my weary eye,
> And the dead were at my feet.

This, the central experience, comes almost at the middle of the poem. It is the nadir of depression to which the earlier stanzas sink; the rest of the poem describes what is in part recovery and in part aftermath. (pp. 335-36)

A usual feature of these states of pathological misery is their apparent causelessness. The depression cannot be rationally explained; the conviction of guilt and worthlessness is out of proportion to any ordinary offence actually committed. In the story of *The Ancient Mariner* Coleridge finds a crime which, in its symbolic implications, is sufficient to merit even his suffering. . . . The Mariner wantonly obliterated something which loved him and which represented in a supernatural way the possibility of affection in the world. . . . (p. 336)

This for Coleridge was the most terrible possibility among the sins.

The depth of meaning it held for him is indicated in the curious self-exculpation with which he ends *The Pains of Sleep*. That poem is a fragment of case-history recounting three nights of bad dreams:

> Fantastic passions! maddening brawl!
> And shame and terror over all!
> Deeds to be hid which were not hid,
> Which all confused I could not know
> Whether I suffered, or I did:
> For all seem'd guilt, remorse or woe . . .

Characteristically, he assumes that these sufferings must be a punishment for something or other. Yet by the standards of waking life and reason he feels himself to be innocent. He never explicitly mentions what the supposed offence might be. But in the last two lines, when he protests his innocence, the terms in which he does so reveal implicitly what crime alone could merit such punishment:

> Such punishments, I said, were due
> To natures deepliest stained with sin . . .
> But wherefore, wherefore fall on me?
> To be beloved is all I need,
> And whom I love, I love indeed.

Why is he innocent of the fatal sin?—because he aims at nothing beyond affection and union with others, gives no allegiance to more individual interests in the outer world which might flaw his complete devotion. It is only in the light of the last two lines that the introductory section of the poem yields its

meaning. Explaining that he is not accustomed to saying formal prayers before going to sleep, Coleridge continues

> But silently, by slow degrees,
> My spirit I to Love compose.
> In humble trust mine eyelids close,
> With reverential resignation . . .

And then one realises that he is protesting against being visited with the horrible dreams *in spite of* cultivating submissive affection and so guarding against the one sin that could merit such punishments.

The Ancient Mariner committed the sin. Yet Coleridge knew that by the ordinary standards of the workaday world his act was not, after all, very terrible. Hence the sarcastic stanzas which show the indifference of the other mariners to the real meaning of the deed. . . . It is not by the ordinary standards of social life, for the breach of ordinary social obligations, that Coleridge or the Mariner could be condemned; as in *The Pains of Sleep,* he protests his innocence by those standards. It is an irrational standard, having force only for him, by which he is found guilty. *The Ancient Mariner* allowed him to indicate something of this by means of the supernatural machinery. The small impulsive act which presses a supernatural trigger forms an effective parallel to the hidden impulse which has such devastating meaning for one's irrational, and partly unconscious, private standards. It is a fiction which permits the expression of real experience.

The total pattern of experience in *The Ancient Mariner* includes partial recovery from the worst depression. The offence for which the dejection and isolation were punishment was the wanton rejection of a very simple social union. One way to recovery is suggested in *The Pains of Sleep*. It is a return to a submissive sense of childlike weakness and distress. . . . (pp. 336-38)

He has to reach complete listlessness—itself a sort of submission—before there is any chance of recovery. His state at the turning point is in significant contrast to the desperate activity, the courageous snatching at hope in the direction from which he personally has decided salvation must come. . . . All this directed effort and expense of spirit is futile in the state of mind which Coleridge describes. Only when his individual striving has sunk to a low ebb does the recovery begin.

This naturally gives the impression, characteristic of such states of depression, that the recovery is fortuitous. It comes unpredictably and seemingly from some trivial accident. This part of the experience Coleridge has paralleled in the supernatural machinery of the tale by means of the dicing between Death and Life-in-Death. To the sufferer there seems no good reason why he shouldn't simply die, since he feels that he has thrown up the sponge. Instead, chance has it that he lives on.

The fact of its being Life-in-Death who wins the Mariner shows how incomplete his recovery is going to be. Nevertheless some degree of recovery from the nadir of dejection does unpredictably occur. It begins with the momentary rekindling of simple pleasure in the things around him. . . . It is the beginning of recovery because what is kindled is a recognition not only of their beauty but also of the worth of their existence and, by implication, of his own. (pp. 338-39)

His returning joy in living things comes, of course, from his changed attitude to himself and his willingness to look differently on the world. (p. 340)

In consistent development of the general theme, the Mariner's recovery leads on to reunion with the very simple and humble kinds of social life. He joins the villagers in the formal expression of atonement with each other, and with the source of love, which he sees in their religious worship. But it would be a mistake to think of this as anything like full recovery. For one thing he never again belongs to a settled community, but has to pass from land to land. . . . More important than [any] sign of imperfect recovery is the contrast between the submissive sociability with which he must now content himself and the buoyancy of the voyager as he first set out. . . . Such a voyage . . . entails a self-reliant thrusting forth into the outer world and repudiates dependence on the comfort of ordinary social ties. But Coleridge's anxieties seem to have shown him this attitude taken beyond all bounds and leading to a self-sufficiency which would wantonly destroy the ties of affection. The albatross is killed, and then the penalty must be paid in remorse, dejection, and the sense of being a worthless social outcast. Only a partial recovery is possible; once the horrifying potentiality has been glimpsed in human nature Coleridge dare not imagine a return to self-reliant voyaging. Creeping back defeated into the social convoy, the Mariner is obviously not represented as having advanced through his suffering to a fuller life; and he no more achieves a full rebirth than Coleridge ever could. (pp. 340-41)

Coleridge's detached, conscious intentions in writing the poem were no doubt mixed. . . . But the achievement, whatever the intention, has unity and coherence. True, the poem is not an allegory. There is no need to think that Coleridge could have paraphrased his theme either before or after writing. . . . [The] fiction Coleridge produced made a special appeal to him and could be handled with special effectiveness because its theme and incidents allowed highly significant though partly unconscious concerns to find expression. This is not to say that he was merely manipulating symbols. The concrete details of the fiction were not *less* but *more* vividly realised because they were charged with something else besides their manifest content. (p. 342)

> *D. W. Harding, "The Theme of 'The Ancient Mariner'," in* Scrutiny, *Vol. IX, No. 4, March, 1941, pp. 334-42.*

ALLEN TATE   (essay date 1941)

[*Tate's criticism is closely associated with two American critical movements, the Agrarians and the New Critics. The Agrarians were concerned with political and social issues as well as literature and were dedicated to preserving the Southern way of life and traditional Southern values. The New Critics comprised one of the most influential critical movements of the mid-twentieth century. Although the various New Critics did not subscribe to a single set of principles, all believed that a work of literature had to be examined as an object in itself through a process of close analysis of symbol, image, and metaphor. Tate's vision of the purpose of literature differed from that of other New Critics. A conservative thinker and convert to Catholicism, Tate attacked the tradition of Western philosophy, which he felt had alienated people from themselves, one another, and from nature by divorcing intellectual from natural functions in human life. In the following discussion of the* Biographia Literaria, *Tate proposes that its theme is "a deep illness of the modern mind." Further, Tate points out the central conflict in Coleridge's poetic principles: that Coleridge "cannot make up his mind whether the specifically poetic element is an objective feature of the poem, or is distinguishable only as a subjective effect."*]

The famous Chapter XIV of *Biographia Literaria* has been the background of the criticism of poetry for more than a hundred years. Its direct influence has been very great; its indirect influence, through Poe upon Baudelaire, and through the French symbolists down to contemporary English and American poets, has perhaps been even greater. This chapter is the most influential statement on poetry ever formulated by an English critic: its insights, when we have them, are ours, and ours too its contradictions. Yet the remarkable "definition" of poetry, which I shall now quote, is not, as we shall presently see, the chief source of the aesthetic dilemma that we inherit today. (That source is another passage.) Here is the definition:

> A poem is that species of composition, which is opposed to works of science, by proposing for its *immediate* object pleasure, not truth; and from all other species—(having this object in common with it)—it is distinguished by proposing to itself such delight from the *whole,* as is compatible with a distinct gratification from each component *part.*

Much of the annoyance and misunderstanding caused by this passage has not been Coleridge's fault; but is rather due to the failure of literary men to observe the accurate use of *species.* For Coleridge is giving us a strict Aristotelian definition of a *species* within a given *genus.* It is not a qualitative statement, and it does not answer the question: *What* is poetry? The *whatness* of poetry does not come within the definition; and I believe that nowhere else does Coleridge offer us an explicit qualitative distinction between poetry and other "species of composition" which may be "opposed" to it.

For what is Coleridge saying? (I have never seen a literal reading of the passage by any critic.) There is the generic division: composition. A poem is a species within the genus; but so is a work of science. How are the two species distinguished? By their immediate objects. It is curious that Coleridge phrases the passage as if a poem were a person "proposing" to himself a certain end, pleasure; so for *object* we have got to read *effect.* A poem, then, differs from a work of science in its immediate effect upon us; and that immediate effect is pleasure. But other species of composition may aim at the effect of pleasure. A poem differs from these in the relation of part to whole: the parts must give us a distinct pleasure, moment by moment, and they are not to be conceived as subordinate to the whole; they make up the whole.

If there is an objective relation of part to whole, Coleridge does not say what it is; nor does he distinguish that relation in terms of any specific poetic work. It is strictly a quantitative analogy taken, perhaps, from geometry. And the only purpose it serves is this: in the paragraph following the "definition" he goes on to say that "the philosophic critics of all ages coincide" in asserting that beautiful, isolated lines or distichs are not a poem, and that neither is "an unsustained composition" of uninteresting parts a *"legitimate* poem." What we have here, then, is a sound but ordinary critical insight; but because it is merely an extension of the pleasure principle implicit in the "definition," we are not prepared by it to distinguish objectively a poem from any other form of expression. The distinction lies in the effect, and it is a psychological effect. In investigating the differentia of poetry . . . we are eventually led away from the poem into what has been known since Coleridge's time as the psychology of poetry.

The difficulties of this theory Coleridge seems not to have been aware of; yet he illustrates them perfectly. In the second paragraph after the famous definition he writes this remarkable passage:

> The first chapter of Isaiah—(indeed a very large portion of the whole book)—is poetry in the most emphatic sense; yet it would be no less irrational than strange to assert, that pleasure, not truth, was the immediate object of the prophet. In short, whatever specific import we attach to the word, Poetry, there will be found involved in it, as a necessary consequence, that a poem of any length neither can be, nor ought to be, all poetry. Yet if an harmonious whole is to be produced, the remaining parts must be preserved in keeping with the poetry; and this can no otherwise be effected than by such a studied selection and artificial arrangement, as will partake of one, though not a peculiar property of poetry. And this again can be no other than the property of exciting a more continuous and equal attention than the language of prose aims at, whether colloquial or written.

This is probably the most confused statement ever uttered by a great critic, and it has probably done more damage to critical thought than anything else said by any critic. Isaiah is poetry in "the most emphatic sense," although his immediate object (effect) is truth. It will be observed that, whereas in the definition our attention is drawn to a species of composition, a poem, we are here confronted with the personage, Isaiah, who does have the power of proposing an object; and Isaiah's immediate object is truth. But are we to suppose that the effect of the poem and the object of the prophet are to be apprehended in the same way? Is our experience of truth the same as our experience of pleasure? If there is a difference between truth and pleasure, and if an immediate effect of pleasure is the specific "property" of poetry (how a property can be an effect it is difficult to see), how can the first chapter of Isaiah be poetry at all? It cannot be, looked at in these terms; and as a matter of fact Coleridge rather slyly withdraws his compliment to Isaiah when he goes on to say that a "poem of any length neither can be, nor ought to be, all poetry." (pp. 45-9)

Coleridge's theory of meter is not quite pertinent here: in the later and more elaborate discussion of meter in **Biographia Literaria** there is the general conclusion that meter is indispensable to poetry. In Chapter XIV, now being examined, he speaks of meter as "an artificial arrangement . . . not a peculiar property of poetry."

There is, then, in Coleridge's poetic theory a persistent dilemma. *He cannot make up his mind whether the specifically poetic element is an objective feature of the poem, or is distinguishable only as a subjective effect.* He cannot, in short, choose between metaphysics and psychology. His general emphasis is psychological, with metaphysical ambiguities.

The distinction between Fancy and Imagination is ultimately a psychological one (see excerpt above, 1817): he discusses the problem in terms of separate faculties, and the objective poetical properties, presumably resulting from the use of these faculties, are never defined, but are given only occasional illustration. (I have in mind his magnificent analysis of "Venus and Adonis," the value of which lies less perhaps in the critical principles he supposes he is illustrating, than in the perfect taste with which he selects the good passages for admiration.) When Coleridge speaks of the "esemplastic power" of the Imagination, it is always a "faculty" of the mind, not an objective poetic order. When he says that a poem gives us "a more than usual state of emotion with more than usual order," we acknowledge the fact, without being able to discern in the merely comparative degree of the adjective the fundamental difference between the poetic and the philosophic powers which Coleridge frequently asserts, but which he nowhere objectively establishes. The psychological bias of his "system" is perfectly revealed in this summary passage of Chapter XIV:

> My own conclusions on the nature of poetry, in the strictest use of the word, have been in part anticipated in some of the remarks on the Fancy and Imagination in the early part of this work. What is poetry?—is so nearly the same question with, what is a poet?—that the answer to the one is involved in the solution to the other. For it is a distinction resulting from the poetic genius itself, which sustains and modifies the images, thoughts, and emotions of the poet's own mind.

There can be little doubt that Coleridge's failure to get out of the dilemma of Intellect-or-Feeling has been passed on to us as a fatal legacy. If the first object of poetry is an effect, and if that effect is pleasure, does it not necessarily follow that truth and knowledge may be better set forth in some other order altogether? . . . The coherent part of Coleridge's theory is the fatal dilemma that I have described. Truth is only the secondary consideration of the poet, and from the point of view of positivism the knowledge, or truth, that poetry give us is immature and inadequate. What of the primary consideration of the poet—pleasure?

Pleasure is the single qualitative feature of Coleridge's famous definition; but it is not *in* the definition objectively. And with the development of modern psychology it has ceased to be qualitative, even subjectively. It is a *response*. The fate of Coleridge's system, then, has been its gradual extinction in the terminology of experimental psychology. The poetry has been extinguished in the poet. (pp. 49-51)

> *Allen Tate, "Literature As Knowledge," in his* Reason in Madness: Critical Essays, *G. P. Putnam's Sons, 1941, p. 20-61.*

G. WILSON KNIGHT   (essay date 1941)

[Knight is primarily known for his Shakespearean criticism, which helped shape the twentieth-century reaction against the biographical and character studies of the nineteenth-century Shakespeareans. In The Starlit Dome: Studies in the Poetry of Vision, *from which the following excerpt is drawn, Knight focuses on various aspects of imagery. His discussions of symbolism are, in fact, considered similar to Coleridge's notion of the symbolic as indefinite with multiple meanings. According to Knight, a poem often has a completely different meaning than the one intended, or understood, by its poet. Here, Knight discusses the central images in Coleridge's poetry and relates them to various Christian symbols.]*

Within a narrow range [**Christabel, The Ancient Mariner,** and **Kubla Khan**] show an intensity comparable with that of Dante and Shakespeare. As with those, strong human feeling mixes with stern awareness of evil, without artistic confusions. Coleridge's main negation tends to a subjective sin-fear: his use of *fear* is, indeed, the secret of his uncanny power, this being the most forceful medium for riveting poetic attention.

Christabel is one nightmare; so, pretty nearly, is *The Ancient Mariner;* and *Kubla Khan* at one point strikes terror. Coleridge is expert in nightmarish, yet fascinating, experience. The human imagination can curl to rest, as in a warm bed, among horrors that would strike pallor in actual life, perhaps recognizing some unknown release, or kinship: as in Wordsworth, who, however, never shows the nervous *tension* of Coleridge. These three poems, moreover, may be grouped as a little *Divina Commedia* exploring in turn Hell, Purgatory, and Paradise.

Christabel is akin to *Macbeth.* There is darkness (though moon-lit), the owl, the restless mastiff. There is sleep and silence broken by fearsome sounds. The mastiff's howl is touched with deathly horror: 'some say she sees my lady's shroud'. Opposed to the nightmarish are images of religious grace. This first part is strangely feminine; the mastiff is a 'bitch', the heroine set between Geraldine and the spirit of her own mother as forces of evil and grace respectively. 'Mary Mother' and 'Jesu Maria' find a natural home in the phraseology. Some sort of sexual desecration, some expressly physical horror, is revealed by Geraldine's undressing. She insinuates herself into Christabel's religious, mother-watched, world; she is mortally afraid of the mother-spirit and addresses her invisible presence with extreme dramatic intensity. As so often a seemingly sexual evil is contrasted with a parental good, yet Geraldine gets her opportunity through Christabel's charity, and when she lies with her is imaged as a mother with a child. Some hideous replacing of a supreme good is being shadowed, with an expression of utter surprise, especially in the conclusion to Part I, that so pure a girl can have contact with so obscene an horror. It is something Christabel cannot confess: she is powerless to tell her father. She is under a spell. The evil is nerve-freezing yet fascinating. There is vivid use of light in the tongue of flame shooting from the dying brands, and before that Geraldine's first appearance in the moonlight is glitteringly pictured. Stealth, silence, and sleep are broken by sudden, fearful, sound. In Part II we get perhaps the most intense and nightmarish use of the recurring serpent-image in our literature: both in Bracy's dream of Christabel as a 'sweet bird' (the usual opposite) with a 'bright green snake' coiled round it and Christabel's tranced hissing later, mesmerized by 'shrunken' serpent eyes. The poem expresses fear of some nameless obscenity. Christabel, we gather, has a lover, but he is of slight importance in the poem as we have it, though there is reason to suppose the conflict between him and Geraldine was to have been made dramatically explicit.

Christabel helps our understanding of *The Ancient Mariner,* which describes the irruption into the natural human festivity of a wedding party of the Mariner's story of sin, loneliness, and purgatorial redemption. These somewhat Wordsworthian elements are set against the 'merry din', the 'loud bassoon'. The wedding guest is agonizedly torn from human, and especially sexual, normality and conviviality.

The story starts with a voyage into 'the land of ice and of fearful sounds'. There is snow and fog. From this the Albatross saves them: it is as 'a Christian soul'. Its snowy whiteness would naturally grip Coleridge: he is fascinated by whiteness. The bird seems to suggest some redeeming Christ-like force in creation that guides humanity from primitive and fearful origins. Anyway, the central crime is the slaying of it and by their wavering thoughts the crew 'make themselves accomplices'; and the dead bird is finally hung round the Mariner's neck 'instead of the cross' as a sign of guilt. Indeed, the slaying of the Albatross in the Mariner's story may correspond to the death of Christ in racial history. It is, moreover, an act of

unmotivated and wanton, semi-sadistic, destruction, explicitly called 'hellish'. As a result the ship is calmed in a tropic sea. Parching heat replaces icy cold. The 'land of ice and snow' may be allowed to suggest primeval racial sufferings or primitive layers in the psychology of man; and yet also, perhaps, something more distant still, realms of ultimate and mysterious being beyond nature as we know it, and of a supreme, if inhuman, purity and beauty. The central crime corresponds to the fall, a thwarting of some guiding purpose by murderous self-will, or to loss of innocence in the maturing personality, and the consequent suffering under heat to man's present mental state. In poetic language you may say that whereas water parallels 'instinct' (with here a further reach in 'ice and snow' suggesting original mysteries of the distant and primeval), flames, fire, and light hold a more intellectual suggestion: they are instinct becoming self-conscious, leading to many agonies and high aspirations. The bird was a nature-force, eating human food, we are told, for the first time: it is that in nature which helps man beyond nature, an aspect of the divine purpose. Having slain it, man is plunged in burning agony. The thirst impressions recall Eliot's *Waste Land,* which describes a very similar experience. The new mode is knowledge of evil, symbolized in the 'rotting' ocean, the 'slimy things' that crawl on it, the 'death-fires' and 'witches oils' burning by night. It is a lurid, colourful, yet ghastly death-impregnated scene, drawn to express aversion from physical life in dissolution or any reptilian manifestation; and, by suggestion, the sexual as seen from the mentalized consciousness as an alien, salty, and reptilian force. It is a deathly paralysis corresponding, it may be, to a sense of sexually starved existence in the modern world: certainly 'water, water everywhere, nor any drop to drink' fits such a reading.

Next comes the death-ship. 'Nightmare Life-in-Death' wins the Mariner's soul. This conception relates to deathly tonings in literature generally, the *Hamlet* experience, and the metaphorical 'death' of Wordsworth's *Immortality Ode.* It is, significantly, a feminine harlot-like figure, and is neatly put beside Death itself. She 'begins her work' on the Mariner. The other sailors all die: observe how he is to endure *knowledge* of death, with guilt. He is 'alone on a wide wide sea' in the dark night of the soul; so lonely—compare Wordsworth's solitaries—that God Himself seemed absent. The universe is one of 'beautiful men dead and slimy things' alive, as in Shelley's *Alastor.* The 'rotting sea' is now directly associated with the 'rotting dead', while he remains eternally cursed by the dead men's 'eyes'. At the extremity of despair and therefore self-less feeling, his eyes are suddenly aware of the beauty of the 'water-snakes' as he watches their rich colours and fiery tracks: 'O happy living things'. The exquisite prose accompaniment runs: 'By the light of the moon he beholdeth God's creatures of the great calm'. A fertilizing 'spring of love' gushes from his 'heart' and he blesses them *'unaware'*—the crucial word is repeated—with unpremeditated recognition and instinctive charity. Immediately the Albatross slips from him and sinks like lead into the sea. An utterly organic and unforced forgiveness of God conditions God's forgiveness of man.

The exact psychological or other conceptual equivalents of poetic symbolism cannot be settled. If they could, there would be no occasion for such symbols, and my use of the term 'sexual' might seem rash to anyone unaware of the general relation of snakes and water to sexual instincts in poetry, as in *Antony and Cleopatra* and Eliot's use of water and sea-life. Christabel's enforced and unhappy silence whilst under Geraldine's serpent spell may be directly related to the water-snakes of *The Ancient Mariner.* She, like the becalmed ship, is helpless; perhaps, in her story too, until a certain frontier, involving spontaneous, but not willed, recognition, is reached. Just as she cannot speak, that is, confess, so the Mariner, when, as it were, saved, spends the rest of his life confessing.

The immediate results of conversion are (i) gentle sleep after feverish and delirious horror, and (ii) refreshing rain after parching heat. These are imaginative equivalents and may be said to touch the concept of *agapé* as opposed to *eros,* and are here logically related to Christian symbols. A sense of purity and freedom replaces horror and sin. Energy is at once released: the wind blows and the dead rise and work, their bodies being used by a 'troop of spirits blest', who next make music, clustering into a circle, with suggestion of Dante's paradisal lives. Now the ship starts to move like Eliot's similar ships in *The Waste Land* and *Ash Wednesday;* yet no wind, but rather the 'lonesome spirit from the South-pole', is causing the motion, and demanding vengeance still. Why? and who is he? Coleridge's prose definition scarcely helps. He works 'nine fathom' deep—in man or creation, at once instinct and accuser, and not quite stilled by conversion. At last he is placated by the Mariner's penance. Next '*angelic*' power' drives on the ship. There is more trouble from the dead men's eyes and another release. As the ship draws near home, each body has a burning seraph upright above it. These seraphic forms that twice seem conditioned by dead bodies, yet not, as individuals, precisely the 'souls' of the men concerned, must, I think, be vaguely identified with the concept of human immortality, the extra dimension of their upright stature over the bodies being pictorially cogent.

At home there is the 'kirk', the woodland 'hermit', and safety. After such fiery experience the normality of the hermit's life, its homely and earthy quality, is emphasized. We meet his 'cushion' of 'moss' and 'oak-stump' and his daily prayers. He is a figure of unstriving peace such as Wordsworth sought, associated with earth and solid fact after nightmare and transcendent vision. Extreme sensual and spiritual adventure has brought only agony. Therefore:

> O sweeter than the marriage-feast,
> 'Tis sweeter far to me,
> To walk together to the kirk
> With a goodly company.

It is an embracing of *agapé* with a definitely lower place, if not a rejection, accorded to *eros;* a welcoming of earth and refreshing rain ('the gentle rain from heaven' is an *agapé*-phrase in Shakespeare) with a rejection of the sun in its drawing, tormenting, heat. I doubt if there is any relieving synthesis implicit in the 'youths and maidens' that go to church at the end of the poem with the Wordsworthian 'old men and babes': the balance is scarcely in favour of youthful assertion. The final lesson is a total acceptance of God and his universe through humility, with general love to man and beast. But the specifically sexual is left unplaced: the wedding-guest is sadder and wiser henceforth, and presumably avoids all festive gatherings from now on; though forgiveness of *reptilian* manifestation remains basic.

This is Coleridge's *Purgatorio,* as **Christabel** is a fragmentary attempt at a little *Inferno.* Whether we can call the central criminal act 'sexual' is arguable; it certainly resembles that in Wordsworth's *Hart-leap Well,* but the Mariner's compulsion to tell his tale suggests rather Eliot's Sweeney and his grim account. One might notice that the imaginative tonings in *Lu-*

crece and *Macbeth* are identical, and that 'sadism' may be only a conscious recognition of a deeper relation than has yet been plumbed: motiveless cruelty is, moreover, a general and most valuable poetic theme, as in Heathcliff's ill-treatment of a dog. Such thoughts help to integrate into the whole the mystery of an unmotivated action which, with the South-pole spirit itself, is left rationally undefined, as Shakespeare leaves the motives of Macbeth and Iago and the pain of Hamlet rationally undefined. The new life comes from acceptance of the watery and the reptilian, at which the sea no longer appears to be 'rotting', that is, dead, though all these drop out of the picture afterwards. The crime, together with rejection of the unrefreshing 'rotting sea' and its creatures, brings parched agony, but acceptance of those brings the other, heavenly and refreshing, water of rain. Also acceptance precedes repentance, not vice versa. A spontaneous, unsought, upspring of love alone conditions the down-flow of grace.

The poem is lively and colourful, as A. C. Bradley has well emphasized. The movement and appearance of sun and moon are described in stanza after stanza; and stars too. The sun peeps in and out as though uncertain whether or not to give its blessing on the strange scene. The poem glitters: the Mariner holds the Wedding Guest with a 'glittering eye', which, if remembered with his 'skinny hand', preserves a neat balance. The light is somewhat ghastly: as in the strange sheen of it on ice or tropic calm, and the witches' oils burning 'green and blue and white'. Green light is a favourite in Coleridge (cp. in **Dejection** 'that green light that lingers in the west'). The snakes move in 'tracks of shining white', making 'elfish' illumination. Their colours are 'blue, glossy-green and velvet black' and by night their every motion pencils 'a flash of golden fire'. The ghost-ship comes barred across the blood-red sun. The 'charmed water' is said to burn 'a still and awful red'. There is a very subtle interplay of light and colour. The Life-in-Death figure is a garish whore with red lips, yellow hair, white leprosy skin; the evil creatures are colourful; the supernatural seraphs brilliant. The whole is dominated by a fearful intensity summed in the image, rather dark for this poem, of a night-walker aware of a demon following his steps. But the play of light and colour helps to give the somewhat stringy stanza succession and thinly narrative, undramatic sequence of events a certain intangible poetic mass. I doubt if the rhyme-links, the metrical rhythms, even the phrase-life, so to speak, would be considered fine poetry without this and, what is equally important, the substance of idea and meaning we have been analysing.

The strangeness and ghastly yet fascinating lights of the experience must guide our judgement of the solution. The experience is of fearful fascination; a feverish horror that is half a positive delight, mental pre-eminently; and the return is a return to earth, the hermits' cell and mossy stone, a return to reality and sanity. Whatever our views of the implied doctrine there is no artistic confusion or lack of honesty. The balancing of symbols, as in the contrast of bird-life and the reptilian, is subtle as Dante's (the *Purgatorio* has a very similarly reiterated observation of the sun in varied position and mood) and Shakespeare's, though without the massive scheme of the one or the sympathetic range of the other. It is a little poem greatly conceived. The supernatural figures dicing for the Mariner's soul suggest, inexactly, the balancing of the Eumenides against Apollo in respect of Orestes in Aeschylus; while the 'lonesome spirit' from the South Pole in its office of accuser performs exactly the function of those Eumenides, furies of guilt and accusation. It is replaced eventually by swift angelic power, as in Eliot's *Family Reunion* the furies of *Sweeney Agonistes* turn into angels.

Poetry of any worth is a rounded solidity which drops shadows only on the flat surfaces of philosophical statement. Concretely it bodies forth symbols of which our ghostly concepts of 'life', 'death', 'time', 'eternity', 'immortality' are only very pallid analogies. They are none the less necessary, if we are to enchain our normal thinking to the creations of great literature, and I next translate the domed symbolism of **Kubla Khan** into such shadow-terms corresponding to the original in somewhat the same way as the science of Christian theology corresponds, or should correspond, to the New Testament.

The pleasure-dome dominates. But its setting is carefully described and very important. There is a 'sacred' river that runs into 'caverns measureless to man' and a 'sunless sea'. That is, the river runs into an infinity of death. The marked-out area through which it flows is, however, one of teeming nature: gardens, rills, 'incense-bearing' trees, ancient forests. This is not unlike Dante's earthly paradise. The river is 'sacred'. Clearly a sacred river which runs through nature towards death will in some sense correspond to life. I take the river to be, as so often in Wordsworth (whose *Immortality Ode* is also throughout suggested), a symbol of life.

Born on a *height,* it descends from a 'deep romantic chasm', a place 'savage', 'holy', and 'enchanted', associated with both a 'waning moon' and a 'woman wailing for her demon lover'. The river's origin blends romantic, sacred, and satanic suggestions. Whatever our views on sex it would be idle to suppose them anything but a tangle of inconsistencies. Moreover, the idea of original sin, the 'old serpent', and its relation to sex is not only Biblical but occurs in myth and poetry ancient and modern. We have not yet compassed the straightforward sanity on this vital issue which D. H. Lawrence said would, if attained, make both nasty sex stories and romantic idealisms alike unnecessary: a certain obscene and savage sex-desecration seems to have fixed itself as a disease in the human mind. That is why we find the virgin-symbol, in both paganism and Christianity, sublimated; especially the virgin mother. Sex is overlaid with both high romantic and low satanic conceptions, complexities, fears, taboos, and worship of all sorts, but the necessity and goodness of pure creativeness no one questions. Our lines here hint a mystery, not altogether unlike Wordsworth's dark grandeurs, blending satanism with sanctity and romance with savagery. They express that mystic glamour of sex that conditions human creation and something of its pagan evil magic; and touch the enigma of the creator-god beyond good and evil, responsible for eagle and boa-constrictor alike.

Whatever our minds make of them, sex-forces have their way. Nature goes on cheerily blasting families and uniting true lovers in matrimonial bonds of 'perdurable toughness', with an equal efficiency working through rake and curate alike, and not caring for details so long as her work be done, Goethe's poetry well presents this seething, torrential, over-mastering creative energy. Look now at our next lines: at the 'ceaseless turmoil', the earth-mother breathing in 'fast thick pants', the fountain 'forced' out with 'half intermitted burst', the fragments rebounding like hail, the 'chaffy grain beneath the flail', the 'dancing rocks'. What riotous impression of agony, tumult, and power: the dynamic enginery of birth and creation. (pp. 83-92)

I come now to the latter movement of our poem, whose form is not unlike an expansion of the Petrarchan Sonnet. This is the sestet. Observe that the metre changes: a lilting happy motion, a shimmering dance motion, replaces heavy resonance and reverberation. Our minds are tuned to a new apprehension, something at once assured, happy, and musical. A higher state of consciousness is suggested: and see what it shows us.

The dome's *shadow* falls half-way along the river, which is, we remember, the birth-death time-stream. This shadow—a Wordsworthian impression—is cast by a higher, more dimensional reality such as I have deduced from other poets to be the pictured quality of immortality. It is directly associated with the 'mingled measure' of the sounds coming from the two extremes. In Wordsworth, and elsewhere, immortality may be associated closely with birth, though that is by way of a provisional and preliminary approach to the greater truth; while in our own thinking it is found most often to function in terms of a life after death. But both are finally unsatisfying; birth and death are both mysteries that time-thinking distorts, and personal life beyond their limits a somewhat tenuous concept. The true immortality is extra-dimensional to all this: it is the *pleasure-dome itself,* arching solid and firm above creation's mazy progress and the 'mingled' sounds of its conflicts, just as in Wordsworth the child's immortality is said to 'brood' over it 'like the day': that is, arching, expansive, immovable.

The 'mingled-measure' suggests the blend and marriage of fundamental oppositions: life and death, or creation and destruction. These 'mingle' under the shadow of the greater harmony, the crowning dome-circle. Observe that it is a paradoxical thing, a 'miracle of rare device'; 'sunny', but with 'caves of ice', which points the resolution of antinomies in the new dimension, especially those of light and heat, for Eros-fires of the mind; and ice, for the coldness of inorganic nature, ultimate being, and death, the ice-caves being perhaps related to our earlier caverns, only more optimistically toned; light instead of gloomy, just as 'sunny' suggests no torturing heat. The 'caves of ice' may also hint cool cavernous depths in the unconscious mind (a usual Wordsworthian cave-association) blending with a *lighted* intelligence: whereby at last coldness becomes kind. These, ice and sun-fire, are the two elemental antitheses of *The Ancient Mariner,* and their mingling may lead us farther. We are at what might be called a marriage-point in life's progress half-way between birth and death: and even birth and death are themselves here mingled or married. We may imagine a sexual union between life, the masculine, and death, the feminine. Then our 'romantic chasm' and 'cedarn cover', the savage and enchanted yet holy place with its 'half intermitted burst' may be, in spite of our former reading, vaguely related to the functioning of a man's creative organs and their physical setting and, too, to all principles of manly and adventurous action; while the caverns that engulf the sacred river will be correspondingly feminine with a dark passivity and infinite peace. The pleasure-dome we may fancy as the pleasure of a sexual union in which birth and death are the great contesting partners, with human existence as the life-stream, the blood-stream, of a mighty coition. The poet glimpses that for which no direct words exist: the sparkling dome of some vast intelligence enjoying that union of opposites which to man appears conflict unceasing and mazed wandering pain between mystery and mystery.

I would leave a space after 'caves of ice'. I am not now so sure about the sonnet form: those six lines are central. So next we have our third and final movement, starting with the Abyssinian damsel seen in a vision playing music. The aptness of a girl-image here is obvious. In Shakespeare and Milton music suggests that consciousness which blends rational antinomies, and so our poet equates the once-experienced mystic and girl-born music with his dome. Could he revive in himself that music he would build the spiritual dome 'in air'; that is, I think, in words, in poetry. Or, maybe, he would become himself the domed consciousness of a cold, happy, brilliance, an ice-flashing, sun-smitten, wisdom. The analogy between music and some form of architecture is not solitary: it receives a fine expression in Browning's *Abt Vogler,* a valuable commentary on **Kubla Khan.** The analogy is natural enough for either music or poetry: we talk of architectonics in criticizing poetry or a novel, for the very reason that literary or musical art bears to rational thought the relation of a solid, or at least an area, to a line. Tennyson's *Palace of Art* is a direct analogy, and Wordsworth compares his life's work to a 'Gothic Church'.

The poem's movement now grows ecstatic and swift. There is a hint of a new speed in the drawn-out rhythm of 'To such a deep delight 'twould win me . . .'. Now the three rhymed lines gather up the poet's message together with his consciousness of its supreme meaning with a breathless expectancy toward crescendo. Next follows a fall to a ritualistic solemnity, a Nunc Dimittis, phrased in long vowels and stately measured motion, imaged in the 'circle' and the eyes dropped in 'holy dread' before the prophet who has seen and re-created 'Paradise': not the earthly, but the heavenly paradise; the 'stately' permanence above motion, the pleasure-dome enclosing and transcending human agony and frustration. To tune out understanding we might go to such a passage as Wordsworth's:

> incumbencies more awful, visitings
> Of the Upholder of the tranquil soul,
> That tolerates the indignities of Time,
> And, from the centre of Eternity
> All finite motions overruling, lives
> In glory immutable.　　(*The Prelude,* III. 116)

Which transmits a similar recognition.

Kubla Khan is a comprehensive creation, including and transcending not only the dualisms of **The Ancient Mariner** ('sun', 'ice', and sexual suggestions recurring with changed significance) but also the more naturalistic, Wordsworthian, grandeurs. Though outwardly concentrating on an architectural synthesis, it has too another, mountainous, elevation suggested in Mount Abora; and indeed the dome itself is a kind of mountain with 'caves', the transcendent and the natural being blended, as so often in Wordsworth. It must be related to other similar statements of an ultimate intuition where the circular or architectural supervenes on the natural: in particular to the mystic dome of Yeats's *Byzantium.* The blend here of a circular symbolism with a human figure (the Abyssinian maid) and images of human conflict may be compared both to Dante's final vision and an important passage in Shelley's *Prometheus.* **Kubla Khan** is classed usually with **Christabel** and **The Ancient Mariner,** both profound poems with universal implications. The one presents a nightmare vision related to some obscene but nameless sex-horror; the other symbolizes a clear pilgrim's progress (we may remember Coleridge's admiration of Bunyan's work) through sin to redemption. It would be strange if **Kubla Khan,** incorporating together the dark satanism and the water-purgatory of those, did not, like its sister poems, hold a comparable, or greater, profundity, its images clearly belonging to the same order of poetic reasoning. Its very names are so lettered as to suggest first and last things: Xanadu, Kubla Khan, Alph, Abyssinian, Abora. 'A' is emphatic; Xanadu, which starts the poem, is enclosed in letters that might well be called

eschatological; while Kubla Khan himself sits alphabetically central with his alliterating 'k's. Wordsworth's line 'of first, and last, and midst, and without end', occurring in a mountain-passage (*The Prelude,* VI. 640) of somewhat similar scope, may be compared. The poem's supposed method of composition is well known. How it comes to form so compact and satisfying a unit raises questions outside the scheme of my study. The poem, anyway, needs no defence. It has a barbaric and oriental magnificence that asserts itself with a happy power and authenticity too often absent from visionary poems set within the Christian tradition. (pp. 93-7)

> *G. Wilson Knight, "Coleridge's Divine Comedy,"*
> *in his* The Starlit Dome: Studies in the Poetry of
> Vision, *1941. Reprint by Barnes & Noble Inc., 1960,*
> *pp. 83-178.*

ROBERT PENN WARREN　(essay date 1946)

[*Warren is considered one of the most distinguished men of letters in America today. His criticism is closely associated with two critical movements, the Agrarians and the New Critics. The Agrarians were concerned with political and social issues as well as literature, and were dedicated to preserving the Southern way of life and traditional Southern values. The New Critics comprised one of the most influential critical movements of the mid-twentieth century. Although the various New Critics did not subscribe to a single set of principles, all believed that a work of literature had to be examined as an object in itself through a process of close analysis of symbol, image, and metaphor. Warren's work is strongly regional in character, often drawing its inspiration from the land, the people, and the history of the South. While he often bases his themes on specific historical events, Warren successfully tran-*

A portrait of Coleridge in 1799.

scends the local to comment in universal terms on the human condition. Warren's deep interest in history and his conception that art is a vital force in contemporary society inform all his work. In Warren's influential reading of "The Ancient Mariner," he argues that John Livingston Lowes (see excerpt above, 1927) has misinterpreted the poem. Lowes rejects the relevance of the poem's moral because of what Warren terms "a literal rather than a symbolic interpretation." Unlike Lowes, Warren contends that the poem has a primary and a secondary theme which are finally fused. The following excerpt deals with Warren's explication of the primary theme, which he terms "the theme of sacramental vision, or the theme of the 'One Life'." The secondary theme, that of the imagination, is "concerned with the context of values in which the fable is presented." Warren proposes that without an acknowledgement of the two themes of the poem, the work is unintelligible.]

What [**The Ancient Mariner**] amounts to seems to be this: (1) Coleridge introduces a theme into his poem merely as a structural device—he did not intend for it to be taken seriously. (2) We would not take it seriously anyway because it violates our moral sense—a man should not have to suffer so much just for shooting a bird.

These pronouncements lead me to a further statement concerning my purpose here: I shall try to establish that the statement which the poem does ultimately make is thoroughly consistent with Coleridge's basic theological and philosophical views as given to us in sober prose, and that, without regard to the question of the degree of self-consciousness on the part of the poet at any given moment of composition, the theme is therefore "intended." I shall also try to establish that the particular ground given by Lowes for the rejection of the relevance of the "moral" is based on a misreading of the poem—a reading which insists on a literal rather than a symbolic interpretation. (p. 65)

Coleridge presumably did connect his poem with dreams.... And we can well believe that a good deal of the *material* for the poem may have come from the poet's opium dreams. But the fact that Coleridge himself made this association between the poem and dreams does little to support the view that he thought of the poem as having no theme with a reference to reality. Coleridge's notion concerning dreams forbids that interpretation. (pp. 65-6)

I am inclined to believe that [Lowes and his school of readers] take the word imagination [in Coleridge's response to Mrs. Barbauld (see excerpt above, 1830)] at their own convenience and not in Coleridge's context and usage. They take it, as a matter of fact, in the casual and vulgar sense, as equivalent to meaninglessness or illusion, or if they don't take it in the casual and vulgar sense, they take it in terms of a poetic theory of illusion for illusion's sake which, as stated, denies significance to the word as fully as does the casual and vulgar sense. But actually, a moment's reflection instructs us that the word was for Coleridge freighted with a burden of speculation and technical meaning. His theory of the imagination, upon which his whole art-philosophy hinges, "was primarily the vindication of a particular attitude to life and reality." And it would be strange if Coleridge, with his lifelong passion for accuracy of terminology and subtlety of distinction, had tossed away that sacred word which stood for the vindication of his most fundamental beliefs as irresponsibly as the merchant in the story of *The Arabian Nights* tosses away the "date shell."

But we must ask here what is the burden of technical meaning with which Coleridge had freighted the word. At the moment we shall not be concerned with a detailed exposition of Cole-

ridge's theory, and certainly not with an account of the stages of its growth and clarification. We shall be, instead, concerned to see how Coleridge's concept would redeem works of pure imagination from the charge, amiable or otherwise, of being in themselves meaningless and nothing but refined and ingenious toys for an idle hour.

The key passage for this purpose is the famous one from the *Biographia Literaria* [see excerpt above, 1817], but we shall group around it other passages drawn from various sources. Here is the key passage:

> The Imagination then I consider either as primary or secondary. The primary Imagination I hold to be the living power and prime agent of all human perception, and as a repetition in the finite mind of the eternal act of creation in the infinite I Am. The secondary Imagination I consider as an echo of the former, coexisting with the conscious will, yet still as identical with the primary in the kind of its agency, and differing only in degree and in the mode of its operation. It dissolves, diffuses, dissipates in order to recreate: or where this process is rendered impossible, yet still at all events it struggles to idealize and to unify.

It is the primary imagination which creates our world, for nothing of which we are aware is given to the passive mind. By it we know the world, but for Coleridge knowing is making, for, "To know is in its very essence a verb active." We know by creating, and one of the things we create is the Self, for a subject is that which "becomes a subject by the act of constructing itself objectively to itself; but which never is an object except for itself, and only so far as by the very same act it becomes a subject." ... Coleridge attributes to imagination this fundamental significance.

But we have been speaking only of what he calls primary imagination, the perception which produces our ordinary world of the senses. Even here we can observe that when "the imagination is conceived as recognizing the inherent interdependence of subject and object (or complementary aspects of a single reality), its dignity is immeasurably raised." But when we turn to his interpretation of the secondary imagination, that dignity is further enhanced. For here we leave creation at the unconscious and instinctive level and define it as coexisting with, and in terms of, the conscious will; here it operates as a function of that freedom which is the essential attribute of spirit.... Reason, as opposed to the understanding, is, in Coleridge's system, the organ whereby man achieves the "intuition and spiritual consciousness of God," and the imagination operates to read Nature in the light of that consciousness, to read it as a symbol of God. It might be said that reason shows us God, and imagination shows us how Nature participates in God.

So, if we look at the phrase, a work of "pure imagination," in the light of Coleridge's theory of the imagination, we see that such a work would be one which not only, to borrow from Coleridge's portrait of the ideal poet, "brings the whole soul of man into activity, with the subordination of its faculties to each other according to their relative worth and dignity," and makes of the reader himself a "creative being" in the image of God, but also gives us a revelation, for "all truth is a species of Revelation." And so that phrase "pure imagination" as applied to **The Ancient Mariner** gives us little excuse to read the poem as an agreeable but scarcely meaningful effusion. (pp. 66-9)

If *The Ancient Mariner* has a meaning, what is that meaning?

It is true that a poem may mean a number of different things. By this I do not intend to say that a poem means different things to different readers. This is, of course, true in one sense, but true, first, only in so far as the poet fails, as fail he must in some degree, in the exercise of his creative control, and second, in so far as each reader must, as a result of his own history and nature, bring to the poem a different mass of experience, strength of intellect, and intensity of feeling. In this second sense we may say that the reader does not interpret the poem but the poem interprets the reader. We may say that the poem is the light and not the thing seen by the light. The poem is the light by which the reader may view and review all the area of experience with which he is acquainted. (pp. 69-70)

In *The Ancient Mariner* I wish to distinguish two basic themes, both of them very rich and provocative, and I shall, in the course of my discussion, attempt to establish their interrelation.

One theme I shall call *primary*, the other *secondary*. I do not mean to imply that one is more important than the other. But the one which I shall call primary is more obviously presented to us, is, as it were, at the threshold of the poem. The primary theme may be defined as the issue of the fable (or of the situation or discourse if we are applying this kind of analysis to a poem which does not present a fable). The primary theme does not necessarily receive a full statement. In fact, in *The Ancient Mariner* it receives only a kind of coy and dramatically naïve understatement which serves merely as a clue—"He prayeth best, etc." But the theme thus hinted at is the outcome of the fable taken at its face value as a story of crime and punishment and reconciliation. I shall label the primary theme in this poem as the theme of sacramental vision, or the theme of the "One Life." The operation of this theme in the poem I shall presently explore.

As the primary theme may be taken as the issue of the fable, so the secondary theme may be taken as concerned with the context of values in which the fable is presented and which the fable may be found ultimately to embody just as more obviously it embodies the primary theme. I shall label the secondary theme in this poem as the theme of the imagination. After having explored the operation of the theme of sacramental unity in the poem, I shall explore the operation of the theme of the imagination, and shall then attempt to define the significance of their final symbolic fusion in the poem.

Before proceeding to the investigation of these themes in the poem, however, I wish to distinguish them from another type of theme which is sometimes emphasized in the discussion of this work. This type is the personal theme; it is concerned with those internal conflicts of the poet which may find expression in the poem. (p. 71)

The poem may very well represent, in one sense, an attempt to resolve [personal] conflicts. The poem, read in this light, may give us a poignant chapter of biography, and as an image of human suffering and aspiration may move us deeply. But we may remember that the poem, even regarded in this light, is not an attempt merely to present the personal problem but an attempt to transcend the personal problem, to objectify and universalize it. (p. 72)

To return to the matter of the objective themes: That more than one theme should be involved, that the poem should operate

on more than one level, would be perfectly consistent with Coleridge's emphasis on diversity within unity. . . . (p. 73)

Coleridge's not infrequent remarks on allegory should have warned the critics. The method of allegory—if by allegory we understand a fixed system of point-to-point equations—is foreign to his conception of the role of the imagination. "A poet's heart and intellect should be *combined*," he says, "intimately combined and unified with the great appearances of nature, and not merely held in solution and loose mixture with them, in the shape of formal similes." But a passage of greater significance on this point deals with the contrast between false and true religion:

> It is among the miseries of the present age that it recognizes no medium between literal and metaphorical. Faith is either to be buried in the dead letter, or its name and honors usurped by a counterfeit product of the mechanical understanding, which in the blindness of self-complacency confounds symbols with allegories. Now an allegory is but a translation of abstract notions into a picture-language, which is itself nothing but an abstraction from objects of sense. . . . On the other hand a symbol . . . is characterized by a translucence of the special in the individual, or of the general in the special, or of the universal in the general; above all by the translucence of the eternal through and in the temporal. It always partakes of the reality which it renders intelligible; and while it enunciates the whole, abides itself as a living part in that unity of which it is the representative.

Allegory is, to adopt Coleridge's terms, the product of the understanding, symbol of the imagination. (pp. 73-4)

Coleridge is using the word *metaphor* really to mean bad metaphor, i.e., a construction which has the form but not the function of metaphor. For the construction which exercises the proper function he reserves the word *symbol*.

Let us try to define some of the qualities which for him a symbol exhibits.

The symbol serves to *combine*—and he italicizes the word—the "poet's heart and intellect." A symbol involves an idea (or ideas) as part of its potential, but it also involves the special complex of feelings associated with that idea, the attitude toward that idea. The symbol affirms the unity of mind in the welter of experience; it is a device for making that welter of experience manageable for the mind—graspable. It represents a focus of being and is not a mere sign, a "picture-language."

The symbol, then, is massive in the above sense. But it is massive in another sense, too. It has what psychoanalysts call condensation. It does not "stand for" a single idea, and a system of symbols is not to be taken as a mere translation of a discursive sequence. Rather, a symbol implies a body of ideas which may be said to be fused in it. This means that the symbol itself may be developed into a discursive sequence as we intellectually explore its potential. To state the matter in another way, a way perhaps more applicable to the problem of interpreting the present poem, a symbol may be the condensation of several themes and not a sign for one. (p. 74)

The symbol is focal and massive, but Coleridge introduces another quality into his description. He says that it is not mechanical (like allegory) and that it "partakes of the reality which it renders intelligible." The same thing is said here in two ways. What is said is that the symbol is not arbitrary—not a mere sign—but contains within itself the appeal which makes it serviceable as a symbol. Perhaps a distinction may help us here. A symbol may avoid being arbitrary in two ways: by necessity and by congruence.

By a symbol of necessity I mean the kind of symbol which is rooted in our universal natural experience. The wind in *The Ancient Mariner* is such a symbol. All phallic symbols, for example, are of this order. When Coleridge speaks of the poet's heart and intellect being intimately combined with the "great appearances of nature," he may be hinting at the idea of necessity. It is true, of course, that he takes these great appearances of nature to be revelatory of a supersensuous reality. For him Nature symbolizes God, though, as a matter of fact, there is also in Coleridge's thought the idea of a projective symbolism in Nature by which man realizes not God but himself. (p. 75)

The symbol is distinguished by being focal, massive, and not arbitrary. Allegory, in the special use of the term by Coleridge, is not focal or massive and is arbitrary. (p. 76)

If we take the poem as a symbolic poem, we are not permitted to read it in the way which Coleridge called allegorical. We cannot, for instance, say that the Pilot equals the Church, or that the Hermit equals the "idea of an enlightened religion which is acquainted with the life of the spirit." The first of these readings is purely arbitrary. The second, though less arbitrary, simply ignores the massive quality of the episode involving the Hermit—considerations such as the Hermit's relation to nature, the function in returning the Mariner to human society, etc., and chiefly the tenor of the whole episode. This allegorical kind of reading makes the poem into a system of equivalents in a discursive sequence. But we must read it as massive, as operating on more than one thematic level. (p. 77)

In this section, I shall look at the poem in terms of what I have called the primary perspective or primary theme—the theme which is the issue of the fable.

The fable, in broadest and simplest terms, is a story of crime and punishment and repentance and reconciliation (I have refrained from using the word *sin*, because one school of interpretation would scarcely accept the full burden of the implications of the word). . . . The Mariner shoots the bird; suffers various pains, the greatest of which is loneliness and spiritual anguish; upon recognizing the beauty of the foul sea snakes, experiences a gush of love for them and is able to pray; is returned miraculously to his home port, where he discovers the joy of human communion in God, and utters the moral, "He prayeth best who loveth best, etc." We arrive at the notion of a universal charity. . . . (pp. 77-8)

[We] have to ask ourselves what is the symbolic reading of the [Mariner's killing of the bird]. And in asking ourselves this question, we have to remember that the symbol, in Coleridge's view, is not arbitrary, but *must contain in itself, literally considered, the seeds of the logic of its extension—that is, it must participate in the unity of which it is representative.* (p. 78)

[The] first problem we must consider is to what extent Coleridge was actually a necessitarian, at least in the poem. (pp. 78-9)

We cannot argue that Coleridge was a systematic necessitarian and that therefore the killing of the Albatross is merely the result of the necessary pattern of things and is not to be taken as sinful *per se* or in extension. The fact seems to be that

Coleridge was early moving toward his later views, that he was not, as he says, committed to any dogmatic system. . . . [In] addition to his living into a transcendental philosophy through the practice and love of poetry, he lived into the guilt of opium long before the Mariner shot the Albatross: he knew what guilt is, and if he longed for a view of the universe which would absolve him of responsibility and would comfort him with the thought of participation in the universal salvation promised by Hartley and Priestley, there was still the obdurate fact of his own experience. It seems that we have in these years a tortured churning around of the various interpretations of the fact, and the necessitarian philosophy is only one possible philosophy in suspension in that agitated brew. And we even have some evidence that in the period just before the composition of *The Ancient Mariner*—before he had struck upon that fable to embody his idea—the poet was meditating a long poem on the theme of the origin of evil. (pp. 80-1)

In his more elaborate and systematic treatment of the subject Coleridge adds another point which is of significance for the poem. Original Sin is not hereditary sin; it is original with the sinner and is of his will. There is no previous determination of the will, for the will exists outside the chain of cause and effect, which is of Nature and not of Spirit. And as for the time of this act of sin, he says that the "subject stands in no relation to time, can neither be in time nor out of time." The bolt whizzes from the crossbow and the bird falls and all comment that the Mariner has no proper dramatic motive or is the child of necessity or is innocent of everything except a little wantonness is completely irrelevant, for we are confronting the mystery of the corruption of the will, the mystery which is the beginning of the "moral history of Man." . . . The [Mariner's] act symbolizes the Fall, and the Fall has two qualities important here: it is a condition of will, as Coleridge says, "out of time," and it is the result of no single human motive. (pp. 81-2)

One more comment, even though I have belabored this point. What is the nature of this sin, what is its content? Though the act which symbolizes the mystery of the Fall is appropriately without motive, the sin of the will must be the appropriate expression of the essence of the will. (pp. 81-2)

The Mariner did not kill a man but a bird, and the literal-minded readers have echoed Mrs. Barbauld and Leslie Stephen [see excerpt above, 1888]: what a lot of pother about a bird. But they forget that this bird is more than a bird. (p. 82)

[The] hunting of the bird becomes the hunting of man. When the bird first appears,

> As if it had been a Christian soul,
> We hailed it in God's name.

It ate food "it ne'er had eat," and every day "came to the mariner's hollo," and then later perched on the mast or shroud for "vespers nine." It partakes of the human food and pleasure and devotions. . . . The crime is, symbolically, a murder, and a particularly heinous murder, for it involves the violation of hospitality and of gratitude (*pious* equals *faithful* and the bird is "of good omen") and of sanctity (the religious connotations of *pious*, etc.). This factor of betrayal in the crime is re-emphasized in Part V when one of the Spirits says that the bird had "loved the man" who killed it.

But why did the poet not give us a literal murder in the first place? By way of answering this question, we must remember that the crime, to maintain its symbolic reference to the Fall, must be motiveless. But the motiveless murder of a man would truly raise the issue of probability. Furthermore, the literal shock of such an act, especially if perverse and unmotivated, would be so great that it would distract from the symbolic significance. The poet's problem, then, was to provide an act which, on one hand, would not accent the issue of probability or shockingly distract from the symbolic significance, but which, on the other hand, would be adequately criminal to justify the consequences. And the necessary criminality is established . . . in two ways: (1) by making the gravity of the act depend on the state of the will which prompts it, and (2) by symbolically defining the bird as a "Christian soul," as "pious," etc.

There is, however, a third way in which the criminality is established. We can get at it by considering the observation that if a man had been killed, we could not have the "lesson of humanitarianism," which some critics . . . have taken to be the point of the poem. But we must remember that the humanitarianism itself is a superficial manifestation of a deeper concern, a sacramental conception of the universe, for the bird is hailed "in God's name," both literally and symbolically, and in the end we have, therefore, in the crime against Nature a crime against God. If a man had been killed, the secular nature of the crime—a crime then against man—would have overshadowed the ultimate religious significance involved. The idea of the crime against God rather than man is further emphasized by the fact that the cross is removed from the Mariner's neck to make place for the dead bird, and here we get a symbolic transference from Christ to the Albatross. Last, there is the crime against God. (pp. 82-3)

We have not yet done with the matter of crime and punishment. There is the question of the fellow mariners, who suffer death. Here we encounter not infrequently the objection that they do not merit their fate. . . . The fellow mariners have, in a kind of structural counterpoint (and such a counterpoint is . . . a characteristic of the poem), duplicated the Mariner's own crime of pride, of will in abstraction. That is, they make their desire the measure of the act: they first condemn the act, when they think the bird had brought the favorable breeze; then applaud the act when the fog clears and the breeze springs back up, now saying that the bird had brought the fog; then in the dead calm, again condemn the act. Their crime has another aspect: they have violated the sacramental conception of the universe, by making man's convenience the measure of an act, by isolating him from Nature and the "One Life." (p. 85)

> *Robert Penn Warren, "A Poem of Pure Imagination: An Experiment in Reading," in* The Rime of the Ancient Mariner *by Samuel Taylor Coleridge, Reynal & Hitchcock, 1946, pp. 59-117.*

C. M. BOWRA (lecture date 1948-49)

[*Bowra, a twentieth-century English critic, is known for his objective approach to literature which reflects his refusal to adhere to any fixed literary tradition. Here, he discusses the realism in "The Ancient Mariner" and its mythic and moral elements. Though Bowra considers the poem, on a basic level, a tale of crime and punishment, he adds that it is much more. The intertwining of the themes of redemption and the supernatural create, in Bowra's eyes, "a myth about a dark and troubling crisis in the human soul." The following is drawn from a lecture which Bowra delivered in 1948-49.*]

The triumph of **"The Ancient Mariner"** is that it presents a series of incredible events through a method of narration which makes them not only convincing and exciting but in some sense a criticism of life. No other poet of the supernatural has quite done this, at least on such a scale and with such abundance of authentic poetry. In his conquest of the unknown, Coleridge went outside the commonplace thrills of horror. Of course, he evokes these, and his opening verses, in which the Mariner stays the Wedding-Guest, suggest that at first Coleridge followed familiar precedents in appealing to a kind of horrified fear. But as he worked at his poem, he widened its scope and created something much richer and more human. To be sure, he chose his subject well. The weird adventures of his Mariner take place not in the trite Gothic setting of a mediaeval castle, which Coleridge used once and for all in **"Christabel,"** but on a boundless sea with days of pitiless sun and soft nights lit by a moon and attendant stars. Nor are his "machining persons" of the same breed as his Geraldine. They are spirits of another sort, who may have their home in some Neo-Platonic heaven, but are transformed by Coleridge into powers who watch over the good and evil actions of men and requite them with appropriate rewards and punishments. The new setting and the new persons with which Coleridge shapes the supernatural give to it a new character. Instead of confining himself to an outworn dread of spectres and phantoms, he moves over a wide range of emotions and touches equally on guilt and remorse, suffering and relief, hate and forgiveness, grief and joy. Nor has his creation the misty dimness commonly associated with the supernatural. What he imagines is indeed weird, but he sees it with so sharp a vision that it lives vividly before our eyes. At each point he anticipates the objection that his is an outmoded kind of composition, and does the opposite of what his critics expect. (pp. 55-6)

It is clear that Coleridge felt about the creations of his imagination something similar to what he felt about dreams. He assumes that while we have them we do not question their reality. **"The Ancient Mariner"** lives in its own world as events in dreams do, and, when we read it, we do not normally ask if its subject is real or unreal. But this is due to a consummate art. Each action, and each situation, is presented in a concrete form in which the details are selected for their appeal to common experience. Coleridge exercises an imaginative realism. However unnatural his events may be, they are formed from natural elements, and for this reason we believe in them. We may even be at home with them because their constituents are familiar and make a direct, natural appeal. Once we have entered this imaginary world, we do not feel that it is beyond our comprehension, but respond to it as we would to actual life.

In other words, though Coleridge begins by appealing to our experience of dreams, he so uses it as to present something which is more solid and more reasonable and more human than the most haunting dreams. He uses the atmosphere of dreams to accustom us to his special world, and then he proceeds to create freely within his chosen limits. At each step he takes pains to see that his eery subject is real both for the eye and for the emotions, that it has both the attraction of visible things and the significance which belongs to actions of grave import. His natural background, for instance, could have been fashioned only by a man who had learned about nature from loving observation and shared the Wordsworths' devotion to it. Amid all these strange happenings nature remains itself, and its perseverance in its own ways sometimes comes in ironical contrast to what happens on the ship, as when, at the moment when the Mariner is haunted by the look in his dead comrades' eyes, the moon continues her quiet, unchanging course:

> The moving Moon went up the sky,
> And no where did abide:

Softly she was going up,
And a star or two beside.

Even when nature breaks into more violent moods, it is still itself, and each touch of description makes it more real, as when Coleridge sketches a storm with something of Turner's delight in wild effects of sky and cloud:

The upper air burst into life!
And a hundred fire-flags sheen,
To and fro they were hurried about!
And to and fro, and in and out,
The wan stars danced between.

In such scenes there is no indeterminacy of dream. Each detail comes from the known world and gives a firm background to the supernatural events which accompany it.

This realistic treatment of the setting is matched by the appeal which Coleridge makes to our emotions in handling his human persons. The Mariner and his comrades are hardly characters in any dramatic sense. They lack lineaments and personality. But perhaps this is well, since what touches us in them is the basic humanity of their sufferings. They are more types than differentiated human beings, and for this reason their agonies are simply and universally human. We feel that what happens to them might in similar circumstances happen to anyone, and we respond readily to their pathos and their misery. And these Coleridge conveys with a masterly directness. . . . Of course, physical sensations play a large part in dreams, but Coleridge describes them as we know them in a waking state, and the lively way in which he handles them creates a powerful emotional effect.

What is true of physical sensations in "The Ancient Mariner" is no less true of mental states. The Mariner passes through an ordeal so weird and so fearful that it might seem impossible to make it real for us. We shrink from asking what such suffering means in conditions so unfamiliar and so hideous as those in the poem. To rise to such an occasion and to give a persuasive and moving account of what the Mariner endures demands a powerful effort of the imagination. Coleridge rises to the full claim of his subject and by concentrating on elementary human emotions makes the most of them. (pp. 59-62)

Coleridge expects us to suppose that his situations are real, and to have some kind of human feelings about them. This is no doubt easy enough when they belong to ordinary experience, but when the supernatural takes command it demands a more unusual art. Then Coleridge makes it look as natural as possible because, however strange it may be, he forms it from elements which are in themselves familiar. (p. 62)

Coleridge's realism is of course much more than an art of circumstantial details. It is a special form of poetry, the reflection of his love for the sensible world and his sensitiveness to its lights and shades and colours and sounds. He possessed to a high degree that cardinal quality of poetry which he calls "the power of exciting the sympathy of the reader by a faithful adherence to the truth of nature." And he has more than "faithful adherence." He is by no means photographic or merely descriptive. His eye for nature is for its more subtle charms and less obvious appeals. . . . Coleridge, for whom the contents of books had a vivid reality, was able to see with the mind's eye, as if objects were literally in front of him. More, too, perhaps than Wordsworth, he evokes the magical associations of sound, whether it be an angel's song or the pleasant noise of the sails. . . . The Romantics knew how to use their senses,

and Coleridge, despite his love of metaphysical abstractions, was in this respect a true member of their company. He used nature to give colour and music, solidity and perspective, to his creations, and it is one of the chief means by which he sustains the enchantment of his poem.

Most of us, when we read "The Ancient Mariner," are content to respond to its magic and to ask no questions about any ulterior purpose or symbolical significance that it may have. It lives so fully by its own rules in its own world that it seems impertinent to ask for more. And in this attitude Coleridge himself seems to support us. . . . Even in his later years, Coleridge seems to have been satisfied if readers of "The Ancient Mariner" supposed his situations to be real and responded to their dramatic truth with appropriate emotions. He must have known that he was successful in doing what he set out to do and that he had carried out his bargain with Wordsworth. It is therefore not surprising that most readers of "The Ancient Mariner" are quite happy that it should be a story of supernatural events and do not wish it to be anything else.

And yet, though this position is natural and reasonable, we cannot but feel doubts about it. How are we to accommodate a poem, which is no more than a work of fancy, to all that Coleridge says about the imagination and its relation to truth and reality? If "The Ancient Mariner" is no more than a glittering fairy-tale, why did Coleridge not take account of this in his many elaborate statements about the nature of poetry? It is of course true that most of these statements were made at a considerable distance of time from his wonderful creative years, and that in the interval he may have changed his views or at least have fitted them not to the poetry which he had written but to that which he vainly hoped to write. Yet it is clear that, even when he wrote "The Ancient Mariner," Coleridge believed in the imagination as a vehicle of truth. (pp. 64-6)

However much we may enjoy "The Ancient Mariner," we must surely feel that there are moments when it breaks beyond illusion and calls to something deep and serious in us. It has after all [this] moral: . . .

He prayeth best, who loveth best
All things both great and small;
For the dear God who loveth us,
He made and loveth all.

Now, whatever its faults may be, this states something which is clearly serious and must be heard. It is not enough to treat it as an archaism, a piece of mediaeval simplicity which Coleridge introduces to complete a poem which has already many old-world themes and phrases. The important thing is that Coleridge thought it necessary to include this moral and did not exclude it, as he did many other verses, when he revised the poem in later life. Of course, it is true that he was unhappy about it in later years and would have liked it to be less emphatic. This means not that he disapproved altogether of it, but that he was not satisfied with the way in which he had stated it. In other words, he still felt that the poem needed a moral, and there is no warrant for thinking that, whatever its form might have been, he intended its substance to be other than what it is. And this is surely of great importance. Coleridge, who thought that the "secondary imagination," with which poetry is concerned, is itself concerned with eternal values, slips into his poem his notion of the values which it represents. It is an all-embracing theory of love between living creatures, and that in some way the poem illustrates. (pp. 66-7)

"The Ancient Mariner" is a myth. It presents in an unusual and lively form certain issues with which we are all familiar and forces us to look afresh at them. It is the advantage of such a myth that it first dissociates certain ideas and then gives a new appeal to them by setting them in new associations. By this means it gives a fresh emphasis to much that we know and takes us to the heart of many matters to which custom has dulled us. By creating an impossible story in impossible conditions, "The Ancient Mariner" draws attention to neglected or undiscovered truths. And this is what Coleridge believed to be the task of poetry. Because through creation the poet reveals the secrets of the universe, especially in the sphere of absolute values, he is often forced to work through myths. They enable him to rearrange familiar material in such a way that we see fundamental issues in their right proportions and in their true nature because of the vivid illumination which the imagination gives to them. To be sure, the myth is only one kind among many kinds of poetry, but it is specially adapted to Coleridge's outlook because it can deal with supernatural issues. It is an extension of the use of symbols. Just as Blake has special symbols for the many mysterious powers which he saw at work in the universe, or Shelley for his far-ranging prophecies, so too Coleridge has his for the mysterious issues which excite him. In "The Ancient Mariner" he shapes these symbols into a consistent whole and subordinates them to a single plan, with the result that his poem is in the first place a story which we enjoy for its own sake, but in the second place a myth about a dark and troubling crisis in the human soul.

Reduced to its lowest terms in the dry language of abstraction, "The Ancient Mariner" is a tale of crime and punishment. It falls into seven sections, and each section tells of a new stage in the process. In each, of course, what counts is the imaginative and poetical effect, the emotional impression which the words make on us. It is this which illuminates the relentless progress from the commission of a crime to its last results. Coleridge puts into his myth the essential qualities which make crime and punishment what they are and shows what they mean to the conscience when it is sharpened and clarified by the imagination. He goes to the heart of the matter in its universal character, and he is able to do this because his myth is so striking that we pay special attention to it. (pp. 67-9)

["The Ancient Mariner"] is a myth of guilt and redemption, but of course it is also much more. Its symbolical purpose is but one element in a complex design. Though Coleridge has his own poetry of a guilty soul, it is not comparable in depth or in insight with the poetry of some other men who have given the full powers of their genius to writing about crime and the misery which it engenders. None the less, Coleridge's introduction of this theme into "The Ancient Mariner" gives to it a new dimension. What might otherwise be no more than an irresponsible fairy-tale is brought closer to life and to its fundamental issues. The myth of crime and punishment provides a structure for the supernatural events which rise from it but often make their appeal irrespective of it. Much of the magic of "The Ancient Mariner" comes from its blend of dark and serious issues with the delighted play of creative energy. Coleridge had good reasons for fashioning his poem in this way. In the first place, the combination of different themes responded to his own complex vision of existence. For him life had both its dark and its bright sides, its haunting responsibilities and its ravishing moments of unsullied delight. He saw that the two were closely interwoven and that, if he were to speak with the full force of his genius, he must introduce both into his poem. In the second place, he saw life not analytically

but creatively, and he knew that any work of creation must itself be an extension and an enhancement of life. He must preserve the mystery and the enchantment which he knew in his finest moments, and for him these came alike from the beauty of the visible world and the uncharted corners of the human soul. The shadow cast by the Mariner's crime adds by contrast to the brilliance of the unearthly world in which it is committed, and the degree of his guilt and his remorse serves to stress the power of the angelic beings which watch over humankind. The result is a poem shot with iridescent lights. (pp. 71-2)

> C. M. Bowra, " 'The Ancient Mariner'," in his The Romantic Imagination, 1949. Reprint by Oxford University Press, 1961, pp. 51-75.

HUMPHRY HOUSE   (essay date 1953)

[*House analyzes "Kubla Khan," "The Ancient Mariner," and "Christabel" and argues that they do not accurately reflect Coleridge's poetic theories as delineated in his critical writings. Further, House contends that the reader should not attempt a precise interpretation of these poems but should, rather, focus on their elements of mystery. House's essay is a slightly expanded version of a lecture he delivered at Trinity College, Cambridge, during the 1951-52 academic year.*]

Coleridge has set us a special problem of critical method. It is obvious that his own creative experience must have deeply affected his critical theories and practice: but he never fully brought the two into relation; he rarely adduced his own poems as instances, and never expounded them. (p. 92)

[The very richness of "The Ancient Mariner"] at once tempts and defeats definiteness of interpretation; as we commit ourselves to the development of one strand of meaning we find that in the very act of doing so we are excluding something else of importance.

An example of this difficulty occurs on the threshold of interpretation, in the opinion we form about the Mariner's relation to ordinary human beings and the relation of the voyage to ordinary human life. (p. 93)

The beginning of the Mariner's own account of the voyage contains no hint that he thought of the voyage as a high spiritual enterprise at variance with current limited social ideas, a conscious seeking of adventure. The ship starts off in an atmosphere of communal agreement and pleasure. . . . The voyage, it seems, began normally, commonly, happily, the crew at one both with the society they left and with each other. (p. 94)

The Mariner, said Wordsworth in rude complaint, "does not act, but is continually acted upon". There is, surely, an important element of truth in this, though it does not in the least derogate from the poem's merits. There are only three points in the poem at which the Mariner may be said to "act"; these are—the shooting of the Albatross; the blessing of the water-snakes; and the biting of his arm. Each of these actions has a very different character. The shooting of the Albatross comes quite suddenly and unexplained; superficially it is unmotivated and wanton. The Mariner himself never makes any explicit attempt to explain it: nor does the poem contain, from his point of view, any defence of it. We shall return to this. In the first phase of his recovery, in the crisis at the centre of the poem, when he blesses the water-snakes, he does so *unaware,* and this word "unaware" is deliberately repeated and occurs each time significantly, emphatically, at the end of the line. That is to say, he did not really know what he was doing; he could find no adequate spring of action in himself, and retrospectively attributed his undeliberate blessing to a supernatural influence on him:

> Sure my kind saint took pity on me.

He himself thought he was more acted upon than acting. Against this must be set the one clear occasion in the poem on which the Mariner does deliberately act. In Part III, when all the crew, including himself, have been stricken dumb by the drought, it is he who sees the sail; it is he who, by a prodigious effort, bites his arm, sucks the blood and finds voice to cry out. This is his one tremendous effort: it is a moment of terrible hope for him and for the whole crew. But the hope is blasted, not just negatively, but positively, appallingly, blasted. The crew all die cursing him with their eyes, and he alone survives.

This is crucial to the whole poem's dramatic effect and, by inference, also to its moral effect. On the one occasion when the Mariner does consciously, deliberately and with all his effort *act,* his action leads ironically to the climax of the disaster. The irony is enforced by the two lines that end this Part:

> And every soul, it passed me by,
> Like the whizz of my cross-bow!

The disastrous anticlimax of this action and this hope is made to throw back to the earlier, unexplained act of the shooting. One main element in the poem's theme is that the Mariner's experience involves a tangle of error, incomprehensibility and frustration. He is certainly not a great courageous spiritual adventurer, though he has a great spiritual experience. He started his voyage in unison with the ordinary world in a common set of values: he comes back as half outcast and half participator. In the poem as a whole a deliberate contrast is certainly presented between the background of the wedding and the Mariner's tale. The interruptions of the Wedding-Guest are meant to point this contrast. His constant fear is that the Mariner is a ghost come back from the dead or even himself some kind of infernal spirit. The contrast is not so much between two types of personality, the normal/conventional and the abnormal/adventurer, but between two aspects of reality, and two potentialities of experience, the visible bodily world of human beings marrying and giving in marriage and an invisible world of spirits and the dead where quite a different system of values is to be learnt. The effect of the interruptions of the Wedding-Guest is to show how these two kinds of reality are always coexistent: the total effect of the poem is to show them interpenetrating. (pp. 94-6)

The Mariner leaves his killing of the Albatross without any full explanation; he does not, cannot or dare not attempt to give his motives. But the description of the bird, its nature and power, taken with the prose gloss, makes it clear that the killing of it was a ghastly violation of a great sanctity, at least as bad as a murder. The bird's human associations appear in the fact that it was hailed as a Christian soul in God's name, it answered the Mariner's hollo, ate human food, and played with the crew.... Furthermore, a function of the bird as a Christian emblem is also hinted at later on, when its corpse is hung round the Mariner's neck "instead of the cross". (pp. 96-7)

What happens in the poem is that the images gather their bearing by progressively rich associations, by gradual increment, and that exact equation is never fully demanded, even though the associations are ordered and controlled. The killing of the Albatross thus becomes a violation of a great sanctity at the

animal, human, and spiritual levels: but these levels are only gradually declared as the poem proceeds, just as the Mariner only gradually discovered the consequences of what he had done. Our enlightenment runs parallel with his. (pp. 97-8)

[The Mariner's] sin may or may not be partly the sin of pride and self-assertion against the order of the universe. As the poem stands it is a sin of ignorance, and links to that half-adumbrated sin of Cain, that he "neglected to make a proper use of his senses etc." It was a wicked ignorance because accompanied by a wildly thoughtless failure to consider what might be the truth about the order of the universe.

This failure to reach the truth, and, to him, the incomprehensibility of what was going on, is made more apparent when the rest of the crew become accomplices in his crime. They do not know whether the fog and mist (along with the Albatross who brought them) are good or bad, or whether the bird belongs more to them or to the breeze: nor do they know whether the sun is good or bad. (p. 98)

At the naturalistic level, both for the mariners and for Coleridge, the tropic sun changed from being a beautiful, pleasant, "good" thing to being an unpleasant, evil thing: this change is a natural quality of the tropic sun, irrespective of the eye of the beholder. The naturalistic error of the crew was not to know that the tropic sun has this double character: and this naturalistic error is an image of their moral and spiritual error. This brings clearly to the front a main feature of "the great appearances of nature" in the poem. . . .

In Part II the becalming and the drought all occur under the influence of the sun; it is under the bloody sun that the deep rots, and that the creatures of the deep are slimy things that crawl with legs upon the slimy sea. (p. 100)

Part IV begins with the crisis of extreme isolation, with the frustrated desire for death, and then moves into the first phase of recovery and redemption.

The parallels here . . . between the spiritual and the natural— the physical imagery not just illuminating but actually conveying the spiritual state—are what most characterise the poem. It is clearest in the landless waste of the sea, the most awful loneliness:

> Alone, alone, all, all alone,
> Alone on a wide wide sea!
> And never a saint took pity on
> My soul in agony.

The transition also from the barren desire for death to the first state of redemption is brought in through the magnificent imagery of the moon and stars. From the helpless repetition of

> the sky and the sea, and the sea and the sky

—the dead, static, unchanging monotony of the spiritual isolation without a specified light—there is a shift by means of the wonderful stanza

> The moving Moon went up the sky,
> And no where did abide:
> Softly she was going up,
> And a star or two beside—

From death to life, or rather from death-in-life, which is so much worse than death that death is longed-for and unattainable. From death-in-life to life. From the flat, unchanging waste of the sea and the sky and the sky and the sea to the ordered, even movement, with grace and hope, of the moon and stars. (p. 101)

The blessing under moonlight is the critical turning-point of the poem. Just as the Albatross was not a mere bird, so these are not mere water-snakes—they stand for all ''happy living things''. The first phase of redemption, the recovery of love and the recovery of the power of prayer, depends on the Mariner's recognition of his kinship again with other natural creatures. . . . (p. 102)

Parts I to IV and the opening stanzas of Part V, taken together with the ending, Part VII, [are] relatively easy to interpret as a tale of crime, punishment and reconciliation, with the recovery of love in the blessing of the water-snakes as its climax. But the remainder of Part V and the whole of Part VI do not seem at first sight to have quite the same coherence and point. (p. 103)

It would be endless to quote all Coleridge's uses of imagery from the moon and stars, clouds, the night-sky and uncertain lights; these examples give some idea of the range. It is certain that, before and after the time of **''The Ancient Mariner''**, such images were used for creativeness both of a wider and of a more specially poetic kind; but they were used also for much else, especially in conjunction with the subtler processes of the mind and the more delicate modes of feeling. They were used especially for the mysteries and uncertainties of mental life which Coleridge was beginning to explore more fully as he became more dissatisfied with the crude associationism represented by Hartley and its ''inanimate cold world'', and as his general ideals of life moved further from those of ''the poor loveless ever-anxious crowd''. It seems to me that the imagery of the mist and the moon and the Albatross in **''The Ancient Mariner''** belongs with this area of experience in general and with Coleridge's exploration of it; indeed the whole poem is part of the exploration, it is part of the experience which led Coleridge into his later theoretic statements (as of the theory of the Imagination) rather than a symbolic adumbration of the theoretic statements themselves.

Within the poem . . . the emphasis is on the mystery and the richness of the mystery. Through the development of the imagery we are gradually led into the realisation that the values of ''the land of mist and snow'' are of the greatest possible concern, but that they are indescribable. They are certainly contrasted with the values which belong to the specious day-to-day clarity of the sun, but they are left to establish themselves in us mysteriously and indefinitely. . . . (pp. 112-13)

''Kubla Khan'' is a poem about the act of poetic creation, about the ''ecstasy in imaginative fulfilment''. Interpretations have diverged to opposite poles of major meaning on the treatment of the emphasis and rhythm of that single line—''Could I revive within me''. If a strong emphasis (and therefore necessarily also a strong metrical stress) is put upon ''could'', the word can be taken to imply ''If only I could, but I can't'', and the whole poem can be made to appear to be about the failure and frustration of the creative power. But if the emphasis on ''could'' is slight, then the condition is an ''open'' condition, like ''Could you make it Wednesday instead of Thursday, it would be easier for me''; and the matter is the very possibility of creative achievement. The word ''once'' in the line ''In a vision once I saw'' then also becomes a light syllable, not implying ''Once, only once and, I fear, never again'', but rather indicating delight, surprise and the sense of unique privilege. (p. 115)

The metre is light and fast; the paragraph moves from delight and surprise, through enthusiasm to ecstasy; no sensitive reader can read it otherwise. The verse is asserting, not denying, the ecstasy. If this were a poem of frustration and failure, the movement would be slow and the stresses heavy. Another verbal detail points the same way—''I would build *that* dome in air''. What dome? Of course, the dome that has been described in the first part. And if it had not there been fully described, the music of the singing and the dulcimer would not have any substantial and evident power. It is just because the first part presents the dome and the river with all its setting so completely, beautifully and finally, that we accept the authenticity of the creative impulse in the second part, and find in the last word ''Paradise'' a fact, not a forlorn hope. **''Kubla Khan''** is a triumphant positive statement of the potentialities of poetry. How great those potentialities are is revealed partly in the description of its *effects* at the ending of the second part and partly in the very substance and content of the first.

The precision and clarity of the opening part are the first things to mark—even in the order of the landscape. In the centre is the pleasure-dome with its gardens on the river bank: to one side is the river's source in the chasm, to the other are the ''caverns measureless to man'' and the ''sunless sea'' into which the river falls: Kubla in the centre can hear the ''*mingled* measure'' of the fountain of the source from one side, and of the dark caves from the other. The river winds across the whole landscape. Nobody need keep this mere geographical consistency of the description prominently in mind as he reads (though once established it remains clear and constant); but I suggest that if this factual-visual consistency had been absent, and there had been a mere random sequence or collocation of items, such as a dream might well have provided—items which needed a symbol-system to establish relations at all—then the absence *would* be observed: the poem would have been quite different, and a new kind of effort would have been needed to apprehend what unity it might have had. Within this main landscape, too, there is a pervasive order. The fertility of the plain is only made possible by the mysterious energy of the source. The dome has come into being by Kubla's decree: the dome is stately; the gardens are girdled round with walls and towers.

It is so often said that **''Kubla Khan''** achieves its effect mainly by ''far-reaching suggestiveness', or by incantation or by much connotation, with little denotation, that it is worth emphasising this element of plain clear statement at the outset, statement which does particularise a series of details inter-related to each other, and deriving their relevance from their inter-relation and their order. Furthermore, the use of highly emotive and suggestive proper names is proportionately no large source of the poem's effect. . . . (pp. 116-17)

Next, the mode of appraisal which relies on suggestiveness is likely to underestimate the strength and firmness of the descriptions. In particular, lines 17-24, describing the source of the river, do not in method employ ''suggestiveness'' at all.

> And from this chasm, with ceaseless turmoil seething,
> As if this earth in fast thick pants were breathing,
> A mighty fountain momently was forced:
> Amid whose swift half-intermitted burst
> Huge fragments vaulted like rebounding hail,
> Or chaffy grain beneath the thresher's flail:
> And 'mid these dancing rocks at once and ever
> It flung up momently the sacred river.

(p. 117)

The whole passage is full of life because the verse has both the needed energy and the needed control. The combination of energy and control in the rhythm and sound is so great, as in

> at once and ever
> It flung up momently the sacred river

that we are even in danger of missing the force of the imagery, as in "rebounding hail" and "dancing rocks". If we miss it, it is our fault not Coleridge's; and it sometimes appears as if readers are blaming or underestimating him because they have improperly allowed themselves, under the influence of the rhythm, to be blind to the "huge fragments" and "dancing rocks" which lay another kind of weight upon it, and to be blind to the construction of the thought, which holds together the continuity and the intermission.

A different kind of clarity and precision in the first part leads us nearer to the poem's central meaning—the consistency with which the main facts of this landscape are treated, the dome and the river. The dome . . . is an agreed emblem of fulfilment and satisfaction, it is breast-like, full to touch and eye, rounded nd complete. In the first part it is mentined three times, as "a stately pleasure-dome" in line 2, as "the dome of pleasure" in line 31, and as "A sunny pleasure-dome" in line 36. Each time the word "pleasure" occurs with it. So too, the word *river* is used three times in the first part, and each time, without fail, it is "the *sacred* river": this is its constant, invariable epithet. The centre of the landscape of this part is . . . the point at which the dome and the river join:

> The shadow of the dome of pleasure
> Floated midway on the waves.

Here, without possibility of doubt, the poem presents the conjunction of pleasure and sacredness: that is the core of Part One. And in Part Two the poet who has been able to realise this fusion of pleasure and sacredness is himself regarded as a holy or sacred person, a seer acquainted with the undivided life: and this part is clinched by the emphatic and final word Paradise. The conditional form of Part Two does not annul the presentation of Paradise in Part One, though it may hold out the hope of a future fuller vision.

What is this Paradise? Those who are intent on making **"Kubla Khan"** either a poem about imaginative failure or a document for the study of opium dreams, remind us that many of the sources for Coleridge's details were descriptions of false paradises. . . . (pp. 118-19)

There is only one answer to those who want to make this a false Paradise—that is, an appeal to the poem as a whole, its rhythmical development, its total effect as a poem of fulfilment, and to say "If you still want to make that experience a spurious experience, do so: 'Thy way thou canst not miss, me mine requires'." Acceptance of the Paradise, in sympathy, is the normal response, from childhood and unsophistication to criticism: to most people rejection would mean a ruinous and purposeless wrench. But what is being accepted?

Positively, it causes a distortion of the poem if we try to approximate this Paradise either to the earthly Paradise which is the ultimate abode of the blest. It may take its imagery from Eden, but it is not Eden because Kubla Khan is not Adam. . . . We may, if we persist in hankering after formal equations, incline to say he *is* the Representative Man, or Mankind in general: but what matters is not his supposed fixed and antecedent symbolic character, so much as his activity. Within the landscape treated as literal he must be of princely scope, in order to decree the dome and gardens: and it is this decree that matters, for it images the power of man over his environment and the fact that man makes his Paradise for himself. Just as the whole poem is about poetic creation at the imaginative level, so, within the work of the imagination, occurs the creativeness of man at the ethical and practical levels. (p. 120)

[The] name Kubla is repeated only once after the first line; and the place of its repetition is significant:

> And 'mid this tumult Kubla heard from far
> Ancestral voices prophesying war!

This is essential to the full unity of the conception: the Paradise contains knowledge of the threat of its own possible destruction. It is not held as a permanent gift; the ideal life is always open to forces of evil; it must be not only created by man for himself, but also defended by him. It is not of the essence of this Paradise that it must be lost; but there is a risk that it may be lost.

About the river, again, we need not aim to be too precise and make equations. Its function in the poem is clear. The bounding energy of its source makes the fertility of the plain possible: it is the sacred given condition of human life. By using it rightly, by building on its bank, by diverting its water into his sinuous rills, Kubla achieves his perfect state of balanced living. It is an image of these non-human, holy, given conditions. It is not an allegorical river which would still flow across that plain if Kubla was not there. It is an imaginative statement of the abundant life in the universe, which begins and ends in a mystery touched with dread, but it is a statement of this life as the ground of ideal human activity.

The "caves of ice" need special attention. Some discussions of the poem seem to imply that they belong with the "caverns measureless to man"; but there surely can be no doubt that in the poem they belong closely and necesarily with the dome.

> It was a miracle of rare device,
> A sunny pleasure-dome, with caves of ice!

The very line shows the closeness by the antithesis, the convex against the concave, the warm against the cold. . . . [This] is a vision of the ideal human life *as the poetic imagination can create it*. Part One only exists in the light of Part Two. There may be other Paradises, other false Paradises too: but this is the creation of the poet in his frenzy. And it is because he can create it that he deserves the ritual dread.

The critique of **"Christabel"** is an entirely different matter: for not only is it inescapably a fragment, but the two parts differ so much from each other, that they scarcely seem to belong to the same poem. (pp. 120-22)

It is generally agreed that the experience of reading the First Part of **"Christabel"** is more an acquaintance with an atmosphere than the apprehension of a poetic unity. This atmosphere is achieved partly through description of the setting, partly by the mystery surrounding Geraldine. (p. 123)

At point after point in **"Christabel"** descriptions are used to heighten the mystery by such suggestions of slight distortion in behaviour, or of contrast, or surprise—

> And wildly glittered here and there
> The gems entangled in her hair.

> in moonshine cold

The brands were flat, the brands were dying,
Amid their own white ashes lying;

But when the lady passed, there came
A tongue of light, a fit of flame;
And Christabel saw the lady's eye

The silver lamp burns dead and dim.

But it is all fragmentary and finally unsatisfying because it leads up to a mystery which is both incomplete and clueless. (pp. 124-25)

> *Humphry House, in his* Coleridge: The Clark Lectures, 1951-52, *Rupert Hart-Davis, 1953, 167 p.*

ELISABETH SCHNEIDER   (essay date 1953)

[*Schneider's* Coleridge, Opium, and "Kubla Khan," *from which the following is drawn, is considered by many scholars one of the most important interpretations of "Kubla Khan" in the twentieth century. Schneider investigates the background of the poem and questions Coleridge's contention that he composed it in a dream. After analyzing the effects of opium documented in medical literature, Schneider is skeptical of Coleridge's claims of semiconscious composition inspired by opium. Instead, the critic argues that Coleridge's proclivity toward daydreaming was as strong an influence as opium. Schneider's study is thought to have overturned a number of traditional concepts concerning Coleridge and "Kubla Khan." Here, Schneider points to "Kubla Khan" as an incomplete fragment and discusses its form and texture that create "the soul of ambivalence, oscillation's very self."*]

A sketch of Coleridge drawn in 1811.

Kubla Khan has been read with equal conviction as cosmic allegory and incantatory nonsense; and with reference to both meaning and form it has been described equally as a fragment and a perfectly rounded complete whole. It has been called the quintessential poem of romanticism, even while its magical virgin birth placed it quite outside literary tradition or pedigree. To the aesthetic purist these may still be peripheral questions; they must be acknowledged, however, to lead at least in the direction of the poetic essence itself. They will serve for a beginning. (pp. 238-39)

[To] one who reads *Kubla Khan* attentively without ulterior motive and without fixed preconceptions, *Kubla Khan* has, throughout, a perfectly normal meaning, one that is as logical and, as far as one can tell, as conscious as that of most deliberately composed poems. This is evident, once we cease to be dazzled by the familiar prefatory note and Kubla's bewitching scenery. Indeed, one hesitates to explain the meaning because of its obviousness and because it must be a commonplace to many. (p. 241)

The first part is merely the picture that everyone knows of the strange and beautiful Paradise or pleasure-grounds, enriched and poeticized ultimately from many sources. The topography of the scene is somewhat unprecise, so that the reader could scarcely draw a map of it. But the actual statement and the separate elements of the picture are perfectly clear. Almost, though not quite literally, like the stream in [John Milton's] *Paradise Lost*, Coleridge's "sacred river" rises from the earth in a fountain, winds through the garden, and sinks again underground. The poet leaves off without finishing or putting to use these pleasure-grounds, either dissatisfied with his presentation of them or unable to continue, or both. In the last eighteen lines ... the poet makes an explicit statement about what precedes. In a vision, he says, he once heard music sung and played by a damsel. Her song was of an earthly Paradise. If he could only revive within himself that music, the joy it would give him would enable him really to re-create the scene of Kubla's Paradise, in poetry that would be truly immortal. He would then be looked upon with awe as one of the inspired great ones, the poet-prophets of the world. ... [The last eighteen lines are] the poet's explanation of his failure to complete the poem. As Coleridge said often in his waking hours, so he says here: he *could* have accomplished something truly worthy of himself, *if only*——.

In part, the thought is related to the later ode *Dejection*. The mood of gloom is not mentioned explicitly, but Coleridge feels the same lack that he described in the ode, a lack of inner joy or delight—what Gerard Hopkins afterward called "the fine delight that fathers thought." This is needed to stir his creative imagination. ... In both poems joy or delight is represented as an inner music that inspires the poet to create; the presence of a woman is imagined; and the epithets for the music, "loud and long" in the one, find echo of both sound and sense in the "strong" of the other. If, then—to return to the direct statement of *Kubla Khan*—the writer, "I," had this inspiration that is rooted in joy, "with music ... I would build that dome ... those caves of ice! And all who heard [my music] should see them [domes, caves] there, And all should cry, Beware! ..." (pp. 242-44)

The idea has been advanced more than once in recent years that the poem is not a fragment but a complete and perfect whole. This view has attracted so many readers and, if sound, would have such real bearing upon the poetic effect of the lines that the basis for it had better be examined. Coleridge himself called the poem a "fragment"; and, haunted as he was by the ghosts of his many unfinished works, I should think it unlikely that he would have added by a deliberate falsehood to the number of that congregation in limbo. He also treated it as a fragment, keeping it, as he did *Christabel,* unpublished for many years, though his usual custom was to publish finished works promptly except for a few obviously intimate ones the publication of which would embarrass himself or others—verses such as those unmistakably addressed to Sara Hutchinson, for example, and *The Pains of Sleep.*

It is difficult, on the other hand, to imagine the poem carried beyond its present close. Conceivably, following a momentary cross-current of thought in the passage that introduces the Abyssinian maid, Coleridge might have written the poem into a hole from which he could not extricate it. He might, that is, have destined the poem to progress in one direction but, having once interrupted this current to comment on the inadequacy of his inspiration, have found he had actually written what must put an end to the work, a continuation of the original being unthinkable afterwards. Coleridge would not be the first poet whose matter had got beyond its inventor's control and taken him where he had not meant to go. But that is not what one means by a finished poem. It is conceivable, too, that he had in mind a three-part musical form with a more beautiful and heightened return to the original garden theme—the Inspired Poet, having recovered his "vision," now demonstrating what he could really do. The poem might then have remained incomplete from Coleridge's inability to transcend what he had already done as the theme would require. On the whole, however, I think this not the most likely reconstruction of Coleridge's intention (though the idea of translating musical into poetic forms had occurred to poets in Germany and might have been familiar to Coleridge). There is nothing like it to be found elsewhere in his work, and I doubt whether *Kubla Khan* represents a departure of that sort from his usual practice.

The most likely explanation of the actual form of the poem would seem to be also the most natural. As it stands, it clearly consists of two parts, the description of Kubla's Paradise gardens and an explanation of why the poet could not after all finish what he had begun, or, to speak within the framework of the dream, why he could not re-create the vision he had seen. The whole reads like a fragment with a postscript added at some later time when it has become obvious to the poet that he cannot finish the piece. The postscript is skilfully linked with the rest by the recurrence of the dome and caves of ice; but these and other devices do not conceal, and I imagine were not meant to conceal, the actually disparate parts. If a man begins a poem, gets stuck, and then adds the comment, "I cannot finish this," even though he versify his comment to match his fragment, he is not likely to produce a whole in the poetic or aesthetic sense, though he does bring his piece to an end beyond which it could not be continued.

To me, at any rate, the poem has never sounded complete in any other sense than this. Several things in it, furthermore, have charm and interest if one reads it as a fragment but are poetically unsatisfactory if one tries to regard it as an organic whole, even a dreamed whole. One of these is Kubla's hearing of the "ancestral voices prophesying war," which Coleridge makes impressive and then drops. It is true that if the poem is read as an actual incoherent and unaltered dream one cannot cavil at the flaw, since the dream produced it; but I do not find enough incoherence for that. So the "ancestral" threat of war is too prominent and at the same time too much out of

key with the other images—too pointless, in fact, since no further use is made of it—to be satisfactory poetically if the fifty-four lines must be regarded as a finished piece; the image remains unassimilated. Only if one reads those words as a hint at something to come in the poem, do they charm the mind as they should with their portentousness.

I think Coleridge would have agreed. On just such a point in *Christabel* a comment survives which was probably Coleridge's in substance and perhaps in language as well. It concerned the lines about the mastiff bitch and Christabel's mother:

> Sixteen short howls, not over loud;
> Some say, she sees my lady's shroud.

These details, so the comment runs, not only give "a prevailing colour or Harmony to the whole," but are "indicative also that my Lady's spirit is to make a principal interest in the after story." They prepare us also for the "visionary and dreamlike manner which pervades the Poem." Christabel's mother, the writer points out, is dropped into the story again, though no structural use is made of her in the fragment as it exists. He justifies and explains these unused references on the specific ground that they would have been an important structural part of the finished poem. Every event in the fragment "is completely in Harmony with the general wildness of the Poem, and is yet consistent with and connected with and dependent upon the other." Coleridge would probably have justified the "ancestral voices" of Kubla, from the poetic standpoint, only by a similar unfulfilled intention of something to come later in the poem. The two lines on the woman wailing beneath a waning moon for her demon-lover also seem poetically in keeping in a fragment but would be out of proportion in a short whole. Shifting the scene from day to night as they do and introducing two figures, obviously not as part of a shifting dream-sequence of irrelevancies but in the language and syntax of a conventional literary comparison, the lines are nearly as much out of drawing as an elaborate Virgilian simile would be in a lyric.

The division of *Kubla Khan* into its two parts also seems fatal to the unity of the poem if it must be regarded as a complete whole. The first part is given over entirely to Kubla's pleasure-grounds, the demon-lover lines being not a new scene but only a comparison. In the last eighteen lines, time, place, and speaker all are changed. The first part is wholly impersonal; the last is written wholly in the first person. The poet enters in the thirty-eighth line unannounced, but, unlike the stars of *The Ancient Mariner,* his place is not prepared and appointed, nor does he enter as a lord that is certainly expected; he rather breaks in. The last eighteen lines terminate but do not fulfil the first part—or so it seems to me. I do not find that the main descriptive portion—the gardens, the fountains, the romantic glen—becomes any different in memory after I have read the concluding lines, for the break remains too complete despite the links in imagery. The conviction does not rush upon me at the end that the split is after all no split; for the end makes the beginning no brighter, no dimmer, deepens the meaning by no tragic implications or irony or illuminating reversal. A fulfilment is still absent at the end, partly because *action,* not pure description, has been left in the air. The place is *being built* before one's eyes. Kubla *decreed* the pleasure-dome; and so the ten miles of ground *were girdled round.* The progression thus started cries out to continue, like an unresolved cadence in music.

On the whole, not only do the first thirty-six lines of the poem refuse to sound as if they had been dreamed; they sound more than anything else like a fine opening for a romantic narrative poem of some magnitude. (pp. 246-51)

[Whatever proportions] went into the making of *Kubla Khan* . . .—we end, as we began, with an awareness of its special character. It may not be the unique and novel synthesis of geographical elements that Lowes thought it [see excerpt above, 1927], and it may not carry a great weight of specific symbols or tell us anything we did not know about unconscious genius. It may not be—and in fact I think is not—among the very greatest achievements of English poetry. Still, it has perfection in its kind; we do not forget it, and we never mistake it for anything else. And some things about the essence of poetry can be perceived more easily, perhaps, in the lesser than in the greater masterpieces.

In part, the special "witchery" of *Kubla Khan* is owing to its odd union of Miltonic verse texture with rather ordinary, conventional Gothic-oriental-tale matter. When Milton himself used Eastern material it succumbed, like all his other sources, to his own severe logic and the firmly organic continuity he gave it. But between his use of it and Coleridge's there intervened the epidemic of oriental and pseudo-oriental tales, which exhibit the wayward structure almost of improvisation. The tales of the *Arabian Nights* themselves seem to Western habits of mind a fabulous sequence of nonsequiturs. . . . Southey composed *Thalaba* as if with a dump truck; despite all the pains bestowed upon his work, the final impression upon the reader is of an indiscriminate pouring-out of large lumps of inert matter animated by no living breath, held together by no structure in the design and no texture in the writing. In *Kubla Khan* the materials are the same. But the Miltonic texture transforms the whole into something altogether different, something that is neither Milton's nor Gothic-oriental. The intricate complexities and unifications of the verse pattern here produce a subtle music that bestows upon ordinarily chaotic—and also stale—material an air of mysterious meaning. It is a new tune; though the texture is Milton's, the voice is the voice of Coleridge.

I do not know any other poem in which the pattern is played primarily with *æ*-sounds. The outlandish proportion of these, along with the Eastern names, is in some measure responsible for the particular flavor of the poem. They are intersprinkled with a good many other short vowel sounds, and most of the long vowels are rather light—either without depth of tone or carried quickly by. Even the other *ō*-sounds, except for the *dome*, are mostly light passing ones that can scarcely be dwelt upon—*momently, holy, float*. Throughout the poem many of the syllables carrying the nominal verse stress are but lightly touched. In the midst of them the "dome" stands out, dominating the poem by pure frequency as well as contrast. This dwelling upon the dome might be thought to justify reading into it such profound symbolic meanings as the "immortality" or the union of male and female. . . . The word *dome* may have had an emotional richness for Coleridge that led him in *Kubla Khan*, half intentionally and half by the accidents of a developing sound pattern, to give it a prominence not fully deserved by its actual meaning within the poem. Set aloft by itself as it is in the opening lines, *dome* is bound, I suppose, wherever it came from, to carry a hint of its cousin *doom*. . . . (pp. 282-85)

This air of importance without visible foundation contributes to the suggestion of mystery about the poem that is part of its charm. A severe critic may object that such charm is factitious and the imputation of it an insult to the poet, but that is not really so. It occurs often enough elsewhere, whether in life or art. An accident of light or shadow along a street may lend an air of mystery to a scene not at all mysterious, transforming an ordinary house front into something as final or portentous as doomsday. (p. 285)

I sometimes think we overwork Coleridge's idea of "the balance or reconciliation of opposite or discordant qualities." I have to come back to it here, however, for the particular flavor of *Kubla Khan,* with its air of mystery, is describable in part through that convenient phrase. Yet the "reconciliation" does not quite occur either. It is in fact avoided. What we have instead is the very spirit of "oscillation" itself. . . . The poem is the soul of ambivalence, oscillation's very self; and that is probably its deepest meaning. In creating this effect, form and matter are intricately woven. The irregular and inexact rhymes and the varied lengths of the lines play some part. More important is the musical effect in which a smooth, rather swift forward movement is emphasized by the relation of grammatical structure to line and rhyme, yet is impeded and thrown back upon itself even from the beginning by the *æ*-inclosed line units. Like the Mariner's ship at the Equator, the verse moves "backwards and forwards half her length," or like tides rocking in a basin. In the middle of the poem the slightly stronger forward movement loses itself altogether in the floating equivocation between backward-turned trochaic and forward-leaning iambic movement. One hears the texture of Milton, whose great will and drive, even in his discursive moments, gives to all he wrote an air of power and singleness of direction, however elaborate and circuitous his form may be. But in *Kubla Khan* one hears this elaboration almost wholly deprived of such will or with only enough will to keep it afloat. (pp. 286-87)

In this forward-flowing movement counterpointed against a stationary-oscillating one, form and meaning are almost indistinguishable. The pleasure-dome is built, then it is unbuilt. The poem is about Kubla, then it is not about him. The oppositions of image are not only the obvious ones of light and darkness, sunny dome and sunless sea or caves of ice, Paradise garden and hints of hell. In the elaborate opening passage *stately, dome, decree, sacred, caverns, measureless,* and *sunless* are all rather solemn words and, except for *stately,* not cheerful-solemn but awful-solemn. Yet the dome is a pleasure-palace; the movement and music of the verse are light rather than solemn. The central statement, through the first half of the poem, is one of bright affirmation. The talk and activity are of building, the pleasure-dome and a delightful Paradise materialize. But even as the words give they take away with half-Miltonic negatives. *Pleasure* itself is rhymed with one of them—*measureless;* deprivation haunts the language. The negations recur in *sunless, ceaseless, lifeless,* a second *measureless.* The demon-lover is not in Paradise; he is an *as-if* brought in to cast his shadow. Images of awe and mystery underlie Paradise in the subterranean river and ocean, and the ancestral threat of war is heard far off. The whole poem oscillates between giving and taking away, bright affirmation and sunless negation, light flowing music that nevertheless stands still and rings the portentous sound of *dome* time after time.

The spirit of the poem, moreover, is cool and rather non-human. One feels no real warmth even in the sunny garden. And though the verse is nominally well peopled, Kubla, the wailing woman, and the Abyssinian maid are not really there, and their half-presence leaves the place less human than if the theme were a poetic scene of nature alone. Even the poet, who is half-present in the end, is dehumanized behind his mask of hair and eyes and magic circle and is only present as mirrored in the exclamations of nebulous beholders—or rather, he *would* be mirrored *if* he had built his dome and *if* there had been beholders. Nor is there any human or personal feeling in the poem; the poet's "deep delight," impersonal enough even if it were there, exists only to be denied.

Here in these interwoven oscillations dwells the magic, the "dream," and the air of mysterious meaning of *Kubla Khan.* I question whether this effect was all deliberately thought out by Coleridge, though it might have been. It is possibly half-inherent in his subject. Paradise is usually lost and always threatened, in Genesis and Milton, in the Paradise gardens of Iem, of Aloadin, of Abyssinian princes. The historical Cubla did not apparently lose his in the end, but it too was threatened with war and dissension and portents. The Paradise of Coleridge's poem was not exactly lost either. What was lost, the closing lines tell us, was the vision of an unbuilt Paradise, an unwritten poem. His Paradise in that sense was truly enough a dream. What remains is the spirit of "oscillation," perfectly poeticized, and possibly ironically commemorative of the author. (pp. 287-88)

> *Elisabeth Schneider, in her* Coleridge, Opium and *"Kubla Khan,"* The University of Chicago Press, *1953, 378 p.*

M. H. ABRAMS   (essay date 1953)

[*Abrams is an American critic best known for his writings on English Romanticism. In* The Mirror and the Lamp: Romantic Theory and the Critical Tradition, *from which the following is drawn, he elaborates on the images of "the mirror" as a metaphor for the classical conception that art must imitate reality, and "the lamp" as representative of the Romantic belief that artists should express personal perceptions through their creations. Using these symbols, Abrams traces the development of Romantic critical theory. Here, Abrams compares Coleridge's criticism to contemporary theories of organicism and biology in order to define his concept of imaginative unity.*]

The historical importance of Coleridge's imagination has not been overrated. It was the first important channel for the flow of organicism into the hitherto clear, if perhaps not very deep, stream of English aesthetics. (Organicism may be defined as the philosophy whose major categories are derived metaphorically from the attributes of living and growing things.) Consider first the antithetic metaphors by which Coleridge, in various passages, discriminates his two productive faculties. The memory is 'mechanical' and the fancy 'passive'; fancy is a 'mirrorment . . . repeating simply, or by transposition,' and 'the aggregative and associative power,' acting only 'by a sort of juxtaposition.' The imagination, on the contrary, 'recreates' its elements by a process to which Coleridge sometimes applies terms borrowed from those physical and chemical unions most remote, in their intimacy, from the conjunction of impenetrable discretes in what he called the 'brick and mortar' thinking of the mechanical philosophy. Thus, imagination is a 'synthetic,' a 'permeative,' and a 'blending, fusing power.' At other times, Coleridge describes the imagination as an 'assimilative power,' and the 'coadunating faculty'; these adjectives are imported from contemporary biology, where 'assimilate' connoted the process by which an organism converts food into its own substance, and 'coadunate' signified 'to grow together into one.' Often, Coleridge's discussions of imagination are explicitly in terms of a living, growing thing. The imagination is, for example, 'essentially *vital*,' it 'generates and produces a form of its own,' and its rules are 'the very powers of growth and production.' And in such passages, Coleridge's metaphors for

imagination coincide with his metaphors for the mind in all its highest workings. The action of the faculty of reason Coleridge compares in detail to the development, assimilation, and respiration of a plant—thus equating knowing with growing and (to borrow a coinage from I. A. Richards) 'knowledge' with 'growledge.'

Indeed, it is astonishing how much of Coleridge's critical writing is couched in terms that are metaphorical for art and literal for a plant; if Plato's dialectic is a wilderness of mirrors, Coleridge's is a very jungle of vegetation. Only let the vehicles of his metaphors come alive, and you see all the objects of criticism writhe surrealistically into plants or parts of plants, growing in tropical profusion. Authors, characters, poetic genres, poetic passages, words, meter, logic become seeds, trees, flowers, blossoms, fruit, bark, and sap. The fact is, Coleridge's insistence on the distinction between the living imagination and the mechanical fancy [see excerpt above, 1817] was but a part of his all-out war against the 'Mechanico-corpuscular Philosophy' on every front. Against this philosophy he proposed the same objection which is found in the writings of a distinguished modern heir of organic theory, A. N. Whitehead. The scheme was developed, said Coleridge, under the need 'to submit the various phenomena of moving bodies to geometrical construction' by abstracting all its qualities except figure and motion. And 'as a *fiction of science*,' he added, 'it would be difficult to overvalue this invention,' but Descartes propounded it 'as *truth of fact:* and instead of a World *created* and filled with productive forces by the Almighty *Fiat*, left a lifeless Machine whirled about by the dust of its own Grinding. . . .' What we need in philosophy, he wrote to Wordsworth in 1815, is

> the substitution of life and intelligence (considered in its different powers from the plant up to that state in which the difference in degree becomes a new kind (man, self-consciousness), but yet not by essential opposition) for the philosophy of mechanism, which, in everything that is most worthy of the human intellect, strikes *Death*, and cheats itself by mistaking clear images for distinct conceptions . . .

Coleridge, with considerable justification, has been called the master of the fragment, and has been charged with a penchant for appropriating passages from German philosophers. Yet in criticism, what he took from other writers he developed into a speculative instrument which, for its power of insight and, above all, of application in the detailed analysis of literary works, had no peer among the German organic theorists. And in an important sense, the elements of his fully developed criticism, whether original or derivative, are consistent—with a consistency that is not primarily logical, or even psychological, but analogical; it consists in fidelity to the archetype, or founding image, to which he has committed himself. This is the contradistinction between atomistic and organic, mechanical and vital—ultimately, between the root analogies of machine and growing plant. As Coleridge explored the conceptual possibilities of the latter, it transformed radically many deeply rooted opinions in regard to the production, classification, anatomy, and evaluation of works of art. The nature of these changes can be brought to light if we ask what the properties are of a plant, as differentiated from those of a mechanical system.

Our listing of these properties is greatly simplified, because Coleridge has already described them for us, in the many, though generally neglected, documents in which he discusses

Coleridge's bedroom and study at Dr. Gillman's home, Highgate. This is the room in which Coleridge died.

the nature of living things. These begin with a long letter written at the age of twenty-four, two years before his trip to Germany and his study of physiology and natural science under Blumenbach; and they culminate with his ***Theory of Life,*** which incorporates various concepts from the German *Natur-Philo-sophen* and from the discoveries and speculations of English 'dynamic' physiologists such as Hunter, Saumarez, and Abernethy. To place passages from Coleridge's biology and his criticism side by side is to reveal at once how many basic concepts have migrated from the one province into the other.

What, then, are the characteristic properties of a plant, or of any living organism?

(1) The plant originates in a seed. To Coleridge, this indicates that the elementaristic principle is to be stood on its head; that the whole is primary and the parts secondary and derived.

> In the world we see every where evidences of a Unity, which the component parts are so far from explaining, that they necessarily pre-suppose it as the cause and condition of their existing *as* those parts; or even of their existing at all . . . That the root, stem, leaves, petals, &c. [of this crocus] cohere to one plant, is owing to an antecedent Power or Principle in the Seed, which existed before a single particle of the matters that constitute the *size* and vis-

ibility of the crocus, had been attracted from the surrounding soil, air, and moisture.

'The difference between an inorganic and organic body,' he said elsewhere, 'lies in this: In the first . . . the whole is nothing more than a collection of the individual parts or phenomena,' while in the second, 'the whole is everything, and the parts are nothing.' And Coleridge extends the same principle to non-biological phenomena: 'Depend on it, whatever is grand, whatever is truly organic and living, the whole is prior to the parts.'

(2) The plant *grows*. 'Productivity or Growth,' Coleridge said, is 'the first power' of all living things, and it exhibits itself as 'evolution and extension in the Plant.' No less is this a power of the greatest poets. In Shakespeare, for example, we find '*Growth* as in a plant.' 'All is growth, evolution, *genesis*—each line, each word almost, begets the following. . . .' Partial and passing comparisons of a completed discourse or poem to an animal body are to be found as early as Plato and Aristotle, but a highly developed organismic theory, such as Coleridge's, differs from such precedents in the extent to which all aspects of the analogy are exploited, and above all in the extraordinary stress laid on this attribute of growth. Coleridge's interest is persistently genetic—in the process as well as in the product; in becoming no less than in being. That is why Coleridge rarely discusses a finished poem without looking toward the mental process which evolved it; this is what makes all his criticism so characteristically psychological.

(3) Growing, the plant assimilates to its own substance the alien and diverse elements of earth, air, light, and water. 'Lo!' cries Coleridge eloquently, on his congenial subject:

> Lo!—with the rising sun it commences its outward life and enters into open communion with all the elements, at once assimilating them to itself and to each other . . . Lo!—at the touch of light how it returns an air akin to light, and yet with the same pulse effectuates its own secret growth, still contracting to fix what expanding it had refined.

Extended from plant to mind, this property effects another revolution in associationist theory. In the elementarist scheme, all products of invention had consisted of recombinations of the unit images of sense. In Coleridge's organic theory, images of sense become merely materials on which the mind feeds— materials which quite lose their identity in being assimilated to a new whole. 'From the first, or initiative Idea, as from a seed, successive Ideas germinate.'

> Events and images, the lively and spirit-stirring machinery of the external world, are like light, and air, and moisture, to the seed of the Mind, which would else rot and perish. In all processes of mental evolution the objects of the senses must stimulate the Mind; and the Mind must in turn assimilate and digest the food which it thus receives from without.

At the same time the 'ideas,' which in the earlier theory had been fainter replicas of sensation, are metamorphosed into seeds that grow in the soil of sensation. By his 'abuse of the word "idea,"' Locke seems to say 'that the sun, the rain, the manure, and so on had made the wheat, had made the barley . . . If for this you substitute the assertion that a grain of wheat might remain for ever and be perfectly useless and to all purposes nonapparent, had it not been that the congenial sunshine and proper soil called it forth—everything in Locke would be perfectly rational.' To Coleridge, the ideas of reason, and those in the imagination of the artist, are 'living and life-producing ideas, which . . . are essentially one with the germinal causes in nature. . . .'

(4) The plant evolves spontaneously from an internal source of energy—'effectuates,' as Coleridge put it, 'its own secret growth'—and organizes itself into its proper form. An artefact needs to be made, but a plant makes itself. According to one of Coleridge's favorite modes of stating this difference, in life 'the unity . . . is produced *ab intra*,' but in mechanism, '*ab extra.*' 'Indeed, evolution as contra-distinguished from apposition, or superinduction *ab aliunde*, is implied in the conception of life. . . .' In the realm of mind, this is precisely the difference between a 'free and rival originality' and that 'lifeless mechanism' which by servile imitation imposes an alien form on inorganic materials. As he says, echoing A. W. Schlegel:

> The form is mechanic when on any given material we impress a pre-determined form . . . as when to a mass of wet clay we give whatever shape we wish it to retain when hardened. The organic form, on the other hand, is innate; it shapes as it develops itself from within, and the fullness of its development is one and the same with the perfection of its outward form.

In this property of growing organisms, Coleridge finds the solution to the problem which, we remember, had worried the mechanists, both of matter and of mind; that is, how to explain the genesis of order and design by the operation of purely mechanical laws. To say, Coleridge declares, that 'the material particles possess this combining power by inherent reciprocal attractions, repulsions, and elective affinities; and are themselves the joint artists of their own combinations' is 'merely to shift the mystery.' Since, by Coleridge's analysis, an organism is inherently teleological—since its form is endogenous and automotive—his own solution of the mystery has no need for the mental equivalent of an architect either to draw up the preliminary design or to superintend its construction. For

> herein consists the essential difference, the contra-distinction, of an organ from a machine; that not only the characteristic shape is evolved from the invisible central power, but the material mass itself is acquired by assimilation. The germinal power of the plant transmutes the fixed air and the elementary base of water into grass or leaves . . .

Parenthetically, it may be pointed out that Coleridge resolved one problem only to run up against another. For if the growth of a plant seems inherently purposeful, it is a purpose without an alternative, fated in the seed, and evolving into its final form without the supervention of consciousness. 'The inward principle of Growth and individual Form in every seed and plant is a *subject*,' said Coleridge. 'But the man would be a dreamer, who otherwise than poetically should speak of roses and lilies as *self-conscious* subjects.' To substitute the concept of growth for the operation of mechanism in the psychology of invention, seems merely to exchange one kind of determinism for another; while to replace the mental artisan-planner by the concept of organic self-generation makes it difficult, analogically, to justify the participation of consciousness in the creative process. We shall see that, in some German critics, recourse to vegetable life as a model for the coming-into-being of a work of art had, in fact, engendered the fateful concept that artistic creation is primarily an unwilled and unconscious process of mind. Coleridge, however, though admitting an unconscious component in invention, was determined to demonstrate that a poet like Shakespeare 'never wrote anything without design.' 'What the plant is by an act not its own and unconsciously,' Coleridge exhorts us, 'that must thou *make* thyself to become.' In Coleridge's aesthetics, no less than in his ethics and theology, the justification of free-will is a crux— in part, it would appear, because this runs counter to an inherent tendency of his elected analogue.

(5) The achieved structure of a plant is an organic unity. In contra-distinction to the combination of discrete elements in a machine, the parts of a plant, from the simplest unit, in its tight integration, interchange, and interdependence with its neighbors, through the larger and more complex structures, are related to each other, and to the plant as a whole, in a complex and peculiarly intimate way. For example, since the existing parts of a plant themselves propagate new parts, the parts may be said to be their own causes, in a process of which the terminus seems to be the existence of the whole. Also, while the whole owes its being to the co-existence of the parts, the existence of that whole is a necessary condition to the survival of the parts; if, for example, a leaf is removed from the parent-plant, the leaf dies.

Attempts to define [the] peculiarities of living systems, or the nature of 'organic unity,' are at the heart of all organismic philosophies. Sometimes Coleridge describes organic relation on the model of Kant's famous formula in the *Teleological Judgment;* in Coleridge's wording, the parts of a living whole are 'so far interdependent that each is reciprocally means and end,' while the 'dependence of the parts on the whole' is combined with the 'dependence of the whole on its parts.' Or, following Schelling, he formulates it in terms of the polar logic of thesis-antithesis-synthesis. 'It would be difficult to recall any true Thesis and Antithesis of which a living organ is not the Synthesis or rather the Indifference.'

> The mechanic system . . . knows only of distance and nearness . . . in short, the relations of unproductive particles to each other; so that in every instance the result is the exact sum of the component qualities, as in arithmetical addition . . . In Life . . . the two component counter-powers actually interpenetrate each other, and generate a higher third including both the former, 'ita tamen ut sit alia et major.'

Alternatively, Coleridge declares that in an organism the whole spreads undivided through all the parts. 'The physical life is in each limb and organ of the body, all in every part; but is manifested as life, by being one in all and thus making all one. . . ,'

These formulae, like the others, are duly transferred from natural organisms to the organic products of invention.

> The spirit of poetry, like all other living powers . . . must embody in order to reveal itself; but a living body is of necessity an organized one,— and what is organization, but the connection of parts to a whole, so that each part is at once end and means!

That function of synthesizing opposites into a higher third, in which the component parts are *alter et idem,* Coleridge attributes, in the aesthetic province, to the imagination—'that synthetic and magical power,' as he describes it in the *Biographia Literaria,* which 'reveals itself in the balance or reconciliation of opposite or discordant qualities. And the affinity of this synthesis with the organic function of assimilating nutriment declares itself, when Coleridge goes on at once to cite Sir John Davies' description of the soul, which 'may with slight alteration be applied, and even more appropriately, to the poetic IMAGINATION':

> Doubtless this could not be, but that she turns
>   Bodies to spirit by sublimation strange,
> As fire converts to fire the thing it burns,
>   As we our food into our nature change.

To Coleridge, therefore, imaginative unity is not a mechanical juxtaposition of 'unproductive particles,' nor a neo-classic decorum of parts in which (as Dryden translated Boileau), 'Each object must be fixed in the due place'—

> Till, by a curious art disposed, we find
> One perfect whole of all the pieces joined.

Imaginative unity is an *organic* unity: a self-evolved system, constituted by a living interdependence of parts, whose identity cannot survive their removal from the whole.

It is a curious attribute of an organismic philosophy that on the basis of its particular logic, in which truth is achieved only through the synthesis of antitheses, it is unable to deny its metaphysical opposite, but can defeat it only by assimilating it into 'a higher third,' as Coleridge said, 'including both the former.' Accordingly, despite Coleridge's intoxication with the alchemical change wrought in the universe by his discovery of the organic analogy, he did not hesitate to save, and to incorporate into his own theory, the mechanical philosophy he so violently opposed. Mechanism is false, not because it does not tell the truth, but because it does not tell the whole truth. 'Great good,' he wrote in his notebook, 'of such revolution as alters, not by exclusion, but by an enlargement that includes the former, though it places it in a new point of view.' Coleridge's fully developed critical theory, therefore, is deliberately syncretic, and utilizes not one, but two controlling analogues, one of a machine, the other of a plant; and these divide the processes and products of art into two distinct kinds, and by the same token, into two orders of excellence.

Again and again, Coleridge uses his bifocal lens to discriminate and appraise two modes of poetry. One of these can be adequately accounted for in mechanical terms. It has its source in the particulars of sense and the images of memory, and its production involves only the lower faculties of fancy, 'understanding,' and empirical 'choice.' It is therefore the work of 'talent,' and stands in a rank below the highest; its examples are such writings as those of Beaumont and Fletcher, Ben Jonson, and Pope. The other and greater class of poetry is organic. It has its source in living 'ideas,' and its production involves the higher faculties of imagination, 'reason,' and the 'will.' Hence it is the work of 'genius,' and its major instances are to be found in the writings of Dante, Shakespeare, Milton, and Wordsworth. For while talent lies 'in the understanding'— understanding being 'the faculty of thinking and forming judgments on the notices furnished by sense'—genius consists in 'the action of reason and imagination.' As part of what it learns from sense-experience, talent has 'the faculty of appropriating and applying the knowledge of others,' but not 'the creative, and self-sufficing power of absolute *Genius*.' The 'essential difference' is that between 'the shaping skill of mechanical talent, and the creative, productive life-power of inspired genius,' resulting in a product modified '*ab intra* in each component part.' (pp. 168-76)

> *M. H. Abrams, "The Psychology of Literary Invention: Mechanical and Organic Theories," in his* The Mirror and the Lamp: Romantic Theory and the Critical Tradition, *Oxford University Press, 1953, pp. 156-83.**

RENÉ WELLEK (essay date 1955)

[*Wellek's* A History of Modern Criticism, *from which the following is drawn, comprises a major, comprehensive study of the literary critics of the last three centuries. Wellek's critical method, as demonstrated in* A History *and outlined in his* Theory of Literature, *is one of describing, analyzing, and evaluating a work solely in terms of the problems it poses for itself and how the writer solves them. For Wellek, biographical, historical, and psychological information are incidental. Although many of Wellek's critical methods are reflected in the work of the New Critics, he was not a member of that group and rejected their more formalistic tendencies. Wellek calls Coleridge one of the few critics outside of Germany who developed "a satisfying theory of poetry . . . which guarded its fences against emotionalism, naturalism, and mysticism and successfully combined symbolism with a pro-*

found grasp of literary history." Here, Wellek traces the influence of August and Friedrich von Schlegel, Friedrich von Schelling, and Immanuel Kant on the philosophy of Coleridge. Wellek contends that Coleridge plagiarized a large portion of his aesthetic theory from them; for example, his "exaltation of art to a metaphysical role" is based on the philosophy of Schelling, while his comparisons of poetry to architecture are borrowed from the Schlegels. Coleridge is much more notable for defining terms of poetic theory, Wellek argues, and is "quite disappointing on the level of genre criticism."]

Coleridge differs from almost all preceding English writers by his claim to an epistemology and metaphysics from which he derives his aesthetics and finally his literary theory and critical principles. He aimed at a complete systematic unity and continuity even though in practice he left wide gaps. But he made an attempt and he insisted rightly on the significance of the attempt. He sometimes speaks of his "disease of totalizing and perfecting" and tells a story about his fanciful impulse to complete the perishable architecture of some smoldering pieces of wood in a fireplace, late at night. But usually he states earnestly and with conviction that the "end and purpose of all reason is unity and system," that the "ultimate end of human thought and human feeling is unity." We must aim at "fixed canons of criticism, previously established and deduced from the nature of man," at a "science of reasoning and judging concerning the productions of literature." Method is Coleridge's constant watchword: it inspired his interests in encyclopedias and the classification of all knowledge. Method means "unity with progression," "that which unites, and makes many things *one* in the mind of man," the "keynote," the "initiative." Coleridge goes to the extravagant length of saying that poetry "owes its whole charm, and all its beauty, and all its power, to the philosophical principles of Method." The statement assumes meaning if we know that method means unity and unifying power and that method is hence identical with the workings of the creative imagination.

These principles, Coleridge argues, must be based on "human nature," i.e. must follow from an analysis of the human mind. Coleridge disconcertingly wavers between a psychological and an epistemological foundation for such an analysis. It is the same basic uncertainty we shall find elsewhere, the same conflict between the tradition of empirical psychology and the dialectics of the German idealists. . . . In the famous definition of poetry in **Biographia Literaria** . . . an appeal is made to the psychic effect on the reader. The poet "brings the whole soul of man into activity, with the subordination of its faculties to each other, according to their relative worth and dignity." Coleridge never elaborated such a psychological scheme; yet he ranked the faculties, beginning with the senses and ascending to reason, in a fairly clear scale, and he used the distinction between imagination and fancy as a value criterion. Elsewhere he more ambitiously tried to "deduce" the position of the arts (and of poetry) from an analysis of the epistemological situation, very much like Fichte's or Schelling's analysis. He proclaims that it is "the office and object of his philosophy" to "demonstate the identity of subject and object." He conceives of nature as identical with that which exists in man as intelligence and self-consciousness. Being is identified with knowing and truth. Art assumes its place as a "mediatress between, and reconciler of, nature and man," as a "union and reconciliation of that which is nature with that which is exclusively human." But this exaltation of art to a metaphysical role which makes it the center of philosophy is merely a reproduction from Schelling and remains isolated in Coleridge's writings. (pp. 158-59)

Coleridge usually ignores the problem of art and discusses beauty. At times he uses the Schellingian vocabulary: Beauty is "the shorthand hieroglyphic of truth—the mediator between truth and feeling, the head and the heart, a silent communion of the Spirit with the Spirit in Nature." But elsewhere he adopts ideas common in Schiller about the union of life and shape as the essence of beauty. In other contexts he lapses into a neo-Platonic mystical terminology; he can speak of "supersensuous beauty, the beauty of virtue and holiness," and of its immediate perception as "light to the eye." Most often he repeats the ancient theory of beauty as harmony, as the one in the many. At other times, he reproduces Kant's arguments for the distinction of the beautiful from the useful and the agreeable. (pp. 159-60)

Coleridge's speculations on the sublime, though various enough, do not hang together and hardly enter his theory of literature. As in Kant, the sublime is considered as subjective: "No object of sense is sublime in itself, but only as far as I make it a symbol of some Idea." Coleridge gives an example: "the circle is a beautiful figure in itself; it becomes sublime, when I contemplate eternity under it." Elsewhere the sublime is considered "neither whole nor parts, but unity as boundless and endless allness," a "total completeness." At other times Coleridge accepts a close relation between the sublime and infinity and like Schelling and the Schlegels applies it to a distinction between ancient and modern literature. Greek literature is finite, Christian romantic literature strives for the infinite. Thus Coleridge can deny sublimity to the Greeks and quote passages from the Bible and Milton as examples of the sublime. But little is made of these conceptions in practice, nor is anything made of such related terms as the "grand" and the "majestic." (p. 160)

[His] different fragments on aesthetics derived from a variety of sources, from Schelling, from Kant, and from 18th-century psychologists, do not give Coleridge an important position in a history of general aesthetic. His specific theory of poetry is far more important, for in it he made a genuine attempt at synthesis. Coleridge tried to work out a scheme that would unify a description of the poet, his equipment and faculties, with a description of the work of art itself and its effect on the reader. Within these three main divisions he tried to apply one and the same logical principle. There is a principle of unity, he argues, but within it there is distinction which must not, however, be complete contradiction and separation. The logic is that of the whole being the sum of the parts but more than the sum of the parts. This "holistic" logic alternates disconcertingly, however, with the application of a triadic scheme of dialectics: the reconciliation of opposites, thesis, antithesis, and synthesis. At other times the elaborate scheme is abandoned and Coleridge comfortably solves his problem by being on both sides at once.

There is first the poet or (almost identical in meaning) genius, e.g. Shakespeare, who is the ideal poet. A long list of qualifications is required in the poet: sensibility, passion, will, good sense, judgment, fancy, imagination, etc. He must be also a good man and "*implicite*, if not *explicite*, a profound metaphysician," a profound philosopher. A poet "is also an historian and naturalist in the light as well as the life of philosophy." Furthermore, he is a religious man. (pp. 161-62)

The inclusiveness of such philosophic requirements is clarified if we realize that genius for Coleridge is always objective, impersonal, directed toward a grasp of the whole universe. A poet is not excited by personal interests. "To have a genius is to live in the universal, to know no self but that which is reflected not only from the faces of all around us, our fellow-creatures, but reflected from the flowers, the trees, the beasts, yea from the very surface of the waters and the sands of the desert. A man of genius finds a reflex to himself, were it only in the mystery of being.'' In Shakespeare's early poems Coleridge sees the promise of genius in a ''choice of subjects very remote from the private interests and circumstances of the writer himself.'' The highest praise is given to Shakespeare for the ''utter aloofness of the poet's own feelings, from those of which he is at once the painter and the analyst.'' Shakespeare is like ''the Spinozistic deity—an omnipresent creativeness.'' This impersonality, this contemplative absorption in rendering reality by creating a new one, requires judgment. Coleridge is tireless in insisting on Shakespeare's genius revealing ''itself in his judgment, as in its most exalted form.'' This genius is so consummate that it reveals itself ''not only in the general construction, but in all the detail.''

From these pronouncements we might conclude that the poet is a philosopher, an impersonal observer, a self-conscious, judicious maker. But Coleridge, with his view of the poet as the whole man, can at the same time say that the poet works ''unconsciously.'' ''There is in genius itself an unconscious activity; nay, this is *the* genius in the man of genius.'' As in Schelling or the Schlegels the poet is both conscious and unconscious. But in Coleridge the poet is also the man of sensibility and the man of passion. He creates in ''an unusual state of excitement,'' in a ''steady fervor'' of the mind. Not only is the poet thus a man of intense feeling: he has preserved this feeling from his childhood. ''The poet is one who carries the simplicity of childhood into the powers of manhood.'' Coleridge does not think the gifts he heaps upon the poet contradictory; the poet is simply everything: both conscious and unconscious, both a philosopher and a child, both constructive and emotional. Coleridge claims for himself an unusual union of intellect and feeling; Wordsworth, another example of a genius not quite so perfect as Shakespeare, is praised for a ''union of deep and subtle thought with sensibility,'' for his ''meditative pathos,'' a quality which combines philosophy and emotion.

Still, while the poet is the whole man, he has a specific faculty which is his alone or is at least shared only by other creators. This faculty is imagination, which is the power of unifying things, of being all things. Coleridge misinterpreted the ordinary German word *Einbildungskraft* to mean ''In eins Bildung,'' which he then translated into Greek as ''esemplastic'' or ''coadunating'' power. Imagination is the power of objectifying oneself, the Protean self-transforming power of genius. . . . Imagination is also the power of changing the possible into the real, ''the potential into the actual,'' the ''essence into existence.'' This notion seems to be derived from Leibniz and provides the bridge between the conception of the poet and the poetry itself. In his famous definition of the imagination as the balance or reconciliation of opposites [see excerpt above, 1817] Coleridge can indiscriminately mix traits descriptive of the poet with contraries observable only in the work of art. ''What is poetry?'' is, in Coleridge's mind, ''nearly the same question with, what is a poet?'' (pp. 162-64)

Coleridge does not always recognize the distinction between the poet and his poetry. Sometimes he wants to reduce the problem of defining poetry to that of describing the poet. He says that ''the most general and distinctive character of a poem originates in the poetic genius itself'' and that a just definition of poetry is possible ''only so far as the distinction still results from the poetic genius, which sustains and modifies the emotions, thoughts, and vivid representations of a poem by the energy without effort of the poet's own mind.'' We would thus abolish the distinction between psychic processes and capacities and the finished product, the work of art, which, in literature, is a structure of linguistic signs. But happily Coleridge *does* in other places discuss the differentia of poetry without the poet.

In the wake of Schiller, the Schlegels, and Schelling Coleridge sometimes extends the term ''poetry'' to all the arts and even to all human creativity. This use has the authority of Plato's *Symposium,* but even in Plato it blurs the distinction between the poet and the philosopher, the legislator and the warrior. (p. 165)

In one place Coleridge tries to introduce a distinction between ''poesy'' and ''poetry'': poesy is to be a ''generic name of all fine arts''; poetry is to be limited to works whose medium is words. Usually, however, he abandons this terminological innovation and talks about music as the poetry of the ear and painting as the poetry of the eye or adopts the ancient view that all the other arts are ''mute poesy.''

In general, however, Coleridge is not much interested in enforcing a view of poetry as basically identical with the other arts. He is not even much concerned with parallelisms and analogies among the arts. He takes from Schlegel the comparison of romantic poetry with Gothic architecture, and ancient poetry with a Greek temple. He draws a parallel between recent poetry and painting, both interested in depicting the minutiae in the background, while Renaissance poetry and painting were supposedly more interested in the beauty and harmony of the whole. . . . But these are isolated insights which show that Coleridge accepted the unity of the arts but paid no particular attention to the problems of their relationship and distinction.

Usually Coleridge speaks of poetry as an art of ''articulate language'' and attempts to determine its differentia from other forms of discourse. He tries to distinguish it from science and morality in terms of its end and function. The immediate end of poetry is pleasure, ''immediate'' implying the lack of practical interest, the aesthetic distance which Kant had described. ''The poet must always aim at pleasure as his specific means''; he must not aim at the useful and good directly, but through pleasure aim at these only as an ultimate end. This end is, on occasion, defined as that of ''cultivating and predisposing the heart of the reader,'' of ''moralizing'' the reader. (pp. 166-67)

[Coleridge] tried to define poetry with very traditional terminology: as pleasure for the reader and passion in the author during composition. But he also wanted to differentiate between poetry and verse and thus to recognize poetry outside of metrical compositions. He argues that there is poetry of the highest kind without meter, and he quotes Plato, Jeremy Taylor, Burnet and Isaiah as examples. But how does this prose-poetry differ from other prose? Coleridge quickly rejects the idea that fictionality makes poetry what it is. ''It is not merely invention: if it were, *Gulliver's Travels* would be poetry.'' We do not call ''novels and other works of fiction'' poems. These are the passages in which Coleridge disposes of a solution which would find much favor today. *Gulliver* is poetry, it is imaginative literature, we would answer without hesitation. Poetry, in a more narrow sense, is only distinguishable by meter.

At the same time, Coleridge tries to draw a line between poetry and verse. He cannot recognize meter itself as the distinguishing characteristic of poetry. He tries to find a tortuous circumlocution for a concept which in effect includes both meter and rhythmical prose. In poetry, as distinct from fiction, "each part shall also communicate for itself a distinct and conscious pleasure," or "the greatest immediate pleasure from each part should be compatible with the largest sum of pleasure on the whole." Though Coleridge repeats this definition with great emphasis several times, it surely offers no solution. Either it is a surreptitious introduction of the pleasures of meter and rhythm or it says merely that poetry is more highly organized than prose, which may not be true in many cases. One must, of course, admit that Coleridge could not have foreseen later developments toward closely patterned poetic fiction. He was content that his criterion of close organization allowed him to group poetic passages in the Bible, Plato, and Taylor with Shakespeare and Milton on the one side, and to put Scott, Defoe, and Richardson on the other. His later attempts at defining the difference ("prose is words in their best order;— poetry is the best words in the best order"; or "good prose is—proper words in their proper places, good verse—the most proper words in their proper places") are even less convincing. They seem to say that poetry is simply better than prose, or that select "best" words are most proper for poetry. These are theories quite untenable on Coleridge's own premises. One must conclude that Coleridge failed in his attempts to define poetry.

While Coleridge hardly succeeds in defining the difference between poetry and verse, he writes an excellent defense of meter against Wordsworth's comparative disparagement of it as a mere "superadded charm." (pp. 168-70)

Coleridge's insistence on the unity of the work of art yields a much more convincing analysis of poetry than his attempts to make either the pleasure principle or the emotion of the poet his criterion. The work of art forms a whole: "language, passion, and character must act and react on each other." Totality works also in the direction of time: "the common end of all narrative, nay, of all poems, is to convert a series into a whole: to make those events, which in real or imagined history move in a straight line, assume to our Understanding a circular motion." Thus conceived, the relation between whole and parts is a version of unity and variety, or as Coleridge prefers to say, of "unity in multeity," and thus an illustration of the workings of the imagination. (p. 170)

In most cases Coleridge keeps hold, so to speak, of both handles: the unity and the things unified, the whole and the parts. The effect depends on the tension, on the reconciliation of opposites, not on sameness or unity in the sense of indistinct totality. There is no contradiction between the reconciliation of opposites, the dialectics of whole and the parts, and the analogy of organism, if the latter is interpreted moderately. They allow Coleridge the contrast between Shakespeare and Beaumont and Fletcher. A play by Shakespeare is like a real fruit, while a play by the two friends is like "a quarter of an orange, a quarter of an apple, and the like of a lemon and of a pomegranate." And again he uses the analogy of a real garden compared with a child's garden of stuck flowers which will wither overnight. Yet such an emphasis on totality can be pushed to superstitious extremes. If we say, as Coleridge does, that "you can't alter a word, or the position of a word, in Milton or Shakespeare" without damage, an impossible ideal of coherence and perfection is postulated. (pp. 171-72)

Whole, organism, unity, continuity are the key terms for the structure of the work of art. But the work of art also represents the world of reality and projects its own fictional world. In what relation is this other world to the great world, and how does art suggest this relation? Coleridge answers again in two ways, keeping the traditional account and adding a new theory. Art is imitation in Coleridge but it is also symbolization. Imitation is, of course, not copying, not naturalism. Imitation is described in terms of the audience reaction as a recognition of likeness in the dissimilar, or, in the terms of the share of the author, as an infusion of the author's own knowledge and talent into external objects. All this is traditional enough: Coleridge himself appeals to such diverse authorities as Petrarch and Adam Smith. What is imitated is not nature but general nature, universal nature. So Coleridge can say that "the essence of poetry is universality." "It was Shakespeare's prerogative to have the universal which is potentially in each particular, opened out to him in the *homo generalis*." Similarly, Robinson Crusoe is praised as the universal representative, as Everyman. "Whatever is not representative, generic, may be indeed most poetically expressed, but it is not poetry." Coleridge thus disparages the merely particular and local. "Poetry is essentially ideal, it avoids and excludes all accident." Wordsworth is criticized for "matter-of-factness," and dramatists other than Shakespeare for depicting transitory manners. At times Coleridge sounds like a good neoclassicist and he himself appeals to Aristotle and Davenant. But of course he sees the problem of the union of the particular with the general, of the concrete with the universal, which is another case of the reconciliation of opposites. (pp. 172-73)

The same tension of interpretations can be found in Coleridge's use of the term "nature." Nature is sometimes the spirit of nature, *natura naturans*, the creativity of nature. . . . Idea and symbol are the two main instruments by which the poet represents this spirit of nature. As in many other writers, "idea" is a slippery term. Coleridge uses it sometimes as the English empiricists do to mean sense datum. At other times he allows the term to assume a supernatural Platonic meaning. But when Coleridge has literary theory in mind, he usually thinks of the "idea" as an instance of the union of the universal and the particular. Idea is the same as essence, is "the inmost principle of the possibility of any thing, as that particular thing." Idea "never passes into an abstraction and therefore never becomes the equivalent of an image." It is neither concept nor image. It cannot be generalized, it cannot be seen, it can only be contemplated. It is a form of being but above form; it is a law contemplated subjectively. It is made accessible, visible to us by symbols.

Law is in the objects; Idea is their essence; it can even be the essence of an individual object (as law could not be). Symbol is the device by which idea is presented. Symbol in Coleridge is contrasted with allegory, in the same way that imagination is contrasted with fancy, the organic with the mechanical. On occasion Coleridge lapses into the old use of "symbol" to mean conventional sign, but usually symbol is to him the union of the universal and the particular. (pp. 173-74)

In his practical criticism Coleridge rarely uses the term "symbol." Yet in speaking of Wordsworth's "Intimations" ode he refers to the "modes of inmost being," which "yet cannot be conveyed save in symbols of time and space." These remarks seem to refute, out of Coleridge's own mouth, the commonsense ridicule he has poured, a few pages before, on the address to the child as "Mighty Prophet! Seer blest." Yet on the whole,

Coleridge seems most disappointing on the question of imagery and symbolization. The distinction between imagination and fancy is used to disparage rhetorical figures which today we would classify as "witty" or metaphysical or simply as figures in which there is only one point of similarity between tenor and vehicle. . . . (p. 175)

Coleridge understands one part of the symbolic, linguistic point of view. He realizes that the emphasis, inherited from the 18th century, on "imagination" as purely visual realization is mistaken. He quotes Kant in support of his distinction between the conceivable and the picturable; he protests against the "despotism of the eye" and the "delusive notion that what is not imageable is likewise not conceivable." Yet he rarely draws the consequences from these insights. Rather he emphasizes imagery which might be called "animating." . . . (p. 176)

Coleridge has least to say about the affective aspect of the aesthetic situation. His clinging to the term "pleasure" prevents him from facing the problem of the ugly or tragic in art. He is content to discuss illusion. . . . Art—he is here mainly thinking of drama on the stage—is not delusion, not a deception such as naturalistic standards require; nor is it, on the other hand, complete consciousness of the artificiality of art. Coleridge accepts a compromise for which he finds the famous phrase, "that willing suspension of disbelief for the moment which constitutes poetic faith." Sometimes he speaks of "negative faith," of voluntary acquiescence in the fiction which shuts out everyday reality. The poet "solicits us to yield ourselves to a dream; and this too with our eyes open; . . . and meantime, only, not to *dis*believe." Sometimes he argues that there is a distinction between our knowing and our feeling. We know, for instance, that Othello and Desdemona are actors, but we do not feel it. Otherwise, we would not say in praise of a good actor that he was "lost in his character; that he appeared and became the very man." It is not true that fiction is known to be always fiction. "It is not felt to be fiction when we are most affected. We know the thing to be a representation, but we often feel it to be a reality." Coleridge suggests that stage-properties diminish illusion, while good acting increases it, an observation which helps to explain his aversion to seeing Shakespeare on the stage of his time. Yet it is hard to see how, even on Coleridge's own terms, knowing could be kept separate from feeling. (p. 177)

The problem of theatrical illusion as discussed by Coleridge is not very different from that of probability or plausibility in an epic or a novel. Coleridge rather frequently uses this criterion, which in a system like Schelling's is quite superfluous. He points out an improbability in Scott's *Rob Roy* which "awakens one rudely out of the day-dream of negative faith." Elsewhere he tries to distinguish between a temporary belief in strange situations and a rejection of moral miracles. . . . Coleridge's general preference is always for objective presentation, for characters speaking in their own tone of voice. In the novel he finds the height of successful illusion in the reproduction of the workings of the minds of the characters. He prefers the method of Richardson to that of Fielding. Richardson has talent for reproducing meditation, Fielding only for external observation, though Coleridge prefers Fielding for his saner morality. (p. 178)

Coleridge thus ascribes little importance to story or plot. It is continually disparaged as merely "interesting." There is, he says, no story interest in *Don Quixote,* Ariosto, the Greek tragedies, or Milton. Indeed, plot is merely a canvas, a scaffolding for a work of art. In enumerating the parts of the

drama—language, passion, character—Coleridge leaves out plot, which Aristotle would have put first. His criticism of Shakespeare is largely character analysis. The play as a play is either ignored or minimized. Psychology of character or of situation, at most the pervading emotional tone of a play, not the play as a piece of stagecraft, is what interests Coleridge.

All that we have been saying explains why Coleridge is quite disappointing on the level of genre criticism or anywhere in the realm between general theory of poetry and practical criticism. (pp. 178-79)

> *René Wellek, "Coleridge," in his* A History of Modern Criticism, 1750-1950: The Romantic Age, *Vol. 2, Yale University Pess, 1955, pp. 151-87.*

J. B. BEER   (essay date 1959)

[*Beer's* Coleridge the Visionary *is widely respected as a solid overview of Coleridge's life and works. In the following, Beer proposes a dialectical interpretation of "Kubla Khan," which he describes as a dually thematic poem divided logically by parts. Beer interprets Coleridge as a visionary poet and "Kubla Khan" as a tragic visionary poem reflecting "all that was unsatisfactory in its author": the futility of his philosophies and the inadequacies of his personality.*]

[*Kubla Khan*] is a poem with two major themes: genius and the lost paradise. In the first stanza the man of commanding genius, the fallen but daemonic man, strives to rebuild the lost paradise in a world which is, like himself, fallen. In the second

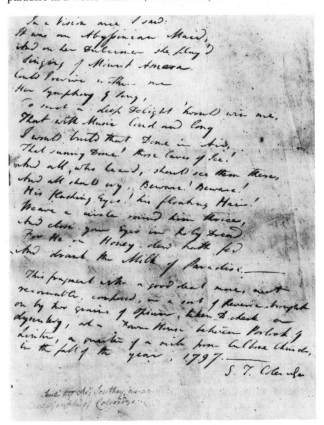

Part of the original manuscript of "Kubla Khan" with the poet's account of its composition. The Granger Collection, New York.

stanza, the other side of the daemonic re-asserts itself: the mighty fountain in the savage place, the wailing woman beneath the waning moon, the daemon-lover. The third stanza is a moment of miraculous harmony between the contending forces: the sunny dome and the caves of ice, the fountain and the caves, the dome and the waves all being counterpoised in one harmony. Finally, in the last stanza, there is a vision of paradise regained: of man re-visited by that absolute genius which corresponds to his original, unfallen state, of the honey-dew fountain of immortality re-established in the garden, of complete harmony between Apollo with his lyre and the damsel with the dulcimer, of the established dome, and of the multitude, reconciled by the terrible fascination of the genius into complete harmony.

In spite of the over-riding pattern of the poem, however, the imagery is so complicated and interwoven that a complete interpretation cannot be presented in one straightforward exposition. Instead, one is forced to establish the dialectic of thesis, antithesis, static harmony and desired consummation in the four stanzas, and then suggest how various images and ideas pass through it. Alph, as the sacred river, runs through measureless caverns to a sterile sea and is thus separated from the fountain, which becomes in its turn destructive; but even in this state, a harmony between fountain and caves is possible, and one may also envisage a re-establishment of the original honey-dew fountain of immortality in a regained paradise. Again, Alph is also Alpheus, the male principle for ever seeking Arethusa the female principle: in this rôle he becomes assimilated with the Kubla of the first stanza and re-emerges in the last stanza in the harmony of the inspired bard with the Abyssinian maid. Or again we may trace in the Cain-like figure of Kubla the Typhonian sun of heat and violence, with the wailing woman beneath the waning moon as his confederate, the usurping Aso of Ethiopia: the harmony of ice and moon figures the redeeming work of Isis, who becomes explicit in the Abyssinian maid, and finally restores Osiris, the sun-god of divine love. As in *The Ancient Mariner,* all these symbols may be translated psychologically. Kubla is the eighteenth-century man of understanding, trying to impose a rational order on the universe, while the second stanza represents that other side of the eighteenth-century mind—the Gothic love of horrible sublimity and powerful destruction—for which the unregenerate Reason can find no place. A powerful genius may impose a harmony even upon these warring elements: but the only true solution lies with the true genius, who in his moment of inspiration is restored temporarily to the state of unfallen man, and so enabled to overcome the sterile conflict between the impotent understanding and the unrestrained energies of destruction by subsuming these elements into the Sun-fountain of the sublime Reason—at once powerful and compellingly attractive. (pp. 266-68)

As a poem, [*Kubla Khan*] was born out of Coleridge's visionary speculations: it was also projected forward as a myth within which much of his later thinking took place. How relevant is either of these facts to poetry or to human experience? (p. 278)

Whether or not we are interested in them depends on whether we prefer our own personal reaction to the poem, or to read it vicariously through the mind of Coleridge, for whom each of the images had associations which bound them together in an intricate logical and sensuous pattern.

Their relevance to human experience is a more complicated issue, and our attitude to it is likely to be associated with our attitude towards Coleridge's thought in general, with its over-riding emphasis upon the importance of the human imagination. For many critics and readers, the human imagination is in the last analysis a peripheral mental function: it has an important biological function, in enabling human beings to deal with situations which cannot for one reason or another be dealt with by direct physical action, but it must be disciplined by the body, and constantly checked against sense experience.

If this view is adopted, *Kubla Khan* is, for all its merits, a tragic poem, and a focusing point of all that was unsatisfactory in its author. It has its basis in a visionary world which even in Coleridge's day was under heavy fire. Evolutionary theories were already abroad, but he refused to listen to them. In the same way, he dismissed as ridiculous the claims of Sanskrit for priority to other languages, because he could hardly believe that Hebrew, or some language immediately prior to it, was not the language taught by God to Adam in Paradise. He spent a good deal of time, all his life, in trying to interpret basic scientific phenomena in terms of theories which he elicited from the Bible. And if he was conservative about the past, he was an impossible idealist concerning the future. His 'Abyssinian maid' was an ideal being who did not and could not exist in this life, and his attempts to find her brought nothing but unhappiness to his wife, his children, his intimate friends and himself. The political scheme of Pantisocracy was a prime example of his inability to see man as he is, weak and potentially vicious, and the best that can be said is that he did at least come to value traditional human institutions more highly in his later thinking. His philosophy as a whole, nevertheless, consisted of a long series of attempts to impose theories on an experience which refused to fit them, and his vision of himself as an inspired genius was a pitiful delusion. (pp. 279-80)

J. B. Beer, in his Coleridge the Visionary, *Chatto & Windus, 1959, 367 p.*

M. M. BADAWI (essay date 1973)

[*Badawi's* Coleridge: Critic of Shakespeare, *from which the following is drawn, is the first book-length study devoted solely to Coleridge's Shakespearean criticism. Badawi states that his intention is "to understand the critical methods and assumptions on Shakespeare and, secondly, to define the nature of his contribution to the criticism of Shakespeare in England." Coleridge inherited a great deal from his eighteenth-century antecedents, Badawi claims, but he also provided new theories for the English interpretation of Shakespeare. Here, Badawi relates Coleridge's Shakespearean criticism to his poetic philosophy as it is delineated in the* Biographia Literaria.]

When we turn from the main bulk of eighteenth-century Shakespearean criticism to that of Coleridge, we realize immediately that we are undergoing a radically different experience. His writings are at once alive and life-giving. We feel more akin to Coleridge even though we may disagree with some of his critical utterances, and that is not solely because we are closer to him in time. In the writings of most of those tireless and voluminous eighteenth-century critics and scholars we wade through a morass of pages in the hope that we may come across some illuminating remark or an important fact to encourage us to proceed on our laborious journey. But it is different with Coleridge. He may not give us the important fact, and as a rule he rarely does; yet we are amply rewarded in other ways.

The strength of Coleridge's Shakespearean criticism, fragmentary as it is, lies in its profoundly systematic nature, in the fine balance achieved in it between guiding principle and spontaneous response; and it is precisely in this quality that eighteenth-century criticism is painfully lacking. Here we encounter a vigorous mind playing freely, and a keen but disciplined sensibility. The reader's impression, true enough, is the starting point . . . ; but it is usually translated into an intelligible statement, which in turn is referred back to some basic principle. In other words, Coleridge's strength as a critic consists in his being a 'philosophic' critic. Not content with simply recording his impressions, as the worst of the romantic critics do, or with forcing a work to fit in with a rigid, preconceived formula, as eighteenth-century critics often try to do, he arranges his various impressions into some sort of system—a system that has its place in a larger system of mind. Opinions may vary as to whether the study of philosophy killed the poet in Coleridge; but there is no doubt that his philosophical preoccupation helped to make him the critic he was. One has to admit that, even if one may dismiss a great part of the philosophy itself.

To be able to see more clearly the systematic nature of Coleridge's criticism of Shakespeare it is necessary to make allowance for some important facts. With very few exceptions Coleridge did not publish his criticism himself; but the great bulk of it has reached us in the form of lecture notes, marginalia, and other fragments. . . . Given that repetition and digressiveness are among Coleridge's mental habits, still a considerable part of the digressions and repetitions may be excused on this score. Likewise his failure to acknowledge at least some of his debts may be due to the inconvenience of so doing in a public lecture room in the presence of a mixed audience of varying intellectual standards and backgrounds.

Yet some critics have suggested that in his practical criticism, or at least in his best criticism, Coleridge disregards his own principles, as if his criticism had no bearing upon his aesthetic theory, which is to be dismissed with the rest of his philosophizing as incoherent, obscure, and sometimes confused. It is strange to accuse a man, who at all times emphasized the need to return to fundamental principles, of taking little notice of such principles himself. The underlying theme of *The Friend, Biographia Literaria,* even *Aids to Reflection,* is a plea for a re-examination of contemporary basic principles in morality, politics, philosophy and criticism, and an attempt to base all of them upon secure foundations. In almost everything, he wrote, Coleridge felt the need to refer to basic principles, and that in spite of his obscurities which are frequently not unjustly complained of. Or perhaps it is because of his incessant desire to go back to such principles, which with him becomes almost an obsession, that he is often tortuous, involuted and obscure.

Biographia Literaria, rambling as it is, stresses the value of principles in literary criticism. In it one of Coleridge's main aims is to point to the chaos in critical writings, both in literary reviews and elsewhere, and the dangers of 'the substitution of assertion for argument', and to advocate a kind of 'philosophical criticism' which sets out by defining its principles. Before he embarked upon the actual criticism of Wordsworth's poetry he thought it wise to explain what he meant by philosophical criticism. I quote the passage in full, for it is important.

> I should call that investigation fair and philosophical, in which the critic announces and endeavours to establish the principles, which he holds for the foundation of poetry in general, with the specification of these in their application to the different *classes* of poetry. Having thus prepared his canons of criticism for praise and condemnation, he would proceed to par-
>
> ticularize the most striking passages to which he deems them applicable, faithfully noticing the frequent or infrequent recurrence of similar merits or defects, and as faithfully distinguishing what is characteristic from what is accidental, or a mere flagging of the wing. Then if his premises be rational, his deductions legitimate, and his conclusions justly applied, the reader, and possibly the poet himself, may adopt his judgement and in the independence of free-agency. If he has erred, he presents his errors in a definite place and tangible form, and holds the torch and guides the way to their detection.

This is the method which Coleridge follows in his criticism of Shakespeare as well. But it is important to realize that Coleridge applies his principles with tact, revealing his awareness that they are not hard and fast rules, but useful tools to guide and clarify his responses to every individual work. First principles of criticism, he says, 'can indeed neither create a Taste nor supply the want of it but yet may conduce effectively to its cultivation and are perhaps indispensable in securing it from the aberrations of caprice and fashion'. The critic is not one who voices his own personal 'opinions', which 'weight for nothing'; he writes about a work 'in such a form, as is calculated either to effect a fundamental conviction, or to receive a fundamental confutation'. (pp. 29-32)

Far from being desultory and impressionistic in his critical pronouncements on Shakespeare, Coleridge in practically every course of lectures on the subject is careful to begin by defining his principles. Some of these principles are involved in his definition of poetry, to which he often devotes the two initial lectures. This is significant. It is not explained away by reference to Coleridge's habit of repeating himself. Nor would it be convincing to say that the impecunious Coleridge found it easy to fill up two lectures with matter which became so familiar to him that it no longer required fresh preparation or previous labour. In the courses of lectures he gave he often had more material than he could dispose of in the allotted number of lectures announced, and on occasions he found it necessary to add one or more free of charge to the number originally planned. It is more probable, and more in keeping with his habits of thought, that Coleridge started his courses on Shakespeare with the discourse on the definition of poetry because of the importance of such a definition, and because of its immediate relevance to the subject in hand. His interest in his principles, and his belief in the intimate relation between them and the main subject of his lectures were such that occasionally one feels that his object in discoursing on Shakespeare was primarily to illustrate his theory of poetry and principles of criticism. (pp. 32-3)

In a sense Coleridge was writing in the English critical tradition when he maintained, as he often did, that the end of poetry is pleasure. Poetry, he said, is opposed to science. (p. 33)

Coleridge's view that poetry has pleasure for its end . . . has a long history behind it. . . . The opposition between poetry and science in Coleridge's definition is the product of eighteenth-century poetics, which equated poetry with pleasure.

In Coleridge's critical theory the pleasure principle was accompanied by its corollary in eighteenth-century criticism, namely the tendency towards naturalism (although in his case it is more often than not successfully counteracted by his less crude conception of 'pleasure' and, more importantly, by his theory of the imagination). In his practical criticism Coleridge was sometimes inclined to look upon Shakespeare's characters as living human beings. In Shakespeare's plays, he said, 'you meet people who meet and speak to you as in real life'; they are 'flesh and blood individuals'.... When Coleridge came to defend Shakespeare's tragi-comedies one of his arguments was as naturalistic as that of the eighteenth-century critics: 'Shakespeare is the Poet of Nature, portraying things as they exist'. (pp. 39-41)

But this is only half the story. And to think that Coleridge's conception of poetry is all included in this definition, which is based upon the opposition between truth and pleasure, is to misunderstand him completely.... Poetic imagination he conceived primarily not as a pleasure-giving faculty, but as one which provides a mode of apprehending reality. But in order to realize the inadequacy of Coleridge's definition (and his own sense of this inadequacy) we must analyse the definition in some detail.

Having attempted the distinction between poetry and science on the grounds of the pleasure-truth opposition, Coleridge realized that his definition would include all manner of writing which does not have truth for its object. He therefore tried to distinguish between poetry and prose by reference to a quantitative and a relational scale of pleasure more in keeping with the eighteenth-century mind than with his own philosophical position. Poetry, we are told, permits 'a pleasure from the whole consistent with a consciousness of pleasure from the component parts'; perfect poetry communicates 'from each part the greatest immediate pleasure compatible with the largest sum of pleasure in the whole'. Supposing that pleasure is the criterion, why this should not apply equally to a well-written novel or prose drama is not clear. Coleridge seems to be thinking here of metre as the element responsible for the pleasure we derive from the parts, but surely, metre exists in good as well as bad verse and in the latter we feel no more pleasure in the parts than in the whole. As he himself says on another occasion, 'rhymes and finger-metre' 'renders poor flat prose ludicrous, rather than tend to elevate it, or even to hide its nakedness'. But he half realizes that he has been trapped by his premise. In *Biographia Literaria,* when he comes to discuss the same point, suddenly the whole discussion collapses and he undermines his own grounds when he declares that 'poetry of the highest kind may exist without metre, and even without the contra-distinguishing objects of a poem', meaning, of course, that poetry may exist in writings which do not propose pleasure for their object. And very soon he shifts the argument from the point of view of the reader and recipient to that of the poet. For, he tells us, after all what distinguishes poetry is not the pleasure we feel in reading it, but that peculiar state and degree of excitement, which arises in the poet himself in the act of composition'.... In order to understand the nature of the excitement the poet suffers during the act of creation, which is after all that which distinguishes what is poetry from what is not, Coleridge seems to ask the reader to put himself in the poet's place, and to try to recreate for himself what the poet actually undergoes. He must first of all possess 'more than common sensibility'. By that is meant that he must feel 'a more than common sympathy with the objects, emotions, or incidents' which form the subject of the poem. In other words, whatever object may happen to be the subject-matter of a poem must obviously *mean* something to the poet. Secondly, he must possess 'a more than ordinary activity of the mind in respect of the fancy and imagination', which means, in plainer language, that the field of the poet's experience must be broad

and inclusive (fancy being the aggregative and collective power) but however widely disparate the component parts of the experience may be, they must be reduced to a real unity of some sort, a unity of vision or interest as Coleridge prefers to call it (imagination being the unifying power). What then results from the coupling of more than usual sympathy with objects and more than ordinary activity of fancy and imagination? A 'more vivid reflection of the truths of nature and of the human heart', which is due to the working of sympathy (for sympathy from the latter part of the eighteenth century onwards becomes a means of recreating the objects upon which it is directed).... Coleridge, indeed, in this particular context does not state that it is the poet's imagination which modifies the truths, but rather says that the truths are modified by 'that sort of pleasurable emotion which the exertion of all our faculties gives in a certain degree'. But from his frequent utterances on the role of imagination there can be no doubt as to what it is that accomplishes the modification. Besides, the pleasurable emotion is only the result of the 'exertion of all our faculties', of the full working of sympathy, fancy and imagination, and it only takes place after all these powers of the mind have done their job in altering the objective world.

This brief analysis indicates that 'pleasure' is only a catch-word which confuses the aim of poetry with its result, or what attends the fulfilment of its function. Poetry is primarily a passionate apprehension of reality. Its object is to recreate human experience imaginatively, to set forth 'values', 'the truths of nature and of the human heart' not as they are in the flux of the world, but reduced to a unified and meaningful pattern. Coleridge himself is aware of this when he forgets about his pleasure principle.... The function of imaginative poetry is to create a unified and significant pattern of the chaos and welter of experience. That is precisely why, as Coleridge says, the whole personality of the poet is engaged in the imaginative process. In imagination, we remember, the moral will is concerned, whereas in fancy it is only what Coleridge calls 'choice', which in his terminology, is something very different from the moral will. Whereas imagination, therefore, is a serious activity, fancy is mere play: it 'plays with counters'. (pp. 41-5)

While he would not abandon the eighteenth-century conception of poetry as having pleasure for its object, somehow at the back of his mind he feels the inadequacy of the conception, and so he always ends his definition by giving a description of the poet in terms of his theory of poetic imagination. We must believe Coleridge when he writes in the same work that his own 'conclusions on the nature of poetry, in the strictest use of the word, have been in part anticipated in the preceding disquisition on the fancy and imagination'. But it is remarkable that Coleridge did not realize that what he said about imagination is incompatible with the view that poetry is opposed to science in having pleasure and not truth for its object [see excerpt above, 1817]. (p. 45)

In Coleridge's analysis of beauty the discussion, we notice, veers significantly towards his conception of the secondary imagination. 'The Beautiful, contemplated in its essentials, is that in which the *many,* still seen as many, becomes one.' The general definition of beauty is 'Multeity in unity', it is the reconciliation of the one and the many; it is essentially 'Harmony': 'The Beautiful arises from the perceived harmony of an object, whether sight or sound, with the inborn and constitutive rules of the judgment and imagination: and it is always intuitive.' So he writes at the conclusion of his essays on the

Principles of Genial Criticism. It is interesting to note that pleasure is not mentioned as an essential in this recapitulation of his thoughts on the subject, but only as an attendant on that perception: 'As light to the eye, even such is beauty to the mind, which cannot but have complacency in whatever is perceived as pre-configured to its living faculties. And the faculty of taste in his treatment at this stage becomes very close indeed to that of imagination: 'Taste is the intermediate faculty which connects the active with the passive powers of our mind, the intellect with the senses. As Coleridge's thoughts on the subject develop, and as he comes under the influence of Schelling, the unity of the manifold, which has constituted his conception of beauty, becomes essentially an *organic* unity, the kind of unity which it is the privilege of imagination alone to create. Art stamps the elements it combines into unity 'in the mould of a moral idea'. The 'common definition of the fine arts' then becomes: 'that they all, like poetry, are to express intellectual purposes, thoughts, conceptions, and sentiments which have their origin in the human mind', and 'a work of art will be just in proportion as it adequately conveys the thought, and rich in proportion to the variety of parts which it holds in unity'. At this moment we cease to hear of pleasure altogether.

Of course, Coleridge's conception of pleasure is not as crude as that of the eighteenth-century literary theorists. The empiricist and associationist idea of pleasure was fraught with all kinds of foreign matter. (pp. 46-7)

Coleridge realized that the end of poetic drama is something more than an emotion. Poetic drama is first and foremost a 'kind' of *poetry*, and as such it has not for its end the mere arousing of emotions. In fact he blames contemporary dramatists precisely for being satisfied with the excitement of emotions in their spectators, without considering whether their works should or should not embody a philosophy of life or a vision of existence. The ancient dramatists both in England and in France, he writes in *The Friend*, considered both comedy and tragedy as 'kinds of poetry'. Their excellence is that 'they excite the minds of the spectators to active thought and to a striving after ideal excellence. The soul is not stupefied into mere sensations by a worthless sympathy with our own ordinary sufferings, or an empty curiosity for the surprising, undignified by the language or the situations which awe and delight the imagination.' (p. 49)

According to Coleridge, great drama undoubtedly should arouse our emotions; but it should do so 'in union with the activity both of our understanding and imagination'. Immediately the understanding and the imagination are introduced we realize that it is not merely a matter of producing an emotional attitude. Coleridge's view of the origin of metre, we must remember, is that although metre demands passion as the stuff and raw material of the experience it also arises from the need to impose order upon that passion. He once described music as 'Poetry in its grand sense', because in it we get not only passion, but 'passion and order' at once; and in hyperbolic language he called poets 'Gods of Love who tame the Chaos'. 'All other men's worlds are the poet's chaos', he said on another occasion. Poetry then is not just the expression of, nor does it result in, mere emotion. It primarily consists in imposing a meaningful pattern upon the flux and chaos of the emotions. In Coleridge's view great poetry is not just 'interesting' or 'entertaining'. Indeed the reporter of his 1811 lectures put it well when he wrote of his treatment of poetry: 'To those who consider poetry is no other light than as a most *entertaining* species of composition, this gentleman's mode of inquiring into its

principles may want attraction.' Without a 'most profound, energetic and philosophical mind', Shakespeare might have become a 'very delightful poet, but not the great dramatic poet'. (p. 51)

Coleridge's celebrated phrase 'the willing suspension of disbelief' suggests something similar to Kierkegaard's observation about the adoption of the right 'mood'. We suspend our disbelief for the sake of poetic faith. Coleridge's use of the words 'disbelief' and 'faith' in this connection is indeed telling. Coleridge did not say the suspension of disbelief for the sake of poetic *belief*. And unless I am very much mistaken the word 'faith' here implies something different from 'belief' or 'disbelief'. In any case, we are told that Coleridge 'used very frequently to insist upon the distinction between belief and faith'. Disbelief is essentially an intellectual matter, whereas in 'faith' the question of values and the whole personality of man (his total faculties with their relative worth and dignity) enters. In *Biographia Literaria* he tells us that this poetic faith is an 'Analogon' of religious faith. I cannot object, as some Coleridge scholars have done, to the use of the word 'willing' in this context. Far from being an unhappy choice, in my opinion, it has an important function to fulfil. To read poetry as it should be read one must adopt the right attitude. . . . We could, if we wished, read parts of [Milton's] *Paradise Lost* as if it were a treatise on astronomy. Coleridge himself, actuated by assumptions about 'pleasure', did read parts of Wordsworth's *Immortality Ode* with the wrong attitude. He chose not to suspend his disbelief for the sake of poetic faith. The suspension of disbelief is therefore an act of will.

Besides there is a historical justification for Coleridge's use of the word 'willing'. 'Willing' is necessary to distinguish the type of activity an ideal recipient is engaged in, according to Coleridge, from the mere passive reading of literature to which associationism leads. . . . [By] stressing the element of choice Coleridge seems to be saying that while we are suspending our disbelief we are not mere 'lazy lookers on' on the world that is revealed to us in poetry. We are not . . . dreaming or even half-dreaming as Coleridge himself suggests at times. Just as the poet himself, while composing, reveals 'judgement ever awake and steady self-possession', so does the ideal reader.

The suspension does not at all imply divorcing poetry from life. On the contrary. It only means that we adopt a specific attitude to human experience—an attitude other than that of science. Our starting point is always human experience. And although the experience itself is transmuted in the creative process into something else, something purer, deeper and more lasting as a pattern than the flux of individual experiences— yet it is with the affirmation of some human value that we always end. . . . [The] values that are affirmed in Shakespearean drama are shown by Coleridge to be in some broad sense moral values, related to man's spiritual life, his joy and suffering, the dignity and grandeur of the human soul, 'the power of destiny and the controlling might of heaven, which seems to elevate the characters which sink beneath its irresistible blow'. That is why it will not do to hold either the naïve assumption that what we see on the stage is something as close as possible to a real event (i.e. complete delusion) or at the opposite extreme, the hard, commonsense assumption that we believe all the time while passing through, for instance, the harrowing experience of *Lear*, that it is nothing but fiction— the two views prevalent in the eighteenth century. The first confuses art with reality, and ignores the vast difference between our responses to a tragedy and our responses to a catastrophic event in everyday life. The latter view suffers from the application of the scientific attitude to what lies outside the realm of science, from a confusion of 'moods'.

Does Coleridge, then, describe adequately the nature of our involvement in drama when he discusses the question of dramatic illusion, or when he deals with the cognate problem of imitation? Does he advance the discussion of the subject a step further than his predecessors? (pp. 53-4)

Coleridge follows his predecessors in holding imitation to be the end of drama. But he differs radically from them in his conception of imitation. In the eighteenth century the Aristotelian *mimesis* acquired the sense of direct copying. Strengthened by scientific influence, this meaning, which held ground throughout the century, was in a large measure responsible for the direction taken by Shakespearean criticism, particularly later in the period. . . . Drama was considered by all the critics to be a copy of human life, and the enjoyment the spectator obtains from it to be derived either from this delusion, that is, from his mistaking it for reality, or from his consciousness that it is only a copy of it. (p. 55)

Coleridge, on the other hand, believed that imitation is not a copy, and the difference between the two consists in a certain degree of difference in the former from the objects imitated. That is why a completely naturalistic view of the characters would be inconsistent at least with Coleridge's principle of imitation. In the discussion of imitation in drama with special reference to Shakespeare, Coleridge shows that he is somewhat aware of the conventionality of Shakespearean drama—though the discussion itself in many parts is far from satisfactory. The copy, he tells us, arouses disgust, whereas a successful imitation causes delight. So far so good. But when he goes on to explain that the quantum of difference that we find in imitation is 'an indispensable condition and cause of the pleasure we derive from it', and almost in the same breath he tells us that while watching a play 'our sense of probability' is in 'slumber' we suspect that the argument is breaking down, particularly as elsewhere, when he comes to analyse the state of dramatic illusion, he tells us that our power of judgement or comparison is suspended. For how can we obtain the pleasure of imitation, i.e. the pleasure arising from the perception of the quantum of difference between imitation and imitated, unless we are in possession of the power of judgement by means of which we can compare the two? 'In all imitation,' says Coleridge, 'two elements must exist, and not only exist but must be *perceived* as existent. He further complicates matters by on the one hand likening the state of dramatic illusion to that of a dream, the explanation given by some eighteenth-century English (as well as German) critical theorists, which is compatible with a passive view of the mind, and on the other hand introducing the Kantian view that the moment we exclaim of a work 'How natural!' we perceive in it a high degree of art. (pp. 56-7)

If observation can only lead to a copy and meditation to an imitation the difference between a copy and an imitation can perhaps be put in this way. In a copy we only meet with the external appearance of the world in which the artist does not enter; whereas in an imitation we get not so much the external world as it appears 'objectively', but rather a vision of the world experienced and felt by the individual poet. The difference therefore between a copy and an imitation is not a difference in degree: in Shakespearean drama we do not get a picture of the world recorded by observation, in which some elements are suppressed and others superadded, as was understood by eighteenth-century critics. It is a difference in kind.

It is, in fact, the difference between the 'primary' and 'secondary' imagination. The world of Shakespearean drama is other than the world of everyday reality. It is an experience of it seen from a particular point of view; it is essentially a world of the spirit, an expression of the value and the meaning the external world held for the poet. That is precisely what we do not obtain from a copy.

Subjective indeed it is, but because the experience does not touch the poet's petty personal self, but arises from the very depths of his being, from 'the unfathomable depths of his own oceanic mind', it has a universal significance. . . . Coleridge again and again points out the impersonal nature of this subjective experience. It is an essential mark of a true genius, he says, that 'its sensibility is excited by any other cause more powerfully than by its own personal interests'. The choice of subjects 'very remote' from personal self is considered by him to be 'a promise of genius'. . . . Coleridge always believed that the greatest artist in literature was Shakespeare, whose impersonal art no other critic pointed out with greater clarity or consistency. As to his critical theory Coleridge's position is sufficiently clear. This complete detachment and negation of self (what Keats calls 'negative capability'), this complete absence of personal interest, may help to explain Coleridge's emphasis on the relation between poetic genius and deep morality. In his *Philosophical Lectures* he says that 'to have a genius is to live in the universal'; meaning that during the act of creation the poet's individuality is 'lost' and with it 'his little unthinking contemptible self'. (pp. 57-9)

From his other writings, particularly from his **'Essay on Method'**, we know the significance Coleridge attached to the distinction between observation and meditation. In observation the mind is a passive recorder of the impressions of the outside world, and is, as it were, a mirror which cannot but produce a copy. Meditation, contrariwise, is an inward recoiling of the mind upon itself: in it the mind is essentially active and imposes its forms on the passive gleanings of the senses, making of them meaning and sense. It is by meditation and not by observation that 'ideas' are born. Truth 'in whatever science', Coleridge believed, originates in the mind. Hence his emphasis on the subjective element in the creative experience: 'For in all that truly merits the name of poetry in its most comprehensive sense, there is a necessary predominance of the ideas (i.e. of that which originates in the artist himself), and a comparative indifference of the materials.' This explains why, in his treatment of Shakespeare, Coleridge's attention is wholly absorbed by an analysis of what is essentially Shakespearean, to a degree such that he tends to isolate him from his age and contemporaries. In the creative act meditation always comes first in the order of importance, and then observation. It is well known that in his approach to Shakespeare's plays Coleridge disregards, nay distrusts, scholarship completely. But it is not sufficiently realized that he does so, as it were, on principle. (p. 59)

Meditation in art is in fact Coleridge's description of that activity of the mind during the creative process which must include the imaginative act in the strictly Coleridgean sense. . . . By meditation Shakespeare 'evolves the germ from within by the imaginative power according to an idea', with the result that his works give the impression that 'the thing said not only might have been said, but that nothing else could be substituted to excite the same sense of its exquisite propriety'. The 'ideas' which are arrived at by meditation, and of which the works of art are the embodiment, are the 'values' which poetic genius reveals in a world 'of which, for the common view, custom had bedimmed all the lustre, had dried up the sparkle and the dew-drops'. . . . If we consider the question of imitation and dramatic illusion from this angle, and Coleridge's theory of imagination invites us to do so, we realize how the 'dream' analogy which Coleridge suggests at times is not only unhappy but misleading. Instead of stressing their 'poetic truth', i.e. the values of which they are the expression, it links the plays to harmful and aberrational forms of self-indulgence, like daydreams or reveries, which Coleridge tirelessly condemns. The fact that the whole state of 'dramatic illusion' depends upon the will ('we choose to be deceived', says Coleridge) should alone be sufficient to make it something qualitatively different from dreaming and to refute the assertion that a dream-like experience is 'the highest degree' of the aesthetic state. But Coleridge seems to be influenced here by sensationalist psychology and the pleasure principle. If the object of poetry is to give us pleasure, then we must do all we can to obtain that pleasure. We must blind our judgement and willingly deceive ourselves. But this will not do. We are not mere passive spectators bewitched or lulled into a state of semi-sleep by a series of events unfolding before our eyes. On the contrary, as Coleridge himself recommends, we respond actively to a play with the whole of our personality engaged—only we do not approach it with the improper attitude, e.g. the attitude of science. If our judgement is suspended it is only suspended in one field or on one level. . . . If we do not judge whether or not the action and events in a play are real in the sense that our presence in the theatre is, we can still judge whether one part of the play is in keeping with another and harmonizes with the whole pattern. We can still ask ourselves such questions as 'What is the meaning of the whole play?' In fact, while watching a play we are in a state of complete vigilance and mental alertness. An apparently insignificant incident, a little remark dropped casually by one of the characters, will perhaps determine our whole response to the play. . . . When we respond to a play rightly we judge and interpret all the time, even though a great deal of our interpretation we do almost unwittingly. Is it too much to say that a sensationalist psychology which has led to the belief that we are completely passive spectators, has also contributed towards blinding the critics to the presence of tragic irony in Shakespearean drama?

Nothing in fact can be more misleading about the nature of drama than this dream analogy. By stressing the element of 'unreality' it suggests a divorce between poetry and life. Once a dream or reverie is over and we apply the reality principle, we forget completely about it. But in the case of our experience of drama, because it brings our whole personality into action, many a good play has altered in some subtle ways one's outlook on the serious business of life. The relation between art and life is an intimate one at all points, and art cannot be divorced from life except to its own detriment. As Coleridge himself says, in good reading we should not judge of books by books, but rather we should refer what we have read to our own experience. (pp. 60-2)

Coleridge himself is not always satisfied with this description of our experience of drama in terms of a dream, in which we suspend our judgement. When he breaks loose from the eighteenth-century sensationalist critical tradition he tells us a different and more convincing story. The experience then becomes, as he describes it, very far indeed from the sickly self-indulgence in pleasant unrealities. Although we do not apply everyday life criteria, no delusion of any kind enters into it, however 'innocent' it may be. (pp. 62-3)

Because Coleridge realizes that the dramatic world is neither the one world nor the other he is driven to the middle state which he styles 'illusion'—a word unfortunate for its association with deception. And in order to describe this state in more intelligible terms, he has to fall back upon the dream analogy, which is the product of the eighteenth-century critical tradition with its passive conception of mind and art and its tendency to relegate poetry, as contra-distinguished from science, to the realm of pleasing dreams and fancies. The result is that instead of clarifying the discussion, the analogy makes it only more muddled and throws it into violent contradiction with Coleridge's other and more valuable principles which are revealed in his theory of imagination.

The question of dramatic illusion is not as purely theoretical as it may seem. In fact it has a direct bearing upon the practical criticism of drama. If the object of a dramatist is to produce as much delusion as possible, then his work will be judged by the degree of its resemblance to everyday life and considerations of form will be ignored. His job will be fulfilled if he manages to portray characters which are true to life. In this case the end of a Shakespearean critic will be only to analyse Shakespeare's characters with a view to pointing out their truth to life, measuring their actions and motives strictly by the moral and psychological criteria we apply in our dealings with our fellow human beings. This is precisely what we have seen eighteenth-century critics do. Coleridge, by denying delusion to drama and acknowledging the middle state, cannot be charged with the same fault. But because his conception of this middle state was in terms of the eighteenth-century views on the subject, he hovered somewhere between their position and a new position of his own. Since he conceived of the 'illusion' as a dream he tended sometimes to attach great value and significance to whatever conduced to this illusion and sustained the slumber. He would say, for instance, that all the 'excellencies of drama' such as 'unity of interest', 'distinctness and subordination of the characters', 'appropriateness of style', 'the charm of language and sentiment' are 'means to this chief end, that of producing and supporting this willing illusion'; but he would also say that 'it is not even always or of necessity an objection to them [i.e. all these excellencies] that they prevent it [i.e. the illusion] from rising to as great a height as it might otherwise have attained; it is enough, if they are compatible with as high a degree as is requisite', or would demand only 'a human interest and a semblance of truth sufficient to procure for these shadows of imagination that willing suspension of disbelief for the moment, which constitutes poetic faith'. Hence in his criticism of Shakespeare we find that he sometimes treats the Shakespearean character as a medium for value, and as a part of the meaning of the whole play as the poet's vision, and at other times, looking upon illusion as an end in itself, he is satisfied as long as a character is psychologically probable, or reveals psychological insight on the part of the poet, instead of considering psychological probability purely as a means. Here again, as in his definition of poetry, we have a mixture of what is the eighteenth-century heritage and what is Coleridge's own.

It is clear . . . that Coleridge's Shakespearean criticism forms part and parcel of his general critical theory. The critical theory itself contains contradictory elements, the result of his attempt to combine what belongs to eighteenth-century sensationalism and what is essentially the product of his own dynamic and idealistic position. On the one hand, we have the view that the object of poetry is to arouse an emotion of pleasure and all that this view entails, from the opposition it draws between science and poetry to the conception of poetry as a pleasant unreality to be willingly indulged in like reveries and day-dreams. On the other, there is the theory of imagination, which regards poetry essentially as a mode of apprehending reality and as the poet's interpretation of existence. (pp. 64-6)

The dichotomy or polarity in his critical position may explain—his constitutional failure to execute his innumerable projects apart—why Coleridge was unable to commit to paper his whole theory of poetry, except in fragments, for his ambitious book on poetry was never written. (p. 66)

> *M. M. Badawi, in his* Coleridge: Critic of Shake-speare, *Cambridge at the University Press, 1973, 222 p.*

A. E. DYSON AND JULIAN LOVELOCK   (essay date 1976)

[*Dyson and Lovelock state that their goal in* Masterful Images: English Poetry from Metaphysicals to Romantics, *from which the following is excerpted, is "to supply a sense of tradition, of the unfolding and continuity of our poetry . . . through close and careful reading of the texts." Asserting that "The Ancient Mariner" is "a drama of betrayal and damnation," they contend that its basis is solidly Christian.*]

CHRISTABEL:

KUBLA KHAN,

A VISION;

THE PAINS OF SLEEP.

BY

S. T. COLERIDGE, ESQ.

LONDON:

PRINTED FOR JOHN MURRAY, ALBEMARLE-STREET,

BY WILLIAM BULMER AND CO. CLEVELAND-ROW,

ST. JAMES'S.

1816.

Title page to the first edition of "Christabel" and "Kubla Khan." The Granger Collection, New York.

['The Ancient Mariner'] starts from the present tense, active, and, as it turns out, irresistible; the tense of absorbed narrative and compulsive confession. It is as if the whole poem is here [in the first stanza] in embryo: narrative vividness, fixed and immediate; human encounter intense yet trancelike; questions, asked in terror or nightmare, needing answers but getting none, for whatever 'answer' there is comes obliquely. It is as if the story comes loose from time, gravitating towards that somehow eternal quality which haunts all its parts—the dramatic violence of sudden storms and appearances, sudden actions. 'By thy long grey beard and glittering eye'—strange invocation, as if feared and hypnotic qualities could be somehow besought! From the start, there is curious double vision; everything is fated and necessary, everything startling and dreadful. Whether 'it is' an ancient Mariner, or an albatross, or a ship of death or a hermit, we encounter the object and it encounters us as in a dream. Everything seems perfectly alive, perfectly unexplained, perfectly inescapable, terribly intense. The poem is full of elementals. Its setting, perhaps the only one possible, is the sea. Its images are calm and storm, sun and moon, life and death; its values are loyalty and betrayal, fear and hope, guilt and deliverance. Everything is extravagant—the extreme case, the ultimate possible image:

> With throats unslaked, with black lips baked,
> We could not laugh nor wail;
> Through utter drought all dumb we stood!
> I bit my arm, I sucked the blood,
> And cried, A sail! a sail!

Is such poetry allegory? Certainly not, in any systematic fashion. Yet it is full of ideas. Is it a dream? Art so highly wrought must originate chiefly in the waking consciousness, radically heightened; yet it has the feel of a dream. Perhaps our best word for it is 'fantasy'—a form of literature which creates a world with its own rules and laws, depending wholly on inner consistency, yet which, at its best, continually draws strength from the 'real' world of human psychology, human intuition and spirituality, and continually feeds its own insights back into that world.

In terms of immediate influence, of course, Coleridge is directly indebted to the ballad form, which had been revived, along with much general feeling for the 'medieval', in the mid-eighteenth century, and which became a highly stylised and consciously 'literary' cult among many later romantics. . . . Most of the best ballads have openings very similar to 'The Ancient Mariner' in their power to arrest attention, to sketch in a situation that bypasses particulars such as names, places, dates, by drawing very immediately on the reader's own intensities. . . . In Coleridge's own categories 'The Ancient Mariner' is poetry of 'imagination', not of 'fancy'; of 'Reason', not of 'understanding'. Perhaps the function of great art is, nearly always, to probe beyond those arguments and reasonings which continually, and rightly, attend man's attempt to make sense of himself, seeking to initiate us rather, intuitively and directly, into psychic and spiritual realities of evil and good. We recognise such an achievement in Sophocles and Euripides, Shakespeare and Milton. Dickens and Dostoievsky, indeed in most literature and drama of high excellence. At a purely speculative level, we will wonder why Iago acts so (as he does himself), we will ponder Oedipus and Satan, Tulkinghorn and Raskolnikov, searching for clues. But, while motives are baffling, the truth is self-evident; no one can doubt the realism of their sufferings and deeds.

Coleridge recognised 'imagination' as the realm of revelation through recreation, the realm where beauty and goodness, and their mighty opposites, are known. (pp. 175-77)

[What] is the best way to start reading **'The Ancient Mariner'**? To our minds, it is best first to release the visual imagination, allowing this to roam through the images. Everything is striking and extraordinary. The visual play suggests a near meeting of dream psychology and conscious image-making, a world close to modern imagism or modern cinema. Something like Walt Disney's *Fantasia* might suggest itself for comparison. If so, could we attempt to match the poem with appropriate music, thereby creating a *Fantasia* in reverse? An approach of this kind has the advantage of directing our attention immediately towards the archetypal image, where the poem's power surely chiefly lives: a solitary man, caught up in a drama of mortal personal guilt and divine deliverance, doomed to roam the world, telling his tale when its moment comes. The affinity is with the wandering Jew, the Flying Dutchman (a possible source for music?), with the exiled Cain even—stories linked only tangentially with religion in its orthodox forms. Perhaps we all have something of the Ancient Mariner in us (as Coleridge himself alleged of Hamlet)?—though if so, mercifully most of us keep him in check.

A legend of this kind attracts material from various sources like a powerful magnet, yet Coleridge's organisation excludes any systematic interpretation of one, definite, kind. (p. 179)

If we look at Coleridge's **'The Ancient Mariner'** with open minds on ... questions of 'intention', certain features are, however, clear. A critic who suggests, as William Empson has done, that the Mariner kills the albatross chiefly to make soup, and that the spiritual punishment of himself and the crew is therefore excessive, signifies a cheerful unwillingness to take the poem seriously at all. That we are indeed faced with a drama of betrayal and damnation, grace and penitence, seems too evident to require much defence. The poem cannot be assimilated to Christian theology by any direct process, yet the religious scheme is present throughout. ... The Spirit who pursues the ship from the north is glossed in the poem's prose commentary in a manner referring us well outside Christian tradition for its source: 'A spirit had followed them; one of the invisible inhabitants of this planet, neither departed souls nor angels; concerning whom the learned Jew Josephus, and the Platonic Constantinopolitan, Michael Psellus, may be consulted. They are very numerous, and there is no climate or element without one or more.' (pp. 181-83)

With this in mind, we can (and must) attempt to trace the poem's central development, whether this is thought of as tentative affirmation, prophetic vision, or as a stream of suggestion flowing gently through fantasy. And here, the present critics should make clear, no doubt, that in this central development the poem is, in their view, evidently and specifically Christian. It is Christian in this sense: that it is written by a Christian; that its most characteristic ideas originate inside Christianity; and that the colour of feeling inherent in the power of the verse would not be found in any writer not profoundly influenced by Christian *experience*. We put the matter in this manner in order to safeguard certain other aspects which modify its Christianity, and defeat any attempt to read it as systematic Christian allegory, some of which have already been touched on. Again, it seems clear that Coleridge, who was not consciously allegorising, would have thought of the poem's truth as universal rather than as sectarian, and would have expected it to speak

first to the imagination, and to the experience, of readers, not to their religious 'beliefs'.

Where, then, are the specific marks of Christianity? First, the albatross is welcomed as a guest, and offered friendship—which is why its betrayal cannot plausibly be glossed in terms of bird soup:

> At length did cross an Albatross,
> Through the fog it came:
> As if it had been a Christian soul,
> We hailed it in God's name.

The 'as if' suggests, of course, analogy rather than anything more definite, and it is obvious that the other mariners think of the bird merely superstitiously, hailing it as a good omen. When this view seems to be confirmed, yet the Mariner none the less kills it, they blame him not for betraying a living creature whom he has befriended, but for killing the bird that 'made the breeze to blow'. For this reason again, they praise him for killing the bird when a further reversal of weather appears now to prove the opposite:

> 'Twas right, said they, such birds to slay
> That bring the fog and mist.

No doubt this is the reason why, later, they simply die, but the Mariner himself is reserved for a different fate. This is nothing to do with a spectacular vengeance from a cruel deity (as William Empson seems to think) but is, rather, an indication of the poem's direction. We are to focus on the plight of the one man who is a moral agent, knowing good from evil, rather than upon the fate of many men excluded from spiritual insight, and so from spiritual life. The crew belongs, to use a phrase of Coleridge's ..., with the 'lethargy of custom'—with that majority among men who miss alike the beauty and the suffering of life, having no eyes to *see*.

The Mariner, however, who has *particularly* offered friendship to the bird, and established trust with it, commits evil in the fullest sense. The bird has come to recognise him, to receive from him, to respond when he calls to it, so the slaying is 'hellish' in the strict, Christian sense. The ancient world, Greek and Christian alike, had accepted duty to a guest as sacred, and believed that to harm a guest or indeed to fail to protect him from evil was a wrong crying to Heaven for vengeance. Above all, duty to a friend was sacred; Dante puts Brutus and Judas Iscariot together, in hell's deepest pit.

It could be argued, of course, that this duty to guests and friends did not extend to animals, yet man's Lordship of Nature is a profoundly Christian belief. The book of *Genesis* asserts it, and Christ himself said that not a bird falls to earth without his Father's knowledge. ... In Wordsworth, the unity of creation is everywhere asserted; and, in **'The Ancient Mariner'**, this insight is, more than anything, the poem's coherence. Because the albatross was really befriended, it was really betrayed; and the Mariner's punishment is precisely that of Macbeth. He passes into inner torment and dereliction, which is hell brought home to him. He cannot pray (one of the traditional signs of damnation), and, like Macbeth, he cannot sleep. When he tells of the killing of the albatross he *looks* demonic (Part I, final stanza), and he knows, as the other mariners do not, that he has done a 'hellish' thing. (The irony is that while the Mariner reports the phrase 'And I had done a hellish thing' as words said to him by his fellows, he alone knows the real meaning of the words, and their full truth.) Later, during his trance, he hears the dialogue between two spirits who direct the stricken ship: and, while these appear to belong to a universe more neoplatonic than Christian in concept, they bring home the moral in a directly Christian way:

> 'Is it he?' quoth one, 'Is this the man?
> By him who died on cross,
> With his cruel bow he laid full low
> The harmless Albatross.
>
> 'The Spirit who bideth by himself
> In the land of mist and snow,
> He loved the bird that loved the man
> Who shot him with his bow.'

The reference to the crucifixion balances the somewhat untheological 'Spirit who bideth by himself', but the final two lines, with their image of a dance of delight and love between Creator and creatures that has been violated, are at once precise and profound. Perhaps the Christian understanding of the nature of evil has seldom been more simply and powerfully captured. There is a chain of love, including the Creator's love for the bird, and the bird's love for the man, which has been totally broken by the man. (pp. 183-86)

When the Mariner kills love, he commits the sin which cuts him decisively from God, and from the life of God, which *is* love, and puts himself in the self-alone, the absence of God, which is hell. Total change comes with the moment of murder. . . . The universe dead and ghastly (a suicide's vision of reality?) is the Mariner's world after his sin. It belongs with Macbeth's world after the killing of Duncan, with the central quality of consciousness conveyed by T. S. Eliot in *The Waste Land,* and indeed with all visions of loneliness and madness in literature, whether specifically Christian or not, where these sufferings are linked, in whatever manner, with man's violation, or loss, of love. But the poem is also about redemption. The Mariner is released from his suffering not through anything he can do himself—above all, he cannot pray even—but through a moment's pure grace. . . . (pp. 187-88)

In 'The Ancient Mariner' Coleridge is moving on the plane of Reason as he defines it; he is depicting realities of good and evil, all probing well beyond the world of 'understanding'. The actual killing of the albatross is no more 'explained' than is the sin of Judas as recounted in the four New Testament accounts of it, or the sin of Eve and Adam as recounted in *Genesis*. 'The man said, ''The woman whom thou gavest to be with me, she gave me of the tree, and I did eat.''' 'The woman said, ''The serpent beguiled me, and I did eat,''' that is all: and, though Milton, in his dramatic presentation, tried to 'understand', tying himself in knots along with the rest of us, *Genesis* simply stops here. So, for Adam and Eve, there is expulsion, and loss of Eden, as God had decreed; they and their seed are to wander in exile for the rest of time. The 'truth' of the story in *Genesis* is, simply, the truth of it; men have eaten the forbidden fruit, do wander in exile, God knows why. Coleridge leaves the Mariner's motives likewise unexplained and mysterious; but they are met by equally unexplained and mysterious operations of grace. The Mariner is in hell (as most men sometimes may be, and some men habitually) and, in human terms, he has no route back. Yet suddenly he sees the water creatures, and they are beautiful; in place of the rot and slime, the horror, there is a dance of delight. Love wells up in his heart; he praises (the moment is entirely given); above all, he blesses them, 'unaware'. 'The self-same moment I could pray.' The universe turns round again, and, for the world of death, a world of life is returned. The water creatures are still the same, in their own reality; it is the Mariner who has changed, or been changed.

Why does human consciousness sometimes inhabit a world of deadness and horror, where life is unbearable, sometimes rejoice in a world radiant with God? If there is one theme that links Blake. Wordsworth and Coleridge, it is this one, the mystery of joy, and dereliction, in the inner soul. (pp. 189-90)

As one would expect, the romantics are keenly aware of different frames of reference, different interpretations, and the tension between joy and fear is at the heart of their *thought*. If God is really there to be seen clearly, why do many men miss him? . . .

It may be that the romantic poets had to declare their strong sense of election in differing fashions, since this sense of election was also their gospel for men. But had they, by grace or purity, achieved particular insight, or were they perceiving in strange, and maybe disordered ways? Were they saner than the excluded majority, or madder, were they driven by divine, or by demonic powers? When their universe went dead, had they sinned exceptionally? Or had their mind broken; or had they merely grown old? (p. 190)

The distinctive character of 'The Ancient Mariner', we are saying, is that it is Christian in its implicit understanding of such questions as these. The mystery is a Christian mystery, and to this degree accessible; while 'good' and 'evil' are not 'explained', they are held under God. The poem offers a clear polarity between a universe where men pray and celebrate and love is paramount, and a universe where blessing is absent and horror prevails. In objective fact the universe is God's, and constant; but sin removes men to a vision where God is absent; to hell. Yet the Mariner receives grace, including the supreme grace of penitence, and is led back to a living, though wounded, destiny in the world of men. In knowing he has done a hellish thing, he makes grace possible; only failure to accept guilt could lock God finally out.

What, then, is the Mariner's destiny? In one sense he seems akin to any poet or artist, or any Christian, who, healed by grace, is driven to tell his tale. Freed from hell, he remains still in Purgatory, and is an object of terror to most whom he meets. The holy hermit is aghast, the Wedding-Guest afraid and reluctant; the Pilot's boy goes mad. The Mariner's destiny is not to start the voyage of sanctity and gradually to mirror holiness, but to remain visibly touched by hell, disturbing and disturbed. . . . The other chief aspect of the poem, which we have not so far touched on, is that its centre is really the Wedding-Guest. At the start, he is picked out by the Mariner, and himself 'arrested'; there are strong suggestions of hypnosis and trance. He fears the Mariner, tries to shake him off, but is held by him; this is *his* moment, with no hope of escape:

> He holds him with his glittering eye—
> The Wedding-Guest stood still,
> And listens like a three years' child:
> The Mariner hath his will.
>
> The Wedding-Guest sat on a stone;
> He cannot choose but hear.

The Wedding-Guest's experience is, in this aspect, related to the Mariner's—especially at the point when, in a trance, the Mariner has heard the two spirits debate. Coleridge is dramatising the moment of encounter when, in the divine will, or the divine capriciousness, *this* man experiences the near approach of God. The encounter is unsought, it is an unwanted distraction, it is terrifying rather than comforting, but, just now, its moment has come. The Mariner's story, his destiny, is now for *this* man entirely, and everything romantic, and fantastic, will converge in its effect.

Coleridge, like Wordsworth, believed that most men are open on their God-ward side only occasionally; that normally, God's presence is ignored, or not even seen. But there are moments when a work of art springs to life, when a relationship crystallises, when something long known is *seen* suddenly—and, at such times, a response, a 'yes' or 'no' must be made. It is surely because Coleridge's poem dramatises this moment in images so bizarre, so altogether unearthly, that it can afford its moral to have the simplicity of a child's hymn. (pp. 191-92)

> *A. E. Dyson and Julian Lovelock, ''Uncertain Hour: The Ancient Mariner's Destiny,'' in their* Masterful Images: English Poetry from Metaphysicals to Romantics, *Barnes & Noble Books, 1976, pp. 175-92.*

L. S. SHARMA (essay date 1982)

[*Sharma assesses Coleridge's Shakespearean criticism and focuses on his treatment of* King Lear *and* Hamlet.]

For Coleridge Shakespeare is the ideal poet, the greatest poet of all time. His treatment of Shakespeare is basically sympathetic, appreciative, rather 'bardolatrous' because he was fully convinced that Shakespeare was the greatest genius the world had ever witnessed. Shakespeare is the consummation of Coleridge's idea of an ideal poet.

An illustration from ''The Rime of the Ancient Mariner.''
The Mariner is seeking absolution for killing the albatross.
Historical Pictures Service, Chicago.

Coleridge was jealously proud of his *Hamlet* criticism where he thought he had done really pioneering work. He did not only psychoanalyse Shakespeare's characters but also vigorously defended and praised Shakespeare for his skilful preparation of the audience for a successful dramatic illusion. The study of the audience-psychology was always a fascinating pursuit for Coleridge. Somehow only his superb character analyses have been so much praised and unfortunately his theatrical preoccupations have been ignored. He was not blind to the merits of the stage like many of his contemporaries, and he was quite fascinated by the adroit way Shakespeare managed the problems of presenting his plays to the audience. The study of manuscript marginalia proves that he is not a one-sided dramatic critic and had genuine sympathy for the technical and theatrical side of the play also. He has tried to prove Shakespeare's mastery of creating the illusion and maintaining it once it was achieved.

Nearly half of his entire attention to the play is concentrated on the first act of *Hamlet* perhaps because of his intense interest in the supernatural and the psychology of the people confronted with ghosts and witches but chiefly because of his interest in the ''exposition''. He is at his very best in the criticism of the first act of *Hamlet*. Apart from the subtle psychological analyses of the character, Coleridge here gives us a sensitive and imaginative insight into the dramatic descriptions and techniques which make the audience conscious of the dramatic illusion. His discussion of Shakespeare's presentation of the ghost in Scenes one and four proves his obsessing interest in the psychology of the audience. This is how he describes the scene one:

> The language is familiar: no poetic descriptions of the night . . . . yet nothing bordering on the comic on the one hand, and no striving of the intellect on the other. It is a language of sensation among men who feared no charge of effeminacy for feeling what they felt no want of resolution to bear. Yet the armour, the dead silence, the watchfulness that first interupts it, the welcome relief of guard, the cold, the broken expressions as of a man's compelled attention to bodily feelings allowed no man,— all excellently accord with and prepare for the after gradual rise into—but above all into a tragedy the interest of which is eminently ad et apud intra, as Macbeth . . . . is ad extra.

He invites our attention to the accuracy of Shakespeare's pictures of watchmen's feeling and then he dwells upon the effect of the feelings of dramatis personae on the spectators. The problem most important to tackle is the belief in the ghost. (pp. 161-62)

Shakespeare attempting a ghost, in an age of disbelief in ghosts, was obliged to make it and the play credible, and therefore he elevates his style. The technique in *Hamlet* includes a gradual introduction in which Horatio, a sceptic who is soon going to be satisfied by the ghost, anticipates the doubts of the spectators. The atmosphere of the scene is established in such a way that even the arch sceptic Hume could not but have faith in the spectre dramatically. The emotion of the audience has been prepared. Bernardo's description of the previous appearance of the spectre also lends an appropriate solemnity and vividness to the scene and also serves to distract the attention of the audience at the last minute from the expected appearance of the ghost to make its return all the more surprising and sudden like its original appearance. There is a most appropriate interruption of the narration at the right moment. Coleridge praises Shakespeare's method in making the watcher's react. Shakespeare's judgement is superb in presenting two persons who have seen the spectre twice before while the sceptic is silent and after being twice addressed by them utters only two hasty syllables, "Most like" and appears horror-stricken. We all feel horror and wonder. Shakespeare, thus, succeeds in doubly bringing home to the audience the experience of seeing the spectre for the first time by their participation in the surprise of the watchmen and then by the contrast between Horatio's reaction and that of Bernardo and Marcellus.

The credibility of the ghost in the fourth scene becomes more difficult because the audience by now has become used to seeing the spectre. Yet Shakespeare once again applies the surprise technique and diverts the attention of the spectators just before the spectre's entry, but does so more elaborately.... Shakespeare hooks the attention of the audience in the nice distinctions and parenthetical sentences of *Hamlet*, and then completely taking them by surprise brings the spectre in with all the suddenness of its visionary nature. Coleridge has great admiration for the subtlety and economy of Shakespeare's art in the first and the fourth scene in preparing the audience for one thing while obviously preparing them for another. He was acutely conscious of the precarious nature of the willing suspension of disbelief by the spectators and therefore praises Shakespeare profusely in maintaining the illusion once he had achieved it. At many places in the Shakespearean plays the action becomes so improbable, distasteful or shocking as to threaten to destroy the illusion. Shakespeare takes great pains to prepare the audience for such trying moments, and maintains the illusion dexterously. As Coleridge observes, "Whatever disturbs this repose of the judgement by its harshness, abruptness, and improbability, offends against dramatic propriety." Sometimes Coleridge admits inspite of his "bardolatry", that Shakespeare's attempts at maintaining the illusion are not entirely successful.

The first scene of *King Lear* does not appear to Coleridge credible enough, yet it seems to him to be important to the play. This kind of improbability is unusual in Shakespeare. "It is", says Coleridge, "well worth notice, that *Lear* is the only serious performance of Shakespeare, the interest and situations of which are derived from the assumptions of a gross improbability." Though in the first scene the conduct of Lear may be incredible, yet the story of the division of the kingdom is a very well-known one rooted in the public mind and taken for granted and therefore without any effects of improbability. And at the beginning of a play the public is normally more tolerant and credulous, and the dramatist has exploited this psychological tendency of the audience to the full. "Many natural improbabilities are", says Coleridge of *The Tempest*, "innocent in the groundwork or outset of the play, which would break the illusion afterwards .... a strong improbability in the story, founded on some known tradition, does not offend in the outset of a play." The action of this scene does not seem to Coleridge essential to the plot. It serves merely as a canvas on which to paint the passions and characters, only an occasion not to be repeated as the cause of the incidents. Even if this scene is lost the interest of the tragedy would not be diminished and it will still be intelligible. The only condition for such scenes to succeed is that "the interest and plot must not depend upon that improbability." Why should then, the first scene have been used at all? Coleridge maintains that in the first six lines the division of the kingdom has been placed in the correct

perspective: "It was not without forethought, and it is not without significance, that the triple division is stated here as already determined and in all its particulars previously to the trial of professions, as the relative rewards of which the daughters were made to consider their several portions." Shakespeare used the opening lines, Coleridge suggests, to discredit Lear's experiment and to tell us that the trial was but a trick and his anger was the direct result of the failure of this silly trick. With great economy of words this idea has been conveyed to the audience and to distract the audience from the improbability of the incident Shakespeare passes without delay to the main agent and prime mover. He introduces Edmund to us with great felicity of judgement and prepares the audience for his character in a casual, easy, and natural way. These are the arguments characteristic of Coleridge. Whenever he is faced with perplexing problems he resolves them by contending that Shakespeare is manipulating the audience for one purpose or another. (pp. 163-65)

> L. S. Sharma, in his Coleridge: His Contribution to
> English Criticism, *Humanities Press, 1982, 235 p.*

ADDITIONAL BIBLIOGRAPHY

Babbitt, Irving. "The Problem of the Imagination: Coleridge." In his *On Being Creative and Other Essays*, pp. 97-133. Boston: Houghton Mifflin Co., 1932.

    A discussion of Coleridge's concept of the imagination. According to Babbitt, "the imagination displayed in 'The Rime of the Ancient Mariner' is qualitatively different from that displayed in poetry that may be rightly regarded as highly serious."

Bate, Walter Jackson. *Coleridge*. Masters of World Literature Series, edited by Louis Kronenberger. Toronto: Macmillan Co., 1968, 244 p.

    An insightful critical biography. Bate devotes particular attention to Coleridge's critical theories and concept of the imagination and traces the genesis of these ideas in Coleridge's life.

Blackmur, R. P. "The Lion and the Honeycomb." In his *The Lion and the Honeycomb: Essays in Solicitude and Critique*, pp. 176-97. New York: Harcourt, Brace & World, 1955.*

    A brief examination of Coleridge's criticism. Blackmur focuses on three words—esemplastic, coadunative, and synergical—as examples of Coleridge's critical terminology and points to their role in the development of modern critical theory.

Bloom, Harold. "Coleridge: The Anxiety of Influence." In *Literary Criticism: Idea and Act*, edited by W. K. Wimsatt, pp. 506-20. Berkeley and Los Angeles: University of California Press, 1974.

    A biographical and critical discussion of Coleridge. According to Bloom, Coleridge, like all poets, suffered from "the anxiety of influence," or the fear that everything worthwhile had already been expressed by earlier poets. Further, Bloom contends that Coleridge's poetry represents an attempt to free himself from the restrictions imposed upon literature by the poet John Milton.

Blunden, Edmund, and Griggs, Earl Leslie, eds. *Coleridge: Studies by Several Hands on the Hundredth Anniversary of His Death*. London: Constable & Co., 1934, 243 p.

    A collection of biographical and historical essays on Coleridge by a number of noted scholars, including George McLean Harper, A. J. Eagleston, and J. H. Muirhead. Most essays combine biographical facts with critical material.

Bostetter, Edward E. "'Christabel': The Vision of Fear." *Philological Quarterly* XXXVI, No. 2 (April 1957): 183-94.

    A discussion of good and evil as depicted in "Christabel." Bostetter parallels the relationship between the two with events in Coleridge's life.

————. ''The Nightmare World of 'The Ancient Mariner'.'' *Studies in Romanticism* I (1965): 241-54.

Questions the interpretations of ''The Ancient Mariner'' by John Livingston Lowes and Robert Penn Warren (see excerpts above, 1927 and 1946). Bostetter argues that both readings are too narrow and offers a new viewpoint, in which he interprets the universe of the Ancient Mariner as grim, medieval, and akin to a religious hierarchy.

Boulger, James D., ed. *Twentieth Century Interpretations of ''The Rime of the Ancient Mariner.''* Englewood Cliffs, N.J.: Prentice-Hall, 1969, 116 p.

A collection of essays on ''The Ancient Mariner.''

Buchan, A. M. ''The Sad Wisdom of the Mariner.'' *Studies in Philology* LXI, No. 4 (October 1964): 669-88.

A discussion of the Mariner's inaction.

Burke, Kenneth. '' 'Kubla Khan', Proto-Surrealist Poem.'' In his *Language As Symbolic Action: Essays on Life, Literature, and Method*, pp. 201-22. Berkeley & Los Angeles: University of California Press, 1966.

A definition of the term ''symbolic action'' and an assessment of ''Kubla Khan'' within the context of that definition. Burke provides a detailed analysis of the poem's diction.

Campbell, James Dykes. *Samuel Taylor Coleridge: A Narrative of the Events of His Life.* 2d ed. London: Macmillan and Co., 1896, 319 p.

The first thorough biography.

Caskey, Jefferson D., and Stapper, Melinda M. *Samuel Taylor Coleridge: A Selective Bibliography of Criticism, 1935-1977.* Westport, Conn.: Greenwood Press, 1978, 174 p.

A bibliography divided into four sections: criticism of individual works, general criticism, biographies, and abstracts and dissertations. The authors provide a bibliography of sources.

Chambers, E. K. *Samuel Taylor Coleridge: A Biographical Study.* Oxford: Oxford at the Clarendon Press, 1938, 373 p.

A biography that focuses on Coleridge's friendships with his contemporaries. Chambers contends that these relationships reveal the development of Coleridge's critical and creative thought.

Coburn, Kathleen. ''Reflexions in a Coleridge Mirror: Some Images in His Poems.'' In *From Sensibility to Romanticism: Essays Presented to Frederick A. Pottle*, edited by Frederick W. Hilles and Harold Bloom, pp. 415-37. New York: Oxford University Press, 1965.

An analysis of various images in Coleridge's poetry and their genesis as documented in his notebooks.

————, ed. *Coleridge: A Collection of Critical Essays.* Englewood Cliffs, N.J.: Prentice-Hall, 1967, 186 p.

A variety of critical interpretations of Coleridge's writings. Critics represented include George Whalley, A. Gérard, Herbert Read, and L. C. Knights.

Colmer, John. *Coleridge: Critic of Society.* Oxford: Oxford at the Clarendon Press, 1959, 229 p.

An analysis of the development of Coleridge's political ideas as detailed in his writings.

Dowden, Edward. ''The Transcendental Movement and Literature.'' In his *Studies in Literature: 1789-1877*, 5th ed., pp. 44-84. London: Kegan Paul, Trench & Co., 1889.*

A discussion of Coleridge in the context of the transcendental and High Church movements in England.

Eliot, T. S. ''Wordsworth and Coleridge.'' In his *The Use of Poetry and the Use of Criticism: Studies in the Relation of Criticism to Poetry in England*, pp. 67-85. London: Faber and Faber, 1948.*

A comparison of the lives of William Wordsworth and Coleridge. Portions of the works of John Livingston Lowes and I. A. Richards form the basis for Eliot's interpretation of *Biographia Literaria*. Eliot discusses Coleridge's theory of poetic diction as well as his doctrine of fancy and imagination.

Emerson, Ralph Waldo. ''First Visit to England.'' In his *English Traits*, edited by Howard Mumford Jones, pp. 1-14. Cambridge: Harvard University Press, Belknap Press, 1966.*

An anecdote recounting Emerson's meeting with Coleridge in 1833. Emerson characterizes Coleridge as ''old and preoccupied'' and assesses their visit as ''rather a spectacle than a conversation, of no use beyond the satisfaction of my curiosity.''

Empson, William. '' 'The Ancient Mariner'.'' *Critical Quarterly* 6, No. 4 (Winter 1964): 298-319.

An interpretation of ''The Ancient Mariner'' from a biographical standpoint.

— Fausset, Hugh I'Anson. *Samuel Taylor Coleridge.* New York: Russell & Russell, 1967, 350 p.

A biography in which the author has attempted to ''explain the poet's achievement in terms of his personality and against a background of his life.''

Frye, Northrop. ''Long, Sequacious Notes.'' In his *Northrop Frye on Culture and Literature: A Collection of Review Essays*, edited by Robert D. Denham, pp. 170-77. Chicago: University of Chicago Press, 1978.

A discussion of Coleridge's notebooks that centers primarily on commentary by the editor of the notebooks, Kathleen Coburn. Frye disagrees with her psychological approach to the notebooks and argues that the most important principle displayed in these writings is Coleridge's concept of imagination and Logos.

Gettmann, Royal A., ed. *''The Rime of the Ancient Mariner'': A Handbook.* San Francisco: Wadsworth Publishing Co., 1961, 183 p.

A collection of useful essays on ''The Ancient Mariner'' from earliest interpretations to modern assessments.

Harper, George McLean. ''Coleridge's Conversation Poems.'' *The Quarterly Review* 244, No. 484 (April 1925): 284-98.

An analysis of what Harper terms Coleridge's ''conversation,'' or friendship, poems. These poems include ''The Eolian Harp,'' ''This Lime-Tree Bower My Prison,'' ''Frost at Midnight,'' ''Fears in Solitude,'' and ''The Nightingale.'' According to Harper, Coleridge composed the poems for specific events and references are made to certain places of deep sentimental value to him. Further, Harper suggests that a knowledge of Coleridge's life is required in order to appreciate fully the allusions made to his friends and family members.

Haven, Richard; Haven, Josephine; and Adams, Maurianne, eds. *Samuel Taylor Coleridge: An Annotated Bibliography of Criticism and Scholarship, 1793-1899, Vol. 1.* Boston: G. K. Hall & Co., 1976, 382 p.

A detailed bibliography of critical writings on Coleridge.

Jackson, J. R. de J. *Method and Imagination in Coleridge's Criticism.* Cambridge: Harvard University Press, 1969, 205 p.

An analysis of Coleridge's critical writings and theories.

————, ed. *Coleridge: The Critical Heritage.* The Critical Heritage Series, edited by B. C. Southam. New York: Barnes & Noble, 1970, 660 p.

A collection of excerpted criticism from the nineteenth century that charts the development of Coleridge's critical reputation. Jackson also provides detailed explanatory notes and annotations that describe the significance of each essay.

James, D. G. ''The Gospel of Heaven.'' In his *The Romantic Comedy*, pp. 155-270. London: Oxford University Press, Geoffrey Cumberlege, 1948.*

A discussion of the religious and mystical elements in English Romanticism. James contends that Coleridge did more than the other Romantics to ''renew Christianity in the nineteenth century.''

Mill, John Stuart. ''Coleridge.'' In his *Dissertations and Discussions: Political, Philosophical, and Historical, Vol. II*, pp. 5-78. New York: Henry Holt and Co., 1874.*

Compares the political and religious philosophies of Coleridge to those of Jeremy Bentham. Though Mill finds little similarity in their beliefs, he defines them both as "'great questioner[s] of things established'."

Muirhead, John H. *Coleridge As Philosopher*. New York: Macmillan Co., 1930, 287 p.
Discusses the influences that informed Coleridge's philosophical convictions and the principles of method that he adopted.

Nethercot, Arthur H. *The Road to Tryermaine: A Study of the History, Background, and Purposes of Coleridge's "Christabel."* Chicago: University of Chicago Press, 1939, 230 p.
A study of "Christabel" that, like John Livingston Lowes's *The Road to Xanadu* (see excerpt above, 1927), probes the historical and literary influences which aided Coleridge in composition.

Praz, Mario. "Coleridge and Wordsworth." In his *The Hero in Eclipse in Victorian Fiction*, translated by Angus Davidson, pp. 37-53. London: Oxford University Press, Geoffrey Cumberlege, 1956.*
A discussion of "Fears in Solitude" in the context of literary history and a brief assessment of *On the Constitution of the Church and State* as a reflection of Coleridge's political and religious beliefs.

Read, Herbert. "Part Two, Essays Ancillary to the Main Theme: Coleridge As Critic." In his *The True Voice of Feeling: Studies in English Romantic Poetry*, pp. 157-88. New York: Pantheon Books, 1953.
A biographical study of Coleridge that traces his development as a critical theorist.

Richards, I. A. *Coleridge's Minor Poems*. 1960. Reprint. New York: Folcroft Press, 1970, 30 p.
An essay based on a lecture given at Montana State University in which Richards examines Coleridge's versification.

Saintsbury, George. "Appendix A: Coleridge and Southey." In his *Essays in English Literature: 1780-1860, second series*, pp. 415-17. London: J. M. Dent & Co., 1895.*
An attempt to defend Robert Southey against charges that his critical essays on Coleridge were overly harsh.

Stephen, Leslie. "Coleridge's Letters." *The National Review* XXV, No. 147 (May 1895): 318-27.
An analysis of Coleridge's life as depicted in his correspondence.

Tillyard, E. M. W. "Coleridge: 'The Rime of the Ancient Mariner,' 1798." In his *Five Poems, 1470-1870: An Elementary Essay on the Background of English Literature*, pp. 66-86. London: Chatto & Windus, 1948.

A detailed study of "The Ancient Mariner." Tillyard discusses the poem both as a moral story focusing on the punishment of crime and as a reflection, in its emphasis on individualism, of Coleridge's age.

Trilling, Lionel. "Samuel Taylor Coleridge, 'Kubla Khan or A Vision in a Dream: A Fragment'." In his *Prefaces to The Experience of Literature*, pp. 226-31. New York: Harcourt Brace Jovanovich, 1979.
A discussion of critical approaches to "Kubla Khan." Particular attention is paid to the interpretation by Elisabeth Schneider (see excerpt above, 1953). While Trilling acknowledges the validity of much of her commentary, he argues that Coleridge's preface to "Kubla Khan" provides the most solid explanation of the poem. According to Trilling, the preface is "not only . . . a kind of manifesto on the working of the poetic mind but also . . . an explanation of how this particular poem is to be responded to."

Whalley, George. "The Mariner and the Albatross." *University of Toronto Quarterly* XVI, No. 4 (July 1947): 381-98.
An interpretation of "The Ancient Mariner" as a personal allegory. Whalley terms the poem "an unconscious projection of Coleridge's early sufferings and a vivid prophecy of the sufferings that were to follow."

———. *Coleridge and Sara Hutchinson and the Asra Poems*. London: Routledge & Kegan Paul, 1955, 188 p.
A discussion of Coleridge's love for William Wordsworth's sister-in-law, Sara Hutchinson. Whalley refers to the poems that Coleridge wrote for Hutchinson as "Asra," an anagram of her first name, and examines the imagery and influences that inform each of them.

Wheeler, K. M. *The Creative Mind in Coleridge's Poetry*. Cambridge: Harvard University Press, 1981, 189 p.
An analysis of the philosophic reflection and self-consciousness that permeate Coleridge's poetry. Wheeler uses Coleridge's own theory of primary and secondary imagination as the basis for an examination of five of his poems, "Kubla Khan," "The Ancient Mariner," "The Eolian Harp," "Frost at Midnight," and "This Lime-Tree Bower My Prison."

Woolf, Virginia. "Sara Coleridge." In her *The Death of the Moth and Other Essays*, pp. 111-18. New York: Harcourt Brace and Co., 1942.

A fascinating study of Coleridge's beloved daughter, Sara, who, Woolf contends, "was a continuation of him, not of his flesh . . . but of his mind, his temperament."

Alexandre Dumas (*fils*)

1824-1895

French dramatist, essayist, novelist, and poet.

Dumas is considered one of the foremost French dramatists of the nineteenth century. Born the illegitimate son of the famous novelist Alexandre Dumas (*père*), he secured his own fame in 1852 with the production of *La dame aux camélias (Camille; or, The Fate of a Coquette)*, a drama based on his novel by the same name. This work, which faithfully portrayed the life of a Parisian courtesan, introduced realism to the modern French stage. Dumas subsequently made important contributions to the theater in his self-proclaimed role as a social reformer: using the stage as a tribunal for such contemporary social problems as adultery and divorce, he pioneered the development of the modern social drama, and he is also credited with raising the *pièce à thèse,* or thesis play, to an unprecedented level of refinement. Dumas's concern with specific social reforms, however, has dated his works. In consequence, he is primarily remembered today for his durable *Camille* and for his influence on Henrik Ibsen and other modern social dramatists.

Dumas was raised by his seamstress mother, Catherine Labay, until the elder Dumas legally recognized his paternity and assumed responsibility for his son's care in 1831. Placed in a succession of boarding schools where he was ostracized because of his illegitimacy, he went on to attend the Collège Chaptal, but left without receiving his degree. Dumas established residence with his father at age seventeen. While he published several volumes of poetry and a lengthy picaresque novel entitled *Aventures de quatre femmes et d'un perroquet* in his early years at the Dumas household, he also adopted his father's extravagant lifestyle and fell into debt. One source of the younger Dumas's insolvency was a two-year liaison with Marie Duplessis, a glamorous young Parisian courtesan who died of tuberculosis shortly after Dumas broke off their relationship in 1846. Duplessis's untimely death inspired Dumas to write the novel *La dame aux camélias (The Lady of the Camellias)*; the success of this work, portions of which are loosely based on the Duplessis-Dumas affair, enabled Dumas to repay some of his debts and to provide for the support of his mother. From 1848 to 1852, he produced a spate of negligible novels in an effort to further recover from his financial losses.

Dumas's first—and greatest—dramatic triumph came in 1852 with the production of his stage adaptation of *Camille* at the Théâtre du Vaudeville. Although censors initially suppressed the play, fearing that audiences would associate Dumas's characters with several of Duplessis's influential admirers and create a scandal, the powerful Duc de Morny interceded on Dumas's behalf, and *Camille* was staged with great success. Dumas sustained this momentum throughout the 1850s, producing such popular social dramas as *Le demi-monde,* a critically acclaimed exploration of the social class existing on the outskirts of respectable Parisian society, and *Le fils naturel,* a complicated intrigue designed to protest the prejudice against illegitimate children. In 1859, he entered into an adulterous relationship with the Russian princess Nadejda Naryschkine. While a daughter was born to the couple in the following year, they falsified the birth certificate and did not acknowledge her as their child until

Naryschkine was widowed and subsequently married to Dumas in 1864. The semi-autobiographical novel *Affaire Clémanceau: Mémoire de l'accusé (The Clemenceau Case)* was Dumas's major production in the mid-1860s. In 1867, he scored a popular success with *Les idées de Madame Aubray,* a drama probing society's treatment of unwed mothers, and also began appending detailed explanatory prefaces to his dramatic works. Dumas courted both controversy and fame in the 1870s. In 1872, for example, he shocked his compatriots by defending the right of husbands to take the life of an unfaithful and unrepentant spouse in the essay *L'homme-femme: Réponse à M. Henri d'Ideville (Man-Woman; or, The Temple, the Hearth, the Street)*; in 1874, he was elected a member of the illustrious Académie française. Dumas continued to address controversial social topics in plays and pamphlets during the 1880s, urging specific legal reforms allowing for divorce and woman's suffrage, but his popularity as a dramatist began to decline. Dumas was admitted to the Légion d'honneur in 1894 and was married to his long-time mistress, Henriette Regnier, after his wife passed away in 1895. He died at Marly-le-Roi in that year.

Dumas aspired to invest his dramas with the insight of the sociological novelist Honoré de Balzac and the technical mastery of the vaudevillian playwright Augustin Eugène Scribe, who invented tightly constructed, fast paced dramas known as "well-made" plays. Thematically, at least, Dumas appears to have fallen short of his ideal, for critics often note that, unlike Balzac, he restricted his observations to his own social milieu, thus earning a reputation as a "specialist" primarily concerned with the manners and problems of a small segment of Parisian society. Dumas virtually devoted his entire dramatic career to exploring the ramifications of illicit love within this circumscribed society. As William Archer explains, the playwright approached his subject not as a moralist, but as a sociologist concerned with the behavior of a select class under definite social conditions. Many other critics have focused on Dumas's reforming zeal and characterized him as a preacher and his dramas as sermons. For his part, Dumas openly acknowledged the didactic nature of his art, stating "If I am forbidden to carry on the stage the big questions that interest a living society, I prefer to stop writing." The subjects of Dumas's dramas were principally matters of law and/or conscience arising from specific situations involving adultery, illegitimacy, and divorce. In *Le demi-monde*, for example, he considers the social implications of a compromised woman's attempt to enter into respectable society via subterfuge and marriage; in *La femme de Claude* (*The Wife of Claude*), he makes a case for legalizing divorce by presenting homicide as its alternative.

Dumas was aided immeasurably in advancing his social theses by a seemingly innate genius for stagecraft. Combining the clever plot devices and intrigues characteristic of Scribe's "well-made" plays with incisive dialogue and a rigorous internal logic, he produced popular and persuasive works that are almost universally admired as models of dramatic efficiency. Dumas is frequently praised in this connection for his masterful and efficient use of moral spokespersons known as *raisonneurs* in such propagandistic "thesis plays" as *Les idées de Madame Aubray* and *The Wife of Claude*.

Ironically, Dumas's best-known play, *Camille*, resists comparison with his other works, for it evinces a sympathy for human frailty and passion rarely encountered in the playwright's other works. Various critical interpretations have arisen concerning this anomaly, most of them focused on the Romantic overtones of the courtesan-heroine's apparent "redemption" through love and suffering, but most critics emphasize that the prevailing effect of the drama was to challenge the hegemony of Romanticism on the French stage. Dumas's drama has the additional distinction of being universally appealing; consistently described as a work of inferior artistic craftsmanship, its longevity testifies to its status as a story of superior dramatic interest. As Henry James observed, "*Camille* remains in its combination of freshness and form and the feeling of the springtime of life, a singular, an astonishing piece of work.... Some tender young man and some coughing young woman have only to speak the lines to give it a great place among the love stories of the world." The composer Giuseppe Verdi seems to have concurred with James's opinion, for he based his popular opera *La traviata* on Dumas's signature piece.

Dumas's remarkable contemporary fame soon gave way to a respectable posthumous reputation as an important figure in literary history. Two developments in particular emerged as significant factors in his decline: his plays quickly lost their topical appeal among audiences, and his Scribean approach to dramatic construction fell into disrepute among the succeeding generation of dramatists who disdained such theatrical conventions. Émile Zola reflected the prevailing attitude of these writers when he stated that Dumas "never hesitates between reality and a scenic exigency—he wrings the neck of reality." In contrast, British and American commentators initially com-

plained that Dumas was realistic to a fault, especially in his frank treatment of sexual and moral transgressions. Modern critics have tended to acknowledge the limitations of his method and interests while emphasizing his contributions to the development of French drama. These contributions were considerable and seem likely to insure his continuing renown and influence. As Neil C. Arvin notes, Dumas was "the first modern dramatist to humanize and socialize the theatre," and in this way he continues to be a vital force in modern social drama.

PRINCIPAL WORKS

La chronique (poetry) 1842
Aventures de quatre femmes et d'un perroquet. 6 vols. (novel) 1846-47
Péchés de jeunesse (poetry) 1847
La dame aux camélias (novel) 1848
  [*The Camelia-Lady*, 1857; also published as *Camille; or, The Camelia-Lady*, 1860; and *The Lady of the Camellias*, 1902]
Diane de Lys (novel) 1851; published in *Diane de lys et Grangette*
La dame aux camélias (drama) 1852
  [*Camille; or, The Fate of a Coquette*, 1853; also published as *The Lady of the Camillias*, 1856]
Diane de Lys (drama) 1853
Le demi-monde (drama) 1855
  [*The "Demi-Monde,"* 1858]
La question d'argent (drama) 1857
  [*The Money-Question* published in journal *Poet Lore*, 1915]
Le fils naturel (drama) 1858
  [*Le fils naturel*, 1879]
Un père prodigue (drama) 1859
L'ami des femmes (drama) 1864
Affaire Clémenceau: Mémoire de l'accusé (novel) 1866
  [*Wife Murder; or, The Clémenceau Tragedy*, 1866; also published as *The Clemenceau Case*, 1890]
Les idées de Mme Aubray (drama) 1867
  [*Les idées de Madame Aubray*, 1965]
La princesse Georges (drama) 1871
  [*La princesse Georges*, 1881]
Une visite de noces (drama) 1871
L'homme-femme: Réponse à M. Henri d'Ideville (essay) 1872
  [*Man-Woman; or, The Temple, the Hearth, the Street*, 1873]
La femme de Claude (drama) 1873
  [*The Wife of Claude*, 1905]
Monsieur Alphonse (drama) 1873
  [*Monsieur Alphonse*, 1886]
L'étrangère (drama) 1876
  [*L'étrangère*, 1881]
Entr'actes. 3 vols. (essays) 1878-79
La question du divorce (essay) 1880
La princesse de Bagdad (drama) 1881
  [*The Princess of Bagdad*, 1881]
Denise (drama) 1885
  [*Denise*, 1885]
Francillon (drama) 1887
  [*Francillon*, 1887]
Nouveaux entr'actes, première série (essays) 1890
Théâtre complet, avec préfaces inédites. 7 vols. (dramas and essays) 1890-93

Théâtre complet avec préfaces inédites: Théâtre des autres.
2 vols.   (dramas and essays)   1894-95

*The plays in this work are dramas Dumas wrote in collaboration with
Auguste Vivier, Émile de Girardin, Anne-Adrien-Armand Durantin,
Alphonse François, Narcisse Fournier, Pyotr Korvin-Krukovski, and
Gustave-Eugène Fould.

BENTLEY'S MISCELLANY   (essay date 1857)

[*Focusing on the dramatist's treatment of sexual morals, the critic
reviews Dumas's early career and comments on* La question d'argent.]

[For a time during the past decade,] the Lorettes reigned supreme in Paris: they were the leaders of fashion, and authors
rushed to pay their allegiance to them. Among others was a
young writer, possessing an historic name in the annals of
literature; for, beyond all question, the novels of Alexandre
Dumas père are amongst the best and healthiest that modern
French literature has to boast. His son, burning to distinguish
himself, set about writing the apotheosis of the Lorette, and
the result was **"La Dame aux Camélias."** As a story, it is poor
and clumsy in the extreme. The introductory portion labours
under a feeling of unreality, and the revolting incident of the
lover exhuming his beloved mistress is very calmly borrowed,
without acknowledgment, from Alphonse Karr's "Sous les
Tilleuls." We dare not attempt to prove that the story, as a
story, is uninteresting, as it is only intended to cast a very thin
veil over the most immoral doctrines; for our ladies, who shed
briny tears over "La Traviata," . . . would regard us as Goths
for enunciating such an opinion. . . . But, stripped of romance,
what interest can be excited in a rightly-constituted mind by
reading the story of a Lorette, who is dying of consumption,
and yet pursuing her old career of reckless depravity? She then
falls a victim to what we presume M. Dumas fils would call
a virtuous attachment, and suffers agonies of remorse at being
compelled to break it off at the will of a stern father, who is
naturally anxious for his son's future well-being, and appeals
to her better feelings to aid him. On this one point of virtuous
resignation Dumas builds up the whole airy scaffolding of his
romance, and bids us admire the wonderful abnegation of a
woman whom stern moralists regard as utterly fallen. But it
seems to us that this is rather begging the question: few would
be disposed to admit that such women are so vitiated that they
cannot do one good action, but it does not follow that, by doing
it, all their past offences are condoned. London criminals are
frequently shown to have done acts deserving the highest praise;
but, unfortunately, their punishment in the cruel eye of the law
is not lessened a bit in consequence. But we will go further,
and assert that the suggestions Marguerite Gauthier makes to
her lover are utterly incompatible with even the slightest spark
of virtue. By the author's own showing, she is thoroughly
infected with the taint of corruption, and in actual life she
would not have given up her lover, except on the reasonable
supposition that he had no money left to support her extravagance. (pp. 347-48)

It is fortunate, then, that Dumas fils has overreached himself
in his much-lauded romance, by displaying the utter worthlessness of the woman he selected as his heroine; or was it
that, while pandering to the popular taste, he was prudently
paving the way for that fiercer onslaught on the Lorettes, which

he commenced at a later date? We would gladly credit him
with the latter object, but, at the same time, we are bound to
protest against the false halo which he has shed round Marguerite, to render her attactive to the undiscriminating reader.
(p. 349)

The same sentiments pervade ["**La Dame aux Perles**"]: the
lady with the pearls is a duchess, who falls in love with an
artist, and dies at the end of a thick volume, in order to excite
that sympathy which the reader would otherwise be inclined to
refuse her. We have had many stories in England written
about wives plagued with bad husbands; but among us the
virtue of the wife is exemplified in the patient endurance of
wrong; in France, on the other hand, it is her bounden duty to
revenge herself in the way most repugnant to husbands. The
lady of the pearls is no exception to the universal rule. . . .
[The duke] treats his wife very badly, it must be confessed;
but an Englishman can hardly blame him for so doing, regard
being had to her conduct. And though it is very deplorable that
there are such things as bad husbands in the world, we can
hardly regard that as a sufficient reason for the wives making
themselves equally bad. And this is the great fault we have to
find with all French novelists; they first begin by establishing
a wrong, and work on the principle that two wrongs must
infallibly make a right. Hence, then, regarding the **"Dame aux
Perles"** from a bigoted point of view, we can only say that
the story is just as unsatisfactory as that of her sister Lorette.

"La Jeunesse à Vingt Ans" can be passed over simply as a
failure, of which M. Dumas fils ought to feel profoundly
ashamed—that is, always supposing he is still affected by that
troublesome feeling. A series of stories relating to the illicit
loves of Parisian students cannot possess any great amount of
attraction, except to the young and thoughtless; and it was
probably for that class this book was written. . . . Apart from
this horrid immorality, however, some of the stories possess
considerable piquency for a certain class of readers; and we
may specially refer to the young student at the Polytechnic,
and his *bonne fortune* [good fortune] at the Bal de l'Opéra,
who turns out to be an elderly lady anxious to obtain a privilege
to sell tobacco. Her husband, the old soldier, is very true to
nature, as, indeed, are most of young Dumas's men; his experience of the other sex, however, is not yet sufficiently rip-
ened. He has only mixed, apparently, with one class; and we
trust that ere long his style may be chastened by contact with
a very different style of feminality. (pp. 349-50)

[In "Les Filles de Marbre,"] the Lorettes were held up to
public execration, and displayed in all their hideous cynicism.
The impetus was thus given, and Dumas thought it advisable
to follow the current of public opinion. His **"Diane de Lys"**
showed in very striking colours the dangers of improper affection. The blow was followed up by M. Emile Augier, with
his "Mariage d'Olympe," and Dumas put the crown on the
whole by his remarkable **"Demi Monde."** . . .

The plot of the **"Demi Monde"** is simple enough; and the play
is only remarkable as the first effective protest against all that
offended the decencies and respectability of society. (p. 350)

It was a horrible condition of things, a species of moral nightmare which brooded over the metropolis of France; and if
Dumas the younger has succeeded in dissipating it, he is one
of the greatest benefactors to his country the age has produced.
But we are afraid the ulcer has only been driven inwardly, . . .
and that, in so far as the race of Traviatas is concerned, France

has imitated England, and fancies itself intensely moral, because vice is now concealed from the public gaze.

At any rate, Dumas fils has flattered himself into the belief that he has been constituted *censor morum* [a censor of morals], and having dealt the death-blow to external profligacy, he has sharpened up his weapons and made a dire attack on another great evil from which France is suffering—a tendency to speculation. And here, again, he is only an imitator; the subject was suggested by the success of Ponsard's "L'Honneur et l'Argent," and he has produced a play under the title of **"La Question d'Argent."** But Dumas is here out of his element, and it is not surprising, therefore, that his last effort has met with very mediocre success. The subject has been worn so threadbare in every age, that it would take a far more clever man than our author to bring forward any novel views. As it is, he has gone over the old ground, and brought together the stock platitudes, and nearly the same class of characters as fretted their brief hour in the **"Demi Monde."** (pp. 351-52)

Dumas's speculation [in the play on married life] go beyond the utmost strictures passed on the matrimonial state by French writers. Even Balzac, who may be allowed to have studied the subject most thoroughly, and to have been led to very unsatisfactory conclusions, would hardly go so far as to suggest that the marriage tie should be abolished because some unions happen to prove unfortunate. And yet, if we follow Dumas's views to their fullest development, we can hardly help feeling that such is the panacea he would suggest for the possible miseries of wedlock. Let us revert to the old system of republican marriage, when husband and wife only agreed to separate: such seem to be the tenets of that modern literary school of which Dumas fils has constituted himself the head. Perhaps, before long, some new prophet will arise in Paris and preach the blessings of Mormonism. (pp. 354-55)

Apart from the lesson taught against playing on the Bourse [stock exchange], M. Dumas's comedy has no special interest, nor should we have devoted so much attention to it had we not wished to show the way in which morality is driven into the Parisians. But if M. Dumas imagines he will gain as easy a victory over the Boursiers as he did over the Lorettes, he is grievously mistaken. . . . The passion for gambling has taken such deep root in Paris at present, that an imperial prophet could not turn the nation from its lust after gold, and years must elapse ere things revert to a healthy condition. Let M. Dumas harangue as he will he cannot alter the views of the age, and he must not anticipate that he will, be able to check the current, even if he write plays far superior to the one at present under consideration. (p. 356)

[M. Dumas the younger] possesses great talent, and could he only tame down his propensity for impropriety, he might yet achieve great things. The momentary success of his first offensive novel appears to have caused him to diverge from the right path, and we sincerely trust that he may yet be able to see the errors of his ways, and try to benefit his fellow-countrymen by drawing his inspiration from a purer fount. As the first step in the right direction, then, we gladly hail his new comedy; and even though it be inferior in sustained interest to others of his literary productions, it has the immeasurable advantage of being in a measure free from those *maculae* [blotches] which have disfigured his previous works. (pp. 356-57)

Let us, therefore, in conclusion, hope that we may see more of M. Dumas fils in future, not as the companion, or even as the assailant of worthless women, but as a man conscious of his innate faculties, willing to sacrifice some portion of his reputation, while gaining the applause and appreciation of the good and the wise among his countrymen. (p. 357)

> *"Dumas the Younger," in* Bentley's Miscellany, *Vol. XLI, 1857, pp. 347-57.*

EDMOND DE GONCOURT AND JULES DE GONCOURT (journal date 1867)

[*The Goncourt brothers were literary innovators who are noted for their diverse contributions to the world of letters. In their best-known work,* Journal des Goncourts, *a diary that contains a detailed record of Parisian literary society, the brothers proved themselves to be adept historians of their age. In the passage below, taken from the Goncourts'* Journal *entry for March 16, 1867, the brothers depict Dumas as a writer who panders to the "commonplace emotions" of a sycophantic group of followers dominated by "whores, speculators, and depraved society women."*]

The opening night of **Les Idées de Madame Aubray,** the first play by Dumas *fils* I have seen since **La Dame aux Camélias.** A special audience, of a kind which I have never come across anywhere else. It is not a play that is being performed, it is a kind of mass being celebrated before a pious congregation. There is a *claque* [a group of sycophants] which seems to be officiating, while the audience writhes with ecstasy, swoons with pleasure, and utters cries of 'Adorable!' at every line. The author writes: 'Love is the springtime, it is not the whole year', and there is a salvo of applause. He goes on, working the idea to death: 'It is not the fruit, it is the flower', and the audience claps more than ever. And so it goes on. Nothing is judged, nothing is appreciated; everything is applauded with an enthusiasm brought along in advance and impatient to express itself.

Dumas has a great gift: he knows how to appeal to his public, this first-night public of whores, speculators, and depraved society-women. He is their poet, and he ladles out to them, in a language they can understand, the ideal of their commonplace emotions. (p. 123)

> *Edmond de Goncourt and Jules de Goncourt, in a journal entry of March 16, 1867, in their* Pages from The Goncourt Journal, *edited and translated by Robert Baldick, 1962. Reprint by Oxford University Press, 1978, p. 123.*

[HENRY JAMES, JR.] (essay date 1873)

[*James was an American-born English novelist, short story writer, critic, and essayist of the late nineteenth and early twentieth centuries. In addition to being regarded as one of the greatest novelists of the English language, James is admired as a lucid and insightful critic. As a young man, he traveled extensively throughout Great Britain and Europe and benefited from the friendship and influence of many of the leading figures of nineteenth-century art and literature: in England, he met John Ruskin, Dante Gabriel Rossetti, William Morris, and Leslie Stephen; in France, where he lived for several years, he was part of the literary circle that included Gustave Flaubert, Émile Zola, Edmond de Goncourt, Guy de Maupassant, and Ivan Turgenev. Thus, his criticism is informed by his sensitivity to European culture, particularly English and French literature of the late nineteenth century. James was a frequent contributor to several prominent American journals, including the* North American Review, *the* Nation, *and the* Atlantic Monthly. *In the essay below he deftly exposes the prejudice and presumption underlying Du-*

mas's moralistic preface to Le Faust de Goethe, *H. Bacharach's translation of Johann Wolfgang von Goethe's* Faust. *For additional commentary by James, see his essays dated 1876, 1877, and 1896.*]

[M. Alexandre Dumas's] readers have of course observed that with the progress of events he has become more and more of a moralist. Every few months, for some time now, he has found himself with something edifying to say, and he has preached his little sermons with increasing gusto and skill. Every one has heard of the pamphlet on adultery ['**L'Homme-Femme**'] in which the writer's wisdom seemed to have said its last word. This last word, it will be remembered, was *Tue-la!*—''Shoot her dead!'' It made quiet thinkers jump, like a pistol-shot at the circus. But the seasons have revolved, and M. Dumas has arrived at new results. This time it is not the treacherous wife that we are to kill, but the author of 'Faust' whom we are to sit and behold ground into small, inanimate pieces before us. M. Dumas frankly confesses that he has never had a finer opportunity to hold his tongue. He is ignorant of the German languge, and he comes after a host of commentators who had eluded this reproach. But his desire to paint a moral is irresistible, and he bravely embarks upon his theme.

M. Dumas is an excellent dramatist. There have been few greater pleasures for the theatre-goers of our time than to listen to the '**Demi-Monde**' and the '**Question d'Argent.**' These are considerable performances, and they imply in their author, in some points at least, a sound judgment and a lively imagination. They prove, certainly, that he knows how to present his ideas. His theory (very well stated in one of his prefaces), that in a drama every word uttered should *count* mathematically, here stands him in excellent stead, and makes him extremely readable. But apart from the presumption that there is something in M. Dumas's ideas, there is a great deal that holds one's attention in his sincerity. Evidently the various items of his philosophy are the result of no small amount of ardent emotion; he believes what he says, and he believes that a foolish generation which does not heed it will go to the bad all the faster for its indifference. For that we are going very directly to the bad, unless we radically amend our morals, is M. Dumas's intimate conviction. We are fatally fond of unclean things, and unless we pull up short in our reckless carnival, we shall find ourselves in the bottomless pit. M. Dumas should know, for he has made an especial study of the unclean; he has an infallible scent for it, and a singularly cunning hand in depicting it. He has apparently received his original impetus in his present undertaking from the discovery that there are a number of unclean things in the history of [Johann Wolfgang von Goethe,] the author of 'Faust.' . . . He made the acquaintance of 'Faust' with a view to judging whether a literal translation of it might be successfully represented in Paris, but he was led to conclusions of a far larger scope. These were in great measure the result of a comparison between the poem and the poet's personal history, and they were flattering, on the whole, neither to the author nor to the man. Goethe, twenty years old, made near Strasbourg the acquaintance of a country parson's daughter; readers of his 'Autobiography' will remember the episode of Frederica. Goethe loved her, seduced her, left her, and carried away the germ of the story of *Margaret;* he loved again repeatedly, and M. Dumas counts off his successive sweethearts on his fingers with a critical commentary worthy of his best performances in this line; but he never loved with the same good faith; everything else was rank grossness; he had got his *Margaret,* his passport to posterity, and this was all he cared about. He began his poem, and wrote a bit here, and a bit

there—having found his legend ready-made to his hand; but on the whole he got on rather lamely, and would very likely have hobbled along into utter oblivion, had not Schiller one fine day made his appearance—Schiller, who, like Dumas, could really serve you up a drama. Schiller set him, poetically, on his feet, prompted, suggested, invented, took charge of him intellectually, to the dénouement. But Schiller, unfortunately, could not last for ever; he died in harness, and left his friend with the second part of 'Faust' on his hands. What Goethe made of it shows us all that Schiller had done for the first part.

> Meanwhile, as death might grow tired of waiting till Goethe found the good (*le bien*), as his intellectual sense became weaker every day, according to the laws of nature, as the moral sense could not come to his assistance and Schiller could no longer advise him, as this poem, commenced with a cry of the heart, ought to have finished with a cry of the soul, as the heart had gone and the soul had never come, Goethe heaped up in his work episodes upon episodes, formulas upon formulas, symbols upon symbols. History, mythology, science, arts, politics, agriculture, industry, everything is summoned, everything comes in without connection, without reason. If Goethe were still living, he would be adding railway, the electric telegraph, chloroform, postal orders, and the *fumier impératif.* What fine verses he would use himself up in making about them all! . . .

M. Dumas gives us the second part of 'Faust' as it should have been, as surely, he declares, as two and two make four. We have no space for his ingenious synopsis, which culminates in the tableau of Faust presenting himself before the Lord, ''holding with one hand Mephistopheles chained at his feet, with the other, Margaret, the eternal spouse, recovered and saved, leaning on his bosom. Humanity,'' the author adds, ''will be thus represented as she is to be some day, after all her errors, revolts, and falls, victorious over evil, man redeemed by his conscience, woman redeemed by her love, making only one in a God integral, eternal, and infinite. This is the fatal, inevitable deduction which the idea contained in the first 'Faust,' imposed upon the second. Good or bad, there was no other, as there is no other solution than *four* to two multiplied by two.'' But the great Goethe was incapable of putting two and two together, having, in the first place, too little imagination, and, in the second, too little morality. (p. 293)

As far as proving a case and settling a question is concerned, M. Dumas's preface is of very small value. His acquaintance with Goethe is evidently of the slightest, and his judgment, even so far as it is based on his meagre information, is ludicrously perverted by national prejudice. The reader who is informed that the author of 'Faust' had no imagination, no intuition, we would recommend simply to read 'Faust' itself. . . . Goethe certainly had an immense respect for reality, and no man was ever a greater collector and conservator, as one may say, of facts; but given the multifarious use he made of them—the mysterious music he drew from them—this was not a limitation but an extension of the poetic faculty. As for his having been or not been a *grand homme,* the question seems to us beside the mark. . . . Very likely he was not; this would be our own impression; but M. Dumas ought to know that it is likely to be a waste of time to look for great men among prolific *littérateurs.* . . . When the reader has followed our advice and refreshed his memory of 'Faust,' let him—we speak without the slightest intention of irony—go and read the **'Demi-Monde.'** This clever drama will suffer, and yet it will not suffer. The reader will find it all form, compactness, roundness, smoothness, polish, art; but he will not find in it, without a rare amount of good will, a single word that echoes in the soul, that provokes the shadow of a reverie. (p. 294)

> [*Henry James, Jr.*], "Dumas and Goethe," in The Nation, *Vol. XVII, No. 435, October 30, 1873, pp. 292-94.**

HENRY JAMES, JR.   (essay date 1876)

[*James expresses extreme disappointment with* L'étrangère, *describing the play as a "rather desperate piece of floundering in the dramatic sea." He charges Dumas with lapses of taste and technique and notes the presence of "that aroma of bad company and loose living which is the distinctive sign of M. Dumas' muse." James's essay originally appeared in the March 25, 1876, issue of the* New York Tribune.]

[Alexandre Dumas's long-expected drama *L'Étrangère*] is pronounced indifferent by some people, and shockingly bad by others. No one, as far as I have observed, has had the originality to call it good. I happened to hear it discussed, a few days since, among several gentlemen who are more or less of the same guild as its author, and it was as pretty a cutting up as one could desire to see. The general verdict was that Alexandre Dumas has so much wind in his sails (from former successes) that he will float safely across his present shallows, but that his decline (since decline it is) will be cumulative; that another piece as bad as *L'Étrangère* will have much worse luck, and that the more gentle the public has been for the author hitherto, the more pitiless it will be when he begins to sink. Has he already begun to sink? I confess that *L'Étrangère* strikes me as a rather desperate piece of floundering in the dramatic sea. . . . [The] Foreigner who gives its title to the piece, . . . is a daughter of our own democracy, Mrs. Clarkson by name. She explains, in the second act, by a mortal harangue—the longest, by the watch, I have ever listened to—that she is the daughter of a mulatto slave girl and a Carolinian planter. . . . Mrs. Clarkson, however, has next to nothing to do with the action of the play, and she is the least successful figure that the author has ever drawn. Why she should be an American, why she should have Negro blood, why she should be the implacable demon that she is represented, why she should deliver the melodramatic and interminable tirade I have mentioned, why she should come in, why she should go out, why, in short, she should exist— all this is the perfection of mystery. She is like the heroine of an old-fashioned drama of the Boulevard du Crime who has strayed unwittingly into a literary work, in which she is out of time with all her companions. She is, on Dumas' part, an incredible error of taste. It must be confessed, however, that her entrance into the play has a masterly effectiveness. The whole first act indeed is an excellent start, though the goal is never really reached. (pp. 86-8)

The real heroine of the play is Mlle. Croizette, who played the Duchess with a great deal of skill and with all that strangely meretricious charm for which she is renowned. She has one really magnificent scene—a scene in which the ill-used (but on her own side by no means unpeccant) heroine, the cup of whose disgust at her husband's turpitude is full, pours it all forth in rage and scorn upon his ignoble head. This is nature caught in the act—Mlle. Croizette's cries and gestures, the passionate reality of her imprecations, electrify the house. The author makes his duchess say things which have never before been said on the stage, but the artistic good faith of the actress carries them off. (pp. 89-90)

On the whole, as I have said, *L'Étrangère* has been a disappointment, and it is unquestionably a very unsatisfactory piece of work for so clever a man as Dumas. It hangs very loosely together, and the story is both extremely improbable and profoundly disagreeable. Disagreeable, above all, for there is not a person in the play who is not, in one way or another, misbehaving grossly. Everyone is in the wrong, and the author most of all. And then his drama is saturated with that aroma of bad company and loose living which is the distinctive sign of M. Dumas' muse. This lady is afflicted with a congenital want of perception of certain rudimentary differences between the possible, for decent people, and the impossible. She has also on this occasion abused her characteristic privilege of indulging in pretentious tirades of the would-be philosophic order—explaining that love is physics and marriage is chemistry, &c. (pp. 90-1)

> Henry James, Jr., "Parisian Affairs," in his Parisian Sketches: Letters to the 'New York Tribune', 1875-1876, *edited by Leon Edel and Ilse Dusoir Lind, New York University Press, 1957, pp. 83-92.*

HENRY JAMES   (essay date 1877)

[*Commenting on* Le demi-monde, *James expresses his admiration for the quiet efficiency of Dumas's craftsmanship and describes the play as the "model" drama of the era. At the same time, he also remarks on the "oddity" of the morality informing the work. James's remarks were originally published in 1877 in a magazine article entitled "Occasional Paris."*]

The **Demi-Monde** of M. Dumas *fils* is not a novelty . . . ; but I quite agree with M. Francisque Sarcey that it is on the whole, in form, the first comedy of our day. I have seen it several times, but I never see it without being forcibly struck with its merits. For the drama of our time it must always remain the model. The interest of the story, the quiet art with which it is unfolded, the naturalness and soberness of the means that are used, and by which great effects are produced, the brilliancy and richness of the dialogue—all these things make it a singularly perfect and interesting work. . . . In seeing the **Demi-Monde** again I was more than ever struck with the oddity of its morality and with the way that the ideal of fine conduct differs in different nations. The **Demi-Monde** is the history of the eager, the almost heroic, effort of a clever and superior woman, who has been guilty of what the French call 'faults,' to pass from the irregular and equivocal circle to which these faults have consigned her into what is distinctively termed 'good society.' The only way in which the passage can be effected is by her marrying an honourable man; and to induce an honourable man to marry her, she must suppress the more discreditable facts of her career. Taking her for an honest woman, Raymond de Nanjac falls in love with her, and honestly proposes to make her his wife. But Raymond de Nanjac has contracted an intimate friendship with Olivier de Jalin, and the action of the play is more especially De Jalin's attempt . . . to rescue his friend from the ignominy of a union with Suzanne d'Ange. Jalin knows a great deal about her, for the simple reason that he has been her lover. . . . [From] the moment that Suzanne sets her cap at Nanjac, Olivier declares war. Suzanne struggles hard to keep possession of her suitor, who is very much in love with her, and Olivier spares no pains to detach him. It is the means that Olivier uses that excite the wonderment of the Anglo-Saxon spectator. He takes the ground that in such a cause all means are fair, and when, at the climax of the play, he tells a thumping lie in order to make Madame d'Ange compromise herself, expose herself, he is pronounced by the author 'le plus honnête homme que je connaisse.' [the most honest man I've known]. . . . An English-speaking audience is more 'moral' than a French, more easily scandalised; and yet it is a singular fact that if the *Demi-Monde* were represented before an English-speaking audience, its sympathies would certainly not go with M. de Jalin. It would pronounce him rather a coward. . . . The point is not that the English-speaking audience would be disposed to condone Madame d'Ange's irregularities, but that it would remain perfectly cold before the spectacle of her ex-lover's masterly campaign against her, and quite fail to think it positively admirable, or to regard the fib by which he finally clenches his victory as a proof of exceptional honesty. The ideal of our own audience would be expressed in some such words as, 'I say, that's not fair game. Can't you let the poor woman alone?' (pp. 279-80)

> *Henry James, in an extract from his* The Scenic Art: Notes on Acting & the Drama, 1872-1901, *edited by Allan Wade, Rutgers University Press, 1948, pp. 279-81.*

THE NATION   (essay date 1881)

[*The critic discusses the public's unfavorable reaction to the first performances of* La princesse de Bagdad *at the Théâtre Français.*]

The first representation of the **"Princess of Bagdad,"** by Alexandre Dumas, is the dramatic event of the day. (p. 127)

The public of the "first representation" is perhaps the most *blasé* public in the world, but it was in turn excited and displeased by this extraordinary Princess of Bagdad, who is pure, and would, in a mere fit of rage, become impure—this honest woman, who exaggerates in a moment the coarseness of a courtesan, who becomes so vulgar as to think of throwing gold-pieces about and of saying things which it was found necessary to suppress at the second representation. This second representation took place before the public of the "Tuesdays." Tuesday is a special day at the Français for season-ticket holders. In the past few years Society, being much deprived of amusements, has adopted the Français; the Tuesday public is the "world" itself, and is, therefore, rather cold and reserved. There was no hissing on Tuesday; the actors were much applauded; but in all the conversations Dumas's play was condemned. The universal question was: "In what world do people behave like this?" The answer might have been found in the play: when *Lionnette,* the Countess de Hun, decides to follow *Nourvady,* she talks confidentially with an old friend, declaring that her fate is just, that she follows her destiny. "I go to vice," says she, "though I love it no more than the rest, as I have gone to marriage, to maternity, without knowing why. No heart! no heart! I am a creature of luxury and of pleasure. . . . You can remember your mother, your wife, your children. Yes, there are indeed mothers, there are women, there are children, . . . and then there are beings who have these same forms, and are called by these same names, and still they are not the same thing."

Here is Dumas's philosophy: he is a Darwinian. He meant to show in the light *Countess de Hun* the hereditary taint, the morbid influences which had prepared her mother to become the mistress of an Asiatic prince, which had made her grandmother, *Madame Duranton,* notorious among the lowest char-

acters of the capital. But if the princess is the victim of heredity, why is she not bad to the end? Why does she become reconciled with virtue? This is the miracle of maternal love. Though she cannot be a wife, she can be a mother. I do not discuss the theory; I set it forth. It is perhaps a pity that Dumas has expressed it so coarsely, with so little management, without any shades, any transitions. His play was written, he says, in seven days—it is only too visible. (p. 128)

> *"Dumas's 'Princess of Bagdad'," in* The Nation, *Vol. XXXII, No. 817, February 24, 1881, pp. 127-28.*

J. BRANDER MATTHEWS   (essay date 1881)

[*An American critic, playwright, and novelist, Matthews wrote extensively on world drama and served for a quarter-century at Columbia University as professor of dramatic literature, the first person to hold that title at an American university. He was also a founding member and president of the National Institute of Arts and Letters. In the following essay, Matthews recognizes Dumas as an important and innovative force in French drama and critiques his best-known plays.*]

With the appearance of M. Alexandre Dumas, *fils,* on the stage, a fresh force came into the French drama. To say this is easy; to qualify this force adequately and to define its limits is no light task. The two other dramatists, each in his way remarkable, who stand to-day with M. Dumas at the head of French dramatic literature, are comparatively simple problems. In M. Sardou we see the utmost cleverness and technical skill, heightened by a girding wit: he continues the tradition of Scribe, adding all the modern improvements. In M. Augier we behold a high and genuine literary value, a humorous and broad humanity; he inherits by right of primogeniture from Molière, and observes mankind with the large frankness of his master. But M. Dumas continues no tradition; he is that rare thing in literature,—a self-made man. He derives from no one; he expresses himself, and with emphasis; he is a personal force. Not condescending to the ingenious trickery of M. Sardou, and never rising to the lofty liberality of M. Augier, his place in the dramatic hierarchy is not so readily fixed as theirs; his character is not so simple,—in fact, it may fairly be called complex, and even contradictory. Here, for instance, is a bundle of inconsistencies. With a real power of creating character, there is no dramatist who has more often and more boldly brought forward the same faces and figures. While declaring in one volume that he knows no immoral plays, but only ill-made ones, in another volume he asserts that the stage in itself is immoral: setting forth in one piece the right of assassinating the erring wife, he sets forth in the next the duty of forgiving her. In comedies inherently vicious he pauses to preach virtue, but with a bluntness of language at times shocking even to vice. He has written the **"Ami des Femmes"** and the **"Visite de Noces,"**—two plays which imply that their author does not suspect what "good taste" means; and yet he has been elected a member of the French Academy, constituted to be a tribunal of taste. The historian of the **"Dame aux Camélias"** and the discoverer of the **"Demi-Monde,"**—a word with which he has enriched the vocabulary of the world,—he has stood forward in the name of the Academy to bestow prizes of virtue. The son of a prodigal father always poor, he himself is wealthy and frugal; and finally, brought up in all the looseness of the lightest Parisian society, he has the Bible at his fingers' ends, and quotes the Scripture as freely as an Orthodox New Englander. With such a character and such a career, M. Dumas is one of the most interesting and curiously complex figures of our century. (pp. 530-31)

The **"Dame aux Camélias"** was at once simple, pathetic, and audacious. It emancipated French comedy, and gave it the right of free speech. To judge it fairly, one must consider the comedies which held the French stage before its coming. There were Scribe and his collaborators, with their conventional and machine-made works; and there were Ponsard and M. Augier with their plays, poetic in intent and finely polished, but as yet reflecting nothing vital and actual. The great merit of the **"Dame aux Camélias"** is that it renewed modern French comedy by pointing out the path back to Nature and the existing conditions of society, and by showing that life should be studied as it was, and not as it had been or as it might be. (pp. 533-34)

As M. Montégut pointed out over twenty years ago in the "Revue des Deux Mondes," the story of a courtesan's love may be a poetic subject if treated with elevation, or it may be a degrading subject if treated realistically; adding that M. Dumas had chosen a middle course, and that the result was little more than a vulgar melodrama. Before M. Montégut wrote, the subject had been treated poetically in M. Hugo's "Marion Delorme"; since, it has been set forth with unspeakable realism in M. Zola's "Nana." In M. Dumas' play we avoid the offensiveness of the latter, but we miss wholly the poetry of the former. On one of its revivals, a competent French critic declared that it bore itself, even in its old age, like a masterpiece; and an almost equally competent American critic recorded that he had had a hearty laugh over its "colossal flimsiness." It is, in fact, not to be taken too seriously. It carries one along by the rush of youthful strength; yet one has time to note phrases horribly out of tune, and to detect a sort of sentimentality run mad. In general its morality is cheap, not to say tawdry. In short, the play seems to me youthful,—in the objectionable sense of the word. And I am half inclined to think that the Dame aux Camélias herself is doing exactly what she is best fitted for when she serves as the heroine of an Italian opera. . . .

["**Diane de Lys**"] is not so direct, simple, or sincere as its predecessor. As M. Dumas himself suggests, the second play is inferior to the first; it cost but a few days' work, and was written to pay off lingering debts. (p. 534)

[The] **"Demi-Monde"** is a masterly play. It stands the threefold test,—it is good in plot, dialogue, and character. The story is one which we follow with interest to the finish with a growing desire to be in at the death. In dialogue it is as brilliant and as metallic as any M. Dumas ever wrote. The characters are splendidly projected against the dim background of a dubious society, and contrasted one against the other with the utmost skill. De Nanjac's heat, for instance, sets off the coolness of De Jalin. In De Thounerins we see a second edition of the old duke invisible in the **"Dame aux Camélias"**; and in Valentine we see the first sketch of the future Iza of the **"Affaire Clémenceau,"** and of the wife of Claude. The chief person of the comedy, Suzanne, is a boldly drawn character, almost worthy of a place by the side of the nobler and more poetic figure of M. Emile Augier's "Aventurière"; four years later she reappears with a hardened outline in the Albertine of the **"Père Prodigue."** (p. 536)

The **"Demi-Monde"** is the model of nineteenth century comedy, just as [Richard Sheridan's] "School for Scandal" is the model of eighteenth century comedy. The contrast of the two plays would be pregnant did space permit. The seemingly careless ease with which Sheridan has sketched his characters, and

the airy humor which informs the whole comedy make us accept a story and special scenes far more dangerous than anything in M. Dumas' piece; and yet the impression left by the "School for Scandal" is pleasant, while the **"Demi-Monde"** is almost a painful spectacle. We cannot help liking some of Sheridan's characters,—Lady Teazle, for instance, and Sir Peter, in spite of his uxoriousness, and Charles, too; while even the scandalous college—after making due allowance for the tone of a by-gone century—is not wholly repulsive. But no woman in the **"Demi-Monde"** should we wish a wife to visit, and no man in it should we care to shake by the hand. (p. 537)

[The **"Question d'Argent"**] is a play of no great value, much inferior in interest to its predecessors, but differing from them in that it is really a comedy. Both M. Dumas' earlier plays were dramas; and even in the **"Demi-Monde"** the situations at times are on the verge of melodrama. But the **"Question d'Argent"** is pure comedy. Its incidents are entirely the result of the clash of character on character; and its central figure, though marred by a touch too much of caricature, is one of which any comedy might be proud. . . . The comedy is less tainted with M. Dumas' views and theories than any other of his plays written before or since. It is more wholesome, and it might be read or seen by any one without damage or danger. Unfortunately the fable is weak, and the figure of the financier who believes that money is absolute monarch, though boldly outlined, is not always artistically filled in. (pp. 537-38)

[The **"Fils Naturel"**] is an admirable specimen of stage-craft; and it is no wonder that two such experts in dramatic art as M. Sarcey and M. Perrin, the director of the Théatre-Français, should incline to consider it M. Dumas' masterpiece. No wonder is it, either, that such praise should revolt at M. Zola, who has a fresh theory of throwing on the stage "nature" raw and crude, as in a photograph. M. Zola holds that M. Dumas "never hesitates between reality and a scenic exigency,—he wrings the neck of reality"; and he says that M. Dumas "uses truth only as a springboard to jump into space." In the **"Fils Naturel,"** for the first time, M. Dumas sought to set a social problem on the stage; and yet nowhere else has he shown so full a share of the constructive faculty which is the birthmark of the true dramatist, but which M. Zola chooses to condemn. (p. 538)

[The **"Père Prodigue"**] is not good. It is overladen with incident; and—as a French critic remarked when it was first acted—it might almost begin with the second act, or the third, or even the fourth. Poor as the play is, it contains one of M. Dumas' most successful characters. The prodigal father is in the true high-comedy vein. By the side of M. Dumas' bull-headed and sentimental heroes, and of his preternaturally witty heroes,—projections of his own impulses and cleverness, and reduplicated to fatigue,—is a series of comic characters of great force and originality. No dramatist of the nineteenth century has enriched literature with more amusing comic portraits. The prodigal father in this play, the self-made speculator in the **"Question d'Argent,"** the broken-down and philosophic artist Taupin, in **"Diane de Lys,"** the clear-headed and good-hearted notary Aristide, in the **"Fils Naturel,"** the outspoken Madame Guichard in **"M. Alphonse,"** and the profligate Duke in the **"Étrangère,"**—these are figures firm on their feet. . . . (p. 539)

[The **"Ami des Femmes"** is] by far the poorest of M. Dumas' plays. There is really little or nothing to admire in it; there is less wit than usual, and no action to speak of. It may be passed over with the remark that its subject was bad, and the taste with which it was treated was worse. Its subject, indeed, is one wholly unfit for state-treatment, unless, as M. Dumas sometimes hints, the theatre ought to be an amphitheatre for gynaecologic clinics. (p. 540)

M. Dumas has always shown the tendency toward mysticism not infrequent in men of his temperament. Even in the **"Dame aux Camélias"** the curtain finally fell on a quotation from the New Testament. Now he frankly takes to preaching, and puts his audacity, his patience, and his ingenuity at the service of the strange system of sociology which he has evolved from his inner consciousness. His skill as a dramatist is bent to the making of purely didactic dramas. He comes forth in the purple and fine linen of the stage to set forth a doctrine of sackcloth and ashes. In the expounding of his new views, his style is harder and more brilliant than ever; and he explains his latest moral kinks with no sign of sweetness or light, but with great rigor and force.

In the **"Idées de Madame Aubray,"** . . . the first fruits of this new philosophy, the preacher fortunately has not yet over-mastered the playwright. The piece is a marvel of polemic literature,—a model in the art of teaching by example. . . . It treats an important subject honestly, and with intellectual seriousness. There is none of the petty begging of the question which disfigures two other works on the same subject,—the "Fernande" of M. Victorien Sardou and the "New Magdalen" of Mr. Wilkie Collins; both clever men, lacking, however, in the courage and the candor needed to face the problem fairly. There is a fourth work of fiction, published not long after M. Dumas', which approaches the subject with the same appreciation of its demands and its difficulties.

This novel is "Hedged In," by Miss Elizabeth Stuart Phelps,—as representatively New England as the **"Idées de Madame Aubray"** is French. It is of course a mere paradox to say that M. Dumas, since his regeneration, appears to me as a typical New-Englander; but he has something of the New England spirit, and he stands at times in the New England attitude. He recalls, in a way, both Nathaniel Hawthorne and Oliver Wendell Holmes. His theology is in essence Unitarian and I have before made mention of his very New England knack of Biblical quotation; and, as his recent volume on **"Divorce"** shows, he is as prone to search the Scriptures for a text wherewith to smite his adversary as are any of those chips of Plymouth Rock who "take to the ministry mostly." Without pushing the analogy too far, it stands out plainly when we set the **"Idées de Madame Aubray"** by the side of "Hedged In," and see that both the American and the French writers, though differing greatly in mental equipment, approach the subject from the same point of view, and give it the same austerity of treatment. (pp. 541-42)

[The **"Visite de Noces"**] is an inquest on the internal corruption of man. Perhaps the verdict is just, in view of the evidence produced; but the impulse of a healthy man would be to let such matter drop into the gutter, where it belongs. To lift it thence is to stir up muddy depths of degradation to no purpose. (p. 542)

Neither the **"Princesse Georges"** nor the **"Femme de Claude"** can be called good plays, or even well-made plays. . . . The thesis in each case has proved too heavy for the plot. In the **"Princesse Georges"** the thesis seems to be the duty of feminine forgiveness; in the **"Femme de Claude,"** the duty of summary justice. I say *seems*, for the exact target of M. Dumas' bullet is not unmistakable, despite much talk about it. Unfortunately the theorist got the better of the playwright, especially

in the **"Princesse Georges,"** in which two ladies of the highest society explain the bad character of the Comtesse de Terremonde at inordinate length and in M. Dumas' own style, with recondite historical and scientific allusions; and shortly after they have done, another of the actors . . . takes up the parable, and preaches another page of the same sort of stuff. After reading these diatribes, with all their pseudo-scientific parade, one can scarcely help wondering whether M. Dumas is not laughing in his sleeve at us. But no, I think his sincerity beyond dispute, only—well, only I wish he would not believe in himself quite so emphatically. If indeed he were not so sincere, there would be only one word to describe his attitude with exactness; and that word, unfortunately, is yet waiting its passport to good society. If I may venture to use it, however, I shall say that M. Dumas has sublime *check*. Now in this very **"Princesse Georges"** the general verdict was that the catastrophe was a mistake. . . . [M. Dumas] defends it by saying that the Princesse Georges would be guilty of cold-blooded murder if she let her husband go to certain death. This is all very true. I do not ask that the Prince should be shot; but I do ask that M. Dumas should not take me in by a petty trick,—that, having led me to think that the Prince was to be killed, he should balk this legitimate expectation by a wrench of probability. M. Dumas can afford to leave such clever devices to M. Sardou; they do not become a teacher and a preacher. (pp. 543-44)

In **"M. Alphonse"** . . . one may note a return to M. Dumas' earlier manner, or at least a temporary cessation of his sociological studies. In spite of its unpleasant subject and its weak-as-water heroine, the play is one of M. Dumas' best. The characters are few and nervously drawn. . . . There is nowhere any feebleness in outline; all M. Dumas' characters, like their creator, believe in themselves. The story, which is simple and pathetic, tells itself plainly. The action is not overladen with philosophical diatribes. M. Dumas for once reaped the benefit of his own improvements in the formula of dramatic construction. We owe to him the cutting short of long-winded expositions and the rapid rush of hurrying action; but unfortunately the inventor of this improved comedy took advantage of the time thus saved for illicit indulgence in metaphysical stump-speeches, and for the promulgation of the gospel according to St. Alexandre. In **"M. Alphonse"** there is little of this skirmishing along the flanks: he sticks close to the issue in hand; and the teaching of the play is only the plainer for this restraint. (pp. 544-45)

[When M. Dumas] rigidly required of himself a moral aim he spoiled his work, . . . as we can see in his latest play, the **"Étrangère"**. . . . I think I can fairly call it the poorest of M. Dumas' plays, and surely—despite its moral intent—the foulest. There is but one decent man or woman in it, and he, like most of M. Dumas' virtuous heroes, is virtuous with a vengeance. He is a good man in the worst sense of the word. For the rest, the duke and the duchess, and the rest of the gang,—the word sounds coarse, but is exactly expressive,—we have no feeling but disgust. All are corrupt; there is a general odor of corruption. A miasma hangs over the stage when the curtain is up, and we breathe more freely when once we get outside. (pp. 545-46)

[In] considering the **"Étrangère"** I cannot help wishing for the hygienic breeze that blows through most of M. Augier's manly plays. There is never a breath of poetry in M. Dumas' dramas,—no touch of imagination. One is never lifted out of matter-of-fact, every-day life. In a measure, the life in his pieces differs from the life around us only in that the people in the plays are rather wittier in speech and worse in character than those in reality. All is hard and dry and brilliant. More than that, everything is narrow. It is a very tiny corner of even the little world of Paris, which serves as the stage of all M. Dumas' dramas. And if one can form a fair idea of Paris from these plays, then one may well wonder and regret that fire and sword left one stone on another. (p. 546)

[M. Dumas concludes his latest work, the divorce pamphlet **"La question du divoree,"** by asking for the passage of a bill] which allows a freedom of separation shocking even to an Illinois or Connecticut legislator.

Among the consequences which would follow the decreeing of divorce in France, M. Dumas tells us, would be a total change in the French drama; for adultery, now the chief stock-in-trade of the stage, would lose its importance in life, and so would see less service in the theatre. If M. Dumas be right, we can only wish that divorce had been established before he began to write; and then perhaps illicit love would not have been found in some form in every one of his plays. There is adultery, or the attempt at it, or the suspicion of it, in eleven out of twelve of M. Dumas' dramas. . . . He is, in short, a specialist; and in literature, as in medicine, a specialist is often dangerous.

All his powers as a playwright are at the service of this peculiar predilection,—his gift of seeing things theatrically; his ability in handling a plot, generally simple, and turning frequently on a single strong situation carefully prepared and provided for, and only postponed to come at last with double force; his gift of characterization; his skill in skating over thin ice; his speech, when needed, vigorous to the point of violence; his knack of breaking the force of all objections to his conclusion by himself advancing them; and his wit, which cannot be denied, though he is far too conscious of it, as any one may see who notes how he scatters it broadcast through his plays . . .—all these remarkable qualifications are held at the beck and call of his desire for the contemplation of illicit love. . . . M. Dumas says he respects the maiden too much to bid her to his plays, and he respects his art too much to write for maidens. There is some reason in this. It is at least an open question whether we do not fetter the artist too tightly when we insist on bringing all literature down to the level of the school-girl. But while we may admit that girls have no business in a dissecting room, we may also protest against always taking the stage for a physiological laboratory. Besides, while true science is clean and wholesome, M. Dumas' is neither. As M. Francisque Sarcey once wrote, "He gives the best advice in the world, in a language which recalls at once the manuals of physiology and the Vie Parisienne of Marcelin." A sceptic is tempted to wonder whether by chance M. Dumas has not picked up his science in the Vie Parisienne. (pp. 547-48)

One may doubt whether M. Dumas knows whether there be any scientific spirit or not. In default of it, he is fertile in hypothesis and theory. Sometimes he gets so entangled in the jungle of his own philosophy, that it is difficult to discover his whereabouts; yet, as a French critic has pointed out, he seems to have had in turn, if not at the same time, these three theories: (1) Love rehabilitates a fallen woman; (2) When she is not capable of rehabilitation, one must kill her; and (3) Woman, anyhow, is a being greatly inferior to man, who indeed may be said to stand intermediate and mediating between woman and God. And it is to prove one or another of these three hypotheses that M. Dumas has written his plays, which, fortunately for us, are most of them of more value than the doubt-ful theories which were the exciting cause of their existence. (pp. 548-49)

J. Brander Matthews, "M. Alexandre Dumas, fils," in The International Review, *Vol. X, June, 1881, pp. 530-49.*

ANATOLE FRANCE   (essay date 1889)

[*France was a French novelist and critic of the late nineteenth and early twentieth centuries. His work is noted for its clarity, control, perceptive judgment of world affairs, and the Enlightenment traits of tolerance and justice. Many of these qualities inform the following essay, in which France argues that Dumas unreasonably expects love to follow the dictates of reason and justice. France's commentary was published in French in 1889 in the first volume of his* La vie littéraire *(On Life and Letters, first series), a collection of articles originally contributed to the journal* Le temps.]

Alexandre Dumas is a moralist as well as a dramaturge. (p. 22)

In morality, it is true, M. Alexandre Dumas has touched only a single point. But it is the point from which all else issues, it is the universal principle. He tells us how we are born, and he shows us that we are born ill; he tells us how we give life and he shows us that we give it badly; and he foretells the end of the world if we do not speedily give

> A stainless bridegroom to a virgin bride.

What he fights against, what he indicts everywhere, is the shameful traffic in love. According to him, prostitution has either publicly or secretly invaded everything. It displays itself in our streets. Marriage has installed it in the homes of the rich. Only among a few courtesans is it not to be seen. It is [depicted in the preface to **"La femme de Claude"** as] the seven-headed Beast whose diadems overtop the loftiest mountains. (p. 26)

He does not merely attack the Beast. He has a grudge against love itself, against love as we ordinarily pursue it. Lebonnard, in the **"Visite de Noces,"** concludes that "that ends by hatred on the woman's part and contempt on the man's." And Lebonnard is no fool. M. de Ryons [in **"L'ami des femmes"**] shows himself still more cruel when he says to Madame de Simerose: "M. de Montègre is going to do you an injury, for he loves you." This M. de Ryons is very impressive. He is the friend of women, and this amounts to saying that he does not love them. "I have pledged myself," he tells us, "never to give either my heart, or my honour, or my life to be devoured by those charming and terrible little beings for whom we ruin, dishonour, and kill ourselves, and whose sole preoccupation, in the midst of this universal carnage, is to dress themselves up sometimes in the form of umbrellas and sometimes of bells." How admirable! It is what the wise Epicurus used to teach in those books which unfortunately have been lost. His pupil, Lucretius, learnt and repeated the lesson with ardour. M. de Ryons is, in his turn, a great philosopher. There is a reason for that; it is because he is not in love. Let him fall in love and immediately his own philosophy and that of Epicurus and that of Lucretius and that of Dumas will be in headlong flight. Our strong man will become a weak man, and he will give all he possesses as a prey to a little being—bell or umbrella.

Oh! I see the evil plainly. The evil is that Love is the oldest of the gods. . . . When he was born neither justice nor intelligence were as yet in the world. The luckless wretch could not find in all the cosmic matter anything out of which he could fashion for himself a brain or eyes or ears. He was born blind and dependent on his instincts, and as he was born, so he is still, and so he will always remain. He has to grope his way about. . . . His real appearance is that of a headless bull. Far from being the child of Venus, he is her father. Look at his labours; they are immense. He has produced everything, but he has done it all without reason, without morality, without intelligence. First, he made living creatures, and what awful creatures they were! Molluscs, fishes, and reptiles. . . . Improving his methods by accident and little by little, he reached marsupials and then viviparous animals. The mammalia cost him a great deal of trouble, and for a long time the monkeys remained his masterpiece. In making man after them, he made no change either in nature or in method. He remained dark, blind, and violent, and did not call reason to his aid. He never will call it. And he is right, for life would soon end if it relied upon intelligence to plant it throughout the earth. He is blind and he guides us. That is the whole evil. And it is an eternal evil, for love will last as long as the worlds. (pp. 27-9)

I do not know whether my mythology is very clear, but I know what I mean. It amounts to saying that there are in man obscure forces, anterior to him, which act independently of his will, and which he cannot always master. Must we on that account have a hatred for life and a horror for man? No, there is good even in the headless Bull himself. We must not abuse him too much. On the whole, he has always done more good than evil. Otherwise he would not survive. What he wants is what nature wants, and nature, after all, is indifferent rather than evil. (pp. 29-30)

Men are better than nature. It is a consoling and an agreeable truth which I shall never weary of repeating.

If they could endow the headless Bull with a little heart and brain, be sure that they would do so at once.

M. Alexandre Dumas believes them to be worse than they are, and he has two good reasons for it: he is a dramatist and he is a prophet.

The theatre lives solely by our woes, and, since the days of Israel, the prophets have proclaimed nothing but misfortune; that is the price of their eloquence.

If M. Alexandre Dumas is right in saying that man is brutal and that woman is absurd, we can, like Musset's Perdican, reply that "there is one holy and sublime thing in the world—the union of two such imperfect beings." (p. 30)

> *Anatole France, "M. Alexandre Dumas, Moralist,"*
> *in his* On Life & Letters, *first series, edited by Frederic Chapman, translated by A. W. Evans, 1911.*
> *Reprint by Dodd, Mead and Company, 1924, pp. 22-30.*

A. B. WALKLEY (essay date 1892)

[*Walkley provides a rather arch account of Dumas's career as a moralist but acknowledges his primacy in the realm of dramatic craftsmanship.*]

How to qualify [Dumas *fils*]? A dramatist who can give Scribe and Sardou points and a beating at their own game; a prophet who has brought down new Tables of the Law from a Sinai hard by Mont Valérien; an apostle whose prefaces, pamphlets, articles, are so many Epistles to the Lutetians; moralist, philosopher, mystic, dabbler in occultism, deist, socialist, conservative—to be thus prodigal of differences is to be a mere

Portrait of Marie Duplessis, the French courtesan who was the prototype of the character Marguerite Gautier in "Camille." The Granger Collection, New York.

centre of perplexity, a rallying point of the bewilderments. To Montesquieu's Persian or Goldsmith's Chinaman his whole theatre would seem one prolonged nightmare, and his pistol-practice a criminal waste of good powder: they would untie the knot of his dramas by tying a knot in a bow-string—or by adding a new wing to the harem. But with the passage from Ispahan to Paris, from polygamy to monogamy, the great conflict of sex passes from a mellay to a duel: a code of honour, seconds, a doctor, and occasionally the police, come upon the ground. Dumas *fils* is always the doctor, sometimes the police, very often the judge. Of course it is the weaker combatant that absorbs his interests—the Eternal Feminine, to wit. He prescribes for her, and when she rejects the drug he throws the Code and the Bible at her head, calls her the Beast of the Apocalypse, the female of Cain, and other hard names—. . . . He began, as the May of youth and the bloom of lustihood will, by putting his head in the Beast's mouth—to show how easily she could be tamed. The result of his experiment was *La Dame aux Camélias.* To the play-going Fifties this seemed, of all things in the world, a realistic play: they took it for a new approximation to the truth. So thinks every generation of its own drama; Sophocles was a realist in the eyes of a people bred on Aeschylus. But *la Dame* is not the beginning of Realism as we know it; rather is it an end—one among many—of Romanticism. Marguerite is a true daughter of [Victor Hugo's heroine] Marion Delorme; and, as you know, she died childless. The play, by its author's admission, is dead; and *Le Demimonde,* masterpiece as it was, is only half-alive. The social half-world it depicts is merged in the general mob. . . . In its time it showed the whips of the elder Duval turned to scorpions in the hands of Olivier de Jalin. But Suzanne d'Ange seems now a more pathetic figure than Marguerite; and Olivier de Jalin—in M. Dumas' eyes 'le plus honnête homme que je connaisse'—has long been voted an egregious cad.

The revolt of the polygamous (or the polyandrous) instinct against the official monogamy of the West: the revolt, its pardon or its punishment—that is the true subject of the living Dumas and his theatre. It is of course the subject of many other dramatists; but in his unswerving devotion, his postponement of every ology to the pathology of love, he is the master of them all. To examine his theatre is an exercise in permutations and combinations. You have so many fixed elements: husband, husband's mistress, wife, wife's lover; you combine these elements in all possible ways, and to each way corresponds a play of Dumas *fils*. The first group of combinations gives the woman taken in adultery. Here that Bible M. Dumas is so fond of quoting would teach him not to throw stones; but that Bible of his does not include the New Testament. He must have blood. At first it was the lover's: in *Diane de Lys* Paul Aubry falls the first victim to his pistol-practice, Diane herself being let off with a fainting fit. Then came the lady's turn: Diane was spared because a something of the old romance still clung about her; she was of the family of the Indianas and Lélias [title characters of novels by George Sand]—a lamb not ready for the shambles. But in the Iza of *l'Affaire Clémenceau* . . . and in the eponymous heroine of *La Femme de Claude* the lamb became the Beast, and Clemenceau's jade-handled dagger, Claude's new patent breechloader, did their work, and the gospel of *tue-la* was preached unto the nations. Then emerged . . . a new theory of the Adulterous Woman: she was to be saved from herself by her superior, Man. . . . [When] started, as so inferior and naturally perverse an animal cannot choose but start, on the high road to adultery, she must not be allowed to reach her destination and so get stabbed like Iza or shot like Claude's wife: she must be pulled up short by a sympathetic, omniscient, omnipotent male friend, who talks like a (boulevard) angel. Jane de Simerose must be saved by M. des Ryons, and restored by stratagem to her husband's arms. Or this weak animal, woman . . . is to be saved by her sympathetic male friend . . . through the latter's Josephic self-denial until what time the husband (who is a brute) shall be conveniently suppressed. That is the strange situation of wife, lover, and husband in *l'Etrangère*.

With the peccant husband the theorist of *l'Etrangère* has a short way. An American *deus ex machiná* . . . kills him "like a little rabbit." Two acts out of three plainly foreshadow the same end for the husband in *La Princesse Georges;* but here M. Dumas at the last moment shirked his own logical conclusion: M. de Terremonde's pistol-shot brings down not the wicked husband but a harmless, unnecessary "walking gentleman." Then came a great change. The Oriental theory of woman's inferiority was suddenly abandoned for another (also Oriental), "an eye for an eye and a tooth for a tooth." This is the actual text quoted by the betrayed wife in *Francillon*. The peccant husband shall not be slain—either personally or vicariously: his wife shall claim the same liberty to break the Seventh Commandment as himself. Here again, however the nothing-if-not-logical Dumas fights shy of his Q.E.D. The wife, put to the touch, does not enforce her claim: she only shows that she could if she would: they kiss again with tears; and the husband, no doubt, goes on *da capo* [as from the start]. One study of adultery M. Dumas has in which there is no question of pardon or punishment: the *Visite de Noces*, a remarkable exposition in one act of the real reason why the husband of a

virtuous woman is tempted to "go Fanti." It stinks in the nostrils of the Philistine; but the fumes of the acid will not blind the judicious to the amazing vigour of the etching.

With a new set of elements, M. Dumas puts down his Bible for his Code. That authority forbids, or forbade, "la recherche de la paternité" [the research of paternity]; so M. Dumas falls to discussing the moral obligation of a father to acknowledge his illegitimate offspring. . . . In *Monsieur Alphonse* [the paternal recognition that] the actual father refuses the mother's husband grants in his own name. In close connection herewith is the question of the *fille-mère*. She is the heroine of two of M. Dumas' most interesting plays, *Les Idées de Madame Aubray;* and *Denise*, in both of which it is the unexpected—the marriage of Dorothy Musgrave not to George Austin but to John Fenwick—which happens. And with such skill does his father's son "prepare" his climax that there is not a man nor a woman in the audience who does not ardently desire this marriage to be made.

For . . . this man's mark of primacy in stage-work is that he has the supreme gift of interesting. No more than his father does he ever shirk the *scène-à-faire*, he invariably "prepares" his situations, he takes you safely over the weak places with a rush, he forces you to accept the most impossible conclusions in spite of your seven senses. It is useless for you to object: the protest you are grumbling to yourself in your stall he puts into the mouth of one of his characters—the fool's for choice—and, lo! you are answered. His style—hard, brilliant, plangent, admirably minted and chased—is the very style for the garish day of the footlights. Its one defect is a tendency to lapse into the jargon of pseudo-science. . . . Science, indeed, has always been his weak point. He believes in table-rapping and chiromancy. You see, he never had a university training, and is perhaps a little too proud of it. . . . But the plain truth is he is a born dramatist, and knows that the "shy" sciences are dramatically effective from their very mystery. As for wit, he is as prodigal of that as his father was of that and money. He lavishes it on all his personages, even on the very lackeys. Sheridan did the same, and you love him none the less for it. In the invention of "bravura" passages, meant to catch the ear of the town, Dumas has no equal. . . . Unlike his father, he works best alone. Who shall say whether he will or will not live? For forty years he has dramatised us every strategic movement, every decisive engagement, all the alarums and excursions, in the great war of Love against Law. The strife will doubtless last "our time," and his fame along with it. For in truth he has practised his art with an abounding sincerity. That is, he has done his best to be great. (pp. 74-9)

A. B. Walkley, "Dumas fils," in his Playhouse Impressions, T. Fisher Unwin, 1892, pp. 74-9.

ARTHUR SYMONS   (essay date 1895)

[*Symons was an English critic, poet, dramatist, short story writer, and editor who first gained notoriety in the 1890s as an English decadent. He takes quick measure of Dumas's stature as a man and as a writer in the following passage, which is excerpted from an account of a visit that Symons and several acquaintances made to Dumas's home two months prior to the playwright's death.*]

[Dumas] left upon us all a certain impression, an impression of largeness, almost of greatness. I do not think he was a great writer. A writer of intellect, of force, of a certain kind of sentiment, he undoubtedly was. Yet he impressed France at large, as he impressed [us] . . . , with the sense of being a great writer, a great man. (p. 725)

Arthur Symons, "A Visit to Dumas Fils," in The Saturday Review, *London, Vol. 80, No. 2092, November 30, 1895, pp. 724-25.*

M. S. VAN DE VELDE (essay date 1896)

[*Van de Velde acknowledges Dumas's prominence as a dramatist and moralist, but he also observes that the playwright's achievement was partially vitiated by narrowness of vision and thematic inconsistencies.*]

Many years ago a French critic said, with some justice and more severity, "Monsieur Alexandre Dumas is a bold painter, a powerful writer, but, unless he changes absolutely, he will never be a moralist." If a moralist is a judge of men and institutions, if he casts a luminous and searching light on every side of a question, if he makes himself master of all the elements it contains, if he weighs and classifies them, then assuredly Alexandre Dumas cannot lay claim to the name. He sees only one aspect at a time, or for a given time. He began by attempting the rehabilitation of the courtesan, and ended by being the implacable censor of the woman of the world. At first he dwelt complacently on the manners and customs of the *demi-monde*—a term he invented, and which has become generic—he affected to believe that the doubtful social centres he depicted under that name were an important portion of French society, and he did not hesitate to bring into the garish light of day the vices that had hitherto done themselves the justice to seek the shade. His unlimited command of language, his sparkling irony, his brilliant wit, his sceptical *verve* enabled him to handle his subject in so fascinating a fashion, to throw so bewildering a glamour on their repulsive realities, that he aggravated the evil he pretended to expose or censure. (p. 94)

Alexandre Dumas openly professed to be a disciple of Balzac; in his scarcely decent way of unveiling social sores he was putting into practice the great novelist's teachings, but he did not, like his master, make these physiological revelations alternate with scenes which would have come as a relief to the alarmed and disconcerted spectators. He aimed—as he says in . . . [a] preface, and these prefaces are not the least interesting portion of his voluminous work—he aimed at "knowing men as Balzac did and the stagelike Scribe," but nevertheless he refused to tread the wider fields of the former, or to confine himself to the Arcadian paths of the latter. He stuck to the narrow road he had selected at his *début,* unmindful of treacherous pitfalls of deep mire and unwholesome malaria.

La Dame aux Camelias is not the story of Marguerite Gautier alone, she merely rises like a dethroned queen over a number of congeners. The ***Demi-Monde,*** a much finer play in many respects, shows a special feature in the habits of the dangerous and malevolent beings dragged on the stage by Dumas for the amusement of a morbidly inquisitive audience. He makes the wretched manoeuvrer lift herself by slow degrees into marriage and public consideration from the impure depths where her snares were laid. But if all the sham countesses and baronesses were struck out of the piece, we should still be confronted by Suzanne weighed down by her past, and, in spite of every effort to throw off the burden, finding it fall back to crush her. The long series of her prevarications, explanations, and deceits form the whole knot of the play.

[It is doubtful whether even birth, rank, and fortune] can wholly protect a woman whose instincts are unconsciously perverse, and who does not possess an innate respect for chastity and virtue. Here again we find a reminiscence of Balzac, who has placed in his picture gallery the portraits of many honest women as debased as courtesans, and of courtesans as virtuous as honest women. (pp. 94-5)

When Dumas had exhausted *Les Dames aux Camelias,* the feminine monsters of the *Demi-Monde,* the women of the world corrupt at heart, he had still some pages of the everlasting chapter to fill with fresh presentments, so he created Albertine, of the *Père Prodigue,* carrying off her splendid spoils; Madame Aubry with her "Ideas," which are but sophistry; Cesarine Rippert, of *La Femme de Claude,* audaciously braving both her husband and her lover, and the depraved girl-wife of *L'Affaire Clemenceau.* Here and there religious and patriotic sentiments, noble and elevated feelings admirable in themselves, couched in magnificent language, are thrust into the dialogue, but they appear too inconsistent with the prevailing tone of the subject to produce their full effect. At the same time audiences in presence of so high and rare a talent, of so profound a knowledge of stage-craft, of ability, imagination, and fecundity, attracted and repulsed by the spectacle offered to them, rose to demand of Monsieur Dumas that he should show what he was capable of if he abandoned scandal for virtue; if he passed from the lower to the higher order, and began to paint humanity, not in its vices, but in its purer aspirations. The author responded to that appeal with the measure of his gifts and his temperament.

It was then that a certain similarity was noticeable between the Dumas heroines and those of Emile Augier. In saying this I do not mean to admit for an instant what has been repeated more than once since the death of the author of *Maître Guerin,* that there is any close analogy between the two dramatists beyond the fact that they are both kings of the modern stage. It was hinted that had Dumas not written ***La Dame aux Camelias,*** and *Le Demi-Monde,* Augier would not have written *Les Lionnes Pauvres.* This is unfair, for every student of humanity must at some tangent or other meet other students of the same subject. (pp. 95-6)

Women occupy the chief place in Dumas' plays. Consciously or unconsciously he struck the key of popularity by awarding them the lion's share; they are creatures of flesh and blood, guilty or vile, no matter; they love, lie and betray as women do in real life; they are passionate, reckless and extravagant with the passion, recklessness and extravagance of real women, and as such they have already been recognised as types. *La Baronne d'Ange* represents all her kind and the circle in which she moves; the title of the play in which she is the baleful heroine—*Le Demi-Monde*—has entered into the current vocabulary of the world . . . as the accepted and euphonious denomination of a class hitherto branded by more brutal names or not mentioned at all.

If some of Augier's heroines have a distant kinship with Dumas', it must be admitted that the former have not as striking an individuality, or as much genuine originality as the latter. Hypercritical judges have attempted to show that *L'Aventurière* is only ***La Dame aux Camelias*** grown older and having forgotten Armand; Olympe the same Marguerite marrying her lover in the expectation of being recognised by his aristocratic family without divesting herself of the *nostalgie de la boue;* and Thérèse of *Les Lionnes Pauvres* likewise distantly related to the same person. But Augier's more effaced heroines are only similar to themselves, which made Albert Delpit say that when he came across one of them in a comedy by the author of *Les Effrontés* he instantly recognised "Mademoiselle Augier." Dumas has minimised the young girl in his works—and for obvious reasons.

When Alexandre Dumas decided to satisfy the demands of the public and to realise the expectations of those who honestly admired and believed in his genius by breaking new ground, he did not repudiate his principles of using dramatic art as a method for pleading a moral thesis. . . . According to his own expression, he inaugurated the Théâtre fonction—the stage going relentlessly to its proposed goal, daring all, risking all, shirking nothing, propounding the problems of life behind the footlights and solving them. (pp. 96-7)

In his more recent works Alexandre Dumas has given drastic advice to the stronger sex. This advice amounts, on the whole, to this: "If you are betrayed by your wife kill her lover (*Diane de Lys*); if she is too callous for repentance kill *her* (*La Femme de Claude*); if it is repugnant to you to stain your hands with blood, drive her out into the world homeless and childless (*La Princesse de Bagdad*). You may stretch out a helping hand to the lost woman who craves to be rehabilitated, but at any cost you must expose and brand the futile, weak, capricious, conscienceless female animal, the calculating, extravagant or mischievous creature whom you have made your wife (*L'Ami des Femmes* and *La Princesse Georges*). When the man does not violently assert his supremacy, when he ceases to rule with a hand of iron, he invariably becomes the pitiful tool of the other sex, commits suicide as in *La Contesse Romani*, disappears like the Duc de Septmomts—the *vibrion* in *L'Etrangère*—or sinks step by step into shameful dishonour like Octave in *Monsieur Alphonse,* and ceases at once to obtain pity for his misfortunes." (p. 97)

Alexandre Dumas says: "An artist only deserves the name when he idealises the reality he sees and realises the ideal he feels." The definition is perfect; he has acted up to it; he poetises, and by so doing he makes the heroines of *Les Idées de Madame Aubry, La Princesse Georges, La Femme de Claude* and *L'Etrangère* doubly dangerous. Mrs. Clarkson, "L'Ange du mal," is the omnipotent personification of feminine despotism, as her stage sisters embody feminine depravity and feminine cupidity. The development of the characters in Dumas' plays is physiological, the development of the action is more romantic than classical or realistic. The situations are often sensational, the *dénouements* too brusque. The spectator experiences the emotions of a sudden surprise, of a terror for which he was not prepared, but these emotions are at the time so forcible and spontaneous that it is only later, when sobered by reflection, that he becomes aware that he has been tricked into them. (p. 98)

[Alexandre Dumas] will not concede that dramatic art is a mere pastime, and whatever opinion may be held on these views it is universally admitted that he has never written a play that did not give food for serious thought, or failed to open a new vista on human lives.

In a letter . . . to M. Francisque Sarcey, he said: "I refuse to have Oscar marry Henriette; I refuse to have Desdemona murdered by Othello; I refuse to have Arnolphe jeered at by Agnes under new names and modern clothes; and if I am forbidden to carry on the stage the big questions that interest a living society, I prefer to stop writing." That he has been allowed

his own way is sufficiently proved by the vast number of plays he has produced since that letter was sent. (pp. 98-9)

[When *Monsieur Alphonse*] first appeared in 1873, it was called by some competent judges one of Dumas' most powerful creations, and it brilliantly avenged the comparative failure of *La Femme de Claude* which had preceded it. Dumas had set himself the ungrateful task of presenting a polished, elegant, egotistical profligate of thirty-three, whose sin and its consequences had left him not only unpunished but cynically indifferent. . . . *Monsieur Alphonse* is more than a thesis; it demonstrates the necessity of reforming the legislation created by the French Revolution, or rather the Civil Code, with regard to paternity and the condition of illegitimate children, but a thesis does not constitute a good play, and it required genius to clothe the bare facts with irresistible dramatic interest, and to enlist the sympathies of the charmed and attentive spectators. In it the author has created a figure which has no prototype on the French stage, and his "Madame Guichard" is a unique and masterly individuality.

La Visite de Noces . . . is a single act rich in sparkling ideas and brilliant dialogue, and in its small compass it contains two distinct subjects. . . . [So] profoundly cynical as to be almost improbable, it is yet so exceedingly cleverly constructed that it astonished even the oldest experts, while it not undeservedly was more severely criticised than any of Dumas' former pieces. The sophistries of Lebonnard do not gloss over the brutality of the crucial situations—the re-awakened passion of a newly-married man for a woman he had loved and left, his brutal avowal of that passion in one short visit, the stratagems employed—and one cannot help feeling that Madame de Morancé's magnificent explosion of contempt and disgust comes somewhat tardily in a woman who has lent herself in a vengeful spirit to so gross a subterfuge. The twice unfaithful and justly punished *roué* fitly ends the play with the cynical remark: "If Madame de Morancé is an honest woman I do not care for her—I have my wife!" (pp. 99-100)

Le Princesse de Bagdad has a strange plot and stranger characters; the dialogue is abrupt . . . , some of the situations are forced, but no one can deny that Alexandre Dumas had in view when writing this play the danger created by the excessive power of money, and its immense influence on the feelings and ideas of the present generation. No one who saw Croizette in the astounding scene where Madame de Hun audaciously pours over her bare shoulders and loosened hair the shower of gold for which she pretends to have sold herself, in her wrath at her husband's suspicions of her, will forget the impression caused by this impassioned acting; the unreality of the situation was obliterated by the realism of the impersonation. As is too frequently the case when the emotions and nerves of an audience have been over-excited by exaggeration, the *dénouement* of the drama seemed an anticlimax. . . .

[*L'Etrangère*] has many grave blemishes, the characters are not sympathetic—repulsive when wicked, they become intolerable when they are not—but as M. de Montégut wrote at the time: "Notwithstanding the unpleasantness, the false morality, the confused motives, the conflict of human passions is sufficient to thrill the audience." . . . Again and again has Dumas made the characters of his plays act up to the famous *Tue la!*—his burning impeachment of sinning wives—and each time he has done so with the energy that seems to create an intoxicating atmosphere. "What makes this atmosphere?" asks M. de Montégut. "The avenging fury with which Dumas pursues the chief offender, and which—a fault in itself—wins the singular, but explicable, success of the piece.'' (p. 100)

[*Denise*], although marking a glorious date on the French stage, and dealing with the vexed question of the possible rehabilitation of a young girl fallen a victim to an unprincipled man, could not by its very nature be a success in England. It contains too much of what is called here ''mere talk''; this verbosity, when it is eloquent as all Alexandre Dumas' dialogue, is grateful to the Parisian cultivated taste; the French public enjoys the delicate literary treat apart even from scenic representation, while no experienced judge could fail to admire the directness of the simple action, the pathetic scenes drawn from life, a kind of life which often crosses ours unawares, but which becomes tragically real to the sagacious observer who dissects it. Without entering into unnecessary detail, it may be said that the gist and pith of *Denise*—as well as the moral of some of Dumas' other comedies—is almost entirely condensed in the lines of Thouvenin. . . . He speaks as follows: ''Do you want to know what absolute truth is? It is *not* the lie you tell, imperilling your honour and your life to save the reputation of the woman whose love you have won; it is *not* to be that woman's lover; *it is* to respect the first woman you have known and loved—your mother—in all the other women you may meet hereafter. It is *not* to make them fall when they stand erect; *not* to drag them down lower when they have already fallen; *it is* to associate yourself for life and eternity with only one woman—your wife—and to have but one motive in marriage—love! This alone is truth! All that assumes the name and is not *this,* has been invented to suit a society which is at once elegant and depraved.''

The sternest moralist in any country would scarcely care to contradict Thouvenin, but we have no evidence as yet that his creed—and presumably Dumas'—has had many disciples; still, it is to the credit of the dramatist that he has dared to voice these beliefs on the stage of Paris, and it may be considered as a favourable symptom that they were listened to not only without demur, but that they elicited genuine applause. (p. 102)

Francillon is virtually Dumas' last play. . . . The Comédie Française has made a hit with *L'Ami des Femmes,* which migrated from its former theatre to take rank in the *répertoire* of the house of Moliére. Monsieur Claretie confidently expected to produce at an early date an important comedy by the author of *L'Etrangère,* in which he had been engaged for some time— which had been erroneously supposed at first to be christened *Le Chemin de Damas.* But it was never intended to have any other title than *La Route de Thèbes.* . . . The *Route de Thèbes* will now never be written, it must for evermore lie buried with all the other fancies and problems of that busy, inexhaustible brain. Rarely—probably never—in the annals of literature and the drama have a father and son triumphantly filled a whole century with their books and plays, and it is not likely that either will find a successor. The author of *La Dame aux Camelias* must hold as unique a place as the author of *Les Trois Mousquetaires.* (p. 103)

> *M. S. Van de Velde, ''Alexandre Dumas fils and His Plays,'' in* The Fortnightly Review, *Vol. LVIII, No. CCCXLIX, January, 1896, pp. 94-103.*

WILLIAM ARCHER (essay date 1896)

[*A Scottish dramatist and critic, Archer is best known as one of the earliest and most important translators of Henrik Ibsen's plays and as a critic of the London stage during the late nineteenth and early twentieth centuries. Archer valued drama as an intellectual product and not as simple entertainment. For that reason he did a great deal to promote the ''new drama'' of the 1890s, including the work of Ibsen and George Bernard Shaw. In the following essay, Archer evaluates Dumas's drama—its technique, style, and moral tendency—with reference to its capacity to serve the interests of the English theater. Significantly, Archer maintains that Dumas's plays are largely predicated on impossible ideals of conduct, thereby making them ultimately immoral; he also predicts that social theater such as Dumas's will soon give way to psychological drama, which he describes as the drama of the future.*]

[Alexandre Dumas *fils* is] recognised by all students of the drama, whether playwrights or critics, as the master-spirit of the modern French stage. . . . We all know him—all who are in any sense specialists—and some of us greatly delight in him. In brief, he is an influence to be reckoned with, to be accepted or rejected. We hope and believe that we are laying the foundations of an original English drama; but that does not mean that we are to shut ourselves off from the rest of the world, and re-discover all the processes of the art. Rather it behoves us to look carefully around, to study the methods and ideals of foreign masters, and to take example by them—or warning. My present purpose is to inquire in which capacity Dumas can best serve us. (p. 364)

First, as to technique. In the preface to **''Un Père Prodigue''** Dumas gives us his technical confession of faith, concluding that ''the dramatist who should know *man* like Balzac and the *theatre* like Scribe, would be the greatest dramatist of all time.'' To which of these summits of science did Dumas himself most nearly attain? I fear we must answer, to the latter. He knew the theatre very like Scribe—too like Scribe. He is commonly said to have overthrown the supremacy of Scribe, and revolutionised the drama; but, great as was the effect produced by **''La Dame aux Camélias,''** it is misleading, I think, to call it a revolution. True, the play itself, ran directly enough in the teeth of the Scribe formula. Written, or rather transcribed from the novel, in a few days, without even the guidance of a scenario, it is absolutely simple in its development, and relies for its interest on character and sentiment alone. But Dumas did not consistently follow up this line of advance, which, indeed, he had chosen at haphazard and not on any preconceived theory. He was too truly the son of his father to resist the allurements of ingenuity. In his first mature work, **''Le Demi-Monde,''** he relapses, to all intents and purposes, not precisely upon the methods of Scribe, but upon those of the plot-school in general. The drama is built on intrigue and counter-intrigue, no less than [Scribe's] ''Adrienne Lecouvreur'' or ''Les Pattes de Mouche,'' though the artificiality of structure is disguised by the extraordinary latitude of disquisition which Dumas permitted himself. By dint of keen observation and an inexhaustible vivacity of utterance, he persuaded the public to let him add a series of social and moral essays to a story conceived and conducted very much on the ordinary lines. That was the real revolution he effected—he did not shatter the Scribe formula, but expanded it so as to make room for any reasonable quantity of generalisation and theorising. And a reasonable quantity did not [always] suffice him. (pp. 364-65)

The intrigue of **''L'Ami des Femmes,''** justly reckoned one of Dumas's most characteristic works, is a . . . flagrant instance of Scribism. De Ryons is for ever divining great matters from small indications, with the sagacity of a Zadig or a Sherlock Holmes, and making predictions which punctually come true, through the intervention of chances which he did not and could not foresee. Dumas's two avowed romances, or melodramas as some prefer to call them, **"L'Etrangère,"** and **"La Princesse de Bagdad,"** are much more simply constructed. In the adroit and highly dramatic awakening of expectancy, the first act of **"L'Etrangère"** is a masterpiece—as good as (but not better than) the first act of [Wilde's] ''Lady Windermere's Fan,'' and the first act of ''The Benefit of the Doubt'' [by Pinero]. . . . **"Le Fils Naturel"** is an unblushing fairy-tale. Dumas's most characteristic pieces of construction, to my mind, are **"Monsieur Alphonse"** and **"Denise,"** In both, the development of the action from a simple and probable starting-point is incomparably rapid and inevitable. Here he rises far above the Scribe level, and gives proof of personal mastery; but even these plays have no very practical lesson for the English dramatist. The mainspring of their mechanism is one which we, on this side of the Channel, are constitutionally chary of employing—and I am Pharisee enough to think our state the more gracious—I mean deliberate, elaborate, and systematic lying. Nowhere in literature, I am convinced, will you find so many lies to the square inch as in **"Monsieur Alphonse."** Everyone concerned, from the god-like Montaiglin to the terrible child, simply wallows in mendacity. Now, we are not all George Washingtons on this side of the Channel; but, whether from hypocrisy or inborn instinct, our gorge rises at such a surfeit of falsehood. (pp. 366-67)

In minor technical points, Dumas is a notoriously bad model. He makes free, and sometimes almost cynical, use of the soliloquy and the aside. For instance, in **"Une Visite de Noces,"** Lebonnard and De Cygneroi are alone on the stage. Lebonnard suggests that if De Cygneroi goes off with Madame de Morancé, Madame de Cygneroi may take revenge in kind for her husband's unfaithfulness. ''She? never!'' replies De Cygneroi. ''It will never enter her mind. Fortunately, she has her religion; and, besides, women like her never have a lover, my dear fellow. It's women like——,'' and here Lebonnard positively *interrupts* him with this aside, containing the moral of the play:

> Admirable! Men think they are jealous of certain women because they are in love with them; and the truth is that they are in love with them because they are jealous of them, which is quite another matter. Prove to them that they have no reason to be jealous, and they at once perceive that they are not in love.

(pp. 367-68)

Even when they are not asides, but form part of the ordinary dialogue, Dumas's interpolated essays can only be regarded as breaches of strict dramatic form, pardonable in him for the sake of their vivacity, but in nowise to be imitated. As for his style, though delightfully supple in quick exchanges of dialogue, it always tends to become heavily rhetorical, antithetical, and literary, in the bad sense of the word, wherever the length of a tirade allows him to develop his periods and work up dialectical or denunciatory fervour. (p. 368)

Let us turn, now, from form to matter, and try to place Dumas in his relation to the general dramatic movement. Here the first thing to be noted, it seems to me, is that he was not properly a psychologist, but rather a sociologist. M. Bourget, in drawing this obvious distinction, uses a different term, and opposes *moraliste* to *psychologue*. I prefer to say ''sociologist,'' because Dumas was not so much concerned with absolute morality as with conduct under definite social conditions. He was always, from **"La Dame aux Camélias"** onwards, either combating or reinforcing prejudices. Moreover, he dealt, not really

with individuals, but with classes. It is characteristic of the tendency of his mind that he gave a name to two social classes, hitherto innominate, at all events for ears polite: he defined the *demi-monde,* and he dissected the genus ''Alphonse.'' Take, for instance, his Suzanne d'Ange in *"Le Demi-Monde"*—she is not an individual woman, but simply a *demi-mondaine*. Of course she has certain characteristics, but they are only the characteristics demanded by the action. It does not for a moment occur to Olivier de Jalin to take her individual nature into account in considering whether he can suffer a *galant homme* like Raymond de Nanjac to marry her. . . . Again, in **"Denise,"** though at this later date Dumas was distinctly verging towards a more intimate and penetrating psychology, he posits in his heroine an ideal character with a single flaw in her record, and then he makes André de Bardannes, not a man, but a nobleman—troubled, that is, as to whether his duty to his name and station permits him to overlook the flaw, not at all concerned as to whether he can banish the recollection of it from his own mind, from his own nerves, sufficiently to love her and be happy in her love. That once taken for granted, the world at large is mightily unconcerned about his duty to his ancestors. The problem becomes one of convention, scarcely even of morality, not at all psychology. Dumas, in short, was always more interested in general rules than in individual cases. He had the lawgiver in his blood. He must have lisped ''Thou shalt'' and ''Thou shalt not'' in his cradle; and the ''thou'' addressed is never an individual, but a member of some determinate social order. And yet, in spite of himself, he establishes his categorical imperatives on the basis of individual character. When he is pleading for leniency, it is a Denise, a Jeannine, a Raymonde that he draws; when he is implacable and rhadamanthine, it is to a Baronne d'Ange, a Femme de Claude, a Duc de Septmonts. Here, again, **"La Dame aux Camélias"** stands out as an exception. Social policy and the Family are victorious over, and through, the very virtues of poor Marguerite. Perhaps it is the sense of injustice with which her fate afflicts us that has led the censorships of the world, official and otherwise, to denounce the play as immoral. Its residual tendency, so to speak, is humane; and, in questions of sex, ''humane'' and ''immoral'' are practically convertible terms.

In one sense, however, the tendency of Dumas's work, as a whole, was really immoral, and should serve as a warning to other would-be moralists. He placed an impassable chasm between the ideal and the actual in conduct. Every play, says Auguste Vitu . . . , should contain *a painting, a judgment, and an ideal*. Now Dumas's pictures were of the life of Paris, or more precisely of a certain sphere of Parisian society, which he represented . . . as fundamentally and almost frenetically polygamous. It was a society, not only based on prostitution, but entirely given over to intrigue and gallantry. And to this picture of unbridled polygamy, Dumas opposed an austerely and rigorously monogamous ideal, which he himself knew and implicitly admitted to be nothing but a pious opinion, far outside the range of practical politics. His magnanimous Gérards, his saintly Claudes, are not the real people of his theatre; they are as fantastic as his father's Monte-Cristo. His Aristide Fressards and his Thouvenins, again, leave us under the impression that virtue and a large family are the concomitants, not to say the rewards, of hopeless provincialism and vulgarity of mind. Dumas himself only pretends to like these personages; he is far from sharing their smug optimisim; it is really with his tongue in his cheek that he claims universal validity for their bourgeois ideals. Yet he throws the whole force of his rhetoric into the doctrine that the only alternative to social corruption, decadence, and ruin is a Puritanic monogamy under legal sanctions. Such a message, addressed to the society he depicts in his plays, must have been worse than useless. It must have left people doubtful of the desirability of virtue, and fully persuaded of its impossibility. (pp. 368-70)

[Dumas's] religion was that most convenient of creeds, the theism of the atheist. Quite unconcerned as to the historical or philosophical evidence of religion, he projected his ideal self upon the veil that enshrouds the fountain-head of Causality, and called the simulacrum God. From such a deity, the counterfeit presentment of Dumas's essentially legislative and dogmatic spirit, there naturally proceeded a hard-and-fast system of commandments to be enforced from without upon a society conceived (in its perfect form) as a stationary mechanism. The idea of a morality evolved from within, a taming, and at the same time an enfranchisement, of the individual will, a gradual remodelling of habits of thought and action in ever subtler accordance with the fundamental needs and aspirations of human nature—such an idea was absolutely foreign to Dumas's impatient and imperious intelligence. I sometimes wonder whether the ghost of General Dumas did not "walk" in his grandson oftener than he perhaps suspected. He was apt to regard himself as the heaven-commissioned drill-sergeant of society. But he fortunately inherited from his father the easy-going temper which taught him to laugh and shrug his shoulders when society paid not the slightest attention to his words of command.

Now it is clearly not the drill-sergeant moralist, not the self-consecrated prophet bringing down from—shall we say Montmartre?—a decalogue graven in stone, that is destined to hold the stage of the future, either in England or in Europe. Social distinctions, legal restraints and anomalies, are slowly but surely passing away. It is right and inevitable that the drama should deal with life under its existing forms; but the dramatist who concentrates his study upon castes, classes and institutions, to the neglect of the individual soul, may do effective work in his day, but will scarcely survive it. . . . More and more—unless the drama is to become merely historical and fantastic—the playwright of the future will be thrown back on individual psychology. He will find in it an inexhaustible mine of matter, if only he have the skill to manipulate it to dramatic ends. "It is in the soul that things happen," says the old man in Maeterlinck's "Intérieur." It is in the soul that the great dramas of the world always have happened and always will. **"L'art pour l'art,"** [art for art's sake], says Dumas, is a formula "absolutely devoid of sense"; and it must be owned that the phrase is rather a discredited one. But if you ask for what other than art's sake [Shakespeare's] "Hamlet," "Macbeth," and "Othello" exist, I am puzzled to inform you. Their direct morality is the veriest commonplace. It needs no Shakespeare to tell us that we ought not to murder our guests, or put instant and implicit faith in the whisperings of reptile malice. Not to enforce such trumpery "theses" were these mighty dramas called into being, but simply to make light in dark plces of the human soul. So, too, with [Racine's] "Andromaque" and "Phédre," with [Goethe's] "Faust" and "Tasso," with [Ibsen's] "Hedda Gabler" and "Bygmester Solness": they are art, if not for art's sake, let us say for light's sake—for the sake of that light which is indispensable to the growth of a beneficent morality. To this abiding and essential illumination Dumas has not greatly contributed. Here and there, and especially in the single act of **"Une Visite de Noces,"** he approached the psychological drama. But, as a rule, he worked

with a scourge or a battering-ram rather than a torch. (pp. 370-72)

William Archer, "Dumas and the English Drama," in Cosmopolis, *Vol. I, No. II, February, 1896, pp. 363-72.*

HENRY JAMES   (essay date 1896)

[*James provides a highly qualified assessment of Dumas's distinction as an artist. While he credits the playwright with remodelling the drama as a vehicle and refreshing it as an art, he also notes that Dumas lacked the transcendent, "poetic" vision characteristic of a master dramatist. James's essay was first published in the February 23, 1896, editions of the* New York Herald *and the* Boston Herald.]

[Alexandre Dumas] has a noble quality of power, a fulness of blood that has permitted him to be tapped without shrinking. We must speak of him in the present tense, as we always speak of the masters. The theatre of his time, wherever it has been serious, has, on the ground of general method, lived on him; wherever it has not done so it has not lived at all. To pretend to be too shocked to profit by him was a way of covering up its levity, but there was no escaping its fate. He was the kind of artistic influence that is as inevitable as a medical specific: you may decline to take it from a black bottle to-day—you will take it from a green bottle to-morrow. The energy that went forth blooming as Dumas has come back grizzled as Ibsen; and under the latter form would, I am sure, very freely acknowledge its debt. A critic whose words meet my eyes as I write very justly says that: "Just as we have the novel before Balzac and the novel after Balzac, the poetry that preceded Victor Hugo and the poetry that followed him, so we have the drama before Alexandre Dumas and the drama after him." He has left his strong hand upon it: he remodelled it as a vehicle, he refreshed it as an art. His passion for it was obviously great; but there would be a high injustice to him in not immediately adding that his interest in the material it dealt with, in his subject, his question, his problem, was greater still than this joy of the craftsman. That might well be, but there are celebrated cases in which it has not been. The largest quality in Dumas was his immense concern about life—his sense of human character and human fate as commanding and controllable things. To do something on their behalf was, for him, paramount, and *what* to do, in his own case, clear: what else but act upon the conscience as violently as he could, and with the remarkable weapons that Providence had placed within his grasp and for which he was to show his gratitude by a perfectly intrepid application? These weapons were three: a hard, prodigious wit, not lambent, like a flame, but stiff and straight like an arrow from a crossbow; a perception not less prodigious of some of the realities of the particular human tendency about which most falsities have clustered; and lastly that native instinct of the conditions of dramatic presentation without which any attempt to meet them is a helpless groping.

It must always be remembered of him that he was the observer of a special order of things, the moralist of a particular relation as the umpire of a yacht-race is the legislator of a particular sport. His vision and his talent . . . were all for the immediate, for the manners and the practices he himself was drenched with: he had none of the faculty that scents from afar, that wings away and dips beyond the horizon. There are moments when a reader not of his own race feels that he simplifies almost absurdly. There are too many things he did not after all guess, too many cases he did not after all meet. He has a certain odour of bad company that almost imperils his distinction. This was doubtless the deepest of the reasons why, among [English-speaking audiences], he flourished so scantily: we felt ourselves to be of a world in which the elements were differently mixed, the proportions differently marked, so that the tables of our law should be differently graven. His very earnestness was only a hindrance—he might have had more to say to us if he had been less practical. This produced the curious dryness, the obtrusive economy of his drama—the hammered sharpness of every outline, the metallic ring of every sound. His terrible knowledge suggested a kind of uniform—gilt buttons, a feathered hat and a little official book: it was almost like an irruption of the police. The most general masters are the poets, with all the things they blessedly don't know and all the things they blessedly invent. It is true that Dumas was splendid, in his way, exactly because he was not vague: his concentration, all confidence and doctrine and epigram, is the explanation of his extraordinary force. That force is his abiding quality: one feels that he was magnificently a man—that he stands up high and sees straight and speaks loud. It is his great temperament, undiminished by what it lacks, that endears him to his admirers. (pp. 300-02)

> Henry James, "On the Death of Dumas the Younger,"
> in The New Review, n.s. Vol. XIV, No. 82, March,
> 1896, pp. 288-302.

EDMUND GOSSE   (essay date 1902)

[*A distinguished English literary historian, critic, and biographer, Gosse wrote extensively on seventeenth- and eighteenth-century English literature. His commentary in* Seventeenth-Century Studies *(1833),* A History of Eighteenth Century Literature *(1889),* Questions at Issue *(1893), and other works is generally regarded as sound and suggestive, and he is also credited with introducing the works of the Norwegian dramatist Henrik Ibsen and other Scandinavian writers to English readers. Gosse comments on two of Dumas's novels,* Affaire Clémenceau *and* The Lady of the Camellias, *in the following essay.*]

It is unquestionable that in his novels [Dumas the Younger] did not, as a·rule, attain to anything like the same beauty of form that he reached in his plays. But among so many failures and half-successes, there stand out two romances from the pen of Dumas which are admirable in the absolute sense. . . . Twice he was strong enough to compose works in prose fiction which had the force, and passion, and unity of his best dramatic masterpieces. When we speak of the younger Dumas as a novelist, we think of two books—of *The Lady of the Camellias,* the novel of his youth, and of *The Clémenceau Case,* the novel of his maturity. In these two books he spoke to the whole world, and he still is speaking. He denounces in each of these books one of the two errors of society which came home to him most acutely—the harshness which excludes the woman of pleasure in her decline from the natural consolations of pity, and the cruelty which avenges on the nameless child the egotism and error of its father. In either case we miss the point of the novelist if we fail to see that his central note is a tender humanity. Dumas is loud, strident, sometimes hard and rough, but he is always dominated by "love for the lovely who are not beloved." Everywhere the ruling quality of pity makes itself felt. (pp. xv-xvi)

The Clémenceau Case is the defence drawn up in prison by Pierre Clémenceau, a French sculptor, who is accused of murdering his wife. . . . In order to set his soul right before his judges and the world, the man writes his life from the begin-

ning, aiming to show that in the turbulence and irony of events, and battered by the terrible sorrows which have befallen him, he could have done nothing else than "execute" his wife. This form of a . . . [defense] gives a writer of the temper of Dumas great advantages, since, without any loss of verisimilitude, he can omit whatever does not interest him, or emphasize whatever excites him. The whole novel is a vast and magnificent pamphlet, and, dealing as it does with violent and open moral obliquity, it is only right to say that, with all the author's Latin license of phrase, we never question for a moment that he brings two cognate issues before us—a sincere hatred of sin, and a pitiful tenderness for the sinner. (pp. xvii-xviii)

It is in this novel that several of the most celebrated formulas of Dumas are first stated. In the early pages we meet with the *"recherche de la paternité,"* which has since bcome so famous. The end of the book is a statement of the *Tue-la,* which became more famous still in the shuddering denouement of *L'Homme-Femme* and *La Femme de Claude.* M. Anatole France, who is something of a Gallio in these grave matters, has detected the germ of weakness in such excess of strength. He has pointed out that Pierre Clémenceau is too good for this world, or too bad, and that, however splendid his intentions, he remains neither more nor less than a murderer. . . . So, indeed, it seems to an Anglo-Saxon mind, which is pleased to find a supporter so brilliant as M. France; the fact being that many of the moral axioms of the younger Dumas are none the less sincere and remarkable for being almost exclusively addressed to the Latin conscience. . . . Such a denunciation of women as is found in the long and brillantly written tirade of Constantin toward the end of *L'Affaire Clémenceau* is as good an example as could be found of the chasm which divides the Latin from the Anglo-Saxon race on questions of sentiment.

Who shall explain by what necromancy Dumas contrived, among the tedious and confused novels of his earliest youth, . . . to produce one romance which has become one of the permanent treasures of the French language and an unquestioned classic? Why is that fortune reserved for the *Lady of the Camellias* which was immediately and finally denied to *Tristan de Roux* and *The Silver Box*? Mainly, no doubt, because . . . Dumas is not a great inventor, and could not be successful until he took to telling simply, clearly, poignantly what he had seen with his eyes and felt with his heart. (pp. xxii-xxiv)

The heroine of this book was closely studied from a real person [Marie Plessis]. . . . (p. xxiv)

[There] seems to have been something singularly winning about her. Janin said of her that "l'ennui a été le grand mal de sa vie" [boredom was the great sickness of her life]. This is rendered in Dumas's novel, where we find expressed, as perhaps nowhere else, the intolerable weariness of what is called "a life of pleasure," its emptiness and insipidity, the irritability and inconsistency it produces in sensitive natures. We are told of Marie Plessis, as of Marguerite Gautier, that what she wished for, above all things, was to be alone, to be in silence, to be calm, to be beloved; and one sees that the irony of her existence was that it resembled that of a small, brilliant macaw in the parrot-house of the Zoological Gardens. She seems to have had many amiable traits. . . . Janin tells us that she hated to disturb family relationships, and that she was no less benevolent than whimsical. Everybody praised her tact and grace, and we are assured that on occasion she could be disinterested. Without the least effort, we can build up an impression of Marie Plessis, a sort of prose version of Marguerite Gautier, very ephemeral but very captivating, and after more than half a century still a bewitching type of lovely woman who has stooped to folly, but is not wholly foolish. (pp. xxvii-xxviii)

[When we] concentrate our attention on what Dumas has to say, we perceive that he stands alone, or almost alone, in modern French literature. He is a prophet-moralist; he is with Carlyle, and Ibsen, and Tolstoi. But he is far less vague than the first of these, and less inquisitive than the second. Mere prophetic denunciation and mere psychological curiosity are not enough for the eminently lucid, practical, and active temperament of Dumas. He is at one with Ibsen and Carlyle in thinking that mankind is gone astray, but he separates himself from them, and forms a kind of alliance with Tolstoi, in not being satisfied until he has suggested a remedy. He presents to us a fervent Latin type of the philosopher who sees that life is full of crookedness and who would like to pull it straight. (pp. xxix-xxx)

Dumas suffers acutely at the aspect of moral pain, and he inculcates pity of it. He does not wish human beings to live like Carmelites, nor, with the later Tolstoi, does he propose to cut off all cakes and ale. Toward the end of his career, like all spiritual teachers who dwell upon a single bunch of theories, he grew more and more severe. He preached, as somebody said, the gospel of chastisement and revoked the pardon of the weeping Magdalen. The worst of his theories was their narrowness. One can not go on forever feeling indignation about the iniquities of the Code Napoléon. His earnestness was never in doubt, but his seriousness sometimes. In the succession of plays and pamphlets with which he bombarded the pleasure-houses of Paris from **Les Idées de Madame Aubray** in 1867 to **Francillon** in 1887, Dumas posed as a kind of fashionable Boadicea, threatening to "cut the Roman boy to pieces in his lust and voluptuousness, and lash the maiden into swooning," but never quite carrying out this fell program, through sheer good-nature, and through sympathy with those who are accustomed to drink in cups of emerald and lie at tables of ebony. Let us admit again that he is with difficulty appreciated, in the fulness of his work, by the logical and unsympathetic Anglo-Saxon mind. He has a conscience, and a very sensitive one, but we must not hope to approximate it to our formidable friend, "the nonconformist conscience." Yet even a Puritan can read with pity and ruth his beautiful, melancholy, passionate story of an unhappy woman whose faults were great and her misfortunes greater. (pp. xxxi-xxxii)

Edmund Gosse, "The Novels of Alexandre Dumas the Younger," in The Lady of the Camellias by Alexandre Dumas, fils, translated by Edmund Gosse, P. F. Collier & Son, 1902, pp. v-xxxii.

CLAYTON HAMILTON   (essay date 1920)

[*After criticizing the view of life, thesis, pattern, and dialogue of* Camille, *Hamilton conjectures that the play continues to hold the stage because it contains "a very easy and exceptionally celebrated part that every ambitious actress wants to play," i.e., the role of Marguerite Gautier.*]

Alexandre Dumas *fils* wrote, first and last, no less than half a dozen dramas which are more important, from the point of view of art, than [**La Dame aux Camélias**]. . . . The faults of **La Dame aux Camélias** are many and apparent. The view of life expressed is sentimental, immature, and in the main untrue. The thesis is immoral, because we are asked to sympathize with an erring woman by reason of the unrelated fact that she happens to be afflicted with tuberculosis. In the famous "big

scene" between the heroine and the elder Duval, the old man is absolutely right; yet the sympathy of every spectator is immorally seduced against him, as if his justified position were preposterous and cruel. The pattern of the play is faulty, because it rises too quickly to its climax—or turning-point—at the end of the second act, and thereafter leads the public down a descending ladder to a lame and impotent conclusion. In the last act, the coughing heroine—like Charles II—is an unconscionable time a-dying. The writing of the dialogue is artificial and rhetorical. Indeed, this noted play exhibits many, many faults.

Why, then, has it held the stage for more than half a century? And why, if it is not a great drama, does **La Dame aux Camélias** still seem destined to enjoy a long life in the theatre? The obvious answer to this question leads us to explore an interesting by-path in the politics of the theatre. This celebrated piece is continually set before the public because every actress who seeks a reputation for the rendition of emotional rôles desires, at some stage of her career, to play the part of Marguerite Gautier.... This part is popular with actresses for the same reason that the part of [William Shakespeare's] Hamlet is popular with actors. Both rôles are utterly actor-proof; and anybody who appears in the title-part of either piece is almost certain to record a notable accretion to a growing reputation. No man has ever absolutely failed as Hamlet; and no woman has ever absolutely failed as Camille. On the other hand, an adequate performance of either of these celebrated parts offers a quick and easy means for adding one's name to a long and honorable list, and being ranked by future commentators among a great and famous company of predecessors.

Here, then, we have a drama which is kept alive because of the almost accidental fact that it contains a very easy and exceptionally celebrated part that every ambitious actress wants to play. **La Dame aux Camélias** is brought back to the theatre, decade after decade, not by reason of the permanent importance of the author, but by reason of the recurrent aspirations of an ever-growing group of emotional actresses. (pp. 72-4)

Clayton Hamilton, "The Career of 'Camille'," in his Seen on the Stage, Holt, Rinehart & Winston, 1920, pp. 70-5.

HUGH ALLISON SMITH   (essay date 1924)

[*Focusing on the significance of* Camille, Le demi-monde, *and* Le fils naturel, *Smith elaborates on Dumas's contribution to the French theater. Considerable portions of Smith's essay were originally published in 1924 in the Oxford University Press edition of* Le fils naturel.*]

More than any other French dramatist of the nineteenth century, Dumas fils was a creator. On most of the roads followed by the French prose drama for the past seventy years he was a pioneer; he even discovered a number of the bypaths into which the theatre has since been occasionally enticed. His restless and independent mind, his self-confidence, and his very lack of background and tradition made him a prolific initiator of new forms, and in most of these his undoubted dramatic gift scored a sensational success. It was inevitable that this originality and this success should impress powerfully his contemporaries and successors. In countries outside of France even, it is surprising how many of his innovations have been followed and exploited during the past fifty years, often without his being given due credit for them, perhaps because so many have

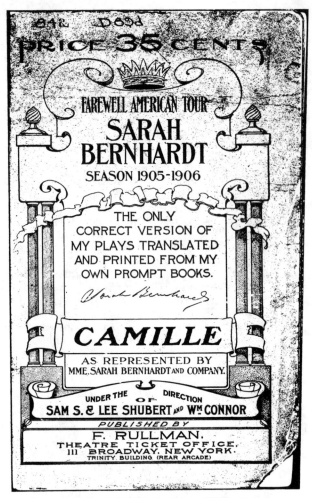

Cover of the Sarah Bernhardt edition of "Camille." Bernhardt was one of the many famous actresses who have played the role of Marguerite Gautier.

and the genealogy of Marguerite Gautier from [Abbé Prevost's] *Manon Lescaut* and [Victor Hugo's] *Marion Delorme* is obvious. It is easy, then, to explain the origin of the work and its philosophy. What is difficult is to account for the great and enduring success of the play.

In this respect, *La Dame aux Camélias* has always been the despair of the critics. The more they have insisted on finding it weak and unhealthy, false to life, and imperfect in its dramatic construction, the more persistently it has continued to live and to inspire its audiences with its nervous and vibrant vitality.

It is not that the critics are wrong in what they have found to blame in it. It is often puerile. The scenes are sometimes thin and ragged, and certainly some are out of date. The life it portrays is doubtless none too true, and even if it were true is worth little enough; its merit in this respect is its striking external realism. It has no philosophy to speak of, and is so far below Dumas's later standards of dramatic construction that he might very well have written it in a dream.

But with all that, it is, or ought to be, one of the finest object lessons in existence, to the critics as well as to others, to show in what consists one of the greatest dramatic resources. It has the power to reach and move an audience,—and an audience of the most varied sort. In fact, take away the critic's pen and shut him in with the thousand others for an evening, and he also will be moved and grow pale in the scenes between Marguerite and Armand, at the ball after their rupture, and will fight against tears in the final act of Marguerite's death.

Probably Dumas's greatest credit in the history of the French stage is his part in creating a theatre of ideas. Here, however, is a living proof that he, himself, did not need ideas to succeed as a playwright. In fact, this play shows why he did so regularly and so strikingly succeed in spite of his ideas. No dramatist ever preached more to his audiences than Dumas. Usually this would have been fatal and all his logic and all the skill and suspense of the *pièce bien faite* [well-made play] would hardly have saved him. *La Dame aux Camélias* explains how the born dramatist, with his father's instinct for all that holds and moves an audience, was able to carry on his nervous shoulders the triple burden of the moralist, of the preacher, and of the social reformer.

The drama has many weapons with which to win over its hearers, but none is so sure to conquer large numbers as passion. The dramatic thrill that is most general and most frequent is the thrill of deep emotion or feeling. Read the climactic scenes between Armand and Marguerite in the third, the fourth, and the fifth acts of this play as a proof. Admit that these persons are Romanticists or even neurotic sufferers. There are, none the less, situations in life when the emotional soul, be it love, longing, grief, despair, seems to rise to the lips and radiate its power. Dumas has known how to find those occasions and to translate *realistically* this emotion into words and dramatic scenes. It is not easy to find another play which shows more clearly the power of passion and feeling in the drama and demonstrates more conclusively that this quality may cover a multitude of dramatic sins.

Le Demi-Monde is probably Dumas's most important play. With it he inaugurated Social drama, a realistic study of the social problems of his day as he saw them manifested in the society of Paris with which he was acquainted. Moreover, in this play he shows clearly what his own attitude is to be toward the kind of social questions which almost exclusively interested

been taken second hand, from contemporary French playwrights. (p. 130)

Of the several plays, then, in which he turned the drama in new directions, there are doubtless three that stand out for the importance of the forms they created. These are *La Dame aux Camélias, Le Demi-Monde,* and *Le Fils Naturel.* In the first of these, he struck again the realistic note which was to lead the drama back onto the firm ground of observation, after its bewilderment in following the noisy and illusory fanfare of Romanticism; with the second, he opened up the new and vast field of the *comédie de moeurs* [comedy of morals], where human nature is studied in connection with, and as affected by, its social environment; and with the third, *Le Fils Naturel,* he created a new model, the *pièce à thèse,* or Thesis Play with which his name is most closely associated. The importance of the forms these three pieces inaugurated warrants a more detailed consideration of the plays themselves.

The theme of *La Dame aux Camélias,* which is the poetization or redemption through love of the courtesan, and its effect, which is to magnify largely the importance of love and passion in life, need no comment other than to remind the reader that Dumas took an exactly opposite stand on this question in his later plays. The attitude here is that of the Romantic school, him. He is no longer a follower of the Romanticists. Although obsessed quite as much as they were by the all-absorbing theme of love and passion, his philosophy is exactly the contrary of theirs. Marguerite Gautier, so sympathetically painted in *La Dame aux Camélias,* and known by so many aliases in Romantic literature, has here become Suzanne d'Ange, incapable of real love, heartless, an adverturess endeavoring to break into honorable society. She is judged and condemned by the sternest of moralists. Her attacks on honest society must be thwarted by all means, even, it would seem, by the most dishonorable.

However, *Le Demi-Monde* is not to be praised simply for creating Social drama and for illustrating the philosophy of its author. It has other good qualities and less common ones. Those mentioned above would alone hardly give it the honor, usually accorded, of being Dumas's masterpiece. It is, from the dramatic standpoint, of of his best constructed plays, the one perhaps in which he has put the largest number of his many striking merits as a dramatist and observer, and the fewest of his several faults as a thinker and moralist.

The dramatic technique of Dumas has been described as pouring the contents of Balzac's novels into the mold of Scribe's comedy. Both of these elements have an undeniable merit. With the first Dumas creates a theatre of ideas; or, more exactly, he restores thought to it after it had been emptied by passing through the hands of Scribe. The merit of the well-made play, to a certain extent at least, for the rigid application of its technique may be objected to, is no less certain. Drama is action, and if this is to mean anything and to interest an audience, it must be action with a purpose and goal; it must have a plot.

The chief weakness in Dumas's drama is not in either of these two elements but in the difficulty of combining the two so that the dual purpose may not mar the unity of the play. This fault is sometimes found in his pieces. The moralist occasionally halts the action to preach, or to expound his theories; the showman frequently holds up the performers while he explains the significance of their actions. In *Le Demi-Monde* this dual purpose is rarely, if at all, apparent. The play is most strongly knit. The attempt of Suzanne d'Ange to break into honorable society, her cleverness and courage and our more or less natural sympathy for a fight against odds form the plot and hold the interest; and it is this same attempt and its frustration that make the social problem of the play. (pp. 137-41)

Of all Dumas's plays, probably the one most characteristic of his manner and interests is *Le Fils Naturel.* In the first place, it deals directly with the subject of the illegitimate child, which, because of his own irregular birth, more constantly than any other subject preoccupies him. However, this drama is mainly significant and interesting in the work of Dumas because it represents, as the first and most perfect model of his thesis plays, the final and inevitable phase of Social drama, not only in the hands of Dumas, but in those of nearly every dramatist who has essayed this genre. It is perhaps not sufficiently recognized that the Thesis Play is an almost certain terminus on the road of Social drama, if it be not the precipice over which its authors often fall.

Certainly no one would think of denying the powerful renewal that came in the drama, as well as in the novel, through the study of man affected by his physical and social *milieu.* The analogy, also, with the aims and methods of natural science, by which the drama was considerably influenced, is generally recognized. None the less, it is easily possible to carry this

analogy too far and to assume that the scientific spirit and method are equally applicable in literature. This mistake has been made, in theory at least, by the extreme realists, by the Naturalists of the novel, such as Zola, and by some of his counterparts in the drama, such as the extremists of the Théâtre Libre. These theorists overlook the fact—to mention but one difference—that the detached and dispassionate attitude of the scientist, who studies a rock or a plant in his laboratory, is entirely impossible for the dramatist, who studies the human heart; in other words, who confesses his soul and the souls of his hearers before a thousand of his fellow men, and for their delectation. Even could he, by the impossible, attain to this scientific detachment, it is certain that it would be before empty seats. A drama, a study of humanity, must warm by its emotion and its sympathy; the degree of coldness of the audience records its failure or its success.

Social drama, such as Dumas wrote, dealt with the important social problems of his day, with marriage, divorce, immorality, illegitimacy, and in general with many questions that come closest to life. Naturally the dramatist, as well as the audience, had his opinions and convictions on such questions. Under these circumstances, it is too much to expect him to be always judicial, an impartial seeker for the truth. He is making a plea before a jury, and his success is to move them and touch their sympathies. Writing, then, on a social question on which he has strong convictions and prejudices, he is tempted, inevitably, to make a plea, to maintain a thesis. Social drama tends naturally to the Thesis Play.

This inherent situation in Social drama and this inevitable state of mind of the dramatist have created the utilitarian theatre and the propaganda play. Admittedly, no one held such a conception of the mission of the theatre more strongly than Dumas fils, or did more to popularize this view. (pp. 142-43)

Dumas was far from being a simple realist. He really escaped from the Romantic fold through being a moralist. But this quality of a moralist, which controls him at all times may not only carry him into realism, but through and beyond it into the realms of imagination and symbolism. The indignant preacher may dwell on his subject until he becomes the inspired, or perhaps the mad, prophet. Nowhere is this clearer than in tracing the development of Dumas with regard to the one character he has so constantly pictured, the courtesan, from her appearance in his first play to his supreme vision of her in *La Femme de Claude.* Marguerite Gautier was borrowed from Romantic fiction and merely staged realistically by Dumas. Before his next play, the moralist had had time to consider her character seriously and he pictures her in her true light, as Suzanne in *Le Demi-Monde,* cold and self-seeking, although still with the paint and charm of her butterfly stage in Marguerite. In *Un Père Prodigue,* she is Albertine, with the paint rubbed off, not only selfish but mercenary; all pretense of love is dropped. She ruins men with indifference to secure money to maintain her effrontery. In Suzanne and Albertine we have the most realistic conceptions, and perhaps Suzanne is truer to life than Albertine.

In Césarine, the wife of Claude, we find the preacher turned prophet and seeing visions. The courtesan has become a symbol of evil, magnified, a monster of the Apocalypse, threatening destruction to all France. This is not an exaggeration, as will be seen from Dumas's own words in the preface to this play, where he explains his vision of this subject. He looks down at Paris and sees it as "a great melting pot where God makes his experiments."

I was at this point in my observations, and I was asking myself what would become of us and whether we should not, in the end, be asphyxiated by these poisoners of our atmosphere, when I saw an enormous bubble appear in the cauldron; and there came forth, not simply from the scum and smoke but from the basic matter of the contents, a colossal Beast, which had seven heads and ten horns, and on its horns the diadems, and on its heads hair of the color of the metal and alcohol which gave it birth.

· · · · ·

At certain moments, this Beast, which I thought to recognize as the one seen by Saint John, gave forth from all her body an intoxicating vapor, through which she appeared radiant as the most beautiful angel of God, and in which came, by thousands, to sport, to tremble with delight, to scream with pain, and finally to evaporate, the anthropomorphic animalcules whose birth had preceded hers.

· · · · ·

This Beast could not be sated. To go faster, she crushed some under her feet, she tore some with her claws, she ground some with her teeth, she stifled some beneath her body.

· · · · ·

Now, this Beast was none other than a new incarnation of woman, resolved to revolt in her turn. After thousands of years of slavery and helplessness, in spite of the conventions maintained by the theatre, this victim of man had wished to overcome him, and thinking to break the bonds of her slavery by breaking those of modesty, she had risen up, armed with all her beauty, all her cunning and all her apparent weakness.

This remarkable passage, we must remember, was written by the same hand which drew Marguerite and her companions so realistically that their prototypes were identified by all Paris and the censor refused to pass the play. It was such plays as the one based on this vision and *L'Etrangère* that caused the Naturalists to attack Dumas's realism, and that led Zola to say that Dumas used observation and reality only as a spring-board from which to leap into the realm of theory and imagination. The accusation is not wholly true, for these are not his most characteristic plays, but such flights of theory were always temptations to Dumas.

Dumas himself would have wished to be judged by his moral effect, although it is certain that his influence is primarily dramatic. Some of the tasks he set were: to reconstruct the family code on the basis of justice, equality and love, and to free the woman and child from unfair laws. He attacks the importance of money as vitiating marriage, and all lack of morals that endangers family life. He wishes to reform the prejudices and laws that seem to him unjust, particularly those concerning marriage and divorce, and he uses the stage as a tribune to propose these reforms. In doing this, Dumas often saw only one side of the question, and his attacks are sometimes unjust and his remedies insufficient, but they are always pre-

sented with dramatic force, and with a logic that is hard to refute if once we accept the premises.

Dumas's character drawing is subordinate to other interests. In fact, this situation is somewhat inherent in Social drama, although we see in a writer such as his contemporary, Augier, that this subordination is in no way necessary. One character, or rather type, which Dumas has created, is of special interest. This is the reasoner, the moralist of the drama, found in most of Dumas's pieces. It is, of course, Dumas himself, showing his actors and pointing out the lessons of the play. Substantially the entire spiritual life of Dumas can be found in this character.

His women are usually fragile, if not deceitful, and good women are rare in his plays. One might say that he has at least popularized, if he has not created, the modern type of the *femme troublante*. His men are perhaps no better morally than his women, being most frequently egotistic, if not odious. Of course, much of this is inherent in his subjects, which for their presentation most often demand the idle, dissipated or pleasure-loving classes.

Dumas's dramatic art is exceptional, and his plays are among the best constructed of the modern stage. Everything leads straight to the dénouement, which according to his own words, should be as inevitable as the answer to a mathematical problem. This faultless, and doubtless over-logical construction has been attacked, particularly by the writers of the Théâtre Libre, about 1880-1890, but it is yet to be proved that it is wrong, except in over-emphasis.

In judging the final value of Dumas's plays, we must say that they do not present any very complete picture of French life. But what he does give is highly dramatic. His plays are moving—perhaps, also, they irritate and exasperate us with their faultless logic, which does not always satisfy and convince. His greatest contribution is to be found in the works of his contemporaries and successors. If his own work has not always lived, much of it does survive in the writings of others, and it is only after considering some of these, and particularly Augier, that we can fairly pass judgment on the real value and possibilities of this drama of which he was the chief creator.

However, while reserving judgment on many of the possibilities in Dumas's drama, we may draw conclusions at once on some outstanding features. He brought drama back to realities, recaptured it from imagination and impulse, restored it to its traditional French guardian, rationalism, and endowed it with serious thought and purpose.

These are inestimable services which outweigh all his faults, of which some at least are obvious and important. He relied too much on logic and not enough on experience, he turned the drama decisively toward propaganda, and his dramatic success in treating immoral love aided in forming a school where any second-rate author could master the triangle play and find a market for his talents. (pp. 145-50)

> *Hugh Allison Smith, "Dumas fils and Realistic Social Drama," in his* Main Currents of Modern French Drama, *Henry Holt and Company, 1925, pp. 122-50.*

H. STANLEY SCHWARZ   (essay date 1927)

[*After carefully qualifying Dumas's position as a realist and discussing his debt to Augustin Eugène Scribe and Honoré de Balzac, Schwarz traces the dramatist's writings through three stages of development: comedies of manners, thesis plays, and symbolist dramas. Schwarz's comments are taken from his* Alexandre Dumas, fils: Dramatist, *a critical work in which he also explores Dumas's dramaturgy and social ideas.*]

[From] his earliest literary endeavors, Dumas *fils* gave every indication of following in the well-trodden paths of the Romanticists. (p. 11)

In spite of its realistic method of treatment, his first play, **La Dame aux camélias,** is impregnated with romanticism; and his second work, **Diane de Lys,** also evinces very definite traces thereof. These, however, [largely] disappear in the remaining plays. . . . (p. 12)

Renouncing romanticism and its methods of expression, Dumas decided "to remain his own master and never write anything that he did not believe to be the absolute truth." That he rapidly adopted the tenets of the realistic school is apparent from his declaration: "Now my methods in matters of the theater were, and are, the following: I write my play as if the characters were alive, and I give them the language of familiar life. Or, to put it into other terms, I mould in plastic clay, and I thus obtain backgrounds of great strength and points of emphasis of great vigor." He likewise states: "I have said nothing about invention, for the excellent reason that invention does not exist for us. We have nothing to invent; we have only to see, to remember, to feel, to coördinate, and to reëstablish, under a special form, that which all spectators must immediately remember having felt or seen without having up to that time been able to take notice of it."

Realism is, nevertheless, a broad term. . . . (pp. 13-14)

It was doubtless Dumas' broad interpretation of realism that caused him, during the latter part of his dramatic career, to fail to heed the call of the naturalistic school which, in the case of the novel, was winning over so many of the realists, and which was also rapidly gaining converts in the drama. Dumas *fils* found that the practises of this school could not very well be adapted to the theater without shocking the audience. "The book is not the stage," he tells us. . . . "The book speaks in low tones, in a corner, with door and windows closed, to one ·single person; it emanates from the alcove and from the confessional. On the other hand, the theater speaks to twelve or fifteen hundred persons in a group and emanates from the public platform and the public square. The painting of truth in public therefore has its limits." . . . "Not only are there words which the spectator does not wish to hear, but there are also situations which he refuses to admit." Frankness is one of the virtues of Dumas *fils;* but, unlike the naturalists, he does not carry it to excess. The extravagances or indecency of a Zola, however characteristic of real life they may be, find no place in the works of Dumas. (p. 15)

[According to Dumas *fils,* the] artist must do more than give an exact reproduction of things as they are: "The artist, the true artist, has a higher and more difficult mission than that of reproducing that which exists; he has to discover and to reveal to us what we do not see in all that which we observe about us every day." In other words, the true artist must idealize the real. . . . (p. 16)

[It is quite evident that certain critics] are not concerned with the purpose of Dumas *fils.* Granted that realism was his goal, they are interested merely in whether or not he completely attained his objective. As we read through the many articles written upon the subject, we notice that the entire question centers upon the human aspect of the characters of Dumas' plays. Fortunat Strowski holds that Dumas *fils* did not succeed

in creating living characters; and René Doumic sums up the case as follows: "What characterizes them is precisely the absence of any individuality. They do not possess any of the signs by which life is recognized. They are walking arguments. . . . Since they have become the mouthpieces of the author, the characters of M. Dumas have become neither less curious, nor less amusing, nor less touching: they have merely ceased to be alive." It is unfortunately true, particularly in the thesis-plays, that the characters of Dumas *fils* are walking arguments, manikins manipulated by the clever fingers of the author; but it is manifestly unjust to state that his characters lack any individuality. Jean Giraud, in **La Question d'argent,** for example, is an excellent rendition of a particular type of *parvenu* [upstart]. What he lacks is certainly not individuality, but greater depth, to make him at the same time individualistic and yet a universal type. (pp. 16-17)

[We must agree with Francisque Sarcey] that Dumas has created no great lasting character, true of all ages: "Excepting de Ryons, that type dear to Dumas, whom he marks with precise, accurate strokes for the excellent reason that he was himself his own model, I do not see that he has created, like Molière or Shakespeare, living characters whose names traverse the ages. Everyone recognizes Desdemona, Othello, and Tartuffe. . . . Dumas, who took such a solicitous interest in women and their destiny, has not succeeded in instilling real life in any one of those whom he has put upon the stage." Sarcey has here indicated the great lacuna in the realism of Dumas *fils.* Realists of genius have succeeded in modeling characters of distinct individuality and also in making them so universally recognizable that they have lived throughout succeeding generations. . . . In the case of Dumas *fils,* we must admit that neither has he created any new character of great universal durability, nor has he succeeded in developing a character used by a former writer so as to make of him a distinct, lasting personality. (pp. 17-18)

Dumas *fils* was a realist of talent, but not a realist of genius. (p. 18)

[The immediate] sources of the drama of Alexandre Dumas *fils* are to be found, as many critics have indicated, in the works of Scribe, the dramatist, and of Balzac, the novelist. Were it not for the fact that literary criticism does not lend itself to mathematical calculation, one might be tempted to say that Scribe plus Balzac equals Dumas *fils.* (p. 26)

Standing aloof from any particular school, [Scribe] sought little more than the production of an amusing, well-made play. One need not look far to discover marked indifferences between his work and that of Dumas *fils.* The latter upbraids society vigorously, the former is optimistically indifferent to social reform; the play is all in all to Scribe, whereas to Dumas it is but the means to an end. Scribe attempts no profound analysis of the passions of his characters; Dumas, on ·the other hand, frequently develops scenes of poignant emotion. And yet, in spite of the differences which exist between these two dramatists, they have much in common; and the influence of Scribe upon Dumas *fils* is indisputable. From Scribe, Dumas derived his attention to subject-matter that would please the public, rapidity of movement, skillful arrangement of scenes to hold the interest of the audience in suspense, and, above all, logical construction of plot.

The influence of Balzac . . . upon Dumas *fils* is equally if not more apparent than that of Scribe. Just as Balzac, with his keen observation, painted in his novels a vivid picture of French life in the middle of the nineteenth century, so Dumas attempted to depict in his plays a panorama of contemporary society. We must bear in mind, however, that the *milieu* of Dumas was that of a restricted society of Paris only. Like Balzac, Dumas *fils* was gifted with a keen observation; but he had had an opportunity of observing a relatively small phase of French life and, lacking the imagination of Balzac, was unable to lend reality to a description of what he had not actually seen with his own eyes. (pp. 26-7)

[In the *Avant-propos* to his *Comédie humaine*,] Balzac attempted to show that men are dependent upon their environment in the same way as are animals. On this system, he pretended to found his *Comédie humaine* in which all of his characters are intimately linked with, and are dependent upon, their environment. Without attempting to make a scientific study of these theories, Dumas embodied them, perhaps unconsciously, in his plays. Thus, instead of presenting to the public a universal and perennial type, such as the Alceste or the Tartuffe of Molière, true of all countries in all ages, Dumas portrays characters existing only in France in the latter half of the nineteenth century. In *La Femme de Claude*, Claude kills his wife because the law permits no divorce. The subsequent passing of the Naquet divorce bill in France thus discontinued the usefulness of the play as a work of social propaganda. While the portrayal of mankind dependent upon a particular environment is most interesting, and propounds many new problems, yet it has the disadvantage of running the risk of ceasing to interest future generations when represented on the stage. (pp. 27-8)

Important as it is, however, environment and man's dependence upon environment do not form the only point of contact between the two writers; for the study of contemporary man himself is an additional great legacy which the novelist bequeathed to the dramatist. The field of Dumas is narrower than that of Balzac and his vision not so broad; but may we not say, having noted these limitations, that, in general, the plays of Dumas *fils* constitute the *Comédie humaine* of the dramatic literature of France during the period between 1852 and 1887? (p. 30)

[Dumas's first four hour plays—*La Dame aux camélias, Diane de Lys, Le Demi-Monde,* and *La Question d'argent*]—are obviously types of the *comédie de moeurs* [comedy of morals], in which the dramatist attempts to put before the eyes of the public the manners and customs of France in his own day. (p. 31)

When Dumas *fils* produced *La Dame aux camélias* in 1852, he swept from the stage with one stroke the marionettes that Scribe had manipulated skillfully for many years before enthralled but somewhat surfeited audiences. (p. 32)

The two central characters think, feel, and speak of nothing but the tremendous love which dominates them, which is at the same time the cause of their greatest joy and their greatest despair. And, in spite of the relentless swiftness of the action, the final catastrophe is ever imminent, holding the spectator breathless lest it break upon its victims and ruthlessly crush them. (p. 35)

[*Diane de Lys*] has little to recommend it. It is curious that *La Dame aux camélias,* written in a week, should be so evidently superior to this play written by Dumas at his leisure. We must remember, however, that, in writing *La Dame aux camélias,* Dumas was putting into dramatic form a theme which, highly dramatic in itself, had appeared several years before in novel form. It represented, furthermore, the recording of events and feelings which the author had seen and felt. *Diane de Lys,* on the other hand, was a play which had to be built. (pp. 35-6)

Weaknesses abound in this second play of Dumas *fils*. The five acts move much less rapidly than those of the preceding play, and evidences of padding are apparent. Nevertheless, the drama is interesting to us in that this second début of the dramatist is his real début; for here we find the genuine Dumas such as he is to reveal himself to us more and more in subsequent plays. *Diane de Lys,* insignificant as a work of dramatic art, foreshadows the author's future greatness and contains many of the elements characteristic of his dramatic system. The characters are more skillfully drawn than those of the later thesis-plays; and Dumas has thereby retained one of the points of strength of *La Dame aux camélias*. Another point of excellence is the attention which the author gives to emotional and dramatic act-endings. This is particularly true at the end of the fourth act where the Count leaves the stage with a threat to kill Paul. . . . [The] promise of a future struggle, this eagerness for battle, is highly characteristic of the entire work of Dumas *fils*.

The coolness of the murder which terminates the play is likewise premonitory of the Dumas of later plays; for we shall find the situation repeated at the conclusion of *La Femme de Claude*. It foreshadows the later work of the dramatist also in that this very coolness on the part of the Count counterbalances the emotionality of Paul throughout the entire play. Dumas was always a great lover of contrasts as we shall later have occasion to indicate. Lastly, the play predicts the Dumas of later plays by its careful attention to detail. Notice that, at the end of the play, Paul takes down *two* swords just before the Count enters. Without a word being spoken, we know that he is to challenge the Count to a duel. Then, suddenly and quite contrary to our expectations, the shot is fired and Paul falls. This detail of the two swords, apparently slight, is a masterstroke in the culmination of the play. (pp. 37-8)

[With *Le Demi-Monde,* Dumas] realized his conception of the *comédie de moeurs*. *La Dame aux camélias* had been a play of this category; but sentiment had dominated it, and the *milieu* of Marguerite had served merely as a background for the main theme, the ever-prevalent love of Armand and Marguerite. The *demi-monde,* on the other hand, is the essence itself of the play that bears its name. *La Dame aux camélias* was a play of love; *Le Demi-Monde* is a play of wits, and in this dramatic mental struggle the *demi-monde* dominates at all times the thoughts and actions of the players. Thus, with this play, Dumas appears as a revolutionary even more than in his first play. He has now rejected practically all of the traditions of the 'conventional' theater, infused in it a realism unknown to previous plays of the nineteenth century, and centered interest upon local social conditions. This latter quality is, perhaps, the play's greatest enemy, for *Le Demi-Monde* is too essentially Parisian to impress an audience unacquainted not alone with Paris, but particularly with the Paris of 1855. (pp. 39-40)

Sarcey claims that it is a thesis-comedy:

> The *Demi-Monde* brought something else which, without being absolutely new, was at least renewed at one stroke. It created the thesis-comedy. The thesis-comedy has always existed in our theater; it is a spontaneous product of our French mind which delights in surrounding a moral idea or a paradox with all of its proofs, with a splendid logical apparatus. *Les Femmes*

savante, Le Tartuffe, Le Misanthrope, indeed almost the entire theater of Molière, enters into the category of the thesis-comedy. The secret of it seemed to be lost; Dumas found it again in the *Demi-Monde.* This is his thesis: that a fallen woman, a comtesse d'Ange, a Suzanne d'Ange, whatever wit, whatever fortune, whatever veneer of good breeding she may have, cannot enter the world of respectable people which must be pitilessly closed to her.

It would seem that Sarcey, in making this criticism, is somewhat ahead of the procession. He wrote the foregoing lines in 1900, after having had the opportunity of investigating the entire dramatic works of Dumas *fils,* and not immediately after the production of the *Demi-Monde,* when he could not know what the future tendencies of the dramatist would be. Had Dumas intended to make this thought the thesis and consequently the main purpose of the play, we should be certain to find greater development of that theme through the spokesman of the play, Olivier de Jalin. It is true that in the last scene he says to Suzanne: "It is not I who prevent your marriage: it is reason; it is justice; it is the social law which insists that an honorable man marry only a respectable woman"; but elsewhere his long tirades are merely descriptive of the *demi-monde....* What is true, however, and what lies included within Sarcey's criticism, is that step by step Dumas was at this time progressing toward the thesis-play. The thesis exists, completely unemphasized, in *La Dame aux camélias;* it becomes more evident in *Le Demi-Monde;* it comes further to the front in *La Question d'argent;* and it entirely occupies the foreground in *Le Fils naturel....* (pp. 40-1)

[With *La Question d'argent,*] Dumas suddenly expanded the *comédie de moeurs* from a delineation of local conditions to a subject of universal scope and interest. (p. 41)

Un Père prodigue is in some measure an off-shoot of the *Demi-Monde,* with the reservation that it is a character rather than the general background that is most emphasized. Despite its sordidness, the plot possesses great possibilities; and the author has handled it with a certain amount of dexterity. At several points during the play, the action might have deviated, to take an entirely different course, and the interweaving of events has been directed with so sure a hand that the audience is ever alert to discover what the final solution is to be. Every act ends with a promise of something to come which will be of vital interest to the spectator, and the actual dénouement is withheld until the curtain is about to fall. Centering interest upon a definite character, the dramatist has supported his play with an action that constantly gains momentum. The ultimate result is the construction of an interesting and very diverting comedy, but unfortunately one of little permanent value. It is a very tolerable comedy of character, a rather good comedy of manners, but not a conspicuously great comedy of any type. (pp. 44-5)

[Between] the years 1858 and 1873, Dumas *fils* develops the thesis-play, in which he uses the stage as a pulpit and preaches his doctrines to the French public, urging it to action, to better living, and to reformation of social laws. More definitely than ever before in his career, does the author appear as a revolutionary. Molière had, in a way, written thesis-plays; Émile Augier was writing social comedies; but Dumas, in his conception of the thesis-play, takes for his theme a contradiction between contemporary manners and the law which governs them, or an incongruity between public opinion and his own viewpoint. With Molière, public opinion was right, and he

who refused to conform thereto fared badly; witness, for instance, Alceste. With Dumas *fils,* public opinion was usually wrong, and should be modified to coincide with true morality; witness, for example, *Les Idées de madame Aubray.* No longer does Dumas at this stage of his career choose a subject purely for the sake of a dramatic situation, or for a particular rôle, as he had previously done in *La Dame aux camélias.* It is now the idea that prevails; and the man of the theater is subordinated to the moralist. Always combatively inclined, he now becomes so to an intense degree. In these plays, as we might expect, the *raisonneur* [quibbler] has a much larger rôle and the dialogue is less dramatic externally; for action must become static as the spokesman preaches to the public. (pp. 46-7)

The timeliness of his topics is an element of great strength in the thesis-play of Dumas; but it is, unfortunately, at the same time a weakness. This type of drama demands social reform; but, once the purpose of the play has been realized and the reform effected, the play ceases to interest the public because the thesis is no longer valid. *La Princesse Georges,* 1871, and *La Femme de Claude,* 1873, lose the force of their preaching when the Naquet divorce bill of 1884 goes into effect; for the problem ceases to be a problem if the hypothesis is invalid. One thing, however, saves the thesis-plays of Dumas from falling into oblivion even though they may fall into disuse as weapons of social propaganda. In the thesis-play, not only did Dumas *fils* excite the intelligence of his audience, but at the same time did he succeed in stirring their emotions. As Émile Faguet observes: "To make one think in the theater and at the same time stir one's emotions has been given to few men. Dumas practically never accomplished the one without the other. That is the reason why the title of thinker as well as that of dramatist is due him and will remain to him. The thinker is not he who draws a conclusion; nothing is easier than that. It is he who leaves behind him a long, a powerful, and perchance a fecund excitation of the public mind." (pp. 47-8)

[Sarcey, however,] took Dumas severely to task for attempting to preach:

> That he try to instruct me, well and good; I even consent to his saddening my soul; but I want this sadness to be open and tender, and I want in this instruction a pleasure of satisfied sensibility; I want ... well, I do not know exactly what I do want. I do know full well, however, what I don't want. I don't want him to annoy me—there—is that understood? Dumas preaches to me incessantly. I listen to his preaching, I find it correct, and I leave the theater not quite so good as when I entered. Corrected? That is not the question. The theater never corrected anybody, and I do not go there to hear a sermon.

In a certain measure, this criticism is justified. Sarcey was a dramatic critic interested above all in the well-made play, and therefore judged a play for its dramatic value. He had praised *La Dame aux camélias* fulsomely because, in that instance, the play was all in all; but, with the thesis-plays, he saw ideas taking precedence over dramatic action; he saw Dumas the thinker dominating Dumas the dramatist, the playwright, the man of the theater. (p. 48)

The first of this group of plays was *Le Fils naturel....* [It is] without doubt the best exposition the author succeeded in giving [the subject of illegitimacy] on the stage. Compared with the other plays of Dumas, the plot is a complicated one; and yet the author has presented his subject with great clarity and with unusual firmness. (p. 49)

[*Le Fils naturel*] is free from most of the drawbacks which a thesis usually entails. In it, dramatic values are not obscured by ideas, even though these theories may be in the ascendency. The characters are well delineated and excellently contrasted. Taken in relation to the rest of the dramatic work of the author, it represents his first great defiance of the Code and his first great challenge to the public. When, in *La Question d'argent*, René informed Jean Giraud at the end of the play that cultured people expected an honest woman to marry an honest man and that therefore Giraud was ineligible, the public applauded for it agreed with the author. In the case of *Le Fils naturel*, however, the spectators were disappointed that Jacques did not fall into his father's arms and accept his name; for they were of the opinion that any other man, in Sternay's place, would have acted precisely as he had done. . . . With its challenge to public opinion, *Le Fils naturel* was the author's great experimental play in a new field. (pp. 51-2)

[In *L'Ami des femmes*, Dumas's] thesis is totally obscured. If we accept it as a problem-play, the main theme indicates that failure to enlighten a bride before her marriage will invite disaster. If this is the author's reason for writing the play, we, the audience, must search diligently before discovering it; and consequently as a thesis-play, it fails to impress us. If we construe it to be a play of observation, we seek in vain to find, from our own experience, any recollection of such a *milieu* as he depicts; and, if he has invented it, we ask ourselves why he did not invent a more interesting or a more artistic one. The truth is that the comedy is what the author least meant it to be, a play of character; for the play is little more than the rôle of de Ryons. (p. 54)

In the preface to [*Les Idées de madame Aubray*], Dumas states: "Two and two make four; four and four make eight. The theater is just as pitiless as arithmetic. If I did not wish to arrive at this dénouement, or rather at this proof, it was my place not to treat the subject. But I treated the subject precisely to arrive at this dénouement, being only too happy to show the logic of the theater in perfect accord, this time, with the Gospel." No other play of the author better illustrates the carrying into execution of this principle. There is not a single scene, or even a single speech, that does not tend toward the ultimate solution. Every event in the play affects Mme Aubray and brings her to the point of making her final decision. Nowhere has Dumas made logic more triumphant; nowhere has he more effectively forced the public to accept a dénouement which it did not wish to countenance. From the point of view of pure theatrical technique, the play is indisputably a masterpiece. (p. 57)

[*Une Visite de noces*] is the dramatist's first treatment of the question of adultery and is the first of a series of three consecutive dramas dealing with this question. . . . [Comedy] is the keynote of the play. In *La Princesse Georges*, . . . tragedy ensues; but the victim is not the person who most deserves to die. In the third play of the series, *La Femme de Claude*, which belongs to the third or symbolistic period of Dumas *fils*, comedy is almost completely eliminated from the play and retribution overtakes the adulteress. (p. 58)

As a thesis-play *La Princesse Georges* is not particularly convincing, and the reason thereof is not difficult to establish. In this instance, logic gives way to poignant emotion, which nowhere in the dramatic work of Dumas *fils* is more fully developed than in the first two acts of this play. Of all the problem-plays, it is perhaps the one most moving and most natural. Cold facts and human emotions are the two elements which the author constantly attempted to resolve into perfect solution: when the facts rose to the surface, the thesis was most apparent, but the play lacked the warmth of life; when human emotions rose to the surface, it was difficult to see below the surface of the mixture and discover the thesis within. (p. 60)

There are marked differences between [*Monsieur Alphonse*], which treats of the illegitimate child, and *Le Fils naturel*, the author's first development of the subject. In *Monsieur Alphonse*, the dramatist has reduced the number of acts from five to three and, instead of a play which covers a span of many years and several localities, has written one in which the three unities are strictly observed. These are, of course, dissimilarities of dramatic procedure. The most striking difference between the two plays, however, is the attitude of the author toward his subject. In *Le Fils naturel*, despite its calm exterior, one notes an undercurrent of indignation. In *Monsieur Alphonse*, on the other hand, no indignation of the author can be detected. . . .

Monsieur Alphonse has several points of excellence. Its simplicity, its celerity of action, its sparkling dialogue, and its splendid portrayal of character recommend it immediately as a superior play. Here the characters are in no wise "walking arguments" but intensely human beings, and each one of them stands out in clear relief. (p. 63)

The first of the two plays characteristic of . . . [the symbolist] stage of the dramatic development of Dumas *fils* is *La Femme de Claude* . . . and, lest we fail to realize its true symbolical portent, the author flatly informs us three times of his intentions, in the document which serves as a preface to the play. First, he says: "Do you see that Claude? He is not merely a mechanic, an inventor, a man; he is Man in the full sense of the word, he is the example; he is what you and I ought to be, to-day more than ever." Then again, he declares: "Claude represents conscience." And finally, he tells us: "In that play *La Femme de Claude*, a purely symbolical work . . . , Claude does not kill his wife, the author does not kill a woman, they both kill the Beast." (In the same preface, Dumas defines the Beast as the prostitute, the adulteress, who is, so he believes, undermining French society.) (p. 66)

In spite of its extravagantly symbolistic conception, *La Femme de Claude* is a well-built play. . . . Throughout the entire work, both the characters are interrelated and the situations interwoven with unusual naturalness. In this drama, the author observed strictly the three unities; and, by means of a small cast, by rapidity of action, by clarity of expression, by clean-cut definition of character portrayal, and by brevity, produced a coherent work of great strength. His next symbolistic play, however, *L'Étrangère*, . . . possesses none of the merits of the former drama and, what is most unfortunate, contains similar defects grossly enlarged. (p. 71)

Francisque Sarcey has so excellently summarized both the defects and the merits of *L'Étrangère* that we cannot do better, in order to complete the picture of the play for the reader, than to quote the final words of his criticism of the drama:

> Such is this curious play which savors of both high comedy and cheap melodrama, an unbelievable mixture of extravagant fantasies, of strange boldnesses, of shocking vulgarities, and of incomparable passages; where two masterly

scenes, that of the introduction of Mistress Clarkson in the first act and that of the discussion with the Yankee in the fifth, stand out against a background of pure inventions which remind one of Ponson du Terrail and of d'Ennery; where, through a confusion of subtle metaphysics, of useless discussions, of unnecessary or ridiculous declamations, there shines forth a group of witty and profound expressions; where, at every moment, in the midst of a wild entanglement, may be discovered delightful bits of clever stage-setting or of witty observation; an uninteresting comedy and yet one which amuses us from beginning to end; badly constructed, made up of broken fragments, and yet one which does not lose its hold upon us for a single instant; in short, a formless monster, always powerful, and at times charming.

As we look back upon *La Femme de Claude* and *L'Étrangère,* two very dissimilar plays, we note that they have one feature in common: distortion. Dumas the realist was still attempting to observe life under his microscope; but he had turned the screw of his lens too far: blurred, distorted images resulted, except in a few points where projecting features of the objects under examination happened to fall into accidental focus. (pp. 74-5)

La Princesse de Bagdad is far removed from the symbolistic plays in which Dumas had previously indulged. The main action is rapid and energetic, and is concentrated upon a very limited number of characters. It manifests, however, a decided leaning toward melodrama. The author has not developed sufficiently the character of Jean de Hun at the beginning to make us accept as plausible his first suspicion of his wife. A man who has been so unsuspicious as to marry Lionnette without investigating her past, who has been so incurious that he has never learned any of these details which are common knowledge to the friends who frequent his own home, a man who is so deeply in love with his wife that he never proffers a word of remonstrance when she plunges him into debt, is hardly the man who will accuse her of having a lover without giving her a chance to offer a single word of explanation. Once we grant the illogical hypothesis upon which the play is constructed, we can admit that the dramatist has executed an excellent piece of work; but it is difficult for us to fail to observe the flimsiness of the substructure upon which a firm building has been erected, and we are tempted to conclude that there is much ado about nothing. (pp. 78-9)

[With *Denise,* Dumas] reverts to the thesis-play and produces an excellent piece of work.... (p. 79)

Denise is assuredly one of the best plays of Dumas *fils.* The thesis—Should one make confession before marriage?—is perfectly apparent; and yet it, at no time, overbalances dramatic equilibrium. By observing the three unities, the author constructs a highly concentrated work and succeeds in postponing the dénouement until the final curtain is about to fall. Francisque Sarcey has remarked: "In a play the essential thing is not necessarily the arrangement of a dénouement that has common sense; it is rather to make the public desire the dénouement which you have prepared, whatever it may be, even if it hasn't a particle of common sense." In *Les Idées de madame Aubray,* Dumas *fils* deliberately forced an unwilling public to swallow the bitter potion which he was administering. In *Denise,* on

the other hand, he deftly brought his public to the point of crying for his sugar-coated pill.

All of the characteristics of Dumas *fils* at his very best are revealed in *Denise;* and, at the same time, his weaknesses are eliminated or reduced to an absolute minimum. Logic dominates the play, but it never becomes preemptive; for, throughout the entire four acts, the action is highly realistic and true to life. Constructing his characters with high relief and exceptional gradation, the author has presented to us a group of people who belie the nomenclature of "walking arguments" which René Doumic has applied to Dumas' characters in general. It is a well-made play. The first act is a remarkable piece of exposition; and the remaining acts are characterized by vigorous movement, together with the intercalation of scenes of great emotion. Throughout these last acts, Dumas, with the hand of a master, seeks not the line of least resistance to reach his climax; rather does he pile up obstacle upon obstacle for the pure joy of surmounting them and of leading to the final goal a breathless public, glowing with the pure joy of the exercise. There is, perhaps, one great store-house that the author did not open in this play; his scintillating wit is conspicuously absent. He has, nevertheless, compensated for this by the interesting quality of the dialogue throughout the entire play. It is a play of uncommon merit, truly Dumasian in every sense of the word. (pp. 82-3)

The more youthful spirit of Dumas again pervades his last play, *Francillon.*... (p. 83)

Although the plot of *Francillon* revolves about a rather unusual incident, nevertheless it is one of the most realistic of the plays of Dumas; granted the plausibility of the escapade of Francillon, the entire action is exceedingly true to life. Dumas has now abandoned all of the stage tricks of Scribe. Furthermore, he has no axe to grind; and, in the absence of any theory to be demonstrated, he has given up his inexorable logic. All of the pleasure which we derive from *Francillon* emanates from the play itself and not from any exterior motive of the author. We no longer feel uneasy or guilty under the preaching of a disciplinary sermon; we no longer feel compelled to travel at a pace faster than we wish to assume; we are left to the complete enjoyment of a play for the play itself. (pp. 84-5)

It is interesting to note that Dumas had written more plausible plays than this trilogy, and yet nowhere more than here was his dramatic technique better evidenced. Here his attention was devoted more perhaps than ever before to the purely well-made play. Youth, energy, swiftness of action, dexterity in dialogue, these are the characteristics which are most conspicuous in the last plays of Dumas *fils* who, even after his sixtieth year, remained a master of stage-craft. (p. 85)

> *H. Stanley Schwarz, in his* Alexandre Dumas, fils: Dramatist, *The New York University Press, 1927, 216 p.*

FRANCIS GRIBBLE (essay date 1930)

[*In the following excerpt from his biographical study* Dumas: Father and Son, *Gribble undercuts Dumas's competence as a philosopher, identifying self-contradiction and sexism as his besetting sins and describing the pro-divorce essay* La question du divorce *as his only redeeming contribution to social philosophy.*]

Sex questions ... were the only philosophical questions which interested Dumas.

Dumas in his later years. The Bettmann Archive, Inc.

He took no interest in religion except when religious leaders contradicted him. He had never heard of the metaphysics of ethics. All transcendental philosophy, from Plato to Hegel, was, for him, a sealed book which he never thought of opening and would have been unable to understand if he had opened it. He excused himself from thinking on such matters by calling himself a freethinker. Life was, for him, simply a tangle of sex questions which it was the task of the philosopher to unravel. Having toyed with those questions in his plays, he proceeded to generalise about them in pamphlets and propagandist works such as **"L'Homme-Femme"** and **"La Question du Divorce."** He derived his conclusions—it would be gross flattery to say that he deduced them—from two sets of premises which contradict each other.

His first premise ... was this: that the normal—and, indeed, invariable—relation between the sexes is a state of war.

There was nothing new in that, however. (p. 264)

[Dumas' generalization gives one the impression] of having been based upon the proceedings of the heroines of comedies—his own, his father's and Scribe's—and it is loosely hung on to Darwin's teaching about the struggle for existence and the survival of the fittest. . . .

Dumas writes,

> the most violent struggle of all is not our struggle against the elements, against barbarism, against famine, or against ambition, war and conquest. Far more violent is the internecine strife between male and female, which is formidable, eternal, of daily recurrence, unceas-

ing, and the more terrible because the combatants begin by adoring each other, or by believing, or at any rate affirming, that they do so. And, let us say it at once—not in woman's praise, for we have something better to do than to praise her, but to her glory—that man, though apparently the victor, is always vanquished in this battle.

Which resonant rhetoric is nonsense, absolutely irreconcilable with either the rhetorician's family circumstances or with other doctrines which he professed at other times. (p. 265)

His mother certainly had not triumphed over his father, when he deserted her, nor had Marie Duplessis gained any triumph over the band of lovers which melted away when failing health destroyed her charms. Nor would Dumas, if he had really seen the sexual life of his time as a contest in which women were better able than men to take care of themselves, have clamoured, as he constantly did, for legislation to protect them. Nor would he have written:

> Society depends upon the family. The family depends upon marriage. The basis of marriage is love.

That is the second premise. It contradicts the first, and, like the first, is clear-cut in form only, and not based upon clear thinking. The statement, put forward as a proposition universally true, that "the basis of marriage is love" confuses the ideal with the actual and challenges a demand, nowhere gratified in Dumas' writings, for a definition of love. For his whole problem arises out of the tricks which love, or what we take for love, plays us, and the unfortunate fact that love is *not* the invariable basis of marriage, can disappear from marriage even when it has originally been its basis, can exist apart from marriage, and may then make marriage an intolerable situation.

Dumas, the dramatist, knew that as well as the next man, and neither saw nor pretended to see any more romance in the "mariage de convenance" [marriage of convenience] than is visible to the rest of us. Dumas, the preacher, displayed quite a different mentality. Instead of deducing his conclusions from his premises, he arrived at his conclusions by instinct and then looked out for premises upon which to base them in the spirit in which the preacher, bent upon admonishing us for some particular sin, searches the Scriptures for a relevant and impressive text for his discourse.

What are the moral rights, and what ought to be the legal rights, of illegitimate children and unmarried mothers? Should the courtesan and the prostitute be the objects of our pity or of our scorn? Ought marriage to be a permanent status or a dissoluble contract? If the latter, what grounds should be held to justify its dissolution? Are men and women under an equal obligation to observe the moral law? What is the proper punishment of an unfaithful wife? Whose business is it to inflict that punishment? Is there any reason why her husband should not kill her? Is not the general recognition of that right of his— proved by so many acquittals in so many *causes célèbres*— the strongest of all imaginable reasons for a revision of the marriage laws and the revival of those divorce laws which the Revolution introduced and the Restoration, with its shameless subservience to clerical influences, abolished?

Those were the main questions to which Dumas addressed himself, in the manner, in the main, of a man who was a philosopher among dramatists and a dramatist among philosophers—inclined, therefore, to take his facts as freely from his imagination as from his experience, and firmly convinced that any utterance which was dramatically effective must necessarily enshrine a profound eternal truth.

We need not follow him through all his answers. If we did, we should find ourselves in a welter of contradictions not less striking than that which compels us to admire the spectacle of Marie Duplessis' favourite lover denouncing prostitution as one admires that of Satan rebuking sin. But one point must be made because it is so characteristic of the man: Dumas' failure to perceive that, as a man as well as a woman must necessarily be a party to any act of sexual irregularity, his thesis requires that the man, as well as the woman, must be punished for it. His agreeable and flattering memories blocked the way: these and that constitutional inability of his to repent in sackcloth and ashes.

That, however, is a stumbling block over which most moralists trip; for none of them—not even our admirable bishops—are ever as hard, in these matters, on men as on women. (pp. 266-68)

We must not, therefore, be too hard on Dumas for an inconsistency which is common to the race of preachers; nor must we be too hard on him because, while calling himself a Feminist—he claimed to have invented the word—he constantly used language which seemed to imply that every married woman was her husband's chattel. That sort of inconsistency always occurs when men begin to preach before they have finished thinking. Dumas was a reformer, in spite of it, and, on the whole, on the side of the angels. (pp. 268-69)

If we postulate that love ought to be of the essence of marriage, and observe that, in fact, it sometimes is not, are we not committed to the conclusion that divorce is the obvious machinery for promoting the greatest happiness of the greatest number by multiplying the marriages which will conform to the ideal?

Dumas thought so. . . . His opponent was a priest—Abbé Vidieu—who had just preached and published a sermon which marshalled all the ecclesiastical arguments for insisting upon the indissolubility of all marriages. He tore those arguments to shreds in a work entitled **"La Question du Divorce"** which carried the war boldly into the enemy's camp.

It is a very brilliant dialectical display, well-documented, as well as well-reasoned, and still worth reading. (p. 270)

[This pamphlet demanding divorce] is, perhaps, the only one of Dumas' contributions to social philosophy which has any real value.

When he generalised about women he constantly lost his way and contradicted himself. When he searched the Scriptures he derived little from the quest except a new prose style which did not become him. But he did handle this one concrete practical problem in a masterly manner. Knowing what he wanted, he got what he wanted, not only for himself, but also for his countrymen. (pp. 271-72)

Francis Gribble, in his Dumas: Father and Son, *Eveleigh Nash & Grayson Limited, 1930, 280 p.**

NEIL C. ARVIN   (essay date 1932)

[*Challenging the "fixed characterization" of Dumas as a realist, Arvin argues that the dramatist is best understood as a writer of*

"mystico-symbolical" plays. In a direct rebuttal, H. Stanley Schwarz argues that Arvin ignores the purport of his and other critics' qualified statements concerning Dumas's realism (see Additional Bibliography and essay above, 1927.)]

[For] seventy-five years no one has seriously challenged the fixed characterization of Dumas fils as a realist. A partial explanation of this curious anomaly is of course to be found in the nature of four or five of his earlier plays, those which, like *La Dame aux Camélias, Le Demi-Monde, Un Père prodigue,* and *Le fils Naturel,* do certainly attempt to portray objectively certain aspects of contemporary social life. And the striking material, or technical, differences between these plays and those of the Romanticists have helped, since the first performance of *La Dame aux Camélias* in 1852, to accentuate in the minds of reader, critic, and spectator their relative realism.

But that there is any significant difference between them and Romantic drama is at least doubtful. The rehabilitation, by love, of the repentant courtesan; the assumption—probably false—that a man can indulge for years in debauchery of the stupidest kind and yet remain essentially ingenuous, and even admirable; the probability that a young man of illegitimate birth, brought up in poverty and obscurity, will inherit 500,000 francs from a total stranger, will "save" his country in a difficult diplomatic bout, will be made a knight of the Legion of Honor and will then marry the wealthy niece of his own aristocratic father, with the latter's consent—such are the themes of some of these early, so-called realistic plays of Dumas. But whatever may or may not be the justification for this formula as applied to those of his plays written before 1865, certainly for *La Femme de Claude, L'Étrangère, La Princesse de Bagdad,* and even for *L'Ami des Femmes,* it is utterly misleading. Indeed the aspect of Dumas' work which is a real innovation in modern French drama, and which probably best represents Dumas himself, is the symbolism, and even the mysticism, which characterizes it after 1865. That these mystico-symbolical plays were less successful at the time than the others, that the public and the critical press were recalcitrant, and that Dumas turned, half-heartedly, late in life to an exasperated kind of naturalism (probably because of the influence of Becque and the Théâtre Libre), does not alter the fact that during more than half of his career he dealt in a medium utterly remote from realism. (pp. 135-36)

An illegitimate child, [Dumas] was for several years persecuted by the most ingenious forms of both physical and mental torment which the refined young ruffians with whom he had to live could invent.... [He] was soon completely terrorized, and, after some months of this treatment, so exhausted that he suffered a severe and prolonged nervous exhaustion which for a time threatened his reason and even his life. Upon his recovery, he fell into a kind of religious exaltation characterized by pitiful acts of self-abasement and even of self-inflicted physical humiliation, and, indeed, soon came to establish in his mind parallels between his own sufferings and those of the saints and of Christ.

These experiences he never forgot and it is certain that many of the essential traits of his character can be traced to them. Moreover, later in life, even after he had won wealth and fame, he appears to have felt the necessity of justifying his social position and of defending himself against adversaries who by that time were wholly imaginary. But his compulsion had in turn brought about an aggressive combativeness which, expending itself upon what was after all an unreal obstacle, merely exhausted without satisfying him. Hence his moralistic and even legislative iconolism. The urge to fight, added to the underlying, subconscious feeling of insecurity, worked for an expenditure into a void of his emotional and intellectual energy and eventually brought him to pathological pessimism. (pp. 136-37)

Fortunately, however, Dumas escaped complete emotional disaster and was saved from too profound a pessimism by finding in mysticism, or more exactly in occultism, the relief which carried him, partially at least, through the difficult readjustments of late maturity.... The manifestations of this spirit are to be seen ... in his interest in physiology and later in phrenology, "typography", and in chiromancy, and in other modern avatars of alchemy and of astrology. This penchant is visible at least as early as the preface to *L'Ami des Femmes,* and becomes more and more pronounced from then on.

It is this aspect of his make-up which, far more than his ability to observe society objectively, colors his later plays.... Commenting on *Le Demi-Monde* Dumas says: "What is the real subject of the play? What is the significance of the struggle between Suzanne and Olivier? Olivier is Man the Organiser; Suzanne is Woman, the Eternal Feminine. The subject of the play is the struggle between expansion and order, between passionate diffusion and rhythm, between primitive forces and moderating laws. Woman, that is to say instinct, does not want to be annihilated; Man, that is to say rule and order, seeks to dominate instinct, to conform it to social exigencies". This seems to be a tremendous responsibility for the rather uninspired characters in question. And *Le Demi-Monde* is one of his first plays; it is indeed the one most frequently cited as an example of the new realism. Ryons, the leading character in *L'Ami des Femmes* was born, so Dumas tells us, "under the influence of Jupiter, Apollo and Mercury: that is to say, his outstanding traits are gayety, a desire to control and dominate, a certain fondness for making a brilliant impression on people, keen intuitive powers, the ability to observe clearly and dispassionately, knowledge of human nature, skill, and the gift of making practical use of his experiences." It seems that Mars, Venus and the Moon have affected him only slightly, and that consequently "he can be an impartial onlooker and judge of all dramatic or romanesque love affairs". In *La Princesse Georges,* Sylvanie de Terremonde is "the Eternal Feminine; her husband, *Passion;* and Séverine de Birac is *Love,* carried to its culmination, forgiveness".

All this is certainly not realism. And yet these are the things that Dumas believed in passionately. Not only in his plays but in his prefaces and pamphlets he continued for years to utter these pronouncements which, as one critic has put it, are "a mixture of Athos, Pathos, and Patmos". And although his last play, *Francillon,* ... is as realistic and as documentary as his early ones, we know from the unfinished manuscripts left at his death that he was working on two plays, *La Troublante* and *La Route de Thèbes,* which were to be highly symbolical interpretations of the fundamental rôle of woman both in the biological and in the social order. Obviously there is more to be said about Dumas than that "he inaugurated realism in modern French drama." (pp. 137-39)

Neil C. Arvin, "Dumas fils a Realist?" in The French Review, *Vol. VI, No. 2, December, 1932, pp. 135-39.*

F. A. TAYLOR   (essay date 1937)

[*Although he acknowledges Dumas's historical importance as the "father of the modern social drama," Taylor expatiates upon the*

author's defects, attributing his flaws in large measure to his moralistic zeal.]

Most critics admit that 1852 was a turning-point in the history of French drama. That was the year of *La Dame aux camélias.* To understand its significance it is necessary merely to compare its subject-matter with that of any play of Dumas's immediate predecessors: Ponsard, Scribe, Legouvé, Ennery, Augier. Now, instead of characters taken from classical antiquity, or puppets dressed up to give a semblance of life, or figures of melodrama, or of bourgeois respectability, the author presents a courtesan dead barely five years before; a woman whom many had known personally and who was known to many others by repute. It was a bold thing to do. When Hugo treated the same theme, he chose *Marion Delorme* from the seventeenth century, and when Didier fell in love with Marion he was ignorant of her past. Augier's *L'Aventurière* was a sixteenth-century Italian figure; but the inexperienced Dumas, greatly daring, had brought a contemporary figure and contemporary life upon the stage. Here was a departure from artifice and convention. For the first time for many years the theatre gave a picture of life as it was. Nor was this all. Granted the unoriginal nature of the theme, treated already in [Abbé Prévost's] *Manon Lescaut* and *Marion Delorme,* none the less as rehandled by Dumas it made a new appeal; for through the whole play ran the note of intimate personal experience, of passion, of human suffering, capable of inspiring thought beyond the immediate limitations of the subject and directing it to social problems of abiding interest.

As to the 'romantic theme' of the rights of passion, this provides a contrast with the realistic background without in any sense invalidating it. At the time Dumas wrote the play he believed in this right of passion; it represented as much the truth of his life as did the picture of Marguerite Gautier and her friends. Also, if it is objected that Marguerite's sacrifice for Armand is pure romance, Dumas warns us that he is not defending the old Romantic paradox, but that this sacrifice was consistent with the character of the woman he knew. All things considered, this play does mark an epoch, in bringing the theatre once more into direct touch with life and with vital problems of permanent human interest. Dumas is the father of the modern social drama. (p. 184)

[A] great deal of Dumas's own experience has found its way into his plays. He has admitted as much often enough himself, and the verification of the fact is sufficient guarantee that in a great deal of his work a basis of realistic observation can be found. ... *Le Demi-monde,* which is an echo of his friendship with a certain Madame Adriani, is a tribute to his exploratory flair in a region of Parisian society hitherto uncharted. Of all his plays it gives the clearest impression of coming from the core of experience, and it is a faithful, grimly suggestive, and realistic picture of a world of failure and spurious values. In *La Question d'argent* Jean Giraud is the type of opportunist financier which every society produces at times of speculation and industrial expansion. Although the study of his type could have been more detailed, he is true enough to life in his unscrupulous manipulation of other people's money and in his desire, after attaining fabulous wealth, to win social consideration by an alliance with a respectable family of assured standing. *Un Père prodigue,* with its contrasted study of two generations, gives a picture of the exuberant and feckless generation of 1830, and of the colder, less spontaneous, less lovable, more disillusioned and cynical generation of 1850. As for *L'Ami des femmes,* it puts on the stage a problem of marital relationships so delicate yet true that all those who demanded reticence in the treatment of certain facts of life were scandalized. . . . M. de Ryons, in his jaunty yet uneasy and irritating self-sufficiency, his wit, his power of intellectual analysis, but principally in his scepticism and lack of faith, is a typical product of the faulty education of the times. Even Olivier de Jalin . . . very probably is a true figure, for there are plenty of men left who still sincerely feel that in the question of sex-morality men and women are not ruled by the same law. . . . In the whole range of French comedy in the nineteenth century there are few more living figures than the dashing but erratic Fernand de la Rivonnière. Who also could be truer, not only of his time, but of all time, than the cunning and unscrupulous M. Alphonse, the perfect *maquereau* [pimp]? He was so true to type—and it is a fairly common type in all countries—that Dumas later confessed that he had dishonoured a hitherto good baptismal name. His intended victim, Widow Guichard, the rough and ready, choleric, suspicious, but honest woman of the people, is equally well observed. . . . And there are quite a number of minor characters, lightly but deftly sketched, who bear the mark of truth: Barantin; Valmoreau, the young rake, but less sinister by far and infinitely more attractive than M. Alphonse or Fernand de Thauzette; Lucien de Riverolles, a spoilt sprig of nobility, sulky and selfish, who claims all the advantages, but rejects the obligations, of marriage; Francillon and the Princesse Georges, two *grandes amoureuses* in the best sense—faithful, loving wives of unfaithful husbands; Albertine de la Borde, the miserly courtesan; Rosalie Michon, another courtesan who does not appear or say a word, whose role is all in narrative but who plays her cards so discreetly that she finally lands that gullible and dyspeptic fish, M. de Carillac, and marries him; M. Mauriceau, the fatuous ex-draper, who sacrificed his daughter's happiness to his ambition. All these characters 'live', to use the hackneyed phrase, although at varying tempos and in different degrees of verisimilitude. Whatever else may be said against Dumas's plays, it is impossible to deny that he had at times that undeniable gift of the true dramatic artist, viz. the ability to create characters and to endow them with vitality.

Quite early in his career the realistic stream of Dumas's observation was joined by a tributary of morality. At first the moral element was subsidiary to the observation. In **La Dame aux camélias** M. Duval, who represents conventional and respectable morality, irrupts into the idyll of Armand and Marguerite, but acknowledges his mistake before Marguerite's death. On one occasion Dumas fell between the two stools of free love and marital duty, and the reader is left guessing as to where he stands—or falls. This was in **Diane de Lys,** where after exploiting his own personal experience with a married woman, Mme. de Nesselrode, he allows moral scruples—or what he calls logic—to inflict death on the lover by the husband, thus violently reversing not only the denouement of his own experience, but the interior harmony and clearness as well as the justice of the play. From middle age onwards the tributary of morality became the main stream; his moral sense gained momentum and took charge of him. When he arrived at this stage he tended more and more to see characters as antitheses of right and wrong. Thus he created that superhuman incarnation of Christian charity, Mme. Aubray; or Césarine, who is La Bête, the spirit of prostitution; or Claude, who stands for Man, Conscience, France; or Mme. de Terremonde, the siren; or Mistress Clarkson, the quadroon ex-slave from America who symbolizes emancipated woman in revolt against man. When the spectator sees characters like this, he is compelled to modify seriously if not to abandon altogether any conceived opinion

about the realist in Dumas. Obviously here there has been no attempt at realistic portraiture. In action, voice, and gesture these characters remind one of nothing seen or heard; the only thing that can be said of them is that they do not belong to Earth. (pp. 185-88)

From the beginning [of his plays, Dumas] will be found throwing the whole of his influence on the side of right. It is one of the written laws of his code of fighting that the right, however sorely tried, must triumph ultimately over wrong, and the battle is unequal because the end has been arranged. The protagonists are not free and fluid, but pawns in the game, rigidly determined to act their appointed part and point their required moral; they are under discipline outside their own control. However much they tried or the audience desired it, they could not kick over the traces and run amok to introduce confusion into the action or corrupt the forces of good with a note of Puckish irresponsibility or fantasy. So when the curtain falls, to the strains of Q.E.D., they have the satisfaction which comes from sinking personality in the cause and agreeing to go where the 'leader' orders. Even in the plays written before the moral inspiration was in full blast, this generalization holds: Paul Aubry will be sacrificed to 'logic'; Suzanne will be prevented from marrying Nanjac, despite the fact that in real life such a woman generally realizes her ambition (**Le Demi-monde**); Hermine will marry Jacques, despite the stigma of his birth and the opposition of the Marquise (**Le Fils naturel**). From these beginnings, results follow automatically. Mme. Aubray will permit her son to marry Jeannine, who has repented of her sin and deserves another chance; Monsieur Alphonse will overreach himself and fail to marry Widow Guichard; Raymonde will be pardoned by Montaiglin and her daughter saved from the clutches of Widow Guichard (**Monsieur Alphonse**); Fernand de Thauzette will not succeed in tricking Marthe, and Denise will reap the reward of her heroism by marrying André (**Denise**). . . . (p. 189)

It is not necessary to have a great experience of life to realize to what an extent this catalogue of results transcends human experience. Dumas was patently concerned much more with what, in his opinion, should be, than with what is. When he claimed that realism was mere work of registration and photography he meant it. As he said in his letter to Sarcey: 'Je ne suis plus simplement un observateur, un poète, je suis un philosophe, un moraliste, un législateur' ['I am no longer simply an observer, a poet; I am a philosopher, a moralist, a lawmaker']. (pp. 189-90)

No one knew better than Dumas what disappointment and tragedy occur in life; how often the good is trampled in the dust; how vice and injustice flourish. But because life was so, Dumas redressed the balance in his art. His *raisonneurs* [quibblers] were agents of a higher justice than that which prevails on earth. This does not mean that any of their qualities were godlike; on the contrary they appear to be very fallible people. The condition of their success was to be pitted against puppets. Only in one case did a *raisonneur* find a tough and intelligent opponent with whom the issue was in doubt, and this was O. de Jalin, who had to measure his powers against Suzanne. In all other cases the denouement presupposed a number of characters, no harder than wax, who could be melted or moulded by the manipulation of the *raisonneur*'s hand. Jane and Montègre were no match for de Ryons; André de Bardannes allowed the words of Thouvenin to drown his legitimate scruples; Cygneroi fell headlong into the trap laid by Lebonnard. However consoling these victories may be, they are not art, but artifice. (pp. 190-91)

[Like Balzac, Dumas tended to think of human nature] as dominated and determined by one strongest instinct, whether of good or evil. As a psychologist he has a totalitarian, one-way mind. For example, when in search of virtue, he can invent Mme. Aubray. Has ever any one met the like? Life would be richer if Mme. Aubray existed; of that there is no doubt, but she is a rare and exceptional figure. . . . Dumas did not get his moral lessons out of normal human beings. Even the pleasant Montaiglin talks more like a priest than a sailor, and as for the women victims, the Claras, the Raymondes, the Jeannines, they lack personality to a marked degree. . . . [They] are mere symbols of repentance and redemption. Despite the undoubted sincerity and nobility of his aims, his constant sympathy with the outcasts and oppressed of life, it is his partiality for 'exceptions' and his failure to use always recognizably human characters to explain and exemplify his message that has impaired the value of his moral teaching. Fallible as human law is, Dumas does his cause no good by creating characters who feel that they are the instruments of divine justice and consequently above the law. He only shows contempt for and impatience with the erring humanity that he wants to help when the Comte de Lys, in obedience to some mysterious 'logic', shoots Paul Aubry. An element of savagery runs through the plays and claims a number of victims. Claude shoots his wife Césarine with no more remorse than if she were a snake. Septmonts is killed in a duel, because he had been diagnosed by a scientist as a vibrion. This disregard for human life is a blemish and an inconsistency in one who claimed the right to raise the fallen. . . . This is a stupid impression to make. Even when the case is less serious and the penalty of death is not in question, it is foolish to leave the moral thesis in the hands of the smug and conceited O. de Jalin, or the equally conceited but more neurotic M. de Ryons. For all his searching and preaching after the ideal, Dumas, to his great misfortune, was unable to create that ideal figure—man or woman—in an attractive form upon the stage. Of the three clever *raissoneurs* whom he created, two were definitely repellent. And if Lebonnard combined sound sense with a taste for practical jokes, he is offset by Thouvenin, a thoroughly worthy person but definitely a bore.

So we come to this conclusion, that just as serious reservations have often to be made against Dumas's observation of life, almost equally serious reservations must be made against the efficacy of his moral teaching, in the interests of which he sacrificed many of his realistic gifts and became a crank. Interested solely in the relationship of the sexes, he has studied only their maladjustments. Whether he thought that the law of life was maladjustment or not, at least he has not shown a single case of successful marriage in the whole of his theatre. (pp. 191-93)

[Dumas] confined his attention to Paris, and to one class mainly in Paris, that of idle society. This, of course, is perfectly legitimate, but the result is that the range, as opposed to the depth, of his observation is not wide. He shows a predilection for noble names, few of the owners of which act up to the motto *noblesse oblige*. Now although it is an illusion to think of the nobility as automatically synonymous with good behaviour; although the Second Empire had a good sprinkling of new creations and spurious titles, it is permissible to doubt whether in this narrow world his picture of the nobility is not distorted. The common cackle of the women of fashion who are the friends of La Princesse Georges; the scandalous and unconcealed association of Fernand de la Rivonnière with a notorious courtesan whom he takes to live in his own, or rather his son's, house; the grotesque instability of M. de Cygneroi,

the depravity of the Prince de Birac, to take only a few examples from this noble world, are far from convincing. These people talk and act more like *déclassés* than well-bred members of good society. Either Dumas did not know the real heart of polite and normal society, or he mixed his knowledge of this society with memories of his youthful experience in the *demi-monde*. Baudelaire, who knew the seamy side of life in Paris well, although perhaps less well than Dumas, once had a glimpse of *le sombre Paris, . . . vieillard laborieux*. If Dumas had seen the same vision, he might have been restored to a saner, less biased view of life. (p. 194)

Speaking, in the preface to *Un Père prodigue*, of the qualities necessary in a dramatist, he says:

> La première de ces qualités, la plus indispensable, celle qui domine et commande, c'est la logique,—laquelle comprend le bon sens et la clarté . . . : la logique devra être implacable entre le point de départ et le point d'arrivée.

Again,

> 'le théâtre est aussi impitoyable que l'arithmétique'.

To this theory objections may be made:

1. The actions of human beings in general are not logical, even in France.

2. Assuming that Dumas has acted in accordance with his theory, will logic always be reconcilable with the moral end to which he is pledged in advance? Obviously not! The pessimism of the analysis of conduct is logically incompatible with the optimism of the denouements. Consider for a moment the denouement of *La Princesse Georges*. The villain of the piece is clearly the Prince de Birac. If any man had qualified for punishment at the hands of an outraged husband it was he. But Dumas saves him, out of respect for his wife, who still loves him; and a comparatively innocent man, M. de Fondette, falls a victim to the outraged husband's gun, just as the Prince de Birac was rushing into the same danger himself. The Prince therefore escapes by an accident. . . . Apart from the objection that this denouement exacts the extreme penalty for a comparatively venial crime, and allows a major criminal to escape, it seems also to infer that the Prince de Birac will in future love his wife. The public was horrified and mystified by what it considered a plain miscarriage of justice, but Dumas claims that 'je t'ai ramené dans la logique éternelle du *toujours*'.

Is not logic of this kind of the transcendental order? Wherein lie the *clarté* and the *bon sens* (not to mention the justice) which logic comprises, on Dumas's own admission?

It would be also pertinent to ask by what logical sequence of events the catastrophe, which is the shooting of Césarine, arrives in *La Femme de Claude*. Whether one works from the beginning to the end, or inversely, as Dumas himself recommends, it is difficult to see why logically the incarnation of Man, or of France, or of Conscience—for that is what Claude is—should choose murder as the only end. (pp. 194-95)

Nothing would have given Dumas greater pain than to hear himself likened to Scribe, whom he criticized with such bitterness; but he took the trouble, like Scribe, to be *un habile dans ce métier*, and, like Scribe again, to achieve *l'ingénieux dans le moyen*, so much so that certain critics and the dramatic generation which succeeded Dumas assert that he was as much addicted to vaudeville as Scribe himself. Nor is the reproach without foundation. Despite all his wit—and there is much strewn throughout the plays: see the whole of the mordant *Visite de noces;* Act I of **Les Idées de Madame Aubray,** with its delightful contrast between the garrulous and fatuous Valmoreau and the caustic Barantin; Act I of **L'Étrangère** with a similar scene between Rémonin and Mauriceau; Albertine de la Borde's final interview with Naton in **Un Père prodigue** . . . ; despite occasional humorous touches (the long speech on smoking by the grotesque M. de Chantrin in **L'Ami des femmes,** and the dialogue between Clara and Sternay . . . in **Le Fils naturel**); despite a fairly wide variety of types of character, some of which, clearly, realistically drawn, are like refreshing oases in the desert of his moralizing; despite concision, energy, lapidary sententiousness, and sometimes grace of language; despite the firm architectural nature of the design, and sometimes a perfect understanding of the art of exposition; despite the noble causes which they champion, the treatment of which roused violent interest and controversy in their time, charming, irritating, dragooning opinion into acquiescence or revolt—it is clear that long before his death Dumas's conception of dramatic art was out of date. It was on the rock of unreality that he came to grief. He had been too *ingénieux dans le moyen.* He had taken too much trouble to arrange life as he wanted it to be, and too little to leave it as it was. As examples it will suffice to cite the presence of the *raisonneur* in so many plays—who is there to say the appropriate word and to give the necessary order when the action needs controlling; coincidences like the fortunate and accidental appearance of the lawyer's clerk in **Francillon;** the role of Clarkson, that *deus ex machina,* in **L'Étrangère;** the ambiguous letter of Jane in **L'Ami des femmes;** the tissue of absurdities in Act I and the wholly unlikely but ingenious situation of Jacques in **Le Fils naturel,** where an illegitimate son forces the whole question of his rights by desiring to marry into his father's family. . . . Accident, coincidence, chance are ingeniously, often too ingeniously, exploited by Dumas. The next generation wanted to look facts more squarely in the face, to show the cruelty, the selfishness, and callousness of life without attenuation, more starkly, dispensing with the tricks of cleverness, spurning the wholly artificial and unconvincing optimism which arranges for the best a situation which in life would bring disaster.

The play which best represents this change of feeling is *Les Corbeaux* of Henry Becque . . .—a plain, untouched, but deeply moving because objective picture of the calamity which falls upon a family when the head of that family has prematurely died. Dumas never attained, because he never wished to attain, objectivity. The whole of the *Théâtre Libre* movement, which is the dramatic expression of the Naturalist school, turned its back upon him for this reason. (pp. 198-99)

[Admittedly, for] good or ill Dumas had set the fashion of social drama, and shown that the stage could be a pulpit too. All those contemporary or later dramatists whose plays deal with moral and social questions are in his debt to some extent. (p. 199)

But even those who seemed to tread in Dumas's steps and who felt that the theatre should be used for the discussion of social questions present these questions in a different way. One has merely to read *La Loi de l'homme* and *Tenailles* of P. Hervieu, which treat the question of marriage and divorce, to see the contrast. Here is a greater simplicity and nakedness, a less rhetorical and emphatic style, a better co-ordination of means with ends, a simpler, clearer, more compelling logic, totally different from the lunar variety in which Dumas indulged.

Brieux is another disciple, sometimes closer to the master than Hervieu. . . . In *Les Avariés* he realizes perfectly the Dumas formula: a theme of more than ordinary importance in social life—the ravages of syphilis; a character, the doctor, whose function is that of *raisonneur;* propaganda for amendment of the law. But there is all the difference in the world between the wit and polish of Dumas's language and Brieux's scorn of literary embellishment and artifice. If not always with success, at least Dumas often attempted to compensate for his didactic purpose by combining the preacher's theme with the language of the devil's advocate, whereas Hervieu and Brieux concentrate principally on the theme. Theirs was not only the more honest but the more effective method.

For there were undoubtedly definite defects in Dumas's dramatic technique. A certain pioneer roughness about him often defeats his moral purpose. He was dogmatic, trenchant, vigorous, controversial, but hardly ever subtle and discreet and understanding. His later followers took advantage of his blazing of the moral trail, but they walked more warily, and they brought to their work a far more delicate psychology. Jules Lemaître's *Révoltée;* Curel's *L'Envers d'une sainte* and *Le Repas du lion;* E. de Porto-Riche's *Amoureuse* (a more realistic version of **Francillon**); M. Donnay's *Le Torrent* (in which a certain Morins plays the part of *raisonneur*) and his other plays *L'Affranchie* and *Les Éclaireuses,* which deal with women's rights, have didactic interludes. Without Dumas's example these plays might well never have been written, but that does not mean that their authors considered themselves members of Dumas's *théâtre utile.* The truth is, they brought not merely idealism but worldly wisdom and common sense to their discussion of social problems, thanks to which Maurice Denier's *Gens de bien* is a useful and necessary corrective to Dumas's **Fils naturel** or **Madame Aubray.** (pp. 199-200)

It seems to be a law of Nature that success in one's lifetime is paid for with oblivion, partial or complete, after death. So it would be idle to deny that for the modern theatre-director and his audience Dumas's name has no longer an appeal. He has ceased to be a talisman; he is definitely in eclipse. The question which naturally arises and must equally naturally be answered is, How far is this eclipse permanent or deserved?

It is not very difficult to give an answer. Dumas's fate is the fate of all those whose eye is fixed on contemporary, and to some extent ephemeral, conditions. Dumas was undoubtedly a very specialized student of certain manners of his time. As those manners evolve, as the reforms which he advocated have been realized, the matter of his plays and their denouements cease to be of dramatic interest. For us they have become antiquated, but they have not yet reached the aesthetic interest of the genuinely antique. He realized himself the risks which he ran. Voltaire had done the same thing before him, and the theatre of Voltaire is dead. But what matter, if Voltaire's influence persists? The parallel is, of course, not exact, and it is flattering to Dumas himself; but that he foresaw the consequences, and claimed to be insensible to them, is true. Enough for him to have helped on the cause of human progress, to have built a badly needed road or bridge, then to be forgotten. If such was his sincere wish, it has largely been granted. A number of examples will make the fact evident. The whole conception of the *honnête homme* and the *homme de coeur,* as personified in Olivier de Jalin, is not only out of date but grotesque. Since the change in the law affecting divorce, the violent denouements of **Diane de Lys, La Femme de Claude,** and **L'Étrangère** correspond to no dramatic necessity to-day.

Even in Dumas's own day the prejudice against illegitimacy was waning, as his own play *Le Fils naturel* proves. On the whole question of the nearer equality of the sexes, of woman's right to a fuller life, to greater charity and justice, public opinion has come round to his view. The ideas which he battled for in *Monsieur Alphonse, La Princesse Georges, Denise,* and *Francillon* are commonplaces now and have lost some of their dramatic appeal. Then there is his idealism. The next generation did not object to idealism as such, as witness the great popularity of Ibsen in the *théâtre libre* and the *théâtre de l'oeuvre*. But that generation differed from Dumas, as the modern generation does, in demanding a greater regard for truth and a stricter correlation of evidence and conclusion. When Dumas forgets to play fair with the characters against whom he is pointing the moral—the Baronne d'Ange, Sternay, the Duc de Septmonts, &c.—we are neither edified nor amused, and we should prefer that he had been less clumsy in the choice of agents who were to bring about his moral ends. (pp. 203-04)

[All that admitted, the] day will come when he will take his place, even if that place is not a big one, among the great names which have made the French theatre illustrious. He is too original to be written off as of no account. Plays like *La Dame aux camélias* . . . , *Le Demi-monde, Un Père prodigue, Les Idées de Madame Aubray, Denise,* and *Francillon* deserve to live because they all have intrinsic dramatic qualities: original character-studies, human sympathy, movement, design, a vigorous command of language. These are the plays in which . . . he keeps closest to life, where his problems are eternal problems, and where his solutions . . . are in accord with the most generous instincts of humanity. (p. 204)

> *F. A. Taylor, in his* The Theatre of Alexandre Dumas fils, *Oxford at the Clarendon Press, Oxford, 1937, 210 p.*

NEIL C. ARVIN (essay date 1939)

[*In the final chapter of his critical work* Alexandre Dumas Fils, *excerpted below, Arvin assesses Dumas's standing in the modern theater. Nothing if not candid, the critic essentially denies the intrinsic significance of Dumas's dramas but insists that the playwright be recognized for his important contribution as the "first modern dramatist to humanize and socialize the theatre."*]

[The] fact is that Dumas in spite of the thirty years during which he almost completely dominated the French stage, had actually had during his latter years very little to say that was new, and that since 1890 he has progressively lost any real significance either to the reader or to the theatre-goer. It is true that *La Dame aux Camélias* is still a dependable war-horse and will almost always make money; that *Le Demi-Monde* has for some time been embalmed in the repertory of the Théâtre-Français; and that there are even yet occasional revivals of two or three of his other plays, especially *Le Fils Naturel* and *Denise*. But no one would seriously maintain that this fragmentary survival is connected with any dramatic, esthetic or social significnce in these plays. *La Dame aux Camélias* is an anomaly whose specious popularity is inexcusable, although not inexplicable, and *Le Demi-Monde* is a museum piece. . . . And it is very doubtful whether any of Dumas's plays are ever read except as historical documents; although *Le Demi-Monde* and even *La Question d'Argent* are still read as specimens of realistic drama.

Dumas is, however, of real importance in the development of modern French drama and especially in the growth of that form

which since 1850 has largely constituted it: the problem, or thesis, or social play. His vigorous over-hauling of the technique of the instrument which had served Hugo, Vigny, Scribe, Sand, and Ponsard gave him and his contemporaries and left to later writers a far more satisfactory medium than they would otherwise have had, and at the same time his insistence upon the moral and social function of the theatre made possible the work of men like Hervieu, Brieux and Curel, in France, and of Ibsen, Strindberg and Wedekind abroad. That his plays are structurally artificial, that his field of observation is restricted, and that his social philosophy is singularly indigent, is not inconsistent with his very real influence upon French drama during his life-time. He had just those gifts of effective expression and of condensation which made an intrinsically meager intellectual, equipment seem, for a time at least, of real significance. The extreme compactness of his dramatic construction is actually as unrealistic as the more turgid technique which it replaced. But it *seemed* more realistic. Becque, Annecy, Julien and the other Naturalists attempted to substitute for the smug and impeccable carpentry of Dumas and of Sardou a less conventional form, but did not get very far. . . . The Dumas formula, artificial though it may be, has proved to be practically far more effective on the stage. The legalistic and social arguments which this highly efficient vehicle was meant to convey seem strangely remote from our contemporary preoccupations. But to Dumas and to his public they were passionately interesting and their highly controversial nature developed a liking for that kind of drama which has lasted until today. (pp. 253-56)

But the doctrinaire style and the controversial themes of Dumas's plays should not make us lose sight of the fact that he, more than any other dramatist of the period, gave to drama the highly efficient framework that became characteristic of French plays and that won for them the epithet *well-made,* meaning often too well-made. That this hardening of dramatic technique and its adaptation to the victorious demonstration and proof of a highly debatable assumption or to the impeccable development of a complicated plot soon succeeded in devitalizing the theatre has been to many a matter of regret. In such a tradition there is no place for fancy or fantasy, for poetic speculation or for real symbolism. Everything is clear, relentlessly explicit, and fits into its place with the precision of a Swiss watch. Once the machinary of the play is set in motion the action proceeds with all the regidity of a mathematical problem, stimulating curiosity as to the manner in which momentary difficulties will be overcome and then satisfying the spectator with a neat and predictable solution. These plays leave one with none of that vague but healthful anguish that a really human problem might create one's aspirations toward the poetic and toward the philosophic are left unsatisfied. (p. 259)

[Imagination?] Warm humaneness? Poetry? Vision? They have no place in his scheme, nor indeed in that of any of his contemporaries. . . . (p. 260)

But an intelligent estimate of Dumas as a dramatist should attempt to meet him as completely as possible on his own ground. Technique and the externals of playwriting were, he considered, highly important, and the brilliance of his own method set the model for at least fifty years of French drama. And yet he always insisted that craftmanship should serve the definite purpose of making drama a tribune from which to attack moral and social evils and to preach reform. One may deplore the unesthetic result of such utilitarianism as it is seen in writers such as Dumas, Hervieu, and Brieux, and yet recognize the real service which the author of *Le Fils Naturel* rendered the French stage. (pp. 261-262)

That Dumas fell short of his objective few can question. For nearly half a century he seemed to have his eye fixed on one small fraction of contemporary society, a pitiful and even tragic fraction it is true, but one which was too special to continue indefinitely to supply really dramatic material. He was unable to detach himself from a kind of grim observation of just one phase of social injustice. But his own failure to breathe into drama a spirit of warm sympathy with human suffering in general or to go from one problem to another, does not alter the fact that he was the first modern dramatist to humanize and socialize the theatre. This gap between his vision of what the theatre should be and what he actually accomplished meant the bitterest kind of disillusionment to the man himself, but does not keep us from seeing what modern drama really owes him. (pp. 262-63)

[One] is forced to recognize that in reality [Dumas] was peculiarly incapable of envisaging or at least of analysing and understanding anything not in some way connected with the moral and social problems involved in love. His interest in the political life of his times was as inarticulate as that of Flaubert. Philosophy and metaphysics were a closed book to him, in spite of his dabblings in occultism. He seems not to have understood or to have been interested in economic theory and practice. Even *La Question d'Argent* is, as a play, the exception that proves the rule, for as a financial study it is quite inadequate. The accomplishment of thirty years of exhausting labor seems to have been fourteen plays all dealing with various aspects of one and the same problem, and several volumes of prefaces and pamphlets repeating or explaining what he had already said in the plays.

Still, in spite of the undeniable paucity of his ideas, it remains true that from the middle of the nineteenth century to the beginning of its last decade he dominated the French stage and that, to a certain extent at least, both the form and the purpose of French drama has remained what it was in his hands: either the flawlessly constructed presentation of moral and social problems or the equally efficient analysis of love. It is difficult to believe that later generations will find any beauty or any intellectual or emotional pleasure in his plays. . . . But no other dramatist of his century succeeded as Dumas did in forcing the public to think about things which it would much have preferred to ignore. Although the tragedy of Dumas lies in the fact that he was incapable of making the public think about more than one thing, and that it was clear to him that fundamentally he had altered nothing, modern drama owes him much both for his unusual dramatic skill and for his insistence upon bringing drama into close contact with life. (pp. 266-68)

> *Neil C. Arvin, in his* Alexandre Dumas Fils, *Presses Universitaires de France, 1939, 268 p.*

MARTIN LAMM (essay date 1948)

[*Lamm analyzes what he regards as the defects and weaknesses of Dumas's problem plays. His remarks were originally published in 1948 in his* Det moderna dramat (Modern Drama).]

[From *Le Fils naturel* (*The Natural Son*) onwards, Dumas] used the stage as a pulpit from which he preached his social sermons. This period of Dumas' play-writing foreshadows the work of Ibsen. But Ibsen succeeded in achieving what Dumas in his last years had bitterly to acknowledge he had failed to do,

namely to make the stage a public platform for the discussion of social problems.

Dumas' failure was due to the defects in his programme as well as to artistic weakness. He went straight into the attack against notorious social injustices, demanding amendment of certain specific sections of the law. Ibsen's greatness lay in posing a problem without giving specific answers. He realized that it was not for him to play the part of a reforming legislator, but rather to stimulate the public conscience. His plays can never become dated, for they deal with fundamental human problems. Dumas' plays, on the contrary, lose their topical significance as soon as the reforms for which he pressed have been carried out. (pp. 25-6)

[Dumas] weakened the effect of his pleas by continually citing extreme and unusual cases. *The Natural Son* is a good instance of this. Diderot before him [in his play by the same name] had endowed his natural son with excessive nobility; for his friend's sake he denies his affection for the girl whom he loves, and who loves him. Dumas' hero is not only equally noble, he is also an intellectual genius, while his father, oddly enough, is a perfect fool. The play ends with a scene where the son, famous now and admired by all France, refuses to acknowledge his father or to use his name. We are left with the undeniable impression that illegitimate children have greater talents than others.

In his later propaganda plays, Dumas avoided the ingenuousness and unevenness which marred *The Natural Son,* but the basic faults were still there. This was true even of the play *Les Idées de Madame Aubray (Madame Aubray's Ideas)* . . . , which the historians of French literature regard as his most mature work. The chief character expresses Dumas' own reforming zeal; Mme. Aubray devotes her life to rescuing fallen girls and to caring for illegitimate children. Her young son is fired by the same zeal, and falls in love with one of his mother's protegees. . . . For a moment Mme. Aubray hesitates—can she accept the practical consequences of her own faith, and respect a woman who in youthful folly committed one error, for which she should not have to pay with a life of misery? In the end, her better instincts win the day and she consents to the marriage. 'This is too much,' are the final words of the play spoken by one of her friends, and that also appears to have been the attitude of contemporary audiences. A present-day reader is probably more disconcerted by an earlier passage, in which the son declares his readiness to accept in marriage, blindfold, a woman who has made a mistake, if his mother desires it. Mme. Aubray and her whole circle, quite contrary to their author's intention, create a comic impression by their determination to meddle with the most intimate affairs of others, and settle them in accordance with their own theories. (pp. 26-7)

Dumas has with reason been compared to Corneille. Like Dumas, Corneille plans his characters in situations which are very difficult to resolve. The conflict in Dumas usually lies between conscience and social conventions. In words which foreshadow Ibsen he says, "there are two moralities, the absolute, and the legal." Dumas was not worried, any more than Corneille had been, when rigorous logic led him to absurd conclusions. With plots constructed in this spirit the characters are bound to display the inflexibility of something cast in one piece. They do not change in the course of the play and there is little light and shade in the drawing of their emotions. . . . When a play is constructed in this way no side issues and no minor episodes can be permitted, for the spectator must be allowed to follow the logical development of the story undistracted. (p. 27)

The strong points of this technique are its clarity and its dramatic concentration; the weaknesses are its rationalism, its crude characterization and its liking for paradox and stage situations which are psychologically improbable and artistically disturbing. It was this logical extravagance which brought about Corneille's fall, and Dumas developed in exactly the same way. (pp. 27-8)

> Martin Lamm, *"French Drama and the Second Empire," in his* Modern Drama, *translated by Karin Elliott, Philosophical Library, 1953, pp. 16-51.**

GEORGE R. MAREK   (essay date 1951)

[*Marek, who compares the prose, dramatic, and operatic versions of* Camille, *testifies to the perennial appeal of Dumas's story.*]

Every time a good Violetta and a believable Alfredo step on to the stage, *La Traviata* glows in all its lambent colours and charms an audience which understands none of the words of the love story but can quite believe the drama itself.

La Traviata is assuredly one of those operas that I would take with me to a desert island. I hold it in special affection. . . . Perhaps the story has something to do with this. Old-fashioned as it may be, it is still more modern than the wildly improbable brother conflicts of *Il Trovatore* and far more neighbourly and close to our lives than the curse of Monterone [in *Rigoletto*].

The story must be good—consider how often it has been told and in how many ways! First it was a real-life story, then it was a novel, then a play, then an opera, then several films. And once it was even a minstrel show! (p. 76)

I have reread the novel [*La dame aux camélias*] recently. It is a masterpiece. It is by no means a bittersweet old confection. Its people and their lives are not merely seen through a stereopticon but they are portrayed in the fullness of life, and what they do and feel is completely believable. This is all the more remarkable because the social problem of the novel is dated. Armand's sister probably could get married to-day without his having to give up Marguerite. . . . [If] the worst came to the worst, Armand might even break loose from his father and go to work. But, in spite of these common-sense objections, Dumas' art is sharp and powerful enough, so that at no time does the book seem like mere camellias and old lace. The atmosphere of passion sweeps one along; one cannot smile at it. Everything about this love is real: the jealousy, the ecstasy, the happiness of their life in the country, the cynical friends, the remorse, and the final simple and heartbreaking letters of Marguerite. (pp. 77-8)

Certainly we must not think of [*La dame aux camélias*] as an old-fashioned romance by an immature novelist. A romance it is, but a fresh and perennially appealing one, written with youthful zest but sure ability. (pp. 78-9)

[The] play, good as it is, is inferior to the novel. It has less imagination, less poetry, less power, though it does retain some of the novel's emotional impact. Dumas wrote a "practical" play. (p. 79)

The libretto [of *La Traviata*] follows the play fairly exactly. It compresses the action and eliminates several scenes and minor characters. For some unfathomable reason Verdi eliminated the poetic last line of the play, "Sleep in peace, Marguerite! Much shall be forgiven you, because you have loved so much."

La Traviata is, then, a faithful musical version of the play. But it is the music, of course, which makes it live and gives it an enchantment beyond anything that Dumas set down. What Henry James said of the play is much more pertinent to the opera: "*Camille* remains in its combination of freshness and form and the feeling of the springtime of life, a singular, an astonishing piece of work. . . . Some tender young man and some coughing young woman have only to speak the lines to give it a great place among the love stories of the world." (pp. 81-2)

> George R. Marek, *"The Lady of the Fictive Camellias," in his* A Front Seat at the Opera, *1948. Reprint by George G. Harrap & Co. Ltd., 1951, pp. 76-82.*

WALTER KERR   (essay date 1956)

[*Kerr, an influential New York drama critic who won the 1978 Pulitzer Prize for drama criticism, dismisses* Camille *as a stiff and antiquated "lavender lollipop" worth knowing only for its historical significance.*]

[At the Cherry Lane Theater, all] the swallow-tailed actors and corseted actresses are standing foursquare on the stage, raising their chins in lofty assurance, and playing Alexander Dumas'

Caricature of Dumas. Mary Evans Picture Library.

lavender lollipop ["**Camille**"] as though it were the most reasonable thing in the world.

This is difficult. Dumas (Fils) was determined that his play should last at least as long as his consumptive heroine (four acts and three relapses), and to this end he worked out a sort of waltz-me-around-again dialogue pattern that is careful to use every word twice. It tends to run like this.

> "Do you wish to be loved?"
>
> "Do I wish to be loved?"
>
> "Eternally?"
>
> "Eternally."

You can get quite a bit of mileage out of that sort of thing, and Dumas did. Every so often he managed to give his impeccably balanced constructions a nice, schmaltzy swing, as in:

> "You must tell him you no longer love him."
>
> "He will not believe me."
>
> "You must go away."
>
> "He will follow me."

But for the most part he has simply bequeathed us velvety catalogues ("I have pawned my jewels, my furs, my carriages"), high-minded denunciations ("This is passion in its most terrestrial and human form"), and the sort of tender imagery ("Say that she crushed her heart between her hands and died of it") that has always succeeded in choking people up, one way or another. . . .

I guess there's just one question to be asked. After you've suppressd the rich purple in the play, and made Dumas sound moderately casual and moderately contemporary, what have you got left? Somewhere along the line a curly-headed character remarks of Camille that she is worth knowing, and worth nothing more. That's probably the answer. If you've never seen "**Camille**," it may be worth knowing—historically, that is. But nothing more.

Walter Kerr, "Dumas' 'Camille' Revived at Cherry Lane Theater," in New York Herald Tribune, *September 19, 1956, p. 18.*

ROGER J. B. CLARK (essay date 1972)

[*Focusing on Act III, Scene IV of* Camille, *in which M. Duval persuades Marguerite Gautier to leave Armand, Clark interprets the play as a symbolic struggle between bourgeois social morality (represented by M. Duval) and individual nonconformity (represented by Marguerite Gautier). Seen in this light, the drama depicts the triumph of social morality over individual passion, thus establishing the anti-Romantic character of the work and aligning it with the ideological viewpoint expressed in Dumas's later works.*]

Considerable debate was aroused from the outset by the question of the moral implications of *La Dame aux camélias*. Many, seeing in it the old Romantic chestnut of the rehabilitation through love of the fallen woman, seeing it in fact as an updated version of [Victor Hugo's] *Marion de Lorme*, interpreted the play not according to what Dumas had put into it but in the light of their own often violent prejudices and personal biases. The Romantics—what was left of them at least—were wildly enthusiastic and chose to read into *La Dame aux camélias* a further attack on bourgeois dogmatism whilst, from the other side, *bien-pensant* [right thinking] critics deplored what they felt to be the antisocial impact of Dumas' work. (pp. 36-7)

As is frequently the case in such circumstances, the cause of the outcry was lost sight of and little attempt was made to evaluate Dumas' own attitude to the moral issues raised by his play and to assess, from inside the work itself, how their creator felt about the rightness or wrongness of Marguerite's and Armand's behaviour. (p. 39)

[In his preface to the play, written in 1867,] Dumas is at pains to highlight those themes and subjects, arguably latent in *La Dame aux camélias,* that were to emerge and be afforded full treatment in such plays as *Le Fils naturel, Un Père prodigue* or *L'Ami des femmes:* the inhumanity of a selfish and materialistic society that encourages the prostitute and feeds on her commerce, and, stemming inescapably from this phenomenon, the corrosive impact of prostitution (which for Dumas included adultery) on marriage, the family and the social structure as a whole. Various solutions are proposed, ranging from simple *recherche de la paternité* to female conscription. (p. 40)

[The ideas developed in the preface] have little to do with what, for the twentieth-century reader, constitutes the interest of *La Dame aux camélias.* But it is also true that these ideas are to be sensed below the play's surface, enabling the critic to reconstruct Dumas' early attitude and thus to show up the consistency of his evolution: present from the outset, the dramatist's ideas themselves undergo relatively little transformation. (pp. 40-1)

It is in the celebrated tête-a-tête between Marguerite and Duval *père,* positioned exactly at the play's midpoint . . . so that it forms its structural and thematic apex, that the ideas to be developed in Dumas' later dramas are most obviously present in *La Dame aux camélias.* In it the writer has sought, for the first time, to debate and resolve the issues, implicit throughout *La Dame aux camélias,* which will become his central ideological preoccupations: the place of marriage and the family in the fabric of society and, especially, the problem of the seemingly irreconcilable opposition between social and individual moralities. The scene comes to life and acquires pathos—unlike many of Dumas' later confrontations—largely because, in the final assessment, the opposition remains unresolved with no neat and comfortable compromise being struck—so that the only remaining answer is for one or other party to give way; because, in fact, neither contender is completely right or completely wrong, because each can see only one facet of the truth. Duval, the incarnation of bourgeois morality and the voice of reason, was clearly conceived of by Dumas as a positive character . . . whose arguments were intended to gain a measure of the audience's approval; indeed his words, both in style and content, frequently come over as a clear prefiguration of the 1867 preface to *La Dame aux camélias* and of Dumas' later prefaces. That the dramatist chose to present his *raisonneur* [quibbler] in a favourable light marks a significant ideological break from the attitude of Romantic playwrights in whose works the representatives of the establishment are invariably portrayed as ridiculous, if not despicable figures (e.g. Don Salluste in Hugo's *Ruy Blas* or John Bell in Vigny's *Chatterton*). Marguerite on the other hand, the paradoxical embodiment of emotion and idealism, stands for the rights of the individual in a ruthless and materialistic society. The opposition between the two is further underlined by the contrast in their styles—the controlled and self-confident rhetoric of

Armand's father versus Marguerite's desperate lyricism—so that the spectator, if intellectually he is meant to see the force of Duval's reasoning, cannot prevent himself at the same time being deeply moved by the cruelty of Marguerite's situation: the clash vividly played out in III, iv between head and heart, reason and emotion, real and ideal lies at the very centre of the drama and is fundamental to an understanding of it. Duval, dark-suited and hat in hand, is as out of place in Marguerite's world as she in his—hence the *dialogue de sourds* quality of the early part of the scene—yet, as this strangely dreamlike *pas de deux* progresses, the two characters move towards each other, swayed in turn by the force of the other's argument (or, more exactly, by the reaction it arouses in them) so that, by the end of the scene, they have come close to reversing their positions, without actually ever making genuine contact.

It is Marguerite who submits, not so much because she is overwhelmed by Duval's arguments, but rather because he succeeds in reawakening in her the voice of her own reason, which she has for so long been endeavouring to quiet; she yields finally to the social argument, which has as its premiss the impossibility of her love for Armand, only because it is an argument that she has already repeatedly put to herself:

> Vous avez raison, monsieur, tout ce que vous
> me dites, je me le suis dit bien des fois avec
> terreur; mais comme j'étais seule à me le dire,
> je parvenais à ne pas m'entendre jusqu'au bout.

Preaching to the converted, Duval *père* appears more as the materialization of Marguerite's rational *alter ego*, and beyond this of middle-class moralism, than as a convincing character in his own right; his disappearance after the conversion of Marguerite is thus perfectly logical since, having done all that needs to be done by providing the required stimulus, he no longer has any role to play.

Social morality emerges triumphant from *La Dame aux camélias* so that there can be little doubt that, in its essence, the play is profoundly anti-Romantic. The Romantic case, given a good airing by Dumas, is in the end shown up as inadequate, its incompatibility with an ordered and disciplined society revealed for all to see. As in *Chatterton,* the individual is reviled then crushed by the mass, rejected from the community; but unlike Vigny's hero who remains defiant to the end, and the difference is paramount, Marguerite resigns herself to her fate, acknowledging that it must be, that her death, however cruel, is morally right and hence inescapable.... Marguerite is redeemed, not just because of the depth and sincerity of her love for Armand, ... but rather because of her heroic renunciation of this love for the sake of Armand and of society, and her acceptance of her punishment, because of her realization that she is wrong and the community right; so that, as she lies dying, all but excised from the social body, Armand may without fear of contamination return to her: "Si ma mort n'eût été certaine, ton père ne t'eût pas écrit de revenir...." Society forgives her only because she accepts to bow to its laws. It is therefore not merely a question of the sinner being punished from outside, which would have turned the play into too obvious a *pièce à thèse,* but more of the sinner acknowledging that she must be punished and virtually wishing the punishment upon herself. The illusion of self-determination that the dramatist succeeds in projecting is a further factor that marks off *La Dame aux camélias* from the rest of Dumas *fils'* output, where retribution comes much more blatantly from the outside,

with the result that the plays become little more than moral theorems, their structures abstract diagrams and their characters mere empty though wordy dummies.

For the actor, the fascination of *La Dame aux camélias* can only be accounted for in terms of the persona of Marguerite Gautier and of the challenge the role presents. For Marguerite is first and foremost a role—i.e. a vehicle allowing the gifted *comédienne* [actress] to express the full range of her talents and which, in return, needs her powerful assistance if it is to be filled out and brought to life on the stage—rather than a character that appears *per se* complex and interesting, and that can be visualized on the printed page before the intervention of the actress. Roles such as that of Marguerite Gautier, in that they leave so much scope for her, seem almost to be defying the actress—which explains why the great French *comédiennes,* almost without exception, as well as many foreign actresses, have been drawn to *La Dame aux camélias,* even though, as a play, it can never hope to rank amongst the greatest. Rose Chéri, Aimée Desclée . . . and Aimée Tessandier, Sarah Bernhardt, Cécile Sorel, Blanche Dufrêne . . ., Ida Rubinstein, Ludmilla Pitoëff, Alice Tissot, Marie Bell, Claudia Victrix and Edwige Feuillière are just a few of the great actresses who, in France, have risen to Dumas' challenge whilst, on the screen, the role has tempted such stars as Norma Talmadge, Yvonne Printemps and, most memorably, Greta Garbo. Infinitely varied, the part of Marguerite demands an actress whose emotional range is sufficiently broad to allow her to reflect the changing moods through which the character moves during the five acts of the play; in turn gay and sad, rhapsodic and elegiac, aggressive and timid, cynical and sincere, hopeful and desperate, she must also be able to interpret the various and very different stages of Marguerite's career: the hard-boiled courtesan of act I must grow into the passionately lyrical lover of acts II and III who must, in her turn, naturally evolve into the pathetic consumption-racked figure of the final acts.

And, in the final analysis, the literary critic too comes back, in order to explain the fascination of *La Dame aux camélias,* to the character of Marguerite. For *La Dame aux camélias* is essentially Marguerite Gautier—Armand seems pale and *déjà vu* besides her—and the pathos the play arouses springs above all from the spectacle of a noble and generous spirit being crushed by an inhuman society, yet accepting its defeat willingly. *La Dame aux camélias* tells the story of the submission of passion to reason, of idealism to reality, of the individual to society: consequently it matters little that Marguerite should happen to be a prostitute . . . for the play, unlike the novel which is too immediately based on the Dumas-Duplessis affair, has a universal significance that transcends the particular events from which it springs.... The play succeeds in moving in that it depicts the plight of an exceptional individual enmeshed in a social order so inflexible that it is unable to cater for exceptions and can only accommodate the likes of Nichette and Gustave, Saint-Gaudens and Prudence. It is a society from which there can be no escape, in which the penalty for non-conformity is death, and whose forbidding moralism and materialism constrict the individual like Lilliputian fetters.... The flight to Auteuil . . . provides only momentary relief for, always and everywhere, there will be a *père* Duval to pull one back, and under. Dumas *fils'* play, in that it so eloquently poses the problem of the antagonism between the individual and the community, can be seen, if one wants, as a final stirring of Romanticism on the stage, but more purposefully, with its firmly anti-idealistic resolution of the dichotomy, as a further foreshadowing of Naturalist theatre and its *comédies rosses.* Seen from this perspective, **La Dame aux camélias** provides, in a different genre, a reflection as revealing of the spiritual and moral ambience of the period as those artistically far greater works, Baudelaire's *Fleurs du mal* and Flaubert's *Madame Bovary.* (pp. 41-8)

> *Roger J. B. Clark, in an introduction to* La dame aux camélias *by Alexandre Dumas fils, edited by Roger J.B. Clark, Oxford University Press, London, 1972, pp. 7-48.*

ADDITIONAL BIBLIOGRAPHY

Finn, Michael R. "Proust and Dumas Fils: Odette and *La dame aux camélias." The French Review* XLVII, No. 3 (February 1974): 528-42.*
  Identifies *Camille* and its heroine, Marguerite Gautier, as sources for certain aspects of Marcel Proust's *Un Amour de Swann* and its heroine, Odette de Crécy.

Fletcher, Jefferson B. "Alexandre Dumas Fils." *The Harvard Monthly* XIII, No. 1 (October 1891): 1-15.
  An incisive contemporary synopsis of Dumas's dramatic art.

Janin, Jules. "A Memoir of Marie Duplessis." In *Camille: La dame aux camélias,* by Alexandre Dumas, *fils,* translated by Edmund Gosse, pp. xv-xxiv. New York: Limited Editions Club, 1955.
  An informal memoir primarily based on Duplessis's public appearances. Dumas remarked that Janin had "a little embellished" this romantic testimonial.

Jerrold, Evelyn. "Alexandre Dumas the Younger." *Temple Bar* LI (November 1877): 392-408.
  Assails the cornerstones of Dumas's literary reputation by impugning the structural integrity of his dramas, the originality of his social themes, and the effectiveness of his logical system of plot development. Jerrold concludes his essay by remarking on the "rows of brazen and bediamonded Messalinas that invariably assist at the first performance of [Dumas's] pieces, all eager to make it appear that they are the heroines of the story." In addition, Jerrold describes Dumas as a "moral charlatan trading on unclean curiosity . . . under the cloak of an evangelist."

Lancaster, Charles Maxwell. "Dumas the Younger and French Dramatic Forms Existing in 1850." *Poet Lore* LI, No. 4 (Winter 1945): 345-52.
  Highlights Dumas's innovativeness as a dramatist. Lancaster credits Dumas with breaking away from the "stilted" Romantic tradition by using drama as a vehicle for attacking contemporary social problems.

Lemaître, Jules. Review of *Le demi-monde,* by Alexandre Dumas, *fils.* In his *Theatrical Impressions,* translated by Frederic Whyte, pp. 33-47. 1924. Reprint. Port Washington, N.Y.: Kennikat Press, 1970.
  A reprint of the critic's April 8, 1890, review of the Comédie-Française production of *Le demi-monde.* After noting the dated quality of the play, Lemaître discusses the attitudes and conduct of Olivier de Jalin apropos of Suzanne d'Ange.

Maguire, C. E. "James and Dumas, Fils." *Modern Drama* X, No. 1 (May 1967): 34-42.*
  Speculation regarding Henry James's review of *L'étrangère* (see excerpt above, 1876). Maguire suggests that similarities between the characters of Mr. Clarkson in Dumas's play and Christopher Newman in James's novel *The American* may have influenced the writer's assessment of *L'étrangère.*

Maurois, André. *The Titans: A Three-Generation Biography of the Dumas.* Translated by Gerard Hopkins. New York: Harper & Brothers Publishers, 1957, 508 p.*

  The standard biography, chronicling the lives of Thomas-Alexandre Dumas Davy de la Pailleterie, Alexandre Dumas, *pere,* and Alexandre Dumas, *fils.* (This book is published in England under the title of *Three Musketeers.*)

Nicoll, Allardyce. "From the Medieval to the Materialistic: The Coming of Realism." In his *World Drama: From Aeschylus to Anouilh,* pp. 485-518. New York: Harcourt, Brace and Co., 1950.*
  Discusses Dumas's contribution to the development of realism in modern European drama.

Perkins, Merle L. "Matilda Heron's *Camille." Comparative Literature* VII, No. 4 (Fall 1955): 338-43.
  Analyzes the differences between Dumas's *Camille* and Matilda Heron's popular nineteenth-century English translation of the play.

Sarcey, Francisque. "Alexandre Dumas Fils." In his *Quarante ans de théâtre,* pp. 169-360. Paris: Bibliothèque des annales, politiques et littéraires, 1901.
  Reprints of highly regarded contemporary essays on *Camille, Le demi-monde, Le fils naturel, Les idées de Madame Aubray, La femme de Claude, Monsieur Alphonse, L'étrangère, Denise, Francillon,* and *Le supplice d'une femme.* Sarcey's commentary is not available in English translation.

Saunders, Edith. *The Prodigal Father: Dumas Père et Fils and "The Lady of the Camellias."* London: Longmans, Green and Co., 1951, 257 p.*
  A popularized account of the Dumas' life and times, with special reference to the production of *Camille.*

Schwarz, H. Stanley. "The Realism of Dumas Fils." *The French Review* VI, No. 4 (March 1933): 312-17.
  Rebuts Neil C. Arvin's remarks concerning Dumas's reputation as a realist (see excerpt above, 1932).

Seidlin, Oskar. "Greatness and Decline of the Bourgeois: Dramas by Schiller and Dumas." *Comparative Literature* VI, No. 2 (Spring 1954): 123-29.*
  Suggests that Dumas patterned *Camille* after Friedrich von Schiller's play *Kabale und Liebe* and contrasts the underlying social and moral philosophies in the two works.

Sewell, J. E. "Dumas with Apologies." *The New Statesman* XXXV, No. 885 (12 April 1930): 13.
  Defends the continuing effectiveness of *Camille* in the course of reviewing an "apologetic" production of the play at London's Garrick Theatre.

Smith, Hugh Allison, and Michell, Robert Bell. Introduction to *La dame aux camélias,* by Alexandre Dumas, *fils,* edited by Hugh Allison Smith and Robert Bell Michell, pp. iii-xii. Oxford French Series, edited by Raymond Weeks. New York: Oxford University Press, 1924.
  A concise introduction to Dumas's characteristics and contributions as a dramatist.

Stanton, Stephen S. Introduction to *"Camille" and Other Plays,* edited by Stephen S. Stanton, pp. vii-xxxix. New York: Hill and Wang, 1962.*
  Discusses *Camille* in the context of the development of the well-made play in France.

Tynan, Kenneth. Review of *La dame aux camélias,* by Alexandre Dumas, *fils.* In his *Curtains: Selections from the Drama Criticism and Related Writings,* pp. 398-99. New York: Atheneum, 1961.
  A reprinted review of Edwige Feuillère's 1957 performance in the role of Marguerite Gautier at the Duke of York's Theatre in London. Tynan also briefly discusses the interpretations of two other well-known leading ladies, Tallulah Bankhead and Eleonora Duse.

Weinberg, Bernard. "Contemporary Criticism of the Plays of Dumas Fils, 1852-1869." *Modern Philology* XXXVII, No. 3 (February 1940): 293-308.
  Analyzes the contemporary critical response to Dumas, empha-

sizing the differences between it and contemporary criticism of Émile Augier and relating Dumas's reception to developments in the French novel.

Young, Stark. "Habima and Sorel." In his *Immortal Shadows: A Book of Dramatic Criticism,* pp. 67-71. New York: Charles Scribner's Sons, 1948.*
    A reprinted review of Cecile Sorel's "divinely callous" performance as Marguerite Gautier in a 1926 production of *Camille.*

Yedlicka, Joseph W. "Speculation in the Second Empire: *La question d'argent* of Dumas Fils." *The French Review* XXI, No. 1 (October 1962): 606-16.
    Treats *La question d'argent* as an expression of the widespread social concern generated by the growth of financial speculation during the Second Empire.

Edward FitzGerald

1809-1883

(Born Edward Purcell.) English translator, poet, essayist, and letter writer.

Best known as the translator of the *Rubáiyát of Omar Khayyám, Astronomer Poet of Persia*, FitzGerald has gained recognition for his unique method of transforming a foreign work into one which preserves the essence of the original. Specifically, FitzGerald did not consider himself a true translator; rather, he viewed his art as "poetic transfusion" and attempted to render each work into a format that would be accessible to the English reader. FitzGerald is also renowned for his correspondence, which critics have come to value for its commentary on society, on literature, and on his relationships with many of the major literary figures of his era.

FitzGerald was born at Woodbridge in the Suffolk area of England to the wealthy Purcell family. His mother was heiress to the affluent Irish FitzGerald family and, after her father's death, the Purcells assumed the FitzGerald name. They spent several years in France before returning to England, where FitzGerald enrolled at the King Edward VI Grammar school at Bury St. Edmunds. Although FitzGerald was not academically ambitious, in 1826 he entered Trinity College, Cambridge, and became friends with such noted literary figures as Alfred, Lord Tennyson, Thomas Carlyle, and William Makepeace Thackeray. After graduating in 1830, FitzGerald traveled to Paris. After a brief visit, he returned to England, however, and although only twenty-one, he announced his intention to retire from society and establish permanent residence in rural Suffolk. FitzGerald remained true to his intent: he established a modest country home, entertained infrequently, and visited friends rarely. His solitude was briefly interrupted in 1856 when he married Lucy Barton, the daughter of his long-time friend Bernard Barton. They were separated a year later, and FitzGerald became increasingly reclusive until his death in 1883.

Beginning in the 1830s, FitzGerald submitted many poems, essays, and reviews to English periodicals, but only one poem, "The Meadows in Spring," was accepted for publication. He anonymously published *Euphranor: A Dialogue on Youth* in 1851 at his own expense. In this work, which is comprised of fictional Platonic dialogues, FitzGerald criticized the English educational system for neglecting to instruct students in physical exercise and practical manners. Both *Euphranor* and FitzGerald's next publication, *Polonius: A Collection of Wise Saws and Modern Instances,* were ignored by his contemporaries. Disillusioned by the poor reception of these works, FitzGerald turned from original writings to translation.

FitzGerald translated works in several languages before he turned to the *Rubáiyát.* His *Six Dramas of Calderón, Freely Translated,* which includes the works of the Spanish dramatist Calderón de la Barca, was the only work to bear FitzGerald's name in his lifetime. Next, he published a translation of *Salamán and Absál* from the Persian poet Jāmī. He also translated several classical Greek dramas, including *Agamemnon* by Aeschylus and *Oedipus Rex* and *Oedipus at Colonus* by Sophocles, which he combined and published as *The Downfall and Death of King*

Oedipus. These works were poorly received by his contemporaries, who charged that FitzGerald had significantly altered the style and tone of the originals by selective editing and excessive use of paraphrase.

FitzGerald's *Rubáiyát,* the work on which his reputation today is based, is perhaps the most celebrated rendering of Persian into the English language. It contains the *rubáiyát,* or quatrains, of the Persian poet, astronomer, and mathematician Omar. In the original manuscripts, Omar's poems consist of individual verses without organization or structure. FitzGerald's version of the *Rubáiyát* illustrates his concept of translation as "poetic transfusion": he imposed a continuity of sequence and grouped Omar's quatrains into consistent patterns of thought. In subsequent editions of the work, FitzGerald carefully revised existing verses, added others, and regrouped them thematically. Often described as elaborate and sensual, the poem depicts the religious turmoil of a simple man who wavers between the appeal of hedonism and his fear of divine justice and who is torn between scientific reasoning and religious mysticism. FitzGerald fashioned the *Rubáiyát* into a work in which the sequence of a day becomes a metaphor for the passage of time: the speaker delights in the dawn and seizes enjoyment from each moment; then, as the day progresses into evening, the narrator associates his fading youth and eventual death with the approach of darkness. According to FitzGerald, the work had great relevance for his era, for the Persian quatrains expressed the doubts, fears, and aspirations of the nineteenth century as clearly as they had expressed the dilemmas common to the eleventh century.

Although the *Rubáiyát* was faulted by critics for many of the same flaws they had found in FitzGerald's earlier translations, his contemporaries generally hailed the work as an original creation. They especially praised his reorganization of Omar's quatrains as a stylistic change that retained the poetic spirit of the original. Twentieth-century commentators echo FitzGerald's early critics and additionally admire the verse form and rhyme structure he imposed upon the work.

In addition to his translations, FitzGerald wrote essays and corresponded prolifically. Though his essays are largely overlooked, critics have recently turned to his letters for their warm and vital portrait of the author, for their appreciations of art, literature, and the rural English countryside, and for their comments on major literary figures of the nineteenth century, many of whom were FitzGerald's correspondents. Despite the contemporary appeal of his letters, however, FitzGerald will be remembered primarily for his original translation of the *Rubáiyát*.

PRINCIPAL WORKS

"The Meadows in Spring" (poetry) 1831; published in journal *Athenaeum*
Euphranor: A Dialogue on Youth (dialogues) 1851
Polonius: A Collection of Wise Saws and Modern Instances [editor] (aphorisms and quotations) 1852
Six Dramas of Calderón, Freely Translated [translator] (dramas) 1853
Salámán and Absál [translator; from *Sáláman and Absál* by Jāmī] (allegory) 1856, 1871, 1879
Rubáiyát of Omar Khayyám, Astronomer Poet of Persia [translator] (poetry) 1859, 1868, 1872, 1879
Agamemnon [translator; from *Agamemnon* by Aeschylus] (drama) 1865
The Downfall and Death of King Oedipus. 2 vols. [translator; from *Oedipus Rex* and *Oedipus at Colonus* by Sophocles] (dramas) 1880-81
Works of Edward FitzGerald (poetry, dramas, essays, and aphorisms) 1887
Letters and Literary Remains of Edward FitzGerald (letters, poetry, and dialogues) 1889

THE ATHENAEUM (essay date 1853)

"Freely translated," says Mr. Fitzgerald [of his *Six Dramas of Calderon*]. There is no doubt of it. By way of apology for so much licence—for a freedom in dealing with his text so unusual—the translator gives an original reason:—"I have not meddled," he says, "with any of Calderon's more famous plays, not one of these on my list being mentioned with any praise or included in any selection that I know of except the homely *Mayor of Zalamca.*" We have not taken the trouble to compare these translations with the originals; holding it quite unnecessary to treat as a serious work a book whose author confesses that he "has sunk, reduced, altered and replaced much that seemed not fine or efficient—simplified some per-

plexities, and curtailed or omitted scenes that seemed to mar the breadth of general effect, supplying such omissions by some lines.''

> A review of "Six Dramas of Calderon," in The Athenaeum, No. 1350, September 10, 1853, p. 1063.

EDWARD FITZGERALD (essay date 1856)

[*In this dedication to* Salámán and Absál, *first published in 1856, FitzGerald defends his translation of the allegory of the Persian poet Jāmī.*]

Had all [Jāmī's Poem *Salámán and Absál*] been like Parts, it would have been all translated, and in such Prose lines as you measure [the Persian poet] Hafiz in, and such as any one should adopt who does not feel himself so much of a Poet as him he translates and some he translates for—before whom it is best to lay the raw material as genuine as may be, to work up to their own better Fancies. But, unlike Hafiz' best—(whose Sonnets are sometimes as close packt as Shakespeare's, which they resemble in more ways than one)—Jámi, you know, like his Countrymen generally, is very diffuse in what he tells and his way of telling it. The very structure of the Persian Couplet . . . so often ending with the same Word, or Two Words, if but the foregoing Syllable secure a lawful Rhyme, so often makes the Second Line but a slightly varied Repetition, or Modification of the First, and gets slowly over Ground often hardly worth gaining. (pp. 42-3)

This, together with the confined Action of Persian Grammar, whose organic simplicity seems to me its difficulty when applied, makes the Line by Line Translation of a Poem not line by line precious tedious in proportion to its length. Especially—(what the Sonnet does not feel)—in the Narrative; which I found when once eased in its Collar, and yet missing somewhat of rhythmical Amble, somehow, and not without resistance on my part, swerved into that "easy road" of Verse—easiest as unbeset with any exigencies of Rhyme. (pp. 42-3)

As for the much bodily omitted—it may be readily guessed that an Asiatic of the 15th Century might say much on such a subject that an Englishman of the 19th would not care to read. Not that our Jámi is ever *licentious* like his Contemporary Chaucer, nor like Chaucer's Posterity in Times that called themselves more Civil. But better Men will not now endure a simplicity of Speech that Worse men abuse. Then the many more, and foolisher, Stories—preliminary Te Deums to Allah and Allah's-shadow Sháh—very much about Alef Noses, Eyebrows like inverted Núns, drunken Narcissus Eyes—and that eternal Moon Face which never wanes from Persia—of all which there is surely enough in this Glimpse of the Original. No doubt some Oriental character escapes—the Story sometimes becomes too Skin and Bone without due interval of even Stupid and Bad. Of the two Evils?—At least what I have chosen is least in point of bulk; scarcely in proportion with the length of its Apology which, as usual, probably discharges one's own Conscience at too great a Price; people at once turning against you the Arms they might have wanted had you not laid them down. However it may be with this, I am sure a complete Translation—even in Prose—would not have been a readable one—which, after all, is a useful property of most Books, even of Poetry. (pp. 43-4)

> Edward Fitzgerald, "Dedication to 'Salámán and Absál: An Allegory'," in his The Variorum and Definitive Edition of the Poetical and Prose Writings of Edward Fitzgerald, Vol. I, edited by George Ben-

tham, Doubleday, Page and Company, 1902, pp. 41-6.

THE ATHENAEUM (essay date 1856)

[The anonymous translation of *Salámán and Absál: an Allegory*] shows some poetic feeling, a diligent use of the dictionary, but a very moderate acquaintance with Persian. The few difficult lines which occur in the poem are passed over without notice, and mistakes are rather numerous. Thus, we have ''Takhalus'' for *Takhallus*, ''parr'' and ''bezann'' for *par* and *bizan*. . . . The translator's efforts in the 'Hiawatha' metre are not successful. What shall we say of such a line as—

Nightingaling thus a noodle;—

or of a couplet like the following:—

Soon as seen, Indecent Hunger
Seizes up and swallows down.

—As a first attempt, however, to make Jámi accessible to the English reader, this little volume is deserving of commendation. (p. 958)

A review of ''Salámán and Absál: An Allegory,'' in The Athenaeum, *No. 1501, August 2, 1856, pp. 957-58.*

RICHARD CHENEVIX TRENCH (essay date 1856)

Six Dramas of Calderon, freely translated, by Edward Fitzgerald, . . . are far the most important and worthiest contribution to the knowledge of the Spanish poet which we have yet received. But, written as they are in English of an exquisite purity and vigor, and dealing with poetry in a poet's spirit, they yet suffer, as it seems to me, under serious drawbacks. Mr. Fitzgerald has chosen, and avows that he has chosen, plays which, with the exception of the noble **Mayor of Zalamea,** can hardly be said to rank among Calderon's greatest, being rather effective melodramas than works of highest art. He does this with the observation—''Such plays as the *Magico Prodigioso* and the *Vida es Sueño* require another translator, and, I think, form of translation.'' In respect of ''form of translation'' I am compelled to agree with him, his version being for the most part in English blank verse; but how little likely Calderon is to obtain a more gifted translator, and how much his modest choice of plays on which to exercise his skill, which are not among his author's best, is to be regretted, I think the reader will own. . . . (pp. 111-12)

Richard Chenevix Trench, ''Calderon in England,'' in his Calderon: His Life and Genius with Specimens of His Plays, *Redfield, 1856, pp. 98-113.**

EDWARD FITZGERALD (letter date 1857)

[*In the following letter to E. B. Cowell, FitzGerald defends his desire to translate Aeschylus's Trilogy into English. Although he admits that the works demand the attention of a better poet, FitzGerald maintains that his ''very free'' translation will provide a readable English version of the Greek dramas.*]

I think I want to turn [Aeschylus'] Trilogy into what shall be readable English Verse; a thing I have always thought of, but was frightened at the Chorus. So I am now; I can't think them so fine as People talk of: they are terribly maimed; and all such Lyrics require a better Poet than I am to set forth in English.

But the better Poets won't do it; and I cannot find one readable translation. I shall (if I make one) make a very free one; not for Scholars, but for those who are ignorant of Greek, and who (so far as I have seen) have never been induced to learn it by any Translations yet made of these Plays. I think I shall become a bore . . . by all this Translation: but it amuses me without any labour, and I really think I have the faculty of making some things readable which others have hitherto left unreadable. But don't be alarmed with the anticipation of another sudden volume of Translations; for I only sketch out the matter, then put it away; and coming on it one day with fresh eyes trim it up with some natural impulse that I think gives a natural air to all. . . . (pp. xiii-xiv)

Edward FitzGerald, in an extract from a letter to E. B. Cowell on May 7, 1857, in his The Variorum and Definitive Edition of the Poetical and Prose Writings of Edward FitzGerald, *Vol. 2, edited by George Bentham, Doubleday, Page and Company, 1902, pp. xiii-xiv.*

EDWARD FITZGERALD (essay date 1865)

[*In the preface to his translation of the* Agememnon *by Aeschylus, first published in 1865, FitzGerald apologizes for the liberties he has taken with the drama, though he maintains that he has preserved the ''Spirit'' of the work.*]

I do not like to put this version—or *per*-version—of Aeschylus into the few friendly hands it is destined for, without some apology, to him as well as to them. Perhaps the best apology, so far as they are concerned, would be my simple assurance that this is the very last *lèse-majesté* I ever shall—or can—commit of the kind.

I suppose that a literal version of this play, if possible, would scarce be intelligible. Even were the dialogue always clear, the lyric Choruses, which make up so large a part, are so dark and abrupt in themselves, and therefore so much the more mangled and tormented by a copyist and commentator, that the most conscientious translator must not only jump at a meaning, but must bridge over a chasm; especially if he determine to complete the antiphony of Strophe and Antistrophe in English verse.

Thus, encumbered with forms which sometimes, I think, hang heavy on Aeschylus himself; struggling with indistinct meanings, obscure allusions, and even with *puns* which some have tried to reproduce in English; this grand play, which to the scholar and the poet, lives, breathes, and moves in the dead language, has hitherto seemed to me to drag and stifle under conscientious translation into the living; that is to say, to have lost that which I think the drama can least afford to lose all the world over. And so it was that, hopeless of succeeding where as good versifiers, and better scholars, seem to me to have failed, I came first to break the bounds of Greek Tragedy; then to swerve from the Master's footsteps; and so, one license drawing on another to make all of a piece, arrived at the present anomalous conclusion. If it has succeeded in shaping itself into a distinct, consistent and animated Whole, through which the reader can follow without halting, and not without some progressive interest from beginning to end, I shall at any rate not have extinguished the Spirit under whatsoever misrepresentations of the Letter; and *that* remains unimpeachable by any treason of mine, inviolate by any but transcriber's errors, in its own imperishable Greek, and undepraved by any wilful alloy of the translator's in more than one English version. (pp. 241-42)

> Edward FitzGerald, in a preface to "Agamemnon: A Tragedy," in his The Variorum and Definitive Edition of the Poetical and Prose Writings of Edward FitzGerald, Vol. 2, edited by George Bentham, Doubleday, Page and Company, 1902, pp. 237-43.

[CHARLES ELIOT NORTON] (essay date 1869)

[In the following passage from the first American review of The Rubáiyát of Omar Khayyám, *Norton highly praises its anonymous translator. He assesses the work favorably, noting that the translator has not only skillfully rendered the poetic form of the work, but has also succeeded in capturing its poetic spirit.]*

[The anonymous translator of *The Rubáiyát of Omar Khayyám, the Astronomer Poet of Persia*] is to be called "translator" only in default of a better word, one which should express the poetic transfusion of a poetic spirit from one language to another, and the re-presentation of the ideas and images of the original in a form not altogether diverse from their own, but perfectly adapted to the new conditions of time, place, custom, and habit of mind in which they reappear. In the whole range of our literature there is hardly to be found a more admirable example of the most skilful poetic rendering of remote foreign poetry than this work of an anonymous author affords. It has all the merit of a remarkable original production, and its excellence is the highest testimony that could be given, to the essential impressiveness and worth of the Persian poet. It is the work of a poet inspired by the work of a poet; not a copy, but a reproduction, not a translation, but the redelivery of a poetic inspiration.

Much in the English work has been simply suggested by the original. Hints supplied by Omar are enlarged; thoughts touched upon by him are completely grasped; images faintly shadowed by him, fully developed. The sequence of the Persian quatrains, depending on the rhyme and not upon the contents of the verse, admits of no progressive development of feeling, and no logical continuity of thought. The poet is compelled by his form into sententiousness, into gnomic sayings, into discontinuous flashes of emotion, and finds himself obliged to recur often to the same idea, in order to present it under a new image or in a different aspect. The English Omar has not troubled himself to follow this peculiarity of his model. He has strung his quatrains together in an order which, if it fail to unite them all in a continuous and regularly developed whole, into a poem formed of the union of the separate stanzas, does at least so bind together many of them that the various portions seem like fragments of an Oriental eclogue. Moreover, a minor key of sadness, of refined melancholy, seems to recur in the English composition more frequently than in the Persian. The sentiment of the original Omar is often re-enforced by the English, is expressed in stronger, tenderer, and more delicate strokes. Every now and then a note of the nineteenth century seems to mingle its tone with those of the twelfth; as if the ancient Oriental melody were reproduced on a modern European instrument. But it is very striking to see, and much more to feel, how close the thought and the sentiment of the Persian poet often are to the thought and sentiment of our own day. So that in its English dress it reads like the latest and freshest expression of the perplexity and of the doubt of the generation to which we ourselves belong. There is probably nothing in the mass of English translations or reproductions of the poetry of the East to be compared with this little volume in point of

value as *English* poetry. In the strength of rhythmical structure, in force of expression, in musical modulation, and in mastery of language, the external character of the verse corresponds with the still rarer interior qualities of imagination and of spiritual discernment which it displays. (pp. 575-76)

> [Charles Eliot Norton], in a review of "Rubáiyát of Omar Khayyám, the Astronomer-Poet of Persia," in The North American Review, Vol. CIX, No. CCXXV, October, 1869, pp. 565-84.

THE NATION (essay date 1877)

[This critic suggests that FitzGerald's translation of Aeschylus's Agamemnon *should be classified as an original work rather than as a translation. Although FitzGerald accurately rendered the tragedy's dramatic passages, he was unable to portray its tender and delicate moments; this fault, according to the critic, detracts from the work's power and impact and diminishes its value as a translation.]*

Mr. Edward Fitzgerald, the translator of that remarkable poem, the **'Rubáiyat,'** . . . has followed that high literary success with a "version or per-version," as he himself calls it of the **'Agamemnon'** of Æschylus. He represents the very opposite pole of the translator's art from the Longfellow school, for he utterly rejects all minute precision and cultivates audacity. He holds, indeed, that in dealing with this most difficult of ancient dramas, "the most conscientious translator must not only jump at a meaning, but must bridge over a chasm very often." This he does with extraordinary power; the trouble is that he sometimes appears to mistake the ocean itself for a chasm to be bridged, and is tempted to fill it in with materials that offer, on the whole, an inadequate substitute for the horizon line. Still, when we consider that the 'Agamemnon' is one of the half dozen masterpieces in the literature of the world, . . . we may well rejoice that a man of such commanding skill as Mr. Fitzgerald has tried his hand upon it.

The **'Agamemnon'** has been called the 'Macbeth' of antiquity: but its text is in such a state that some lovers of Greek literature have abandoned, in a kind of despair, the attempt to read it. This naturally gives to Mr. Fitzgerald a peculiar justification for his mode of dealing with the tragedy; and he frankly avows, in his preface, what his method has been:

> This grand play, which to the scholar and the poet lives, breathes, and moves in the dead language, has hitherto seemed to me to drag and stifle under conscientious translation into the living; that is to say, to have lost that which I think the drama can least afford to lose all the world over. And so it was that, hopeless of succeeding where as good versifiers and better scholars seem to me to have failed, I came first to break the bounds of Greek tragedy; then to swerve from the Master's footsteps; and so, one license drawing on another to make all of a piece, arrived at the present anomalous conclusion. . . .

Anomalous it is not, however, though somewhat wild and irregular, and needlessly wayward on some points, especially in regard to rhymes. One covert design that runs through its structure is evidently to reproduce by metre the effect contributed by music on the Greek stage. (p. 310)

Most American readers will have to come to Mr. Fitzgerald by the way of his previous poet—Omar Khayyám; and their first interest will be to learn, if possible, by a comparison of the two works, how much of the 'Rubáiyat' was contributed by the Persian and how much by the Englishman. If much of the present book proves to coincide in flavor with its predecessor, it awakens suspicions or confirms them. As a matter of fact, while the general tone of the two is very unlike, we now and then encounter a passage, interpolated into the Greek, which has singularly the flavor of the astronomer-poet. Take, for instance, the following:

> But thus it is: All bides the destined Hour;
>   And Man, albeit with Justice at his side,
> Fights in the dark against a secret Power
>   Not to be conquer'd—and how pacified? . . .

Or this, where the 'Rubáiyat' flavor is still stronger:

> Call not on Death, old man, that call'd or no
>   Comes quick; nor spend your ebbing breath on me
> Nor Helena; who but as arrows be
>   Shot by the hidden hand behind the bow. . . .

There is absolutely nothing of this in Æschylus, except the words "Call not on Death" and an allusion to Helena. If there is so much of Fitzgerald in this quatrain, how much is there in those attributed to Omar Khayyám? It may be said that it is no great matter, so long as the wine is good, to enquire too closely from what cask it came. It is a satisfaction to know the brands apart; but, after all, if a vintage proves to be contemporary with ourselves, there remains the hope that we may have more of it.

This question answered, we turn to ask if there is power enough in this English poet to give us something of the grasp and strength of Æschylus? There certainly is; and it is, indeed, in this quality that he eminently shines. The grander soliloquies and descriptions in the 'Agamemnon' have never been so well rendered; we may almost say that they have never before been rendered at all. Take, for instance, the magnificent passage which describes the flashing from hill to hill, by signal-fires, of the news that Troy has fallen:

> And first . . .
> Did Ida fire her forest-pine, and, waving,
> Handed him on to the Hermaean steep
> Of Lemnos; Lemnos to the summit of
> Zeus-consecrated Athos lifted; whence,
> As by the giant taken, so despatcht
> The Torch of Conquest traversing the wide
> Aegean with a sunbeam-stretching stride,
> Struck up the drowsy watchers on Makistos;
> Who, flashing back the challenge, fla-h d it on
> To those who watch'd on the Messapian height.
> With whose quick-kindling heather heap'd and fired
> The meteor-bearded messenger refresht,
> Clearing Asopus at a bound, struck fire
> From old Kithaeron; and, so little tired
> As waxing even wanton with the sport,
> Over the sleeping water of Gorgopis
> Sprung to the Rock of Corinth; then to the cliffs
> Which stare down the Saronic Gulf, that now
> Began to shiver in the creeping Dawn;
> Whence, for a moment on the neighboring top
> Of Arachnaeum lighting, one last bound
> Brought him to Agamemnon's battlements

Or take this fine burst from the lips of Clytemnestra, on the arrival of the herald to confirm the news first told by the signal fires:

> CLYTEMNESTRA. "I sang my song of triumph ere he came,
> Alone I sang it while the City slept,
> and these wise Senators with winking eyes,
> Look'd grave, and weighed mistrustfully my word,
> As the light coinage of a woman's brain.
> And so they went their way. But not the less
> From those false fires I lit my altar up,
> And, woman-wise, held on my song, until
> The City taking up the note from me,
> Scarce knowing why, about that altar flock'd,
> Where, like the Priest of Victory, I stood,
> Torch-handed, drenching in triumphant wine
> The flame that from the smouldering incense rose.
> Now what more needs? This Herald of the Day
> Adds but another witness to the Night;
> And I will hear no more from other lips
> Till from my husband Agamemnon all"

Thus much for Mr. Fitzgerald's power of picturesque and vigorous rendering. These are soliloquies, but in the most thrilling dramatic passage of the poem his boldness has secured for him an equal success. It is a scene which might have been regarded by a Greek spectator, in the performance, with some such hushed expectancy as that which awaits on our stage the approach of Lady Macbeth in her sleep-walking trance—the unsealing of the lips of Cassandra. Poor Cassandra, the daughter of King Priam, and now the slave and concubine of Agamemnon—she who in her pride of beauty and innocence had refused the love of a god, and had been doomed in return to the fatal gift of unbelieved prophecy—here she stands in presence of an enraged queen, her vengeful rival and future murderess. . . . [The] scene goes on, drawing from Cassandra, in a wild whirl of passion, whose circles expand every moment, a revelation of past, present, and future more powerful and fearful than any Dantean terror—and all transacted, be it understood, at the very moment when Agamemnon is approaching his doom. Another instant and the curtain or stage-scene is drawn aside, revealing Clytemnestra by the body of her slain husband. There is no scene in Macbeth of more tremendous power; and although all this, as here quoted, is rather a transfusion than a translation, yet it gives more of the real sense of the original than all previous translations put together.

But, after this, it must be said that it is the stirring and dramatic passages in which Mr. Fitzgerald is strongest, and that in the more delicate and tender descriptions his touch is not always gentle enough to satisfy. It is one of the extraordinary features of this great drama that the Promethean Æschylus here introduces phrases and passages as soft and beautiful as any in Shakspere's songs, and it is in rendering these that Mr. Fitzgerald is least satisfactory. . . . Sometimes Mr. Fitzgerald omits the passage altogether, as with the celebrated description of Helen's entrance into Troy—perhaps the most exquisite miniature-painting of womanly beauty to be found in literature—a passage which can scarcely be translated without being spoiled, but in which every syllable seems to thrill with the consummate loveliness it describes. . . . It is a serious charge against a translator, or even an imitator, to say that he omits a passage like this, and that he also omits the greater part of the lovely picture of poor Iphigenia at the altar. . . . The greater the power of Æschylus the less we can afford to lose these passages; it is as if a translator of Shakspere should omit his songs. (p. 311)

We should say, on the whole, that while Mr. Fitzgerald's **'Agamemnon'** is a far more heroic and stimulating work for the English reader than [some other versions]. . . , yet the lover of AEschylus must prepare himself for occasional resentment as well as gratitude; and he who wishes to know AEschylus in English must still combine several parallel translations for each passage from the Greek. It would be safest to say that this remarkable poem is not to be placed in the department of translations, but rather of original works, and that it is Greek only in the sense in which Keats' 'Hyperion' is Greek, or the sublime audacities of Marlowe, whose mighty genius touched the self-same ancient theme of love and wrong. (p. 312)

> *"Fitzgerald's 'Agamemnon',"* in The Nation, *Vol. XXIV, No. 621, May 24, 1877, pp. 310-12.*

J. A. SYMONDS   (essay date 1877)

[*Symonds was a noted nineteenth-century English critic, poet, historian, and translator. Although primarily remembered for his translations of the Greek poets, Symonds is also known for his aesthetic theory and impressionistic essays. In his assessment of FitzGerald, Symonds considers his translation of* Agamemnon *a fine example of Greek poetry in English form; yet he contends that FitzGerald should have followed the Greek version more consistently and translated the entire drama.*]

Those of us who for many years past have known Mr. Fitzgerald's version of the **Rubaiyat of Omar Khayyam** by heart, and who have felt that in those quatrains, at once melodious and pointed, a real poet had revealed himself beneath the garb of a translator, received the announcement of his **Agamemnon** with no common interest. The command of language and metre displayed in the smaller work, its spontaneity of music, and its depth of thought and feeling, inclined us to expect much of the greater: for, though it does not follow that the versifier who can render with consummate skill the epigrams of a Persian poet-sage should be able to cope with the difficulties of the first Greek dramatist's most perfect tragedy, yet the translator's choice of phrase and mastery of handling made it evident that nothing from his' pen could be commonplace. Nor was this expectation frustrated. Whatever deductions may have to be made by the student, who feels that in the **Agamemnon** Mr. Fitzgerald has done less than a more sustained effort of his singular powers might have produced, it will be acknowledged by all competent judges that his translation separates itself at once from merely meritorious work, and takes a place apart among all English versions of Greek poetry. It is almost trivial to say that the diction of a modern author is Shaksperean. The phrase seems to mean much; but, when analysed, it conveys an indistinct impression. Yet Mr. Fitzgerald's style in the finest passages of this great torso has a weight, a compactness, and a picturesqueness, to find the proper parallel for which we must look back to Shakspere's age. The strong sonorous verse has the richness and the elasticity of Marlowe's line; and for the first time, after so many attempts, the English reader catches in his translation a true echo of the pompous Aeschylean manner. (pp. 4-5)

[It] may be well at once to state what constitutes the specific character of this new version, and why I have ventured to call it a torso. Mr. Fitzgerald describes his drama on the title-page as *a tragedy taken from Aeschylus,* and in the preface he styles it *a version or per-version of Aeschylus* [see excerpt above, 1865]. He does not, therefore, pretend that it is a faithful translation. Convinced of the impossibility of presenting the Greek play in its integrity to English readers, and doubtful of

his power to succeed where "as good versifiers, and better scholars," had seemed to him to fail, he determined to re-cast the **Agamemnon** of the Attic poet, adhering in parts to the original, and in parts diverging from it, according to his sense of fitness. The result is that, while the whole poem is profoundly penetrated with the Aeschylean spirit, which it reproduces with wonderful vividness, and while certain portions are accurate transcripts from the original, the Greek student will find many of the most impressive passages suppressed, and some most carefully prepared effects omitted. The long dialogue between Cassandra and the Chorus, for example, is curtailed and re-modelled in such a way as to sacrifice the dramatic terror produced by the gradually increasing lucidity of the prophetess, and by the dreadful details of her visions. The cry of Agamemnon, sounding from behind the scenes at the moment when expectation is strained to its utmost pitch of tension, is again exchanged for exclamations from the Chorus, implying that they have heard their master's death-shriek. Thus Mr. Fitzgerald deliberately omits a dramatic incident, which for its force and suddenness is scarcely to be rivalled. . . . We do not want to be told what the ancient Councillors have heard, but to hear with our own ear—if only with the ear of the mind in reading—that shriek which reveals the ruin of the house of Atreus in this supreme catastrophe. In like manner it might be observed that the final altercation of Clytemnestra and Aegisthus with the Chorus, fine as it is in its rapidity of movement and energy of passion, has suffered by transposition and curtailment.

The language throughout the drama, even in the passages which may seem to have been injured by compression, is so grandiose, and the imagery is so Aeschylean, that it is impossible not to regret the author's disinclination to grapple with the Greek more closely. Where he has adhered to the original most faithfully, as in Clytemnestra's description of the courier fire, and her reception of Agamemnon, the success has been so thorough as to make us feel that the whole drama might have been presented with equal force and splendour. Is it quite beyond hope that Mr. Fitzgerald should reconsider his decision and complete the play upon the strictly Aeschylean outlines? He may argue that to reproduce the Choruses exactly would be beyond the power of any modern versifier; and his poet's tact is, perhaps, in this point right. Yet even here we might reply that where the original has inspired him to attempt a tolerably faithful rendering of choice passages—as in the description of Helen's flight from Sparta to Troy, her reception by the Trojans, and the grief of abandoned Menelaus—he has done his best. In a word, the most perfect portions of the tragedy are those which represent the Greek with most fidelity; the modern poet proving his ability to bear the whole Titanic weight if he had chosen, by the energy with which he has disposed of certain favoured passages. (p. 5)

In conclusion, it may be permitted to hope that this *Agamemnon* is only the first of a series; and that the poet who possesses such rare powers of reproductive and re-creative translation may trust them so far upon another trial as to render his original in all its fullness. (p. 6)

> *J. A. Symonds, in a review of "Agamemnon," in* The Academy, *Vol. XII, No. 270, July 7, 1877, pp. 4-6.*

ALFRED TENNYSON   (poem date 1883)

[*Tennyson was a prominent nineteenth-century English poet and a long-time friend of FitzGerald's. His poem "To E. FitzGerald,"*

An undated watercolor portrait of FitzGerald by William Makepeace Thackeray. The Bettmann Archive, Inc.

excerpted below, was written in two parts in 1883. The first part, a tribute to the poet-translator written for FitzGerald's seventy-fifth birthday, was initially published as a dedication to Tennyson's ''Tiresias.'' The second part was written a few weeks after FitzGerald's death and originally appeared as an epilogue to the same poem.]

Old Fitz, who from your suburb grange,
    Where once I tarried for a while,
Glance at the wheeling Orb of change,
    And greet it with a kindly smile;
Whom yet I see as there you sit
    Beneath your sheltering garden-tree,
And while your doves about you flit,
    And plant on shoulder, hand and knee,
Or on your head their rosy feet,
    As if they knew your diet spares
Whatever moved in that full sheet
    Let down to Peter at his prayers;
Who live on milk and meal and grass;
    And once for ten long weeks I tried
Your table of Pythagoras,
    And seemed at first 'a thing enskied'
(As Shakespeare has it) airy-light
    To float above the ways of men,
Then fell from that half-spiritual height
    Chilled, till I tasted flesh again
One night when earth was winter-black,
    And all the heavens flashed in frost;

And on me, half-asleep, came back
    That wholesome heat the blood had lost,
And set me climbing icy capes
    And glaciers, over which there rolled
To meet me long-armed vines with grapes
    Of Eshcol hugeness; for the cold
Without, and warmth within me, wrought
    To mould the dream; but none can say
That Lenten fare makes Lenten thought,
    Who reads your golden Eastern lay,
Than which I know no version done
    In English more divinely well;
A planet equal to the sun
    Which cast it, that large infidel
Your Omar; and your Omar drew
    Full-handed plaudits from our best
In modern letters, and from two,
    Old friends outvaluing all the rest,
Two voices heard on earth no more;
    But we old friends are still alive,
And I am nearing seventy-four,
    While you have touched at seventy-five,
And so I send a birthday line
    Of greeting; and my son, who dipt
In some forgotten book of mine
    With sallow scraps of manuscript,
And dating many a year ago,
    Has hit on this, which you will take
My Fitz, and welcome, as I know
    Less for its own than for the sake
Of one recalling gracious times,
    When, in our younger London days,
You found some merit in my rhymes,
    And I more pleasure in your praise.

· · · · ·

'One height and one far-shining fire'
    And while I fancied that my friend
For this brief idyll would require
    A less diffuse and opulent end,
And would defend his judgment well,
    If I should deem it over nice—
The tolling of his funeral bell
    Broke on my Pagan Paradise,
And mixt the dreams of classic times,
    And all the phantoms of the dream,
With present grief, and made the rhymes,
    That missed his living welcome, seem
Like would-be guests an hour too late,
    Who down the highway moving on
With easy laughter find the gate
    Is bolted, and the master gone.
Gone into darkness, that full light
    Of friendship! past, in sleep, away
By night, into the deeper night!
    The deeper night? A clearer day
Than our poor twilight dawn on earth—
    If night, what barren toil to be!
What life, so maimed by night, were worth
    Our living out? Not mine to me
Remembering all the golden hours
    Now silent, and so many dead,

And him the last; and laying flowers,
   This wreath, above his honoured head,
And praying that, when I from hence
   Shall fade with him into the unknown,
My close of earth's experience
   May prove as peaceful as his own.

(pp. 1317-21)

Alfred Tennyson, "To E. FitzGerald," in his The
Poems of Tennyson, *edited by Christopher Ricks,
Longmans, 1969, pp. 1317-21.*

EDMUND GOSSE (essay date 1889)

[*A distinguished English literary historian, critic, and biographer,
Gosse wrote extensively on seventeenth- and eighteenth-century
English literature. His commentary in* Seventeenth-Century Stud-
ies *(1883),* A History of Eighteenth-Century Literature *(1889),*
Questions at Issue *(1893), and other works is generally regarded
as sound and suggestive. In the following brief survey of Fitz-
Gerald's best-known works, Gosse considers the* Rubáiyát *of
FitzGerald's finest achievement, but praises his minor writings
as well. For additional commentary by Gosse, see excerpt below,
1902.*]

FitzGerald more than any other recent translator of poetry,
carried out that admirable rule of Sir John Denham's, that the
translator's business is not "alone to translate language into
language, but poesie into poesie; and poesie is of so subtle a
spirit, that in pouring out of one language into another, it will
all evaporate, if a new spirit be not added in the translation."
FitzGerald's versions are so free, he is so little bound by the
details of his original, he is so indifferent to the timid pedantry
of the ordinary writer who empties verse out of the cup of one
language into that of another, that we may attempt with him
what would be a futile task with almost every other English
translator—we may estimate from his versions alone what manner of poet he was.

In attempting to form such an estimate we are bound to recognise that his best-known work is also his best. The *Omar Khayyám*
of FitzGerald takes its place in the third period of Victorian
poetry, as an original force wholly in sympathy with other
forces, of which its author took no personal cognisance. Whether
it accurately represents or no the sentiments of a Persian astronomer of the eleventh century is a question which fades into
insignificance beside the fact that it stimulated and delighted
a generation of young readers, to whom it appealed in the same
manner, and along parallel lines with, the poetry of Morris,
Swinburne, and the Rossettis. . . . That FitzGerald was ignorant
of, or wholly indifferent to the existence of these his compeers
did not affect his relationship to them, nor their natural and
instinctive recognition of his imaginative kinship to themselves. The same reassertion of the sensuous elements of literature, the same obedience to the call for a richer music and
a more exotic and impassioned aspect of manners, the same
determination to face the melancholy problems of life and find
a solace for them in art, were to be found in the anonymous
pamphlet of Oriental reverie as in the romances, dramas, songs,
and sonnets of the four younger friends. (pp. 65-6)

[To judge] of his manner as a translator, or rather as a para-
phraser, we must examine not merely the most famous and
remarkable of his writings, but his treatment of Spanish and
Greek drama, and of the narrative of Jámí. It appears that he
took Dryden's licence, and carried it further; that he steeped
himself in the language and feeling of his author, and then

threw over his version the robe of his own peculiar style. Every
great translator does this to some extent, and we do not recognise in Chapman's breathless measure the staid and polished
Homer that marches down the couplets of Pope. But then, both
Pope and Chapman had, in the course of abundant original
composition, made themselves each the possessor of a style
which he threw without difficulty around the shoulders of his
paraphrase. In the unique case of FitzGerald—since Fairfax
can scarcely be considered in the same category—a poet of no
marked individuality in his purely independent verse created
for himself, in the act of approaching masterpieces of widely
different race and age, a poetical style so completely his own
that we recognise it at sight as his. The normal instances of
this manner are familiar to us in *Omar Khayyám.* They are
characterised by a melody which has neither the variety of
Tennyson nor the vehemence of Swinburne, neither the motion
of a river nor of the sea, but which rather reminds us, in its
fulness and serenity, of the placid motion of the surface of a
lake, or of his own grassy estuary of the Deben; and finally
by a voluptuous and novel use of the commonplaces of poetry—
the rose, the vine, the nightingale, the moon. There are examples of this typical manner of FitzGerald to be found in
Omar Khayyám, which are unsurpassed for their pure qualities
as poetry, and which must remain always characteristic of what
was best in a certain class of Victorian verse. Such are:—

Alas, that spring should vanish with the rose!
That youth's sweet-scented manuscript should close!
   The nightingale that in the branches sang,
Ah, whence and whither flown again, who knows!

and (a gem spoiled in recutting, after the first edition, by the
capricious jeweller):—

Thus with a loaf of bread beneath the bough,
A flask of wine, a book of verse,—and thou
   Beside me singing in the wilderness—
And wilderness is paradise enow.

Nothing quite so good, perhaps, as these and many more which
might be quoted from the *Omar Khayyám,* is to be found in
the other translations, yet wherever the latter are happiest they
betray the same hand and murmur the same accents. It is in
The Mighty Magician [from *Six Dramas of Calderon*] that we
meet with such characteristic stanzas as this:—

Who that in his hour of glory
   Walks the kingdom of the rose,
And misapprehends the story
   Which through all the garden blows;
Which the southern air who brings
It touches, and the leafy strings
   Lightly to the touch respond;
And nightingale to nightingale
   Answering on bough beyond—
Nightingale to nightingale
   Answering on bough beyond.

while the following passage, perhaps the richest and most memorable in FitzGerald's minor writings, is found in the *Salámán
and Absál:*—

When they had sail'd their vessel for a moon,
And marr'd their beauty with the wind o' the sea,
Suddenly in mid sea reveal'd itself
An isle, beyond imagination fair;
An isle that was all garden; not a flower,
Nor bird of plumage like the flower, but there;

Some like the flower, and others like the leaf;
Some, as the pheasant and the dove, adorn'd
With crown and collar, over whom, alone,
The jewell'd peacock like a sultan shone;
While the musicians, and among them chief
The nightingale, sang hidden in the trees,
Which, arm in arm, from fingers quivering
With any breath of air, fruit of all kind
Down scatter'd in profusion to their feet,
Where fountains of sweet water ran between,
And sun and shadow chequer-chased the green,
This Iram-garden seem'd in secrecy
Blowing the rosebud of its revelation;
Or Paradise, forgetful of the dawn
Of Audit, lifted from her face the veil.

In reading these sumptuous verses the reader may be inclined to wonder why *Salámán and Absál* is not as widely known and as universally admired as the *Omar Khayyám*. If it were constantly sustained at anything like this level it would be so admired and known, but it is, unfortunately, both crabbed and unequal. (pp. 66-8)

[The story is] told in three parts, with a moral or transcendental summing-up at the close. The metrical form chosen for the main narrative is blank verse, with occasional lapses into rhyme. These, in all probability, respond to some peculiarity in the Persian original, but they are foreign to the genius of English prosody, and they produce an effect of poverty upon the ear, which is alternately tempted and disappointed. There are, moreover, incessant interludes or episodical interpolations, which are treated in an ambling measure of four beats, something like the metre of *Hiawatha,* but again with occasional and annoying introductions of rhyme. It is obvious, at the outset, that we do not see FitzGerald here exercising that perfect instinct for form which he afterwards developed; he was trammelled, no doubt, by his desire to repeat the effects he discovered in the Persian, and had not yet asserted his own genius in what Dryden called metaphrase. Nevertheless, *Salámán and Absál* contains passages of great beauty, such as that in which the poet, in wayward dejection, confesses that his worn harp is no longer modulated, and that—

Methinks
'Twere time to break and cast it in the fire:
The vain old harp, that, breathing from its strings
No music more to charm the ears of man,
May, from its scented ashes, as it burns,
Breathe resignation to the harper's soul.—

(p. 69)

Of FitzGerald as a prose writer there has hitherto been little known. His correspondence now reveals him, unless I am much mistaken, as one of the most pungent, individual, and picturesque of English letter-writers. Rarely do we discover a temperament so mobile under a surface so serene and sedentary; rarely so feminine a sensibility side by side with so virile an intelligence. He is moved by every breath of nature; every change of hue in earth or air affects him; and all these are reflected, as in a camera obscura, in the richly-coloured moving mirror of his letters. It will not surprise one reader of this correspondence if the name of its author should grow to be set, in common parlance, beside those of Gray and Cowper for the fidelity and humanity of his addresses to his private friends. (pp. 69-70)

Edmund Gosse, "Edward FitzGerald," *in* The Fortnightly Review, *n.s. Vol. XLVI, No. CCLXXI, July 1, 1889, pp. 57-70.*

THE NATION   (essay date 1889)

[FitzGerald's works] are well known in the circle that cares for literature of the highest order. Original genius he did not possess, but his appreciativeness of excellence was sound and true; whenever he praises, one is compelled to assent. He spent the most of his energy in endeavoring to render foreign classics into English in such a way as to make them effective to modern taste. He did not write for those who could read the originals. He professed only to make adaptations rather than translations, and he cut and modified with a free hand. Scholars have praised his work for what it strove to accomplish, accepting the limitations which his taste imposed upon it. Taste, however developed and refined, is still not genius, and it must be frankly acknowledged that he has not given us just what Calderon, Aeschylus, and Sophocles created. His Persian translations vary even more widely from the originals. **'Omar Khayyám'** is a celebrated work in his version, but it is largely his own work, and it may be hoped that the other translations will become better known, for, without having the commanding qualities of Omar, they are studded with charming stories in verse, and not encumbered with Eastern moods of thought so much as to disturb a Western mind; to us they are more pleasing. The two poetical speeches of the English and Roman generals, with their fine movement, are also a kind of translation—from prose to verse, though nearer to original composition. The dialogue of **'Euphranor'** is the most considerable work of his own hand, and reaches what seems to be his ideal of writing—fine feeling in fine English. His name, however, is linked indissolubly with literature, in all probability, only in one work, the Omar; his memory will always be associated with the Tennyson group; besides, and by virtue of it, he will long be remembered by those who prize simplicity, refinement, and moral worth above the more vulgar quality of distinction. (p. 114)

"The Translator of 'Omar Khayyám'," in The Nation, *Vol. XLIX, No. 1258, August 8, 1889, pp. 112-14.*

MELVILLE B. ANDERSON   (essay date 1889)

Judging from the pure wine of poetry which, in the capacity of a translator, [Fitzgerald] has added to our literature, and from the sanity, the sense of style, the vigor of intellect, and the large imaginative grasp of his thought everywhere apparent in his versions, one may fairly doubt whether his self-supposed inferiority to the Tennysons and Carlyle and Thackeray was not a matter of ambition rather than of native capacity. At all events, the translator who, by the fine originality and daring creativeness of his renderings of such various poets, has fairly earned a right to the title of prince of translators since old Chapman, may safely be said to have deserved better of his language and of future memory than any secondary poet of his time. It is only when we consider that really great translators are even rarer than poets who can pass awhile for great, that we are capable of doing justice to the modest genius of him who made great Sophocles, mighty Aeschylus, sad Omar, and impassioned Calderon, clasp hands across the centuries and speak with living force in English words. He has made these masters speak upon his page, perhaps not just as they would have spoken had they been Englishmen, but with a music and a power scarcely inferior to their own. He has done for them, in short, what Chaucer did for Boccaccio, what Coleridge did for Schiller. The quatrains from Omar [*The Rubáiyát of Omar Khayyám, the Astronomer Poet of Persia*] seem to be little less original with FitzGerald than is the *Elegy* with Gray, and perhaps the one poem will live as eternally as the other. If this be true, or even half true, then "dear old Fitz," with his "innocent [life] . . .," concerning which he was apt to be so remorseful, has after all left his countrymen a legacy which they will prize when the Swinburnes and Morrises and Mrs. Brownings shall be remembered, if at all, like Waller and Marvell and Donne, by a few tuneful lines in old anthologies. Better were it for the fame of some such poets, would they but devote themselves, as FitzGerald did, to rescuing, for the benefit of English readers, the great masterpieces of the literatures from the clutches of dismal pedants, whose versions keep the word of promise to the letter and break it to the spirit. FitzGerald will have the reward he neither sought nor expected. (p. 164)

> Melville B. Anderson, "The Translator of Omar Khayyám," in The Dial, *Vol. X, No. 115, November, 1889, pp. 161-64.*

THE ATLANTIC MONTHLY   (essay date 1890)

[*In the following review of* Letters and Literary Remains of Edward FitzGerald, *the critic discusses FitzGerald's views of some of his contemporaries, praises the style of the letters, and assesses the importance of his translations.*]

Edward Fitzgerald gave a new classic to English literature in his translation of Omar Khayyám. His letters may prove to have, in their own sphere, an interest not less enduring. They comprise a lifelong correspondence upon matters which will continue to engage the minds of men, and these are treated from a unique personal point of view. Mr. Fitzgerald advanced but one claim to be considered by his friends. He was, he said, a man of taste, whether in poetry, art, or music; he brought to his subject the touch-stone of that criticism which depends rather on feeling than on reason; he did not care to ask the why and wherefore of his judgment, and in those cases in which he found himself dull to masterpieces approved by other highly cultivated minds he was merely nonplused at his incapacity to appreciate. He was, however, gifted with a rare degree of independence and also of candor, which permitted him to hold and express views of literature with admirable sincerity, so that he does not offend even when he departs most widely from popular opinions. He disparages Tennyson with the freedom of a friend, but other modern poetry meets with [scanty consideration]. . . . He cannot take to Hawthorne, though he acknowledges him to be the most distinct genius which America has produced. He has a very incomplete faith in Carlyle; with the best disposition to admire him and with some sympathy, he does not finally pass muster. His praise of Thackeray, though at the last ungrudging, strikes one as tardy. . . . So one might continue the long list. Perhaps it is as well to admit at once that he was a man of prejudice as well as of taste. The root of the matter is that he was out of sympathy with the modern age. It was not for nothing that he found his favorite reading in the classics and in Boccaccio, Cervantes, and Scott. He was not an idealist; imagination and passion were both lacking in him; he was attached to life as it presents itself to the eye,—the passing spectacle, with humor and pathos met at random, with no sentiment except of the natural feelings. He was a true lover of poetry, but there was quite enough in old English verse to satisfy him. So far as our own time is concerned, he represents

that discontent with the Victorian literature which is interesting because it is rare. . . . It is well enough known what liberties he took with his text. What his success was will be variously estimated. It cannot be maintained that his [translations entitled *Six Dramas of Calderon*] ever would hold its own as an English classic for its own sake, as undoubtedly his Omar must. The other Persian translations will be favorites with a few. The Greek plays, which he rendered in the same way, do not represent the originals either in kind or in power; and judged as English dramas, they are rather curious than excellent. It is singular to observe that his literary faculty concerned itself with poetical philosophy most successfully, while his critical taste declared itself for dramatic realism. (pp. 133-34)

A nature so simple and a fortune so uneventful do not require many phrases to describe them, but in the writer's expression of himself and description of his surroundings there is a rich variety. He had command of a remarkably pure style. From the literary point of view, the style is really the one quality in which [his] letters excel. Clear, rapid, and entirely without pretense, yet with a certain distinction in the utterance and sense of selection in the words, with an abundant natural flow and plenty of humor and even a dash of wit, the writer goes on to the end of his paper in a vein of which one never tires; and his matter is worthy of so ready a tongue. Whether it is some blowing breeze on the buttercups, or the blare of Handel's trumpets, or Constable laying the old Cremona down on the sunshiny grass, . . . there is always something on the various pages which one is glad to have read, and to have come in touch with so fine a mind in the reading; and not with him only, but also with Tennyson, who was almost from college days Mr. Fitzgerald's friend; with Thackeray, who valued him second to none in affectionate remembrance; and with Spedding, at whom these two aimed their good-humored fun, though they respected him none the less for that. Others, too, in more humble stations, add variety to the characters, and increase the human interest which enlivens and relieves the whole.

A more entertaining volume, one that brings the mind into contact with what refines and elevates it with the sense of the higher interests of culture, and at the same time affords companionship with a simple and strong nature in its daily life, has not been added to the shelves of pure literature in many a year. Indeed, it stands by itself, and possesses an originality, a flavor, and character of its own, which those who hereafter examine the Victorian time will not willingly spare. Mr. Fitzgerald himself occupies a peculiarly distinct position as the translator of Omar, which must continue to draw attention; as a member of the Tennyson group of literary friends, from whom delightful glimpses of their comradeship are to be obtained, he appeals to the never-dying curiosity of men in regard to the private life of genius; as a man who seems to have avoided notice by choice in an age when to get into the public view is the object of such universal effort, he stimulates the desire to know him. On these several accounts his memoir was sure to be sought; and now that, on its appearance, it exhibits such rare qualities that its greatest value proves to be intrinsic, we have reason to anticipate for its author the great prize of a slowly matured fame, like that of a half dozen other English gentlemen whose distinction in literature came without self-seeking. He wins, after death, a place in English letters equal to the good fortunes of his friendships in early life, among, if not beside, his old comrades; and, notwithstanding their neighborhood, his life will be valued for itself, as an expression of the old English virtues of "high thinking and plain living." (pp. 134-35)

"Edward FitzGerald," in The Atlantic Monthly, *Vol, LXV, No. CCCLXXXVII, January, 1890, pp. 133-35.*

ARTHUR PLATT   (lecture date 1896)

[In the following excerpt, originally delivered as a lecture in 1896, Platt praises FitzGerald for his accurate rendering of the spirit of Omar Khayyám's Rubáiyát. *He also praises FitzGerald's letters, saying "there are no other letters like them in English."]*

Persian scholars will tell one that FitzGerald palmed off a very inferior article on the English market [in his translation of Omar's *Rubáiyát*]; that he dressed up his Omar out of all recognition, making him appear taller than he really was. . . . And they are quite indignant about it, looking upon us admirers of Omar just as we look on the benighted inhabitants of Continental Europe who persist in admiring Lord Byron long after *we* have exploded him. But, for all that, it appears that Omar really did strike FitzGerald as the most interesting of the Persian poets. It was just because he felt a certain kinship with him that he was able to make such a success out of him. For FitzGerald wandered in the same valley of darkness himself. He, too, was naturally of a religious turn of mind; on his tomb are inscribed, by his own wish, the words: "It is He that has made us, and not we ourselves," and yet he, too, failed to find any world but this. In Omar he could find that same idea of resignation to that which "has made us and not we ourselves.". . . (pp. 29-30)

[His] is not a lofty or heroic strain, no doubt; many persons are sure always to be shocked by it, and to say that it is nothing but the despairing cry: "Let us eat and drink, for to-morrow we die." "I know you will thank me," writes FitzGerald to a friend, when sending him a copy, "and I think you will feel a sort of 'triste Plaisir' [sad pleasure] in it, as others besides myself have felt. It is a desperate sort of thing, unfortunately at the bottom of all thinking men's minds; but made music of." In those words he exhausts all criticism of his own poem. Never, surely, did any poet more justly weigh his own work in a single sentence.

But FitzGerald's way of making the best of this world was very different from the easy Epicurean philosophy which Omar professed, and which he appears to have, to some extent, practised. Assuredly Omar was no vulgar Epicurean himself . . . but, for all that, the burden of his song is simply:

> Drink!—for, once dead, you never shall return.

Strange, indeed, that such a doctrine should be popularised in England by the man whose motto was Plain Living and High Thinking. . . . (p. 31)

Now for a word on FitzGerald's principles of translation. The unhappy translator is always being impaled on the horns of a dilemma. If he translates literally, he produces stuff no mortal can read. "I am sure," says FitzGerald elsewhere of another poem. "I am sure a complete translation, even in prose, would not have been a *readable* one, which, after all, is a useful property of most books, *even of poetry*." If, on the other hand, he makes a good and readable thing of it, then arise all the people who know the original, and begin to peck at it like domestic fowl. If one steers a middle course, one pleases nobody. FitzGerald boldly adopted the principle that what is wanted in a translation is *this*: To give people who don't know the original a sort of idea of the effect it produces on people who do. For this end we must throw all attempt at a *literal* translation to the wind. We must soak ourselves in the spirit of an author,

and reproduce that spirit in as good poetic style as we may be master of. So, not only with Omar, but with his other translations too, he omits whole passages, puts in bits of his own, modifies and arranges everything, and makes—a poem. (p. 32)

[Let] us thank the gods that we know no Persian, and try to estimate the position of this Omar purely as *English* literature. I always think of Gray's *Elegy* in connexion with it. (p. 35)

On a close comparison [between FitzGerald and Gray], I think—I am afraid—the palm must be yielded to Gray. His *Elegy* is better arranged as a whole—naturally, when one thinks how the other was pieced together out of the chaotic heap of the original Omar. And taking stanza for stanza, line for line, there are better stanzas and better lines in Gray. He has not the same natural easy flow as FitzGerald, whether melancholy or humorous or whimsical, but he has more weight and dignity and power. He took himself more seriously. Modesty is a good thing, or so they say who understand about it, but FitzGerald was perhaps *too* modest; if he had been more ambitious he might have taken even more pains than he did, and insisted deliberately on making a treasure for ever, as Gray did. Yet, perhaps he would have spoilt it, so we had better be content. Then, too, when we compare the two, we must allow for the lapse of time. Time has laid a decaying finger here and there upon Gray. There are bits of the *Elegy* which are written in the poetic slang of the day. . . . And how do we know how much poetic slang of the *nineteenth* century there may not be in FitzGerald? At any rate, as Omar has it, "One thing is certain, and the rest is Lies"—the Persian allusions in FitzGerald are a nuisance. (p. 36)

[The work of FitzGerald's which seems] to live best after Omar is the *Letters*—one series to different friends and another to Fanny Kemble. Which of the two is the more delightful I do not know; but I think there are no other letters like them in English. Pieces of delightful literary criticism—often fearfully unorthodox; but what a joy it is to meet a man who says what he thinks, and does not feel bound to admire what he doesn't admire. (p. 40)

But I hear two objections taken to the Letters—they are too feminine, and the Capital Letters are used in a chaotic way at the beginning of words. Well, the Capitals can be left alone. He always had a Fancy for Them; but, as to the other charge, is it not just that feminine quality which gives the Letters their charm? In a general of division or an anatomist or a New Woman to be feminine may be a mistake; but here what have we to do with that? One does not want a man to write letters in the spirit in which he would lead a charge of cavalry! It is just that feminine quality in his nature which makes the man himself and his letters so lovable. "One loves Virgil somehow," he says, after quoting him in one of them, and is it not just the same with Virgil, whom the Neapolitans nicknamed the Maid? It is that gentle melancholy temperament which gives its charm to the verse of both. The letters of Horace Walpole may be infinitely more brilliant and sparkling, they may have more amusing stories in them, but one does not love Walpole—not a bit. (p. 41)

Arthur Platt, "Edward FitzGerald," in his Nine Essays, *Cambridge at the University Press, 1927, pp. 23-42.*

JOHN HAY   (lecture date 1897)

[The following excerpt was taken from a lecture delivered to the Omar Khayyám Club in December, 1897. The club, formed after

FitzGerald's translation of the Rubaiyat *appeared, was primarily a social organization which boasted such literary figures as A. C. Swinburne and Edmund Gosse as members.*]

I can never forget my emotions when I first saw Fitz-Gerald's translation of the Quatrains. (pp. 176-77)

The exquisite beauty, the faultless, the singular grace of those amazing stanzas, were not more wonderful than the depth and breadth of their profound philosophy, their knowledge of life, their dauntless courage, their serene facing of the ultimate problems of life and of death. Of course the doubt arose, which has assailed many as ignorant as I was of the literature of the East, whether it was the poet or his translator to whom was due this splendid result. Could it be possible that in the Eleventh Century, so far away as Khorassan, so accomplished a man of letters lived, with such distinction, such breadth, such insight, such calm disillusion, such cheerful and jocund despair? My doubt lasted only till I came upon a literal translation of the "Rubáiyát," and I saw that not the least remarkable quality of Fitz-Gerald's poem was its fidelity to the original. In short, Omar was an earlier Fitz-Gerald, or Fitz-Gerald was a re-incarnation of Omar.

It is not to the disadvantage of the later poet that he followed so closely in the footsteps of the earlier. A man of extraordinary genius had appeared in the world, had sung a song of incomparable beauty and power in an environment no longer worthy of him, in a language of a narrow range; for many generations the song was virtually lost; then by a miracle of creation, a poet, a twin brother in spirit to the first, was born, who took up the forgotten poem and sang it anew with all its original melody and force, and all the accumulated refinement of ages of art. It seems to me idle to ask which was the greater master, each seemed greater than his work. Omar sung to a half barbarous province; Fitz-Gerald to the world. Wherever English is spoken or read, the **"Rubáiyát"** have taken their place as a classic.

Certainly our poet can never be numbered among the great popular writers of all time. He has told no story. He has never unpacked his heart in public, he has never thrown the reins on the neck of the winged horse, and let his imagination carry him where it listed. But he will hold a place for ever among that limited number, who, like Lucretius and Epicurus, without rage or defiance, even without unbecoming mirth, look deep into the tangled mysteries of things, refuse credence to the absurd and allegiance to arrogant authority, sufficiently conscious of fallibility to be tolerant of all opinions, with a faith too wide for doctrine and a benevolence untramelled by creed, too wise to be wholly poets, and yet too surely poets to be implacably wise. (pp. 177-80)

> *John Hay, in an extract from a lecture delivered at the Omar Khayyám Club in December, 1897, in* The Life of Edward Fitz-Gerald *by John Glyde, C. Arthur Pearson, Ltd., 1900, pp. 176-80.*

HOLBROOK JACKSON (essay date 1899)

One approaches FitzGerald's translation of Omar Khayyám as one would Carey's "Dante" or Chapman's "Homer," with that degree of reverence due to the classical, and I use this word in its broadest and best sense, not meaning that which is merely approved of pedants or any conventional recognition, but as Sainte-Beuve has finally put it, that which "has enriched the human mind, increased its treasure and caused it to advance a step."

The art of translation is not facsimile reproduction, that is impossible. To convey the sense expressed in one language into another may be accomplished, but to translate the method of expression is quite another matter and by the very nature of things impossible. . . . The question as to how far FitzGerald has succeeded in rendering the ideas of his subject, is difficult of solution to one who is unacquainted with the original language, but . . . I have come to the conclusion that not only does FitzGerald convey Omar's ideas identically, but with excellent taste and consummate art he has succeeded in condensing the sense contained in upwards of five-hundred unarranged quatrains into an exquisite sequence of little over one hundred. . . . [No] translation conveys more of the philosophy of Omar, with the exception that FitzGerald lays less emphasis on the amorous side of Omar's character than is evidently the case, and in no other translation is such poetic beauty made manifest as in that which entitles the earliest to the first place. (pp. 17-19)

Other translators may come, but it is more than probable that the *Rubáiyát* of Omar Khayyám rendered into English verse by Edward FitzGerald will ever be the sun around which all others will revolve, lesser planets, drawing their light from him, yet paled by his greater rays. Some things are done as if by magic, with finality stamped upon them at birth. The first quatrain in FitzGerald's version is an example:—

> Awake! for morning in the bowl of night
> Has flung the stone that puts the stars to flight:
> 　　And lo! the hunter of the East has caught
> The Sultan's turret in a noose of light.

And for quaintness and apt turning of a vagrant phase the following is a good example:—

> Into this universe, and why not knowing,
> Nor whence, like water willy-nilly flowing:
> 　　And out of it like Wind along the Waste,
> I know not whither, willy-nilly blowing.

This is that combination of music and poetry which defies Time. (p. 21)

> *Holbrook Jackson, in his* Edward FitzGerald and Omar Khayyám: An Essay and a Bibliography, *1899. Reprint by Folcroft Library Editions, 1974, 41 p.*

THE ACADEMY (essay date 1900)

To some FitzGerald without Omar may seem like "Hamlet" without the Prince, but that is a ludicrous misconception impossible to anyone who knows FitzGerald's Letters. We firmly believe that these Letters [in the *Letters of Edward FitzGerald*] have been overshadowed by the *Rubáiyat,* and are by no means so widely read and loved as they would be if their claims had not been thus obscured. They are among the best in their world, and one might make all sorts of comparisons between them and the letters of Byron, Cowper, Lamb, and the rest—from which they would emerge wearing still their own peculiar charm. They are, perhaps, the most natural letters in the language. They are packed with matter, yet are perfectly easy, almost lazy, in their movement. . . . Books are the theme of FitzGerald's Letters. He digresses to pictures, to boats, and to village lore, but the principal events in his life are the opening of new books or old ones. His Letters are an inspiring record of quiet, thorough, personal, unpretentious reading, such as, one fancies, is scarce enough nowadays. Whatever Fitz-Gerald's achievements as a writer may be, they are not more

An early depiction of Salámán and Absál as they reach an island refuge. Courtesy of the Freer Gallery of Art, Smithsonian Institution, Washington, D.C.

valuable than the example of his wise reading. Ever ready to laugh at the "mob" of writers, FitzGerald found that word entirely to his taste when he discussed reading. . . . It was in this spirit of freedom and self-choosing that FitzGerald read his books and rapped out his little judgments. His Letters are an education in personal enjoyment of books. He is not unconscious nor un-proud of this freedom. (p.75)

> *"FitzGerald sans Omar," in* The Academy, *Vol. LIX, No. 1473, July 28, 1900, pp. 75-6.*

THE ACADEMY (essay date 1901)

[*In the following review of* More Letters of Edward FitzGerald, *the critic finds FitzGerald's letters, in contrast to the letters of most writers, unique in their appeal as everyday correspondence. According to the critic, "FitzGerald's letters are the most comfortable reading in the world."*]

[All] FitzGerald's Letters are of the friendly human kind, and we may say at once that the Letters in [*More Letters of Edward FitzGerald*] seem to us to be exactly like those already published, and that we are well content that they should be so. . . . The important thing to note is that these Letters have an intercalary relation to those in the two volumes of *Letters* [*of*

Edward FitzGerald] and the volume of *Letters to Fanny Kemble.* They will be read by careful readers in connection with these. They are of the same progressive dates, they have the same topics and complexion; in a word they merge with the earlier *Letters* as wine from the same decanter.

What is the peculiar charm of FitzGerald's Letters? We should say it is their essential normality. They are, in intention and in scope, such *Letters* as the ordinary well-read man wishes to write, could in a measure write, but does not write. They are his own written or would-be written Letters raised to the nth power. They transcend on the same plane. Hence they have a charm which is not one of the charms of Lamb's Letters—as why should it be? Lamb's Letters are, if you please, the finest in the language—though of all forms of literature Letters are least amenable to the "mark" system of merit—but Lamb's Letters are essentially Lamb's, and not yours transfigured. His elaborate humorous poses, his mystifications, his plots, surprises, premeditated fun, and his bursts of familiar eloquence are removed from everyday correspondence. The finest letters in the language, if you please, but not the nighest to your letter-writing self. Similarly, Byron's Letters are essentially Byron's, the rushing wind of his opinions that rather invigorates than detains. In both Lamb and Byron there is a further removal from the norm to be noted. Both of them fall into strains in which the epistolary character is rather lost. . . . In FitzGerald you never lose the epistolary feeling. As letters, and only as letters, these pages appeal to you. Involuntarily you visualise the hand-writing, hear the paper crinkle, and are conscious of the envelope and the stamp. You approach each letter with the little thrill which an unopened letter communicates. You read it once, twice, and find nooks of interest in it to explore again; it is all easy, interesting, and touched with mind; you put it into your breast pocket. FitzGerald's letters are the most comfortable reading in the world. We can never read them without laughing at the idea that his was an incomplete or half-lived life. To have written these Letters, that so surely warm and entertain; that survey the world of culture, yet domesticate you in a Suffolk countryside; that bring the idea of leisure and ripening predilections before eyes tired with the changes and unprofitable eagerness of life at the centre;—to have written these Letters was, we say, a great unconscious achievement. . . .

[No] new note is struck in the volume. The same delightful air of "puddling among books and pictures," the same burly inexactness, the same purpose within vagary, and care within carelessness, are present in every page. The man's honest blunderings and easy contentments are a perpetual joy. He buys a mop for his kitchen, and, liking the colour of its head, keeps it in his study as a decoration. He buys and cleans pictures, but never seems to hang them: "the Truth is, they look so much better on the Floor." . . . These potterings at Woodbridge or elsewhere are endlessly amusing in a man who in the next sentence is going to say a fine thing about a new book, or on a question of style, or on life's difficulties. And through all the interests of to-day—the doings of Tennyson and Browning, Carlyle and Thackeray, the clash of reviews, the box from Mudie's, the fragments of art and scholarship—you hear the North Sea blowing on shore, or the chimes of Woodbridge Church playing "Where and oh where is my Soldier Laddie gone?" every three hours. . . .

With all his seclusion and delightful incapacities, FitzGerald had in him a curious strain of the editor. Not the editor of daily contacts and weekly or monthly task-work, but the editor who, giving his thoughts the benefit of leisured rumination, sees what this man can best do, or in what mistaken direction he is being drawn, and seeks to set him right and extract his best. . . . One could pick many a passage in which he appears as an inspirer or jealous guardian of excellence. (p. 583)

So he rambles on from the thirties to the eighties of last century, ever putting aside what could not serve him, ever cherishing what could, and storing unsuspected honey for us all. How acceptable, how uncloying, is this repast!—nothing fiery, nothing toilsome—but the best and cleanest of each day, and then: "Now for a Pipe in my Garden—to think over all these little things." (p. 584)

> *"Thrice Welcome," in* The Academy, *Vol. LXI, No. 1545, December 14, 1901, pp. 583-84.*

W. F. PRIDEAUX (essay date 1901)

[*In the following excerpt from a letter to the editor of the* Academy, *Prideaux responds to the author of a review of Fitzgerald's letters (see excerpt above, 1901).*]

You justly say that all FitzGerald's Letters are of the friendly human kind, and I do not think that . . . [the critic], in making this qualification, meant to imply that the former series was of a different brand from those contained in the new volume. But the "note" of FitzGerald is that, while not abstaining from criticism in a candid-friendly way, he is intensely human in his treatment of his old associates, thus differing from the candid-friendly inhuman kind, which, Iago-wise, puts on the trappings of affection in order to stab its friends more surely in the back. FitzGerald kept his causticity—and he could be caustic at times—for those he didn't love. (p. 619)

> *W. F. Prideaux, "'More Letters of Edward Fitz-Gerald'," in* The Academy, *Vol. LXI, No. 1546, December 21, 1901, pp. 619-20.*

EDMUND GOSSE (essay date 1902)

[*In the following introduction to a 1902 edition of FitzGerald's complete works, Gosse defends FitzGerald's method of translation. For additional commentary by Gosse, see excerpt above, 1889.*]

What FitzGerald could do in prose we know from his correspondence and from **"Euphranor."** It has stately passages, and the final page no doubt deserves the high commendation of Tennyson; it possessed to the Cambridge men the charm of recalling with delicate local colour the dialectics of their youth, but when all is said and done it remains a little lifeless and unrealized, a little uninteresting, to tell the blunt truth. In its form and setting, it seems to follow the "Alciphron" of Berkeley, but at how great a distance! To turn from **"Euphranor"** to the **"Letters"** is to prepare to assert FitzGerald's real claim as a prose writer. In these unaffected documents he lays bare his innocent and beautiful temperament. His command over the quieter forms of language, over all the homely stops of the instrument, is here so complete that without the least strain or effort, without raising his voice, all is said as he alone would say it, with an incomparable rustic felicity. What phrases he has, in his unaffected and confidential utterances to his friends! "I remember you did not desire to hear about my garden, which is now gorgeous with large red poppies, and lilac irises—satisfactory colouring; and the trees murmur a continual soft chorus to the solo which my soul discourses within." In casual

passages, like this, in the **"Letters"** we have the whole FitzGerald nature suddenly revealed to us as though his body robed itself, as he wrote, with a mild irradiating lustre.

Of the translations, there is this to be said: they must never be read without regard to the poet's peculiar and perhaps unique conception of the translator's duty, but which no one less inspired with tact and delicacy should ever dare to imitate. When he undertook to "translate" a Persian poem, for instance, he made a more or less free paraphrase of such parts as he thought charming, and then he ingeniously tesselated the fragments into whatever he desired to produce, perhaps "a sort of Epicurean Eclogue in a Persian Garden." He did not believe—and he was certainly right—that an exact translation of any poem can continue to be a poem in the new language. He thought that all the fragrance faded from it in the transit, as from a violet sent by post. So he was ready with great courage to omit from Calderon, for instance, all that was surprising or shocking, anything which, by its want of intelligibility, might "check the current of sympathy" in English readers. To carry out his theory, he stuck at nothing; he would reduce, alter and expand, omit whole scenes and supply such omissions by passages of his own.

The result of all this was that to people mainly interested in a precise study of the original text, or even to people uninterested in FitzGerald himself, his translations have always been unsatisfactory, and even annoying. We see an instance of this in the absurd multiplication of versions of Omar Khayyám, produced by worthy persons who are mystified by the overwhelming popularity of the **"Rubáiyát"** and cannot get it into their heads that it is not in the least Omar Khayyám, but FitzGerald, in whom lovers of poetry are interested. These excellent translators cry aloud to the public, "We bring you much closer and more trustworthy renderings of your favourite Omar, and yet you obstinately return to the vague, inexact and garbled quatrains of FitzGerald." Precisely, and so the world of taste will always continue to return, because for Omar Khayyám the historical and the veraciously-interpreted, none of us care sixpence; it is FitzGerald who clothed these dry old bones with poetry. And what is true of Omar Khayyám is in some modified measure true of all the works on which FitzGerald laid his curious hand in paraphrase. The versions he offers us must never be compared with the original, or treated as translations at all. They should be judged on their own merits as poems, always—of course—bearing in mind the highly-important restriction that it is only the diction in them which is FitzGerald's. And this brings us, perhaps, to our final point, that it is in his faultless delicacy of diction, his Sophoclean appropriateness of phrase, that FitzGerald lives preëminently among the poets. No writer has defended more strenuously in his phraseology the axiom that Beauty is the main object of the arts. (pp. xxv-xxviii)

> *Edmund Gosse, in an introduction to* The Variorum and Definitive Edition of the Poetical and Prose Writings of Edward Fitzgerald, Vol. I *by Edward Fitzgerald, edited by George Bentham, Doubleday, Page and Company, 1902, pp. ix-xxviii.*

[FRANCIS THOMPSON] (essay date 1903)

[*Thompson, an English poet, critic, essayist, and biographer, is considered one of the most important poets of the Catholic Revival in nineteenth-century England. In the following brief assessment of FitzGerald's translations of* Six Dramas of Calderon, *Thompson praises the author for his ability to make the Spanish dramas into "breathing English plays."*]

It can scarce be accident, indeed, that FitzGerald's selection [of plays in *Six Dramas of Calderon*] hardly at all displays the famed poetical quality of Calderon's drama. Manifestly (we think) he desired to commend the great Spaniard's fitness for the English stage; and therefore he chose pieces with the maximum of stage-quality, the minimum of that poetry which the modern theatre hates as the gates of Hades. This preoccupation with acting-possibilities is shown in more than one note. It is a pity, because his selection gives no complete suggestion of Calderon, does not even (from a literary standpoint) present the Spaniard at his highest. . . .

But we must take Calderon as FitzGerald has chosen to give him us, and be glad to get him. FitzGerald's Omar was more FitzGerald than Omar; and in a less degree, his Calderon suffers a FitzGeraldine change. If the Omar was FitzGerald-Omar, the Calderon is Calderon-FitzGerald. It was part of FitzGerald's strong personality to impose it on the authors he translated; and precisely from this process springs the vitality of his translations. . . . FitzGerald's Calderon is less changed from the original than his Omar. It is also less miraculous. But not because of the less freedom; rather because he had to do with a far greater master, on whom he could work no artistic improvement. He attempts such improvement—it was in the man; but it is countervailed by the inevitable loss of translation from a great genius. He attempts too much improvement, takes too much liberty; as when a Frenchman docks Shakespeare of all which—justly or unjustly—rasps a Gallic taste. Yet, with all that may rightly be brought against it, the translation remains a work of genius, vital as scrupulously respectful versions of Calderon are not vital. These are breathing English plays— and to compass that is a feat. (p. 536)

[*Francis Thompson*], *"FitzGerald and Calderon," in* The Academy and Literature, *Vol. LXIV, No. 1621, May 30, 1903, pp. 536-37.*

THE ACADEMY (essay date 1905)

No one can regard Edward FitzGerald as anything but an amateur, however brilliant, and yet after a lapse of more than fifty years we have a reprint of his remarkable tractate on education [*Euphranor: a Dialogue on Youth*], which, as far as the spirit of it is concerned, might well have issued from the press but yesterday. There is hardly a doctrine that seems out of date; time has but mellowed some of the ideas which, if neither harsh nor crude, may well have seemed a little startling to the shallow and incurable optimists of the early 'fifties. The work itself is an ideal sketch of the education of the "classes dirigeantes" in England, the benefits of which FitzGerald would be glad to extend to the lower orders. . . . For [FitzGerald] as for Aristotle, whom he quotes, youth is the real, the inexhaustible fountain of the heroic spirit. It says much for the rare quality of his thought that the long extract he gives from the Greek philosopher, instead of staring at us like a gaudy patch on a background of shoddy and fustian, serves as an attractive border to the bright fabric of his own fancies. . . . We have here in brief a sort of English "Émile." If it lacks the stupendous paradoxes of Rousseau, it largely makes up for them by its never failing flow of common sense. FitzGerald is in this respect a lineal descendant of Locke. (p. 1330)

Many will read this charming reprint of a forgotten book not for its educational, but for its literary charm, for in it FitzGerald proved himself a master of the two crafts. The old-world picture of the cultured undergraduate of the 'fifties, the Verdant Green with a serious turn, the delightful conventional setting of the story, a May day after Chaucer's own heart, the high literary excellence and naturalness of the dialogue, and, last but not least, the final scene with its description of the boat-race, which Tennyson much admired, and its haunting close about the nightingale singing "among the flowering chestnuts of Jesus" are but a few of the attractions that must render the book fascinating to every lover of English prose. [The editor] has done a great service in restoring the lost treasure trove to its rightful place in the thesaurus of national masterpieces. (p. 1331)

"De Juventute," in The Academy, *Vol. LXIX, No. 1755, December 23, 1905, pp. 1330-31.*

A. C. BENSON (essay date 1905)

[*Benson was an English essayist, poet, and scholar of the late nineteenth and early twentieth centuries. In the following survey, taken from his book-length study of FitzGerald, Benson contends that the author translated the works of others rather than composing his own because he had little imaginative power. While Benson considers most of FitzGerald's work "second-rate, the product of a gifted and accomplished amateur," he does praise the* Rubáiyát *and the letters.*]

FitzGerald's mind was deficient in the imaginative quality. He had a strong spectatorial interest in life, a kind of dark yet tender philosophy, which gave him his one great opportunity: but even there he had, like Teucer, to shoot his arrows behind the shield of Ajax. He had, of course, an extraordinary delicacy of perception; but on the critical side. His strength lay in his power of expressing, with a sort of careful artlessness, elusive thoughts, rather than in strength or subtlety of invention. His timid, fastidious imagination shrank from the strain of constructing, originating, creating. The *Euphranor* . . . is the only experiment that he made in the direction of fiction, and there is no dramatic grasp in it, no firm delineation of character; one feels that he is moving puppets to and fro, and the voice of the showman is speaking all the time. He had, too, a certain feminine irritability, a peevish fastidiousness which would have dogged his steps if he had embarked upon a larger subject; he would never have been satisfied with his work; he would have fretted over it, and abandoned it in despair.

He was deficient, too, in the patience requisite for carrying work through. "To correct is *the* Bore," he wrote to Cowell. Yet the bulky volumes of extracts and selections and abridgements . . . testify to a certain laboriousness, an acquisitiveness, a species of diligence which cannot be gainsaid. One may wonder, too, that so desultory a student contrived to translate so much as FitzGerald did; but his mind was in a sense active; he could not be unoccupied, and yet had not the vigour necessary for original work. To such a man it is a comfort to have work which demands no expenditure of vital force, which may be taken up and laid down at will, and where the original supplies the literary impulse.

But what is perhaps at the root of the matter is that FitzGerald always subordinated Art to Life. He had little of the fierce, imperative, creative impulse. Art seemed to him not a thing apart, but an accessory of life; and therefore a single touch of nature was to FitzGerald a higher thing than the highest achievement of art.

Thus he had a great tenderness for worthless little books, if they only revealed some gentle and delicate trait of character,

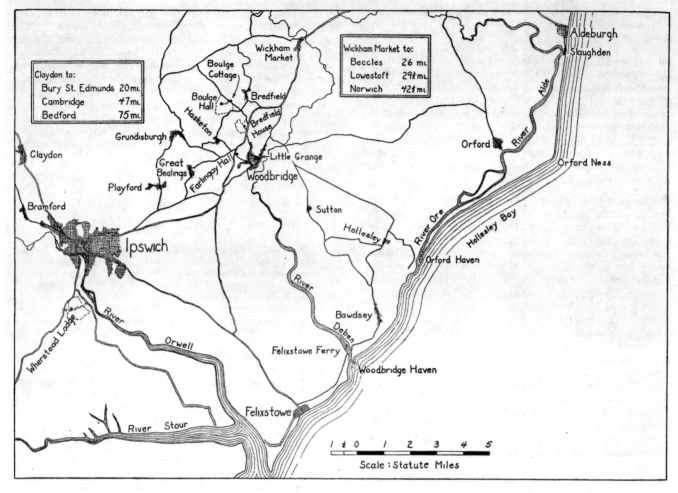

A map of FitzGerald's Suffolk.

some small piece of wistful individuality. A great conception, a broad and vigorous motive, often bewildered and stupefied him. His idea of the paradise of art was as of a place where you could wander quietly about picking a flower here and there, catching a little effect, watching a pretty grouping of trees and water, the sunlight on a grassy bank or a gable-end. He lived and thought in a series of glimpses and vistas, but the plan of the place, its avenues and terraces, was unregarded by him. And thus there was a want of centrality, of combination, of breadth, about his mind. Art was to him not an impassioned quest, but a leisurely wandering in search of charm, of colour, of subtle impressions. (pp. 86-8)

Salámán and Absál is an allegory over which FitzGerald spent much time and care; it is idle to speculate why, when the work is compared with *Omar,* the achievement appears to be so slight. Yet so it is. The truth is, I conceive, that FitzGerald put so little of himself into the poem, but was content to ride, as it were, in Jámí's chariot. (p. 89)

There is a certain Oriental splendour about this [translation]; but it is loosely put together, and there are obvious faults both of metre and language.

The whole translation, it must be confessed, is a languid performance. The figure of FitzGerald seems to move and pace as it were uneasily, embarrassed and encumbered by the rich and pictorial draperies. One feels that he was following the original too closely, and had not the courage boldly to discard the Eastern imagery, as he did in *Omar,* where he selected enough to give his version an Oriental colouring while he escaped from the weight of the unfamiliar and over-loaded texture. (pp. 93-4)

The *Salámán and Absál* is indeed interesting only in the light of *Omar,* as revealing the process whereby rich results were attained, though it is hard to repress a sense of wonder that the uncertain hand which penned the *Salámán* can have worked in the same material with such firm and easy strokes as were employed in the *Omar.* (p. 94)

[In his translation of *The Rubáiyát of Omar Khayyám,* Fitz-Gerald] was enabled to chase and chisel his delicate stanzas, like little dainty vessels of pure gold. He brought to the task a rich and stately vocabulary, and a style adapted to solemn and somewhat rhetorical musings of a philosophical kind. FitzGerald's love of slow-moving verse adorned by beautiful touches of natural observation and of pathetic presentment stood him in good stead. The result was that a man of high literary taste found for once a subject precisely adapted to his best faculty; a subject, the strength of which was his own strength, and the limitations of which were his own limitations.

Moreover, the poem was fortunate both in the time and manner of its appearance; there was a wave of pessimism astir in the world, the pessimism of an age that dares not live without pleasure, in whose mouth simplicity is a synonym for dulness. . . . (p. 96)

Further, it was fortunate in the manner of its appearance. If FitzGerald had presented the world with an original poem of dreary scepticism and desperate philosophy, he would have found but few hearers. But the sad and wasted form of his philosophy came slowly forwards, dimly smiling, draped in this rich Oriental fabric, and with all the added mystery of venerable antiquity. It heightened the charm to readers, living in a season of outworn faith and restless dissatisfaction, to find that eight hundred years before, far across the centuries, in the dim and remote East, the same problems had pressed sadly on the mind of an ancient and accomplished sage. They did not realise to what an extent FitzGerald had concentrated the scattered rays into his burning-glass; nor how much of the poignant sadness, the rich beauty of the thought had been overlaid upon the barer texture of the original writer by the far more sensitive and perceptive mind of the translator. It was as though FitzGerald had found some strict and solemn melody of a bygone age, and enriched it with new and honeyed harmonies, added melancholy cadences and sweet interludes of sorrow. (p. 97)

There is little that need be said, little indeed that can be said, about the style which FitzGerald adopted for his *Omar.* It is not due to any special poetical tradition; the poem is written in a grave, resonant English of a stately kind, often with a certain Latinity of phrase, and yet never really avoiding a homely directness both of diction and statement. His aim appears to have been to produce melodious, lucid, and epigrammatic stanzas, which should as far as possible follow the general lines of the original thought; but at the same time he did not hesitate to discard and suppress anything that interfered with his own conception of structure; no doubt the exigencies of rhyme to a certain extent influenced the line of his thought, because the triple rhyme which he employed is bound to impose fetters on the fancy; but he seems to have given no hint as to how he worked; the wonder rather is that anything which is of the nature of a paraphrase should succeed in achieving so profound an originality. (pp. 97-8)

[In his translations of the Greek dramas *Agamemnon* and *Oedipus*] FitzGerald gives but little idea of the original. Half the charm, so to speak, of these ancient human documents is their authenticity. Not only the archaic form, the statuesque conventionality of the Greek stage, the traditions of a once-living art, are sacrificed; but, what is more important still, the very spirit of Greek Tragedy, the unshrinking gaze into the darkest horrors of life, the dreadful insistence of Fate, forcing men to tread unwillingly in rough and stony paths—these are thrown aside. And thus the force, the grim tension, which are of the essence of Greek tragedy are replaced by a species of gentle dignity, which leaves the stiffness of movement without the compensating strength, and the austere frigidity without the antique spirit. A kind of flowing and even Shakespearian diction takes the place of the gorgeousness of the original, but without any of the modern flexibility of handling.

It seems that there are two possibilities open to the translator: the first, to make a literal and dignified version. . . . Or else, to produce a frankly modern play, just following the lines of the ancient drama, and endeavouring to represent movement and emotion rather than language. FitzGerald has fallen between these two possibilities. The plays are frigid but not archaic; timid where the ancient plays were bold; gentlemanly where the originals were noble. They are as like Greek plays

as the Eglinton Tournament was like a mediaeval Joust; a revival in which the spirit, the only thing which justified and enlivened the ancient sport, has somehow evaporated.

In the version of the *OEdipus,* FitzGerald allows himself great licence, but in the *Agamemnon* his method is still more luxuriant. For instance, when the Herald from the host describes the miseries of the life of the camp, he says:—

> Not the mere course and casualty of war,
> Alarum March, Battle, and such hard knocks
> As foe with foe expects to give and take;
> But all the complement of miseries
> That go to swell a long campaign's account,
> Cramm'd close aboard the ships, hard bed, hard board:
> Or worse perhaps while foraging ashore
> In winter time; when, if not from the walls,
> Pelted from Heav'n by Day, to couch by Night
> Between the falling dews and rising damps
> That elf'd the locks, and set the body fast
> With cramp and ague; or, to mend the matter
> Good mother Ida from her winter top
> Flinging us down a coverlet of snow.
> Or worst perhaps in Summer, toiling in
> The bloody harvest-field of torrid sand,
> When not an air stirr'd the fierce Asian noon
> And even the sea sleep-sicken'd in his bed.

There is no doubt that this is a fine passage. But what is the source of it?—

> For if I were to tell of the toils and the hard quarters, the narrow ill-strewn berths—nay, what day-long privation too did we not have to bewail? and then again on land—where danger was ever at hand, for we couched close by the walls—from heaven and earth alike the meadow dews down-drizzling crept, the constant rotting of our raiment, breeding evil vermin in our very hair; and if one were to tell of the winter that slew the birds themselves, the intolerable cold that the snows of Ida brought, or the heat, when the unstirred ocean fell and slept in his windless bed.

Perhaps it is ill to quarrel with a method deliberately adopted; but it will be seen that it ends in a mere wrapping up of the ancient simplicities in an embroidered modern robe; one who studies FitzGerald's *Agamemnon* may do so for its own sake, but he must not think that he is getting near either to the spirit or the form of the original. (pp. 119-21)

This is still more noticeable in the lyrical translations of the choruses of the *Agamemnon,* in which FitzGerald seems to be hobbling in fetters, dealing with ideas and words that have no native existence in our own language except as pedantic attempts to represent in an English form thoughts which have no real counterpart in English thought. This terrible jargon, well-known to schoolmasters, this attempt to transvocalise, so to speak, Greek expressions, and to squeeze the juice out of the ancient language, strikes dreariness into the mind. Such a passage as the following from one of the grandest choruses will suffice to illustrate my meaning:—

> But now to be resolved, whether indeed
>   Those fires of Night spoke truly, or mistold
>   To cheat a doating woman; for behold
> Advancing from the shore with solemn speed,

A Herald from the Fleet, his footsteps roll'd
In dust, Haste's thirsty consort, but his brow
Check-shadow'd with the nodding Olive-bough;
    Who shall interpret us the speechless sign
    Of the fork'd tongue that preys upon the pine?

Who indeed? This passage is like a turbid stream in flood. It is muddy with Greek, it bears Greek particles, like river-wrack, floating on its surface. But it is neither Greek nor English. It can give no sense of pleasure to an English reader; and to any one who can appreciate the original, it only brings a dim sense of pain.

The two versions of the *OEdipus* are even less satisfactory than the *Agamemnon;* for there the serene and even flow of Sophocles' diction is converted into what it is difficult to distinguish from dulness. And here indeed FitzGerald has taken a licence which it is hard to condone; for he has transplanted entire into his pages the translation of the choruses by [the eighteenth-century translator] Robert Potter . . . , in a mellifluous classical verse, of the school of Gray. . . . And he has gone further still by practically omitting two of the principal characters in the two plays, Creon almost entirely in the first and Ismene entirely in the second, for no better reason than that the intrusion of characters whom he has the misfortune to dislike had appeared to him to be inartistic. And this is, I think, a really serious blot; because it is the very dissimilarity of the Greek point of view to our own, the different artistic standard, that contribute to give these plays their bewildering value. The whole essence of the culture which depends upon familiarising oneself with the best products of the human spirit, is that one should try to put oneself in line with the old. To admire a Greek play for the modernity which may be found in it, is, I believe, to misapprehend the situation altogether. (pp. 122-23)

The play in FitzGerald's hands simply ceases to represent the original.

With regard to the Calderon plays we are on very much the same ground. Calderon was essentially a lyrical poet, and without being ungenerous to his art it may be doubted whether, with all his mastery of ingenious stage-craft, he was really altogether at home in dramatic form.

However indulgently one may try to judge FitzGerald's versions of Calderon, they cannot be reckoned among his literary successes. It is probable that FitzGerald did not really understand Calderon, and it is not unfair to say that we have here a marked instance of FitzGerald's friendships biassing his studies. (p. 124)

FitzGerald can hardly have cared instinctively for the Spanish dramatist, for it is impossible to conceive two temperaments that were more radically unlike. . . . Calderon was conventional, magnificent, worldly-minded, with a background of mysticism. FitzGerald hated conventionality in every form, clung to the simple and retired life, feared and hated the din of the great glittering world. Again, where Calderon was mystical, FitzGerald was agnostic. It is surely significant that in the 1853 volume, containing versions of six of Calderon's plays, FitzGerald admits that, with the exception of *The Mayor of Zalamea* (which is in reality a play of Lope's recast), none of Calderon's masterpieces are attempted. A man who could begin with the inferior works of the author he was translating could not have been greatly in earnest about his task. He did afterwards attempt two of the undoubted masterpieces, *The Mighty Magician* and *Beware of Smooth Water;* but these were an afterthought.

Again, it must be borne in mind that Calderon was a very artificial writer, and belonged to an extremely definite school. He abounds in preciosities and what may be called affectations both of manner and of thought. In the first place he is what would be called in English "Euphuistic"; his style is full of audacities and conceits, and of subtle refinements of thought. These are far from being the best part of Calderon; but the texture of his writings is so impregnated by them that they may be held to be absolutely essential to his style. FitzGerald omits and compresses, with the result that the airy grace and the fine elegance disappear; some of the poetry remains, but it is transposed into a different key; it is as when a bass sings a rearranged air intended for a tenor; it is quiet and homely instead of lustrous and brilliant. The result is that no one could really gain any idea of the characteristic manner of Calderon from FitzGerald's version.

FitzGerald thus makes no pretence about the matter; he says frankly that he omitted these things because he did not care for them. But when we remember that Calderon cared for them, and that the whole Spanish nation cared for them, and that they represent an unbroken literary tradition of two centuries and a half, the confession is tantamount to saying that FitzGerald did not really care for Calderon. It remains then that by getting rid of what he called bombast, and recklessly throwing overboard unfamiliar idioms, FitzGerald is really shirking his most formidable difficulties. (pp. 125-26)

It may be noted that FitzGerald's knowledge of Spanish was very limited. . . . [It] is clear that FitzGerald is very unsure about quantities, and that the accent shifts, in the proper names he uses, from syllable to syllable in a perplexing way. This shows that he was not really very familiar with the language; and lastly, it appears that he had frequent recourse to his dictionary even when reading Cervantes. If this was so with Cervantes, it must have been far more the case with Calderon, whose vocabulary is much richer and more complex. But the conclusion that is forced upon us is that FitzGerald's equipment in Spanish was such as to make it impossible for him to be an adequate interpreter of a writer both intricate and difficult in a language in which he was never really more than an enthusiastic learner. (pp. 127-28)

Next to the *Omar Khayyám,* there is little doubt that FitzGerald's best title to literary fame will be derived from his letters. The *Omar* forms, as it were, a pedestal for his fame; without it FitzGerald's other works would not have received, and, it may be frankly said, would hardly have deserved attention. (p. 136)

FitzGerald's letters will please by a sort of confiding and child-like wistfulness, which is never undignified, combined with a delicate humour, a shrewd eye for all that is characteristic, an admirable power of brief and picturesque description, and by a style which is at once familiar and stately: The earlier letters have more stateliness than the latter, and the only sign of youth in them is a sort of deliberate quaintness and even pomposity, which fell away from him in his later years. His letters, like Charles Lamb's, are full of echoes, echoes of books and voices and the sweet sounds of nature. The letters are never dull; even the most detailed and domestic have that evasive quality called charm; and the style, though it is seldom elaborate, always walks with a certain daintiness and precision. There are many little mannerisms in the letters, which, like all mannerisms, please if the personality pleases. Such are FitzGerald's use of initial capitals to indicate emphatic substantives—"I like plenty of Capitals," he used to say—and his unique punctuation, which brings the very gradations of voice and pauses of thought before the reader. (p. 137)

FitzGerald's management of paragraphs is another salient characteristic; and he has, moreover, a peculiar delicacy in his use of paragraph endings, which close the passage as it were with a certain snap, leaping briskly from the page, instead of dying feebly away into silence.

Again, FitzGerald's handling of anecdote is another salient characteristic of his style. Nowadays letterwriters are, as a rule, far too much in a hurry to deal in anecdotes. But FitzGerald tells a story with delighted zest, repeating it to different correspondents frequently. He had, too, a marvellous sense of pathos; not the superficial pathos which depends upon accidents, but the pathos which has its root in the *lacrimoe rerum* [tearful reality of life]. (p. 138)

But beside the humanity of the letters there is a grateful sense of leisureliness about them. These letters are not written in the train, like the letters of eminent Bishops, nor dashed off against time, as by statesmen waiting to keep an appointment; they are rather written gently and equably in the firelit room, with the curtains drawn, and the cat purring beside the hearth; or in the pleasant summer, with the windows open, and the scent of roses in the air. They are not written with any motive, except to have a confidential talk with an absent friend; and, what is one of the greatest charms of good letters, they are not written *to* a correspondent but *from* the writer. They are not replies; but with a gentle egotism, they give picture after picture of the simple life FitzGerald was leading. They preserve the moment, the hour, the scene; they indicate the thought just as it rose fresh in the author's mind. I imagine that FitzGerald had one special felicity in framing these letters; he was not a conversationalist of a high order; his reflective mind did not move briskly enough. But one cannot resist the feeling that his mind worked exactly as fast as he wrote; the thought never outruns the expression: the expression never lags behind the thought.

Another great charm of the letters is their inimitable humour; it is not wit in FitzGerald's case so much as a subtle, permeating medium which penetrates a whole passage and lends it a delicate aroma. (pp. 138-39)

Of course the letters will not suit every one. Readers who are in search of definite facts and definite anecdotes, who prefer precise scandal about historical personages to subtle revelations of character and personality, may think there is much sauce and little meat. But FitzGerald's letters, though they contain interesting incidental reminiscences of distinguished persons, will be read more for the subtle aroma which pervades them than as solid contributions to the literary history of the time. He himself set no great value on his letters. . . . Yet, if only FitzGerald could thus have taken the whole world into his confidence, instead of a few dear friends only, he might have proved a great and moving writer; but he needed the personal relation, the individual tie, to call out his tender, melancholy thought.

It is a task of great difficulty to endeavour to fix the position of FitzGerald with regard to the literary tradition of the age. The truth is that he was essentially an amateur; he was enabled by a curious conjuncture of fortunate circumstances to give to the world one minute piece of absolutely first-rate work. But the *Omar* cannot be said to have affected the stream of English poetry very deeply; it has not turned the current of poetical thought in the direction of Oriental verse; moreover, the language of the *Omar,* stately and beautiful as it is, has no mod-

ernity about it; it is not a development, but a reverting to older traditions, a memorable graft, so to speak, of a bygone style.

FitzGerald's position with regard to the poetry that was rising and swelling about him is as that of a stranded boat on a leeshore. He could not bring himself into line with modern verse at all; he had none of the nineteenth-century spirit. Yet he is in the forefront of those who, standing apart from the direct current of the time, seem destined to make the Victorian age furnish a singularly rich anthology of beautiful poetry. (pp. 143-45)

With FitzGerald it may be plainly said that, with the exception of *Omar* and *The Meadows in Spring,* all the rest of his deliberate work in verse is second-rate, the product of a gifted and accomplished amateur.

But, in prose, there still remain the wonderful letters; and these have a high value, both for their beautiful and original literary form, for the careless picture they give of a certain type of retired and refined country life, for their unconsidered glimpses of great personalities, and for the fact that they present a very peculiar and interesting point of view, a delicate criticism of life from a highly original standpoint. The melancholy which underlies the letters is not a practical or inspiring thing, but it is essentially true; and it carries with it a sad refinement, a temperate waiting upon the issues of life, a sober resignation, which are pure and noble. (p. 145)

> *A. C. Benson, in his* Edward FitzGerald, *Macmillan & Co., Limited, 1905, 207 p.*

MAY HARRIS (essay date 1926)

[FitzGerald was] the last of the Epicureans. He belonged—scholar-gipsy that he was—to the day of philosophy which regarded happiness as the highest aim of humanity, and inclusive in its ethical content of prudence, honor, and justice, as well as of pleasure. The doctrine of responsibility to others does not enter into this concept; it was flawless for gods, but otherwise for mortals. FitzGerald was prisoned in an alien age, but he was able always to maintain his aloofness, his freedom as an individual; keeping back the pressure of the outside world with his roses and nightingales—his barriers for a peace that never became a solitude. He took life on his own terms; ordered Little Grange as he pleased, and was gracious and charming when he chose to be so. It was when his orbit touched that of other people that the troubled note comes in. (p. 310)

> *May Harris, "A Victorian Pagan," in* The Sewanee Review, *Vol. XXXIV, No. 3, Summer, 1926, pp. 309-17.*

A. Y. CAMPBELL (essay date 1932)

FitzGerald was the Gray of the nineteenth century; a sensitive and scholarly recluse, a fine critic and letter writer, a dilettante, a sad man; warm and yet wistful in his friendships; author of the only other comparable elegy. His poem is as Oriental in colouring as [Gray's "Elegy"] is English; yet the stuff of its sentiment is, in a sense, more durable; our native rusticity is extinct; but the hedonist, the philosopher, the lover—these in their widely different reactions will remain throughout all ages confronted with the fact of mortality. The quatrains (the "heroic" and the Persian) wind their lovely sustained rhythms through either composition with equal mastery and range. There is nothing in the *Rubáiyát,* certainly, to rival the grave, deep harmonies, and richly sensuous evocation, of those five great opening stanzas which immortalize an English evening. But there is mystery, which the other has not. And if the poignant and searching wit of parts of FitzGerald's monody must have been alien to all the majesty of Gray's, there is yet also a plangency unattainable by any eighteenth-century poem, there is a sympathetic sincerity and vibrant individual tone, sensible in every modulation and indeed in every characteristic line of this exquisitely melodious testament of a Victorian pagan. . . . FitzGerald's [poem begins] with the dawn: "Awake! for Morning in the Bowl of Night"—in that opening stanza the almost breezy call of his incense-breathing ashes excites youth to a sensitivity that, in measure as it saddens, enhances and itself enriches this our brief and only life.

Such is in fact FitzGerald's achievement; the contemporary of Tennyson and Browning, he left to posterity one of the most beautiful long poems of the Victorian age; a poem highly original, for all it was a translation, because so new and so peculiar; a poem, whatever its limitations, purely, and one may even say flawlessly, poetical. And for everyone but the specialist, he did virtually nothing else. (pp. 177-78)

[FitzGerald's *Rubáiyát*] is unique, not merely in the Victorian period, but in literature. The quality of its grief is nowhere flawed with bitterness, not even in the stanzas in which Man forgives his iniquitous taskmaster. The poetry of hedonism has been sometimes mutinous and sometimes mundane, according as the soul had been beaten or drugged. The *Rubáiyát* by contrast is always sensuous and always melancholy. It never lets us forget the sadness of life, it never disturbs our sense of the enjoyment of the moment. In it one seems to find the most perfect fusion of artistic rapture with the spiritual pang. If the rest that can be told of its author may seem to our strenuous epoch merely a pathetic waste, we must remember, not only that every fine friendship or affection is itself an achievement, and one which posterity can seldom or never appraise, but that to produce some kinds of poetry it is probably necessary to submit to no other intellectual harness. (pp. 187-88)

> A. Y. Campbell, "Edward FitzGerald," in The Great Victorians, *edited by H. J. Massingham and Hugh Massingham, Doubleday, Doran & Co., Inc., 1932, pp. 177-88.*

CORNELIUS WEYGANDT   (essay date 1936)

Omar Khayyam is one of the miracles of English literature. That is, it is a work of art of high power written by a man who has, in that department of art, poetry, written no other book, and for that matter no other single poem, of high power. It is true, of course, that as a letter-writer Fitzgerald takes a first place, a place by Lamb and Cowper. There are, too, passages in the letters of Fitzgerald that are lyrical, with a good deal of the lift of poetry. Yet even these best passages are not of the perfection of form, the inevitability of phrase, the heart's-cry of the *Rubaiyat.*

It is easy to say that Fitzgerald made a success of the adaptation of Omar because he was in sympathy with his original. That he was in sympathy with Omar is true, but he was just as sympathetic, through other sides of his nature, with Calderón and Aeschylus and Sophocles, plays of all of whom he adapted. Yet neither *Six Dramas of Calderón* . . . , nor *Two Dramas from Calderón* . . . , was a success; nor the *Agamemnon* . . . from Aeschylus, nor *The Downfall and Death of King Oedipus* . . . from Sophocles.

A frontispiece to a twentieth-century edition. From Rubaiyat of Omar Khayyam, *by Edward Fitzgerald. Illustrated by Eugene Karlin. Thomas Y. Crowell Co., Inc. Illustration copyright © 1964 by Harper & Row, Publishers, Inc. Reproduced by permission of Harper & Row, Publishers, Inc.*

The *Rubaiyat* is a miracle on a par with the miracle of Walton's *Compleat Angler,* of White's *Natural History of Selborne,* of Clare's asylum poems. That is, it is the work of a man who was slow coming to any power at all in literature, who was not from his youth destined for success in literature, who was not looked upon by those who knew him as sure, by the quality of him, to one day amount to something as a writer, who suddenly achieved by a visitation of power that can only be described as miraculous. (pp. 256-57)

Fitzgerald was of a very individual cast of mind, with a style as individual. He was weightier perhaps in his verse than in his prose, more aware of the brevity of life and of all that is sweet in life. The prose, like the verse, has much in it that is Anacreontic, Epicurean, Horatian, Omarian. Prose and verse both are of the marrow of the man who made them. They are the man as his friends knew him transmuted into art. They are the very essence of him. Their outward show is of taking things lightly, of shrugging the shoulders at life, and letting it go at that. Inwardly, quatrains and letters alike reëcho with the world-old plaint of man over the little time he has to know the beauty of the world. They are original, their like was not before they were. The quatrains of *Omar Khayyam* are not only the first things of their kind in English poetry, but in all the poetry of the West. Minor though they are, the verses of the *Rubaiyat* mark the beginning of a mode in English poetry. Best of all they are in themselves things of beauty, building up into a "golden Eastern lay," as Tennyson called it, such as men will find pleasant and easy to the mind as long as men are human. (p. 258)

> *Cornelius Weygandt, "Of Fitzgerald and the East,"
> in his* The Time of Tennyson: English Victorian Po-
> etry As It Affected America, *D. Appleton-Century
> Company Incorporated, 1936, pp. 243-58.*

HOXIE NEALE FAIRCHILD   (essay date 1957)

[FitzGerald's] *Rubáiyát,* though extremely free, is not an original poem in the same sense as [Tennyson's] *In Memoriam.*
Very frequently [FitzGerald] alters, rearranges, or adds wholly
new matter to Omar's quatrains, but even then we cannot be
sure that he is speaking for himself. Much of the "freedom"
may be unintentional mistranslation; many of the additions may
be attempts to impart coherence to the fragmentary original
without unfaithfulness to Omar's spirit and manner.

Some of the divergencies from Omar, however, are too striking
to justify the supposition that the poem is a mixture of free
translation and impersonal dramatic monologue from beginning
to end. (pp. 421-22)

If we assume that [FitzGerald] admired Omar's irreligious quatrains with . . . aesthetic neutrality and detachment, we are at
a loss to explain why they inspired the only good poetry he
ever wrote. Other Persian poets did not stir him to genuine
creativity, nor did Aeschylus, Sophocles, or Calderón. Despite
the already acknowledged ambiguity of the whole situation, it
seems more reasonable to suppose that FitzGerald's *Rubáiyát*
represents what he himself wanted to say. The conjecture may
be valid not only for the passages in which he executes a free
fantasia on Omar's theme but for those in which he translates
the congenial text with relative faithfulness. . . . The gazelle-
eyed girl and the jug of wine are taken over merely as interestingly exotic symbols of escape from the pressure of unanswerable questions. We find more and more of FitzGerald
himself, I believe, the further we move behind the factitious
sensuality into the doubt and pain which constitute the real
substance of the poem

> A Moment's Halt—a momentary taste
> Of being from the Well amid the Waste—
>   And Lo! the phantom Caravan has reach'd
> The nothing it set out from—Oh, make haste!
>
> (p. 424)

[Neither] in fictitious sensuality nor in wit was there surcease
from the misery of being flung

> Into this Universe, and *Why* not knowing
> Nor *Whence,* like Water willy-nilly flowing;
>   And out of it, as Wind along the Waste
> I know not *Whither,* willy-nilly blowing.
>
>   • • • • •
>
> There was the Door to which I found no Key;
> There was the Veil through which I might not see:
>   Some little talk awhile of me and thee
> There was—and then no more of thee and me.

That is the real message of the poem. "Come, fill the Cup"
is traditional hedonistic swagger, not a solution. (p. 425)

> *Hoxie Neale Fairchild, "Frustrated Romanticism,"
> in his* Religious Trends in English Poetry: Christi-
> anity and Romanticism in the Victorian Era,

1830-1880, Vol. IV, *Columbia University Press, 1957,
pp. 405-32.**

JOANNA RICHARDSON   (essay date 1960)

The *Rubáiyát,* with its doubts of religion, shocked and fascinated an age of religious upheaval. Its themes remain our constant preoccupations. But, as FitzGerald recognized, it has been
the music that has sung the *Rubáiyát* into English literature.
We may talk of alliteration, metaphor and scansion, but such
analyses do not explain why so many English people find,
suddenly, that they know so much of the poem by heart. Whatever the merits of the original, FitzGerald's *Rubáiyát* is a great
English poem; and, as he once wrote, 'only God, who made
the Rose smell so, knows why such Poems come from the
Heart and go to it'. (p. 26)

FitzGerald has a double claim to immortality. The translator
of Omar Khayyám has, perhaps, received his due; the letter-
writer remains to be discovered. There is no definitive edition
of FitzGerald's correspondence, and this ommission is strange
and unjust, for he holds so high a place among the English
letter-writers that at times he is reminiscent of Keats. One
cannot, it is true, trace the same god-like growth of soul and
intellect; and yet one can understand why, to FitzGerald, 'poor
Keats' little finger' was 'worth all the body' of Shelley. He
found, in Keats, his own best genius magnified. FitzGerald's
letters, like the letters of Keats, reveal the living, sensual man,
with his griefs and humours and pleasures, the lover of life
and nature and literature, the possessor of a sharp and loving
visual sense, and sometimes they recall the poet by a sudden
turn of phrase, by sheer verbal felicity. (p. 30)

[Although FitzGerald's letters contain many passages of literary criticism,] we do not read the letters of FitzGerald to
discover his criticism of the arts; we read them, especially,
because they reveal himself: serene, detached, unhurried, slightly
wistful, with a humour, a modesty, a poetry of his own that
touches the heart. And revelation is not, perhaps, the word to
use of FitzGerald; for it has been truly said that 'there is a
sense of kindly mystery about him, and we don't want to
account for him. We are glad to have him as he is.' 'I think',
wrote FitzGerald himself, 'I shall become rather a Bore, for I
certainly do write Letters which I should not if I had proper
occupation. . . .' His diffidence is part of his charm; to read
FitzGerald's letters is, inescapably, to love him.

Of the quoting from FitzGerald there is no end. His sudden
poetry, his Romantic melancholy, his touching modesty, his
Elian, Keatsian humours: they make his letters constantly alive.
True, he discusses the great men of his time; but such portraits
remain unimportant beside the authentic picture of himself.
FitzGerald is always a man of sensibility; he is rarely self-
conscious, he is always sincere. He scribbles (it seems that he
talks) on the spur of the moment: he writes, as he once described it, 'whatever-about-ly'. His thoughts 'go floating about
in a gossamer way'. He is a man of taste and genius who likes
'to sail before the wind over the surface of an ever-rolling
eloquence'. But his letters are not merely fine because they
are admirable prose. They are masterly because they come from
the heart.

It is difficult to place him in English literature. In time (and
in certain features) he was eminently Victorian. . . . And yet,
so often, as one reads his translations or his letters, one discerns
the Romantic born out of his time: his *mal du siècle,* his pastoral

and exotic interests, his morbidity, his humour and chivalry. FitzGerald was no Victorian philosopher. . . . (pp. 36-7)

FitzGerald, like all great men of letters, cannot be neatly classified. He belongs to, and stands apart from, his age. . . . Tennyson, in the birthday poem addressed to him, acclaimed 'Old Fitz' as a divine translator, and the *Rubáiyát* as a golden poem, 'a planet to the sun which cast it' [see excerpt above, 1883]. FitzGerald himself, with his usual diffidence, decided: 'I have not the strong inward call, nor cruel-sweet pangs of parturition, that proves the birth of anything bigger than a mouse. . . . I am a man of taste, of whom there are hundreds born every year.'

FitzGerald's judgement was quashed by his contemporaries; it will always be contradicted by posterity. His *Rubáiyát* is indeed a golden poem; his letters sometimes touch the epistolary heights. When he called himself a man of taste, he had perhaps forgotten his own aphorism; taste is the feminine of genius. (p. 38)

> *Joanna Richardson, in her* Edward FitzGerald, *British Council, 1960, 42 p.*

C. M. BOWRA (lecture date 1961)

[The following excerpt is taken from a lecture originally delivered in 1961.]

FitzGerald loved words and had a natural gift for their use, but he lacked the mastering, driving impetus which makes a truly creative writer. Though he enjoyed the practice of writing, as his letters abundantly show, and though he was an acute and exacting critic of the work of other men, he was incapable of forming a large design for any literary undertaking of his own. His gift was for sensibility and the niceties of observation, for finding the right, unassuming words for what caught his fancy in nature or books or human relations. His refusal to join in the ardours and struggles of other men meant that he had very little to write about, and his emotional life, confined as it was to his friends, gave him no inspiration. (p. 174)

Poetry was the art which FitzGerald most loved and admired and wished to practise. Recognizing that he could not be a great poet in his own right, he decided to devote himself to the translation of poetry, and with this for the rest of his life he was mainly occupied. (p. 176)

In translating from Spanish and Greek FitzGerald's methods were very much his own. He translated eight plays of Calderon, the *Agamemnon* of Aeschylus, and the *King Oedipus* and the *Oedipus at Colonus* of Sophocles. The results are always readable, even distinguished, but the methods are certainly eccentric. First, FitzGerald thought nothing of omitting passages which did not appeal to him. This might not matter if the omitted passages were unimportant either for their own sake or because they did not contribute to the structure of a complete work of art. However, if they bored FitzGerald, or for some reason he took against them, they were left out. Secondly, he took more than legitimate liberties with the text when he fused two separate and quite different plays of Sophocles into a single play. The two plays about Oedipus differ in manner, in intention, in tragic interest, in the actual quality of their poetry, and to make them one, FitzGerald had to leave out important characters, soften the asperities of the first play, obscure the age of Oedipus, who is a young man in one play and an old man in the other, spoil the detective interest of the first play and the religious interest of the second. Thirdly, FitzGerald disliked anything too elaborate and mannered, and this did not make

him an ideal translator of Calderon, who wrote in the high manner of Spanish rhetoric, or even of Aeschylus, with his bold, unexpected phraseology and his complex, metaphorical lessons. If these got in the way, FitzGerald pushed them aside and simplified and lowered the more musical and more melodious passages of Aeschylus and the tone of the text. Fourthly, FitzGerald was not a lyrical poet, and the more melodious passages of Aeschylus and Sophocles were beyond his reach. He reduced the first to much less than their full scale; the second he did not attempt to translate but used instead the poor versions of an eighteenth-century rhymer called Robert Potter. His gift was much more for philosophic or reflective verse than for lyrical or even dramatic poetry, and though his lines have always a noble resonance and often a real sweep and splendour, they are not dramatic. We can read them with pleasure, but we cannot imagine that they could be spoken successfully on the stage. He prefers the fine sweep of noble sentiment to human situations, and general remarks about the human state to particular instances of it. All this means not merely that he was an unfaithful translator, but that he did not really find the right medium for his own views. Tying himself, as he did, to drama, he shirked the issues that in fact most troubled and most interested him. The result was not a faithful version, and FitzGerald did not intend it to be one; but in that case, it was equally not an independent work of art which conveyed the richness and the oddity of FitzGerald's own personality. (pp. 177-78)

> *C. M. Bowra, "Edward FitzGerald," in his* In General and Particular, *Weidenfeld and Nicolson, 1964, pp. 173-91.*

ADDITIONAL BIBLIOGRAPHY

"The Omar Cult." *The Academy* 59, No. 1472 (21 July 1900): 55-6.
  Contends that FitzGerald's *Rubáiyát* had a significant impact on the moral and religious tenets of the nineteenth century.

Arberry, A. J. *FitzGerald's "Salámán and Absál."* Cambridge: Cambridge at the University Press, 1956, 206 p.
  A study commemorating the centenary of *Salámán and Absál*'s first publication. Arberry discusses FitzGerald's theories of translation as well as the events leading to the publication of FitzGerald's work.

―――. *The Romance of the "Rubáiyát."* London: George Allen & Unwin, 1959, 244 p.
  A concise examination concerning FitzGerald's writing of the *Rubáiyát*. Arberry traces the poem's history and discusses the events leading up to FitzGerald's translation.

Blyth, James. *Edward FitzGerald and "Posh": "Herring Merchants."* London: John Long, 1908, 199 p.
  An account of the friendship between FitzGerald and the master of his fishing boat, whom FitzGerald considered the ideal man. This book provides insight into FitzGerald's eccentric personality.

Borges, Jorge Luis. "The Enigma of Edward FitzGerald." In his *Other Inquisitions: 1937-1952*, translated by Ruth L. C. Simms, pp. 75-8. Austin: University of Texas Press, 1964.*
  Compares Omar with FitzGerald. Borges notes that although the two men were culturally and spiritually different, FitzGerald reflected both their personalities in his translation of the *Rubáiyát*.

Cadbury, William. "FitzGerald's *Rubáiyát* As a Poem." *ELH* 34, No. 4 (December 1967): 541-63.
  A structural analysis of the *Rubáiyát*.

Draper, John W. "FitzGerald's Persian Local Color." *West Virginia University Philological Papers* 14, No. 4-2 (October 1963): 26-56.
    Analyzes FitzGerald's depiction of Persian culture in his translation of the *Rubáiyát*.

FitzGerald, Edward. *The Letters of Edward FitzGerald*. Edited by Alfred McKinley Terhune and Annabelle Burdick Terhune. 2 vols. Princeton: Princeton University Press, 1980.
    A comprehensive source for FitzGerald's correspondence that includes biographical profiles of FitzGerald and his correspondents.

James, C. W. "Edward FitzGerald on Music and Musicians." *Macmillan's Magazine* 85, No. 509 (March 1902): 330-37.*
    Comments on FitzGerald's concept of music.

Khayyám, Omar. *The Rubáiyát of Omar Khayyám*. Translated by Robert Graves and Omar Ali-Shah. Harmonsworth: Penguin, 1972, 95 p.
    A new translation of the *Rubáiyát* that includes critical notes and an appendix of FitzGerald's translation as well. Graves and Ali-Shah claim that FitzGerald's translations of the poems of Omar are misleading and inaccurate. The editors base their charges on a twelfth-century edition of the *Rubáiyát*, owned by Ali-Shah, that has since proved to be a hoax.

More, Paul Elmer. "Kipling and FitzGerald: *The Seven Seas* and *The Rubáiyát*." In his *Shelburne Essays*, second series, pp. 104-25. New York: G. P. Putnam's Sons, 1907.*
    Compares Rudyard Kipling's *The Seven Seas* with FitzGerald's *Rubáiyát*. More claims that FitzGerald's work possesses a psy-chological awareness that reflects the mood and spirit of the Persian culture.

Ralli, Augustus. "Edward FitzGerald and His Times." In his *Critiques: Critical Essays on English Writers*, pp. 171-83. 1927. Reprint. Port Washington, N.Y.: Kennikat Press, 1967.
    Discusses FitzGerald and his works in relation to the era in which he lived.

Saintsbury, George. "FitzGerald's *Omar Khayyám*. In his *A Saintsbury Miscellany*, pp. 89-99. New York: Oxford University Press, 1947.
    Discusses FitzGerald's translation of the *Rubáiyát*. Saintsbury suggests that although the translation itself is not as literal as many critics would hope, FitzGerald has captured the essence of the work.

Shojai, D. A. "The Structure of FitzGerald's *Rubáiyát of Omar Khayyám*." *Papers of the Michigan Academy of Science, Arts, and Letters* LII (1967): 369-82.
    A detailed structural analysis of FitzGerald's *Rubáiyát*.

Sundaresa Iyer, K. V. *Dust & Soul of FitzGerald's "Omar Khayyám."* Tiruvanmiyur, India: Kalakshetra Publications, 1977, 91 p.
    An introduction to the *Rubáiyát* that focuses on Omar's philosophy and purpose in the original Persian work.

Terhune, Alfred McKinley. *The Life of Edward FitzGerald, Translator of "The Rubáiyát of Omar Khayyám."* New Haven: Yale University Press, 1947, 373 p.
    The standard biography.

Joseph Joubert

1754-1824

French critic and essayist.

A minor critic, philosopher, and transitional figure in the movement from Classicism to Romanticism, Joubert is remembered primarily for his *pensées,* or maxims, on metaphysics, aesthetics, and language, which reflect his classically inspired desire to put "a whole book into a page, a whole page into a sentence, and that sentence into a word." Although Joubert adopted the classical *pensée,* a literary form established by such seventeenth-century French authors as Blaise Pascal, Jean de la Bruyère, and the Duc de la Rochefoucauld, commentators note that in addition to echoing classical stylistic preferences, a number of Joubert's maxims prefigure the literary and poetic philosophies of the Romantics. Joubert considered art the concrete product of inspiration, and he attempted to formulate new concepts to explain the imaginative faculty. Because he was interested in the musicality of language and used a dense yet concise style, several critics maintain that he was a distant predecessor of the nineteenth-century Symbolists and Formalists whose aesthetic theories were developed by a diverse group of literary figures including Charles Baudelaire, Gustave Flaubert, Stéphane Mallarmé, and Edgar Allan Poe.

The eldest son of a provincial doctor and his wife, Joubert was born in Montignac, France. He studied law and the Greek and Roman classics at a Jesuit *collège* in Toulouse until 1774 when, bedridden, he began a journal of comments on his varied reading. Upon his recovery Joubert visited Paris where he met the philosophers Jean de la Harpe, Jean d'Alembert, and Denis Diderot, the last of whom encouraged the young student's interest in art and literature. Eventually, Joubert settled permanently in Paris, where he frequented literary salons. There he became the friend and mentor of François Chateaubriand and gained the reputation of an erudite and witty scholar. Although Joubert undertook many writing projects, none of them come down to posterity in complete form, and his reputation as a critic and philosopher is based solely on records of his compelling personality, correspondence, and *pensées* and essay fragments from his notebooks. After Joubert's death in 1824, his wife asked Chateaubriand to assemble and edit Joubert's journals and the various *pensées* he had jotted on scattered scraps of paper. In 1838, *Recueil de pensées de Joubert,* a slim volume of Joubert's maxims, was published and circulated privately. Despite the eventual publication of his complete works, *Pensées de Joseph Joubert,* and an English translation of selected maxims and letters, *Pensées and Letters of Joseph Joubert,* Joubert's writings have received limited critical attention.

Although Joubert is frequently labeled a moralist, critics focus primarily on his aesthetic theories and critical method. He did not write a treatise on poetics; yet commentators maintain that throughout his *pensées* on aesthetics and language he evinced a poetic style that reflects the classical attributes of moderation, concision, and clarity and often presages the Romantic emphasis on emotion.

Beginning in the 1790s, such Romantic theorists as Samuel Taylor Coleridge in England and August and Friedrich von Schlegel, Johann Gottfried von Herder, and Johann Wolfgang von Goethe in Germany were developing poetics which stressed imagination and intuition as well as the emotional content and expressivity of language. Because Joubert read only French and Latin, critics suggest that it is unlikely that he was aware of the growing Romantic movement. However, at the end of the eighteenth century, when the classical style of clarity, harmony, and rationality continued to rule French letters, Joubert was the only French author or theorist whose work demonstrated affinities with Romantic aesthetic theories. Several commentators acknowledge Joubert's foresight in his insistence on the suggestive qualities of language. Yet he did not expound a philosophy of "pure poetry" but believed instead that a statement's meaning takes precedence over its form. Joubert contended that literature, like all art, is an expression of a higher reality that cannot be apprehended solely by reason. Therefore, he adopted a non-mimetic, or non-imitative, view of literature, and favored instead a more expressive theory of art, which became a fundamental characteristic of both the Romantic and Symbolist aesthetic. Critics generally agree that many of the approximately eight thousand *pensées* and several dozen letters that comprise the bulk of Joubert's literary contribution exemplify his philosophy of moderation, concision, and clarity. Yet despite their regard for Joubert as a masterful stylist, they fault the fragmentary nature of his work, its occasional preciosity, and elaborate metaphors.

Joubert's critical method was appreciative and intuitive. However, few commentators agree with his evaluations of individual authors and works, and some note the narrowness of his vision and perception when discussing the works of others. Joubert's great interest in the classics, coupled with his habit of excising from his library those works, or the sections of them, with which he disagreed have prompted some critics to suggest that his scope was too narrow and that the influence of the past too prevailing. Though Joubert is generally regarded as a minor French critic who is often better known for his association with Chateaubriand than for his works, he continues to attract the attention of literary historians who attempt to define his role in the development of Romanticism and Symbolism.

*PRINCIPAL WORKS

Recueil de pensées de Joubert (meditations) 1838
Pensées, essais, maximes, et correspondance de Joseph Joubert (meditations, essays, and letters) 1842
Pensées de Joseph Joubert (meditations) 1922
Pensées and Letters of Joseph Joubert (meditations and letters) 1928
Les carnets de Joseph Joubert (meditations) 1938
Sur la poésie (meditations) 1958
Pensées (meditations) 1966

*All selections from Joubert's private notebooks were published posthumously.

C. A. SAINTE-BEUVE (essay date 1849)

[*Sainte-Beuve is considered to be the foremost French literary critic of the nineteenth century. Of his extensive body of critical writings, the best known are his "lundis"—weekly newspaper articles which appeared every Monday morning over a period of several decades, in which he displayed his knowledge of literature and history. In the following excerpt from the "lundis," originally published in December, 1849, Sainte-Beuve appraises the style and critical content of Joubert's pensées.*]

[As a young man M. Joubert chatted] with famous people of letters; he knew Marmontel, La Harpe, D'Alembert; he knew especially Diderot, by nature the most gracious and the most hospitable of spirits. The influence of the latter upon him was great, greater than one would suppose, seeing the difference in their conclusions. Diderot had certainly in M. Joubert a singular pupil, one who was pure-minded, finally a Platonist and a christian . . . ; studying and adoring piety, chastity, modesty, and never finding, to express himself upon these noble subjects, any style sufficiently ethereal, nor any expression sufficiently luminous. However, it is only by that contact with Diderot that one can fully explain the inoculation of M. Joubert with certain ideas, then so new, so bold, and which he rendered truer by elevating and rectifying them. M. Joubert had his Diderot period when he tried everything; later, he made a choice. Always, even at an early day, he had tact; taste did not come to him till afterward. "Good judgment in literature," said he, "is a very slow faculty, which does not reach the last point of its growth till very late." Reaching that point of maturity, M. Joubert was sufficiently just to Diderot to say that there are many more *follies of style* than *follies of thought* in his works. It was especially for his interest and initiation in art and literature that he was indebted to Diderot. But, in falling into a soul so delicate and so light, those ideas of literary reform and of the regeneration of art, which in Diderot had preserved a kind of homely and prosaic, a smoky and declamatory character, were brightened and purified, and assumed an ideal character which approximated them insensibly to the Greek beauty; for M. Joubert was a Greek, he was an Athenian touched with the Socratic grace. "It seems to me," said he, "much more difficult to be a modern than to be an ancient." He was especially an ancient in the calmness and moderation of his sentiments; he disliked everything that was sensational, all undue emphasis. He demanded a lively and gentle agreeableness, a certain internal, perpetual joy, giving to the movement and to the form ease and suppleness, to the expression clearness, light and transparency. It is principally in these that he made beauty consist:

> The Athenians were delicate in mind and ear. They never would have endured a word fitted to displease, even though one had only quoted it. One would say that they were always in good humor when writing. They disapproved in style of the austerity which reveals hard, harsh, sad, or severe manners.

(pp. 187-88)

Upon [the nineteenth-century sculptor] Pigalle and modern statuary as opposed to the ancient, one might cite from him thoughts of the same kind, whole pages which mark at once and very clearly in what respect he agrees with Diderot, and wherein he separates from him. Thus, then, about the epoch of '89, there was in France a man already at maturity, thirty years old, eight years older than André Chénier, and fourteen years older than Chateaubriand, who was fully prepared to comprehend

them, to unite them, to furnish them with incitements and new views, to enable them to extend and complete their horizon. This was the part, indeed, of M. Joubert touching M. de Chateaubriand. . . . [M. Joubert] encouraged him in an undertone, or murmured to him sweet counsel in a contradiction full of grace. The best, the finest criticism to be made upon the first and great literary works of M. de Chateaubriand, might still be found in the *Letters and Thoughts of M. Joubert.* (pp. 188-89)

An English poet (Cowley) has said: "One concludes by doubting whether the milky-way is composed of stars, there are so many of them!" There are too many stars in the heaven of M. Joubert. One would like more intervening spaces and more repose. "I am like Montaigne," said he, "unfit for continuous discourse. Upon all subjects, it seems to me, I either lack intermediate ideas, or they weary me too much." These intermediate ideas, if he had given himself the trouble to express them, would not have wearied us, it seems, but would rather have given us repose in reading him. One is conscious in his writings of an effort,—often happy, yet an effort. "If there is a man," he says, "tormented with the accursed ambition of putting a whole book into a page, a whole page into a phrase, and that phrase into a word, it is I." His method is always to express a thought in an image; the thought and the image make, for him, but one thing, and he believes that he has grasped the one only when he has found the other. "It is not my phrase that I polish, but my idea. I stop till the drop of light which I need is formed and falls from my pen." This series of thoughts, then, are only drops of light; the mind's eye is at last dazzled by them. "I would like," says he, defining himself with marvellous correctness, "I would like to infuse exquisite sense into common sense, or to render exquisite sense common." Good sense alone wearies him; the ingenious without good sense rightly appears to him contemptible; he wishes to unite the two, and it is no small undertaking. "Oh! how difficult it is," he cries, "to be at once ingenious and sensible!" La Bruyère, before him, had felt the same difficulty, and had avowed it to himself at the beginning: "All is said, and one comes too late, now that there have been men for seven thousand years, and men, too, that have thought." M. Joubert recognizes this likewise: "All the things which are easy to say well have been perfectly said; the rest is our business or our task: painful task!" I indicate at the outset the disadvantage and the fault; these books of maxims and of condensed moral observations, such as that of La Bruyère, and especially such as M. Joubert's, cannot be read consecutively without fatigue. It is the mind distilled and fixed in all its sugar; one cannot take much of it at once.

The first chapters of the first volume [of the *Letters and Thoughts of M. Joubert*] are not those which please me most; they treat of God, of creation, of eternity, and of many other things. To the peculiar difficulty of the subjects is added that which springs from the subtlety of the author. Here it is no longer with Plato that we have to do, but with Augustin [*sic*] in large doses, and without any connection in the ideas. Unquestionably it will be well, one day, to make of all these metaphysical chapters a single one, much abridged, into which shall be admitted only the beautiful, simple, acceptable thoughts, rejecting all those which are equivocal or enigmatical. (pp. 195-96)

It is when he returns to speak of manners and of arts, of antiquity and of the century, of poetry and of criticism, of style and of taste,—it is in treating all these subjects that he pleases and charms us, that he appears to us to have made a notable and novel addition to the treasure of his most excellent predecessors. Taste, for him, is *the literary conscience of the soul*. Not more than Montaigne does he love the book-like or bookish style . . . , that which savors of ink, and which one never employs except when writing: "There should be, in our written language, voice, soul, space, a majestic air, words that subsist all alone, and which carry their place with them." This life which he demands of the author, and without which style exists only on paper, he wishes also in the reader: "The writers who have influence are only men who express perfectly what others think, and who reveal in minds ideas or sentiments that were striving to come forth. It is in the depths of minds that literatures exist." Again, he who relished the ancients so well, the antiquity of Rome, of Greece, and of Lewis XIV, does not demand impossibilities of us; he will tell us to appreciate that antiquity, but not to return to it. In respect to expression, he prefers again the sincere to the beautiful, and truth to appearance:

> *Truth* in style is an indispensable quality, and one which suffices to recommend a writer. If, upon all sorts of subjects, we should write today as men wrote in the time of Lewis XIV, we should have no truth in style, for we have no longer the same dispositions, the same opinions, the same manners. A woman who would write like Madame de Sevigné would be ridiculous, because she is not Madame de Sevigné. The more the way in which one writes partakes of the character of the man, of the manners of the time, the more must the style differ from that of the writers who have been models only by having manifested preëminently, in their works, either the manners of their epoch or their own character. Good taste itself, in that case, permits one to discard the best taste, for taste, even good taste, changes with manners.

(pp. 197-98)

What M. Joubert demands, above all, of the moderns, is, not to insist upon their faults, not to follow their inclinations, not to throw themselves in that direction with all their strength. The visionary and fickle nature, the sensual, the bombastic, the colossal, especially displease him. We have had a high opinion for some years of what we call force, power. Often when I have chanced to hazard some critical remark upon a talent of the day, one has replied to me: "What matters it! that talent has power." But what kind of power? Joubert is going to reply for me: "Force is not energy; some authors have more muscles than talent. Force! I do not hate it nor do I fear it; but, thanks to Heaven, I am entirely disabused in regard to it. It is a quality which is praiseworthy only when it is concealed or clothed. In the vulgar sense Lucan had more of it than Plato, Brebeuf more than Racine." He will tell us again: "Where there is no delicacy, there is no literature. A writing in which are found only force and a certain fire without splendor, announces only character. One may produce many such, if he has nerves, bile, blood, and boldness." M. Joubert adores enthusiasm, but he distinguishes it from explosiveness, and even from fervor . . . , which is but a secondary quality in inspiration, and which *excites* . . . whilst the other *moves* . . . "Boileau, Horace, Aristophanes, had fervor; La Fontaine, Menander, and Virgil, the gentlest and the most exquisite enthusiasm that ever was." Enthusiasm, in that sense, might be defined a kind of *exalted peace*. Fine works, according to him, do not intoxicate, but they enchant. He exacts agreeableness and a certain amenity even in the treatment of austere subjects;

he requires a certain charm everywhere, even in profundity: "It is necessary to carry a certain charm even into the deepest investigations, and to introduce into those gloomy caverns, into which one has penetrated but for a short time, the pure and antique light of the ages that were less instructed but more luminous than ours." Those words *luminous* and *light* reappear frequently in his writings, and betray that winged nature that loved the heavens and high places. The brilliant, which he distinguishes from the luminous, does not seduce him: "It is very well that thoughts should shine, but it is not necessary that they should sparkle." What he most of all desires in them is splendor, which he defines a quiet, inner brilliancy, uniformly diffused, and which penetrates the whole body of a work.

There is much to be drawn from the chapters of M. Joubert upon criticism and upon style,—from his judgments upon different writers; in these he appears original, bold, and almost always correct. He astonishes at the first impression; he generally satisfies when one reflects upon his sayings. He has the art of freshening stale precepts, of renewing them for the use of an epoch which holds to tradition only by halves. On this side he is essentially a modern critic. In spite of all his old creeds and his regrets for the past, we distinguish immediately in him the stamp of the time in which he lives. He does not hate a certain appearance of elaborate finish, and sees in it rather a misfortune than a fault. He goes so far as to believe that "it is permissible to avoid simplicity, when to do so is absolutely necessary for agreeableness, and when simplicity alone would not be beautiful." If he desires naturalness, it is not the vulgar naturalness, but an exquisite naturalness. Does he always attain it? He feels that he is not exempt from some subtlety, and he excuses himself for it: "Often one cannot avoid passing through the subtle to rise and reach the sublime, as to mount to the heavens one must pass through the clouds." He rises often to the highest ideas, but it is never by following the high-roads; he has paths that are unseen. Finally, to sum all up, there is singularity and an individual *humor* in his judgments. He is an indulgent *humorist*, who sometimes recalls [Laurence] Sterne, or rather Charles Lamb. He has a manner that leads him to say nothing, absolutely nothing, like another man. This is noticeable in the letters he writes, and does not fail to be wearisome at last. It appears by all marks that Joubert is not a classic but a modern, and it is by this title that he appears to me fitted, better perhaps than any other person, to give emphasis to good counsel, and to pierce us with his shafts. (pp. 198-200)

On the whole, if we must characterize M. Joubert, he had all the delicacy which one can desire in a mind, but he had not all the power. He was one of those meditative and fastidious minds that "are incessantly distracted from their work by immense perspectives and distant prospects of celestial beauty of which they would like to show everywhere some image or some ray." He had in too high a degree the sentiment of the perfect and of the complete: "To perfect one's thought," cried he, "that takes time, that is rare, that imparts an extreme pleasure; for perfected thoughts enter minds easily; they need not even be beautiful to please, it suffices that they be finished. The condition of the soul which has had them communicates itself to other souls, and conveys to them its own repose." He had sometimes that sweet enjoyment of finishing his thoughts, but never that of joining them together and forming a monument. (pp. 201-02)

C. A. Sainte-Beuve, "Joubert," in his Monday-Chats, *edited and translated by William Mathews, S. C. Griggs and Company, 1877, pp. 185-204.*

JULES LEMAÎTRE (essay date 1880)

[*A prominent French critic of the late nineteenth and early twentieth centuries, Lemaître is known for his highly subjective and impressionistic criticism. In his essay on Joubert, originally published in 1880 in the French periodical the* Revue bleue, *Lemaître briefly treats Joubert's literary criticism, metaphysics, and political views.*]

[Joubert] is more of a Platonist than Plato. The universe for him is a very exact system of symbols in which he endeavours to seize hold of the correspondences between the real and the ideal, the reflection of God in things. Where this reflection is lacking, he closes his eyes. He does not allow matter to exist only in so far as it is a representation of something spiritual. In itself it disgusts him. Accordingly, he reduces it as much as he can. He only admits that at the most it has the thickness of an onion-peel; he regards the world as a prodigious piece of gold-beater's skin. This is literally the case. 'A grain of matter,' he says, 'has been enough to create the world. . . . This mass which frightens us is nothing more than a grain of matter which the Eternal has created and set to work. By its ductility, by the hollows which it holds, and by the Workman's art, it presents a sort of immensity in the decorations that have proceeded from it. . . . By taking back His own breath, the Creator could reduce its volume and easily destroy it.'

Like his metaphysics, his literary criticism is nothing but metaphors, comparisons, and allegories. He says of Voltaire: 'Voltaire, like a monkey, has charming movements and hideous features.' He says of Plato: 'Plato loses himself in the void, but one sees the play of his wings, one hears their noise.' He tells us that 'Xenophon writes with a pen made from a swan's feather, Plato with a pen of gold, and Thucydides with a stylet of bronze.' One is tempted to go on thus: 'Corneille writes with a pen made from an eagle's feather, Racine with one made from the feather of a turtle-dove . . . , Chateaubriand with a pen made from a peacock's feather, Joubert himself with one made from the feather of an angel.'

In politics he is for that form of government into which most artifice enters. What displeases him in democracy is that force and power finding themselves in the same hands, that is to say in those of the greatest number, 'there is no art, no equilibrium and political beauty.' He wants power to be separated from material force and from number, and to hold them in check. It is in this fiction that he sees beauty: 'Fiction is wanted everywhere. Even politics are a sort of poetry.'

His psychology is also made up of images. He remarks that man *lives* only in his head and his heart; that language is a *cord* and speech an *arrow;* that the soul is a *lighted vapour* of which the body is the *torch;* that certain souls have no *wings,* nor even *feet* for stability, nor hands for work; that the mind is the *atmosphere* of the soul, that it is a *fire* whose thought is the *flame;* that imagination is the *eye* of the soul. Farther on, I see that the mind, which just now was an atmosphere and a flame, is a *field,* and then a *metal;* that it can be *hollow* and *sonorous,* or that its *solidity* can be *plane,* so that thought produces on it the effect of the *blow of a hammer;* then that it resembles a *concave* or a *convex* mirror; that it is *cold,* and it is *warm;* that modesty is a *net-work,* a *piece of velvet,* a *cocoon,* etc., etc.

Do you feel nature's revenge. This, for a despiser of matter, is a very material imagination. It is the same with all those overfastidious persons.

With all this, Joubert is very 'special.' His quintessential subtleties, his virginal Epicureanism, and what I call his 'angelicism' can still give us, here and there, rather pleasant little throbs of the soul. By a thousand mysterious affectations, by his elaborate and delicious bad taste, he remains close to us. This modest sensitive writer is one of the most distinguished of those prettily whimsical artists who are, as it were, on the margin of literatures.

Only I ought to confess that Joubert always indicates both terms of his comparisons; and it is this, among other things, which distinguishes him from, for instance, M. Stéphane Mallarmé. That does not prevent the relationship from existing. I wished to show our Symbolist poets that they have an unexpected but authentic ancestor. (pp. 301-05)

Jules Lemaître, "Joubert," in his Literary Impressions, *translated by A. W. Evans, Daniel O'Connor, 1921, pp. 299-305.*

EDITH SICHEL (essay date 1895)

[*The following is a brief laudatory review of Joubert as a philosopher.*]

[Joubert was] a Benvenuto Cellini of thought: no great sculptor, but a carver of gems, creating his maxims and reflections with infinite care and fancy.

Nobody, perhaps, who has written so little has been so much written about by the few who make up the inner circle of literary men; nobody has been better loved by them. . . . To his contemporaries his work was one with his personality, for his private *Journals of Thoughts and Maxims* were the flower of his daily philosophy. He was essentially the king of friends; he was as essentially the true critic—the interpreter—who has the poet in him, and knows first of all how to appreciate. Joubert was the critic, the interpreter of life, with insight so vivid as to seem almost like creative imagination. It was the same quality which made of him both friend and critic. When he judged a book or an idea, he passed into it, taking it from its own point of view; and when he came into close relationship with human beings, he passed into *them,* leading their lives with them and insisting upon a minute knowledge of their daily existence—their walks, their diet, their books, their friends, their conversation.

Yet his heart was rather ardent than passionate; tender as a woman's; wide as a man's; gay as a child's. Basking in hospitality and good company, he contrived to combine simplicity with fastidiousness; glowing indulgence and gracious playfulness with a certain austerity of mind: the result, not of asceticism, but of the pursuit of truth and beauty which dominated his tastes and existence, and made him reject all the furbelows of life and of speech. Superfluous words he detested. (pp. 180-82)

[Joubert] never kept his discoveries for himself; the sunlight of his wit played half tenderly, half keenly, on everything it touched, making the rare seem obvious, and the obvious rare. (p. 183)

"To converse and to know" was [Joubert's] motto as well as Plato's, and his amiable manners no less than his distinguished intellect soon gained access for him to the society of Marmontel, La Harpe, d'Alembert, and, above all, Diderot, whose "most hospitable of minds" immediately acquired a strong influence over him. He has been called Diderot's "purified pupil"; and indeed it is strange to find Joubert, who was "finally both a Platonist and a Christian in love with ideal beauty and holiness,'' at this moment under the Encyclopaedist's sceptre. Its sway passed before long, but its influence, we are told, may be traced in the sympathy he always had for new ideas; whilst in later days, when his judgment was ripe, he still kept his old admiration, and maintained that Diderot had ''more follies of style than follies of thought.'' (pp. 185-86)

Edith Sichel, ''Pauline de Beaumont: Chapter II,'' in her *The Story of Two Salons*, Edward Arnold, 1895, pp. 180-212.*

RICHARD ARTHUR (essay date 1897)

[*Arthur indicates his admiration for Joubert and attempts to define the goal of his critical writings.*]

[In Joubert] the man of letters was ever hidden behind the warm flesh-and-blood-and-soul human being. He loved literature and art, but recognised the great truth overlooked by many that the whole is greater than the part, that life with its first considerations of love and friendship comes before literature and art and science and commerce and whatever else; that these are for life, and that life is not solely for them. (pp. 528-29)

If Joubert ever had any misgivings . . . as to his place in life he must have cast them out very early. . . . His *Letters* and *Thoughts* give little evidence of anxiety on this score. He seems to have had no other ambition than to cultivate his being to the utmost, without any ulterior object in view, without ever casting a side glance at renown, without ever seeking to attract the eyes of the world to his own person. If he sometimes speaks of his failure to produce literary work, it is in a calm and contented, almost playful mood, not at all despairingly, hardly regretfully. ''My ideas!'' he says; ''it is the house to lodge them in that costs me dear to build;'' and, ''I tried to get along without words: the words are now revenging themselves by coming to me with difficulty;'' and again, ''Ah, if I could express myself in music, in dancing, in painting, as I express myself in words, how many ideas I should have which I have not, and how many feelings that will ever be unknown to me!''

Joubert's aim was: in life, the development and full exercise of his human feelings, the refinement of his whole nature, by the cultivation of them and of his mind, the peaceful passing of his days in piety and wisdom, the encouragement and sustenance of his friends; in literature, to have vague, mystic, instinctive notions of the unknowable, and clear precise ideas of the tangible, visible, and thinkable. He loved to ponder over anything that interested him until it became a transparent image and suggested its proper form of expression. ''It is not my phrase I polish,'' he tells himself, ''but my thought.'' His total unconcern with renown or success put him in the happy position of being able to forego all obedience to conventional literary mandates of his own or any other time which would have restricted the free movement of his individual characteristics, and so he was enabled to be thoroughly himself, to do what his nature prompted him to do in the way that suited him, and to leave undone whatever did not rise up in him spontaneously. He played for no stake, and was not therefore disquieted or turned aside by having to adjust his game. Not only in his writings, but in his reading, did he exercise an entire disregard for the highways: he made all sorts of excursions along unfrequented, obscure, grass-grown pathways. He applied himself to long studies of orators, poets, and philosophers, impatient ''to be quit of others' opinions, to know what had been known,

and to be able to be ignorant in entire security of conscience.'' With this end in view he attacked science, studied ''fire, the earth, heaven, and the waters of the earth, without embarrassing himself too much with the tools of science. . . . (pp. 529-30)

A volume of epigrams and another of friendly letters seems a small output for a highly-endowed, richly-cultivated mind, active during the prescribed length of man's days. But the maxims are all spirit; there is no superfluous flesh about them. Joubert gives ten ideas, often double ones, clear-cut crystal ideas, on a page, whereas your fifty-volume author often expands himself loquaciously over ten pages without getting a single idea into them. (pp. 530-31)

[*Thoughts* is] distinguished by the absence of all sign of haste and fever and irresolution, by the strong, even, onward river-movement, the clarity and conciseness, that mark the classic. Some writers walk round their subjects; many look at them from one side; some get underneath, and look up at them: Joubert found his view-point above them, away up in the sky—sometimes, indeed, too far up. He is not unconscious of a certain subtlety, and takes the trouble to excuse it. ''Often, in order to lift ourselves up and reach the sublime, we cannot help proceeding by way of the subtle, just as to get to·heaven we must pass by the clouds.'' But, with all his aërial flights, there reigns in whatever he did a sound good sense and a wide tolerance. He is emotional, but calmly; enthusiastic, but temperately; elated, but soberly; and in all his writings the thermometer of reason scarcely shows one degree of fever-heat. He worshipped at the shrine of beauty and was intoxicated by virtue, but differed from those of his fellows, the disciples of the Art for Art's sake doctrine, and from those others who profess to follow Art simply for truth's sake, in that, for him, beauty and truth were interdependent, reciprocal, inseparable.

Both in his way of looking at things and his manner of expressing thoughts Joubert was very original. His style is for the most part a daring imagery, in which . . . a double impression is conveyed. . . .

His judgment of literary men and books ancient and modern was remarkably keen and to the point, appreciative, sympathetic, and tolerant, but pitiless and stinging where he thought he saw any charlatanry or insincerity. (p. 531)

Joubert's letters, few in number, are free, graceful, and natural, full of sympathy, warm-heartedness, and bonhomie. Their language is limpid and supple, and lets us see the man through it everywhere.

A glance at the headings under which Joubert's maxims fall gives an idea of the diversity of his interests. He was an objective more than a subjective thinker and writer, judging other men and outward objects, it is true, by reference to the law he found written in his own inward being, but never giving himself up to a long and morbid dissection, vivisection, of his psychologic existence. . . .

Joubert seldom approached anything like a probing analysis of his parts. He often surveyed himself, but with a curious, interested eye, seeming to say complacently, ''without pride and without modesty,'' *that appears to be the sort of fellow I am,* and it never occurred to him to quarrel with himself for not being other than he was made, or to wish to be anything else. The secret of his happy life lay in that unquestioning acceptation of himself as he found himself and in his fidelity to his fundamental nature. (p. 532)

Richard Arthur, *"Joseph Joubert,"* in The Westminster Review, *Vol. CXLVIII, No. 5, November, 1897, pp. 524-36.*

GEORGE SAINTSBURY (essay date 1904)

[*Saintsbury was an English literary historian and critic of the late nineteenth and early twentieth centuries. A prolific writer, Saintsbury composed a number of histories of English and European literature as well as several critical works on individual authors, styles, and periods. In the following excerpt from an essay originally published in 1904, Saintsbury investigates Joubert's statements on literature, style, and literary criticism.*]

In literature, with an exception to be noticed presently, his time exerts remarkably little influence on Joubert. This is not the case elsewhere; in his religious, political, moral, social judgments we feel . . . the pressure, and the shadow, and the sting, of the Revolution everywhere. . . . Joubert was born in mid-eighteenth century, and he died just as the Romantic movement was in full bud and had begun to burst, with [Victor Hugo's] *Odes et Ballades*. But he is neither a hard and fast classic, nor a revolter of the extreme kind against classicism, nor, like those not uninteresting contemporaries of his . . . , blown hither and thither by the wind of this or that doctrine. He betrays, indeed, the enfranchising and widening influence of Diderot; but he has worked this out quite independently, and with a "horizontality" and comparative range of view in which the early Romantics themselves . . . were conspicuously lacking, and which even Sainte-Beuve never fully attained. (pp. 118-19)

The fault of the "Pensée" itself in general, is that, in human necessity, it will miss, or only go near ten times (perhaps a hundred) for once that it hits; and it is easy enough for a hostile critic in turn to hit the misses. But it is the hits that count. . . . (p. 120)

Taking them together, [the Poetry Section of the *"Pensées"* contains] more truth—more stimulating, suggestive, germinal truth—about poetry, than any other single treatise from Aristotle down to the present day. This is the way a man must think of poetry if he is to be saved; though not every clause of the Joubertian creed is thus Athanasian.

The Style section is equally astonishing. I think I first read Joubert about thirty years ago; I know his ancestors and his successors much better now; but he astonishes me just as much as ever. In another rather longer stretch you have the best things in Aristotle, Longinus, and others—some at least of which he pretty certainly had neither read nor heard of—revised and applied; you have the principles and the practice of Hugo, Gautier, Saint-Victor, Flaubert, of Ruskin, Arnold, Pater, put plumply or by suggestion beforehand in eighteen pages.

Here is everything: the necessity of choice which is the condition of good style, and which works so differently in ancient and modern times; the powers of "the word" in all their varied bearings . . . ; the right to reinvest an old word with new meaning; the "science of names"; the placing of words; the freedom which the reader possesses of improving on his author by keeping his word and adding to his sense; the difference between musical and pictorial style; the impossibility of literature when words are used with an absolutely fixed value; the unpardonable sin of mere purism; the natural and justifiable idiosyncrasy of dictionary and even grammar in good writers, with the due guards against its excess; the variety of degree in which ancient authors are to be followed; the value and the danger of idioms.

These and a hundred other things will all be found, sometimes of course (the fault of the form again) put too absolutely; sometimes, though very rarely, intermixed with things more dubious—but always present at short, at all but the shortest notice. Never, I think, did any critical writer enter so much into the marrow of things in so limited a space. . . . (pp. 120-21)

These two sections [on poetry and style] form the *aureus libellus* [excellent little book] of Joubert—if I knew a wealthy and sensible, intelligent and obliging bibliophile, they should be printed on vellum and adorned by the greatest decorative artists of the age, and bound in the simplest but the most perfect coat obtainable. We decline slightly with the two remaining chapters—though there is still plenty of gold to be found—and the decline is continuous. (p. 121)

[In] a fashion which is nearly unique in this history, but which is priceless in its únicity—the disadvantages which have been powerless to affect his general conceptions [of literature] recover their hold upon him, to some extent, in particulars. He is still sound on what the *general* merits of poetry and of literature should be; but he sees those merits in the wrong place. At first sight, to an English reader who is not thoroughly broken to the ways of our difficult art, it may seem impossible, inconceivable, a bad joke, that the author of [aphorisms] as to the necessity of "transport," the power of words, and all the rest of it, should admire Delille and not admire Milton. But remember, he understood the *words* of Delille—they had, feeble as they were, the power to excite, according to his own true and profound theory, that poetry which was ready to answer and magnify them in his own soul. He did not understand the *words* of Milton, and they could not touch him. . . . (p. 122)

Some further instances, however, may and must be given of the working of this curious state of things, which makes a critic equal to the very greatest we have met in abstract appreciation of poetry and literature, the inferior of many we have met—if not of most who were good critics at all—in his appreciation of individuals. . . . His few remarks on Molière argue, as we should expect, a rather lukewarm admiration; but he is among the highest praisers of La Fontaine, ranking him as (of course this is before the nineteenth century) fuller of poetry than any other French author. (Note again that his means, "fuller of poetry *which can bring itself into contact with Joubert's mind.*") He admits that his beloved Delille has only "sounds and colours" in his head, but then they are the sounds and colours that Joubert can see and hear, and he knows rightly that sounds and colours make more than half of poetry. As for the ancients, he remarks with great truth, that Cicero, whom nevertheless he admired much, has "more taste and discernment than real criticism." (pp. 123-24)

He is very valuable on Rousseau, but that "a Voltaire is good for nothing at any time," though he had acknowledged many literary gifts and graces in this Voltaire, is not merely unjust, but *saugrenu* [preposterous]. (pp. 124-25)

It will be seen that while he is free from [the] hasty generalisations and indigestible "philosophy of literature" [exemplified in Madame de Staël's novel *Corinne*], while he has a less extended knowledge of literatures (though probably a much more accurate one) than hers, he actually far transcends her in real philosophy of view, that he takes a sight of all poetry, all literature, and their qualities, which is aquiline alike in sweep and searchingness. Further, that though his knowledge is again more accurate than Chateaubriand's, it is more circumscribed, and that he cannot relish some particular things which Chateaubriand could, yet that once more he excels his friend in clearness, ideality, comprehension, and depth. That finally . . . , in comparison with all the other Empire critics, from Fontanes and Geoffroy downwards, a similar *distinguendum* [distinction] has to be observed. One Joubert—the Joubert of the general views and of the sections on style and poetry—is far over their heads, out of their sight and reach. The other Joubert—the Joubert of the particular judgments—is very much nearer them, though he is sometimes, not always, their superior. (p. 125)

> George Saintsbury, "*Diderot and the French Transition*," in his A History of Criticism and Literary Taste in Europe from the Earliest Texts to the Present Day: Modern Criticism, Vol. III, *William Blackwood and Sons, 1904, pp. 89-140.**

IRVING BABBITT   (essay date 1912)

[*Babbitt was one of the founders of the New Humanism (or neo-humanism) movement which began during the second decade of the twentieth century. The New Humanists believed that the aesthetic qualities of a work of art should be subordinate to its moral and ethical purpose. Here, Babbitt briefly treats Joubert's political and religious views and appraises the style and critical content of his* pensées.]

The literary **"Pensées"** [or **"Thoughts"**] show such a fine quality of critical insight that Joubert has come to be regarded as the critics' critic. . . . He has that gift of ornate conciseness which he himself declared to be the supreme beauty of style. It is not, however, his phrase that he polishes, he says, but his idea. . . . His ambition was so to express the exquisite as to give it general currency. Now it is not easy to imagine a continuous discourse made up entirely of the exquisite and we are not surprised when Joubert says he is unfitted for continuous discourse. (p. 35)

The danger for a critic who aims solely at the exquisite . . . and who lacks intermediary ideas, is that he may become affected and obscure, and Joubert does not altogether avoid these penalties of oversubtlety. . . . [I] should not agree with those critics who prefer his **"Letters"** to the **"Thoughts"** because of their greater simplicity and naturalness. The **"Letters,"** however, do reveal one essential side of Joubert far more completely than the **"Thoughts."** They are pervaded by a fine vein of whimsical humor, an habitual sportiveness. . . . It seemed to Joubert an important part of wisdom to distinguish the very few things that are to be taken seriously and then to take all other things playfully. . . . He is at the opposite pole from those "serious and gloomy spirits who have very futile doctrines"; a sentence that inevitably calls to mind many modern reformers.

Possibly the danger of a sort of transcendental *préciosité* [fastidious refinement] in Joubert appears most clearly in some of his thoughts on religion. He recognizes the existence of matter only by courtesy. If the Creator withdrew his breath from the world, he says, it would "become what it was before time, a grain of flattened metal, an atom in the void, even less than this: a mere nothing." . . . One is tempted to say that in both the literal and figurative sense, Joubert lacked body. He himself admitted the justness of Madame de Châtenay's remark that he seemed a pure spirit who had stumbled on a body by chance and made the best he could of it.

Though we can detect in Joubert something of the shrinking of the valetudinarian from the rough and tumble of life, we cannot insist too strongly that his spirituality is true spirituality

and not the Rousseauistic imitation. The words that he traced almost with his dying hand really sum up the effort of his whole life: "22 March, 1824. The true, the beautiful, the just, the holy!" He is far removed from a man like Coleridge who retired from his actual obligations into a cloud of opium and German metaphysics. (pp. 35-7)

The danger of Joubert's avowed dislike for mere reality . . . is not so much a romantic retreat into the tower of ivory as an undue sympathy for certain conceptions of the noble style and the grand manner. . . . His attitude towards the opposite school of art appears in his remark that the novels of Lesage "seem to have been written in a coffee-house by a player of dominoes just after leaving the theatre."

Joubert's shrinking from *l'affreuse réalité* [mere reality] is also to be connected with the fact that he had lived through the Reign of Terror. "The Revolution," he says, "drove my spirit from the real world by making it too horrible for me." (pp. 38-9)

But even without the Revolution Joubert would never have been a thorough-going modern. The ancients, he says, were appealed to by the magic of the past and not like the moderns by the magic of the future, and he was in this respect a true ancient. (p. 39)

What the eighteenth century wanted, according to Joubert, was not religious liberty, but irreligious liberty. It was for discarding as mere prejudice everything that did not make itself immediately intelligible either to reason or feeling. . . . The other extreme towards which Joubert himself inclines is to impose the past too despotically on the present. Though he vivifies tradition with insight, more perhaps than any other French reactionary, he is nevertheless too resolutely traditional. Such has been the revolutionary stress of the past hundred years that it has rarely failed to disturb the poise even of the most finely tempered spirits. Joubert tends to see only the benefits of order. . . . (pp. 39-40)

Joubert is . . . consistent in his severe handling of the two great leaders of eighteenth century thought, Voltaire and Rousseau. He can, to be sure, imagine good coming from a reformed Rousseau, but can conceive of no circumstances in which a Voltaire would be of any profit. (p. 41)

If Joubert leans too much to the side of reaction in his politics and religion he preserves in the main a remarkable poise in his literary opinions. He was placed between an age that had been rational in a way to discredit the reason and an age that was going to be imaginative in a way to discredit the imagination. He protests against the excess of the past and utters a warning against the excess that was to come. Yet nothing would give a false notion of Joubert's work than to look on it primarily as a warning or a protest, or upon his rôle as only negative and restrictive. For the French he is not merely the author of the **"Pensées"** but, along with Fontanes, the literary mentor of Chateaubriand. Now of these two "guardian angels" of Chateaubriand, as Sainte-Beuve calls them, Joubert was the one who inspired and encouraged, whereas Fontanes was rather inclined to caution and hold back. In his attacks on formalism, in his plea for hospitality of mind and feeling, Joubert had his face turned towards the future. (pp. 41-2)

Joubert is constantly vindicating the claims of the imagination against both the formalists and the rationalists. "Nothing that does not enrapture is poetry; the lyre is so to speak a winged instrument." No view of life is sound that lacks imaginative wholeness. "Whatever we think, we must think with our whole selves, soul and body,'' and above all avoid one-sidedness. ''Man is an immense being in some sort, who may exist partially but whose existence is delectable in proportion as it becomes full and complete.'' It would not be easy to find an utterance more satisfying than this from the point of view of the humanist. Above all Joubert is severe upon the one-sided intellectualists.... He warns us to distrust words in philosophical books that ''have not become generally current and are fit only to form a special dialect.'' (pp. 42-3)

Joubert, according to Chateaubriand, wanted his philosophy to be at the same time painting and poetry. A philosophical thought, as Joubert believed, when it got thoroughly matured lost its abstract rawness, as it were, and took on atmosphere, form, sound, light, color. Possibly his unwillingness to speak abstractly, even when abstraction is plainly indicated, is responsible for the somewhat over-luxuriant metaphor.... He seems very modern in his insistence that words should not be treated as mere algebraic signs after the fashion of the eighteenth century, that they should not be robbed, so to speak, of their aura of suggestiveness. He felt and encouraged the subtle emotional interplay and blending of the different arts that was to figure so largely in the romantic movement. ''Beautiful verses,'' to quote one of his many utterances on this subject, ''are exhaled like sounds and perfumes,'' and this should seem good doctrine to a follower of Verlaine. ''We should not portray objects,'' to cite another advanced saying, ''but our feelings about objects''; and this should satisfy even a post-impressionist.

But Joubert was careful to follow his own rule and never utter a truth without at the same time putting forth its complementary truth. He did not, like so many moderns, go mad over the powers of suggestiveness.... [After] saying that when ''you understand a word perfectly, it becomes, as it were, transparent, you see its color and form, you feel its weight,'' etc., he admits that the main thing in a word is not its color or its music, but its meaning; and that when words are so chosen and arranged as to express the meaning most clearly, they are likely also to seem the most harmonious. ''What is wanted,'' he says, ''is not merely the poetry of images but the poetry of ideas.'' ''When the image masks the object, and you make of the shadow a body, when expression gives such pleasure that you no longer tend to pass beyond, to penetrate to the meaning, when the figure in fine absorbs the whole of your attention, you are held up on the way and the road is taken for the goal, because a bad guide is conducting you.'' This hits severely many of the French romanticists, Gautier certainly, and I should not hesitate to add, Hugo. (pp. 43-5)

Joubert is nowhere more original than in his ideas about the rôle of illusion in life and art. Here if anywhere he justifies his boast that he is more Platonic than Plato.... He defends art and literature against Plato by arguments that are themselves highly Platonic. The artist should not be satisfied with copying the objects of sense, for in that case his works would fall under Plato's censure of being at two removes from reality, mere ''shadows of a shadow world.'' He should, on the contrary, so use the objects of sense as to adumbrate a higher reality; so as to produce a cast, a hollow cast as it were, of a heavenly archetype. Now this adumbration of a higher reality can only be achieved by the medium of imaginative illusion. By imaginative illusion communication may be established between the reality of sense and the reality of spirit. We may be made to ''imagine souls by the means of bodies.'' ''Heaven, seeing that there were many truths which by our nature we could not

know, and which it was to our interest, nevertheless, not to be ignorant of, took pity on us and granted us the faculty of imagining them. We can perceive the truth in this sense only through a veil of illusion, and it is the grace of the truth to be thus veiled. This intimate blending of illusion and wisdom is the charm of life and of art. ''God deceives us perpetually and wishes us to be deceived; and when I say that he deceives us,'' Joubert adds, ''I mean by illusions and not by frauds.'' Illusion thus conceived becomes an integral part of reality, and we must not strive to see anything in its nakedness.... (pp. 46-7)

Joubert has remarks of extraordinary penetration not only on the right use of imaginative illusion, but on its misuse by the Rousseauists, on what one may call the false illusion of decadence. If Rousseau did not relate illusion to the reality of spirit, he did relate it in a way to the reality of sense; he used it to throw a sort of glamour over earthly impulse, especially the master impulse of sex. In his attitude towards this master impulse, Joubert not only departs from Rousseau, but is one of the least Gallic of Frenchmen. ''By chastity,'' he says, ''the soul breathes a pure air in the most corrupt places, by continence it is strong whatever may be the state of the body; it is royal by its empire over the senses; it is fair by its light and peace.'' Reason may suffice for ordinary virtues, according to Joubert, but religion alone can make us chaste. (pp. 47-8)

[Taste,] like most other desirable things, is dualistic in its nature, is a mediation between extremes; but the selective and restrictive aspect of taste that Joubert emphasizes is not only the most important in itself, but it is the aspect which the moderns from Rousseau to Signor Croce have most persistently neglected and denied. ... Madame de Staël tended to identify genius with taste, and to make both purely expansive. Joubert inclines rather to the extreme of concentration. ''If there is a man,'' he writes, ''tormented by the accursed ambition to put a whole book in a page, a whole page in a phrase, and that phrase in a word, it is I.'' ... Joubert attacks repeatedly another closely related naturalistic vice, the worship of mere force or energy, the literary Napoleonism of which Sainte-Beuve accused Balzac. ''Without delicacy,'' says Joubert, ''there is no literature.'' ''To write well a man should have a natural facility and an acquired difficulty.'' We are more familiar perhaps with the exact opposite, with the man who had little natural facility, but who has at least succeeded in acquiring the sterile abundance of the journalist. Joubert has not a trace of our modern megalomania. (pp. 49-50)

Though Joubert was in a high degree judicial and selective, the standards by which he judged and selected were not formal, but intuitive. ''Professional critics,'' he says, expressing his disdain for the formalists, ''can distinguish and appreciate neither uncut diamonds nor gold in the bar. They are merchants and know in literature only the coins which have currency. Their criticism has balances and scales but neither crucible nor touchstone.'' (pp. 50-1)

Though he possessed the critical touchstone of which he speaks I am not setting up Joubert himself as infallible.... That he could be insufficiently on his guard against formalism even in poetry where he is usually most at home, is shown by his comparison of Milton with the Abbé Delille, which is not only bad but almost monumental in its badness. Perhaps his blindness here is an instance of the potency of the *Zeitgeist* [the moral or historical reality of the country in which it has been created] which he was one of the first to define adequately.

Still his critical intuition puts him on his guard as a rule even against the *Zeitgeist*. Perhaps indeed Joubert may be most adequately defined in contradistinction to the formalist, as the intuitive critic. (p. 51)

To say that Joubert is spiritually intuitive is to put him in the class of sages; a class, the representatives of which are recognizable through the infinitely diverse accidents of time and space by their agreement on essentials. It would, for example, be easy to collect a list of parallel passages from Joubert and Emerson. (p. 54)

Joubert's quality as a critic is revealed especially by the fact that he not only had standards but held them fluidly. His insistence on the fixed and the permanent is nearly always tempered by the sense of change and instability. (p. 56)

Though Joubert is thus willing to concede a great deal to the element of relativity he is not ready to go to the point of seeing in literature merely an expression of society. (p. 58)

> *Irving Babbitt, "Joubert," in his* The Masters of Modern French Criticism, *Houghton Mifflin Company, 1912, pp. 34-59.*

MARCEL PROUST   (essay date 1919?)

[*A French novelist and critic, Proust is best known for his multi-volume novel,* À la recherche du temps perdu (Remembrance of Things Past), *which is considered one of literature's greatest achievements. In the following excerpt from his miscellaneous criticisms, Proust provides a brief discussion of Joubert's correspondence. Although* Proust the Reader *was originally published in French in 1957 as* Contre Sainte-Beuve, *it is thought that Proust wrote it in 1919.*]

One can see that Joubert's letters were intended to please.... The wish to make a good impression on one's friends is compensatory, so to speak, to ambition; and those who, like Joubert, have renounced the thought of fame because deficient health, deficient talent too, may be, and lack of determination and driving force prevented them from working for it, are on the other hand stimulated into minor exploits, impromptus or little more, in order to make the most of themselves in the sight of younger members of their circle whom they would like to be admired by. And so we find in Joubert an abstemious distinction whose accents tell of solitude ... and yet, for all that, something perpetually sociable, all letter-writing and talking and allusions to his own Joubertian self, and assumptions that man is a social animal.... Nevertheless, what he says is coloured from within by his latent genius, and one understands how, feeling so superior and yet being unrecognised and having produced nothing, he set himself to prove his worth in the letters to Fontanes, and Molé, and Mme. de Beaumont, if nowhere else. (p. 371)

> *Marcel Proust, "Proust the Reader: Joubert," in his* Marcel Proust On Art and Literature 1896-1919, *translated by Sylvia Townsend Warner, Meridian Books, Inc., 1958, pp. 371-72.*

H. P. COLLINS   (essay date 1928)

[*Collins explicates Joubert's critical method and ranks him unfavorably with his contemporaries.*]

It has been customary to derive the essential characteristics of [Joubert's] thought from his early and lifelong devotion to the great philosopher, [Plato], but this is an assumption in which some caution is needed. If Plato was the dominant intellectual influence upon him, his moral nature was more, and his whole spiritual nature quite as much, conditioned by orthodox Christianity, of which the expression was not always tempered by the keenest intellectual stringency. His sayings on local and contemporary matters, in which his recoil from the spirit of the *philosophes* and the horrors of the Revolution (he connected the two) affected his view most strongly, are a rather curious blend of reason and conventional piety; but a blend less curious than it might have been had the time not been one in which piety was itself a form of "la raison." Joubert valued "la raison"; and he was probably aware that it must be sought upon various planes if it is to be made applicable to all things. In questions of literature, of high philosophy, in which he passed more or less beyond the sphere of his religious certitude, he is very obviously inspired by ancient and timeless wisdom; mainly embodied, for him, in Plato. But a consideration of his views on social, political, and domestic questions will show that they are deeply tinctured with the attitude ... bred of the culture of the *ancien régime;* a culture formalized, semi-Augustan, traditional, narrow, and singularly persuasive, from which nobody but the Rousseauists had escaped. With the Rousseauists Joubert, for all his "hospitality" of mind, could have nothing lasting in common. It is a great distinction of Joubert that, finding himself at a parting of the ways, he turned neither to the right nor to the left, but still went forward.... Joubert's delicate constitution, physical and mental, induced a certain fastidiousness; but "behind his weakness there was strength." Reactionary he was, though not very often, and never *statically* so. For, it must be remembered, occasional tracts of ignorance that seem strange to us were hardly to be escaped by the rarest French intellects of his age; and Joubert in any case had no pretensions to the intellectual vigour and indiscriminate hunger for knowledge of a Diderot or a Madame de Staël, nor perhaps half the facilities for reading that Sainte-Beuve quite soon after turned to so good account. He had a finer, subtler feeling for the essentials of literature, of the human spirit itself, than any of them; but Dante and Shakespeare meant nothing to him. Homer, he said, *is* poetry, as Plato is metaphysics.

It is to this limitation, rather than to his Platonism (which is usually left to mean a transcendentalism and idealism that have been fatal to so many purely critical thinkers) that should be traced the disparity between Joubert's almost supreme quality in aesthetic generalization and the inadequacy or partiality of his judgments on some writers. This disparity has been slightly exaggerated—even by so great an authority as Dr. Saintsbury [see excerpt above, 1904]. For it must be borne in mind that Joubert did not write for publication; that he made no sustained survey even of French literature; and that nearly all his judgments are touched with the over-emphasis of the aphorism. On the Greeks and the Romans (confining the question for the moment to pure literature) he is very original, considering his time and his nationality: he is no neo-classic. His love of Virgil has something of the idolatry of the Renaissance; his criticisms are wholly on the *positive side,* but so far they are both sound and stimulating. (pp. 225-26)

Joubert was to some extent, in a complex and rather negative way, the product of his own century: his comment on the earlier and greater French writers is a little disappointing. A certain fastidious exclusiveness seems to limit his scope.... What Joubert ... did *not* write is, of course, negative evidence; but he has more than one mention of Molière, and he is wholly insignificant on that great writer. Of Rabelais he does not speak. Rabelais was not very Platonic, and Joubert was openly distrustful of "vigour"; but it is to be feared that he had no stomach for this fight. His greatest admirations seem to be for Bossuet, which is explicable enough, and La Fontaine, whom he thinks the most poetical of Frenchmen. He also rates highly Amyot, Corneille, La Bruyère, and Fénelon—though his reservations on the last are both strong and discriminating. Yet he thinks Balzac (he of the *Lettres*) "un de nos plus grands écrivains" [one of our greatest writers], which seems a lapse into the unconscious aestheticism which led to his notorious (though too much preached-on) admiration for the Abbé Delille and the "Descriptive" school. What he respects in Corneille is a nobility that transcends his works, which are "less perfect" than Racine's. Of Racine . . . Joubert had a poor opinion . . . , [though] neatly expressed. But a Frenchman of perfect sincerity who calls Racine "the Virgil of the ignorant" is giving a very real indication of the uncommonness of his own mind. (pp. 226-27)

Joubert was not an idealist or a transcendentalist in his aesthetic criticism. Being by no means a pure romantic, he had no "absolute" in art. Deeply spiritual by nature, his literary values, at least on their highest plane, are spiritual ("it is above all in spirituality of ideas," he says, "that poetry consists"); but his absolute does not lie solely in the highest manifestations of the human spirit in art. Though he may concede that *la religion* is the metaphysics of the simple, his certainty of a personal God (of Whom "space is the stature") and the further conviction of a better world to come lead him fundamentally to see human life as a passage, and, therefore, even the highest concerns of this life as subordinate, *in the individual,* to something beyond. But his Catholicism does not generally condition his literary judgments: it is clear that his intelligence has had to temporize. There is something higher than any spiritual apprehension possible to the individual man . . . ; but the soul of mankind is itself real, and real only. . . . So the literature which is but the expression of a transient phase of society; the literature which merely records *l'affreuse réalité* [mere reality]; and the literature that springs from what is exaggerated in the romanticism of Rousseau must all pass. The Platonic leaven is here clearly at work in the son of the *dixhuitième* and of the college at Toulouse. (p. 227)

Joubert's perfectionism in art (this is closely related to what has been said of his religion) concerns the ideal state, not of the creator, but of the critic, the reader. A writer is enduring not because what he gives is perfect, but in so far as he contributes to the process of inward self-perfection by the sensitive reader. At this perfection Joubert aimed; and though the attitude may sound "precious," it almost never became so in him. "Light!" was his cry, as it was to be Matthew Arnold's after him; and one can best suggest why this also was not precious by pointing out that his demand for the writer to carry us, first and essentially, into the realms of light means very much the same thing as does Longinus's desideratum of "the Sublime." Coming when it did, from Joubert as from Longinus and from Arnold, it was a necessary protest against a thickening spiritual darkness.

This self-perfecting aim of Joubert's is, of course, only an ideal formulation of the critical spirit itself, of the motive of all criticism. On deeper examination, indeed, the two things are identical. But unfortunately, self-perfection in aesthetic criticism has never been considered as a way of complete morality.

Joubert's humanism is quite as remote from the naturalism of Rousseau as from the most formalized pseudo-Aristotelianism of the previous age. He respects the dignity of man, but he has no illusions about liberty. "Universal justice will be liberty

enough." It has been very aptly said that he differed from Mme. de Staël in seeing morality as a bridle and not as a spur. He concedes to the Romantics that literature needs passions; but adds that it is restrained passions which avail. He wishes to control instinct by reason, and to subdue reason and unite it with a higher, more spiritual wisdom that is partly Platonic and partly religious; deriving as much from the humility of man as from his dignity. Joubert would have man achieve his highest nature not by discarding reason, but by subordinating himself to reason and reason to a higher impulse.

The *essence* of things is a kind of order; and it is by orderly contemplation of order that their nature is apprehended and conveyed. Whatever conforms to "universal order" is beautiful. As a natural consequence of this view, Joubert's conception of education (and particularly his justification of religious teaching as a part thereof) is based mainly upon the idea of order as the only way of life for the average mind. Joubert being comparatively practical, his "order" is not in all things the transcendent harmony of Plato's *Er* [a character in *The Myth of Er the Son of Aremius*]; but his lowering of its plane in political and domestic matters is justifiable both as intelligence and as utilitarian ethic. (pp. 228-29)

The tendency of Joubert's criticism at its highest was to "platonize" the poetic consciousness—it was Coleridge's too—but they both platonized it unawares; holding the one a not wholly assimilated religious dogma and the other a wholly intractable metaphysical conscience, which both were too scrupulous knowingly to abandon. Joubert, though centuries of the Christian tradition came between him and direct acceptance of Greek thought, remains one of the most perfect exemplars of the power of Plato's spirituality to inspire a truly poetic conception of poetry. It must be noted here that Joubert had entertained both the idea that "la métaphysique" could be more poetic than poetry and the idea that the poet could find more truths in his quest of beauty than could the philosopher in quest of truth.

He does not rank with Coleridge and two or three others. The first reason, naturally, that strikes one is his lack of sustained reasoning, the fragmentary form in which we have his opinions, and the never *perfectly* final finality of the aphorism. The second reason, also evident, and hardly separable from the first, is the faint air of over-delicacy which pervades his responses to the stimulus of high literature; it is accentuated by his very metaphorical expression; and the whole effect is capable of irritating, slightly and not unjustly, one who comes to him in a mood of passionate surrender to great poetry—a mood which, on the other hand, could, or should, find entire satisfaction in Coleridge on the Imagination. One who feels that poetry touches the highest comprehension of life, of the nature of things, and the mystery of things, that human vision has glimpsed may feel at difference with Joubert's conscious perfectionism *as expressed*. As expressed, we must say: Joubert's attitude almost certainly sprang from an unconscious impulse deeper than itself.

A third limitation of the Joubertian Poetic, if not directly due to the seeming disregard of Dante and Shakespeare that has already been noted, is certainly implicit in his reluctance for intimate experience with work that was, roughly speaking, anti-Platonic. Like many men who combine robust common-sense in practical matters with extremely refined aesthetic taste, he had an aversion to the art that concerns itself mainly with a valiant inclusion of the grosser elements of life. . . . [He] apparently did not realize that the wider, the more various, the more uncongenial is the experience that is comprehended and subdued, the greater is the sublimation. His austere judgment and taste consistently rejected bad work: it is another thing to reject any kind of experience prematurely because it has been made the material of bad work. (pp. 230-31)

The fourth limitation of Joubert's criticism is of a less obvious kind. . . . Joubert's knowledge of the nature of great art was a "religious knowledge." That is essential; for a critical comprehension that is religious (the word will not be misunderstood), however imperfect, is nearer to reality than any which wants for one of the greatest impulses of the human soul. Yet Joubert's approach to the poetry that is religion and the religion that is poetry, is incomplete. Let us put it this way: the aspiration (spiritual, intellectual and emotional) of man to ultimate truth is in the last resort one and indivisible: it is monistic. Joubert, though he would have been pained to recognize it, formulates a dichotomy—which is, of course, remote from and unconnected with the metaphysical dualism he disliked. The reality on which he said so many excellent things, is an incomplete reality. There is "la réalité" and there is God. . . . To Joubert, God must be unknown: human reality is divine also, but of a second order of divinity. "Order"; the "reason which is the rule of rules"; these, be they never so entirely spiritualized, "of essence and not of existence," be they even insurpassable as means of critical integration, are imperfect philosophical concepts when not fully derived, as Joubert does not derive them, from their origin. He specifies reality without specifying in comparable terms the nature of God; he does not achieve a moral identity between devotional truth and ultimate aesthetic truth. This does not affect the duality either of his piety or of his aesthetic judgment; but it does impair the value of his philosophic legacy. (p. 231)

H. P. Collins, "The Criticism of Joubert," in The New Adelphi, Vol. I, No. 3, March, 1928, pp. 225-32.

PAUL J. STURM   (essay date 1941)

[*Sturm interprets Joubert's* pensées *as an expression of his personality. For further commentary by Sturm, see Additional Bibliography.*]

[Joubert's] notebooks were a register for the ideas that occurred to him; they allowed him to test incompletely conceived notions, for he was never sure of all there might be in a thought until he had written it down. Here he analyzed the qualities of his mind and feeling, not with the desire to publicize them, but because he could never escape the problems hinging on the close relation of his thought and personal idiosyncrasies.

There are not a few literary works of intrinsic value, whose greater interest lies in the personality of the author they reveal; it even may happen that an author's masterpiece, whether he suspects it or not, is himself. That was Joubert's case, and his *Pensées* are primarily notes on life and art as experienced by a remarkably subtle and subjective intelligence. Though he wrote much that is valid in any context, his work cannot avoid being first considered as the expression of a personality. (p. 345)

[Joubert] has been seen as a moralist, even a moralizer, rather more prim than we like men to be. Too much place was given in the *Pensées* to his religious and moralistic dicta, for his real originality does not lie in theological or philosophical ways. He added nothing there, unless it be the spectacle of a highly sensitive man reacting in his own fashion to eternal questions. Joubert is to be considered most attentively when he speaks of

taste, of literary ideas, of esthetic principles, and no less carefully when he speaks of himself. Many things . . . escape the professional psychologist. The scientific method does not disengage those facets of character most subtly significant, nor yet those movements of the heart unamenable to cold charting. That is the artist's province, and one Joubert adorned in the portrait of himself.

For his psychological dicta he was his own subject most often, and indeed in the whole of the *Carnets* are few pages that do not in some measure add to the self-portrait to which he devoted such minute attention. It is not possible in a single article to study all that intellectual autobiography, but one aspect may serve to indicate how faulty the representation of Joubert has been, and how much, both because and in spite of [the work of Beaunier, Joubert's biographer], remains to be treated. In the *Carnets* it is to be noted that as Joubert's attention shifted from broad philosophic questions to matters closer at hand, more immediately connected with the living of life, he became more curious about the workings of his mind. As the notebooks became more exclusively personal, he entered many reflections on his character, temperament and spirit. (pp. 349-50)

[Joubert's] writing, which grew so personal in implication, depended to an extraordinary degree on the kind of man he was. While that is of course true of all authors, in the case of some the subjective aspect attains an importance outweighing all other considerations. The *moraliste* especially is preoccupied with the impact of society on himself, and is constrained to probe as deeply as he may into the nature of his relations with the world. That is not to deny the trait to authors of another sort, or to limit the application of what personal truths the *moraliste* may discover. The bias of a writer's thought may present variations in externals which are less significant than they appear, but it is still true that in a certain category of authors we look first for the artist, while in another we cherish the man and against his, measure our own experience of the world. In Joubert's case there is further reason to study his self-analysis. The many fine fragments that came from his pen remain unfused, and he was curious to resolve the paradox of his talent for original and brilliant statement, which he could never submit to the discipline through which it might have found complete expression. That problem lay at the root of all the *pensées* on himself, which with few exceptions treat of three main subjects: his art, the characteristics of his mind, and himself as a social being. More intimate remarks occupy little space, for though Joubert willingly bared his mind, he would not dissect his heart even in the privacy of his journals. Much of his fascination lies in that reticence. There can hardly be a more fruitful field to investigate the workings of genius than a mind so richly endowed, but denied . . . any complete success. (p. 351)

He considered [his] unpublished art with as much earnestness as if it were known to all France, rather than to himself alone, and with close scrutiny analyzed his attainment and his ideal. In 1799 he formulated his purpose; already conscious that he could not appeal to a wide public, he was yet unsure how to use his talents and undecided as to his medium of expression. The next year he noted succinctly that he would wish his books to be read like a poem; that is, meditatively, for they would be but the essence of his thought, and poetically, for their conception would be that of poetry. He was born with a hatred of abstraction which grew deeper with age, and led him to imagine a style far removed from the dryness that repelled him in the writings of Condillac, Locke and Malebranche. He aspired to clarity, not of a banal sort, but that of the perfect image, entirely congruous to his thought and beautiful in itself. Clarity implied to him not only the abandonment of a specialized philosophic terminology, but a positive effort toward making common language serve a purpose at once poetic and philosophic. Factual statement was meaningless to him; he had in each case to find the exact image.

The question of form plagued him always. It seemed impossible to reconcile what he desired to say with any artistic pattern he commanded. Ideas he considered most highly came expressed in too definitive shape, and it was never easy to find their proper setting. The limitations of his naturally lapidary style hampered him, as he had too many forms of thought for it to accommodate. Joubert recognized his mania for condensation as a quality and a defect. He seems to have alternated between the inclination to cultivate his rich but narrow gift, and the urge to push back the bounds that hemmed him in. At times he appeared to accept the maxim as his native form of expression, and wish only to perfect it, declaring he sculpted and engraved his thoughts, and so spoke to his reader's memory. This art-form he viewed neither wholly as prose nor as poetry, but as something between. . . . Joubert rarely suggested he had found his ultimate formula; on occasion he indicated satisfaction with one or another effect achieved, but that only seldom. He had many half-conceptions, intuitions that delighted his mind, but often so vague there could be no question of setting them to paper, and these pleased him more than what he wrote.

With the years his problems became less of form than of thought. As that grew more rarified, less communicable in ordinary terms, he dreamed of doing without words, for they troubled him seriously. Later still he found that the words he had scorned took revenge by becoming ever more difficult and expressing less and less of what he wanted to say. He observed in himself tendencies to preciosity; that distressed him, for he protested it was never a phrase he polished, but his idea. His instinct to distill all but the essence led to difficulties, for it meant that each idea became an entity in itself and far from easy to incorporate with others. Joubert ended by realizing what he had suspected all the while, that he could never construct "a dwelling to house his ideas."

Yet much of his writing he thought worthy of communication; though his thoughts might never be synthesized, they were individually excellent. He perceived each thing he wrote to be touched with himself and possessed of considerable elevation. Some twenty years before his death Joubert seems to have renounced thinking in terms of publication, but he did not for that reason cease to think of his *pensées* as an artistic expression. He continued what, in effect, he had always done, to write for himself. There is fatigue and a measure of regret in the final notes of self-criticism: he could write well only slowly and with distressing consequences to his body. Heaven had given him for eloquence only some beautiful words, and with those he had hoped to build a structure which they proved unfit to support.

One may not say that at a given moment Joubert realized himself incapable of writing a book, and consequently gave over thinking of it. It merely appears from the *Carnets* that during the decade 1795-1805 he was most hopeful of setting his ideas in their proper form, and hence most intent in criticizing their literary qualities. Before the end of that period he had recognized that his problems were not so much literary as psychological; it was by the nature of his mind that he met literary success or failure. Remarks on his habits of thought

entered the *Carnets* later than the literary *pensées,* and continued in greater abundance until the end. They deal with the same basic problem, and after 1800 Joubert made no distinction between them.

When he became convinced that his difficulties must lie in the very fabric of his mind, he began probing for what lay at the source both of his originality and impotence. Early in the search he discovered a fundamental characteristic that must color all else: what seemed false, that is, what offended his heart, ceased to exist as far as he was concerned. This peculiarity, which few admit so frankly, obviously limited his speculation, admirable though it may have been for the uses of personal contentment. The Revolution, he said, drove his mind from the real world by making it too horrible; thereafter it could function only in an atmosphere from which all unfavorable elements had been excluded. Revolution or no, there is small reason to believe he would not in time have made his own new world from those fragments of the old that pleased him. He well knew himself unadapted to the brutal things of this world, and though he did not always remain in his shelter, it was there against his need.

It was a mind he saw to be quite unendowed for abstract thought, demanding concreteness and clarity. . . . He stood always in need of sympathy, could never talk before antagonistic persons, had no gift for argumentation, and expanded only in the presence of his warm friends. Such a mind is not closely bound to the earth, and Joubert felt the need of imposing fetters so it might retain some contact with ordinary reality. But these were not often applied; he rejoiced in the lightness and buoyancy of his spirit that would prevent its ever bogging down in dullness. That same character made it incapable of ever penetrating to the heart of any philosophic system. Joubert realized himself to be an eclectic, indeed he gloried in the attribute.

He came to recognize, also, the futility of judging his *pensées* by literary standards, for they were less literature than the expression of his whole self and the foundation of his life. He remarked that his spirit had long been deprived of what he came to regard as its proper sustenance. Once that was found, purely literary considerations lost in importance; what mattered was to procure his own spiritual nourishment. In embracing an orthodoxy that might spare him the search for basic doctrines, he reserved the privilege of meditating on the dogma he had accepted, never to examine its ultimate validity, but to adjust it more nearly to his spirit. In his mature years he never came to grips with fundamental problems of philosophy and religion. He felt unequipped for that through lack of intermediary ideas which either failed, or else fatigued, him. He exercised his talents, rather, on the periphery of great questions, and often saw keenly into matters of detail. (pp. 352-55)

His aspirations at the end were not literary; he desired to lift himself to an ever higher spiritual level, and he groaned that his mind too often failed him in that. (p. 356)

[From] the *Carnets* it is evident that at different times Joubert's study of himself centered about different characteristics. Before 1805 he made few specific observations on his moral nature but in the years following these are found in abundance. They corroborate other testimony to the effect that Joubert, despite a strong cast of other-worldliness, was a distinctively social being who recognized his duties as a member of society and was markedly successful in performing at least a part of them. There was about him a natural amenity which, for those in whose company he felt at ease, made his companionship a unique delight. Half-measures were not for him; he threw himself whole-heartedly into all he undertook. . . . Ambitious of perfection, he tried to moderate his zeal, sought to prevent the too-frequent disturbance of his nervous organization by imposing a rule of calm he only too often broke. . . . If he was violent in denouncing whatever incurred his displeasure, he found it easy to extend the warmest charity to most individuals who crossed his path. No pleasure gratified him more than to give pleasure, and even his personally administered criticism he desired to be so kindly as to give no offense. . . . (pp. 356-57)

There is most charm and light in these judgments on his moral nature. That is perhaps due to the subject, for though he was an imperfect artist, there can be no question that as a man he had a peculiar and refreshing genius. In the *pensées* on his character there is a serene frankness untainted by false pride. He had spent the greater part of a lifetime closely observing the movements of his heart, and though he may have had reason to withhold complete approval from what he wrote, he had none to be displeased with his delicately balanced moral nature. He was never pleased to note others' shortcomings, but rather gratified to discover in his fellows any trace of that perfection he had set as his goal. He took pride in never having "learned to speak ill, to execrate." (p. 357)

It is surely rare to come upon a mind of this sort, singularly clear, capable of sensing much that lies beyond its ken, able even to formulate objections to everything most in harmony with its nature, and yet with the capacity of sweeping aside all obstacles to its even course. Joubert was never blind to the evils of the world, but experience of systems and codes he found alien to his nature led him to establish principles as a measure for all ideas. Happiness for him depended on the rather severe limitation of his thought, but one feels an awareness on his part of what lay beyond the pale, as if he kept it just enough in mind never to forget the wisdom, even necessity, of that choice. If he sometimes regretted he was not otherwise, he more often accepted himself, even with a show of complacence. (p. 358)

> Paul J. Sturm, "Joseph Joubert's Self-Portrait," in *The Romanic Review, Vol. XXXII, No. 4* (December, 1941), pp. 345-58.

MARGARET GILMAN   (essay date 1949)

[*Gilman traces the evolution of Joubert's thought from his early association with the French philosopher Denis Diderot to the development of his own aesthetic theories and critical methods.*]

It is only since the publication in 1938 of a large portion of [*Les Carnets de Joseph Joubert*] that it has been possible to realize fully how dear poetry was to Joubert, how much thought he devoted to it, and how rich the *Carnets* are in observations on it. [The *Carnets*] shows how Joubert's thought developed and changed in the long period from 1774 to 1824. . . . At times the interest in poetry seems nearly submerged by Joubert's moral and religious and political preoccupations, but never completely so.

This interest in poetry is shown very early in the *Carnets*, and particularly in the fragments of the essay on *La Bienveillance universelle*, composed between 1779 and 1783. . . . After his arrival in Paris he had come to know Diderot well, and had worked with him until Diderot's death in 1784. Later on he renounced his early master, and many passages of the *Carnets*

contain violent contradictions and criticisms of Diderot. But even without Joubert's own statement the influence of Diderot on his early thinking is obvious. The notes for the unfinished essay on *La Bienveillance universelle* are impregnated with Diderot's ideas, including those on poetry and imagination. Joubert, like Diderot, is writing not of the poet in the limited sense, but of the "maker," the creative writer. . . . Aesthetic questions are discussed only incidentally in *La Bienveillance universelle*, but Joubert's ideas on them, as on other subjects, seem almost without exception to be derived from Diderot. The interesting thing is to follow the persistence of certain of these ideas in later years, when Joubert was vehemently renouncing Diderot and all his works. (pp. 251-52)

In the years just after 1800 the *Carnets* are especially rich in ideas about poetry. Joubert, with his personal religious problem solved, with the establishment of what seemed a stable government, turned his thoughts to literature again. These are the early years of his friendship with Chateaubriand, and the discussion of the "Poétique du christianisme" section of [Chateaubriand's] *Génie du christianisme* may have stimulated his own thinking. But, sympathetic though he was with Chateaubriand, their ideas on poetry have little in common. For Chateaubriand the great question is the influence of Christianity on poetry in its widest sense, while Joubert is forever pursuing the tantalizing question, "What *is* poetry?" (p. 253)

[For] Joubert there is no poetry without enthusiasm, no poetry without imagination. If this were all, one might be tempted to see in him no more than a docile and thoughtful disciple of Diderot, and to deny him any great originality. However, when Joubert considers the poet not only as the maker, the creative writer in general, but as the maker of the special kind of writing we call poetry, his remarks, although there are still echoes of Diderot, have a more individual and personal note. Above all he stresses a quality in poetry which is not mentioned by Diderot before him nor the romantics after him: concision. (p. 256)

The poet can by his labor make any material poetic. It is evident how far Joubert is at this point from any theory of pure inspiration. Here is a conscious construction, the work of an architect, of an artist. Yet the finished work is no solid structure, but light as air, aglow with color and light. . . . [Joubert] seems to be on the fringes of the modern doctrine of pure poetry. (pp. 257-58)

It is in the years around 1805 that Joubert established his conception of poetry. The little he says of it in later years tends to repeat and develop what had been said earlier. During these years the moralist is again uppermost, and poetry and piety are once more allied. . . .

[If] one takes all that Joubert says at its face value one has somewhat the impression of a potpourri of ideas past and to come: a classic belief in order and clarity, in painstaking labor; a romantic faith in inspiration and enthusiasm; a conception of the imagination as both a storehouse and a creator of images which is close to Diderot's, and at moments seems to foreshadow Baudelaire's; an emphasis on poetry as an architecture of words which even suggests Mallarmé and Valéry; and a final vision of poetry akin to "la poésie pure" [pure poetry]. All this is intriguing, but again one must beware of the temptation to read into Joubert's words all the significance that more than a century of discussions of poetry can suggest. One possible test of their true meaning is to ask what poets Joubert admired, whether any poet he knew corresponded to his conception of poetry, or whether he was dreaming rather of what poetry should be. (p. 258)

[What] we find in Joubert is not so much a prophecy of poetry to come as a sure judgment of the poetry he knew and loved, and an ability to deduce from that poetry an "art poétique" [poetic art] of his own. His ideas come both from his early acquaintance with Diderot and his reading of poetry itself. Without Diderot he would hardly have arrived at his conception of the nature and importance of imagination, accompanied on the one hand by enthusiasm, on the other by conscious labor. And his conception of poetry itself owes more than a little to Diderot, without, however, achieving the amazing insight into the wellsprings of poetry that Diderot had. Diderot's exaltation of Homer as the supreme poet, and Joubert's elevation of La Fontaine to the rôle of the French Homer, may well serve as a measure of the distance that separates them. It is to his own reading of poetry, and his special love of La Fontaine, that Joubert's idea of poetry owes most. For him poetry is a special language by means of which the poet etherealizes and lightens the images supplied by the imagination, and expresses them in concise and perfect form. He reached, I believe—and here lies his importance—a more valid conception of poetry than the somewhat vague and hazy one of the romantics who followed him. On the other hand, to see in him even a remote ancestor of the symbolists seems to me to misread his meaning, to forget that he found in La Fontaine the exemplification of his poetic ideal. Joubert is not dreaming of a poetry of obscurity and mystery, he is cherishing a poetry of clarity and harmony. (p. 260)

> *Margaret Gilman, "Joubert on Imagination and Poetry," in* The Romanic Review, *Vol. XL, No. 4 (December, 1949), pp. 250-60.*

THE TIMES LITERARY SUPPLEMENT (essay date 1954)

Joseph Joubert owes his peculiar prestige among critics to his sense of the Golden Mean. If his fastidiousness declined at times almost into the cult of the exquisite, he never lost his moral anchorage in religion or his Platonic range of sensibility. He was the earliest and perhaps the most penetrating critic of the Romantic revival in France, while at the same time he repudiated his own *dixhuitième* [eighteenth century] with an almost neurotic emphasis. . . . Nothing illustrates Joubert better than his comic avoidance of Madame de Staël . . . , who conceived morality as a spur and not as a bridle. For many years after his death the self-effacing invalid was remembered in France mainly as the friend and mentor of Fontanes and Chateaubriand, and in a sense it remains his most noteworthy achievement to have kept on terms with them, personally and intellectually, at all. . . .

In an ultra-psychological age the question of Joubert's bodily and mental health at once comes to the fore; and here up-to-date biographers have not greatly helped. There is no indication that, until he was approaching seventy, Joubert suffered any serious physical illness: and it seems that his valetudinarian way of life was either a nervous retreat or traceable to mild psycho-somatic ailments. His fineness of character and his spiritual integrity lend all his evasions of experience a consistency, an air of authenticity, rarely associated with neurosis; but there can be no doubt that he *was* more than normally evasive. He has been called a prig, and Madame de Duras found him "affected"; but his letters exhibit a fine sense of humour, a subtle gift for self-criticism, and a completely common-sense view of all questions of personal conduct. The strain of inertia, the difficulty in concentration, the abnormal sensitiveness to physical unpleasantness of any kind, all point to a genuine neurosis. He repeatedly complains of his incapacity for sustained thought. . . . His inability to compose anything long enough to publish would be abnormal in a writer of his gifts unless nervous energy were deficient. What is remarkable is the positive discipline imposed by moral culture, his sustained poise, his intolerance of any but balanced emotion. Waiting for the drop of light to form and fall from his pen, he seems to have achieved a complete critical detachment from the more terrifying aspects of a world that could nurture a Catullus, a Rabelais, a Madame de Staël. . . .

Specially Joubertian are the terseness, the metaphorical expression, and the hint of a flight into the empyrean. Always with Joubert the exactness of perception is closely related to a quest for the less tangible, more rarefied aspects of reality. If his feet never quite leave the earth, his eyes are reluctant to look lower than the skies. His grasp of the essentials of literature, of the nature of the imagination, is as firm as his sensibility is fragile: he is in the line of the great critics in his centrality, but he is the least of them in capacity for self-development. He cannot expand; he can only refine. He is tormented by the desire to say finer and finer things in a shorter and shorter space, but always on the same subjects: he has no passion to leave the familiar experience for the unfamiliar. The great drawback to new books, he says (only half humorously), is that they keep us from the classics. Thus he comes quite deliberately to value all things for their quality of permanence, . . . rather than for their originality. All good writing "resembles Homer's" (or Bossuet's); but Joubert is a true critic and remembers just in time that a good writer is only good when he is also himself, and is creating something out of his difference from Homer or Bossuet as well. Even here the traditionalist guards himself. Your true writer, he says—very finely—has a natural facility and an *acquired* difficulty. . . .

Joubert could understand the creative imagination while all the time a little afraid of it. . . . [The] artist has his own laws which are free of other laws. Plato's banishment of the poet is magnificently countered. The poet (rejoins the critic) is supreme not only in the realm of images, but in the realm of ideas. He is the interpreter and champion, not merely of sordid reality, but of the divine in man; of the idea itself as well as of the "copy of a copy of the idea."

The Platonic vein which gave wings to his discernment also lent dangerous plausibility to his exclusions. His tolerance is bounded: his comments on foreign literature—as apart from foreign philosophers—show limitations which are not purely linguistic. . . .

He is sounder in theory than in application. His reflections **"Du Style"** are criticism of the purest, which is the more surprising since the aphorism is not by its nature final: the author has to find the bull's-eye, so to speak, by over-shooting the mark. What first strikes one about Joubert's remarks on style is their unclouded realism. Unlike most professed realists, he is never sentimental about *writing*. Nor does he ever confound the word and the "objective correlative." He can observe at the same time that words, like spectacles, obscure everything they do not clarify, and that there is a great art in introducing pleasant ambiguities into one's phrasing. Sometimes the vague word is preferable to the exact one. Joubert perceives the equal authenticity of the writer whose style induces a particular way of writing and him whose style induces a particular way of thinking. Almost too artfully he counsels us, before using a fine word, to make a place for it. The logic of style (he claims) exacts a sounder judgment and finer intuitions than are needed to construct a system of philosophy. There is a certain looseness possible in the connecting of ideas, but words admit only one single possible point of correspondence and contact. Language must be visible as well as audible. In really effective expression, pronounced symmetries are mingled with blurred symmetries, and over-lively with subdued metaphors. Imagery may be employed to clarify conceptions; but it is no way to sum up opinions.

Joubert's neatness, his concentrated relevance, may smack of the aesthete; but his life's jottings as a whole show him no votary of art for art's sake. The reality revealed by creative art is never identified with the reality which is God. Joubert acquiesces, even glories, in the belief that God deceives us and wishes us to be deceived. Again and again he stresses that heavenly things are not to be questioned as are profane things. . . .

Perhaps it is not damaging to say of Joubert what he said rather damagingly of Racine, that his genius lay in his discernment. His definition of criticism (his true bent) as the methodical exercise of discrimination, hints a limitation: criticism is far more than that. His discernment of quality was always acute, but notably more acute when the issue was beyond the reach of dogma. His astringent mind was not of an order to romanticize, and so relax, the hold of Catholicism. He could to some extent poetize Plato: he could not poetize God. So for once he fell foul of Chateaubriand over the *Génie du Christianisme*. The two men were united by a deep distrust of the century of reason. But Chateaubriand must expand into the conception of a God whom he could, if not recreate, at least interpret. Joubert had long disclaimed, almost with horror, any desire to do either. God wishes us to be deceived.

"Joseph Joubert, the Critic's Critic," in The Times
Literary Supplement, *No. 2727, May 7, 1954, p. 299.*

RENÉ WELLEK   (essay date 1955)

[*Wellek's* A History of Modern Criticism *is a major, comprehensive study of the literary critics of the last three centuries. Wellek's critical method, as demonstrated in* A History *and outlined in his* Theory of Literature, *is one of describing, analyzing, and evaluating a work solely in terms of the problems it poses for itself and how the writer solves them. For Wellek, biographical, historical, and psychological information is incidental. In the following excerpt from* A History, *Wellek provides a brief overview of Joubert's critical theories.*]

Only one writer of the time, and he stood completely apart, had an insight into an imaginative conception of poetry: Joseph Joubert. . . . But he was hardly a critic in a public sense; he was rather a writer of aphorisms in the great French tradition. His papers were published only in 1838—and then only in a small selection—and thus could not affect the development of critical ideas at that time. Many of the admired sayings of Joubert on poetry formulate the usual emotional reaction to 18th-century rationalism. "There is no poetry without enthusiasm." "The lyre is, so to speak, a winged instrument." "Beautiful verses are exhaled like sounds or perfumes." "Anybody who has never been pious shall never become a poet." Joubert is exceptional only when he speaks of the poet as "purging and emptying the forms of matter" with the help of certain rays. "He makes us see the universe as it is in the mind of God." This Platonism is based on an insight into the role of imagination in art and life. "Imagination is the faculty of making sensuous what is intellectual, of making corporeal what is spirit: in a word, of bringing to light, without depriving it of its nature, that which in itself is invisible." Here the problem of the symbol in art is glimpsed without the term; the synthesis of the particular and the universal, the task of rendering in material language what is mental and spiritual. Joubert distinguished—as did Rivarol, many Germans, and Coleridge—between two kinds of imagination. "The imaginative, the animal faculty, [is] very different from imagination, the intellectual faculty." The first is "passive." The second is "active and creative." Most of his remarks are about imagination as a "species of memory," on "memory as the storehouse on which imagination draws," on imagination as a "painter." "It paints in our soul and outside for the soul of others. It clothes with images." It is substantially the visual imagination of Addison and the whole of the 18th century, with a glimpse, here and there, of its creativeness.

There are other remarkable sayings in Joubert's commonplace books: The poet should return the physical and primitive meaning to words, "polish, remint the money and renew its original markings." Another saying shows that Joubert understood the conciseness of poetry and its difference from rhetoric. "The character of the poet is to be brief, that is to say, perfect, *absolutus* as the Latins said; that of the orator is to be flowing, abundant, spacious, extended, varied, inexhaustible, immense." Joubert speaks of the poet "making words light and giving them color, making them fly about," though he can also speak of the "architecture of words" or the "pure essence" with which verse should be seasoned. All these are occasional metaphorical sayings which show that Joubert had learned from Diderot, whom he knew personally.

In spite of these theoretical insights, Joubert's literary opinions (we cannot speak of criticism) are not particularly coherent or independent. He disliked Racine, who seems to him sufficient only "for poor souls and poor spirits." Racine "made poetic the most middle-class sentiments and the most mediocre passions." Of all French poets Joubert admired La Fontaine most, calling him "our real Homer; the Homer of the French." His horror of reality was such that he frequently sided with the conventional and even inane. He preferred the Abbé Delille to Milton and defended Corneille's grand style by saying, "We should rise above the trivialities of the earth, even if we have to mount on stilts." Delicacy, even preciosity, his valitudinarian's shrinking from issues, will always impede a deeper impact of Joubert's fine observations. (pp. 243-44)

René Wellek, "Stendhal and Hugo," in his A History of Modern Criticism, 1750-1950: The Romantic Age, *Vol. 2,* Yale University Press, 1955, pp. 241-58.*

ALBERT S. GÉRARD   (essay date 1964)

[*Placing Joubert in the context of European Romanticism, Gérard treats the critic's aesthetic theories.*]

One of the reasons why Joseph Joubert increasingly appears as a significant, although minor, figure in early nineteenth-century French literature is that, in the midst of the preromantic Chateaubriand generation, he alone seems to have grasped some of the fundamentals of European romanticism. In this, he was totally out of touch with the prevailing literary mood of his own country, and it is not surprising that his aristocratic fastidiousness, his craving for lucidity and harmony, his contempt for egotism and sensationalism, should have earned him at first the reputation of a latter-day classicist. . . .

Sainte-Beuve was apparently the first critic to acknowledge that Joubert was modern in a deeper sense than the so-called "romantics" of his time [see excerpt above, 1849]. Indeed, as one studies Joubert's *Carnets,* one grows more and more convinced that he was the only Frenchman of his time to realize that the new trends involved a thorough going reappraisal of the poetic faculty and even of the nature of knowledge in general. And his aphoristic notes were, at the time, the only French expression of a new insight into the nature of poetry that was being fully developed in England and in Germany. (p. 158)

[There] is no doubt that Joubert, like his German and English contemporaries, felt the philosophical need to re-examine the current assumptions about the nature of knowledge in its relation with art. And he alone, among the French *hommes de lettres* [men of letters] of his day, took a share in the idealistic movement which received its main impetus from poets and students of poetry who found in the aesthetic experience and in the artistic faculty a way out of the rationalism and the sensationalism of the eighteenth century. From the feeling that such parts of the truth as were conveyed by the senses or by abstract reasoning were valueless and dead arose the psychology of the imagination, which was the main contribution of Coleridge and Wordsworth to the corpus of romantic thought as well as to the romantic theory of poetry. And, although Joubert in his early writings was apt to entertain the old and the new views of imagination simultaneously . . . he soon came out decisively on the side of imagination, asserting that art was a mode of knowledge capable of quenching the deep thirst of man where reason fails piteously. . . . But like Coleridge, and indeed before him, Joubert soon came to feel that the accepted terms and concepts of traditional psychology—although he was sometimes constrained to use them in their neoclassical sense— were unable to account satisfactorily for the distinguishing features of the poetic experience and of poetic creation. It is therefore by no means surprising that he too should have tried to redefine conventional words, to frame new distinctions, so as to give conceptual existence to the faculty that must be responsible for forms of experience which the older psychology of art had overlooked or denied. So it is that, just as Coleridge was to establish his famous distinction between primary imagination, secondary imagination, and fancy, Joubert, several years earlier, was already toying with the notion of various faculties or modes of the mind's activity. (pp. 159-60)

Joubert's use of "phantaisie" and "imaginative," like the lake poets' use of "fancy," was . . . a way of denoting at least three inferior kinds of poetry: poetry that relied on the mere collocations of sense images without submitting them to the unifying and idealizing power of a central idea; poetry that is purely subjective and arbitrarily reads human moods and emotions into natural objects through the device that came to be known as "pathetic fallacy"; poetry that resorts to personification, allegory, and mythology, purporting to make the invisible visible by the arbitrary and mechanical construction of concrete correlatives for abstract entities. . . . It is true that, in comparison with the achievements of his German and English contemporaries in this field, Joubert's efforts appear feeble, patchy, and inordinately confused. From the point of view of comparative literary history, however, they deserve some consideration, because nobody else in France at the time was so uneasily conscious of the wider issues involved in what may

have appeared to many as a mere turn in literary taste. His discrimination of the poetic faculties was a step forward in the revaluation of creative imagination, a process which had begun with Diderot but was not to reach its climax until Baudelaire's *L'Art romantique.* (p. 166)

> *Albert S. Gérard, "'Fancy' in Joubert: Modes of Imagination in Romanticism," in* Comparative Literature, *Vol. XVI, No. 2, Spring, 1964, pp. 158-66.*

PATRICIA A. WARD   (essay date 1980)

[*In this excerpt from her book-length study,* Joseph Joubert and the Critical Tradition: Platonism and Romanticism, *Ward comments on Joubert's Platonism and defines his role in the Romantic movement.*]

As a Platonist living in France between 1754 and 1824, Joubert's intellectual interests were concentrated . . . on metaphysics, aesthetics, and language. His struggles to articulate an idealistic philosophical outlook and to define the essence of beauty and of poetry ran directly counter to eighteenth-century associationist and materialist systems of philosophy and psychology. He rejected these as did others of his contemporaries in Germany and England. But in France Joubert was largely a generation ahead of his time. . . . Joubert worked out his intuitions and insights quite alone. While clinging to a Platonic position and resisting the Kantian answer to Hume, he reflected on issues which were to intrigue idealistic aestheticians from Schelling and Hegel to Croce. While remaining true to the poets and writers of the Empire, Joubert articulated a conception of poetry which was expressive, musicalized, and formalized. While admiring the great classical writers of Greece and of seventeenth- and eighteenth-century France, he adopted a non-mimetic view of the imagination which was most "unclassic". Consequently, this rather obscure notebook writer constitutes a prototypal example of the impact that Platonism had on early Romantics searching for a new aesthetic of creativity and a new definition of poetry.

Yet, Joubert the man defies almost all attempts to label him. Perhaps the only descriptions which fit are those of "Platonist" and "perfectionist". . . . Joubert was dominated by the desire to find a perfect expression for his ideas, but he rarely achieved this union of idea and external form except in an abbreviated fashion. His inability to externalize his inner ideas and feelings haunted him, but his notebooks constitute a remarkable record of the workings of his mind. More than any piece of extended prose, the entries are an organic expression of Joubert's Platonic way of apprehending truth and of approaching the act of writing. There may well have been a coalescence of personality and philosophical bent in Joubert's search for perfection. (pp. 11-12)

[Although] his Platonic roots have always been recognized, critics have failed to pursue Joubert's claim that he was more purely Platonic than Plato himself. Joubert's brilliant aesthetic insights can almost all be traced back to [his] idealism. As one reads the private *carnets,* one is impressed by the remarkable glimpses of the nature of beauty in a man so imbued with a classical training. Like the Romantics, he saw art as expressive of the inner soul and feeling but composed of formal ideals. He was also aware that the roots of creativity do not lie in the conscious and that the world of art is not the world of reality. (p. 19)

Joubert's influence during his life-time was limited; his impact on literature occurred primarily during the brief years of his close contact with Chateaubriand. Paradoxically, his idealistic aesthetics, although unknown until after the publication of the 1838 edition of his *pensées,* broached the same problems that German and English Romantic poets and critics were discussing. These ideas did not enter the mainstream of French literature until the 1820's and 1830's, and then mainly through translation and interpretations of German thought. The basic appeal of Joubert's Platonic thought to the latter half of the century lay in its idealism, but the idealism which became popular as the century wore on in France owed less to the rediscovery of Plato and Plotinus . . . than to the initial discovery of Kant, Schelling, and Hegel. (p. 139)

In his notebooks, Joubert occasionally recreates moments which constitute visionary or imaginative experiences; in them he expresses the magical transformation of nature at dusk or in the rain. He knew what *rêverie* and *contemplation* were, but philosophical and aesthetic inquiry took the place of poetic creativity in his personal world. His aesthetic theory is a correlate to the new poetics of Romanticism and Post-Romanticism. His vision of the beautiful was basically Neo-Platonic, for beauty is an idea particularized as form and intuited as such in the mind of the creator via the imagination. The artist or poet inculcates form into matter or unites it with its medium so that inner form is the determinant of beauty. Art is not an imitation in the Aristotelian sense, and Joubert rejects the normative aesthetics of Classicism in which art is the mimesis of representative human action or of Nature. The act of creation is much more the particularization of an intuition of the beautiful. Obviously, any later nineteenth-century idealist could find aspects of Joubert's aesthetic theory with which to identify: with the consuming drive to achieve a perfect expression of ideal beauty, with the belief that an idea can only be expressed as form, and with the theory of the creative imagination which intuits and expresses beautiful forms.

Joubert diverges from Romanticism in one major way. He does not conceive of Nature as vital, as impregnated by living Form. Nor does he conceive of a parallel between form in Nature and form in art. The aesthetic experience is a microcosm of the *metaphysical* universe for Joubert; it is a particularization of the universal. For Romantics like Schelling or Coleridge, Nature shows what the universe is like because the Universal is particularized as living form. As in Nature, the art object is symbolic and organic, the universal permeates the particular, and living form shapes matter. . . . Joubert's Platonism leads him only to a partial articulation of the Romantic understanding of the relation of form to matter. The missing ingredients— the redefinition of the relationship between the knowing subject and object, as first outlined by Kant, and the vitalization of Nature, as developed by Fichte and Schelling—are excluded

by Joubert's unyielding Platonism. Later writers who had been exposed to Hegelian ideas and articulated a purely formalist aesthetic, devoid of the parallel with nature, frequently sound like Joubert. For this reason, he has been interpreted frequently as a precursor of later nineteenth-century poetics. (pp. 140-41)

> *Patricia A. Ward, in her* Joseph Joubert and the Critical Tradition: Platonism and Romanticism, *Librairie Droz S.A., 1980, 153 p.*

ADDITIONAL BIBLIOGRAPHY

Arnold, Matthew. ''Joubert; or, A French Coleridge.'' In his *Essays in Criticism,* pp. 170-202. New York: J. H. Sears & Co., n.d.*
> The earliest English introduction to Joubert's *pensées,* originally published in London's *National Review* in 1864. Arnold compares Joubert's personality, interests, and literary preferences to those of Samuel Taylor Coleridge and considers Joubert a precursor of Romanticism.

Evans, Joan. *The Unselfish Egoist.* London: Longmans, Green, and Co., 1947, 202 p.
> A short biography of Joubert based on André Beaunier's extensive biographies, *La jeunesse de Joubert, Joseph Joubert et la révolution,* and *Roman d'une amitié: Joseph Joubert et Pauline de Beaumont.*

Fairclough, G. Thomas. *A Fugitive and Gracious Light: The Relation of Joseph Joubert to Matthew Arnold's Thought.* University of Nebraska Studies, n.s. no. 23. Lincoln: University of Nebraska Press, 1961, 79 p.*
> A detailed comparison of the religious, literary, and societal theories of Joubert and Matthew Arnold. Fairclough concludes that Joubert's *pensées* significantly shaped Arnold's life and thought.

Poulet, Georges. ''Joubert.'' In his *The Interior Distance,* translated by Elliott Coleman, pp. 65-96. Baltimore: Johns Hopkins Press, 1959.
> Explicates Joubert's concepts of time and space as evinced in his statements on metaphysics, memory, silence, and imagination.

Sturm, Paul J. ''Joubert and Voltaire: A Study in Reaction.'' In *Studies by Members of the French Department of Yale University,* edited by Albert Feuillerat, pp. 185-220. Yale Romanic Studies, edited by Albert Feuillerat, vol. XVIII. New Haven: Yale University Press, 1941.*
> Discussion of the many references to Voltaire in Joubert's notebooks. Sturm notes that while Joubert repudiates Voltaire as a philosopher, he praises him as a stylist.

Ward, Patricia A. ''Joseph Joubert on Language and Style.'' *Symposium* XXXI, No. 3 (Fall 1977): 256-70.
> An examination of Joubert's statements on the aesthetics of language.

———. ''Joseph Joubert on the Creative Process in Art.'' *The French Review* LI, No. 2 (December 1977): 204-11.
> A detailed analysis of Plato's influence on Joubert's aesthetic philosophy.

Joseph Sheridan Le Fanu

1814-1873

(Also wrote under the pseudonym of Charles de Cresserons.) Irish novelist, short story writer, poet, journalist, and editor.

Although Le Fanu is regarded as a minor Victorian novelist, he is considered a significant writer of Gothic literature. Critics consistently praise his short stories and novels for their typically Gothic characteristics, including evocative descriptions of physical settings, foreboding atmosphere, and supernatural elements. Yet these works also represent a departure from the Gothic tradition because of their emphasis on psychology and finely drawn characters. By exploring the subconscious motivations of his main characters, Le Fanu created works distinguished by an approach previously unknown in Gothic works.

Born in Dublin, Le Fanu was a precocious child, and at an early age began to entertain his family with readings from his verse. He was privately educated by his father, Dean of the Irish Episcopal Church, until entering Trinity College, Dublin, in 1833. There, Le Fanu studied law, although he never practiced; instead, he launched a joint career in journalism and literature. He contributed regularly to the *Dublin University Magazine* and gained recognition with his short stories and his ballads "Phaudrig Crohoore" and "Shamus O'Brien." In 1839, Le Fanu bought three Dublin periodicals and combined them to form the *Evening Mail,* a conservative publication in which many of his early works appeared. During this period, he published two historical novels, *The Cock and Anchor, Being a Chronicle of Old Dublin City* and *The Fortunes of Colonel Torlogh O'Brien,* as well as his first collection of short stories, *Ghost Stories and Tales of Mystery.* These early works, however, were virtually ignored. Le Fanu married Susanna Bennett in 1844, and together they became prominent in Dublin social and cultural circles. Le Fanu was considered a brilliant conversationalist and was a popular member of society until his wife's death in 1858. His anguish caused him to withdraw from his companions, who labeled him "The Invisible Prince." The period of mourning and seclusion proved fruitful artistically, however, for during this time Le Fanu produced the four novels for which he is best known: *The House by the Church-Yard, Wylder's Hand, Uncle Silas: A Tale of Bartram-Haugh,* and *Guy Deverell.* In addition, he became the editor of the *Dublin University Magazine* in 1859, and, in 1861, assumed its proprietorship as well. Le Fanu continued managing and editing the publication until a few months before his death.

Critics have described Le Fanu's short stories and novels as a successful combination of the elements of the Gothic tradition and those of the modern horror story. While commending their supernatural atmosphere, critics also praise his works for their accurate depiction of Irish life. His earliest short stories feature elements common to Gothic fiction, including an aura of anticipation and terror, violence, and foreboding settings. As his writing progressed, however, Le Fanu, unlike his predecessors, sought to portray the thoughts and inner conflicts of his characters. Critics praise this analysis and understanding of his characters as Le Fanu's lasting contribution to Gothic literature.

Le Fanu rarely depended on the stock devices of Gothic literature to further his eerie plots; rather than relying on such

elements as sliding doors and descending ceilings, he left many incidents in his stories unexplained. This technique, many critics believe, made his stories more suspenseful. Unlike earlier horror fiction, there are no ghosts in Le Fanu's works; instead, his characters are haunted by phantasms that are solely the creations of their imaginations. Also central to the effectiveness of Le Fanu's writing is his narrative method: he often employed first person narration to convey an individual's experience of terror as well as complex plots to progressively build suspense. Critics consistently note that Le Fanu's realistic settings, skillfully imbued with a sense of menace, lend credibility to his stories and contribute to their dramatic impact.

Le Fanu's short stories also evidence his developing narrative technique. In his first collections, *Ghost Stories and Tales of Mystery* and *The Purcell Papers,* Le Fanu relied heavily on supernatural incidents. Commentators contend that although the stories achieve and maintain a high level of suspense, their overall success is hindered by contrived plots and wooden characters. The five longer stories in the later collection entitled *In a Glass Darkly,* however, are widely praised by critics. In these stories, Le Fanu relied less on the supernatural and instead depicted human wickedness as the primary source of evil. He also portrayed the subtle subconscious conflicts of both the victim and the villain through first-person narration. In addition, Le Fanu here refined his use of the recurrent character:

Dr. Hesselius, a therapist specializing in mental disorders, is introduced in each of the stories to provide the reader with a prefatory "case history" of each victim. This technique allowed Le Fanu to successfully link the stories and to explore the psychology of the characters.

Of Le Fanu's fourteen novels, critics agree that his finest are *The House by the Church-Yard*, *Wylder's Hand*, *Uncle Silas*, and *Guy Deverell*. These works are characterized by the taut construction and psychological insight that inform the stories of *In a Glass Darkly*. *The House by the Church-Yard* represents an intermediate stage between Le Fanu's earlier historical novels and his later tales of mystery, and although its plot is often considered episodic and confusing, this work marks his first attempt at psychological analysis. *Wylder's Hand* is regarded by many critics as the most uncomplicated of Le Fanu's mysteries, and some have termed it his masterpiece. By including fewer characters in this work, Le Fanu was able to more fully develop the character of Wylder. *Uncle Silas*, perhaps Le Fanu's best-known work, is praised for its clear narrative and simplified structure. In this work, often described as the first psychological thriller, Le Fanu deftly manipulates the level of suspense, gradually elevating the reader's anticipation and sense of horror. *Guy Deverell*, the last of Le Fanu's critically acclaimed novels, is noted for its mysterious atmosphere.

During his lifetime, Le Fanu's works were popular successes, although they received little critical attention. With the appearance of *Uncle Silas*, however, some reviewers complained that Le Fanu had exceeded the boundaries of Gothic mystery writing and charged him with sensationalism, a contention that is still discussed today. In 1864, in a postscript to the last serial installment of *Uncle Silas*, Le Fanu defended himself against this claim by comparing his work to the celebrated romances of Sir Walter Scott. Following Le Fanu's death, his reputation suffered a gradual decline as readers and critics lost interest in Gothic fiction. In the 1920s, however, the prominent horror story writer M. R. James drew attention to Le Fanu by writing introductions to several newly-issued volumes of his out-of-print works. V. S. Pritchett and Elizabeth Bowen also wrote lengthy essays championing Le Fanu as one of Gothic literature's foremost figures. In 1978, Jack Sullivan summarized the opinion of modern critics in his assessment of Le Fanu's influence on horror literature: "Beginning with Le Fanu, one of the distinctive features of modern ghostly fiction is . . . [the] synthesis of psychology and supernaturalism." While he is not well-known today, Le Fanu is noted by those acquainted with his work as an innovative and masterful writer of psychological horror fiction.

(See also *Dictionary of Literary Biography*, Vol. 21: *Victorian Novelists Before 1885*.)

*PRINCIPAL WORKS

"Phaudrig Crohoore" (ballad) 1837; published in journal
    Dublin University Magazine
The Cock and Anchor, Being a Chronicle of Old Dublin City
    [as Charles de Cresserons] (novel) 1845
**"Shamus O'Brien" (ballad) 1850; published in journal
    Dublin University Magazine
Ghost Stories and Tales of Mystery (short stories) 1851
The House by the Church-Yard (novel) 1863
Uncle Silas: A Tale of Bartram-Haugh (novel) 1864
Wylder's Hand [as Charles de Cresserons] (novel) 1864

Guy Deverell (novel) 1865
Checkmate (novel) 1871
In a Glass Darkly (short stories) 1872
Willing to Die (novel) 1873
***The Purcell Papers* (short stories) 1880
The Poems of Joseph Sheridan Le Fanu (poetry) 1896
The Collected Works of Joseph Sheridan Le Fanu. 52 vols.
    (novels, short stories, and poetry) 1977

*Many of Le Fanu's works were originally published serially in periodicals.

**This work was written in 1837.

***The short stories in this work were written in the years 1838 to 1840.

SAMUEL LOVER (letter date 1846)

[*Lover was a popular Irish novelist and songwriter of the early nineteenth century. During the 1840s he toured the United States giving readings from his works. At these recitations he also introduced his American audiences to Le Fanu's ballad "Shamus O'Brien." In the following letter to Le Fanu's brother William, Lover praises the ballad and requests permission to publicly acknowledge Le Fanu as its author.*]

In reading over your brother's poem [**"Shamus O'Brien"**] while I crossed the Atlantic, I became more and more impressed with its great beauty and dramatic effect—so much so that I determined to test its effect in public, and have done so here, on my first appearance, with the greatest success. Now I have no doubt there will be great praises of the poem, and people will suppose, most likely, that the composition is mine, and as *you know* (I take for granted) that I would not wish to wear a borrowed feather, I should be glad to give your brother's name as the author, should he not object to have it known; but as his writings are often of so different a tone, I would not speak without permission to do so. It is true that in my programme my name is attached to other pieces, and *no* name appended to the recitation; so far, you will see I have done all I could to avoid *'appropriating,'* the spirit of which I might have caught here, with Irish aptitude; but I would like to have the means of telling all whom it may concern the name of the author to whose head and heart it does so much honour.

> *Samuel Lover, in a letter to William Le Fanu on September 30, 1846, in* Temple Bar, *Vol. L, August, 1877, p. 512.*

J. S. LE FANU (essay date 1864)

[*In his preface to* Uncle Silas, *Le Fanu first explains that the novel is an elaboration of a short story previously published as* "A Passage in the Secret History of an Irish Countess." *In the following excerpt from his preface, Le Fanu defends himself against critics' charges that his works are sensational by comparing his novels to the romances of Sir Walter Scott. The preface was originally published as a postscript to the last serial installment of* Uncle Silas *in the December, 1864 issue of the* Dublin University Magazine.]

May [the writer of this Tale] be permitted a few words . . . of remonstrance against the promiscuous application of the term "sensation" to that large school of fiction which transgresses no one of those canons of construction and morality which, in producing the unapproachable *Waverley Novels,* their great author imposed upon himself? No one, it is assumed, would describe Sir Walter Scott's romances as "sensation novels"; yet in that marvellous series there is not a single tale in which death, crime, and, in some form, mystery, have not a place.

Passing by those grand romances of *Ivanhoe, Old Mortality,* and *Kenilworth,* with their terrible intricacies of crime and bloodshed, constructed with so fine a mastery of the art of exciting suspense and horror, let the reader pick out those two exceptional novels in the series which profess to paint contemporary manners and the scenes of common life; and remembering in the *Antiquary* the vision in the tapestried chamber, the duel, the horrible secret, and the death of old Elspeth, the drowned fisherman, and above all the tremendous situation of the tide-bound party under the cliffs; and in *St. Ronan's Well,* the long-drawn mystery, the suspicion of insanity, and the catastrophe of suicide—determine whether an epithet which it would be a profanation to apply to the structure of any, even the most exciting of Sir Walter Scott's stories, is fairly applicable to tales which, though illimitably inferior in execution, yet observe the same limitations of incident, and the same moral aims.

The author trusts that the Press, to whose masterly criticism and generous encouragement he and other humble labourers in the art owe so much, will insist upon the limitation of that degrading term to the peculiar type of fiction which it was originally intended to indicate, and prevent, as they may, its being made to include the legitimate school of tragic English romance, which has been ennobled, and in great measure founded, by the genius of Sir Walter Scott. (pp. 27-8)

> *J. S. Le Fanu, "A Preliminary Word," in his* Uncle Silas: A Tale of Bartram-Haugh, *1864. Reprint by The Cresset Press, 1947, pp. 27-8.*

CHARLES LEVER   (letter date 1864)

[*Lever was a popular nineteenth-century novelist and an editor of the* Dublin University Magazine.]

I cannot wait for the end of . . . your story [**Wylder's Hand**], to tell you of a very serious blunder you have made in it—a mistake perhaps more palpable to myself than to many of your readers; but which, recognised or not, is still grave. Your blunder was in not holding back your novel some twelve or fifteen years, for you will never beat it—equal it you may, but not pass it. It is first rate, and I feel assured it will have a high success. The two women are beautifully drawn, and the touches of nature in your blackest characters attract the sympathy of the reader to individuals who, if handled by an inferior artist, would have repelled by their cold rascality. In this day of serial deluge, one is driven to hourly comparisons; and I tell you frankly, that at my fire-side you carry off the palm from all competitors. . . . Though I said it will be hard for you to beat *Wylder's Hand,* by all means try, at all events. Write on and write fast. I am sure that the imaginative faculty is never the better for lying fallow, and if you be able to falsify my prediction and do a greater work, none of your friends will be more rejoiced than myself. (pp. 160-61)

> *Charles Lever, in a letter to Joseph Sheridan Le Fanu in 1864, in* Wilkie Collins, Le Fanu, and Others *by S. M. Ellis, Constable & Co. Ltd., 1931, pp. 160-61.*

[ALFRED PERCEVAL GRAVES]   (essay date 1873)

[*Le Fanu began contributing short stories and ballads to the* Dublin University Magazine *in 1833 and eventually became its editor and proprietor. The following obituary notice, attributed to the popular Irish poet Alfred Perceval Graves, briefly assesses Le Fanu's literary contributions. For additional commentary by Graves, see excerpt below, 1877.*]

[Le Fanu's] earliest contributions to literature appeared in this Magazine, of which, years afterwards, . . . he became proprietor and editor. Amongst his earliest articles were several stories, some serious, others replete with wit and humour, and highly illustrative of the habits and feelings of the Irish peasantry. Amongst his contributions to the Magazine were also many short poems, some full of tenderness and feeling, others of powerful dramatic effect. Foremost amongst the latter were **"Shamus O'Brien"** . . . and **"Phaudhrig Crohore,"** two of the best specimens of Irish ballad poetry, abounding in rollicking humour and vivid description, combined with touches of the deepest pathos. . . . To the public he was scarcely known apart from his books. . . . **"Uncle Silas"** was, perhaps, the best of his works, the plot the most skilfully contrived, the interest the most absorbing. Of his latest work, **"Willing to Die,"** the last pages were written a few days before his death. He was a man who thought deeply, especially on religious subjects. To those who knew him he was very dear. They admired him for his learning, his sparkling wit and pleasant conversation, and loved him for his manly virtues, his noble and generous qualities, his gentleness, and his loving, affectionate nature. His death has left in many hearts a void which cannot be filled up. (p. 320)

> [*Alfred Perceval Graves*], "Joseph Sheridan Le Fanu," *in* The Dublin University Magazine, *Vol. LXXXI, No. CCCCLXXXIII, March, 1873, pp. 319-20.*

[ALFRED PERCEVAL GRAVES]   (essay date 1877)

[*In this appraisal of Le Fanu's ballads and prose works, Graves favorably compares the author's writings to those of Sir Walter Scott and Wilkie Collins. For additional commentary by Graves, see excerpt above, 1873.*]

[Le Fanu's ballad '**Phaudrig Croohore**'] has the disadvantage not only of being written after [Sir Walter Scott's] 'Young Lochinvar,' but also that of having been directly inspired by it; and yet, although wanting in the rare and graceful finish of the original, the Irish copy has, we feel, so much fire and feeling that it at least tempts us to regret that Scott's poem was not written in that heart-stirring Northern dialect without which the noblest of our British ballads would lose half their spirit. Indeed, we may safely say that some of Le Fanu's lines . . . are finer than any in 'Young Lochinvar,' simply because they seem to speak straight from a people's heart, not to be the mere echoes of medieval romance. (p. 508)

Few will deny that ['**Shamus O'Brien**'] contains passages most faithfully, if fearfully, picturesque, and that it is characterised throughout by tragic intensity, a profound pathos, and an abundant though at times a too grotesquely incongruous humour. (p. 512)

There are evidences in '**Shamus O'Brien**,' and even in '**Phaudrig Croohore**,' of a power over the mysterious, the grotesque, and the horrible, which so singularly distinguish him as a novelist. (pp. 514-15)

There are about Le Fanu's narratives touches of nature which reconcile us to their always remarkable and often supernatural incidents. His characters are well conceived and distinctly drawn, and strong soliloquy and easy dialogue spring unaffectedly from their lips. He is a close observer of Nature, and reproduces her wilder effects of storm and gloom with singular vividness; while he is equally at home in his descriptions of still life, some of which remind us of the faithfully minute detail of old Dutch pictures.

Mr. Wilkie Collins, amongst our living novelists, best compares with Le Fanu. Both of these writers are remarkable for the ingenious mystery with which they develop their plots, and for the absorbing, if often over-sensational, nature of their incidents; but whilst Mr. Collins excites and facinates our attention by an intense power of realism which carries us with unreasoning haste from cover to cover of his works, Le Fanu is an idealist, full of high imagination, and an artist who devotes deep attention to the most delicate detail in his portraiture of men and women, and his descriptions of the outdoor and indoor worlds—a writer, therefore, through whose pregnant pages it would be often an indignity to hasten. And this more leisurely, and certainly more classical, conduct of his stories makes us remember them more fully and faithfully than those of the author of the 'Woman in White.' Mr. Collins is generally dramatic, and sometimes stagy, in his effects. Le Fanu, while less careful to arrange his plots so as to admit of their being readily adapted for the stage, often surprises us by scenes of so much greater tragic intensity that we cannot but lament that he did not, as Mr. Collins has done, attempt the drama, and so furnish another ground of comparison with his fellow-countryman, Maturin (also, if we mistake not, of French origin), whom, in his writings, Le Fanu far more closely resembles than Mr. Collins, as a master of the darker and stronger emotions of human character. But, to institute a broader ground of comparison between Le Fanu and Mr. Collins, whilst the idiosyncracies of the former's characters, however immaterial those characters may be, seem always to suggest the minutest detail of his story, the latter would appear to consider plot as the prime, character as a subsidiary element in the art of novel writing. (pp. 515-16)

> [Alfred Perceval Graves], ''An Irish Poet and Novelist: Joseph Sheridan Le Fanu,'' in Temple Bar, Vol. L, August, 1877, pp. 504-17.

T. W. ROLLESTON (essay date 1887)

Le Fanu was a poet as well as a novelist, and he was a poet *as* a novelist. Unfortunately his powers, though great, were limited, or rather he chose to exercise them too much in one particular groove. In taking up a novel of Le Fanu's we enter a region of mystery and terror, the region whose secrets such writers as Wilkie Collins, the late Hugh Conway, and too many others, have devoted themselves to bringing to light. But Le Fanu is incomparably superior to any of these. Where, in the best of them, do we find his wit, his learning, his sense of beauty, his passion, his mastery of language, his creative power? His characters in his best books are real human beings, in whom we can take interest apart from the tale in which they figure. . . .

Of all [Le Fanu's] works *The House by the Churchyard* seems to us to exhibit the richest and most varied power. For intensity of excitement nothing can match *Uncle Silas*. And yet in *Uncle Silas* one feels that Le Fanu has adopted a *métier*, and narrowed the sphere of his art. He defended this novel in express terms

against the charge of sensationalism [see excerpt above, 1864], and it certainly contains much that the usual sensational novel does not aim at. But on the whole it must be confessed that it and most of the author's other productions aim at working on the nerves, not on the spirit of the reader. This, however, cannot be said of *The House by the Churchyard.* It is true that in the latter the main interest is of a sinister kind, centering upon the fortunes of a criminal, and linked with circumstances of physical horror. But though such is the motive of the story, and such it must appear in any bare narration of the plot, yet there is so much beauty and dignity in some of the characters, so much pathos and noble passion, so much healthy humour and mirth, and vivid description of simple things and people, that the dark thread which runs through the whole fabric is rarely seen. The picture which this book gives of Irish society about the middle of the eighteenth century, is as brilliant an example as could well be found of the imaginative power which can revive a past epoch, and make it seem as real to us as our own. The plot is simple enough, although enveloped in mystery until near the end. . . .

Artists in general, writers of fiction included, may be divided into two classes—those who make the main interest of their work centre on what is high, lovable, beautiful; and those who seek to impress us with revelations of the sinister, the malignant, the appalling. All great artists belong to the first order, nor is there any other way of being great than theirs. Le Fanu, on the whole, and judging him by his most powerful and impassioned work, belongs to the second order. But in this order he stands high, he stands among the highest; and he stands there, in spite of a too diffuse and erratic manner of conducting his plots, mainly by virtue of his splendour of style and imagination. And he has traits of the higher school which ennoble his work, and make the ineffaceable impression which it leaves in our memory something better than a haunting horror.

> T. W. Rolleston, ''Joseph Sheridan Le Fanu,'' in Irish Fireside, n.s. Vol. I, No. 9, February 26, 1887, p. 133.

S. M. ELLIS (essay date 1916)

> [In this brief discussion of Le Fanu's literary techniques, Ellis claims that of all his varied literary works Le Fanu's greatest achievement was his horror fiction. For additional commentary by Ellis, see excerpt below, 1931.]

[Le Fanu] at different times was a writer of ballads voicing the aspirations and romance of Irish national life; a journalist expressing High Tory views; an historical romance writer; a writer of squibs and satires; a fine poet; and a supreme author of ghost stories and novels of murder and mystery. In these last categories he is pre-eminent, and his success is almost entirely achieved by his art of *suggesting* evil presences and coming horrors. Very rarely is there an actual, visible ghost in his stories. His was not the old school of traditional apparitions, in white or grey, with blue fire, clanking chain, and wailing cry. His spectres—far more terrible—are in the brain of the haunted. Demoniacal possession, and the resultant delusional apparition, or concrete crime—these are the bases of Le Fanu's finest stories. For the actual details of a murder it is true he had rather a morbid partiality, and spared no particulars about the wounds and blood and the aspect of the mangled or strangled corpse. Like Ainsworth, he was distinctly macaberesque, and both seem to have had a sort of flair for scenes of human torture and physical pain. There is a description in **''Torlogh**

O'Brien'' of the death of a man by the strappado which makes painful reading, so particular are the details of the agony. But, after all, this is merely realism, and realism is not unknown or unprofitable to romance writers of to-day. However realistic Le Fanu may be, there is over all his scenes of horror a softening veil of romance and mystery; and if Death is all too prominent in his books—why so it is, unhappily, in real life, and Le Fanu's chief exemplar is but a reminder of that inexorable enemy from whom no poor mortal may escape at the last. (p. 21)

S. M. Ellis, ''Joseph Sheridan Le Fanu,'' in The Bookman, *London, Vol. LI, No. 301, October, 1916, pp. 15-21.*

M. R. JAMES (essay date 1923)

[*A popular writer of horror stories in his own right, James wrote introductions for several twentieth-century reprints of Le Fanu's works. In the following excerpt from his prologue and epilogue to Le Fanu's* Madam Crowl's Ghost, and Other Tales of Mystery, *James assigns Le Fanu to the ''first rank'' of ghost story writers while discussing the strengths and weaknesses of his work.*]

Joseph Sheridan Le Fanu, . . . was in his own particular vein one of the best story-tellers of the nineteenth century; and the present volume [*Madame Crowl's Ghost, and Other Tales of Mystery*] contains a collection of forgotten tales by him, and of tales not previously known to be his.

There have always been readers and lovers of Le Fanu's works, though not so many as those writings deserve. To these I know that the addition which I bring to their stock will be welcome. But the larger public, which knows not this Joseph, may be glad to be told what they are to expect in his stories.

He stands absolutely in the first rank as a writer of ghost stories. That is my deliberate verdict, after reading all the supernatural tales I have been able to get hold of. Nobody sets the scene better than he, nobody touches in the effective detail more deftly. I do not think it is merely the fact of my being past middle age that leads me to regard the leisureliness of his style as a merit; for I am by no means inappreciative of the more modern efforts in this branch of fiction. No, it has to be recognized, I am sure, that the ghost-story is in itself a slightly old-fashioned form; it needs some deliberateness in the telling: we listen to it the more readily if the narrator poses as elderly, or throws back his experience to ''some thirty years ago.'' (p. vii)

• • • • •

Anyone who reads through the whole range of . . . [Le Fanu's works] will be struck by certain habits of the writer, quite apart from any question of style or quality. I shall enlarge upon two of these. One very marked one is his *penchant* for rewriting a story in a different setting, and for developing a long story out of a short one.

Take examples of this. *The Cock and Anchor,* his first novel, was . . . reissued with some changes as *Morley Court.* But there—it is a story of the eighteenth century. In 1870 the plot and many of the incidents reappear in *Checkmate* in a nineteenth century setting. True, another, and a very striking thread is now interwoven with them: the coarse villain of *The Cock and Anchor* is replaced by the refined, but far more formidable figure of Walter Longcluse; and the atmosphere is of Le Fanu's most impressive. But the earlier story has been incorporated into the later. (pp. 271-72)

I do not defend or repudiate [Le Fanu's tendency to repeat characters or plots in his works]; I merely record it as a marked feature in Le Fanu's work and pass on to call attention to another equally curious. That is, my author's fondness for repeating a certain *motif*—again in varied contexts—so varied that I think the reader need not resent it. The theme is this: the villain of the piece returns after the lapse of many years to surroundings where some who knew him of old still live, and, until the catastrophe, passes unrecognized. In most cases his old crime has been committed before the book begins—we are only told of it as a past event and we only see the criminal in his new avatar. (p. 273)

Le Fanu himself, who lets a year or two lapse after using this favourite theme before he touches it again, may well have applauded himself for his moderation. To the critic who reads the whole series of his works from start to finish, he may well seem to have indulged his predilection for it (predilection I am sure it is, and not poverty of invention) too much. Personally I find the settings of the theme so satisfactorily varied that I do not resent its recurrence. But if any one is inclined to cavil, I cannot put up a very strong defence. Only, I would represent that Le Fanu is pretty obviously one who writes stories for his own (and his readers') pleasure: he has no axe to grind; no cause to champion; no crusade to preach; in none of his books do I find any *tendency*—unless it be in the one in which he makes fun of spiritualism. His object is to tell a story, usually one that will mystify and alarm his reader, and in his favourite theme he sees the possibility of many effective variations. I do not blame him for making trial of them.

There are, to be sure, really weak places in his armour. For one thing he is certainly a hasty and rather careless writer. His text admits of many small emendations, which shows him to have been a bad proof reader: there are a certain number of definite mistakes and inconsistencies in the stories, and you may often find sentences which are not only too long, but do not construe. That is one blemish, due, I cannot doubt, in part to the conditions under which he wrote—I mean the serial form which he employed for twelve out of his fourteen novels.

A more serious fault affects the texture of the work: it is what I will call his mawkishness. He can write of sad things with true and moving pathos; he can write love-scenes that appeal as genuine; but he does, now and again, also indulge in a sentimentality which calls the blush to the cheek. (pp. 274-75)

[Of the later novels], six are markedly superior to the rest. These are: *The House by the Churchyard, Wylder's Hand, Uncle Silas, Guy Deverell, Tenants of Malory, Checkmate.*

Uncle Silas and *The House by the Churchyard* divide the honours of the first place. Probably the first-named is too well known to require description; but the second, I think, is not, and it is a book which seems to me to bring together in a concentrated form all Le Fanu's best qualities as a story-teller. . . .

From the prologue, in which the scene is set and the tale started by the digging-up of a strangely battered skull in the churchyard, you pass to an amazingly fine description of a dark night of storm and a funeral, and these strike the note of ominous mystery which runs through all the book. Not that the book is a gloomy one: it is full of live, gay people, and there is rollicking farce of excellent quality, side by side with ghosts and murders, and a sombre ballad (unsurpassed in its way) which has a decisive bearing on the catastrophe. In short, this is a book to which I find myself returning over and over again and with no sense of disappointment.

The other four novels all have strong points. The intrigue in *Wylder's Hand* defies detection; *Guy Deverell* is full of good small character sketches; *Checkmate* has moments of breathless interest; *Tenants of Malory* is marked out by the glorious talk of Mr. Dingwell. . . . (p. 276)

Personally I find the remaining [novels] . . . worth reading, but I do not wish persons unacquainted with Le Fanu to approach him by way of *A Lost Name* or *All in the Dark*. Let them begin with *In a Glass Darkly*, where they will find the very best of his shorter stories, and go on to *Uncle Silas* and *The House by the Churchyard*. It is on these three volumes that I principally base the claim I make for Le Fanu, that he is one of the best story-tellers of the last age. (p. 277)

> *M. R. James, "Prologue" and "Epilogue," in* Madam Crowl's Ghost and Other Tales of Mystery *by Joseph Sheridan Le Fanu, edited by M. R. James, G. Bell and Sons, Ltd., 1923, pp. vii-viii, 265-77.*

E. F. BENSON (essay date 1931)

[*In his assessment of* In a Glass Darkly, *Benson discusses Le Fanu's method of creating atmosphere and building suspense.*]

The writer of ghost stories and of tales which are designed to make the flesh creep embarks on hazardous voyages. If he does not scare his readers or inspire in them those precious uncomfortable impulses that cause them to glance hastily round in order to make sure that the creaking board or the wail of the wind did not betoken some dreadful presence even now making itself manifest to their horrified eyes, he has failed more ruinously than can any other class of narrator. (pp. 263-64)

[There] is one author, far too little known by those in search of creepy lore, who seldom fails in his high mission: his name is Sheridan Le Fanu. He produces, page for page, a far higher percentage of terror than the more widely read Edgar Allan Poe, and whether he deals in ghosts direct or in more material horrors, his success in making his readers very uneasy is amazing. Though we may already know the story we select to give us some insupportable moments on a lonely evening, there is a quality about most of his tales which seldom fails to alarm: familiarity with them does not breed comfort. Many ghost stories are efficacious for a first reading, but few, when we already know the worst that the author has to tell us, preserve untainted the atmosphere of horror as do the tales in *In a Glass Darkly*. The best of these, **"Green Tea," "The Familiar,"** and **"Mr. Justice Hartbottle,"** are instinct with an awfulness which custom cannot stale, and this quality is due, as in [James's] *The Turn of the Screw*, to Le Fanu's admirably artistic methods in setting and narration. They begin quietly enough, the tentacles of terror are applied so softly that the reader hardly notices them till they are sucking the courage from his blood. A darkness gathers, like dusk gently falling, and then something obscurely stirs in it. . . .

This quiet, cumulative method leading up to intolerable terror is charcteristic of all Le Fanu's best work, and it is that which makes him so wholesale a fear-monger. He employs this technique not only in his short stories, but when he is engaged on a full-length novel. Far the best of these, to my mind, is *Uncle Silas*, which in skill of narration, of gradual crescendo towards that most hideous chapter called **"The Hour of Death,"** is a sheer masterpiece in alarm. The book is a long one: it is not till we come to the four hundred and fiftieth page or thereabouts that the climax arrives, but from the first page onwards there

is no pause in the relentless drip, drip, drip of ominous and menacing incident. Without the aid of the supernatural (though we are once or twice, rather unfairly, threatened with a ghost that does not mature), Le Fanu piles up, in the growing dusk, chapter by chapter, the horror of great darkness. Out of this dusk, intermittently at first, peer the grim faces of the French governess, of Dudley Ruthyn, of Uncle Silas, creatures of flesh and blood, but more ghastly than any ghost. Occasionally, as when Madame de la Rougierre is sent about her business, or when Dudley has apparently sailed for Australia, or when Uncle Silas seems like to die, we try to persuade ourselves that the darkness is lifting, but we are aware in our quaking consciousness that we are but buoying ourselves up with idle hopes. We do not see them for the moment because night is gathering, but we are sure that they are awfully whispering together in that shroud of blackness from which they will presently emerge for some murderous business. We cannot close the book, we cannot skip a word, we are altogether in the author's grip, and these compulsions are due to the consummate art with which he handles and develops his hideous theme. . . . Already, after a dreary period of fiction in which so many of our eminent writers have seemed to aim at producing flat and interminable chronicles, there are signs that the public craves for stories again, and, if such signs portend a change, we may be sure that among the authors of the mid-nineteenth century Le Fanu will come into his own, for technically, as a story-teller, his best work is of the first rank, while as a flesh-creeper he is unrivalled. No one else has so sure a touch in mixing the mysterious atmosphere in which horror darkly breeds. (p. 264)

> *E. F. Benson, "Sheridan Le Fanu," in* The Spectator, *Vol. 146, No. 5356, February 21, 1931, pp. 263-64.*

S. M. ELLIS (essay date 1931)

[*In the following discussion of Le Fanu's stories and novels, Ellis concentrates on Le Fanu's descriptive ability and evocation of horror. For additional commentary by Ellis, see excerpt above, 1916.*]

[Le Fanu's collection *Ghost Stories and Tales of Mystery*] included *The Evil Guest* and *The Watcher* (which was later entitled *The Familiar* when reprinted in *In a Glass Darkly*). For sheer terror, the haunting of the unhappy protagonist of this tale has no equal. It is a crescendo of horror. At first he is conscious of footsteps dogging him at lonely spots. They intensify. In time, the malignant Watcher becomes visible. Then the appalling death scene, where the author skilfully leaves to the imagination what supreme terror finally wrested poor Barton's shuddering soul from his body. (p. 156)

[*The House by the Churchyard*] is surely one of the greatest romantic narratives in our language. Herein the author conjured up and related with the art of a consummate story-teller all the romantic conditions, legends, and traditions of his native Chapelizod, that village set so picturesquely by the beautiful region of the Phoenix Park. I have never seen the place, but it is as familiar and actual by Le Fanu's printed word as old Paris from the descriptions of Victor Hugo and Italy from the glowing lines of Byron. In *The House by the Churchyard* there is, further, a sense of impending and immutable tragedy that compels attention throughout the long length of this story with all its varied wealth of picturesque detail and scenic description. Light episodes may intervene, but ever the *motifs* of murder and retribution press to the front with a sort of stately inevitable-

An illustration from the horror story "Green Tea."

ness. At the outset, at the very opening of the first chapter, the right key-note is struck with supreme artistry. The influences of Nature are attune with the atmosphere of menace which is to envelop the story. . . . (p. 157)

There is no need for me to point out how powerfully the sombre and dramatic flow of incident continues in this tale and the vivid grim characterisation that gives life to Dangerfield, Sturk, Black Dillon, and many another. I will only add that in *The House by the Churchyard* I find the most terrifying ghost story in the language. (pp. 157-58)

The House by the Churchyard was succeeded immediately by *Wylder's Hand* . . . , the story which shows Le Fanu still at the height of his powers, for I place it before *Uncle Silas,* generally regarded as his masterpiece. The plot is more probable and powerful; the dread secret of sombre Redman's Dell is kept unrevealed until almost the end with infinite art that holds the reader attuned to expectation and excitement; this is, in truth, one of the few books that compel the reader to sit up till the small hours, for he cannot retire until he has solved the mystery. This is a bizarre tale, and it is told with a raw, jagged power that is suggestive of [Emily Brontë's] *Wuthering Heights,* and, indeed, Captain Stanley Lake is of the same implacable breed as Heathcliff. The scenic descriptions, too, are all in tone— the sad yellow evening light over the dells and wooded slopes of Brandon Park; the sombre old house whose windows looked

'toward the distant sunset horizon, piled in dusty gold and crimson clouds against the faded, green sky—a glory that is always melancholy and dreamy,' or at night:

> A cold bright moon was shining with clear sharp lights and shadows. Everything looked strangely cold and motionless outside. The sombre old trees, like gigantic hearse plumes, black and awful. The chapel lay full in view, where so many of the strange and equivocal race, under whose ancient roof-tree I then stood, were lying under their tomb-stones.

It must ever be a matter for regret that Le Fanu's stories were not illustrated by the great contemporary artists who excelled in this kind of work. (p. 159)

I agree with Lever that Le Fanu never surpassed *Wylder's Hand,* or, I would add, *The House by the Churchyard,* though in general estimation the author's best work is *Uncle Silas.* . . . This book contains some of Le Fanu's most descriptive writing. (p. 161)

In this book it is again the sense of impending tragedy and horror long drawn out which is almost overwhelming in its cumulative effect. The imagination is excited and dilated to such a pitch that when the actual scene of the murder is reached it is nearly an anticlimax. In the original short form of the story it was the heroine's girl cousin who was murdered, and hence its title when reprinted in *Ghost Stories* . . . —*The Murdered Cousin.* In *Uncle Silas* the victim was changed to Madame de la Rougierre, the weird Frenchwoman who was perhaps Le Fanu's most powerful creation. (p. 163)

Guy Deverell [is] an exciting story with clever characterisation. . . . To me, [the work] appears to have two faults, namely that the reader is kept too long in an uncertain state as to what the mystery is, and that the great scene in The Green Chamber, to which fifty-seven expectant chapters have led, is not actually related but left to the imagination. But it has much power, particularly in the sense of presentiment of coming retribution which ever and anon assails Sir Jekyl Marlowe—'he had come within the edge of the shadow of judgment, and its darkness was stealing over him, and its chill touched his heart.' (pp. 165-66)

The books of Le Fanu have a remarkably wide appeal and apparently are read with pleasure by the most differential types of mind. . . . One must predicate that Le Fanu's readers possess some measure of culture, for he writes with the outlook of a gentleman; his books attest literary allusion and classical knowledge. He is indeed an archaeologist, and I think it is his blend of learning with mystery and crime which created romances that hold the attention of readers who would have no liking for the ordinary sensational novel. For in Le Fanu's work there is something akin to the panoramic pilgrimage of human life, the sunshine and the shadows, the joy and the tragedy, the happy song and the dirge of sorrow, the high lights of the hills of romance and the dark valley through which all must shudderingly pass ere they reach the oblivion of the tomb. (pp. 178-79)

> *S. M. Ellis, "Joseph Sheridan Le Fanu," in his* Wilkie Collins, Le Fanu and Others, *Constable & Co. Ltd., 1931, pp. 140-91.*

MONTAGUE SUMMERS (essay date 1932)

[*Summers finds that the distinguishing feature of Le Fanu's genius was his extraordinary "sense of place." He also explores the atmosphere Le Fanu creates with his descriptions of settings.*]

It is, I think, almost universally acknowledged that the super-natural stories of Joseph Sheridan Le Fanu are unsurpassed, I will even add unsurpassable. . . .

There is one aspect of Le Fanu which must not be overlooked—his marvellous versatility. (p. 296)

I cannot attempt to apprize which is the best of Le Fanu's stories, short or long. Each of his admirers will probably declare for his own favourite. . . . What I wish to do is to endeavour very briefly to discuss (I dare not say to discover) wherein lies the peculiar quality of Le Fanu's genius, that extraordinary and essential feature which sets him apart from and above the majority of writers in this kind. I would suggest that there are few, if any, other writers of supernatural fiction who have been imbued with so keen a sense of place, who are able to create so vividly, and so realistically to convey the haunted house. Le Fanu's houses are full of horror, of impending doom, of a personal terror which is lurking very near, which is able to and may reveal itself most fearfully and most cruelly under some frightful guise that well nigh bids to shake fair reason on its throne. His heavy old-fashioned mansions even on the printed page have a strange vampirish power which seems to drain the reader's vitality and reduce his resistance to the lowest ebb. They are sunless and sombre as the dark folk who inhabit them; outside the rain is always falling, falling; the wind is ever soughing drearily through the leafless trees. This atmosphere is produced in just a few swift strokes. A sentence or two, and there before us looms the haunted house.

No elaboration, no accumulation of detail could give this effect. Brick may be piled upon brick, we may be led from room to room upstairs and downstairs, our attention may be called to each bureau, to each cabinet, to every canvas on the wall, and we carry away but a blurred and indistinct picture. (p. 297)

Every lover of Le Fanu will readily remember the first sight of Bartram-Haugh from the post-chaise window [in *Uncle Silas*]. . . . Equally admirable is the description of Malory in *The Tenants of Malory*, and the church of Cardyllian-Beaumaris. . . .

In *Guy Deverell*, which has always seemed to me one of Le Fanu's best stories, the whole mystery of the plot lies in the secret of the architecture of the Green Chamber, and tragedy begins to stalk abroad from the moment when Beatrix shows Monsieur Varbarriere the handsome red leather portfolio on the side of which in tall golden letters were the words: "Views and Elevations of Marlowe Manor House. Paulo Abruzzi, Architect, 1711."

Checkmate, again, opens with a magnificent description of Mortlake Hall, "a singular and grand old house," standing in gardens surrounded by "tall yew hedges, quincunxes, leaden fauns and goddesses, and other obsolete splendours." It may be said that neither Bartram-Haugh, nor Malory, nor Mortlake Hall . . . were haunted in one sense of the word; yet haunted indeed they were, haunted by the thick-mantling shadows of guilty deeds, of destiny and doom. . . . All these houses, and a dozen more of which Le Fanu has written, were haunted by malignant apparitions ready and quick to work evil, spirits who, as the wise man of Ecclesiasticus saith, "are created for vengeance, and in their fury they lay on grievous torments." (p. 298)

Montague Summers, "*Joseph Sheridan Le Fanu and His Houses*," in Architectural Design & Construction, Vol. II, No. 7, May, 1932, pp. 296-99.

ELIZABETH BOWEN   (essay date 1946)

[*In her introduction to* Uncle Silas, *written in 1946, Bowen analyses in detail the novel's style, plot, character, and setting.*]

Uncle Silas is a romance of terror. Joseph Sheridan Le Fanu lets us know that he expanded it from a short story (length, about fifteen pages) which he wrote earlier in his literary life and published, anonymously, in a magazine—under the title of *A Passage in the Secret History of an Irish Countess*. . . . [It holds] the germ of the later novel—or, at least, of its plot. But about that plot itself there is little new. The exterior plot of *Uncle Silas* is traditional, well worn by the time Le Fanu took up his pen. What have we? The Wicked Uncle and the Endangered Heir. I need not point out the precedents even in English history. Also, this is the Babes in the Wood theme—but in *Uncle Silas* we have only one babe—feminine, in her late adolescence, and, therefore, the no less perpetual Beauty in Distress. Maud Ruthyn has her heroine-prototype in a large body of fiction which ran to excess in the gothic romances but is not finished yet—the distraught young lady clasping her hands and casting her eyes skyward to Heaven: she has no other friend. . . . No, it is hard to see that simply uncle and niece, her sufferings, his designs, compressed, as they were at first, into a number of pages so small as to limit "treatment" (Le Fanu's *forte*) could have made up into anything much more than the conventional magazine story of the day.

What *is* interesting is that Le Fanu, having written the story, should have been unable, still, to discharge its theme from his mind. He must have continued, throughout the years, to be obsessed, if subconsciously, by the niece and uncle. More, these two and their relationship to each other became magnetic to everything strangest and most powerful in his own imagination and temperament. The resultant novel, our *Uncle Silas,* owes the pressure, volume and spiritual urgency which make it comparable to [Emily Brontë's] *Wuthering Heights* to just this phenomenon of accretion. Accretion is a major factor in art. Le Fanu could not be rid of the niece and uncle till he had built around them a comprehensive book. (pp. 7-8)

Uncle Silas is, as a novel, Irish in two . . . ways: it is sexless, and it shows a sublimated infantilism. It may, for all I know, bristle with symbolism; but I speak of the *story,* not of its implications—in the story, no force from any one of the main characters runs into the channel of sexual feeling. The reactions of Maud, the narrator-heroine, throughout are those of a highly intelligent, still more highly sensitive, child of twelve. This may, to a degree, be accounted for by seclusion and a repressive father—but not, I think, entirely: I should doubt whether Le Fanu himself realized Maud's abnormality as a heroine. She is an uncertain keyboard, on which some notes sound clearly, deeply and truly, others not at all. There is no question, here, of Victorian censorship, with its suggestive gaps: Maud, on the subject of anything she *does* feel, is uninhibited, sometimes disconcerting. And equally, in the feeling of people round her we are to take it that, child-like, she misses nothing. The distribution of power throughout the writing is equal, even: the briefest scene is accorded brimming sensuous content. We must in fact note how Maud's sensuousness (which is un-English) disperses, expends itself through the story in so much small change. She shows, at every turn, the carelessness, or acquiescence, of the predestined person: Maud is, by nature, a bride of Death. She delays, she equivocates, she looks wildly sideways; she delights in fire and candlelight, bedroom tea-drinking, cosy feminine company, but her bias is marked. The wind blowing her way from the family mausoleum troubles our heroine like a mating cry. Her survival after those frightful hours in the locked bedroom at Bartram-Haugh is, one can but feel, somewhat ghostly: she has cheated her Bridegroom only for the time being. Her human lover is colourless; her marriage—unexceptionable as to level and in felicity—is little more than the shell of a happy ending. From the parenthesis in her "Conclusion" (Maud writes down her story after some years of marriage) we learn that the first of her children die.

Is, then, *Uncle Silas* "morbid?" I cannot say so. For one thing, morbidity seems to me little else than sentimentality of a peculiar tint, and nothing of that survives in the drastic air of the book. For another, Maud is counterpoised by two other characters, her unalike cousins Monica Knollys and Milly Ruthyn, who not only desire life but are its apostles. And, life itself is painted in brilliant colours—colours sometimes tantalizing, as though life were an alternative out of grasp; sometimes insidious, disturbing, as though life were a temptation. I know, as a matter of fact, of few Victorian novels in which cosiness, gaiety and the delights of friendship are so sweetly rendered or play such a telling part. Le Fanu's style, translucent, at once simple and subtle, is ideal for such transitions. He has a genius for the unexpected—in mood as well as event. One example—a knowing twist of his art—is that Maud, whose arrival at Bartram-Haugh has been fraught with sinister apprehension, should, for the first few months, delight in her uncle's house. After Knowl—overcast, repressive, stiff with proprieties—Bartram-Haugh seems to be Liberty Hall. She runs wild in the woods with her cousin Milly; for the first time, she has company of her own age. Really, it is the drama of Maud's feelings, the heightening of conflict in her between hopes and fears, rather than the melodrama of her approaching fate, which ties one to *Uncle Silas,* page after page, breathless, unwilling to miss a word.

Le Fanu either felt or claimed to feel uneasy as to the reception of *Uncle Silas.* . . . [In his "Preliminary Word" (see excerpt above, 1864)] he enters a plea that the novel be not dismissed as "sensation" fiction. *Uncle Silas* was published in 1864: the plea would not be necessary to-day. *Sensationalism,* for its own sake, does, it is true, remain in poor repute; but sensation (of the kind which packs *Uncle Silas*) is not only not disdained, it is placed in art. The most irreproachable pens, the most poetic imaginations pursue and refine it. The status of the psychological thriller is, to-day, high. *Uncle Silas* was in advance of, not behind, its time: it is not the last, belated Gothic romance but the first (or among the first) of the psychological thrillers. And it has, as terror-writing, a voluptuousness not approached since. (It was of the voluptuousness in his own writing that Le Fanu may, really, have been afraid.) The novel, like others of its now honoured type, relies upon suspense and mystification. . . . [The] real suspense of the story emanates from the characters; it is they who keep the tale charged with mystery. The people in *Uncle Silas* show an extraordinary power of doubling upon or of covering their tracks. Maud seldom knows where she stands with any of them; neither do we. They are all at one remove from us, seen through the eyes of Maud. The gain to a story of this nature of being told in the first person is obvious (but for the fact that the teller, for all her dangers, must, we take it, survive, in order to tell the tale). All the same, it is not to this device that Le Fanu owes the main part of his effects—you and I, as readers, constantly intercept glances or changes in tones of voice that Maud just notes but does not interpret aright. No, Maud has little advantage over you or me. Temperamentally, and because of her upbringing, she is someone who moves about in a world of

strangers. She is alternately blind and unnecessarily suspicious. Her attitude towards every newcomer is one of fatalistic mistrust; and this attitude almost, but not quite (which is subtle) communicates itself to the reader. We do not, for instance, know, for an unreasonably but enjoyably long time, whether Milly, for all her rustic frankness, may not at heart be a Little Robber Girl, or Lady Knollys a schemer under her good nature. (pp. 9-11)

In the main, it could be a charge against [Le Fanu] that too many of the characters in *Uncle Silas* are overcharged, and that they break their bounds. There is abnormal pressure, from every side; the psychic air is often overheated. And all the time, we must remember, this is a story intended to be dominated by the figure of *one* man: Uncle Silas. All through, Uncle Silas meets competition. He is, I think, most nearly played off the stage by Madame de la Rougierre. Apart from that he is (as central character) at a disadvantage: *is* he, constantly, big enough for his own build-up? Is there or is there not, in scenes in which he actually appears, a just perceptible drop into anticlimax? Le Fanu, in dealing with Uncle Silas, was up against a difficulty inherent in his kind of oblique, suggestive art. He has overdrawn on his Silas in advance. In the flesh, Uncle Silas enters the story late: by this time, his build-up has reached towering heights. It is true that most of the time at Bartram-Haugh he remains off stage, and that those intervals allow of batteries being recharged. At Knowl, still only a name, he was ever-present—in the tormented silences of his brother, the hinting uneasy chatter of Lady Knollys, and Maud's dreams. (pp. 12-13)

Of the French governess, what is one to say? She is Uncle Silas's rival or counterpart. She is physical as opposed to metaphysical evil. No question of "semi-transparent structure" here—the Frenchwoman is of the rankest bodily coarseness: one can smell her breath, as it were, at every turn. In the *Uncle Silas* atmosphere, bleached of sex, she is no more woman than he is man; yet, somehow, her marelike coquetry—that prinking with finery and those tales of lovers—is the final, grotesque element of offence. *As* a woman, she can intrude on the girl at all points. She is obscene; and not least so in the alternate pinchings and pawings to which she subjects Maud. While the uncle gains in monstrousness by distance, the governess gains in monstrousness by closeness.

Madame de la Rougierre is unhandicapped by a preliminary build-up: she enters the story without warning and makes growth, page by page, as she goes along. Le Fanu, through the mouths of his characters, is a crack marksman in the matter of epithets: nothing said of the governess goes wide. He had, it is true, with this Frenchwoman a great vein to work on: with Wilkie Collins and Dickens he could exploit the British concept of the foreigner as sinister. Her broken English (with its peculiar rhythm, like no other known broken English, specially coined for her) further twists, in speech, the thoughts of her hideous mind. Like Uncle Silas, Madame de la Rougierre is, morally, of an unrelieved black: considering how much we are in her company it is wonderful that she does not become monotonous—the variations Le Fanu *has* contrived to give her are to be admired. "When things went well," we are told, "her soul lighted up into sulphureous good-humour." The stress is most often upon this woman's mouth—a "large-featured, smirking phantom" is Maud's first view of her, through the drawing-room window. We have her "wide, wet grin". She would "smile with her great carious teeth".

This creature's background is never fully given. Indeed, her engagement, as his daughter's companion, by Mr. Ruthyn of Knowl, is, with his obstinate tolerance of her presence, one of the first anomalies of the plot.

Uncle Silas, as a novel, derives its power from an inner momentum. In the exterior plot there are certain weaknesses—inconsistencies and loose ends. In this regard, the book has about it a sort of brilliant—nay, even inspired—amateurishness; a sort of negligent virtuosity in which Le Fanu shows his race. This may be the reason why *Uncle Silas* has never yet quite made the popular grade. It has not *so far,* that is to say, moved forward from being a favourite book of individual people into the rank of accepted Victorian classics. (pp. 14-16)

[*Uncle Silas* is] defenceless in its simplicity: it has no sub-plots and contains comparatively few people. The writing is no less simple: this, its beauty apart, is its great virtue. The effect of the simplicity is, that every sentence of Le Fanu's—or, at least, its content—incises itself deeply upon one's memory: one can forget not the slightest hint or statement or question. And, the excitingness of the story keeps one on the stretch, at once watchful and challenging, like a child listener. Like the child, one finds oneself breaking in, from time to time, with: ''But—?... But, I thought you *said*—?''

The omissions or inconsistencies of the plot are not psychological; they are practical or mechanical. They do not, to my mind, detract from or injure the real story, because they are not on its reallest plane. (p. 16)

The plot is obfuscated (sometimes, one may say, helpfully) by an extraordinary vagueness about time. This is a book in which it is impossible to keep a check on the passage of weeks, months, years. The novel is dominated by one single season in whose mood it is pitched: autumn. Practically no other season is implied or named.... The whole orchestral range of the novel's weather is autumnal—tranced, dripping melancholy, crystal morning zest, the radiance of the magnified harvest moon, or the howl and straining of gales through not yet quite leafless woods. The daylight part of Maud's drive to her uncle's house is through an amber landscape. The opening words of the novel are, it is true, ''It was winter....'' But our heroine, contradictory with her first breath, then adds: ''the second week in November''. By this reckoning Maud, in telling Lady Knollys that Madame de la Rougierre had arrived at Knowl ''in February'' is incorrect. The Frenchwoman, we had been clearly told, arrived ''about a fortnight'' after the opening scene.... No, there is nothing for it: one must submit oneself to Le Fanu's hypnotizing, perpetual autumn. One autumn merges into another: hopeless to ask how much has happened between! Yet always, against this nebulous flow of time stand out the moments—each unique, comprehensive, crystal, painfully sharp.

The inner, non-practical, psychological plot of *Uncle Silas* is, I suggest, faultless: it has no inconsistencies. The story springs from and is rooted in an obsession, and the obsession never looses its hold. Austin Ruthyn of Knowl, by an inexorable posthumous act, engages his daughter's safety in order to rescue his brother's honour. Or rather, less Silas's honour than the family name's. (p. 17)

> I think [Austin says to his daughter] little Maud would like to contribute to the restitution of her family name.... The character and influence of an ancient family is a peculiar heritage—sacred but destructible; and woe to him who either destroys or suffers it to perish.

Call this *folie de grandeur* [delusions of grandeur], or a fanaticism of the Almanach de Gotha. It is the extreme of a point of view less foreign to Le Fanu than to his readers. It was a point of view that they, creatures of an industrialized English nineteenth century, were bound to challenge, and could deride. It could only hope to be made acceptable, as mainspring and premise of his story, by being challenged, criticized—even, by implication, derided—in advance, and on behalf of the reader, by a person located somewhere *inside* the story. The necessary mouthpiece is Dr. Bryerly. Dr. Bryerly's little speech to Maud is a piece of, as it were, insurance, on Le Fanu's part. ''There are people'', remarks Dr. Bryerly, ''who think themselves just as great as the Ruthyns, or greater; and your poor father's idea of carrying it by a demonstration was simply the dream of a man who had forgotten the world, and learned to exaggerate himself by his long seclusion''. True—and how effective. The reader's misgivings, his fear of being implicated in something insanely disproportionate, have been set at rest. He is now prepared to lean back and accept, as Le Fanu wished, the idea on one—but that a great—merit purely: its validity for the purposes of the tale.

One more comment, before we leave the plot. In the disposition of characters ... about the field of the story, Le Fanu shows himself, as a novelist, admirably professional, in a sense that few of his contemporaries were. Not a single, even the slightest, character is superfluous; not one fails to play his or her part in the plot, or detains us for a second after that part is played. One or two (such as the house party guests at Elvaston) are merely called in to act on Maud's state of mind. But Maud's mind, we must remember, reflects, and colours according to its states, the action of the interior plot. No person is in the story simply to fill up space, to give the Victorian reader his money's worth, or to revive flagging interest—Le Fanu, rightly, did not expect interest to flag.

The background, or atmosphere, needs little discussion: in the first few pages one recognizes the master-touch. The story of *Uncle Silas* is ... divided between two houses: Knowl and Bartram-Haugh. The contrast between the two houses contributes drama. Knowl, black and white, timbered, set in well-tended gardens, is a rich man's home. It is comfortable; fires roar in the grates; pictures and panelling gleam; the servants do all they should. As against this, [Bartram-Haugh] is overcast, rigid, haunted: Mr. Ruthyn is closeted with dark mysteries; there are two ghosts, and, nearby, the family mausoleum, in which Maud's young mother lies and to which her father is to be carried under the most charnel circumstances of death. (pp. 18-19)

The psychological weather of those first Bartram-Haugh chapters is like the out-of-doors weather: gay and tingling. Till Milly is sent away, nothing goes wholly wrong.

From *that* point, the closing in is continuous. The ruined rooms, the discovery of the ogress-governess in hiding, introduce the beginning of the end.... All through Le Fanu's writing, there is an ecstatic sensitivity to light, and an abnormal recoil from its inverse, darkness. *Uncle Silas* is full of outdoor weather—we enjoy the rides and glades, cross the books and stiles, meet the cottagers and feel the enclosing walls of two kingdom-like great estates. Though static in ever-autumn, those scenes change: there is more than the rolling across them of clouds or sunshine. Indeed we are looking at their reflection in the lightening or darkening mirror of Maud's mind. (p. 20)

[Since the publication of *Uncle Silas,*] human susceptibilities have altered—some may have atrophied, others developed further. The terror-formula of yesterday might not work to-day. Will *Uncle Silas* act on the modern reader?

I think so, and for several reasons. Le Fanu's strength, here, is not so much in his story as in the mode of its telling. *Uncle Silas,* as it is written, plays on one constant factor—our childish fears. These leave their work at the base of our natures, and are never to be rationalized away. Two things are terrible in childhood: helplessness (being in other people's power) and apprehension—the apprehension that something is being concealed from us because it is too bad to be told. Maud Ruthyn, vehicle of the story, *is* helpless apprehension itself, in person: this is what gets under our skin. Maud, simplified (in the chemical sense, reduced) for her creator's purpose, is, we may tell ourselves, an extreme case. She has a predisposition towards fear: we are to watch her—and *be* her—along her way towards the consummation of perfect terror—just as, were this a love story, we should be sharing her journey towards a consummation of a different kind. (pp. 20-1)

Maud had suspected in Dr. Bryerly a supernatural element of evil: his influence on her father appeared malign. This brings us to another terror-ingredient: moral dread. . . . In *Uncle Silas,* there is no supernatural element in the ordinary sense—the Knowl ghosts exist merely to key Maud up. The genuine horror is the non-natural. Lady Knollys, in her chatter, suggests that Silas may be a non-human soul clothed in a human body.

What Maud dreads, face to face with Silas, is not her own death.

Physically, Maud's nerve is extremely good. She stands up to Madame de la Rougierre, to whom her reactions are those of intense dislike, repugnance and disdain. She is frightened only of what she cannot measure, and she has got the governess taped. . . . Were she, in fact, a goose or weakling, the story would lack the essential tension: *Uncle Silas* would fail. As it is, we have the impact of a crescendo of hints and happenings on taut, hyper-controlled and thus very modern nerves. *Is* there to be a breaking-point? If so, why, how, when? That, not the question of Maud's bodily fate, sets up the real excitement of *Uncle Silas.*

The let-up, the pause for recuperation, even the apparent solicitude: these are among the sciences of the torture chamber. The victim must regain his power to suffer fully. The let-ups in *Uncle Silas*—the fine days, the walks, the returned illusions of safety—are, for Maud and the reader, artfully timed. Nothing goes on for long enough either to dull you or to exhaust itself. And the light, the open air, the outdoor perspective enhance, by contrast, the last of the horror-constants—claustrophobia. On the keyboard of any normal reader *Uncle Silas* will not, I think, fail to strike one or another note: upon the claustrophobic it plays a fugue. The sense of the tightening circle, the shrinking and darkening room. (pp. 21-2)

> *Elizabeth Bowen, in an introduction to* Uncle Silas: A Tale of Bartram-Haugh *by J. S. Le Fanu, The Cresset Press, 1947, pp. 7-23.*

V. S. PRITCHETT　(essay date 1947)

[*Pritchett, a modern British writer, is respected for his mastery of the short story and for what critics describe as his judicious, reliable, and insightful literary criticism. He writes in the conversational tone of the familiar essay, approaching literature from the viewpoint of an informed but not overly scholarly reader. Pritchett's critical method is to stress his own experience, judge-*

An illustration from the horror story "Mr. Justice Harbottle."

ment, and sense of literary art as opposed to following a codified critical doctrine derived from a school of psychological or philosophical theory. In his discussion of Le Fanu, first published in 1947, Pritchett praises the style and narrative technique of the author's short stories. He also contends that because Le Fanu's was primarily a "talent for brevity" he never achieved the same level of success in his novels as he did in his short stories.]

In mid-Victorian literature Le Fanu is crowded out by Dickens and Thackeray, talked off the floor by Lever, that supreme raconteur, surpassed or (should one say?) by-passed on his own ground by Wilkie Collins: yet he has, within his limits, an individual accent and a flawless virtuosity. . . . [His] books show that, like so many talented Irishmen, he had gifts, but too many voices that raise too many echoes.

Le Fanu brought a limpid tributary to the Teutonic stream which had fed mysterious literature for so long. I do not mean that he married the Celtic banshee to the Teutonic poltergeist or the monster, in some Irish graveyard; what he did was to bring an Irish lucidity and imagination to the turgid German flow. Le Fanu's ghosts are the most disquieting of all: the ghosts that can be justified, blobs of the unconscious that have floated up to the surface of the mind, and which are not irresponsible and perambulatory figments of family history, mooning and clanking about in fancy dress. The evil of the justified ghosts is not sportive, willful, involuntary or extravagant. In Le Fanu the fright is that effect follows cause. Guilt patters two-legged behind its victims in the street, retribution sits adding up its account night after night, the secret doubt scratches away with malignant patience in the guarded mind. We laugh at the headless coachman or the legendary heiress grizzling her way through the centuries in her nightgown; but we pause when we recognize that those other hands on the wardrobe, those other eyes at the window, those other steps on the landing and those small shadows that slip into the room as we open the door, are our own. It is we who are the ghosts. Those are *our* own steps which follow us, it is *our* "heavy body" which we hear falling in the attic above. We haunt ourselves. Let illness or strain weaken the catch which we keep fixed so tightly upon the unconscious, and out spring all the hags and animals of moral or Freudian symbolism, just as the "Elemental" burns sharp as a diamond before our eyes when we lie relaxed and on the point of sleep.

Some such idea is behind most of Le Fanu's tales [in *In a Glass Darkly*]. They are presented as the cases of a psychiatrist called Dr. Helvetius, whose precise theory appears to be that these fatal visitations come when the psyche is worn to rags and the interior spirit world can then make contact with the external through the holes. A touch of science, even bogus science, gives an edge to the superstitious tale. The coarse hanging judge is tracked down by the man whom he has unjustly hanged and is hanged in turn. The eupeptic sea captain on the point of marrying an Irish fortune is quietly terrorized into the grave by the sailor whom, years before, he had had flogged to death in Malta. The fashionable and handsome clergyman is driven to suicide by the persecutions of a phantom monkey who jumps into his Bible as he preaches, and waits for him at street corners, in carriages, in his very room. A very Freudian animal this. Dark and hairy with original sin and symbolism, he skips straight out of the unchaste jungle of a pious bachelor's unconscious. The vampire girl who preys on the daughter of an Austrian count appears to be displaying the now languid, now insatiate, sterility of Lesbos. I am not, however, advancing Le Fanu as an instance of the lucky moralist who finds a sermon in every spook, but as an artist in the dramatic use of the evil, the secret, and the fatal, an artist, indeed, in the domestic insinuation of the supernatural. With him it does not break the law, but extends the mysterious jurisdiction of nature.

Le Fanu might be described as the Simenon of the peculiar. There is the same limpid narrative. He is expert in screwing up tension little by little without strain, and an artist in surprise. The literature of the uncanny scores crudely by outraging our senses and our experience; but the masters stick to the simple, the *almost* natural, and let fall their more unnerving revelations as if they were all in the day's work. And they are. The clergyman in *Green Tea* is describing the course of his persecution, how it abates only to be renewed with a closer menace.

> I traveled in a chaise. I was in good spirits. I was more—I was happy and grateful. I was returning, as I thought, delivered from a dreadful hallucination, to the scene of duties which I longed to enter upon. It was a beautiful sunny evening, everything looked serene and cheerful and I was delighted. I remember looking out of the window to see the spire of my Church at Kenlis among the trees, at the point where one has the earliest view of it. It is exactly where the little stream that bounds the parish

passes under the road by a culvert; and where it emerges at the roadside a stone with an old inscription is placed. As we passed this point I drew my head in and sat down, and in the corner of the chaise was the monkey.

Again:

> It used to spring on a table, on the back of a chair, on the chimney piece, and slowly to swing itself from side to side, looking at me all the time. There is in its motion an indefinable power to dissipate thought, and to contract one's attention to that monotony till the ideas shrink, as it were, to a point, and at last to nothing— and unless I had started up, and shook off the catalepsy, I have felt as if my mind were on the point of losing itself. There are other ways [he sighed heavily] thus, for instance, while I pray with my eyes closed, it comes closer and closer, and I see it. I know it is not to be accounted for physically but I do actually see it, though my lids are closed, and so it rocks my mind, as it were, and overpowers me, and I am obliged to rise from my knees. If you had ever yourself known this, you would be acquainted with desperation.

And then, after this crisis, the tortured clergyman confides once more to his doctor and makes his most startling revelation in the mere course of conversation. The doctor has suggested that candles shall be brought. The clergyman wearily replies:

> All lights are the same to me. Except when I read or write, I care not if night were perpetual. I am going to tell you what happened about a year ago. The thing began to speak to me.

There is Henry James's *second* turn of the screw.

We progress indeed not into vagueness and atmosphere, but into greater and greater particularity; with every line the net grows tighter. Another sign of the master is Le Fanu's equable eye for the normal. There is a sociability about his stories, a love of pleasure, a delight in human happiness, a tolerance of folly and a neat psychological perception. Only in terms of the vampire legend would the Victorians have permitted a portrayal of Lesbian love, but how lightly, skillfully and justly it is told. Vigilance is a word Le Fanu often uses. We feel a vigilance of observation in all his character drawing, we are aware of a fluid and quick sensibility which responds only to the essential things in people and in the story. He is as detached as a *dompteur* [tamer]; he caresses, he bribes, he laughs, he cracks the whip. It is a sinister but gracious performance.

One doesn't want to claim too much for Le Fanu. . . . He is known for two of his many novels: *Uncle Silas* and *The House by the Churchyard*. *Uncle Silas* has ingenious elements. Le Fanu saw the possibility of the mysterious in the beliefs and practices of the Swedenborgians, but the book goes downhill halfway through and becomes a crime puzzle. A good man dies and puts his daughter in his brother's care, knowing his brother is reputed to be a murderer. By this reckless act the good man hopes to clear his brother's name. On the contrary, it puts an idea into his head. This brother, Uncle Silas, had married beneath him, and the picture of his illiterate family has a painful rawness which is real enough; but such a sinister theme requires quiet treatment, and Le Fanu is too obviously sweating along in the footsteps of Dickens or Wilkie Collins. Lever is another echo. It is his voice, the voice of the stage Irishman which romps rather too nuttily about *The House by the Churchyard*, into which Le Fanu seems to have thrown every possible side of his talent without discrimination. There are ghosts you shrink from, ghosts you laugh at, cold murder is set beside comic duels, wicked characters become ridiculous, ridiculous ones become solemn and we are supposed to respect them. It is all a very strange mixture, and Sterne and Thackeray, as well as Lever, seem to be adding their hand. A good deal is farcical satire of the military society in eighteenth-century Dublin, and Le Fanu is dashing and gaudy with a broad brush:

> Of late Mrs. Macnamara had lost all her pluck and half her colour, and some even of her fat. She was like one of those portly dowagers in Nubernip's select society of metamorphosed turnips, who suddenly exhibited sympathetic symptoms of failure, grew yellow, flabby and wrinkled, as the parent bulb withered and went out of season.

His comic subalterns, scheming land agents and quarreling doctors, his snoring generals and shrill army wives, are drawn close up, so close up that it is rather bewildering until you are used to the jumpy and awkward angles of his camera. One gets a confused, lifesize impression, something like the impression made by a crowded picture of Rowlandson's, where so much is obviously happening that one can't be sure exactly what it is and where to begin. Le Fanu was spreading himself as Lever had done, but was too soaked in the journalist's restless habits to know how to define his narrative. He became garrulous where Lever was the raconteur. He rambles on like some rumbustious reporter who will drop into a graceful sketch of trout fishing on the Liffey or into fragments of rustic idyll and legend, and then return to his duels, his hell-fire oaths and his claret. I can see that this book has a flavor, but I could never get through it. The truth is that Le Fanu, the journalist, could not be trusted to *accumulate* a novel. You can see in *Uncle Silas* how the process bored him, and how that book is really a good short story that has unhappily started breeding. His was a talent for brevity, the poetic sharpness and discipline of the short tale, for the subtleties and symbolism of the uncanny. In this form Le Fanu is a good deal more than a ghost among the ghosts. (pp. 122-27)

> *V. S. Pritchett, "An Irish Ghost," in his* The Living Novel & Later Appreciations, *revised edition, Random House, 1964, pp. 121-28.]*

NELSON BROWNE   (essay date 1951)

> [*Browne's book-length study is a critical survey of Le Fanu's short and long prose works. In the excerpt below, Browne discusses Le Fanu's greatest novels,* The House by the Churchyard, Uncle Silas, Wylder's Hand, *and* Guy Deverell, *and compares them favorably with his short stories. Browne also argues that Le Fanu was indeed a "sensation-monger"—a view that Le Fanu had defended himself against (see excerpt above, 1864) and that Michael A. Begnal disputes (see excerpt below, 1971).]*

The House by the Churchyard divides with *Uncle Silas* the award for first place amongst Le Fanu's novels. (p. 36)

The House by the Churchyard contains not one clearly defined plot but several which are interrelated and which converge, or, rather, are unified as the crisis of the story approaches. There is, first, the story of the melancholy Mervyn, really the Lord

Dunoran, whose misfortunes date from his father's disgrace and death in prison while awaiting execution of sentence of death for murder. Subsidiary to Mervyn's ultimately successful attempts to vindicate his father and re-establish his own fortunes, is his secret romance with Miss Gertrude Chattesworth, and this is a little history in itself. Next, there is the mysterious disappearance of Charles Nutter, Lord Castlemallard's Irish agent, the descent of the baleful Mary Matchwell upon the sorrowing Mrs. Nutter, Nutter's reappearance and his arrest upon a capital charge, and finally his triumph over the designing Mary Matchwell and the complete proof of his innocence. (pp. 37-8)

These three themes provide the dramatic elements. For the rest, there is pathos in the unhappy romance of Captain "Gipsy" Devereux and the Rector's daughter, Lilias Walsingham; there is dash and rattle, conviviality and skylarking in the lively picture of garrison life, and there is the humorous progress of certain rather absurd courtships. (pp. 38-9)

It is, however, the main plot, the Paul Dangerfield—Charles Archer villainy, which gives the novel its distinctive force. Everything else is made accessory to this transcendent iniquity. From the first encounter at the dinner given in Dangerfield's honour by General Chattesworth when Sturk is strangely disturbed by a dim recollection that he had seen "that high forehead, gleaming silver spectacles, hooked nose, grim mouth," somewhere before, until we are told that even in death Dangerfield's "jaundiced features were stamped with the ironical smile they had worn in life," we are fascinated by a personality that both attracts and repels. (p. 39)

In a costume novel there is always the attraction of the picturesque, and in addition there is all the grace and dignity of the old times in *The House by the Churchyard*, the noble hospitality and the courtly manners. Le Fanu obtains, moreover, that delicate suggestion of something a little faded, a little antiquated in a genteel way, but infinitely gracious, in the style of his leisurely sentences, which preserves the illusion that we are indeed reading pages from the past. This novel is the last in which Le Fanu returns to the past for his theme and settings, and though its excellence is sufficient to make it remarkable, it does, nevertheless, represent an intermediate stage between the old historical romance of the *Torlogh O'Brien* type, with its Ainsworthian flavour, and the kind of story that he was to make peculiarly his own, the story of crime, remorse and punishment, played under the mellow lamp-light and amid the heavy, dark mahogany of the early Victorian drawing-rooms. (pp. 41-2)

[*Wylder's Hand*] is a masterpiece of mystery-story writing. . . . (p. 42)

Mark Wylder himself is one of the most complete character studies ever attempted by Le Fanu, and is surpassed only by Silas Ruthyn. None of his foibles is concealed from us—his conceit, his showy vulgarity, his atrocious manners, his disreputable past, his braggartry, his materialism, to which are added a streak of buffoonery allied to a dangerous, calculating shrewdness.

Conveyed with hundreds of delicate strokes and hints, the character of the man dominates the drama as completely when he is, so to speak, off the stage, as when in the opening chapters he swaggers right in front of the footlights. His mysterious disappearance, his callous treatment of Dorcas, the threats contained in his brutal, bombastic letters, the secrecy with which his movements are surrounded, the havoc caused by the mere mention of his name or by speculations about his prolonged absence—these things make him a simulacrum of the invisible enemy of mankind himself, working in darkness and making mischief always. (p. 44)

Uncle Lorne with very little shifting of emphasis might very readily have been a figure of fun—his ravings, for instance, taken from their context, are melodramatic almost to the point of absurdity—but the great virtue of this character is the way Le Fanu uses him as a kind of chorus, introducing him when the action reaches a point where excitement and tension are greatest. Oddly enough, most of Uncle Lorne's spectral appearances occur when de Cresserons is at Brandon Hall and this fact increases their sensational value since Le Fanu has contrived that those portions of the story—they are the most critical portions—in which de Cresserons is in personal contact with the main characters are narrated in the first person by de Cresserons himself. (pp. 45-6)

Since the novel is less complex than *The House by the Church-yard* and the number of characters fewer, Le Fanu concentrates all his powers to produce a uniform plot in which, from the outset, the reader is shown the working of a destructive force, not personalized in either Mark Wylder or Stanley Lake, though each in his own way is the agent of it. It is a force somehow identified with the houses of Wylder and Brandon, with the peculiar history of the two estates so inextricably united in weal and woe, and with the demoralizing taint of great riches.

An atmosphere of doom saddens everything and everyone in the story. Even the beauty of the two heroines is unlucky; their friendship is almost, their happiness is completely, blighted. (pp. 46-7)

Uncle Silas is the only novel of Le Fanu's which is still fairly well known. It has more unity than the two preceding novels and the story gains in concentration from being told in the first person, a form of narration that always brought to Le Fanu a notable accession of power. On the whole the modern reader has grown used, where sensational literature is concerned, to receiving his shocks by the most direct, if not always by the most subtle methods. There is directness in *Uncle Silas,* but the subtlety with which Le Fanu tightens and relaxes the springs of suspense, his immense power of characterization, and his unrivalled command of what we may term the vocabulary of terror, with all its shades and nuances of nervous suggestion, combine with this directness to make it a novel that is a delight to the connoisseur of sensational fiction. (pp. 47-8)

Of all Le Fanu's types of human iniquity Uncle Silas is the most fearful and most awe-inspiring. Infinitely more polished than Dangerfield, who one feels was not quite a gentleman by Le Fanu's standards, he is yet more pitiable in that he is obliged to live at Bartram-Haugh in a kind of private hell of his own making, for ever excluded from the cheerful bustle of the world. A tarnished reputation, penury, guilt, all conspired to present the melancholy spectacle of something a trifle wasted, a little gone to seed, but with some traces of former pomp and vanity remaining in the elegance, the graceful conversation, the valetudinarian airs and graces. (p. 50)

If we can believe in the dominion of terror exercised by Uncle Silas, what of Madame de la Rougierre? Ghoulish, grotesque, unimaginably wicked, incredibly vain, amorous and intemperate, she is as hateful as she is horrible. From the moment when Maud catches sight of her, grimacing and curtseying outside the library window at Knowl, she is the embodiment of evil and one feels that in "the deep damnation of her taking-

off" there was a fatal justice. For ever harping on death, the grave, hauntings, "Monsieur Cadavre and Monsieur Squelette," she is truly what she calls herself, "Madame la Morgue—Mrs. Deadhouse."

The character of Dudley Ruthyn is interesting for the skill with which Le Fanu presents the indefinable type of man whose good looks do not neutralize an inherent lowness and a corresponding vulgarity—a vulgarity which pervades his dress, his demeanour, even his walk. The boorishness of Dudley Ruthyn, his clumsy brutality, are, of course, strongly contrasted with the refined viciousness of his father. The rustic beauty of his sister Milly, seen through the condescending eyes of Maud Ruthyn, is, on the other hand, genuinely attractive. On the whole she is a more likeable character than her splendid cousin, for despite manifold disadvantages of heredity and breeding, she is naturally kind-hearted and sincere. (pp. 51-2)

Mr. E. F. Benson has commended "the quiet cumulative method leading up to intolerable terror" as characteristic of all Le Fanu's best work, and instances *Uncle Silas* as the best example of the use of this technique [see excerpt above, 1931]. (p. 52)

It is undoubtedly this gradual onset of a hideous storm of terror which gives this novel its merciless hold upon the reader. With the deceptive intervals of calm and repose, the story brings us gagged and bound with suspense and fear to that awful scene in the third-floor room at Bartram-Haugh, powerless like Maud herself to parry the blow that must descend. Like her, rooted to the spot in a place of concealment, we behold the mystery of Charke's murder being solved as prelude to another bloody deed. We feel the inrush of the frosty night air as the window swings wide in one mass, bars and all. We witness Dudley's stealthy approach to the bed where the sleeping Frenchwoman lies in her drugged stupor; we hear those crunching blows, the unnatural shrieks, that dreadful sound "like the shaking of a tree and rustling of leaves"; we see the entry of "that frail, tall, white figure, with the venerable silken locks that resembled those upon the honoured brow of John Wesley." We can almost feel the touch of his thin white hand, he passes so near, and as we close the book the smell of perfumes and ether lingers in imagination still.

Compared with its predecessor *Guy Deverell* seems deficient in grim horror, but this deficiency serves to emphasize the other excellent qualities which are part of Le Fanu's equipment as a novelist.

The fact that the action takes place at a house-party in a large country mansion imposes a strict observance of the unity of place, if not that of time also, yet *Guy Deverell* is not so unitary in design and purpose as *Uncle Silas.* For this the long-winded nature of the narrative is chiefly to blame, but there is, too, an indeterminate quality about the mystery itself, as if the author could not quite make up his mind whether or not it was worth while to unravel the knot of intrigue. Further, there are moments when we are left doubting as to which of the two most striking characters—Sir Jekyl Marlowe or M. Varbarrierre alias Herbert Strangways—is to play the villain's part. These things weaken the dramatic force of the story.

It is not the plot with its *motif* of revenge, its family skeletons which inhabit the mysterious "Green Room" in preference to the traditional cupboards, but the masterly character-drawing and the brilliant table-talk which make *Guy Deverell* a pleasure to read. (pp. 53-4)

Sir Jekyl's house-party affords Le Fanu a convenient opportunity to practise his gift of caricature. His touch is so light that though we are amused by his vignettes we are also aware that he has not betrayed his faith in class distinctions. Sir Jekyl's guests may be various kinds of fools and humbugs, but they are ladies and gentlemen, too. The fact is that whether or not Le Fanu is describing a villain or a poltroon he invariably builds up a character from without inward. . . . Facial expressions, mannerisms, tricks of speech, the whole outer bearing of a man or woman give clues to the psychic nature, and by these means Le Fanu gives at least a picturesque actuality to his characters, and this faculty is seen to perfection in *Guy Deverell,* in *Uncle Silas,* in *Wylder's Hand,* and in *The House by the Churchyard.* (p. 56)

Le Fanu more than once apologizes for his self-indulgence in the mysterious and horrible, sometimes, perhaps, with his tongue in his cheek, but in . . . [his preface to *Uncle Silas* (see excerpt above, 1864)] he appears sincerely anxious to disassociate himself from the Horror School, and to plead in advance for the literary respectability and moral integrity of the type of sensationalism which is found in *Uncle Silas.* But it will not do! Le Fanu is a sensation-monger in a manner that Scott, in spite of the elements of Gothicism which his novels undoubtedly reveal, never would have emulated.

In appealing to the honourable example of Scott, however, Le Fanu was acknowledging, if not a debt, certainly an affinity.

With more perseverance, without the impediment of divided political loyalties which enfeebled and confused his patriotism, he might have repeated in Ireland what Scott achieved for Scotland. He had all Scott's reverence for antiquity; he had, too, the same youthful enthusiasms, and much the same haphazard, yet wholly liberal, education, the same prodigality of genius, the same indefatigable industry, the same instincts of the *grand seigneur* [great lord]. But he lacked Scott's gusto, his vitality, his humanity and, above all, his power to shape characters that were stereoscopically real, solid-seeming in virtue, in vice, or even in oddity.

Le Fanu's most striking characters are for the most part either actuated by vengeance or tormented by remorse. Further, most of them are in some way abnormal—set apart from the generality of their fellow-creatures by some defect of temperament, by great wealth, by some distinguishing mark of beauty or ugliness, or by their susceptibility to influences outside the range of normal experience. Thus his portrayal of human nature is more or less limited to those examples which present some mental or spiritual deformity, or to those whose reactions to the stimulus of terror he can describe with the precision of an alienist. (pp. 107-08)

There is much in Le Fanu that suggests a comparison with Poe—the House of Usher that falls at last, the morbid sensibility to night terrors, the love of the macabre, the fear of death—but the comparison, though inevitable, is not really helpful. In the first place, Poe had a poetic imagination which achieved its richest expression in his verse, though it is also revealed in the glowing yet sombre imagery of his prose. Further, Poe's imaginative flights have in them something erratic and wild, though never disorderly because they are constrained by a powerful intellect.

The nature of Le Fanu's imagination is fundamentally dramatic rather than poetic, and it finds adequate expression in prose which never strains beyond the limits of prose composition, though within these limits he is a dexterous and effective writer.

Le Fanu equals, even surpasses, Poe when it comes to creating an atmosphere of stark terror: sensationalism after all was his *forte.* But the greatness of Poe is measured by intellectual, rather than by emotional, standards. The question as to which of the two writers is the greater literary artist may be decided on the grounds of personal taste, but while conceding Le Fanu's superiority in two things—his power to create and maintain suspense and his skill as a necromancer—the decision on general grounds (taking into account his greater range of genius and his power to concentrate his talents effectively) must be given in favour of Poe. (pp. 109-10)

Anyone who has read Le Fanu's works extensively cannot fail to be struck by certain habits of composition which have an interest completely unconnected with any questions concerning style or quality. One of the most consistent of these habits is . . . his practice of rewriting a story, giving it a completely new setting and introducing some novel elements into the plot. (pp. 110-11)

Another habit is the repetition, with ingenious variations, of one particular theme, the most common being the one in which the chief actor in some former drama of crime or intrigue returns many years afterwards to mix, unrecognized, with many of those who knew him in another place, under another name, and in a totally different aspect. The unravelling of the mystery becomes all the more absorbing as the reader, from hints that he is given, identifies the criminal with the man whose misdeeds of twenty years before still cry for vengeance. Sometimes the character presented thus is not wholly unregenerate. Strangways, who poses as the Frenchman Varbarriere in *Guy Deverell,* is an avenger of wrong and, similarly, Mr. Dingwell, the great Greek merchant in *The Tenants of Malory,* is the means of justice being done. (p. 111)

Just as Le Fanu reproduces old incidents and returns to a familiar theme, he also shows an inclination to repeat the use of certain names for characters and of certain localities for his settings. . . .

His practice of repeating themes and names may, of course, be explained and excused as one of the results of the serial habit of writing and the urgency and haste which such a habit renders inevitable. Still, his contemporaries subject to the same tyranny do not exhibit the same reactions to its constraint. (p. 112)

As for less pardonable blemishes, these again may be attributed to his hasty, piecemeal methods of composition. He was a remarkably careless proof-reader and his novels are so full of printer's errors that it is obvious the faults are the outcome of his own negligence. . . .

The snail's pace at which Le Fanu's novels proceed is to my mind by no means a deterrent to the reader's enjoyment of such masterpieces as *The House by the Churchyard* or *Wylder's Hand.* Indeed the nature of these stories is such that any acceleration of the pace of the narrative would be inartistic and out of keeping with the deliberately gradual process of harrowing the reader which was the author's purpose. This is not to say that the novels are uniformly presented in slow motion. The crises when they come have the sudden animation of a flash of lightning, and they are correspondingly more shocking and demoralizing by contrast with the almost imperceptible darkening of the horizon which has been clouding over from the very first. (p. 113)

Naturally, in all but the very best of Le Fanu's novels there is tedium and after the publication of *Haunted Lives* ... when his powers as a novelist seemed to wane, the tedium grows. Of the five novels written after 1868 none, except *Checkmate,* have much to recommend them even to the enthusiast who might be satisfied with even the smallest dram of the familiar brew. Paradoxically, his skill as a short-story writer instead of diminishing during these last years appears to have augmented, and for proof we have only to turn to *In a Glass Darkly.* This suggests the criticism that Le Fanu's real field was the short story and that he had not the essential talents of the novelist. ... I feel that the short stories, on the whole, show him at his best more consistently than the novels, and that all those qualities so justly admired in the latter appear with even more striking prominence in the former. Certainly the impatient reader is likely to take more kindly to the short stories. Yet to ignore ... [his] great novels, *The House by the Churchyard, Uncle Silas, Wylder's Hand,* [and] *Guy Deverell* ... , would be an injustice since in these books the author's talents are found in their fullest expression, proving that the merits of his short stories *are* capable of being sustained with no diminution of power or impressiveness throughout a three-volume novel. (pp. 114-15)

Nelson Browne, in his Sheridan Le Fanu, *Roy Publishers, 1951, 135 p.*

E. F. BLEILER (essay date 1963)

[*In this excerpt from his introduction to a collection of Le Fanu's short stories, Bleiler discusses the supernatural element in Le Fanu's work. This essay was composed in 1963.*]

Of all the Victorian authors who wrote ghost stories, only LeFanu seems to have recognized that there must be an aesthetic of supernatural terror. He obviously thought deeply about the nature of fictional supernaturalism and was aware of the implications that supernaturalism would have for the other dynamics of the story. Most of his fellow authors felt that they had done enough if they declared a house haunted; from this there followed automatically ghosts dragging chains, shrieking phantoms, or spirits of the dead who made actual physical attacks upon the stalwart hero or fainting heroine. Or they thought of a ghost as a compulsive personality fragment that insisted upon reenacting (often to sad music and pallid lighting) the murders or other crimes that it had committed; or else they peopled the countryside with spirits of missing persons who stalked around evenings, pointing out to the curious the places where their bodies had been hidden. LeFanu seems to have been alone in rejecting these crudities; to him alone it occurred that the personality of the beholder could be just as important and perhaps just as supernatural as the manifestation itself.

In his best work LeFanu was primarily a psychologist, although not in the modern understanding of the term. His mode of thought hearkened back to the earlier nineteenth century, where theorists like Schubert and Carus were dividing the mind into conscious and unconscious levels, and seeing in dream, madness, and vision emergences of both a hidden "nightside of nature" and the supernatural. And like the early nineteenth-century philosophers he was greatly interested in the barrier between the ego and the non-ego, in the manner that each creates the other, and in the osmotic process which can penetrate the seal between the two areas of existence. LeFanu was concerned with penetrating the hidden recesses of the psyches of his characters and mapping out the strange areas where the sense of reality can manifest itself to cover equally what is perceived and not-perceived. Within his better fiction LeFanu so blended and intertwined the natural and the supernatural that his work is a fugue of strange states of consciousness, linkages between the outside world and man, and a hidden, often diabolic morality, that will not suffer evil to go unavenged or unbetrayed. As a result there is nothing else in contemporary literature quite like the effects and symbolism that sweep through **"Green Tea," "The Haunted Baronet,"** or **"Squire Toby's Will,"** just as there is nothing comparable to the perverse eroticism of **"Carmilla"** or the strange sexuality of **"Schalken the Painter."**

Within his later work LeFanu developed ever more strongly a rationale of supernaturalism that permitted him to invade both the mind and the manifestation. In the tales grouped together loosely by the analytical lens of Dr. Hesselius in *In a Glass Darkly,* the supernatural is an unconscious element in the mind and it may leap into emergence when the barriers protecting the conscious ego are temporarily broken down, in one case by a drug, in another case by a sense of guilt. Yet this is not all, for the larger implications of the mind as a microcosm of the universe also loom out, and potentially evil mental fragments may become hypostatized into semi-independent existence, to ally themselves with larger evil forces of which we are fortunately unaware. Obviously, such concepts are likely to strain the fabric of a story, and in some of LeFanu's later work, like **"The Haunted Baronet,"** the story becomes almost a symbolic organism or passion, in which the characters, instead of being people, are forces or small nodes and concentrations in a larger fabric which twists and strains through a uniquely haunted universe. It is probably significant that **"The Haunted Baronet,"** together with Hoffmann's *Devil's Elixir* ... , is the final, typologically extreme spiritualization of the basic Gothic and Romantic plot of the disinherited hero.

In all this LeFanu took, essentially, the opposite road from his contemporaries. He strove to create an artistically consistent world where the supernatural was a natural manifestation; sometimes this was the world of philosophical and psychological speculation; sometimes it was a folkloristic world where faith in the Devil and his workings can account for his presence. LeFanu's fellow writers ... , on the other hand, usually dragged occasional and erratic supernaturalism into our everyday life. ... [Their works] all show the same classical separation of the real and unreal. Only LeFanu seems to have equated the haunted swamps and strange fluttering birds and fierce ancestral portraits with the guilt layers of a man's mind.

Why did LeFanu differ so greatly from his fellows? The difference is not just a matter of quality. ... It is more a matter of an attitude, a point of view, and a quality of emotion. Obviously, the answer lies in part in LeFanu's own unusual personality, which combined the gentle weaknesses and terrible dreams of the visionary with the strengths of the very competent business man. Both the sensitivity to perceive an emotion and the strength and rigor to analyze and reproduce it were present. Partly, it may have been a matter of personal belief. The supernatural had a personal meaning for LeFanu which did not exist for his more or less orthodox fellow writers. ... [LeFanu] is often writing a story of the early nineteenth century, and paradoxically, because of his peculiar time lag is often quite modern. (pp. vii-ix)

E. F. Bleiler, in an introduction to Best Ghost Stories of J. S. LeFanu *by J. S. LeFanu, edited by E. F. Bleiler, Dover Publications, Inc., 1964, pp. v-xi.*

FREDERICK SHROYER (essay date 1966)

[*In this excerpt from his introduction to* Uncle Silas, *Shroyer outlines the elements that contribute to that novel's atmosphere of terror.*]

[Since Le Fanu's death, most of his] fourteen novels have been largely forgotten, but not his masterly terror novel, *Uncle Silas.* Rereading it . . . , I was again reminded of how very good it is, and to me there seems no mystery involved in both its longevity and perennial appeal. Simply, it is one of the most effective, gripping novels of terror—a true Gothic novel—ever written.

Today, as in the past, *Uncle Silas* continues to serve diabolically well to chill the reader's psychic bones. It begins gently and discursively enough as the narration of a lady who remembers what it was that surrounded her as a girl—her isolated home, her dour, withdrawn father, and their servants—and then, little by little, it draws the reader into an insidious, one-way tunnel of fear wherein crouches murder most foul.

Uncle Silas is definitely not a novel to be read alone in a creaking, deserted house late at night. Indeed, in the malign glow of its bloody foxfire, most other novels of terror dim quickly toward extinction. Nor should the reader be comforted overmuch by its relatively quiet, almost prosaic beginning. Rather let him heed the cry of the winter winds outside the ghost-whispering old manse of Knowl, forewarned that it is that, and the encroaching darkness of a winter's night, that most truly presage the true nature of the horror awaiting him at the narrative's next turning.

We are all a little afraid of death, and *Uncle Silas* is, above all, a novel in which death prowls the pages. Maud Ruthyn, the narrator, is peculiarly obsessed with night thoughts, and though she may at times philosophize sentimentally about death, she lives in the awful shadow of its presence and, indeed, at times seems half in love with it. Her death-obsessed father, Austin Ruthyn, a Swedenborgian, knowing that he is a dying man, half-yearns for the opening of the gate through which, he believes, he will pass into a landscape littered with signs and wonders.

But all of this is, in itself, not enough to make *Uncle Silas* the outré [exaggerated] experience it is. LeFanu, death-haunted himself, . . . knew that unrelieved darkness loses in time its effect, and thus all through the novel, as murder and terror accumulate, he scatters small diamonds of wit, sunlight and satire upon the novel's vast shroud. Just as *Macbeth* is made infinitely more terrible by the interpolation of the gate-keeper scene, so is the basic terror of *Uncle Silas* amplified by Le-Fanu's occasional introductions of warm fireside scenes and episodes which serve, briefly, seemingly to move Maud away from the bloody death for which she is destined. Thus, too, from time to time, pleasant, frequently comic characters are introduced to serve as shafts of sunlight in an ever darkening room: Maud's cousin, Milly, the simple, slangy daughter of Silas Ruthyn; the worldly, witty, heart-of-gold Lady Knollys; and even Silas's son, Dudley, especially when he jigs, smokes his church-warden and presents Maud with a parrot.

Still, LeFanu does not dally long with the comic and the whimsical. It is a darker, bloodier draught that he brews, and in its making he draws upon the blacker, more disturbing manifestations of nature to froth it with terror. Indeed, *Uncle Silas* begins with a touch of this sort of thing, and in the following quotation from the beginning of the novel, it should be noted

that even when he contrasts the wildness of a winter's night outside with the warm candle-lit rooms within Knowl, LeFanu brings something of the external gloom into the rooms by the use of such words as 'sombre,' 'black,' 'ebony,' 'grim,' and 'pale':

> It was winter—that is, about the second week in November—and great gusts were rattling at the windows, and wailing and thundering among our tall trees and ivied chimneys—a very dark night, and a very cheerful fire blazing, a pleasant mixture of good round coal and spluttering dry wood, in a genuine old fireplace, in a sombre old room. Black wainscoting glimmered up to the ceiling, in small ebony panels; a cheerful clump of wax candles on the tea-table; many old portraits, some grim and pale, others pretty, and some very graceful and charming, hanging from the walls.

On another occasion, after the death of her father, Maud's depression and growing apprehension are orchestrated and amplified again by the seeming shouts of phantom riders galloping through a nighted storm:

> And so it was like the yelling of phantom hounds and hunters, and the thunder of their coursers in the air—a furious, grand, and supernatural music, which in my fancy made a suitable accompaniment to the discussion of that enigmatical person—martyr—angel—demon—Uncle Silas—with whom my fate was now so strangely linked, and whom I had begun to fear.

> 'The storm blows from that point,' I said, indicating it with my hand and eye, although the window shutters and curtains were closed. 'I saw all the trees bend that way this evening. That way stands the great lonely wood, where my darling father and mother lie. Oh, how dreadful on nights like this, to think of them—a vault!—damp, and dark, and solitary—under the storm.'

The above description of a storm leads quickly, it will be noted, into gloomy speculations about the finality of death, and, as it has been intimated before, LeFanu comes unerringly to the matter of death to contribute to the horror and accumulating drifts of creeping doom and darkness in his novel. Not infrequently in LeFanu's fiction does death forsake the anonymity of an abstraction to become, in fact, an actual entity. (pp. v-vii)

LeFanu seldom fails to utilize the supernatural as a device to darken most effectively the atmosphere of terror he creates. *Uncle Silas* is not a novel of the supernatural, but what is one to make of the gypsy girl's prophetic utterances when she is accosted by Maud on her way to Uncle Silas's decaying manse? Or of the voice that Maud hears 'near the hearthstone, as I thought, say in a stern whisper, "Fly the fangs of Belisaurius"'? Or of Lady Knollys's chilling comment upon Uncle Silas when she says, 'Perhaps other souls than human are sometimes born into the world and clothed in flesh, venerable, fiery-eyed'? (p. viii)

[Though] LeFanu's marvelous creation, the grotesque, unforgettable Madame de la Rougierre, who repeatedly asserts that she is in love with death and all of its sombre accoutrements, says that she has seen one of Knowl's ghosts, it is not important really if she has or not. By his descriptions of the ghosts that may or may not haunt Knowl, and by Madame's statement, LeFanu has achieved the effect he sought: he has made us all a little afraid, and like the witty French lady who, when asked if she believed in ghosts, replied, 'No, but I'm afraid of them,' we, too, find ourselves whistling a little too loudly as we glance apprehensively over our shoulders. (p. ix)

> *Frederick Shroyer, in an introduction to* Uncle Silas:
> A Tale of Bartram-Haugh *by J. S. LeFanu, Dover*
> *Publications, Inc., 1966, pp. v-xiii.*

MICHAEL H. BEGNAL   (essay date 1971)

[*In his book-length study of Le Fanu, Begnal concentrates on Le Fanu as a novelist and places him within the scope of Victorian literature. In the following excerpt, Begnal specifically addresses the relation of Le Fanu's works to the nineteenth-century Gothic tradition.*]

Sheridan LeFanu has been praised for many years as a creator of suspense and of the supernatural, and it is true that a good part of his work is squarely in the nineteenth-century Gothic tradition. In his short stories, especially, he makes great use of the miraculous and the spine-tingling, and Horace Walpole, Charles Maturin, and Edgar Allan Poe are obviously among his literary ancestors. (p. 27)

Like [Maturin's] Melmoth and [Emily Brontë's] Heathcliff, most of the protagonists of the stories are men divided against themselves. They are creatures of violently shifting moods, unable to control the extreme forces in their natures. Byronic in character, they plumb the depths and soar to the heights, and ultimately they are the cause of their own destruction. Much in the manner of Poe's, LeFanu's tales oscillate between the poles of supernatural horror and suspenseful detection. . . . The central difference with the Irishman, however, is that in his development he will break out of the usual ghost story mold to deal with a new dimension, and, as in his novels, to relate his insights to his own society.

Ghost Stories and Tales of Mystery . . . was LeFanu's first collection of stories of the shadowy and mysterious. . . . Two of the pieces, **"The Watcher"** and **"Schalken the Painter,"** are based on horror, while the other two [**"The Murdered Cousin"** and **"The Evil Guest"**] are essentially detective thrillers.

[The emphasis in these stories] is on suspense rather than the psychological, and LeFanu is fascinating and shocking his audience rather than instructing them. He is analyzing terror rather than character. The basic elements of this volume . . . are conventionally Gothic, and though some of the stories are well done, they offer little that is extremely out of the ordinary.

What these Gothic tales do represent is LeFanu's fascination with horror and brutality, a fixation which is to continue throughout his writings. The violence and despair of his protagonists seem to follow in almost a direct line from Charles Robert Maturin's *Melmoth the Wanderer* . . . with its emphasis on the darker and seamier sides of life. In LeFanu's tales too, rarely are we granted glimpses of hope or of happiness, and certainly love can have little power over the forces of darkness. (p. 31)

Nelson Browne states (quite unfairly it should be noted) that "LeFanu is a sensation-monger in a manner that Scott, in spite of the elements of Gothicism which his novels undoubtedly reveal, never would have emulated" [see excerpt above, 1951].

In his preface to ***Uncle Silas*** [see excerpt above, 1864], the novelist refutes this charge which was first made in his own time, and it would seem that he is justified in his defense. The scenes of violence, and even occasionally of grotesquerie, are not meant to hold the reader's attention for their own sake or on their own fantastic merit. Rather they are meant to inject a note of realism into the work which is to bring home the immediacy of what the story is attempting to convey. LeFanu is not content to hint at passions or to leave horror and terror to the reader's imagination. In a time of pleasant Victorian optimism in society's slow but progressive movement toward the perfection of the individual and his place among his peers, it is the real, the present, state of the world which has been overlooked. While this may not be a completely valid excuse for the presentation of the violent, it is at least a justification which LeFanu may bring to bear against his critics.

Rather than seeing his protagonists as strikingly abnormal and saving his scenes for times when we wish to scare ourselves to sleep, we are to realize that the only thing unreal here actually is the exaggeration of their predicaments. Alienation is much more characteristic of the individual than is contentment and homogeneity, and confusion rather than rationality lies at the center of human affairs. Also, as was the case with Melmoth, it is the evils of existence which drive a man into his own despairing corner; he does not choose this alienation of his own accord. Relationships are torn apart by blind circumstance, and rarely is a hope or a solution to be found. All are isolated by an uncaring and uninterested public life in which each must go his own separate way, never really able to maintain a close touch with another. Here is the true horror of which a man can rarely speak.

Horror, then, becomes an artistic device which LeFanu consciously manipulates in his construction of a given tale. On one level it is meant to entertain, to interest and involve the reader in the events which begin to unfold, and perhaps the critic should remind himself that pleasure is an essential facet of any artistic production. LeFanu is a master at the creation of supernatural event and narrative, and he can usually at least partially convince his reader that what is being witnessed might possibly be true. . . . (pp. 32-4)

[With his narrative technique] LeFanu can be assured of the reader's attention, and the thrust of the theme attains an even greater power. With Conan Doyle, for example, and even with Wilkie Collins to a certain degree, a distance is maintained between the reader and the event, for everything is related in a very calm and cool mannner. We view crime and sin in a detached, deductive way, as a puzzle which Sherlock Holmes may solve as an intellectual exercise but not as something which affects him or us very much. It is this very detachment which LeFanu is trying to avoid in his work. . . . In LeFanu's work the horror is always drawn up close, and life forces itself upon us. There is an enigma in **"The Evil Guest,"** as there is in **"The Murdered Cousin,"** but the emotions of the characters in the stories never allow the reader to abstract himself from the immediate circumstances.

Then too, the forces of evil which confront us are implicit and inherent in ordinary people who are quite like ourselves—not Asiatic fanatics á la Fu Manchu or evil Teutonic scientists and madmen who threaten the existence of the universe. They are sailors, artists, adolescent girls who reflect LeFanu's conviction that evil does not spring from some murky shadowland, but exists right here among us. . . . No one seems to be safe from the touch of the terrible, and there seems no way in which one might protect himself. The technique of narrating most of the tales in the first person heightens the tension even more. Here lies LeFanu's skill, and here too is the basic motivation for his judicious demonstration of the ghostly and the monstrous.

As his work develops, he begins more and more to take us inside his characters, to take a psychological interest in what is happening within the minds of those who are terrorized and victimized by forces which they cannot control. Evil may be dramatically described from the outside, but its delineation can be even more striking when the artist works from the inside out. Thus as his writing continued, especially in the short story, LeFanu came to consider not only the origins of evil but also its effect on the individual human consciousness. Here is his most decisive departure from a tradition which had been content with descriptions of action and outer forms to achieve its objects. The culmination of this development . . . is *In A Glass Darkly,* and certainly LeFanu is, in these stories, no longer at all involved with the Gothic for its own sake. The center of his investigations is always the human psyche, and only from here may significant or valuable statements be made about the human condition. The conscious and the subconscious are inextricably locked together, and only from a description of these separate entities and an understanding of their interaction can a total vision be accomplished.

The supernatural with which LeFanu is concerned is a universal as well as a particular phenomenon, transcending individual time and place, so that we find in his work little use of the banshee, leprechaun, or other manifestation of Irish folklore. . . . His phantoms are essentially unnameable, mainly because each tormented inmate of LeFanu's fiction creates his persecutor out of himself. In the latter part of his career, actually, he seems to relinquish any hearty belief in a spirit world that exists outside the human community, and comes to believe that the individual or the society is responsible for the demon or the monster. No longer does this society or the "common good" contain the answer or solution which can assuage the misery of the individual, so that paradoxically and perversely one becomes one's own torturer. Unfulfilled desires, incomplete aspirations, all contribute to the moral and spiritual decay of the man who once could trust and believe in his God and his country. It is only a step from here to the insights which Freud and Jung were to categorize and expand in succeeding generations, and it is but the same step to the Dubliners whom James Joyce was to paint with so much love and so much hate.

Thus Sheridan LeFanu, in the best of his stories, expects that what he has written will operate on two levels at the same time. The immediacy of the description is meant to bring home the close relationship or kinship between reader and character, while the reader must also view what he is experiencing as something of a psychological case study. When these two facets of his art are working well together, we have LeFanu at his best, pleasing and instructing . . . at one and the same time. His dealings with the supernatural are not the dilettantish dabblings of a Walpole, for always we are brought back to ourselves and to our own time. To LeFanu, the problem of the writer is a serious one, and there is no room for the indulging of one's own foibles and fantasies. (pp. 35-8)

Michael H. Begnal, in his Joseph Sheridan Le Fanu, *Bucknell University Press, 1971, 87 p.*

DAVID BROWNELL   (essay date 1976)

[*In this general discussion of several of Le Fanu's major novels, Brownell considers the overall effectiveness of Le Fanu's mystery and supernatural fiction.*]

Le Fanu's ghost stories have an economy usually absent in his novels—many of which are expansions of plot elements found in his ghost tales. In fact, Le Fanu is a great self-plagiarist: in character types, plots, and terrors he has a narrow range, and his continual recycling of his materials is irritating to anyone who reads several Le Fanu works in succession.

Le Fanu's territory as a writer is the realm of the unpleasant. His characters are almost invariably unpleasant people, and often very evil ones indeed. Le Fanu seems to know very well what evil lurks in the hearts of men, and to be more interested by his villains than by his heroes and heroines. His settings too are often unpleasant places, which exude a damp suggestion that horrible events have left a mark. An eerie unpleasantness surrounds the actors, and sometimes Le Fanu suggests the horrible with one economical phrase, as in the somehow terrible apparition of a "fat white hand" [in **"The Haunting of the Tiled House"** and *The House by the Churchyard*].

Le Fanu seems to feel that tales of the supernatural cannot be set in his own period. He distances them by setting them at least one long life before his own time. Perhaps a ghost in contemporary costume will always seem funny: spooks don't wear bikinis or bermuda shorts. But another reason exists for this distancing of the setting of Le Fanu's ghost stories: like the mystery story, the ghost story often finds the explanation

An 1895 illustration of The Cock and Anchor *by LeFanu's son, Brinsley LeFanu.*

of puzzling present events in actions that took place in the past. The shared assumption seems to be that a past wrong-doing will come out, and a balance of justice must be restored. But Le Fanu's world does not usually involve the restoration of order. . . . In Le Fanu's mysteries and ghost stories the innocent often suffer severe punishment along with the guilty, and the world around them is not at all beneficent. (p. 191)

The first of [Le Fanu's early novels], *The Cock and Anchor*. . . , is set in the Ireland of 1710, with Le Fanu's characteristic fondness for stories set in the past. It is not a good historical novel, as it tells us little about the period in which it is set and makes no use of that period other than to offer a few melodramatic scenes of anti-English conspiracies which are not essential to the plot. Le Fanu seems to use the past only in order to lend plausibility to various family death-warnings and other supernatural tokens not acceptable in a contemporary setting.

Le Fanu seems uncertain of what he wants to do in this book— a fault that recurs in his works, which rarely aim at or achieve any artistic unity. Here he seems to be trying to write a tragic novel, in which the hero and heroine die of frustrated love; but he includes the usual tedious and allegedly comic Irish servant. Scott's *The Bride of Lammermoor* is the model of the sort of thing Le Fanu may have had in mind; but Scott's tragedy works because the lovers are separated for reasons which are real in their state of society. Here, if a few coincidences which separate the pair were removed, nothing would keep them from marrying and living happily ever after. So not fate but the author seems cruel. But since Le Fanu, unlike Scott, fails to interest the reader in any of the characters, the reader's sufferings are minimal. (pp. 191-92)

Some critics consider *The House by the Churchyard* . . . Le Fanu's greatest novel, but I think it inferior to *Wylder's Hand* both as a mystery and as a novel because of its uncertainty of tone. Again Le Fanu seems not quite sure of what he is trying to do. The uncertainty can be found from the novel's very beginning, which displays Le Fanu's characteristic awkwardness in choosing his narrative structure and point of view—an awkwardness found in the works of many English writers of twenty years earlier. . . .

The House by the Churchyard should, I think, properly be described as a novel rather than a mystery: although there is a mystery which has to be cleared up, the story is not dependent on the mystery and its solution. The novel offers a picture of a vanished Ireland and of its upper-class society, with the mystery and a ghost story thrown in for a bonus. (p. 193)

[*Wylder's Hand*] is a genuine mystery: the whole story depends on the discovery of what has happened to Mark Wylder. . . .

The novel's atmosphere is often spooky: an insane uncle of [Wylder's fiancée] Dorcas roams about the landscape, believing himself to be the family ghost, and offering Dantesque visions of Mark Wylder confined in hell. . . .

Is Mark Wylder dead? The reader may think he knows, as Larkin thinks he does: but then Le Fanu contrives two jolting surprises which force you to reconsider all that you have believed you knew. . . . The novel is written with greater technical skill than Le Fanu usually shows. While his choice of a first-person narrator seems more awkward than useful, and de Cresseron fades into omniscience after Wylder's disappearance, he does add something by experiencing personally the mysterious visitations of the ghostly Uncle Lorne. Le Fanu manages well his actual deceptions of the reader, providing unexplained sit-

uations in which the characters' remarks are legitimately ambiguous. . . .

[In] *Uncle Silas*, Le Fanu chose to concentrate on the eerie atmosphere of menace which had formed a part of *The House by the Churchyard*. No doubt finding his invention flagging under the pressure of constant writing, he recycled an old plot: a story had appeared . . . [as] **"An Episode in the Secret History of an Irish Countess,"** and had been revised . . . as **"The Murdered Cousin."** . . . (p. 194)

[*Uncle Silas* is often called a Gothic mystery:] I would add that the Gothic predominates over the mystery. The reader knows pretty well what to expect when he learns that the heroine, Maud Ruthyn, is an attractive young girl, shy, emotional, and indecisive, raised in seclusion by a peculiar father, and that on her father's death she will become the ward of his brother Silas, who is believed by most of the world to have murdered a bookmaker to whom he owed large sums of money. . . .

There is no real mystery about the outcome: as the story is told in the first person, we assume Maud will escape. Her cousin Milly is her only helper. . . . Such doubts as may exist about the reality of Silas's religion don't keep us guessing long. The question of whether and how the bookmaker was murdered in a locked room is a very subsidiary one, and when the locked room mystery is finally explained, the solution lacks the ingenuity of those Wilkie Collins finds for similar problems.

Nor are the characters brilliantly portrayed. Maud is simply a standard heroine, of the foolhardy and not too bright variety, although she is less inclined than most Victorian heroines to be hypocritical about her interest in attractive and well-to-do members of the opposite sex. Le Fanu's villains are usually more interesting than his virtuous people: but Madame de la Rougierre, Maud's corrupt governess, and the other subordinate villains are merely grotesque. Uncle Silas himself has the cold power of the best Le Fanu villains, but if Le Fanu had tried to do what Dickens planned in *Edwin Drood*, and shown from within a hypocrite's view of his own hypocrisy, the book might have been more interesting.

Why, then, has this book such a reputation? Its atmosphere explains its fame. *Uncle Silas* is more about death than about its characters. Le Fanu, like the heroine's father, was fascinated by the Swedenborgians; but instead of finding comfort in a sense that the world around him was linked by a thousand ties to an unseen and brighter world, he seems to have found everywhere death in the midst of life. The book is filled with sinister dreams and apparitions, some of which are rationally explained, some not.

The essence of Gothic, of course, is a vaguely pornographic concentration on a helpless heroine, surrounded by threats and menaces, usually of a sexual nature. She is never violated, but always about to be; unspeakable things are suggested, but never clearly seen or performed: in the midst of terror she is powerless.

The powerlessness of such a heroine surrounded by vague menaces seems rather like that reported by opium addicts as a characteristic of their dreams, and the atmosphere of *Uncle Silas* is often reminiscent of the opium world described by Thomas De Quincey, and glimpsed in such other nineteenth century addicts as Coleridge, Crabbe, and James Thomson. I have not seen the suggestion made by any previous critic, but it seems possible to me that in his later years Le Fanu may have been addicted to some opiate. Several of his characters are—among them Stanley Lake, Uncle Silas, and the villain of *Checkmate*—and perhaps such an addiction might explain why the novels after *Uncle Silas* deteriorate and become more filled with terrible incoherent dreams, just when one would expect that Le Fanu had hit his stride as a novelist. (p. 195)

In *Checkmate* (whose title is misleading; Le Fanu does nothing with the chess metaphor) we are concerned once again with the recurrent Le Fanu family: here, the Ardens—Sir Reginald, a gouty and extravagant ill-tempered old baronet; his gambling-mad son Richard; his beautiful, innocent, and rather sappy daughter Alice; and also Sir Reginald's brother David, a wealthy benevolent old merchant still concerned with avenging the murder more than twenty years ago of another brother, Henry.

During most of the book the reader is most puzzled by trying to figure out what the mystery of the title is; but the question that has to be solved is what has become of Yelland Mace, one of Henry Arden's murderers. . . .

Checkmate is loosely assembled, and a rather perfunctory piece of work. The scenes which Le Fanu had used before in *The Cock and Anchor* are less vivid here, and less fully imagined. But the book is full of the characteristic Le Fanu atmosphere: supernatural portents attend the deaths of the wicked, and many of the characters suffer from very bad dreams indeed. One or two scenes have a fine nightmare quality: Alice is dogged by Longcluse during a performance of Handel's *Saul* in Westminster Abbey, during which the action is matched to the text of the oratorio. But in general the book represents a decay of Le Fanu's powers. (p. 196)

Le Fanu does not use a detective as the central personage of his stories, nor does he confine himself, as a modern mystery writer would, to setting up a problem to be explained; instead he ranges into ghost stories, history, romance, Gothic adventures, and social satire—sometimes all in the same book.

But these defects do not destroy Le Fanu's occasional successes: at his best he continues to be well worth reading. In *Wylder's Hand* the reader can still be fascinated by the various duels of wit which occur between characters, in which one slip on either side may lead to fatal results: Mark Wylder against Stanley Lake, Lake against the solicitor Larkin, Lake against his wife, and, finally, Lake against his sister. Tension continually increases: in a sense the whole novel becomes a duel of wits between the reader and the author, as the former seeks to learn what has really happened, and Le Fanu withholds understanding until he is ready for it. And at certain climactic moments Le Fanu manages the effect he desires to produce in the reader—a surprise, even a shock, mingled with a sense of cold horror. Le Fanu does not deserve to be forgotten. (pp. 196-97)

> *David Brownell, "Wicked Dreams: The World of Sheridan Le Fanu," in* The Armchair Detective, *Vol. 9, No. 3, June, 1976, pp. 191-97.*

GLEN ST JOHN BARCLAY (essay date 1978)

[*Barclay assesses Le Fanu's use of the symbols of "psychological repression" and eroticism and maintains that his use of the unconscious anticipates Freudian theory.*]

One of the major merits of [Le Fanu's] short stories of the occult [in *In a Glass Darkly*] is . . . the fact that they embody symbols of psychological repression which positively anticipate the work of Freud. For example, in *Green Tea*, . . . an apparently harmless and well-intentioned old clergyman is driven to his death by the apparition of a monkey which keeps materializing before him whenever his constitution is weakened by excessive consumption of green tea. He has no idea how to deal with the apparition, because he has no idea what it represents. Nor does Le Fanu himself attempt to define precisely the symbolism of the monkey. The post-Freudian reader however easily recognizes the hideous, hairy little animal as an image of the old cleric's repressed sexual desires, which have been banished to his unconscious for so long that he has literally forgotten that he ever had them.

The idea that nature, denied normal expression, will reassert itself in an abnormal and indeed unrecognizable form, is given even more subtle, and thus more effective expression in *The Familiar*. Captain Barton has once caused the death of a sailor by having him flogged with excessive violence, apparently to stop the man from bothering Barton about the fate of his daughter, who had loved the captain and been abandoned by him. Barton returns home, becomes engaged to another girl, and is thereupon haunted by a phantasm of the dead sailor, whose physical appearance is far smaller than the actual body of the man when he was alive. The figure is obviously a hallucination of Barton's tremendous and repressed feelings of guilt over his treatment of both the sailor and his daughter. The altered size of the figure may simply be intended to serve as a reminder that it is in fact something outside the limits of normal nature. Also, to the extent that it represents Barton's conscience, it might symbolize the fact that in the past at least his conscience was far less powerful than his desires. (pp. 30-1)

The other short stories of the occult generally lack this element of symbolism. Tales such as *Madame Crowl's Ghost, Mr Justice Harbottle* and *Some Strange Disturbances in an Old House in Aungier Street* are in essence simply superbly told tales, written with restraint, a flawless ear for dialect and humour, and a well-nigh perfect prose style which is graceful, lucid, idiomatic, musical and above all controlled. It is indeed this extreme sensitivity and fastidiousness of expression that makes Le Fanu's obsession with crude physical horror all the more incongruous and disturbing. Probably no writer of any literary pretensions has exhibited a more clinical concern with the physically repellent, and the subtlety with which he treats this aspect on occasion makes it only the more ugly. For example, the horror of the episode in *Uncle Silas* where Dudley Ruthyn stoves in Madame de la Rougierre's head with a geological hammer is intensified by the fact that the narrator does not actually witness the event, but instead hears the attendant noises. In the same manner, one hears rather than sees the trepanning operation in *The House by the Churchyard*.

But Le Fanu can also be extremely explicit in visual details. The episode in *Checkmate* where the wicked baron shows David Arden the plaster masks, mementoes of the gruesome plastic surgery which transformed the handsome murderer Yelland Mace into the hideously fascinating Mr Longcluse, is as ugly as precision can make it. But Le Fanu can be more clinical still. Colonel Gaillarde, in *The Room at the Dragon Volant*, is described as having 'the palest face I ever saw. It was broad, ugly and malignant. . . . Across the nose and eyebrow there was a deep scar, which made the repulsive face grimmer'. The Colonel apparently acquired his complexion at Ligny, where 'a bit of a shell cut me across the leg and opened an artery. It was spouting as high as a chimney and in half a minute I had lost enough to fill a pitcher. . . . I lost so much blood, I have been as pale as the bottom of a plate ever since'. (pp. 31-2)

One could hardly deny that Le Fanu had a taste for the morbid. (p. 32)

It is perhaps not precisely accurate to say that Le Fanu was obsessed by lesbianism. The position is rather that he seems to have been virtually incapable of conceiving any kind of erotic or even emotional relationship in anything other than lesbian terms. He is admittedly not the only Victorian novelist to be preoccupied with the physical expression of emotional relationships between women. . . . Le Fanu, however, carries this approach to the point of making his heroes sound like transvestites; in fact he has no heroes in the conventional sense. There are instead strange, ostensibly male figures, insistently androgynous, and also characteristically instruments of destruction. For example Guy Deverell, in the book of that name, is described as being 'tall, slender, rather dark, and decidedly handsome', with a voice 'sweet but peculiar', and 'a clear, melancholy face, with . . . large eyes and wavy hair'. Deverell is also a symbol of ferocious and unrelenting vengeance, wielded by the monstrous Varbarriere. Stanley Lake in *Wylder's Hand,* which is quite literally a story of lesbian love, is 'rather handsome', with 'eyes very peculiar both in shape and colour, and something of elegance of finish in his other features, and of general grace in the *coup d'oeil'*. He also has 'a singularly pale face', is physically small and delicate, is lacking 'in a few manly points of character', and is a crook and a murderer. (p. 33)

There was really no need for anybody ever to write another vampire story [after Le Fanu's *Carmilla*]. Everything composed since has been only a variation on the themes developed in the novelette. Everything composed since has in fact been only plagiarism, conscious or otherwise. All the ingredients are present in classic form. There is the young, beautiful and incredibly unintelligent heroine; the quaint old Gothic family *schloss* somewhere in Eastern Europe; the equally beautiful female predatory demon, the descendant of a vanished aristocratic family; the dear old general, whose own daughter had been an earlier victim of the demon; and the wise old doctor, skilled in the lore of the vampire and the strategy of coping with this particular menace, or epidemic as it is technically termed. All the physical and hydraulic absurdities are also present: the vampire has a grasp which paralyses human limbs; it has the power to rise spotless and fragrant, without bathing or changing its clothes, after lying all day in seven inches of blood, which interestingly never coagulates; and it can be put down only by having a stake driven through its heart and then being decapitated. There is also of course the phoney historical background, expounded with a sense of style and conviction which Le Fanu's imitators could never approach.

Above all there is also the element of erotic symbolism. This is explicit to a degree which can only be termed fantastic, in the context of the times. (pp. 34-5)

Le Fanu repeatedly makes the vampire speak unambiguously about her love for the heroine: she loves only her; she wishes to spend her whole life loving her; and she wishes to continue to possess the heroine after death, whether she receives only hatred in return or not. Carmilla also speaks of her 'humiliation', which may imply the physical nature of the act through which her love has to be expressed, but more likely simply refers to the totality of her obsession with the heroine. These, one might note, are sentiments most uncharacteristic of a vampire: the nature of the species from all other accounts is to be motivated only by thirst, and its sole concern for the welfare of the victim is that the victim should not die too soon, thereby depriving the vampire of the means of slaking its thirst. A vampire does not experience emotions. Carmilla on the other hand is both predatory and emotionally involved. The truth of the matter is that Carmilla is obviously conceived not as a demon, but as a woman, totally absorbed, physically and emotionally, by her passion for another woman. Nor is the heroine herself wholly unresponsive to Carmilla's advances: she is fascinated by her beauty, and enjoys stroking and playing with her hair. (p. 36)

[The vampire legend] takes flight through the medium of Le Fanu's art, as a symbol of predatory lesbianism and . . . sex. There is also a slight but explicit undercurrent of social commentary, in that the vampire-lady is an aristocrat, who preys on her social inferiors after death, as she and her ancestors preyed on them while they were among the living. This subtheme is indeed not fully developed. . . . It is not really important. What is important is that Le Fanu should have devised a totally effective erotic symbol with consummate literary art, permitting the presentation of themes which could not possibly even be alluded to under the social aesthetic conventions of the time. The treatment of physical passion between women could be permissible in Victorian times only if it were made clear that one of the women was dead. Now that the theme can be discussed, we presumably have no further need of the symbol. Permissiveness has made the vampire story obsolete, even if Le Fanu's art had not already made it superfluous.

One should not however rate Le Fanu's achievement too highly. He has undoubtedly a great deal to offer, much of it unavailable in other writers of his time. He has an almost perfect, muted, musical prose style, immensely evocative without recourse to rhetoric. His treatment of dialect is impeccable and his eroticism is the most seductive in Victorian fiction. He has written some of the best stories of occult and also of high adventure in English. At the same time, his own baffling temperament can only limit his appeal. One rapidly becomes dissatisfied with a novelist who seems to be concerned with eroticism in any sense only in terms of lesbians, transvestites and child molesters. It is not entirely unfair to Le Fanu that he should be remembered largely as the man whose stories have inspired almost as many worthless and sadistic books and films as [Bram Stoker's] *Dracula* itself. It was the kind of company he kept. (pp. 37-8)

Glen St John Barclay, "Vampires and Ladies: Sheridan Le Fanu," in his Anatomy of Horror: The Masters of Occult Fiction, Weidenfeld and Nicolson, 1978, *St. Martin's Press, Inc., 1979, pp. 22-38.*

JACK SULLIVAN (essay date 1978)

[*In this excerpt from his study of the English ghost story, Sullivan discusses in detail Le Fanu's short stories. He first introduces "Green Tea" as the archetypal ghost story and then explores Le Fanu's development as a writer. Sullivan emphasizes the differences between the author's early and late tales and analyzes at length the unusual blend of sensualism and vampirism in "Carmilla."*]

[Le Fanu's short story] **"Schalken the Painter"** was as revolutionary in execution as in the peculiar nature of its two ghosts. The story tells of the abduction, rape, and final seduction of a young woman by a living corpse, all from the point of view of the girl's befuddled uncle and horrified fiance. Le Fanu handled both the necrophilia and the supernaturalism in the tale with a new anti-Gothic restraint. As if reluctant to reveal its sordid and marvelous secrets, the plot develops itself entirely through suggestion and indirection, building toward an extraordinary dream sequence involving the transformation of a coffin into a Victorian four-poster bed. It is a chilling performance.

Yet **"Schalken the Painter"** is not the most refined or the most representative of Le Fanu's tales. It is rather the promising start of a long, influential career in ghostly fiction. The culmination of that career is **"Green Tea,"** a late tale which represents the new ghost story in its most uncompromising form. **"Green Tea,"** the story of a man who literally has a monkey on his back, can serve as an ideal introduction not only to Le Fanu's other tales, but to the entire ghostly school that he spawned. It is a thoroughly modern tale, and its modernity, so unexpectedly daring, is the key to understanding the contradictions between plot and theme in more ambivalent tales such as **"The Mysterious Lodger"** and **"The Familiar."** (pp. 11-12)

The structure of **"Green Tea"** is a perfect illustration of M. R. James's model for the modern ghost story:

> Let us, then, be introduced to the actors in a placid way; let us see them going about their ordinary business, undisturbed by forebodings, pleased with their surroundings; and into this calm environment let the ominous thing put out its head, unobtrusively at first, and then more insistently, until it holds the stage.

Le Fanu was the first to use this strategy, and he applies it with particular deftness here. The victim in **"Green Tea,"** the Reverend Mr. Jennings, is introduced to the reader by the central narrator, Dr. Martin Hesselius, who in the course of the tale becomes Jennings's therapist. (pp. 12-13)

Although Jennings is a reserved, "perfectly gentleman like man," he has a few revealing quirks. For one thing, he has a peculiar tendency to flee from the pulpit during his own sermons. . . . The situation becomes so critical that Jennings resorts to having an alternate clergyman waiting in the wings "should he become thus suddenly incapacitated." Hesselius also notices a "certain oddity" in Jennings's dinner conversation: "Mr. Jennings has a way of looking sideways upon the carpet, as if his eye followed the movements of something there." . . . The final oddity is revealed by the hostess, Lady Mary Heyduke, when she remarks that she used to quarrel with Jennings over his addiction to green tea. Hesselius agrees that Jennings was once "extravagantly" addicted to the stuff, but insists that "he has quite given that up." . . . (p. 13)

Le Fanu, a careful artist, was undoubtedly aware of the ludicrousness of all this. The notion that humor is anathema to horror is one of the persistent cliches of anthology introductions. It is also one of the most erroneous, as anyone who has read Bierce or Hartley can attest. Humor, particularly when ironic or absurd, is inextricably fused with supernatural horror in fiction. I have found the linkage to be consistent throughout the field: the reader automatically integrates the two elements as he reads. In **"Green Tea,"** the first apparition scene skirts the same arbitrary borderline between the laughable and the horrible as the clues which anticipate it. The absurdity of the premise—the lethal apparition is, after all, a monkey—weakens the impact not at all; indeed the strange power of the tale lies in the irony that something intrinsically ridiculous can drive a man to destroy himself.

Jennings, of course, is not amused by this creature. His account of the first apparition is peculiarly unnerving and deserves to be quoted at length as a paradigm of Le Fanu's apparition scenes:

> "The interior of the omnibus was nearly dark. I had observed in the corner opposite to me at the other side, and at the end next the horses, two small circular reflections, as it seemed to me of a reddish light. They were about two inches apart, and about the size of those small brass buttons that yachting men used to put upon their jackets. I began to speculate, as listless men will, upon this trifle, as it seemed. From what centre did that faint but deep red light come, and from what—glass beads, buttons, toy decorations—was it reflected? We were lumbering along gently, having nearly a mile still to go. I had not solved the puzzle, and it became in another minute more odd, for these two luminous points, with a sudden jerk, descended nearer and nearer the floor, keeping still their relative distance and horizontal position, and then, as suddenly, they rose to the level of the seat on which I was sitting and I saw them no more.

> "My curiosity was now really excited and before I had time to think, I saw again these two dull lamps, again together near the floor; again they disappeared, and again in their old corner I saw them.

> "So, keeping my eyes upon them, I edged quietly up my own side, towards the end at which I still saw these tiny discs of red.

> "There was very little light in the 'bus. It was nearly dark. I leaned forward to aid my endeavour to discover what these little circles really were. They shifted position a little as I did so. I began now to perceive an outline of something black, and I soon saw, with tolerable distinctness, the outline of a small black monkey, pushing its face forward in mimicry to meet mine; those were its eyes, and I now dimly saw its teeth grinning at me.

> "I drew back not knowing whether it might not meditate a spring. I fancied that one of the passengers had forgot this ugly pet, and wishing to ascertain something of its temper, though not caring to trust my fingers to it, I poked my umbrella softly towards it. It remained immovable—up to it—*through* it. For through it, and back and forward it passed, without the slightest resistance.

> "I can't in the least, convey to you the kind of horror that I felt." . . .

Throughout this passage the emphasis is on the way Jennings perceives the apparition rather than on the apparition itself. Jennings's reaction is the important thing, as is the reader's: we are forced to see this strange abomination exactly as Jennings sees it. It scarcely matters whether the thing is "real" or hallucinated; in a good horror tale this distinction is effaced. Supernatural horror in fiction has little to do with the materiality or immateriality of spooks. What counts is the authenticity of the experience. The scene works because of the intricate perspectival character of the writing, a technique which anticipates Henry James's *The Turn of the Screw.* . . . The most remarkable aspect of Le Fanu's perspectivism is his use of synecdoche, a poetic mechanism which allows him to straddle the boundary between the explicit and the indirect. (pp. 13-15)

As an intentionally fuzzy narrative, "Green Tea" is similar to several tales in Ambrose Bierce's *In the Midst of Life* and *Can Such Things Be?* Like Bierce's "The Moonlit Road" and "The Suitable Surroundings," "Green Tea" seems arbitrarily burdened with narrators and editors. Yet the seeming arbitrariness of the narrative scheme imparts a unique atmosphere to these tales. Le Fanu anticipates Bierce in his evocation of a world where things refuse to fit together, where terrible things happen to the wrong people for the wrong reasons, where horrors leap out of the most trivial or ridiculous contexts. The disjointedness of the narrative pattern reinforces our sense of a nightmare world where everything is out of joint. Why should we expect aesthetic order when monkeys can chase people into their graves, green tea can cause damnation, and therapists can suddenly drop out of sight when patients are on the precipice of suicide? Besides instilling a sense of underlying chaos, the filtering device also gives the impression of narrative distance, a useful effect in any kind of ironic fiction, but particularly necessary in the ghost story, where too much narrative directness can instantly blunt the desired impact. Jennings must seem like a thoroughly helpless creature, dwarfed by diabolical forces beyond his comprehension (let alone control) and gradually receding from our vision into hell. What could serve this purpose better than to have his narrative manipulated by three verbose doctors who are more concerned with selling their theories than with protecting his sanity?

Le Fanu's complicated narrative skein also helps create the "loophole" of ambiguity mentioned by M. R. James. It is at least *possible* that Hesselius's claims are justified, that his unorthodox medications would have banished Jennings's monkey, and that his infallibility is "absolutely certain." (Although this certainty would not efface the supernatural element in the story, it would have the disappointing effect of a natural explanation: demonic forces might still exist in some sense, but would be so easily subdued by infallible German doctors as to be in effect naturalized.) . . . [Yet] we doubt Hesselius's word: the easy way out is a remote possibility but "not quite practicable." Even if Hesselius were believable as the medical equivalent of a Dickensian benefactor (dispensing cures instead of money at the end), we would still be left with the terrible irony of Jennings destroying himself just as he is about to be delivered.

Either way, "Green Tea" is a horror tale. It is Le Fanu's most extreme, yet most controlled performance. Although the "well managed crescendo" admired by M. R. James occurs in most of his tales, nowhere is it more attenuated and cumulative than in "Green Tea." In "Schalken the Painter," "Chief Justice Harbottle" and others, the initial apparition comes fairly quickly; here the "journey" is more leisurely and spread out; the distance travelled is greater. By taking his time, Le Fanu makes Jennings's "doors of perception" experience all the more painful and catastrophic. Similarly, the heavy use of ambiguity and dramatic irony suggest a dislocated, strangely modern world where reality is grim enough to outpace our most exaggerated fantasies. (pp. 29-31)

[Le Fanu's development as a writer] lacks a sense of cumulative progression. An erratic writer, Le Fanu leaped ahead as frequently as he doubled back on himself: the distribution of continuities and contrasts between the early and late tales is haphazard, precluding easy generalizations about early, middle, or late "periods" in his career. He was as capable of writing the masterful "Schalken the Painter" in 1839 as he was of writing the awkward, unconvincing "Dickon the Devil" in 1872. Nevertheless, the Hesselius tales (all of which are collected in *In a Glass Darkly*) have a sense of assurance, control, and maniacal intensity which are absent in most of the earlier work. The Hesselius tales also segregate themselves from the other tales by their denser narrative texture and the more clinical tracing of supernatural "stages." Even so, they cannot be said to represent a definitive "late manner," for none of the other late tales exhibit these characteristics. What they do represent is a noticeable thickening and development of motifs from the earlier work.

A sense of grim absurdity, for example, is apparent in the earliest tales. In "Schalken the Painter," . . . the innocent sixteen-year-old Rose Velderkaust is remorselessly and inexplicably victimized, much as Jennings is. Her forced marriage to the corpselike (but wealthy) Minheer Vanderhausen seems profoundly uncalled-for and undeserved. Rose never escapes from this otherworldly rapist either in this life or, as Schalken's dream vision implies, in the next. The "arch smile" she displays as she draws the black curtains on the four-poster coffin—revealing "the livid and demoniac form of Vanderhausen"—suggests she has eternally succumbed to his advances. She hardly has any choice in the matter.

This sense of helplessness in a malign universe, the major theme of *In A Glass Darkly,* appears throughout the earlier tales, although sometimes obliquely. (pp. 37-8)

[The] quality of threatening inscrutability injects even the non-apparitional early tales with a dark stream of supernatural horror. Though there is nothing overtly supernatural in "The Last Heir of Castle Connor" . . . , the suicidal death of the young hero at the hands of a mysterious professional dueller has a mesmeric, choreographed quality suggestive of a diabolical ritual. It is only when he is at "the very verge of the fathomless pit of death" that the victim suddenly becomes keenly alert, as if awakening from a nightmare into something far worse:

> Never before or since have I seen horror so intensely depicted. It seemed actually as if O'Connor's mind had been unsettled by a shock: the few words he uttered were marked with all the incoherence of distraction; but it was not words that marked his despair most strongly; the appalling and heart-sickening groans, I might almost say *howls*, that came from the terror-stricken and dying man must haunt me while I live; the expression, too, of hopeless imploring agony with which he turned his eyes from object to object, I can never forget.

This is easily one of the most dreadful death scenes in Le Fanu, equalling if not transcending the final agony of James Barton in "The Familiar." The vision of death as a "fathomless pit" is communicated with far greater authenticity and conviction than the reconciliatory message delivered by O'Connor's mother at the end of the tale. . . . [The] tension between the artificially injected faith in Christian redemption and the more dramatically realized terror of the void reflects a painfully divided consciousness. (pp. 38-9)

Le Fanu's tales suggest a world in which we are unbearably alone in situations of escalating awfulness: our friends desert us, not when they would be useful, but when they are indispensable.

Le Fanu makes us feel this sense of aloneness through the use of constant ironies. In **"The Familiar,"** James Barton, a former agnostic, seeks the help of a "famous clergyman"; he is told by this august spiritual advocate that the demon pursuing him is merely an hallucination caused by "the undue action or torpidity of one or other" of Barton's "bodily organs." . . . This is a typical Le Fanu reversal. When the atheists in these stories are awakened by demons in their beds, they undergo rapid conversions; but the spiritual advisors whose help they seek and whose theology they embrace suddenly assume the role of hard-line materialists, rebuffing them with Hobbesian severity.

It is significant that Le Fanu's first published ghost story, **"The Ghost and the Bone Setter"** . . . , is his most intensely farcical. This delightful story tells of the havoc unleashed by the ghost of an old squire who bootlegs cold water to "allay the burning thirst of purgatory." To obtain the much-sought-after liquid, he periodically comes down out of his picture. . . . The squire is not content to go after water; he also raids the liquor cabinet, pitching a noisy, bottle-smashing drunk before staggering back to his frame.

The brief introduction, which explains the Irish superstition behind the story, is almost as comical as the story itself. According to the superstition, "the corpse last buried" in a given churchyard, is "obliged" to supply "his brother tenants with fresh water." This belief has resulted over the years in much grim hilarity:

> Fierce and desperate conflicts have ensued in the case of two funeral parties approaching the same churchyard together, each endeavoring to secure to his own dead priority of sepulture and in consequence immunity from the tax levied upon the pedestrian powers of the last comer. An instance not long since occurred, in which one of two such parties, through fear of losing to their deceased friend this inestimable advantage, made their way to the churchyard by a *short cut,* and in violation of one of their strongest prejudices, actually threw the coffin over the wall, lest time should be lost in making their entrance through the gate.

The objection may be raised that this is merely a whimsical story, in an entirely different category from the later, more serious tales. But the difference, is one of degree and context only. Had the squire been a malignant rather than a harmless ghost, he would be not unlike the drunken phantom in **"The Sexton's Adventure,"** a tale as dark and horrific as any, but also studded with grotesque humor.

The climax of this tendency is **In A Glass Darkly,** tales which are consistently ironic, which open vistas of cosmic horror from trivial or laughable premises. **"Mr. Justice Harbottle,"** **"The Familiar,"** and **"Carmilla"** are trickier than **"Green Tea"** in that the moral elements give the illusion of moving toward a manageable allegorical resolution. In **"Mr. Justice Harbottle"** the illusion is short-lived. It is the most violent of

Le Fanu's tales, with a torture scene clinical enough to arouse the most sadistic reader. But it also conjures up a deeper, more comprehensive cruelty which undermines its didactic surface.

"Mr. Justice Harbottle" was one of Le Fanu's final convulsing visions. (pp. 43-5)

At first glance, the plot has a more comforting logic than the plot of **"Green Tea."** The central character, Harbottle, is a law-and-order hanging judge, "as dangerous and unscrupulous" as he is corrupt, a sadist who delights in sending innocent men to the hangman. . . . Going a step further than Dickens in *Bleak House,* Le Fanu presents Harbottle as a typical administrator of the English criminal code, which he envisions as "a rather pharisaical, bloody, and heinous system of justice.". . . (p. 45)

The modern ghost story conjures up an inexplicably horrible world whose inhabitants follow their own mysterious rules. The only principle of consistency seems to be a self-referential system of cruelty, capable of constantly regenerating itself as it seeps into the natural order of things. Occasionally, as in **"Mr. Justice Harbottle,"** a story will show it operating with equal intensity in both worlds, in which case the supernatural disturbance echoes what is already apparent in everyday reality. Even in this case there is not necessarily a rational, causal relation between abominations in this world and the next: Harbottle, an inhabitant of the normal, empirical world, incarcerates and kills people, largely because he enjoys it; he is then apprehended by similarly fiendish figures from another world who revile, torture, and kill him also because they enjoy it. The two events are joined together by mechanical elements in the plot, but the memorable thing is the gleeful cruelty inherent in each event. The symbolic center of this world is brilliantly visualized in the "gigantic gallows" which tower in the darkness of Harbottle's dream: replete with an endless supply of dangling corpses and an eager hangman who shakes a rope and cries out at Harbottle with "a voice high and distant as the caw of a raven hovering over a gibbet," this eternal death machine is a perfect metaphor for Le Fanu's vision of reality. . . .

Structurally, **"Mr. Justice Harbottle"** bears many similarities to **"Green Tea."** Although Hesselius does not appear as a character, his diagnosis of the case appears in the prologue. . . . (p. 49)

[The prologue] confirms what it wants to deny—that the Harbottle horrors are unexplainable. In its failure to codify and explain, the prologue reveals the irrelevance of anticipated arguments for and against "natural" or "supernatural" interpretations of the story. The difference between psychological ghosts and real ghosts is eliminated because the story forces us to glimpse a world in which such nice distinctions do not have any relevance. Skulking through that world—and breaking through into ours—are unearthly energies which are neither material nor spiritual, but a hideous synthesis resistant to classification and analysis. By trying to separate the "spirit world" from the "proper domain of nature," Hesselius actually shows that the two lose their individuality once the "intrusion" takes place. The perception of otherworldly beings by several characters can no more be used to support a "supernatural" interpretation of this tale than Jennings's perception of the monkey can be used to support a "psychological" version of **"Green Tea."** In both stories, the line separating such categories is smudged. Beginning with Le Fanu, one of the distinctive features of modern ghostly fiction is precisely this synthesis of psychology and supernaturalism. The dissolving of distinctions is connected with the overall rupture of causality, the failure of the story to reveal any underlying rationale behind the supernatural mechanism even though the mechanism itself is minutely described. (pp. 50-1)

Le Fanu's insistence on narrative distance . . . is sometimes excessive in the late tales. Even more than **"Green Tea," "Mr. Justice Harbottle"** is a jumble of editorial insertions, paraphrased letters, and introductions to introductions. The familiar heavy hand of an unknown editor (presumably the Hesselius "enthusiast" who edited **"Green Tea"**) is much in evidence: his narrative introduces another narrative which in turn introduces a letter from an unnamed friend of the second narrator; the letter introduces memories of childhood tales "heard recounted at the fireside at home, with so delightful a horror." . . .

Although there is perhaps some attempt in all this to achieve a mythical or at least folkloric perspective, the attempt is undercut by the clinical separation of each thread in the narrative fabric, as well as by the patently artificial medical jargon crammed in by the editor to cover for the loss of a more accurate "scientific" version. If the purpose of myth is to interpret and clarify fundamental experiences, these tales can almost be seen as antimythical: they move toward shadowy uncertainty rather than clarification. There is something almost Conradian in the seemingly senseless confusion of tales within tales, in the endless circling around an experience which becomes progressively murky. Like Conrad twenty years later, Le Fanu sees life as having an opacity, a heart of darkness. As the metaphor for a world view, Le Fanu's supernaturalism is not as far from Conrad's skepticism as we might think; they are simply different ways of pinpointing vertigo and disorder. (p. 52)

[**"Carmilla"** is] Le Fanu's sole contribution to the vampire myth. Le Fanu's treatment of vampires is consistent with his usual approach to the supernatural in the late tales. His main concern, as always, is with repetitive cycles of victimization. Unlike the more straightforward vampire tales of Prest, Polidori, and Stoker, **"Carmilla"** does not have a neat resolution in which evil is banished. The obligatory staking scene is as dramatic and explicitly gruesome as Stoker's but it only ambiguously ends Carmilla's ghostly existence; more important, it fails to contain the larger forces of which she is only a single manifestation. In its open-endedness and irresolution, **"Carmilla"** looks forward to later vampire tales. . . . (p. 60)

The most intriguingly problematic of the late tales, **"Carmilla"** reveals its full weirdness only after several readings. It raises a variety of dark questions, but seldom directly. The most immediately perplexing question is what actually happens to the vampire. Since Carmilla is not only staked through the heart, but also decapitated, cremated, and scattered onto the current of a river, we can assume that she is efficiently disposed of. But that does not end the matter. Unlike Bram Stoker's Lucy, who attains heavenly release when the stake pierces her heart, Carmilla is denied transcendence. Her former lover leaves behind "a curious paper to prove that the vampire, on its expulsion from its amphibious existence, is projected into a far more horrible life.". . . . The nature of this remoter dimension of suffering is not explained. This is an odd variation on the vampire theme, but one thoroughly characteristic of Le Fanu. Since Lucy has been bitten by Dracula, she is obviously more victim than monster; Stoker therefore balances the moral equation by having her otherwise hideous death end in ultimate peace. Attacked in her sleep by an unknown vampire, Carmilla

is as much a victim as Lucy, yet Le Fanu denies her salvation, dooming her to "a far more horrible life." (pp. 60-1)

Since the narrator, Laura, is one of Carmilla's victims, her final status is also ambiguous. Laura is in the unique position of being the only Le Fanu character who is both the narrator of a tale of pursuit and its object. That she survives the ordeal is also singular and seemingly explains her position as narrator: like Melville's Ishmael, she is the only one who survives to tell the tale. In what form she survives, however, is questionable. . . . Her doctor tells her she has recovered from the disease, but anyone who has read **"The Familiar"** or **"Mr. Justice Harbottle"** knows how much Le Fanu's doctors can be trusted.

Laura herself is not an entirely trustworthy narrator, any more than Hesselius in **"Green Tea."** She seems capable of thoroughly blocking out reality. . . . Her obtuseness may well be a function of her surrender to Carmilla's considerable charms, sexual as well as vampiric.

In any case, we cannot rely on her to diagnose her own vampirism even if the symptoms are obvious. That she may well have finally succumbed to the disease is slyly hinted at in the Prologue: the editor, anxious to reopen the correspondence with Laura commenced by the late Dr. Hesselius, discovers that she has died. The cause of her death is not divulged, but the final sentence of her narration hauntingly indicates that—at least psychologically—she is far from free of the plague of vampirism: "It was long before the terror of recent events subsided; and to this hour the image of Carmilla returns to memory with ambiguous alterations—sometimes the playful, languid, beautiful girl; sometimes the writhing fiend I saw in the ruined church; and often from a reverie I have started, fancying I heard the light step of Carmilla at the drawing room door.". . . For Le Fanu, this is a singularly chilling and evocative ending, accomplishing through a rendering of inner experience what other tales awkwardly attempt through editorial addenda. As usual, the ending does not end things but suggests the circumference of a diabolical circle. There is no release, either in this life or the next.

In other ways as well, **"Carmilla"** displays Le Fanu's technique at its most sophisticated. One unusual feature of the story is the luxury of a direct angle of perception: we *see* Carmilla; she is the only supernatural force which Le Fanu allows us to observe directly, in scene after scene. This clarity is necessary if we are to identify Carmilla as both victim and victimizer; though ostensibly the otherworldly pursuer, she is also a typical Le Fanu victim, doomed to unending cycles of agony by seemingly random, meaningless events. It is enormously difficult to use a frontal approach in writing a ghost story. . . . Yet Le Fanu manages to invest Carmilla with the same aura of infernal mystery that we experience from less tangible spectres.

One of the ways he accomplishes this is through the substitution of ghostly eroticism for ghostly indirection. The yoking of sensuality with malignance is of course not unusual: the apparitions in **"Schalken the Painter," "The Fortunes of Sir Robert Ardagh,"** and **"Green Tea,"** among others, conspicuously project both qualities, suggesting the author's abhorrence of physicality more than they build toward a conscious theme. Here, however, sensuality is more than a string of lurid adjectives (though "languid" is used a number of times); it is a powerfully ambivalent experience, a balancing of ecstasy and torment. (pp. 61-3)

Ambivalence is the controlling principle throughout the story: pleasure vies with revulsion, love with death. A fractured consciousness reveals itself through persistent balances in the language: Carmilla speaks sadomasochistically of "the rapture of my enormous humiliation," "the rapture of that cruelty which yet is love". . . ; like most vampires, she speaks constantly of the sweetness of death, longing for annihilation, yet feverishly clinging to what Yeats called "death-in-life and life-in-death." "Everyone must die and all are happier when they do" is her constant refrain. Perpetually in a state of death, she is capable of extending this unearthly happiness which, because she is not dead at all, is also unearthly suffering. (p. 64)

In its blending of lesbianism, sadomasochism, necrophilia, and vampirism, **"Carmilla"** seems exotically pornographic. There is an inherent connection between ghost stories and pornography in that both attempt to produce an actual physical reaction in the reader. Pornography, however, is an episodic form, banking everything on a series of isolated scenes which are not obliged to add up to a convincing whole. In the ghost story, the whole is always greater than the sum of its parts; cumulative impact is everything. In **"Carmilla,"** Le Fanu's dark, ambiguous eroticism is a means toward making his vampire seem eerie and mysterious. Once this end has been accomplished, Le Fanu drops the eroticism altogether. After the "gloomy triumph" of the doctor's diagnosis, the nightly attacks cease: the remaining third of the story builds toward the horrifying "ordeal and execution" of Carmilla. (p. 65)

All this is not without its comical aspects; **"Carmilla"** has an exceptionally heavy dose of grotesque humor, even for *In A Glass Darkly*. There are incidents and exchanges as farcical as those in purely comical tales such as **"The Ghost and the Bone Setter"** and **"My Aunt Margaret's Adventure."** In one of the better exchanges, a travelling dentist comes closer to the truth than he realizes when he comments on the extraordinary ugliness of Carmilla's teeth. He offers to "blunt" them, but Carmilla sullenly declines the offer. Dramatic irony crops up in many Le Fanu tales, but it becomes endemic here. (p. 66)

Along with gallows, there is much gallows humor. Beckett's "mirthless laughter," the inevitable response to constant encounters with disaster, echoes through these tales with resounding hollowness. Le Fanu's apparitions leer and grin at their victims as if gloating over a private joke. Along with less subtle agonies, Le Fanu's victims must endure the pain of continually missing the point of a grim joke which is being perpetrated on a cosmic level at their expense. On the level of ghost story aesthetics, the purpose behind the "atrocious plan" must remain a mystery. But the crucial point appears to be that there is no point at all. . . . These are distinctly modern ghosts, the manifestations of random impulses in the universe. They are apparitions from the void. (p. 67)

Le Fanu has been called a Romantic and a mystic, but his stories suggest that he was at least as appalled as he was fascinated by the prospect of an enlarged human consciousness. If there is any message at all in these stories, it is that the world—both inner and outer—is inexplicably hostile. The best we can do is keep our distance and hope we never see any glowing red eyes. (p. 68)

Jack Sullivan, " 'Green Tea': The Archetypal Ghost Story" and "Beginnings: Sheridan Le Fanu," in his Elegant Nightmares: The English Ghost Story from Le Fanu to Blackwood, *1978. Reprint by Ohio University Press, 1980, pp. 11-31, 32-68.*

ADDITIONAL BIBLIOGRAPHY

Bayer-Berenbaum, Linda. *"Uncle Silas* by J. S. Le Fanu." In her *The Gothic Imagination: Expansion in Gothic Literature and Art,* pp. 107-19. Rutherford, N.J.: Fairleigh Dickinson University Press; London: Associated University Presses, 1982.

 A discussion of style in Le Fanu's novel *Uncle Silas.* Bayer-Berenbaum specifically addresses Le Fanu's use of such concepts as elongation, asymmetry, and black and white color imagery.

Bleiler, E. F. Introduction to *Ghost Stories and Mysteries,* by J. S. Le Fanu, edited by E. F. Bleiler, pp. iii-ix. New York: Dover Publications, 1975.

 A general survey of Le Fanu's works.

Briggs, Julia. "Ancestral Voices: The Ghost Story from Lucian to Le Fanu." In her *Night Visitors: The Rise and Fall of the English Ghost Story,* pp. 25-51. London: Faber, 1977.*

 A general discussion of the various narrative techniques employed in ghost stories throughout the development of the genre. Briggs argues that Le Fanu's works are distinguished by his "intuitive understanding and vivid portrayal of fear, guilt, and anxiety."

Diskin, Patrick. "Poe, Le Fanu and the Sealed Room Mystery." *Notes and Queries* 13, No. 9 (September 1966): 337-39.*

 Theorizes that Le Fanu's short story "Passage in the Secret History of an Irish Countess" may have inspired Edgar Allan Poe's short story "The Murders in the Rue Morgue."

Kenton, Edna. "A Forgotten Creator of Ghosts: Joseph Sheridan Le Fanu, Possible Inspirer of the Brontës." *The Bookman,* New York LXIX, No. 5 (July 1929): 528-34.*

 Asserts that the source of inspiration for Charlotte Brontë's novel *Jane Eyre* was Le Fanu's short story, "A Chapter in the History of the Tyrone Family." Kenton further maintains that chapters from Emily Brontë's *Wuthering Heights* resemble the plots of several of Le Fanu's stories.

Lozès, Jean. "Joseph Sheridan Le Fanu: The Prince of the Invisible." In *The Irish Short Story,* edited by Patrick Rafroidi and Terence Brown, pp. 91-101. Gerrards Cross, England: Colin Smythe; Atlantic Highlands, N.J.: Humanities Press, 1979.

 Divides Le Fanu's stories into three categories, "humorous Irish stories, realistic stories and stories of the irrational" and contends that his mystery stories were his most successful.

McCormack, W. J. *Sheridan Le Fanu and Victorian England.* Oxford: Clarendon Press, 1980, 310 p.

 An extensive detailed biography of Le Fanu.

Nethercot, Arthur H. "Coleridge's 'Christabel' and Le Fanu's 'Carmilla'." *Modern Philology* 47, No. 1 (August 1949): 32-8.*

 A comparison of Samuel Taylor Coleridge's poem "Christabel" and Le Fanu's short story "Carmilla" that focuses on the vampire imagery in both works.

Penzoldt, Peter. "Le Fanu." In his *The Supernatural in Fiction,* pp. 67-91. London: Peter Nevill, 1952.*

 Discusses Le Fanu's importance to the history and development of the Gothic novel.

Sullivan, Kevin. *"The House by the Churchyard:* James Joyce and Sheridan Le Fanu." In *Modern Irish Literature: Essays in Honor of William York Tindall,* edited by Raymond J. Porter and James D. Brophy, pp. 315-34. New York: Twayne Publishers, 1972.*

 Compares James Joyce's novel *Finnegans Wake* with Le Fanu's *The House by the Churchyard.* Sullivan suggests that Joyce may have been influenced by Le Fanu's novel.

Coventry Kersey Dighton Patmore

1823-1896

English poet, essayist, and aphorist.

Patmore occupies a minor but conspicuous place in Victorian literature as the poet of both married and mystical love. The chief source of his reputation as the laureate of wedded devotion is *The Angel in the House,* his four-volume tribute to middle-class courtship and marriage. This work, which was immensely popular among Patmore's contemporaries, has come to be valued by modern critics primarily as the domestic precursor to *The Unknown Eros,* a series of odes in which Patmore employs conjugal love to symbolize the mystical attraction between the soul and God. As the subject of *The Unknown Eros* suggests, Patmore was a highly individualistic thinker whose ideas on love, religion, and social themes frequently set him apart from the mainstream of nineteenth-century thought. Nevertheless, as a convert to Catholism he partook in its great nineteenth-century revival in England and is therefore frequently mentioned in connection with Gerard Manley Hopkins, Francis Thompson, and other prominent Catholic poets.

Patmore was born to Eliza Patmore and Peter George Patmore, an English writer who was a familiar figure in early-nineteenth-century literary affairs. Patmore's formal education was minimal, consisting of a private tutorial in the French language at the Collège de France at St. Germains in 1839, but the experience allowed him to meet the leaders of Parisian literary society, and he soon began writing poetry. Selections from his youthful verse were published in a volume entitled *Poems* in 1844. Generally regarded as a premature work—Patmore afterward described it as "the first little volume of rubbish, done to please my father"—it nonetheless drew encouraging remarks from the writer Edward Bulwer-Lytton, and also won the admiration of the Pre-Raphaelite brotherhood, who subsequently solicited his writing for publication in their journal, *The Germ.* In 1846, the poet Richard Monckton Milnes arranged for Patmore's appointment as assistant librarian to the British Museum. He held this position for some twenty years, concurrently making frequent contributions to the *North British Review* and other leading British periodicals.

Patmore married Emily Augusta Andrews, the first of his three wives, in 1847. Their married life was evidently a source of great personal satisfaction to him and coincided with the production of his second collection of verse, *Tamerton Church-Tower and Other Poems,* and the domestic love poetry of *The Angel in the House. The Angel* was originally published in four separate volumes: *The Angel in the House: The Betrothal* and *The Angel in the House Book II, The Espousals,* highly detailed narrative accounts of the courtship and marriage of the fictional lovers Felix Vaughan and Honoria Churchill, and *Faithful for Ever* and *The Victories of Love,* a series of letters in verse recounting the emotional and marital fortunes of Honoria's rejected suitor, Frederick Graham. Apparently, Patmore abandoned plans to continue the poem when his wife died of consumption in 1862. Emily Patmore's influence on her husband was profound and may have extended to his later writings on mystical love. According to Basil Champneys, his friend and biographer, Patmore's "consistent purpose was to present a perfect picture of womanhood by means of knowledge revealed

to him through his wife. . . . When she died, it brought about the transition from Love in earthly fruition to Love in the realm of spiritual aspiration, in which sphere it becomes more closely identified with that Divine Love which is the main and almost exclusive subject of his later work.''

Most of his later poetry belongs to the period of his marriage to Marianne Caroline Byles, a pious Catholic whom he met in Rome shortly before his conversion in 1864. The comfortable circumstances of their marriage—Marianne Patmore's wealth enabled him to resign from his post at the British Museum and to purchase a magnificent country estate—seem to have had a tonic effect on the poet's spiritual and aesthetic life. Specifically, he stated that he experienced sudden flashes of spiritual inspiration for his poetry, and he also devised the distinctive ode form which became the technical trademark of his later verse. *The Unknown Eros* is the principal work reflecting this development. Patmore's critical reputation, however, did not fare as well as his spirits; in 1890, a reviewer for the *Spectator* epitomized contemporary repugnance at the religious and political antipathies vented in several odes in its complaint that Patmore was "too fierce, too unjust to the many forms of belief which [he] assails, and too unconscious of the many vulnerable points in the forms of belief which he adopts." The idyll *Amelia* may be said to be Patmore's last significant original verse work.

Following its publication, Patmore's poetic activity mainly involved revising poems for subsequent collections.

Marianne Patmore died in 1880. The next year, Patmore completed and published *St. Bernard on the Love of God*, her unfinished translation of the mystical writings of St. Bernard of Clairvaux, and married Harriet Robson. Thereafter he worked mainly as an essayist. Encouraged by Frederick Greenwood, an editor of the *St. James Gazette* who admired his conservative political opinions, Patmore contributed nearly one hundred articles to the journal, many of which were later published in *Principle in Art* and *Religio Poetae*. Reviewers of these works again assailed Patmore's opinions, indignantly challenging his narrow interpretations of religion and the relationship between the sexes, but they also began to recognize him as one of the most independent thinkers of his day. According to Arthur Symons, he represented "one of the few surviving defenders of the faith, and that alone gives him an interesting position among contemporary men of letters." Patmore's last work was *The Rod, the Root, and the Flower*, a collection of aphorisms reminiscent of those of the French philosopher Blaise Pascal. This work, chiefly concerned with religious subjects, was his last publication before he died of heart disease.

Frank Harris once stated that love was "Patmore's religion, the faith by which he lived and died." This devotion is reflected in Patmore's poetry, in which he focused on the love existing between husband and wife, God and the soul. Patmore's critics have remarked that each of these types of love is given a distinctive expression as poetry. In *The Angel in the House*, Patmore uses everyday language, incidents, and emotions to realistically portray the ideal love relationship between ordinary people. The meter and form of the poem are similarly prosaic—iambic lines grouped in quatrains with regularly occurring rhymes. Patmore's only excursion into more ethereal realms in *The Angel* occurs in reflective passages entitled "The Accompaniments" and "The Sentences," which are interspersed throughout the poem. In contrast to the resolute commonness of *The Angel, The Unknown Eros* aspires to the metaphysical and the mystical. Death, mourning, and political concerns are represented in the ode cycle, but critical interest has centered on the "Psyche Odes," a group of three poems in which the love shared between God and the soul is symbolized by the sexual relationship between Psyche and Eros. The meter and form of this work are regarded as inspired and adventurous—iambic lines of widely ranging lengths arranged in an unpredictable rhyme pattern. Despite the differences between *The Angel* and *The Unknown Eros*, Patmore considered the works expressions of the same truth. He stated: "I always think of the relation between husband and wife as the relation of the soul to Christ, an intimacy of supernal joy, of highest inspiration; I regard this merging of one's self in a supreme unity as the passionate symbol of the love of the soul for God. This to me is the truth of truths, the burning heart of the universe." Patmore wrote a prose treatise on this subject known as the *Sponsa Dei*, but burned it, maintaining afterward that Gerard Manley Hopkins, who had read it in manuscript form, had counseled him against "telling secrets."

Patmore's daring in spiritual matters was frequently surpassed by the audacity of his political and social pronouncements. Essentially, he was a dogmatic authoritarian who preached the ascendancy of the few over the many in political and religious affairs and the superiority of the male over the female in worldly matters. In the poem "1867," published in *The Unknown Eros*,

for example, he categorized the enfranchisement of the British working class as "the great crime"; in the essay "The Weaker Vessel," published in *Religio Poetae*, Patmore scorned sexual equality as absurd and explained his belief in the natural inferiority of women; Arthur Symons's statement that the essay "Christianity and Progress", which was published in *Religio Poetae*, represented "the closest and most cogent statement of Christianity as an aristocracy . . . that has been made since the democratic spirit made its way into the pulpit" indicates the potency of Patmore's prose, but also suggests the archaism of some of his ideas. As early as 1894, a critic for the journal *Poet Lore* described Patmore as something of a living anachronism, "an interesting and most representative remnant and specimen of the days that knew not the illumination of Evolution and Democracy."

Sardonic comments such as this indicate a marked departure from Patmore's early renown as the benign laureate of wedded love. Indeed, the critical perspective on Patmore and his works has undergone several significant changes since the publication of his first collection of poems. Regarded originally as a pale but promising Tennysonian love poet, Patmore earned a reputation for moral and artistic courage in championing married women and married love in *The Angel in the House*. Several reviewers, however, lamented the absence of spiritual elevation and true poetic "fire" in Patmore's prosaic verse, and his friend Alfred, Lord Tennyson registered a common complaint when he observed that parts of *The Angel* seemed to have been "hammered up out of old nail-heads." With the publication of *The Unknown Eros*, critics began to regard him as a visionary poet capable of creating bold, unconventional verse, yet they also denounced him as a wrong-headed reactionary in his approach to political, religious, and social issues. Similar criticisms were leveled against *Religio Poetae* and *The Rod, the Root, and the Flower*, even as Symons and other commentators considered him an eccentric representative of old-guard authoritarianism. Patmore's posthumous reputation has been fairly stable. Significantly, such major critics as Symons, Arthur Quiller-Couch, and Herbert Read have characterized *The Angel in the House* as a bastardized form of the novel, pointing out the inherent inadequacy of placid domestic affection as the subject for an epic-length poem, and they have elevated *The Unknown Eros* to the highest place in Patmore's oeuvre. Most modern commentators concur that *The Unknown Eros* has merits as mystic literature, yet few have taken a serious interest in Patmore's poetry. The fact that no critic has added substantially to Patmore scholarship since the publication of J. C. Reid's 1957 study is a telling commentary on the current state of the poet's popularity.

As Percy Lubbock and other critics have noted, Patmore was too unusual an artist for his works to be neatly ranked beside Tennyson, Hopkins, or any of his other poetic peers. Instead, they are commonly regarded as a testament to a peculiar temperament that has drawn a select group of admirers. Edmund Gosse appears to have anticipated the fate of Patmore's reputation in 1905, when he wrote of his friend: "The peculiar beauty of his verse is not to everyone's taste; if it were he would have that universal attractiveness which we have admitted that he lacks. But he wrote, with extreme and conscientious care, and with impassioned joy, a comparatively small body of poetry, the least successful portions of which are yet curiously his own, while the most successful fill those who are attuned to them with an exquisite and durable pleasure."

PRINCIPAL WORKS

Poems (poetry) 1844

Tamerton Church-Tower and Other Poems (poetry) 1853; also published as *Tamerton Church-Tower and Other Poems* [revised edition], 1854

*The Angel in the House: The Betrothal (poetry) 1854

*The Angel in the House: Book II, The Espousals (poetry) 1856

The Angel in the House: Book I, The Betrothal; Book II, The Espousals (poetry) 1858

*Faithful for Ever (poetry) 1860

*The Victories of Love (poetry) 1862

Odes (poetry) 1868

The Unknown Eros and Other Odes, I-XXXI (poetry) 1877; also published as *The Unknown Eros and Other Odes, I-XLVI* [enlarged edition], 1878

Amelia (poetry) 1878

Amelia, Tamerton Church-Tower, Etc., with a Prefatory Study of English Metrical Law (poetry and essay) 1878

Poems. 4 vols. (poetry) 1879

St. Bernard on the Love of God [translator, with Marianne Patmore; from the treatise *De Diligendo Deo* by St. Bernard of Clairvaux] (prose) 1881

**Poems. 2 vols. (poetry) 1886

Principle in Art (essays) 1889

Religio Poetae (essays) 1893

The Rod, the Root, and the Flower (aphorisms) 1895; also published as *The Rod, the Root, and the Flower* [enlarged edition], 1950

Poems (poetry) 1906

The Poems of Coventry Patmore (poetry) 1949

*These works were published as *The Angel in the House* in 1863.

**This work also includes poems written by Henry Patmore.

E[DWARD] B[ULWER-] LYTTON (letter date 1844)

[*Bulwer-Lytton was one of the most popular and versatile English writers of the nineteenth century. Although he was prominent in many fields of literature, including drama, poetry, and history, he made a special mark as a novelist, publishing* Pelham; or, The Adventures of a Gentleman, The Last Days of Pompeii, *and many other works occupying a middle ground between popular and serious fiction. In the following letter, Bulwer-Lytton counsels Patmore on improving his performance in* Poems. *His concerns regarding such technical matters as meter selection and variation, line endings, and diction are shared by many critics of Patmore's early verse.*]

[The pages of your *Poems*] with unmistakable testimonials of no common genius;—not one which does not proclaim the mind and heart of a Poet.—I honestly, and without compliment, think the promise you hold out to us—is perfectly startling, both from the luxuriance of your fancy, and the subtle and reflective inclinations of your intellect. It rests with yourself alone to fulfil that promise,—for no less honestly, I may say, tho' with respect, that I doubt if very large and material alterations in the faculty we call taste, are not essentially necessary to secure you the Wide Audience and the permanent Fame which must root themselves in the universal sympathies, and the household affections of men.—As yet you seem to me

to lean more towards that class of Poets who are Poets to Poets—not Poets to the Multitude.—Such were men like Peile Carew [*sic*], Herbert, perhaps even Cowley—and in later days— Coleridge, Shelley, Keates, and one or two living writers I could name. These are writers whom the young Poets are apt to over-estimate—and, without imitating them precisely, their vein runs too much into similar channells—In Poetry as in life there must be something Practical kneaded up with the ideal— in order for our work to become solid.—However costly the materials for building, we cannot well dispense with cement. This practical power it is which the greatest Poets—(and those below the greatest who have been most popular, and cherished), eminently possess. It is a something wholly independent of what the Germans call "form"—and should please and interest even if turned into prose and into any language—The "form" shows the Poetical gift and the substance is more than the Gift— it is the Manhood or the Godhead behind it.—I should earnestly recommend to a poet like yourself, the diligent cultivation of the *constructive* faculty, that which gives strong human interest to all that it builds up. . . . (pp. 54-5)

With regard to form. While you seem to me to excell, and perhaps to exuberate in original felicity of phrase and expression I doubt if you have attended sufficiently to variety and sustained music in rhythm. Most of your poems are really in almost the same metre, and that one which has too fatal a facility for that enjoyment in art which is derived from difficulty overcome, and which makes us prefer the marble statue to the wax figure. It is little more than the Printer's division of one line into two that distinguishes the metre of **"Lilian"** from that of the **"River."**—In **"Hubert,"** and others, the running the sense into lines over the rhym, is not only too often, but to my poor judgment, too inartistically indulged.—These you call trifles, but Form is never a trifle and while you obviously over cultivate form to a degree that some Enemies might call affectation, you also permit yourself a luxurent carelessness in it, which (pardon me) is a worse affectation of the two. Nor do I like a repeated indulgence of that extra-plainness which Wordsworth introduced for a scientific purpose but which he and others have strangely abused, which introduces into the midst of the eloquence *natural* and becoming to the dullest of us when elevated by sentiment and feeling—a triteness that jars upon all the strings the Poet has just awakened.—Such lines for instance as:

> Endues the chairs and tables
> With a disagreeable life,

might furnish critics not disposed to be unfair with much that might help to thwart popularity by ridicule.—All simplicity that fails to *touch* us by being simple, appears but conceit— This is what we understand by the slang word 'Cockneyism.'

A more material point which I strongly urge you to reconsider is in that part of your Art which relates to *details*.—It seems to me that in common with Tennyson, you cultivate details to the injury of the broad clear whole.—The **"River"** is indeed a most exquisite poem—but it is by the details alone that you make it so.—Had you paid equal attention to the elaboration of a great conception—[in] which, after all, the details would have stood out clear, single and luminous at the close—you would have tripled the beauty and popularity of the piece. On the other hand, you have shown how well you can manage this art of detail in Sect. VI. of **"Hubert,"**—in which line after line of that swelling and most beautiful passage, conduces almost like a gradual Drama, to the burst at the close—the appearance of Mabel.—This passage is, with one or two slight exceptions, deserving of the highest and most unqualified admiration.

From all I can conjecture from your poetry and your youth, I should say that you have only to aspire to be a Poet *to the Masses*—to be more practical in that sense of the word in which it was applied by Goethe to Schiller, to cultivate the power of enchaining human interest, to bring down your fancy to a level with the Heart and understanding—in order to achieve a very high destiny. (pp. 55-7)

> E[dward] B[ulwer-]Lytton, *in a letter to Coventry Patmore on July 27, 1844, in* Memoirs and Correspondence of Coventry Patmore, Vol. I *by Coventry Patmore and Basil Champneys, edited by Basil Champneys, George Bell and Sons, 1900, pp. 54-7.*

[JAMES FERRIER]   (essay date 1844)

[*Ferrier excoriates Patmore's* Poems *and scorns his verse as "the life into which the slime of the Keatses and Shelleys of former times has fecundated." The attack was probably motivated by literary politics involving Ferrier's publisher,* Blackwood's Edinburgh Magazine. *Keats and Shelley were members of a group that the* Blackwood's *critics had labeled the "Cockney School" of poets, against whom* Blackwood's *had crusaded because of their literary "vulgarity" and other alleged faults. Patmore became associated with the feud because of his father—Peter George Patmore had fraternized with some of the "Cockney" poets and had further antagonized* Blackwood's *by acting as a second in a duel between representatives of* Blackwood's *and another magazine.*]

Had Mr Patmore's injudicious friends not thought proper to announce him to the world as the brightest rising star in the poetical firmament of Young England, we would probably have allowed his effusions [in **Poems**] to die of their own utter insignificance. But since they have acted as they have done, we too must be permitted to express our opinion of their merits; and our deliberate judgment is, that the weakest inanity ever perpetrated in rhyme by the vilest poetaster of any former generation, becomes masculine verse when contrasted with the nauseous pulings of Mr Patmore's muse. Indeed, we question whether the strains of any poetaster can be considered vile, when brought into comparison with this gentleman's verses. His silly and conceited rhapsodies rather make us sigh for the good old times when all poetry, below the very highest, was made up of artifice and conventionalism; when all poets, except the very greatest, spoke a hereditary dialect of their own, which nobody else interfered with—counted on their fingers every line they penned, and knew no inspiration except that which they imbibed from Byssh's rhyming dictionary. True that there was then no life or spirit in the poetical vocabulary—true that there was no nature in the delineations of our minor poets; but better far was such language than the slip-slop vulgarities of the present rhymester—better far that there should be no nature in poetry, than *such* nature as Mr Patmore has exhibited for the entertainment of his readers.

The first poem in the volume, entitled **"The River,"** is a tale of disappointed love, terminating in the suicide of the lover. Poor and pointless as this performance is, it is by far the best in the book. (p. 331)

The common practice of writers who deal with stories of love, whose "course never did run smooth," is to make their heroes commit suicide, on finding that the ladies whom they had wooed in vain were married to other people. But in the poem

before us, Mr Patmore improves upon this method; he drowns his lover, Witchaire, because the lady, whom he had never wooed at all, does not marry him, but gives her hand (why should she not?) to the man who sues for it. . . .

On a fine day in the following summer, the poet brings the lady to the banks of [the river where Witchaire drowned]. His evident intention is, to raise in the reader's mind the expectation that she shall discover her lover's body, or some other circumstance indicative of the fatal catastrophe. This expectation, however, he disappoints. The only remarkable occurrence which takes place is, that the lady does *not* find the corpse, nor does any evidence transpire which can lead her to suppose that the suicide had ever been committed; and with this senseless and inconclusive conclusion the reader is befooled. (p. 332)

"The Woodman's Daughter" is a story of seduction, madness, and child-murder. These are powerful materials to work with; yet it is not every man's hand that they will suit. In the hands of common-place, they are simply revolting. In the hands of folly and affectation, their repulsiveness is aggravated by the simpering conceits which usurp the place of the strongest passions of our nature. He only is privileged to unveil these gloomy depths of erring humanity, who can subdue their repulsiveness by touches of ethereal feeling; and whose imagination, bouyant above the waves of passion, bears the heart of the reader into havens of calm beauty, even when following the most deplorable aberrations of a child of sin. Such a man is not Mr Patmore. He has no imagination at all—or, what is the same thing, an imagination which welters in impotence, far below the level of the emotions which it ought to overrule. The pitfalls of his tale of misery are covered over with thin sprinklings of asterisks—the poorest subterfuge of an impoverished imagination; and besotted indeed is the senselessness with which he disports himself around their margin. Maud, the victim, is the daughter of Gerald, the woodman; and Merton, the seducer, is the son of a rich squire in the neighbourhood. (p. 333)

[In the course of the poem, the woodman] suspects that his daughter is with child, and taxes her with it. Maud confesses her shame; upon which, as we are led to conjecture, old Gerald dies brokenhearted—while the girl is safely delivered under a cloud of asterisks. She is deterred from disclosing her situation to Merton, the father of the child—and why? for this very natural reason, forsooth, that

> He, if that were done,
>   Could hardly fail to know
> The ruin he had caused; he might
>   Be brought to share her woe,
> Making it doubly sharp.

So, rather than occasion the slightest distress or inconvenience to her seducer, she magnanimously resolves to murder her baby; and accordingly the usual machinery of the poem is brought into play—the asterisks . . . being now converted into a very convenient pool, in which she quietly immerses the offspring of her illicit passion. And the deed being done, its appalling consequences on her conscience are thus powerfully and naturally depicted—

> *Lo! in her eyes stands the great surprise*
>   *That comes with the first crime.*

> She throws a glance of terror round—
>   There's not a creature nigh;
> But behold the sun that looketh through
>   The frowning western sky,

Is lifitng up one broad beam, *like*
A lash of God's own eye.

Were we not right in saying that there is nothing in the writings of any former poetaster to equal the silly and conceited jargon of the present versifier? Having favoured us with the emphatic lines in italics, to depict the physical concomitants of Maud's guilt, he again has recourse to asterisks, to veil the mental throes by which her mind is tortured into madness by remorse: and very wisely—for they lead us to suppose that the writer could have powerfully delineated these inner agitations, if he had chosen; but that he has abstained from doing so out of mercy to the feelings of his readers. (pp. 334-35)

["**Lilian**"] is an echo, both in sentiment and in versification, of Mr Tennyson's "Locksley Hall;" and a baser and more servile echo was never bleated forth from the throat of any of the imitative flock. There are many other indications in the volume which show that Mr Tennyson is the model which Mr Patmore has set up for his imitation; but "**Lilian,**" more particularly, is a complete counterpart in coarsest fustian of the silken splendours of Mr Tennyson's poem. It is "Locksley Hall" stripped of all its beauty, and debased by a thousand vulgarities, both of sentiment and style. The burden of both poems consists of bitter denunciations poured forth by disappointed and deserted love; with this difference, that the passion which Mr Tennyson gives utterance to, Mr Patmore reverberates in rant. A small poet, indeed, could not have worked after a more unsafe model. For while he might hope to mimic the agitated passions of "Locksley Hall," in vain could he expect to be visited by the serene imagination which, in that poem, steeps their violence in an atmosphere of beauty. (p. 335)

The indignant passions of [Mr Patmore's] unrequited lover [in "**Lilian**"] are, indeed, passions of the most ignoble clay—not one touch of elevated feeling lifts him for a moment out of the mire. The whole train of circumstances which engender his emotions, prove the lover, in this case, to have been the silliest of mortal men, and his mistress, from the very beginning of his intercourse with her, to have been one of the most abandoned of her sex. "**Lilian**" is a burlesque on disappointed love, and a travestie of the passions which such a disappointment entails. We know not which are the more odious and revolting in their expression—the emotions of the jilted lover, or the incidents which call them into play. (pp. 335-36)

The author of "**Lilian**" evidently piques himself on the fidelity with which he has adhered to nature in his treatment of that story. But there are two ways in which nature may be adhered to in verse; and it is only one of these ways which can be considered poetical. The writer may adhere to the truth of *human* nature, while he elevates the emotions of the heart in strains which find a cordial echo in the sentiments of all mankind. Or, if his whole being is sicklied over with silliness and affectation, he may adhere to the truth of *his own* nature, and while writing perfectly naturally *for him,* he may unfold his delineations of character in such a manner as shall strip every passion of its dignity, and every emotion of its grace. Now, it is only by reason of their adherence to the latter species of nature, that "**Lilian**" and the other compositions of Mr Patmore can be considered natural, and, viewed under this aspect, they certainly are natural exceedingly. (p. 339)

[This], then, is the pass to which the poetry of England has come! This is the life into which the slime of the Keateses and Shelleys of former times has fecundated! The result was predicted about a quarter of a century ago in the pages of this Magazine; and many attempts were then made to suppress the nuisance at its fountainhead. Much good was accomplished: but our efforts at that time were only partially successful; for nothing is so tenacious of life as the spawn of frogs—nothing is so vivacious as corruption, until it has reached its last stage. The evidence before us shows that this stage has been now at length attained. Mr Coventry Patmore's volume has reached the ultimate *terminus* of poetical degradation; and our conclusion, as well as our hope is, that the fry must become extinct in him. His poetry (thank Heaven!) cannot corrupt into any thing worse than itself. (p. 342)

> [*James Ferrier*], *"Poems by Coventry Patmore,"* in Blackwood's Edinburgh Magazine, *Vol. LVI, No. CCCXLVII, September, 1844, pp. 331-42.*

THE ATHENAEUM (essay date 1853)

Some nine years ago . . . Mr. Coventry Patmore delivered himself of a small volume of considerable merit [*Poems*], but deformed by conceits and mannerisms. As the latter appeared to be due to a certain school in which he had chosen to graduate, rather than to any tendencies on the part of the poet himself, we ventured to think that nothing but resolution on his part was needed to the removal of what had proved offensive,— and were prepared to welcome the promise of amendment implied in the assurance, at the opening of the present volume, that alterations had been made in the earlier poems. This act of will, we find, has been only partially performed. The labour of correction has more evidently been expended on the ballads which had previously appeared than on the leading work now for the first time before us [*Tamerton Church-Tower and Other Poems*]. The latter still manifests an occasionally provoking perversity in its style and treatment, which impairs its really great merit.

'**Tamerton Church-Tower**' is a ballad which affects a blending of the gay and grave—the former quaint, and the latter mystic:—an affectation which results in a production, however beautiful in parts, somewhat grotesque. The poet's intention was, to intensify the pathetic and the moral;—unfortunately, he has directed attention principally, and not auspiciously, to the manner. Instead of the thoughts and feelings shining through the diction as through a transparent medium,—the mind is arrested on its way to the meanings in order to analyze the language in which they are conveyed. In all this there is much ingenuity exhibited; but an ingenuity that takes the place of that pure simplicity without which a ballad composition cannot be thoroughly successful. (p. 442)

In a poem entitled '**Hope against Hope,**' Mr. Patmore expresses his faith in the regeneration of the world, from the modern tendency to the revival of old forms. Somehow or other, these "old forms" in his opinion include the old spirit,—which he believes will seek its ancient dwelling places on their revival. Here we detect Mr. Patmore's weakness, and also, in an appreciable sense, his strength. The ancient ballad form of poetry is evidently his delight:—and he emulates even its uncouth ruggedness, as if there were a charm in that to resuscitate the long-lost and peculiar power of the minstrel ballad. That power, however, he will permit us to tell him, resided not in out-of-the-way phrases or sudden unexpected resemblances, but simply in simplicity. The most natural expressions of feeling, or of natural phenomena, are the spells that most affect us in reading the Percy collection. These are not to be caught by study, but most come unsought, if at all. Mr. Patmore has accordingly been compelled, like many other imitators of the old ballad style, to substitute these natural and untaught graces by startling lines, conspicuous for anything but their simplicity—frequently remarkable from their oddity alone. For instance, the uncle of the narrator of . . . ['**Tamerton Church-Tower**'] is described as "learned and meek,"—

> A soul, in strangest truth,
> As wide as Asia and as weak (!) . . .

The reader will be astonished to find how arbitrary is the title of this poem. Its quaintness agrees harmoniously enough with the spirit of the composition; yet it will be well with the author if, both at the head and in the body of his poem, it do no more than induce his readers to pause and think, and not to resent the affectation. . . .

It may be generally said, that Mr. Patmore's verses are suggestive:—but we are not allowed to be sure that this quality is the result of the poet's art. In one instance he confesses to a suggestion having been unintentional. '**A Sketch in the Manner of Hogarth**,' previously published, led many readers of the verses so entitled to believe that Mr. Patmore was an advocate for the abolition of capital punishments:—but he now repudiates the implication. He distinctly states in a note,—"I had no such intention in publishing them." What other possible intention, then, had he?—or had he none at all? In like manner, of an Ode entitled '**The Caves of Dahra**,' and published in 'Punch,' we confess that we have conceived a political interpretation:—but we dare not say that any such was within Mr. Patmore's design. True art has nothing to do with these mysteries and ambiguities; and as we hope to meet with Mr. Patmore again, we trust that he will disabuse his mind of all such caprices of purpose and manner,—and, thus setting it free, do justice to the poetic genius which, in spite of his faults, it is evident that he possesses. (p. 443)

> *A review of "Tamerton Church-Tower, and Other Poems," in* The Athenaeum, *No. 1328, April 9, 1853, pp. 442-43.*

A[LFRED] TENNYSON   (letter date 1854)

[*Tennyson was an extremely popular and influential nineteenth-century English poet; he held the post of English Poet Laureate from 1850 until his death in 1892 and is currently regarded as one of the most representative writers of the Victorian era. Patmore admired Tennyson greatly. The two writers enjoyed a close friendship for a number of years until a misunderstanding arising from Emily Patmore's death dampened their relationship in 1862. Tennyson appraises* The Angel in the House: The Betrothal *with a friend's frankness and good will in the letter excerpted below.*]

Many thanks for [*The Angel in the House: The Betrothal*]. I still hold that you have written a poem which has a fair chance of immortality; tho' I have praised (Landor-like) so many poems that perhaps my praise may not be thought much of: but such as it is, accept it, for it is quite sincere. There are passages want smoothing here and there; such as:

> 'Her powers makes not defeats but pacts,'

a line that seems to me hammered up out of old nail-heads.

Others want correcting on another score as

> 'I slid
> My curtain,'

which is not English. You mean I made my curtain slide and that (even so exprest) would not be good. There is nothing for it but

> 'I *drew* my curtain.'

Little objections of this calibre, I could make; but, as for the whole, I admire it exceedingly, and trust that it will do our age good, and not ours only. The women ought to subscribe for a statue for you.

> *A[lfred] Tennyson, in a letter to Coventry Patmore on October 30, 1854, in* Memoirs and Correspondence of Coventry Patmore, Vol. I *by Basil Champneys, George Bell and Sons, 1900, p. 165.*

THE ECLECTIC REVIEW   (essay date 1855)

[*In reviewing* The Angel in the House: The Betrothal, *the critic for the* Eclectic Review *welcomes Patmore as a poet of wedded love, but finds fault with the tone and versification of the work.*]

The author [of the '**Angel in the House: The Betrothal**'] is happy in his choice of a subject for his song, differing in this respect from some of our young singers. He is fortunate in finding an almost unoccupied domain in the choicest of all the realms of poesy, that is, wedded love. We have had plenty of love-singers, but the greatest love-poet of all, the world has never yet seen. Him who should set a worthy crown on woman's queenly brows we have long waited for. Maiden and mistress have been lauded and decked and jewelled in innumerable strains, but it was all love before marriage; and few have dared or been fitted to go higher. They have been like loose gallants, they have wooed the virgin to the very door of the sanctuary, and then turned aside. Woman as wife and mother,—love kneeling at her feet in the little world of home,—love as a religious chivalry,—these have never yet been fittingly sung. (pp. 547-48)

Of all [the English poets since the reign of Charles II] who have ever essayed the theme of love, Alfred Tennyson has sung some of the sweetest, purest, and more precious things. But Coventry Patmore is the first to attempt a sustained poem in woman's praise and honour, with such definite earnestness, such serious sweetness, such fine thought and feeling, and such manifest capacity for the work. We have cleared a large space for him, we have raised high expectations; let us see how he fills and fulfils them. . . . This first part of the '**Angel in the House**' only takes us through the phase of courtship, to leave us, like true lovers, eager for what is to come. . . . It is planned coolly and carefully by a man who looks on life with a serene eye; but we think in unfortunate that it should so evidently bear the impress of the same serene cool spirit in working it out. It has a little too much the look of courtship as the author would court now. To us, the rich flushes and warm golden lights of that happy Nevermore—that Eden of Love's past—are too much subdued by the cold cloistral colour of his present contemplation. . . . We could have wished a little more warmth of colour; and it is not necessary that the blood-flush be hectical—it may be the rose of health. Nevertheless, this very treatment many indicate all the more fitness, on the part of the author, for the future portions of his poem which relate to wedded love. We have also to complain of the metre. We think the author should have at once taken that of Tennyson's 'In Memoriam,' which is one of the most melodious, plastic, full, and satisfying in the whole metrical repertoire for the expression of tenderness, pathos, piety, all gentle feeling, and lowly or subtle beauty; it is just a linked sweetness long drawn out. Once it has obtained possession of the ear, the alternate rhymes sound like a feeble inversion of it, monotonous as a solo on the drum. There is also another drawback. Mr. Patmore frequently puts an extra foot into his lines, over which we continually stumble. For example—

Gave thanks that when we *stumble* and fall.

Fatal in force yet *gentle* in will.

Some work of fame and *labour* immense.

If the rhythm had been more lyrical and leaping, the extra syllable might have been rendered effective; but the rhythm of this poem has a conscious loftiness and a stately movement, so that these leaps which have to be taken are as out of place as a polka hop in the midst of a minuet. Enough of fault-finding. (pp. 548-50)

[Mr. Patmore] sings of woman the pure, the worshipful, the incentive to great deeds and noble lives. He nurses up grand conjectures and hopeful prophecies of her future, which is luminous with the beauty of promise. She that has accomplished so much, what may she not accomplish? He does not disguise her failings, but his flatteries are very sweet, and sure to conquer. She should be proud of such a poet.

The **'Angel in the House'** is somewhat shy, and must be approached with gentleness. In a crowd, or in the presence of a brusque, hard critic, she would be shrinking as a sensitive maiden, who broods over the sweet secret of first love amidst her rude and importunate brothers. But only win her regards by kindred sympathy, and then sit down for a long, quiet, loving talk, and she will become eloquent; her discourse is full of true wisdom and sweet human tenderness, it sparkles here with quaint fancies, and is again stately with its innate nobility of thought. She has watched the storms and conflicts of life with a patient eye of faith, like one who sees behind the veil. She believes that wherever love hath nestled there is good still: it did not even fly without shaking down some dews of heaven from its wings; and that there are none so dark, and cold, and narrow of heart, but love will warm and brighten, and quicken them into larger life. her words are healthful as the embrace of mountain air and the draught from mountain springs; and many things that she utters will long remain in memory with an abiding beauty. (pp. 555-56)

> *A review of "The Angel in the House: The Betrothal," in* The Eclectic Review, *n.s. Vol. IX, May, 1855, pp. 546-56.*

T[HOMAS] CARLYLE   (letter date 1856)

[*A noted nineteenth-century essayist, historian, critic, and social commentator, Carlyle was a central figure of the Victorian age in England and Scotland. In his writings, he advocated a Christian work ethic and stressed the importance of order, piety, and spiritual fulfillment. Known to his contemporaries as the "Sage of Chelsea," Carlyle exerted a powerful moral influence in an era of rapidly shifting values. He praises both the conception and the execution of* The Angel in the House: Book II, The Espousals *in the letter excerpted below. A special feature of his commentary is his reference to the presence of "metaphysical" passages in the poem. For a fuller discussion of the metaphysical properties of Patmore's verse, see the essays by John Holloway, W. H. Gardner, and Mario Praz listed in the Additional Bibliography.*]

Certainly it is a beautiful little Piece, this **"Espousals"**; nearly perfect in its kind; the execution and conception full of deli-

cacy, truth, and graceful simplicity; high, ingenious, fine,—pure and wholesome as these breezes now blowing round me from the eternal sea. The delineation of the thing is managed with great art, *thrift* and success, by that light sketching of parts; of which, both in the choice of what is to be delineated, and in the fresh, airy, easy way of doing it, I much admire the genial felicity, the real *skill*. A charming *simplicity* attracts me everywhere: this is a great merit which I am used to in you.—Occasionally (oftenest in **"The Sentences"**) you get into an antique *Cowleian* vein, what Johnson would call the "Metaphysical," a little; but this too, if well done, as it here is, I like to see,—as a gymnastic exercise of wit, were it nothing more. Indeed, I have to own, the whole matter is an "ideal"; soars high above reality, and leaves the mud of fact (mud with whatever *stepping stones* may be discoverable therein) lying far under its feet. But this you will say is a merit, its poetific certificate—well, well. Few books are written with so much conscientious fidelity now-a-days, or indeed at any day; and very few with anything like the amount of general capability displayed here. I heartily return many thanks for my share of it. (pp. 311-12)

> *T[homas] Carlyle, in a letter to Coventry Patmore on July 31, 1856, in* Memoirs and Correspondence of Coventry Patmore, Vol. II *by Basil Champneys and Coventry Patmore, edited by Basil Champneys, George Bell and Sons, 1900, pp. 311-12.*

GEORGE BRIMLEY   (essay date 1857?)

[*Brimley sympathizes with Patmore's plan to write a poem on the subject of married love but expresses keen disappointment with the first two parts of* The Angel in the House. *The objects of his criticism include the length of the poem, the ratio maintained between action and reflection, and the tone of the work. The composition date of Brimley's essay is unknown; he died in 1857.*]

The volume published last year, with the title of ***The Angel in the House, Part I.***, inspired us with the hope that a poet of no ordinary promise was about to lay down the leading lines [on the subject of married love], in a composition half narrative and half reflective, which should at least shew, as in a chart, what its rich capabilities were, and give some indication of the treasures that future workers in the same mine might have gathered in, one by one. But two Parts have been already published, and he has only got as far as the threshold of his subject; while the age is no longer able to bear poems of epic length, even with, and much less without, epic action. He has encumbered himself besides with the most awkward plan that the brain of poet ever conceived. The narrative is carried on by short cantos—idyls he calls them—in which, however, the reflective element largely prevails; and between each of these are introduced, first, a poem wholly reflective, and as long as the corresponding narrative canto, upon some phase of passion not very strictly connected with the narrative, and then a set of independent aphorisms, which are often striking in sentiment and sense, and frequently expressed with admirable terseness and force, but which convey the impression that the writer is resolved not to lose any of his fine things, whether he can find an appropriate place for them or not. We doubt whether any excellence of execution would have won great success for a poem written on such a plan, and threatening to extend to such a formidable length. But had the writer really set about singing his professed theme, and not wasted his strength and the patience of his readers in this twofold introduction, he possesses many of the qualities requisite for success. His conception of feminine character is that of a high-minded, pure-hearted, and impassioned man, who worships and respects as well as loves a woman. His delineation of the growth of love in the woman's heart is delicate and subtle, and the lofty aspirations and unselfish enthusiasm he associates with the passion of his hero no less true to the type he has chosen. And as we conceive him not so much to intend to relate the story of an individual man and woman, as to embody in a narrative form a typical representation of what love between man and woman should be, he cannot be censured for selecting two persons of a nature higher-toned and circumstances richer in happy influences than fall to the lot of most of us in this world. Had it been the purpose of our paper to review *The Angel in the House,* we could have found many admirable passages in which sentiments of sterling worth and beauty are expressed with great force and felicity of langauge. Perhaps the only very prominent fault of execution lies in the writer's tendency to run into logical puzzles by way of expounding the paradoxical character of love, which, like wisdom, is yet justified of her children. This tendency betrays him not only into prosaic and even scholastic phraseology, that gives frequently a ludicrous turn to his sentiments, but tempts him too often into the smartness of epigram, varied by the obscurity of transcendental metaphysics. To the same feature of his mind, as shewn in the fondness for this way of expressing his subject, we are inclined to attribute the jerkiness of the verse, which often reads like a bit of [Samuel Butler's] *Hudibras* slightly altered, and is very dissonant from the innermost spirit of the poem. If we might venture to offer a bit of advice by way of conclusion, we should say to him, forget what you have done; treat these two parts as an experiment that has partially failed; begin at the real subject—married love—on a different plan and in a different key. Let the narrative, the drama, occupy a more prominent position; reject every phrase, every turn of thought, that appears to you to be particularly smart and clever, and adopt a measure that cannot run into jingle, but will flow with a calm delicious melody through the pleasant lands along which its course will lie. And if we add one exhortation more, it will be to guard against over-refinement; not to be afraid of the warm blood and beating pulse of humanity; to remember that the angel in the house is, as the least sensuous of poets remind us—

> An angel, but a woman too.

(pp. 286-89)

George Brimley, "'The Angel in the House'," in his Essays, *Rudd & Carleton, 1858, pp. 251-89.*

[AUBREY DE VERE] (essay date 1858)

[*De Vere, a prolific Anglo-Irish poet, critic, and essayist, was on fairly intimate terms with Patmore; his invitation to the newly widowed poet to accompany him on a trip to Rome in 1864 eventuated in Patmore's conversion to Catholicism. In the essay excerpted below, De Vere gives a resounding endorsement to the first two parts of* The Angel in the House, *simultaneously broaching two major issues concerning the poem: the appropriateness of dedicating verse to prosaic subjects and the relationship which such verse shares with the novel.*]

[Of those poems] which attempt to describe the finer emotions of modern society, the most original and the most artistic which we have seen is Mr. Coventry Patmore's **'Angel in the House'** [Books I and II].... Mr. Patmore's hero does not hide his nineteenth century extraction in tartan or plaid, or even in 'homely russet brown;' he is a young man of good birth and gentle breeding; has won university honours, and lectured at the neighbouring institute. The lady of his love is one of the three daughters of a Dean of Salisbury. The scene lies in the cathedral close or near to it, and the incidents of the poem never rise above the familiar occurrences of English domestic life. The task Mr. Patmore has undertaken to perform is to trace, with no other colouring and no more elaborate decorations than these, the ebb and flow of those feelings which are in every rank of life the well-head of poetry.

The **'Angel in the House'** is a tale in verse, the hero of which sings the wooing and winning of his bride. The interest of the poem is studiously rendered independent of vicissitudes; the merit of it consists entirely in its careful and ingenious execution. Such a mode of treatment, while it increases the difficulty of the performance, in proportion as it foregoes the excitements derived from romantic adventure, is doubtless necessitated by the author's desire to illustrate ordinary, not exceptional, modern life. This necessity has been turned . . . to no small account. Renouncing the stimulus of curiosity, the poet has derived the interest of his work from higher sources, the philosophic analysis of the affections, and a descriptive power equally harmonious and vivid. (pp. 123-24)

[Our] interest is riveted, throughout the bulk of the poem, by those moral relations and affections which belong to no age and no place in particular, and into the true character of which Mr. Patmore evinces so profound an insight. (p. 130)

Mr. Patmore's work is entirely free [from the blemish of animal passions]; his Honoria is the Castara of the nineteenth century; her unsullied purity is heightened by the strain of affectionate tenderness pervading the poem; but she attains the utmost refinement without effort and without affectation. In its manly and healthy cheer, the **'Angel in the House'** is an effectual protest against the morbid poetry of the age, as, in its serenity, it dissents from that 'spasmodic school' which delights in jerks and jolts, and tolerates no music that has not a dash of discord in it.

Another attribute of Mr. Patmore's style seems to us yet more remarkable than his descriptive skill. His habit of justly balanced observation and reflection is constantly breaking forth in couplets of quaint and sententious subtlety. . . .

In the first edition of the poem this reflective vein presented itself in the more salient form of poetical aphorisms, under the name of **'The Sentences,'** appended to the descriptive passages. . . . The present edition is much improved by the rejection of these passages, and would, we think, be further improved by the rejection of some of them which have been allowed to remain in an altered form. (p. 131)

Novels have been frequently regarded as serious rivals in our day to poetry, stepping as they do into the field of imaginative literature, but demanding from the reader a less sustained exercise of the attention. In the work before us, as in [Elizabeth Barrett Browning's] 'Aurora Leigh,' poetry has in turn crossed the border and made reprisals. Nothing can be more slight than the texture of these compositions; but they have a sort of novelty derived from the poetic form they give to well-known objects; and Mr. Patmore's style of versification is remarkable for the qualities of smoothness and refinement in which Mrs. Browning is so lamentably deficient. We trust, however, that he will not allow his poetic talent to degenerate into mannerism; and that if he cherishes the domestic interests and familiar incidents of life, he will not carry these predilections to excess. (p. 133)

[Aubrey De Vere], in a review of "The Angel in the House," in The Edinburgh Review, *Vol. CVII, No. CCXVII, January , 1858, pp. 121-33.*

THE SOUTHERN LITERARY MESSENGER (essay date 1859)

[The critic for the Southern Literary Messenger *objects to* The Angel in the House *on classical grounds, characterizing the first two parts of the poem as works sufficient in Truth but deficient in Beauty.]*

["**The Betrothal**" and "**The Espousal**"] have, no doubt, been largely read with pleasure, and we heartily commend them to all lovers of pure and gentle feeling. They treat their subject, love, with the utmost delicacy and highmindedness. They present a better analysis of the emotion than we remember to have seen elsewhere at all. They abound with useful practical thought, tersely expressed, and the principles they develope are broad and sound. And this is the extent of the praise which can be accorded them. We do not find the "thoughts that breathe and words that burn." We are charmed with the neatness of the sentiment, but we are never carried away by the divine fury. We are constantly compelled to acknowledge the justness, the keenness of thought; we are never lifted into the atmosphere of rapture. Indeed, the poet seems to aspire to the praise rather of an instructor. (pp. 415-16)

It is not the business of the "bard," we suggest, to instruct us. We have not only minds to be developed. We unfortunately need something more than bare statements of duty. We are apt to forget this when comparisons between ancient and modern poetry present the superior scientific accuracy of the latter. The divorce of the True and the Beautiful is unfortunate, if it be necessary; but one is no less important to us than the other. (p. 416)

We may add that the metre, (Iambic Dimeter, or eight-sylla-bled,) seems to us unsuited to great elevation. The formal pauses and returns, the necessary stiffness, sometimes give the appearance almost of doggerel. The author moves with great ease in his alternate rhymes, and asserts that rhyme, so far from clogging the poet, only adds vigour to his flight. We do not ignore the naturalness and agreeable effect of rhyme, but we doubt if it can ever be applied to the highest poetry—if it can serve any but a familiar, it may be pleasant and piquant, but certainly not sublime purpose. (p. 417)

"Coventry Patmore," in The Southern Literary Messenger, *Vol. XXVIII, No. 26, June, 1859, pp. 415-19.*

LITTELL'S LIVING AGE (essay date 1860)

This is not an age in which, speaking generally, men, who claim the sacred name of poet, care to live laborious days, and scorn delights to build the lofty rhyme. There is, however, a pleasant gossiping sort of muse, with a touch of modern philosophy and modern sentiment, with whom the poets of the hour, not unprofitably flirt. Such appears to us to be Mr. Patmore's favorite muse; a thoughtful, graceful, semi-celestial, semi-terrestial, demi-angelical, demi-feminine lady who glides in ball-rooms, dreams in verandahs, feeds peacocks, talks romances under tented trees with her courtly admirers,—Mr. Patmore among others,—whom "she knights with her smile"— and then floats away into purple mist, rosy twilight, starry exhalation, and the seventh heaven of saintly heroic, self-renouncing, yet passive, visionary love.

Such a muse, it is pleasant to know. Such poems as Mr. Patmore can produce, under her inspiration, it is agreeable to read and not difficult to forget. For they have merit, undoubted merit; but not we fear of a high order. Such extremely facile verse,—with its prtty negligences, its charming undress qualities, and its noble Christian platonism, as we find in this little volume [*Faithful for Ever*], may be once murmured gratefully over, in some still afternoon, when the kind heavenly powers send us a sunny sky, a happy half-holiday, and a genial mood, in those golden moments, when, in our poet's phrase,—

> —— life is mere delight
> In being wholly good and right.
>
> (p. 766)

"'Faithful for Ever'," in Littell's Living Age, *Vol. LXVII, No. 864, December 22, 1860, pp. 764-66.*

THE BRITISH QUARTERLY REVIEW (essay date 1861)

[The critic for the British Quarterly Review *focuses on the technical demerits of* Faithful for Ever.]*

[*Faithful for Ever*] consists of a series of letters in rhyme. Nothing can be more removed from our idea of the ease and nature proper to a good letter, than the art and elabortion proper to good poetry. Mr. Patmore's correspondents write to each other in a style of such studied subtlety and finished beauty, as would be deemed strange, very strange, were any of our friends so to address us. Here and there, indeed, as if this departure from nature were beginning to be felt, we have, in verse, as plain prose as can be written, even in the case of persons who in the next page take us far into the Fairy land of poetry. But even this is not so much a relief as a mistake. Such alternations of differences, if not of opposites, come upon us like discord, and never unity. (p. 142)

The metre which Mr. Patmore has chosen is not to our taste. There is an abrupt monotonous tone about it which is not pleasant, and the poet has made it much less agreeable than it might have been, by so frequently ending a line with the first word, or words, of a sentence which is to have its conclusion somewhere below, but where you must not attempt to guess— you must wait and see. Here is an example of what we mean:—

> A wonder!   Ere these lines were dried,
> Vaughan and my Love, his ten-days' Bride,
> Became my guests.   I look'd, and, lo,
> In beauty soft as is the snow
> And powerful as the avalanche,
> She lit the deck.   The Heav'n-sent chance!
> She smiled, surprised.   They came to see
> The ship, not thinking to meet me.
> At infinite distance she's my day!
> What then to him?   Howbeit they say
> 'Tis not so sunny in the sun
> But men might live cool lives thereon!

Surely, with a little effort, sound and sense might be made to go more musically together than in such lines. Poetry in this form can never be popular. It does not come as from the harp. It does not address itself to the natural ear, but to an artificial one. And as the artificial are the few, so the admirers of such poetry will be the few. It is quite open to a poet to conform himself to a conventional and passing taste in this manner, but he must bear the costs. It is due, however, to Mr. Patmore to say, that the passages are many in which the cadence is unbroken, and the beautiful thought is wedded to harmonious verse. (pp. 144-45)

In our modern poetry there is a much deeper and wiser teaching than in the poetry of the age of Byron and Scott. It is in this respect, and in the nice presentation of the more subtle and profound forms of thought, that poets like Mr. Tennyson and Mr. Patmore have a ground of their own. But we hold our modern seers to be greatly inferior to the last generation in real bardic power. Their verse has not the ring of the true metal in anything like the same high tone and bounding continuity. They have thought, refinement, fancy—but the fire! Where is that? Their metres are often such that they seem to have been devised for the purpose of marring poetry rather than making it; and the example of Wordsworth has taught them to confound prose with poetry in a manner which the whim or fashion of the hour may tolerate and admire, but which certainly will not meet with acquittal before the permanent tribunal of taste. In literature, tastes vary almost as much as in millinery, especially in poetry. But there are clear landmarks between poetry and prose, and the poet who disregards them will do so at the peril of his reputation in the future, whatever may be its fate in the present. (p. 149)

> *A review of ''Faithful for Ever,'' in* The British Quarterly Review, *Vol. XXXIII, No. LXV, January 1, 1861, pp. 142-50.*

THE SPECTATOR   (essay date 1877)

[*The Unknown Eros and Other Odes, I-XXXI*] is singularly unlike much of the poetry which of late years appeared among us. Against that of the Epicurean order, of which we have had too much, it may almost be regarded as a protest. It consists of a series of poems, most of them odes, in the stricter sense of the term, others in a laxer sense, embodying trains of very lofty and occasionally of somewhat mystical thought, in subtle, expressive, and musical language. Their chief characteristics are continuity of meditation and richness of illustrative imagery, but they also abound in passion, that is, passion in its intellectual and imaginative, not its sensuous form.... These Odes are written not in stanzas, but in an irregular metre, varying from very short to very long lines, the elastic modulations of which are in harmony with thoughts which rise and fall obedient to no external law, and yet, like the cadences of an Æolian harp, follow a law of their own. (p. 538)

[This style of poetry is] now rare among us. Occasionally it reminds us of Crashaw, though the resemblance is less than the dissimilarity, his exaggerated quaintnesses never occurring, while his rich diction and impassioned metrical cadences are combined with a larger imagination and with deeper thought. By many the work will be called obscure. Against several of the poems that charge may, we think, be justly brought, though by no means against all those which for their appreciation require both cultivated minds and careful attention.... [The author] has not always borne in mind that where the subject of a poem is abstruse there is the more need that the language should be as unequivocal as words can be made. Where the topic is familiar, the reader's guess—a thing far more often necessary than is commonly known—at once interprets the doubtful expression; but where the reader deals with a profound subject, or one new to him, he must follow, not correct his guide. A doubtful ''antecedent,'' a word that may be used either as a verb or a substantive, or an allusion not explained, any one of these accidents may turn the reader's feet into

labyrinthine paths, and add to the perplexities of a journey which at best must be often under shade.... He is a captious reader who quarrels with occasional obscure passages in meditative poetry, but the general scope of a poem should always be plain. It will otherwise lose in passion and power, as well as in light. (p. 539)

> *A review of ''The Unknown Eros, and Other Odes,'' in* The Spectator, *Vol. 50, No. 2548, April 28, 1877, pp. 538-40.*

CATHOLIC WORLD   (essay date 1877)

[*The critic for* Catholic World *treats* The Unknown Eros *as a milestone in Patmore's career, lauding the impressive range of his thought and the versatility of his newfound style but objecting to the pessimism and prejudice expressed in some of his controversial politically oriented verse. ''The Standards'' and ''1867'' were the most controversial poems in* The Unknown Eros. *In ''The Standards,'' Patmore suggested that an anti-Vatican pamphlet issued by Prime Minister William Gladstone presaged the persecution of English Catholics; in ''1867'' he lamented recent extensions of the franchise to the English working class as the ''great crime,'' expressing his patrician sympathies by describing the once sovereign English aristocracy as the ''outlawed Best.'' For a detailed discussion of Patmore's class prejudices, see the excerpt by Reverend Duncan C. Tovey (1886).*]

In the author of **The Unknown Eros** we find a man who has certainly something new to say; who follows no leader; who has thoughts, and a mode of expressing them, all his own; who cares less for how than for what; whose work compels attention, and who depends in nowise on the jingle of words, the tricks of adjective and rhyme—the ballet-dancing, so to say, of the English language—for his attraction. Indeed, in respect of form he is far behind the other poets of the time. He almost disregards it. Yet, ... the strange dress that he has chosen for his creation fits it admirably, and moulds itself at will to the strenuous freedom of the combative athlete, the scorn of a man of fine feelings and bright intelligence, the meditative mood of the student, or the softer movements of a lover. (p. 703)

Between his earlier work and the present there is no comparison.... [**The Angel in the House** was] nothing more than the story, told with all the fond minuteness of a gentle, ardent, intelligent, and chivalrous young lover, of his first true love.... The verse is sweet and pleasant and flowing as the subject; but it is a song to while away a drowsy hour, not to cause us to halt and listen in the busy march and fierce strife of life....

These later poems are of a far different and more solemn nature. The poet has lived much, felt much, suffered much, joyed much, thought and meditated much in this long interval. (p. 705)

We think that three characteristics will strike the readers of these odes: 1, the high spiritual nature of many; 2, the deep pathos and human love of others; 3, the lofty scorn and fierce sarcasm displayed, mistakenly sometimes, in certain of the odes.

The poet is an Englishman of Englishmen, and, only for his Catholic faith, it seems to us that he would be one among the prophets of despair, whose name is legion and whose day is the present.

O, season strange for song!

he cries in the "**Proem**";

> Is't England's parting soul that nerves my tongue
> As other kingdoms, nearing their eclipse,
> Have, in their latest bards, uplifted strong
> The voice that was their voice in earlier days?
> Is it her sudden, loud and piercing cry,
> The note which those that seem too weak to sigh
> Will sometimes utter just before they die?

(p. 708)

In the sixth ode, entitled "**Peace,**" he returns to this theme:

> O England, how hast thou forgot,
> In dullard care for undisturbed increase
> Of gold, which profits not,
> The gain which once thou knew'st was for thy peace!
> Honor is peace, the peace which does accord
> Alone with God's glad word:
> 'My peace I send you, and I send a sword.'

• • • • •

> Beneath the heroic sun
> Is there then none
> Whose sinewy wings by choice do fly,
> In the fine mountain-air of public obloquy,
> To tell the sleepy mongers of false ease
> That war's the ordained way of all alive,
> And therein with good-will to dare and thrive
> Is profit and heart's peace?

• • • • •

> Remnant of Honor, brooding in the dark
> Over your bitter cark,
> Staring, as Rispah stared, astonied seven days,
> Upon the corpses of so many sons,
> Who loved her once,
> Dead in the dim and lion-haunted ways,
> Who could have dreamt
> That times should come like these!

We do not altogether go with Mr. Patmore in this invective, however much we may admire its form. . . . [We] may have some very hard things to say against England for not drawing the sword in certain cases; yet between the nation that is too ready to fight and the nation that guards severely what are strictly its own primary interests without fighting, we certainly prefer the latter. The bloody road is a sad road to glory, and its end is never seen. While, then, we may for the moment side with the passionate poet who sits down in his studio and hurls his wrath in words of flame against the ministry for not leading the country into war and reviving ancient glories, as they are called, on second thoughts, while still, perhaps, thoroughly disgusted with the ministry and the meanness of their ways, we become gradually reconciled to the situation, and thank Heaven, though of course not the ministers, that we can sleep quietly in our beds. (pp. 708-09)

There is another peace against which Mr. Patmore declaims in no measured terms in "**The Standards.**" This was written soon after the launching of Mr. Gladstone's first pamphlet, not so much against "the English Catholics," as the author states in a note—he would do well to remember that the world is a little larger than England—but against *Catholics:* against the Catholic Church and its chief. . . .

This call is most spirited and trenchant and bold. . . .

"**1867**" is a poem strongly written and of marked character, but with which we cannot agree. It was called out apparently by the passage of the bill extending the suffrage by the conservative ministry under the leadership of Mr. Disraeli. It is—so we read it, and we see no possibility of reading it otherwise—a direct and bitter attack on a rational extension of the popular liberties, which we take to be radically wrong in conception. . . . (p. 709)

Let us here say that if a man cannot attack Mr. Disraeli, or the Earl of Beaconsfield, on higher and fairer ground than on that of his being "a Jew," he may as well let that statesman alone. A man who adopts this very small, very cheap, and very common mode of attack is not worthy the hearing of sensible men. Addressing the "outlawed Best"—by the bye, the poet is very arbitrary and perplexing in his use of capitals—England's nobles, presumably, Mr. Patmore says:

> Know, 'twas the force of function high,
> In corporate exercise, and public awe
> Of Nature's, Heaven's, and England's Law,
> That Best, though mix'd with Bad, should reign,
> Which kept you in your sky!

Does he mean that the "Best" are restricted to the English nobility? If he does mean this, he is quite wrong; if he does not mean it, then the lines immediately following are meaningless:

> But, when the sordid Trader caught
> The loose-held sceptre from your hands distraught,
> And soon, to the Mechanic vain,
> Sold the proud toy for naught,
> Your charm was broke, your task was sped,
> Your beauty, with your honor, dead.

And so the ode goes on to hope that

> Prayer perchance may win
> A term to God's indignant mood
> And the orgies of the multitude,
> Which now begin. . . .

We cannot help thinking, if God's name must be introduced in the matter, that he is not especially indignant with Mr. Disraeli and the English nobles and people at the extension of the suffrage, and that for this reason to stigmatize 1867 as "the year of the great Crime" is nonsense. As for "the sordid Trader," there has always been a considerable admixture of the "Trader" in the composition of the English government, noble or ignoble. . . . [And] never was that government, at least since Reformation times, so pure and its members so honest as to-day, when "the sordid Trader" has a large hand in the administration. We do all honor to the spirit of chivalry; we do not object to class distinctions in countries where such distinctions are historic and hereditary; but we recognize manhood wherever we find it, and set it above all accidents of time or clime or artificial restrictions. (pp. 709-10)

We could linger with delight over many passages in these odes, and dwell with pleasure on the peculiar depth, conciseness, and expressiveness of the phrases used, the mere words often which the poet chooses. His power of condensation and deep philosophic comprehension and observation constantly strikes one. The concealed art of the whole is marvellous. (p. 710)

[The] more we read the odes the more we find in them, the more we admire them, and the clearer they become. Though independent of each other, a secret string of purpose, of aim and aspiration, of a yearning after something that the poet has not yet quite caught or cannot as yet fully express, becomes apparent. To this is due much of the obscurity and dimness that at first offend the eye. Closer study, however, reveals a throbbing passion, a high ideal, gleams of light from heaven, the flashes of a bright intelligence warmed by a pure heart and looking from and through all things earthly heavenwards. We have seen no man of late who can lash the follies and lay bare the falsehoods of the time so thoroughly. A man of intense and rooted convictions, he may make mistakes sometimes, but at least he makes them nobly. (p. 711)

We hope to hear again and soon from Mr. Patmore. (p. 712)

> *A review of "The Unknow Eros," in* Catholic World,
> *Vol. XXV, No. 149, August, 1877, pp. 702-13.*

[EDMUND GOSSE]   (essay date 1886)

[*A distinguished English literary historian, critic, and biographer, Gosse wrote extensively on seventeenth- and eighteenth-century English literature. His commentary in* Seventeenth-Century Studies *(1883),* A History of Eighteenth Century Literature *(1889),* Questions at Issue *(1893), and other works is generally regarded as sound and suggestive, and he is also credited with introducing the works of the Norwegian dramatist Henrik Ibsen and other Scandinavian writers to English readers. Gosse knew Patmore personally, publishing a full-length critical memoir of the poet in 1905 (see excerpt below). The following review of* Poems, *which includes his often-quoted reference to Patmore as "this laureate of the tea-table, with his humdrum stories of girls that smell of bread and butter," conveys Gosse's sense of Patmore as a poet of limited appeal but enduring interest.*]

There can be no doubt that to Mr. Patmore it is difficult to do exact justice. There are few writers with whom the reader feels that it would be so useless to contend, few whose attitude towards life and literature has been so persistent from youth to old age. It is difficult for those who do not look at human affairs from Mr. Patmore's dogged outpost not to be angry with him or misunderstand him. So admirable an artist has rarely been content to do so little with his art; so brilliant and pungent a thinker has perhaps never been content so long to dwell on the very borderland of insipidity. Born with a gift which we believe would have enabled him to adorn a wide circle of themes, he has almost obstinately confined himself to the embroidery of one. Dowered with a rare ear for metrical effect, educated in all the niceties of metrical science, he has of set purpose chosen the most sing-song of English metres as the almost exclusive vehicle of his ideas. This laureate of the tea-table, with his humdrum stories of girls that smell of bread and butter, is in his inmost heart the most arrogant and visionary of mystics. There is no figure more interesting or more difficult to analyze on the poetic stage of our generation.

The secret of Mr. Patmore's poetic aims and quality is given, we think, in one of the preludes to **'Sarum Plain'** [in *The Angel in the House*]. It is a little piece which might serve as the motto of his collected works:

> An idle poet, here and there,
>   Looks round him; but, for all the rest,
> The world, unfathomably fair,
>   Is duller than a witling's jest.
> Love wakes men, once a lifetime each;
>   They lift their heavy lids, and look;
> And lo! what one sweet page can teach,
>   They read with joy, then shut the book.

> And some give thanks, and some blaspheme,
>   And most forget; but, either way,
> That and the Child's unheeded dream
>   Is all the light of all their day.

The delicate truth of these lines must be patent to every reader, but we may go further and make them a text on which to hang our exposition of their author's entire works. From his earliest verses, written . . . at sixteen, to the magnificent octosyllabics called **'The Three Witnesses,'** . . . the same strain is ever repeated. Nothing interests Mr. Patmore except that "book" out of which impassioned lovers are apt, as he says, to read only what "one sweet page can teach." He has never "shut the book"; it is the only one he cares to read. He is the deepest student our literature has ever had of that extraordinary condition of mind and body which is called "falling in love." Its smallest symptoms absorb him; its pathology has no hallucinations which are beneath his care; he notes down with scientific accuracy and scientific enthusiasm the minutest characteristics of this pathetic and ludicrous disease. From the known he passes to the unknown Eros, and from heaven back to earth. (p. 771)

It is in this obsession that Mr. Patmore takes so unique a position. We have had love-poets before, but never one who was so exclusively absorbed in his subject. . . . For an equal insight into the subleties and perversities of the lover's disease we must go where the conventional admirer of Mr. Patmore would hardly dare to follow, into the musky alcoves of the long-drawn stories of Crébillon and his compeers. It is not merely an idle paradox to say that there are pages of 'Les Liaisons Dangereuses' which read like cantos of **'The Angel in the House'** with the seamy side turned outwards; for Laclos holds just the same relation to Mr. Patmore that a poacher holds to a gamekeeper.

We believe that from this peculiarity Mr. Patmore's hold upon the reading public will always fluctuate. To those who are passing through the lover's fever, to those whose daily and hourly experience for the moment is expressed in such subtle and lovely verses as these:—

> Your name pronounced brings to my heart
>   A feeling like the violet's breath,
> Which does so much of heaven impart
>   It makes me amorous of death;
> The winds that in the garden toss
>   The guelder-roses give me pain,
> *Alarm me with the dread of loss,*
>   *Exhaust me with the dream of gain;*
> I'm troubled by the clouds that move;
>   Tired by the breath which I respire;
> And ever, like a torch, my love,
>   Thus agitated, flames the higher,—

to these it will seem that nothing so appropriate, nothing so insidious, was ever penned. The saint again, in *his* moments of unearthly rapture, will find no pages in English poetry more thrilling with nard and spices than certain in **'King Cophetua the First'** and in **'Deliciæ Sapientiæ de Amore.'** But who is saint or lover long enough to support so great a strain? The poet is still ardent, still sincere, but the reader's mood is changed, and the glamour of admiration has passed. The common man, even the common reader of poetry, asks himself how far this sustained and curious study of the symptoms of amorosity is useful and healthful, and in his impatience he is, perhaps, unjust to the very remarkable talent of the writer. In the end poetry meant for the most austere of mystics finds its way to the shelves of schoolgirls. (pp. 771-72)

We need hardly say that we offer a warm welcome to these two little volumes [of Mr. Patmore's *Poems*]. They represent the life-work of one whose verse is very far from being of uniform interest, but who at his best appeals with singular originality and with undeniable charm to a chord in human nature which will never go out of fashion. When time begins to weed out the names and subdue the pretensions of the writers of the Victorian age, we believe that Mr. Patmore, holding, perhaps, at length a very attenuated roll of verses, will nevertheless be among the last to disappear altogether. (p. 772)

> [*Edmund Gosse*], in a review of ''Poems,'' in The Athenaeum, *No. 3059, June 12, 1886, pp. 771-72.*

THE SPECTATOR   (essay date 1886)

[*In reviewing* Poems, *the critic appraises Patmore's skill and stature as a poet. Significantly, Patmore's preoccupation with the theme of love is considered a literary liability.*]

Mr. Patmore writes,

> I believe that I am closing my task as a poet, having traversed the ground and reached the end which in my youth I saw before me. I have written little, but it is all my best; I have never spoken when I had nothing to say, nor spared time or labour to make my words true. I have respected posterity; and should there be a posterity which cares for letters, I dare to hope that it will respect me.

A preface more dignified than this, or one that expresses more concisely the aspirations of a life-time, could not be written by a poet. From his youth to the present hour, Mr. Patmore has had a clear purpose before him, and these two volumes [entitled *Poems*] show how far he has been able to achieve it. We cannot suppose he has altogether reached his ideal. What poet ever does reach it? But no one who studies his verse with the attention it deserves will question the assertion that he has spared neither time nor labour to make his words ture. A hasty glance, indeed, at "**The Angel in the House**" might lead the reader to class Mr. Patmore with the fluent versifiers who write easily, and therefore write negligently. A large portion of his poetry is composed in a metre which beyond all others lends itself to carelessness and monotony. We do not generally look for condensation in a story written in octosyllabic verse, and in Mr. Patmore's verse there are passages which, at a first glance, convey the impression of laxity and of over-much familiarity. The reader, if in an unsympathetic mood, may even pronounce such lines as the following, and many similar in character might be quoted, to be worthy of the chit-chat in a third-rate novel:—

> My Housekeeper, my Nurse of yore,
>   Cried, as the latest carriage went,
> 'Well, Mr. Felix, Sir, I'm sure
>   The morning's gone off excellent!
> I never saw the show to pass
>   The ladies in their fine fresh gowns,
> So sweetly dancing on the grass
>   To music with its ups and downs.
> We'd such work, Sir, to clean the plate;
>   'Twas just the busy times of old.
> The Queen's room, Sir, looked quite like state.

> Miss Smythe when she went up, made bold
> To peep into the Rose Boudoir,
>   And cried, ''How charming! all quite new;''
> And wondered who it could be for.
>   All but Miss Honor looked in, too.
> But she's too proud to peep and pry.
>   None's like that sweet Miss Honor, Sir!
> Excuse my humbleness, but I
>   Pray Heav'n you'll get a wife like her! . . .

Mr. Patmore may sometimes mistake commonplace realism for simplicity, but he never ceases to be an artist, and there is, perhaps, no poet of the day who at times has written with more subtle skill. This will be evident to every student of *The Unknown Eros,* under which title will be found poems less popular than "**The Angel in the House**," but reaching a higher level, and as remarkable for happiness of expression as for nobility and grace of thought. In these odes, Mr. Patmore stands at times upon the mountain-heights of poetry, and the reader feels he is in the presence of a thinker as well as of a singer. Not from *The Unknown Eros,* however, has the English public formed its opinion of Mr. Patmore as a poet. He has gained his laurels in another, and a less exalted, field of art. Yet if in his method he is a realist, in his aims he is an idealist, and in the harmony of the two we see the secret of his success. (p. 934)

Mr. Patmore is the poet of lovers, the profound student of woman, and one whose reverence grows by what it feeds on. And although he writes:—

> A woman is a foreign land,
>   Of which, though there he settle young,
> A man will ne'er quite understand
>   The customs, politics, and tongue,—

we are persuaded that if ever man was born who can understand these customs and these politics, Mr. Patmore is that man. And his treatment of the theme is neither morbid nor sentimental,—that is to say, not from the lover's standing-point. To him, falling in love is the profoundest truth in life; and so it is to the poet, who has gauged every variety of the complaint, and finds in this knowledge his richest inspiration. (pp. 934-35)

Mr. Patmore's work has been before the public for thirty years, and again and again it has passed through the ordeal of criticism. There is little new, therefore, to be said about it; but this, after so long an experience, may be said with confidence, that the reputation of the poet, so far from diminishing, has strengthened with the years. It would be rash to prophesy as to the place posterity will assign to him among the singers of our century. Yet we may venture to observe that if that place is not among the highest, the cause will be due not so much to deficiency of genius, as to choice of subject. The land which Mr. Patmore has selected for his territory is rich in beauty and one in which all poets have loved to wander, but its range is restricted, and the air is not sufficiently bracing for a permanent residence. The poet who makes love his sole theme is in danger, especially when unmoved by strong passion, of conveying a one-sided or a false view of life. There is much in Mr. Patmore's verse which the man of mature age rejects, not because it is not true, but because for him it has necessarily lost its charm. On the other hand, young men and maidens will delight in its revelations, and more than tolerate its weaknesses. (p. 935)

> ''Mr. Patmore's Poems,'' in The Spectator, *Vol. 59, No. 3028, July 10, 1886, pp. 934-35.*

Coventry Patmore's first wife, Emily Augusta Patmore; from an 1851 portrait by Sir John Everett Millais.

REV. DUNCAN C. TOVEY   (essay date 1886?)

[*In reviewing* Poems, *Tovey maintains that Patmore's later poetry is vitiated by class prejudice. The ode "1867" serves as the focus of his argument: citing a passage in which Patmore alludes to occasional instances of suppression of the lower classes and unchecked license among the nobility as pardonable abuses of aristocratic rule, he condemns the poet's "invertebrate" morality, arguing that Patmore's "ignoble" moral standards exclude his poetry from serious artistic consideration. The* Spectator (1890) *also criticizes Patmore's class attitudes. Tovey's essay was originally published in the* Guardian, *most likely in 1886.*]

[The] lower classes of society, as far as they appear at all in the **"Angel in the House,"** bask in the rays reflected upon them by their social superiors. As long as they remain in this *quasi*-feudal relation they are respectable, though ungrammatical, objects of interest. The prattle of the housekeeper faithfully represents this character:

> Well, Mr. Felix, Sir, I'm sure
>   The morning's gone off excellent!
> I never saw the show to pass
>   The ladies, in their fine fresh gowns
> So sweetly dancing on the grass
>   To music with its ups and downs.
> We'd such work, Sir, to clean the plate, etc.

Here a certain graphic power is observable—the same power which we notice in **"The Girl of All Periods"** and **"Olympus"**—but conditioned here by the form and subject of the poem. The question which Coventry Patmore's subsequent writings suggest is whether his sympathies are not permanently hampered by the prejudice of class. With refined thought, and *wide* sympathies, and the poet's eye for the world of nature, we should have the elements of great poetry ready to hand. What is it then that makes us feel that **"The Unknown Eros,"** etc., so great a contrast to Coventry Patmore's earlier poems, as belonging more distinctly to the literature of power, falls

short of the same measure of success in its own province? His theme, in both of its main aspects, is a noble one; comparable, indeed, to Dante's. He has his Florence and his Beatrice; his degenerate countrymen; his earthly love foreshadowing a love celestial and ideal. Dante is an evidence that it is possible for genius to make political and even personal antipathies immortal. But Dante has done this by a faculty quite independent of the passion which sets it to work; the man "who had seen hell," and Purgatory to boot, had a tremendous machinery at his command. He does not succeed by making us share his animosities; rather the terror and pity which he excites are all in the interest of his victims. . . . But a modern poet, with a kindred intensity of conviction, has an uphill task if his readers are not at the outset in sympathy with him. The commencement of the poem "**1867**"—

> In the year of the great crime
> When the false English Nobles and their Jew,
> By God demented, slew
> The Trust they stood twice pledged to keep from wrong—

which has appended to it the note:

> In this year the middle and upper classes were disfranchised by Mr. Disraeli's Government, and the final destruction of the liberties of England by the Act of 1884 rendered inevitable—

is the statement of a particular view of very modern politics, a statement crude in itself, and needing an explanation, which, however, is cruder still; a direct slap in the face to perhaps two-thirds of Coventry Patmore's readers, by way of encouraging them to do justice to what follows. This is a drawback to which the poet himself is something less than indifferent; we, who are but looking on, and trying to estimate his work on purely critical grounds, cannot but see that it is a drawback of a very serious kind. For the indignation that finds its vent in poetry must interest us either because we share it, or because it makes appeal to a moral truth deeper than the occasion which excites it, or because it is manifested in the plastic power of a great imagination, presenting scenes which fascinate us when judgment and sympathy are inert or even adverse. Thus the Hebrew Prophet lives still, as the witness to a righteousness independent of time and place, for those who have a very imperfect acquaintance, or no acquaintance at all, with the circumstances of his mission; Dante lives because his Heaven and Hell and Purgatory have been made almost visible to our eyes, and he has made us believe for a while that what we have seen there are the judgments of God, little as we care now for Dante's opinions, his loves or hates. . . . What conditions of success analogous to these does Coventry Patmore start with? When the decadence of England is a fact manifest to all men, how many will attribute it precisely to "the disfranchisement of the upper and middle classes by Mr. Disraeli's Government in 1867, and the final destruction of the liberties of England by the Act of 1884"? And yet that this, and nothing but this, is the explanation of our downfall, Coventry Patmore assures us, in a passage which we will quote at length, because it seems to us to summarize his political creed:

> Ah, Land once mine
> That seem'd to me too sweetly wise,
> Too sternly fair for aught that dies,
> Past is thy proud and pleasant state,
> *That recent date*
> When, strong and single, in thy sovereign heart,
> The thrones of thinking, hearing, sight,

The cunning hand, the knotted thew
Of lesser powers that heave and hew,
And each the smallest beneficial part,
And merest pore of breathing, beat
Full and complete,
The great pulse of thy generous might,
Equal in inequality,
That soul of joy in low and high;
When not a churl but felt the Giant's heat,
Albeit he simply call'd it his,
Flush in his common labour with delight,
And not a village-maiden's kiss
But was for this
More sweet,
And not a sorrow but did lightlier sigh
And for its private self less greet,
The whilst that other so majestic self stood by!
Integrity so vast could well afford
To wear in working many a stain
To pillory the cobbler vain
And license madness in a lord.
On that were all men well agreed;
And, if they did a thing,
Their strength was with them in their deed,
And from amongst them came the shout of a king.

The corruptions by which a nation is ruined are of long standing, and particular enactments are their consequences and not their causes. If we understand this passage aright, up to a recent date all Englishmen were agreed that the integrity secured by the governing classes could safely tolerate the excesses of the aristocracy, whilst it punished the free expression of opinion on the part of the artisan. It would be easy to disprove the fact of this *consensus* of opinion; still easier to expose a theory so crude as this, or to denounce a moral standard so ignoble and invertebrate. But it is sufficient to say that no *great* poetry can be built upon such a foundation; that the theme being what it is, all the art, were it ten times as great as it is, employed in embellishing it would be worse than thrown away. The topic is worthy of the political and literary capacity of Theodore Hook; the morality would have been warmly applauded by the followers of the Prince Regent. When greater gifts are enlisted in such a service we can only exclaim with Jaques, "O knowledge ill-inhabited, worse than Jove in a thatched house!" Let the poet regret, if he pleases, the transference of power; let him anticipate, by representing as already full-grown, the evils which every change accomplished without social convulsion, only gradually develops; let him idealize the past, and put a *nimbus* round the heads of the privileged few, and he may compel our admiration, if not our assent; but it is an artistic blunder of the worst kind to foist the mad but licensed lord and the conceited and pilloried cobbler into this goodly company; to mingle harsh realities with pleasant fictions, to tempt us to dream and suddenly shake us up to think. It is as if some unkind hand were to introduce into Mr. Dicksee's "Passing of Arthur" the sketch of a Mohawk fighting a watchman. And who can help reflecting, at our poet's instigation, that the stains here noted as accidental and negligable were radical defects in our "vast integrity"; that he who tells the now "outlawed Best":

Know 'twas the force of function high
In corporate exercise, and public awe
Of Nature's, Heaven's, and England's law
That Best, though mixed with Bad, should reign
Which kept you in your sky!

should be the last to suggest that a system based upon this principle could afford to license a contempt of that virtue which is its very essence? The naïve revelation of a class-feeling at the very point where a lofty morality should supersede it deprives these poetical jeremiads of any weight or impressiveness; they are Latter-day Pamphlets in which spleen and bitter contempt, and a prejudice essentially vulgar, have usurped the place of moral earnestness. Rhadamanthus, though his methods are not ours, though, as Virgil tells us, he first punishes and then hears, may be an august and venerable figure; but a Rhadamanthus in plush inspires no reverence or respect. (pp. 158-64)

Rev. Duncan C. Tovey, "Coventry Patmore," in his Reviews and Essays in English Literature, 1897. Reprint by Kennikat Press, 1970, pp. 156-68.

THE SPECTATOR (essay date 1890)

The difficulty [with Mr. Patmore's book] is to find sufficient unity of thought among the different pieces to qualify them to be collected under the title of *The Unknown Eros*. We should ourselves have thought that they were more closely connected together by their consistent attacks on "the modern spirit," whether political or religious, than by anything else; and these irregular ode metres lend themselves admirably to invective of that kind; indeed, nothing can be more different from the sweet shocks of his earlier verse then these stiletto thrusts of scorn. On the whole, however, we find the general effect too fierce, too unjust to the many forms of belief which Mr. Patmore assails, and too unconscious of the many vulnerable points in the forms of belief which he adopts. There is more bitterness in the volume than sympathy, and yet there is too much passion. Whether the Eros be "unknown" or not, to our minds there is too much of it. "**Cupid and Psyche,**" for instance, and "**De Natura Deorum,**" rather repel us. They are powerful in their way, no doubt, and are intended to have a purely religious drift; but they dwell too much on the analogies of earthly passion, and we not unfrequently find ourselves agreeing entirely with Psyche,—

Ah me! I do not dream,
Yet all this does some heathen fable seem!...

We will give an instance of what we mean in regard both to Mr. Patmore's political and his religious feeling. Nothing can be more vigorous than the attack [in the poem "**1867**"] on the Tory policy of "dishing the Whigs" in 1867. But vigorous as it is, it is the vigour not of justice, but of one-sided scorn. . . . The truth, of course, is that it was not "the Best, though mixed with Bad," who reigned, before the democratic wave overwhelmed them, but only the most cultivated,—a very different matter indeed. And unquestionably there was a narrow selfishness in the rule of the cultivated which alone would have ensured its doom. Had the aristocracy in power been a true aristocracy of virtue, we should have had a much earlier and nobler educational system for the poor than any we succeeded in getting till the poor got votes. Moreover, we should not have had to wait for their sympathy with the manifold removable, or at least more or less attenuateable miseries of the poor, till the poor had obtained a substantial weight in our political system. Say what Mr. Patmore will of the subserviency to ignorant and selfish popular demands which democracy has brought us, he ought not to ignore what it was that hastened the access of that subserviency,—namely, the indifference of the select few to the wretchedness and sufferings of the ignorant many. That brilliant invective of Mr. Patmore's breathes a hard and exclusive scorn, a scorn which should at least have been as truly earned by the rule of what he euphuistically calls "the Best," as by the rule of that "progressive" party whom he terms, in a later and still more scornful poem on "**1880-85**," "the Gergesenian swine,"—gladly rushing to their destruction. After all, is there so much moral difference between the common average man, and the select few of higher culture but often deeper and more fastidious selfishness, whom Mr. Patmore chooses to style "the Best"? We prefer the high culture, and admire it greatly when it is combined with the higher moral qualities; but we fear that the select and the elect are a very different class: and so Mr. Patmore thinks also in his finer moods, at least if we understand aright the meaning of the poem headed "**Let be!**" (p. 513)

[What] we have said of the bitterness of Mr. Patmore's political fastidiousness, we must say also of the bitterness of his religious denunciations. He is a thoroughgoing Vaticanist, and can see nothing noble in Protestantism or any other form of religious creed. Indeed, he is so bitter on the subject that [in the poem "**The Standards**"] he treated Mr. Gladstone's anti-Vatican pamphlet as evidence that a great persecution of the Roman Catholics was approaching in England. . . . Nobody can say that the drift or purpose of that pamphlet was to stimulate to persecution of the Roman Catholics, and, as a matter of fact, it had no such effect. Mr. Gladstone's pamphlet was written with the sort of eagerness and ardour which he throws into all he does, be it the Home-rule agitations, the defence of "exclusive dealing," or the argument against the absolutism of Rome; but he had a perfect right to express his opinion on the tendencies of the Infallibility decree and its ecclesiastical bearing, and Mr. Patmore had no more justification for his adjective, than he had for calling uncultivated people generally "Gergesenian swine." We contend that Mr. Patmore's fierce partisanship has itself the incendiary spirit, though that spirit is fortunately limited by the imaginative character of his often very beautiful and exalted verse. (p. 514)

> *A review of "The Unknown Eros," in* The Spectator, *Vol. 64, No. 3224, April 12, 1890, pp. 512-15.*

THE ATHENAEUM (essay date 1890)

[*The critic for the* Athenaeum *takes issue with the versification and polemicism of the odes in a later edition of* The Unknown Eros.]

The new poems [in this edition of **The Unknown Eros**] are in structure and expression and mode of thought so thoroughly of the type of their precursors as to offer no internal evidence whatever of their difference in date. Mr. Coventry Patmore, having advisedly adoped that ode rhythm which he prefers to call "catalectic verse," has in its use adhered consistently to his first manner. We so far regret this that we think he might well have glided into a second manner in which he would have no less continued to carry out his metrical principles in the ode and would, without losing the dignity of his versification, have given it ease and the charm of melody. . . . That peculiarly pliant form of verse which, as Mr. Patmore notices in his preface, is by some even accused of lawlessness, should be above all things flowing and musical, but by introducing constraint and severe abruptness Mr. Patmore makes his "catalectic" verse, law-abiding though it be, create a sensation of irregularity and jerkiness which would not be produced by catalectic verse more euphoniously modulated, even if it were far less correctly measured. The abruptness is mainly caused

by the use of the pause as a sudden dead stop in the rhythm instead of as a rhythm punctuation, but sometimes is due to short lines which really are not lines, but only portions of the preceding or the following line—short pausing lines which do not by their meaning or their sound allow of the natural stress of the pause, and which are thus made breaks in the pace rather than true pauses. Mr. Patmore's object in this method of versification is, of course, to avoid the triviality which is the peril of the ode; and, although we think he might have attained that object with less sacrifice of charm, we cannot but admit that he has fully attained it. His utterance has always a marked dignity and self-possession; if it never becomes impassioned it never becomes phrenetic, and never inept, and its importance, if sometimes a little beyond the need, gives appropriate emphasis to the quiet fervour of sentiment and intentness of thought which distinguish most of this volume. (p. 693)

'**Eros and Psyche**,' '**Psyche's Discontent**,' '**De Natura Deorum**' are each and all a corollary to the original title-poem, '**To the Unknown Eros**,' and thus strengthen its claim, previously very doubtful, to be name-father to the book. They attempt a mingled mystic and sensuous explanation of the conjugal union, the "bond I know not of nor dimly can divine" foreshadowed in the mind of the speaker in ['**To the Unknown Eros**']; but, while that ode is "so thinks the boy," these examine the revelation as if from the woman's side, in the personage of Psyche. They are of too distinct an importance among the contents of the volume to pass unnoticed, but they are of less value than their less psychological-physiological companions. This is not because of the nature of their theme, for Mr. Coventry Patmore is able to treat it with reverence; but because it is impossible to accept his Psyche. Considered as representing a human being, she is dramatically false; considered as a substitute for a treatise on marriage, she is misleading. *Could* a creature possessed soul and body by love as this Psyche is intended to be investigate and criticize her feelings and sensations, discuss them with the lover, with herself, with an old Juliet's-nurse of a Pythoness? In the confidences between the girl and the crone, the '**De Natura Deorum**,' a tone of jocularity enhances the incongruity. And, be it said, this jocularity has other faults: it is artistically unbefitting the generally exalted style and diction, and it defiles the nuptial love of Psyche, which should be a sacred thing.

In '**Sponsa Dei**' and '**To the Body**' we have the conjugal theme of the Eros poems with a deeper mysticism—a mysticism Christian, devotional, and even, in spite of its erotic presentment, ascetic. These two new odes seem to have a direct and intentional connexion of doctrine with the reprinted '**Deliciæ Sapientiæ de Amore**.'. . .

There are several—"a good several"—of the poems which cannot by any interpretation be traced to Eros at all. Some of these are too much the scolding rhetoric of the platform, the mad gallop to nowhere of political or polemical passion. Such windy violence is no more poetry than it is argument; and as to these diatribes of Mr. Patmore's there is moreover the drawback that the reader cannot always find out from their context what they are about, and may have forgotten, or not have known, the immediate circumstances which provoked them. '**The Standards**,' that singular Jeremiad and Ecstasy about a storm of persecution which Mr. Patmore somehow persuaded himself in 1874 that he saw breaking over his [Catholic] co-religionists, has at this distance of time become almost unintelligible and quite without any appearance of common sense it may have once possessed. Even in 1877 it was strange that its author should have chosen to let it figure in the volume, an evidence of how polemic fever can daze a sane man; it is stranger still that he should wish it remembered now. We are helped to some comprehension of **'The Standards'** by a footnote stating [when] it was written. . . . Surely Mr. Coventry Patmore ought to be able to see that the need of notes to express the purport of his controversial odes shows that they are not of lasting stuff, that they cannot survive their occasions, and, being dead, should be decently buried. All living verse says for itself what it is about. We rejoice that, though Mr. Patmore has retained those and other irascible disputations, he has added to them but one. That one, which he entitles **'1880-85,'** has its tale told in the foot-note to **'1867.'** In the haste of his vehement execrations, he has even less than usual set forth the cause of them; he relies on his readers' recollections of an epoch so recent as that of the last extension of the franchise. But, whether as a poem or as a contribution to political history, the piece is faulty in not conveying in itself any suggestion of what was the deed he rails at. Nor are redeeming beauties to be found in the ode to set against this primary defect: it is very angry, that is all. (p. 694)

> *A review of "The Unknown Eros," in* The Athenaeum, *No. 3291, November 22, 1890, pp. 693-94.*

THE SPECTATOR (essay date 1893)

[The essays in **Religio Poetae**] are on various subjects, and are for the most part detached, except for the religious standpoint from the Roman Catholic point of view, which links them together. In his essay on **"The Weaker Vessel,"** Mr. Patmore undertakes to teach men and women, but more especially women, their right places in the scheme of the Universe, and to show cause why they should be very thankful for the position which he believes to have been assigned to them; but we are doubtful whether the more thoughtful women of the day will like to be taught after this manner:—

> To maintain that man and woman are equals in intelligent action, is just as absurd as to maintain that the hand that throws a ball and the wall that casts it back are equal. The woman has exquisite perception and power of admiring all a man can be or do. She is the 'glory' of his prowess and nobility in war, statesmanship, arts, invention, and manners; and she is able to fulfil this, her necessary and delightful function, just because she is nothing in battle, policy, poetry, discovery, or original intellectual or moral force of any kind. The true happiness and dignity of woman are to be sought, not in her exaltation to the level of man, but in a full appreciation of her inferiority and in the voluntary honour which every manly nature instinctively pays to the weaker vessel.

We are quite at one with Mr. Patmore in thinking it a grave mistake for women to attempt to be *manly,* that is to say, to ape the tone, manners, and dress of men; but, on the other hand, we do not think that a very vivid sense of inferiority would be likely to promote any great degree of real happiness among them. Mr. Patmore is really very unsparing in his attempts to reduce woman to a proper sense of humility. He tells her that,—

> She has not the strength for, or, indeed, the knowledge of, true virtue and grace of character

unless she is helped to that knowledge and strength by the man. . . .

> She only really loves and desires to become what he loves and desires her to be; and beauty, being visible or reflected goodness, can only exist in woman when and in proportion as man is strong, good, and wise.

The fact is that Mr. Patmore, in his anxiety to prove woman the "weaker vessel," forgets that men and women are so closely connected and so dependent on each other, that what is said of one may, as a rule, with almost equal truth be said of the other. Every one must be able to call to mind at least one marriage among his acquaintance, where it is decidedly the woman who possesses both the "strength for, and the knowledge of, true virtue and grace of character," and who has been able, generally quite unconsciously, to raise her husband to a very much higher moral and spiritual level than he could ever have reached by himself. Browning evidently does not share Mr. Patmore's views when, after speaking of his death to his wife "Leonor" in "By the Fire-side," he suddenly exclaims:—

> Oh, I must feel your brain prompt mine,
>   Your heart anticipate my heart,
> You must be just in front, in fine,
>   See and make me see, for your part,
> New depths of the divine.

If "the strength for, and the knowledge of, true virtue and grace of character" are only to be gained by women through men, the fate of the many women whom circumstances or inclination have debarred from any close intimacy with them must indeed be hopeless both in this world and in the next. The whole of the great social and educational movement among women seems to us to disprove the accusation that they have "no original moral force." . . . Mr. Patmore airily dismisses this movement in these words:—

> The happiest result of the 'higher education' of woman cannot fail to consist in rendering her weakness more and more daintily conspicuous. How much sweeter to dry the tears that flow because one cannot accede to some demonstrable fallacy in her theory of variable stars, than to kiss her into conformity as to the dinner-hour or the fitness or unfitness of such-or-such a person to be asked to a pic-nic! . . . It is a great consolation to reflect that, among all the bewildering changes to which the world is subject, the character of woman cannot be altered; and that so long as she abstains from absolute outrages against Nature—such as divided skirts, free-thinking, tricycles, and Radicalism—neither Greek, nor conic sections, nor political economy, nor cigarettes, nor athletics, can really do other than enhance the charm of the sweet unreasonableness which humbles the gods to the dust, and compels them to adore the lace below the last hem of her brocade! It is owing to this ineradicable perfection that time cannot change, nor custom stale, her infinite variety.

This "sweet unreasonableness" that Mr. Patmore admires so much in woman, is said to have such a positive character about it, that "it is elevated from a defect into a sacred mystery." He should really be more careful how he writes. In this one unconsidered sentence, he may have placed in the hands of the "weaker vessel" a most dangerous weapon. Some lady may, after reading this, solemnly assure her husband that he is in the presence of a "sacred mystery" the next time he feels constrained to take her to task for being unreasonable; and what answer will he find to that? (pp. 116-17)

[It] is only fair to add that Mr. Patmore is, like many people, better than his creed, as he shows by the genuine admiration and respect with which he writes of Madame de Hautefort and Lady Russell in his charming little sketch of the former, and in his very appreciative essay on Mrs. Meynell's prose-writings.

He further modifies his condescending attitude towards women in the essay, **"Dieu et ma Dame,"**—an essay, by-the-way, in which it might have been better had he adhered to his own wise rule of not always speaking of personal feelings on religious subjects, lest the doing so should appear profanation, or be perilous to those who are unsympathetic on such matters. We have only been able to notice one of the subjects on which Mr. Patmore writes [in *Religio Poetae*]; but any one who takes up this pleasantly written little volume of essays will find in them many wise, true, and poetical thoughts. (p. 117)

> *"Mr. Patmore's Essays," in* The Spectator, *Vol. 71, No. 3395, July 22, 1893, pp. 116-17.*

FRANCIS THOMPSON (essay date 1893)

[*Thompson, an English poet, critic, essayist, and biographer, is considered one of the most important poets of the Catholic Revival in nineteenth-century literature. He defends Patmore's theories concerning religious language and symbolism in the following essay, which was first published as part of a review of Patmore's* Religio Poetae *in the periodical* Merry England *in September, 1893. Thompson submitted his essay, originally entitled "A Poet's Religion," under the pseudonym "Francis Tancred."*]

Vox clamantis in deserto [a voice crying out in the desert] is the sentence which the non-Catholic papers would probably have passed upon Mr. Coventry Patmore's new volume of Essays, *Religio Poetæ*, had it been written by a less eminent man. As it is, some of them have sub-expressed it. A man of genius, in this nineteenth century, who quotes the Fathers as living authorities; says that the "amount of substantial poetry" to be found in St. Augustine, St. Bernard, St. Thomas, St. Francis of Sales, St. John of the Cross, "is ten times greater than is to be found in all the poets of the past two thousand years put together"; declare that "Aquinas is to Dante as the Tableland of Thibet is to the Peak of Teneriffe"; and is a symbolist after another fashion than that of M. Mallarmé and his school—prodigious! "Does not life consist of the four elements?" asks Sir Toby Belch [in William Shakespeare's play *Twelfth Night*]. "Faith, so they say; but I think it rather consists of eating and drinking," answers Sir Andrew. "Right!" exlaims Sir Toby: "thou art a philosopher; let us therefore eat and drink." And a good part of the nineteenth century, agreeing with Sir Toby that Sir Andrew was a philosopher, is by no means likely to think Mr. Patmore one. . . . [These] essays deal with mysteries of spiritual experience such as those of which Clemens Alexandrinus said that there were some to which he was unwilling to allude even in words, much more in writing, lest he should be placing a sword in the hands of a child. Since then we have had the writings of the great Spanish mystic Saints; but no one, so far as we are aware, has thought a magazine the proper place for their intimate discussion, nor

do we conceive that the effect would be a wholesome one upon the average simple Christian. What Mr. Patmore says is deducible from that profoundly mystic passage of St. Paul: "The husband is the head of the wife, as Christ is the head of the Church. He is the Saviour of His body. . . . So also ought men to love their wives as their own bodies. He that loveth his wife, loveth himself. For no man ever hated his own flesh, but loveth it and cherisheth it, as also Christ doth the Church." He who completely understands this passage may study Mr. Patmore's book for himself. But there are two of the more esoteric essays on which we may comment. One is **"The Precursor."** The other is **"The Language of Religion."** . . . In the latter Mr. Patmore is mainly concerned to enforce two things. Firstly, that the whole system of the Church's language and rites proves that there is a body of knowledge which ought not to be, and cannot be, effectually communicated to all. The language in which the Church adumbrates this knowledge, says Mr. Patmore, like the religious language both of the Jewish prophets and of the heathen mythologies, is symbolic.

No one has ventured to touch Mr. Patmore's assertions regarding the symbolic meanings of the Breviary, the Scriptures, or the mythologies; for the unfortunate reason, we fear, that symbolism in this age of Strauss and Renan has become a dead language to English Catholics. But his mention of a body of knowledge not communicable to all aroused unintelligent opposition. Read in its place among the other essays, we doubt whether it would even have excited comment. For it is clear that Mr. Patmore spoke of that science of the Saints which is hardly to be called teaching, since it is rather learned than taught. Of this science, doubtless, it was that the Alexandrian doctor spoke in the passage we quoted above; and even the most intimate of Catholic mystic writers, although writing a language hardly to be understood of the multitude, a language of "liquefactions, exolutions, ecstasies, and the kiss of the spouse," have, it is not to be doubted, respected the "secret of the King."

The second point is that the Church has largely borrowed the language of the ancient mythologies in figuring her own mysteries; and he particularly insists on Egypt as the source to which she was of old indebted. If anybody should be scandalised at this, it merely shows how little Catholics know their own writers—the Abbé Ancessi, for example. This was a commonplace of knowledge with the early Christian writers. (pp. 204-06)

In **"The Precursor"** Mr. Patmore seeks to show that St. John the Baptist represents natural love as the precursor of Christ, the Divine Love. He is careful to add that both loves find their fulfilment in Christ; the special type of Divine love apart from natural love being St. John the Divine. Most modern Christians will certainly boggle at this. "Why do you paint the tree?" asked Rousseau's pesant; "the tree is there, is it not?" "Why do you allegorise these men?" will ask the modern Christian; "the men were real men, were they not?" To which we answer; firstly, as regards the principle. It is an established canon of Catholic Scriptural exegesis that while man allegorises only through words and things, God allegorises also through persons and events. Let it not be forgotten that the Divine Word is Himself a Person. The ideal Saint speaks no idle word; and so God cannot direct or fashion an event or person that is not charged to the full with manifold significances. Secondly, as regards the proof of this principle. We have the testimony both of Christ and the Apostles that the leading personages of the Old Testament had a typical and allegorical significance. Thirdly, as regards the application of the principle to the personages of the New Testament. The Fathers sanction the belief that the two St. Johns and St. Peter had a deep mystic meaning, besides their direct import as historical personages. Mr. Patmore expressly disclaims the intention to exclude any other interpretations of the Baptist's mystical import: therefore we the less hesitate to express our conviction that his interpretation is *a* truth, whether or not it be the total truth. (pp. 208-09)

The water which the Baptist drank Mr. Patmore also interprets as signifying "the life of the external senses, or nature." Let him who doubts this turn to the prayer over the mingled wine and water in the Mass. In the original Gelasian Sacramentary it ran: "Grant us, we pray, to become partakers of His Godhead, Who was pleased to share in our human nature." But this was not explicit enough for those who adapted it to the Common of the Mass. So they inserted: "Grant us, *by the secret signification of this commingling of wine with water,* to become, *etc.*" In other words, the union of water with wine means the union of natural humanity with the Divinity. . . . Similar is the imagery of the Marriage of Cana. The changing of water into wine signified the changing of the natural into the Divine; and its *special* significance is pointed by the circumstances under which the miracle was worked—at a marriage feast. In other words, it meant the ultimate transformation of the natural Sacrament of Marriage into the Divine Sacrament of the Marriage of the Lamb. The *ultimate*, not the *immediate* transformation; for He "kept the best wine to the last." We may add that this use of natural love as a gradual preparation for Divine love, on which Mr. Patmore insists as at least *a* meaning of the Precursor's personality, is directly alluded to in the Canticle: "Under the apple tree I raised thee up." St. Augustine's interpretation of the Baptist is that he signifies the Old Law as the forerunner of the New. (pp. 209-10)

We may add a word as to the style of the book. It is severely pregnant to a degree which some will call bald. But we do not call a countenance "bald" because it is rased of the "excrement" (to speak Shakespeareanly), which hides the play of facial expression. [Mr. Patmore] desires exposition, not the softer graces. Indeed, his subject matter is such, that the cultivation of beauty for beauty's sake would but obscure what is in itself difficult enough. The beauty of precision is the only legitimate beauty in such a case. Accordingly, imagery is used only for illustration or deeper expression. Few would see beauty in the style of Aquinas. Yet De Quincey justly says that St. Thomas's is a style admirably fitted to its peculiar purpose. Is not this the supreme justification of all style? Let it be the justification of Mr. Patmore's. One who has had a purely literary training, and has afterwards passed to the treatment of such subjects as occupy *Religio Poetæ,* must have experienced a disagreeable surprise. He discovers that the style of literary beauty which had been the pride of his heart, is as useless for his new objects as a butterfly-net for deep-sea fishing. (p. 211)

> *Francis Thompson, "Victorian Age: Patmore," in his* Literary Criticisms, *edited by Rev. Terence L. Connolly, S.J., E. P. Dutton and Company Inc., 1948, pp. 203-11.*

[ARTHUR SYMONS] (essay date 1893)

[Symons was an English critic, poet, dramatist, short story writer, and editor who first gained notoriety in the 1890s as an English decadent. Eventually, he established himself as one of the most important critics of the modern era. Symons provided his English contemporaries with an appropriate vocabulary with which to define the aesthetic of symbolism in his book The Symbolist Movement in Literature; *furthermore, he laid the foundation for much of modern poetic theory by discerning that conceiving of the symbol as a vehicle by which a "hitherto unknown reality was suddenly revealed" could become the basis for an entire modern aesthetic. As a reviewer, Symons expressed both impatience with and enthusiasm for Patmore's work. His ambivalence is reflected in the following essay, in which he praises* Religio Poetæ *as a nearly perfect book and describes its author as one of the most essential poets of his generation, yet disparages* The Angel in the House *as a work founded on "dinner-table domesticities." (See excerpt below by Symons, 1897, for a detailed discussion of* The Unknown Eros *and* The Angel in the House.)]*

[*Religio Poetæ*] contains twenty-three short essays—many of them rather sermons than essays—on such topics as **'Peace in Life and Art,' 'Ancient and Modern Ideas of Purity,' 'Emotional Art,' 'Conscience,' 'Distinction.'** There is nothing which marks it as of the present but an occasional personality, which we could wish absent, and a persistent habit of self-quotation. There is absolutely no popular appeal, no extraneous interest in the timeliness of subject or the peculiarities of treatment; nothing, in fact, to draw the notice of the average reader or to engage his attention. To the average reader the book must be nothing but the vainest speculation and the dullest theory. Yet, in many ways, it is one of the most beautiful and notable works in prose that have appeared in recent years. It is a book, argumentative as it is, which one is not called on so much to agree with or dissent from as to ponder over, and to accept, in a certain sense, for its own sake. Mr. Patmore is one of the few surviving defenders of the faith, and that alone gives him an interesting position among contemporary men of letters. He is a Christian and a Catholic, that is to say, the furthest logical development of the dogmatic Christian; but he is also a mystic; and his spiritual apprehensions are so vivid that he is never betrayed into dogmatic narrowness without the absolution of an evident vision and conviction. And, above all, he is a poet; one of the most essential poets of our time, not on account of the dinner-table domesticities of **'The Angel in the House,'** but by reason of the sublimated love-poetry of **'The Unknown Eros,'** with its extraordinary subtlety of thought and emotion, rendered with the faultless simplicity of an elaborate and conscious art. His prose is everywhere the prose of a poet. Thought, in him, is of the very substance of poetry, and is sustained throughout at almost the lyrical pitch. There is, in these essays, a rarefied air as of the mountain-tops of meditation; and the spirit of their pondering over things, their sometimes remote contemplation, is always, in one sense, as Mr. Pater has justly said of Wordsworth, impassioned. Each essay in itself may at once be said to be curiously incomplete or fragmentary, and yet singularly well related as a part to a whole, the effect of continuity coming from the fact that these are the occasional considerations of a mind which, beyond that of most men, is consistent and individual. Not less individual than the subject-matter is the style, which, in its gravity and sweetness, its fine, unforbidding austerity, its smooth harmony—a harmony produced by the use of simple words subtly—is unlike that of any contemporary writer, though much akin to Mr. Patmore's own poetic style.

The subjects with which these essays deal may be grouped under three heads: religion, art, and woman. In all, Mr. Patmore's attitude is intensely conservative and aristocratic—fiercely contemptuous of popular idols and ideals, whenever he condescends to notice them. The very daring and very logical essay on **'Christianity and Progress'** is the clearest and most cogent statement of Christianity as an aristocracy, in opposition to the current modern view of it as a democracy, that has been made since the democratic spirit made its way into the pulpit. (pp. 902-03)

We are concerned neither to defend nor to contend against [the attitude revealed in these essays], admitting only that, granted the premises (which, no doubt, can be taken on certain grave and ancient warrants), the deductions from those premises are strictly logical, and, at the present day, as novel as they are logical. Mr. Patmore is inclined to be petulant, and he occasionally rides a hobby-horse so recklessly as to commit himself to incredible fallacies. But a book which attains perfection has never yet been produced, and Mr. Patmore's is close, very close indeed. (p. 903)

> [*Arthur Symons*], *in a review of "Religio Poetæ,"*
> *in* The Athenaeum, *No. 3453, December 30, 1893,*
> *pp. 902-03.*

ALICE MEYNELL (essay date 1893)

> [*Meynell was a turn-of-the-century English poet, essayist, and critic whom Patmore befriended late in his life. She criticizes several elements of Patmore's principles and practices of versification in the following essay, but otherwise vouches for the consummate artistry of* The Unknown Eros.]

To most of the great poets no greater praise can be given than praise of their imagery. Imagery is the natural language of their poetry. Without a parable she hardly speaks. But undoubtedly there is now and then a poet who touches the thing, not its likeness, too vitally, too sensitively, for even such a pause as the verse makes for love of the beautiful image. Those rare moments are simple, and their simplicity makes one of the reader's keenest experiences. Other simplicities may be achieved by lesser art, but this is transcendent simplicity. There is nothing in the world more costly. It vouches for the beauty which it transcends; it answers for the riches it forbears; it implies the art which it fulfils. . . . The loveliness that stands and waits on the simplicity of certain of Mr. Coventry Patmore's Odes, the fervours and splendours that are there, only to be put to silence—to silence of a kind that would be impossible were they less glorious—are testimonies to the difference between sacrifice and waste. (pp. 89-90)

[Yet transcendent] simplicity could not possibly be habitual. Man lives within garments and veils, and art is chiefly concerned with making mysteries of these for the loveliness of his life; when they are rent asunder it is impossible not to be aware that an overwhelming human emotion has been in action. Thus [such poems in *The Unknown Eros* as] *Departure, If I were Dead, A Farewell, Eurydice, The Toys, St. Valentine's Day*—though here there is in the exquisite imaginative play a mitigation of the bare vitality of feeling—group themselves apart as the innermost of the poet's achievements.

Second to these come the Odes that have splendid thought in great images. . . . Emotion is here, too, and in shocks and throes, never frantic when almost intolerable. It is mortal pathos. If any other poet has filled a cup with a draught so unalloyed, we do not know it. Love and sorrow are pure in *The Unknown Eros;* and its author has not refused even the cup of terror. Against love often, against sorrow nearly always, against fear always, men of sensibility instantaneously guard the quick of their hearts. . . . But through nearly the whole of Coventry Patmore's poetry there is an endurance of the mortal touch. Nay, more, he has the endurance of the immortal touch.

That is, his capacity for all the things that men elude for their greatness is more than the capacity of other men. He endures therefore what they could but will not endure and, besides this, degrees that they cannot apprehend. Thus, to have studied *The Unknown Eros* is to have had a certain experience—at least the impassioned experience of a compassion; but it is also to have recognised a soul beyond our compassion.

What some of the Odes have to sing of, their author does not insist upon our knowing. He leaves more liberty for a well-intentioned reader's error than makes for peace and recollection of mind in reading. That the general purpose of the poems is obscure is inevitable. It has the obscurity of profound clear waters. What the poet chiefly secures to us is the understanding that love and its bonds, its bestowal and reception, does but rehearse the action of the union of God with humanity—that there is no essential man save Christ, and no essential woman except the soul of mankind. When the singer of a Song of Songs seems to borrow the phrase of human love, it is rather that human love had first borrowed the truths of the love of God. (pp. 90-2)

The art that utters an intellectual action so courageous, an emotion so authentic, as that of Mr. Coventry Patmore's poetry, cannot be otherwise than consummate. Often the word has a fulness of significance that gives the reader a shock of appreciation. This is always so in those simplest odes which we have taken as the heart of the author's work. Without such wonderful rightness, simplicity of course is impossible. Nor is that beautiful precision less in passages of description, such as the landscape lines in *Amelia* and elsewhere. (pp. 93-4)

If Mr. Patmore really intends that his Odes shall be read with minim, or crotchet, or quaver rests, to fill up a measure of beaten time, we are free to hold that he rather arbitrarily applies to liberal verse the laws of verse set for use—cradle verse and march-marking verse. . . . Liberal verse, dramatic, narrative, meditative, can surely be bound by no time measures—if for no other reason, for this: that to prescribe pauses is also to forbid any pauses unprescribed. Granting, however, his principle of catelexis, we still doubt whether the irregular metre of *The Unknown Eros* is happily used except for the large sweep of the flight of the Ode more properly so called. [John Milton's] *Lycidas,* the *Mrs. Anne Killigrew,* the *Intimations* [of William Wordsworth], and Emerson's *Threnody,* considered merely for their versification, fulfil their laws so perfectly that they certainly move without checks as without haste. So with the graver Odes—much in the majority—of Mr. Coventry Patmore's series. A more lovely dignity of extension and restriction, a more touching sweetness of simple and frequent rhyme, a truer impetus of pulse and impulse, English verse could hardly yield than are to be found in his versification. And what movement of words has ever expressed flight, distance, mystery, and wonderful approach, as they are expressed in a celestial line— the eighth in the ode *To the Unknown Eros?* When we are sensible of a metrical check it is in this way: To the English ear the heroic line is the unit of metre, and when two lines of various length undesignedly add together to form a heroic line, they have to be separated with something of a jerk. And this adding—as, for instance, of a line of four syllables preceding or following one of six—occurs now and then, and even in such a masterly measure of music as *A Farewell.* It is as when a sail suddenly flaps windless in the fetching about of a boat. In *The Angel in the House,* and other earlier poems, Mr. Coventry Patmore used the octosyllabic stanza perfectly, inasmuch as he never left it either heavily or thinly packed. Moreover those first poems had a composure which was the prelude to the peace of the Odes. And even in his slightest work he proves himself the master—that is, the owner—of words that, owned by him, are unprofaned, are as though they had never been profaned; the capturer of an art so quick and close that it is the voice less of a poet than of the very Muse. (pp. 94-6)

Alice Meynell, "Mr. Coventry Patmore's Odes," in her The Rhythm of Life and Other Essays, *1893. Reprint by John Lane/The Bodley Head, 1896, pp. 89-96.*

POET LORE   (essay date 1894)

It is not of the religion of the poet that Mr. Coventry Patmore writes in **'Religio Poetæ,'** but rather of the poetry or mystic symbolism of dogma. To him "the amount of substantial poetry, of imaginative insight into the noblest and loveliest reality," to be found in the works of Saint Augustine, Saint Bernard, Saint Thomas Aquinas, Saint Frances of Sales, Saint John of the Cross, for example, "is ten times greater than is to be found in all the poets of the past two thousand years put together." This statement at the start of this little book indicates much of its subject-matter and temper.

That which these saintly seers of the church have in common with the poet is the mystical habit of perceiving and vitalizing the things of thought by analogies. Mr. Patmore has much of the same gift, and it allures the reader to follow his blindest irrationalities with interest and appreciation of this fine quality. But that which the great secular poet has, in distinction from the most poetic of the Fathers, is a humanity-loving ardor, untethered to dogma and free to develop its faculty and direct its vision where it will. It is this, also, which Mr. Patmore, like his admired Fathers, lacks. There are two or three stakes to which his mind seems to be tied; and with all his agility, keenness, almost penetration, the reader soon knows his limitations, perceives his "congenital incapacity" to examine the present, actual and dynamic phenomena that alone could correct his static formulas in art, letters, religion, and life, and henceforth looks upon him as an interesting and most representative remnant and specimen of the days that knew not the illumination of the ideas of Evolution and Democracy.

In the various short essays, . . . both in those which are more and those less closely linked with the initial essay, **'Religio Poetæ,'** the object is to trace the correspondence of matters of art, sex, and life with the Church's prefiguring of the sacramental. In this exposition, the very pith of the process depends upon one or two obsolescent counters of speech being taken, not only for current coin, but genuine substance.

The authority and excellence of the few over the many, the nullity and unreason of "the feminine," forever subordinate to the entity and reason of "the masculine," as symbolized in the relation of the Celibates, or "Brides of the Church," to God, are the very alphabet by which he thinks of art and life,—in fact, they are his thought. So if it is "Christianity" and "Progress" which he is discussing, he returns to his formula of the authority and excellence of the few over the many, to clear Christianity of any concern for "the greatest happiness of the greatest number," and hence of any failure in doing what she did not profess to do, "to improve bad or even indifferently good peole who form the mass of mankind." Or if it is a question of "the Emotional in Art" or "Peace in Art," he brings up again the "masculine" and "feminine" fixed symbolism, the one ever in utter mastery over the other,

to decree no good in the modern qualities of unrest, emotion, and aspiration in Art or Letters. But since the development of the People tends to bring in question the authority and excellence of the few, and the development of woman to show that reason is not all unfeminine, nor unreason all unmasculine, his very alphabet and substance of thought is imperilled by current facts. So, in his lively essays on **'The Weaker Vessel'** and on **'Distinction,'** in which he inveighs against the doctrine of the equality of man and woman as a "damnable heresy," and against Democracy as civilization "gone to rot" . . . , he must needs shut his eyes and repeat his alphabet louder than ever and with an arrogance that is amusing when one sees how very tight shut his eyes are. (pp. 269-70)

P., in a review of "Religio Poetæ," in Poet Lore, *Vol. VI, No. 5, 1894, pp. 269-70.*

THE ATHENAEUM   (essay date 1895)

[*The Rod, the Root, and the Flower*] is a wonderful medley of religious ecstasy, poetical extravagance, scientific nomenclature, and metaphysical abstraction that is submitted to us in the cold blood in which we approach a collection of aphoristic lore. Had it been presented in a wholly poetical form, there would be little to be said, and much to admire; for there is much that will pass in that form that cannot be accepted out of it. If we do not like poetry, we can at least refrain from arguing about its ideas; while in the form of prose they appear to challenge dispute and contention on every page.

It seems here and there as though Mr. Patmore were fully conscious of the obvious objection that may be taken to many of these aphorisms. In No. 147 of the **"Aurea Dicta"** he admits that "the highest and deepest thoughts do not 'voluntary move harmonious numbers,' but run rather to grotesque epigram and doggerel." Surely this is true of such an utterance as "God is infinite; all else is indefinite, except woman, who alone is finite"; or "The Soul's shame at its own unworthiness of the embraces of God is the blush upon the rose of love." Stated in plain prose, these and the like are sentiments that fail to charm or even to amuse, and only annoy and irritate. This loss of temper is all the more certain and justifiable, the deeper the reader's insight into Mr. Patmore's delicate perceptions of spiritual truth, and the conviction which he produces that, when he will, he can clothe a spiritual truth in words that are neither grotesque nor extravagant, possibly as well as any other living writer. But it pleases him sometimes to luxuriate in full-flavoured rhapsodies and mystifications of thought and language which are apparently quite intentional; though if they are meant to enlighten, they must, with the great mass of men, defeat their object. . . . [In] spite of a tendency to lapse into "wild hyperboles," . . . there are many of these aphorisms which are not far from perfection either in thought or form. "It is one thing to be blind, and another to be in darkness"; "There are not two sides to any question which really concerns a man, but only one"; "The ardour chills us which we do not share," are, for instance, good *aperçus* [insights], and well expressed. Some of the articles are too long to merit the title of aphorism, and are, rather, brief essays, and it is perhaps here that Mr. Patmore is at his best. For a fine example of the humour which is often the nicest appreciation of truth, the reader may be commended to No. 14 of the **"Magna Moralia,"** on the outward behaviour of the true saint. . . . (p. 862)

This is so pre-eminently the right tone to adopt, and so much the most effective method of "digging again the wells which the Philistines have filled''—and such is Mr. Patmore's professed endeavour—that he would have done well to indulge his genius a little further in this direction, and restrain it in some of its wilder flights. For he is alive to the fact that if his readers cannot share all his ardour, some of it will chill them; and the experience is apt to detract from the enthusiasm which they might otherwise feel for what is good, and even excellent, in this volume. (p. 863)

> *A review of "The Rod, the Root, and the Flower,"*
> in The Athenaeum, *No. 3556, December 21, 1895,*
> *pp. 862-63.*

RICHARD GARNETT   (essay date 1896)

[*Garnett evaluates Patmore's performance as a literary critic, identifying "intuitive discernment and convincing statement of novel and yet simple truths" as his chief virtue and "indifference to persons in comparison with principles" as his chief vice. Garnett bases his criticism on pertinent essays and aphorisms in* Principle in Art, Religio Poetæ, *and* The Rod, the Root, and the Flower.]

Mr. Coventry Patmore is among those of the critics of his time who have earned the right to criticise the considerable performances of others by considerable performances of their own. No one, it is to be supposed, will now dispute either the significance or the permanency of the addition which he has made to the poetical literature of his century, or question that among its characteristics is a strength of intellect which should entitle his critical utterances to a respectful hearing. It cannot be denied that some of the early judges of his poems, including even so sane and mature a censor as Matthew Arnold, were far from impressed with this intellectual force, but the cause was simply . . . impatience with certain prosaic constituents of his poetical work, feeble, no doubt, if regarded in themselves, but rather examples of misdirected strength if viewed in connection with the masculine energy and penetrating sagacity of the far more extensive and important portions of **"The Angel in the House."** It is, indeed, somewhat startling to find such loftiness and gravity not seldom in perilous propinquity to the ludicrous, but this is a symptom of the curious duality that runs through Mr. Patmore's work, and sometimes almost seems to part both the poet and the critic into twain. . . . [Just] as there is a duality in **"The Angel in the House,"** a sphere of strong sense, intense feeling, and exquisite description contrasted with one of prosaic commonplace; so in the **"Odes"** pure spiritual rapture and marvellous spiritual introspection contrast with unlovely see-things of political passion. In the critical department of Mr. Patmore's work a corresponding duality exists, perhaps best defined by the remark that he belongs to the exceedingly small class of men who have a stronger hold upon and a more lively apprehension of principles existing in the abstract than of principles embodied in individuals. With ordinary men it is different; such can seldom so much as see a principle until it is incarnated in a person. Mr. Patmore is an extraordinary man, and few things in him are more extraordinary than his constant and quiet enunciation of subtle truths, which a discerning reader receives with thankfulness as invaluable additions to his own intellectual store. At the same time, his imperfect grasp of, or frigid indifference to, the actual works which he professes to be criticising render him much happier in the exposition of such principles than in the application of them. (p. 180)

Among his essays is one on William Barnes, the Dorsetshire poet, one of the most exquisite of our singers, but whose poems, being written in a provincial dialect, are but little known.

Mr. Patmore reveals his own high appreciation of Barnes in the title of his essay, **"A Modern Classic,"** and this is literally nearly all that he does for him. There are several pages of admirable remarks about the principles of art in general, and just two pages about Barnes himself, in which he is rather damaged than otherwise by a wholly gratuitous comparison of his poetry to Spenser's "Epithalamium." There is praise, to be sure, but it is all *ipse dixit* [according to his own authority], not a single line of Barnes himself is quoted in confirmation of illustration, and, unless the reader has much more respect for *ipse dixits* than he ought to have, his case can only be that of the man who beholds his natural face in a glass. The essay closes very inconsistently with a complaint that people do not read Barnes, but how can they be expected to go out of their way to master an unfamiliar dialect unless convinced that it is worth their while? and can they be convinced by two pages of mere assertion? The essay, therefore, is wholly ineffective as concerns its professed purpose, and we can attribute the failure to nothing but Mr. Patmore's indifference to persons in comparison with principles. . . . His admiration for Barnes is sincere, but tepid; the man is nothing to him in comparison with the views which he can be made to suggest. A critic like Macaulay or Carlyle would have got rid of generalities as soon as possible, tackled the man himself, drawn a picture of him which would have set the world gazing, and expatiated upon his beauties in a way to send their readers after his books. . . .

Critics far inferior to Mr. Patmore have given more adequate accounts of many of the writers treated by him, and the reason, if we mistake not, is that they have made up in sympathy for what they lacked in discernment. Most profoundly does Wordsworth declare concerning the man of genius:—

> You must love him, ere to you
> He will seem worthy of your love.

This essential qualification, unfortunately, is almost always absent from Mr. Patmore in his relation to the ostensible subjects of his criticisms. He is, indeed, far from incapable of generous admiration. We meet ever and anon with gleams of cordial appreciation of Dante, of Goethe, of Hegel, of the Spanish mystics, but, unfortunately, these are the people he is *not* criticising. Were he to give us detailed studies of any of these, we should expect work of the most satisfactory character and of the highest value. But, unhappily, his critical energy has been mainly spent in reviewing authors whose high standing in the republic of letters he must acknowledge, but whom, nevertheless, he can only bring himself to half admire. To employ one of his own quaint similes, it is as impossible to produce great criticism under such conditions as to breed a whale in a duckpond. A good example of his dealings with a great writer imperfectly apprehended, because imperfectly relished, is his treatment of Rossetti. As he seems on the point of winding up an essay containing many just remarks, but pitched throughout in far too low a key, it suddenly occurs to him that something remains to be said. "In much of his work there is a rich and obscure glow of insight into depths too profound and too sacred for clear speech, even if they could be spoken." Most true! but surely this was the saying to have put into the forefront of the battle. It should have been the text from which the whole sermon was preached, instead of an ornamental appendage at the extremity. . . . And so it would, have Mr. Patmore in his dealing with his great contemporary been able to summon to his aid the "love that when wisdom fails makes Cythna wise"; nor would he then have committed himself to the astounding assertion that the wonderful "Burden of Nineveh'' might have been written by Southey! This reserved attitude may in a measure be excused as a reaction against the extravagant adulation of writers who show any sort of promise, a nuisance never more obnoxious than now. But the caution which is certainly in place when immature critics pronounce on writers of dubious position is needless when writers of Rossetti's established fame are sifted by men of the intellectual calibre of Mr. Patmore. (p. 181)

[Now] we may turn from the ungrateful but needful task of fault-finding, and accompany Mr. Patmore to the ground where he is stronger than any living English critic. No one has a gift like him for the intuitive discernment and convincing statement of novel and yet simple truths. As in his poetry, so in his criticism, his exquisitely uttered prayer has been granted.

> Thou primal Love, who grantest wings
> And voices to the woodland birds,
> Grant me the power of saying things
> Too simple and too sweet for words.

It is true that these inspired utterances are sometimes exaggerated into paradoxes, and, though irrefragable in the realm of general principle, are often grievously distorted in their application to individual cases and circumstances. But this is merely the tribute which every artist and thinker must in some department or other of his work pay to mortality. Mr. Patmore's special limitation, as it appears to us, is the difficulty he finds in bringing himself down from the ideal to the concrete. The greater should by rights include the less, but with him clear comprehension of an aesthetic or spiritual truth is no guarantee for its correct application to the case of the next author, or institution, or social tendency that he may happen to encounter. This does not in the least detract from the beauty and value of the original enunciations. How great this is, we may be allowed to establish by a few examples. . . .

> The follies of a Blake or a Hartley Coleridge are venial when compared with those of the thoughtful and prudent fool—the fool in respect of great things, as the other is in respect of small.
>
> It is a peculiarity of the very highest work of every kind that it is not the result of painful labour, but that it is easier to do it than not to do it, when it can be done at all.
>
> A wise or tender phrase in the mouth of a Byron or a Moore will be despised, where a commonplace of morality or affection in that of a Wordsworth or a Burns will be respected. . . .

In this air of authority, this habit of propounding striking truths which frequently have no very close connection with the ostensible argument of his essay, and are just as likely to occur in a generally unsatisfactory essay as in a conclusive one, Mr. Patmore resembles a great writer whom he unreasonably disparages—Emerson. Neither are powerful reasoners; they hardly seem capable of carrying on a sustained argument from definite premises, they seldom persuade by eloquence or convince by logic, but they announce and illuminate. Notwithstanding great apparent differences, they have much actual resemblance; and the differences chiefly arise from the Englishman's mind being steeped in the dyes, or stains, as the reader pleases, of a host of traditional ideas of which the American knows nothing. . . . Mr. Patmore's style never attains the exquisite beauty of Emerson's at its best, but it is, perhaps, of more uniform excellence.

It hardly ever rises to eloquence, although the conclusion of the essay on **"Peace in Life and Art"** is exceedingly impressive. But it never seems to attempt eloquence, or to care whether it is eloquent or not. With all its wealth of felicitous remark, which might well excuse some apparent self-consciousness, it always conveys the impression that, with the writer, matter is before manner; that, though aware that he has fine things to say, he is not writing for the sake of saying them. It possesses two great and by no means usual virtues, the continual intimation of a reserved power, which conveys the pleasant assurance to the reader that he is drinking, not draining, a perennial fountain; and that which Aristotle says all good poetry should exhibit, a continual slight novelty, which stimulates attention at every sentence, and keeps the mind on the alert, without putting it upon the rack. (p. 182)

> *Richard Garnett, "Living Critics: Mr. Coventry Patmore," in* The Bookman, *London, Vol. IX, No. 54, March, 1896, pp. 180-82.*

ARTHUR SYMONS (essay date 1897)

[*Symons contrasts* The Angel in the House *and* The Unknown Eros *as love poetry, categorizing the former poem as a prose-like work informed by affection and the latter work as a genuinely poetic expression of passion. According to Symons,* The Unknown Eros *is distinguished as "the most devout, subtle, and sublimated love-poetry" of the nineteenth century.*]

The most austere poet of our time, Coventry Patmore conceived of art as a sort of abstract ecstasy, whose source, limit, and end are that supreme wisdom which is the innermost essence of love. Thus the whole of his work—those "bitter, sweet, few, and veil'd" songs, which are the fruit of two out of his seventy years—is love-poetry; and it is love-poetry of a quite unique kind. In the earlier of his two books, *The Angel in the House,* we see him, in the midst of a scientific generation (in which it was supposed that by adding prose to poetry you doubled the value of poetry), unable to escape the influence of his time, desperately set on doing the wrong thing by design, yet unable to keep himself from often doing the right thing by accident. In his later book, *The Unknown Eros,* he has achieved the proper recognition of himself, the full consciousness of the means to his own end; and it is by *The Unknown Eros* that he will live, if it is enough claim to immortality to have written the most devout, subtle, and sublimated love-poetry of our century.

Patmore tells us in *The Angel in the House,* that it was his intention to write

> That hymn for which the whole world longs,
> A worthy hymn in woman's praise.

But at that time his only conception of woman was the conception of woman as the lady. Now poetry has nothing whatever to do with woman as the lady; it is in the novel, the comedy of manners, that we expect the society of ladies. Prose, in the novel and the drama, is at liberty to concern itself with those secondary emotions which come into play in our familiar intercourse with one another; with those conventions which are the "evening dress" by which our varying temperaments seek the disguise of an outward uniformity. . . . But the poet who endeavours to bring all this machinery of prose into the narrow and self-sufficing limits of verse is as fatally doomed to failure as the painter who works after photographs, instead of from the living model. At the time when *The Angel* was written, the heresy of the novel in verse was in the air. Were there not, before and after it, the magnificent failure of [Elizabeth Barrett Browning's] *Aurora Leigh,* the ineffectual, always interesting, endeavours of Clough, and certain more careful, more sensitive, never quite satisfactory, experiments of Tennyson? Patmore went his own way, to a more ingenious failure than any. *The Angel in the House* is written with exquisite neatness, occasional splendour; it is the very flower of the poetry of convention; and is always lifting the trivialities and the ingenuities to which, for the most part, it restricts itself, miraculously near to that height which, now and again, in such lines as *The Revelation,* it fully attains. But it is not here, it is in *The Unknown Eros* alone, that Patmore has given immortality to what is immortal in perishable things.

How could it be otherwise, when the whole force of the experiment lies in the endeavour to say essentially unpoetical things in a poetical manner? . . . The subtlety, the fineness of analysis, the simplified complexity, of such things as *The Changed Allegiance* [from *The Angel in the House*], can scarcely be overpraised as studies in "the dreadful heart of woman," from the point of view of a shrewd, kindly, somewhat condescending, absolutely clear-eyed observer, so dispassionate that he has not even the privilege of an illusion, so impartial that you do not even do his fervour the compliment of believing it possible that his perfect Honoria had, after all, defects. But in all this, admirable as it is, there is nothing which could not have been as well said in prose. It is the point of view of the egoist, of the "marrying man," to whom

> Each beauty blossomed in the sight
> Of tender personal regards.

Woman is observed always in reference to the man who fancies she may prove worthy to be his "predestinated mate," and it seems to him his highest boast that he is

> proud
> To take his passion into church.

At its best, this is the poetry of "being in love," not of love; of affection, not passion. Passion is a thing of flame, rarely burning pure, or without danger to him who holds that windblown torch in his hand; while affection, such as this legalised affection of *The Angel in the House,* is a gentle and comfortable warmth, as of a hearth-side. It is that excellent, not quite essential, kind of love which need endure neither pain nor revolt; for it has conquered the world on the world's terms.

Woman, as she is seen in *The Angel in the House,* is a delightful, adorable, estimable, prettily capricious child; demonstrably finite, capturable, a butterfly not yet Psyche. It is the severest judgment on her poet that she is never a mystery to him. For all art is founded on mystery, and to the poet, as to the child, the whole world is mysterious. . . . [To the true lover, the true poet,] woman is as mysterious as the night of stars, and all he learns of her is but to deepen the mystery which surrounds her as with clouds. To him she is Fate, an unconscious part of what is eternal in things; and, being the liveliest image of beauty, she is to be reverenced for her beauty, as the saints are reverenced for their virtue. What is it to me if you tell me that she is but the creature of a day, prized for her briefness, as we prize flowers; loved for her egoism, as we love infants; marvelled at for the exquisite and audacious completeness of her ignorance? Or what is it to me if you tell me that she is all that a lady should be, infinitely perfect in pettiness; and that her choice will reward the calculations of a gentleman? If she is not a flame, devouring and illuminating, and if your passion for her is not as another consuming and

refining flame, each rushing into either that both may be commingled in a brighter ecstasy, you have not seen woman as it is the joy of the poet and the lover to see her; and your fine distinctions, your disentangling of sensations, your subtleties of interpretation, will be at the best but of the substance of prose, revealing to me what is transitory in the eternal rather than what is eternal in the transitory. The art of Coventry Patmore, in *The Angel in the House,* is an art founded on this scientific conception of woman. But the poet, who began by thinking of woman as being at her best a perfect lady, ended by seeing her seated a little higher than the angels, at the right hand of the Madonna, of whom indeed she is a scarcely lower symbol. She who was a bright and cherished toy in *The Angel in the House* becomes in *The Unknown Eros* pure spirit, the passionate sister of the pure idea. She is the mystical rose of beauty, the female half of that harmony of opposites which is God. She has other names, and is the Soul, the Church, the Madonna. To be her servant is to be the servant of all right, the enemy of all wrong; and therefore poems of fierce patriotism, and disdainful condemnation of the foolish and vulgar who are the adversaries of God's ordinances and man's, find their appropriate place among poems of tender human pathos, of ecstatic human and divine love. And she is now, at last, apprehended under her most essential aspect, as the supreme mystery; and her worship becomes an almost secret ritual, of which none but the adepts can fathom the full significance. (pp. 71-4)

Out of this love-poetry all but the very essence of passion has been consumed; and love is seen to be the supreme wisdom, even more than the supreme delight. Apprehended on every side, and with the same controlling ardour, those "frightful nuptials" of the Dove and Snake, which are one of his allegories, lead upward, on the wings of an almost aerial symbolism, to those all but inaccessible heights where mortal love dies into that intense, self-abnegating, intellectual passion, which we name the love of God.

At this height, at its very highest, his art becomes abstract ecstasy. . . . [Emotion] may take any shape, may inform the least likely of substances. Is not all music a kind of divine mathematics, and is not mathematics itself a rapture to the true adept? To Patmore abstract things were an emotion, became indeed the highest emotion of which he was capable; and that joy, which he notes as the mark of fine art, that peace, which to him was the sign of great art, themselves the most final of the emotions, interpenetrated for him the whole substance of thought, aspiration, even argument. Never were arguments at once so metaphysical and so mystical, so precise, analytic, and passionate as those "high arguments" which fill these pages with so thrilling a life.

The particular subtlety of Patmore's mysticism finds perhaps its counterpart in the writings of certain of the Catholic mystics: it has at once the clear-eyed dialectic of the Schoolmen and the august heat of St. Teresa. Here is passion which analyses itself, and yet with so passionate a complexity that it remains passion. Read, for instance that eulogy of *Pain,* which is at once a lyric rapture, and betrays an almost unholy depth of acquaintance with the hidden, tortuous, and delightful ways of sensation. Read that song of songs, *Deliciæ Sapientiæ de Amore,* which seems to speak, with the tongue of angels, all the secrets of all those "to whom generous Love, by any name, is dear." . . . Read those perhaps less quint-essential dialogues in which a personified Psyche seeks wisdom of Eros and the Pythoness. And then, if you would realise how subtle an argument in verse may be, how elegantly and happily expressed, and yet not approach, at its highest climb, the point from which these other arguments in verse take flight, turn to *The Angel in the House,* and read *The Changed Allegiance.* The difference is the difference between wisdom and worldly wisdom: wisdom being the purified and most ardent emotion of the intellect, and thus of the very essence of poetry; while worldly wisdom is but the dispassionate ingenuity of the intelligence, and thus of not so much as the highest substance of prose. (pp. 74-6)

Arthur Symons, ''Coventry Patmore,'' in The New Review, *Vol. XVI, No. 92, January, 1897, pp. 71-7.*

SIR ARTHUR QUILLER-COUCH   (essay date 1901)

[*Quiller-Couch was a distinguished English critic, editor, and novelist. He records his response to Patmore's major works in the following essay, which features commentary on the suitability of nuptial love as a subject for art, the disparity between Patmore's attitude toward women in his prose and in his poetry, and his difficulties in applying critical principles to writers and their works. Quiller-Couch's remarks originally appeared in 1901 in the* Monthly Review *as part of a review of Basil Champneys's* Memoirs and Correspondence of Coventry Patmore (*see Additional Bibliography*).]

[Of Patmore's first collection of Verse, *Poems,*] I am only acquainted with those poems which Patmore allowed to reappear in later collections; but these on the whole awaken no regret for the lost ones. Their author used afterwards to speak of them as trash and an object lesson in faults of style and subject. Yet on the whole the critics received them with respect, and there are lines and even whole stanzas in *The River* and the *Woodman's Daughter* (both written at sixteen) which unmistakably declare the poet. The scenery in the former is aptly and easily painted, and gives us an early assurance of a gift which Patmore afterwards hid somewhat obstinately, yet refined in secret, until, when we come to the *Odes,* we hardly know whether to admire more his penetrating vision for ''natural'' beauty or his classical economy in the use of it. Nor could a youth without the root of poetry in him have found so exquisite a phrase for girlhood as

The sweet age
When heaven's our side the lark.

But weak in choice of subject, and loose in their grip of it, these poems undoubtedly are. And (to anticipate a little) I find the same feebleness, poorly disguised by wayward abruptness and obscurity, in *Tamerton Church Tower.* It would be false for me to pretend that, after several readings, I understand that poem, or even know precisely what it is all about. . . . I am far from saying that in the ill-told and apparently aimless story of *Tamerton Church Tower* there is nothing to be understood; but I certainly do not find the intelligible portion of it either so pleasant or so profitable as to awaken the smallest desire to explore the rest. It is, let me grant, a ''noticeable'' poem; but it is also a very callous one, and (worse than this) it treats of women with a short-sighted vulgarity most singular to find in a young poet destined to become the singer of wedlock and married love. (pp. 125-26)

I hinted just now that *Tamerton Church Tower* . . . was a most inauspicious performance. On second thoughts ''inauspicious'' is not the word. The wine was there, though turbid and even muddy. In the *Angel* it has been clarified by time and quiet thinking; the lees have settled; the liquor is drained off bright and pure. The one poem tells us little and tells it darkly; the

other attempts far more, yet remains exquisitely perspicuous. . . . [The *Angel*] dealt with emotions through which most of us pass at one time or another, and in passing through which (as almost any breach of promise case will prove) the most prosaic of God's creatures finds a temporary solace in the Muse. Patmore looked into these emotions with clear eyes, but he spoke of them with a decency which was even more gratifying to a race accustomed to value decency above insight. (pp. 129-30)

[The poem's popularity is based on] its entire sincerity. The story is simple and pleasant, yet to persons unaccustomed to poetry I do not think the book can be easy reading. It contains (especially in the Preludes) a large amount of abstract thought. Patmore's Muse, when she *did* alight or tread the earth, was as yet (for I am speaking of the *Angel,* not of the *Odes*) apt to go flat-footedly; and an untrained reader dislikes and shirks abstract thought. By its strength the author's emotion lifts the reader over these difficulties; by its clearness of conviction it provides him with eyes. It achieves, and surely in its climax transmits, the true lover's thrill. And it leaves you with an after-taste of hours spent in company both amiable and profitable, an impression which I may liken to a memory of some sunny morning-room, fresh, habitable, and decorously gay with English flowers. (pp. 130-31)

[Patmore remained convinced] that nuptial love contains the key, for men and women, of spiritual truth; that, things which are unseen being apprehended from things which are seen, the love between man and woman is the true stair by which alone we can mount to an apprehension of the love of God. Extending this belief into art and literature, he held that in nuptial love the painter and the poet must find the highest of all themes. I state this view of his not so much to contest it, as to point out some conditions imposed on it by the material and methods of art. We regard nuptial love at its best as peaceful, as normal, as a state in which two different natures with two separate wills acquiesce in equipoise. Now, no one has spoken more weightily than Patmore of the value of peace in art, of that restfulness which abides in the normal, in order, in law, and (subjectively) in obedience to law. But arts such as painting and poetry illustrate law by means of its exceptions, vindicate the normal by means of man's deflections from it, teach peace by bringing it triumphant out of conflict. They work, in short, by comparison and contrast. [Patmore says:]

> Shakespeare . . . evolves peace from the conflict of interests and passions to which the predominance and victory of a moral idea give unity. That idea is never embodied in any single conspicuous character, though it is usually allowed an unobtrusive expression in some subordinate personality, in order to afford a clue to the 'theme' of the whole harmony. Such theme-suggesting characters are, for example, the Friar in *Romeo and Juliet,* and Kent in *King Lear,* who represent and embody the law *from which all the other characters depart more or less, with proportionate disaster to themselves.*

In other words, the normal is art's standard and point of reference rather than its subject-matter. (pp. 131-32)

If this be true, then nuptial love, treated absolutely, is as poor a subject for art as, treated relatively, it is a good one. . . . I cannot help thinking that, pleasant as we find it when Felix and Honoria arrive in port after their gentle agitations, Patmore would have found it extremely difficult to build a poem on their subsequent bliss, and that with the *Victories of Love*—in which their happiness forms a point of rest—he discovered in the less complacent yoke of Frederick and Jane a far better subject, if he had only handled it well. (p. 132)

One word more about the *Angel* and *Victories of Love*. I have always found it difficult to reconcile the deep and tender homage paid to woman in these poems, and notably in the lines beginning

> Why, having won her, do I woo?

and ending—

> Because her gay and lofty brows,
>   When all is won that hope can ask,
> Reflect a light of hopeless snows
>   That bright in virgin ether bask;
> Because, though free of the outer court
>   I am, this temple keeps its shrine
> Sacred to Heaven; because, in short,
>   She's not and never can be mine,

with the opinions on the natural subjection of woman persistently held by Patmore, and expounded in his prose essays. In them he never tires of scoffing at the view of woman as man's equal, though dissimilar. She is the "weaker vessel," "the last and lowest of all spiritual creatures," made to be ruled and strictly ruled: "No right-minded woman would care a straw for her lover's adoration if she did not know that he knew that after all he was the true divinity"—with much more to the same effect. How, then, does man arrive at paying homage and reverence to that which is of so much less worth and dignity than he? Apparently by a magnificent act of condescension. (pp. 133-34)

[It] is, I confess, a disappointment to discover that the exquisite homage paid to Honoria by her poet-husband was, [according to Mr. Champneys], polite humbug. "Everybody knew what he meant in thus making a divinity of her," etc. Did everybody? I—alas!—for years understood him to be saying what he believed. (p. 135)

[It] must be owned that the *Odes* are of very unequal inspiration. Roughly, they fall into two classes, the one concerned with principles, the other with persons. And here we may bring the *Odes* and the *Prose Writings* under a common criticism. No writer of his generation had a clearer vision than Patmore for truth of principle: I had almost said a vision comparable with his. There are passages in the two little books, *Principle in Art* and *Religio Poetæ*, which every young follower of art should commit to memory and bind for a phylactery on his forehead. But they jostle with passages of the ineptest criticism; for this seer into mysteries was constitutionally incapable of applying the principles he discovered, and of bringing either fair judgment or temperate language to bear upon men and their works. . . . So with the *Odes*.—It is well to begin by separating those which take hold of the doors of Heaven from those [political odes] which exhaust themselves in constructive damnation of Mr. Gladstone. (pp. 139-40)

[In the non-political odes]—*Saint Valentine's Day, Wind and Wave, Winter, The Day after To-morrow, Tristitia, The Azalea, Departure, The Toys, If I Were Dead, Tired Memory*, and the *Psyche Odes*—we listen to a very different voice. He is the seer now, and his utterances pierce and shake as few others in our whole range of song since Wordsworth declined from his best. And because this assertion is likely to be challenged, and

certain to be misunderstood, I hasten to avow my conviction that Tennyson and Browning, Arnold, Swinburne—yes, and Meredith—are more excellent poets than Patmore. He was a learned theorist in metre, but neither a gifted singer nor an expert one. He could tell us most wisely that the language of poetry "should always seem to *feel*, though not to *suffer from*, the bonds of verse," and that metre never attains its noblest effects when it is altogether unproductive of "beautiful exorbitancies on the side of the law." But these beautiful exorbitancies were not for him: his thoughts carried an exquisite sense of measure in speech and pause, but not their own music. His pace was ever the iambic. He called the metre of the *Odes* "catalectic" which may mean anything (except perhaps, "cataleptic") or nothing. "The system," says Mr. Champneys, "cannot be explained by analysis." In point of fact, there is no system at all, unless we call it system to break up the iambic line into irregular lengths according to the lift and fall of the poet's emotion. But music is something more than perfect measure; and though Patmore, in the *Odes*, paces, like Queen Elizabeth, "high and disposedly," he does not sing. Nor has he the steady, comprehensive poetical vision of the great ones I have named. He praises apprehension at the expense of comprehension, and upon apprehension he narrowed his aim. Yet now and then, beside his penetrating flashes, Browning's experimental psychology wears but a half-serious look, as of a clever game; Tennyson's *In Memoriam* keeps, indeed, its seriousness, but as the pathetic side of its inadequacy to its theme; while even the noble philosophies of Arnold and Meredith (though we return to them) are momentarily stunted in a glimpse of more tremendous heights. (pp. 140-41)

> *Sir Arthur Quiller-Couch, "Coventry Patmore," in his* Studies in Literature, *third series, G. P. Putnam's Sons, 1930, pp. 122-42.*

EDMUND GOSSE (essay date 1905)

[*Gosse analyzes his friend's significance in the following essay, which is excerpted from the conclusion of his critical biography* Coventry Patmore.]

We see [Patmore] as the type, in recent English literature of a high order, almost the solitary type of absolute faith. He was no propagandist; he made no efforts of any conspicuous kind to communicate his belief to others. It was enough for him to enjoy with emphasis his perfect and spontaneous confidence in God. He was not touched by curiosity or doubt, and positive knowledge, of a scientific kind, was without attraction to him. (p. 208)

He lived in a contemplation of eternity, and he saw the whole of existence in relation to it. There were no softened outlines in his landscape; he perceived as he thought, but two things, the radiance of truth, crystalline and eternal, and the putrescence of wilful and hopeless error.

The "difficulties" which assail the modern man did not approach him. His only trouble was lest the flame of love should burn low upon his personal altar. Excessive in all things, he lived in an atmosphere of spiritual glory, haughty, narrow, violent in the extravagance of his humility.

He was all prejudice, in one sense, and yet he had, in another, no prejudices. He embraced the unexpected in his scheme of Catholic symbolism, and in life he was profoundly indifferent to criticism of his lines of thought. Strictly orthodox as it was his pride to be, those who listened to his conversation were

Coventry Patmore; from an 1894 portrait by John Singer Sargent.

smaller, and of a radiance less extended. Star differeth from star in magnitude, but a light is not necessarily extinguished because it is of the second species. Patmore will be preserved by his intensity, and by the sincerity and economy with which he employed his art. Like Gray, like Alfred de Vigny, like Leopardi . . . , he knew the confines of his strength; he strove not to be copious but to be uniformly exquisite. He did not quite reach his aim, but even Catullus has scarcely done that. The peculiar beauty of his verse is not to every one's taste; if it were he would have that universal attractiveness which we have admitted that he lacks. But he wrote, with extreme and conscientious care, and with impassioned joy, a comparatively small body of poetry, the least successful portions of which are yet curiously his own, while the most successful fill those who are attuned to them with an exquisite and durable pleasure.

It is much to his advantage that in a lax age, and while moving dangerously near to the borders of sentimentality, he preserved with the utmost constancy his lofty ideal of poetry. His natural arrogance, his solitariness, helped him to battle against what was humdrum and easy-going in the age he lived in. He was not in any sense a leader of men. He lacked every quality which fills others with a blind desire to follow, under a banner, any-whither, for the mere enthusiasm of fighting. It was difficult even to be Patmore's active comrade, so ruthless was he in checking every common movement, so determined was he to be in a protesting minority of one. Yet his isolation, looked at from another point of view, was a surprising evidence of his strength, and it is not difficult to believe that pilgrim after pilgrim, angry at the excesses of the age that is coming, and wild to correct its errors, will soothe the beating of his heart by an hour of meditation over the lonely grave where Coventry Patmore lies, wrapped for ever in the rough habit of the stern Franciscan order. (pp. 211-13)

> *Edmund Gosse, in his* Coventry Patmore, *Charles Scribner's Sons, 1905, 213 p.*

PERCY LUBBOCK   (essay date 1908)

[*Lubbock was an early-twentieth-century editor, critic, historian, and biographer. His most renowned critical work,* The Craft of Fiction, *is a detailed analysis of the works of Leo Tolstoy, Gustave Flaubert, and Henry James. Lubbock explicates the philosophy and poetics of love informing* The Angel in the House, The Victories of Love, *and* The Unknown Eros *in the following essay.*]

The austere figure of Coventry Patmore stands strangely apart from the other poets of the Victorian age. He owed next to nothing to his predecessors, and he has scarcely at all affected the poetry of later days. He stalked in his own narrow field, casting hardly more than an indifferent glance at the work of his contemporaries. His poetry has an individuality so deep and so curious that its appeal must always be as dumb to most people as it is intense to a few. He raised a new flower, unique in its bold shape and colour, but he contrived to spread round it a desert which effectually deters the casual adventurer. And yet this grim recluse, who appears to stamp so summarily upon any conciliatory overture from the world at large, stands almost alone in literature for the interpretation and the defence of one of the most normal and least recondite elements of human life.

From the beginning of art the deepest-seated of man's passions has been celebrated in every aspect save one, that one being precisely the aspect which the world agrees, on the whole, to consider the most estimable and the most conducive to its welfare. If it is strange that marriage, for all its admitted claim

often startled by luminous appreciation of things which seemed to lie far removed from the simplicity of faith. This was because his imagination was so candid that each image and object made an entirely new impression upon it, unaffected by conventional tradition. His hatreds were impulsive and instinctive; he encouraged them because he looked upon them as an expression of the force with which he repelled evil. If he disliked anything it must be because it was evil, and he indulged his hatred as being the very crown of his love of good. He had no doubt about the path that he was destined to traverse, nor about his lovely and sufficient Guide along it. He stood up against the world, secure in his faith in God, and in poetry which is the handmaiden of God. (pp. 209-10)

[Patmore] does not stand quite in the central stream of the age in which he lived. He will not be inevitably thought of as representative of the intellect of his time, like Tennyson, nor as a spreading human force, like Browning, nor as a universal stimulant and irritant, like Matthew Arnold. His contributions to the national mind will be far less general than theirs, mainly because of his curious limitations of sympathy. . . . Patmore was narrow, and he was hard; there is that in his genius which refuses to dissolve.

Yet there is no reason why his fame should be less durable than that of Tennyson and Arnold, although it must always be upon the world's gratitude, should have been found thus destitute of lyrical quality, it is infinitely more of a paradox that the one voice raised in real fervour on its behalf should give the effect of keeping the majority scornfully at bay. That a passion which is strictly 'honourable' in its intentions, whose domesticity is not a mere fortunate accident, but its very essence, is possible material for poetry of the most rapturous kind, Patmore, at any rate, has abundantly proved. (pp. 356-57)

[To Patmore,] the bond itself is the very crown and glory of the whole theme. It is not a mere compromise struck between the world on one side, and the strength of man's passions on the other, with a view to securing some measure of peace and order, but an original and eternal disposition of nature. . . . [His] ardour has so little in common with the general respect given to honourable love that, in spite of the everyday nature of his theme, his poetry is profoundly esoteric. He is the one writer who has found his chief source of inspiration in this most familiar of life's phases; and yet the final result is that his appeal is limited, his air forbidding, his doctrine remote and inaccessible. (p. 357)

Patmore's earlier poetry, though, like everything else that he said or did, in reality quite unrelated to his period and environment, accidentally corresponded with a taste of the time. **'The Angel in the House,'** by the fact that it was anecdotic and domestic, won a large audience in the fifties—an audience which those very qualities have now lost for it. The parochial felicities, the tea and talk, the ingenuous croquet of the mid-century, were all akin in sentiment to the narrative parts of the poem. The romance of Felix and Honoria was so pre-eminently 'nice' in tone that it won its way to many thousands of blameless hearts, who could understand the innocence of the story, if not the far more characteristic interludes in which Patmore expounds his theory of love. . . . [It] might be expected that the **'Angel'** would by this time have at any rate the charm of quaintness. But this, curiously enough, in spite of the courageous realism of the picture, it somehow contrives to miss. Perhaps the reason is that Patmore himself was really very far from being a mild and amiable young man, handing bread-and-butter at tea on the lawn, such as he portrays. He had a theory of what true love should be; and tea on the lawn was the appropriate setting for it. But he was not nearly enough the child of his age to love the setting for its own sake; indeed, he would have been exceedingly out of place in it himself. He describes the orderly life of Sarum Close from the outside; and his description is too deeply tinged with his own peculiarities—his obscurity, his strained use of words, his mixture of verbosity and extreme compression—to be generally typical. (pp. 358-59)

The warm love and romance which underlay that idyllic life Patmore knew to its remotest depth; but its manners, its amusements, its very language were entirely alien to him. He could not prevent an occasional infusion of his own more pungent liquors into that milky cup. The result is satisfactory from neither point of view; the narrative is too flat, or it is too rugged. The characterisation is conventional, the plot a mere shadow. Patmore's outlook had no breadth; nor had he, save in one connexion, to be indicated presently, any power of placing himself outside his own point of view. His gift was purely lyrical and individual.

But, though Patmore perhaps would not have allowed as much, the essential part of the **'Angel in the House'** is not the story at all, but the 'preludes which are prefixed to the cantos of the poem, two or three to each, in which he develops his own proper theme through endless dainty and intricate modulations.

They form together what is in one way the most singular series of love-lyrics in the language. No one but Patmore, it may safely be said, has written upon the subject with such depth of mystical conviction, and yet with such airy and unclouded gaiety. The lightness and brightness of the tone, far from being a sign of unreality, is the expression of a peculiar point of view, held with impassioned earnestness by an exceptionally forcible nature. 'The cruel madness of love,' which the hero of [Tennyson's poem] 'Maud' prayed to escape, would have been to Patmore a totally meaningless phrase. The course of romance might run smoothly or roughly; but, rough or smooth, it is a blissful vision, an 'aura of delight,' which no uncertainty or even jealousy can wholly mar. . . . The pangs and fevers are indeed described; but their bitterness is swallowed up in the pervading sunshine which, for accepted and rejected alike, clings to the thought and the presence of woman. . . . The beloved object moves in a rosy mist of virtues, fresh with purity mild with kindness, sparkling with modest joy. But we see her no more clearly than that; nor, it seems, does the poet. The effect upon the reader is to make the whole emotion appear to be generalised—not concentrated upon one glowing point, but a kind of universal admiration, the less interesting for being so all-embracing. Patmore, the self-confident individualist, the arrogant, the masterful, seems here to be not quite individualist enough. And yet it is impossible to say that the emotion is indefinite or languid. On the contrary, it revels in minute discriminations, and is never betrayed by its ingenuity into falling below the pitch of rapturous ecstasy. (pp. 359-61)

The emotion of these poems differs from the hungry, jealous fever of other natures for the reason that this poet, so complex in his simplicity, can see through the eyes of the woman even more clearly than through his own; or, if not quite that, at least that the whole and absolute beauty of the drama appeals to him even more strongly than its special relation to himself. The exquisite and joyful completeness of a perfect union—the idea of this exists for him side by side with the thought of the individual happiness, and it is even the more vivid of the two. Moreover, the woman's relation to this central miracle is fully as absorbing as the man's. Indeed her more ethereal, more instinctive, more impressionable nature, as he regards it, makes her share by so much the subtler and the finer. In such poems as **'The Chace'** and **'The Changed Allegiance,'** the progress of a woman's love is traced with a daring firmness of touch which, directed by a sensibility one hair's breadth less perfect, might well have overshot the limit of fatuity. It is perilous, to say the least of it, for a man to be so acutely alive to the blessing of a fortunate romance from the woman's point of view. But Patmore had, in this one and only instance, the power of detachment. The whole picture, exceeding and including the two individual aspects, stood out clearly before him; so clearly that its steady light became in later years the one all-explaining symbol. In the **'Angel in the House'** its full meaning was not yet so exhaustively explored, nor the picture so suffused with mysticism. The idea is there, but it is still in its first simplicity—the idea of love, not as a leaping flame, obscuring the rest of life for a moment and then dying down as life resumes its course, but as a steady and pervading glow, in whose warmth alone the world has meaning and coherence. (p. 362)

When all is said, the fact remains that the **'Angel in the House,'** in spite of the 'preludes,' is by no means widely known or read. (p. 363)

Most of all, it is the sentiment which fails somehow to appeal. If, at first sight, it has the appearance of being a rather sugary exaggeration of the homeliest kind of emotion, it proves on a closer study to be an intricate development of an emotion both intangible and unfamiliar. It is deeply felt, and yet is not simply personal. It is preoccupied with the thought, not indeed of its own beauty—for that would effectually destroy its value—but of the whole treasure of poetry which permeates the world when the spring sun shines and the sluggish blood begins to freshen. Behind the warm, direct impulse, which for most people usurps the whole field, there lurks a sense of satisfaction, of inviolable content, which refuses to be caught into the narrowing channel of one single fulfilment. That is enough, as jealous human beings are constituted, to give the emotion—and the more so that it is obviously so real—a sense of remoteness. And yet there are a few moments when it approaches very close, when something so intimately true as to be inexpressible appears to slip into words without an effort. Here is one:

> Not in the crises of events,
>   Of compass'd hopes, or fears fulfill'd,
> Or acts of gravest consequence,
>   Are life's delight and depth reveal'd.
> The day of days was not the day;
>   That went before, or was postponed;
> The night Death took our lamp away
>   Was not the night on which we groan'd.
> I drew my bride, beneath the moon,
>   Across my threshold; happy hour!
> But, ah, the walk that afternoon
>   We saw the water-flags in flower!

But this absolutely simple note is rare. The real heart of the poem keeps aloof, uttering a deceptively familiar strain, which yet, as we listen closely, becomes unexpected and evasive. Popular it can hardly be, but, in virtue of its utter originality and of a kind of fresh, unearthly brightness, it cannot surely be forgotten.

'The Victories of Love,' a second series of narrative poems, designed as a continuation of the first, has all the weaknesses of the 'Angel,' and few of its beauties. The 'preludes' disappear; and the story is told by means of letters exchanged between the various characters, written in octosyllabic couplets. Patmore was far too destitute of the power of characterisation to be successful in such a form. He would not himself allow that his gift was not for sustained flights of song, but for short and lyrical outbursts. He was always planning to reveal his constantly expanding theory of love in long, connected poems; but, as a matter of fact, the set of his genius was exactly in the opposite direction. He was entirely without the power of writing steadily and regularly. He waited on the impulse, and was content to wait for years, if necessary, before it came. (pp. 363-65)

[Patmore's tendency towards mysticism eventually] carried him into the Roman Catholic Church; but he did not leave behind him that preoccupation with the love of woman and man with which he had started. (pp. 368-69)

He found in the passionate, overwrought pages of [St. John of the Cross] a vision of the ecstatic union of the human soul with the Divine Presence, which offered such daring analogies with earthly passion as must inevitably seem unintelligible, not to say repellent, to the average human being. To Patmore, however, although his own mysticism was so securely grounded upon natural emotion, the lack of any such foundation in the writers to whom he was now turning for guidance did not vitiate

the doctrine which they taught. It must indeed seem a further tribute to the amazing purity of his own ideal that he could feel these disembodied passions to be entirely ethereal in origin. For the ordinary mortal, it must make all the difference whether or no they spring from a robust and natural soil, such as that on which Patmore's feet were firmly planted. The great beauty of such poems as 'Sponsa Dei,' and the 'Child's Purchase' might even have a certain taint if they had not been preceded by the poems of his youth.

However that may be, there is certainly no sickliness in the stately irregular odes in which Patmore so fearlessly traces the analogy between human and divine love, or rather, he would have said, their identity. He seems in them to have mastered the secret of uniting the most honied sweetness with extreme severity of line. The metre he adopted—iambic lines of unequal length, with rhymes recurring at irregular intervals—is not in itself a very good one, for it depends for its whole effect upon the taste and ear of the writer; unskilfully used, it becomes ragged and shapeless at once. But in the right hands it is of course capable of much finer effects than the too facile numbers he had used before. Patmore handled it with great skill, and made fine use of the endless modulations which become possible through such varied choice in the disposition of rhymes and length of line. In his earlier work his peculiar and highly mannered diction, even though it was there less marked, had often seemed too heavily weighted for his material; but in the longer odes, with their more dignified metre and more abstruse subjects, it has a singular fitness—the stiff-robed angular beauty of some lean effigy of medieval bishop or saint. With all this, and somehow without sacrificing the effect of severity, Patmore contrived to unite a strain of sweetness as voluptuous as that of Crashaw. (pp. 369-70)

The essential quality of these poems, the quality which singles them out among poetry, and gives them their curiously unmistakable ring, is perhaps this union of severity—a certain noble gauntness—with a sensuousness that lavishes itself in such lovely and minute detail. Both in beauty of this kind and in beauty of pathos Patmore seemed able to pass in all security far beyond the limit at which, in more languid hands, these things become over-ripe and sentimental. Not even so, however—to leave the simpler poems for the present out of account—is it easy to explain the profound impression which the 'Unknown Eros' makes upon many to whom the transcendentalism by which it is inspired is entirely alien. In the most characteristic of the poems, such as the three 'Psyche Odes' or 'The Contract,' Patmore threads his way through a maze of delicately adjusted discriminations to his final vision of perfect love—that complete union in which strong and weak meet and are satisfied, the weak subject to the strong and yet exerting over the strong an even more potent mastery, both finding their fulfilment in a mutual bond, not imposed on them from without, not a concession to weakness, but joyfully and freely embraced as something without which the very flower of love would be wanting. Moreover, through every line runs the current of symbolism; and, to read the poems aright, we must in every word see through and past the actual picture under our eyes, to the vision of that other marriage of the soul, which few have drawn as this poet, out of the depths of his fearless strength and faith, dares to draw it.

It is small matter for wonder if most of those who read cannot hope to follow him thus far. Perhaps it is, after all, no more strange that, even for those to whom the whole train of thought seems most unreal, the poems should yet remain revelations of deep and magic beauty. Poetry to the making of which has gone such pure fire and austere art can scarcely end, wherever its way lies, in coldness of appeal. Those who have thus felt the beauty of Patmore's great odes will find it difficult to speak of them without the appearance of exaggeration. No doubt it is impossible to claim for them the highest place; reasons for this—their lack of clarity, their frequent harshness, their violent transitions—are easy enough to single out. But they have a place apart, a peculiar niche, where they stand removed from the possibility of comparison with other poetry, greater or less. In writing of Patmore there is no danger of indulging in that favourite game of critics . . . which consists in sorting and arranging poets in order of merit, like schoolboys in a class. Patmore's genius, whatever its scope may be, is far too original and solitary to be treated like this. Mr Gosse predicts for it an increasing influence upon future generations [see excerpt above, 1905]; and it is indeed probable that, as time goes on, his lonely individuality, so far removed from all the aspirations of his own age, will stand out more and more clearly. Even now its appeal, though naturally limited, probably penetrates deeper than that of many more dominating names. (pp. 371-72)

Percy Lubbock, "Coventry Patmore," in The Quarterly Review, *Vol. CCVIII, No. CDXV, April, 1908, pp. 356-76.*

DESMOND MacCARTHY (essay date 1932)

[*MacCarthy, who served for many years on the staff of the* New Statesman *and edited the journal* Life and Letters, *is considered one of the foremost English literary and dramatic critics of the twentieth century. He extols Patmore's virtuosity as a religious poet in the following essay, describing him as "the greatest religious poet in English literature since the seventeenth century."*]

[Coventry Patmore] is the greatest religious poet in English literature since the seventeenth century, not excepting Christina Rossetti, and perhaps greater than Crashaw, with whom, of all other English religious poets, he has most affinity. (p. 75)

[It is] shocking to the Protestant religious sense that anyone should assert that the goal of life is not to love God, but to be "in love with" Him, and that such passion is reciprocal. Yet to Patmore that was a fact. It was the key to the mysteries of his religion; it was the burning core of the Universe, and in the light which it shed he interpreted the love between man and woman; thus he became both a mystical-religious and a mystical-amorous poet.

Eternal peace and tempests of delight tax language to the uttermost, and Patmore knew that "views of the unveiled heavens" have seldom inspired poets; he noticed also that "the most ardent love is rather epigrammatic than lyric," and that the saints abound in epigrams. But the supreme merit of his most splendid Odes is that he did blend in them lyric impetus and passionate concentration. The Odes are filled with a "great rejoicing wind," yet every phrase in them clings to a thought. The verse-form he chose, with its uneven lines and dramatic pauses, had no independent form apart from emotion. It was such a means of direct communication as some modern poets are now seeking. How finely he used his freedom cannot be well shown except by quoting a whole poem; so perfectly and invariably do alternate pause and rush lead to a final climax or

diminuendo [a gradual reduction of force or loudness]. But perhaps the following fragment may suggest his skill:

> She, as a little breeze
> Following still Night,
> Ripples the spirit's cold, deep seas
> Into delight;
> But, in a while
> The immeasurable smile
> Is broke by fresher airs to flashes blent
> With darkling discontent:
> And all the subtle zephyr hurries gay,
> And all the heaving ocean heaves one way,
> T'ward the void sky-line and an unguess'd weal.
> Until the vanward billows feel
> The agitating shallows, and divine the goal,
> And to foam roll.
> And spread and stray
> And traverse widly, like delighted hands,
> The fair and fleckless sands;
> And so the whole
> Unfathomable and immense
> Triumphing tide comes at the last to reach
> And burst in wind-kiss'd splendours on the deaf'ning
>   beach,
> Where forms of children in first innocence
> Laugh and fling pebbles on the rainbow'd crest
> Of its untired unrest.

The loveliness of the metrical change at:

> She, as a little breeze
> Following still night

can only be fully felt when the opening of the poem is also before one; but no ear is likely to miss the skill with which, from that point onwards, these irregular lines are conducted to their climax, nor I hope, that sense of *effort,* so subtly audible in the slow, difficult lines which precede and prepare the relief of the explosion:

> And so the whole
> Unfathomable and immense
> *Triumphing tide comes at the last to reach,*
> And burst in wind-kiss'd splendours on the deaf'ning
>   beach.

(pp. 75-7)

It matters little in expounding Coventry Patmore's poetry whether we approach him as a love-poet or a religious poet. He was a Catholic. He accepted the dogmas of his religion, but he interpreted some of them in a mystical sense based on intense personal experience. (p. 77)

[From] what Coventry Patmore wrote, both in prose and verse, there is no doubt what those spiritual experiences were. The like of them is to be found in the records of not a few saints, in the Spanish Catholic mystics, and in the particular (I am told) in the works of St. John of the Cross. Their nature can be suggested by saying that the ultimate goal of spiritual life, the union of God and the Soul, differs only in intensity and completeness, not in kind, from the most perfect imaginable union between lovers. It follows that the vocabulary of human passion is the one approximation to a language fit to express the extreme experience. To speak of it in other terms is, to these mystics, a faithless base timidity; and yet unless their minds are, when they speak of it, white as a furnace in a thorough blast, their most precious things may "become a post the passing dog defiles''. Because Coventry Patmore in *The Unknown Eros* and other odes has attained to that incandescent austerity, he must be ranked in his proper place, not, please, among the interesting but lesser of the Victorians, but among the religious poets of the world. Of course, there are other kinds of religious poetry in which poets have reached an equal or greater excellence, but in his own tongue and on his own spiritual ground who is his match? (pp. 77-8)

> *Desmond MacCarthy, ''Coventry Patmore,'' in his* Criticism, *Putnam, 1932, pp. 74-80.*

HERBERT READ   (essay date 1932)

[*Read was a prolific English poet, novelist, and critic whose commentary on poetry is often informed by his definition of two basic poetic forms, the organic and the abstract. According to Read, organic form is that in which imagination dictates the form of a poem and fuses structure and content, as in free verse; abstract forms are those in which structure follows a fixed pattern, as in sonnets. Read's preference for organic form is evident in the following essay on Patmore, in which he distinguishes between the ''apt but uninspired expression'' of* The Angel in the House *and the ''daring . . . impetuosity'' of his unconventional, irregularly-metered odes.*]

Defect of presentation explains why *The Angel* is not read today; and I can imagine no posterity which will reverse our present inclination in this matter. This poem has become and will remain a literary curiosity, not justified by any remarkable beauties even of texture or expression. For it has to be admitted that Patmore, at this stage of his inspiration, was no inevitable poet. He chose a simple metre for his simple subject—iambic octosyllabic—and laboured hard to make it smooth. But as Tennyson said, some of his lines seemed ''hammered up out of old nails'' [see excerpt above, 1854], and though such lines were pointed out to him, he was often incapable of seeing anything wrong with them, and there are plenty left in the final version. That would not matter so much if there were corresponding jewels of highest light, to outshine these defects; but actually the texture is sustained at an even level of apt but uninspired expression. It is wit-writing of an extremely competent and felicitous kind, but it is not, and perhaps never pretended to be, lyrical poetry of any emotional intensity. (pp. 358-59)

Patmore's poetic technique received an immense impetus from his invention of what was virtually a new verse-form—the ''Ode.''. . . (p. 360)

[The Patmorean Ode is] an iambic measure (like that of *The Angel in the House),* which, however, breaks away from the regularity of the octosyllabic couplet or quatrain to indulge in what Patmore himself called ''the fine irregular rock of the free tetrameter.'' The verse in these Odes moves ''in long, undulating strains'' which are modulated by pauses and irregularly occurring rhymes, the rhymed words determining the length of the lines which vary arbitrarily from two to ten or even twelve syllables. It is therefore a metre of extraordinary freedom and impetuous force—which only needed the freedom of stress introduced by Patmore's friend Hopkins to give us all the constituents of modern free verse. (pp. 361-62)

One cannot help regretting the destruction of . . . [Patmore's *Sponsa Dei*], but actually I doubt if much of the substance of Patmore's doctrine has been lost. It is all implicit in the Odes, and in that book of maxims which is one of the greatest of Patmore's achievements, *The Rod, the Root, and the Flower*

(an English work which it is not wholly ridiculous to compare with Pascal's *Pensées*). The . . . Ode, *To the Body,* may be given as an example of the daring, and the impetuosity (there are only three sentences in it), and the final intensity of Patmore's poetry. . . . (p. 366)

Even at its best Patmore's poetry is spoilt by ugly inversions and elisions, inexcusable considering the freedom of the form. But in these last Odes we are hardly aware of such faults: the thought is irredeemably fused in the expression, and the result is true poetry of the rarest and perhaps the highest kind—metaphysical poetry such as has been written by Lucretius, Dante, Donne, Crashaw, and Wordsworth. Those who limit poetry by a narrow lyrical conception of the art will find little to charm their indolence in Patmore. But those who are braced to the highest levels of the art, where the flowers are few and fugitive, where Nature and Humanity, to adapt a saying of Patmore's, are beautified and developed instead of being withered up by religious thought, will find in the best of the Odes a fund of inspired poetry for which they would willingly sacrifice the whole baggage of the Victorian legacy in general. And they will find this poetry amply supported by Patmore's prose, to which justice is not often done—prose which has ''the virile qualities of simplicity, continuity, and positiveness.'' (p. 368)

> *Herbert Read, ''Coventry Patmore,'' in* The Great Victorians, *edited by H. J. Massingham and Hugh Massingham, Doubleday, Doran & Company, Inc., 1932, pp. 355-69.*

FREDERICK PAGE   (essay date 1933)

[*Page was a respected Patmore commentator who defended the poet's fame in* Patmore: A Study in Poetry. *He attempts to justify Patmore's controversial use of a conventional contemporary social setting in* The Angel in the House *in the excerpt below.*]

Patmore was domestically happy, he was concerned politically with his own time; it was domestic and political happiness, with religious sanctions, that he could offer to others: he would therefore show what domestic happiness is, realistically, and he would accept the costumes and furniture of his own time and place. (p. 88)

[It is] the costumes and furniture of the poets' own times and places that the conventional decorums of narrative poetry never have accepted, not even in Chaucer. . . . Nor is poetry without reason in this. All poetry is concerned with the soul, and refuses to stress costume and furniture. In lyric poetry there is nothing but the soul. . . . Narrative poetry insists upon the costume and furniture that reveal the soul: its courage, in sword and plume; its magnificence, in pomp; its pathos, in those modes which Revolution is to destroy. But contemporary costume and furniture are the prose of our daily life, and so far unfriendly to the soul. Therefore lyric, drama, monologue, satire, may be modern, but a narrative poem may not—till there has been shown that it may be.

Emerson had looked in vain for the poet he described. 'We do not, with sufficient plainness, or sufficient profoundness, address ourselves to life, nor dare we chant our own times and social circumstance. If we filled the day with bravery, we should not shrink from celebrating it.' Emily and Coventry Patmore filled the day with bravery, and he addressed himself to celebrating their life [in *The Angel in the House*], with sufficient plainness in the idyls, with sufficient profundity in the preludes. (pp. 91-2)

[Patmore elucidates his point of view in the following passage:]

The human ideal—that is to say the heroic, which is directly or indirectly the subject of all poetry—is continually advancing. To the prowess of Achilles a succeeding age adds the chastity of Sir Galahad; and a still later age demands that its hero shall be able, not only to overcome his enemies and keep himself "pure in work and will", but also to entertain happy, honourable, and beneficial relations of various kinds with the world in which he lives, and to become, in fact, the "modern gentleman". Similarly with womanhood; to the bright cheeks of [the Homeric heroine] Briseis is added, in course of time, the bright soul of [Dante's] Beatrice; and the woman receives a further perfection from the thorough social culture of the "modern lady". The hero and the heroine of the nineteenth century are waiting to have their portraits taken; but it seems the painter who is worthy of the work is not forthcoming. Our Goethes, Heines, and Tennysons, indeed, appear to discern the truth, but they have not had confidence and courage to face it fully and act upon it. They have painted in their best productions strictly modern life, but not modern life with its most poetical characteristic,—namely, a capacity of elaborate social beauty. Hermann, Alexis, Eustace, the heroes of "Locksley Hall", and the "Gardener's Daughter", Dora, Dorothea, Amy, and the rest, are modern young men and women, indeed; but they are either so slightly sketched, or in so humble a scale of life, that they in no way deserve to be regarded as even approximate delineations of the modern heroic, as it actually exists in England and elsewhere.

'Or in so humble a scale of life': the implication is anti-democratic, it is not anti-plebeian.

We are not allowed to doubt but that the poor and suffering most often are what "the rich should be, right-minded"; and that they therefore, more frequently than the rich, have the foundation of right manners. Nevertheless, spiritual loveliness when found in conspicuous places, and "clothed upon" with extraordinary personal and intellectual gifts, while it is more impressive than humble worth in the sight even of the best, as being exposed to subtler temptations to deny itself, is made visible to many who would refuse to acknowledge the same lustre were it shining in a dark place, and is more imposing to all, not only because all are naturally delighted with the extraordinary occurrence of harmony between the apparently hostile realms of grace and nature, of fortune and desert, but also because such harmony explains, exalts, and really completes its seemingly-opposed elements, and grace, expressing itself with thorough culture and knowledge of the world, becomes natural, and nature, instructed in its true perfection, gracious.

(pp. 93-4)

[That] is Patmore's justification of the social setting of *The Angel in the House*.

Is *The Angel in the House* an artistic presentation of a certain mode of life, or does it fall below the dignity of poetry? They are almost but not quite two distinct questions, if art is one thing and poetry another. The objections to the poem made on behalf of the dignity of poetry are two: that which rejects the poem totally, and that which objects to it in detail.

The first objection says that happy domestic life in materially ideal circumstances is not a fit subject for poetry; and there is this much justification, that it lacks the excitement both of tragedy and comedy. But it was to remedy this, and to be true to life, that Patmore balanced the peace and plenty of Felix and Honoria with the vicissitudes and narrow means of Frederick and Jane. He has secured the atmosphere of comedy without a comic story; and he has related his little story to the whole of life, including its unjoyful possibilities, in the preludes. But so far as the total rejection of *The Angel* is motived by an ungrateful or dishonest refusal on the part of its critics to admit that happiness is or was offered to them in their daily circumstances, Patmore would reject his judges with at least as much scorn as they reject him; and so also if they despise or blaspheme domestic happiness, and, in envy or perversity, hate its materially ideal circumstances.

The second objection is that *The Angel in the House* falls below the dignity of poetry incidentally. If it does, it is now from a defective sense of the ridiculous, and anon from an excessive sense of humour, and in one and the other from the possession of a sense of the humane—that deeper and higher humour which, in George Saintsbury's phrase, 'takes all life as its province—which is the humour of humanity'.

But that is just the trouble. Nothing is more uncertain than the sense of humour. Offer the public . . . [Alexander Pope's] *Rape of the Lock* in the same pair of covers as [his] *Essay on Man and Woman*, and they are all at sea. A man will write to the editor of *Fraser's Magazine* to cancel his subscription if [Thomas Carlyle's] *Sartor Resartus* be not discontinued.

Richard Garnett said that Patmore had no perception of the sublime in other men's writings, or of the ridiculous in his own. It was not quite that: he distrusted the sublime, thinking it unhuman, and he liked what was human even when it was ridiculous.

> Shall I, the gnat that dances in Thy ray,
> Dare to be reverent?

his Psyche ask [in *The Unknown Eros*]. And how much less dare to be sublime! And as for the ridiculous:

> Know'st thou not, Girl, thine Eros loves to laugh?
> And shall a God do anything by half?
> He foreknew and predestinated all
> The Great must pay for kissing things so small,
> And ever loves his little Maid the more
> The more she makes him laugh.

Patmore's practice then was quite conscious:

> from his exaltation still
> Into his ocean of good-will
> He curiously casts the lead
> To find strange depths of lowlihead.

It will still be objected that he lapsed from the dignity of poetry. The satirists shall be heard, but not without Mr. Chesterton's retort: 'It is the supreme proof of the man's being prosaic that he always insists upon poetry being poetical.'

> The ladies rose; I held the door,

there's a line of poetry for you! 'The shop-girl fitted on the sandshoes': there's epic incident! To which one might reply: 'Go, bid thy mistress when my drink is ready, She strike upon the bell.' And it ought to be as little a matter for complaint that the 'business' in *The Angel in the House* is versified, as that the stage-directions in *Macbeth* are not. But let Patmore continue to sink through another quatrain (it is from the description of a honeymoon journey):

> A florin to the willing Guard
>   Secured, for half the way,
> (He lock'd us in, ah, lucky starr'd,)
>   A curtain'd, front coupé.

And now let the critic magnanimously concede what he can. 'When Patmore is not occupied with the railway guard and the shop-assistant, and when he discards pure narrative for philosophical reflection, he is a poet of the first and indisputable rank.' Very well:

> I sighed, as her retreating grace
>   Assured me that she always wore
> A heart as happy as her face,—

this is reflection, as philosophical as one can expect from a yet-unaccepted lover, and is, surely, indisputably, poetry.

> How light the touches are that kiss
>   The music from the chords of life!—

this is a philosophical reflection. But reflections must reflect something, and the first reflects the departure of Honoria and her sisters:

> The ladies rose. I held the door,

and Felix is left alone with the Dean, whom he is going to ask for his daughter's hand. And what could the second reflect but one of the 'touches' it speaks of?

> I, while the shop-girl fitted on
>   The sandshoes, look'd where, down the bay,
> The sea glow'd with a shrouded sun.
>   'I'm ready, Felix; will you pay?'
> That was my first expense for this
>   Sweet stranger, now my three days' Wife:
> How light the touches are that kiss
>   The music from the chords of life!

That the incident was historically true of Coventry and Emily Patmore, and was not invented for Felix and Honoria Churchill, is a proof of Patmore's philosophical reflectiveness. And for the rest, the reader . . . will feel that he is much more occupied, in obedience to one of his predilections, with the sea and the sun than with the shop-girl, and critic as well as reader will accept the poetry of

> Sweet Stranger, now my three days' Wife.

And the railway guard? The critic is letting Patmore off too lightly, he should have cited Briggs,

> Factotum, Footman, Butler, Groom,
>   Who press'd the cyder, fed the pigs,
> Preserv'd the rabbits, drove the brougham,
>   And help'd at need to mow the lawns,
> And sweep the paths and thatch the hay.

Let me put in evidence another quatrain, from that same honeymoon journey, and then consider in one group these three further examples of the art of sinking.

> I loved that girl, so gaunt and tall,
>   Who whisper'd loud, 'Sweet Thing!'
> Scanning your figure, slight yet all
>   Round as your own gold ring.

Obviously what is common to the three passages is the mutual goodwill of the people concerned. Patmore was indeed occupied with the railway guard—for the space of one line; and for that space he puts by his anticipation of the *solitude à deux*, to recognize 'the friend of the bridegroom, which standeth and heareth him, rejoicing greatly because of the bridegroom's voice', and to acknowledge his congratulation. And the bride too must have her bridesmaids: the virgins that are *not* her fellows shall bear her company. 'I loved that girl' and all the more that her celestial unselfishness was set off by her ungainliness. And Briggs doubtless stands for this goodwill too, though he is here for another purpose. It is part of the poetry of marriage (we have read it in Patmore's notebook . . .) that it shall be conditioned by small or great economies: the accents or the syllables in its lines must be counted; and it is the poetry of marriage that it is part of universal goodwill. Briggs's multiplication of duties was an economy, and he must have been at least as 'willing' as the guard: the tone of the poems secures our suspension of any belief in the sullenness of Briggs or mercenariness in the guard. The three passages illustrate Patmore's 'gratitude': expressed in bounty, in love, in laughter. And they illustrate what I will for once call, colloquially, his democracy, the only egalitarianism compatible with universal goodwill, because it is goodwill. Felix claimed that he and Frank

> Were perfect in the pleasant half
>   Of universal charity.

I claim this for Patmore, and I repeat that he did nothing by halves. (pp. 94-9)

There is another instinctive opposition to *The Angel in the House* to be taken note of, and I am fortunate in being able to state it, and its corrective, in the words of Mr. T. S. Eliot. He is speaking of a prejudice which for long kept him from enjoying the *Purgatorio* [of Dante] and the *Paradiso* as he enjoyed the *Inferno*:

> the prejudice that poetry not only must be found only *through* suffering but can find its material only *in* suffering. Everything else was cheerfulness, optimism, and hopefulness, and these words stood for a good deal of what one hated in the nineteenth century. It took me many years to learn that the states of improvement and beatitude are still further from what the modern world can conceive as cheerfulness, than are his states of damnation.

> (pp. 101-02)

Frederick Page, in his Patmore: A Study in Poetry, *Oxford University Press, London, 1933, 184 p.*

CLAUDE COLLEER ABBOTT   (essay date 1938)

[*Abbott suggests that Patmore's mysticism, particularly as it is expressed in the "Psyche Odes," is tainted by chauvinistic sensuality. His commentary was first published in his introduction* to the 1938 edition of Further Letters of Gerard Manley Hopkins, Including His Correspondence with Coventry Patmore.]

In order [for one] to appreciate his work [Coventry Patmore] must be granted his version of Milton's lines,

> For contemplation hee and valour formd,
> For softness shee and sweet attractive Grace,
> Hee for God only, shee for God in him,

a version in which the place of woman is that of an inferior being whose purpose is to delight her lord and master. This attitude is even more stressed in the **"Psyche Odes"** than in *The Angel in the House.* They are not, in essence, divine poems, but, first of all, amorous poems with Patmore as the dominant lover. Psyche speaks thus to the Pythoness about her god, Eros.

> Because he loves so marvellously me,
> And I with all he loves in love must be,
> How to except myself I do not see.
> Yea, now that other vanities are vain,
> I'm vain, since him it likes, of being withal
> Weak, foolish, small!

To make this concession to Patmore's convention, despite the reasoned pleas of those who find him to be an original and great poet, is not easy. There is a smallness about his conception of sanctified love that runs through all his work in verse and prose, profound and exquisite though he often is. To call him a mystic is, surely, to misuse the term. Mystics never want the best of both worlds. Here, for me, is the flaw in Patmore. That, possibly, is why his best poems are those which are most written out of his own suffering and transcend his thesis, brilliantly rounded though it be. (pp. xxix-xxx)

> *Claude Colleer Abbott, in an introduction to* Further Letters of Gerard Manley Hopkins, Including His Correspondence with Coventry Patmore, *edited by Claude Colleer Abbott, revised edition, Oxford University Press, 1956, pp. xxi-xl.*

J. C. REID (essay date 1957)

[*In his study* The Mind and Art of Coventry Patmore, *excerpted below, Reid attempts to fortify Patmore's critical reputation by demonstrating the depth and unity of his thought and work. He focuses on these aspects of* The Unknown Eros *in the following essay, explicating the series of odes as a "coherent organic whole" concerned with the entire range of love's meanings and effects.*]

[The] final sequence of the poems [in *The Unknown Eros*], as it appeared in the collected edition, is the result of a thorough rearrangement of the original order. In this reshuffling [Patmore] was seeking to impart a significant progression to the poems, to turn them from a miscellany into a coherent organic whole with a gradually unfolding theme. The ultimate shape the work assumed reveals a definite development of thought and mood; it sums up all his hopes and ideals, it surveys the whole field of his philosophy, and leads upwards to **'The Child's Purchase'** as climax. (p. 284)

The Unknown Eros consists of a Proem and two books, the first containing twenty-four odes, the second eighteen. . . . [The] first deals mainly with what is 'natural' in man—his sorrows, his trials, his communion with Nature, his response to human love, his aspirations; the second chiefly with the 'supernatural' in him—his awareness of the Divine chastisement, his apprehension of God's presence, his desire for a deeper understanding of God's love, and the mystical union. Throughout both books are disposed poems which link them together—poems of philosophical speculation, poems of ordinary religious experience and others dealing with the nature of poetic utterance. Five main themes are woven into the first book—nature as a symbol of love, and the part it plays in man's spiritual progress; human love both in its concreteness and as a premonition of divine love; the life of man in society, and its effect on the maturing soul; the consideration of the nature of truth, order and law; and finally, the theme of penitence, and of the spiritual preparation of the soul to receive the influx of divinity. (pp. 284-85)

The first three odes are all Nature poems, concerned with the seasons, spring, summer and winter, in which a Wordsworthian vision of living things is fused with his own vision of love. In each poem the season symbolizes one aspect of the phases of love. . . . [In 'St. Valentine's Day,' spring is] seen as a parable of the transformation of the cold austerity of virginity into the warm, fruitful response of mature love. . . . 'Wind and Wave', which follows, is a poem of the summer sea, with the 'immeasurable smile' of sunlight breaking on the heaving waves. In the image of the ocean responding at first in gentle ripples to the little breeze, gaining force and momentum and finally crashing on the beach, Patmore depicts the fruition of love, its consummation in marriage, and its surging on to the 'void skyline and an unguess'd weal'. . . . On another level, this poem may be taken as symbolizing the surge, climax and repose of the sexual act itself. . . . (pp. 285-86)

'Winter' depicts the blanketed silence of the season as 'not death but plenitude of peace'. Here is the spirit of love released from bodily desire, wrapped in the profound calm of the contemplation of God, and content with the assurance of a new birth. The tone is one of profound stillness, of immensely quiet serenity, beneath which the heart still beats strongly. The subject is quite simply the transformation of human love into contemplation, the consummation of the virginity of the spirit. (p. 286)

Having dealt with love through the images of Nature in the first three poems, the poet turns to consider human love directly, and ten odes which follow show its pathos, its joys, its revelations and its consolations. . . . [They] present the crises of human love, and show the revelation of its inwardness under the impact of grief, as well as the purgative effect of pain on the soul. They represent the apotheosis of the philosophy of *The Angel in the House;* the transcendence of death by love, the relationship between 'Life, Death, Terror, Love', the divine nature of love revealed as plainly in its sorrows as in its joys.

'Beata', one of the original nine odes, gains special significance from its place in the sequence. The single sentence which constitutes the poem develops the image of white light broken up by a prism into its constituent colours. The rays of infinite Heaven striking upon woman

> Renounced their undistinguishable stress
> Of withering white,
> And did with gladdest hues my spirit caress,
> Nothing of Heaven in thee showing infinite,
> Save the delight.

Like the opening lines of **'Wind and Wave'**, **'Beata'** states Patmore's conviction that the Incarnation was necessary to teach men the nature of God, that love, no abstract thing, expresses itself in the concrete, and that to be knowable, all infinite things must be bounded by the finite. (pp. 286-87)

Nine odes which follow distil the sadness of lonely, remembering love after the death of the beloved. **'The Day After Tomorrow'** is, as Alice Meynell called it, a 'magnificent ode of reunion' [see Additional Bibliography]. Separated from his wife by death, the poet remembers the past delights of love, and sees them as an earnest of reunion in eternity. And in lines which suggest the time between Christ's death and resurrection he says:

> One day's controlled hope, and then one more,
> And on the third our lives shall be fulfill'd!

Here the terror of death is dissolved in the joy of eternal life. At the very beginning of the poetic consideration of love, therefore, Patmore sees married love as finding its perfect consummation in the Beautific Vision. **'Tristitia'** . . . is another declaration that love continues after death, and that in the certainty of the happiness of the beloved, even the most bitter agony will be tempered. . . . In logical sequence comes the beautiful ode **'The Azalea'**, in which the husband, dreaming that his wife is dead, wakes, in the happy realization that it was a dream, then to the blinding awareness that she *is* dead. This poem is filled with the pain of separation, and the poignant agony of recollected joy. But the perfume of the azalea which pervades it is yet another symbol of the continuity of love. (pp. 287-88)

'The Toys', one of the most familiar of the odes and the one which perhaps comes closest to sentimentality, gives, on the human level, a concrete instance of the widower's apprehension of the sustaining power of woman's love in the difficulty he finds in understanding his motherless children. Regret for a harsh dismissal of his child takes him to the nursery, where, gazing upon the boy's pathetic collection of treasures, he thinks of the greater charity of God towards the greater childishness of man. In its context, this poem is less 'soft' than it might appear in isolation, for it carries a stage further the conviction of the sustaining grace of God, and the awareness that all human love is a shadow of Eternal Love. **'Tired Memory'**, another very human poem, is full of remorse at the fading of the sharpness of love's recollection. . . . In the heart, 'dead of devotion and tired memory', a new movement of sensuous delight is felt which compels him to examine the old love and the new in relation to each other. Patmore's psychological subtlety is nowhere more evident than in this poem. With complete absence of equivocation, the poet scrutinizes his own motives, recognizing the human weaknesses which flaw human love, and the impossibility of man, in this middle state, retaining unchanged the pristine memory of even the most perfect human love. (pp. 288-89)

Recollections of this earthly love are to come again later, in two odes, **'If I Were Dead'** and **'A Farewell'**, as if sometimes, in man's concern with the external world and with mystical contemplation, memories of past love disturbingly intrude. (p. 289)

These two poems are interspersed among four odes which deal with 'public weal', and in which Patmore considers man's life in the community and the operation of God's providence therein. **'Magna Est Veritas'** rejects the 'world's cause'. Yet it is not a pessimistic poem, but an expression of trust in Providence, for

> The truth is great, and shall prevail,
> When none cares whether it prevail or not. . . .

'1867', **'Peace'** and **'1880-1885'** are dominated, too, by Patmore's concept of national honour, one which we accept in Shakespeare, and in the mood of war-time, but which many readers have been unable to accept from Patmore, since it is mingled here with political pessimism and intransigent Toryism. The intemperate tone of these odes forms a striking contrast to the dignified poignance of the immediately preceding poems. Yet they have a legitimate place in the plan of *The Unknown Eros*. Since Patmore was always aware of the social implications of love and its fundamental importance in the State, he could not, in a work concerned with the whole range of love's meaning and effects, ignore the milieu in which love was lived. The difficulty is that the political odes strike a partisan, rather than a universal, note. Instead of showing how love operates in public life as it does in private life, he offers mostly bitter recriminations. The tone is wrong; and reveals a marked defect in his sensibility. Yet these odes are not wholly lost in the lava of Patmore's prejudices, Based upon a passionate dislike of tyranny and a sense of the importance of individual freedom, they are not black Jeremiads, for they assert the conviction of future restoration and the certainty that God's will operates in history. (pp. 289-90)

[In] the next two odes Patmore examines alternatives to his own concept of man and his destiny. **'The Two Deserts'** rejects the claims made for science as a substitute for the spiritual vision. . . . In **'Crest and Gulf'**, where the mood is more bitter, he pours scorn on 'the bitter jest of mankind's progress'. Yet, even here, we find, instead of a mere sterile cynicism, a vivid contrast between the transitory nature of earthly aims and the permanent world of eternal values where final issues are decided. (pp. 290-91)

A preparation for the revelation of Book II, and a bridge between the contemplation of Nature and human life and the contemplation of the Deity, [the final five odes of Book I] reveal the spiritual resources of the soul undergoing the purgation essential as a preliminary to union with the divine. **'Let Be!'**, a meditation on the impossibility of judging others, serves to temper the apparent hauteur of the political odes by showing Patmore's more truly charitable side:

> But not all height is holiness,
> Nor every sweetness good;
> And grace will sometimes lurk where who could guess?
>
> . . . Why should I clear myself, why answer thou for me?

Indications, too, are here of Patmore's struggle with himself in subduing his passions to his religion, his attempt, in a sense, to sublimate his sensuality:

> And that which you and I
> Call his besetting sin
> Is but the fume of his peculiar fire
> Of inmost contrary desire.

The mystery of grace is the theme of **'Faint Yet Pursuing'**, an ode which movingly states the sense of imperfection which comes to the most earnest seeker, and is analogous to the spiritual dryness of which St. John of the Cross speaks. **'Victory in Defeat'** develops the same theme further, recording the alternations of success and failure which mark the soul's progress towards asceticism, and recognizing, with psychological acuteness, the pain that comes after the first ecstasy of surrender:

> Ah, God, alas,
> How soon it came to pass
> The sweetness melted from thy barbed hook
> Which I so simply took;
> And I lay bleeding on the bitter land.
>
> (pp. 291-92)

'**Remembered Grace**' reaffirms trust in God's mercy. Even in the depths of apparent deprivation the soul remembers past evidences of God's love and cannot but see the marks of His power and His providence in the sacramental signs of nature. (p. 292)

At the end of Book I '**Vesica Piscis**' gives a glimpse of the rewards of the faithful soul, in the first intimations of the immediate presence of God. Purged by its suffering, faithful in its trials, the soul is ready to approach the Deity directly. Patmore's image for the struggles of the dedicated spirit is Peter's unsuccessful fishing before his casting of the net in obedience to Christ's command once more filled his boat with the 'quick, shining harvest of the Sea'; and the discovery of the coin in the fish is man's discovery of God living in his own flesh.

In Book I of *The Unknown Eros*, then, Patmore moves logically from love found in Nature to love found in the flesh, in its dual aspects of joy and pain, thence to the social and philosophical referents of such a view of love, finally to the pursuits of divine love, in terms of human failings and aspirations, up to the first faint stirrings of the divine spirit felt in the soul of man.

The way is now prepared for a poetic exploration of the mysteries of the love of God. '**To the Unknown Eros**', which opens Book II, shows by its joy and tranquility a deepening of the mood of the work and a serene sense of approaching fulfilment. With the words

> What this breeze
> Of sudden wings
> Speeding at far returns of time from interstellar space
> To fan my very face,
> And gone as fleet,
> Through delicatest ether feathering soft their solitary beat

the soul recognizes the presence of the messengers of God, and prepares to respond to the will of the divine lover. At first the messages are enigmatic and only hint at

> A bond I know not of nor dimly can divine

but she knows that the way to union must lie in a detachment from earthly love, in a sacrifice for a greater gain. All the longing which she thought once to satisfy in Nature and in earthly love she now realizes can be satisfied only in God. '**The Contract**' develops the notion of the attainment of divine love by sacrifice of earthly love through the presentation of the 'virgin marriage' of Adam and Eve. . . . [As] part of the general plan of *The Unknown Eros*, '**The Contract**' refers to the spiritual strength that comes from a voluntary renunciation of sexual intercourse, and, on another level, to that virginity of mind essential in all love, whether physical or divine. Like most of the other odes, it has also an immediate psychological significance; at its centre lies the idea generally described today as 'sublimation'. It is not to be taken as a serious exegesis of

the first chapters of Genesis, but as a parable, using the story of Adam and Eve to describe the difference between pure love and lust, and to point up the weakness of man's flesh inherited from the choice of Eve. The last lines look forward to the fulfilment of the original pledge of Adam and Eve when 'a heaven-caress'd and happier Eve' will bring forth

> No numb, chill-hearted, shaken-witted thing,
> 'Plaining his little span,
> But of proud virgin joy the appropriate birth,
> The Son of God and Man.

In '**Arbor Vitae**' and '**The Standards**' Patmore expressly draws attention to the fact that, for the Christian, there is a guide from whom he may learn the way of God and by whose instruction he can confirm the truth of his own intuitions. (pp. 292-94)

[Patmore then] turns directly to the vision of the soul as spouse of Christ, and since man is a duality, to the role of the body in the apprehension of God.

> What is this Maiden fair
> The laughing of whose eye
> Is in man's heart renew'd virginity?

he asks in '**Sponsa Dei**'; and replies:

> What if this Lady be thy Soul, and He
> Who claims to enjoy her sacred beauty be
> Not thou, but God.

With this ode, we enter the highest reaches of Patmore's poetry. . . . '**Sponsa Dei**' and six of the odes that follow, including the Psyche poems, represent the most complete poetic expression of the 'burning heart' of his nuptial philosophy.

'**Legem Tuam Dilexi**' sings of the joy that succeeds man's acceptance of the bonds of law, and the repudiation of the word horrible—'infinite'. It is logical that '**To the Body**' should follow, for the body, 'wall of infinitude', and 'foundation of the sky', is the glorious limit of man. In his most mystical poems Patmore is still the humanist, accepting the wonder of the body and singing the Incarnation; and in this splendid ode he obeys the counsel of St. Paul, 'Glorify and bear God in your body.' But he also hymns the resurrection of the body; for man is complete only when the soul is reunited to its 'old abode'. . . . After thanking God for the pleasures he has known in the body, Patmore turns in '**Deliciae Sapientiae de Amore**' to celebrate the glory of virginity, including . . . all who are virginal in mind, and all the blessed in Heaven, for

> Love makes the life to be
> A fount perpetual of virginity.

No other poem of Patmore's so movingly expresses his conviction of the purity of love in law, and of the mystical dignity of virginity. Yet he is humble before his great theme, and no trace of the arrogance of the political odes enters in to flaw this piece of sustained lyricism. But the poems immediately before and after '**Deliciae Sapientiae de Amore**' show his continual awareness of his age and of his physical surroundings. The placing of these odes seems designed to indicate that there is no reason why the mystic should be divorced from actuality; and that Patmore is quite aware of the need for the speculative mystic to keep his feet on the ground lest he lose himself in misty subjectivism. (pp. 294-95)

Although '**The Cry at Midnight**', which follows '**Deliciae Sapientiae de Amore**', is satirical in tone, it has a direct relation to the mystical poems. It rebukes the deists and agnostics who cannot conceive that the Creator—if there be a Creator—could possibly be concerned with the love of man, and think it blasphemy that some should say 'Our Bridegroom's near!' What, Patmore asks, is their norm?. . . God's ways are not man's. He, not man, is the measure of all things, and His love for His creature is a mystery which neither philosophy nor science can solve. **'Auras of Delight'** presents a calculated contrast to positivist thinking, this time in terms of a personal conviction of grace, a recollection of the intimations of divinity which come to man, particularly in childhood. At times, especially during the crises of adult life, the vision seems to have vanished, but never do they altogether die,

> Those trackless glories glimps'd in upper sky,

so that the sense of the holiness of pure love always determines, for those who have experienced it, their revulsion from lust.

Thus prepared for, the **"Psyche Odes"** now crown the spiritual pilgrimage recorded in the earlier pages. Purged by suffering, disciplined by obedience to God's law, aware of the immensity of God and of her own insignificance, yet possessed by love for Him and convinced of His reciprocal love, the soul reaches out to embrace her God, and finds peace and the fulfilment of her destiny in union with Him. . . . In the full flood of mystical-erotic expression the odes explore the nature of God's love, the intimacy between Creator and created, the mystery of His infinite condescension and the resources of the soul. . . . As [the radiance of Eros's love] begins to permeate Psyche, she cries at first:

> O, too much joy; O, touch of airy fire;
> O, turmoil of content; O, unperturb'd desire,

but submits completely to the will of her Lover, so that when He leaves her she is content in a love which, however widely shared, remains for her unique. (pp. 296-97)

Psyche tells the Pythoness, in **'De Natura Deorum'**, of the visit of Eros, and of her fear that, if he does not return, she may be unable to remain faithful to him, for she remembers her past failings. . . . But as the Pythoness reminds her of her own littleness and her immeasurable inferiority to Eros, she realizes that the especial joy of their union comes from this disparity. Only deliberate rejection of His love will hinder God's coming. He will forgive all else. And Psyche now knows that the severity and apparent harshness of Eros are salutary for herself and for her love. This Eros is not

> Our People's pompous but good-natured Jove,

that is, he is not the God of Victorian convention, the benevolent schoolmaster of sentimental piety. Although reverence in man's relation with God is neccessary, inability to realize. His love may cause excessive reverence to turn into fear:

> Knowst thou not, Girl, thine Eros loves to laugh?

Throughout this particular ode, Patmore strives to achieve a tone appropriate to the reverent gaiety of Psyche. But he writes with a colloquial playfulness which often falls short of what he intends. . . . Perhaps this in part reflects the difficulty Patmore found in visualizing himself as the receptive rather than the dominant partner in a love-relationship.

The final **"Psyche Ode"**, **'Psyche's Discontent'**, finds the soul seeking respite from the love which has almost engulfed her.

She begs that she be allowed to prove her love by her diligence in bearing

> The fardel coarse of customary life's
> Exceeding injucundity.

But her God-Lover replies that what he seeks for in her is not service, but love:

> Yea, Palate fine,
> That claim'st for thy proud cup the pearl of price,
> And scorn'st the wine,
> Accept the sweet, and say 'tis sacrifice!

Sharply and clearly, with reverence and yet with total involvement, the odes convey the intimacy of divine love. Despite an occasional touch of false rhetoric and now and then an incongruity of tone such as was noted in **'De Natura Deorum'**, they show, in the main, a combination of delicacy of feeling and subtlety of intellect.

It is a mark of Patmore's sense of proportion that he should follow the Psyche poems with the ode on **'Pain'**, which opposes the Christian concept of the cleansing power of pain to both the Hedonism of some nineteenth-century writers and the algolagnia of Swinburne. Patmore is never concerned only with the fruits of the spiritual life, but always remembers their roots in human effort and in daily living. In this poem, he brings us back from the heights of mystic contemplation to the realities of human life, and yet goes beyond the fact of pain to the mystery of its relationship to 'joy and heart's delight'. The poet prays for strength and prudence, for help to resist the temptation to turn from pain to its 'pale enemy', pleasure. Here again we see Patmore's psychological perception in his realization of the thin barriers which separate bliss and suffering.

'Prophets Who Cannot Sing', which introduces **'The Child's Purchase'**, speaks of the inadequacy of poetry to do justice to the hidden life of the spirit. He is approaching his great final subject with humility. Although the tone is characteristically Patmorean, the theme of this ode has a good deal in common with those passages in the *Four Quartets* in which Eliot considers the limitations of language in the rendering of religious experience. Patmore's 'prophets who cannot sing' are not those without a vision to record, but those with a vision of the 'unveil'd heavens' so intense that it is inexpressible. (pp. 297-99)

With this warning in our ears, we come to **'The Child's Purchase'**, his final poetic word on love and virginity. In the Blessed Virgin Mary he sees the perfection of virginity, of married love and of the love of God, as well as the supreme expression of the meaning of the Incarnation. . . . Since every ordinary marriage is the symbol of union with God, the Blessed Virgin, the Mother of God, is the perfect exemplification of Patmore's nuptial philosophy and of his concept of limits. In the magnificent litany which is the core of the poem, he calls her:

> Our only savior from an abstract Christ.

Echoes from Dante, St. Bernard and the Bible are mingled in this hymn of praise to the Blessed Virgin, not only as the Mother of Christ, but also as the Second Eve forecast in **'The Contract'**, she in whom all womankind is raised up and glorified. Patmore is now ready to surrender his work to the judgment of Heaven, recognizing that, behind all that he has written of love, stood the hitherto unapprehended figure of the Virgin.

> When clear my Songs of Lady's graces rang,
> And little guess'd I 'twas of thee I sang!

She is the final paradox of all paradoxes, the 'rainbow complex in bright distinction of all beams of sex'; to whom God is 'Husband, Father, Son and Brother'. The 'rinsed and wrung' language of this ode, its dignity and its fusion of intelligence and sensibility make it a great religious poem, sincere, humble, yet full of daring insights.

The whole work closes with the eighteen lines of **'Dead Language'**. . . . Should not such thoughts as this book expresses be 'decently cloak'd in the Imperial Tongue'? [Patmore] imagines his monitor asking, to which he replies, 'Alas, and is not mine a language dead?' While in this final poem Patmore acknowledges the rejection of his later poetic vision by his age, it also, in the plan of *The Unknown Eros,* indicates his coming abandonment of poetry and his dedicating himself to religious and mystical speculation. It is not a lament over a lack of understanding, but a renewed assertion that the real significance of the odes lies hidden beneath the symbols, as the mysteries of the liturgy are hidden in the Latin.

Far from being a mere miscellany, then, . . . *The Unknown Eros* is a unified work, based upon a plan to which each ode contributes and in the context of which they gain richer significance. Together the odes outline 'the whole pedigree of love'. Love as symbolized in Nature, love in its human reality, love in terms of social action, and philosophy, love as penitence, are the themes of the first book. The second expresses lyrically the ecstasies of union with God, from the first intimations of His presence through the consciousness of the need for guidance, for self-abnegation, and the acceptance of pain, to the fullness of union. Both books are interspersed with reflections on the fluctuations of the spiritual life and on the duality of man. Full of 'wit' and of curious paradoxical turns of thought, which do not eliminate pathos but reinforce it, *The Unknown Eros* is a poem unique in its age. (pp. 299-301)

The highest points of *The Unknown Eros* make Patmore a poet of the order of Donne, Crashaw, Hopkins and Herbert. Yet the work contains that dross which is the evidence of the intensity of his personal struggle. Throughout he is disturbed by memories of his first wife, which his later married happiness could not wholly eradicate; he is conscious of the difficulty of transmuting the experience of earthly love into divine love; he suffers not a little from the responsibility of his expanding knowledge of human passion. So paradoxes, invective, sardonic jests, difficult sayings, and rhetorical exaggeration break into the poems. A closer look at a characteristic ode from *The Unknown Eros* may give us a clearer idea of important aspects of Patmore's poetic sensibility. **'Sponsa Dei'** is not one of his best odes; it does not reach the height of the widower's' odes, nor of the best Psyche poems, but neither does it sink as often as the political odes. Representative of his average level of achievement in this volume, it shows the faults as well as the virtues of his later poetic style. (p. 303)

The themes of this ode, that human love is a shadow of divine love, that the never-to-be-satisfied element in love comes from an instinctive awareness of this, and that all souls are feminine to God, are among those which appear in not dissimilar form in *The Angel in the House.* And the same kind of paradox as is found in the earlier work is also here, the idea that beneath the mundane details of love and courtship is 'the burning heart of the universe'. Yet the tone is more elevated, and its control calls for a different kind of tact than that which governed the gentle playfulness of *The Angel.* The lines

> If she does something but a little sweet,
> As gaze towards the glass to set her hair,
> See how his soul falls humbled at her feet!

which might not have been out of place in the lover's ecstasy in *The Angel,* lend a touch of the commonplace to the higher statement of the ode. (pp. 304-05)

Some of the epithets are from stock—'sweet', 'fair', 'gentle' and 'divine'; and, save perhaps in the lines

> A reflex heat
> Flash'd on thy cheek from His immense desire,

the imagery barely escapes triteness. Patmore's analogy for the soul's delight in its own beauty when it is loved by God:

> Such as a Bride, viewing her mirror'd charms,
> Feels when she sighs, 'Ah, these are for his arms!'

hints at a streak of coarseness in his sensibility. Although, in the odes, he had largely passed beyond the clichés of the popular religious vocabulary, he was not able wholly to dissociate himself from conventional epithets of other kinds, which lend a touch of literary vulgarity to some of the odes. One is tempted to attribute this element to the state of the poetic vocabulary in the mid-Victorian times. Patmore was not the only one among writers of power and outstanding ability to fall foul of the 'vocabulary of the heart'. For the present, it is relevant to note in **'Sponsa Dei'** the touches of rhetorical exaggeration:

> To die unknown for her were little cost,

for instance; and the lack of concrete poetic detail. Patmore's tendency towards generalization, marked in this poem, is both a strength and a weakness. In **'Legem Tuam Dilexi'** and **'Deliciae Sapientiae de Amore'** and other odes, the poetico-philosophical abstractions have a genuine impressiveness, because the philosophy from which they proceed is felt as a passionate experience rendered with fitting dignity and breadth. But elsewhere, as in **'Sponsa Dei'**, there is something of the verbal gesture, of the easy-way-out in language.

On the other hand, the virtues of his style are evident in this ode, too. One of these is the clarity of the central concept, the stiffening which his philosophy gives to the idea, the poetic logic with which the relationship between man's love for his 'Margaret, Maude, or Cecily' and God's love for man is worked out and the smoothness with which the experiences are linked. In the early part of the ode, we have an imaginative description of the exaggerated mood of the worshipping lover, who, even in his elation, recognizes that his beloved cannot satisfy his desire. Then, with the lines

> And what this sigh
> That each one heaves for Earth's last lowlihead
> And the Heaven high
> Ineffably lock'd in dateless bridal-bed

the transition is made between earthly and divine love, with the Incarnation seen as the great proof of the relationship.

The language is seldom inflated, and some of the phrasing is poetically inventive—'a frantic flight of courtesy', 'thy sick fire', 'tear-glad Mistress', 'a reflex heat'. More than this, the rhetorical control rarely wavers throughout. The opening lines are particularly sure in their statement. Among them

> With hope of utter binding, and of loosing endless
> dear despair?

is especially interesting. It contains a slightly clumsy inversion, yet its compressed paradoxical statement of Patmore's basic idea of the joy of limits shows the strong intellectual control behind the ode.

As a whole, **'Sponsa Dei'** is greater than the sum of its parts, and the same is true of many of the other odes. The most memorable of them are usually the most concrete, the 'widower's' odes and the **'Psyche'** group, which deal with a particular situation, rather than with an abstract idea. Elsewhere **The Unknown Eros** indicates the difficulty Patmore found in expressing an intellectual experience in emotive terms. If **The Unknown Eros** is compared with the poems of St. John of the Cross, we see the difference between the work of a speculative mystic and that of a true mystic who was also a great lyrical poet. But the problem of the abstract subject is not the whole answer. There is a flaw in Patmore's sensibility, not one gross enough to invalidate his poetry, but apparent enough to keep his work in the second rank. It is partly a matter of emotional temper, partly one of too great a selectivity of experience, of over-assurance that he knew precisely what a valuable experience was, a touch, if you will, of spiritual complacency.

Yet, overriding this, throughout **The Unknown Eros** is the sense of struggle, of the battle to achieve harmony of thought and feeling, harmony of flesh and spirit; and finally, a confidence, trust and knowledge that ultimate peace will succeed the 'weary life's campaign'. And such knowledge is humble, not arrogantly haughty; it is a measure of the success of Patmore's war against himself that he can say, with manifest sincerity:

> Mother, who lead'st me by unknown ways,
> Giving the gifts I know not how to ask,
> Bless thou the work
> Which, done, redeems my many wasted days,
> Makes white the murk,
> And crowns the few which thou wilt not dispraise.

The Unknown Eros, then, is as complex and as serious a work as was written in England in the nineteenth century. It speaks to the twentieth century with a clearer voice than it spoke to Patmore's own age. The marks of strain and tension in it, and the struggle towards personal integration, give it an immediacy which most contemporary readers fail to find in Browning or Tennyson. The discipline Patmore exercises over his poetic expression in the odes is indicated by the demands he makes on his readers. His long, carefully-wrought sentences require close attention. Their syntax is rarely involved, but the thought is tightly-knit, closely-woven rather than uttered in lyrical outbursts. From this discipline and the organization of the thought, as much as from subject-matter, form and language, comes the curiously individual ring of the odes. . . . (pp. 305-07)

The very seriousness of Patmore's spiritual quest accounts equally for the disturbed and disturbing qualities of the odes and for their tender dignity. The revelation in **The Unknown Eros** of a complex spirit, individual, self-reliant, proud and even crotchety, struggling to submit himself to God, makes the work one of the most moving of religio-poetic expressions. Because they are so daring in their aim, the odes are at times extravagant, at others teeter on the edge of the absurd; yet the purity of Patmore's intention preserves them for banality. At their best they are in truth 'wedded light and heat'. Sometimes there is a storm of feeling here rather than a flooding of the spirit; sometimes thought and emotion are not fused; but in the better odes, and they are many, the poet seems to be poised on the brink of eternal silence, to be about to attain that divine tranquillity whose pursuit is so movingly recorded in this extraordinary work. (p. 307)

> *J. C. Reid, in his* The Mind and Art of Coventry Patmore, *Routledge & Kegan Paul, 1957, 358 p.*

JOHN J. DUNN   (essay date 1960)

[*Dunn discusses the nature of Patmore's Catholicism, describing him as a believer whose insular traditionalism and individualism run counter to the mainstream of modern Church thought. (For additional commentary by Dunn, see excerpt below, 1969).*]

Patmore was, consistently, a great traditionalist. Long before his conversion [to Catholicism], he painstakingly evolved that ideal of British life expressed in **The Angel in the House**. . . . In this vast, novel-like poem, Patmore evokes the orderly, conservative world of **"Sarum Close,"** a world strictly governed by the religious, social and political conventions of the Victorian upper middle class. Whatever the limitations of such an idyllic world, it was Patmore's vision of what constitutes English greatness:

> A tent pitch'd in a world not right
> It seem'd, whose inmates, every one,
> On tranquil faces bore the light
> Of duties beautifully done,
> And humbly, though they had few peers,
> Kept their own laws, which seem'd to be
> The fair sum of six thousand years'
> Traditions of civility. . . .

As the years passed, Patmore saw the nicely balanced hierarchy of values integral to this gracious, leisurely way of life threatened by material progress, "godless" science, and the rise of what Marx called the proletariat. The ominous shadow of Victorian liberalism hovered over the manicured lawns and the gracious young ladies in crinoline. The long-cherished conservative religious and political principles enshrined in the rule of the many by the dedicated few seemed doomed, while anarchy walked upon the earth. (pp. 239-40)

A great deal of Patmore's pessimism concerning nineteenth century liberalism and progress resulted from a deep-seated mistrust of the masses. He believed strongly in rule by a talented aristocracy, preferably Catholic, which would guard ancient values while ministering to the needs of a docile body politic. But he foresaw the inevitable success of the "unwashed" masses, whom he referred to contemptuously by such terms as "dross and draff," "Gergesenian swine," "bad corpses" (**"1880-85"**); "forest-pigs" (**"Arbor Vitae"**); "sordid Trader," "Mechanic vain" (**"1867"**). In **"Crest and Gulf,"** he summarized his rudimentary political philosophy in a line: "The Many's weedy growth withers the gracious Few!" . . .

Because he envisioned England as a wasteland desolated by materialistic science and the rise of democracy, he viewed Catholicism as the last embattled rampart of the traditionalism in which he so strongly believed. In **"Arbor Vitae,"** for example, he depicted the Church as the sole source of spiritual life in a Darwinian wilderness:

> Rich, though rejected by the forest-pigs,
> Its fruit, beneath whose rough, concealing rind
> They that will break it find
> Heart-succouring savour of each several meat,
> And kernell'd drink of brain-renewing power, . . .

In **"The Standards,"** written in 1874 during the hostility toward the Church engendered by the pronouncements of the Vatican Council, he imaged a beleaguered group of English Catholics, attacked by Gladstone and liberalism, aided only, as he somewhat grudgingly admits, by "many a faithful rogue /

Discrediting bright-Truth with dirt and brogue.'' . . . The heroic minority stands ready, even willing, to endure martyrdom:

> Lo, yonder, where our little English band,
> With peace in heart and wrath in hand,
> Have dimly ta'en their stand, . . .
>
> (p. 242)

In his enthusiasm, however vigorous and honest, he ran counter
to the sounder trend of Catholic intellectualism in the nineteenth
century. Unlike Newman and Manning and their disciples, he
adopted the fierce polemicism of a latter-day prophet who was
thirsting to die in defense of the Church, which was, to him,
the last great repository of the traditional values of British
civilization. Instead of beholding the Church as a steadying
force in the movement toward political and economic liberalism, as a dynamic agent in shaping the powerful movements
boiling up from the lower classes, he identified it with his own
obstinate insularity. His was a classic example of the ghetto-
mentality which has frequently hampered the Church in the
modern world.

What was the nature of the faith which Patmore defended so
fervently? Here lies a seeming paradox. The man who asserted
trenchantly the objective, absolute truth of Catholic dogma in
an anarchic universe was himself highly individualistic in his
fulfillment of the demands of his new religion. Possessing no
bent for missionizing or for changing the corrupted world, he
was much more a mystic than an apologist; he was more vitally
concerned with the personal relationship of the soul to its Creator than with the sacraments or the liturgical life of the Church.
(p. 243)

Central to Patmore's mysticism was the doctrine of the incarnation, a mystery which he considered even more basic than
the redemption. The intrusion of the divine and the eternal into
human history he regarded as the foundation of man's mystical
relationship with God. Without Christ, no possible contact
could have been made between an infinite Creator and a finite
creation. Christ, by taking on flesh, also sublimated human
littleness, the human body, human love; Christ saves man from
the sterile madness of contemplating a merely infinite God:

> The 'Infinite!' Word horrible! at feud
> With life, and the braced mood
> Of power and joy and love. . . .

Throughout *The Rod, the Root and the Flower* the incarnation
is delineated as the basis for man's repugnance toward infinity
and his joyous acceptance of the body and its functions and
even limitations. In poems such as **"To the Body"** and **"Pain"**
Patmore lauds man's physical bonds, the incarnation having
given significance and dignity to such bonds. (pp. 243-44)

Certainly Patmore's emphasis on the incarnation is orthodox
and, given the poet's strong, virile, almost sensual personality,
understandable. He undoubtedly wanted justification for his
intense enjoyment of the vibrant physical currents which flowed
through his own being. But his belief in this doctrine did not
express itself in conventional sacramental and liturgical outlets;
on the contrary, it led to a highly personal mysticism. Just as
God could fetter himself to a human body and feel both delight
and pain in that body, so God would descend into a receptive
soul, adapting his vastness to the limited capabilities of that
soul. This concept Patmore referred to as the ''Sacrament of
the Manifest Presence,'' for which the whole corporate dogma,
liturgy, and organization of the Church was an ''external sanction.''

At this point Patmore's emphasis again differs from that of the
mainstream of modern Catholic liturgical theory, which has
more and more come to stress the common worship possible
through a proper use of the sacraments and the liturgy. Patmore,
always the uncompromising individualist, wanted a basically
personal relationship with a God who would manifest himself
in what might be called a private love affair with the human
soul. (p. 244)

[The] three **"Psyche Odes"** form the daring culmination of the
poet's mysticism. In these poems he shadows forth, through
the myth of Eros and Psyche, the strong personal ties which
unite the soul, pictured as feminine and passive, with a god
who finds joy in her very limitations. The doctrine of the
manifest presence and the Patmorean interpretation of the
meaning of the incarnation focus in these odes, which form an
allegory, in the strong language of connubial love, for the
whole gamut of emotions to which the mystic is subject—
passion, pain, hope, exaltation, despair. (pp. 245-46)

> *John J. Dunn, ''The Insular Catholicism of Coventry
> Patmore,'' in* The American Benedictine Review,
> *Vol. XI, Nos. 3 & 4, September & December, 1960,
> pp. 239-48.*

JOHN J. DUNN (essay date 1969)

[*Focusing on the ''post-conversion'' poetry, Dunn explains and
critiques Patmore's use of erotic love to symbolize the mystical
union of God and the individual. For additional commentary by
Dunn, see excerpt above, 1960.*]

[A fruitful way of] assessing what Patmore's conversion meant
for his poetry is a brief examination of his emphasis on the
Incarnation. While this doctrine is also a keystone of Protestant
theology, Patmore seems not to have fully contemplated its
significance until he viewed it through the eyes of the Catholic
Church. No other doctrine is stressed as heavily by Patmore,
who saw in the Incarnation the central truth of man's religious
experience. (p. 205)

[In *The Rod, the Root, and the Flower,* Patmore maintains that
from] the individual's standpoint, the significance of the Incarnation is that man's nature is glorified. In every human
being destined for redemption the drama of the Incarnation is
enacted anew. . . .

Man's body as well as his soul shares in the transfiguration
effected by Christ's assumption of human nature: ''The Soul
is the express Image of God, and the Body of the Soul; thence,
it, also, is an Image of God, and 'the human form divine' is
no figure of speech'' (**"Homo"**. . .). (p. 206)

Because redeemed human nature participates in the continuing
miracle of the Incarnation, the man who fervently embraces
that doctrine discovers that every act he performs takes on the
colors of eternity. When the genuinely religious man is living
most fully in time, his experiences are occurring simultaneously
on the level of eternity. . . . It is not difficult to see why a
vigorous sensualist like Patmore embraced this theology of the
Incarnation. It provided his powerful urges with a convincing
rationale, since there could be no intemperance or excess in
pleasures which were habitually viewed *sub specie aeternitatis*
[in their essential nature].

According to Patmore, given the crucial importance of the
Incarnation, there is only one experience which is powerful
enough to embody both man's divinity and God's humanity.

Only love, to Patmore the one total fulfillment in human existence, can perpetually renew the blessed mystery first signified when the angel spoke to Mary at Nazareth. Love is the continuation of the Incarnation throughout human history.

Thus, human love is understandable only when its most intense physical ecstasies are solemnized by the realization that God's presence has exalted man's flesh. Furthermore, divine love can be apprehended solely through the acceptance of God's habitation in the body and soul of man. Therefore, the Incarnation is the key to a vital understanding of both human and divine love and their relationship to each other. In the Incarnation, human and divine love meet and fuse: man's love is deified, and God's love is humanized. The love of man for woman and the love of God for man become analogous to one another because of that critical moment when humanity and divinity were joined in a single integrated and exalted essence. (pp. 206-07)

Such a doctrine leads naturally and logically to Patmore's contention that the intimate details of a man's love for a woman form the best available symbolic language for expressing God's analogous love for the soul. (p. 207)

[Because] "all knowledge, worthy of the name, is nuptial knowledge" . . . , the mystical odes in Book II of *The Unknown Eros* [including the **"Psyche Odes"**] inevitably revolve around the symbolic imagery of a human marriage. The profane "nuptial knowledge" embodied in the love imagery of *The Angel in the House* becomes, as a result of Patmore's conversion and his meditation on the Incarnation, the heavenly "nuptial knowledge" of his religious odes. (p. 208)

To Patmore, one important parallel between divine and human love lies in the fact that all love is mysterious and arbitrary. God's all-powerful love for the elected soul, e.g., as described in the ode **"To the Unknown Eros,"** is as irresistible and unfathomable as the sudden growth of human love recorded in *The Angel in the House*. The soul cannot will the presence of her divine lover any more than a man can determine arbitrarily to fall in love with some appropriate female. . . .

As long as Psyche tries to will the presence of her divine lover, Eros remains aloof. But as soon as she resigns herself completely to his will, he is in her bed. (p. 209)

The satiated Psyche longs to understand her Eros as well as enjoy his caresses. The enigmatic and deliberately anti-intellectual Pythoness, Psyche's spiritual advisor, comforts her by saying that the God's love is no more mysterious that the affections of a human lover. Love should simply be enjoyed without restraint. Analysis cannot explain it and often succeeds only in chilling its ardor. . . .

Thus, both human and divine love begin in mystery and perplexity and end in resignation and acceptance. Love is too powerful to be resisted, too mysterious to be completely understood. (p. 210)

Mystery and the blissful conjunction of the great with the small characterize God's relationship to the soul, just as they typify, to a lesser degree, the love of a man for a woman. A third and central similarity between human and divine love is the overwhelming ecstasy which results when love is consummated. All other pleasures pall in the bliss of that encounter, whether it takes place between two human lovers or between God and the soul.

To the author of *The Angel in the House,* the highest possible human experience is the fusion of two separate beings in the act of marriage. So intense is the delight which results from the fusion that every act, every object, the landscape itself is luminous with the warmth and light thereby engendered. Accordingly, to the author of *The Unknown Eros,* the joyousness attendant upon God's marriage with the soul can be expressed most effectively by borrowing the strong imagery through which lovers convey the bliss of their intercourse. No more potent language is available to body forth the "intolerable delight" experienced by the soul which is subjected to the sudden, even violent caresses of God's love. . . .

This imagery, which shocked many nineteenth-century readers by its frankness, occasionally disturbs the modern reader by its awkwardness. The symbolic function of the imagery is made clear enough by the titles of the poems and in the conversations of Psyche with Eros and the Pythoness, but the symbolism often seems strained and mechanical. The real interest of the poet frequently seems to lie in the erotic imagery itself, not in the mystical union which it prefigures. (p. 212)

Again and again in *The Rod, the Root and the Flower* Patmore labors to justify the use of [his] explicit sensual imagery. For example, Psyche's reaction . . . in **"Psyche's Discontent"** reflects, according to Patmore's interpretation, the soul's feeling of inadequacy in the presence of its creator. . . . Somehow, however, the symbolism incorporated in the sensual imagery seldom flows as smoothly and spontaneously from that imagery as Patmore undoubtedly intended. there is never quite the ceremonious dignity of the Song of Songs nor the extravagant but convincing fervor of a John of the Cross. (p. 213)

In the **"Psyche Odes"**, Patmore attempts to express the healthy joy of love through the gay irreverence of Psyche and the humorous raillery of the Pythoness. The implication is that the unpretentious and private gaiety of a sexually successful marraige corresponds to the soul's delighted response to her divine lover. Alluding vaguely in *The Rod, the Root and the Flower* to "certain hints" in the lives of the saints, Patmore declares that God's "love raises the spirit above the sphere of reverence and worship into one of laughter and dalliance" (**"Aurea Dicta,"** XXXIX . . .). (pp. 213-14)

No one would deny the necessity of joy and laughter in any marriage, even in the solemn nuptials of the soul and God, but the levity in the **"Psyche Odes,"** is too often clumsy. It requires a real wrench of the reader's sensibility to see the symbolic connection between the repartee of Eros and Psyche and the joyousness which accompanies God's presence in the chosen soul.

An instance of this questionable use of "laughter and dalliance" occurs in the last of the **"Psyche Odes,"** **"Psyche's Discontent."** Psyche wants to be a wife rather than a mistress, and she requests, as a relief from excessive pleasure, the "fardel coarse of customary life's / Exceeding injocundity." After delivering herself of these melodious lines, Psyche playfully engages her lover in a dialogue. Eros begins

"Thus irresistibly by Love embraced
Is she who boasts her more than mortal chaste!"
"Find'st thou me worthy, then, by day and night,
But of this fond indignity, delight?"
"Little, bold Femininity,
That darest blame Heaven, what would'st thou have or be?'

'Shall I, the gnat which dances in thy ray,
Dare to be reverent? Therefore dare I say,
I cannot guess the good that I desire. . . .

To many readers, an arrogant and patronizing lover relishing
the piquancy of a kittenish rebellion against his tyranny is not
a satisfying image of the relationship between God and the
soul. (p. 214)

The final similarity which Patmore sees between marriage and
God's relationship with the soul is the necessity of pain. . . .
Vicissitudes are, obviously, as inevitable in the soul's union
with God as they are in any marriage, and in either case they
can strengthen the bond of love. Patmore records the "dark
night of the soul" in such tradition-oriented odes as "**Let
Be!**," "**Faint Yet Pursuing**," "**Victory in Defeat**," and
"**Remembered Grace**."

But Patmore is also clearly contending that pain actually enhances the delight which flows from the act of love. Love
without pain is inconceivable to him. (p. 215)

Patmore's ode "**Pain**" is, at first glance, a conventional statement on the value of pain as a "medicine of sin," a "pangful,
purging fire" to cleanse away "luxury, sloth and hate." But
a closer reading of the poem revelas that the poet regarded pain
as having a positive attraction of its own. . . .

> When thou lov'st, I am at first afraid
> Of thy fierce kiss,
> Like a young maid;
> And only trust thy charms
> And get my courage in thy throbbing arms.
> And, when thou partest, what a fickle mind
> Thou leav'st behind,
> That, being a little absent from mine eye,
> It straight forgets thee what thou art,
> And ofttimes my adulterate heart
> Dallies with Pleasure, thy pale enemy.
> O, for the learned spirit without attaint
> That does not faint,
> But knows both how to have thee and to lack,
> And ventures many a spell,
> Unlawful but for them that love so well,
> To call thee back. . . .

The imagery in the "**Psyche Odes**" is less reticent than the
veiled language of "**Pain**," but there is a similar ambiguity.
Is the pain both suffered and desired by Psyche necessary for
her purification, or does it contribute directly to the pleasure
which she enjoys in the embraces of Eros? At times, the suggestion seems merely to be that pain provides a good discipline.
(pp. 215-16)

More often, however, the pain lauded in the "**Psyche Odes**"
seems an integral part of love's complex fulfillment. Pleasure
without pain is sweet and cloying. Psyche cries out that she is
being suffocated by an excess of pleasure.

> Bitter be thy behests!
> Lie like bunch of myrrh between my aching breasts.
> Some greatly pangful penance would I brave.
> Sharpness me save
> From being slain by sweet!   ("**Eros and Psyche**" . . .)

Only through the contrast to pain, it seems, is it possible to
define the full meaning of pleasure. (pp. 216-17)

While pain and sex images are often combined in the writings
of mystics to objectify intense delight, Patmore seems to be
using such images almost literally. Pain is itself somehow
pleasurable, not merely a symbol of enjoyments that are too
intense to be defined in ordinary language. There is almost too
much fervor in Psyche's readiness to endure pain if Eros demands it.

> Should'st thou me tell
> Out of thy warm caress to go
> And roll my body in the biting snow,
> My very body's joy were but increased;
> More pleasant 'tis to please thee than be pleased.
> Thy love has conquer'd me; do with me as thou wilt,
> And use me as a chattel that is thine!
> Kiss, tread me under foot, cherish or beat,
> Sheathe in my heart sharp pain up to the hilt,
> Invent what else were most perversely sweet.
>   ("**Eros and Psyche**" . . .)

Such a passage can presumably be considered a symbolic embodiment of the soul's unquestioning obedience to the dictates
of a divine lover, but phrases like "perversely sweet" suggest
that the moralistic Victorain poet, learned in all the ways of
domestic felicity, was casting an amorous eye on forbidden
fruit.

Even more explicit is the imagery in the dialogue between
Psyche and the Pythoness.

> —But whence these wounds? What Demon thee enjoins
> To scourge thy shoulders white
> And tender loins!
> "'Tis nothing, Mother. Happiness at play,
> And speech of tenderness no speech can say!"
> "How learn'd thou art!
> Twelve honeymoons profane had taught thy docile heart
> Less than thine Eros, in a summer night!
>   ("**De Natura Deorum**" . . .)

It is small wonder that the Victorian middle class which had
so warmly accepted the inanities of love in a deanery rebelled
against such unorthodox "happiness at play," however much
the author might protest that what appeared to be sadism and
masochism were in reality the imaging forth of God's intimacy
with the soul.

The symbolic function of pain in the "**Psyche Odes**," then, is
ambiguous at best. Sometimes pain is used for contrast, sometimes to express strong physical or emotional experiences and
sometimes, as in the above passages, to hint that it is in itself
a source of strange delight. Like the rest of the erotic imagery
in the "**Psyche Odes**," the pain imagery may not entirely succeed in conveying the edifying mystical truths which it purports
to represent. (pp. 217-18)

[What] Patmore was trying to do with his love imagery is
obvious enough. Because of the Incarnation, human love becomes the prototype of divine love and, therefore, serves as
its most appropriate symbol. The msytery, inequality, erotic
intensity, and healthy mingling of gaiety and pain characteristic
of the love between a man and a woman are analogous, in
Patmore's mind, to those higher but similar conditions which
define God's passion for the soul.

How well Patmore succeeded in his symbolic use of love and
eroticism is open to question. . . . The imagery, taken as a
whole, does suggest the mystery and fervor of the mystic's
rapture. Human love, it is reasonable to suppose, is that earthly
experience which can best serve as a symbol and percursor of

the ineffable exhilaration which fills the mystic who believes that he has enjoyed communion with God.

But Patmore's imagery, however appropriate it may be in the abstract, does not always succeed in its symbolic intent. Patmore seems unable to conceive of any love which is not composed of the same elements as the strongly sexual if sentimentalized marriage which he describes so exhaustively in *The Angel in the House.* In that poem, no trivial domestic detail is too small to be illumined by the radiance of the lover's passion. Similarly, in the odes, no detail of the art of love, however erotic or even perverse it may seem, is considered unworthy to embody some nuance of the mystic's ecstatic union with God. The **"Psyche Odes,"** particularly, dwell so lovingly on these details that symbolism is sometimes submerged in eroticism. When Patmore does lose control of his symbolic love imagery, the reader's whole attention is focused on the physical love-making of Eros and Psyche, not on the exalted truths which that love-making supposedly symbolizes. In such unsuccessful passages, the imagery of an intensified and prolonged sexual enjoyment fails to transcend itself and thereby, for many readers at least, fails to evoke effectively the mystical experience which it is intended to represent. Such failures are perhaps only occasional, but they do make questionable the ranking of Patmore's odes in the very first order of mystical poetry. (pp. 218-19)

> *John J. Dunn, "Love and Eroticism: Coventry Patmore's Mystical Imagery," in* Victorian Poetry, *Vol. VII, No. 3, Autumn, 1969, pp. 203-19.*

ADDITIONAL BIBLIOGRAPHY

Burdett, Osbert. *The Idea of Coventry Patmore.* London: Oxford University Press, Humphrey Milford, 1921, 213 p.
    A detailed explication of Patmore's philosophy of love as revealed in his poetry and his prose. *The Angel in the House* and *The Unknown Eros* command Burdett's special attention.

Cadbury, William. "The Structure of Feeling in a Poem by Patmore: Meter, Phonology, Form." *Victorian Poetry* IV, No. 4 (1966): 237-51.
    A discussion focused on Patmore's poetic technique. Cadbury examines Patmore's use of meter and sound to express feeling in a segment of *The Angel in the House* entitled "Love at Large."

Champneys, Basil. *Memoirs and Correspondence of Coventry Patmore.* 2 vols. London: George Bell and Sons, 1900.
    The standard biography. In addition to chronicling the poet's life, Champneys publishes material from Patmore's private papers, including an enlightening autobiographical account of his conversion to Catholicism.

Cohen, J. M. "Prophet without Responsibility: A Study in Coventry Patmore's Poetry." *Essays in Criticism* 1, No. 3 (July 1951): 283-97.
    A consideration of Patmore's literary accomplishments. Cohen suggests that Patmore's writing was adversely affected by his "fear of passion."

Evans, Ifor. "Coventry Patmore and Allied Poets: Coventry Patmore, Francis Thompson, Alice Meynell." In his *English Poetry in the Later Nineteenth Century,* 2d ed., pp. 154-87. New York: Barnes & Noble, 1966.*
    Characterizes Patmore as a prominent figure in the development of religious and philosophical verse in late nineteenth-century England. Evans provides a detailed discussion of content and method in Patmore's major works.

Gardner, W. H. "The Achievement of Coventry Patmore: Parts I and II." *The Month* n.s. 7, Nos. 2, 4 (February 1952; April 1952): 89-98, 220-30.
    A revaluation of Patmore's writings. As a poet, Gardner declares Patmore to be the sometime equal of George Herbert, Richard Crashaw, and John Keats.

Gosse, Edmund. "Coventry Patmore: A Portrait." *Contemporary Review* LXXI (February 1897): 184-204.
    A posthumous biographical sketch derived in large measure from Gosse's personal acquaintance with Patmore.

Harris, Frank. "Coventry Patmore." In his *Contemporary Portraits, third Series,* pp. 191-210. 1920. Reprint. New York: Greenwood Press, Publishers, 1969.
    A contemporary character sketch.

Holloway, John. "Patmore, Donne, and the 'Wit of Love'." In his *The Charted Mirror,* pp. 53-62. London: Routledge & Kegan Paul, 1960.*
    Compares and contrasts Patmore's verse with the poetry of John Donne.

Hopkins, Gerard Manley. "Correspondence with Coventry Patmore." In his *Further Letters of Gerard Manley Hopkins, Including His Correspondence with Coventry Patmore,* 2d ed., edited by Claude Colleer Abbott, pp. 295-393. London: Oxford University Press, 1956.
    Comments on Patmore's poetry, prose, and prosody. A large portion of Hopkins's letters are concerned with technical criticism of poems that Patmore had sent to Hopkins as he was revising his collected works.

Hough, Graham. "Hopkins and Patmore." *The Spectator,* London 197, No. 6705 (28 December 1956): 936-37.*
    A review of E. J. Oliver's *Coventry Patmore* (see annotation below) and *Further Letters of Gerard Manley Hopkins, Including His Correspondence with Coventry Patmore* (see annotation above). Hough deftly contrasts the intellectual, temperamental, political, and spiritual outlooks of two of England's most famous Catholic converts and poets—Patmore and Gerard Manley Hopkins.

Meynell, Alice. "Coventry Patmore." In her *The Second Person Singular and Other Essays,* pp. 94-109. London: Oxford University Press, Humphrey Milford, 1922.
    A reprint of a reverential tribute to Patmore.

Oliver, E. J. *Coventry Patmore.* London: Sheed and Ward, 1956, 211 p.
    A general biographical and critical study.

Patmore, Derek. *The Life and Times of Coventry Patmore.* London: Constable, 1949, 250 p.
    A biography written by Patmore's great-grandson. The book is an enlarged and revised version of the author's 1935 study, *Portrait of My Family, 1783-1896.*

Patmore, Francis J. "Coventry Patmore: A Son's Recollections." *The English Review* LIV (February 1932): 135-41.
    Anecdotal reminiscences of Patmore's later years written by his youngest son.

Praz, Mario. "Appendix I: The Epic of the Everyday, Coventry Patmore's *The Angel in the House.*" In his *The Hero in Eclipse in Victorian Fiction,* translated by Angus Davidson, pp. 413-43. London: Oxford University Press, 1969.
    Identifies and discusses two major influences in *The Angel in the House:* Patmore's intention to convey the atmosphere of everyday life and the "metaphysical influence" of John Donne and other seventeenth-century poets.

Rossetti, William Michael. "The P.R.B. Journal, 1849-53." In *Pre-raphaelite Diaries and Letters,* edited by William Michael Rossetti, pp. 205-309. London: Hurst and Blackett, 1900.*
    Chronicles the activities of the Pre-Raphaelite Brotherhood from 1849 to 1853. The journal includes numerous references to Patmore's interaction with the group.

Shuster, George N. "Poetry and Three Poets." In his *The Catholic Spirit in Modern English Literature*, pp. 104-26. 1922. Reprint. Essay Index Reprint Series. Freeport, N.Y.: Books for Libraries Press, 1967.*
     An assessment of Patmore's achievement as a Catholic poet.

Symons, Arthur. "Coventry Patmore." In his *Figures of Several Centuries*, pp. 351-75. London: Constable and Co., 1916.
     Personal and critical reflections on Patmore's thought and work.

Thompson, Francis. "Patmore." In his *The Real Robert Louis Stevenson and Other Critical Essays by Francis Thompson*, edited by Rev. Terence L. Connolly, S.J., pp. 14-21. New York: University Publishers, 1959.
     Reprinted review of Edmund Gosse's *Coventry Patmore* (see excerpt above, 1905). Thompson comments on Gosse's criticism and offers his own assessment of Patmore's career.

Weinig, Mary Anthony, S.H.C.J. *Coventry Patmore*. Edited by Herbert Sussman. Twayne's English Author Series, no. 331. Boston: Twayne Publishers, 1981, 153 p.
     A reconsideration of Patmore's poetic career. In the course of her study, Weinig addresses numerous issues raised by previous scholars.

Jones Very

1813-1880

American poet and essayist.

Although he left only a small body of work, Very was a prominent figure in the American Transcendentalist movement. He is best known for his deeply religious sonnets which deal with the theme of complete submission to God. In his own time, such critics as Ralph Waldo Emerson, Margaret Fuller, Richard Henry Dana, William Channing, and Nathaniel Hawthorne considered Very one of the most accomplished poets in the United States. Today critics value Very's works for their stylistic mastery and highly individual poetic vision, though his limited range of subjects has prevented greater recognition.

Very was born in Salem, Massachussetts, a descendent of a long line of sea captains. Working as a cabin boy from an early age, he accompanied his father on many sea voyages to such destinations as Louisiana, Denmark, and Russia. Very attended the Salem Public Grammar School until 1827, but discontinued his education to work as an errand boy and later as a teacher at the Fisk Latin School in Salem. With the financial help of an uncle, he entered Harvard College as a sophomore in 1834 and achieved distinction as a classical scholar. He won the prestigious Bowdoin Prize for essay writing in two consecutive years, 1835 and 1836. After graduating from Harvard, Very remained at the college as a Greek tutor and entered Harvard Divinity School. One of his Greek students was an undergraduate named Henry David Thoreau.

In 1838 his Bowdoin Prize essays came to the attention of Elizabeth Palmer Peabody, a close associate of the Transcendentalists and Hawthorne's sister-in-law. She was so impressed that she showed them to Emerson, whom she later introduced to Very. Emerson admired Very's poetic ability and critical acumen and encouraged him to become a professional writer. Along with Peabody, he arranged for Very to lecture at the Concord and Salem Lyceums. Later in 1838, Very claimed that he had religious visions and that all his poetry was dictated to him directly by the Holy Spirit. He attempted to popularize through his writings and lectures his belief in a "will-less existence," in which the individual is guided entirely by God's will. The cost of adhering to his religious convictions was high. He was asked to resign from his post at Harvard after he exhorted his students to "Flee to the mountains, for the end of all things is at hand"; in addition, the college trustees compelled Very to enter the McLean Asylum in Somerville, Massachusetts. Very stayed there one month but returned to Salem undeterred. Emerson and his fellow Trancendentalists attested to Very's claim to sanity and he remained for a while a respected figure in their circle. However, his beliefs directly conflicted with those of the Transcendentalists, and his friendship with Emerson ended in 1840 when Very tried to convert him to his radical religious views.

Little is known about Very's life after 1840. His contemporaries considered him mildly insane, morbid, and overly critical of society, and he spent most of his life in isolation from the people and events around him. Although he never received his degree from the Harvard Divinity School, he became licensed to preach as a Unitarian minister in 1843 and held temporary

pastorates in Massachusetts and Maine until he retired in 1858. For the remainder of his life he lived in Salem with his sisters and contributed poetry and essays to various magazines.

Only one collection of Very's works appeared during his lifetime—the *Essays and Poems*, edited by Emerson. The volume includes poetry, the two Bowdoin Prize essays, and an additional critical essay entitled "Shakespeare." Two posthumous editions of this work, published in 1883 and 1886, include poems written after 1839. In his essay "Epic Poetry," Very describes his theory of life and poetry; "Hamlet" is a character study, influenced by Romantic Shakespearean criticism, in which Very views Hamlet as an artist in conflict with society; in "Shakespeare," Very challenges those critics who charged the dramatist with immorality. He adds that, although they are good people, Shakespeare's characters cannot be considered virtuous because they are not Christian. Almost all of Very's religious poems are composed in the Shakespearean sonnet form, the medium in which reviewers have judged him most comfortable and most competent. Many of his sonnets grow directly out of Very's own profound piety, mysticism, and quietism, and through them he discusses his philosophy of will-less existence. Much of Very's poetry focuses on this surrendering of one's will to God's and on nature as a means of divine revelation. Critics attribute the impassioned tone of Very's sonnets to his use of the unusual device of assuming the voice of God. His use of diction is often compared to that of the English metaphysical poets, especially George Herbert. Yet Very's later poetry lacks much of the depth and variety of his earlier work. The years between 1833 and 1840 are generally considered Very's most productive, and scholars believe that after 1840 the quality of his poetry declined. Although much of the later verse is collected in the 1883 and 1886 editions of his works, some poems as well as letters and sermons have still not been published.

Early critics of Very's writings frequently prefaced their discussions with an explanation of his religious views and a defense of his sanity. The remarks of James Freeman Clarke, Emerson, and William P. Andrews imply that in the nineteenth century Very excited as much curiosity for his religious fanaticism as he did for his poetry. By the turn of the century, starting with Gamaliel Bradford's lengthy study, critical attention shifted to the style and content of his writings. Yvor Winters's 1936 essay, in which he placed Very in the context of American literary history and concluded that he is "one of the greatest devotional poets in English," marked the turning point of the critical assessment of Very's writings. Some critics still continued to subscribe to Emerson's dictum that Very had no style, but many more demonstrated a lively interest in the various aspects of Very's poetic manner. Later critics have explored his themes, symbolism, and poetic structure. They agree that Very was a highly proficient stylist whose visionary poetry was nourished by deeply felt religious beliefs. Scholars point out that in his later years Very's poetry became monotonous and dogmatic. According to some critics, his poetry was sometimes too narrow in range because of the single-mindedness of his convictions. Modern interpreters of Very—especially Nathan Lyons, Anthony Herbold, and Lawrence Buell—have devoted increasing attention to the intellectual content of the nature poetry and have traced his roots to Transcendentalism and Unitarianism. Bradford and Winters, however, have proposed that his style is more similar to Puritan and Quaker writers. The most recent critics of Very have begun to explore his unpublished sermons and epistles.

Since undergoing a dramatic transformation in the 1930s, Very's literary reputation has remained strong. Critics praise his handling of the sonnet form, his diverse poetic persona, and the intensity of his religious and nature lyrics. Today, scholars examine Very's poetry in an effort to establish his relation and importance to the Transcendental movement.

[See also *Dictionary of Literary Biography*, Vol. I: *The American Renaissance in New England*.]

PRINCIPAL WORKS

Essays and Poems   (essays and poetry)   1839
Poems (poetry)   1883
Poems and Essays (poetry and essays)   1886

[JAMES FREEMAN CLARKE]   (essay date 1839)

[*Clarke was the editor of the journal* The Western Messenger, *where Very's poetry was first published. Here, Clarke introduces Very to the readers of* The Western Messenger, *discussing his mental state and likening his sonnets to "wells of thought, clear and pellucid."*]

[Mr. Very's sonnets] have been read by ourselves with no common emotions of interest, and we trust will be equally interesting to our readers.

We hope it will not be considered indelicate if we introduce them with a few words about their author, as some acquaintance with his mental history and experience seems indispensible to a just comprehension of their meaning. If possible, we should place ourselves upon his standing point of thought, in order to be aware of their significance.

We had the pleasure of meeting Mr. Very, a few months since, in the city of Boston. We had heard of him before, from various quarters, as a young man of much intelligence and of a remarkably pure character, whose mind had become extremely interested within a few months, upon the subject of religion. He was said to have adopted some peculiar views on this important theme, and to consider himself inspired by God to communicate them. Such pretensions had excited the fears of his friends, and by many he was supposed to be partially deranged. The more intelligent and larger sort of minds, however, who had conversed with him, dissented from this view, and although they might admit a partial derangement of the lower intellectual organs, or perhaps an extravagant pushing of some views to their last results, were disposed to consider his main thoughts deeply important and vital.

And here we may remark that the charge of Insanity is almost always brought against any man who endeavours to introduce to the common mind any very original ideas. And especially is this the case with moral and religious truths. (pp. 308-09)

[The] intense contemplation of any vast theme is apt to disturb the balance of the lower intellectual faculties. While the Reason, which contemplates absolute truth, is active and strong; the understanding which arranges and gives coherence to our thoughts, may be weakened or reduced to a state of torpor. When this reaches an extreme point, it becomes delirium or mono-mania.

But even in these cases it may be a question which is the *worst* delirium, that by which a man, possessing some great truth, has lost the use of his practical intellect—or that other widespread delirium, in which the mind is enslaved to the lowest cares and meanest aims, and all that is loftiest and greatest in the soul is stupified and deadened in worldliness. When, for instance, we have seen a man in whose intellect all other thoughts have become merged in the great thought of his connexion with God, we have had the feeling very strongly, which we once heard thus expressed, "Is this MONO-MANIA, or is it MONO-SANIA?"

With respect to Mr. Very, we have only to say that the intercourse we have ourselves had with him has given no evidence even of such partial derangement. We have heard him converse about his peculiar views of religious truth, and saw only the workings of a mind absorbed in the loftiest contemplations, and which utterly disregarded all which did not come into that high sphere of thought. We leave it to our readers to decide whether there is any thing of unsoundness in [his] sonnets. To us, they seem like wells of thought, clear and pellucid, and coming up from profound depths.

Mr. Very's views in regard to religion, as we gathered them from himself, were not different from those heretofore advocated by many pure and earnest religionists. He maintains, as did Fenelon, Mme. Guion and others, that all sin consists in self-will, all holiness in an unconditional surrender of our own will to the will of God. He believes that one whose object is not to do his own will in any thing, but constantly to obey God, is led by Him, and taught of him in all things. He is a Son of God, as Christ was *the* Son, because he *always* did the things which pleased his Father. He professes to be himself guided continually by this inward light, and he does not conjecture, speculate or believe, but he *knows* the truth which he delivers. In this confidence however there is nothing of arrogance, but much modesty of manner. (pp. 309-10)

> [James Freeman Clarke], "Religious Sonnets," in
> The Western Messenger, *Vol. VI, No. 5, March, 1839,*
> *pp. 308-14.*

[MARGARET FULLER]   (essay date 1840)

> [A distinguished critic and early feminist, Fuller played an important role in the developing cultural life of the United States during the first half of the nineteenth century. She wrote social, art, and music criticism, but she is most acclaimed as a literary critic; many rank her with Edgar Allan Poe as the finest in her era. In this review of several newly published books, written in the form of a dialogue between Prof. P. and the Rev. Mr. N., Fuller praises Very's poems for their "elasticity of spirit," "genuine flow of thought," "nobleness," and "purity." Though she also sees merit in Very's essays, she posits that they are not "just criticism." For later assessments of Very's essays see the excerpts by Rufus Wilmot Griswold (1852), Gamaliel Bradford (1906), William Irving Bartlett (1942), and Perry Miller (1950).]

Prof. P.—. . . Here is another little volume for you.

Rev. Mr. N.—**"Poems and Essays by Jones Very"**—. I do not remember ever to have heard of it.

Prof. P.—Its circulation is limited, its merits unobtrusive. But in these little poems, though unfinished in style, and homely of mien, you will find an elasticity of spirit, a genuine flow of thought, and an unsought nobleness and purity almost unknown amid the self-seeking, factitious sentiment, and weak movement of our overtaught, and over-ambitious literature, if, indeed, we can say we have one. The essays, also, are full of genuine thought, but not, I think, of just criticism. The author seeks too resolutely for unity, and loses sight of condition. Especially is this the case in the Essays on Shakspeare and Hamlet. He has not found the centre of the Shakspearean circle, and he has strained many points in the attempt.

Rev. Mr. N.—Singular! how little worthy criticism exists on Shakspeare.

Prof. P.—Surely, a dozen or more fineries by Schlegel, two or three just views by Goethe, and some invaluable hints by Coleridge, are all I know of. Amid such destitution, Mr. Very's observations seem well worth considering. His view, whether you agree with it or not, boasts a height and breadth not unworthy of his subject; and in details, he is delicate and penetrating. (p. 132)

> [Margaret Fuller], "'Chat in Boston Bookstores—
> No. I'," in The Boston Quarterly Review, *Vol. III,*
> *No. IX, January, 1840, pp. 127-34.**

[RALPH WALDO] EMERSON   (essay date 1841)

> [Emerson was one of the most influential figures of the nineteenth century. An American essayist and poet, he founded the Transcendental movement and shaped a distinctly American philosophy which embraces optimism, individuality, and mysticism. His phi-

losophy stresses the presence of ongoing creation and revelation by a god apparent in everything and everyone, as well as the essential unity of all thoughts, persons, and things in the divine whole. He was also Very's friend and the editor of his Essays and Poems. In this review of the collection, he asserts that although Very's poems have a narrow range and "no pretension to literary merit," they embody "an extraordinary depth of sentiment." Later critics who discuss style in Very's poetry include Gamaliel Bradford (1906), Yvor Winters (1936), William Irving Bartlett (1942), and Nathan Lyons (1966).]

[The genius of Jones Very's **Essays and Poems**] is religious, and reaches an extraordinary depth of sentiment. The author, plainly a man of a pure and kindly temper, casts himself into the state of the high and transcendental obedience to the inward Spirit. He has apparently made up his mind to follow all its leadings, though he should be taxed with absurdity or even with insanity. In this enthusiasm he writes most of these verses, which rather flow through him than from him. There is no *composition*, no elaboration, no artifice in the structure of the rhyme, no variety in the imagery; in short, no pretension to literary merit, for this would be departure from his singleness, and followed by loss of insight. He is not at liberty even to correct these unpremeditated poems for the press; but if another will publish them, he offers no objection. In this way they have come into the world, and as yet have hardly begun to be known. With the exception of the few first poems, which appear to be of an earlier date, all these verses bear the unquestionable stamp of grandeur. They are the breathings of a certain entranced devotion, which one would say, should be received with affectionate and sympathizing curiosity by all men, as if no recent writer had so much to show them of what is most their own. They are as sincere a litany as the Hebrew songs of David or Isaiah, and only less than they, because indebted to the Hebrew muse for their tone and genius. This makes the singularity of the book, namely, that so pure an utterance of the most domestic and primitive of all sentiments should in this age of revolt and experiment use once more the popular religious language, and so show itself secondary and morbid. These sonnets have little range of topics, no extent of observation, no playfulness; there is even a certain torpidity in the concluding lines of some of them, which reminds one of church hymns; but, whilst they flow with great sweetness, they have the sublime unity of the Decalogue or the Code of Menu, and if as monotonous, yet are they almost as pure as the sounds of surrounding Nature. (pp. 130-31)

> [Ralph Waldo] Emerson, in a review of "Essays and
> Poems," in The Dial, *Vol. II, No. I, July, 1841,*
> *pp. 130-31.*

RUFUS WILMOT GRISWOLD   (essay date 1852)

> [Griswold was an anthologist, magazine editor, and an advocate of "Americanism" in literature.]

[Very's] essays entitled **"Epic Poetry," "Shakespeare,"** and **"Hamlet,"** are fine specimens of learned and sympathetic criticism; and his sonnets, and other pieces of verse, are chaste, simple, and poetical, though they have little range of subjects and illustration. They are religious, and some of them are mystical, but they will be recognised by the true poet as the overflowings of a brother's soul. (p. 405)

> Rufus Wilmot Griswold, "Jones Very," in his The
> Poets and Poetry of America, to the Middle of the
> Nineteenth Century, *revised edition, Carey & Hart,*
> *1852, pp. 405-07.*

WILLIAM P. ANDREWS (poem date 1881)

[*Andrews was a friend of Very's and the editor of* Poems. *The following is a poetic tribute to Very composed in 1881.*]

We thought: the morning birds have ceased to sing,
   We hear but songs from out a gilded cage;
When to our August noon a breath of Spring
   Brought us a strain from out another age:
The sultry airs no longer round us blew,
   The whole wide earth took on a living green;
Flowers bloomed again where erst in Spring they grew,
   And beckoned where the sun-dried heath had been.
O Purest Poet of our world-worn time!
   Thy gentle spirit breathed that quickening lay;
Thy rapt soul heard the harmonies sublime,
   And sang the music of a loftier day:
THE SOUL of all things in thy pulses stirred,
And soared in praises like the morning bird.

(pp. 111-12)

William P. Andrews, "Jones Very," in Lowell,
Whittier, Very and the Alcotts among Their Contem-
poraries, edited by Kenneth Walter Cameron, Tran-
scendental Books, 1978, pp. 111-12.

THE LITERARY WORLD (essay date 1883)

[*In this review of* Poems, *the critic discusses Very's mysticism and commends the "neatness and delicacy" of his style.*]

Pure mysticism, and that of the deeply religious kind, we do not easily associate with the American life of today. For such a plant our society seems to afford neither soil, climate, nor other favorable conditions. A certain mystical vein is found in Longfellow, and still more clearly in Whittier, but in each case it is touched and changed by sober Saxon sense until it lies within the appreciation of the practical mind. But our poetry has one mystic of the Old World type, a brother in spirit to Tauler and Madame Guyon, who, like them, lost the present in the unseen, and transfigured the homely scenes of a common life with a glow as of Hebrew inspiration. This solitary soul was Jones Very, a name to most readers unknown, yet deeply revered by the choice spirits who came within his modest, but profound, influence. . . .

[It is George Herbert that Very's] verses first suggest, but George Herbert with a decided difference. The same pure, sweet, spiritual fervor breathes through both, joined with the same devoutness in tone. But Very has nothing of that mere verbal quaintness which must have struck even the contemporary reader of Herbert. He never plays with words, and his fancy commits no freaks in her flight. In fancy indeed he seems almost deficient, as Hawthorne says he was deficient in humor. The peculiar, striking qualities of his verse lie far below the words. In childlike, unconscious simplicity of expression, he reminds one of William Blake. Yet in the naturalness and facility with which he pierces through the material, outward fact, to the spiritual lesson beneath, he rivals the dictionary of correspondences, and deserves the name of a poetic Swedenborg. To those who have ears to hear, his words will prove what he delighted to style them, a Message and a Call, and many readers will be grateful for this introduction to a genius so impressive and so unique. The neatness and delicacy of [*Poems by Jones Very*] are in full accord with the retirement of the poet's spirit. . . .

"Jones Very," in The Literary World, Vol. XIV,
No. 13, June 30, 1883, p. 203.

THE ATLANTIC MONTHLY (essay date 1883)

[Very's] essays would scarcely attract attention now, in the altered condition of literary estimate; many of the poems [in *Poems*, by Jones Very] are commonplace; some are but feeble repetitions of sentiments that had been better expressed before. One or two of those here presented to the public might have been dropped, as being tame or diluted; but the best give evidence of original power, genuine feeling, and unconscious art, if art can be said ever to be unconscious. At all events, they betray a peculiar tone of religious emotion, expressed in suitable language, always simple, often beautiful, sometimes ravishingly sweet and touching. (p. 123)

[Mr. Very] was unique and peculiar. His vein was narrow, but deep. He had not the piercing insight of Emerson, the keen observation of Bryant, the warm human sympathy of Longfellow, the artistic feeling of Lowell, or the hilarity of Holmes. But he possessed a profound sense of the reality of divine things as symbolized in nature. He had but one thought, that of the immanence of God. He had but one emotion, a desire that the Spirit might be witnessed and confessed. He had but one interest, that men should turn their eyes towards the light. He was a mystic, but not of the German type; more Christian than Emerson, rather Greek than Latin in the style of his devoutness. (p. 127)

[Very's] poems can hardly be popular in an age like ours,— an age fond of change, diversion, variety, amusement, color; an age of external decoration, averse to meditation, inclined to criticise rather than to believe. But there must be many devout souls who will welcome this beautiful volume with delight, as expressing lofty thoughts in musical phrase. (p. 128)

"Jones Very," in The Atlantic Monthly, Vol. LII,
No. CCCIX, July, 1883, pp. 123-28.

GEORGE BATCHELOR (essay date 1883)

[*Batchelor points to a revival of interest in Very's work. He also suggests that the "disordered perception" created by Very's self-righteousness considerably diminished his poetic accomplishment.*]

Among the minds stirred about half a century ago by the impulse of Transcendentalism, one of the least conspicuous, and since that time one of the least known, was one which now fairly promises to be foremost in the poetic interpretation of the movement. As the personal influence of men and women disappears with their exit from the stage on which they played their parts, and their works only remain to praise them, many singular changes are wrought. A charming presence, a moving voice, a persuasive smile, are indications of character and legitimate means of influence. But in literature they have no value, excepting some slight attractiveness which they add to work which is undeniably good as it stands in the unflattering black and white of the printed page. On the other hand, however unattractive be the personality of a thinker, and however small his power to use eye, hand, voice, and presence, as a means of communication, good work once committed to the press will win its way and justify its author.

Therefore it happens that Jones Very, for forty years past one of the most reserved, modest, retiring, and unknown of literary men, now slowly comes to the front. . . . (p. 58)

[In **Poems,** by Jones Very,] we have the brief story of his life and an enlarged edition of his poems. It seems to me not exaggeration to say that, for the one thing in which they excel—the spiritual interpretation of nature—these poems have no rivals in American literature, and are to be compared only with the best work of Wordsworth in the same department. The "sense sublime of something far more deeply interfused," which gave Wordsworth his power of interpreting nature, was to Very a reality to such an extent that his language ceases to be metaphorical. Tropes and figures which, used by other poets, would be regarded as "poetical," come from his pen as simple statements of fact. When he says:

> The flowers I pass have eyes that look on me,
> The birds have ears that hear my spirit's voice,
> And I am glad the leaping brook to see,
> Because it doth at my light step rejoice,

he means literally that he and the birds, the streams, and the flowers, have means of a mutual understanding denied to other men, because they refused to become submissive to the Divine will as he had done. (pp. 58-9)

Natural genius and the finest classical culture had given him unerring good taste and command of the Shakspearean sonnet as a means of communicating his thought to the world, and the uninstructed reader would never suspect that he was reading the words of a man "beside himself" according to the standard of what we call "common sense." His was uncommon sense . . . , a higher mood of sanity, to which few men ever attained.

In one way only does the exaggeration of his statement indicate a disordered perception. No man but himself was "right." He tried to say to Emerson that he was right, but he told him "The Spirit said you were not right; it is just as if I should say, it is not morning, but the morning says it is morning." To the message of the morning, Very listened, and he believed that no one else did. Hence an exaggerated condemnation of his fellows and a turning away from all that we call modern progress. He says:

> I walk the streets, and though not meanly drest,
> Yet none so poor as can with me compare;
>
> • • • • •
>
> In only ask the living word to hear
> From tongues that now but speak to utter death;
> I thirst for one cool cup of water clear,
> But drink the riléd stream of lying breath;
> And wander on, though in my Fatherland,
> Yet hear no welcome voice and see no beckoning hand.

He heard nothing, or but now and then a note of "the still, sad music of humanity" which came to the ears of Wordsworth mingled with the songs that nature sang to him. Yet there is a verse which hints at possibilities of a larger life for him:

> As the years come gliding by me,
> Fancy's pleasing visions rise,
> Beauty's cheek, ah! still I see thee,
> Still your glances, soft blue eyes!

One would like to know whether he wrote this "by permission, not by commandment," and we must regret that by some mis-

carriage of his genius he was reduced to the singing of one sweet song to nature when clearly he might have been a poet of humanity whose verses would have moved the world to listen. (p. 59)

*George Batchelor, "A Poet of Transcendentalism,"
in* The Dial, *Vol. IV, No. 39, July, 1883, pp. 58-9.*

MARY FISHER   (essay date 1899)

[*Fisher proposes that Very's poetry has been overrated by critics. Though she condemns his dreaminess and "monotonous circle of ideas," Fisher singles out Very's "The Arab Steed" as an unusually successful poem.*]

[Very's] love for nature never rises above a comfortable sensation of being undisturbed in his self-communings. This drowsy comfort is expressed in . . . **"The Columbine."** . . . (p. 128)

With the exception of the religious sonnets and hymns, the subjects of Very's poems are mostly natural objects met in his rambles, notably flowers and trees; as **"The Yellow Violet," "The Houstonia," "The Oak and the Poplar," "The May Flower," "The Wind Flower," "The Sabbatia,"** etc.

Jones Very thought himself a reed through which the Master Musician spoke. The monotonous burden of his rhymes is, "I am the Lord's: He speaks through me; I am but a passive instrument of His will." But never was there more foolish overrating of a humble power of rhyming. He has not written a quotable line, unless it be the opening lines of the sonnet entitled **"The True Light,"** which are a pretty rhetorical rendering of the familiar thought that the kingdom of God is within you:—

> The morning's brightness cannot make thee glad,
> If thou art not more bright than it within,
> And naught of evening's peace hast thou e'er had,
> If evening first did not with thee begin.

Once only did he break through the monotonous circle of ideas to which he gave expression, and write true poetry, and that was when he wrote **"The Arab Steed."** Perhaps for this one poem he deserves grateful remembrance. There is in it a fire, a swift energy, an imaginative vigor of which he gives no proof elsewhere. His weakness is the weakness of the monotone,—the weakness of the man in whom is lacking that fine common-sense born of experience, and who has nothing, therefore, to hold him back from yielding to the extreme conclusions of his theories. His love of God crowded from his heart the love of man. He was pure; but his purity was that of white, dry sand in which not even a nettle will grow; and so "our brave saint," as Emerson calls him, has done less for the world than many a sinner with the gift of song. (pp. 129-30)

Jones Very represents wholly the dreamy poetic side of Transcendentalism with its coloring of religious mysticism. (p. 130)

Mary Fisher, "Transcendentalists and the Transcendental Movement in New England—George Ripley, Amos Bronson Alcott, Jones Very, Sarah Margaret Fuller Ossoli," in her A General Survey of American Literature, *A. C. McClurg and Company, 1899, pp. 113-42.**

G. M. HAMMELL   (essay date 1901)

[Very] is not the poet of the crowd; and he sometimes wrote verse which no criticism, however sympathetic, can pronounce poetic. Not always was he inspired. He wrote, as Wordsworth often wrote, by habit or by volition; and it is no dishonor to say of him, as it has been said of Wordsworth, that a selection of his poetry is essential to his place in literature.

He was, first of all, the poet of transcendentalism, that unique intellectual movement of the early nineteenth century, which, subordinating the Hebrew-Christian sacred books to the monitions of the spirit, sought truth by new attitudes of independent or self-dependent insight and inquiry. An old Concord villager, whom the writer found mowing grass in the yard that surrounds the abandoned Hillside Chapel, where the School of Philosophy used to meet, remarked that the Concord philosophers endeavored to know more than God himself knows.

There is a quality of mysticism, therefore, in Very's verse which sets him forever apart and makes him the poet of those who seek the spirit in hidden places. He was characteristically a recluse spirit, an unpopular poet, speaking to the few, but to them with a voice of authority. (pp. 20-1)

It has been alleged that transcendentalism lifted him, then left him, and that, after his exaltation and descent, he never came to his own. It is certain that he never became a "practical man;" political economists class him as a "consumer;" materialistic critics pronounce him infertile, a mere parasite. (p. 23)

He was thrust aside from the strong currents of native life, his career was doomed to the narrow circles of an eddy—but he bore in noble, uncomplaining silence the burden of a seeming failure. Emerson predicted for him a large and growing audience, but Very's audience was never large, and for a decade it has not grown. In the great public libraries there is no demand for his "work," and critics cannot agree as to his place in the world of American literature. (p. 25)

[Very's] sonnets are consummately perfect in form and possessed of that subtle power which Ruskin pronounced the paradox of art—"the power to stay what is fleeting, to enlighten what is incomprehensible, to incorporate the things that have no measure, and immortalize the things that have no duration." . . . To Very himself there was a kind of mystery about his writing; he regarded himself simply as a medium. Whatever may be the correct psychology of his poetic activity, literary criticism, if it be true to its own canons, must admit that the sonnets, at least, exhibit more than a "humble power of rhyming." If Jones Very—the Very of 1839—was only "a humble rhymer," then Curtis, Emerson, Hawthorne, Dana, and Bryant were mistaken in their panegyric. His was more than a "slender rill;" at his best he was one of our truest, greatest poets to whom nature opened her secrets. (p. 27)

[Very was] a poet whose verse is the voice of a pure spirit, dedicated to Him who is all and in all. (p. 30)

G. M. Hammell, "Jones Very—A Son of the Spirit," in The Methodist Review, *n.s. Vol. XVII, No. 1, January-February, 1901, pp. 20-30.*

WILLIAM P. TRENT   (essay date 1903)

The sun of transcendentalism did not awaken large choirs of poets in New England, but besides stirring into life the master spirits . . . , it also inspired a few minor but true poets to sing out their gentle souls. . . . [Jones Very] was probably the most complete religious mystic of the epoch—a clergyman so spiritual that he almost passed over the bounds of sanity. He published but one book, a small volume of *Essays and Poems,*

which appealed only to a select audience that has not grown greatly since new editions have been given to the world. His favourite metrical form was the Shakespearean sonnet, and in expressing his love of God and nature he often struck a note that seemed a far-off echo of some of the greater poet's truest strains. But his lack of variety and of broad human appeal stood in Very's way, and thus such strongly imaginative sonnets as that entitled "**The Dead,**" although preserved by the anthologies, can scarcely be said to be familiar to lovers of poetry. (p. 346)

William P. Trent, "Transcendentalism—Its Interpreters," in his A History of American Literature: 1607-1865, *D. Appleton and Company, 1903, pp. 314-48.**

GAMALIEL BRADFORD   (essay date 1932)

[*Bradford is best known as a biographer and critic who rejected the chronological biographical approach in literary criticism in favor of what he termed "psychography," or profiling a personality by means of anecdotes and quotations. In the following essay, which is the first extensive study of Very's work, Bradford traces the evolution of his writings. He focuses on Very's style and asserts that mysticism and love of nature are the most notable features of his writings, concluding that his is "a name which ought not to be forgotten." For later treatments of Very's style see the excerpts by Yvor Winters (1936), William Irving Bartlett (1942), and Nathan Lyons (1966). Other critics who assess Very's Shakespearean criticism are Margaret Fuller (1840), William Irving Bartlett (1942), and Perry Miller (1950). This essay first appeared in a different form in the* Unitarian Review *in 1887.*]

[While Very's prose] is filled with the same spirit which pervades the poetry, and so forms a good introduction to that, I myself do not find in it the same artistic touch, the same lightness and ease which make the charm of the verse. The difference is that between a man's working with tools for which he was born, and again with others which are not natural to him.

When, however, we come to examine the three essays, in the order in which they are printed, we shall find between the first and last of them something of the same difference which exists between the prose as a whole and the verse; so much so, indeed, that one might almost conceive of a gradual progress from one to the other, and believe that the genius of the man had in this way followed its own law of development. It is true that a comparison of dates will hardly bear us out in this view; and yet, so often, the internal life cannot be measured by the times and limits of the external: one may see the youth and the man dwelling in the same soul side by side. And it seems to me that the history of many minds can be understood and written only by a chronology of the spirit different from that of the body.

The essay on Epic Poetry, in this order, comes to us first; and here, I believe, we have the earliest of Very's works, both in its manner and in its date. In this he attempts to prove that the epic, from its nature, belongs to a past age and all efforts to reproduce it under modern conditions must fail. He has put originality into his work. Even here, we begin to find a theory of poetry, a theory of life, entirely new. Already Very has begun to treat nature and the human soul in his own way, viewing everything in the relation which his own mind had established between itself and God:

The effect of Christianity was to make the individual mind the great object of regard, the centre of eternal interest, and transferring the scene of action from the outward world to the world within, to give all modern literature the dramatic tendency—and as the mind of Homer led him to sing of the physical conflicts of his heroes with *visible* gods *without;* so the soul of the modern poet, feeling itself contending with motives of Godlike power *within,* must express that conflict in the dramatic form, the poetry of sentiment.

Here and elsewhere one touches the note which makes Very true and noble: his insight into the history and nature of the soul. The inquiry in regard to Epic Poetry, moreover, does not lack interest. And yet one feels a certain sense of effort through it all. It is the work of a man born to affirm and not to compare; and affirmation is not the office of criticism. The style, too, is weak. One finds occasionally a strong, nervous sentence after the manner of Emerson, a manner so easily caught by those who read him, and so dangerous to anyone who cannot use it. Yet this manner, keen, trenchant, vigorous, is not Very's own: it has not grace enough, has not enough of the true artist's touch. What Very's manner is, we shall see best when we come to his poetry, but in this first essay the style is tentative, doubtful, perhaps hampered by the same sense of effort which one cannot but feel in the matter of the piece also:

> The poets of the present day who would raise the epic-song, cry out like Archimedes: "Give me a place to stand on and I will move the world."

To write like that is not to have a bad style. It is worse: to have no style at all. And Very's first essay is full of such sentences.

When we come to his essays on Shakespeare and Hamlet, we are treading on other ground. If the same defects of manner are occasionally visible, one cannot help feeling that the man is speaking with an inspiration. And to an inspiration can we not pardon anything? The two essays may very well be considered together. They are both of them a development in the same line of the one idea that was beginning to take possession of Very's life: the idea that the human soul had no object and no aim but to identify itself with God, that in this union of our will with his was to be found the satisfaction, the highest fulfillment of all desires. Without that, as he thinks, we must be forever miserable, all the more miserable, if we are ignorant of the cause of our pain. (pp. 189-92)

At least the thesis is original. I do not think that the riddle of Avon has been tried in that way before. Certainly I do not say that Very has solved it; but in trying to explain Shakespeare, he explains himself. That is all we ask of him.

In the same strain he continues. Genius is but an increased activity, a more universal capacity for growth, a larger unconscious sympathy with all nature, animate and inanimate. It is by this that Shakespeare felt as he did the harmony between the evil and the good which must be unperceived by us:

> Like the ocean his mind could fill with murmuring waves the strangely indented coast of human existence from the widest bay to the smallest creek; then, ebbing, retire within itself, as if form was but a mode of its limitless and independent being.

Shakespeare, too, in Very's idea of him, though hating decay and all the outward signs of death, though thrilled perpetually with the joy and beauty of the world, felt instinctively the eternity of his existence, felt it, perhaps, the more by reason of the passionate life that was within him. Hence his indifference to fame and his carelessness in the preservation of his works. 'For,' says Very, 'fame can only be a motive to those who have no practical belief in the next world, or to whom it is an uncertainty.' Certainly that is cutting the knot; but, after all, weaker explanations have passed current for the same thing. (pp. 193-94)

And Very goes on to mark the difference which consists in Shakespeare's power of depicting life as it really is, as he sees it about him, while he is incapable of creating an ideal outside of life. The difference is clear, and the distinction not new. It is the explanation which is new and worth our attention, as it seems to me.

> Homer and Shakespeare were without a struggle the natural representatives of this action; and their language was a universal one through which all things found expression.... Such minds, as we have before said, seem to be exceptions, for wise purposes, to the rest of our race; exhibiting to all the natural features of the soul in the unconscious and childlike state of innocence.... In Wordsworth and Milton, on the contrary, we see the struggle of the child to become the perfect man in Christ Jesus. Their constant prayer is, "Not my will, Father, but thine be done." They are striving for that silence in their own bosoms, that shall make the voice that created all things heard.

There are people who will call this fantastic. In truth, it is not the tone of America in the twentieth century, yet I cannot but think there is something near Christianity in it, nearer, perhaps, than some of us dream.

I must quote one passage more before we leave this essay, as much for the style, which shows Very's prose at its best, clear and refined, though never vigorous, as for the summing up of his idea of Shakespeare which it presents:

> Shakespeare, though at times he may have been possessed of his genius, must, in far the most numerous of his days and years, have been possessed by it. Lost in wonder at the countless beings that thronged uncalled the palace of his soul and dwelt beneath its "majestical roof fretted with golden fires"; he knew not, or, if he knew, forgot that even those angel visitants were not sent for him merely to admire and number; but that knowing no will but His who made kings His subjects, he should send them forth on their high mission, and with those high resolves which it was left for him to communicate. Had he done this, we might, indeed, reverence him as the image of his God; as a sharer in His service, whose service is perfect freedom.

I do not say that that is great, but it is the work of a man who had thought and felt. Many of us may learn something from it.

I have quoted enough to show the vein. In the essay on Hamlet, it is in the main points the same. There is the same interest for us that there was in the essay on Shakespeare: a new and strong interpretation of a hackneyed subject. And that is a great recommendation here and today. There is the same explanation of external phenomena by internal, of the world by the soul. There is the same depth and seriousness of treatment. Only, perhaps, here the author is further advanced. He has grown more at ease with his materials. He begins to find himself at home.

To Very's mind, as to that of all critics, Hamlet is the sun, the efflorescence of Shakespeare's genius; but the application of Very's theory in regard to this genius makes clear in Hamlet many things which have puzzled others. In Hamlet, he thinks, we have Shakespeare for a minute stopping to question this mighty stream of activity which elsewhere glows forth in him unbounded and unchecked. He stops suddenly. He examines himself. He asks himself the why of all these things; and the very power he has of feeling everything makes the question more tremendous, more unanswerable. According to Very, it is the great defect of Shakespeare that he cannot find the answer. All the disorder, all the ugliness, which is caused by the separation of the soul from God—this man could understand it all. But the solution of the riddle was not given to him.

Fantastic again! Fantastic or not, is there not thought here? (pp. 193-97)

I have spoken thus at length of Very's prose, because in it one sees the man apart from the artist, and it is interesting to begin with that. It is not often that one has a chance to see so clearly the foundation before one examines the structure that is built on it, and the opportunity should be improved when it comes. But the beauty and the charm are not there after all. One must go higher for them. (pp. 197-98)

Sainte-Beuve, speaking of Maurice de Guérin, observes delicately that the worship of Nature and the worship of Christ cannot go together: 'The Cross bars more or less the free view of Nature; the divine Pan has nothing to do with the divine crucified One.' At first sight, Very, like Wordsworth and some others, may seem a contradiction of this; but I do not think we shall find it so if we look carefully. True, he speaks again and again of Christ, often with love and almost adoration; and yet, to me he does not seem to look upon him as Christians looked upon him two hundred years ago. Jesus is to him a friend, a teacher, a brother, nay, in a certain sense, a savior, if you will; never, I think, a God. For God he looks above Calvary and beyond it, or rather he looks forward and not back, within and not without. In his idea, the God in Christ is in us too. 'He does not make Christ a man, but all men Gods,' or, better, part of God. Certainly, if this is not so, Sainte-Beuve is, in this case, wrong. First and foremost in Very comes his love of Nature, his power of interpreting her; and though, at minutes, he separates himself from her, feels an enmity between her and God, he always returns to her. She is his hope, his consolation, the real mediator between him and the divine:

Nature! my love for thee is dearer far
Than strength of words, though spirit-born, can tell.

That is the note. Again and again he turns to it. The best of his poems deal with it directly, and in all the others it is the ground-tone running through, side by side with his passionate desire to be at one with God. Indeed, his longing for Nature becomes often the best expression for this desire which he can find.

The first three divisions of the poems, which are made in the edition of 1883—'The Call,' 'The New-Birth,' 'The Message'—are concerned chiefly with the peculiar mission which he felt himself called to, and its communication to others. In 'The Call' he speaks repeatedly of his newly discovered communion with God, of the joy and peace which is to be found there:

So does my spirit wait thy presence now
To pour thy praise in quickening life along,
Chiding with voice divine man's lengthened sleep,
While round the unuttered Word and Love their vigils keep.

Observe here the lengthening of the last line, an innovation common in Very's sonnets, which adds a certain largeness, as it seems to me. One sees in this and in many other places in this part of the book that peculiar sense of his own inspiration which makes Very so remarkable. It is not the confidence of Petrarch: 'Know me whoever can, I know myself.' Nor is it the confidence of Shakespeare:

For I am that I am, and they that level
At my abuses reckon up their own.

Compared with that one might almost call it the confidence of Jesus:

To him who hath, to him my verse shall give,
And he the more from all he does shall gain.
(pp. 197-200)

Very has been several times compared to George Herbert; but the comparison does not seem to me apt. They both were what are called 'religious poets,' to be sure. So was Watts. Very, moreover, has an occasional line in the manner of Herbert, as:

Then hast me fenced about with thorny talk.

But Herbert was an epigrammatist, I had almost said a wit; at any rate an Elizabethan, as full of conceits and word-plays as Shakespeare or Chapman himself. To compare him with Emerson would be juster. Very is the farthest possible removed from conceits of any kind. He is no Elizabethan of the seventeenth century, but rather suggests an Italian or a German of the thirteenth. . . . (p. 201)

In 'The Message' we find collected sonnets which deal, for the most part, with Very's performance of his mission in rebuke and appeal to other men. I do not think that his highest claim to consideration lies in this; but perhaps it is the most original point in him, the point least to be paralleled in the literature of which he forms a part. Emerson, to be sure, exhorts, encourages, instructs; but the tone of Very is different. There is a certain sternness in it, a flavor of absolutism, which carries one back a thousand, two thousand years, out of modern skepticism and doubt where men at best do no more than find conviction for themselves. 'He spoke as one having authority, and not as the Scribes and Pharisees.'. . . It is Emerson who compares Very to David and Isaiah [see excerpt above, 1841]. In this point of his character the comparison is just. By his passionate sensibility to Nature, by his broad and spiritual view of God, he stands apart from them; but he has in common with them, if in a far less degree, that authority and prophetic sternness, that austerity and severity of purpose, which laid the scourge again and again on the backs of the wayward and disobedient Jews. And he has also, in common with them, a sense of wrath and scorn at the meanness and pettiness of men around him, a feeling of isolation in the midst of a people who have fallen off from God.

> My heart grows sick before the wide-spread death
> That walks and speaks in seeming life around;
> And I would love the corpse without a breath
> That sleeps forgotten 'neath the cold, cold ground. . . .

Is it not the same desolate cry which comes always from the inspired lips: 'He came unto his own and his own received him not'? And not from the saints only, but from the poet and from the sage, every man who sees without the emptiness and folly and frivolity of the world, and within the intense reality of things. It is by this chord that Very is in sympathy with many men of his century who are otherwise so different from him, men like Shelley and Leopardi; or [Sénancour,] the strange and forlorn author of *Obermann,* men bound together, not by beliefs or creeds, but by a common hatred of the meanness and pretension by which so many souls are chained, men who stand side by side regardless of their differences. . . . (pp. 202-04)

After man let us take Nature. It is the refuge which many a weary heart has sought before us, and many more will seek it after. I know few better guides to it than Very. Not that he is one of the great word-painters. He does not show us the external world in a rich, sensuous glamour like Keats, nor does he idealize it into a dream like Shelley, nor clothe it in purple, sunset splendor, like Byron. His rendering of it is more that of Wordsworth, a seizing of delicate points and making them stand out before the eye almost unobscured by the veil of language; but Wordsworth at his best moments has far more inspiration than Very, more illumination, if I may use the word; and at his worst he has far less sympathy. This is what makes Very so singular and so precious: his identification of himself with Nature, his losing himself in pure adoration. He forgets to write for the sake of writing, but lets his feelings flow directly from his pen.

> Nature! my love for thee is deeper far
> Than strength of words, though spirit-born, can tell;
> For while I gaze they seem my soul to bar,
> That in thy widening streams would onward swell,
> Bearing thy mirrored beauty on its breast.

This figure of a river seems especially to charm him. He turns to it again and again, delighting himself with the calmness of it:

> A motion that scarce knows itself from rest.
> Amid the fields I am a child again,
> The spots that then I loved, I love the more,
> My fingers drop the strangely-scrawling pen
> And I remember nought but Nature's lore.

'Strangely-scrawling pen' is somewhat forced, but we can feel the note. The group of sonnets called **'Nature'** is all in this strain. . . . Nature is touched and lighted up by the presence of the soul. Seeing the snow which covers and purifies all, he hears man bid it cover his heart also:

> But all in vain: its guilt can never hide
> From the quick Spirit's heart-deep searching eye;
> The barren plains and caverns yawning wide
> Lie ever naked to the passer-by;
> Nor can one thought deformed the presence shun,
> But to the Spirit's gaze stands bright as in the sun.

Read 'The Violet':

> The nearest neighbor of the creeping vines.

In such lines as that one sees Very's best vein. No splendor of Miltonic inversion, no sublimity; a feeling moulding its own words, and admirable simplicity. Simplicity! We hear of it often nowadays. I am a little weary of the phrase myself. We forget so readily that between simplicity and commonplace there is an immense gulf fixed. (pp. 204-06)

I spoke a little while ago of Very's entire identification of himself with Nature. The phrase is something overworn; but in his case it had reality. With him it means far more than an after-dinner admiration of rainbows and the sunset glow, more even than a careful study of Nature and a poetical interpretation of her. There are minutes when he seems to enter into her being, to breathe her breath, to throb, himself, with that mysterious life which we have all of us, at minutes, a faint intuition of, but which few, it seems to me, have felt as he did. At least few have given such utterance to that feeling of it. One sonnet, that to **'The Columbine,'** is especially noticeable for this. . . . (p. 207)

All the sonnets in this section **'Nature'** are interesting. One finds an occasional awkwardness and carelessness of expression; but the average is Very's best. Just the reverse is the case with the division entitled **'Song and Praise.'** One finds there some of his weakest work, and, side by side with it, some of his greatest. . . . **'The Prayer'** at the beginning, **'The Fossil Flower,'** the **'Lines to —— on the Death of His Friend'**—there are few things in the whole book finer than these. But on the other side, we have **'The Tenant'** and **'The Sight of the Ocean'**:

> I turned from the dark and rocky height,
> With grateful heart to my hearthstone bright.

That recalls Wordsworth in his bathetic fits, or I do not know what hymns of our childhood. Here again one sees his lack of literary skill. The truth is, Very wrote wholly by his inspiration. When that failed him, he had no talent to keep him up, and he wrote very poor stuff indeed.

The book closes with eight or ten sonnets collected under the title of **'The Beginning and the End.'** . . . All of them, I think, are worthy of their author: they have hardly any of his characteristic weaknesses. Indeed, it seems as if the Shakespearian sonnet were Very's true instrument. In that he is at home, and can do what he will. With other lyrical forms he cannot feel at ease. (pp. 208-09)

I shall be asked why I have dwelt thus long on a man so little known as Jones Very. To be sure, he is not and never can be one of the great figures in literature. His breadth is not sufficiently great in proportion to his depth. Moreover, the outward forms of current religious phraseology, in which he clothed his profound spiritual life, are to a certain degree repulsive to many men of this generation; and on the other hand, his passionate idealism does not altogether please comfortable orthodoxy. Yet I cannot help thinking that there are two points in Very, which ought to give him a place, permanent, at least, if not prominent, in our literature: his love of Nature and his mysticism. I know well that with our vast material civilization the love of Nature and mysticism have little to do. Yet I, myself, have a belief, perhaps unwarranted, in certain deeper sides of human nature, which makes me think that one day our vast material civilization, as it at present exists, may be all gone—

> Like what seemed corporal, melted into thin air;

and then the world may be inclined to find a small place even for such men as Jones Very. (pp. 211-12)

Very at the age of twenty-four.

[Very's is] a name, certainly, not of the greatest, and yet, as it seems to me, a name which ought not to be forgotten. (p. 212)

> *Gamaliel Bradford, "Jones Very," in his* Biography and the Human Heart, *1932. Reprint by Books for Libraries Press, 1969; distributed by Arno Press, Inc., pp. 185-212.*

YVOR WINTERS   (essay date 1936)

[Winters was a twentieth-century American poet and critic. He was associated with the New Criticism movement and gained a reputation as one of the most stringently anti-romantic critics of his period. Maintaining that a critic must be concerned with the moral as well as the aesthetic import of a work of art, he also believed that poetry ought to provide rational comment on the human condition, with the poet "seeking to state a true moral judgment." His critical precepts, usually considered extreme, include an emphasis on order, dignity, restraint, and morality. They are embodied in In Defense of Reason, *his best known collection of essays, which includes "Maule's Curse," a study of nineteenth-century American literature. In the following essay, which marked a turning point in Very criticism, Winters analyzes Very's style and argues strongly for a reassessment of his place in American Literature, deeming him "one of the greatest devotional poets in English." For other studies of Very's style see the excerpts by Gamaliel Bradford (1906), William Irving Bartlett (1942), and Nathan Lyons (1966).]*

In the past two decades two major American writers have been rediscovered and established securely in their rightful places in literary history. I refer to Emily Dickinson and to Herman Melville. I am proposing the establishment of a third [, Jones Very]. (p. 159)

Very was about ten years younger than Emerson and about four years older than Thoreau. He preached at times in the Unitarian pulpit; he is commonly listed as one of the minor Transcendentalists; yet both facts are misleading. He was a mystic, primarily, whose theological and spiritual affiliations were with the earlier Puritans and Quakers rather than with the Unitarians or the friends of Emerson; and if a minor writer, he was at least not one in relationship to the Transcendentalists. (p. 160)

That Very should so long have been neglected, that he should be left, a century after the production of most of his best poetry, to the best defense that one, like myself, at every turn unsympathic with his position, is able to offer, is one of the anomalies of literary history. Of the sincerity of his profession, we can hold no doubt. His poems are as convincing, and as excellent, as are the poems of Blake, of Traherne, or of George Herbert. His contemporaries, those who regarded him not only in spirit, but in the flesh, paid his sincerity the highest tribute that men can pay to that of any man: they adjudged him insane. . . . It was during his stay at the asylum that he finished his three essays in literary criticism, which, whatever their faults, are beautifully written and display great penetration and perfect presence of mind. (pp. 165-66)

[While] recognizing that Very's mystical poetry is imperfectly relevant to us, we may get what we can from it, and since that which we can obtain is frequently of great value, we can scarcely be losers in the relationship.

To the fine anguish which Very suffered from his sense of defilement in a sinful world, and to the strange conflict which must have lived within him between this feeling and the real humility which appears in many of his poems, we may obtain a clue in the extraordinary poem entitled **"Thy Brother's Blood"**. . . . (p. 169)

To give a better indication of the power and purity of statement to which Very attains, I shall quote a few . . . poems and passages. The quotation of brief passages is largely unjust, for Very is not a poet of separable moments; his poems are reasoned and coherent, and the full force of a passage will be evident only when one meets it in the context. Further, there is a feeling of intense personal conviction in Very, a kind of saturation with his subject and his feeling, which one tends to lose in a brief passage; it is a conviction so extraordinary that in some of his secondary achievements it is able to carry a considerable weight of stereotyped language without the destruction of the poem. To appreciate the finer shades of his statement one should be familiar, moreover, with his work as a whole, for he is essentially a theological poet, and his references to doctrine are on the one hand fleeting and subtle, and on the other hand of the utmost importance to a perception of his beauty; and in addition, his finest effects are the result of fine variations in tone, the appreciation of which must of necessity depend in a large measure upon a consciousness of the norm from which the variations occur. (pp. 170-71)

"The Garden", is restrained and precise in its imagery, and may conceivably find few admirers; an appreciation of its beauty depends upon a realization of the mystical significance, or some part of it, back of the description; though my own sympathy with the author's religious views is largely one of a kind of hypothetical acquiescence, the poem nevertheless seems very fine to me. . . . **"The Lost"**, is one of the author's four or five most beautiful; it appears to go close to the heart of the mystical experience, and in spite of the obscurity resulting is unforgettable. The subject is that of identity with God, and hence with all time and place, of the divine life in the unchanging present of eternity; or rather the subject is the comparison of that life with the life of man, "the lost". The mysterious and subdued longing expressed in the poem culminates, perhaps, in lines five and six, and again in lines nine and ten, and the reader may possibly work his way into the poem best by concentrating for a moment on these lines; the poem, however, is a unit and impeccable:

> The fairest day that ever yet has shone,
> Will be when thou the day within shalt see;
> The fairest rose that ever yet has blown,
> When thou the flower thou lookest on shalt be;
> But thou are far away among Time's toys;
> Thyself the day thou lookest for in them,
> Thyself the flower that now thine eye enjoys,
> But wilted now thou hang'st upon thy stem.
> The bird thou hearest on the budding tree,
> Thou hast made sing with thy forgotten voice;
> But when it swells again to melody,
> The song is thine in which thou wilt rejoice;
> And thou new risen 'midst these wonders live,
> That now to them dost all thy substance give.

The same subject reappears in the poem entitled **"Today"**, a lovely but less finished performance, of which I quote the first half:

> I live but in the present,—where art thou?
> Hast thou a home in some past, future year?
> I call to thee from every leafy bough,
> But thou art far away and canst not hear.
>
> Each flower lifts up its red or yellow head,
> And nods to thee as thou art passing by:
> Hurry not on, but stay thine anxious tread,
> And thou shalt live with me, for there am I.

"The New Man", a companion-piece to **"The Lost"**, . . . treats the converse of this theme, or the experience of salvation. (pp. 171-73)

Much of Very's Nature poetry, especially of his later work, is merely dull; the best of it resembles that of Blake, but is less excellent. Nature, as in Blake, is seen through a daze of beatitude and with only occasional clarity of outline. Nevertheless, there are lovely passages. . . . In **"Autumn Flowers"**, the natural description becomes a firm moral allegory; the poem is nearly one of the best and tempts one to compare it with Bridge's "The birds that sing on autumn eves." (pp. 173-74)

But Very seldom preached, like Emerson; rather, he gave us his life: he is a mystic, not a sectary and a reformer. Emerson, if he was to concern himself with mysticism at all, could do no other than reform, for he had no mystical life to give: if we are to judge him by his writing, he never experienced that which he recommended, and judged in his own terms he was a failure. His poetry deals not with the experience, but with his own theory of the experience; it is not mystical poetry, but gnomic or didactic poetry, and as the ideas expounded will not stand inspection, the poetry is ultimately poor in spite of vigorous phrases. Or to put the difference another way, Very

speaks with the authority of experience, whereas Emerson claims to speak with the authority of thought, but he lacks that authority.

Yet the measure of Emerson's failure may seem at times the measure of the superiority of at least a little of his poetry to Very, at any rate to those of us who inhabit the lower room, the chamber of illusions, and endeavor to keep it in order that the mystic on the floor above us may suffer as little inconvenient disturbance as possible. For Emerson's failure drove him to examine at odd moments the broken shards and tablets buried in his character from an earlier culture. He was by accident and on certain occasions a moral poet, and he was by natural talent a poet of a good deal of power. When we come from the more purely mystical works of Very to "The Concord Hymn" or to "Days", we may feel that we are entering a world of three dimensions, of solid obstacles, and of comprehensible nobility.

But we have not done with Very so easily. Emerson at the core is a fraud and a sentimentalist, and his fraudulence impinges at least lightly upon everything he wrote: when it disappears from the subject, it lingers in the tone. Very at the core is a saint, and the impeccable rightness of his judgement emerges in many and curious ways. When he brings his character to bear upon matters that we can understand, we find ourselves, for all our doubts, in the presence of one of the greatest devotional poets in English. . . . **"The Created"**, is probably the best single poem that Very composed. . . . We have here perfection of structure, perfection and power of phrase, great moral scope, and sublimity of conception. Equally perfect, but of less power, is a hymn entitled **"The Visit"**; nearly as perfect is a song, **"The Call"** . . . ; less perfect still, and less compact, but of a magnificence comparable at moments to that of Henry Vaughan, is a hymn entitled **"The Coming of the Lord"**. There are other poems of less importance, because of imperfections or of limitations of scope, but still worthy of examination: **"The Still-Born"**, . . . **"The Son"**, **"In Him We Live"**, **"The Earth"**, **"The New Birth"**, **"The New World"**, **"The Morning Watch"**, **"The Dead"**, **"The Prison"**, **"Enoch"**, and **"The Cottage"**; and there are doubtless others.

Very numbered among his admirers Emerson, Channing, Clarke, Andrews, Charles Eliot Norton, Bryant, and other persons of distinction; his contemporaries repeatedly compared him to George Herbert, and it would appear with reason. Yet for fifty years he has rested in oblivion, except as a name, incorrectly described, in the academic summaries of his period. It is now fifty-six years since his death, and a hundred years since he first entered upon his full poetic power; in a year or two we shall have the centenary of his commitment to the McLean Asylum. In this last, at least, it should be possible to find some significance that will justify our recalling him to memory. Perhaps the moral is merely this: that it is nearly time that we paid him the apology long due him and established him clearly and permanently in his rightful place in the history of our literature. (pp. 175-78)

> *Yvor Winters, "Jones Very: A New England Mystic," in* The American Review, *Vol. 7, No. 1, April, 1936, pp. 159-78.*

WILLIAM IRVING BARTLETT   (essay date 1942)

[*Bartlett's study is an overview of Very's Shakespearean criticism, poetry, and spiritual development. Although he comments that*

Very's poems are often overly didactic, Bartlett maintains that his uniqueness "lies in his humility, his complete simplicity of expression, and his rich, mystical communion with his God." For other appraisals of Very's Shakespearean criticism see the excerpts by Margaret Fuller (1840), Gamaliel Bradford (1906), and Perry Miller (1950); for further commentary on his style see Gamaliel Bradford (1906), Yvor Winters (1936), and Nathan Lyons (1966).]

[Very's **"Epic Poetry"** is] a scholarly essay, clearly and logically constructed, and written in a style of pleasing maturity. One senses immediately Very's love of the classics, but the flavor of the essay is literary rather than "bookish." Besides the writers of epic poems already mentioned, one discovers Cicero, Aristotle, Plutarch, Sallust, Voltaire, Lamartine (*The Pilgrimage*), Monti, Ariosto, Girandi Cinto, Trissino, Bacon, Shakespeare, Wordsworth, Coleridge, Carlyle (*Sartor Resartus*), Schiller, Lord Kames, Pollok, and Wilkie.

But particularly refreshing is the Greek spirit permeating this essay. Even a casual reader must feel Very's intense love for and sympathy with Greek life—its devotion to nature and to physical beauty, its eager expression of patriotism, its yearning "after a life beyond the narrow limits of its earthly existence." Very's knowledge of the Greek language, his understanding of Greek literature, and his psychological interpretation of the nobility and dignity of Greek heroism offer proof that he was indeed an inspiring teacher at Harvard and a stimulating companion for both Thoreau and Emerson. It is pleasurable for an admirer of Very to reflect that the germ of **"Epic Poetry"** originated and partly developed before the religious frenzy possessed its creator, and that the work bears unmistakable evidence of a youthful, almost pagan, delight in things Greek. This early joy was like a strong plant; its roots sank deep in the rich soil of Hellenism, drank from its fountains of beauty, and drew forth a sustenance so potent that it was stamped indelibly with the thing that nurtured it. Later fires might wither and sear, strong blasts might twist and gnarl; but always there would remain a bit of green from an early spring, and a suggestion of grace and symmetry from a form once known as beautiful.

The essays **"Shakespeare"** and **"Hamlet"** should be considered together, as Very himself suggested. **"Shakespeare"** is Very's most important prose work; as compared with **"Epic Poetry,"** it is longer, is more intensely unified because of strict adherence to its one central theme, is more felicitous and pungent in its style, and is almost perfectly constructed. (p. 76)

Very's criticism of Shakespeare smacks of much that the Romantic critics—particularly Coleridge, and to a less degree Lamb and Hazlitt—have said. But Very leaves the stamp of his own individuality even on a critique of Shakespeare. This appears in the form of a condemnation of what he contends is Shakespeare's marked deficiency: the dramatist had not surrendered his will to God, had not been baptized with the Holy Ghost. Consequently, even though Shakespeare's characters are great and natural, they are only unconsciously so. His mind was a pure and spotless mirror reflecting nature, but only a nature of pure and spotless innocence—never of virtue. "Had that love of action which was so peculiarly the motive of Shakespeare's mind, been followed also as a duty, it would have added a strength to his characters which we do not feel them now to possess. Since Shakespeare acted from impulse rather than principle, he should not be regarded as a man so much as a phenomenon. "'Twas God's care only that the mind he sent labored not in vain." This, in short, is Very's explanation of the peculiar genius of Shakespeare.

"Hamlet" is Very's amplified repetition of his theory of Shakespeare's mind and character. Taking a single play for an example, Very attempts to demonstrate further that Shakespeare's master passion was the love of intellectual activity for its own sake, and that, in consequence, "his continual satisfaction with the simple pleasure of existence must have made him more than commonly liable to the fear of death," or at least must have intensified his interest in the subject of death. *To be or not to be* forever, was a question which Hamlet yearned to settle; all else faded into nothingness before the all-absorbing importance of the question of existence. Very's belief was that Hamlet's mind was one which "could never reach that assurance of eternal existence which Christ alone can give"; in this very fact lay the materials that created the remarkable tragedy of Shakespeare's popular hero. The action, therefore, was mental, and was so intense as completely to absorb even all physical energy. Hamlet was not, therefore, as Dr. Johnson has said, weak and cowardly, but was rather admirably courageous. His thinking had reached a stage when the ephemeral, earthly life failed to satisfy; his whole nature suffered the insatiable thirst for perpetuity. The "dread of something after death"—perhaps even annihilation—tortured him. So, though loving not this life, he endured it and clung to it because he was uncertain about another, and his whole existence seemed to an onlooker only as a tragedy of passive indecision. Very naturally finds the "to be or not to be" soliloquy the key to interpretation of the entire play. He rides his theory so hard as almost to exhaust it, and he errs in ignoring the influence of environment and attending circumstances in influencing Hamlet's state of mind. Yet one is impressed with this essay. It is nearly perfect in structure—more so than **"Epic Poetry"**—and has a pleasing literary flavor. Very disagrees, not only with Dr. Johnson in his interpretation of Hamlet's mind and character, but also with Goethe, with Coleridge, and with Goldsmith.

Both **"Shakespeare"** and **"Hamlet"** are characterized by spontaneity and mastery of expression. The reader never gets the impression that Very labored to construct good, sonorous sentences or turn apt phrases; the diction is exact, the sentences are admirable, but both the language and the structural pattern seem effortless. (pp. 77-9)

But perhaps even more prevalent than the element of spontaneity is the genuine ring of conviction in Very's Shakespearean essays. Both are products of that period of his strongest mental exaltation, and both were composed with the same seriousness that marked the creation of his religious sonnets. He clung tenaciously to the belief that he was God's messenger and that what he wrote concerning Shakespeare, therefore, was divinely communicated. Hence, to doubt the truth of his essays or to suggest their lack of divine inspiration was faithlessness on the one hand and sacrilege on the other. He once said very simply to a friend that it was "given him to know" about Shakespeare and that what he wrote was not only "the true word, but the best word that had been spoken on the subject." (p. 79)

With such an understanding of Very's belief in his divine inspiration, one can turn to the **"Poems"** with the feeling that he is comfortably prepared to give them just and adequate interpretation. (p. 80)

[In **"To the Humming Bird,"**] one discovers Very in his most pleasant and appealing mood—simple, kind, unaffected, gentle, intensely sympathetic with animal life, and personal in his reaction to nature. In spirit the poem reminds one of Freneau's "The Wild Honey Suckle," and in both mood and structural pattern it suggests Burns's "To a Mouse." Indeed, as one reads the stanzas, one senses the essence of pure nature poetry; and one can easily imagine Wordsworth as responding happily to Very's sincerity of emotion and simplicity of diction.... Gone, indeed, are the earlier tendencies of Very to use the heroic couplet and the stilted personification and conventional language of the Classicists. Pope has been supplanted by Wordsworth and other Romantics; "nature methodized" has become nature emotionalized.

Very's love of the birds is represented by two further poems, both of which are in the Shakespearean sonnet form, with an extra foot in the last line. **"To the Canary Bird"** voices artistically an intense sympathy with a creature imprisoned from its natural habitat. Speaking to the bird, Very says:

> I cannot hear thy voice with others' ears,
> Who make of thy lost liberty a gain;
> And in thy vale of blighted hopes and fears
> Feel not that every note is born with pain....

[In **"The Robin,"**] Very illustrates a tendency which grew into an unfortunate habit—the wrenching of a sonnet begun with simple observation and pure adoration of the common yet picturesque aspects of nature into stern and ugly moralizing. Thus the poem begins—

> Thou need'st not flutter from thy half-built nest,
> Whene'er thou hear'st man's hurrying feet go by—

and continues through the second quatrain with proof of Very's close observation of the robin's habits. But the third quatrain and the couplet concentrate a sermon:

> All will not hear thy sweet out-pouring joy,
> That with morn's stillness blends the voice of song,
> For over-anxious cares their souls employ,
> That else upon thy music borne along
> And the light wings of heart-ascending prayer
> Had learned that Heaven is pleased thy simple
> joys to share.

Such an obsession with what to some readers is a repellent phase of religion, suggests the poems of Anne Bradstreet almost two hundred years earlier, and, to a greater extent, those of Very's older contemporary, William Cullen Bryant. Indeed, Very's application of the ethical at the close of some of his poems more closely resembles Bryant's "moral tag" than the didactic treatment employed by any other American poet. The nature poetry of the two men is alike in many respects. One has only to compare the poems glorifying American birds and flowers to see that each man is a Puritan, that he passionately loves his subjects, and that he enjoys a deep communion with nature. But Bryant is generally more majestically calm and solemn, more melancholy, more frigid in his association than is Very. The crowning glory of Very is his spirituality; unlike Bryant, he finds a strong mystic meaning in nature, and the realization of this discovery frequently so permeates his being as to melt his Puritanical reserve and inflame his soul into an intense and passionate interpretation of the spiritual significance of nature. The expression of such spirituality, then, is Very's unique contribution to American literature. His exceedingly simple diction and his almost total lack of conscious rhetoric or of stylistic device are a fitting garment for his sincerity, and accentuate the reverential attitude he bears towards his subject. In truth, Very's poems seem often the essence of spiritual nature transmuted into the language of a devout disciple.

Such are **"The Painted Columbine"** and **"The Columbine,"** both of which glorify Very's favorite flower. The latter poem is important, for it expresses Very's belief in the mystical identification of himself with nature. As he lovingly examines the columbine, he loses almost all conscious identification with the flesh, and becomes absorbed in the object of his devotion.... It is doubtful whether the verse of any other poet in American literature conveys so completely the mystical unity of man with nature, and if one turn to English literature, only the Romantics offer possible comparisons. The lines,

> Nodding our honey-bells mid pliant grass
> In which the bee half hid his time employs,

suggest the sensuous languor of Keats, but the complete absorption with nature is more like Wordsworth or even Shelley.

The columbine poems have companion pieces in **"The Wind-Flower"** and **"The Violet."** Though neither of these sonnets represents Very's pure absorption with nature, both glow with a genuine warmth of emotion, and reveal the intimate relationship and deep understanding which exists between Nature and him who loves her. Certainly, one senses in these poems that deep personal feeling Very experienced toward nature, so that to him loneliness was almost impossible. Flowers, birds, and trees were to him companions even as they were to Wordsworth and Thoreau, and his communion with nature was just as real as that with men, and was generally more satisfying because less disappointing.... [Lines such as those in **"The Violet"**] represent Very at his best, for they combine his two dominant traits—love of nature, and love of God. These, blended with an extremely simple diction, unadorned style, and regular structural pattern, make him, indeed, the unique spiritual interpreter of nature in American poetry.

And yet in spite of Very's intense spirituality and his conviction, as expressed to Emerson and others, that his words were divinely inspired, he sometimes admitted the inability of language to convey his feeling. Often, like Wordsworth, with whom he found greatest joy, he profoundly felt himself to be a part of all he saw and heard; and so mystical was the union that it broke through the barriers of rhetoric and illuminated his simple diction until the reader's imagination and emotions were stirred and he was enabled to expand and glorify the meager record until he, too, approached Very's original rapture. Such a poem is the beautiful sonnet, **"Nature."** ... (pp. 81-6)

In somewhat similar vein is **"The Tree,"** another sonnet in which Very communes with nature and finds the assuring proof of God's eternal cycle of creation and love. The reader of this poem senses without effort the reverence Very felt for nature and for God; he realizes that Emerson and Alcott rightly saw in this mystical poet a purity of life and an unworldliness which stamped him as a saint. **"The Tree"** is a tenderly expressed sonnet, simple in style, genuine in emotion, fresh and clean as winter snow. Less spiritual but equally as impressive are the sonnet, **"The Latter Rain"** and the blank verse piece, **"To the Fossil Flower."**

Reference to these poems leads naturally to the consideration of one sonnet, **"The Song,"** unmarked by any touch of the sternly religious or of the didactic. Beginning with an attempt to lyricize his praise of nature, Very quickly admits his inability to achieve his purpose, and at length indulges his remembrance of a past but happy youth, now somewhat idealized.... One regrets that Very did not voice such moods oftener, and one wishes that life might have affected him less seriously, that it might have made him less repellently and sternly Puritanical, less unrelentingly just. But once he was possessed by the religious ecstasy, he gave himself to it wholly and willingly, returning at rare, and then often melancholy, intervals to his first interest—nature. (p. 87)

Perhaps no sonnet better illustrates Very's early attitude toward the spiritual than the poem, **"Life."** Herein he expresses his hunger for a stronger, firmer faith, his thirst for the very Fountain Head, his passion for actual absorption with God, and a life rich in its fruitage. Nature furnishes the imagery, but religion supplies the treatment; the tree is Very, but the earth, sky, sun—all elements that give life—are God.... Such a poem demonstrates no great spiritual struggle and suggests no turmoil of doubt; it merely expresses definitely that humble, unostentatious, complete devotion to God which characterized Very's life from youth to death.

This early devotion brought a richer spiritual experience. Very gradually felt that his life was becoming absorbed with that of the Spirit; and he became firmly convinced that the more will-less he grew, the more abundantly the streams of God-love might flow through his being. Grateful for the revelation of divine presence and now unshakably certain of the value of will-lessness, he grew more eager for self-effacement and yearned for an absorption so complete as to suggest the Mysticism of the Orient. The sonnet, **"In Him We Live,"** splendidly represents such a mental attitude.... (pp. 88-9)

As Very's mysticism deepened, he became more physically passive, more spiritually active. So intense was his feeling of communion with God that he saw the Divine Presence in every material object, and thought of matter, not in terms of science, but in terms of religion. Perhaps in **"The Presence"** one discovers the very quintessence of mysticism in American literature.... (p. 91)

In later years Very's poetry was to be compared to that of Donne, of Herbert, of Herrick, of Vaughan, and even of Blake; but in no case is the comparison very apt. Perhaps any religious poem, because of its mood if for nothing else, will remind one of other religious poems; but Very's verse is unlike that of any other poet, English or American. His piety may suggest Herbert; his simple diction and childlike faith may remind a Blake enthusiast of Blake; his intense fervor and his mysticism may faintly suggest Herrick's "His Litany, to the Holy Spirit," Vaughan's "The World," or Donne's "A Hymn to God the Father" or "Holy Sonnets": but Very's sonnets display none of Donne's fondness for literary conceits; none of Vaughan's cogitations over metaphysics; no lament over the loss of primal innocence, such as Herrick expressed; none of the intricacy and subtlety of thought which are found in Blake; and certainly nothing of the elaborate and conscious workmanship and literary brilliance which dominate "The Temple" of Herbert. What uniqueness Very possesses lies in his humility, his complete simplicity of expression, and his rich, mystical communion with God. Others have possessed these virtues, but no other has owned them in exactly the same proportion. Perhaps every one of the English poets with whom Very has been compared is a greater poet than the New Englander; but no one of them has lived more humbly, or has written with less thought of literary effect, and no one of them has revealed so close, so constant, or so strong a communion with God. (p. 95)

[Very] felt that he was God's messenger, and he was eager that men know it. But he chose to prove his representation of divinity, not by a verbal crusade, but by an unmistakable ex-

ample; his life should be so pure and holy that men would recognize him as God's spokesman. They should be inspired, first to true will-lessness, and secondly to passionate unity with the spiritual. In **"The Earth"** he voices his willingness to be an instrument used by God for spreading the Message. (p. 96)

The ideal of willing instrumentality is expressed also in a different type of figure. Very would be a mere holder of the pen, through which God's message might flow into words for men to read and hear. In **"Who Hath Ears to Hear Let Him Hear,"** he compares his songs to those of a bird, and he imagines the joy which they may bring to the "willing heart." ...

Very found this mystical union to be constantly and increasingly satisfying, and he gave himself completely to it. He was the willing and pliable clay in the hands of God the potter, chanting rapturously [in **"The Clay"**]:

> Thou shalt do what Thou wilt with thine own hand,
> Thou form'st the spirit like the moulded clay.

The theme occurs often in Very's later poems, indeed so often as to become monotonous, but it is highly important because it offers some explanation of the four poems of autobiographic significance in Very's first edition. (p. 97)

[The sonnet **"Beauty"**] represents that great emotional upheaval in the poet's life and clearly represents a struggle between natural human passion and divine, spiritual love. In the first two quatrains his lyric beauty and intensity remind one of the Elizabethans:

> I gazed into thy face,—and beating life
> Once stilled its sleepless pulses in my breast,
> And every thought whose being was a strife
> Each in its silent chamber sank to rest;
> I was not, save it were a thought of thee,
> The world was but a spot where thou hadst trod,
> From every star thy glance seemed fixed on me,
> Almost I loved thee better than my God....

One who had so thoroughly mastered human passion could sincerely write the other two autobiographic poems, **"Thy Beauty Fades"** and **"Love,"** in both of which the ephemeral quality of earthly love is contrasted with the soul-satisfying, everlasting quality of divine love. For to Very only the spiritual life was a vital reality; the body and its fleshly hungerings must be conquered by a supreme will-lessness that annihilated the barriers to communion with the Father. To this state Very the mystic had attained at the time his *Essays and Poems* was published. (pp. 98-9)

> *William Irving Bartlett, in his* Jones Very: Emerson's *"Brave Saint," Duke University Press, 1942, 237 p.*

PERRY MILLER (essay date 1950)

[*An American historian, Miller is considered a pioneer in recording and interpreting the literature and culture of seventeenth-century New England. In this excerpt from his* The Transcendentalists: An Anthology, *Miller places Very's essays in the context of American intellectual history. For other essays on Very's Shakespearean criticism see Margaret Fuller (1840), Gamaliel Bradford (1906), and William Irving Bartlett (1942).*]

If Jones Very was indeed mad, his madness had in it something of the method of the great romanticists. His essay on the epic is practically unique in American criticism because it is an effort to capture the distinction—more carefully investigated in Germany—between the modern and the romantic as being the complex and the dramatic, in contrast to the primitive and the classic, which is characterized by the simple and by the epic. It was an attempt, far from unsuccessful, to domesticate in America the kind of romantic theorizing that flourished in Germany, particularly with the Schlegels; yet, because it also grew out of the peculiar pressures of the New England society, the essay could contend that the root of modern complexity of consciousness is Christianity—though not liberal Unitarianism! It challenged the Protestant culture of America by a startling reading of a classic to which lip-service was still paid; the Byronic Satan was hardly yet recognizable in America of 1838. (p. 343)

[Very's essay entitled **"Shakespeare"** can] be taken as the essence of the romantic conception of Shakespeare and so of the artist, of the great artist capable of the wise passivity that permits "Nature" to speak through him. There was always the danger, of course, that these impulses might come from below rather than from on high, and Emerson had announced that he would live from the Devil if he were the Devil's child. There clearly was much that was Devilish—or at least lewd—in Shakespeare; Very girded the New England conscience for the struggle and proved that Shakespeare's obscenities, because they are as natural as any impulse from the vernal wood, are basically innocent. (p. 346)

The character of Hamlet was as fascinating to American romantics as to the English and German. Jones Very struck the pure romantic note, and although distressed that Hamlet was not a Christian, he still saw in him the perfect symbol of the

The manuscript copy of Very's poems "Eternal Life" and "The Redeemed."

sensitive poet in conflict with a crass and Philistine world. (p. 353)

Perry Miller, "The Movement: 'Literary and Critical'," in The Transcendentalists: An Anthology, *Cambridge, Mass.: Harvard University Press, 1950, pp. 331-421.**

NATHAN LYONS   (essay date 1966)

[Lyons's introduction to Jones Very: Selected Poems, *from which the following is excerpted, is a balanced, in-depth study of the poet's style and ideas. Lyons argues that Very's religious sonnets are his most notable achievement, but that his "world is illiberal, with a monotonic purity." Other critical assessments of Very's style are offered by Gamaliel Bradford (1906), Yvor Winters (1936), and William Irving Bartlett (1942).]*

The Quietist image will not admit much exploration, in deference to its ethic as well as its scope. Very's stylistic canon is therefore sharply limited. The Shakespearean sonnet is his predominant form; curt Biblical syntax and regular meter encourage slow, measured reading; paradox, simple metaphor, and metonymy are the principal figures; chaste imagery supplies the slightest color and animation to his verse.

Very's poems are without drama; for drama is of the world, and Very is hardly a creaturely poet. Paradox provides the only drama of Christian mysticism: he that will save his life, must first lose it; he that will lose his life for Christ's sake, shall find it; the last shall be the first; when man is weak, then is he strong; in death begins eternal life; to him who hath shall be given. As a poet and an intense Christian mystic, Very has sure recourse to this rich lode. But his poems are rarely mystical; though many were written in what he claims was mystical communion, they generally only state his mystical paradoxes.

Very's paradox is never pointed or sharp. The oxymoron of Crashaw's epigrams or Donne's Holy Sonnets demonstrate an intellectual, even an emotional, vigor opposed to Very's Quietism; poetic success in these terms would have undermined the man. Very resolves traditional quarrels between matter and spirit, motion and rest, life and death, not by violently yoking them, but by quiet and authoritative reconciliation. He uses antithetical parallels within one line, or in one line against the next—closer, in this, to neoclassic than metaphysical prosody. At their worst, Very's paradoxes are merely undistinguished echoes of Biblical passages: "For those who worship Thee there is no death." At their best, they convince, leisurely establishing the central paradox of passive-seeking:

These when they come, the man revealed from heaven,
Shall labor all the day in quiet rest.

("**The New Man**")

and,

It is the way unseen, the certain route,
Where ever bound, yet thou art ever free.

("**The Hand and Foot**")

Very's is a hidden God. For communion with Him, the poet cherishes only the intangible. In one sermon, he speaks of "this tyranny of what is seen"; self-denial is prayer; and one can pray only when he prays inwardly. In **"Enoch,"** the poet looks to find a man who walked with God:

> But soul forgetful of her nobler birth
> Had hewn Him lofty shrines of stone and wood,
> And left unfinished and in ruins still
> The only temple He delights to fill.

Like the Wesleyan and the Quaker, Very insists upon firsthand religion: there can be neither physical nor personal intermediaries.

For communion, and to find the "meat" that does not perish, man must be reborn. But first he must be "self-forgetting." From this proceeds Very's special concept of surrender. It has not the sponge-like quality of Whitman's loafing. It is a "wise-passiveness," but it excludes Wordsworth's connotation that what is received from nature is a principal source of ethical knowledge. Very differs with the Indian religions, particularly Buddhism, in that he expects no noetic satori, no sudden perception of an ultimate reality. Very's surrender is the motion of thought within rest, the peace of "traveling" on his "Maker's river": but mainly it is a disinterested act of devotion to the Father.

Such a surrender implies a willful decision to be will-less. . . . But this scarcely invalidates the premises of Very's Quietism. **"The Hand and Foot"** is the perfect inscription to Very's religion, and it remains a focal poem for the study of his central paradox. Though the first two lines imply an initial conscious choice, the focus is upon the process once initiated.

> The hand and foot that stir not, they shall find
> Sooner than all, the rightful place to go.

There is a kind of justification by selflessness. Such a view is not Calvinist, for it implies no elected soul; the soul is set free through its peculiar holiness, its total surrender, as any other soul might be set free. Very sought and contributed to his salvation; it was not an imputed righteousness.

"Rightful place" might imply that no other path is possible; but such stress would be wrong. The phrase states, not that no other choice exists, but that this absolute can be reached by a process, at this moment extrinsic to choice. All movement and thought might imply conscious exercise of will, even the movement of a hand or the conjuring of an idea. But in Very's canon, thought is simply received, and acts are directed; this, after the initial, general abandonment. "Thou wilt my hand employ," he begins **"The Disciple"**; and "I idle stand that I may find employ," he affirms in **"The Idler."** Though Knox can caution that in the mystical state man has the illusion that he is an automaton, the "other power" directing Very to the "rightful place" was a paramount assumption. Again, only the initial submission could be willed: "The morning comes to those who willingly would see." And selflessness could be willed: "We must by an effort of the will, by prayer, and meditation, turn the mind from vanity and worldliness, before the Truth can interest us, enter into and fill the soul."

Consequently, spiritual vigor is constantly contrasted to restless and selfish physical labor; the decrease in the latter is requisite to the initiation of any spiritual moment. Very's unseen God cannot be found in outward activity; repeatedly, busyness keeps man from communion.

> Nor here nor there, where now thy feet would turn,
> Thou wilt find Him who ever seeks for thee.
>
> ("The Created")

Only stillness evokes the knowledge of direction:

> My body shall not turn which way it will,
> But stand till I the appointed road can find.
>
> ("The Idler")

The only zeal is within the calm:

> Till to the light restored by gentle sleep
> With new-found zeal I might Thy precepts keep.
>
> ("Change")

And by seeking Him, one finds himself:

> His way is hidden that thine eye may seek,
> And in the seeking thou thyself may find.
>
> ("To All")

While at rest, man sees by "inward light things hid before"; from the unheard God one learns to speak.

Very's symbols are actually little more than simple metaphors, at time metonymies; these become themes, repeated fugally throughout his work. Often the symbols originate in a Biblical image or phrase, and retell it, expanding and sustaining the original figure. The figure is often in the title itself. It may combine mild paradox and metonymy: **"Christmas"** refers more to Easter, to a new birth of Christ, a resurrection in those who were spiritually dead; **"The Jew"** quarrels with the "thorny talk" of form and convention which Very equates with Old Testament laws and the rejection of Christ. **"The Journey"** is a spiritual pilgrimage; **"The Unfaithful Servants"** are hands, eyes, and souls that serve themselves, not God; **"The Garden"** is a state of communion with God. **"The Slaveholder"** profiteers with God's free gifts and holds the day in bonds; **"The Children"** remain children of the Father, but have lost all childlike simplicity, humble love, and thanks. Eye, ear, hand, foot, fox, and bird—among Very's few physical images—become emblematic of the poet's quarrel with sense. A most interesting metonymy is "room," in **"The Absent."** Because they are separate, and designed for special purposes, rooms are metaphorically compared to men whose lives reflect specialized passions rather than the wholeness of living in the "mansion" of Christianity: "Within thy sleeping room thou dost abide, / And thou the social parlor dost prefer."

The morning, a much used and central image, is spiritual awakening; it comes to those who "willingly would see." **"The Clouded Morning"** is a time when man should awaken, but does not. In **"The Morning Watch,"** Very follows the physical day from pre-dawn darkness to the flooding of windows with "the awakening light"; but all slumber, there is no faithful herald or watchman to proclaim the dawn, no Christian community—"No friends from house to house their neighbors greet"; all slumber on in sluggard trances; finally, the "day's bright gates" close, and all chance of awakening has passed. The rich sonnet **"Morning"** first discloses an image of the new day with its noisy workmen, busy laborers in the fields, and an embarking traveler; this Very contrasts to an inner awakening, where too a "light breaks gently." But here,

> The forge and noisy anvil are at rest
> Nor men nor oxen tread the fields of corn,
> Nor pilgrim lifts his staff—it is no day
> To those who find on earth their place to stay.

"The Eagles," a less simply conceived, more rigorously sustained symbolic effort, allegorizes Matthew 24:28: "For wheresoever the carcass is, there will the eagles be gathered together." Eagles are depicted gathering at "the place of death," the air tainted with their "noisome breath." But the poem is not a total metaphorical equivalent for the destruction of the unregenerate; Very slips fluidly into direct statement with justifying abruptness: "But all unburied lies the naked soul," and "The battened wills beneath their talons bleed." He returns to the central image, depicting "whitening bone," "pestilence," and the carcasses; then he becomes suggestively obvious in "half formed prey," and finally the iron beaks pursue their slaughter relentlessly until the field is cleared of those "who worshipped idol gods." The sonnet is graphically mordant; the slaughter fitted to the animality Very eschews; but the evil or sin itself—self-will—is abstract, and never particularized.

Of Very's total poetic achievement—over seven hundred poems—more than 80 per cent are Shakespearean sonnets. Use of a form he did not create probably made the process of writing seem less willful, and may have added to its attractiveness for one who wished to surrender. An early mastery of the form, a respect for order, and the fear of "the weight of too much liberty," are possible reasons for its adoption. Invariably the sonnets are metrically regular (occasionally too facile, even monotonous) and the rhyme correct. Very's basic unit of thought is the line, or more usually, a pair of unrhymed lines. He seems to have built his sonnets by interlocking couplets; first he set down two unrhymed lines, then he found a set to match them.

Very's line is firm and economical; the line is curt, but never, as in Donne, shrewdly so. There is a marked absence of caesuras—in **"The Lost,"** **"In Him We Live,"** and in most other poems. Sometimes Very syncopates an object, "To want is there to be where I am not" (**"The Sower"**). Often he reverses standard word order. Very likes the Latinic verb-last structure, common to the Protestant hymn; its flexibility helps to explain his ease in the sonnet form, for with it he more easily maintains meter and meets the rhyme. Very pads frequently, often without major damage, in the usual ways, by the use of redundant clauses, and the contrived use of awkward verb forms: "Mid tombs and ruined piles in death to dwell." The end verbs allow him to shift emphasis structurally; at times he juxtaposes related images by use of a subject-object or double object grouping, followed by the verb. Note the rapid succession of object after subject and the suspended verb in, "And long thy life my body shall sustain"; the use of a split verb with a lengthy object inserted, "They cannot from their path mistaken stray"; and the quick repetition of key terms, here a double object in similar construction—"I cannot find in mine own work my joy." The concision of Very's line aptly supports his thrifty religion.

In Very's best poems, the epithets are singularly lean: cunning fox, aged chair, skulking mouse, dim lamp, and thorny talk. His diction is Biblically tight, and often homely. He relies chiefly on one- or two-syllable words. Thee, thou, thine, this, that, here, there, where, He, and Him are used with an accusing directness. Very makes remarkable use of the pronoun, demonstrative and personal, as in the superb poem, **"The Created"**: "Nor here nor there, where now thy feet would turn, / Thou wilt find Him who ever seeks for thee." These strikingly simple lines, which pronounce the threat to spiritual salvation incurred by hurriedness, are equally lean:

> While thou wert busy here and there
> So He was here and He is gone
> Thou oft had time enough to spare
> But He thy Lord and Master now.

Very's success in these last lines suggests that tetrameter quatrains might have proved a more flexible form for him than the sonnet. Though a poet who would pad a sonnet might also pad a quatrain, the freer line of Emily Dickinson, or the abrupt distich of the German mystic Angelus Silesius seem more reasonably germane to Very's method; the weight of more liberty might have encouraged closer fidelity to the apocalyptic.

But Very's sonnets, when there is enough matter for the form, are firm and enduring. Among his best are **"The Presence,"** **"The Hand and Foot,"** **"The Journey,"** **"In Him We Live,"** and **"The Absent."** **"The Presence"** begins with the ingenuous,

> I sit within my room and joy to find
> That Thou who always lov'st art with me here.

The moment is a state of recognition and quiet thankfulness set in a common scene with some few bare objects. No reason is given for the Divine presence; though there is a watch, there is no sensation of time: there is only unhurried satisfaction in ritual quiet. Very does not prove the presence of God. His authority usually manifests itself in direct statement, neither argued nor debated, often shown. He is master of the abrupt, affirming start: he will bear direct witness to his experience. "I saw the spot where our first parents dwelt," he begins **"The Garden"**; "I am thy other self"; "I do not need thy food, but thou dost mine"; "I have no brother." Although there is no conscious drama, there is a profound dramatic effect in the unusual juxtaposition of God's indwelling and the perfect stillness of the scene. God's presence (not God) originates in the poet's soul. . . . For Very, God is external to man; he speaks from without; "but it is *outward from within*," after a man has gently encouraged God's entrance into him. There are parallels to Hinduism and Emerson's "Brahma" in **"Thou art the eyes by which I see"**; the poet looks with God, and therefore the fire burns brighter. The unadorned things, "The aged chair, that table, watch and door," are part of his large estate, and are sufficient.

The five members of the sonnet are brief and unaffected: the middle three, each neatly of two lines, distinctly note common acts, sights, and things. The nouns are characteristically plain; "aged," the lone adjective, is hardly an extravagance. Very speaks of essentials that do not change, that perform the necessary tasks for man with a quiet holiness, the door that enables him to leave or remain secluded, the table for written thoughts; he ignores fashion; progress for him meant only "new depths of truth within the holy word."

"The Hand and Foot," **"The Journey,"** **"In Him We Live,"** and **"The Absent,"** are more typical sonnets; they do not depict an actual scene, as do **"The Fair Morning,"** and the nature poems: they particularize an idea. The little variety they do contain usually takes the form of alternate images for the central idea.

In **"The Hand and Foot,"** the initial paradox is maintained throughout, restated in different ways, in somber, patient insistence upon the need to submit wholly. Partial parataxis keeps the phrases and members in a delicately elliptical relationship, and encourages the imaginative turning and developing of the first image into distinct images. The slight disruption of word order and the elimination of usual grammatical links in the fifth member enhances the characteristic tightness.

> The bird has not their hidden track found out,
> The cunning fox though full of art he be.

The first image then grows to include the idea that the path is not theirs (is, itself, not willfully chosen); that it is unseen, beyond, as it were, the vision of bird and cunning fox; that it is a bondage that makes them free; and finally, that it is His path, a path thus perfect, for it is made by Him whose perfect law of love "Bids spheres and atoms in just order move."

"The Journey" and **"In Him We Live"** are more abstract, yet the spare Verian abstract even here reports a convincing belief. Very tells of journeys where he daily walks. Though there is "no end in view," there is an unwillingness to act or plan:

> I know nowhere to turn, each step is new
> No wish before me flies to point the way.

Very never wanted to know the Divine Plan. The conflict here, between man's inevitable ignorance and his need of an absolute path, is resolved, as before, by delivering oneself over to God's will. Though man, "all houseless," knows "not where to dwell," God knows the turnings of the road, "where this way leads and that."

"In Him We Live" has a gently dialectical progression held within the direct affirmation of the first and last two lines. Initially, Very praises the Father, and offers thanks that "in each motion" he is "made rich" with Him. Then there is a development of essentially abstract sense images: a glance, movement of the body, song, movement of the hands. This stately body, Very says, cannot move, "save I/Will to its nobleness my little bring." To sing, he must "consent" to every note; he "must conspire" with every effort to move his hands. But even these little acts of cordial cooperation with the Father are too much: they show him how "little" he possesses, and even that "little," more than he desires.

"The Absent" has a precious intimacy. Its scene, always and obviously metaphoric, is built by domestic and local images. Those who are "not yet at home" have "one hole like rat or skulking mouse," and are blind to all others; they prefer the sleeping room, the parlor, and,

> All others wilt in the cupboard hide,
> And this or that's the room for him or her.

With these homely images, Very connotes the security that accompanies finite man who trusts, and the paltriness of any worldly vision.

Rejection of the incarnated world prevented Very from entering, like his Shakespeare, into the lives of others or of things. There are no characters in his poems, no explicit conflicts, and few scenes. The intangible, alone permanent and holy, reigns supreme. Nature, as for Emerson, is a "differential thermometer," a way of registering man's departure from the natural; and with Swedenborg, Very could say that the visible world was created for our instruction; but the poet's correspondences are too often flat and without form.

Appreciation of natural beauty, as Very implies in **"The Lost,"** **"The True Light,"** and **"To the Pure All Things Are Pure,"** depends upon man's inner awakening, his "sweet obedience of the will." And in **"The Lost,"** Very firmly states that then man can enter into nature:

> Thyself the day thou lookest for in them,
> Thyself the flower that now thine eye enjoys.

But nature was, for Very, more often a source of comfort than revelation and communion, and he rarely entered the portal beyond appearance: nature supplied a ragbag of images from which to draw morals in the manner of the medieval bestiary. The nature poems, although generously praised by some of

Very's few admirers, are prosaic and littered with poetic commonplaces and stale epithets; they generally lack the apocalyptic proof of the religious sonnets. In **"The Columbine,"** for example, where Very graphically attempts to show communion with a specific plant, we are not convinced that he and the flower are actually nodding their honey-bells together 'mid pliant grass. And such epithets as "mirrored beauty," "pictured flowers," "boundless main," "morning's golden darting beam," and "stream of life" further mar the nature poems. **"The Latter Rain,"** attempting something less alien to the poet's spirit, is a refreshing exception:

> The rain falls still—the fruit all ripened drops,
> It pierces chestnut burr and walnut shell,
> The furrowed fields disclose the yellow crops,
> Each bursting pod of talents used can tell.

Perhaps because Very did not seek communion, or illumination from Nature's "mystic book," the image has, quite simply, a pristine concreteness.

Some of Very's hymns also have real merit. **"The Coming of the Lord"** is among the best, with strong avowal of abiding faith:

> Come suddenly, O Lord, or slowly come,
> I wait Thy will, Thy servant ready is;

and its vigorous, taut, conclusion:

> Lord, help me that I faint not, weary grow,
> Nor at Thy coming slumber too, and sleep;
> For Thou hast promised, and full well I know
> Thou wilt to us Thy word of promise keep.

"Faith and Sight" richly echoes the morning images:

> The comings on of Faith,
>   The goings out of Sight;
> Are as the brightening of the morn,
>   The dying of the night.

And **"The Prayer,"** with its plaintive questioning, and final assurance, and **"The Fox and the Bird,"** which gnomically affirms the primacy of the unseen, are superior performances. **"The Coming of the Lord"** and **"The Immortal"** have affinities with the hymns of Isaac Watts, and Cowper's *Olney Hymns*—"Walking With God," for example; the others are more peculiarly Very's.

But it is the religious sonnets which, in theology and style, are unparalleled. Very's theological beliefs were altogether unlike Blake's, with whom he has wrongly been compared. For Blake, finding sex and violence chief ingredients of his world, stated that "God wants not man to humble himself," and persistently argued with brittle and acid pith that life is will. Charles Eliot Norton suggested that Very's poems are "as if written by a George Herbert who had studied Shakespeare, read Wordsworth, and lived in America." Very could be homelier than Herbert, but he lacked Herbert's dazzling variety, his exacting architectonics; more pertinently, Herbert was not a Quietist, and Very was not a metaphysical poet. The Wordsworth of "Expostulation and Reply" and "Michael" is surely a source, but only vaguely a counter-part, particularly not in the religious sonnets or hymns; moreover, Very vitalized conventional devotion, while Wordsworth rejected it; Very was more abstract, more consistently bound to one paradox, and he employed a more static form. Very specially praised William Cullen Bryant's "The Future Life"; his moral nature poems belong, but hardly compare in quality, to the tradition of "To the Fringed Gentian'' and ''To a Waterfowl.'' But Bryant's religious poems are more sustained, rhetorical, and aureate. Often Very's flights are so low as to resemble the frequent flat statement of Coventry Patmore, William Collins, and Cowper, but he differs significantly from each. Each voice threatens to, and often does, become dull, trite, and complacently pious. None becomes so laconic as Very, so sure in a few devotional forms, so abjuring of all emotions but one.

Very's failures are obvious and revealing. Though he may seem more a medium than a maker, Very could not have written his sonnets without stringent literary training in his youth. Very's theology falters when it is commonplace or too abstract, but the main flaw is merely faulty poetics. Emerson asked, ''Cannot the Spirit parse and spell?'' To be faithful to the Spirit which ''dictated'' his poems—and which has, no doubt a hand in all genuine poetry—Very did not necessarily need to accept its first promptings, but should have argued each poem into a ''fidelity to its own nature,'' however long that might have taken. Knox's observation is apt: ''total abandonment to the Divine will is not inconsistent with having, and with expressing wishes of one's own''; and, it may be added, neither is it inconsistent with artistic awareness. Yeats would have said that Very was too honest. But the act of faith that sometimes cheated Very's art is also the instrument of his great individual achievements. (pp. 18-33)

This is Jones Very's world. It is narrow, but it can be calm and deep. There is no physical joy, no sustained ecstasy; Very is deaf to sex and humor. His voice admits no Dickinsonian playfulness; it is at turns patient, thankful, warning, and praising. Sometimes the voice is interior prayer, scarcely audible; but it can acutely chide; always it is sweet, somber, or grave. Unlike Blake's insistence, in poems such as ''London,'' on a broad canon and the specifics of evil, Very's evil is narrow and abstract, limited chiefly to self-will. Very is a dualist, and he does not attempt Thomistically to reconcile the active and the contemplative lives: he explores and extols the motion of contemplation. Very's world is a paean to love of the unseen, and to submission to the Father; we leave it not with a broad theology, but an image of life solitary and without compromise, intense yet calm, of one carrying his cross without gripe or cheat.

If we live in the incarnated world but neglect it for spiritual aspirations, we are in danger of becoming split, deracinated, transformed, forced into strange skins and deep burrows; if we neglect the spiritual world we court the eagles. Very lives in an upper room, a prophet's or a priest's chamber, and is specially able within a limited class of emotions. But he is antidote and complement to materialism, and frigid witwork, and indecision. Very's world is illiberal, with a monotonic purity. His deep quiet encourages a tight marshalling of inner forces, and within our frantic hurry an intense stillness. (pp. 33-4)

> *Nathan Lyons, in an introduction to* Jones Very: Selected Poems *by Jones Very, edited by Nathan Lyons, Rutgers University Press, 1966, pp. 3-34.*

ANTHONY HERBOLD (essay date 1967)

[*Herbold discusses the two opposing views of nature in Very's poetry: nature as ''finite, contingent, imperfect,'' and nature as ''infinite, self-generating, perfect.'' Influenced simultaneously by Romantic and Calvinist doctrine, Very, Herbold contends, was unable to reach a unified concept of nature. Herbold stresses that what is remarkable about Very's use of nature is ''his transmu-*

tation of concept into technique.'' For another discussion of Very's stance toward nature see the essay by Carl Dennis (1970).]

The poetry of Jones Very seems pure. It seems alarmingly (or boringly) simple. True, Very chronicled a psychomachy: self and will versus God and Providence; but God's victory was assured. The chronicle lacks drama. Here is a warrior we envy—or endure. So consistent, so uncomplicated!

If that is how we read Jones Very's verse, we are not, I believe, reading what Very wrote. Or rather, we are reading one Very. There were several Verys: the Hellenist, the belletrist, the ''preacher of the Gospel,'' the martyr of the Holy Ghost, the enthusiast and prophet, the nature poet. And each of these Verys was articulate. (p. 244)

There are two reasons for this tendency to reduce Very, for finding *the* Very. If we hear two voices in a poet, and if the voices not only differ but contradict each other, we usually assume, naturally, that one of the voices is only apparent, ''merely dialectical,'' the other the true voice. Further, we usually assume, rightly, that a poet knows what he is doing. With Jones Very, neither assumption is legitimate. We find Verys disagreeing with Verys, and all the while Very the poet seems unaware of these disagreements. The will-less stenographer of the Spirit lived in peaceful coexistence with the Harvard humanist; the Calvinist was protected from the Transcendentalist by a spiritual *apartheid*.

These conflicts of self with self are typified by Very's concepts of nature. He held two mutually incompatible concepts simultaneously, and they can be found side by side in his verse. Moreover, this conflict caused other conflicts. Nature means here what it usually meant to Very and his contemporaries. It is used, not in a humanistic, but in a quasi-naturalistic sense. Hence the word refers, not to universal human nature, but to things ''out there''—brooks and birds and the cosmos. This is an elusive definition, and thus a definition that fits. Were nature defined more precisely, it would not be the nature found in Very's poetry.

The first nature was finite, contingent, imperfect. In **''Philosophy and Religion''** nature kills men, while religion

> with its heavenly voice,
> Speaks to the suffering, dying sons of men!
> It bids their sinking hearts in hope rejoice;
> Declares that man, though dead, shall live again;
> Points to the Saviour, who, e'en from the grave,
> Has power, above all nature's might, to save. . . .

Furthermore, nature is a poor teacher [as in **''The Cemetery''**].

> Nature with faithful trust restores the grain
> Which man unto her bosom doth commit,
> But tells us not that man shall live again,
> Or only in dim type obscurely speaks,
> By revelation taught, we learn indeed
> The hidden meaning of her countless forms; . . .

This ''glimmer of things'' (**How Long?''** . . .) seldom informs the soul. As Very wrote in an unpublished sermon, ''the testimony of the natural world is external to ourselves and cannot fully enlighten the mind.''

Very here conceived of nature, not as an Oversoul, not as visible deity, not even as what Carlyle (translating Goethe) called ''the living Garment of God''; Very conceived of nature as something inert. The concept is not pantheistic. Thus it was that he warned us in **''The Forms of Nature and the Unity of**

Their Origin" not to seek in "outward things," for it is the Lord we seek, and

> in the wind the Lord was not
> Nor in the earthquake dire
> Which shook the solid mountain's base,
> Nor in the flaming fire. . . .
>   ("**The Still Small Voice**" . . .)

Although Very said that "outward things" proclaim His power ("**The Child's Answer**" . . .), although man should "commune with things which God has made" ("**Nature's Help for the Soul**" . . .), implicit in all such assertions is a distinction between the "works and wonders of the Almighty's hand" ("**The Winter Night**" . . .) and the Worker. Creator and creation are not to be (con)fused. Nor should man dwell on nature.

The second of Very's natures was infinite, self-generating, perfect. When he claimed that "each plaintive wave mourned" for Arabella Johnson . . . , he was indulging in a variety of pathetic fallacy that transcends poetic license. A fallacy becomes an outlook. Thus, in "**Nature**" . . . , trees, clouds, and stars shared in the poet's feelings; and in "**Man in Harmony with Nature**" . . . , a leaping brook rejoiced at the poet's light step. Such poems turn feeling into idea; pathetic fallacy becomes pantheism. In another poem, also entitled "**Nature**" . . . , heaven's glory is *in* the skies; in "**The Tree**" . . . the celestial bodies "brighter beam when most we need their love"; and in "**The Swift**" it is nature, not God, that cares "for e'en the humble sparrow's fall." Clearly, nature has displaced God. . . .

What caused this polarity of nature as things and Nature as deity? And why did the poet allow these conflicting dogmas to split his verse down the middle, split it even within the bounds of a single sonnet? Why was the middle road—nature good but not divine—so rare? I think the cause is to be sought in Very's double heritage. He was both a Calvinist and a Romantic by birth. And however incompatible these bequests, both entailed an irrationalism which nurtured conflicts in their heir. Very may have seen the contradictions within him, but he seldom reasoned himself out of them.

According to the Christianity that Very inherited, nature was not only imperfect but "upset." (pp. 244-47)

Stated in its mildest form, this concept precluded meaningfulness in mere nature. To have anything one must have God. . . . Nor did Very stop here. He claimed, not only that Christ is "the only lasting trust" once the world has "vanished" for us ("**'Tis Finished**" . . .), but that the song he heard was not a song "of sense or earth" ("**The Birthday of the Soul**" . . .). Very vowed to oppose without compromise what in his essay "**Epic Poetry**" he called "the power of materiality." . . . Homer, he said, found only "conflicts *without* to describe"; Christian poets had risen to the "description of . . . internal conflicts." . . . (p. 247)

This was the dualist in Very, the Platonist who looked upon matter as the enemy of soul. His was not, however, that idealism which considers the world illusion: the world was there, substantially—and the world was evil. The orders of nature and grace were thus opposed. In his essay on Shakespeare, Very wrote that Shakespeare's spirit was "the antagonist of matter". . . . Elsewhere Very said the same of his own spirit and of all spirit. For it is Satan who "reigns on earth" ("**The Serpent**" . . .). Men are not at home here in nature. This life

is an exile, a pilgrimage. Until we "return home" ("**The Will**" . . .), we wander here

> sad and lone,
> As in a foreign clime,
> Till we again shall meet our own,
> Beyond the shore of time. . . .

Because of this heritage, Very warned us, indefatigably, that world defiles soul and that nature is a threat to the inner life. . . . The good was invisible; the visible, evil. To the dualist, it was that simple. (pp. 247-49)

This deep-rooted antipathy to nature explains Very's technique no less than his message. He was not a creaturely or a mimetic poet. His images are few, and hardly particularized. Very was steeped less in nature than in abstraction. He seems never to have shared the young Wordsworth's commitment to "nature and the language of the sense." As Very wrote of himself, he saw not with the eye and heard "not with the ear" ("**Thy Brother's Blood**" . . .). And as Channing is reported to have said of him, he "suppressed his senses."

A poem that clearly portrays this first Very is "**The World.**" . . . (p. 249)

This essentially Calvinistic view of nature, though modified by the Arianism of Channing and contradicted by Very's second view, gained (or regained) ascendancy as the years went by. . . .

But there was a second view. Whatever we call it—Pelagian, Rousseauist, Romantic, Transcendental—it was clearly an optimistic view of nature. It was also an idealistic view, in both the popular and the philosophical sense. We know that Very devoted pages of his commonplace books to Wordsworth's ideas of nature, and we know that Emerson accepted Very as the Transcendentalists' "brave saint." (p. 250)

Joseph Warren Beach has shown that the cult of Nature was a substitute religion that bridged faith and atheism. It is therefore one of history's ironies that a Jones Very should have worshiped at the shrine. Whenever Very "went a-whoring after Baalim" he proved that, with God, he had no need of gods. (Such, perhaps, is the paradox of Baal.) Very seldom recognized Nature for what it was; so he adopted, alongside his first concept, the concept of an unfallen, perfect nature. He still considered man fallen, but man had fallen because he had "left Nature." It followed that man must not turn from things to eternity—the lesson derived from Very's first concept; he must re-establish his lost harmony with nature. (p. 251)

In working out a technique to embody this second concept, Very performed several of the rites of the Church of Nature, among them child-worship. The best way to recapture the childlike innocence of Shakespeare's mind, he wrote, is to recall "to our thoughts the days of our childhood, before we had been schooled by the selfishness of sin, when the tides of life flowed on with no will but His who was pouring them through our souls." . . . The "tides of life," like Wordsworth's "impulse from a vernal wood," are divine emanations which, by an unexplained body-soul osmosis, we imbibe from nature. In the same essay, Very referred to the tide of happiness which flowed naturally into Shakespeare "from the consciousness of being." We have "strayed from the paths of our youth"; we must return to innocence by returning to Nature. Apparently, the child was somehow exempt from original sin, and the "tides of life" replaced baptism. (pp. 251-52)

Very sometimes advised [a mystical unity between man and nature]. To do so, he had to blur the distinctions between nature and human nature that he elsewhere insisted upon. But once Very had assimilated the dogma of an All, distinctions blurred easily. To an orthodox Christian, to the "other Very," this union of man and nature was a pseudomysticism in which man would not rise into the ether of superrationality but fall into a pit of subrationality; he would not become pure Spirit, which is above human nature, but mere matter, which is below it. It is therefore surprising to find that the Calvinist in Very did not blink with astonishment when Very's Romantic *persona* said that the bubbling brook leapt up when he went by (**"Nature"**). . . .

[The] language with which Very embodied nature did not condone pantheism, it sanctified it.

Such sanctification presupposes a metaphysic of monism. (Logically, monism denies the *meta*physical, but logic was a "scholastic rationalism" the Transcendentalists transcended.) The union of man with nature was based on an assumed premise, that nature is united with God: we should be in nature because goodness is in nature; goodness is God; ergo, God is in nature—*is* Nature. The transition from the dogma of Creation ("And God saw everything that he had made, and, behold, it was very good") to the dogma of pantheism ("Everything is good, is God") required the leveling of a single distinction. It was only an iota here or there which distinguished matter as a manifestation of spirit from matter as spirit. And why not simplify the equation—since truth is always simple? Again, an appeal to the All did the leveling. God got lost in the process, but to nineteenth-century pantheists He was going already, or gone. Nature could take His place until naturalism came along—an even simpler solution, for it considered idea and spirit cobwebs in the brain and swept them away. Even with Very, who seems never to have doubted God's presence, and who probably never foresaw the advent of naturalism, the transition from nature to Nature was relatively easy, for he was given to the use of intense personification and, again, to extreme forms of pathetic fallacy. (pp. 252-53)

Granted this second concept of nature, and the poetic technique which it gave rise to, our surprise gives way to understanding when we find Very first damning and then praising the senses, or teaching that "sense poetry" is inferior poetry and then counseling us to yield to impulse. (p. 254)

Did Very find a synthesis? Was he able to hold on to both concepts of nature, yet somehow work out a technique which would eliminate or make use of the contradictions they entailed? No. Perhaps the two concepts could be fused. There is no fusion in Very's poetry. This is not to say that there is no syncretism, that Very did not consciously or unconsciously attempt a synthesis. In **"The Intuitions of the Soul"** . . . , he took a Trancendentalist way out: the same thoughts "of God, Of Beauty, or of Wisdom, Power, or Love" that he found within himself he found also "in Nature." Nature, like man, is "divine." But this apotheosis of nature proved a troublesome doctrine. (pp. 254-55)

Late in life, Very sometimes assumed, or backed into, a quite different stance: he preached Natural Law. This shift is first noticed in his political and occasional verse, where he found an appeal to Reason convenient. Nature became valuable for the lessons it taught, so long as it did not blind the disciple to supernature. But Very's stance was unsteady. In **"Interpreting Nature"** . . . , he was vague about what nature teaches; and in

"The Soul's Opportunities" . . . , he told men to learn nature's lessons, without telling them how. When he did offer a rudimentary pedagogy, he made a flower trust in God . . . or asserted that fireflies, by obeying "their varying mood," offer men a guide. . . .

When Very wrote that nature shows the Divine Will, he seems to have stood on firmer ground. And it is here that nature became more significant as technique than as concept. He was relying on his first concept of nature. In its most attenuated form, the concept was worked out in metaphors or in traditional symbols. . . . More often, Very wrought nature into poems by means of Swedenborgian "correspondences." But again, he often seems to have compromised his integrity. (pp. 255-56)

Most successful are those poems in which Very worked, not by symbol or by correspondence, but by sign. "As to the corporeal world," wrote Jonathan Edwards, "though there are many other sorts of consents [within the world itself, or with the supreme being], yet the sweetest and most charming beauty of it is its resemblance of spiritual beauties." Like Edwards, Very found signs of Providence in nature. By interpreting these signs, he found sermons in stones.

> The beast, the bird, the fish, the shell,
> The flower, the crystal from the mine,
> Have each some word of truth to tell
> Of the Creator's vast design. . . .

[In **"Welcome,"** quoted above,] the poet was not vague. He found something definite in nature, design, and from this he found the Designer. In **"My Garden"** . . . , Very found Providence and God's love as well.

This seeking after nature's signs also gave Very his types: the dryness of sin, the warmth of morning, the stream of grace. Equally typological, and less conventional, are "whitening fields," "winter in the godless heart," God's eagles feeding on carrion will, and the sunrise of the soul. This poetry is successful because the correspondences are not faked. In **"Nature Teaches Us of Time and Its Duration"** . . . , Very wrote that nature was made in order to teach: nature is not a conscious teacher; and it teaches not impossible but real lessons—here, that time must have a stop. In **"Autumn Leaves,"** a sonnet which deserves to be known, Very saw in nature a hint of immortality. Significantly, he closed the poem with "the unseen hues of immortality." . . . The hues are *unseen*. There is no sentimentality here, no confusion. What he saw helped explain what he did not see. He did not claim to see what he did not see. In these poems, a resolution—though not a synthesis—was achieved, not by fusing the second concept of nature with the first, but by subordinating the second concept. (pp. 257-58)

Jones Very's poetry is more than a dialectic between self and God, will and will-lessness. It is also a dialectic between nature and Nature. When both voices speak at once, they weigh his poetry down with contradiction, obscurity, vagueness, disunity, unparticularized images, confused correspondences, lost distinctions, and logical fallacies. When the Calvinist subordinates the nature poet, Very's verse is usually substantial, often illuminating, sometimes even powerful. . . .

Jones Very inherited both the Calvinism of his forebears and the Romanticism of his contemporaries. This double heritage was not his alone: it can be found in works of Melville and Hawthorne, and no doubt in the works of Emerson as well.

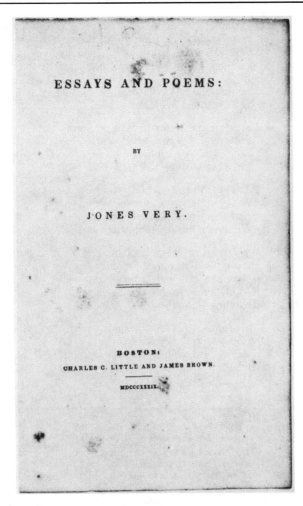

The frontispiece to the first edition of Very's Essays and Poems.

Unique was Very's use of nature, his transmutation of concept into technique. (p. 259)

> Anthony Herbold, *"Nature As Concept and Technique in the Poetry of Jones Very," in* The New England Quarterly, *Vol. XL, No. 2, June, 1967, pp. 244-59.*

CARL DENNIS   (essay date 1970)

[*Through his analysis of the similarities between Very's and Emerson's nature poetry, Dennis concludes that Very was influenced more by Emerson's interpretation of nature than by the ideas of English Romanticism. For another discussion of Very's stance toward nature see the excerpt by Anthony Herbold (1967).*]

Emerson's aesthetic is paralleled very closely by Very's own poetic theory and practice. Not only does Very regard the poet as receiving direct inspiration from the ultimate source of truth, but he also regards the poet's tasks as awakening man's spiritual life by revealing the moral truths expressed in the material world. For like Emerson, Very sees nature as a source of analogues for the highest laws of the mind, as a language to be read by an inspired interpreter. He adopts, in other words, Emerson's theory of correspondence.

Perhaps the best way to keep in mind the essence of Emerson's theory of correspondence in this discussion is to distinguish it from the attitudes to nature advocated by the British Romantics. Both Emerson and the Romantics agree that nature is good, that man is benefited by its society; but they see this benefit accruing in different ways. The British poets tend to alternate between two distinctly different conceptions of the mind's relation to nature. On the one hand, they see nature as an active force beneficently shaping the mind of a passive observer, a view which they rooted partly in the empirical psychology of Locke and his followers. On the other hand, they see nature as passive matter to be shaped and colored by man's creative imagination, a view which they bolstered by tenets of German idealism. When they regard nature as active, they celebrate man's receptivity, his "wise passiveness"; when they regard it as passive, they speak of the mind's "esem-plastic" powers molding nature to express human emotion. Neither of these attitudes to nature is adopted by Emerson. The key concept of his aesthetic is "correspondence," the notion that nature bodies forth by analogy spiritual truth. And the implications of this concept preclude either a re-creation of nature or a passive submission to it. The Transcendental poet need not mold nature because God has already made all natural facts analogues of spiritual facts; and he cannot submit to nature, because nature is not a power but a language requiring active study and translation. This rejection of both submission and manipulation is one of the controlling principles of Very's poetic theory and practice. (pp. 251-52)

To see how Very presents nature in his poetry we may begin by examining a few of those poems written with the specific intention of formulating the theory of correspondence. The sonnet, **"Man in Harmony with Nature"** . . . , comes close to being a full poetic statement of the central tenets of the essays. . . . The harmony between man and nature described in the first quatrain is that of a mutual responsiveness. Nature reveals kinship with man's "spirit voice," rejoicing in his presence; and man, in his joy, reveals his awareness of the spiritual aspects of nature. The harmony does not appear to be the result of man's submissiveness to nature, or of nature's submissiveness to man's manipulation, but the result of nature's being made like man, with the power of expressing ideas and emotions. The poet clarifies the relation in the second quatrain by attributing his harmony with nature to "the sweet obedience of the will." This submission of the poet's mind is not to nature but to God; it is that state of selflessness which makes possible a full receptivity to divine inspiration. The poet who is "formed" by God can "learn" this submission by going out into nature because nature is created completely passive to God's will, being bidden by God to "live and play." Once man has humbled himself he will be in harmony with submissive nature, and his selflessness will allow him to see his own spiritual life in all things. With this power of understanding and identification all creatures will seem his fellows and the world will appear as it is, formed to fit his spirit, "another house." The key concept of the poem is that of nature as companion, which is expressed explicitly in the final line. Nature helps to show man what true submissiveness means, but once man has learned the lesson, has read the message, he and nature are spiritual equals, serving God in a harmony that they are "born" to establish.

Most of the poems elaborating Very's theory of nature stress either the necessity of submission to God or the spiritual aspects of physical objects, rather than combining both complementary assertions in one poem as we find in **"Man in Harmony with**

Nature." On the one hand, we have poems asserting the doctrine of inner illumination. They reject the notion that submission to nature leads to harmony with nature, and insist rather on the need of achieving an enlightened activity of the mind through a selfless humility under God's guidance. The poem entitled "The True Light," for example, begins by distinguishing the inner light of the spirit from the outer day-light of nature, and asserts that the day can become a comfort to man, can become a metaphor for the light of the soul, only when man has developed his spiritual resources. . . .

> And naught of evening's peace has thou e'er had,
> If evening first did not with thee begin.
> Full many a sun I saw first set and rise,
> Before my day had found a rising too;
> And I with Nature learned to harmonize,
> And to her times and seasons made me true. . . .

In asserting that the brightness of the morning and the peace of the evening must begin in man before man can take pleasure in nature, the poem may seem to be asserting that these qualities are actually imparted to nature by the mind. But the goal presented here is harmony and not recreation. The intention of these lines is simply to assert that this harmony does not result from absorbing nature's qualities but from an inner awakening which allows one to read natural phenomena as mental analogues. The meaning of nature becomes visible when man has submitted himself to God's will.

Another poem of this kind, "The New Birth," specifically sets forth the notion that the flow of man's thought is the result of God's direct inspiration, and indirectly opposes the poet's state of inner illumination to a submission to outward impulses.

> The portals open to the viewless wind
> That comes not save when in the dust is laid
> The crown of pride that guilds each mortal brow,
> And from before man's vision melting fade
> The heavens and earth. . . .

The insistence here on the primacy of the inner life is extreme; for the lines suggest that the senses are a distraction and that the physical world has to be left behind completely. Rejecting nature as a power, Very seems here to reject it as a source of truth. But the attitude is atypical. For though Very's poems consistently contend that God directly infuses the humble mind, they also affirm that nature can help man remember God's holy laws.

Many poems stress the symbolic uses of natural facts in the most specific terms. In the poem appropriately entitled "The Revelation of the Spirit Through the Material World" the reader is encourged to overcome an enslavement to "gross material eyes" and to observe in all objects "a beauty and grandeur not of earth" since God has filled all objects with spirit:

> The Spirit with its rays illume[s]
> Their inmost depths, from matter now refined;
> That man may thus with it communion hold,
> And learn of higher things than sense has told. . . .

Here it is clear that leaving the senses behind does not mean leaving nature behind, but rather using nature as a metaphor made by "Spirit" for man's moral instruction. The symbolic theory is again asserted in the poem called "Nature Intelligible," but this time not against materialists but against both religious mystics who would dispense with nature as a phan-

tasm (as Emerson sometimes does) and skeptical agnostics who regard nature as inscrutable. The world, the poet asserts, is not a "vain illusion to the sight" as "the Hindoos say"; nor is it a "wildering maze, without a plan." Rather it is a glorious mansion built for man,/The work of One Eternal Mind." . . . Because nature embodies God's creative thought, it is constantly giving us spiritual insights:

> Summer and Autumn, Winter, Spring,
> Each season of the varied year,
> Doth each for us a lesson bring,
> If we but turn the listening ear.
>
> Awake, O man! and face to face
> With Nature stand, a living soul;
> And every word and letter trace,
> Written on her mysterious scroll. . . .

This image of nature as a scroll or book to be read by the inquiring student, it will be remembered, is Emerson's favorite metaphor to describe man's right relation to nature. And the same notion of nature as language is again set forth in Very's poem "Interpreting Nature":

> The sights we see, the sounds we hear,
> Are fitted to the eye and ear;
> They're not a dumb, unmeaning show,
> But speak a language all men know.
>
> • • • • •
>
> Daily the sights and sounds return,
> Till we the lesson taught shall learn
> That Nature everywhere doth teach,
> Though not in words of human speech.

A great body of Very's nature poetry can be described as specific readings of natural facts. The readings are almost always obvious and explicit, requiring little interpretation to reveal what the facts symbolize. Many are based on time-honored comparisons. But though the poems are simple, our awareness of the poet's use of the theory of correspondences helps us to understand their special qualities.

One of the most commonly anthologized of Very's poems, "To the Canary Bird," is a good example of a kind of reading quite common in Very's poetry. . . . (pp. 257-61)

The poem develops one clear comparison. The canary emprisoned in its cage is presented as the analogue of the soul's longing for heaven. As a song bird the canary also suggests the religious poet, and his gilded cage the world's attempts to make him forget his religious commitment. In establishing the figurative meaning of the bird, the poem is extremely explicit. The first eight lines personify the canary as they describe it, so that its application is suggested at once. The next four lines place the situation in human terms; and the last two bring the bard and the bird together through the images of the gilded cage and native sky, which apply literally to one and figuratively to the other. What is most distinctive about the poem is not so much the meaning of the analogy as the poet's attitude to it. The poet identifies himself with the bird as he reads it. He does not simply use the bird as a means to express his own predicament, but rather uses his own predicament to empathize with the bird. The first line of the poem, "I cannot hear thy voice with others' ears," establishes at once that the poet's relation to the bird is distinctive; and the rest of the poem may be regarded as the poet's attempt to prove to the canary that his empathy is sincere, that the likeness of his situation to the canary's enables him to identify himself with its pain. The canary, then, is the poet's fellow; and by the end of the poem the identification is so complete that there is some doubt in the reader's mind as to whether the canary too is seen as having heavenly longings. The final effect, then, is to present not only an example of a reading of nature, but of the quality of mind necessary to enable the reading to take place. That is, the poem develops the notion stated in the essays that comprehension is based on love, on the ability to identify oneself fully with the life without.

We find a similar kind of empathetic reading in "The Tree." . . . One theme of this poem is the dependency of all things on God. The tree is presented as an instance of dependency in the natural world and as an analogue for man's necessary submission to God. Like man, the tree makes a hesitant and cautious beginning in life, then becomes in its prime the protector of the weak, and finally, in misfortune and age, stript bare, holds up its "leafless arms" to heaven in an attitude of humble supplication. In one sense the poem is a celebration of the poet's ability to put one natural fact to several uses. He can use the tree as as source of aesthetic pleasure; he can use it as a model of submissive dependence and humility. But the poet loves the tree as well as uses it, and his triumph of insight is also presented as a triumph of fidelity. He refuses to abandon the tree physically after the tree has ceased to serve physical uses. Instead of looking for comfort elsewhere, turning away from the tree to God, he looks "through" its branches at heaven, and so makes the tree his fellow-worshiper. The poem, then, is best understood as affirming Very's belief in the unity of vision and love. The poet's love for the tree is dependent on his ability to give it moral meaning, and this ability is dependent on his love.

The spiritual quality which Very most commonly ascribes to natural objects in his poetry is unconscious submissiveness and dependence. Like the tree, nature is usually an example not of conscious and mature humility but of a childlike thoughtless passivity and trust. And often the poet who observes nature is presented as yearning for its thoughtless innocence. . . . [In "The Columbine"] the poet's identification with the natural fact is expressed in even stronger terms than in "To the Canary Bird" and "The Tree." The poet wishes to become a flower, to forget his maturity for innocence, and refers to himself as the columbine's fellow, dew-sprinkled, rooted, and budded. The completeness of the poet's identification with the columbine helps to establish the plant's symbolic meaning. The flower is not personified; it is literally rooted, blown, sunned, and folded. Rather, the poet naturalizes himself, and in his ability to see himself as the flower the meaning of the columbine as a way of life emerges. As in the poems on the canary and the tree, insight is here a function of love. The poet's ability to see meanings in nature depends on his ability to cast out the selfconsciousness and selfishness that prevents sympathetic identification. And in this poem there is an especially close correlation between selflessness and insight because what the poet sees when he has rejected egoism and become submissive and loving is the unconscious, submissive dependence of the flower. . . . Very's ability to read the flower is a proof that he already possesses the virtue of the flower, and has therefore understood its highest use as a moral analogue. And the tone of the poem, despite the poet's expressed desire to "forget that I am called a man," is consequently one of calm and quiet rather than of uneasy longing. The poet's identifi-

cation with the flower is not the result of his losing himself in the life of the flower, but of seeing the life of the flower in himself.

Many of the poems which are specific readings of nature are less personal and empathetic than the readings discussed above. Although the ability to identify with the life without is for Very the poet's main virtue, the readings are often presented less as the product of the poet's particular involvement with an object than as a simple, objective description of observable facts. The tendency of such readings is to suggest the ease with which facts can be interpreted and their general applicability to all men. Nature's meanings are so clear that the barest descriptions make them evident. Some of these poems end with interpretive stanzas which draw the analogy for the reader; but others rely simply on the metaphoric overtones of the description to bring the figurative meaning home to the reader. (pp. 261-65)

Of all Very's allegoric poems, the one that is most crucial to students of his theory of nature is the sonnet entitled "The Lost," a poem that attempts to relate the metaphoric uses of nature to man's powers of empathy. . . . (p. 268)

[The] poem is an attempt to put nature clearly in its place, to define its uses as spiritual instruction, while insisting on the dangers it possesses as a potential source of distraction. The first quatrain affirms not only that man must be spiritually awake before he can use nature as language, as does the "Inward Morning," but also that man's beauty is far superior to nature's since it is moral. To say that man must regard himself as the brightest day or fairest flower is not to say that man and nature have some mysterious, ineffable tie, but only to affirm metaphorically that natural beauty is inferior to beauty of the soul. Because man now delights in temporal, physical forms, we are told in the second quatrain, and has forgotten that their beauty only shadows forth what he himself actually possesses, he has impaired his own spiritual health, has wilted his "petals." In the sestet the theme is complicated as the notion of nature's subordination to man is related to the doctrine of the good man's empathetic involvement in the life without. The point made here is that the theory of correspondence, though it asserts man's primacy, nevertheless, does full justice to nature's intrinsic holiness. Just as nature improperly regarded can distract man from his inner life, so a defective inner life, a life of pride and selfishness, results in a distortion of nature's language. When man is spiritually lost, . . . he does not hear the song of the bird but rather unconsciously forces his own song upon it, the bird being "made" to sing with the poet's "forgotten voice." But when the bird is allowed to sing its own "melody," when the listener is no longer selfish, man can make the song truly his own by an empathy which allows him to see himself in all things. This empathy produces joy not only because the song of the bird is joyous in its subscription to God's law, but because man by casting out selfishness attains a state of similar submission to God. By not giving his "substance" to nature, by not allowing himself to be distracted from the pursuit of inner holiness, man can more fully comprehend nature's "wonders," since he can see nature's holy utility as God's language. (pp. 268-69)

In all the poems we have discussed so far which work on the theory of correspondence of mind and nature, the meanings of natural facts appear easily accessible to the poet. The poet is never confused or hesitant; nature is never cryptic; and the language of the poetry is correspondingly clear, free of paradox and ambiguity. To the reader who comes to Very's poetry from

Very's home in Salem, MA. From Jones Very: Emerson's ''Brave Saint'' *by William Irving Bartlett, p. 120. Copyright © 1942 Duke University Press, Durham, NC. Reproduced by permission of the publisher.*

a reading of Emerson's, it is this clarity of statement and simplicity of language that is most striking; for Emerson believes that nature, though always full of meaning, is often inscrutable; and the language of his poetry is often correspondently ambiguous. It is true that Emerson agrees with Very in asserting that full insight into nature may be gained by moral regeneration, but he often presents himself, along with the rest of mankind, as lacking the illumination of the reason and struggling to regain it. Very, on the other hand, consistently presents himself in his poetry as a man who has successfully submitted himself to the direction of God, who has cast out selfishness, made himself a child again, and gained the power of reading spiritual meanings in nature. His poems, therefore, though they often are personal and religious, do not display the internal conflict that distinguishes the work of Herbert or Donne. Very does not wrestle with the devil, the world, and the flesh. When he speaks of sin and darkness, he speaks as a virtuous man to a sinful world, urging men to awake and remember their true natures. Both Very and Emerson, then, subscribe to the theory of correspondences, but Very's poetry resembles Emerson's simple ''The Apology'' more than Emerson's ''The Sphinx'' because Very almost always presents himself as a man fully inspired.

What separates Very's poems from Emerson's even more obviously than their consistent simplicity is their structure, the

fact that most of them are sonnets, deviating from the Shakespearean form only by the occasional use of a closing Alexandrine. Where a characteristic feature of Emerson's ''ecstatic'' poems is an excess of illustrative material piled on in couplets or cross rhyme, Very's use of an enclosed form imposes a comparatively strict ordering of his material, each sonnet proceeding in a slow but logical development of a single theme through direct statement and a limited number of figures. In attempting to explain Very's choice of the sonnet form one might possibly argue that since the meanings of nature are always accessible to Very, he can state his themes easily within the confines of a tight form; whereas Emerson, who often presents himself as groping towards the truth, needs more expansive and flexible forms to arrive at an interpretation of nature. But although this fact may allow Very to use the sonnet, it does not make the choice necessary. And the formal rigor of a sonnet seems more appropriate to the poet who attempts to impose order on nature than to the poet who reads a nature which corresponds to the mind. Perhaps Very's choice in part results from his celebrating virtues different from those that Emerson exalts, from his emphasis on self-submission rather than self-reliance. While for Emerson the sonnet would be an unbearable restriction of self-expression, for Very it might serve as an aesthetic instance of the mind's submission to imposed laws. . . . [His] conservatism might have prompted

Very's use of the sonnet not simply as a form of self-discipline but as a way of placing his poetry within the tradition of the English religious lyric, which from the sixteenth century had established the sonnet as an important formal mode of devotional utterance.

But neither a desire for discipline nor a respect for tradition can explain another obvious feature of Very's prosody, the lack of craftsmanship in the writing of many individual lines, especially the frequent inversions that twist the natural order of speech for the sake of rhyme. Almost every sonnet is marred in some way by this device, which not only makes the lines sound forced but also sometimes obscures the argument. Thus in **"The Lost,"** the inversion in the second and fourth lines momentarily clouds the relation of man to the day and the flower, a particularly unfortunate clumsiness since the poet has set out to clarify the distinction through complicated metaphor. This lack of polish may simply result from Very's inability to see the greater forcefulness of natural word order; but it may also result from his belief that true poetry is not the result of the poet's will and craft but of God's voice working through him, that it is "the word of God uttered throught the soul as it ever speaks through inanimate creation." . . . To rework a line would be to alter God's dictation. (pp. 270-72)

Although the structural characteristics of Very's verse can't be deduced directly from the theory of correspondence, their probable causes are nevertheless more consistent with the theory than with the alternative views of nature posited by the English Romantics. Just as with Emerson's poet, the inspiration which Very's poet receives comes from within or from above, and not from physical nature. And the formality of the verse is probably not meant to be seen as an imposition of form on a disordered material, but as an expression of the same submission to law which is bodied forth by a correspondently submissive nature. (pp. 272-73)

> *Carl Dennis, "Correspondence in Very's Nature Poetry," in* The New England Quarterly, *Vol. XLIII, No. 2, June, 1970, pp. 250-73.*

COLETTE GERBAUD (essay date 1977)

[*Characterizing Very as "a soundly practical man" rather than as a mystic out of touch with the present, Gerbaud argues that his idea of rebirth is realistic, traditional, and conservative. She posits that Very's language is "reminiscent of the hermitic language of the alchemists," for he attempts to convey an extraordinary state of mind using ordinary diction and imagery. This essay was first presented as a paper read at a symposium in 1977.*]

[Jones Very] invites the reader to follow him and discover "the new life" which a "new birth" alone makes possible.

"The new life" is not a myth as that of a paradise that one is looking backward to. It is a reality that one should be looking forward to, and strive to bring about. The idea of a Paradise, of a Promised Land is not absent from Very's poetry, but it is not a dream. In spite of what misinformed people may have said, Very was no madman, and no dreamer, but a soundly practical man. (pp. 43-4)

[In his **"Epistles,"**] Very had undertaken the next to impossible: namely to convey by means of words what takes place inside man's mind and body when he passes from the usual state of life, to an exceptional state of being: who could understand him? Certainly not those who had not made the trip,

as he knew and stated himself. Only those who have known or mastered, or passed through and out of a state can know what that state is. Those who are in that state are unaware of it and cannot either judge it, nor know it since awareness implies a critical position towards oneself. In other words perspective is necessary for a good understanding and a fair appraisal. Very's language, although different in terms and formulas, is however reminiscent of the hermetic language of alchemists, who referred to things apparently remote and strange, but actually so near us that our eyes cannot see them in their normal, physical condition. (p. 47)

[At] first sight Very's mystic labor seems illusory. Yet he clears our vision and shows what efforts self-conquest may cost, and what suffering must be experienced before the agents of sin can be crushed:

> The child must suffer what thou sufferest too,
> And learn from him Thou sent e'en so to die;

In this work a non earthly help is necessary:

> In Thee I trust . . . . secure from sin,
> For Thou hast conquered every foe within.
>   **"The Disciple"**

The God Very praises is essentially masculine, as it is in many Christian countries. Unlike Oriental mysticism, or Catholic devotion to the Holy Virgin, Very's religious fervour is based on the worship of the Father. Religious fervour may be part of a mystic quest, but mysticism is more inclusive. Very's direct and repeated appeal to the Father adds a sentimental, personal note to his poetry. . . . But the feminine phase of the regenerative process is not forgotten. The passive and compulsory state of the body at night allows the unfolding and strengthening of the higher consciousness, whose watch is perpetual:

> I thank Thee, Father, that the night is near
> When I this conscious being may resign;
>
>   • • • • •
>
> And while within her (dark-robed night's)
>   darkened couch I sleep,
> Thine eyes untired above will constant vigils keep.
>   **"Night"**
>   (pp. 53-4)

The body of Jones Very's inspiration, that is his word, is in the image of his own person: tall and lean, dressed in black, with no ornaments, like a puritan church. So, one is free to leave the earth without any regret, unhampered by unnecessary flesh, and soar on the wings of the Spirit. Very was a famous hymnologist in his time and country. His poetry never attracted the worshipper inordinately to the point of making him forget the purpose of his worship. It does not draw the attention onto itself but invites to prayer, and meditation. It reminds the reader of the Bible in its admonitory tone, its paradoxes, its parables, its use of the personal pronoun in, the second person singular. This is no doubt part and parcel of a very traditional religious poetry. But inside this chosen, iron frame, Very's inspiration flows at ease: it tells of his joy, of his exhilarating joy, shooting its light to the sky in an irresistibly ascending movement:

> There is no death with Thee! each plant and tree
> In living haste their stems push onward still,

Youth and vigour, the vigour of "the new man" his refreshed view of everything lend themselves to a poetic form of a special kind: exhortation, which ranges this poetry with the didactic verse. It unites idealism and realism for Very's avowed purpose to awaken the ''unborn'' forbids him to side with the dreamers, or even with the utopians, in spite of appearances. A poetry singing rebirth such as his obeys several very strict rules: this can be seen in the use of tenses for instance: as a poetry of annunciation it sometimes uses the future, or the near future tense, but this tense, just as the past tense, is used only in relationship with a superior present tense, which might be at the apex of a triangle the first or left angle of which would be the past, and the right angle the future: for the present tense is the only possible tense for actuality in both acceptations of the word. Reality alone must be the ruling principle and its dictate is: ''hic and nunc''; this implies immediacy: it therefore banishes all imaginary pushing back or forwarding of the present into a distant time: everything is contained here and now, so that it also rules out all places, distant places; places cannot be distant in the spirit. In the spirit there is *no* distance, there is no past nor future, but a unique and eternal NOW. Very's mystic poems are in the present tense; past and future are only used as references for the imperfect states that will disappear; the future is used to herald the coming of a new being. The apparent lack of concreteness comes from the fact that Very does not talk about a particular place, but of the non-temporal place 'par exellence': our mind, our soul, the dwelling of the spiritual spark in each of us. This reality rules out all minor realities of the world, and his poems may appear monotonous to some readers. But the sun then also might appear monotonous, for it is the orb that Very celebrates, as he does the dawn, the morning, or the night. The direction of his poetry is vertical, in depth, and in elevation, as opposed to the passive, horizontal, sprawling, still-born life movement. (''**The Living God**''). Colors are rare, for they belong to the realm of the senses: whereas the Spirit is light, includes all colors, and drives away gloom. Very is interested in the principles, in the laws of life and those can reduce to the one Principle, the one Law: God; all the rest, all manifestations are secondary phenomena, and *he,* Very, is out to make us discover the Unique Principle; hence the states of being he depicts are: awakening, rejoicing, peace, freedom as opposed to sleep, suffering, and spiritual death. The symbol inscribed in his message is that of growth, and expansion, according to the Biblical command: ''Be fruitful and multiply'', but the way to this growth is the narrow way, for ''strait is the gate that leadeth unto life'', so Very's verse is terse, bare of ornaments, and the form he chose to write in most of the time is the most difficult and strict: the sonnet form.

Jones Very's conception of the second birth or rebirth is quite in keeping with the traditional practice such as it is reported by the experiences and writings of mystics throughout the centuries. These experiences and writings vary in form, but not in content. If Jones Very has been ranged with minor poets, as a mystic he should be classed among the most authentic that the United States have produced. His very failures and limitations served him to reach the highest summit that a life can reach. . . . Very was conservative even in his most violent and youthful outbursts against orthodox preaching, and his poems prove as much. He returned to the age-old method of uniting the useful and the beautiful. But he is not for all that an outmoded thinker: quite the reverse: his call to awaken, to become more conscious of ourselves, to be present in each look, word, act, is answered by the many contemporary movements, or by specialists in human behaviour or health: psychoanalysis, parapsychology, dianetics, meditations of all kinds and denominations, etc. . . People talk endlessly of alienation, loss of

identity, loneliness, drug addiction, and what not, all of which might be alleviated, if not magically cured, by the regular reading of such poetry. Under an apparently simple form a great density reveals itself and forces the attention. In a time when so many doctrines are given up or revised, his conception of rebirth and resurrection deserves to be called back to memory: the poem entitled ''**The New Body**'' is an echo of his sermon on I Cor. XV, 44. . . . In this sermon he very simply explains the sense of the resurrection which starts already here and now, whose real purport is the Transfiguration, and during which the physical body too is regenerated. No poem can perhaps suggest more pathetically the plight in which the ''unborn'' may be, than ''**The Lost**'', for instance, and no poem perhaps is more difficult to penetrate, and more far-reaching in its implications. It includes the secret of the second birth, if ever there is any; no word can adequately express it, but only suggest it: and this is: oneness—, when oneness is achieved, then: ''Each object throws aside its mantle dim,''

(''**The Eye and Ear**'')

and:

> The bird thou hearest on the budding tree,
> Thou hast made sing with thy forgotten voice;

(''**The Lost**'').
(pp. 55-8)

Colette Gerbaud, ''Jones Very's Mystic Conception of Rebirth,'' in Proceedings of a Symposium on American Literature, *edited by Marta Sienicka, Uniwersytet im. Adama Mickiewicza w Poznaniu, 1979, pp. 43-58.*

PHYLLIS COLE (essay date 1982)

[Cole analyzes the Calvinist, Puritan, Neoplatonic, and Romantic elements in Very's ''Epistles,'' essays which he wrote to introduce and explain his poems, but which Emerson chose not to publish in Essays and Poems. *She maintains that these essays are primarily important for their illumination of Very's pietism and interest in language.]*

[Very's] ''**Epistles**'' provide a crucial text for understanding [his] highly personal pietism and obsessive interest in the language of the Bible. Much of the last forty years' scholarship on Very has debated the particular quality of Calvinist conviction that informs his writing, even though this writing was produced within a Unitarian and Transcendentalist setting. And evangelical Calvinism, it has concurrently been seen, is one of the enduring patterns of American culture at least into the nineteenth century, constituting both a major pole of the ''Protestant Temperament'' broadly construed and an important way into Romantic sensibility more particularly. Very's ''**Epistles**'' reveal him as a Calvinist both by temperament and by literary vocation. By temperament he pursues a radical perfection, explaining how the soul must be born again not once but twice out of the original ''still-birth'' of the body through a life of constant self-denial. And this spiritual ascent finds expression in literary work too, in a particular kind of reading and speaking, of Scriptural exegesis and prophecy. ''Birth'' takes place through a mystically informed reading of the ''words of *God*,'' and this birth in turn enables one to speak as the word, with the truth-telling power of Paul and John and even of Christ. (pp. 169-70)

In his insistence on the new birth and the absolute truth of Scripture, Very was . . . a ''Calvinist.'' But in both respects Very's statement is idiosyncratic and personal, a romantic vision and not a doctrinal stance. The **"Epistles"** are in part a narrative of conversion, one which would have found a readier audience on the circuits of Second Great Awakening evangelism than in Cambridge or Concord. . . . [The] **"Epistles"** recast the experience of conversion into a more formal, personally distant imaginative structure. Here Very asserts the existence of three absolute "spheres" or "states" in an essentially Neoplatonic cosmology. He speaks in the first person with a claim to knowledge of all three, but presents the result rather than the experience of that knowledge. Each state, he emphasizes, includes a language and level of understanding of its own; and failures of communication are seen as separations of state. What the unborn consider "natural"—the realm of bodily enjoyment—is really "unnatural"; the truly "natural" must be a "body of denial," a gift of birth. Similarly, "world" is to the born a special place and meaning, one which unborn readers "know not." Very articulates the relationship among these states largely through a series of Scriptural figures and conceptual paradoxes. And as speaker he claims at least in the present the sole right to interpret such paradoxes: "Remember therefore," he warns, "that with the real meaning of Scripture, as with the commonest thing around you, *you* can as yet have nothing to do."

The "real meaning" of Very's Bible is then absolute but elusive. . . . The great New Testament texts on resurrection are his center; he echoes both Christ's parables of the kingdom and Paul's hymn to the coming time when "the dead shall be raised incorruptible, and we shall all be changed." Most fundamentally of all, though, he follows the drama of resurrection through the gospel of John: like Christ to Nicodemus in John 3, he tells how a man must be "born from above" to see the kingdom of God; and he ends by proclaiming, like Christ to Lazarus in John 11, "I am the Resurrection and the Life."

In claiming to be Christ Very is inviting the reader to be Christ too, for such identity is the essential attribute of all reborn or eternal life. At the same time, however, he does not imagine easy ways to the divine state any more than easy readings of Scripture; the burden of his argument is warning as well as encouragement. "You are permitted to see" the born, but "you are no more, ignorantly, to exult yourselves to their spheres, than you physically would do to those of the bright *shining* globes, which to your night-vision roll over your heads." Emotionally Very is, unlike Emerson, a separatist and preparationist. His system demands a reprobate, a large unborn multitude who will never transcend "night-vision;" the judgmental anger of his earlier outburst is not after all so far under the surface of this writing. And even in forwarding the work of resurrection Very insists on the traditional Puritan paradox of preparation for grace: though you must not "exult yourselves" upward, still spiritual growth is "dependent upon yourself"; the soul must "be willing," "quickening" through desire, sowing "bare grain" with no certainty that a harvest will follow. This is the work of self-denial, of clearing a place in the soul for grace to enter rather than moving toward grace. Nowhere is Very more a traditional American Puritan than in these emphases on election and preparatory self-denial; for in his immediate culture Unitarians and Transcendentalists, Awakening evangelists and Swedenborgians, alike affirmed a more Arminian doctrine of the soul's capacity to will its own salvation.

In fact Very, in this drama of birth through denial, is recreating a Puritan imitation of Christ; and this imitation becomes the key to his quite un-Puritan proclamation of self as Christ. In the first Epistle the repudiation of body and sexual origin appears to be a rather traditional way of ascetic discipleship, of *following* Christ; in fact Very echoes Christ's injunction that whoever will follow must "*deny himself.*" But by the second Epistle self-denial has become self-crucifixion, full mystical participation in the "true body of Jesus Christ." And this body is "lifted up" (another Johannine term) in resurrected glory as in crucifixion. Humility, rather than Emerson's seizure of possibility, becomes a way to Emerson's end of godlike knowledge and power. . . . The compelling interest of Very's Puritan Romanticism is that it recapitulates [the Romantic "American Self"] within its own rhetoric.

The personal center of this Romanticism, at once neurotic and brilliantly original, is the account of Very's own power as Christ, his own work saving the unborn. No soul can "exult" itself upward through his spheres, but once "lifted up" to Birth and Rebirth the soul can exert immense power downward to "draw all who are dead . . . to life." Such "action of the soul" is called "Prayer," the title of the second Epistle. Prayer is a continuation of self-denial and self-crucifixion, but now it is an act of love, of giving oneself for the life of others: "For this cause, says Jesus, I sanctify *myself; that* they also may be one even as we are one." In thus quoting Christ's priestly prayer from John, Very lays claim to atoning as well as self-redeeming power in his own habitual asceticism. "Love" as an "action of the soul" is not manifest in good works or communal relationships; it is a private contemplative condition "for the health of others." It acts as a magnetic emanation from the higher sphere to the lower, a sort of energy of divine love exerted directly by born and reborn God-Man. Very's figure for this life of Prayer—for his own life—is a tree rooted in decay and therefore green and fresh as it grows toward the upper air, "so that the influence of life shall ever be thrown around you, and be for the healing of the nations." This healing influence then extends outward and downward, back toward its own source in decay but now with the power of God on the Last Day to call upon the dead to "come forth."

Very's reborn soul is not self-reliant in Emerson's sense, because its absolute need and vindication is this saving work on behalf of others. On the other hand Very does not easily imagine a communion of saints, a joyfully reborn society. There is no room in his thought for truly collective experience. The crux, one which emerges explicitly in the final **"Epistle on Miracles,"** is Very's yearning from his uppermost sphere for encounter with the other single souls that he will resurrect. Biblical metaphors multiply as he reaches out toward these unborn: he is their begetter and they his children; he stands as a stranger at their door and knocks; he is a fisher of men, a net thrown into the sea to catch "abundantly of every kind." Very projects a mask of unassailable authority in his ascetic quietism. He stands in an "unseen relation" to his intended converts and speaks to them "from within" as an "external influence," that is an influence from a higher sphere of being. Communication is mystical, not open to disproof. But when the "Miracle" of conversion takes place its test will be acknowledgment of Very's own mission and authority, "face to face" meeting between Very and the soul he has converted. (pp. 171-74)

Alone among American Romantics, Very dares to imagine the face-to-face meeting from God's perspective; it is recognition of the divinity *in him* that will constitute the apocalyptic event. Very insists (as Christ did not) that he is the father of all who follow him, and as he looks for face-to-face recognition he assumes both a parental and a godlike position of strength for himself. Very is never the petitioner. But when this as-yet-unfulfilled moment of resurrection takes place, the risen Lazarus will "minister unto" Very the father-Christ. The emotional need behind the mask of authority emerges most painfully in this demand for recognition and ministering love.

Indeed in an important sense Very's **"Epistles"** read as documentation of a personal pathology; his imagination has worked to create unambiguous, unassailable conditions of power for himself.... Very's effort to ordain the conditions of human speech and meaning was, of course, a failure both personally and culturally: ambiguity rather than closure would become the more viable mode for discerning truth in literary and religious America. But Emerson saw too that this "exaggerated and detached pietism" was "true in itself ... speaking things in every word"; only a bridge was needed "between Very and the Americans." And with our longer retrospect, these **"Epistles"**—quintessential expression of Very's truth—appear even more integral to Very's America. Both their grandeur and their pathological quality belong to the history of the American "deific creation *ex imaginatio.*" (pp. 174-75)

Phyllis Cole, "Jones Very's 'Epistles to the Unborn'," in Studies in the American Renaissance: 1982, *edited by Joel Myerson, Twayne Publishers, 1982, pp. 169-83.*

HYATT H. WAGGONER (essay date 1984)

[*Waggoner asserts that Very perhaps "most completely embodied the quality the Transcendentalists valued highest, absolute trust in the inward vision," yet he acknowledges that Very sometimes lacked the ability to communicate that vision.*]

Very remains today an interesting minor poet. If he had been a better one, more imaginative and linguistically resourceful, he would remind us of Hopkins. As it is, generally only the themes of the two are similar—God shining out through nature, present everywhere even in the humblest circumstances and least "sacred" objects; man dependent on Him always, even as he moves and breathes. If he had been more witty and "metaphysical" in the literary sense, he would more often remind us of Edward Taylor. The *ideas* of the two are often indistinguishable, except when Very is writing directly about the objects of nature, when it becomes clear that *his* view of it is truly sacramental, while for Taylor nature is generally just illustrative.

Very seems to have had trouble meeting people, but his contacts with nature were true "meetings" in the sense which Martin Buber has given to the term. It was, unfortunately, generally quite true, as he wrote, that "Nature! my love for thee is deeper far / Than strength of words, though spirit-born, can tell," yet now and then he found the words to suggest to us what nature meant to him. **"The Columbine"** was a favorite of his contemporaries and deserves to be better known today. In it his feeling for the flower is that of one created being for another. The sympathy does not seem affected or arch: He knows very well what dryness means and can say without coyness, "And here will drink with thirsty pores the rain." He does not suppose that the flower is "wiser far than human seer," as Emerson thought "the humble bee." He does not appropriate the flower as an illustration of a doctrine, or use it for any ends of his own. He simply accepts it as real, valuable, and alive,

as *he* is. We are close here to St. Francis, and close to Thoreau, too; and, oddly enough, as it may seem, to a good many *haiku* poems and to one of the dominant characteristics of our own newest poetry, the poetry of the 1960's. Very's poetry anticipates thematically—though not of course formally—contemporary "objectivist" poetry: He moves toward the transcendent through the senses—without benefit of LSD.

Very's poetry is repetitious and very often bare of anything but the doctrines he wishes to express. Convinced that it was his role merely to listen to the Voice within and write down what he was "told" ("You hear not mine own words, but the teachings of the Holy Ghost," he once wrote), he was unwilling—or unable?—to try to perfect a style—to sacrifice, as it would seem to him, inspiration for the sake of mere effect. He was the living example of what Emerson, in "The Problem," had said must be true of any great artist: He wrote "in a sad sincerity: / Himself from God he could not free." He thought he merely took dictation, now and then perhaps missing a word, but never letting "vain or shallow thought" affect what he was doing. The Holy Ghost, it would be possible to conclude, if we took Very on his own terms, often writes very awkwardly and dryly.

Yet when he found the words to make *us* hear what he heard and the images to enflesh the doctrines he believed, he wrote poems that have value beyond their use as devotional aids. Never a master of language and too often dependent on the time-worn verbal formulas of orthodox faith, so that much of his verse not labeled "hymns" *reads* like hymns, still, syntactical awkwardness and all, his very best poems remind us of the first-rate minds and best artists of his own time and foreshadow those of our time. They earn for him the right to take his place in the long line of American poets who, beginning with Edward Taylor, have defined the American style in poetry. Of his very best poems this is *true*, we say; I had not realized how true. We feel ourselves in the presence of a first-rate mind and authentic experience.

For instance, **"The Mind the Greatest Mystery."** The mind in this poem is imaged first as a cavern, then as the sea. The inversions are awkward and the language perhaps too bare. Very does not conceive of himself as creating an effect, as Poe would, but of having something important to say and saying it as plainly as possible. He begins

> I threw a stone into a cavern deep,
> And listening heard it from the floor rebound;
> It could not from my thought its secret keep,
> Though hidden from the sight its depth I found,

and ends

> But when, from these, I turned to explore the mind,
> In vain or height or depth I sought to find.

Here as last, by a circuitous route, we come back to Emerson. The mind is immeasurable, and in the mysteries of both its depth and its height we find God. Very preached as Emerson once said Jesus did *ab intra,* from within, as one *in-spired;* he preached both in Unitarian pulpits throughout New England and through the medium of poetry as the language best suited to the Spirit. Except in the specific content of his faith, he was everything Emerson said the poet should be. If in the end he reminds us more of Hawthorne and Thoreau and Edward Taylor and John Woolman, it is because he really *was* true to the Voice he heard within and not to the voices he heard, but would not follow, saying more fashionable things. Instead, like Taylor, he made of both his life and his work a long "preparatory meditation." Though he is often merely tediously devout, and though he speaks in a voice that seems always close to a stammer, Very is perhaps the American poet who most completely embodied the quality the Transcendentalists valued highest, absolue trust in the inward vision. As a result, his poems often bring to at least partially adequate expression insights not available to him in the literature and learning of his time. **"The Dead,"** with its wasteland imagery, anticipated Eliot, as does **"The Hand and Foot." "Soul-Sickness"** anticipates Freud and contemporary psychiatry. **"The Columbine"** and other poems show his understanding of the possibility of an I-Thou relationship with nonhuman things, long before Buber.

To praise him in more "absolute"—that is, aesthetic—terms, by comparing his accomplishment with that of poets of his own time, I think we should remember his poems on the Fugitive Slave law and on the completion of the transcontinental telegraph as not only the best ever written by any poet on these subjects but as good reading today. His sonnet **"On Visiting the Graves of Hawthorne and Thoreau"** is surely better than Longfellow's on Hawthorne's funeral. **"The New Man"** and **"The New World"** *almost* express the inexpressible timeless dream of a new heaven and earth when time shall be at an end.

Not long after editing Very's poems, Emerson wrote, in "The Poet," that he found nothing "of any value in books excepting the transcendental and extraordinary." He went on to say, "If a man is inflamed and carried away by his thought, to that degree that he forgets the authors and the public and heeds only this one dream which holds him like an insanity, let me read his paper, and you may have all the arguments and histories and criticism." It seems likely that he was not thinking of Very when he wrote these words, but every specification in them would apply more perfectly to the work of the Salem mystic than to many of Emerson's own verses. What is generally missing in Very is only that "adequate expression" that Emerson took for granted as the gift of the poet. (pp. 126-29)

> Hyatt H. Waggoner, "Ecstasy in Concord and Salem," in his American Poets: From the Puritans to the Present, *revised edition, Louisiana State University Press, 1984, pp. 115-29.*

ADDITIONAL BIBLIOGRAPHY

Andrews, William P. "Memoir." In *Poems by Jones Very*, pp. 3-31. Boston: Houghton Mifflin and Co., 1883.
    A brief overview of Very's life and career, written by a friend. Andrews's memoir includes a section on early critical reception of Very's works. In addition, the memoir contains one of the earliest discussions of Very's concept of "will-less existence."

Arner, Robert D. "Hawthorne and Jones Very: Two Dimensions of Satire in 'Egotism; or, The Bosom Serpent'." *New England Quarterly* XLII, No. 1 (March 1969): 267-75.*
    Suggests that Nathaniel Hawthorne modeled Roderick Elliston in his short story "Egotism; or, The Bosom Serpent" on Very. Arner proposes that Hawthorne perceived Very as "the perfect type of the isolated individual" and satirized his estrangement from everyday life.

Baker, Carlos. "Emerson and Jones Very." *The New England Quarterly* VII (March 1934): 90-9.*
    Traces Very's friendship with Ralph Waldo Emerson from their meeting in 1838 to their parting because of philosophical differences a year later. According to Baker, Emerson was unable to condone Very's belief in an existence without individual free will.

Berthoff, Warner B. "Jones Very: New England Mystic." *The Boston Public Library Quarterly* 2, No. 1 (January 1950): 63-76.
    Discusses Very's religious views within the context of the theological controversy in New England during the 1830s. Berthoff states that Very was never able to resolve the dualism inherent in his belief that "man was either dead in the flesh or alive in the spirit" and that Very's quietism removed him from the social questions of his day.

Brooks, Van Wyck. "Emerson in Concord." In his *The Flowering of New England: 1815-1865*, pp. 196-209. New York: E. P. Dutton, 1936.*
    A brief description of Very's sonnets. Brooks refers to them as "frosted orbs of electric light."

Buell, Lawrence. "Transcendental Egoism in Very and Whitman." In his *Literary Transcendentalism: Style and Vision in the American Renaissance*, pp. 312-30. Ithaca, N.Y.: Cornell University Press, 1975.*
    An analysis of Very's depiction of self in his poetry. According to Buell, Very used several poetic voices—divine, prophetic, and human—in a "conscious manipulation of the persona for literary effect."

Cameron, Kenneth Walter. "Jones Very." In his *Transcendental Reading Patterns*, pp. 200-10. Hartford, Conn.: Transcendental Books, 1970.
    A list of books borrowed by Very from the Harvard College Library between 1834 and 1838. Cameron considers the list a valuable tool for studying influences on Very's writing.

Fone, Byrne R.S. "A Note on the Jones Very Editions: Parts I and II." *American Notes and Queries* VI, Nos. 5, 6 (January 1968; February 1968): 67-9, 88-9.
    A comparative study of the three major editions of Very's works. Fone documents their overall strengths and weaknesses as well as their textual variations.

Gittleman, Edwin. *Jones Very: The Effective Years, 1833-1840*. New York: Columbia University Press, 1967, 436 p.
    A biography of Very that focuses on his intellectual and artistic development through the age of twenty-seven. Gittleman concludes that had Very "died in 1840 instead of 1880 the basis for present interest in him would not be affected in the least." The book also includes a selected bibliography of Very criticism.

Marovitz, Sanford E. "Emerson's Shakespeare: From Scorn to Apotheosis." In *Emerson Centenary Essays*, edited by Joel Myerson, pp. 122-55. Carbondale: Southern Illinois University Press, 1982.*
    Relates the evolution of Ralph Waldo Emerson's understanding and appreciation of William Shakespeare to Very's Shakespearean criticism. According to Marovitz, Very led Emerson to a consideration of Shakespeare in more "specifically religious terms."

Reeves, Paschal. "Jones Very As Preacher: The Extant Sermons." *ESQ*, No. 57 (IV Quarter 1969): 16-22.
    An analysis of Very's religious beliefs as reflected in his sermons written after 1842. Reeves stresses Very's "surprisingly wide spectrum of knowledge," the diverse influences on his theological doctrine, and his insistence upon social responsibility and "the dignity of human nature."

Robinson, David. "Jones Very, the Transcendentalists, and the Unitarian Tradition." *Harvard Theological Review* 68, No. 2 (April 1975): 103-24.
    An exploration of Very's attitudes toward Transcendentalism and Unitarianism as reflected in his poetry. Robinson asserts that Very eventually sided with the Unitarians because his "more traditional piety" conflicted with the tenets of Transcendentalism.

————. "Jones Very: An Essay in Bibliography." *Resources for American Literary Study* V, No. 2 (Autumn 1975): 131-46.

A bibliographical essay in which Robinson surveys the various editions and bibliographies of Very's works as well as biographies and criticism of the author. In addition, Robinson discusses Very's manuscripts and the historical context of his works.

————. "Four Early Poems of Jones Very." *Harvard Library Bulletin* XXVIII, No. 2 (April 1980): 146-51.

Discusses four of Very's unpublished poems dating from the mid-1830s. Robinson points out that these early poems, which are "in general markedly secular," form an interesting contrast to Very's later, mystical verse. In his early poetry, Robinson asserts, Very "was experimenting with several themes and voices before his spiritual rebirth."

Richard Wagner

1813-1883

German dramatist, essayist, and composer.

Recognized as an outstanding nineteenth-century composer, Wagner also distinguished himself as a dramatist and theoretician whose works profoundly influenced modern literature. Wagner's many operas and innovative dramatic theories, as well as his powerful personality, have consistently elicited substantial commentary. *Der Ring des Nibelungen (The Nibelung's Ring)*, his most widely acclaimed work, embodies many of his theories, including the use of cyclic structure, leitmotiv, and myth. Wagner's conception of Greek tragedy and interpretation of the pessimistic and materialistic philosophies of Arthur Schopenhauer and Ludwig Feuerbach also inform his operas. Like the ancient Greek dramatists, Wagner combined myths, symbols, and various art forms to express human and national aspirations. His primary goals were to create *Gesamtkunstwerk,* or unity of the arts, through a synthesis of music, poetry, and dance, and to portray the ideal human being.

Wagner was born in Leipzig, Germany. His father died when he was six months old, and a year later his mother married the actor and artist Ludwig Geyer, whose theatrical background influenced the young boy. Wagner was schooled in liberal arts at the Dresden Kreuzschule, where he displayed a keen appreciation for Greek drama and, by the age of fourteen, he had already attempted to write a classical tragedy. In 1828, Wagner began an independent study of harmony and composition and three years later entered Leipzig University as a music student. By his early twenties, Wagner had already earned a reputation as an egocentric and eccentric musician. His marriage to the German actress Christiane Planer in 1836 was the first of a series of tumultuous and influential liaisons that would affect his art and life. It was at this time also that Wagner's extravagant way of life resulted in unmanageable debts which would continue to plague him.

Wagner's operas, the first of which he composed as a student, can be divided into three categories: early, Romantic, and mature. The use of a librettist and the traditional Italian operatic style characterize such early works as *Die Feen, Das Liebesverbot; oder, Die Novize von Palermo,* and *Rienzi.* Since musicians and artists were dependent upon the patronage of the wealthy, in 1837 Wagner traveled to Paris, hoping to attract financial backing with a successful staging of *Rienzi.* Yet Wagner was unable to find a producer, and as a result of his careless spending, he was imprisoned briefly before moving to the Parisian suburb of Meudon. There he wrote *Der fliegende Holländer (The Flying Dutchman)*, which is recognized as the best of his early works and as a transitional opera between the early and Romantic phases. The first opera for which he composed both the libretto and music, *The Flying Dutchman* is also the first in which Wagner incorporated the mythic sources that became a hallmark of his Romantic and mature works.

The middle phase of Wagner's artistic development spans the years 1848 to 1853, during which he served as the court choir director in Dresden. During this period Wagner wrote what are generally considered his most Romantic operas: *Tannhäuser*

(Tanhauser) and *Lohengrin. Tanhauser* depicts the medieval legend of a knight's love for a beautiful woman, while *Lohengrin* portrays the saga of a mysterious lover whose identity must be hidden from the beloved. These works are considered Romantic for their poetic themes, sensual appeal, and dynamic dramatic construction. They also represent Wagner's achievement of an original style, including the use of myths and his own librettos, and demonstrate his increasing ability to combine several art forms.

Although Wagner wrote many essays on a variety of topics throughout his life, he presented his most prominent aesthetic theories in three works composed during his Romantic period: *Die Kunst und die Revolution (Art and Revolution), Das Kunstwerk der Zukunft (The Artwork of the Future),* and *Oper und Drama (Opera and Drama).* In *Art and Revolution,* Wagner discussed the revolutionary nature of art. Maintaining that all art is an expression of communal joy, he asserted that it should be accessible to everyone. He considered classical Greek tragedy the most perfect art form; like the Greeks, he wished to inspire an intense emotional response that would be enhanced by the union of drama and music. In *The Artwork of the Future,* Wagner developed his concept of *Gesamtkunstwerk.* He contended that the artist should strive, through a synthesis of music, poetry, and dance, to represent perfected human nature, and he considered the ''music-drama,'' as he called his operas, the most effective vehicle. In *Opera and Drama,* Wagner elaborated on his conception of music-drama. Since he found mythology continually relevant and universal in its ability to move an audience, he theorized that it was the most suitable source for dramatic themes. These themes were enhanced through the use of leitmotives, melodic phrases associated with recurring ideas, characters, and verbal patterns, which could be combined, juxtaposed, and developed to provide structural unity and psychological nuances.

During Wagner's last creative period, in which he produced such works as *The Nibelung's Ring, Tristan und Isolde (Tristan and Isolde),* and *Die Meistersinger von Nürnberg (The Mastersingers of Nuremberg),* his theoretical interests encompassed political as well as aesthetic concerns. He saw himself as a hero who would redeem the materialistic and base through art. Attracted to socialism as a means for reform, he befriended the Russian revolutionary Mikhail Bakunin. During the 1849 Dresden uprising, Wagner was in the center of revolutionary activity that later prompted his escape to Switzerland. There he began writing the dramatic poem that gradually evolved into his first mature work and the one which most fully embodied his concept of *Gesamtkunstwerk.* His masterpiece, *The Nibelung's Ring,* comprises four operas: *Das Rheingold (Rhinegold), Die Walküre (Valkyrie), Siegfried,* and *Götterdämmerung.* Written in reverse order beginning with *Götterdämmerung* and finishing with *Rhinegold,* the *Ring* cycle is based on the Scandinavian Edda, a collection of ancient myths and legends, and the Volsunga Saga, a medieval Icelandic epic concerning the story of the Volsungs. Wagner's rendition of these myths and legends depicts a struggle among gods, giants, men, and dwarfs. He imbued the *Ring* with epic elements—characters of heroic proportions, the evocation of legendary action of national and historical importance, and supernatural forces—combined in a work of vast scope and setting. Although the texts were published collectively in 1853, Wagner did not complete the music until much later. From its first performance, the impact of this work was immediate and intense, and the *Ring* cycle has consistently inspired strong sentiment. Many early reviewers disapproved of its mythological subject matter and what they considered poor characterizations and implausible rhetoric. The Russian novelist Leo Tolstoy labeled it "counterfeit art." George Bernard Shaw, the English dramatist and music critic, interpreted the *Ring* cycle as an allegory of class struggle, and twentieth-century commentators have provided a wide variety of readings, including Freudian interpretations. Several scholars have focused on its incorporation of Schopenhauer's pessimism and emphasis on renunciation and redemption, and others have treated the influence of Greek tragedy. In the 1930s, the German novelist Thomas Mann, one of Wagner's foremost admirers, emphasized the psychological depth and inspired treatment of myth, which, he asserted, elevated it above all other opera. A recent critic, Hugh Ridley, suggested that the *Ring* cycle could not have been written without Feuerbach's positive materialism, for Wagner derived his evaluation of sensuality and concept of myth from Feuerbach's philosophy. Of Wagner's works, the *Ring* cycle continues to attract the most enduring interest.

Another work of Wagner's late period, *Tristan and Isolde,* is based on the Arthurian legend of Tristan de Leonis. Scholars now recognize this opera as one of Wagner's finest, though many nineteenth-century commentators condemned it as sensual, overly long, and verbose. Others, however, praised its dramatic qualities; the German philosopher Friedrich Nietzsche, in particular, considered it a modern embodiment of Greek tragedy. Twentieth-century scholars focus on such aspects as its depiction of pessimism and the influence of Schopenhauer's philosophy of denial of the will. On the basis of what he described as its obscure symbols, eloquent text, and metaphysical elements, Norbert Fuerst labeled *Tristan and Isolde* the first German Symbolist poem.

In 1862, Wagner was pardoned for his revolutionary political activities and returned from exile alone to Saxony, for his wife had broken off their relationship a year earlier. His financial and artistic aspirations soon met with a sympathetic patron when King Ludwig II of Bavaria offered to subsidize his efforts. Wagner then settled in Munich, where he concentrated on writing and composing. For some time, Cosima von Bülow, daughter of the pianist and composer Franz Liszt and wife of Hans von Bülow, a principal conductor of Wagner's operas, had maintained a liaison with Wagner. After giving birth to several of the composer's children, she left her husband and lived openly with Wagner. Wagner's first marriage ended with his wife's death in 1866, and when Von Bülow eventually obtained a divorce, Cosima and Wagner were married.

Another of Wagner's mature works, the comic opera *The Mastersingers of Nuremberg,* appeared in 1867. Although it is unlike the majority of Wagner's works because it depicts history rather than myth, the opera does reflect his dramatic theories. Many commentators note Wagner's resemblance to his main character, Hans Sachs, who espouses revolutionary musical ideas. While some scholars praise the work's humor and local color, others fault its plot and diction. Yet, *The Mastersingers of Nuremberg* remains one of Wagner's most popular operas.

Wagner had long envisioned a special theater in which only his works would be performed, and in 1872, with the patronage of Ludwig II, he supervised the construction of the innovative Bayreuth *Festspielhaus.* The building influenced twentieth-century theater design: opera boxes were eliminated, allowing the audience to focus on the stage; the musicians were relegated to an orchestra pit; and the best available stage machinery was installed. The premiere of the *Ring* cycle in 1876 inaugurated the first Bayreuth Festival, and by 1883, with the first production of *Parsifal,* a tradition of yearly performances had been established. Though early commentators criticized the mingling of sacred and profane love in this legend of a knight's love for and renunciation of a beautiful seductress, *Parsifal* is acknowledged today as one of Wagner's most prophetic works, particularly for its linking of the themes of love and death. Declaring *Parsifal* his last effort, Wagner traveled to Venice, where he died of a heart attack.

Wagner's operas and aesthetic theories have consistently inspired great critical controversy. During his lifetime, Wagner was simultaneously rejected as a modernist whose operas and aesthetics were incomprehensible and untenable and hailed as a prophetic dramatist and composer whose works would revolutionize modern art. Several periodicals were founded exclusively to discuss his works, and by the early twentieth century, more than ten thousand books and articles had been written about him. Wagner's popularity steadily increased until World War I, when anti-German sentiment prevented the performance of his works outside his native land. In the 1930s and 1940s, Adolf Hitler's friendship with Wagner's daughter Eva and the use of his works as propaganda for the Nazi movement contributed significantly to the decline of the composer's reputation. Criticism of this period noticeably reflects commentators' repugnance for Wagner's nationalism and anti-Semitism, which were embraced by the Nazis. Modern literary scholars, however, largely deem the parallels between Wagner and the Nazi movement extraliterary and focus instead on the works' dramatic qualities and philosophical sources.

Today Wagner is considered a foremost nineteenth-century dramatist and composer whose works have influenced myriad artists and artistic traditions, embracing music and literature. His impact on modern literature has been profound and pervasive. His artistic theories, particularly his use of myth and his concept of the leitmotiv, have influenced many authors who sought to replicate the effect of recurring themes, characters, and structural motifs in their prose, as Wagner had done in his music-dramas. Among the many notable novelists and poets affected by Wagner's works are D. H. Lawrence, Virginia Woolf, Émile Zola, Paul Verlaine, Stéphane Mallarmé, Thomas Mann, and Gabriel D'Annunzio. Wagner's importance as a literary model, the wealth of criticism on his works, and the continuing popularity of his operas attest to his lasting appeal.

PRINCIPAL WORKS

Das Liebesverbot; oder, Die Novize von Palermo   (opera) 1836
Rienzi (opera) 1842
  [*Rienzi*, 1914]
Der fliegende Holländer (opera) 1843
  [*The Flying Dutchman*, 1895]
Tannhäuser (opera) 1845
  [*Tanhauser*, 1900]
Die Kunst und die Revolution (essay) 1849
  [*Art and Revolution* published in *Richard Wagner's Prose Works*. 8 vols., 1893-99]
Das Kunstwerk der Zukunft (essays) 1850
  [*The Artwork of the Future* published in *Richard Wagner's Prose Works*. 8 vols., 1893-99]
Lohengrin (opera) 1850
  [*Lohengrin*, 1881]
Oper und Drama. 2 vols. (essays) 1852
  [*Opera and Drama* published in *Richard Wagner's Prose Works*. 8 vols., 1893-99]
Der Ring des Nibelungen (librettos) 1853
  [*The Nibelung's Ring*, 1877]
Tristan und Isolde (opera) 1865
  [*Tristan and Isolde*, 1886]
Die Meistersinger von Nürnberg (opera) 1868
  [*The Mastersingers of Nuremberg*, 1889]
Das Rheingold (opera) 1869
  [*Rhinegold* published in *The Nibelung's Ring*, 1877]
Die Walküre (opera) 1870
  [*Valkyrie* published in *The Nibelung's Ring*, 1877]
Götterdämmerung (opera) 1876
  [*Götterdämmerung* published in *The Nibelung's Ring*, 1877; also published as *The Twilight of the Gods*, 1911]
Siegfried (opera) 1876
  [*Siegfried* published in *The Nibelung's Ring*, 1877]
Parsifal (opera) 1882
  [*Parsifal in English Verse*, 1899]
***Die Feen* (opera) 1888
Richard Wagner's Prose Works. 8 vols. (essays and poetry) 1893-99
Mein Leben (autobiography) 1911
  [*My Life*, 1911]
Richard Wagners Briefe in Originalausgaben. 17 vols. (letters) 1911-13

Richard Wagners gesammelte Schriften. 14 vols.   (essays and poetry) 1914

*This work is comprised of the librettos for the operas *Das Rheingold, Die Walküre, Siegfried,* and *Götterdämmerung.*

**This work was completed in 1834.

EDUARD HANSLICK   (essay date 1846)

[*Hanslick was a prominent Viennese music critic, who, after championing Wagner's early works, became one of his most fierce detractors. This early positive review of* Tanhauser, *written when he was a law student, introduced Hanslick to the Viennese public as a music critic. Hanslick received a lengthy letter of appreciation from Wagner for this review, which appeared in German in eleven consecutive issues of the* Weiner Musikzeitung *during November and December 1846. For further commentary by Hanslick, see excerpt below, 1874.*]

If there is anyone among contemporary German composers from whom we can expect something distinguished in the field of serious grand opera, it is he. Richard Wagner is, I am convinced, the greatest dramatic talent among all contemporary composers.

The first work with which he presented himself to the world was the big, five-act opera, *Rienzi*. It was first given in Dresden, with the utmost brilliance, and was received with noisy jubilation. Listeners were so enraptured by the freshness of this new music, and so dazzled by its impact, that there was a general tendency to regard the young composer as a suddenly revealed regenerator of dramatic music, the Messiah of German opera. Richard Wagner was the man of the hour, and his fame was established overnight. A superficial examination of the score sufficed to convince the critic that here was, indeed, a great musical talent, an uncommon gift for dramatic expression. The work was animated by a youthful vigour and enthusiasm which carried the listener away. But with regard to strictly artistic requirements it was inadequate, and I was thus unable to join in the enthusiastic praise which even Liszt, himself a genius, uttered in my presence.

Wagner's second opera, *The Flying Dutchman*, aroused sympathy right at the outset, if only because of its uncommonly poetic, exotic substance. It represents unqualified progress beyond *Rienzi*. The characters are drawn more simply and with greater repose; the situations are more tightly compressed and more confidently represented. The musical forms still lack the ultimate finish, and the instrumentation lacks moderation here and there. But in both respects a significant improvement is undeniable. *The Flying Dutchman* alone would have sufficed to assure Richard Wagner a seat and a voice among contemporary dramatic masters. (pp. 34-5)

The *Tannhäuser* libretto has a rich dramatic plan and the virtue, significant for a grand opera, of taking place within the framework of a familiar folk legend and a no less familiar national-poetic institution, the Wartburg Song Contest. The element of the supernatural, without which no grand opera is quite complete, appears in fortunate concord with the content of the whole. Pictorial fantasy, sentiment, medieval atmosphere, German character and customs—all are included and, even more important, all are capable of musical expression and development. (pp. 36-7)

Eduard Hanslick, " 'Tannhäuser'," in his Music
Criticisms: 1846-99, *edited and translated by Henry
Pleasants, revised edition, Peregrine Books, 1963,
pp. 33-45.*

[GEORGE ELIOT]   (essay date 1855)

[*The English novelist and essayist Eliot elucidates Wagner's dramatic theories and praises his operas.*]

Much cheap ridicule has been spent on the 'music of the future;' a ridicule excused, perhaps, by the more than ordinary share Herr Wagner seems to have of a quality which is common to almost all innovators and heretics, and which their converts baptize as profound conviction, while the adherents of the old faith brand it as arrogance. It might be well, however, if the ridicule were arrested by the consideration that there never was an innovating movement which had not some negative value as a criticism of the prescriptive, if not any positive value as a lasting creation. The attempt at an innovation reveals a want that has not hitherto been met, and if the productions of the innovator are exaggerated symbols of the want, rather than symmetrical creations which have within them the conditions, of permanence—like an Owenite parallelogram, an early poem of Wordsworth's, or an early picture of Overbeck's—still they are protests which it is wiser to accept as strictures than to hiss down as absurdities. Without pretending to be a musical critic, one may be allowed to give an opinion as a person with an ear and a mind susceptible to the direct and indirect influences of music. In this character I may say that, though unable to recognise Herr Wagner's compositions as the ideal of the opera, and though, with a few slight exceptions, not deeply affected by his music on a first hearing, it is difficult to me to understand how any one who finds deficiencies in the opera as it has existed hitherto, can give fair attention to Wagner's theory, and his exemplification of it in his operas, without admitting that he has pointed out the direction in which the lyric drama must develope itself, if it is to be developed at all. Moreover, the musician who writes librettos for himself, which can be read with interest as dramatic poems, must be a man of no ordinary mind and accomplishments, and such a man, even when he errs, errs with ingenuity, so that his mistakes are worth studying.

Wagner would make the opera a perfect musical drama, in which feelings and situations spring out of *character*, as in the highest order of tragedy, and in which no dramatic probability or poetic beauty is sacrificed to musical effect. The drama must not be a mere pretext for the music; but music, drama, and spectacle must be blended, like the coloured rays in the sunbeam, so as to produce one undivided impression. (p. 49)

[Wagner states that the] ascent from the warbling puppets of the early opera to the dramatic effects of Meyerbeer, only serves to bring more clearly into view the unattained summit of the true musical drama. An opera must be no mosaic of melodies stuck together with no other method than is supplied by accidental contrast, no mere succession of ill-prepared crises, but an organic whole, which grows up like a palm, its earliest portion containing the germ and prevision of all the rest. He will write no *part* to suit a *primo tenore,* and interpolate no *cantata* to show off the powers of a *prima donna assoluta;* those who sing his operas must be content with the degree of prominence which falls to them in strict consonance with true dramatic development and ordonnance. Such, so far as I understand it, is Wagner's theory of the opera—surely a theory

worth entertaining, and one which he has admirably exemplified so far as the libretto of his operas is concerned. (p. 50)

Certainly Wagner has admirably fulfilled his own requisition of organic unity in the opera. In his operas there is a gradual unfolding and elaboration of that fundamental contrast of emotions, that collision of forces, which is the germ of the tragedy; just as the leaf of the plant is successively elaborated into branching stem and compact bud and radiant corolla. The artifice, however, of making certain contrasted strains of melody run like coloured threads through the woof of an opera, and also the other dramatic device of using a particular melody or musical phrase as a sort of Ahnung or prognostication of the approach or action of a particular character, are not altogether peculiar to Wagner, though he lays especial stress on them as his own. (pp. 51-2)

Wagner has wisely gone for the themes of his operas to the fresh and abundant source of early German poetry and legend, and the mode in which he expands and works up these themes shows a deep and refined poetic feeling. (p. 52)

[*George Eliot*], "*Liszt, Wagner, and Weimar,*" in
Fraser's Magazine, *Vol. LII, No. CCCVII, July, 1855,
pp. 48-62.**

CHARLES BAUDELAIRE   (essay date 1861)

[*A French poet and critic, Baudelaire is best known for his collection of poems,* Les fleurs du mal (The Flowers of Evil), *which is ranked among the most influential works of French poetry. In* The Flowers of Evil *Baudelaire analyzes, often in shocking terms, his urban surroundings, erotic love, and conflicts within his own soul. Underlying these topics is Baudelaire's belief that the individual, if left to his own devices, is inherently evil and will be damned. Only that which is artificial can be construed as absolutely good. Poetry, according to Baudelaire, should in turn serve only to inspire and express beauty. This doctrine forms the basis of both his poetry and his criticism. Twentieth-century critics maintain that Baudelaire's extensive critical writings on nineteenth-century art are as valuable as his poetry. According to Baudelaire, criticism allows one to contemplate art; he contended that every great artist would one day become a critic. Literary historians consider Baudelaire's positive review of* Tanhauser, *excerpted below, a seminal response, for its author was among the first French writers to actively support Wagner's music. In a letter to Wagner dated February 17, 1860, Baudelaire expressed his admiration: "I owe you the greatest musical enjoyment I have ever experienced." Here, Baudelaire expresses admiration for the universal elements of Wagner's operas and his ability to create variations within an architectural framework. He also points out that Wagner combines Classic and Romantic qualities with Medieval mysteries. The following essay, which appeared in French as "Richard Wagner" in the April 1 issue of the* Revue européene, *was written March 18, 1861, five days after the Paris premiere of* Tanhauser.]

The destiny of Wagner was determined by [his] absolute, despotic taste for a dramatic ideal in which everything, from a declamation marked and underlined by the music with so much care that the singer cannot omit a single syllable—a veritable arabesque of sounds delineated by passion—to the most painstaking care about staging and sets, in which, as I say, all the details should at all times contribute to the totality of the effect. With him, that was in effect a permanent postulation. Since the day when he freed himself from the old routines of the libretto and when he courageously repudiated his *Rienzi,* an opera of his youth which had been honored by a great success, he has marched straight ahead, without the slightest deviation, toward this imperious ideal. Therefore I was not at all surprised to find in those works that have been translated, particularly in *Tannhäuser, Lohengrin* and *The Flying Dutchman,* an excellent method of construction, a spirit of order and division that recalls the architecture of ancient tragedies. But the phenomena and the ideas which occur periodically through the ages always take on at each resurrection the complementary character of variance and circumstantiality.... [The] poems of Wagner, although they reveal a sincere taste for and a perfect understanding of classic beauty, also contain a considerable amount of the Romantic spirit. If they evoke the majesty of Sophocles and Aeschylus, at the same time they compel our minds to recall the medieval *Mystery Plays,* developed when the plastic arts dominated Roman Catholic expression. They are comparable to those great visions which the Middle Ages painted on the walls of churches or wove into magnificent tapestries. Their general aspect is definitely legendary: *Tannhäuser,* legend; *Lohengrin,* legend; *The Flying Dutchman,* a legend. And it is not merely an inclination natural to every poetic mind that led Wagner to this apparent specialty; it is a formal, deliberate decision determined by the study of the conditions most favorable to lyric drama.

He himself has carefully explained the question in his books. The fact is that not all subjects are equally suited to provide the basis for a comprehensive drama endowed with a universal character. Obviously there would be great danger in translating the most delightful and the most perfect genre picture into a fresco. It is above all in the universal heart of man and in the history of that heart that the dramatic poet will find pictures that are universally intelligible. In order to be perfectly free to construct an ideal drama, it will be wise to eliminate all the difficulties that might arise from technical, political or even too specific historic details. I shall let the master himself speak:

> The only picture of human life that may be called poetic is that in which the motives that have meaning only to abstract intelligence are replaced by the purely human impulses which govern the heart. This tendency (which relates to the finding of a poetic subject) is the sovereign law that controls poetic form and presentation.... The rhythmic arrangement and the almost musical ornament of rhyme are for the poet the means of giving lines and musical phrases a power that is as dominating as a spell and that governs feeling as it wishes. This tendency, so essential to the poet, leads him to the limits of his art, limits which directly border on music; and, consequently, the most complete work of the poet should be that which in its final realization would be perfect music.

> Hence I found myself led necessarily to designate *myth* as the ideal material for the poet. Myth is the original and anonymous poem of the people, and in every age we find it revived, recast once again by each succeeding generation of great poets in cultivated periods. Myth, indeed, almost completely strips human relations of their conventional form, intelligible only to abstract reason; it reveals what is truly human in life, what is eternally comprehensible, and reveals it in that concrete form, free of all imitation, which gives to all true myths their individual character, recognizable at the first glance.

And elsewhere, returning to the same theme, he says:

> Once and for all I abandoned the terrain of history and established myself on that of legend.... I was able to put aside all the detail necessary to describe and represent historic fact and its accidents, all the detail that is required for the complete understanding of a remote and special period of history, and that contemporary writers of historical plays and novels deduce, for that reason, in such a circumstantial manner.... Legend, regardless of the period or nation to which it belongs, has the advantage of including nothing except what is purely human in that period or nation, and of presenting it in a form that is strikingly original and therefore intelligible at the first glance. A ballad, a popular song suffice to represent in an instant this character in its most fixed and its most striking features.... The character of the scene and the tone of the legend together contribute to cast the mind into that *dream* state which soon carries it to the point of full *clairvoyance,* and the mind then discovers a new relationship among the phenomena of the world that its eyes had not been able to perceive in the ordinary waking state.

How could Wagner fail to understand admirably the sacred, divine character of myth, he who was at once a poet and a critic? I have heard many persons draw from the very range of his faculties and from his high critical intelligence a reason to distrust his musical genius, and I think that this is a propitious occasion to refute a very common error whose principal root is perhaps the ugliest of human feelings, envy. "A person who reasons so much about his art cannot produce beautiful works in a natural way," say some, who thus deprive genius of its rationality and assign to it a purely instinctive and practically vegetable function. Others are disposed to consider Wagner as a theoretician who produced operas solely to verify *a posteriori* the value of his own theories. That is not only completely false, since the master began when he was quite young, as we know, by producing various kinds of poetic and musical composition, and only gradually succeeded in creating an ideal of the lyric drama for himself, but it is even something that is absolutely impossible. It would be a very novel occurrence in the history of the arts for a critic to become a poet—a reversal of all psychic laws, a monstrosity; on the other hand, all great poets naturally and inevitably become critics. (pp. 205-08)

[We have] two men in Richard Wagner, the man of order and the man of passion. Here we are concerned with the passionate man, the man of feeling. His personality is so vividly inscribed in the slightest passage of his work that the search for his chief quality will not be very difficult. From the beginning one thing had struck me very forcibly: in the voluptuous and orgiastic portion of the overture of *Tannhäuser,* the artist had put as much force and had developed as much energy as he had in painting the mysticism that characterizes the overture of *Lohengrin.* ... [In] his choice of subjects and in his dramatic method, Wagner resembles antiquity, by the passionate energy of his expression, he is today the truest representative of modern nature. And all the knowledge, all the efforts, all the studied arrangements of this rich mind are, to tell the truth, only the very humble and very zealous servants of that irresistible passion. The result, regardless of the subject that he uses, is a superlative solemnity of tone. By means of that passion he adds something superhuman to everything; by means of that passion he understands everything and makes everything understood. Everything that is implied in the words: *will, desire, concentration, nervous intensity, explosion,* is felt and is sensed in his works. I do not believe that I am deceiving either myself or anyone else in affirming that I see therein the principal characteristics of the phenomenon that we call *genius;* or at least that we find the above mentioned characteristics in the analysis of everything that until now we have rightly called *genius.* (pp. 222-23)

> *Charles Baudelaire, "Richard Wagner and 'Tann-häuser' in Paris," in his* Baudelaire As a Literary Critic, *edited and translated by Lois Boe Hyslop and Francis E. Hyslop, Jr., The Pennsylvania State University Press, University Park, 1964, pp. 188-231.*

FRIEDRICH NIETZSCHE   (essay date 1872)

[*Nietzsche, a nineteenth-century German philosopher, essayist, poet, and autobiographer, exercised a great influence on modern philosophy, particularly in the area of existential thought. His first published work was a highly influential study of Greek art,* Die Geburt der Tragödie aus dem Geiste der Musik (The Birth of Tragedy) *in 1872, from which the following excerpt is taken. Nietzsche believed that before Socrates, Greek culture exhibited two tendencies: the Apollonian, marked by a concern with restraint, harmony, and measure, and the Dionysian, characterized by a primitive resistance to structure and reason. The first tendency found expression, according to Nietzsche, in Greek sculpture and architecture, while the second found its outlet in the drunken orgies of the Dionysian festivals and the music associated with them. Nietzsche's view of Wagner varied considerably, from the unqualified praise evidenced here and in his review of the 1876 Bayreuth festival (see excerpt below), to his repudiation of Wagner evinced in his "The Case of Wagner" (1888) and in his review of* Parsifal *(1888). Critics speculate that Nietzsche felt betrayed by what he interpreted as Wagner's refutation of his former artistic principles. In the following excerpt, Nietzsche expresses his belief that Wagner's music drama embodies the theories of Hellenic tragedy and rhapsodizes on the rebirth of the ancient form in* Tristan and Isolde. *Other critics who consider Wagner's use of myth include Alfred A. Wheeler (1883), W. E. Walter (1904), Thomas Mann (1933 and 1937), Theodor Adorno (1937-38), and Norbert Fuerst (1966).*]

I ask the question of . . . genuine musicians: whether they can imagine a man capable of hearing the third act of **Tristan und Isolde** without any aid of word or scenery, purely as a vast symphonic period, without expiring by a spasmodic distention of all the wings of the soul? A man who has thus, so to speak, put his ear to the heart-chamber of the cosmic will, who feels the furious desire for existence issuing therefrom as a thundering stream or most gently dispersed brook, into all the veins of the world, would he not collapse all at once? Could he endure, in the wretched fragile tenement of the human individual, to hear the re-echo of countless cries of joy and sorrow from the "vast void of cosmic night," without flying irresistibly towards his primitive home at the sound of this pastoral dance-song of metaphysics? But if, nevertheless, such a work can be heard as a whole, without a renunciation of individual existence, if such a creation could be created without demolishing its creator—where are we to get the solution of this contradiction?

Here there interpose between our highest musical excitement and the music in question the tragic myth and the tragic hero—in reality only as symbols of the most universal facts, of which music alone can speak directly. If, however, we felt as purely Dionysian beings, myth as a symbol would stand by us absolutely ineffective and unnoticed, and would never for a moment prevent us from giving ear to the re-echo of the *universalia ante rem* [the importance of the universal before the particular]. Here, however, the *Apollonian* power, with a view to the restoration of the well-nigh shattered individual, bursts forth with the healing balm of a blissful illusion: all of a sudden we imagine we see only Tristan, motionless, with hushed voice saying to himself: "the old tune, why does it wake me?" And what formerly interested us like a hollow sigh from the heart of being, seems now only to tell us how "waste and void is the sea." And when, breathless, we thought to expire by a convulsive distention of all our feelings, and only a slender tie bound us to our present existence, we now hear and see only the hero wounded to death and still not dying, with his despairing cry: "Longing! Longing! In dying still longing! for longing not dying!" And if formerly, after such a surplus and superabundance of consuming agonies, the jubilation of the born rent our hearts almost like the very acme of agony, the rejoicing Kurwenal now stands between us and the "jubilation as such," with face turned toward the ship which carries Isolde. However powerfully fellow-suffering encroaches upon us, it nevertheless delivers us in a manner from the primordial suffering of the world, just as the symbol-image of the myth delivers us from the immediate perception of the highest cosmic idea, just as the thought and word deliver us from the unchecked effusion of the unconscious will. The glorious Apollonian illusion makes it appear as if the very realm of tones presented itself to us as a plastic cosmos, as if even the fate of Tristan and Isolde had been merely formed and moulded therein as out of some most delicate and impressible material.

Thus does the Apollonian wrest us from Dionysian universality and fill us with rapture for individuals; to these it rivets our sympathetic emotion, through these it satisfies the sense of beauty which longs for great and sublime forms; it brings before us biographical portraits, and incites us to a thoughtful apprehension of the essence of life contained therein. With the immense potency of the image, the concept, the ethical teaching and the sympathetic emotion—the Apollonian influence uplifts man from his orgiastic self-annihilation, and beguiles him concerning the universality of the Dionysian process into the belief that he is seeing a detached picture of the world, for instance, Tristan and Isolde, and that, *through music,* he will be enabled to *see* it still more clearly and intrinsically. (pp. 161-64)

> *Friedrich Nietzsche, "'The Birth of Tragedy'," in his* The Complete Works of Friedrich Nietzsche: The Birth of Tragedy; or, Hellenism and Pessimism, Vol. 1, *edited by Oscar Levy, translated by William A. Haussmann, 1909. Reprint by the Macmillan Company, 1924, pp. 21-187.**

J. K. PAINE   (essay date 1873)

[*Paine outlines the artistic theories Wagner presented in his* Art and Revolution, The Artwork of the Future, *and* Opera and Drama *and relates them to Wagner's own operas. He discusses particularly Wagner's concept of the unity of arts in his music dramas.*]

In **"Art and Revolution"** [Wagner] draws a picture of modern civilization the reverse of flattering, for he says it is founded on hypocrisy. He draws a parallel between the artistic life of the ancient Greeks and that of the present age, to the total denial, of course, of the existence of true art in modern times. Ancient art was the expression of national life; our art and

Woodcut of the Dutchman in The Flying Dutchman.

literature are matters of luxury. He maintains that the development of genuine art is incompatible with Christian belief and consciousness. The past two thousand years belong to philosophy, and not to art. "Christianity," he declares, "justifies an ignominious and miserable existence of man upon earth, out of the wonderful love of God, who has created him, not for a joyful life on earth, as the aesthetic Greeks erroneously believed, but has imprisoned him here, as it were, in a loathsome dungeon, in order that after his death, as a reward for his self-abasement, he shall have prepared for him an endless state of unoccupied and indolent glory."

"The Christian cannot turn to nature or the senses, for is not sensuous beauty to him a vision of the Devil?" Therefore Christianity is incapable of true art, which in Wagner's eyes is the highest activity of man in harmony with himself, as a sensuous being, and with nature.

"Hypocrisy," he continues, "is the most prominent feature,—nay, the true physiognomy of all the Christian centuries up to the present day; and this vice stands out more and more glaringly and shamelessly as mankind, out of an unconquerable, inward source, and in spite of Christianity, refreshes and reinvigorates itself and moves onward to the true solution of the problem of life." Moreover, he asserts that the industry of modern nations is perverted, being a worse enemy to art than

the Church. "Art has been betrayed into the hands of the god of the modern world, the high-born god of five per cent."

"Modern art draws its strength from money speculations; its moral object is the pursuit of wealth, its aesthetic excuse, entertainment for the victims of ennui."

"The public art of the Greeks, as it reached its apex in the tragedy, was the expression of the deepest and noblest thoughts and sentiments of the whole people; the deepest and noblest of our modern consciousness is just the reverse, the denial of our public art."

"The ancients, then, had real art, the moderns have mere *artistic handicraft*. With the fall of Greek tragedy the drama no longer embraced a union of the fine arts; but, henceforth, each art went on its own separate way, and though great and noble minds have for centuries raised their voices in the wilderness, yet we have not listened to them; we tremble before their fame, yet laugh in the presence of their art; for a great and genuine work of art could not be created by them alone; our co-operation with them was essential. The tragedy of Æschylus and Sophocles was the work of Athens."

"Only a great revolution of mankind can prepare the ground for a new art, such as the Greeks had." This is the substance of Wagner's first pamphlet.

In his next pamphlet, **"The Future Work of Art,"** the author is no longer destructive, but, on the contrary, eminently and ingeniously constructive. He teaches that man is his own god and stands above nature, and in his inward and outward life, as an observing and impressionable creature, corresponds perfectly to that grand and complete art which is the result of a combination of all the separate branches or modes of art. Each of the arts, poetry, music, painting, sculpture, architecture, and dancing, contributes its share to the result, in a measure corresponding to the several artistic faculties of man. Thus the emotional nature is expressed by music, the understanding by poetry, and the bodily man by dancing. The union of these three "purely human" expressions of art pre-exists in the drama, in which man represents himself, personally, in the highest degree of completeness, with the assistance of the imitative arts of painting and sculpture. Painting supplies the landscape or natural scene, in the midst of which man moves; sculpture lives in man himself, and architecture furnishes the place in which the artistic representation takes place. The object, in a word, is to reunite the various branches of art as they were united in ancient Greece, but on a higher plane and with infinitely richer materials.

In his longest writing, **"The Opera and Drama,"** Wagner proceeds to make a special application of these principles. He reviews the opera and drama of the past with sharp, unsparing criticism. He announces his brief formula, which appears to him so self-evident that it seems as though the world would have adopted it long ago. It is as follows: "The opera was an error, since in that species of art the means of expression (music) has been made the object, while the true object of expression (the drama) has been made the means." This is the key-note of the first part of the succeeding discussion, in the course of which he draws an historical sketch of the opera as a branch of art which has been developed in two directions: first, "in a *serious* direction, through Gluck, Mozart, Cherubini, Méhul, Spontini, and all those masters who felt the weight of responsibility which fell to music when it announced for itself alone the aim of the drama; second, in a *frivolous* direction, through all those musicians like Rossini, Meyerbeer, and others, who, impelled by the instinct of the impossibility of solving an unnatural problem, turned their backs upon it, and, thinking only of enjoying the advantages that opera has gained from its extended publicity, gave themselves up to an unmixed system of musical experimentalizing.'' At the close of this lengthy discussion, the author fancifully, though not altogether tastefully, compares the modern Italian opera to a courtesan, the French opera to a coquette, the new romantic German opera to a prude, Mozart's opera to a lovely and beautiful woman,—having previously stated that music is a woman. And now he stops to ask, Who is the man that shall implicitly love this woman? It is the poet. In other words, poetry and music must be equally and happily wedded, in order to constitute the ideal work of art. In the next part, Wagner examines the causes why we have had no true theatre. The English drama of Shakespeare is drawn from real life, but represents it in an incomplete form. Shakespeare did not feel the necessity of giving a representation wholly true to the surrounding scene; he therefore condensed and sifted the manifold materials of the romance, and treated them dramatically simply in the degree required for the necessities of a contracted stage and a limited plot.

Neither his, nor the Italian and French drama which seeks to reproduce the finished forms of ancient classical tragedy, but has nothing in common with modern life, nor the vacillation between these extremes that characterizes the German drama of Goethe and Schiller, fulfils the highest mission of dramatic art.

Wagner consequently would abolish the literary drama as well as the opera, and substitute for them a work of art addressed to our sensuous nature. ''In the drama,'' are his words, ''we are made wise by feeling.'' He wholly rejects the literary standpoint, and will have only a ''direct, living art of representation.'' He addresses not the reason and imagination, but the totality of the senses. We must not be educated to understand a work of art, but to enjoy it.

The third part of **''Opera and Drama''** is devoted to a statement of the true relation of music to poetry. Wagner denounces what is commonly termed melody, or the traditional form of the *air,* that is, the rising and falling musical phrases whose motives or subdivisions are repeated in certain modified imitations, in order to establish a necessary identity or individuality in the musical thought, and preserve a unity of design, without which the aesthetic sense of proportion and beauty cannot be gratified and the emotions powerfully affected. This form of melody must be done away with, and what he calls *infinite melody,* hinted at vaguely in Beethoven's last compositions, must be substituted. The only genuine melody, he asserts, is that which arises from the heartfelt delivery of the language,—melody that does not attract any attention on its own account except as the sensuous expression of a sentiment that is clearly manifest in the language.

Such an infinite melody is, or should be, the creation of the poet; and within it exists the germ of the accompanying harmony, though unexpressed.

Through the medium of the orchestra the harmony knows no arbitrary limits. The family of keys must be made one in spirit and agreement. The independent members of the whole round of keys must be permitted to move here and there with perfect freedom.

As regards the employment of the chorus, Wagner will not give any place to *polyphony;* and the traditional style of opera chorus, as a mass of united voices, he would also dispense

with. ''A mass of people can never interest, but merely confuse the hearer; only distinctly distinguishable individualities can gain his attention and sympathy.''

The actions and gestures of the personages of the play hold the same relation to the language of the drama as the flexible movements of the orchestra do to the melody,—as a powerful agency for enhancing the effect and meaning of the vocal part. The orchestra gives powerful expression to all the utterances of the actor, and sustains and explains him in every way. As far as the expression of emotion is concerned, the modern orchestra will occupy a position in the future drama similar to that held by the ancient chorus in the Greek tragedy. (pp. 220-25)

I have stated the principal points of the arguments that Wagner has sought to illustrate more or less completely in his operas. He did not attempt, however, to apply these principles to their full extent at the outset. He was too shrewd for this. In the operas of **''Rienzi''** and **''The Flying Dutchman''** he approached his aim only at a remote distance. In **''Tannhäuser''** he advanced nearer, but still retained the air, concerted pieces, and other traditinal forms. He drew closer to the ultimate goal of his desires in the opera of **''Lohengrin,''** since he selected for the first time a mythical subject: it being his creed that the myth is the beginning and end of all true poesy. As Greek art sprang from Greek mythology, so must future German art be founded on the German myths. Such is the Wagnerian logic. The characters of mythology being endowed with superhuman qualities, miracle is indispensable to the future drama; not, however, with the object of making us *believe,* but *feel* directly the inner connection of actions, without the aid of imagination or reflection.

The opera of **''Tristan and Isold''** . . . was the first complete attainment of Wagner's ideal. (p. 225)

Wagner's wholesale denunciation of modern civilization, his declaration that our present religion and social and political life must be completely revolutionized before his ideal work of art can be appreciated, is so far removed from any possibility of realization, that we may dismiss the subject as the vagary of a wild dreamer. ''This dream of a reform of the world,'' observes Ambros, ''can never be realized, because it contains irreconcilable contradictions, such as absolute freedom in single details, and conformity to law as a whole. . . . These ''irreconcilable contradictions'' distinguish Wagner's writings throughout; for they are a strange mixture of truth and error, in which the error predominates. His total and irreverent denial of the inestimable good which Christianity has done and will continue to do for humanity; his vain attempt to persuade men to return to the naturalism of earlier times, at least to a conduct of life in which nature and the senses are to be the chief guide; his arrogant attitude towards the art of mediaeval and modern times, the true spirit of which he ignores when he asserts that it is not the outgrowth of Christianity and the Renaissance, and that it is not art, but artistic handicraft; these and other statements are errors which demonstrate to every rational and sober-minded reader that the author's judgment is partial and warped, and that he is to be classed with other violent agitators and enthusiasts with heated imaginations who seem out of joint with the world. Wagner's scheme of uniting all the fine arts in order to constitute a grand, comprehensive art or drama, such as the Greeks are supposed to have had, looks promising enough for the moment, but reflection does not lend wings to our faith. There is in truth nothing eminently new or original in the idea.

Music, poetry, and dancing have from time immemorial appeared conjointly in the drama, in one form or another, accompanied to some extent by the other fine arts. As regards the triple alliance of poetry, music, and dancing, the latter, which hitherto, in all the higher forms of dramatic representation, has deservedly held a subordinate place, finds itself in Wagner's *scheme* suddenly raised to an equality with the two most spiritual of arts; a position which in Wagner's *operas* it does not and cannot maintain.

As far as the place which painting, sculpture, and architecture shall occupy in the drama, the first cannot amount to anything more than mere decorative painting; and, unless statues are placed in niches or grouped on the stage, sculpture will have to be left out of the account; for it is absurd to talk of the actors representing this art by their figures and attitudes. The very idea of sculpture is a perfect physical form and action in repose; and unless the actors are models of physical beauty, and can be grouped so as to assume attitudes perfectly statuesque, it cannot be acknowledged that plastic art has anything to do with the future drama. In the Greek tragedy this was possible. The actors wore huge masks, which, according to ancient ideas, were absolutely essential; for the fidelity of the representation was of less consequence than its beauty. (pp. 225-27)

As to the share which architecture is to have in the future drama, can it do more than furnish an appropriate surrounding in which the action is to take place? Architecture requires forms that imply solidity of structure. The material thrusts itself upon our attention, and the sham show of the stage columns, arches, walls, etc. does not merit the name of architectural art.

No one can deny the intimate relation which the arts hold to each other, but it is quite another matter to accept the theory of a grand unity of all the fine arts. Even the Greeks did not combine them equally. "In the tragedy," says Schlegel, "the poetry was the chief object, and everything else was held strictly subservient to it. Their dancing and music had nothing common with ours but the name." We have neither the spirit nor object of such a drama. The modern play concerns itself chiefly with the representation of the actions of human life, while the ancient drama had a supernatural and religious aim. Moreover, the modern way of speaking or reciting poetry is wholly unlike the ancient musical declamation, which is foreign to the genius of modern speech. Music, consequently, will henceforth be employed as an artifice introduced into the drama for its own ends. If the time ever comes in real life when men shall make love, quarrel, or die in vocal melody or declamation, as they do at present on the operatic stage, then music will cease to be an artifice; but until then it will not be introduced into the play merely to serve a subordinate place in clothing or coloring the words. Music will be kept out of the way altogether, or else made to realize its highest object, which is to express, in accordance with the principles of musical art, the various moods of feeling prompted by the conflict of the play, without laying particular stress on its essential *naturalness* in the drama. (pp. 227-28)

Every fine art is complete in itself. "A complete dramatic poem and an equally independent and artistically developed musical composition do not blend, but on the contrary *conflict* with each other, for each follows its own peculiar laws."

A great play like "Hamlet," teeming with profound thought and philosophy, or "Macbeth," with its predominance of terror and rapidity of action, must sacrifice its most characteristic scenes and passages in order to meet the requirements of the musical drama. On the other hand, if music were made subservient to the words of a poem, it would lose the very essence of its being; it would degenerate from its present free position among the foremost arts; it would no longer be the powerful language of the emotions, but, like Greek music, would have no higher object than merely to color the declamation.

Now Wagner aims to strike a middle course. Poetry must concede pure, reflective thought and all superfluous imagery; in other words, the literary stand-point must be resigned, and *feeling* made the object of the drama, which music must enhance without enjoying any real independence of its own. It is evident that such an equal concession must rob each art of its highest prerogative, and just in the degree with which the combination of the various materials grows more manifold, so will the intellectual conception lose its clearness and force. The conception of a universal art interests us on account of its superficiality rather than its profundity. It provides a greater variety, but less warmth of inspiration; it is less artistic than abstract.

One statue like the Venus of Milo, one picture like the Dresden Madonna, one poem like Faust, or one musical composition like Beethoven's Fifth Symphony, will singly outweigh and outlive the representative drama of Wagner, as realized in his last operas, simply for the reason that each art appears to complete advantage only when it is unshackled, or left entirely free to work out its highest object by itself. The only exception is the union of music and poetry, as it has been employed traditionally in church and secular music; in this case the words, however beautiful and significant they may be as poetry, resign their prominence in order that the structural form and lyric flow of the music may not be impeded. It matters not how intimate the modern alliance of poetry with music may be, the real interest of a mass, oratorio, or opera centres in the music. (pp. 228-29)

Gluck and Wagner have sought to wed poetry and music in perfect equality; but the result is not satisfactory, for the reason that the movement of the feelings, through the agency of music, is far more expanded in duration than the motive supplied by the words. A dramatic text cannot content itself with a repetition of the same thought, but must proceed from one thought to another, in order to sustain the progress of the action. Now if the music follows the poem strictly, syllable after syllable, word after word, without the privilege of dwelling here and there upon the sense of a passage, it cannot fulfil its highest object, which is to express the emotional principle to the utmost; and the orchestra cannot provide for this want by the rhythmical flow and coloring of the instrumental accompaniment. (p. 230)

The Nibelungen Song cannot be too highly prized, when considered from a literary or philological stand-point, and the Germans are justly proud of their great epic; but it is a difficult if not an impossible matter to convert its principal incidents into a permanent dramatic form for the modern stage; and this is especially the case as Wagner has conceived the subject. He has thrown over it the glamour of sensuality, the true expression, it may be, of his own subjective nature, yet not of the mythological characters in general. He has interwoven with the natural, human element of the German myth the more Northern or Scandinavian features, the preternatural world of gods, Nibelungen, Valkyrias, giants, dwarfs, and water-sprites, with their wild manners and freakish actions, in such a way that the human element is rendered unnatural, if not almost unrecognizable, and we long for a return to the society of everyday men. These ancient Northern myths seem far less in harmony with modern civilization than even the gods and demigods of Greek mythology, or the heroes of the Iliad. And who wishes to revive these personages on the modern stage? Neither will the allegorical or symbolical significance with which Wagner has sought to invest these characters suffice to convince us of the real need of such a drama. How can we accept his or any other theory as to the origin and meaning of these myths, when there reigns so complete a difference of opinion concerning them in the minds of modern scholars? (p. 234)

If the texts of Wagner's operas are open to grave criticism as dramatic subjects, they deserve severe censure with respect to their rhetoric and versification. Even Wagner's most determined admirers cannot maintain that he possesses a good literary style; for he has dispensed with this. It would be absurd to compare the words of his operas with the dramatic poetry of Goethe, Schiller, or any illustrious name of German literature. According to Wagner's intention, neither the words nor the music can be separated from the scene and action. In the portrayal of character Wagner fails to display any great originality or power. His personages generally lack those individual traits that distinguish one dramatic character from another. As a dramatic poet, therefore, Wagner cannot be classed with the great masters of the art; nor as a musician will he ever occupy an equal rank with Bach, Handel, or Beethoven. What, then, is the secret of Wagner's present popularity and ascendency?

Wagner is a consummate master of all the externals of the stage. He has made the splendid show and brilliant pomp of the theatrical spectacle an indispensable adjunct to his operas. One grand effect succeeds another in logical and natural sequence; yet nothing, apparently, is introduced for the sake of mere effect. In this respect Wagner is much the superior of Spontini, Meyerbeer, and his other predecessors of the modern French stage, who introduce magnificence and splendor into the play without any real cause, merely to dazzle and astonish the beholder. But the action and substance of the play are obscured and injured instead of enhanced by such a jumble of accessories. In Wagner's operas the rich variety and contrast of the scenes make a vivid impression upon the spectator, because nothing appears to be superfluous, or to be introduced without the object of benefiting the play. (pp. 235-36)

[We have abundant proof] of his masterly skill in the management of the stage, and of his fertile imagination as a decorative artist. Many of these scene-pictures are truly poetical. . . . (p. 236)

Wagner has displayed equal skill and originality in the treatment of the action of the play. He is true to the dramatic object in all points of detail. In a word, the action, scenic display, words, and music are combined, so as to produce a remarkable unity of effect, though not without the sacrifice of the real independence of each of the several arts thus combined. (p. 237)

Time alone will decide the question of Wagner's place in musical history, and how much truth and merit belong to his works. Meanwhile the unprejudiced critic must acknowledge that Wagner is a man of wonderful energy and talent,—at the same time one whose head and heart are not entirely right. His erroneous theory has marred all his recent music. He has tried to institute a reform or revolution through the intellect rather than by the spontaneous and gradual growth of concrete musical thoughts, the offspring of real musical genius. (p. 239)

J. K. Paine, in a review of "'Gesammelte Schriften',' in The North American Review, *Vol. CXVI, No. CCXXXIX, April, 1873, pp. 217-45.*

EDUARD HANSLICK   (essay date 1874)

[*Hanslick provides a balanced review of* The Mastersingers of Nuremberg *in which it is conjectured that he was caricatured as the coarse and vulgar pedant Beckmesser. The 1874 version of his article, excerpted below, is a revision of an 1868 review of the opera's Munich premiere. For additional criticism by Hanslick, see excerpt above, 1846.*]

Friends and foes are well aware that a new opera by Wagner means something extraordinary, something to occupy the fantasy and the intellect in all respects. *Die Meistersinger* is, indeed, a remarkable creation, uniquely consistent in method, extremely earnest, novel in structure, rich in imaginative and even brilliant characteristics, often tiring and exasperating, but always unusual. It is of compelling interest, if only as a phenomenon; whether one is pleased or repelled depends upon one's conception of musical and dramatic beauty. Its virtues cannot be denied—nor its faults; there are scenes which rank among Wagner's most fortunate musical inspirations, surrounded by long, unrewarding stretches of dull or disagreeable music. And as a theatrical spectacle alone it is worth seeing.

If we give the synopsis, as can be done in a few words, it will be difficult to understand how an opera longer than [Giacomo Meyerbeer's] *Le Prophète* or *Les Huguenots* could be made of it. Its greatest fault is in the over-elaboration of a small, meagre plot which, with neither intricacies nor intrigue, is continually at a standstill and would normally offer barely enough material for a modest two-act operetta. One can hardly give an apt description of the tenacious verbosity of the dialogue, with all the domestic altercations and dry instruction. (pp. 111-12)

Apart from the tiresome way Wagner has handled it, the plot [of *Die Meistersinger*] indicates progress towards a better and healthier attitude. Contrary to his theory (which accepts only mythology as a proper source of plots), but following a good instinct, Wagner has returned from his abstruse submarine and superterranean legends to the real theatre. At long last he has turned his back on his dwarfs, giants, and Valkyries. He has set foot in the midst of the real world and given us lively pictures of the life of the German people of the Middle Ages. These artisans of Nuremberg, with their simple, philistine adventures and plain doggerel verses, are preferable to the ecstasies and bombastic, stuttering alliterations of *Tristan and Isolde* or *Das Rheingold*. In the colourful description of the national festival on the Nuremberg meadows, Wagner has had a particularly fortunate poetic inspiration. It is also the first time that he has stooped again to the term 'opera'; in *Tristan and Isolde,* he still saw fit to ennoble the subject with the vague term 'action'.

Aside from the description of medieval national life, it is the conflict between free poetry, spontaneously inspired, and spiritless, pedantic versification which constitutes the intellectual and emotional core of the work. Walther represents the one, the guild of the Nuremberg masters the other. A poet of genius against a dozen pedantic masters who cannot understand him and yet dare to judge him. Do you get it? Actually, the superiority of the genius who creates his own laws is fervently defended in each act—and all too long-windedly—against the strait-jacket of scholarship. . . . Wagner's safety valve is Hans Sachs who, as an unprejudiced third person and intermediary, stands between the two parties. Brought up on the school rules of the singers' guild, and suddenly enlightened by Walther's 'free poetry,' he is a kind of converted Mozartian who dares deliver a special vote on behalf of the 'music of the future'.

For a comic opera—and that is what *Die Meistersinger* is, according to its exposition and its two pronounced buffo parts—Wagner's talent seems inadequate, particularly with respect to humour. The conversational tone which dominates the first two acts is never easy and fluent. Quite the contrary, it is expressed through an awkward, contrived, continuously restless music, with a noisy and complex instrumentation. The most trivial questions and answers, commonly expressed in normal tones, are shouted above the tumult of the orchestra. To this false colouring is added a false design by a declamatory style characterized by leaps contradictory to all rules of diction. (pp. 117-18)

> *Eduard Hanslick, "'Die Meistersinger'," in his* Music Criticisms: 1846-99, *edited and translated by Henry Pleasants, revised edition, Peregrine Books, 1963, pp. 111-22.*

EDVARD HAGERUP GRIEG   (letter date 1876)

[*Grieg was a Norwegian composer and pianist, who, after studying in Germany, returned to Norway where he wrote songs and dances based on folk melodies, most notably his* Peer Gynt Suite. *In 1876, Grieg attended the Bayreuth Festival as the correspondent for the Norwegian journal* Bergensposten, *in which the reviews of* The Nibelung's Ring, *excerpted below, appeared between August 20 and September 3.*]

[For us Norwegians the sources Wagner used for the *Ring* stories] have special significance in that Wagner has taken the Volsunga Saga and the Older Edda as well as the German Nibelungenlied and, with poetic licence, has interwoven these elements all together for his drama. Wagner must be given credit for having kept to Nordic sources and, above all, to those of the older period, untainted as these are by the Christian outlook and ethic. Because of this we now have the myth in its true and original greatness. That is why this work is of importance to the Scandinavian.

Wagner has taken the characters' names from the Edda but, in place of the Nordic forms, he has given them a Germanic tone; thus, not Sigurd but Siegfried; not Gunnar but Gunther; not Odin but Wotan and not Loki but Loge, and so on. In writing his poetry he has followed the Edda in employing alliteration rather than rhyme.... I shall not pass judgment on this text but point out one thing that is strange—the Prologue takes the form of a drama played out on the stage; this is not really necessary because in Norse epics there was always something which went before. Also, it is difficult to become involved with these mermaids, giants, gods and goddesses—one can observe them, one can admire their display on the stage but one can not, as a human being, respond to and share their emotions. (p. 62)

Wagner's special ability to describe scenes such as occur in *Rheingold* causes the spectator to be carried away by the effect and to forget the lack of drama in them. Long dialogues such as the gods have cannot be consistently interesting; no matter how much the music sustains them, they still become quite tedious. Again, Wagner writes better for the giants and dwarfs than he does for the gods and goddesses—he does not have the elevated serenity and noble simplicity that the character of Wotan demands. (p. 63)

•　•　•　•　•

The second act [of *Die Walküre*] is one of those endless dialogues that cannot help being tiresome; the pity is that the action is not of much interest and the words meaningless. Such dialogues embody the principles of Wagner's dramatic composition and he is always ready to defend them passionately—they do need a champion of genius for they have little to say for themselves. Even the music, I am sorry to say, cannot give form to these passages, for Wagner has overestimated its ability to underline and characterise the spoken word. His dialogues are indeed put together like the long dialogues of Schiller or Goethe—with the difference that in the plays of these authors the listener can at least hear every word. Wagner's passages of dialogue, I have realised, were added at a late stage of composition and are lacking in real inspiration when compared with the scenes full of action which they link together. (pp. 64-5)

•　•　•　•　•

There is no doubt that *Götterdämmerung* is the most effective of the dramas and the one with the most compelling action. In it all that has gone before is resolved and the fates of the gods and of men are fulfilled. The use of a chorus seems to involve all of mankind—and what an effect it makes! By allowing the Rhine-maidens to recover the gold in the end Wagner underlines the message that, in the hands of man, it is a force for evil and intrigue. It further shows that *Der Ring des Nibelungen* is the only possible title for the cycle. (p. 65)

It is the mortals in the *Ring* that interest us and move us. Wagner's portrayal of these characters is more sympathetic than that of the gods. We identify with them from start to finish. (p. 66)

•　•　•　•　•

Whatever the shortcomings of detail [in the *Götterdämmerung*], one thing is certain—Wagner has created a great work, full of audacious originality and dramatic merit. He has, in his new lively way, brought out old material, little known in Germany, and by means of his clever musical-dramatic treatment has breathed new life into it. (p. 69)

The ethical background that Wagner has given the material, one that is in harmony with current philosophies, may also be of importance for the future of the work outside its own sphere of music theatre. This may be whatever it will—the result of this occasion is boundless in its range. An important new chapter in the history of the arts has been written by Wagner. The thousands who have taken part in this Festival will be able to tell the world that German art at Bayreuth has celebrated a triumph that is unique of its kind. (pp. 69-70)

> *Edvard Hagerup Grieg, from five letters to the editor of "Bergensposten" from August 6, 1876 to August 18, 1876, in* Bayreuth, the Early Years: An Account of the Early Decades of the Wagner Festival As Seen by the Celebrated Visitors & Participants, *edited by Robert Hartford, Cambridge University Press, 1980, pp. 61-70.*

FRIEDRICH NIETZSCHE   (essay date 1876)

[*Nietzsche traces Wagner's evolution as a "dithyrambic dramatist" and discusses Wagner's role as a "revolutionist of society." As in* The Birth of Tragedy *(see excerpt above, 1872), Nietzsche here extols Wagner's creative imagination and dramatic output. This essay was published in German as* Wagner in Bayreuth *in 1876. For further criticism by Nietzsche, see excerpt below, 1888.*]

The characters an artist creates are not himself, but the succession of these characters, to which it is clear he is greatly attached, must at all events reveal something of his nature. Now try and recall Rienzi, the Flying Dutchman and Senta, Tannhäuser and Elizabeth, Lohengrin and Elsa, Tristan and Marke, Hans Sach, Woden and Brunhilda,—all these characters are correlated by a secret current of ennobling and broadening morality which flows through them and becomes ever purer and clearer as it progresses. And at this point we enter with respectful reserve into the presence of the most hidden development in Wagner's own soul. In what other artist do we meet with the like of this, in the same proportion? Schiller's characters, from the Robbers to Wallenstein and Tell, do indeed pursue an ennobling course, and likewise reveal something of their author's development; but in Wagner the standard is higher and the distance covered is much greater. In the *Nibelungen Ring,* for instance, where Brunhilda is awakened by Siegfried, I perceive the most moral music I have ever heard. Here Wagner attains to such a high level of sacred feeling that our mind unconsciously wanders to the glistening ice- and snow-peaks of the Alps, to find a likeness there;—so pure, isolated, inaccessible, chaste, and bathed in love-beams does Nature here display herself, that clouds and tempests—yea, and even the sublime itself—seem to lie beneath her. Now, looking down from this height upon Tannhäuser and the Flying Dutchman, we begin to perceive how the man in Wagner was evolved: how restlessly and darkly he began; how tempestuously he strove to gratify his desires, to acquire power and to taste those rapturous delights from which he often fled in disgust; how he wished to throw off a yoke, to forget, to be negative, and to renounce everything. The whole torrent plunged, now into this valley, now into that, and flooded the most secluded chinks and crannies. In the night of these semi-subterranean convulsions a star appeared and glowed high above him with melancholy vehemence; as soon as he recognised it, he named it *Fidelity—unselfish fidelity.* Why did this star seem to him the brightest and purest of all? What secret meaning had the word "fidelity" to his whole being? For he has graven its image and problems upon all his thoughts and compositions. His works contain almost a complete series of the rarest and most beautiful examples of fidelity: that of brother to sister, of friend to friend, of servant to master; of Elizabeth to Tannhäuser, of Senta to the Dutchman, of Elsa to Lohengrin, of Isolde, Kurvenal, and Marke to Tristan, of Brunhilda to the most secret vows of Woden—and many others. It is Wagner's most personal and most individual experience, which he reveres like a religious mystery, and which he calls Fidelity; he never wearies of breathing it into hundreds of different characters, and of endowing it with the sublimest that in him lies, so overflowing is his gratitude. It is, in short, the recognition of the fact that the two sides of his nature remained faithful to each other, that out of free and unselfish love, the creative, ingenuous, and brilliant side kept loyally abreast of the dark, the intractable, and the tyrannical side. (pp. 110-12)

[Wagner has not] learned to look for repose in history and philosophy, nor to derive those subtle influences from their study which tend to paralyse action or to soften a man unduly. Neither the creative nor the militant artist in him was ever diverted from his purpose by learning and culture. The moment his constructive powers direct him, history becomes yielding clay in his hands. His attitude towards it then differs from that of every scholar, and more nearly resembles the relation of the ancient Greek to his myths; that is to say, his subject is something he may fashion, and about which he may write verses. He will naturally do this with love and a certain becoming reverence, but with the sovereign right of the creator notwithstanding. And precisely because history is more supple and

more variable than a dream to him, he can invest the most individual case with the characteristics of a whole age, and thus attain to a vividness of narrative of which historians are quite incapable. In what work of art, of any kind, has the body and soul of the Middle Ages ever been so thoroughly depicted as in *Lohengrin*? And will not the *Meistersingers* continue to acquaint men, even in the remotest ages to come, with the nature of Germany's soul? Will they not do more than acquaint men of it? Will they not represent its very ripest fruit—the fruit of that spirit which ever wishes to reform and not to overthrow, and which, despite the broad couch of comfort on which it lies, has not forgotten how to endure the noblest discomfort when a worthy and novel deed has to be accomplished?

And it is just to this kind of discomfort that Wagner always felt himself drawn by his study of history and philosophy: in them he not only found arms and coats of mail, but what he felt in their presence above all was the inspiring breath which is wafted from the graves of all great fighters, sufferers, and thinkers. Nothing distinguishes a man more from the general pattern of the age than the use he makes of history and philosophy. . . . Wagner is most philosophical where he is most powerfully active and heroic. It was as a philosopher that he went, not only through the fire of various philosophical systems without fear, but also through the vapours of science and scholarship, while remaining ever true to his highest self. And it was this highest self which exacted *from his versatile spirit works as complete as his were,* which bade him suffer and learn, that he might accomplish such works. (pp. 117-21)

[Wagner] rivets and locks together all that is isolated, weak, or in any way defective. . . . And in this respect he is one of the greatest civilising forces of his age. He dominates art, religion, and folklore, yet he is the reverse of a polyhistor or of a mere collecting and classifying spirit; for he constructs with the collected material, and breathes life into it, and is a *Simplifier of the Universe.* (p. 123)

Wagner concentrated upon life, past and present, the light of an intelligence strong enough to embrace the most distant regions in its rays. That is why he is a simplifier of the universe; for the simplification of the universe is only possible to him whose eye has been able to master the immensity and wildness of an apparent chaos, and to relate and unite those things which before had lain hopelessly asunder. Wagner did this by discovering a connection between two objects which seemed to exist apart from each other as though in separate spheres—that between music and life, and similarly between music and the drama. Not that he invented or was the first to create this relationship, for they must always have existed and have been noticeable to all; but, as is usually the case with a great problem, it is like a precious stone which thousands stumble over before one finally picks it up. Wagner asked himself the meaning of the fact that an art such as music should have become so very important a feature of the lives of modern men. . . . A single great artist might certainly be an accident, but the appearance of a whole group of them, such as the history of modern music has to show, a group only once before equalled on earth, that is to say in the time of the Greeks,—a circumstance of this sort leads one to think that perhaps necessity rather than accident is at the root of the whole phenomenon. The meaning of this necessity is the riddle which Wagner answers.

He was the first to recognise an evil which is as widespread as civilisation itself among men; language is everywhere diseased, and the burden of this terrible disease weighs heavily upon the whole of man's development. (pp. 131-33)

It is the voice *of Wagner's art* which . . . appeals to men. And that we, the children of a wretched age, should be the first to hear it, shows how deserving of pity this age must be: it shows, moreover, that real music is of a piece with fate and primitive law; for it is quite impossible to attribute its presence amongst us precisely at the present time to empty and meaningless chance. Had Wagner been an accident, he would certainly have been crushed by the superior strength of the other elements in the midst of which he was placed. But in the coming of Wagner there seems to have been a necessity which both justifies it and makes it glorious. Observed from its earliest beginnings, the development of his art constitutes a most magnificent spectacle, and—even though it was attended with great suffering— reason, law, and intention mark its course throughout. Under the charm of such a spectacle the observer will be led to take pleasure even in this painful development itself, and will regard it as fortunate. He will see how everything necessarily contributes to the welfare and benefit of talent and a nature foreordained, however severe the trials may be through which it may have to pass. (pp. 145-46)

[The] observer who is confronted with a nature such as Wagner's must, willy-nilly, turn his eyes from time to time upon himself, upon his insignificance and frailty, and ask himself, What concern is this of thine? Why, pray, art thou there at all? Maybe he will find no answer to these questions, in which case he will remain estranged and confounded, face to face with his own personality. Let it then suffice him that he has experienced this feeling; let the fact *that he has felt strange and embarrassed in the presence of his own soul* be the answer to his question. For it is precisely by virtue of this feeling that he shows the most powerful manifestation of life in Wagner— the very kernel of his strength—that demoniacal *magnetism* and gift of imparting oneself to others, which is peculiar to his nature, and by which it not only conveys itself to other beings, but also absorbs other beings into itself; thus attaining to its greatness by giving and by taking. As the observer is apparently subject to Wagner's exuberant and prodigally generous nature, he partakes of its strength, and thereby becomes formidable *through him and to him.* And every one who critically examines himself knows that a certain mysterious antagonism is necessary to the process of mutual study. . . . [In] Wagner the whole visible world desires to be spiritualised, absorbed, and lost in the world of sounds. In Wagner, too, the world of sounds seeks to manifest itself as a phenomenon for the sight; it seeks, as it were, to incarnate itself. His art always leads him into two distinct directions, from the world of the play of sound to the mysterious and yet related world of visible things, and *vice versâ.* He is continually forced—and the observer with him— to re-translate the visible into spiritual and primeval life, and likewise to perceive the most hidden interstices of the soul as something concrete and to lend it a visible body. This constitutes the nature of the *dithyrambic dramatist,* if the meaning given to the term includes also the actor, the poet, and the musician; a conception necessarily borrowed from Æschylus and the contemporary Greek artists—the only perfect examples of the dithyrambic dramatist before Wagner. . . . [If] it were sought to associate Wagner's development with an inner barrier of . . . [some] kind, it would then be necessary to recognise in him a primitive dramatic talent, which had to renounce all possibility of satisfying its needs by the quickest and most trivial methods, and which found its salvation and its means of expression in drawing all arts to it for one great dramatic

display. But then one would also have to assume that the most powerful musician, owing to his despair at having to appeal to people who were either only semi-musical or not musical at all, violently opened a road for himself to the other arts, in order to acquire that capacity for diversely communicating himself to others, by which he compelled them to understand him, by which he compelled the masses to understand him. (pp. 147-50)

Wagner's actual life—that is to say, the gradual evolution of the dithyrambic dramatist in him—was at the same time an uninterrupted struggle with himself, a struggle which never ceased until his evolution was complete. His fight with the opposing world was grim and ghastly, only because it was this same world—this alluring enemy—which he heard speaking out of his own heart, and because he nourished a violent demon in his breast—the demon of resistance. When the ruling idea of his life gained ascendancy over his mind—the idea that drama is, of all arts, the one that can exercise the greatest amount of influence over the world—it aroused the most active emotions in his whole being. It gave him no very clear or luminous decision, at first, as to what was to be done and desired in the future; for the idea then appeared merely as a form of temptation—that is to say, as the expression of his gloomy, selfish, and insatiable will, eager for *power and glory.* Influence—the greatest amount of influence—how? over whom?—these were henceforward the questions and problems which did not cease to engage his head and his heart. He wished to conquer and triumph as no other artist had ever done before, and, if possible, to reach that height of tyrannical omnipotence at one stroke for which all his instincts secretly craved. With a jealous and cautious eye, he took stock of everything successful, and examined with special care all that upon which this influence might be brought to bear. With the magic sight of the dramatist, which scans souls as easily as the most familiar book, he scrutinised the nature of the spectator and the listener, and although he was often perturbed by the discoveries he made, he very quickly found means wherewith he could enthral them. These means were ever within his reach: everything that moved him deeply he desired and could also produce; at every stage in his career he understood just as much of his predecessors as he himself was able to create, and he never doubted that he would be able to do what they had done. . . . Wagner's ability, his taste and his aspirations—all of which have ever been as closely related as key to lock—grew and attained to freedom together; but there was a time when it was not so. What did he care about the feeble but noble and egotistically lonely feeling which that friend of art fosters, who, blessed with a literary and aesthetic education, takes his stand far from the common mob! But those violent spiritual tempests which are created by the crowd when under the influence of certain climactic passages of dramatic song, that sudden bewildering ecstasy of the emotions, thoroughly honest and selfless—they were but echoes of his own experiences and sensations, and filled him with glowing hope for the greatest possible power and effect. Thus he recognised *grand opera* as the means whereby he might express his ruling thoughts; towards it his passions impelled him; his eyes turned in the direction of its home. The larger portion of his life, his most daring wanderings, and his plans, studies, sojourns, and acquaintances are only to be explained by an appeal to these passions and the opposition of the outside world, which the poor, restless, passionately ingenuous German artist had to face. Another artist than he knew better how to become master of this calling, and now that it has gradually become known by means of what ingenious artifices of all kinds Meyerbeer succeeded in preparing and achieving every one of his great successes, and how scrupulously the sequence of "effects" was taken into account in the opera itself, people will begin to understand how bitterly Wagner was mortified when his eyes were opened to the tricks of the *métier* which were indispensable to a great public success. I doubt whether there has ever been another great artist in history who began his career with such extraordinary illusions and who so unsuspectingly and sincerely fell in with the most revolting form of artistic trickery. And yet the way in which he proceeded partook of greatness, and was therefore extraordinarily fruitful. For when he perceived his error, despair made him understand the meaning of modern success, of the modern public, and the whole prevaricating spirit of modern art. And while becoming the critic of "effect," indications of his own purification began to quiver through him. It seems as if from that time forward the spirit of music spoke to him with an unprecedented spiritual charm. As though he had just risen from a long illness and had for the first time gone into the open, he scarcely trusted his hand and his eye, and seemed to grope along his way. Thus it was an almost delightful surprise to him to find that he was still a musician and an artist, and perhaps then only for the first time.

Every subsequent stage in Wagner's development may be distinguished thus, that the two fundamental powers of his nature drew ever more closely together: the aversion of the one to the other lessened, the higher self no longer condescended to serve its more violent and baser brother; it loved him and felt compelled to serve him. . . . The limits of the interval separating the preceding and the subsequent ages will be described historically in two sentences: Wagner was the *revolutionist of society;* Wagner recognised the only artistic element that ever existed hitherto—*the poetry of the people.* The ruling idea which in a new form and mightier than it had ever been, obsessed Wagner, after he had overcome his share of despair and repentance, led him to both conclusions. Influence, the greatest possible amount of influence to be exercised by means of the stage!—but over whom? He shuddered when he thought of those whom he had, until then, sought to influence. His experience led him to realise the utterly ignoble position which art and the artist adorn; how a callous and hard-hearted community that calls itself the good, but which is really the evil, reckons art and the artist among its slavish retinue, and keeps them both in order to minister to its need of deception. Modern art is a luxury; he saw this, and understood that it must stand or fall with the luxurious society of which it forms but a part. This society had but one idea, to use its power as hard-heartedly and as craftily as possible in order to render the impotent—the people—ever more and more serviceable, base and unpopular, and to rear the modern workman out of them. . . . [Wagner's] thoughts concentrated themselves upon the question, How do the people come into being? How are they resuscitated?

He always found but one answer: if a large number of people were afflicted with the sorrow that afflicted him, that number would constitute the people, he said to himself. And where the same sorrow leads to the same impulses and desires, similar satisfaction would necessarily be sought, and the same pleasure found in this satisfaction. If he inquired into what it was that most consoled him and revived his spirits in his sorrow, what it was that succeeded best in counteracting his affliction, it was with joyful certainty that he discovered this force only in music and myth, the latter of which he had already recognised as the people's creation and their language of distress. It seemed to him that the origin of music must be similar, though perhaps more mysterious. In both of these elements he steeped and healed his soul; they constituted his most urgent need:—in this way he was able to ascertain how like his sorrow was to that of the people, when they came into being, and how they must arise anew if *many Wagners* are going to appear. What part did myth and music play in modern society, wherever they had not been actually sacrificed to it? They shared very much the same fate, a fact which only tends to prove their close relationship: myth had been sadly debased and usurped by idle tales and stories. . . . Music had kept itself alive among the poor, the simple, and the isolated. . . . Here the artist distinctly heard the command that concerned him alone—to recast myth and make it virile, to break the spell lying over music and to make music speak: he felt his strength for drama liberated at one stroke, and the foundation of his sway established over the hitherto undiscovered province lying between myth and music. His new masterpiece, which included all the most powerful, effective, and entrancing forces that he knew, he now laid before men with this great and painfully cutting question: "Where are ye all who suffer and think as I do? Where is that number of souls that I wish to see become a people, that ye may share the same joys and comforts with me? (pp. 155-63)

[The] genius of dithyrambic drama doffs its last disguise. He is isolated; the age seems empty to him; he ceases to hope; and his all-embracing glance descends once more into the deep, and finds the bottom: there he sees suffering in the nature of things, and henceforward, having become more impersonal, he accepts his portion of sorrow more calmly. The desire for great power which was but the inheritance of earlier conditions is now directed wholly into the channel of creative art; through his art he now speaks only to himself, and no longer to a public or to a people, and strives to lend this intimate conversation all the distinction and other qualities in keeping with such a mighty dialogue. During the preceding period things had been different with his art; then he had concerned himself, too, albeit with refinement and subtlety, with immediate effects. . . . [All] he desired now was to come to terms with himself, to think of the nature of the world in dramatic actions, and to philosophise in music; *what desires* he still possessed turned in the direction of the *latest philosophical views.* He who is worthy of knowing what took place in him at that time or what questions were thrashed out in the darkest holy of holies in his soul—and not many are worthy of knowing all this—must hear, observe, and experience ***Tristan and Isolde,*** the real *opus metaphysicum* of all art, a work upon which rests the broken look of a dying man with his insatiable and sweet craving for the secrets of night and death, far away from life which throws a horribly spectral morning light, sharply, upon all that is evil, delusive, and sundering: moreover, a drama austere in the severity of its form, overpowering in its simple grandeur, and in harmony with the secret of which it treats—lying dead in the midst of life, being one in two. And yet there is something still more wonderful than this work, and that is the artist himself, the man who, shortly after he had accomplished it, was able to create a picture of life so full of clashing colours as the ***Meistersingers of Nürnberg,*** and who in both of these compositions seems merely to have refreshed and equipped himself for the task of completing at his ease that gigantic edifice in four parts which he had long ago planned and begun—the ultimate result of all his meditations and poetical flights for over twenty years, his Bayreuth masterpiece, the ***Ring of the Nibelung!*** He who marvels at the rapid succession of the two operas, ***Tristan*** and the ***Meistersingers,*** has failed to understand one important side of the life and nature of all great Germans: he does not know the peculiar soil out of which that essentially German gaiety, which characterised Luther, Beethoven, and

Wagner, can grow, the gaiety which other nations quite fail to understand, and which even seems to be missing in the Germans of to-day—that clear golden and thoroughly fermented mixture of simplicity, deeply discriminating love, observation, and roguishness, which Wagner has dispensed, as the most precious of drinks. . . . (pp. 163-66)

His work would not have been complete had he handed it to the world only in the form of silent manuscript. He must make known to the world what it could not guess in regard to his productions, what was his alone to reveal—the new style for the execution and presentation of his works, so that he might set that example which nobody else could set, and thus establish *a tradition of style,* not on paper, not by means of signs, but through impressions made upon the very souls of men. (pp. 167-68)

If art mean only the faculty of communicating to others what one has oneself experienced, and if every work of art confutes itself which does not succeed in making itself understood, then Wagner's greatness as an artist would certainly lie in the almost demoniacal power of his nature to communicate with others, to express itself in all languages at once, and to make known its most intimate and personal experience with the greatest amount of distinctness possible. His appearance in the history of art resembles nothing so much as a volcanic eruption of the united artistic faculties of Nature herself, after mankind had grown to regard the practice of a special art as a necessary rule. It is therefore a somewhat moot point whether he ought to be classified as a poet, a painter, or a musician, even using each these words in its widest sense, or whether a new word ought not to be invented in order to describe him.

Wagner's *poetic* ability is shown by his thinking in visible and actual facts, and not in ideas; that is to say, he thinks mythically, as the people have always done. No particular thought lies at the bottom of a myth, as the children of an artificial culture would have us believe; but it is in itself a thought: it conveys an idea of the world, but through the medium of a chain of events, actions, and pains. The *Ring of the Nibelung* is a huge system of thought without the usual abstractness of the latter. (pp. 172-73)

[If] the heroes and gods of mythical dramas, as understood by Wagner, were to express themselves plainly in words, there would be a danger . . . of our finding ourselves transported from the world of myth to the world of ideas, and the result would be not only that we should fail to understand with greater ease, but that we should probably not understand at all. Wagner thus forced language back to a more primeval stage in its development, a stage at which it was almost free of the abstract element, and was still poetry, imagery, and feeling; the fearlessness with which Wagner undertook this formidable mission shows how imperatively he was led by the spirit of poetry, as one who must follow whithersoever his phantom leader may direct him. Every word in these dramas ought to allow of being sung, and gods and heroes should make them their own—that was the task which Wagner set his literary faculty. Any other person in like circumstances would have given up all hope; for our language seems almost too old and decrepit to allow of one's exacting what Wagner exacted from it; and yet, when he smote the rock, he brought forth an abundant flow. Precisely owing to the fact that he loved his language and exacted a great deal from it, Wagner suffered more than any other German through its decay and enfeeblement, from its manifold losses and mutilations of form, from its unwieldy particles and clumsy construction, and from its unmusical auxiliary verbs. All these

are things which have entered the language through sin and depravity. On the other hand, he was exceedingly proud to record the number of primitive and vigorous factors still extant in the current speech; and in the tonic strength of its roots he recognised quite a wonderful affinity and relation to real music, a quality which distinguished it from the highly evolved and artificially rhetorical Latin languages. Wagner's poetry is eloquent of his affection for the German language, and there is a heartiness and candour in his treatment of it which are scarcely to be met with in any other German writer, save perhaps Goethe. Forcibleness of diction, daring brevity, power and variety in rhythm, a remarkable wealth of strong and striking words, simplicity in construction, an almost unique inventive faculty in regard to fluctuations of feeling and presentiment, and therewithal a perfectly pure and overflowing stream of colloquialisms—these are the qualities that have to be enumerated, and even then the greatest and most wonderful of all is omitted. Whoever reads two such poems as *Tristan* and the *Meistersingers* consecutively will be just as astonished and doubtful in regard to the language as to the music; for he will wonder how it could have been possible for a creative spirit to dominate so perfectly two worlds as different in form, colour, and arrangement, as in soul. This is the most wonderful achievement of Wagner's talent; for the ability to give every work its own linguistic stamp and to find a fresh body and a new sound for every thought is a task which only the great master can successfully accomplish. (pp. 173-75)

[Wagner,] who was the first to detect the essential feeling in spoken drama, presents every dramatic action threefold: in a word, in a gesture, and in a sound. For, as a matter of fact, music succeeds in conveying the deepest emotions of the dramatic performers direct to the spectators, and while these see the evidence of the actors' states of soul in their bearing and movements, a third though more feeble confirmation of these states, translated into conscious will, quickly follows in the form of the spoken word. All these effects fulfil their purpose simultaneously, without disturbing one another in the least, and urge the spectator to a completely new understanding and sympathy. . . . Because every essential factor in a Wagnerian drama is conveyed to the spectator with the utmost clearness, illumined and permeated throughout by music as by an internal flame, their author can dispense with the expedients usually employed by the writer of the spoken play in order to lend light and warmth to the action. . . . [When] passions are rendered in song, they require rather more time than when conveyed by speech; music prolongs, so to speak, the duration of the feeling, from which it follows, as a rule, that the actor who is also a singer must overcome the extremely unplastic animation from which spoken drama suffers. He feels himself incited all the more to a certain nobility of bearing, because music envelopes his feelings in a purer atmosphere, and thus brings them closer to beauty. (pp. 177-78)

In Wagner the man of letters we see the struggle of a brave fighter. . . . In his writings he is always the sufferer, because a temporary and insuperable destiny deprives him of his own and the correct way of conveying his thoughts—that is to say, in the form of apocalyptic and triumphant examples. His writings contain nothing canonical or severe: the canons are to be found in his works as a whole. Their literary side represents his attempts to understand the instinct which urged him to create his works and to get a glimpse of himself through them. If he succeeded in transforming his instincts into terms of knowledge, it was always with the hope that the reverse process might take place in the souls of his readers—it was with this intention that he wrote. . . . I know of no written aesthetics that give more light than those of Wagner; all that can possibly be learnt concerning the origin of a work of art is to be found in them. He is one of the very great, who appeared amongst us a witness, and who is continually improving his testimony and making it ever clearer and freer; even when he stumbles as a scientist, sparks rise from the ground. Such tracts as **"Beethoven,"** **"Concerning the Art of Conducting,"** **"Concerning Actors and Singers,"** **"State and Religion,"** silence all contradiction, and, like sacred reliquaries, impose upon all who approach them a calm, earnest, and reverential regard. Others, more particularly the earlier ones, including **"Opera and Drama,"** excite and agitate one; their rhythm is so uneven that, as prose, they are bewildering. Their dialectics is constantly interrupted, and their course is more retarded than accelerated by outbursts of feeling; a certain reluctance on the part of the writer seems to hang over them like a pall, just as though the artist were somewhat ashamed of speculative discussions. What the reader who is only imperfectly initiated will probably find most oppressive is the general tone of authoritative dignity which is peculiar to Wagner, and which is very difficult to describe: it always strikes me as though Wagner were continually *addressing enemies;* for the style of all these tracts more resembles that of the spoken than of the written language, hence they will seem much more intelligible if heard read aloud, in the presence of his enemies, with whom he cannot be on familiar terms, and towards whom he must therefore show some reserve and aloofness. The entrancing passion of his feelings, however, constantly pierces this intentional disguise, and then the stilted and heavy periods, swollen with accessary words, vanish, and his pen dashes off sentences, and even whole pages, which belong to the best in German prose. But even admitting that while he wrote such passages he was addressing friends, and that the shadow of his enemies had been removed for a while, all the friends and enemies that Wagner, as a man of letters, has, possess one factor in common, which differentiates them fundamentally from the "people" for whom he worked as an artist. Owing to the refining and fruitless nature of their education, they are quite *devoid of the essential traits of the national character,* and he who would appeal to them must speak in a way which is not of the people—that is to say, after the manner of our best prose-writers and Wagner himself; though that he did violence to himself in writing thus is evident. But the strength of that almost maternal instinct of prudence in him, which is ready to make any sacrifice, rather tends to reinstall him among the scholars and men of learning, to whom as a creator he always longed to bid farewell. He submits to the language of culture and all the laws governing its use, though he was the first to recognise its profound insufficiency as a means of communication.

For if there is anything that distinguishes his art from every other art of modern times, it is that it no longer speaks the language of any particular caste, and refuses to admit the distinctions "literate" and "illiterate." It thus stands as a contrast to every culture of the Renaissance which to this day still bathes us modern men in its light and shade. (pp. 192-95)

No artist, of what past soever, has yet received such a remarkable portion of genius; no one, save him, has ever been obliged to mix [the] bitterest of ingredients with the drink of nectar to which enthusiasm helped him. It is not as one might expect, the misunderstood and mishandled artist, the fugitive of his age, who adopted this faith in self-defence: success or failure at the hands of his contemporaries was unable either to create or to destroy it. (pp. 197-98)

Friedrich Nietzsche, "Richard Wagner in Bayreuth," in his The Complete Works of Friedrich Nietzsche: Thoughts Out of Season, Part I, Vol. 4, *edited by Oscar Levy, translated by Anthony M. Ludovici, The Macmillan Company, 1909, pp. 99-204.*

EDWARD ROSE   (essay date 1879)

[*After briefly discussing Wagner's aesthetics, Rose presents a critical survey of his operas and charts his development in the music drama.*]

That Wagner deserves the most careful and thorough criticism is, I think, unquestionable. He has done a great work for the operatic stage, not merely in his abolition of the commonplace recitative, and other absurd conventionalities, but in his entire reform of the language and style of plot of musical plays. If we compare his libretti with those of Scribe, or the best of his contemporaries, we find an astonishing difference. As a rule, though Scribe's plots were finer than those of the average librettist, and his construction was good, his language was wanting in poetry and distinction, and his stories were those of ordinary plays, by no means specially and exclusively suited for music. Of all faults, these are the ones with which Wagner can least be charged: there can be no question that the legends of the *Flying Dutchman,* of *Tannhäuser,* of the *Walküre,* are distinctively adapted for the lyric stage. . . . There is no want of poetry in him—rather, perhaps, a want of the prose of life, common sense and steady strength.

His work bears, indeed, a strong likeness to certain schools of painting and of poetry now fashionable in England—to the productions of Burne Jones and of Swinburne. Like theirs, his technical knowledge is very great; like them, he avoids as the one deadly fault commonplaceness of style; and like them he often chooses subjects interesting rather to minds trained to art than to the mass of mankind—to a certain extent, perhaps, he holds the creed of 'art for art's sake,' though, like most who profess it, he loses no chance of exemplifying his own ultramodern system of morals. (pp. 519-20)

It would be unfair, and indeed absurd, to judge Wagner by the standard of Shakespeare; a better comparison is with the Greek tragedians, to whom he is as like in some respects as he is singularly unlike them in others. Take the one trilogy of Æschylus which we know; in many ways Wagner seems to have followed its manner and tried to reproduce its effects. (pp. 520-21)

What Wagner himself would probably consider the great distinction between his work and that of his predecessors—Greek, English, or German—is the fact that with him the opera is professedly a combination of all the arts: music, the drama, and painting have each their share—and it may be said that in his latest work their shares are almost equal: at Bayreuth, in the *Nibelungen* tetralogy, the scenery played nearly as important a part as the singers. This characteristic has grown as his genius has developed—his theory has been formulated and perfected gradually. Music, he says, was not made to live alone. All our artistic senses should be appealed to at once. . . . (p. 521)

A brief chronological sketch of the dramatic works of Wagner, from the first published, *Rienzi,* to *Parsifal,* of which the music is as yet only partly composed, may help to show the growth and changes of his mind. . . .

[It] is to be remarked that Wagner when he wrote . . . *Liebesverbot* ('The Veto on Love') was completely under the influence

Costume designs for Kundry in Parsifal. *Created by Gustav Klimt. Reproduced by permission of Office du Livre.*

of the 'Young Europe' school in morals, and that he turned Shakespeare's serious story [*Measure for Measure*] into a merry glorification of sensuality at the expense of asceticism. (p. 522)

The admirable construction of this story, the swift and dramatic action, need hardly be pointed out: nor the fact that, except perhaps in the sensuousness, there is hardly anything in it which reveals to us the presence of Wagner, as we know him from his later works. Like almost all his plays, however, it opens remarkably well—with a picturesque and spirited group: so begin *Rienzi, Tannhäuser, Lohengrin,* and the *Meistersinger.* It is perhaps also worth noticing that Wagner has chosen for adaptation nearly the least pleasant in story of all Shakespeare's comedies. . . .

[*Rienzi*] was distinguished from most of its contemporaries by its breadth of purpose, and in many parts of its music the Wagnerian style was already distinctly perceptible; but the story, founded on real history—as interpreted in Bulwer's novel—differed altogether in tone from his later legendary plots.

The first and second acts were completed, music and words, early in 1839, and between them and the rest of the play, written after the first enthusiasm was past, there is a very perceptible difference. As a fact, the plot of the novel, amply sufficient in the earlier part, fails towards the end in the coherence and strength needed for the theatre; but this fault of beginning far better than he ends is a very common one with Wagner, as with many poet-dramatists. In *Tannhäuser, Lohengrin, Tristan,* the opening gives a splendid promise, which is not altogether

fulfilled, and which causes some feeling of disappointment. The poetry of situation with which the drama opens is not always followed by sufficient poetry of event; and we miss the *crescendo* necessary on the stage, where simple beauty should lead up to powerful interest. (p. 523)

[The libretto of *Rienzi*] has great merits and great faults, but neither are distinctively Wagnerian, except perhaps the strong and simple construction of the early acts, the fine choice of scene throughout, and the mistake of giving so prominent a place to a character so vacillating as Adriano is here made. Wagner's chief people are indeed very seldom heroic—Tannhäuser is far from an estimable person; Senta is untrue to Erik, her first love; Elsa wants faith; Tristan is false to his friend; Adriano not to be relied upon, and the people in *Parsifal* by no means 'nice.' His nominal heroes are generally mere lay figures—Lohengrin, even the Dutchman, nay, Tannhäuser himself, make very little individual impression on us; while Siegfried, though distinct enough, is little more than a jolly boy, quite unworthy of his Walküre bride. On the other hand, Senta, Elsa, Elizabeth, and Brünnhilde, have each a rare charm, a distinct and especial beauty.

The stride from *Rienzi* to the *Flying Dutchman* is very great, though the one was first performed within a month or two of the other. (p. 524)

Here, for once, Wagner gives us an opera solely depending on the music, and the weird tone of the story; and here he has—also for once—felt that so simple a plot must be developed briefly: the *Flying Dutchman* is really a short opera. It is purely Wagneresque, and its effect—though sometimes obtained by means too obvious—is very striking. . . .

[The] *Flying Dutchman* does not show us Wagner fully developed—it is a transition opera. The story is weird, but it is perfectly human; it is even one which other dramatists have used. The incidents are thoroughly tragic, and the tendency to introduce the lighter as well as the graver events of legend among situations of the deepest human interest is not yet apparent. In *Tannhäuser* what one may call the fairy-tale element begins—the bringing-in of the blossoming cross has a strange effect amid scenes of death and despair: still odder seems the visible transformation of the magic swan in *Lohengrin:* while in the *Nibelungen* tetralogy we are in sheer fairy-tale, among talking birds and magic helmets, intermingled with an occasional flash of savage human passion like that in the hut of Hunding. . . .

As a poem, [*Tannhäuser*] stands very high indeed among Wagner's works; but it is essentially a poem, a legend, rather than a stage play. It contains many fine situations, but hardly one of them has the full effect on the stage it would seem to deserve, and all are quite at the mercy of the scene painter; . . . and this constant danger would seem to tell against Wagner's theory of a combination of arts. An independent art is much safer; and, while *Macbeth* and *King Lear* may gain as much from good scenery as *Lohengrin* and *Tannhäuser,* they lose comparatively little by bad. (p. 525)

Wagner describes [the scenery of *Tannhäuser*] very finely and very minutely in his stage directions, and it is almost doubtful whether any painted pictures could call up so surely and so exactly as poetical words the ideas he wishes to convey. Eloquent stage directions are, indeed, a bad sign; they are, to begin with, false art—a play is essentially a thing to be seen and heard, not read. But here, as in other things, Wagner seems greedily to attempt to combine all claims to glory; and this, like his other characteristics, grows upon him from play to play.

The splendid story on which *Tannhäuser* is founded is well known—and is told, almost perfectly, in the overture, one of Wagner's grandest achievements; the conclusion to the legend formed by the miracle of the flowering cross is, I believe, entirely Wagner's addition—I do not know that the two stories have ever been combined before. Taking the whole as a legendary poem, the effect is good; but the second story is quite undramatic—it is certainly not one of the few miracles suited for theatrical representation. Yet the pilgrims chanting on their way to Rome add another to the rich contrasts of this work, perhaps the most varied and vivid in colouring of its author's creations. (pp. 525-26)

Tannhäuser is full of picturesque situations, but they are not all good stage situations, and the story, as a whole, has not the compression and strength needed for the theatre.

In this respect his next opera was much stronger, and it has accordingly proved of all his works the most effective on the stage. There is probably no more perfect act on the lyric stage than the first of *Lohengrin;* the story is striking, compact, and stately, and is worked out with an admirable clearness. The rest is perhaps not so good; the second act contains only one incident—Ortrud's sudden burst of pride on the cathedral steps—and that is in no way necessary to the story; and similarly the incident brought in to relieve the over-simplicity of the last act—Telramund's attack on Lohengrin—has no result what-

ever. This is a characteristic of many poets who attempt to write plays suited for the stage; they introduce a good deal of action, but it is action dragged in at random, and is no indispensable result of the plot.

Yet *Lohengrin* is dramatically the best of Wagner's operas, and is, it need hardly be said, incomparably superior to the ordinary libretto. All Wagner's works are, indeed, those of a poet, and of a man with most unquestionable dramatic instinct; and there is not one in which traces, at least, of a very high order of power may not be found. Only it may be doubted whether his genius is of that complete and sound order which alone can produce a thoroughly satisfactory work. If it be, and if he have written any one thing wholly successful, this is certainly *Lohengrin.*

A feature in this opera very characteristic of its author is the night-effect, followed by daybreak. . . .

The effect is a fine one, though it is perhaps too much and too often relied on by Wagner; there is such a dawn in the first act of *Rienzi,* and there are scenes in almost all his plays which depend a great deal upon their 'night-feeling'—or their dawn or sunset feeling—for their effect. This is particularly noticeable in the *Walküre,* the *Meistersinger,* and, above all, *Tristan and Isolde*—*Lohengrin's* successor, . . . in which the very backbone of the second and third acts is the contrast between the poetry of night and of day. (p. 527)

The excess of talk over action has come to a climax in [*Tristan*], as, indeed, Wagner avows, in a defence of the growing length (and diminishing incident) of his works. In his early operas, he says, he allowed for the frequent repetition of words common in lyric dramas; later, 'the whole extent of the melody is indicated beforehand in the arrangement of the words and verses.' He chooses legendary plots, he tells us, because 'the simple nature of their action renders unnecessary any painstaking for the purpose of explanation of the course of the story: the greatest possible portion of the poem can be devoted to the portrayal of the *inner* motives of the action.' When he composed *Tristan* his theories were perfected, and he absorbed himself 'with complete confidence in the depths of the inmost processes of the soul, and fearlessly drew from this inmost centre of the world their outward forms.' This view of the duties of a dramatist—if to a slight extent to be paralleled in some works of the Greek tragedians—will generally be considered a wrong and an impracticable one; its curious opposition to the tendency of modern philosophy is worth noticing—the great musical reformer and innovator would seem to hold reactionary views in science. (pp. 528-29)

[In 'local colouring' the *Meistersinger*] is charming, and in indication of dramatic position; and the life of a German town in the busy, cheery days of Hans Sachs is pleasantly painted. Some isolated pictures are especially quiet and true, as the sunny Sunday morning of the third act, with the poet-shoemaker reading his big Bible; but these ordinary merits of Wagner are here opposed to more than his ordinary defects of overlength, want of invention of incident, and of what I may call *sturdiness*—strength and common sense—of plot. These, and the sense of humour which prevents absurdity, are great necessities in a dramatist; and unfortunately Wagner has them not.

A fault from which the *Meistersinger,* perhaps from the nature of its story, is comparatively free, is one very usual with Wagner—a constantly strained feeling, a never-ceasing tension. . . .

[In the *Nibelungen* tetralogy] the interest excited by that which is nominally the mainspring of the story—the fate of the gods—is very languid. To begin with, it is not at all clearly set before one; the gods are not present at the conclusion, and the effect it will have upon them is by no means evident. The light fairy-tale tone of a great deal of the story—especially in the Prelude and in the Second Day—is no doubt intended as a relief to the tragic incidents; but I think the whole would gain greatly if the story, instead of being relieved by the introduction of these passages, were shortened by their omission. . . . (p. 529)

As a fact, however, the main plot of the poem is the fate, not of the gods, but of Brünnhilde; this is what must catch the attention of every audience, as of every reader, who cannot but feel that the play proper is contained in Acts II. and III. of the *Walküre,* the end of *Siegfried,* and the *Götterdämmerung:* in considerably less, that is to say, than one-half of the te-tralogy; and that all which does not closely concern Brünnhilde is really episodic. This applies especially to the one powerful act devoted to the history of Siegmund and Sieglinde, whose very strength—superb, though feverish and unhealthy—is its worst fault, as it directs the interest of the audience into a wrong channel, which leads nowhere. But it must be said that Brünnhilde is a magnificent picture—a thing which has a place apart, of its own, in literature; which we meet now for the first time and can never forget. The whole effect of the Walküren, shouting from rock to rock, galloping on their wild horses, is unique and grand. That this effect is to some extent obtained, as in the *Flying Dutchman,* by too obvious means is true; there is more than enough of 'Hoyotoho! Hoyotoho! Heiaho!'—but this, and an accompanying consciousness of the effect he is producing, is a constant characteristic of Wagner. So, too, is a certain straining after originality, an attempt to be unlike other people, which too often produces mere eccentricity. (p. 530)

[When] we look through the list of poets who have written for the stage, the number whose works have proved to possess the power of really moving the crowds of men and women who fill our theatres is so very small, that to have succeeded as well as Wagner is hardly the lot of one true poet in a thousand. Of modern writers, whom have we whose work ranks high with the scholar and can also win favour on the public stage? Besides Wagner, perhaps only one living man, the brilliant, flashy, enthusiastic, intensely 'theatrical' poet of the Parisians, Victor Hugo—with whom, as a comrade essentially like, in spite of all his French unlikeness, I leave the ultra-German Richard Wagner. (p. 532)

> *Edward Rose, "Wagner As a Dramatist," in* Fraser's Magazine, *n.s. Vol. XIX, No. CXII, April, 1879, pp. 519-32.*

ALFRED E. WATSON   (essay date 1882)

[*The following excerpt from the May 27, 1882 issue of the satirical periodical* Punch *is an example of the persiflage to which* The Nibelung's Ring *was sometimes subjected.*]

Few men have made more noise in the world than Herr Richard Wagner, and if anybody doubt it, let him try the ***Ring des Nibelungen; or, Panto-Mime and the Three Merry Maidens of the Rhino.*** The *Nibelungen* is made up of ''motives,'' but Herr Wagner's motives are often hard to understand. ''Blow it all!'' says Herr Wagner (they have trombones, *and they all do it*), ''here goes!'' Herr Wagner's rule is, ''When in doubt, play the drum.'' This raises a spirit of emulation in the bosom of the gentleman who has been entrusted with the cymbals. Bang

they go! The violins tremble with indignation. Herr Seidl waves his arms to the ophicleides; at it go the horns, and the singers yell in another key, to show that they are not to be put down by the odds against them. Half-a-dozen ''motives'' have been going on—if one could only have picked them out.

The *Nibelungen* opens with a view of some queer fish in an Aquarium. Here are the Rhine Maidens with Our New Patent Self-instructing Swimming Apparatus fitted on them, trying to remember that pretty little thing they heard last night. They don't recollect the proper words, so *Woglinde* sings the tune, which seems to be badly recollected from MENDELSSOHN, to the thrilling words:

> Weia! Waga! Waga la Weia!
> Wallala, weiala weia!

Then ''Gin a body meet a body coming through the Rhine.'' Everybody joins in chorus.

These bodies are taking care of the Rheingold, or Rhino, as it is generally called, and a bad young man, *Panto-Mime's* brother, comes and walks about in the water; to which these bold young minxes do not object until he goes up the ladder, which has been incautiously left, from the bottom of the Rhine to the shelf on which the Rhino rests, and walks off with the treasure. Then they let off the steam—which, by the way, they do on every possible occasion. Before the steam has quite evaporated, and while there is still a good deal of Hot-bathy smell about the place, the gauze rises, and discovers about as coarsely a painted scene as we ever remember. Here *Wotan,* the King of the Gods, is in a very low state of mind, because the Giants have built him a palace and are coming to ask for their money. The *''Can't-pay-the-Rent-and-don't-know-what-I-shall-do-about-the-Taxes Motive''* expresses *Wotan's* sorrow, after which, to some good old pantomime music, in come the giants *Fafner* and *Fasolt.* You know they are giants directly, because it is stated so in the bill; though, as a matter of fact, dwarfs, giants, and gods are all the same size. To their *''Now-then,-Gov'nor,-are-you-going-to-weigh-in? Motive?''* *Wotan* replies that he really shall be very much obliged if they will kindly make it convenient to call again, and off they go, taking with them the goddess *Fry-a,* so named because she acts as a sort of plain cook and bakes the apples, which is all that keeps the gods young. For these gods are in a very bad way altogether. *Wotan,* who is a disreputable old man, then goes off on an expedition to steal the Rhino from *Panto-Mime's* brother, who is very good at conjuring tricks; and, at the bad old man's request, transforms himself into a crocodile, which makes the god very nervous, and he hits at him with his spear to the *''I-say,-you-know,-no-larks Motive.''* The performer then changes himself into a toad, and to the *''Halloa!-now-I've-got-you Motive,''* *Wotan* treads on him and steals the ring and the money. The Giants call again, *Wotan* settles their little account, and then, to the *''Schlog-him-on-the-kop Motive,''* *Fafner* settles his brother. (pp. 105-06)

> *Alfred E. Watson, '' 'The Prize Ring des Nibelungen; or, Panto-mime and the Three Merry Maidens of the Rhino','' in* The Wagner Companion *by Raymond Mander and Joe Mitchenson, W. H. Allen, 1977, pp. 105-08.*

M. G. VAN RENSSELAER   (essay date 1883)

[*In this laudatory review, Rensselaer praises Wagner's dramatic techniques which for this critic reached their zenith in* Parsifal.]

Wagner's title to have originated an entirely new development in lyrico-dramatic art does not rest upon his music in itself considered. He has been a musical innovator to an extraordinary degree, a creator of novel expressional methods without the aid of which he could not have put his novel aims in shape. But he has been an innovator, a creator, in a wider sense than this. He is the first operatic composer who is above all things a *dramatist* in the highest, noblest meaning of the word. His point of departure is not the music, but the kernel of the drama properly so called—the main idea he wishes to express. He conceives this with extreme clearness, and elaborates it with perfect singleness of aim by every means of expression at his command—words, music, action, and stage settings. No slightest musical ornament or motive, no dramatic situation or accessory, is planned or allowed without strict reference thereto. With a greater variety of expressional means than have ever before been used by any dramatist, Wagner secures a strength and unity of effect unapproached on the modern stage. And his conceptions, moreover, are of so large and deep a sort as to put him in the very first rank among poetical creators. It is well known that he writes his own text-books. But it is not to their verbal structure that I would point to confirm these words. He conceives as do the greatest dramatic writers. But he elaborates, as I have said, in a novel fashion of his own—not with words only, but with words and music both. Therefore we find in his printed texts a finely impressive plan, admirably calculated developments and situations, clearly defined personalities, with only just so much dialogue, and dialogue of only just such a sort, as will give an outline of his intentions. The filling up which other poets do with words, he does with the plastic, thrilling, marvellously expressive language of sweet tones.

Planning for the musical drama, Wagner plans in the same broad way as did the Greeks when writing for their equally artificial mode of presentation—for the open-air theatre, the chorus, mask, and buskin. He simplifies and solidifies his story much more than do other modern dramatists, gives us but a few important figures, and avoids all sub-plots and minor threads of interest. And he does something still more important and still more Greek than this. Speaking through music chiefly, he must speak to the *feelings,* and not to the reasoning powers. So he must speak broadly, strongly, and plainly, and only of things which may be expressed by emotional appeals without the aid of intellectual definitions and subtle details. Therefore he avoids all even comparatively petty themes, all tales of transient interest or importance, all characters of local shape or flavor. He falls back upon the fundamental passions of humanity; deals with perennial facts and ever-living situations; typifies in his characters the main forces and the leading impulses, desires, and fatalities of our race. Such a broadly human theme is the struggle in man's heart between impure love and pure, which he has painted in *Tannhäuser.* Such is the lesson that innocence and love make shipwreck if unsupported by faith and trust, which he has taught in *Lohengrin.* For certain artistic reasons connected with scenery and costume, and with the advisability on the lyric stage of avoiding too close a comparison with every-day life, he puts his creations in the distant past, and sometimes outside of the natural world of prose. But not for these reasons only. Dealing with the realms of fable, legend, and mythology, he has at command the poetic atmosphere, the larger psychical types, the primitive passions, the variety of circumstance and catastrophe, his aims demand. He gets outside of conventionalities, of trivialities, of lesser laws—of all bounds and limitations save such as art prescribes. Yet with all this his characters are not unsubstantial myths, or typical abstractions, or puppets of any sort, allegorical or other. With all their fabulous environment, their superhuman stature, they are men and women like ourselves—only painted on a larger, bolder scale, to suit the large, bold nature of his art. They are warm with life and passion—not so much types as incarnations of good or evil; men of old time or of no time, but distinctly individualized kinsmen of our own, governed by the same impulses and swayed by the same influences that sway and govern us. To thus make a work of art broadly human instead of local or transient in its theme, to infuse it with a deep and vital meaning below its palpable story, and yet keep the outer form living, coherent, and artistically self-sufficient, is the noblest thing in art. (pp. 544-46)

To his grasp of deep tragic motives Wagner adds a wonderfully dramatic instinct for situation, an instinct unparalleled, it has often been said with truth, since Shakespeare's day. Much more is left to be explained and emphasized by action than is usual on the contemporary stage, whether lyrical or not. Of course his demands upon his singers are proportionately great. . . . [This] new lyrico-dramatic style, heroic in mood, with its large methods of interpretation, was almost unknown before Wagner's day. It is a creation of his own, or, rather, a complementary art which has sprung up in response to the demands of his.

Parsifal is of especial importance among Wagner's dramas, because while the latest in time, it is also the deepest in theme and the completest in execution, showing his musical methods in their highest development and his intellectual force in its greatest strength. In it we have a play typical not only of some of the most fundamental passions of humanity, but of some of the deadliest and divinest. Its music is more complicated yet more consistent, its symbolism more important and more clearly shown. In it Wagner approaches as near to allegory as is possible in work which is to keep its artistic balance and perfection. (pp. 546-47)

The history of Christ is never referred to during the drama, for Wagner writes no such inartistic things as "allegories." But it is, of course, suggested—as are certain ceremonies of the Christian religion—by various scenes which occur quite naturally in the dramatic evolution of the visible characters. But the work has a still deeper intention than to suggest the facts and beliefs of any one creed. The visible Parsifal, the suggested Christ, are alike types of redeeming love and goodness; the visible Kundry, the suggested Magdalen, of sin, suffering, and salvation. All are used as means of impressing the eternal law—felt through all religions or in spite of none—the law that evil brings a curse behind it; that remorse alone will not undo its work; that love and good deeds are the only salvation of a sinful world. The lesson is a deep one—deeper than any Wagner had taught before. His thought has never been so profound, his music never so divine, as in this last drama. (p. 555)

M. G. Van Rensselaer, "'Parsifal'," in Harper's New Monthly Magazine, *Vol. LXVI, No. CCCXCIV, March, 1883, pp. 540-56.*

ALFRED A. WHEELER (essay date 1883)

[*In this positive assessment of Wagner's operas, Wheeler discusses the dramatist's use of myth, universality, mastery of form, and the fusion of the musical and dramatic arts. For further commentary on Wagner's use of myth, see excerpts by Friedrich Nietzsche (1872), W. E. Walter (1904), Thomas Mann (1933 and 1937), Theodor Adorno (1937-38), and Norbert Fuerst (1966).*]

The great lesson of the [Nibelungen] trilogy is that Wagner is first of all a dramatist. All his revolutions in the forms of music have proceeded first and solely from the needs of drama. Drama is the end, music the means. To express the inmost spirit of the dramatic action at the very moment it is passing before the eyes of the spectator, Wagner summons to his aid the power of music. The music is thus the revelation of the drama, just as the drama is also the definition of the music. (p. 331)

"**The Nibelung's Ring**," in common with all but one of Wagner's dramas, is the outgrowth of a myth. The distinctive feature of all myths of a genuinely popular origin is the purely human quality of their interest. This very element is the vital principle in drama, and no mere portrayal of historical incidents, however vivid and true to fact, can supply its place. If a historical drama win success, it is by virtue of its truth to nature rather than its truth to history. (pp. 331-32)

It will not be supposed that, in thus ascribing the germs of his dramas to sources outside of himself, one iota of diminution from the original potency of Wagner is or could be intended. It is the poet's privilege to take and make his own whatever serves his purposes, and it is no more possible to discover Wagner's dramas in the legends from which he derived them than it is to account for "Hamlet," "Othello," or "Lear," by reference to the early plays or stories which gave the first hint of them to Shakspere. . . . It is this free use of materials, this imaginative dealing with them, guided by the highest sense of dramatic design, which puts the stamp of ownership on everything Wagner touches. . . . (p. 332)

It is noteworthy, however, that he does not discard those elements in a legend which give it a local habitation. Human feeling without them would be vague and meaningless. For the sake of local color, of picturesque effect, of the proper setting of dramatic action, many elements are necessary which depend for their success upon the antiquarian, prior to the poetic, spirit. The life and manners at the court of the *Landgrave* in "**Tannhäuser**," or of *King Mark* in "**Tristan**," are instances of this. But never is anything of this sort depicted for its own sake, or allowed any position but one wholly subservient to the purely human interest of the action. There is abundant matter in "**The Nibelung's Ring**" which seems to contradict this. The whole tragedy, for example, turns on the possession of a ring, which not only has the extraordinary power of giving its owner the mastery of the world, but is also endowed with a curse that brings destruction upon everybody but its original possessor. Here, certainly, are elements of the supernatural, which, far from exhibiting those purely human qualities belonging to mankind in all countries and at all times, are products of an age of superstition and witchcraft. True, antiquarian these features assuredly are, and in the highest degree; but not on this account do they detract one particle from the human interest of the drama. (pp. 332-33)

It is the purely human interest of scenes like the meeting of *Siegmund and Sieglinde*, their miserable fate, *Brünnhilde*'s compassion, *Siegfried*'s buoyant youth and love, the terrible snare that involves his death, and *Brünnhilde*'s glorious self-sacrifice, which transcends and banishes all thought of merely antiquarian details. What the spectator carries away with him from a performance of "**The Nibelung's Ring**" is *not* the consciousness that he has just beheld a splendid picture of a by-gone age, but the overpowering conviction that the characters before him were moved by the very feelings that most deeply stir and thrill his own soul. This is the touchstone of poetic worth. (pp. 333-34)

Without dwelling longer upon the dramatic contents of "**The Nibelung's Ring**," I pass to the consideration of its dramatic form. Here Wagner shows himself the veritable artist. He has solved the problem which Goethe and Schiller so long debated—the problem of uniting Greek beauty of form with the spirit of modern life. (p. 334)

[The] structure of such works as "**Lohengrin**," "**The Mastersingers of Nuremberg**," "**Tristan and Isolde**," or "**The Valkyrie**," affords the most perfect example in modern times of the assimilation, without imitation, of the lessons of the Greeks. . . . This is the praise of Wagner, that, since the Renaissance awoke an interest in Greek art, he is the first poet who has taken the lesson of Greek dramatists so thoroughly to heart, that, without imitating such essentially Greek but now meaningless and external features as the introduction of the Chorus, he has made their unrivaled dramatic method his own, and has bequeathed it as a living and fructifying principle to the modern world. Greek he frequently is not, when long epic narratives in the midst of his dramas overcome that sense of proportion which at other times makes his action advance swiftly to its culmination. Many of the narratives in "**The Nibelung's Ring**" are of unmeasured prolixity; and the account in "**The Mastersingers**" of the various kinds of singing in which one must be skilled before attaining admission to the guild is as wearisome as the Homeric catalogue of ships. But taken at its best—as in that matchless tragedy of "**Tristan**," which will yet be regarded as a landmark in the world's history of the drama—Wagner's work sustains its high claim to mastery of form. (p. 335)

Thus far, in considering the contents and structure of one of Wagner's dramas, we have discovered no qualities which might not belong with advantage to any play intended simply to be acted. When, however, we examine the diction of his dramas, it becomes evident that his versification is not complete in itself, but is purposely designed to reach completeness only upon being united to music. Whatever pleasure is derived by the lover of poetry from regularity of metrical structure and the melodious sequence of words will be found for the most part wanting in the perusal of one of Wagner's dramas. It is evident that, in the union of poetry to music, the new melody of the music supersedes almost entirely the old melody of the words; and the important question, therefore, arises as to how much of the character of pure poetry should be relinquished by words intended for musical partnership. . . . This question I do not think has reached its final solution at Wagner's hands. Three distinct methods of solving it are evident in his works. From "**Rienzi**" to "**Lohengrin**" he followed the precedent of librettists of Italian opera, and made his characters express themselves in purely lyrical forms of verse (such as quatrains of alternate rhymes), which were often crudely executed. After "**Lohengrin**," the four dramas of "**The Nibelung's Ring**" were finished in 1852, and in them recourse was had to the mediaeval form of alliterative verse, in which the place of rhyme is taken by a certain assonance of consonants. It is noteworthy, however, that although this experiment was partially repeated in "**Tristan and Isolde**," yet in his last two works, "**The Mastersingers**" and "**Parsifal**," alliterative verse (in the ancient sense) has been practically abandoned. If his last work may be supposed to embody his ripest opinion in this matter, Wagner had determined to indulge every caprice of versification consistent with giving his words a rhythmical impulse to musical utterance. For in "**Parsifal**" lines of all lengths, rhymed, unrhymed, and alliterative, follow each other without law. The effect, in reading, is jarring on the par; but when the music adds to each syllable its proper emotional emphasis, the irreg-ularity vanishes and the completeness of the diction stands unquestioned. (pp. 335-36)

> *Alfred A. Wheeler, "Wagner As a Dramatist," in* Overland Monthly, *n.s. Vol. I, No. 4, April, 1883, pp. 331-36.*

ALGERNON CHARLES SWINBURNE   (poem date 1883)

[*Swinburne was an English poet, dramatist, and critic. Though renowned during his lifetime for his lyric poetry, he is remembered today for his rejection of Victorian mores. His explicitly sensual themes shocked his contemporaries: while they demanded that poetry reflect and uphold current moral standards, Swinburne's only goal, implicit in his poetry and explicit in his critical writings, was to express beauty. Swinburne was a member of a group of English Wagnerians which included Francis Hueffer and Arthur Symons. The following eulogy appeared in the 1883 collection* A Century of Roundels.]

Mourning on earth, as when dark hours descend,
Wide-winged with plagues, from heaven; when hope
   and mirth
Wane, and no lips rebuke or reprehend
      Mourning on earth.

The soul wherein her songs of death and birth,
Darkness and light, were wont to sound and blend,
Now silent, leaves the whole world less in worth.

Winds that make moan and triumph, skies that bend,
Thunders, and sound of tides in gulf and firth,
Spake through his spirit of speech, whose death
   should send
      Mourning on earth.

The world's great heart, whence all things strange and
   rare
Take form and sound, that each inseparate part
May bear its burden in all tuned thoughts that share
      The world's great heart—

The fountain forces, whence like steeds that start
Leap forth the powers of earth and fire and air,
Seas that revolve and rivers that depart—

Spake, and were turned to song: yea, all they were,
With all their works, found in his mastering art
Speech as of powers whose uttered word laid bare
      The world's great heart.

From the depths of the sea, from the well-springs of
   earth, from the wastes of the midmost night,
From the fountains of darkness and tempest and
   thunder, from heights where the soul would be,
The spell of the mage of music evoked their sense, as
   an unknown light
      From the depths of the sea.

As a vision of heaven from the hollows of ocean, that
   none but a god might see,
Rose out of the silence of things unknown of a
   presence, a form, a might,
And we heard as a prophet that hears God's message
   against him, and may not flee.

Eye might not endure it, but ear and heart with a
   rapture of dark delight,
With a terror and wonder whose care was joy, and a
   passion of thought set free,
Felt only the rising of doom divine as a sun-dawn
   risen to sight
      From the depths of the sea.

(pp. 576-77)

> *Algernon Charles Swinburne, " 'The Death of Rich-ard Wagner'," in his* The Works of Algernon Charles Swinburne: Poems, *Vol. 1, David McKay Publisher, 1910, pp. 576-77.*

STÉPHANE MALLARMÉ   (poem date 1886)

[*A renowned French poet and essayist, Mallarmé formulated the theories of the French Symbolist movement and composed mu-sical, evocative poems of innovative syntax and complex meta-phor. His poem "Hommage à Wagner," which first appeared in the January 8, 1886 number of the* Revue wagnérienne, *is expli-cated by its translator C. F. MacIntyre: "1. Wagner is dead, the house of his art is draped with funereal palls; tomorrow his fame will be forgotten and sink. 2. But all our old music, with its familiar strains and tricks that make quiver the riffraff, you can stick that away in some old clothespress. 3. The crowd did not take to Wagner at first, but the very bulk of his loud brass makes everybody feel faint and sentimental. 4. Then out hops Wagner, grinning like a Chessy cat, feeling himself a god being anointed. Even the ink of a bad press can't quite choke off those last prophet-ic sobbings: that his music will still go on for a while—an evil prophecy!"*]

The silence already funereal of a moiré
arranges more than one fold on the table
which when none remembers any more
a sinking of the main leg will let crumble.

Our so old conquering zest of conjuring,
hieroglyphics giving the thousands an ecstasy
to propagate the familiar thrill of a wing!
Stick all that in an old clothespress for me.

From the smiling fracas original and hated
very loud trumpets of gold that swooned
   on the vellums
among those of masterly clarities has gushed

as far as the parvis born for their simulacrum,
the god Richard Wagner radiant, self-consecrated,
by ink in sibylline sobs but badly hushed.

(p. 95)

> *Stéphane Mallarmé, "Hommage [à Richard Wag-ner]," in his* Selected Poems, *translated by C. F. MacIntyre, University of California Press, 1957, pp. 94-5.*

FRIEDRICH NIETZSCHE   (essay date 1888)

[*As a young man, Nietzsche had greatly admired Wagner and highly praised his creative nature and works in "The Birth of Tragedy" (1872) and "Wagner in Bayreuth" (1876). However, Nietzsche eventually broke off his friendship with Wagner and harshly criticized his works. In the following satirical appraisal of Wagner as an artist, Nietzsche characterizes Wagner as an "artist of the decadence" and accordingly treats the dramatic style, themes, and staging of his operas. This essay, written in May 1888, was published in German as* Der Fall Wagner: Ein

The Bayreuth Theater in 1876.

Musikanten-Problem *in 1889. For further commentary by Nietzsche, see excerpt below, 1888.*]

[I] was one of the most corrupt of the Wagnerians. . . . I was capable of taking Wagner seriously. . . . Ah, this old magician, to what extent has he imposed upon us! The first thing his ingenuity furnishes is a magnifying-glass. We look into it, we don't trust our eyes—everything becomes great, *even Wagner becomes great*. . . . What a wise rattlesnake! All his life he has rattled before us about "devotion," about "loyalty," about "purity"; with a panegyric on chastity he withdrew from the *corrupt* world! And we have believed him. . . . (p. 369)

There is nothing on which Wagner has meditated more profoundly than salvation; his opera is the opera of salvation. Some one always wants to be saved in Wagner's works; at one time it is some little man, at another time it is some little woman—that is *his* problem. And with what opulence he varies his leading motive! What rare, what profound sallies! Who was it but Wagner taught us that innocence has a preference for saving interesting sinners? (the case in *Tannhäuser*). Or that even the wandering Jew will be saved, will become *settled*, if he marries? (the case in the *Flying Dutchman*). Or that corrupt old women prefer to be saved by chaste youths? (the case of *Kundry* in *Parsifal*). Or that handsome girls like best to be saved by a cavalier who is a Wagnerian? (the case in the *Mastersingers*). Or that even married women are willingly saved by a cavalier? (the case of *Isold*). Or that "the old god," after he has compromised himself morally in every respect, is finally saved by a freethinker and immoralist? (the case in the *Nibelung's Ring*). Admire especially this last profundity! Do you understand it?

I take good care not to understand it. . . . That other lessons also may be derived from these works I would rather prove than deny. That one can be brought to despair by a Wagnerian ballet—*and* to virtue! (once more the case of *Tannhäuser*). That the worst consequences may result if one does not go to bed at the right time (the case of *Lohengrin*). That one should never know too exactly whom one marries (once more the case of *Lohengrin*). *Tristan and Isold* extols the perfect husband, who on a certain occasion has only one question in his mouth: "But why have you not told me that sooner? Nothing was simpler than that!" Answer—

> In truth I cannot tell it,
> What thou dost ask
> Remains for aye unanswered.

Lohengrin contains a solemn proscription of investigation and questioning. Wagner, accordingly, advocates the Christian doctrine, "Thou shalt *believe,* and must *believe*." It is an offence against the highest and holiest to be scientific. . . . *The Flying Dutchman* preaches the sublime doctrine that woman makes even the most vagabond person settle down, or, in Wagnerian language, "saves" him. Here we take the liberty to ask a question. Granted that it is true, would it at the same time be desirable? What becomes of the "Wandering Jew," adored and *settled down* by a woman? He simply ceases to be the eternal wanderer, he marries, and is of no more interest to us. Translated into actuality: the danger of artists, of geniuses—for these are the "Wandering Jews"—lies in woman—*adoring* women are their ruin. Hardly anyone has sufficient character to resist being corrupted—being "saved"—when he finds himself treated as a god; he forthwith *condescends* to woman. Man is cowardly before all that is eternally feminine; women know it. In many cases of feminine love (perhaps precisely in the most celebrated cases), love is only a more refined *parasitism,* a nestling in a strange soul, sometimes even in a strange body. Ah! at what expense always to ''the host''! (pp. 369-70)

[The *Nibelung's Ring*] is also a history of salvation, only, this time, it is Wagner himself who is saved. For the half of his life Wagner has believed in *revolution,* as none but a Frenchman has ever believed in it. He sought for it in the Runic characters of myths, he believed that he found in Siegfried the typical revolutionist. ''Whence comes all the evil in the world?'' Wagner asked himself. From ''old conventions,'' he answered, like every revolutionary ideologist. That means from customs, laws, morals, and institutions, from all on which the old world, old society rests. ''How does one get rid of the evil in the world? How does one do away with the old society?'' Only by declaring war against ''conventions'' (traditional usage and morality). *That is what Siegfried does.* He commences early with it, very early: his procreation is already a declaration of war against morality—he comes into the world through adultery and incest. . . . It is *not* the legend, but Wagner who is the inventor of this radical trait; on this point he has *corrected* the legend. . . . Siegfried continues as he has commenced; he follows only the first impulse, he casts aside all tradition, all reverence, all *fear.* Whatever displeases him he stabs down. He runs irreverently to the attack on the old deities. His principal undertaking, however, is for the purpose of *emancipating woman*—''saving Brunnhilde.'' . . . Siegfried and Brunnhilde; the sacrament of free love; the dawn of the golden age; the twilight of the gods of the old morality!—*evil is done away with.* . . . Wagner's vessel ran merrily on this course for a long time. Here, undoubtedly, Wagner sought *his* highest goal. What happened? A misfortune. The vessel went on a reef; Wagner was run aground. The reef was Schopenhauer's philosophy. Wagner was run aground on a *contrary* view of things. What had he set to music? Optimism. Wagner was ashamed. In addition, it was an optimism for which Schopenhauer had formed a malicious epithet—the *infamous* optimism. He was still more ashamed. He thought long over it; his situation seemed desperate. . . . A way out of the difficulty finally dawned on his mind. The reef on which he was wrecked—how would it be if he interpreted it as the *goal,* the ultimate purpose, the real meaning of his voyage? To be wrecked *here*—that was a goal also. . . . And he translated the *Nibelung's Ring* into Schopenhauerism. Everything goes wrong, everything goes to ruin, the new world is as bad as the old.—Nothingness, the Indian Circe, makes a sign. . . . Brunnhilde, who, according to the earlier design, had to take leave with a song in honour of free love, solacing the world in anticipation of a Socialistic Utopia in which ''all will be well,'' has now something else to do. She has first to study Schopenhauer; she has to put into verse the fourth book of the ''World as Will and Representation.'' *Wagner was saved.* . . . In all seriousness, that *was* a salvation. The service for which Wagner is indebted to Schopenhauer is immense. There first did the *philosopher of the decadence* give *himself* to the artist of the decadence.

To the *artist of the decadence*—that is the word. And it is here that my seriousness commences. I am not at all inclined to be a quiet spectator, when this decadent ruins our health—and music along with it. Is Wagner a man at all? Is he not rather a disease? He makes everything morbid which he touches,— *he has made music morbid.*

A typical decadent, who feels himself necessary with his corrupt taste, who claims that it is a higher taste, who knows how to assert his depravity as a law, as progress, as fulfilment.

And nobody defends himself. Wagner's power of seduction becomes prodigious, the smoke of incense steams around him, the misunderstanding about him calls itself ''Gospel''—it is by no means the *poor in spirit* exclusively whom he has convinced.

I should like to open the windows a little. Air! More air!

It does not surprise me that people deceive themselves about Wagner in Germany. The contrary would surprise me. The Germans have created for themselves a Wagner whom they can worship; they have never been psychologists, they are thankful they misunderstand. But that people also deceive themselves about Wagner in Paris! where people are almost nothing else but psychologists. And in St. Petersburg! where things are still divined which are not divined even in Paris. How intimately related to the entire European decadence must Wagner be, when he is not recognised by it as a decadent. He belongs to it: he is its Protagonist, its greatest name. . . . (pp. 371-73)

I give prominence to this point of view: Wagner's art is morbid. The problems which he brings upon the stage—nothing but problems of hysterics—the convulsiveness of his emotion, his over-excited sensibility, his taste, which always asked for stronger stimulants, his instability, which he disguised as principles, and, not least, the choice of his heroes and heroines regarded as physiological types (a gallery of morbid individuals!): altogether these symptoms represent a picture of disease about which there can be no mistake. *Wagner est une névrosé* [Wagner is a neurotic]. Nothing is perhaps better known at present, at any rate nothing is studied more than the Protean character of degeneracy, which here chrysalizes as art and artist. Our physicians and physiologists have in Wagner their most interesting case, at least a very complete case. Just because nothing is more modern than this entire morbidness, this decrepitude and over-excitability of the nervous mechanism, Wagner is the *modern artist* par excellence, the Cagliostro of modernism. In his art there is mixed, in the most seductive manner, the things at present most necessary for everybody—the three great stimulants of the exhausted, *brutality, artifice,* and *innocence* (idiocy). (pp. 373-74)

[Wagner was] a typical decadent, in whom all ''free will'' was lacking, all whose characteristics were determined by necessity. If anything is interesting in Wagner it is the logic with which a physiological trouble, as practice and procedure, as innovation in principles and crisis in taste, advances step by step, from conclusion to conclusion.

I confine myself this time solely to the question of *style.* What is the characteristic of every *literary* decadence? It is that the life no longer resides in the whole. The word gets the upper hand and jumps out of the sentence, the sentence stretches too far and obscures the meaning of the page; the page acquires life at the expense of the whole; the whole is no longer a whole. But that is the simile for every style of decadence; always anarchy of the atoms, disgregation of will, in the language of morality, ''liberty of the individual,'' widened to a political theory, ''*equal* rights for all.'' Life, the *equal* vitality, the vibration and exuberance of life pushed back into the most minute structures, the rest *poor* in life. Everywhere paralysis, distress, and enervation, or hostility and chaos, always becoming more striking, as one ascends to ever higher forms of organization. The whole has ceased to live alogether, it is composite, summed up, artificial, an unnatural product.

There is hallucination at the commencement in Wagner—not of tones, but of gestures; for these he only seeks the appropriate semeiotic tone. If you want to admire him see him at work here; how he separates, how he arrives at little unities, how he animates them, inflates them, and renders them visible. But by so doing his power exhausts itself, the rest is worth nothing. How pitiable, how confused, how laic is his mode of "developing," his attempt to pierce at least into one another, things which have not grown out of one another! . . . That Wagner has masked his incapacity for creating organically under the guise of a principle, that he asserts a "dramatic style" where we assert merely his incapacity for any style, corresponds to an audacious habit which has accompanied Wagner all his life; he posits a principle where he lacks a faculty. . . . Once more, let it be said that Wagner is only worthy of admiration and love in the invention of minutiae, in the elaboration of details. (pp. 376-77)

[Wagner] is quite a great stage-player. Does there at all exist a more profound, a more *oppressive* effect in the theatre? . . . Wagner's art presses with the weight of a hundred atmospheres: bow yourselves just, nothing else can be done. . . . Wagner the stage-player is a tyrant, his pathos overthrows every kind of taste, every kind of resistance. Who has such convincing power of attitude, who presents the attitude so definitely before everything else? This holding the breath of Wagnerian pathos, this unwillingness to let an extreme feeling escape, this dread-inspiring *duration* of conditions where momentary suspense is enough to choke one!

Was Wagner a musician at all? In many cases he was something else in a *higher degree*, namely, an incomparable histrio, the greatest mime, the most astonishing theatrical genius that the Germans have had, our *scenic artist* par excellence. His place is elsewhere than in the history of music, with the grand true geniuses of which he is not to be confounded. Wagner *and* Beethoven—that is a blasphemy—and in the end an injustice even to Wagner. . . . He was also as a musician only that which he was in other respects: he *became* a musician, he *became* a poet, because the tyrant in him, his stage-playing genius, compelled him to it. One finds out nothing about Wagner as long as one has not divined his domineering instinct.

Wagner was *not* a musician by instinct. He proved this himself by abandoning all lawfulness, and—to speak more definitely—all style in music, in order to make out of it what he required, a theatrical rhetoric, a means for expression, for strengthening attitudes, for suggestion, for the psychological picturesque. Wagner might here pass for an inventor and an innovator of the first rank—*he has immeasurably increased the speaking power of music;* he is the Victor Hugo of music as a language. (p. 378)

Friedrich Nietzsche, "The Case of Wagner," in The Fortnightly Review, *n.s. Vol. LVIII, No. CCCXLV, September, 1895, pp. 367-79.*

FRIEDRICH NIETZSCHE   (essay date 1888)

[*In this brief discussion of* Parsifal, *Nietzsche rejects the opera as a possible parody and labels it "a bad work." This essay, excerpted below, was written in December 1888 in German as* Nietzsche contra Wagner: Aktenstücke eines Psychologen. *For additional commentary by Nietzsche, see excerpts above, 1872, 1876, and 1888.*]

[Was] Wagner in earnest with Parsifal? . . . We should like to believe that "Parsifal" was meant as a piece of idle gaiety, as the closing act and satyric drama, with which Wagner the tragedian wished to take leave of us, of himself, and above all *of tragedy,* in a way which befitted him and his dignity, that is to say, with an extravagant, lofty and most malicious parody of tragedy itself, of all the past and terrible earnestness and sorrow of this world, of the most *ridiculous* form of the unnaturalness of the ascetic ideal, at last overcome. For Parsifal is the subject *par excellence* for a comic opera. . . . Is Wagner's **"Parsifal"** his secret laugh of superiority at himself, the triumph of his last and most exalted state of artistic freedom, of artistic transcendence—is it Wagner able to *laugh* at himself? Once again we only wish it were so; for what could Parsifal be if he were *meant seriously?* Is it necessary in his case to say . . . that **"Parsifal"** is "the product of the mad hatred of knowledge, intellect, and sensuality?" a curse upon the senses and the mind in one breath and in one fit of hatred? an act of apostasy and a return to Christianly sick and obscurantist ideals? And finally even a denial of self, a deletion of self, on the part of an artist who theretofore had worked with all the power of his will in favour of the opposite cause, the spiritualisation and sensualisation of his art? And not only of his art, but also of his life? Let us remember how enthusiastically Wagner at one time walked in the footsteps of the philosopher Feuerbach. Feuerbach's words "healthy sensuality" struck Wagner in the thirties and forties very much as they struck many other Germans—they called themselves the young Germans—that is to say, as words of salvation. Did he ultimately *change his mind* on this point? It would seem that he had at least had the desire of *changing* his doctrine towards the end. . . . Had *the hatred of life* become dominant in him as in Flaubert? For **"Parsifal"** is a work or rancour, of revenge, of the most secret concoction of poisons with which to make an end of the first conditions of life; *it is a bad work.* The preaching of chastity remains an incitement to unnaturalness: I despise anybody who does not regard **"Parsifal"** as an outrage upon morality. (pp. 71-3)

Friedrich Nietzsche, "Nietzsche contra Wagner," translated by Anthony M. Ludovici, in his The Complete Works of Friedrich Nietzsche: The Case of Wagner, *Vol. 8, edited by Oscar Levy, translated by Anthony M. Ludovici and J. M. Kennedy, 1911. Reprint by The Macmillan Company, 1924, pp. 53-82.*

LEO N. TOLSTOY   (essay date 1896)

[*Tolstoy was a celebrated nineteenth-century Russian novelist, dramatist, and essayist whose novels* War and Peace *and* Anna Karenina *are considered all-encompassing documents of human existence and supreme examples of the realistic novel. Unable to sit through an entire performance of* Siegfried *in Moscow, Tolstoy expressed his dissatisfaction with Wagner's art in this essay. Tolstoy's major concern is to distinguish bogus art, which he called an elitist celebration of aesthetics, from universal art, which he claims successfully "infects" its recipient with the highest sentiment an artist can transmit—that of religious feeling. On the basis of these principles, Tolstoy labeled Wagner's operas "counterfeit art." This essay was originally published in Russian in 1896 as* Chto takoe iskusstvo *and later translated as* What Is Art?.]

To what an extent people of our circle and time have lost the capacity to receive real art and have become accustomed to accept as art things that have nothing in common with it is best seen from the works of Richard Wagner which have latterly come to be more and more esteemed, not only by the Germans, but also by the French and the English, as the very highest art, revealing new horizons to us.

The peculiarity of Wagner's music, as is known, consists in this, that he considered that music should serve poetry, expressing all the shades of a poetical work. (p. 118)

Wagner wishes to correct the opera by letting music submit to the demands of poetry and unite with it. But each art has its own definite realm which is not identical with the realm of other arts but merely comes in contact with them; and therefore, if the manifestation of, I will not say several, but even of two arts—the dramatic and the musical—be united in one complete production, then the demands of the one art will make it impossible to fulfil the demands of the other, as has always occurred in the ordinary operas where the dramatic art has submitted to, or rather yielded place to, the musical. Wagner wishes that musical art should submit to dramatic art and that both should appear in full strength. But this is impossible; for every work of art, if it be a true one, is an expression of intimate feelings of the artist, which are quite exceptional and not like anything else. Such is a musical production, and such is a dramatic work, if they be true art. And therefore, in order that a production in the one branch of art should coincide with a production in the other branch, it is necessary that the impossible should happen: that two works from different realms of art should be absolutely exceptional, unlike anything that existed before, and yet should coincide and be exactly alike.

And this cannot be, just as there cannot be two men, or even two leaves on a tree, exactly alike. Still less can two works from different realms of art, the musical and the literary, be absolutely alike. If they coincide, then either one is a work of art and the other a counterfeit, or both are counterfeits. Two live leaves cannot be exactly alike, but two artificial leaves may be. And so it is with works of art. They can only coincide completely when neither the one nor the other is art, but only cunningly devised semblances of it. (pp. 118-19)

Wagner is not only a musician, he is also a poet, or both together; and therefore, to judge of Wagner, one must know his poetry also—that same poetry which the music has to subserve. (p. 121)

From an author who could compose [the] spurious scenes [of *The Nibelungen Ring*], outraging all aesthetic feeling, as those which I had witnessed, there was nothing to be hoped; it may safely be decided that all that such an author can write will be bad because he evidently does not know what a true work of art is. (p.124)

But why did people go, and why do they still go to these performances, and why do they admire them? The question naturally presents itself: How is the success of Wagner's works to be explained?

That success I explain to myself in this way: thanks to his exceptional position in having at his disposal the resources of a king. Wagner was able to command all the methods for counterfeiting art which have been developed by long usage, and, employing these methods with great ability, he produced a model work of counterfeit art. The reason why I have selected his work for my illustration is that in no other counterfeit of art known to me are all the methods by which art is counterfeited—namely, borrowings, imitation, effects, and interestingness—so ably and powerfully united.

From the subject, borrowed from antiquity, to the clouds and the risings of the sun and moon, Wagner, in this work, has made use of all that is considered poetical. We have here the sleeping beauty, and nymphs, and subterranean fires, and dwarfs, and battles, and swords, and love, and incest, and a monster, and singing-birds—the whole arsenal of the poetical is brought into action.

Moreover, everything is imitative; the decorations are imitated and the costumes are imitated. All are just as, according to the data supplied by archaeology, they would have been in antiquity. The very sounds are imitative; for Wagner, who was not destitute of musical talent, invented just such sounds as imitate the strokes of a hammer, the hissing of molten iron, the singing of birds, etc.

Furthermore, in this work everything is in the highest degree striking in its effects and in its peculiarities: its monsters, its magic fires, and its scenes under water; the darkness in which the audience sits, the invisibility of the orchestra, and the hitherto unemployed combinations of harmony.

And besides, it is all interesting. The interest lies not only in the question who will kill whom, and who will marry whom, and who is whose son, and what will happen next.... (pp. 127-28)

[It is the] poeticality, imitativeness, effectfulness, and interestingness which, thanks to the peculiarities of Wagner's talent and to the advantageous position in which he was placed, are in these productions carried to the highest pitch of perfection, which act on the spectator, hypnotizing him as one would be hypnotized who should listen for several consecutive hours to the ravings of a maniac pronounced with great oratorical power. (p. 129)

[Thanks] to the masterly skill with which [*The Nibelungen Ring*] counterfeits art while having nothing in common with it, a meaningless, coarse, spurious production finds acceptance all over the world, costs millions of rubles to produce, and assists more and more to pervert the taste of people of the upper classes and their conception of what is art. (p. 130)

> *Leo N. Tolstoy, in a chapter in his* What Is Art? *translated by Almyer Maude, 1899. Reprint by The Bobbs-Merrill Company, Inc., 1960, pp. 118-30.*

ERNEST NEWMAN   (essay date 1898)

[*The following, by Wagner's chief biographer, is a harshly negative assessment of Wagner's philosophic powers. Newman explicates Wagner's operas through an examination of his artistic theories as expounded in his prose works and letters. In addition, Newman comments on the possible influence of Arthur Schopenhauer on Wagner; Pierre Lasserre (1917) and Jack M. Stein (1947) pursue a similar line of inquiry. For further criticism by Newman, see Additional Bibliography.*]

[The] best way to study Wagner's theories is in connection with the circumstances of his own life. It was characteristic of him throughout that he should try to elevate his own idiosyncrasies into forms of thought and action for the rest of the world. It was so with his ideas on the respective spheres of the arts; for the careful reader can detect in his prose works, along with those remarkable notions as to the functions of poetry, music, and the other arts, the cerebral abnormality that gave birth to these notions. Nothing was more characteristic of Wagner than his passion for holding up his own peculiar and *à priori* ideas as laws of life for others, in the most perfect unconsciousness that his ideas were born of an organism not only abnormal in many ways, but radically incapable of plain objective thinking. From first to last he presents a pathetic picture of the hopeless idealist in conflict with external forces too vast and too complex for him to understand. His writings on social subjects—particularly his early ones—are *à priori* to the verge of absurdity; scarcely another man could have been found in Europe to advocate so earnestly, with such sincere conviction, a return to the social and artistic ideals of the Greeks. That vain dream, held to by Wagner with extraordinary tenacity, is typical of the unreal, fantastic cloud-land in which the great musician lived. . . . [He] built the strange philosophy of life and art that appears in *Art and Revolution* and *The Art-work of the Future,* and that has gone so far to reveal the incompetence of his mind to deal with questions of the positive and the actual. There can be no dispute as to the dependence of this social creed upon his own congenital ideas and his pecuniary circumstances. . . . One brings, of course, no charge against him of casuistry or deliberate self-seeking; the very *naïveté,* both of the theories themselves and of their correspondence with his own personal needs, is conclusive as to Wagner's sincerity in the matter. He was simply a brain of enormous musical power, filled with peculiar notions as to the importance of the musical drama in the development of culture, and with too little objective outlook upon the world and too little capacity for impersonal reason to allow of his seeing the utter unreality and apriorism of his theories for all other men. In later life he partly came to recognise some of his deficiencies in this respect, admitting to Roeckel, for example, that though he read and wrote so much of philosophy, he had little head for philosophic thinking. . . . But taking his prose works and his letters on their face-value, the most cursory reading suffices to show how abnormal he was in many respects, how he dwelt with exaggerated emphasis upon theories and suggestions that appear to us hopelessly *à priori,* how he argued in the most sincere unconsciousness from the desires and needs of Richard Wagner to the supposed desires and needs of civilised mankind.

All this is of the utmost importance, not only in the diagnosis of his character, but in the attempt to comprehend his musical works. One has only to become acquainted with his correspondence during the twenty-three years he spent upon *The Ring,* to realise that he meant that work to be something more than a mere opera, a mere story of gods and men, of love and hate, and life and death; that he intended it as a serious contribution to the philosophy of the universe. Hence the need of studying *The Ring* in connection with some of the theories expressed in his prose-works and elsewhere. (pp. 868-70)

The "problem" of the drama . . . is the revolt of the "natural individual" against constituted authority as embodied in conventions and formulas. (p. 870)

[Without] reading into the *Ring* more pseudo-philosophy than it has the misfortune to contain already, one can see clearly enough that in that drama Wagner was preaching a social evangel which, with characteristic seriousness, he held to be of prime importance to mankind.

Now one has only to go back to his prose-works and his correspondence to see the theories of the *Ring* in all their *naïveté,* free from the glamour in which they are enveloped, in the tetralogy itself, by the wonderful art of the musician. Hearing or studying the music, one almost feels inclined to subscribe to the theorems of Wagner, just as *Tristan* tempts to Nirvana and *Parsifal* to asceticism; one gets a clearer notion of the ideas and their objective value by contemplating them in their plain prose expression. And looking at the matter in this way, one sees at once that Wagner was a man of high spirit and generous

sympathies, acutely sensitive both to his own miseries and those of others, but quite incapable of thinking any social problem out, or of doing anything more than offer the most *à priori* solutions of it. . . . [In 1849] he wrote to his correspondents in terms that show clearly the personal character of the philosophy and the portraiture of the *Ring.* In his correspondence with Uhlig, for example, he not only foreshadowed the theories of his *Art and Revolution* and *The Art-work of the Future,* but unconsciously sketched out, as it were, the problem of the *Ring* and some of the characters. Just as we can recognise much of Wagner himself in Walther of *The Meistersingers,* so one can see that Siegfried in the tetralogy is just a peg whereon to hang certain of the musician's theories as to the wholesome vitality of the "free individual."

> You see, dear friend, . . . it is such trifles as conventional fame-seeking and anxiety for daily bread which threaten to exert—and in a decisive manner—their august modern sovereignty over the true, free sphere of man's art. But can there be a choice here? Certainly not; not even if persons like you begin to be prudent and practical. I will be happy, and a man can only be that if he is free; but that man only is free who is what he can and, therefore, must be. Whoever, therefore, satisfies the inner necessity of his being, is free; because he feels himself alone with himself; because everything which he does answers to his nature, to his true needs. Whoever follows a necessity, not from within, but from without, is subject to compulsion; he is not free, but an unfortunate slave. The free man laughs at oppression from without if only inner necessity be not sacrificed to it; it can cause only fly-stings, not heart-wounds.

That is a kind of philosophising that has gone sadly out of fashion, the day being past when vaporising about the free individual, and inner necessity, and man being that which he is by virtue of his inner essence, and the rest of the windy jargon of the dreamer, can do much more than make us yawn. The passage is only of interest for the light it throws upon the philosophical scheme of the *Ring.* At the end of *A Communication to my Friends* . . . , when Wagner was relating the steps of his musical and intellectual development, he told how, in the drama as he had then worked it out, he had found expression for his inmost philosophy of life.

> With the conception of Siegfried, . . . I had pressed forward to where I saw before me the human being in the most natural and blithest fulness of his physical life. No historic garment more confined his limbs; no outwardly-imposed relation hemmed his movements, which, springing from the inner fount of Joy-in-life, so bore themselves in face of all encounter, that error and bewilderment, though nurtured on the wildest play of passions, might heap themselves around until they threatened to destroy him, without the hero checking for a moment, even in the face of death, the welling outflow of that inner fount; or ever holding anything the rightful master of himself and his own movements, but alone the natural outstreaming of his restless fount of life. It was Elsa who had taught me to unearth this man; to me he

was the male embodied spirit of perennial and sole creative instinct *(Unwillkür),* of the doer of true deeds of *Manhood* in the utmost fulness of its inborn strength and proved loveworthiness. Here, in the promptings of this man, love's brooding wish had no more place; but bodily lived it there, swelled every vein and stirred each muscle of the gladsome being, to all-enthralling practice of its essence.

This was the type of man Wagner had held up for admiration in his writings and in his letters; it was the type to which he himself wished to conform. He was oppressed with a sense of the hardness of the world and the restraint our modern society, based on commerce and industrialism, imposes upon the artist; and he longed vaguely and nebulously for a condition of things more favourable to art. Thousands before and after him have felt the same weariness and cherished the same desires; but him they impelled to random philosophising, to weaving cloudy schemes of social and political and artistic improvement. There is from first to last in his works—outside the department of music—hardly one suggestion as to art and life that is worth attention—or at least any more attention than one usually renders to the earnest and sincere but unpractical prophet. . . . He lived, we must always remember, in a time of social and political ferment, and in a country where the tendency has always been to philosophise *in abstracto.* Everything—his own nature, his training, his associates, his enemies—combined to make him a mere declaimer upon themes that require anything but declamation to elucidate them. He always states just that half of any problem which serves the ends of his own artistic theories; anything like a sanely comprehensive view of the intermixture of good and evil in the world is impossible to him. "Our God is Gold," he cried; "our Religion the Pursuit of Wealth." "Our Modern Art is a mere product of Culture, and has not sprung from Life itself; therefore, being nothing but a hot-house plant, it cannot strike root in the natural soil, or flourish in the natural climate of the present." There is no meaning in talk of this kind; it is windy rhetoric, pure and simple—the mere sad declamation of a frustrated artist, in a world of dark complexities whose meaning and whose interconnection he cannot fathom.

The mood in which Wagner thought out the philosophy of the *Ring,* then, was one of emotional revolt against the resistance of modern life to the impulses of the artist—a revolt determined in its forms and theories by the musician's idealism and lack of objective vision and of impartial reason. The part played by the *Ring* itself in the tetralogy can be clearly seen to be an expression of Wagner's own passion for attributing most of the evils under which art now suffers to its dependence upon gold and commerce. "This is Art as it now fills the entire civilised world!" he cried in *Art and Revolution.* "Its true essence is industry; its ethical aim the gaining of gold; its aesthetic purpose, the entertainment of those whose time hangs heavily on their hands." (pp. 870-73)

And finally, among his theories of this period was that of the necessity of the downfall of the State. In *Opera and Drama,* after a long "interpretation" of the *Œdipus* of Sophocles, in which the action of Antigone is taken to mean "the annulling of the State by her love-curse," he proceeds in a passage that shows how prone he was to read extraneous meanings into artistic products, and at the same time throws light upon the kind of subtle theorems he tried to incorporate in his own dramatic works. (p. 873)

It was in this misty way tht Wagner dealt with the problems of the philosophy of history, launching forth a number of pseudo-propositions that explain simply nothing. It is a typically Teutonic manner, requiring for its most perfect exhibition nothing more than a half-comprehension of any question under the sun. It is somewhat strange that Wagner's panegyrists should have followed his lead so blindly in discussions of this kind, and have sung paeans in his praise as a great and original thinker. Nothing could more clearly prove Wagner's incompetence to handle a philosophical question than this *banal* rhetoric about the "annulling of the State," "the free self-determining individual," and the rest of it. . . . [No] one with a grain of philosophical ability will set about the business in the manner of Wagner, retailing foolish platitudes instead of arguing, and maundering for pages together about those precious entities "the State," "Society," and "the individual." There is no special merit in multiplying darkness in this way in quarters where there is already too little light; and it is a hopeless absurdity for a musician, with no ratiocinative ability to begin with, no habits of cool, persistent, objective thought, and no training in the special subjects he is so fain to meddle with, to inflict his frothy rhetoric upon an unoffending world. One blames him and his thoroughgoing worshippers only in so far as they attempt to handle subjects with which they are quite incompetent to deal; and one's objection to their voluminous writings is not that they expound wrong or doubtful theories, but that their pseudo-demonstrations are mere shoddy, having as little relation to the subjects they are actually concerned with as a seventeenth-century divine's commentary on Genesis has with modern Darwinism. With the best will in the world, indeed, and with all one's admiration for Wagner's stupendous musical genius, it is sometimes hard to feel well-disposed towards him when reading his prose works. To say that the root of all our social misery is money, and that in "property" originate "all the crimes in myth and in history," is to place oneself almost outside the pale of serious discussion. (pp. 874-75)

[In] the *Ring* Wagner was simply preaching a scheme of philosophy purely personal to himself. All artists, of course, tend to express in their works their own congenital or acquired leanings towards this or that view of life. The difference between these and Wagner is, however, enormous. One does not urge it against any artist that he sings his own moods and desires, so long as these are capable of being bent towards and comprehended in an artistic effect. . . . A novel that is a tract is bad enough; a poem that is a tract is infinitely worse; but what shall be said of a musical drama that is a tract? The thorough-going Wagner-worshipper may object to the term as being irreverent, and missing its mark by over-statement; he would prefer to speak of the "philosophy" of the *Ring.* "Philosophy," however, is a somewhat more dignified word than suits the occasion. Most artworks that set out to "prove" something are flawed at the commencement; if you take them as works of art, ignoring the argumentation, the latter seems somewhat superfluous; while if you ask yourself whether the premises of the work really lead to the conclusion the author has aimed at, you are as likely to disagree as to agree with him. (pp. 875-76)

Now the scheme of the *Ring,* in so far as it leaves the broad currents of human passion, and affects to preach a social or philosophical evangel, is essentially a childish one. Wagner has shown considerable art in the way he has welded the various sagas together in his poem; it was not an easy task, and he has performed it for the most part with signal success. The music, again, in its best moments is unapproachable, and even in its lapses from that high standard is worthy of the admiration due to a triumph almost achieved. But Wagner would have been offended at the suggestion that the *Ring* was to be looked upon merely as a good dramatic poem, set to immortal music. If there was one point upon which he was more positive than any other, it was the stupidity of regarding his works as mere operas—a mere combination of music and poetry. They were *Dramas;* and not merely dramas in the ordinary sense of the word, but lights upon man and the universe, elucidations of problems of life and art and conduct. He was a born preacher; and if you did not care to pay attention to his sermon, he did not wish you to listen to his words as you would simply to an oratorical performance. . . . [Wagner] held that a piece of psychological portraiture that was impossible to the mere actor, dependent as he is upon mere words, was rendered possible to the singer by the expressive power of music.

> I declare . . . that not even the most eminent actor, of our own or bygone times, could solve the task of a perfect portrayal of Tannhäuser's character on the lines laid down in the above analysis; and I meet the question: 'How could I hold it possible for an opera-singer to fulfil it?' by the simple answer that to *music* alone could the draft of such a task be offered, and only a dramatic *singer,* just through the aid of music, can be in the position to fulfil it. Where a player would seek in vain, among the means of recitation, for the expression wherewithal to give this character success, to the singer that expression is self-offered in the music.

And that this passage bears out the interpretation I have put upon it—that it correlates with a hundred other passages of unconscious self-revelation—may be seen from the fact that Wagner regarded *the music* of the *Ring* as affording the true key to the comprehension of its philosophy.

> I now realise myself . . . how much of the whole spirit and meaning of my poem is only made clear by the music; I cannot now, for my life, even look at the words without the musical accompaniment.

This does not mean merely that by the system of leading motives a light that would otherwise be lacking is thrown upon certain scenes and incidents. One has only to understand the peculiar psychology of Wagner, and the exaggerated stress he laid upon the power of music in the drama, to see that to *his* mind the philosophy of the *Ring* was not only revealed by the music, but made clearer, more convincing, more universal than could possibly have been done by words.

Upon this point Wagner certainly deceived himself. At the risk of repetition, let me say once more that from beginning to end of his career, he laid down for universal acceptance ideas and theories that were purely personal to himself, and that he was unable to conceive how the whole world, when it came to its senses, could think differently from him. He avowed to Uhlig his belief that the poem of the *Ring* was "the greatest ever written"; and to Roeckel he wrote that he was certain the hearer would see the philosophy of the drama as the composer had conceived it. His faith in his own philosophical ideas, his belief in their importance for the regeneration of the universe, would be grotesque if it were not so pathetic. His purely musical gift, which has never been equalled among men, he seemed to lay comparatively little stress upon; while he constantly troubled

himself, his correspondents, his readers and his hearers, with speculations in philosophy and other subjects for which he had only the most mediocre capacity. . . . [This] was the man, and this the mind, that preached in season and out of season upon questions of philosophy, and economics, and history, and aesthetics, and sociology; that really felt a mission to give to the world, not only in prose but in a drama, the true solution of the problem of human existence.

For that, finally, is what the *Ring* pretends to do. . . . [Wagner] was living, as he always did, in a mental world of fog and mist, wherein everything took the strangest of forms. His essay on the *Nibelungen,* written at that time, is still worth reading as an example of the most approved Teutonic apriorism; a purely historical subject is treated from the point of view of the most abstract dialectics, and historical events, depending upon all kinds of economic, social, and military forces, are made to stand as "moments" in a development that follows its dialectical course like a piece of pre-arranged clockwork. He was not alone in this manner of writing history in Germany just then; other men were doing it almost as serenely and as absurdly as himself. The only things worth wondering about are, first, how a musician who could treat history and sociology in this, the easiest, the most primitive, the most *banal* of all possible methods, could ever have been held up to our adoring gaze as a great thinker; and, second, how it is that those who have shrugged their shoulders in quiet tolerance over Wagner's philosophy, as expresed in the *Nibelungen* and other prose works, should have failed to pass a similar criticism upon the philosophy of the *Ring*.

For surely one has only to read that poem with one's eyes open to be convinced that Wagner was labouring under the most pathetic delusion when he thought he was contributing anything of the slightest value to the intellectual store of the race. It is quite unnecessary for his disciples to take such infinite pains to prove that Wagner was a Schopenhauerite before ever he read a line of Schopenhauer. That is just the trouble; he had already certain vague innate notions as to renunciation and redemption, and Schopenhauer, so far as Wagner could understand him, gave a support to these notions. He took the philosopher up, not because of his interest in philosophy, but because of his interest in his own ideas. (pp. 876-80)

[The *Ring*] was, in fact, simply a moral treatise on the wrongness of wrong and the rightness of right—not a particularly illuminative philosophy. As he went on, however, he discovered, according to his own account, that he was "unconsciously being guided by a wholly different, infinitely more profound intuition, and that instead of conceiving a phase in the development of the world, I had grasped the very meaning and essence of the world itself in all its possible phases and had realised its nothingness; the consequence of which was, that as I was true to my living intuitions and not to my abstract ideas in my completed work, something quite different saw the light from what I had originally intended." This "something quite different" was the making of Wotan the centre of the whole drama, as the embodiment of the principle of renunciation. Wagner, in fact, was suffering from a very bad attack of Schopenhauerism, partly congenital, and partly induced. There is undoubtedly a touch of old-world grandeur even in the more metaphysical portions of the *Ring;* but that effect is produced mainly by the nobility of the music. On the purely philosophical side, upon which Wagner laid so much stress, the scheme is hopelessly mediocre in conception; it is just a very dull sermon on liberty and law. Fricka, as the representative of conventional law and order, is as hopeless a lay figure as one could meet; and all the other characters, in so far as they do not interest us on the purely human side, in so far as they merely pose as symbols of various parts of the social structure, are not only dull but foolish. (pp. 880-81)

That the so-called "philosophy" of the *Ring* is merely the mediocre sentiment of a man incapable of thinking out the great problems he was interested in, must, I think, be the verdict of every one who considers it on its merits, apart from the glamour of the music. (p. 882)

> *Ernest Newman, "Wagner's 'Ring' and Its Philosophy," in* The Fortnightly Review, *n.s. Vol. LXIII, No. CCCLXXVIII, June 1, 1898, pp. 867-84.*

BERNARD SHAW   (essay date 1898)

[*Shaw is generally considered the best-known dramatist to write in the English language since Shakespeare. He is closely identified with the intellectual revival of the British theater, and in his dramatic theory he advocates eliminating romantic conventions in favor of a theater of ideas, grounded in realism. During the late nineteenth century, Shaw was a prominent literary, art, music, and drama critic, and his reviews were known for their biting wit and brilliance. Here, Shaw interprets* The Nibelung's Ring *as an allegory of class struggle.*]

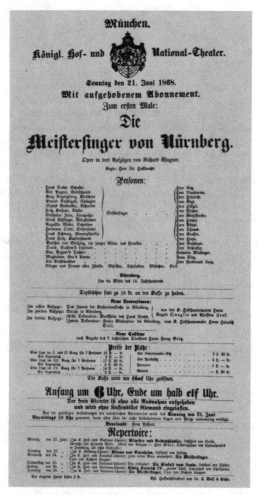

Playbill announcing the premiere of The Mastersingers of Nuremberg.

[*The Ring*], with all its gods and giants and dwarfs, its water-maidens and Valkyries, its wishing-cap, magic ring, enchanted sword, and miraculous treasure, is a drama of today, and not of a remote and fabulous antiquity. It could not have been written before the second half of the nineteenth century, because it deals with events which were only then consummating themselves. Unless the spectator recognizes in it an image of the life he is himself fighting his way through, it must needs appear to him a monstrous development of the Christmas pantomimes, spun out here and there into intolerable lengths of dull conversation by the principal baritone. Fortunately, even from this point of view, *The Ring* is full of extraordinarily attractive episodes, both orchestral and dramatic. (pp. 1-2)

[The] curtain goes up and you see . . . the depths of the Rhine, with three strange fairy fishes, half water-maidens, singing and enjoying themselves exuberantly. They are not singing barcarolles or ballads about the Lorely and her fated lovers, but simply trolling any nonsense that comes into their heads in time to the dancing of the water and the rhythm of their swimming. It is the golden age; and the attraction of this spot for the Rhine maidens is a lump of the Rhine gold, which they value, in an entirely uncommercial way, for its bodily beauty and splendor. Just at present it is eclipsed, because the sun is not striking down through the water.

Presently there comes a poor devil of a dwarf stealing along the slippery rocks of the river bed, a creature with energy enough to make him strong of body and fierce of passion, but with a brutish narrowness of intelligence and selfishness of imagination: too stupid to see that his own welfare can only be compassed as part of the welfare of the world, too full of brute force not to grab vigorously at his own gain. Such dwarfs are quite common in London. He comes now with a fruitful impulse in him, in search of what he lacks in himself, beauty, lightness of heart, imagination, music. The Rhine maidens, representing all these to him, fill him with hope and longing; and he never considers that he has nothing to offer that they could possibly desire, being by natural limitation incapable of seeing anything from anyone else's point of view. With perfect simplicity, he offers himself as a sweetheart to them. But they are thoughtless, elemental, only half real things, much like modern young ladies. That the poor dwarf is repulsive to their sense of physical beauty and their romantic conception of heroism, that he is ugly and awkward, greedy and ridiculous, disposes for them of his claim to live and love. They mock him atrociously, pretending to fall in love with him at first sight, and then slipping away and making game of him, heaping ridicule and disgust on the poor wretch until he is beside himself with mortification and rage. They forget him when the water begins to glitter in the sun, and the gold to reflect its glory. They break into ecstatic worship of their treasure; and though they know the parable of Klondyke quite well, they have no fear that the gold will be wrenched away by the dwarf, since it will yield to no one who has not forsworn love for it, and it is in pursuit of love that he has come to them. They forget that they have poisoned that desire in him by their mockery and denial of it, and that he now knows that life will give him nothing that he cannot wrest from it by the Plutonic power. It is just a if some poor, rough, vulgar, coarse fellow were to offer to take his part in aristocratic society, and be snubbed into the knowledge that only as a millionaire could he ever hope to bring that society to his feet and buy himself a beautiful and refined wife. His choice is forced on him. He forswears love as thousands of us forswear it every day; and in a moment the gold is in his grasp, and he disappears in the depths, leaving the waterfairies vainly screaming ''Stop thief!'' whilst the river seems to plunge into darkness and sink from us as we rise to the cloud regions above.

And now, what forces are there in the world to resist Alberic, our dwarf, in his new character of sworn plutocrat? He is soon at work wielding the power of the gold. For his gain, hordes of his fellow-creatures are thenceforth condemned to slave miserably, overground and underground, lashed to their work by the invisible whip of starvation. They never see him, any more than the victims of our ''dangerous trades'' ever see the shareholders whose power is nevertheless everywhere, driving them to destruction. The very wealth they create with their labor becomes an additional force to impoverish them; for as fast as they make it it slips from their hands into the hands of their master, and makes him mightier than ever. You can see the process for yourself in every civilized country today, where millions of people toil in want and disease to heap up more wealth for our Alberics, laying up nothing for themselves, except sometimes horrible and agonizing disease and the certainty of premature death. All this part of the story is frightfully real, frightfully present, frightfully modern; and its effects on our social life are so ghastly and ruinous that we no longer know enough of happiness to be discomposed by it. It is only the poet, with his vision of what life might be, to whom these things are unendurable. If we were a race of poets we would make an end of them before the end of this miserable century. Being a race of moral dwarfs instead, we think them highly respectable, comfortable and proper, and allow them to breed and multiply their evil in all directions. If there were no higher power in the world to work against Alberic, the end of it would be utter destruction.

Such a force there is, however; and it is called Godhead. The mysterious thing we call life organizes itself into all living shapes, bird, beast, beetle and fish, rising to the human marvel in cunning dwarfs and in laborious muscular giants, capable, these last, of enduring toil, willing to buy love and life, not with suicidal curses and renunciations, but with patient manual drudgery in the service of higher powers. And these higher powers are called into existence by the same self-organization of life still more wonderfully into rare persons who may by comparison be called gods, creatures capable of thought, whose aims extend far beyond the satisfaction of their bodily appetites and personal affections, since they perceive that it is only by the establishment of a social order founded on common bonds of moral faith that the world can rise from mere savagery. But how is this order to be set up by Godhead in a world of stupid giants, since these thoughtless ones pursue only their narrower personal ends and can by no means understand the aims of a god? Godhead, face to face with Stupidity, most compromise. Unable to enforce on the world the pure law of thought, it must resort to a mechanical law of commandments to be enforced by brute punishments and the destruction of the disobedient. And however carefully these laws are framed to represent the highest thoughts of the framers at the moment of their promulgation, before a day has elapsed that thought has grown and widened by the ceaseless evolution of life; and lo! yesterday's law already fallen out with today's thought. Yet if the high givers of that law themselves set the example of breaking it before it is a week old, they destroy all its authority with their subjects, and so break the weapon they have forged to rule them for their own good. They must therefore maintain all all costs the sanctity of the law, even when it has ceased to represent their thought; so that at last they get entangled in a network of ordinances which they no longer believe in, and

yet have made so sacred by custom and so terrible by punishment, that they cannot themselves escape from them. Thus Godhead's resort to law finally costs it half its integrity—as if a spiritual king, to gain temporal power, had plucked out one of his eyes—and it finally begins secretly to long for the advent of some power higher than itself which will destroy its artificial empire of law, and establish a true republic of free thought.

This is by no means the only difficulty in the dominion of Law. The brute force for its execution must be purchased; and the mass of its subjects must be persuaded to respect the authority which employs this force. But how is such respect to be implanted in them if they are unable to comprehend the thought of the lawgiver? Clearly, only by associating the legislative power with such displays of splendor and majesty as will impress their senses and awe their imaginations. The god turned lawgiver, in short, must be crowned Pontiff and King. Since he cannot be known to the common folk as their superior in wisdom, he must be known to them as their superior in riches, as the dweller in castles, the wearer of gold and purple, the eater of mighty feasts, the commander of armies, and the wielder of powers of life and death, of salvation and damnation after death. Something may be done in this way without corruption whilst the golden age still endures. Your gods may not prevail with the dwarfs; but they may go to these honest giants who will give a day's work for a day's pay, and induce them to build for Godhead a mighty fortress, complete with hall and chapel, tower and bell, for the sake of the homesteads that will grow up in security round that church-castle. This only, however, whilst the golden age lasts. The moment the Plutonic power is let loose, and the loveless Alberic comes into the field with his corrupting millions, the gods are face to face with destruction; since Alberic, able with invisible hunger-whip to force the labor of the dwarfs and to buy the services of the giants, can outshine all the temporal shows and splendors of the golden age, and make himself master of the world, unless the gods, with their bigger brains, can capture his gold. This, the dilemma of the Church today, is the situation created by the exploit of Alberic in the depths of the Rhine.

From the bed of the river we rise into cloudy regions, and finally come out into the clear in a meadow, where Wotan, the god of gods, and his consort Fricka lie sleeping. Wotan, you will observe, has lost one eye; and you will presently learn that he plucked it out voluntarily as the price to be paid for his alliance with Fricka, who in return has brought to him as her dowry all the powers of Law. The meadow is on the brink of a ravine, beyond which, towering on distant heights, stands Godhome, a mighty castle, newly built as a house of state for the one-eyed god and his all-ruling wife. Wotan has not yet seen this castle except in his dreams: two giants have just built it for him whilst he slept; and the reality is before him for the first time when Fricka wakes him. In that majestic burg he is to rule with her and through her over the humble giants, who have eyes to gape at the glorious castles their own hands have built from his design, but no brains to design castles for themselves, or to comprehend divinity. As a god, he is to be great, secure, and mighty; but he is also to be passionless, affectionless, wholly impartial; for Godhead, if it is to live with Law, must have no weaknesses, no respect for persons. All such sweet littlenesses must be left to the humble stupid giants to make their toil sweet to them; and the god must, after all, pay for Olympian power the same price the dwarf has paid for Plutonic power.

Wotan has forgotten this in his dreams of greatness. Not so Fricka. What she is thinking of is this price that Wotan has consented to pay, in token whereof he has promised this day to hand over to the giants Fricka's sister, the goddess Freia, with her golden love-apples. When Fricka reproaches Wotan with having selfishly forgotten this, she finds that he, like herself, is not prepared to go through with his bargain, and that he is trusting to another great world-force, the Lie . . . , to help him to trick the giants out of their reward. But this force does not dwell in Wotan himself, but in another, a god over whom he has triumphed, one Loki, the god of Intellect, Argument, Imagination, Illusion, and Reason. Loki has promised to deliver him from his contract, and to cheat the giants for him; but he has not arrived to keep his word: indeed, as Fricka bitterly points out, why should not the Lie fail Wotan, since such failure is the very essence of him?

The giants come soon enough; and Freia flies to Wotan for protection against them. Their purposes are quite honest; and they have no doubt of the god's faith. There stands their part of the contract fulfilled, stone on stone, port and pinnacle all faithfully finished from Wotan's design by their mighty labor. They have come undoubtingly for their agreed wage. Then there happens what is to them an incredible, inconceivable thing. The god begins to shuffle. There are no moments in life more tragic than those in which the humble common man, the manual worker, leaving with implicit trust all high affairs to his betters, and reverencing them wholly as worthy of that trust, even to the extent of accepting as his rightful function the saving of them from all roughening and coarsening drudgeries, first discovers that they are corrupt, greedy, unjust and treacherous. The shock drives a ray of prophetic light into one giant's mind, and gives him a momentary eloquence. In that moment he rises above his stupid gianthood, and earnestly warns the Son of Light that all his power and eminence of priesthood, godhood, and kingship must stand or fall with the unbearable cold greatness of the incorruptible law-giver. But Wotan, whose assumed character of law-giver is altogether false to his real passionate nature, despises the rebuke; and the giant's ray of insight is lost in the murk of his virtuous indignation.

In the midst of the wrangle, Loki comes at last, excusing himself for being late on the ground that he has been detained by a matter of importance which he has promised to lay before Wotan. When pressed to give his mind to the business immediately in hand, and to extricate Wotan from his dilemma, he has nothing to say except that the giants are evidently altogether in the right. The castle has been duly built: he has tried every stone of it, and found the work firstrate: there is nothing to be done but pay the price agreed upon by handing over Freia to the giants. The gods are furious; and Wotan passionately declares that he only consented to the bargain on Loki's promise to find a way for him out of it. But Loki says no: he has promised to find a way out if any such way exist, but not to make a way if there is no way. He has wandered over the whole earth in search of some treasure great enough to buy Freia back from the giants; but in all the world he has found nothing for which Man will give up Woman. And this, by the way, reminds him of the matter he had promised to lay before Wotan. The Rhine maidens have complained to him of Alberic's theft of their gold; and he mentions it as a curious exception to his universal law of the unpurchasable preciousness of love, that this gold-robber has forsworn love for the sake of the fabulous riches of the Plutonic empire and the mastery of the world through its power.

No sooner is the tale told than the giants stoop lower than the dwarf. Alberic forswore love only when it was denied to him

and made the instrument for cruelly murdering his self-respect. But the giants, with love within their reach, with Freia and her golden apples in their hands, offer to give her up for the treasure of Alberic. Observe, it is the treasure alone that they desire. They have no fierce dreams of dominion over their superiors, or of moulding the world to any conceptions of their own. They are neither clever nor ambitious: they simply covet money. Alberic's gold: that is their demand, or else Freia, as agreed upon, whom they now carry off as hostage, leaving Wotan to consider their ultimatum.

Freia gone, the gods begin to wither and age: her golden apples, which they so lightly bargained away, they now find to be a matter of life and death to them; for not even the gods can live on Law and Godhead alone, be their castles ever so splendid. Loki alone is unaffected: the Lie, with all its cunning wonders, its glistenings and shiftings and mirages, is a mere appearance: it has no body and needs no food. What is Wotan to do? Loki sees the answer clearly enough: he must bluntly rob Alberic. There is nothing to prevent him except moral scruple; for Alberic, after all, is a poor, dim, dwarfed, credulous creature whom a god can outsee and a lie can outwit. Down, then, Wotan and Loki plunge into the mine where Alberic's slaves are piling up wealth for him under the invisible whip.

This gloomy place need not be a mine: it might just as well be a match-factory, with yellow phosphorus, phossy jaw, a large dividend, and plenty of clergymen shareholders. Or it might be a whitelead factory, or a chemical works, or a pottery, or a railway shunting yard, or a tailoring shop, or a little ginsodden laundry, or a bakehouse, or a big shop, or any other of the places where human life and welfare are daily sacrificed in order that some greedy foolish creature may be able to hymn exultantly to his Plutonic idol:

> Thou mak'st me eat whilst others starve,
> And sing while others do lament:
> Such unto me Thy blessings are,
> As if I were Thine only care.

In the mine, which resounds with the clinking anvils of the dwarfs toiling miserably to heap up treasure for their master, Alberic has set his brother Mime—more familiarly, Mimmy—to make him a helmet. Mimmy dimly sees that there is some magic in this helmet, and tries to keep it; but Alberic wrests it from him, and shows him, to his cost, that it is the veil of the invisible whip, and that he who wears it can appear in what shape he will, or disappear from view altogether. This helmet is a very common article in our streets, where it generally takes the form of a tall hat. It makes a man invisible as a shareholder, and changes him into various shapes, such as a pious Christian, a subscriber to hospitals, a benefactor of the poor, a model husband and father, a shrewd, practical independent Englishman, and what not, when he is really a pitiful parasite on the commonwealth, consuming a great deal, and producing nothing, feeling nothing, knowing nothing, believing nothing, and doing nothing except what all the rest do, and that only because he is afraid not to do it, or at least pretend to do it.

When Wotan and Loki arrive, Loki claims Alberic as an old acquaintance. But the dwarf has no faith in these civil strangers: Greed instinctively mistrusts Intellect, even in the garb of Poetry and the company of Godhead, whilst envying the brilliancy of the one and the dignity of the other. Alberic breaks out at them with a terrible boast of the power now within his grasp. He paints for them the world as it will be when his dominion over it is complete, when the soft airs and green mosses of its valleys shall be changed into smoke, slag, and filth; when slavery, disease, and squalor, soothed by drunkenness and mastered by the policeman's baton, shall become the foundation of society; and when nothing shall escape ruin except such pretty places and pretty women as he may like to buy for the slaking of his own lusts. In that kingdom of evil he sees that there will be no power but his own. These gods, with their moralities and legalities and intellectual subtlety, will go under and be starved out of existence. He bids Wotan and Loki beware of it; and his "Hab' Acht!" is hoarse, horrible, and sinister. Wotan is revolted to the very depths of his being: he cannot stifle the execration that bursts from him. But Loki is unaffected: he has no moral passion: indignation is as absurd to him as enthusiasm. He finds it exquisitely amusing—having a touch of the comic spirit in him—that the dwarf, in stirring up the moral fervor of Wotan, has removed his last moral scruple about becoming a thief. Wotan will now rob the dwarf without remorse; for is it not positively his highest duty to take this power out of such evil hands and use it himself in the interests of Godhead? On the loftiest moral grounds, he lets Loki do his worst.

A little cunningly disguised flattery makes short work of Alberic. Loki pretends to be afraid of him; and he swallows that bait unhesitatingly. But how, enquires Loki, is he to guard against the hatred of his million slaves? Will they not steal from him, whilst he sleeps, the magic ring, the symbol of his power, which he has forged from the gold of the Rhine? "You think yourself very clever," sneers Alberic, and then begins to boast of the enchantments of the magic helmet. Loki refuses to believe in such marvels without witnessing them. Alberic, only too glad to show off his powers, puts on the helmet and transforms himself into a monstrous serpent. Loki gratifies him by pretending to be frightened out of his wits, but ventures to remark that it would be better still if the helmet could transform its owner into some tiny creature that could hide and spy in the smallest cranny. Alberic promptly transforms himself into a toad. In an instant Wotan's foot is on him; Loki tears away the helmet; they pinion him, and drag him away a prisoner up through the earth to the meadow by the castle.

There, to pay for his freedom, he has to summon his slaves from the depths to place all the treasure they have heaped up for him at the feet of Wotan. Then he demands his liberty; but Wotan must have the ring as well. And here the dwarf, like the giant before him, feels the very foundations of the world shake beneath him at the discovery of his own base cupidity in a higher power. That evil should, in its loveless desperation, create malign powers which Godhead could not create, seems but natural justice to him. But that Godhead should steal those malign powers from evil, and wield them itself, is a monstrous perversion; and his appeal to Wotan to forego it is almost terrible in its conviction of wrong. It is of no avail. Wotan falls back again on virtuous indignation. He reminds Alberic that he stole the gold from the Rhine maidens, and takes the attitude of the just judge compelling a restitution of stolen goods. Alberic, knowing perfectly well that the judge is taking the goods to put them in his own pocket, has the ring torn from his finger, and is once more as poor as he was when he came slipping and stumbling among the slimy rocks in the bed of the Rhine.

This is the way of the world. In older times, when the Christian laborer was drained dry by the knightly spendthrift, and the spendthrift was drained by the Jewish usurer, Church and State, religion and law, seized on the Jew and drained him as a Christian duty. When the forces of lovelessness and greed had built up our own sordid capitalist systems, driven by invisible proprietorship, robbing the poor, defacing the earth, and forcing themselves as a universal curse even on the generous and humane, then religion and law and intellect, which would never themselves have discovered such systems, their natural bent being towards welfare, economy, and life instead of towards corruption, waste, and death, nevertheless did not scruple to seize by fraud and force these powers of evil on pretence of using them for good. And it inevitably happens that when the Church, the Law, and all the Talents have made common cause to rob the people, the Church is far more vitally harmed by that unfaithfulness to itself than its more mechanical confederates; so that finally they turn on their discredited ally and rob the Church, with the cheerful co-operation of Loki, as in France and Italy for instance.

The twin giants come back with their hostage, in whose presence Godhead blooms again. The gold is ready for them; but now that the moment has come for parting with Freia the gold does not seem so tempting; and they are sorely loth to let her go. Not unless there is gold enough to utterly hide her from them—not until the heap has grown so that they can see nothing but gold—until money has come between them and every human feeling, will they part with her. There is not gold enough to accomplish this: however cunningly Loki spreads it, the glint of Freia's hair is still visible to Giant Fafnir, and the magic helmet must go on the heap to shut it out. Even then Fafnir's brother, Fasolt, can catch a beam from her eye through a chink, and is rendered incapable thereby of forswearing her. There is nothing to stop that chink but the ring; and Wotan is as greedily bent on keeping that as Alberic himself was; nor can the other gods persuade him that Freia is worth it, since for the highest god, love is not the highest good, but only the universal delight that bribes all living things to travail with renewed life. Life itself, with its accomplished marvels and its infinite potentialities, is the only force that Godhead can worship. Wotan does not yield until he is reached by the voice of the fruitful earth, that before he or the dwarfs or the giants or the Law or the Lie or any of these things were, had the seed of them all in her bosom, and the seed perhaps of something higher even than himself, that shall one day supersede him and cut the tangles and alliances and compromises that already have cost him one of his eyes. When Erda, the First Mother of life, rises from her sleeping-place in the heart of the earth, and warns him to yield the ring, he obeys her; the ring is added to the heap of gold; and all sense of Freia is cut off from the giants.

But now what Law is left to these two poor stupid laborers whereby one shall yield to the other any of the treasure for which they have each paid the whole price in surrendering Freia? They look by mere habit to the god to judge for them; but he, with his heart stirring towards higher forces than himself, turns with disgust from these lower forces. They settle it as two wolves might; and Fafnir batters his brother dead with his staff. It is a horrible thing to see and hear, to anyone who knows how much blood has been shed in the world in just that way by its brutalized toilers, honest fellows enough until their betters betrayed them. Fafnir goes off with his booty. It is quite useless to him. He has neither the cunning nor the ambition to establish the Plutonic empire with it. Merely to prevent others from getting it is the only purpose it brings him. He piles it in a cave; transforms himself into a dragon by the helmet; and devotes his life to guarding it, as much a slave to it as a jailer is to his prisoner. He had much better have thrown it all back into the Rhine and transformed himself into the shortest-lived animal that enjoys at least a brief run in the sunshine. His case, however, is far too common to be surprising. The world is overstocked with persons who sacrifice all their affections, and madly trample and batter down their fellows to obtain riches of which, when they get them, they are unable to make the smallest use, and to which they become the most miserable slaves. (pp. 7-24)

> Bernard Shaw, in his The Perfect Wagnerite: A Commentary on the Niblung's Ring, 1898. Reprint by Dodd, Mead & Company, 1936, 151 p.

[H. H. STATHAM]   (essay date 1899)

[Statham explicates Wagner's theory of a composite work of art as expressed in The Artwork of the Future.*]*

The essay on **'The Art-work of the Future' ('Das Kunstwerk der Zukunft')** is a kind of reasoned rhapsody on the future conditions of art, which it was no doubt a *tour de force* to have turned off in two months, and which, in spite of its exaggerated and sometime almost frenzied tone both of thought and diction, is a really remarkable production. The two leading ideas pervading it are—first, that the great and true art-power of the future lies in the people, *das Volk* (a word which the translator chooses to represent by 'Folk,' which, in spite of philological relation, is not the true English analogue of *Volk*); and secondly, that the part of music acting alone had been played out, and the future chance for artistic production lay in the combination of what he calls 'the three varieties of Humanistic art'—Dance, Tone, and Poetry, or the union of movement, music, and speech combined in one artistic conception. The first position is of course the same doctrine which William Morris was incessantly preaching in regard to architecture and the decorative arts, and which Utopian and Socialist architects continue to preach; a prophecy of a glorious resuscitation of architecture when the artisans *en masse* shall be the true designers or makers of architecture, each executing his portion of the design under his own free inspiration. Wagner does not follow out and face this result in regard to music—he perhaps instinctively felt in what paradoxes it would land him, and he stops short at generalities. The most forcible point he makes— one which compels one to pause and consider at all events— is that the bane of art is that it should be regarded not as a need, but as a luxury—'this crack-brained need-without-a-need,' as he calls it; and that '*want,* which shall teach the world to recognise its own true need,' is to deliver us from this artificial state:—

> Want will cut short the hell of luxury; it will teach the tortured, need-lacking spirits whom this hell embraces in its bounds the simple, homely need of sheer human physical hunger and thirst; but in fellowship will it point us to the health-giving bread, the clear sweet springs of Nature; in fellowship shall we taste their genuine joys, and grow up in communion to veritable men. In common, too, shall we close the last link in the bond of holy necessity; and the brother kiss which seals this bond will be the *mutual Art-work of the Future*.

This sounds, no doubt, very beautiful and human (or humane), as a general conception, but it is only really applicable to artisans' art, the art of making things for actual use. So far Morris was quite right; there was a time when a man making a lock-plate or a chair or any other such object had a sort of

need to fashion it with beauty or character to his own liking, and at present he commonly has not. But the higher and more intellectually perceived forms of art have always been, and, until mankind attain all the same level of intellectual development, always will be, the enjoyment of the most cultured minority. There is an esoteric circle of those who really perceive their intellectual beauty, and delight in it and long for it . . . ; there is a pretty large circle of those who simulate the same enjoyment because they think that it is right, and that they ought to enjoy great works of art; and there is the large mass of people who neither understand nor pretend to care about art. This is sad, but it is the truth; and the fact is that an art which appealed to the 'simple and homely needs' of human nature would be but a simple and homely art.

The second and far longer portion of the essay, that which sketches the course by which the three separate forms of artistic expression are supposed to have at last blended into one, is full of interesting passages in spite of a good deal of rhodomontade, and contains thoughts of real value. As to one point in it, the idea that dance-rhythm sought to 'find again and know her own true nature in the art of tone,' and was therefore its parent, we have before observed that there seems no good reason to assume that the dance preceded the tune; in fact, the experience of everyday life suggests the contrary: it is the music which awakens the desire to dance, even with unsophisticated children, much more often and more imperiously than the act of dancing awakens the desire to sing or play an accompaniment to the movement. So that here we think the historic conception is at fault, or at least open to much question. It is a singular discrepancy between theory and practice, too, that while Wagner affirms that as rhythm is the *mind* of Dance, the abstract summary of corporeal motion, so is it, on the other hand, 'the moving self-progressive *skeleton* of Tone' . . . , yet in his own operas he showed a continually increasing effort to shake off the fetters of rhythm from the music; even employing complicated devices of syncopation to break up and elude the bar-accent. And when we arrive at the conclusion to which this long essay leads up, it is difficult to avoid the conviction that instead of the conclusion being the result of the argument, the argument was consciously framed to conduct to a foregone conclusion—one which would fortify his own position. Wagner never had any genius for, any grasp over, artistic form in instrumental music on a large scale; he had occasionally essayed such work, but never with much success, as he must himself have felt and indeed may be said to have tacitly admitted. But he had great ambition, a passionate determination to play a great part in the world in connexion with music; by assiduous study and practice he had become a mastercraftsman in the marshalling of harmonic combinations and in the knowledge of what could be done with instruments of all kinds; he had a strong perception of scenic effect; and if he had no literary faculty of style, he had dramatic and poetic ideas. If he could do nothing with extended musical form, he could handle with great effect episodical music dependent on and suggested by dramatic action and situation, and he would undertake to prove to the world that the form which he could not handle was no longer worth handling. (pp. 105-07)

[In] many essays longer and shorter, and under varying titles, we seem to find much the same thing said over and over again in slightly different language, and always with a diffuseness which serves rather to obscure than to emphasize the author's meaning. The essay on **'Art and Revolution,'** which in the main is only another statement of the Socialistic view of Art already referred to in connexion with the **'Art-work of the**

Future,' closes, however, with a definite and concisely stated creed, viz. that we should 'erect the altar of the Future, in Life as in the living Art, to the two sublimest teachers of mankind:— Jesus, who suffered for all men; and Apollo, who raised them to their joyous dignity'; in other words, Greek beauty and joyousness, and Christian sympathy and seriousness; or we might take the two as representative of objective and subjective art. The question is whether such two altars can ever be erected in one temple of the human race; whether they do not represent ideals of worship, or of Art, which are mutually exclusive; either may be predominant at one period or another of human developement, but one may doubt whether Christ and Apollo can ever sincerely be worshipped simultaneously. (pp. 108-09)

[*H. H. Statham*], *"The Writings of Wagner,"* in The Edinburgh Review, *Vol. CLXXXIX, No. CCCLXXXVII, January, 1899, pp. 96-118.*.

W. E. WALTER (essay date 1904)

[*Emphasizing Wagner's skill as a composer and dramatist, Walter discusses Wagner's treatment of the Grail legend. For additional discussions of Wagner's use of myth, see excerpts by Friedrich Nietzsche (1872), Alfred A. Wheeler (1883), Thomas Mann (1933 and 1937), Theodor Adorno (1937-38), and Norbert Fuerst (1966).*]

In his very interesting *A Study of Wagner,* Ernest Newman, speaking of *Parsifal* says: "Looking at the strange group of beings the like of which have scarcely been seen on the stage before or since, one becomes vividly conscious of the genius of the man who could breathe musical life into them, and of the immense superiority of his dramatic gift to that of any other musician." This, perhaps, is the first feature to be impressed upon one who has studied this curious music-drama with a mind moderately free from prejudices, for or against. And the more deeply one goes into it, the better acquainted one becomes with the sources from which Wagner derived his theme, the greater becomes the wonder at his achievement. *Der Ring des Nibelungen* is a mighty work, a tremendous monument to the memory of the genius who created it. *Tristan und Isolde* is one of the most beautiful and majestic structures ever reared by musician or dramatist. By almost common consent *Parsifal* is the equal, musically and dramatically, of neither of them. Yet it is quite the most wonderful when one considers the theme and the problems it presents, both to the musician and to the dramatist. . . . [*Tristan and Isolde*] contains all the primitive merits of the Siegfried legend with the additional and very important one of singleness and simplicity of theme and action. Its theme is love, which has the most universal appeal of all. Its action, so simple in its progress, involves few problems for the dramatist to deal with. No warring gods and knavish gnomes, no mixture of the divine and the human are there to raise almost insoluble complications. There are a man and a woman who love when they should not and pay the penalty of their mutual sin. All else is subordinate.

But when one turns to *Parsifal,* how different are the conditions! Is there anything seemingly more undramatic in its form, substance, or essence than the Legend of the Holy Grail as it has come to us from the past? Did ever man set at a more hopeless task than Wagner when he began to make a drama out of the inchoate mass of incident which Wolfram von Eschenbach could not relate in less than twenty-five thousand lines? The very idea seems preposterous. Yet Wagner did it, and so successfully that he can hold one in breathless interest for four hours. The spell he casts about one dissipates quickly,

but in the presence of the work there is no denying its potency. In writing *Parsifal,* Wagner has done the impossible, he has wrought a miracle and placed a final crown of glory on his fame. (pp. 499-500)

It has often been said that if the Legend of the Holy Grail was to have been prepared for stage use, either with or without music, the work needed a man with Wagner's curious combination of mental traits. In other words, Wagner is the only man that has lived who could see the possibilities in such a theme, and he was able to do so because he read into the story, perhaps unconsciously, certain ideas concerning life which he wished to give to the world. And he was able in a measure to realise these possibilities in his drama first, because he was a musician of very individual genius, and second, because he was born with an instinct for the stage almost as strong as his musical impulse. He was instinctively a playwright and master of theatrical effect, and it is this side of his genius that seems not yet to have received its due share of credit. We are told on the one hand that Wagner saw and thought in the terms of music; in other words, while he believed that in selecting a theme he worked only for his symmetrical and well-balanced combination of the musical, dramatic, and plastic arts, reduced to its essence, he chose and arranged everything subordinate to the musical impulse which was striving within him. He was first and foremost a musician with his other qualities secondary to that. We are told also that he was first and foremost a philosopher who had certain messages he would give to the world and that music and drama were merely the humble servants of this purpose. This in substance is the creed of that school of extreme Wagnerists who look on him as one of the great philosophic minds of the world, by some strange trick of fortune, enabled to supplement his ponderous treatises and essays with musicodramatic illustrations.

It is dangerous to attempt the analysis of the artistic impulses of any genius, and Wagner's whole nature was of such complexity, and contained so many contradictions that with him the task is more than usually difficult. Yet it is impossible to admit the merit of the theory that he was above all else a philosopher—even setting aside the question whether he was a good or a bad one.

Undoubtedly when he finally began to write the poem of *Parsifal* he was wrapped up in certain ideas of renunciation, of redemption by pity, of vegetarianism and the like. He was at last completely under the influence of Schopenhauer, with the tinge of mysticism which had always been in him of deeper hue than ever. Yet it is a fair question to ask if it is not possible he would still have used this theme had he had quite another lot of ideas to give to a waiting world.

Wagner was one of those happy individuals whose ideas however changeable they may be, are always the only correct ones. He had complete and absolute confidence in himself, and he always saw the world and all within it through the windows of the opinion or creed he happened to be holding. He moulded everything into the form which at the moment coincided with his views. If he changed his views, he had ample dexterity with which to change the form, altogether unconscious of this mental process. But if this was true of his philosophy and of his life in general, it was not true of his music nor his stagecraft. From the time he abandoned the operatic formalities of *Rienzi,* his musical progress was steady and unbroken until it reached, in his last work, its point of perfection as a system. And so, too, during all the years he wabbled about in a philosophic swamp, seeking a panacea for human woes and miseries, his surety in dramatic construction, developed along a single line, gained continually until it reached a point of mastery that enabled him successfully to dramatise the Grail Legend.

It is a beautiful theory that Wagner hit upon the Grail Legend and used it solely because it was best fitted to be a vehicle for his philosophical disclosures. It is particularly beautiful because on it rests the assertion that *Parsifal* is a "sacred" drama. But a study of the drama in connection with its music, together with a study of the sources from which he took his material and of the manner in which he handled other mediaeval legends compels one to doubt very seriously the merit of that idea. The belief gradually but surely will come to one that it was not Wagner, the philosopher, the sociologist, that chose these subjects, but Wagner, the musician and playwright. It is a fair presumption that sooner or later he would have reached the Grail Legend, whatever his opinions as to the redemption of mankind might have been. (pp. 500-01)

Parsifal or some treatment of the Legend was all but inevitable from the time he first turned his attention to mediaeval literature. It has in a superior degree all those qualities which appealed to him as a musician. Richly romantic, strongly tinged even in its least ascetic form with old world mysticism and magic, exhibiting on the one hand the highest ideals of chivalry, and on the other the highest ideals of mediaeval religious belief, how could it help appeal to a man so richly endowed with romance and mysticism, whose music reached its highest levels in the expression of these qualities?

Moreover, we see now, since Wagner realised them, the dramatic possibilities of the theme. Putting aside the philosophy, the theology, and all the other didactic elements which he and his commentators have injected into the work, and considering it merely as an art-work, we have left a great drama in which the mediaeval atmosphere is preserved to emphasise an eternally young theme—the yielding to temptation by a man of high estate, the penalties he suffers, and his final redemption through the sacrifice of another. It is but a new way of stating a proposition found in all of Wagner's music-dramas, from *Tannhäuser* on. (p. 501)

In what way does the mystic—or magic—element in *Parsifal* differ essentially from the potion in *Tristan und Isolde?* The latter is a purely theatrical device made possible by the mediaeval atmosphere which encompasses the theme. The potion is a symbol conveniently at hand by means of which the dramatist retains the sympathy of his audience for his hero and heroine in their guilty love. It is a trick, but legitimate because it is in harmony with the atmosphere of the drama. It does not violate the verities because the audience has before it an ancient and familiar theme in which the potion is present, though really serving a different purpose.

His whole treatment of the Grail Legend betrays the feeling and instinct of the dramatist and skilled playwright in far greater degree than it does that of the philosopher. The philosophical impulse was undoubtedly there. Wagner undoubtedly believed that it was the only one which moved him, but it was decidedly subordinate, first to the musical impulse and then to the dramatic. The process could not have been other, since he was first a musician, then a dramatist, and then—at least as he considered himself—a philosopher.

It was this feeling for the stage which enabled him to make so free with the legend. He twisted it, and turned it, and distorted it in whatever way suited his purpose, just as he treated the Siegfried legend for his *Ring*.... Was it Wagner the philosopher, Wagner the preacher, who brought Klingsor, the Chateau Merveil and the Lady Orgeluse into his drama, or was it Wagner the dramatist, who was making a libretto? And how came it, if Wagner was concerned only with proclaiming anew the beauties of an ancient, sacred theme, that he shoved aside the versions which were really religious in motive and intent and took one which was purely a romance of chivalry, of an uncommonly high moral tone to be sure, but none-the-less purely a romance, in the modern sense, a novel of adventure. It cannot be that he did not know the *Joseph of Arimathea* and the *Perceval* of Robert de Boron, or the *Grand Saint Graal* and the *Queste del Saint Graal.* They were easily procurable, at least in very full synopses, and *Parsifal* contains much evidence that he was familiar with their substance. The chances are that the dramatic instinct within him compelled him to see the greater possibilities in Wolfram's version, all the more so, since that instinct had taught him that nothing is holy to the hand of the playwright when it comes to the question of devising a situation.

The final and convincing proof of this seems to be the wonderful second act, the scene of Parsifal's temptation. It is a commonplace that music without contrast loses the greater portion of its effectiveness, however inspired its themes may be. It is equally a commonplace that the vital spark of drama is the clash of interests, in its higher forms, of good and evil. Even in Wolfram's version of the Grail Legend contrast, so far as his Parsifal is concerned, is all but completely absent. (pp. 501-02)

Wagner must have realised at once that there was no drama in this Parsifal's career, nor opportunity for music. Something had to be done and his first work was to transpose the atmosphere of the monkish legend to Wolfram's poem. That alone gave him the material for his first and third acts. Then he had to provide musical contrast and dramatic interest. The musician and dramatist in him saw that the sombre beauty of the first and third acts without some relief would be unendurable. He needed a scherzo, something brisk, lively, and if wicked, all the better. He also needed a clash of interests to make his drama a vital work. Before such needs what strength have legendary traditions, however sacred and holy? With the keen scent of the playwright he finds exactly what he wants in Gawain's most celebrated adventure, the Chateau Merveil, where Klingsor, a magician through necessity, has imprisoned a large number of unfortunate ladies. Wagner lifts this bodily into his work. He eliminates the gallant Gawain; transforms such very respectable women as King Arthur's mother and her handmaidens into sirens who will lure Knights of the Grail to sin and to destruction; makes Klingsor who probably never heard of the Grail, a candidate for the brotherhood who, after paying a fearful price for admittance, failed of election, and is therefore eternally at war with it, with the sirens as his weapons; and then Wagner combines the lovely Lady Orgeluse with Kondrie, the Sorceress, the Loathly Damsel who rides on a mule and gives Parsifal several unpleasant moments. This is masterly, it is a stroke of genius, but it makes it difficult to see where Wagner has preserved his reverence for a sacred legend. Like any other artist he hesitates at nothing to make his work as nearly perfect as possible, and thus he gets a scherzo for his music and a clash of interests for his drama. It is the artist, the musician, the dramatist that has done this, not the philosopher and sociologist. To be sure he is enunciating through his work his own individual views of sin, its punishment and the redemption of the sinner; but it seems impossible to take them seriously as a part of the drama. They are not essential, whether one agrees with them or not. They merely confuse and distract, taking away from the interest of the drama itself. This bare fact, that they are unessential, tends to compel one to believe that even in Wagner's brain they were of secondary importance, although he himself might not have been and probably was not conscious of it. (pp. 502-03)

What do the various sociological theories contained in it add to *Der Ring des Nibelungen?* What does Schopenhauerism add to *Tristan und Isolde?* In the end, reduced to their essence, they are operas, all of them, the most artificial and exotic of all forms of art, the furthest removed from nature and the realities of life. Being operas, they must stand or fall primarily through their music, secondarily through their librettos. . . . The effect of the music is heightened if the drama around which it is written is good, but a poor book does not necessarily mean and unsuccessful opera.

Moreover, it is a very debatable question whether the infusion of the didactic element does not always harm an opera. It is a question whether those who patiently seek after the meanings of the *Ring, Tristan,* and *Parsifal,* get as much delight out of them as those who regard them simply as works of art. As such they are able to stand alone, needing no flying buttresses of philosophy to support them. If one listens to *Parsifal,* regarding it simply as a work of art, as an extraordinarily beautiful and poignant version of the most beautiful legend the past has bequeathed to us, he is likely to be more greatly the gainer, than he who goes with his head full of the queer, distorted notions which came from the none-too-well balanced brain of a man who in his field was the greatest musical genius the world ever had. *Parsifal* is a lasting example of how a man may be great in spite of himself. Wagner put enough extraneous and foreign matter into it to ruin a half dozen operas or dramas; but such was the might of his musical and dramatic genius that it rose triumphantly over all obstacles placed in its way and conquered in spite of them. Those who want to delve into *Parsifal* for esoteric meanings and get pleasure in doing so can find endless opportunity for the exercise of their ingenuity. But in the end, it will be with them as it has always been with others where music and drama are concerned. The final appeal will be purely aesthetic, and in the strength of that *Parsifal* must stand or fall. (p. 503)

> W. E. Walter, *"Wagner and the Grail Legend,"* in The Bookman, *New York, Vol. XVIII, No. 5, January, 1904, pp. 499-503.*

HOUSTON STEWART CHAMBERLAIN   (essay date 1915)

[*Chamberlain was an English writer and Wagnerian who married the composer's daughter Eva. In this excerpt from his book-length appreciation of Wagner as a dramatic poet, Chamberlain traces his father-in-law's developing dramatic skill as seen in his early operas,* Die Feen, Das Liebesverbot, *and* Rienzi.]

[I] do not deny that Wagner had the express intention of writing operas; but it is impossible for us to come to a proper appreciation of the works of the first period, both for themselves, as well as for the rôle they play in Wagner's development, if we do not realise the fact that in their innermost being they are distinct from everything which we generally understand by opera. A clear appreciation of this fact is the first and most important realisation with regard to these works of the first period. (pp. 46-7)

Portrait of Parsifal by Aubrey Beardsley.

In the first work, **"The Fairies,"** we already find the purely-human motive of Redemption through Love as foundation and subject of the work. In this first work, thanks to a marvellous disposition of Providence, it is music which accomplishes this redemption by its miraculous function, representing in this case a force which is termed "the godlike in mortal." Through Arindal's fault his wife, Ada, has been changed into a stone. With his cry of "Love conquers!" Arindal has already put to flight the infernal powers of darkness,—but how is he to release the stone from its enchantment? In despair he sinks to the ground, when he hears a celestial voice, which bids him "Seize thy lyre!" "Heavens! What do I hear!" exclaims Arindal;

"yes, I possess the power of gods! I know the power of sublime tones, of that divinity which mortal man possesses!" He sings; his song breaks the spell and his beloved wife sinks into his arms. This work, which was only performed for the first time after Wagner's death, appears like a prophecy. In his later life Wagner said that "he could not conceive of the spirit of music otherwise than as love." Here we find the redemption of woman, in other words, of the inner being, brought about by song as a gift of love,—that is of the spirit of music,—given to the active, "exterior man."

The redemption of music through the drama! . . . [The] most important thing for us is, that "**The Fairies,**" without there being any necessity for the pointing of symbols, already shows a drama born of the spirit of music in the form of an opera.

But in order fully to comprehend "**The Fairies,**" we must consider in connection with it the work which immediately followed, namely, "**Das Liebesverbot.**" Here the fundamental theme of the drama is also redemption, and that in a form which anticipates "**Tannhäuser,**"—the redemption of a sinful man through a pure maiden. It is, moreover, an admirable trait that in this case fraternal love consummates the work. But it is the absolute contrast of the working out of the "**Liebesverbot**" compared with that of "**The Fairies**" which most of all arrests our attention. Such a similarity in the main themes and such a difference in the works themselves! Wagner himself once remarked: "Whoever should happen to compare '**Das Liebesverbot**' with '**The Fairies**' must find it hard to understand how such a striking change in direction could have been brought about in so short a time!" But perhaps we can after all understand it. In these first two works we already see that which was to be repeated in the later works, appearing in pairs, and which I have designated by the handy explanation "it is here a case of conflict between poet and musician."

Doubtless the two works have been born of the spirit of music; that is sufficiently proved by the two purely-human themes which run through both; but the conscious recognition of the way in which poet and musician can blend into one is not yet apparent. In the case of "**The Fairies**" the poem is diffuse and uncompact; it was evidently intended that music was to complete everything singlehanded; little care also has been expended on verse and diction. In "**Das Liebesverbot,**" on the other hand, the action is at once rich, interesting and clear, and diction and versification are correspondingly carefully worked out. The work might, in fact, very well be performed without music. In "**Das Liebesverbot**" we also find the comic element represented in several excellent scenes. The impression in short is, that in the first work the text was merely intended to serve as a vehicle for the music, whereas the second is a work, carried through with a swing, to which music was to give an intenser vitality. A reason for this is doubtless to be found in the subjects themselves, "**The Fairies**" being modelled on a fairy-tale of Gozzi's, "**Das Liebesverbot**" on a comedy by Shakespeare. This, however, does not bring us very far, for the very choice of these subjects is significant, and, furthermore, we see Wagner in both cases already working out his conceptions with such creative freedom that his complete independence cannot be questioned. No, we must look deeper than this, and in so doing we shall reach the following conclusion, namely, that in "**The Fairies**" a sufficient scope was not allowed the poet. Now we have seen that wherever the poet has not sufficiently "formed," the music is impeded in the development of its power of expression. Consequently the work had fallen short of Wagner's own artistic ideal, and that is why he now unconsciously chose

a subject in which the creative function of the poet had necessarily to be a much greater one, namely, the subject of "**Das Liebesverbot.**" But in doing so he fell into the other extreme, inasmuch as this work does not necessarily seem to require the co-operation of music. (pp. 47-51)

[In "**The Fairies,**"] the weaker of these two productions, with its ill-defined contours, the idea of the redemption through love appears with far greater force and lucidity than in the sharply delineated work "**Das Liebesverbot**" with its manifold action. How is this to be explained? The reason is, that "**The Fairies**" complies in a far greater degree with the law which demands that the theme which alone can and should be treated by the Word-Tone-Poet is the Purely-Human, freed from all convention. In these very first works we already find examples which prove the truth of this later revelation: only the Purely-Human can be represented in the perfect art-work. A second realisation, which a study of these works would afford us, I can unfortunately only put forward as an hypothesis. . . . [It] would be the following: that as a result of the better text of "**Das Liebesverbot,**" the music would in many cases considerably excel that of "**The Fairies.**" If this be really the case, as indeed a knowledge of the later works puts beyond all doubt, then we should have already here at the outset the proof, which later recurs so frequently, that the more the poet has let the spell of his poem control his eye and understanding, the more forcible is the development of his music. But there is no need for us to have recourse to hypotheses: a study of "**The Fairies**" is in itself sufficient. The more "operatically" a scene is treated, the weaker does also the music become,—the more dramatic it is, in the deepest sense of the term, the more significant becomes the music. I would refer principally to the scene of Arindal's madness, which is almost perfect in beauty. But also in other passages, wherever the poem inevitably breaks away from the definite form, we find a diction so masterful and unique that the mighty Word-Tone-Poet of later days seems bodily to stand before us.

"**Rienzi**" stands in such an interesting relation to the first two works that unless we have studied their essential traits, we can hardly comprehend the former in its peculiar construction. The two directions which we saw indicated in the first two works, Wagner in this case endeavours to combine. In common with "**Das Liebesverbot,**" "**Rienzi**" shows us a manifold characterisation and dramatic emotion . . . ; the endeavour to express everything in and through music shows the relationship with "**The Fairies.**" But as a result of these advantages, "**Rienzi**" also displayed the shortcomings of the former works in an intensified form. The fault in the poem of "**Das Liebesverbot**" was that the conventional factor pervaded the whole piece, that is, the conventional with regard to manners and customs. In "**Rienzi**" it is the historically-formal factor which threatens everywhere to smother the purely-human theme underlying the work. If "**The Fairies**" did not satisfy Wagner, this was owing to the fact that in the true and perfect drama, after which he was unconsciously striving, the essential foundation for the development of the music is the poem, and no music, however excellent, can cover up the defects of the former,—on the contrary, it is just the music which shows up these defects. Moreover, in "**Rienzi**" an even greater rôle is imputed to music than in the case of "**The Fairies.**" For if we wish to sum up in one word the essential character of "**Rienzi,**" we must admit that of all Wagner's works it is the one which most observes the designation of "music-drama." . . . The poet has, to be sure, chosen a purely-human theme: the liberation of one's country, self-sacrifice in behalf of the generality, and already in "**Rienzi**" we see that fine poetic device whereby the same thing is exhaustively depicted by being impersonated in different characters: Rienzi, Irene, Adriano,—the work in fact abounds in poetry. But this purely-human theme the poet presents for us in a rich, historically-formal garb, such as would suit a spoken drama, and this whole he then hands over to the musician and demands that he shall "realise" the drama on the stage. Even the diction, as Wagner confessed himself later, is "remarkably neglected." ... The result was a work of indisputable grandeur, in which the possibilities of music were extended to their utmost. (pp. 52-6)

> Houston Stewart Chamberlain, in his The Wagnerian Drama: An Attempt to Inspire a Better Appreciation of Wagner As a Dramatic Poet, *John Lane/The Bodley Head, 1915, 240 p.*

PIERRE LASSERRE (essay date 1917)

[*Surveying Wagner's major works, and focusing particular attention on* The Nibelung's Ring, *Lasserre explores Wagner's philosophic concerns, their source and development, and their revelation in his operas. The influence of Schopenhauer on Wagner, discussed here, has also been studied by Ernest Newman (1898) and Jack M. Stein (1947). This essay was originally published in 1917 in French as "L'esprit de la musique française."*]

We find in *Lohengrin* that part of the theme is truly poetic, stamped with real humanity and lacking in its developments neither simplicity nor grace. Take for example all the part dealing with the feelings of Elsa towards Ortrude, her deadly enemy. Ortrude has contrived a diabolical plot for the ruin and dishonour of Elsa. Unmasked and defeated she appeals to the girl's pity and begs her to restore her in the eyes of the world by reconciliation: but this is only in order to find opportunity for the hideous vengeance she is meditating. Elsa is far more sorry for her wickedness than for her misfortune . . . , and grants her not only pity but friendship; rendered happy by love she thinks she would be ungrateful for her own good fortune if she hardened her heart even against this wicked woman. Everyone knows well the charm of the setting devised by the poet's scenic inventiveness for the expression of these feelings. The ingenuous raptures of Elsa's love for her knight have a charm no less natural and pure. And the triumph of this love in the splendour and glory of nuptial pomp provides not merely a scene and a spectacular effect; there is wafted by the pageant of these celebrations a breath of youth and untroubled enthusiasm. (p. 153)

This drama has, according to Wagner, a high philosophic trend. But there is one strange point—or rather, it is only too comprehensible—to which I cannot too emphatically draw attention. What we find infantile in his theme is precisely what he himself, when he undertakes to annotate it and bring out its philosophic meaning, thinks greatest. And those elements of invention of which we can scarcely make sense are the very ones to convey, according to him, the most precious and sublime meanings. (p. 155)

[Despite Wagner's explanation,] *Lohengrin* (and one must say the same of *Tannhäuser* and the *Phantom Ship*) presents itself as a sufficiently simple work. In it the author follows almost line for line the incidents of the old mediaeval legend, heightening them with straightforward and sometimes beautiful poetic developments. We could read and re-read the text and suspect none of the extraordinary meanings which his commentary would have us discover in them. But had he thought of putting those meanings in it himself? Did he not introduce them after the work was done? There are very strong reasons for thinking that he did so. The strongest is obtained from a comparison of dates. *Lohengrin* is three years earlier than the year 1848. The *Communication to my friends,* which gives the commentary on it, is two years after that date. . . . The so-called explanation of the meaning of his first dramas is in reality a manifesto of his new thoughts. But as he became from this moment a passionate theorist, without however, ceasing to be a poet, we find him no longer relegating the expression of his theories to the annotations on his dramas; he propagates them in the dramas themselves. That is the new characteristic of the *Nibelungen Ring* as compared with *Lohengrin*.

This new bent of his mind, which henceforth remained for Wagner, subject to slight variations, a definite tendency, has however no originality. It gives no evidence of any personal effort of reflection. It is a beaten track, but he follows it with as much feverish ardour as if he had hewn it out by his own initiative. He embraces his ideas with passion, but he is not in any sense their creator. He received them from the ambient air. In German philosophic and literary circles of the nineteenth century there were no ideas more widely received; the source from which he draws them occupied in German thought of that century the position of an ordinary commonplace. That commonplace consists in what might be called the cult of the primitive, in the identification of the primitive with the ideal. The supposition, or the dream, is that all the creations of thought and of the human soul, all the institutions of human life, poetry, religion, morality, law, once had a primitive state, a primitive form, superior to all the forms they have subsequently assumed, which is the excelling type by which all the rest must be judged, and to which a return must be made. (pp. 157-59)

Being the work of the ideologue as much as of the poet, the *Nibelungen Ring* or *Tetralogy* generally passes for a very obscure composition. (p. 163)

Side by side with its symbolic meanings, which themselves are only partially, not wholly, wrapped in darkness, it offers us a story that is very clear and easily understood as soon as one stops looking too eagerly for symbolism. Its clearness is of two sorts according to which of two themes one chooses to study. One is the sort of clearness which is proper to fanciful stories and fairy tales. . . . The other is somewhat out of range of the young, but is no more difficult to understand than a novel or drama in the fashion of 1830, a novel or drama by Georges Sand or Dumas, such as *Lelia, Indiana, Jacques* or *Antony,* inspired by the defence of free love and the rights of nature against the slavery and prejudice of marriage and laws. It does not really aggravate the difficulty, that the characters in this romance instead of being taken from the lower-middle classes of France and Germany are taken from Germanic mythology and prehistoric legend; especially when, from above the clouds or out of the abysm of time they address us in the language in use yesterday or the day before and quite familiar to us. In these two senses the *Ring* is a very clear work. The fantastic on a vast scale, a chain of wonderful stories put on the stage, and a romance modelled on the old romantic themes of sentimental anarchism, the whole mixed with certain riddles of metaphysical terminology, that for my part I think are only too easily deciphered, such are the elements of which the invention of the Tetralogy is composed. (pp. 164-65)

The subject matter of [the *Ring*] was borrowed by Wagner from the old Germanic-Scandinavian poem of the Nibelungen. One can understand the attraction it must have exercised, apart from all philosophic and symbolic aims, on a composer of operas the bent of whose mind led him in the direction of spectacular opera. For such is indeed the trend of Wagner's mind, at any rate such is one of the faculties that constituted his genius; he has a passionate taste for theatrical decoration and the composition of scenic effects; he adores their fascination, and he has a wonderful aptitude for their processes and artifices. . . . Among the attractions which he found in the fable of the *Nibelungen*, not the least was the quality of the scenic effects to which it lent itself. The under-water Rhine caves, with the gambolling of the water sprites, the palace of the gods in the clouds, the cavern of the Nibelungen and the metamorphoses of Alberich, the rides of the Valkyrs, the combat of Siegfried and the dragon, Brünnhilde sleeping surrounded by a rampart of flames, the crumbling of Valhalla and its fall through space, all these combinations of marvels and landscape, of magic and nature, lent themselves to rich and wondrous imagery mounted on cardboard and wire, and promised rich entertainment to the eyes of spectators. (pp. 171-72)

[All] this decorative part of Wagner's operas has not merely a perceptible attraction. It has also an element of poetic value if not in itself at any rate in the allurements that it holds out to the richest inspirations of the musician. Wagner as a musician excels in painting great landscapes; or more exactly in evoking for the imagination the hidden springs and profound rhythms of the natural forces manifested in the powerful undulations of a river's volume, the graceful or majestic course of the clouds, the murmurs of the trees, the play of light and shadow. His fantastic scenes are developed in the midst of these phenomena of nature, which may be said to take no less important a part in them than the characters themselves.

Yet it is very necessary that the latter should hold their own place in the scheme. Whatever influence picturesque or musical considerations may have had on the turn given by Wagner to the story of the *Nibelungen*, he was bound, since he was making a drama out of it, to be pre-occupied with representing human nature. But to what extent could this preoccupation be reconciled with the double intention guiding the artist's pen, to display a scene of fantasy and to symbolise ideas? Characters who must at one and the same time take part in marvellous deeds of fable, and incarnate abstract ideas, surely cannot possibly preserve to any extent worth mentioning the liberty of feeling and thinking like natural beings. (pp. 173-74)

There are in the *Tetralogy* a few expressions of real humanity, some natural touches drawn from life. Fricka really does resemble a jealous wife, domineering and of narrow outlook, and her domestic scenes with Wotan are sometimes good comedy—not divine, but middle-class. There is a spirit of pleasantry in the dialogues of Mime and Siegfried, which though very Germanic does not lack wit or relief; they have the moralist's touch. Siegfried is agreeable, if one puts aside the anarchic signification of his personality; but the author too has been careful not to let that be explained to him. This young Hercules charms not only by the splendour of his physical youth, but also by a certain child-like quality of heart. Brünnhilde is tiresome, with her final prophesy, to which nothing led up in her career as wild amazon, artless lover or even as betrayed wife, for she was only that in a roundabout way, and the experience cannot have taught her much about humanity. . . . Take them all round, all these figures are pretty elementary. To us these persons give the effect of elements quite as much as persons. There remains, it is true, Wotan, the complexity of whose thoughts and sentiments might make a

real moral personality and introduce into the drama a really human interest.

Poor Wotan! His title of monarch of the gods, his lance, the mystery of his single eye, confer on him a seeming majesty. But strip him of these external attributes, and what a fall is there! From beginning to end his role is nothing but one long lament. And what does he lament? Some misfortune that has befallen him? Not at all, but his faults, and especially the fundamental irresolution of his mind, which knows not how to will or to refuse. In a mere mortal this complaining would be wearisome. Is it less so in a god? One may certainly say that it is very incongruous on his lips. Treated in a humorous or satiric vein the character might be excellent. . . . [Wagner] has made up his mind to attribute greatness to him, a greatness superior to that of gods and kings who believe in the principles of their trade as rulers and who practise it with conscience and conviction. But why should I pretend not to understand? Wotan is indeed great from the point of view of anarchist philosophy. For such a philosophy what is next greatest after the open and declared enemy of Law? The guardian of the laws who applies them while groaning over them.

To grasp, as far as possible, Wagner's intention we must understand Law in the most general sense—political laws, social laws, laws of morality, intelligence and thought, rules, institutions, discipline of every kind; these are what Wotan personifies, these are what must perish with the power and reign of Wotan. All this general body of principles of order Wagner sums up somewhere in one word. He calls it "the Monumental." He desires and foretells the crumbling away of the Monumental, and contrasts its detestable fixity with what . . . he calls "Life." Like all romantic and revolutionary natures, he is incapable of understanding that the "Order" which offers itself and acts as a destroyer of living forces is not Order, but Routine; that real Order is the support and mainstay of spontaneous energies, and that the latter if not guided and kept in their channel by fixed elements are doomed to sterility and wretched waste. This error shows the violence of impulses where reason is weak. (pp. 174-76)

If we wished to probe further into the dark places of the *Tetralogy*, we should have to scrutinise the allusions which occur in it to the previous phase of Wotan's existence. But upon what a confused region we should have to enter! It appears that before Wotan became master of the world, the founder and guardian of the laws, he too had lived the free life of Love—unfortunately he wearied of it, and this fatigue is symbolised in a ridiculous fashion by the quarrels of the elderly divine household. He conceived an ambition for Power, a desire for Gold and for Knowledge. To satisfy the last he sought the help of Erda, who is primitive and eternal Wisdom (Ur-Weisheit). But by doing this he worked for his own ruin. Power, Gold and Knowledge are the joint agents of destruction, the inseparable powers of death. Here let us recognise in a peculiarly muddled and deliquescent form the absurdities of Rousseau's discourse against civilisation. . . . [The] thread of ideas is not Wagner's only guide in the world of ideas. He is guided quite as much by considerations of the picturesque. If the arrangement of some of his episodes is prompted by reasons of symbolism, others are what they are only for reasons of scenic picturesqueness, but take on a symbolic meaning after completion. This point shows the child-like simplicity and lack of common-sense of those critics who enquire too seriously what were Wagner's thoughts. The fairy story of the *Ring* is wrapped in clouds, some arising from the author's intentions, others emanating from the story itself. (pp. 176-77)

The action of *Tristan* is wrapped in a poetry whose charm is at once heady and lugubrious. The frame within which it is developed, the circumstances of each scene add to the tragedy of guilty passion a sort of magical effect in which may be recognised the old Celtic imagination that invented this story of love and death. The vessel at sea, the fond tender avowal made over the symbolic abyss of the waters at the very mouth of the harbour where the royal bridegroom, already betrayed, awaits his bride, the meeting by night in the park, where far away are heard the muffled sounds of hunting calls, the torch waved from the top of the tower as a danger signal, Tristan on his bed of pain spending his days looking out to sea for the white sail that will tell him of Yseult's return,—it would be idle to deny the poignancy and strength of the hold on our feelings exercised by all these images, animated as they are by powerful and pulsing music. It is wiser to point out their dangers, and ask whether the extreme attractions of this poetic atmosphere do not serve as a deceptive wrapping for contents that are by no means proportionately valuable.

Let us consider by themselves the themes of the action. There is one of these that is of low quality, one might almost call it brutal; by repercussion it lowers the quality of all the others. This is the philtre, the love potion poured out for Tristan and Yseult by Brangaine. True, it is not this potion which gives birth to their passion. The natural movement of their hearts and their youth was already throwing them into each other's arms. But sooner than yield to it, sooner than commit a triple felony against a husband who is his king, and who has entrusted to his honour the protection of his beloved wife, Tristan, and with him Yseult drawn in to share his sacrifice, would prefer to die. A violent solution, and very short, so to speak.—An infinitely preferable one, I will not say from the moral point of view, but from the point of view of art, which would gain from it far greater richness, real pathos and variety, would be the struggle of will against desire. But it is not even this solution which is adopted. It is a worse one. Inspired by a criminal devotion, the nurse Brangaine substitutes for the poison prepared for the joint suicide the irresistible love philtre. These noble lovers, imagining they are drinking death from the cup, drink delirium. When they put down the empty cup they have lost their moral liberty, that is to say their moral grandeur itself. They step down from the ship drunk and staggering with passion. They are no longer masters of themselves. They become frenzied victims of hallucination. Their souls undergo a terrible simplification.

And the philtre not only delivers them over to this fury of a passion whose sinful character they are no longer capable of realising. It has another effect on them, not less inhuman but far more extraordinary, it gives them over without any intellectual protection to the extreme suggestions of Schopenhauer's philosophy, or at least the philosophy of Schopenhauer as interpreted by Wagner. The reading of this philosopher had marked an epoch in his life; no sooner had he made his acquaintance than he swore by no other guide; from that time he never ceased to mingle his teaching with everything, to resolve all kinds of problems after his principles. But what is most singular, and what gives one of the most characteristic signs of the gulf that exists between German and French natures, is that Schopenhauer's ideas set their stamp upon the late ardent and painful love passion which he experienced in his forty-third year, and which inspired him to write *Tristan*. There worked in him, in his sentiments and sensations, a combination of Schopenhauerian metaphysics, and amorous delirium which seems to us far from natural, and yet it acquired an explosive force in this Germanic soul. Schopenhauer's morality counsels the annihilation of desire, promising us as the goal of this effort entrance into some undefined state of divine slumber, some kind of pantheistic paradise in which all the movements of life expire and individuality disappears. And it would seem at first sight that nothing could be more opposed to this passion for the void than the exaltation of love.

But neither Wagner nor his heroes feel it thus. For Tristan and his beloved, love's supreme cry is a summons to the void; the expiration of desire in death is the very object of desire carried to its paroxysm. And this is not as one might suppose a sudden flash of imagination quickly dying out, that crosses their brains under the stroke of sensual madness. It is a steadily maintained idea. It is their one idea. It is the theme of their outpourings. They turn it over and over in all its aspects, which are terribly lacking in variety. They shout to ''Day,'' that is to say Life, to be gone, and to ''Night,'' which is the Kingdom of Death, to descend upon them and wrap them round. They dream of the delights of perfect union by the annihilation of individual conscience. They analyse these delights with unrestrained and minute dialectic; they harp on them with a kind of incandescent monotony. (pp. 178-81)

I have called Wagner's works dramas, but the term applies to their external appearance rather than to their nature and true quality. There is no drama where there is not living and active humanity, and . . . there is little humanity in Wagner's dramatic inventions. Take away from them all the rubbish of symbolic significations, foggy abstractions obscuring ideas that are more childishly simple than is usually supposed, and what remains of these strange compositions ought to be called by its true name, poetic fantasies. They remind one of frescoes or rather of moving tapestries that unroll before our view natural and fantastic scenes of a heavy and expensive colouring, figures of strong and outstanding picturesqueness, but almost without life. This essentially German art form has its charm; it is free from vulgarity. There is no error of taste in taking pleasure in it, so long as it is only a petty pleasure. (pp. 184-85)

> Pierre Lasserre, "Wagner, the Poet," in his The Spirit of French Music, *translated by Denis Turner, E. P. Dutton & Co., 1921, pp. 148-85.*

THOMAS MANN (lecture date 1933)

[A novelist, short story writer, essayist, and critic, Mann is regarded as the major German novelist of the twentieth century. His novels and stories, including such famous works as Buddenbrooks *and* The Magic Mountain, *demonstrate his great skill as a narrator and are shaped by a number of recurring themes: the isolation of the artist in society, the nature of time, and the modern fascination with decadence and death. His essays on literature are recognized for their critical perception. Mann's lengthy essay ''The Sufferings and Greatness of Richard Wagner,'' from which this excerpt is drawn, is considered the best piece of appreciative criticism on Wagner. Mann explores many facets of Wagner's dramatic and theoretical works, including his use of psychology and mythology. In addition, Mann questions the validity of Wagner's aesthetic theories and explains his conception of nationalism. Other commentators who examine Wagner's use of myth include Friedrich Nietzsche (1872), Alfred A. Wheeler (1883), W. E. Walter (1904), Theodor Adorno (1937-38), and Norbert Fuerst (1966). Originally given as a lecture at the University of Munich on February 10, 1933, this essay was first published in German as ''Die Leiden und Grosse Richard Wagners'' in the April 1933 issue of the* Neue Rundschau. *For additional criticism by Mann, see excerpt below, 1937.]*

Suffering and great as that nineteenth century whose complete expression he is, the mental image of Richard Wagner stands before my eyes. Scored through and through with all his century's unmistakable traits, surcharged with all its driving forces, so I see his image; and scarcely can I distinguish between my two loves: love of his work, as magnificently equivocal, suspect and compelling a phenomenon as any in the world of art, and love of the century during most of which he lived his restless, harassed, tormented, possessed, miscomprehended life. (p. 15)

Zola and Wagner, the *Rougon-Macquarts* and the **Ring of the Nibelungs**—fifty years ago who would have thought of putting them together? Yet they belong together. The kinship of spirit, aims and methods is most striking. It is not only the love of size, the propensity to the grandiose and the lavish; not only, in the sphere of technique, the Homeric leit-motif that they have in common. More than anything else it is a naturalism that amounts to the symbolic and the mythical. (p. 17)

[What is it that raises the works of Wagner to a] plane so high, intellectually speaking, above all other musical drama? Two forces contribute, forces and gifts of genius, which one thinks of in general as opposed, indeed the present day takes pleasure in asserting their essential incompatibility. I mean psychology and the myth. Indeed, psychology does seem too much a matter of reason to admit of our seeing in it anything but an obstacle on the path into the land of myth. And it passes as the antithesis of the mythical as of the musical—yet precisely this complex, of psychology, myth and music, is what confronts us, an organic reality, in two great cases, Nietzsche and Wagner. A book might be written on Wagner the psychologist, on the psychology of his art as musician not less than as poet—in so far as the two are to be separated in him.

The technique of the motif had already been used on occasion in the old opera; it was now gradually built up, by the profoundest virtuosity, into a system which made music more than ever the instrument of psychological allusion, association, emphasis. Wagner's treatment of the love-potion theme [in **Tristan and Isolde**], originally the simple epic idea of a magic draught, is the creation of a great psychologist. For actually it might as well be pure water that the lovers drink, and it is only their belief that they have drunk death which frees their souls from the moral compulsion of their day. From the beginning Wagner's poetry goes beyond the bounds of suitability for his libretto—though not so much in the language as precisely in the psychology displayed. "The sombre glow" sings the Dutchman in the fine duet with Senta in the second act [of *The Flying Dutchman*]:

> The sombre glow I feel within me burning—
> Shall I, O wretch, confess it for love's yearning?
> Ah, no, it is salvation that I crave—
> Might such an angel come my soul to save!

The lines are singable; but never before had such a complex thought been sung or been written for singing. The devoted man loves this maid at first sight; but tells himself that his emotion has nothing to do with her. Instead it has to do with his redemption and release. Then confronting her again as the embodiment of his hopes for salvation, he neither can nor will distinguish between the two longings he feels. For his hope has taken on her shape and he can no longer wish it to have another. In plain words, he sees and loves redemption in this maiden—what interweaving of alternatives is here, what a glimpse into the painful abysses of emotion! This is analysis—

and the word comes up in an even bolder and more modern sense when we think of the youthful Siegfried, and the way Wagner vitalises, in his verse and against the significant background of the music, the spring-like germination, the budding and shooting up of that young life and love. It is a pregnant complex, gleaming up from the unconscious, of mother-fixation, sexual desire and fear—the fairy-story fear, I mean, that Siegfried wanted so to feel: a complex which displays Wagner the psychologist in remarkable intuitive agreement with another typical son of the nineteenth century, the psychoanalyst Sigmund Freud. When Siegfried dreams under the linden tree and the mother-idea flows into the erotic; when Mime teaches his pupil the nature of fear, while the orchestra down below darkly and afar off introduces the fire-motif: all that is Freud, that is analysis, nothing else—and we recall that Freud, whose profound investigation into the roots and depths of mind has been, in its broadest lines, anticipated by Nietzsche, shows an interest in the mythical, precultural and primeval which is narrowly associated with the psychological.

"Love in fullest reality," says Wagner, "is only possible within sex; only as man and woman can human beings love most genuinely, all other love is derivative, having reference to this or artificially modelled upon it. It is false to think of this love (the sexual) as only one manifestation of love in general, other and perhaps higher manifestations being presumed beside it." This reduction of all love to the sexual has an unmistakably psychoanalytical character. It shows the same psychological naturalism as Schopenhauer's metaphysical formula of the "focus of the will" and Freud's cultural theories and his theory of sublimation. It is genuine nineteenth century.

The erotic mother-complex appears again in **Parsifal**, in the seduction-scene in the second act—and here we come to Kundry, the boldest, most powerful creation among Wagner's figures—he himself probably felt how extraordinary she was. Not Kundry but the emotions proper to Good Friday were Wagner's original point of departure; but gradually his ideas more and more took shape about her, and the decisive conception of the dual personality, the thought of making the wild *Gralsbotin* (messenger of the Grail) one and the same being with the beguiling temptress, supplied the final inspiration—and betrays the secret depths of the fascination that drew him to so strange an enterprise.

"Since this occurred to me," he writes, "almost everything about the material has become clear." And again: "In particular I see more and more vividly and compellingly a strange creation, a wonderful world-demonic female (the *Gralsbotin*). If I manage to finish this piece of work it will be something highly original." Original—that is a touchingly subdued and modest word for the result he actually produced. Wagner's heroines are in general marked by a trait of lofty hysteria; they have something sleep-walking, ecstatic and prophetic which imparts an odd, uncanny modernity to their romantic heroics. But Kundry herself, the Rose of Hell, is definitely a piece of mythical pathology; her tortured and distracted duality, now as *instrumentum diaboli,* now as salvation-seeking penitent, is portrayed with clinical ruthlessness and realism, with a naturalistic boldness of perception and depiction in the morbid realm, that has always seemed to me the uttermost limit of knowledge and mastery. And Kundry is not the only character in **Parsifal** with this excessive type of mentality. The draft of this last work of Wagner says of Klingsor that he is the demon of the hidden sin, he is impotence raging against evil—and here we are transported into a Christian world that takes cognisance of recondite and infernal soul-states, in short, into the world of Dostoiewsky.

Our second phenomenon is Wagner as mythologist, as discoverer of the myth for purposes of the opera, as saviour of the opera through the myth. And truly he has not his like for soul-affinity with this picture-world of thought, nor his equal in the power of invoking and reanimating the myth. When he forsook the historical opera for the myth he found himself; and listening to him one is fain to believe that music was made for nothing else, nor could have any other mission but to serve mythology. Whether as messenger from a purer sphere, sent to the aid of innocence and then, alas, since faith proves inconstant, withdrawing thither whence it came; or as lore, spoken and sung, of the world's beginning and end, a sort of cosmogonic fairy-tale philosophy—in all this the spirit of the myth, its essence and its key, are struck with a certainty, an elective intuition; its very language is spoken with a native-bornness that has not its like in all art. It is the language of "once upon a time" in the double sense of "as it always was" and "as it always shall be"; the density of the mythological atmosphere—as in the scene with the Norns, at the beginning of the *Götterdämmerung,* where the three daughters of Erda indulge in a solemn-faced gossip about the state of the world, or in the appearances of Erda herself in the *Rheingold* and *Siegfried*—is unsurpassable. (pp. 22-7)

[What] left me cold—was Wagner's theory. It is hard for me to believe that anyone ever took it seriously. This combination of music, speech, painting, gesture, that gave itself out to be the only true art and the fulfilment of all artistic yearning— what had I to do with this? A theory of art which would make *Tasso* give way to *Siegfried*? I found it hard to swallow, this derivation of the single arts from the disintegration of an original theatrical unity, to which they should all happily find their way back. Art is entire and complete in each of its forms and manifestations; we do not need to add up the different species to make a whole. (pp. 28-9)

Wagner, as an impassioned man of the theatre—one might call him a theatromaniac—inclined to such a belief, in so far as the first desideratum of art appeared to him to be the most immediate and complete communication to the senses of everything that was to be said. And strange enough it is to see, in the case of his principal work, *The Ring of the Nibelungs,* what was the effect of this ruthless demand of his upon the drama, which after all was the crux of all his striving, and of which the fundamental law seemed to him to be precisely this utter, all-inclusive sense-appeal. . . . Wagner's masterpiece owes its sublimity to the epic spirit, and the epic is the sphere from which its material is drawn. The *Ring* is a scenic epic; its source is the dislike of the previous histories that haunt the stage behind the scenes. . . . (pp. 29-30)

His relation to the single arts out of which he created his "composite art-work" is worth dwelling upon. It has something peculiarly dilettantish about it. . . . In fact, not only the superficial but the admiring and empassioned observer might well say, at risk of being misunderstood, that Wagner's art *is* dilettantism, monumentalised and lifted into the sphere of genius by his intelligence and his enormous will-power. There is something dilettante in the very idea of a union of the arts; it could never have got beyond the dilettante had they not one and all been ruthlessly subordinated to his vast genius for expression. There is something suspect in his relation to the arts— something unaesthetic, however nonsensical that may sound. (pp. 31-2)

[He] has made [a] mighty contribution to poetry, she is much the richer for his work—always bearing in mind that it must not be read, that it is not really written verse but, as it were, exhalations from the music, needing to be complemented by gesture, music and picture and existing as poetry only when all these work together. Purely as composition it is often bombastic, baroque, even childish; it has something majestically and sovereignly inept—side by side with such passages of absolute genius, power, compression, primeval beauty, as disarm all doubt; though they never quite make us forget that what we have here are images that stand not within the cultural structure of our great European literature and poetry, but apart from it, more in the nature of directions for a theatrical performance which among other things needs a text. Among such gems of language interspersed among the boldly dilettant, I think in particular of the *Ring* and of *Lohengrin*—the latter, purely as writing, is perhaps the noblest, purest and finest of Wagner's achievements.

His genius lies in a dramatic synthesis of the arts, which only as a whole, precisely as a synthesis, answers to our conception of a genuine and legitimate work of art. The component parts— even to the music, in itself, not considered as part of a whole— breathe something irregular, over-grown, that only disappears when they blend into the noble whole. Wagner's relation to his language is not that of our great poets and writers, it wants the severity and delicacy displayed by those who find in words the highest good and the most trusted medium of art. That is proved by his occasional poems; the sugared and romantic adulations of Ludwig II of Bavaria, the banal and jolly jingles addressed to helpers and friends. One single careless little rhyme of Goethe is pure gold—and pure literature—compared with these versified platitudes and hearty masculine jests, at which our reverence for Wagner can only make us smile rather ruefully. Let us keep to Wagner's prose, to the manifestos and self-expositions on aesthetic and cultural matters. They are essays of astonishing mental virility, but they are not to be compared, as literary and intellectual achievements, with Schiller's works on the philosophy of art—for instance, that immortal essay on *Naive and Sentimental Poetry*. They are hard to read, their style is both stiff and confused, again there is something about them that is overgrown, extraneous, dilettante: they do not belong to the sphere of great German and European prose; they are not the work of a born writer, but the casual product of some necessity. With Wagner everything was like that, always the product of necessity. Happy, devoted, complete, legitimate and great he is, only in the mass. (pp. 33-5)

His acquaintance with the philosophy of Arthur Schopenhauer was the greatest event in Wagner's life. No earlier intellectual contact, such as that with Feuerbach, approaches it in personal and historical significance. It meant to him the deepest consolation, the highest self-confirmation; it meant release of mind and spirit, it was utterly and entirely pertinent. There is no doubt that it freed his music from bondage and gave it courage to be itself. (p. 57)

Never probably in the history of the mind has there been so wonderful an example of the artist, the dark and driven human being, finding spiritual support, self-justification and enlightenment in another's thought, as in this case of Wagner and Schopenhauer.

[Schopenhauer's] *The World as Will and Idea:* what memories of one's own young intoxications of the spirit, one's own joys of conception, compact of melancholy and gratitude, come up at the thought of the bond between Wagner's work and this great book! This comprehensive critique and guide, this poesy of knowledge, this metaphysics of impulse and spirit, will and idea as conceived by the artist, this marvellous thought-structure of ethical, pessimistical and musical elements—what profound, epoch-making, human affinities it displays with the score of the *Tristan!* (pp. 58-9)

The official works on Wagner assert in all seriousness that *Tristan* was not influenced by the Schopenhauerian philosophy. That seems to me a curious lack of insight. The arch-romantic worship of the night embodied in this sublimely morbid, consuming, enchanting work, deep-dyed in all the worst and highest mysteries of the romantic essence, has about it nothing specifically Schopenhauerian. The sensuous, super-sensuous intuitions in the *Tristan* come from a remoter source: from the perfervid and hectic Novalis, who writes: "Union joined not only for life but for death is a marriage that gives us a companion for the night. Love is sweetest in death; for the living death is a bridal night, a sweet mysterious secret." And in the *Hymns to Night* he complains: "Must morning always come? Does the domain of the earthly never cease? Will it never be that love's sweet sacrifice shall burn for ever on the altar?" Tristan and Isolde call themselves the "Night-consecrate"— the phrase actually occurs in Novalis: "Consecrated to the night." And still more striking from the point of view of literary history, still more significant for the source of *Tristan,* for its emotional and intellectual bases, are its associations with a little book of evil repute, I mean Friedrich von Schlegel's *Lucinde.* (pp. 61-2)

Its cult of the night, its execration of the day, are what stamps the *Tristan* as romantic, as fundamentally affiliated with all the romantic aspects of emotion and thought—and as such not needing the Schopenhauerian sign-manual. (p. 63)

[When] the Wagner authorities say that *Tristan* is a love-drama, as such contains the strongest affirmation of the will to live, and in consequence has nothing to do with Schopenhauer; when they insist that the night therein celebrated is the night of love . . . , and that if this drama has a philosophy at all then it is the exact opposite of the doctrine which would deny the will, and that precisely on that ground it is independent of the Schopenhauerian metaphysics—it seems to me that all this betrays a strange psychological insensitiveness. The denial of the will is the moral and intellectual content of Schopenhauer's philosophy, of secondary significance and not the crucial point. His philosophic system is fundamentally erotic in its nature, and in so far as it is that the *Tristan* is saturated with it. . . . Wagner is mythological poet not less in *Tristan* than in the *Ring;* even the love drama deals with a myth of the origin of the world. "Often," so he writes from Paris in 1860, to Mathilde Wesendonck, "I look with yearning toward the land of Nirvana. But Nirvana soon becomes *Tristan* again. You know the story of the Buddhistic theory of the origin of the world? A breath troubles the clearness of the heavens"—he writes the four chromatic ascending notes with which his *opus metaphysicum* begins and ends, the g-sharp, *a, a*-sharp, *b*-natural— "it swells and condenses, and there before me is the whole vast solid mass of the world." It is the symbolic tone-thought which we know as the "*Sehnsuchtsmotif,*" and which in the cosmogony of the *Tristan* signifies the beginning of all things, like the E-major of the Rhine motif in the *Ring.* It is Schopenhauer's "will," represented by what Schopenhauer called the "focus of the will," the yearning for love. And this mythical equating of sexual desire with the sweet and fatal world-creating principle that first troubled the clear heaven of the

inane—that is so Schopenhauerian that the refusal of the experts to see it looks like obstinacy. (pp. 64-5)

Nowhere does Wagner's skill at mimicry triumph more magically than in the style of the *Tristan*—this not as a matter of language merely, by phraseology in the spirit of the court epic; for with intuitive genius he is able to saturate his word and tone painting in an Anglo-Norman-French atmosphere, with a discernment which shows how completely the Wagner soul is at home in the pre-national sphere of European life. The divorce from history, the free humanisation, takes place only in the field of speculative thought, and then in the service of the erotic myth. For its sake heaven and hell are cut out. Christianity too, since it would amount to historical atmosphere. There is no God, no one knows Him or calls upon Him. There is nothing but erotic philosophy, atheistic metaphysics: the cosmogonic myth in which the *Sehnsuchtsmotif* evokes the world. (pp. 66-7)

Wagner's power of concentrating the intellectual and the popular in a single dramatic figure, is nowhere better displayed than in the hero of his revolutionary phase—in Siegfried. . . . [He] is a clown, a sun-god and an anarchistic social revolutionary, all rolled into one, what more can the theatre demand? And this art of combination is simply an expression of Wagner's own mingled and manifold nature. He is not musician and not poet, but a third category, in which the other two are blended in a way unknown before; he is a theatre-Dionysius, who knows how to take unprecedented methods of expression and give them a poetic basis, to a certain extent to rationalise them. But in so far as he *is* poet, it is not in a modern, literary and cultivated spirit, not out of his mind and consciously, but in a much deeper and devouter way. It is the folk-soul that speaks out of him and through him. . . . At least, this is the correct and accepted theory of his artistic position, and it is supported by a kind of unwieldy awkwardness which his work betrays when considered as literature. And yet he can write: "We should not underestimate the power of reflection; the unconsciously produced work of art belongs to periods remote from ours, and the art product of the most highly cultivated period cannot be produced otherwise than in full consciousness." That is a blow between the eyes for the theory which would ascribe an entirely mythical origin to his works; and indeed, though these indubitably bear in part the marks of inspiration, of blind and blissful ecstasy, yet there is so much else, so much cleverness, wittiness, allusiveness, calculated effect; so much dwarfish industry accompanies the labours of gods and giants, that it is impossible to believe in trance and mystery. The extraordinary understanding displayed in his abstract writings, does not indeed act in the service of spirit, truth, abstract knowledge; but to the advantage of his work, which it labours to explain and justify, whose pathway it would smooth, both within and without. (pp. 71-3)

[The] vast universal effectiveness of this art had, originally and personally speaking, very pure and spiritual sources. This was first of all due to its own lofty plane, where no deeper scorn is known than that for effect, for "effect without cause." And next because all the imperial, demagogic and mass-effective elements must be conceived in a quite ultra-practical and ideal sense as having reference to all too revolutionary conditions yet to be achieved. In particular the innocence of the artist comes in play, where the will to rouse enthusiasm expresses itself, powerfully instrumented, in a national appeal, celebrating and glorifying the German spirit, as happens quite directly in *Lohengrin,* in King Henry's "German Sword" and in the *Meistersinger* on the honest lips of good Hans Sachs. It is thoroughly inadmissible to ascribe to Wagner's nationalistic attitudes and speeches the meaning they would have to-day. That would be to falsify and misuse them, to besmirch their romantic purity.

The national idea, when Wagner introduced it as a familiar and workable theme into his works, that is to say, before it was realised, was in its heroic, historically legitimate epoch. It had its good, living and genuine period; it was poetry and intellect, a future value. But when the basses thunder out at the stalls the verse from the "German Sword," or that kernel and finale of the *Meistersinger:*

> Though Holy Roman Empire sink to dust
> There still survives our sacred German art

in order to arouse an ulterior patriotic emotion—that is demagogy. It is precisely these lines . . . that attest the intellectuality of Wagner's nationalism and its remoteness from the political sphere; they betray a complete anarchistic indifference to the state, so long as the spiritually German, the *"Deutsche Kunst,"* survives. Even so he was not thinking of German art, but rather of his music-theatre. . . . (pp. 85-6)

[The Germanness of Wagner's works] is deep, powerful, unquestionable. The birth of drama from music, as it is consummated, purely and enchantingly, at least once, at the height of Wagner's creative powers, in the *Tristan,* could only spring out of German life; and as German in the highest sense of the word we may also characterise its tremendous sense-appeal, its mythological and metaphysical tendencies, above all, its profoundly serious consciousness as art, the high and solemn conception of the art of the theatre, with which it is filled and which it communicates. But in and with all that, it has a universal rightness and enjoyability above all German art of this high rank. . . . (pp. 90-1)

Wagner is German, he is national, in the most exemplary, perhaps too exemplary, way. For besides being an eruptive revelation of the German nature, his work is likewise a dramatic depiction of the same; a depiction the intellectualism and the poster-like effectiveness of which is positively grotesque, positively burlesque. . . . [This] Germanness, true and mighty as it is, is very modern—it is broken down and disintegrating, it is decorative, analytical, intellectual; and hence its fascination, its inborn capacity for cosmopolitan, for world-wide effectiveness. Wagner's art is the most sensational self-portrayal and self-critique of the German nature which it is possible to conceive; it is calculated to make Germany interesting to a foreigner even of the meanest intelligence; and passionate preoccupation with it is at the same time passionate preoccupation with the German nature which it so decoratively criticises and glorifies. In this its nationalism consists; but it is a nationalism so soaked in the currents of European art as to defy all effort to simplify or belittle it. (pp. 91-2)

A last word upon Wagner's relation to the past and to the future. For here too there reigns a duality, and interweaving of apparent contradictions, similar to the antithesis of Germanness and Europeanism which I have just analysed. There are reactionary traits in Wagner, traces of reversion and cult of the dark past; we might interpret in this sense his love of the mystical and mythological; the Protestant nationalism in the *Meistersinger;* as well as the Catholic spirit in *Parsifal;* his general fondness for the Middle Ages, for the life of knights and princes, for miracles and perfervid faith. And yet my feeling for the true nature of this artist phenomenon, conditioned

Brünnhilde's awakening in Siegfried; *by Knut Ekwall, 1876.*

through and through as it was by renewal, change and liberation, strictly forbids me to take literally his language and manner of expression, instead of seeing it for what it is, an art-idiom of a very figurative sort, with which something quite different, something entirely revolutionary, keeps pace. This stormily progressive creative spirit, so charged with life despite all its soul-heaviness, its bond with death; this man who gloried in a world-destroyer born of free love; this bold musical pioneer, who in *Tristan* stands with one foot already upon a-tonal ground—to-day he would probably be called a cultural Bolshevist!—this man of the people, who all his life long and with all his heart repudiated power and money, violence and war; whose dream of a theatre—whatever the times may have made of it—was one set up to a classless community; such a man no retrograde spirit can claim for its own; he belongs to that will which is directed toward the future. (pp. 95-6)

> *Thomas Mann, "The Sufferings and Greatness of Richard Wagner," in his* Past Masters and Other Papers, *translated by H. T. Lowe-Porter, Alfred A. Knopf, 1933, pp. 15-96.*

THOMAS MANN   (lecture date 1937)

[*Here Mann treats Wagner's concept of mythology and poetic ability as manifested in* The Nibelung's Ring. *Wagner's use of myth has also been discussed by Friedrich Nietzsche (1872), Alfred*

A. Wheeler (1883), W. E. Walter (1904), Theodor Adorno (1937-38), and Norbert Fuerst (1966). Mann's essay was originally given as a lecture at the University of Zurich on the occasion of a performance of The Nibelung's Ring *at the Zürich Stadttheater in 1937. For additional commentary by Mann, see excerpt above, 1933.]*

Wagner's personal approach to the myth—that is to say, his development away from a practitioner of the traditional opera form to a revolutionary in art and inventor of a new species of drama born of myth and music, calculated vastly to heighten the intellectual status, the artistic value of the operatic stage, and to lend it a truly German seriousness—this approach, this development, is always worth fresh consideration, it will always remain highly remarkable and in the history of art and the theatre well worth thinking about. And the human interest is great as well. For with its aesthetic and artistic impulses are united moral and social ones, which alone give it its full emotional value. What we have here is a catharsis, a process of purifying, cleansing, intellectualizing, which is to be valued humanly so much the higher because this was the most passionate conceivable nature, ravaged by violent and obscure compulsions to powerful effects and enjoyments, under which he laboured, in which he fulfilled himself.

We know how the pressure of this artist nature, versatile to the point of danger, first concentrated upon the great historic opera, and in the traditional form familiar to the public achieved a triumph with *Rienzi,* which would have decided any other man to continue on this well-trodden path. What prevented Wagner was the soundness of his intellectual conscience, his capacity for disgust, his instinctive, still unformulated repugnance to the insipid role of luxurious entertainment played by the musical theatre in the prevailing bourgeois society about him. It was, in particular, his own relation to music, too reverent, too German, in an old and high sense of the word, not to feel its true essence betrayed by "grand opera." He found it simply a shame that it should serve as a sounding flourish, an aural ornamentation to a pompous middle-class spectacle; in him music yearned for purer, more appropriate dramatic associations. His fruitful borrowings into the romantic field of the saga are equivalent to the conquest of that purely human element which he considered, by contrast with the historical and political, to be the true and native sphere of music. But at the same time it meant for him the rejection of a bourgeois world of cultural decadence, false education, money rule, sterile scholarship, and mindless tedium, in favour of a folkishness, a folk-reality, which, as he came more and more to feel, was the social and artistic, the redeeming and purifying future state.

Wagner experienced modern culture, the culture of bourgeois society, through the medium and in the image of the opera-theatre activity of his time. The position of art, or of that which as an artist was his concern, became to him in this modern world a criterion for the value of bourgeois culture as a whole. Is it surprising, then, that he learned to hate and scorn it? He saw art debased to a means of luxurious enjoyment, the artist become a slave to wealth. He saw shallowness and jog-trot apathy where he wanted to see serious devotion and consecration. He saw, with rage and chagrin, the waste of enormous resources—not to lofty ends, but for what he as an artist most despised, for effect. And finding nobody who minded all that as he did, he deduced the worthlessness of the political and social conditions that produced it and were linked up with it. He deduced the need of revolutionary change.

So Wagner became a revolutionary. He became one as an artist, because he promised himself that from the alteration of all

things happier conditions for art, for his art, the mythical-musical folkplay, would flow. He had always denied that he was a political-minded man, and never concealed his dislike of the activities of political parties. When he accepted the Revolution of 1848 and took part in it, he did so out of revolutionary sympathy in general, scarcely at all on account of its concrete goals, for his actual dreams and hopes went far beyond them—went, indeed, *beyond the bourgeois epoch itself.* We must be clear on this point: a work like the *Ring,* which Wagner conceived after *Lohengrin,* was composed as a challenge to the whole of bourgeois culture and civilization as it had been in the ascendant since the Renaissance; its mingling of primevalness and futureness addresses itself to a classless folk-world that did not exist. The resistance it met, the indignation it aroused, was not so much directed at what was revolutionary in its form, the fact that it broke with the rules of a form of art (opera) and publicly came out against them. No, the hostility had another and quite different source. The German "Goethe-man," who knew his *Faust* by heart, raised angry and contemptuous protest, a highly respectable protest, whose source was the still existent bond with the cultural world of German classicism and humanism, from which this work declared itself free. The cultivated German laughed at all this Wagalaweia, all these alliterations, as a barbaric innovation; if the word had existed at that time he would have called Wagner a "*Kultur*-Bolshevist"—and not without all reason. The enormous, one may say planetary success which, notwithstanding, the bourgeois world vouchsafed to this art, thanks to its appeals to nerves, senses, and brain, is a tragicomic paradox; it must not make us forget that it was conceived for quite a different public and has social and moral aims reaching far beyond the capitalistic and bourgeois order into a brotherly humanity founded in love and justice and freed from the madness of power and gold.

The myth, for Wagner, is the language of the still creative folk—hence he loves it, and as artist gives himself utterly to it. The myth: for him that is simplicity, anti-culture, nobility, purity—in short, what he calls the purely human—and what, at the same time, is the uniquely musical. Myth and music, that is drama, that is art itself; for only the purely human seems to him the proper field for art. How unavailable for art—or for what he understands by the word, all the formally historical and derivative, by contrast with the purely human, pure as a spring is pure—he only rightly understands when he finds himself faced with the choice between two sources of material, which have been possessing his consciousness even during the composition of *Lohengrin:* Friedrich Barbarossa and Siegfried's death. There is a long struggle and much delving into theory over the decision between these two themes. How the saga of the primitive hero triumphed over the imperial story, Wagner himself relates in the great *Communication to My Friends,* written later, in Switzerland, altogether the most revealing contribution of all that we owe to our great artist's love of confession. In it he explains how just because of its historical and political character he could only have dealt with the Barbarossa material (which had attracted him as a theme out of Germany's past) in the form of spoken drama and would have had to relinquish the music, which after all he needed as a rounding out and fulfilment of his creative nature. When he wrote *Rienzi,* when he was still a composer of opera, he might have been able to think of a Friedrich drama set to music. But he was no longer a composer of opera and could feel no desire to return to that stage—the less so because he always naïvely equated his own personal success with that of art itself, being convinced that opera, like spoken drama, after he had overcome it, would simply disappear forever; that the novel thing he was contributing—namely, the myth-music theatre—was the art form of the future. But for his purposes, only the unhistorical, the "purely human," freed from all convention, would serve his turn. Then how happy was he that as he penetrated deeper and deeper into his material, the Siegfried saga, he found that he could dredge out more and more historical dross, free the subject from successive layers of disguises, and take it back to where it issued newborn, a purely human manifestation of the poetic folk-soul. This extraordinary revolutionary was just as radical about the past as about the future. The saga was not enough for him; it must be the saga in its most primitive form. The mediaeval *Nibelungenlied* was already modern, distorted, dressed up; it was history, far from being early and folkish enough to serve the art he had in mind. He must penetrate back to the original sources, back to the pre-German, Scandinavian, early Germanic Eddaroots: these alone were the sacred depths of the past, corresponding to his sense of the future. He did not yet know that even within his work he would not be able to bring himself to stop at any beginning already somehow weighed down by history, and to start from that point . . . ; that here too he would be by a magnificent compulsion forced back to the beginning and arch-beginning of all things, the primeval cell, the first contra E-flat of the prelude to the prelude; that it would be laid upon him to erect a musical cosmogony, yes, a myth-cosmos, himself, and endow it with profound organic *bios,* the singing spectacle-poem of the beginning and end of the world. But so much he did already know, that in his insatiable burrowings into the ultimate depths and dawns he had found the man and hero whom he, like Brünnhilde, loved before he was born, *his* Siegfried, a figure that enchanted and gratified as well his passion for the past as his avidity for the future, for it was timeless: the human being—they are his own words—"in the most natural, blithest richness of his sense-endowed manifestation; the masculine embodiment of the spirit of unique, eternal, procreative instinctiveness; veritable doer of deeds; in the fullness of the highest, most immediate power and most unquestioned loveliness." This unconditioned, untrammelled figure of light, then, this unsafeguarded, independent, self-responsible being, relying upon his own strength alone, radiant with freedom, fearless, guiltless doer and fulfiller of destiny, who by the noble and natural event of his death brought about the twilight of old, worn-out world powers, redeemed the world by lifting it to a new level of knowledge and morality—him Wagner makes the hero of the drama conceived as belonging to the music, which, no longer in modern verse, but in the alliterative accents of his Old Norse sources, he sketched and called *Siegfried's Death.* (pp. 357-61)

[The *Ring* is] a work without compare, one may say with no exaggeration or disloyalty to other art-creations, from other, perhaps purer spheres. For it is *sui generis,* a work apparently departing from the modern, and yet in the subtlety, the awareness and developed lateness of its resources extremely modern, primitive in its emotion and its romantic, revolutionary intent; a world-poem overgrown with music and soothsaying nature, where the primeval elements of being are the actors; Night and Day hold speech together; mythical, primitive types of humanity, the blond, golden-haired children of joy, meet together with the brood of hatred, affliction, and revolt, in the depths and windings of the fairy-tale plot. The pendant to Siegfried is Hagen, a figure that for sinister power towers over all earlier or contemporary conceptions, from the Hagen of the *Nibelungenlied* down to Hebbel's. Wagner's creative and theatrical power of character-drawing triumphs as perhaps nowhere else in the figure of the half-gnome; and the words of the text contribute

mightily to its success. As when Hagen, in answer to the question why he did not share in the brother-oath, mockingly characterizes himself:

> Mein Blut verdärb' euch den Trank!
> Nicht fliesst mir's echt
> und edel wie euch;
> störrisch und kalt
> stockt's in mir;
> nicht will's die Wange mir röten.
> Drum bleib' ich fern
> vom feurigen Bund.
>
> My blood would curdle your drink!
> Not flows it in me
> True and noble like yours;
> Sullen and cold
> It thickens in me,
> Will no redden my cheek.
> So I stand off
> From the fiery bond.

That is a picture, a mythical character-mask for the stage, compressed into words. Hagen talking in his sleep, in the night conversation with Alberic; Hagen keeping the hall alone, while the free sons and joyous comrades must fetch him the ring of world-dominion; above all, Hagen as the wild and grotesque herald to Gunther's unblest marriage—the theatre knows nothing nearer to the daemonic than these scenes.

To have doubts of Wagner's gift as a poet has always seemed absurd to me. What could be more fine and profound, poetically speaking, than Wotan's relation to Siegfried; the paternally superior bantering of the god, his weakness for his destroyer, the surrender of the old power for love of the eternally young? The wonderful music which the composer has found to express all this, he owes to the poet. But again, what all does the poet not owe to the musician? How he seems often only to understand himself when he calls to his aid his other supplementary and explanatory language, which in simple truth is for him the kingdom of subliminal knowledge, unknown to the Word up there! Mime's attempt to teach Siegfried to fear, his malicious description of the shivering and shaking, is painted over a cellarage of the darkly distorted fire-music and the equally discoloured and distorted motif of the sleeping Brünnhilde. Accompanying the dwarf's description of fear is the sound of that which in the *Ring* is the symbol of all frightful things, that which is fear and terror itself, *par excellence;* that which guards the rocks: fire, which Siegfried will not fear, for he will break through without learning it. But at the same time, down in the darkness, the music haunts and hints at the thing which is really to teach him fear: the memory of the sleep-banned one, of whom he knows naught, but whose awakener he is fated to be. The audience, gazing and listening, will be brought back to the end of the evening before: it will understand that in the depths of Siegfried's soul, so hard of understanding in the matter of fear, there stirs a feeling, a guess at the actual source of fear: love, which the stupid youth has not yet learned either but is to learn along with fear, for the two are musically and emotionally the same.—Earlier, under the linden tree, he had dreamed of how his mother looked: his mother, a human being and a woman. The motif of love of woman . . . from Loki's narrative in the second scene of the *Rheingold,* rises from the orchestra. Again it is the same complex of mother-image and women's love that breaks out in words when Siegfried frees the Walküre from the cuirass and discovers "That is no man!"

''Fiery fear fixes my eyes, my senses swing and sway! Whom call I to aid, who shall help me—Mother, be mindful of me!''

Nothing can be more Wagnerian than this mixture of mythical primitiveness and psychological, yes, psychoanalytical modernity. It is the naturalism of the nineteenth century, consecrated through the myth. Yes, Wagner is not only an incomparable painter of external nature, of tempest and storm, rustling leaves and dazzle of waves, rainbows and dancing flames. He is also a great seer of animate nature, the eternal human heart: about the rocks of virginity he sets the ring of fiery fear, to be broken through by the primitive male, driven by his awakening creative mission; who then at sight of all he longs for and fears breaks out in his cry for help addressed to the sacred feminine principle from which he sprang, the mother. In Wagner's work and world the great and only thing is emotional primitive poesy, the first and simplest, the pre-conventional, pre-social; only this seems to him at all suitable for art. His work is the German contribution to the monumental art of the nineteenth century, which in other countries appears principally in the form of the great social novel-writers: Dickens, Thackeray, Tolstoy, Dostoyevsky, Balzac, Zola. Their works, towering up in the same moral loftiness, are *European* nineteenth-century, literary and social critique, social world. The German contribution, the German manifestation of this greatness, knows and wants to know nothing of the sociological; for it is not musical, and above all certainly no subject-matter for art. The only true material is the mythical, the purely human, the unhistorical, timeless primeval poesy of nature and the heart; it is truly the flight from the social and the antidote for all its corruption; from its depth the German spirit creates what is perhaps the loftiest, most compelling art the century has to offer. (pp. 368-70)

Thomas Mann, ''Richard Wagner and the 'Ring','' in his Essays of Three Decades, *translated by H. T. Lowe-Porter, Alfred A. Knopf, 1947, pp. 353-71.*

THEODOR ADORNO (essay date 1937-38)

[*In the essay excerpted below, Adorno examines Wagner's concept of myth and its relation to bourgeois ideology, psychology, law, and violence. For further discussions of Wagner's use of myth, see excerpts by Friedrich Nietzsche (1872), Alfred A. Wheeler (1883), W. E. Walter (1904), Thomas Mann (1933 and 1937), and Norbert Fuerst (1966). Adorno's essay was originally published in German in his book-length study of Wagner entitled* Versuch über Wagner, *which was written between autumn 1937 and spring 1938.*]

[Wagner found] himself reduced to a stratum of subject-matter that acknowledges neither history nor the supernatural nor even the natural, but which lies beyond all such categories. Essence is drawn into an omnisignificant immanence; the immanent is held in thrall by symbol. This stratum, where all is undifferentiated, is that of myth. Its sign is ambiguity; its twilight is a standing invitation to merge irreconcilables—the positivistic with the metaphysical—because it firmly rejects both the transcendental and the factual. Gods and men perform on the same stage. After *Lohengrin,* Wagner actually banned authentic historical conflicts from his work. The world of chivalry in *Tristan* and *Parsifal* provides only the emotional colouring of a reality that has receded into the mists of time, and the exception of *The Mastersingers* really does just prove the rule. The mythical music drama is secular and magical at one and the same time. This is how it solves the riddle of the phantasmagoria.

However, the attempt to legitimate this hybrid form by appealing to the multiple meanings inherent in the myths has its limits. If Wagner's idea of an unvarying human nature turns out to be an ideological delusion then that delusion will be destroyed by the power of the myths as these assert themselves in his works against his will. The elective affinity that impels him towards the myths undermines the humanity in which he still believes: staunch bourgeois as he is, his conception of himself crumbles before his very eyes. No doubt his impotence benefits to a certain extent from the negative truth, from a dawning awareness of the chaos underlying the bourgeois order—but it is to this chaos that he is inexorably drawn back. This is the objective reason for Wagner's regression. The pure human being turns out to be an ideal projection of the savage who finally emerges from the bourgeois, and he celebrates him as if, metaphysically, he really were the pure human being. With whatever justice Wagner's music may be called psychological, the same claim can scarcely be made for his texts, which merely re-enact at a primitive, literal level those vestiges of the imagination that live on in the psychological subject. The dramatist of the *Ring,* and in effect all the mature works, scorns to 'develop' his characters. The Wagnerian tendency towards exteriorization, which always subordinates subjective animation to the tangible gesture and the outward effect, thereby manages to expose something of the ephemeral nature of subjectivity itself. The motives of the characters are presented with almost exaggerated bluntness. Their behaviour changes with lightning rapidity. They barely retain their identity, and Siegfried is not even fully aware of his identity. . . . Love is something that occurs only at first sight and never as inward stillness; this was the case as early as the *Dutchman,* and it applies with equal truth to Siegmund and Sieglinde and to Walther and Eva. The fact that, for all his German nationalist ideals, Wagner always remains free from a stuffy philistinism is something he owes to an unspoilt view of sex. This alone allows him to create the moving scene in which Brünnhilde wishes to preserve her maidenhood for the sake of her beloved, but where she yet gives herself without restraint. Of course, her love later changes to hate with equal rapidity. No reflection leads her to see through the mechanics of the intrigue; and later still, after Siegfried's death, her hate is as abruptly transformed back into love—here, too, without any attempt to resolve the logic of the plot. Once Gutrune has told her about the potion that made Siegfried forget her, she wastes no further time on it. It is as if Wagner had anticipated Freud's discovery that what archaic man expresses in terms of violent action has not survived in civilized man, except in attenuated form, as an internal impulse that comes to the surface with the old explicitness only in dreams and madness.

At the same time, however, Wagner's indifference towards the inner life of the individual reveals traces of a political awareness of the way the individual is determined by material reality. Like the great philosophers he mistrusts the private. His preoccupation with totality is not just totalitarian and administrative; it points also to the fact that the universe is an interlocking system in which the more ruthlessly the individual tries to prevail, the less he succeeds. The attempt to change the world comes to nought, but changing the world is what is at issue. Siegfried does not suffer from the Oedipus complex; instead he smashes Wotan's spear. If in the historical world the primordial conflict is sublimated into dream, in the Alberich-Hagen scene in *The Twilight of the Gods,* the transition takes place visibly on the stage. This concrete sensuousness, and its implied contrast with inwardness, stamps the mythological subject-matter with the mark of history to a much greater degree than Wagner's aesthetics would have us believe. Myth and culture succeed each other in phases, and in this way the mythic origins of culture come into view. As a dramatist Wagner can see how myth and law interlock. The 'contrasts' to which the *Ring,* following Schopenhauer, attaches such importance are predicated on anarchy. The war of all against all is resolved only with difficulty by the legal order emerging from it. It constantly breaks out anew wherever no explicit system of contracts exists to prevent it. Wotan is ready for any act of violence as long as he is not bound by codified agreements. Moreover, these very agreements, which impose restrictions on an unenlightened state of nature, turn out to be fetters that deprive him of the freedom of movement and hence help to re-establish chaos. In Wagner, law is unmasked as the equivalent of lawlessness. The *Ring* could have as its motto the statement by Anaximander . . . : 'Wherever existing things have their origin, there too they must of necessity perish, for they must pay the penalty and be condemned for their iniquity, in accordance with the order of time.' The law that defined itself as punishment for lawlessness comes to resemble it and itself becomes lawlessness, an order for destruction: that, however, is the nature of myth as it is echoed in pre-Socratic thought, and Wagner adopts it not just as subject-matter, but in its innermost aesthetic consequences. The archaic idea of Fate presides over the seamless web of universal immanence in the *Gesamtkunstwerk.* . . . (pp. 115-18)

If in the *Ring* mythic violence and legal contract are confounded, this not only confirms an intuition about the origins of legality, it also articulates the experience of the lawlessness of a society dominated in the name of law by contract and property. The aesthetic criticism of Wagner, that as a modern he had violated the ancient and, as a profane person, offended against myth, may well be justified. But, equally, it must be pointed out that a regressive aesthetic practice is not a matter of individual choice or psychological accident. He belongs to the first generation to realize that in a world that has been socialized through and through it is not possible for an individual to alter something that is determined over the heads of men. Nevertheless, it was not given to him to call the overarching totality by its real name. In consequence it is transformed for him into myth. The opacity and omnipotence of the social process is then celebrated as a metaphysical mystery by the individual who becomes conscious of it and yet ranges himself on the side of its dominant forces. Wagner has devised the ritual of permanent catastrophe. His unbridled individualism utters the death sentence on the individual and its order.

As he searches for the cause of his own entanglement in the ground of the world, an understanding is reached between the present and the mythical. Wagner has not conjured up the myths simply as metaphors: beneath his gaze everything becomes mythological, and this applies with particular force to the only modern subject he ever treated. *The Mastersingers* flirts with that convention that used to operate in painting, according to which pictures of events remote in time and space could be peopled with the inhabitants of the modern world. . . . [The] anachronism is more than a pretended naivety and a pleasure in archaizing pastiche. In that light-hearted opera every element of the present sounds as if it were a reminiscence. The expression of sweet nostalgia merges with the allure of the familiar, the promise of security at home, together with the feeling, 'When was I here before?', and the archetypes of the bourgeois find themselves invested with the nimbus of what is long since past. Ultimately, the work captivates its audience much more because of this than because of its nationalist self-

idolization and its bestial sense of humour. Each listener has the feeling that it belongs to him alone, that it is a communication from his long-forgotten childhood, and from this shared *déjà vu* the phantasmagoria of the collective is constructed. The atmosphere distilled in this witches' kitchen is irresistible because it stirs up, gratifies and even legitimates ideologically an impulse that adult life has only laboriously and not wholly successfully managed to master. It relaxes everyone's limbs, not just Sachs's, and, as the demagogue of the feelings, the composer demonstrates the right reactions in which everyone then joins. Nowhere is Wagner more mythological than in the modernity of such pleasures. He can adapt to the most subtle nuances of individuality, but he does so in order to prepare the listener for the amorphous bliss of a pre-individual condition. The promise of happiness that gingerbread holds out to the Nuremberger is shown to be a divine realm of ideas. Whatever truth this contains, however, is subordinated to a lie. Wagner fraudulently presents the historical German past as its essence. In this way he has invested concepts such as 'ancestors' and 'the people' with that absoluteness which was subsequently unleashed in an outburst of absolute horror. This manipulated awakening of memory is the exact opposite of enlightenment. . . . [We] find in Wagner a strange confusion of the moonlit night and the smell of lilac (whose romantic charm was unknown in the sixteenth century) with sadistic brutality. The lambent quality of the music, the tone of the *Venusberg,* encourages its hearers to cast off not just their mundane reality, but also their humanity, and to give free rein to their destructive impulses. With the diabolical relish that is inseparable from the simple good humour it claims to be, the theatre-goer who takes pleasure in the brawl at the end of Act II is really gloating at a miniature foretaste of the violence to come.

All Wagnerian ambiguity stems from his relationship to archaic images. His talent for calling up the past pursues the inflections of the soul down to their real models and so illuminates their regressive element; at the same time, however, he entrusts himself to this element as if it were primordial truth and so he regresses too. Aesthetically he anticipates tensions that became explicit only with the disagreements between Freud and Jung. His 'psychoanalytic' motifs—incest, hatred of the father, castration—have been pointed out often enough; and Sachs's apothegm about 'true dream interpretation' seems to bring the work of art close to the analytic ideal of making the unconscious conscious. At moments of the process of becoming conscious, Wagner's language anticipates that of Nietzsche thirty years before *Zarathustra:*

> Descend then, Erda, Great Mother of fear,
> Great Mother of sorrow!
> Away, away to eternal sleep!

And from the same perspective Siegfried replies:

> Bravery or bravado—how do I know!

However, the formula is itself mythical. The gesture of challenge contained in that 'bravery and bravado' comes to resemble the archaic powers, and the 'how do I know?', with its persistent blankness, easily succumbs to them once again. Siegfried is not just the individual laboriously freeing himself from an unconscious state of nature. He is already the fool who will be celebrated in *Parsifal,* the 'childish hero' the 'idiot', who does not overcome fear by achieving a knowledge of self, but who merely does 'not know' what fear is, and when he finds out, from his experience of sex, forgets it again. When Wotan dismisses Erda, the Great Mother of fear, she does not lose her power and neither does he gain his liberty. On the contrary, in the Norn scene he succumbs to their sentence against his will and the Norns descend to the Great Mother when the rope snaps. The only function of consciousness is to complete the circle of unconsciousness. The cosmogonist Klages rejects Wagner; but there is more of his philosophy in the Erda passages than there is of psychoanalysis. Even his theory of knowledge, the notion of drifting organic images as opposed to conscious thought, is to be found in rudimentary form in *Siegfried.* Erda's sleep is said to be 'brooding' and she says of herself:

> My sleep is dreaming,
> My dreaming meditation,
> My meditation mastery of wisdom.

As in Klages, the disenfranchisement of the earth signifies metaphysical calamity:

> I am confused since I awoke:
> Wildly and awry the world revolves!

Whoever takes action against blind fate stands condemned as the demonic antagonist of the soul: the world ash-tree is mortally wounded by the God who cut his spear from it. It is Wagner who starts the process of transforming Schopenhauer's metaphysical concept of the Will into the more manageable theory of the collective unconscious. Ultimately this turns into the 'soul of the people', in which a brutality borrowed from the overbearing individual combines in an explosive mixture with the amorphous masses who have been solicitously protected from any thoughts of an antagonistic society. (pp. 119-23)

> *Theodor Adorno, in his* In Search of Wagner, *translated by Rodney Livingstone, NLB, 1981, 159 p.*

ERIC BENTLEY   (essay date 1944)

[*In this study of modern literary heroes, originally published in 1944, Bentley analyzes such Wagnerian characters as Siegfried, Tristan, and Parsifal in relation to the theories of the hero expounded by Nietzsche and Thomas Carlyle. For additional commentary by Bentley, see excerpt below, 1946.*]

In his early operas, Wagner examines the efforts of heroes to push back the boundaries of necessity, but he finds the hero doomed at the start (*The Flying Dutchman*) or misunderstood in the end (*Lohengrin*). The major spiritual problem, as most would admit, was faced only in *The Ring Cycle*, which, whether it is the most perfect, is certainly the richest and the most problematic of Wagner's works. (p. 150)

In *The Ring* Wagner sought, or so at first it seems, to embody the new heroic religion which, with Carlyle and Nietzsche, he found to be a necessary successor to the Christian epoch. Wotan, the old god whose tenure has always been insecure, is dethroned by Siegfried, the hero who can neither be helped nor hindered by the gods. The theme is worked out with the utmost variety of character and incident.

The old world, as Wotan explains to Mime . . . , consists of the dwarfs and of Alberich; of the giants, Fasolt and Fafnir; of the gods and Wotan. The earth contains riches which are innocent enough when in the protection of the auroral Rhinemaidens but which, in the hands of the loveless dwarfs and giants, became the cause of endless and purposeless strife. Wotan, who heads the hierarchy of the gods, is not omniscient or omnipotent. He forfeits one eye as the price of marriage with Fricka, whose dowry is the power of Law. He forfeits the Rhinegold and the magic ring in order to have his castle

built without losing Freia, Fricka's sister, whom he has pledged to the builders of the castle, the giants. Freia is a symbol of love—she possesses golden apples—and godhead has been able to retain the attribute of love (Freia) and law (Fricka) only by humiliating barter. So much for the limitation of Wotan's power. His wisdom is limited by his unruly temper, which drives him to quarrel with the giants who thus learn that he is not perfect. The giants represent stupid insurgent humanity as the dwarfs represent shy, treacherous humanity. (pp. 150-51)

When, assisted by his cynical intelligence, personified by Loge, the god gives away the Rhinegold, Fafnir kills Fasolt rather than share the booty, transforms himself by the use of the Tarnhelm, a magic helmet, into a dragon and sits guarding the gold. That is: the richness and the meaning of the earth were, in the course of history, claimed by man himself, but, far from rising to wisdom and nobility, man became a slavish and sleepy monster while God was an increasingly harassed elder statesman. Man has bought the ring and the gold by sacrificing love.

The symbols are primordial. The ring is a time-honored symbol for man's goal, his union with what he most needs. It is often a female sexual symbol—as in the final lines of [Shakespeare's] *The Merchant of Venice*—but, here in Wagner, the ring is what Fafnir prefers to woman: namely, the key to worldly power. The helmet represents the dexterity and adaptability of man, a dexterity and adaptability which can easily be misused. . . . It is important to note how Wagner demonstrated the necessity of godhead's preserving love and handing over earthly power to mankind. Erda, Mother Earth herself, the personified lifeforce, rises from her bed, warning Wotan to yield the ring to Fafnir. The demands of the life-force are final. *Das Rheingold,* which I have been sketching, closes with rejoicing over Freia. Intelligence (Loge) has the last word on the gods: "They hurry to their end, who boast of such great strength."

The Christian story passes from the failure of Adam to the triumph of the second Adam. In *Die Walküre* and *Siegfried,* Wagner describes a not wholly dissimilar process, the failure of Wotan and the triumph of Siegfried.

Feeling the insecurity of his position, Wotan buttresses his divine power with a bodyguard of fallen heroes whom his Valkyries have borne to Valhalla from the battlefield. These buttresses of Deity symbolize the churches or any organized support of the old order. Fearing that Alberich will wrest the ring from Fafnir, Wotan prepares plans for the future. His conclusion is that only a higher nature than has previously existed can recover the ring. This higher creation is the hero, the germ of whom he feels in his own godhead. The Wagnerian hero, like the Carlylean and the Nietzschean, is the legitimate successor of the old god. As Zarathustra strives towards superhumanity by his love of the earth, Wotan impregnates Erda herself. The fruit of this union is not the hero but true will, directive *Wille zur Macht* (as against the merely rational Loge). True will, which is also the eternal image of woman drawing men on to high endeavor, is called Brünnhilde.

The breeding of the hero is indirect and slow. Wotan cannot father him. He fathers, by a mortal woman, the twins Siegmund and Sieglinde. Contravening human laws against adultery, for Sieglinde is by this time married to Hunding, and contravening also holy ordinance against incest, the pair engender the hero, Siegfried: the old order is broken by immoralists. The sexual potency and creative power of Siegmund are suggested by the myth, familiar to readers of Malory, of the sword which can be drawn only by the hero. But Siegmund has to atone for his temerity by death; and (a highly imaginative stroke) Brünnhilde flees carrying on her war-horse the fragments of Siegmund's broken sword and Sieglinde pregnant with the hero. Siegmund's death, required by the ancient law (Fricka), was redeemed by the resentful will of Brünnhilde.

Brünnhilde's rebellion, threatening the status of Wotan and the old order, is punished, not with death, for Wotan cannot kill the emanation of his own union with the life-force, but by her being thrown into a deep sleep. Like Snow White and other heroines of the folk imagination, Brünnhilde can be awakened only by the advent of the hero. The creative will of humanity is imprisoned, though the circle of flame that encloses her is a mirage. Since only the hero has courage, a mirage is enough to deceive unheroic mankind.

The delivery comes in *Siegfried.* Wagner portrays his hero as the iconoclast. By a Christian criterion, he is too loud, too violent, too arrogant: an unregenerate pagan devoid of compassion. Siegfried agrees with Carlyle that one need not act charitably to the contemptible and treats Mime as roughly as his anvil. But the *hubris* which the ancients considered a fault is a virtue for Wagner, as for Nietzsche; and it is by his boundless confidence that Siegfried recreates Nothung, the sword of Siegmund. Siegfried is a crude emanation of the vital energy which for Carlyle, Nietzsche, and Wagner has superseded the divine idea. He is irreverent and, like Zarathustra, is more at home with the beasts, and especially the birds, of the forest than with men. For Nietzsche, men were a cross between monster and phantom; for Wagner, at this time, they were either dolts or knaves. Siegfried slays the dragon, seizes the ring and helmet, leaving the earth's riches undespoiled. A friendly bird whispers to him in sleep that on a mountain peak Brünnhilde awaits him within a ring of fire.

The climax of the death of Fafnir is prefatory to a higher climax. At the foot of Brünnhilde's mountain, Siegfried meets Wotan. They converse and Siegfried explains that he has a healthy contempt for the old and effete. Wotan summons all his divine grandeur to impress the youth. But Siegfried reverses the fate of his father (who had broken Nothung across the spear of Wotan) by breaking the spear of Wotan with Nothung. After this, Wotan disappears from human history. God, as Nietzsche put it, is dead. We await the superman. The myth of Heroic Vitalism ends in the prologue of *Götterdämmerung,* where Siegfried and Brünnhilde exchange symbols, a male one for a female, Brünnhilde's horse for Siegfried's ring. The quest is achieved. On the horse of Brünnhilde, Siegfried is master of the world. Meanwhile Wotan has tried to mend his spear with a bough from the World Ash. The ash withers, for now that the hero has freed mankind from divine shackles, its day is done. Wotan's heroes cut it down and prepare to burn Valhalla with the faggots. Night will fall on the gods. (pp. 151-54).

[*Götterdämmerung*] is Wagner's palinode. It is a picture of life after the triumph of heroism. The hero finds himself the dupe of villainy and corruption, because he carries with him the ring and its curse. The ring is a symbol of power as the gold is a symbol of wealth. Alberich is economic man, the victim and incarnation of Mammonism; Siegfried is power man, the hero of the new post-capitalist epoch. According to the Wagner of *Götterdämmerung* power man is doomed no less than economic man. Siegfried is given a chance to restore the ring to the Rhine-maidens, but he is too proud or too ignorant to yield to their entreaties. Moreover, night has not yet fallen on the gods. They linger on until the final consummation. And the final consummation is reached through the sacrificial love of Brünn-

hilde. In the closing bars of *Götterdämmerung* is heard the motif of redemption by love. The ring returns to the Rhine, and reconcilement is reached through love and sacrifice. The Siegfried-ideal, evidently, is not enough. (pp. 154-55)

Wagner did not, as many since Nietzsche have imagined, evolve from world-embracing Heroic Vitalism to Buddhistic nihilism. The two opposite philosophies or attitudes, Heroic Vitalism and Buddhist-Christian religion, coexisted in his breast as they did in Carlyle's and Nietzsche's. (p. 156)

The two Wagnerian philosophies are brought together in *The Ring* by a device as daring as the maestro's musical technique. Since the Siegfried story is nowadays known to us chiefly through Wagner, we tend to forget his most audacious act: the conflation of the myth of Siegfried with the myth of the fall of the gods. The twilight of the gods was not part of a story imposed on Wagner by his sources. It is an alien element which only an urgent sense of purpose and a considerable genius could fuse. The idea that heroism is ultimately worthless, that the "innocence of becoming" can only be restored through sacrifice, is what Wagner substitutes for the happy ending which Shaw rightly ridicules. But why does Shaw ignore the meaning of the substitution? Perhaps because he could not see how a man can affirm and deny the life-force in the same work. Shaw himself was to be a "perfect Wagnerite," a Wagner without negation or nihilism, without Schopenhauer, Buddha, and *Götterdämmerung.* But Wagner remained an imperfect one.

Siegfried is, manifestly and *par excellence,* the hero of Heroic Vitalism. How does Wagner interpret him and how did he arrive at his conception? (pp. 156-57)

Through the fog of Wagner's prose, one can dimly descry the intention. The Flying Dutchman, Tannhäuser, and Lohengrin are all seeking redemption (*Erlösung*) through the eternal feminine. Wagner's magniloquence—Senta is "the Woman of the Future," Tannhäuser "the spirit of the whole Ghibelline race," Lohengrin, "the type of the only really tragic material, of the tragic element of our modern life"—convinces us at least of his serious intentions. The Siegfried idea came from the heroine of *Lohengrin,* Elsa. She made Wagner, he says, a full-fledged revolutionary. He was yearning for redemption through the spirit of the Folk, and Elsa was the incarnation of that spirit.

Elsa was the incarnation of Wagner's personal and social ideals, of all his life-affirming ideals. At last he had arrived at a conclusion. But Elsa was a woman, and Elsa's life was a failure. It was necessary to present the idea again. The Ring Cycle springs from this need. The character of Siegfried was a necessity of Wagner's development, Siegfried the hero in his fullness, the doer of deeds, the complete man. "It was Elsa," Wagner says, "who taught me to discover this man." (pp. 157-58)

"Siegfried," [Wagner] wrote, "is the man of the future whom we have wanted and desired but who cannot be made by us and who must create himself through our annihilation." This conception has been well digested by those who write about Wagner and Hitler. One thing is forgotten: that Wagner himself rejected it. *Siegfried* has one of the grimmest, most ironical endings in all drama, no less ironical for the fact that the audience goes home thinking it has witnessed a happy ending. . . . The words of Siegfried and Brünnhilde are ambiguous. Consider the final line: "*Leuchtende Liebe, lachender Tod* [Gleaming love, laughing death]!" This means that salvation is to be found in love and death, love being associated with light, and death not with decay but with laughter. The statement as it stands is not very different from the conclusion of the whole tetralogy. But the context is different. Siegfried is not yet the dead hero who has paid the price. He is overcome with *hubris;* he is on the brink of his downfall at Gunther's court. The irony here consists in his utter unawareness. Brünnhilde on the other hand is, until the last moment, overcome with foreboding. Each ecstatic thought of Siegfried's she has capped with a despairing thought. He speaks of life, light, day, creation; she of death, darkness, night, annihilation. Logically there is no contradiction, because he is speaking of their own future, she of the end of the gods. But the gods cannot die while Siegfried keeps the ring. Brünnhilde knows this and cries out in deliberate forgetfulness, Siegfried in involuntary joy: *"Leuchtende Liebe, lachender Tod!" Götterdämmerung* is foreshadowed.

Ambivalence is the cardinal characteristic of Wagner's mind, and the natural outlet for such ambivalence is irony. Irony and *double-entendre* are carried over into the music itself when the orchestra plays such themes as World's Heritage at the very time when Brünnhilde, full of foreboding, feels that she will not inherit the world. *The Ring* concludes with the leitmotif of redemption through love. Whether Wagner rejects his Siegfried philosophy or merely moves away from it would be hard to determine. (pp. 158-59)

For most people *Tristan* is the quintessence of Wagnerism; for the musician it is the great step towards modern atonality. For the historian, however, it represents—unlike *The Ring*—only one side of Wagner: Wagner the nihilist. That it should be precisely this opera that brought Nietzsche to Wagner is of course a paradox, and we must assume that it spoke to the nihilist who was resident also in Nietzsche's spirit. *Tristan* speaks in a voice of command. You have either to flee or capitulate. An early German Romanticist had described music as "the land of faith where all our doubts and our sorrows are lost in a sea of sound." None but Wagner ever quite realized this idea, and he nowhere but in *Tristan.*

The piece is a landmark also in the history of the drama. The bourgeois epoch, since Lessing and Diderot, had developed its own non-tragic drama based upon two psychological factors: the Illusion that the characters on the stage were real, and Suspense as a magnet to draw the audience. Far from restoring that tragic dignity which sets the audience at a distance, Wagner exploited the technique of illusion and suspense to the utmost. His stage at Bayreuth was known for its "mechanical wonders" and its realism. Effect is piled on effect to secure the surrender of the audience. It is a total surrender, a surrender of all the faculties, to a magician. (pp. 159-60)

We are confronted with Tristan, a great example of a hero whose existence justifies life, "the miracle of all kingdoms," as Brangaene says, "the highly praised man, the hero without peer, the treasury and seat of fame." But from the first he moves in an atmosphere of fret and fever, of billowing, sinister emotion and talk of feud and death. The time-honored conflict of love and honor is transmuted into something macabre and morbid, for though honor remains honor, love is equated with death and, worse still, is found the better for being equated with death, just as the love of Siegmund and Sieglinde grows more confident and ecstatic when they know it is incestuous. Tristan stands to Frau Minne, the divine patroness of love, as Tannhäuser did to Venus, but Wagner's Tristan not only surrenders as did the Tannhäuser of mediaeval tradition, he surrenders in the belief that she is not only deadly but the more exciting and desirable for being deadly. This is Wagner's very

un-Nietzschean transvaluation of values. Darkness and night, primordial symbols of evil, become symbols of goodness, which is equated with extinction; day is an object of dread. This inversion of symbols is not limited to the famous *"unbewusst, höchste Lust"* ("highest joy, to be unconscious"), it is the imagery of the whole drama. Its meaning is brilliantly hit in a single sentence of Nietzsche's in which he isolates the essence of passionate pessimism: *"Denn der Mensch will lieber noch das Nichts wollen als* nicht *wollen"* ("For man would rather desire nothingness than *not* desire"). The Buddhistic-Schopenhauerian philosophy advocated the annihilation of desire; and Wagner was soon desiring annihilation.

Tristan has a crude sexual basis. The world knows how it had its origin in Wagner's love for the wife of a silk merchant, Otto Wesendonk. But that is not all. The love duet is a not very indirect representation of the sexual act. More than that: the idea of ecstasy followed by extinction follows the sexual pattern. The whole of *Tristan* is a celebration of the sexual act in the terms of music-drama, as *Lady Chatterley's Lover* is such a celebration in realistic terms. The celebration might be cleanly pagan as in primitive, ancient, and Renaissance poetry. But in Wagner it is not. His love is greasy with self-conscious sex. He performs moral gymnastics and ends standing on his head. Which is no doubt what critics mean by inverted puritanism.

What happens to the Wagnerian hero? He goes to his death not with Hellenic cheerfulness but with orgiastic pleasure. Wagner's "religious" resolution to extinguish desire led him to an attitude that was neither pagan nor religious. He took what was piquant in both schemes of life and accepted the responsibilities of neither. His hero is not a great exemplar of *any* view of life. His heroic tragedy is neither tragic nor heroic. (pp. 160-61)

Parsifal is ostensibly the completest renunciation of worldliness and thus of nineteenth-century civilization. It is a return to that defense of spirituality as against the flesh and the devil which had been the subject of *Lohengrin* and *Tannhäuser*. Like Lohengrin, the hero is a stainless, saintly knight with an aura of the supernatural about him. Like Tannhäuser, he is tempted by a sensual sorceress. Unlike both other heroes, however, Parsifal succeeds in his mission, and the drama ends with the very Wagnerian words:

> Höchsten Heiles Wunder
> Erlösung dem Erlöser!
>
> [Miracle of highest salvation,
> redemption to the redeemer!]

Parsifal is of all Wagner's works the most extraordinary and the most unacceptable. In *Tristan* the code of chivalric heroism is fused with nineteenth-century sex and nineteenth-century nihilism; in *Parsifal* it is chivalric religion which he fuses with these. In *Tristan* the Launcelot-type is degraded, in *Parsifal* the Galahad-type is degraded. The second degradation is the more drastic and the more disastrous.

Like most Wagnerian protagonists, Parsifal is searching for redemption (*Erlösung*); like them, he relies upon miracles (*Wunder*); like them, he lives in a world of phantasmagoria, the strange Wagnerian world where everything is mythic and unreal yet solid and substantial as a Victorian drawing-room. Redemption, in this context, has less the force of a religious experience than of a superb thrill. The miracles which bring redemption have less the force of sublimity than of magic for magic's sake. One has the feeling that an obsession with this sort of redemption, a dependence upon this sort of miracle, a penchant for this sort of phantasmagoria are fundamental traits of Wagner's mind, reflecting his compromise with his age. They offer solace without solution, excitement without order.

In *Götterdämmerung* we see Wagner in retreat from Heroic Vitalism; in *Parsifal* we see him stating an alternative that reveals only his mental confusion. The virtues by which Parsifal succeeds are: virginity, simplicity, and compassion. These qualities Wagner most sadly lacked. The virginity is like the renunciation of Hans Sachs, a piece of wishful thinking. The simplicity is also a fantastic overcompensation. The compassion comes oddly from the man who cracked jokes when four hundred Jews were burnt to death in a theatre fire. Perhaps if Wagner had really been capable of making sacred drama out of virginity, simplicity, and compassion, we could take these virtues seriously. But he was not. He could not even imagine what the words meant. Why, then, was he interested in them? The immoralist, in search of the abnormal and the illicit, makes of vice his first subject of study, but when in time vice becomes normal, virtue in its turn acquires a morbid fascination, and normality seems Bohemian. This is the stage Wagner has reached in *Parsifal*. Once his conception is taken seriously, it is a matter not for the church or the theatre, but for the clinic. (pp. 162-63)

The Composite Artwork (*Gesamtkunstwerk*)—the Wagnerian conception *par excellence*—did not quite come off. Wagner was not much of a poet; he was still less of a philosopher. His music, for all its influence, is more a résumé of the past than a model for the future. There is truth in Nietzsche's withering words: "Wagner as musician is reckoned among painters, as poet among musicians, as artist generally among actors." Yet though Wagner's mind was fundamentally a theatrical one, his greatest achievement was not in the sphere of drama but in the sphere of music. That is one typically Wagnerian paradox. Another is that, despite waves of nihilism and vulgar Teutonism, he could on occasion affirm life, crave excellence, and admire the hero. That is why the term Heroic Vitalist fits him better than the term proto-Nazi. (p. 163)

> Eric Bentley, "Richard Wagner, Siegfried, and Hitler," in his The Cult of the Superman: A Study of the Idea of Heroism in Carlyle and Nietzsche, with Notes on Other Hero-Worshipers of Modern Times, Peter Smith, 1969, pp. 147-63.*

ERIC RUSSELL BENTLEY   (essay date 1946)

[*Bentley is considered one of the most erudite and innovative critics of the modern theater. He was responsible for introducing Bertolt Brecht, Luigi Pirandello, and other European playwrights to America through his studies, translations, and stage adaptations of their plays. In his critical works, Bentley concentrates on the playwright and the dramatic text, rather than on the production aspects of the play. In the following excerpt from* The Playwright As Thinker, *Bentley interprets Wagner's dramatic theories and discusses how his* Tristan and Isolde *and* The Mas-

Rock of the Valkyries in Valkyrie. *After an original sketch by Joseph Hoffmann.*

Depiction by Arthur Rackham of the Rhine maidens in Wagner's Rhinegold. *From* The Ring of the Niblung, *translated by Margaret Armour. William Heinemann Ltd., 1939. Reproduced by permission of the publisher.*

tersingers of Nuremberg *reflect them. Bentley also analyzes Wagner as a product of his times, examining his relationship to German Romanticism and noting the representation of the middle class and its effect on art. For additional commentary by Bentley, see excerpt above, 1944.*]

In Wagner's theoretical works . . .—*Art and Revolution, The Art-Work of the Future,* and *Opera and Drama*—the national character of [a] new art is emphasized *ad nauseam.* Art is *of* the Folk, *for* the Folk, and, since the artist is a magical mouthpiece, *by* the Folk. As Wagner grew older his nationalism took on the color of the times and he became a Reich-German, anti-French, anti-Semitic, and proto-Nazi.

A Nazi critic once wrote that Bayreuth was Nazi Germany in little, and indeed there is a true, though indirect, connection between the demagogue of Bayreuth and the demagogue of Berchtesgaden. The idea of a national German art begins as lofty idealism and has ended—for the present—with Nazism. But Bayreuth has more significance than that. Eighteenth-century opera had catered either directly to the court or to other similar groups in a courtly society. Bayreuth was an attempt to give social function to the opera in "a century of vile bourgeoisie." Despite the blandishments of the Bavarian king, Wagner knew that to be a court musician in 1870 was to be the lackey of a lackey. Despite the apparent loss of status which

the artist was supposed to have undergone in the nineteenth century, Wagner resolved to be more of a monarch than poor King Ludwig.

The romanticists had claimed primacy for the artist in the ideal world; Wagner proceeded to realise their ideal in actuality. The romanticists had called themselves unacknowledged legislators of the world; Wagner would be an acknowledged legislator. It is rightly said that Wagner made only too solid and tangible what romantic poets had left to the fancy. The theater at Bayreuth is itself a romantic fancy made solid and tangible. It is not only a nationalist symbol but also a symbol of aestheticism, the Palace of Art, Axel's Castle, the ivory tower itself. (p. 82)

In his essay *Opera and Drama* Wagner has expounded his pseudo-ideas of theater. Ignoring his arbitrary "Teutonic" antitheses and the involutions, at first baffling and in the end disgusting, of his argument, we can extract from this document the assurance that Wagner was abundantly aware of the unsatisfactory status of the theater in modern life, that he saw abundantly that even Goethe and Schiller had not really succeeded in the theater, and that he shared the hope of those who saw a future in "music drama" with mythological subject matter. Myth, Wagner thinks, is always true; it is elemental; it springs from the Folk; it can be expressed in "tone-speech," that is, language that is meant to be musically enunciated (as against verses whch happen to be set to music later). The Wagnerian "music drama" has a more closely knit dialogue than the despised Grand Opera. It avoids pretty songs and pretty stanzas. In "music drama" with no recitatives the dialogue is continuous like the melodic line, and because of this Wagner slows down his voices and gives the impression of speed with his orchestra. Hence the typically Wagnerian pattern of slow vocal melody against a complex, often bewilderingly fast and tempestuous, symphonic background.

Wagner proposed to replace the Grand Opera of Meyerbeer and Scribe with the Composite Art Work, and for that reason one prime fact has been overlooked by all but the anti-Wagnerites: Wagner's own theater technique is to a great extent that of Meyerbeer and Scribe. (pp. 85-6)

Wagner's objections to conventionality and artificiality are not so much objections to Scribe as to the late classicism of the eighteenth century, which Scribe had previously rebelled against. Wagner wished to simplify the drama of his operatic predecessors, to reduce it to bare essentials, to organise and centralise it, so that the effect might be strong and direct. That had been Scribe's idea too. (p. 86)

[Wagner's] early works, as far as *Tannhäuser* and even *Lohengrin,* are still Grand Opera of a kind that the audiences of Scribe and Meyerbeer would understand, at least dramatically (though the vehement criticism all Wagner's works met with shows they had something in them more challenging or at least more puzzling than the Scribe-Meyerbeer commodity.) . . . Wagner did not produce a full-fledged Wagnerian "music drama" till *Der Ring des Nibelungen.* For all its longueurs and needless repetitions, for all the flaws and inconsistencies which mar the final libretto, *The Ring* is one of the most significant products of the nineteenth century, at once a criticism and a mirror of the age, less great than [Goethe's] *Faust* or even [Ibsen's] *Peer Gynt,* yet less of the closet and more of the theater than either of these.

Wagner's greatest works are *Tristan* and *Die Meistersinger,* for only in these is the conglomeration of elements a real synthesis. *Tristan* is a great drama, and it is great music; but it is marred by a diffuseness which would have ruined a work of lesser genius. In each of his works Wagner creates a special and unmistakable atmosphere appropriate to his conception; even when he works at several operas at once, he keeps them as far apart in atmosphere as separate worlds. That is one of the great things about Wagner. Now none of Wagner's manners or atmospheres is as markedly peculiar as the manner of *Tristan.* It can be recognised wherever you drop the phonograph needle. The *Tristan* manner consists (among other things) of regularly and rapidly undulating waves of sound, developed chromatically, and sweeping or fading into space. The result is very curious. So much does one feel the manner as an endlessly repeated pattern that *Tristan* seems overrepetitious and long *however much you cut it.* (pp. 87-8)

The astonishing thing is that *Tristan* is great all the same, great not as an expression of the "eternal truth of myth," but as an expression of European nihilism, one of the deepest trends in nineteenth century thought and sensibility. In its symbolism (it is one long representation of the sexual act), in its equation of love and death, its apotheosis of darkness and its renunciation of light, it is the Anti-Faust, the decadent poem *par excellence.*

If *Tristan* is the favorite of the Wagnerites, *Die Meistersinger* is the favorite Wagnerian opera of the non-Wagnerites. Yet *Die Meistersinger* is just as essentially Wagnerian and just as authentically of the period. (p. 88)

The nineteenth century saw the ascendancy of the middle class, and as all the champions of genuine culture realised, this meant an ascendancy of the middle-class mind; it meant the apotheosis of mediocrity. In nineteenth century literature, therefore, we find, since the artist is by nature an aristocrat in the sense of a seeker after excellence, a series of portraits of mediocrity, a type which had not previously been common in literature. Aristotle had defined the tragic character as being above life size, and the comic character as being below life size, and literary tradition had been chiefly concerned with these two types; but the nineteenth century, especially through the novel but also in drama, was interested in the middle-sized or average man. . . . Wagner does not portray the type; he embodies it; he is its mouthpiece; through his genius, lack of genius becomes vocal; which means (and this is Wagner's "betrayal" of culture) that he confers upon mediocrity the favors of its opposite, genius. Hence Nietzsche's hostility to his former friend and idol. Nietzsche found out that Wagner was the spokesman of the new age in its most negative aspects. *Tristan* is grandiose illusion; *Die Meistersinger* is incarnate *gemuetlichkeit,* the middle-class substitute for serenity. (pp. 88-9)

Wagner is the prime instance of a compromised genius, of one who in criticising his age came to terms with it, of one who in his very denunciation of falsehood himself proved a liar. His gifts were extraordinary. The potency of his magic is unsurpassed in the history of music. That, Nietzsche maintained, made him all the more dangerous. None saw Wagner's merits more clearly than Nietzsche, even after the breach of friendship, for Nietzsche knew that Wagner was the only man who, uncompromised, might have brought grandeur and sublimity back to the world. "I had no one," he lamented, "but Richard Wagner." Nietzsche saw not only Wagner's potentiality but also his nature and his historical meaning:

> I understand perfectly if today a musician says: "I hate Wagner, but I cannot endure any other music." But [?And] I would also understand a philosopher who explained: "Wagner epito-

mises modernity. It can't be helped, one must first be a Wagnerite.''

To follow Nietzsche in the matter, and it is wise to do so, is not to become a rabid anti-Wagnerite; it is to see very sharply the pro and the con; it is the pro and the con for a whole complex of ideas and meanings. (p. 89)

> Eric Russell Bentley, "Wagner and Ibsen: A Contrast," *in his* The Playwright As Thinker: A Study of Drama in Modern Times, *1946. Reprint by Harcourt Brace Jovanovich, Inc., 1967, pp. 75-106.*

JACK M. STEIN (essay date 1947)

[*In this in-depth discussion of the influence of Arthur Schopenhauer's aesthetic theories on Wagner, Stein contends that after reading Schopenhauer's* Die Welt als Wille und Vorstellung *and* Parerga und Paralipomena, *Wagner reworked his conception of* Gesamtkunstwerk, *or union of the arts. Stein posits that these new theories inform Wagner's later works, including* Siegfried, Tristan und Isolde, Tanhauser, The Mastersingers of Nuremberg, Götterdämmerung, *and* Parsifal. *Other critics who have discussed the possible influence of Schopenhauer on Wagner include Ernest Newman (1898) and Pierre Lasserre (1917). For further commentary by Stein, see Additional Bibliography.*]

Over and over again since the first appearance of the poem of Wagner's *Tristan und Isolde* . . . , Schopenhauerian ethics, his famous doctrines of pessimism, renunciation, etc., have been read into and out of the works of Wagner by philosophers, musicologists, historians, and Wagner specialists. The violence of this academic controversy has forced into obscurity a matter of greater significance, the influence on Wagner of Schopenhauer's aesthetic theories, and particularly his metaphysics of music. This neglect has caused the critical fact to be overlooked that acceptance of these theories effected a sweeping revision of Wagner's conception of the *Gesamtkunstwerk* only a few years after it had first become crystallized in his mind. And because this has been overlooked, all aesthetic discussions of that part of Wagner's theory or of the music dramas written after Wagner's contact with Schopenhauer are subject to extensive revision and correction.

A few chronological details will present the picture more clearly. In 1851, when Wagner was thirty-eight years old, he published the three-volume essay, *Oper und Drama,* which contained a detailed blueprint of what he called *Das Kunstwerk der Zukunft,* a theoretical work of art presenting a genuine organic synthesis of poetry, visual drama, and music. . . . It is this essay which all discussions of Wagner incorrectly assume to be his ultimate theoretical formulation of the *Gesamtkunstwerk,* and hence the only theoretical pattern for all the major works.

But in 1854, only three years later, Wagner was introduced to the works of Schopenhauer. He read both volumes of *Die Welt als Wille und Vorstellung,* as well as the two volumes of *Parerga und Paralipomena,* and accepted most of what he read with great enthusiasm. There is abundant proof of this in his letters, his prose works, and his music dramas. Scholars have most clearly and repeatedly recognized his acceptance of the Schopenhauerian metaphysics and ethics. But Wagner's own system of aesthetics was so precisely and so fully stated in *Oper und Drama* that they have failed to recognize the importance of his subsequent acceptance of Schopenhauer's aesthetics. If it can be successfully demonstrated that Wagner was impelled to recast his theory of the *Gesamtkunstwerk* under the influence of Schopenhauer, an aesthetic revaluation of everything Wagner wrote after 1854 is indicated. Such a re-examination of theory and practice would involve much of the theory, and all of the major works, except *Das Rheingold* and *Die Walküre;* in other words, *Siegfried, Tristan und Isolde*, the Paris revisions of *Tannhäuser, Die Meistersinger, Götterdämmerung*, and *Parsifal.*

In order to make clear the extent to which the theories in *Oper und Drama* were later revised, Wagner's formulation of the *Gesamtkunstwerk* in that essay must first be sketched briefly. In it, Wagner rejects poetry, music, and drama individually, and denies their validity as independent forms of art. He refers to them as incomplete phases of the one true art form, an organic synthesis of all three.

At the time of writing *Oper und Drama*, Wagner was strongly influenced by the sensationalism of Ludwig Feuerbach; hence his *Gesamtkunstwerk* is predicated on the assumption that it must appeal to the senses, and through them exclusively to the emotions. Reason, the mind, everything conceptual and intellectual are to be eliminated.... [The] most urgent problem was to free the poetic dialogue from its contact with reason and the intellect; in other words, to devise a means of emotionalizing the intellectual content of the poetic verse. This Wagner proposed to do in two ways: first by intensifying the emotional appeal of the words themselves, and secondly, by uniting the poetic verse with vocal melody in such a fashion that the melodic line would be felt as an extension of the specific emotional content inherent in the poetic verse.

By means of a discussion of the origin of language which owes much to Herder and the early Romanticists, Wagner emerges with a new type of verse form, the three most prominent characteristics of which are alliteration, condensation, and a free rhythm. Alliteration, he contends, can—and in more primitive times, did—express an intuitive perception of the relationship between different objects or qualities. Condensation of the language permits a higher percentage of root syllables, which derive from the early intuitive stages of language development, and eliminates to a large extent elements like conjunctions and prepositions, which bear no emotional quality. Free rhythm replaces the arbitrary pulsation of most poetry with the normal speech accent, thus making possible an endless degree of subtlety in accentuation for purposes of emotional shading.

It is when Wagner launches upon the task of uniting this theoretical verse with a vocal melody that he produces the most amazing discussion of musical prosody that has ever been written. Even if we should discount all the rest of Wagner's theory as purely personal rationalization with no general validity and make no claim that it offers any original contribution to art theory or to philosophic thought, this synthesis of word and music must be acknowledged as an epochal contribution which has not ceased to have a tremendous influence.

For his *Gesamtkunstwerk* Wagner needed an organic union of melodic line with poetic verse. One must not interpret this to mean simply setting a poetic text to music. Wagner demanded a melodic configuration at every point so intimately fused with the poetic verse that the melody would be felt as the actual musical counterpart of that text, or better, as the musical portion of an indivisible unit, which Wagner called *die Versmelodie.* By this fusion, the vocal line, drawing on the immense resources of music, would complete the emotionalization of the poetic line demanded by Wagner's original premise of an exclusive appeal to emotion. (pp. 92-5)

The harmonic and instrumental resources of the orchestra in general are to be employed at all times by the poet-composer as a . . . means of underlining the emotional content of the melodic verse. A second function of the orchestra is to provide what Wagner calls *Erinnerungsmotive*. Whenever the melodic verse incorporates a reflective reference, expressed or implied, to something which has previously occurred or been said, the orchestra can articulate this thought in emotional terms by repeating the characteristic melodic and harmonic contour of the original melodic-poetic verse. The restatement can be either exactly like the original or altered melodically, rhythmically, or harmonically, in order to express subtle emotional variations, but in any case, it is to be sufficiently like the original to be immediately recognized by the listener. The use of these motifs of reminiscence is to be entirely functional. They are not to be used as a stop-gap at moments when the dramatic interest lags. A single motif used without proper justification is sufficient to destroy the unity. A third important function of the orchestra is to underline the stage action, especially gestures—which, incidentally, Wagner recommends be used sparingly so that significant visual details can be transmitted aurally as well.

This, in brief outline, is the aesthetic side of the *Gesamtkunstwerk* in *Oper und Drama*. For the present discussion, it is important to note the focal position of the melodic verse, the synthesis of poetic verse and vocal line. It is to be the structural center. . . . Everything else in the entire work converges toward it, and is derived from it. The functions of the orchestra are at all times conditioned by it, the motifs of reminiscence are drawn directly from the contour of the melodic verse. The stage action and gestures interpet to the emotions through the visual sense what the poetry and music are transmitting aurally. There must be no chorus; there must not even be simultaneous singing by the principal characters, for only one melodic verse can be fully projected at one time. (p. 97)

After *Oper und Drama* Wagner began his *Ring* cycle, composing *Das Rheingold* and *Die Walküre* in the manner newly devised in the essay. But in the autumn of 1854 came the contact with Schopenhauer. Even though this was a philosophical system which in all its phases was about as diametrically opposed to Wagner's former optimistic, materialistic sensationalism as could be imagined, he immediately made the necessary about-face and became an unhesitating pessimistic, phenomenalistic transcendentalist. He easily succeeded in convincing himself that he had been one all along, and had needed only Schopenhauer to make his own position clear to him. Much can be said in support of this, and a great deal has been written on whether Schopenhauer's point of view came as a revolution or a revelation to Wagner.

Wagner found Schopenhauer's view of art, and especially his unique position with respect to music, too fascinating to resist. In the first pages of Book Three of *Die Welt als Wille und Vorstellung*, Schopenhauer identifies the Kantian *Ding an sich*, which is the ultimate reality behind the world of phenomena, as the metaphysical Will, and sets up the Eternal Ideas or Unchanging Forms of Plato as direct objectifications of this Will, a kind of generic mid-point between the Will and the phenomenal world, independent of the laws of time, space, and causality. There would seem to be a good deal of meretricious theorizing involved in this somewhat eclectic epistemological manipulation, but the arguments pro and con are not essential here. All forms of art, except music, continues Schopenhauer later in Book Three, are revelations in terms of phenomena of these Eternal Ideas. Music alone is independent of the world as representation, since it does not derive its material from phenomena and is an objectification, not of the Eternal Ideas, but of the metaphysical Will itself. . . . Music is to Schopenhauer then a kind of Eternal Idea itself; in fact, he asserts that music could exist even if the phenomenal world were non-existent.

Now, in endorsing such a point of view, Wagner was faced with some very perplexing problems. Schopenhauer, of course, rejected the possibility of any genuine synthesis of music with the other arts, because of their intrinsic inequality. But the *Gesamtkunstwerk* was a form to which Wagner was definitely committed. Therefore, it was imperative for him to reconcile Schopenhauer and the *Gesamtkunstwerk* somehow or other. To fit this transcendental concept of music into any *Gesamtkunstwerk* was difficult, but to fit it into his own recently attained sensationalistic synthesis of music, poetry, and visual drama . . . was impossible. It is the central argument of this article that he could not do this, and that he therefore was compelled to devise a completely new concept of the *Gesamtkunstwerk* to replace that of his **Oper und Drama.**

Beethoven, the essay in which the new theory of the *Gesamtkunstwerk* receives its definitive statement, appeared in 1870, a full sixteen years later. In the meantime, **Tristan und Isolde,** the Paris version of **Tannhäuser, Die Meistersinger,** and **Siegfried** had been completed. All of these works reflect in many ways the gestation that was in process in Wagner's mind after his contact with Schopenhauer. They thus represent various stages in the disintegration of the idea of the *Gesamtkunstwerk* found in **Oper und Drama,** which was ostensibly the pattern upon which they were constructed.

In its most essential form, the new theoretical *Gesamtkunstwerk* of the essay **Beethoven** is a synthesis of music and visual action as complementary revelations, or objectifications, of the metaphysical Will. In this dualistic synthesis, dialogue—that which in the new *Gesamtkunstwerk* corresponds extrinsically to the melodic verse of **Oper und Drama**—is relegated to a subordinate position, as a mechanical aid to clarifying the mimetic action. Such a synthesis of poetic verse and vocal line as formed the very root of the earlier theory is declared an impossibility. (pp. 97-9)

The importance of the disintegration of the melodic verse cannot be overestimated. For if poetic verse and melodic line are no longer to be fused, then all of the many details involving prosody and voice leading, poetic and melodic alliteration, modulation, motifs of reminiscence, etc., cease to be an integral part of the *Gesamtkunstwerk*.

These matters are not discussed at all in **Beethoven,** which is concerned only with the metaphysical justification of the synthesis of visual drama and music. The new *Gesamtkunstwerk* is established only on broad philosophical lines. There is none of the concrete detail and practical suggestion which were so abundant in **Oper und Drama.** This is undoubtedly one of the reasons why **Beethoven** has not received the attention it deserves in this connection. One error begets another. Because **Beethoven** has been largely disregarded, the theories it embodies have been allowed no importance in Wagner study. Because the theories of **Beethoven** have not been considered important, those of **Oper und Drama** have been accepted as the final statement of Wagner's aesthetic position. And, finally, because the validity of **Oper und Drama** has been extended throughout Wagner's entire mature period, the music dramas

have all been measured by it. This series of errors can be rectified only by attacking them at the point of origin. (pp. 99-100)

[Volume One of *Parerga und Paralipomena*] contains a rather long essay, entitled *Versuch über das Geistersehn und was damit zusammenhängt,* which was not at all intended by Schopenhauer to be related with his theory of art, but which Wagner used as a kind of catalytic agent to unite Schopenhauer's metaphysics of music with Wagner's own conception of the *Gesamtkunstwerk.*

It is not as strange as it might seem on first thought that Wagner should have used this discussion for his artistic purposes. In numerous passages throughout *Die Welt als Wille und Vorstellung,* Schopenhauer reveals his belief in the transcendental nature of dreams and clairvoyance. To relate this to art, which for the romantic was also revelatory, is a comparatively obvious step. (p. 100)

In this essay, Schopenhauer attempts an idealistic explanation of clairvoyance and the phenomenon of dreams. Since perception is basically intellectual and not sensory, a function of the brain and not of the senses, which only stimulate the brain to action, says Schopenhauer, it is perfectly possible for some extra-sensory force also to cause the brain to function. Because this force is usually at work during either normal or clairvoyant sleep, Schopenhauer calls it *das Traumorgan.* Ordinary dreams are the result of the action of the *Traumorgan,* but the strongest excitation by the *Traumorgan* results in clairvoyance, where direct contact is made with the metaphysical Will. Dreams in deep sleep are of this same nature. But these clairvoyant visions or revelatory dreams are not transmissible as such to our consciousness, since our consciousness is bound to phenomenal laws. Therefore, says Schopenhauer, they are sometimes interpreted by the brain just before we awaken, in what he terms an allegorical dream whch approaches the phenomenal world closely enough to be perceived by our conscious self. These are the prophetic dreams which, he says, have been reported by trustworthy sources at all periods of history and from all parts of the civilized world.

Music, says Wagner, can be compared with this allegorical dream, since it likewise is a revelation of the Will in terms which are perceptible to our waking consciousness. For, just as the allegorical dream is an intermediate step between clairvoyance and wakefulness, approaching the phenomenal world sufficiently to perform its function of transmitting the Will, but not coinciding with it, so music establishes contact with the conceptual world, while not coinciding with it as the other arts do. Whereas all other forms of art deal with phenomena, music alone is not bound to the phenomenal world, and is a direct objectification of the Will. Through rhythm, however, music is related to the laws of time, and since rhythm is derived originally from the dance, to the laws of space as well. Thus music, like the allegorical dream, has a partial connection with the conceptual world; hence the validity of the analogy.

Wagner establishes the contact between visual drama and the Will by relating it to the perception of apparitions, which Schopenhauer considers analogous to clairvoyance. According to Schopenhauer's hypothesis, while the body is in a state of partial wakefulness, the dream organ projects its visions into the brain at the same time as the brain is registering external phenomena through the mediation of the senses. But this dual stimulation interferes with the normal sensory stimulus, and the effect of the latter is not as strong as usual. The inner vision, called forth by the dream organ, is superimposed upon the vaguely discerned phenomenal surroundings, and the result is an apparition or vision.

The apparition or vision, Wagner compares with drama, which is likewise an intermediate revelation of the inner clairvoyant vision of the poet, expressed in terms of time and space, and projected into the surrounding of the waking consciousness, while the senses, particularly the sense of sight, are in a partial state of depotentiation. This depotentiation of the senses, which is a necessary postulate for the perception of the vision, is accomplished for the drama by music. Wagner here refers to the effect which music has on a sympathetic listener in a concert hall. One who is absorbed in the music, with his eyes wide open, sees none of the distracting sights upon which his eyes are resting.

Now, when the composer and the dramatist are one and the same person, his clairvoyant vision of the essence of the universe is the single impulse which is simultaneously transmitted to us in two complementary ways, in terms of visual drama and in terms of music. Each is therefore in its own way an expression of the same clairvoyant vision of the metaphysical Will.

This is Wagner's new *Gesamtkunstwerk,* a transcendental mimetic-musical dualism, in which each of the phases, music and visual drama, is an identical and concurrent statement of the other. (pp. 101-02)

The dissolution of the synthesis of word and tone as represented by the melodic verse, which is the basis for his earlier theory, is nowhere directly acknowledged. Wagner always found it impossible to retract anything he had ever written or said. However, not only does the very existence of the new theory automatically negate the melodic verse, but a careful reading of *Beethoven* and later essays reveals numerous statements which also make the conclusion inescapable. (p. 102)

The theory of *Oper und Drama* is best exemplified by *Das Rheingold* and *Die Walküre,* which are nearest it chronologically, and that of *Beethoven* by the two latest works, *Die Meistersinger* and *Parsifal.* Several aspects of these two pairs of works are contrasted briefly here in order to indicate the parallelism between theory and practice.

The poems of *Das Rheingold* and *Die Walküre,* having been written within a year after *Oper und Drama,* contain many examples of functional alliteration, a high percentage of root syllables, and a system of accentuation based on the irregularity of normal speech, principles which Wagner evolved in *Oper und Drama* for the emotionalization of the poetic verse. The poems of *Die Meistersinger* and *Parsifal* stand in direct contrast to this. *Die Meistersinger* is written throughout in *Knittelvers,* in imitation, often for comic effect, of the verse form of the Mastersingers, with no suggestion of alliterative cross-relationships, condensation, or any other element prescribed in *Oper und Drama.* Wagner is here not concerned with a synthesis of poetic verse with melodic line, as he was in *Das Rheingold* and *Die Walküre.* The liveliness and, at times, brilliance of the dialogue are to be considered a part of the scintillating stage action, not of a musical-poetic synthesis. *Parsifal,* the only poem written after *Beethoven* had crystallized Wagner's new conception of the *Gesamtkunstwerk,* contains everything from free verse to rhymed couplets, including a negligible smattering of alliteration. It is the poorest—as well as the shortest—of the poems, and shows admirably Wagner's substitution of the dual synthesis of mimetic action and music for the former threefold synthesis of poetry, music, and scenic action. In no other

music drama by Wagner are the words as inessential as in *Parsifal.*

In *Das Rheingold* and *Die Walküre,* the vocal line is fused with the poetic line by application of the various techniques discussed in *Oper und Drama* to form genuine *Versmelodie.* In *Die Meistersinger* and *Parsifal,* melodic verse is almost nonexistent. It is replaced either by vocal melody, periodic in design, and fitted only in a general way to the rhythm and meter of the poetic line (such as the *Werbelied* in Act One, or the Prize Song in Act III of *Die Meistersinger,* and the many concerted numbers in both *Die Meistersinger* and *Parsifal*), or by a kind of bare recitative, where the music of the vocal line is reduced to the negative function of not interfering with the rapid delivery of the mimetic dialogue. Both these techniques can be correlated readily with the mimetic-musical dualism of the theory of *Beethoven,* the former submerging the poetic line for musical purposes, while the musical counterpart of the visual scene is to be found in the orchestra. (pp. 103-04)

Perhaps the most striking exemplifications of the later theory, which represents stage action and music as independent but complementary revelations of the metaphysical Will, are the frequent scenes in *Parsifal* where no words are sung at all, but where there is only a moving pantomime with rich orchestral accompaniment, or the massed scenes of *Die Meistersinger,* particularly the final scenes of Acts One and Two, where at times as many as sixteen different groups of people are speaking simultaneously, so that Wagner could not possibly have meant the words to be comprehended. The aesthetic effect of scenes like these is altogether independent of the words. They are mimetic sequences with full orchestral accompaniment, where the poetry plays no part. (p. 105)

> *Jack M. Stein, "The Influence of Schopenhauer on Wagner's Concept of 'Gesamtkunstwerk',"* in The Germanic Review, *Vol. 22, No. 2, April, 1947, pp. 92-105.*

FRANCIS FERGUSSON   (essay date 1949)

[*Fergusson is one of the most influential drama critics of the twentieth century. In his seminal study,* The Idea of a Theater, *he claims that the fundamental truths present in all drama are defined exclusively by myth and ritual, and that the purpose of dramatic representation is, in essence, to confirm the "ritual expectancy" of the society in which the artist works. Fergusson's method has been described as a combination of the principles of Aristotle's* Poetics *and the principles of modern myth criticism. Here Fergusson closely examines the dramatic structure of* Tristan and Isolde *and explores Wagner's principles of composition.*]

If one thinks of *Tristan und Isolde* as simply another love-story, one can see that it is plotted on the serviceable principles of the well-made play. The first act is an exposition of the basic conflict, that between the love of Tristan and Isolde and their moral obligations, especially to King Mark. It ends with an incident which raises the suspense: they kiss just as the ship docks, and the curtain falls with a burst of musical excitement. The second act is built on top of the first, and shows the overt deed which the first act promised. This act also ends with an exciting event, the betrayal and the stabbing; and the second act curtain marks the "climax" of the conflict. The third act is the denouement: all is resolved, or dissolved, in death.

The single purpose of this scheme, thus abstractly understood, is to hold and excite the audience by means of the *facts* of the story. It would have been equally useful as the framework for a drama of ethical motivation, like Racinian tragedy; the same facts, in the same order, might have been used to present the life of the reasoning soul in its struggle with inclination, instead of the invisible life of passion transcending rationalizable reality altogether. Thus the plot of the opera as "intrigue" shows something about Wagner's relation to the audience, and something about the well-made play, but very little about his real principles of composition.

In order to investigate these, one must, as usual, consider the plot as the first form which the action (in this case the "action of passion") takes; i.e., as the "soul of the tragedy." It is then clear how the first act may be regarded (on the ritual analogy) as initiation; the second as the struggle of passion in its worldly prison, and the third as fated fulfillment, or the passionate transcendence of the world altogether. Wagner has so arranged the incidents of the story as always to show on stage passionate moments. These successive moments constitute a sequence, or rhythm of feeling, or (if one thinks of them together, instead of in the temporal succession in which we get them) a spectrum of emotions generated by absolute passion in its struggle out of the illusory world. We are led from the remote nostalgic aspiration of the beginnings of Act I, to the close violence of the lovers' night in Act II, and thence to the physically spent, but paradoxically comforted, release of the love-death.

What Wagner is "imitating" by means of these events is a passion which knows no bounds, in spite of its physical involvements. But the plot is only the "first actualization," and Wagner also imitates or expresses the life of passion by means of his personages, the ideas they express, and the imagery of the poetry and of the stage-setting.

When the curtain rises after the overture, we see Isolde and her faithful Brangaene moping in a curtained part of the ship, and we hear a young sailor, aloft in the rigging, sing the following words:

Westwarts	Westward
Schweift der Blick;	your eyes stray;
ostwarts	eastward
streicht das Schiff.	the ship flies.
Frisch weht der Wind	Fresh blows the wind
der Heimat zu;	toward home;
mein irisch Kind,	my Irish child,
wo weilest du?	where are you lingering?

The words define the beginnings of the objectless movement, and the insubstantial scene, of passion. Isolde is looking one way, and going another. She is leaving home, on a ship going home; and on the other hand she is not moving at all, but "lingering." These willful paradoxes do not cohere logically; but the sensations of getting nowhere with the utmost speed; of leaving and coming at once, all in a languor of gloom, do compose to define a moment of feeling with great accuracy. It is the beginning of that course of passion which is the life of the drama.

Isolde, in despair and anger, tells Brangaene the story of her relations with Tristan: his present black aloofness, staring at the sea; the savagery and self-pity of their first meeting, with Tristan wounded and Isolde bent on murder; and finally the sinister fatality which brings them together on the ship. Wagner continues to develop this relation as though passion created both the characters and the circumstances. To follow this development, with its "logic of feeling," one must feel the passion directly—excluding the perspectives of reason on pain of

having it all break up in absurdity. Would Isolde's and Tristan's passion be satisfied by lust, murder, or suicide? Suicide seems to the lovers the most promising means of release, and they drink the cup which they think will be their death. When it turns out to be in fact a love-potion, their kiss seems equally right and equally obedient to the otherworldly fate which commands them. So Wagner contrives to bring the passion, which first appeared far off, like an airplane on the horizon, roaring over us with all its power. (pp. 78-80)

[Qualitative progression well describes] the principles on which Wagner's music-drama is composed: he composes, not with real and substantial persons and things, but with qualities. Thus the ship which carries Isolde is not a ship in its own right, but only those aqueous and unfixed qualities which it shares with the lost beginnings of passion. As for the wind, it would ruin everything to know its velocity in knots; it is (like Isolde's sighs) merely one of the dreamlike emanations of passion. Even the characters are not to be thought of as real, but only as shifting moral qualities which express passion—or, from the point of view of the audience, induce passion. By thus composing with qualities only (sensuously and emotionally charged appearances) passion becomes the one reality in the drama. If you think realistically of Wagner's act of composition, you might say that he selected only such qualities of persons and things as would convey the passion he intended. But if you think of his creative art as German idealism would describe it—as Nietzsche, following Schopenhauer, describes it, and as Wagner himself often thought of it—you would say that Wagner's passion created, or "dreamed up" out of itself, all of the visible and intelligible elements of the drama. And this is the feeling one should ideally have at a performance: the shifting pictures on stage seem to come directly and solely from the emotion which the music has induced in the audience.

Tristan owes its significance partly to the fact that it is the most perfect instance of drama as "the expression of emotion": the doctrine which identifies action with passion. (p. 81)

In Act II, after the initiation of Act I, Wagner comes closest to presenting passion itself—no mean feat in the case of an emotion to which nothing is adequate. The basic symbolism, both in the setting and in the poetry, is that of Night versus Day. The Night is the lovers', and it feels to them and to us secret, true, unitive, and holy, in direct contrast to public, illusory, divisive, and evil Day. All physical light, even that of the torch, is violently rejected, along with all that it stands for—the light of reason, the actual circumstances of the lovers, and their moral obligation to King Mark. And Night is sought as eagerly as the death, love and primordial oneness for which it stands. Wagner has these words for their first culmination of utter obedience:

BOTH	bricht mein Blick sich	My sight broken
	wonn'-erblindet,	blinded in bliss
	erbleicht die Welt	the world goes pale
	mit ihrem Blenden:	in all its dazzling:
ISOLDE	die uns der Tag	which deceitful Day
	trügend erhellt,	lighted for us,
TRISTAN	zu täuschenden Wahn	Raising against us
	entgegengestellt,	its lying illusion—
BOTH	selbst dann	only now
	bin ich die Welt:	am I the world:
	Wonne-hehrstes-Weben,	Majestic web of joy,

Liebe-heiligstes Leben	Most holy life of love,
Nie-wieder-erwachens	The never-more-waking
wahnlos	undeluded
hold bewusster Wunsch.	longing benign and
	known.

To reason, these ecstatic cries seem even more nonsensical than the words of the sailor's song at the beginning of Act I; but, given the passion Wagner intends and induces with his music, they are exact, and every word is meant. Tristan, Isolde, the performers on stage and in the orchestra, and the audience, are all identified with the one passion, and all could say, if they had the strength, "I am the world." (pp. 82-3)

[Tristan] and Isolde wish never to wake; they do not want to see the daylight world in a truer way, but to get rid of it altogether. And in the opera the symbol of Night stands, not for a transitional moment of human experience, and for one among many modes of knowledge, but for the threshold of the void of truth itself.

It has often been pointed out that the music of Act II unmistakably mounts the lovers "for the hot encounter." Passion is here manifested in desperate sensuality, and the mystic annihilation-in-oneness of the climax . . . is figured by implication in the sexual act—which is said to provide a little death of the spirit. But these meanings are (for the pessimistic other-worldly faith in passion) erroneous, because sensual and physical. We are not yet at the end of the act, the end of the action, the end of the story, or the more terrible loss of self which passion demands. What, then, is the dramatic content of the third act? How does Wagner convey the anomalous triumph of the void?

He conveys it of course by the music. . . . (pp. 83-4)

The motive of the third act is still ostensibly that "love" which has possessed Tristan and Isolde all along, and thus the last act in a sense continues the movement of the first two. But "love" is to be sought, this time, not by way of sensuality but by way of death, and for this ultimate effort of passion new beginnings are required. The opening sequences of the last act show the approaching triumph of death as equivalent to the triumph of love, which the erotic violence of Act II just failed to reach. This approach is the more painful for being pleasurable, and the more pleasurable for being painful; and now, at last, we understand that the fated and true end is near. But the beginning of this movement is nostalgic and far-off, like the beginning of Act I, and Isolde's vigil at the beginning of Act II. The empty sea, Tristan's fatal wound, his dark and ruinous "home," and the inexpressibly dreary and seductive sound of the shepherd's pipe, combine to produce the most disquieting version of the paradox of getting nowhere with the utmost speed—for now "nowhere" is reality itself.

Tristan's fatal wound is necessary for the "intrigue." It serves to account for his death rationally, in case there should be a mind in the audience still capable of demanding facts and logic. But what Wagner is presenting here is Tristan's pleasurable-painful, willing-unwilling death-seeking action, and this he conveys dramatically by means of the symbols he has assembled. Tristan has come home—to the shadowy tree, tall walls, and empty ocean of his childhood. These elements have their immediate effect and they also serve, with the sound of the pipe, to induce a Proustian *intermittence du coeur*: Tristan feels again the most devastating moments of his early experience, the death of father and mother. . . . This backward rush of Tristan is still further speeded and intensified by Kurwenal, who spoils and caresses him with uncomprehending and help-

less maternal solicitude, like that which Isolde, with her woman's hands and voice, will presently lavish upon him, expressing the painful pleasure of dissolution: of leaving everything for good, and of judging the whole course of life since the cradle as a mistake and an illusion.

It is in the analysis of the third act that one is most tempted to substitute a Freudian mythology for the one which Wagner offers, in the effort to understand the meaning of the opera. One might say that Tristan's progress in this act is a fine example of pathological regression, from a thwarted love affair back through the morose introversions of childhood to the thrillingly irrational demand for the impermeable gloom of the womb itself. But the Freudian vocabulary merely begs the ultimate questions which few in our time venture to answer. It does not tell us (for all its play with the death wish and the pleasure principle) in what direction the reality of the human situation is to be sought; and when applied to the opera it leaves out the power of the faith which informs it. For **Tristan** fulfills Bergson's requirements for a true mystic experience: its emotions are suffered "in the expectation of a transformation," and its images "as symbolic of what is being prepared," sinister though this preparation feels to us here below. Wagner provides a dramatic form and psychological documentation for his gloomy act of faith; but its true power and scope can only be felt in the work as a whole, and especially and most directly in the music.

I do not attempt to raise the technical question of the nature and merits of Wagner's music as music. But if one is to understand Wagner's dramaturgy, it is essential to consider the crucial role which Wagner and his closest disciples thought that music played, or should play, in the art of drama. (pp. 84-6)

The music defines with the greatest exactitude an "arabesque of passion," determining not only the performers' tiniest movements of feeling, but also the last detail of the setting and staging. . . . The music conveys directly the "action of passion," and from it the story, the characters, and everything on-stage is to be deduced, by an inexorable esthetic logic, in complete obedience to the artist's will. (pp. 86-7)

Francis Fergusson, "'Tristan und Isolde': The Action and Theater of Passion," in his The Idea of a Theater: A Study of Ten Plays, the Art of Drama in Changing Perspective, *Princeton University Press*, 1949, pp. 68-97.*

AUDREY WILLIAMSON (essay date 1961)

[*Williamson's is a positive appraisal of characterization in* The Nibelung's Ring. *This excerpt was taken from "The Ring and Its Characters," which originally appeared in* High Fidelity *in November, 1961.*]

Der Ring des Nibelungen is in one sense a vast sociological symbol, a depiction of the greed for power and the tragedy it brings not only on the world but to those who succumb to it. But in another sense it is a study of individual human characters in relationship to this and to each other—a merging, as it were, of the symbol with the psychological forces behind it. (p. 271)

[Wagner's dramas] show a characteristic blending of the Shakespearean humanities and the Greek symbol, and the Greek source . . . can occasionally be traced across 2,000 years of theatre from Euripides, through Shakespeare, to Wagner.

Thus the great and moving father-daughter reconciliation scene between King Agamemnon and Iphigenia, in Euripides' *Iphi-*

Caricature commemorating the centenary of Wagner's birth.

genia in Aulis, reappears with King Lear and Cordelia and again with Wotan and Brünnhilde, and in all cases it closes the rebellion of the most-loved child against the father's tyranny, with the daughter representing his inner conscience. (In larger symbol it is, of course, a dramatization of the eternal rebellion of youth against its elders' mistakes in state and government.) Again, in the recognition scene of the long-parted brother and sister, Siegmund and Sieglinde, we see an echo of the even more famous "recognition" scene between Electra and her brother Orestes, which stems from Aeschylus, the father of all drama as the modern theatre understands it.

Das Rheingold is the one opera in ***The Ring*** cycle which contains no purely human characters—only gods, giants, dwarfs, and Loge, the strange being who had no allegiance to any of them, a sower of mischief whose isolation Wagner has brilliantly depicted in his sardonic withdrawal at the crossing into Valhalla. . . . (pp. 271-72)

For Wotan in ***Rheingold*** has already stepped down from his godhead and become defiled by human fallibility; by stooping to Alberich's level in his grasp for the gold and power it represents, he has sacrificed the integrity of his own laws and, therefore, his right to rule. That it is a personal as well as a political tragedy Wagner emphasizes in Wotan's own realization of his degradation. Wotan moves through bitterness and dejection to an attempt, through another, to create a better world order, and finally to total abnegation of power.

In between—for Wotan is the true tragic hero of ***The Ring***—he must experience some of the deeper sufferings of human loss and frustration, in his love for his son Siegmund and daughter Brünnhilde. For, if he descends to the evil qualities of humanity, he is still essentially noble.

Siegmund, a victim of Wotan's own outmoded laws, he must betray to his death; and both music and dramatic action combine with great subtlety to reveal the depth of Wotan's grief at this bereavement. Weary, numb with the sense of his loss, he is graphically depicted in the curt dismissal of Hunding—*"Geh! Geh!"*—the first "Go" marked not savagely but softly in the score. . . .

Wagner wrote no more psychologically penetrating scenes than that final one with the boy Siegfried, Siegmund's successor, where we get in turn a dramatic web of Wotan's emotions—his pride in the boy (the pride of Creator and grandfather, God and man); his amusement at Siegfried's disrespect and importunity, hardening in spite of himself into resentment and impatience; the sudden pang of jealousy for Brünnhilde, whom he must lose to this all-conquering youth. The Wotan who stoops and picks up his shattered spear is a tragic and superseded human being, not only a symbol of power abused and authority laid low. . . . (p. 272)

For Wotan grows in the cycle from flawed godhead to renunciation, thus fulfilling all the needs of the greatest poetic drama. And the irony and humor he develops in ***Siegfried*** are signs of this mature wisdom and detachment from the scramble for power.

In between, we get the great scenes with Brünnhilde in ***Die Walküre***. Wotan is tyrannous when thwarted, all the more because of his recognition that she expresses his own true longings and twists the knife in his own wound. The analogy here is not only with Euripides and Shakespeare, but also with Mary Shelley's Count Frankenstein, creator of a being who has developed a will and personality outside the creator's own control. *"Aus meinem Angesicht bist du verbannt"* is one of Wotan's most revealing cries, comparable with that wonderful last scene when Brünnhilde pleads for his clemency and probes his own agony by reminding him of her attempt to save Siegmund. . . . (pp. 272-73)

It is with such touches of psychological insight that Wagner builds up his finest scenes, working towards the poignancy of the god's eventual capitulation to the love he cannot suppress. Into "der freier als ich der Gott!" is packed the essence of Wotan's personal tragedy.

The actor of Wotan must have majesty, nobility and rage but it is only a half-interpretation if it excludes the many moments of melting tenderness or human suffering that Wagner has woven into the character and music. . . . Wotan is the King Lear of opera, demanding an actor of the same stature and emotional range.

Brünnhilde also must develop, from goddess to woman: in the *Todesverkündigung* scene she is Fate, a messenger of death. . . . But she quickens to her first understanding of human love at the end of this scene, and, in ***Siegfried***, how sensitively Wagner has shown her fears and doubts on awakening to womanhood.

Siegfried himself is something more than the "inspiriting young forester, a son of the morning" of Shaw's fine description. Wagner has shown considerable imagination in describing the innocent attempts of the child of nature to apply the lessons of the field to human life, of which he knows nothing, and depicts his hero as affectionate by nature in such touches as the sad strain at his mother's death . . . and in his loneliness for his own kind. It is a flaw in *The Ring* that in *Götterdämmerung* this affection and loyalty become traduced, not by his own character development, but by the mechanical device of the drugged potion—unusual for Wagner, whose use of magic (as in *Tristan*) is normally always an external symbol of some deep inner psychological conflict.

The Electra-Orestes recognition scene of the ill-starred Wälsungs, Siegmund and Sieglinde, has already been mentioned. It is an elaborate dramatic revelation of half-memories and illusions (Sieglinde's recognition of Siegmund in her own face in the forest pool, and his voice in hers echoing in the woods, are two of the many imaginative details). Yet the twins are sharply contrasted. Like other Wagnerian women . . . , Sieglinde is not above taking the initiative in the love affair; but it is the grave, lonely Siegmund, scarred and hardened by suffering, who achieves . . . a tender kind of peace, resignation and security in his love, while the girl—not unlike Shakespeare's Lady Macbeth—cracks under the strain of guilt and fear.

In *Götterdämmerung* we move almost entirely among human beings, with the hybrid Hagen brooding like some morose Iago over the lives around him, twisting them to his purpose as Iago twisted Othello.

Yet the whole Gibichung household is human and alive, not the least in its unspecified implications of psychology and background. Hagen is perhaps even more Edmund in *King Lear* than Iago: the bastard of a great house who also seems to have become strangely ascendant in it, trusted like Edmund by the legitimate family. Yet, as in Edmund too, we have the secret, poisonous glint of inferiority complex and resentment, flashing out with dark suddenness in Hagen's response to the invitation to share in Siegfried's and Gunther's oath of blood-brotherhood. His blood is not noble enough, he says; and in that *"mein Blut"* we have the one revealing glimpse into the corroding force of his envy.

That his hatred is unsuspected and unshared by the legitimate brother and sister, Gunther and Gutrune, arouses our curiosity as to the background of this fascinating household. How did he come to gain this position of domination and respect? Did it stem from the mother, whom they mention with respect? Wherein lies his charm? The sudden joviality he shows with the vassals is perhaps a clue, yet is almost more frightening than his moroseness. (pp. 273-74)

Part of Hagen's fascination and power lies, as it does in many creations of great writers, in the unsolved mystery of his psychology: the mystery of evil. It is intensified in his traumatic brooding by the Rhine. (Is Alberich here real, or a figment of his dreams and ambitions?) And his curt last word of "Retribution," when asked by the shocked Vassals why he has killed Siegfried, adds to his mystery as he strides, a lonely, enigmatic figure, away across the horizon.

Part of his power, of course, springs from the psychology of Gunther and Gutrune. On his knowledge of this, Hagen hazards all. For Gunther, too, is a complex character, weak enough to be led into evil, but proud and masculine in his first scene, with a flash of envy at Siegfried's prowess and a curious need to have Hagen's reassurance of his own valor. They are a lonely couple, this brother and sister, leaders of a great race, yet turning to the bastard half-brother for guidance. It is interesting that both seem in need of a hero to love and follow; was it the

secret of Hagen's success. They yield instantly to Siegfried's charm, and, in spite of the Brünnhilde plot, Gunther appears genuinely to value Siegfried's friendship and, indeed, shows a good deal more feeling for him than for his unknown bride. . . . (pp. 274-75)

Certainly the tragedy for Gunther is his disillusion at Siegfried's apparent betrayal of him; it bores into his own loyalty and explains—more than mere weakness—his reluctant capitulation to the two stronger characters, Hagen and Brünnhilde. Nevertheless, he has a revealing moment of doubt: *"Verrieth— er mich?"* And *"so wär' es Siegfrieds Ende!"* is surely . . . a poignant stab of regret. Never free from remorse, he lives just long enough to realize his mistake; and his restrained grief and sudden final challenge of Hagen's authority bring him movingly into dramatic focus. Both brother and sister seem gentle, naturally affectionate creatures, closely knit as a family; equally betrayed, they have their own place in the development of the tragedy.

As for Brünnhilde, in the great second act of *Götterdämmerung* she moves from the lowest range to which she can fall as a goddess—a woman loving deeply, suffering and betrayed—to the heroic proportions of Greek tragedy and a final spiritual tranquility. Her revenge is the reaction of Wotan's daughter, a reflection of his Olympic rage *(Zorn);* it springs from a cutting wound and is at least not ignoble in scale. But her passion moves us less than does her bewilderment in a human world whose values she cannot understand—*"Wo ist nun mein Wissen?"*

Characteristically, her admiration of Siegfried still burns fiercely under the anguish and rage; when Hagen suggests he shall overcome Siegfried, she lashes him with her scorn: *"An Siegfried? du?"* . . . Hagen forces himself to accept her taunt, but at this further stab to his envy Wagner leaves us guessing. The whole of this wonderful trio is a seething psychological cauldron of motive and countermotive, an interplay of character moving to a climax of Sophoclean scale. Dramatically it transcends the final Immolation of Brünnhilde. . . . (p. 275)

Audrey Williamson, "The Ring and Its Characters," in Penetrating Wagner's Ring: An Anthology, *edited by John Louis DiGaetani, Fairleigh Dickinson University Press, 1978, pp. 271-78.*

MORSE PECKHAM (essay date 1962)

[*Treating Wagner's operas from* The Flying Dutchman *to* Parsifal *as a single work in ten acts, Peckham discusses their common theme: the artist's role in and relationship to society. Peckham also argues caution in linking Wagner with the philosophy of the Nazi movement.*]

The hysterical adulation and the furious hatred which have always been the norm of judgments of Richard Wagner's music dramas are alone almost enough to mark him as a transcendental artist. . . .

But there are more marks of his transcendental origins, his unique, novel, and extravagant style, his youthful conception of himself as a world-redeemer, his control of musical meaning by literary analogues, and especially his idea of the *Gesamtkunstwerk*, a fairly common idea of German transcendentalism. The notion of a work of art that would synthesize all the arts is a logical consequence of the transcendental notion that each of the arts says the same thing in a different way, but that each of those ways is necessary because each corre-

The frontispiece from an early edition of Tristan and Isolde. *Cercle National R. Wagner.*

sponds to a different facet of human behavior. If the work of art is to be fully functional, it must appeal to and make use of the whole range of human personality and behavior. (p. 240)

[Wagner] was not one of the creators of transcendentalism, as the slightly older and more rapidly maturing Schumann was, but rather, by growing up in the transcendental ambience, was highly sensitive to the problem of how the heroic redeemer could fulfill his destiny without exerting morally irresponsible power. Even before he had fully realized the question and worked out the implications he was somehow aware that the transcendental attempt to redeem society was not going to work.

Here, perhaps, a word of explanation is necessary. Wagner has been so identified in the popular mind and among high-level anti-Wagnerians with Hitler and Nazism that he has become almost a kind of symbol of the brutal and irresponsible wielding of social power. Actually, a graver mistake, a more erroneous misreading of Wagner's libretti would be impossible to imagine. If the Nazis had understood Wagner they would have banned him; if they had been capable of believing him, they would never have been Nazis. (p. 241)

[Few] nineteenth-century artists have been so grossly misunderstood, as much by his adorers as by his haters. Actually, he was concerned with only one problem, though with endless ramifications of it: Art, through the artist, is the source of human value. The artist cannot re-enter society. How is the

value of which he is the bearer to be made socially valid? The gap between artist and society cannot be closed; neither can it be permanently bridged. How can it be crossed? Is it the artist's responsibility to cross over to the public? Is it the public's responsibility to cross over to the artist? Must the lightning the artist wields be tamed, channeled, masked, perhaps, to make it available to others? And if it should be, how can that ultimate responsibility of the artist be discharged?

All of Wagner's creative career and of his practical career, as a man of the theater, as a public figure, was devoted to this one problem. Nor is he in this sense atypical. From the beginning, . . . the nineteenth-century thinker, in making the distinction between self and role, makes the distinction between moral responsiblity and morality. (pp. 242-43)

[It] can be said that his ten major works from *The Flying Dutchman* to *Parsifal* in reality compose one gigantic work in ten acts. (p. 243)

Wagner's creative life . . . was virtually continuous for more than forty years; and it was devoted to an exhaustive exploration of a single intellectual problem and of a single musical problem. (pp. 243-44)

[*The Flying Dutchman*] revives an older symbol and gives it a new significance. The Dutchman is an outcast and a wanderer, modeled on the Ancient Mariner-Harold-Manfred tradition. He is cursed to sail forever, with no hope of death. But there is a difference from the older figure. His crime is known and he has hope of redemption. He refused to submit to the arbitrary and cruel jokes of nature and of God; he will be saved if he can find a woman who will be true to him even to death. Every seven years he is permitted to come to land and seek such a woman, but he has never found her. He is, then, alienated from society and isolated in a universe which derives no meaning from either nature or nature's God. The ocean, in a fairly well-established tradition, is a symbol of the valueless self; the land, of the valueless society, in which the bad are strong and the good are powerless.

Senta, however, whose father is willing to sell her to the Dutchman, has long loved his portrait and his story. When her father brings the Dutchman to her, she swears undying love; but the suspicious Dutchman, overhearing a conversation between Senta and Erik, her now rejected suitor, misunderstands the distinction between Senta's love for Erik, which is of the land, of society, only a social role, and her love for him, which is of the ocean, of the self. He rushes back to the sea; Senta leaps after him into the waves. The ship sinks, and he and Senta soar upward over the wreck, in each other's arms. The wreck of the accursed ship and their salvation above the sea indicates that the ocean is itself cleansed and redeemed. That is, the self is redeemed and made radiant with value, while the land remains valueless. What appears to be death to the onlooking landsmen is in actuality life, the life of the self, redeemed by love.

Nor is it by any means an accident that the staging requires the audience to be of the party of the landsmen, of social death. They think of the Dutchman as a terrible and cursed ghost, something supernatural. Only Senta is capable of escaping that orientation and recognizing the Dutchman's human identity, a spiritual redirection which she is able to achieve only because she is familiar with the song of the Dutchman . . . and with his portrait. That is, her redemption from society, which accomplishes the Dutchman's redemption from the valueless self, is brought about by her contemplation of works of art.

Redemption through woman and woman's love is one of the great themes of transcendentalism.... Woman was selected as the proper symbol because of her power to love in spite of society, of her biologic and economic necessity to think more in terms of individuality than of collectivity. That it was not a matter of erotic love is apparent from the frequency with which a friend of the same sex performs the necessary act of recognizing the self beneath the role.... (pp. 244-45)

In spite of the fact that art releases Senta, and Senta redeems the Dutchman's selfhood and sense of value, the outcast is still dependent upon a force within society for his redemption. Although Wagner has gone beyond the point where social re-entry is seen as the consummation of redemption, he is not free of social dependence. How was redemption to be achieved independently of social recognition? He returned to the problem in *Tannhäuser*. Here the protagonist is an artist, specifically a musician and poet, like Wagner himself. It is Wagner's most intensely personal work. At the same time it marks another step out of the transcendental position; the symbolism is almost entirely Christian and it is extremely easy to give it a traditional Christian interpretation as a conflict between profane and sacred love.... Wagner here begins to use a solution to the problem of the gap between artist and society which others of his contemporaries, Tennyson, for example, also adopted. It is an exoteric-esoteric device; that is, it presents to society a perfectly consistent structure of meanings which conforms with its dominating orientative symbolism; but on the other hand, it holds an interior meaning which is quite different, indeed, quite opposed.

Tannhäuser replaces the ocean with the cave, and Senta with Venus-Elisabeth. As the work opens, Tannhäuser is in the cave of Venus; he is the self-in-hiding in the paradise of total gratification—but he can't stand it. Urged by the drive toward reality, he rejects paradise and returns to the world. There at the contest of song he mocks the sentimental eroticism of the Minnesingers (the knightly love singers) and praises the erotic realities of Venus. Horrified and shocked, the knights would destroy him, but he is saved by Elisabeth, who insists that he have the chance to redeem himself by going to Rome. The pope, equally horrified at his worship of a pagan goddess, condemns him to hell. Bitterly, Tannhäuser sets out to return to Venus, but the utterance of the name of Elisabeth stops him, and her death permits him to die, while the chorus sings of her entry to heaven and her pleading before God for Tannhäuser's soul. He is saved. He is saved not because of institutionalized Christianity but in spite of it. Elisabeth, it turns out, not only loves Tannhäuser; she empathizes with him. In her prayer to the Virgin she admits to precisely those same erotic desires which the sentimental knights refuse to accept, and it is the stifling of those desires, their denial, which kills her. To clinch this, the dead staff of the pope, which he said could no more put forth leaves than Tannhäuser could be saved, is brought in at the end by the young pilgrims; it is in full leaf.

Tannhäuser, then, dies because there is no one left in the real world who can accept him with his erotic desires, in the totality of his personal identity. From Tannhäuser's point of view, the Venusberg, the paradise of erotic fulfillment, is a bore, but at least it is better than the sentimentalities and falsehoods of society. Nevertheless, Elisabeth's position is equivocal. On the one hand she wishes to return Tannhäuser to society; on the other, her identification with Tannhäuser kills her. Further, Wagner still has not resolved the problem of making the hero independent of someone within society who will confirm his

sense of identity and release him from egocentricity. He has to re-examine the problem in *Lohengrin*.

This work is a political drama. The transcendental hero descends into the world at a time of political-social crisis, when the heathen hordes are attacking the old Holy Roman Empire from the east, and the concealed heathens within Brabant have spirited away the heir to the throne. Only when the crisis within Brabant has been solved can its resources be added to the empire's and the threat to European civilization be met. Emerging from the realm of pure value, Lohengrin at first appears to solve the crisis by saving Elsa from the false accusation that she murdered her brother, and by his marriage to Elsa becoming himself the ruler of Brabant and the ally of the emperor. Nevertheless he fails. Elsa insists on knowing his name and his origin; that is, she demands his authority as a representative of society and the heir of its leadership.

At this point Wagner perceives the limitation of the transcendental effort to redeem the world. Elsa the Christian has been seduced into doing what she promised not to by Ortrud, the secret pagan. They are, in short, sisters under the skin. Between paganism and Christianity there is no difference. Both are merely instruments by which society exerts its control over mankind. Both are implements of social power. The failure in *Lohengrin* is dual. When the hero at last achieves complete independence from society, his redemptive power is compromised by his lack of authority. At the same time the orientations of society are seen as invalid. Wagner attempts to resolve the problem by having Lohengrin restore the Prince, whom he had saved from Ortrud by turning him into a swan, and give him his own sword, horn, and ring, standing for a prince's power and duty to defend his people, to summon them to cooperation, and to pledge his life to the values of Lohengrin.

The transcendental hero, then, cannot himself redeem society, but he can make the natural leader—as Balzac and Carlyle hoped—into a redemptive instrument. Yet this solution also leaves unsolved difficulties. If society stubbornly resists redemption by the hero, why cannot it just as well resist the hero's representative and surrogate? And further, is not Lohengrin's preservation of the Prince in the shape of a swan somewhat equivocal? If Ortrud had not uttered her triumph, would not the Prince have remained a swan? Is not Lohengrin, then, exerting arbitrary power? Is he not violating another identity in order to wield social power? And does not this compromise his whole position?

To answer these questions Wagner set out to write another work, which developed into a tetralogy and took him nearly thirty years to complete and bring to the stage. To do so he had to create a new kind of singer, a new kind of orchestra and orchestral conducting, a new kind of theater—the best theater for opera ever built—and a new kind of financing, the festival. (pp. 245-48)

To root out the cancer of humanity's social life, Wagner uses ancient German and Scandinavian mythology and legend [in the *Ring*], just as in *Tannhäuser* and *Lohengrin* he had used Christian mythology. In the manner of Feuerbach, whom he had just read, he sees all mythologies as equivalent. Before he finishes the *Ring*, he will see none as valid. For the moment, in the tradition of Herder, he sees German mythology as particularly appropriate for a German artist and a German public. The second point is to note the order in which the *Ring* was written. It is not enough to say, as is often said, that he wrote it backward. Actually he wrote backward, forward, and sideways. After he had worked from *Siegfried's Death* back to *The Rhinegold,* he reworked the tetralogy, changing *Siegfried's Death* to *The Twilight of the Gods* and to it adding a prologue which explains events before *The Rhinegold* begins. The work would be more immediately comprehensible had he preceded *The Rhinegold* with another short work called *The World Ash Tree.* For the events of the *Ring* really begin when Wotan breaks off a branch from the tree that supports the world, shapes it into a spear, and carves on it his runes of world governance.

The meaning of the *Ring* emerged slowly, over many years, and the history of its composition is the history of how Wagner, who thought symbolically before he conceptualized his insights, worked out the problem he had set himself. The original ending was to have Siegfried reconciled with Wotan, in Valhalla, and this reconciliation was to symbolize the solution of society's ills, the successful excision of its cancer, the patient restored to health. The Wotan-Siegfried relationship is a repetition of the Lohengrin-Prince of Brabant dualism, the self-conscious transcendental hero and his unself-conscious instrument. (pp. 249-50)

Wagner begins, then, at exactly the point *Lohengrin* leaves off, with the morally equivocal problem which was left hanging in the air as Lohengrin returned to Monsalvat, the realm of pure value. It is no surprise to discover that the sword, the horn, and the ring, are carried over from *Lohengrin* into the next work. To them is added the spear. But after Wagner's encounter with Schopenhauer's philosophy, which crystallized conceptually what he had already begun to see symbolically—indeed had felt even in *The Flying Dutchman*—the whole character and point of the work changed. In the new ending there is no redemption of society, no reconciliation between Wotan and Siegfried, no afterlife for Siegfried and Brünnhilde in Valhalla; Valhalla is itself destroyed, and the ring goes back to the Rhine, from which it had been torn. The writing of the *Ring* is the history of Wagner's solution of the problems posed by *Lohengrin:* that solution is the failure of the transcendental hero, the impossibility of an adequate society.

The *Ring* is usually discussed as if Siegfried were the transcendental hero. But Siegfried is unself-conscious, unable to use the sudden insights he occasionally has, fearless only because he is ignorant and stupid. No, Wotan is the transcendental hero who attempts to introduce pure value into society by his control over the ultimate source of human and social energy, unconscious psychic life, the ash tree that supports the world. By identifying the transcendental artist-hero we can understand that this shaping of the spear broken from the ash tree symbolizes how the transcendental poet-hero controls the world by controlling the human imagination. In the terms of this book, whoever controls the shaping power of men's orientations controls society. Yet Wotan desires to use this power responsibly; he carves upon the spear the laws that bind him to man's service, laws which sustain his power. If he transgresses those laws, his power is lost. Wotan symbolizes, then, one kind of social power, from which he successively creates social order, freedom, and love.

But there is another kind of power in the world also, economic power, the treasure of gold guarded by the daughters of the river Rhine. It is natural power. The ash tree supports the world, true. The world is, in Schopenhauer's form of Kantianism, representation (or idea). But this is no Platonic idealism. The world is there, it exists. Man cannot know it, but he experiences it through the will, and above all through the frustration of the will. Alberich, the gnome, baffled, mocked, and humiliated by the Rhine daughters, whom he attempts to love, seizes upon the gold as compensation for his frustrated eroticism. (The significance of the erotic problem in *Tannhäuser* is thus clarified and made certain: sexuality is a reality which cannot be idealized away.) The desire for economic power over society takes its origin from the frustration of the human will as it expresses itself in erotic love. Freud himself could say no more on the subject.

Wotan is now faced with an appalling paradox. There are two kinds of power in the world, imaginative and economic (or natural). Economic power cannot of itself become morally responsible; it is compensation for frustration, and no compensation can ever make up for what frustration loses. Imaginative power, Wotan thinks, can be made morally responsible by self-limitation. But because it is limited, such power cannot endure the existence of any other kind or source of power. *All* power must be under control. Wotan, too, has been motivated by love for man and by his desire to create for man a satisfactory world. His love is now frustrated; to overcome that frustration he must break his own laws; he must win the gold from Alberich by thievery and trickery. His moral position is now fatally compromised. His paradox is this: to be morally responsible, power must be self-limiting; but limited power is a contradiction, a paradox. Power, therefore, cannot be made morally reponsible. Erda, the earth goddess, the goddess of things as they are, the goddess of the impregnable resistance of reality to human desire and will, warns Wotan that he must give up the ring or lose his power; and that even if he does, he will lose his power anyway. (pp. 250-52)

[Wagner] exhibits the kind of thinking we have seen before, and seen as one of the central ideas of the nineteenth-century vision; not the reconciliation of opposites and antinomies but the full exposure to them and acceptance of them in all their irreducible polarity—this is the task of the thinker-artist.

Once the paradox of Erda's warning is grasped, the rest of the *Ring* is comprehensible. Wotan himself, however, does not, cannot, understand her. He will refuse to accept the unacceptable. He is determined to find a solution to the unsolvable. He gives the ring to the giants—he turns over the economic nexus of society to the workers, who have so little idea of what to do with it that one giant kills the other and makes off with it, to become a dragon and sleep on it forever, if possible. But Wotan enters the newly built Valhalla from which he hopes his power will emanate to establish order and value in the world. And as he and the gods march over the rainbow bridge the Rhine daughers sing from below that only in their world is the true, that the world of the gods is false and cowardly.

With this much understood, the rest of the story, the working out of the consequences, can be examined rapidly. Wotan first establishes social order among men and then attempts to create a hero (Siegmund) who will be the instrument of his will and capture for him the ring. But as Fricka, the goddess of social morality, points out, in doing so he has violated his own laws. Wotan realizes that he has deceived himself. He has destroyed the very social order he has created. (The Lohengrin-Prince of Brabant equivocation is here finally admitted.) He cannot create a free man. His will simultaneously desires social freedom and social slavery. The paradox of reality has invaded the personality of the transcendental hero. He thinks now of only waiting for the end, and he sets out to destroy his will, Brünnhilde, his daughter by Erda, the offspring of the union of idea and reality. But once again he deceives himself, for he thinks that by releasing his will into society, by freeing it of its responsibility to him, he can enable it to control the free hero, the child of Siegmund, who is an accidental result of Wotan's attempt to create a redeemer. (pp. 252-53)

[The] shift from Siegmund to Siegfried corresponds to the cultural shift by which the transcendental hero stepped back from attempting to control society directly to attempting to control it indirectly. His power over the imagination conceals itself behind freedom—Siegfried—and love—Brünnhilde—the two forms of the hidden will. Yet love in its boundless desire to have complete control over its object, destroys freedom; woman, in her determination to make man submit to biological necessity, destroys his autonomy. And freedom, in its fearless and blind and stupid conviction that it is adequate to the conditions which reality imposes upon man, destroys love; man destroys woman in the effort to maintain his autonomy. To gratify man's free exercise of his power over reality, one woman is as good as another; Gutrune can serve Siegfried's purposes as well as Brünnhilde; to gratify woman's biological drives, only one man will do.... Siegfried consequently underestimates the capacity of reality to frustrate his will; he is destroyed through the machinations of Hagen, the son of Alberich. In fact, Hagen, whom in his fearless illusion of adequacy Siegfried has failed to understand, kills him; the uncontrollable and frustrated desire for economic power destroys the instrument of the transcendental hero, Wotan. Wotan can no longer avoid recognizing his self-deceptions and the unresolvable paradox of reality. Love achieves its only gratification possible, death. The ring returns to the Rhine daughters, who drown Alberich in the flooding waters of their river. Valhalla burns; the gods are destroyed. In the orchestra the theme of the will-to-live finally reaches a resolution on a major chord, which dies away into silence. The will can be gratified only when the world of man ceases to exist; that is, it can never be gratified.

In a word, or a few, Wagner's point is this: the transcendental hero cannot redeem society. Not because he does not have access to value; he does. But that value cannot be realized in a world impregnable to morality. The attempt to make social power morally responsible only reveals the morally irresponsible power of nature. From the power of the imagination imposed upon reality flow social order, love, and freedom, but the imaginative and value-laden will, when it encounters the unshakable amorality of nature, can only destroy the very values of order, love, and freedom which it has created. The transcendental hero cannot solve the problems of society because the problems of society, since it is a natural product, are unsolvable.

To clarify what has happened to the nineteenth-century vision, let me summarize the developing issues as sharply as I can. After the negative phase, value was found immanent in the self, and symbolically in nature. It was then drained from nature and found only in the self, but capable of being embodied in society. At the end of the *Ring* society and nature are placed in the same category, valueless, unredeemably resistant to being impregnated with value. Nor is this all. The gods die. Wotan, unlike Lohengrin, does not leave the world; he is destroyed with it. The transcendental vision of value is shorn of its transcendental authority, of its divinity, of its godhead. The question now remaining is this: Does value exist at all? Or are we back to the total negation of Werther and Manfred? Does the world offer no gratification for the orientative drive? (pp. 253-54)

Tristan and Isolde was written after Wagner had composed the *Ring* through the second act of Siegfried. Immediately before him lay Siegfried's awakening of Brünnhilde and their love.

Since this love was to lead to disaster, and love was to be revealed as destructive, Wagner had to run counter to the whole transcendental tradition of erotic love, which was, as one might expect, one of the few transcendental notions which had penetrated deeply into the public mind. In a society which was becoming steadily more puritanical, any thing that sanctified sexuality by coloring it with a quasi-religious light was bound to be popular. That the public still does not comprehend the real meaning of transcendental love is plain when one examines middle-class fiction today, particularly as it appears in magazines and moving pictures. *Tristan,* as a result, has always been the most completely misunderstood of all of Wagner's works. One of Freud's least popular remarks is his statement that he regarded love as the model psychosis; Wagner would have agreed with him, and he said as much in *Tristan.*

Yet when he came to the third act of *Siegfried,* he himself still accepted the tradition. *Tristan* is an exploration of its significance. Once and once only ... does Wagner's real meaning come through explicitly. In the third act, Tristan curses the drink, the love potion, which ostensibly was the cause of his and Isolde's fatal passion. But then he penetrates to the perception that he himself brewed the drink, that the poison of love in it came from his father's need and his mother's sorrow. And he curses the drink, and he who brewed it—himself. The sorrowing Kurvenal bends over his master's prostrate body and cries out against love, "the world's fairest illusion." Erotic love, then, is a projection, a self-created mask which the lover places over the face and the form of the beloved. Lovers do not see each other at all. They see only themselves. Thus Tristan reaches an emotional consummation of his love when Isolde is not with him, and he is dying; and Isolde reaches her ecstasy when Tristan is dead, though she is firmly convinced, to the moment of her own death, that he still lives. Further, the climax of her emotion is identical with her total loss of identity and her merging with nothingness.

Thus, the love scene in the garden is entirely an analysis of how two lovers exploit each other's emotions. Their whole effort is to merge their two identities and together vanish away into night and nothingness, to become one with the universe. Unfortunately reality intrudes, as it always does. Death is the only gateway that leads to this goal, but when you are dead you can scarcely enjoy the loss of identity. Transcendental erotic love, then, is an unrealizable ideal, because it pursues a symbol and not a reality. It is an insanity. Far from being an apotheosis of love, *Tristan* strips the mask from one of mankind's most cherished orientative gratifications and reveals it as an illusion. But even more is involved.

The weakness of transcendental love, even when, as it often was, it was recognized as a symbol, was that it was a resolution to the problem of transcendental authority. As we have seen, if the beloved confirmed the identity of the transcendentalist by loving him in return, thus confirming him as a bearer of divine value, the lover then became dependent upon the beloved. The situation exhibits the same pattern as the transcendental heroic redeemer whose unself-conscious representative and instrument is within society. The lover is therefore exploiting the beloved; at the same time his dependency upon her denies the very thing his love is designed to achieve, a confirmation of his independent identity and selfhood. The pattern has the weakness of all forms of transcendentalism; it imagines that the not-self can in fact be redeemed into value by the activities of the self at the level of the social role. A dual violation takes place. The lover violates the beloved by exploiting her as a symbol; and he violates himself by making his identity depend upon a symbol. If identity can be affirmed only by affirming another's identity, transcendental love is unable to turn the trick.

Attention, therefore, shifts to the reason for this inconsistency; and it is what we have already seen: the need for authority, the need for the confirmation of the divinity of the self. Wagner has taken the whole problem of the *Ring* and narrowed it down to the relation between two people. This pinpointing enables him to see that the illusion of love is caused by the illusion of divinity. Consequently, the divine world of value which Tristan and Isolde strive to reach cannot be reached, because it doesn't exist. The divine, unconscious ground of the universe is mere night and nothingness. The problem he had to solve in the *Ring* is now clear, but to finish it he had first to write *The Meistersinger*. (pp. 255-57)

The symbolic structure [of *The Meistersinger*] is extraordinarily complex. Hans Sachs, for instance, is also God, John the Baptist, the self-conscious nineteenth-century artist free from transcendental illusions, and the mature Wagner. Walther is Adam, Christ, the unself-conscious nineteenth-century artist still caught in the illusions of religion and love, and the young Wagner. This is just a bit of it, and to work it all out is a delightful—and instructive—exercise in literary interpretation. But the whole thing is masked in an adept historical realism. To distinguish it from transcendental realism I shall call it objectist realism. . . . [This] kind of realism is the artistic expression of seeing transcendental divinity as pretension and illusion. For this orientation there is no divine ground to the universe, no opening out of the unconscious self into the Godhead. Since the artist cannot claim a transcendental authority for his style, he must turn elsewhere, outside of art, or to earlier art, for a model. . . . (p. 258)

The theme is *Wahn*, illusion. The question of the opera is how a new art is to supersede an old art, when the old art has the political and social power and the new art has none. Clearly, put in this form, the problem is one that Wagner struggled with all his life. But it is also to be noted that this, the problem of social power, is precisely the problem of the *Ring*. Hans Sachs is the transcendental hero shorn not only of any hope of redeeming society but also stripped of transcendental illusions. Not only does society refuse to recognize his authority; he himself refuses. Consequently it is only with the utmost hesitation, doubts, self-questionings, and modesty that Sachs interferes with the situation at all, to unite the young lovers, Eva and Walther, and to have Walther's genius recognized. But he has one powerful weapon. Stripped of illusions he can recognize and identify the illusions of others, particularly those illusions which persuade people who have social power that they ought to have social power because they deserve it. In his great monologue he says, "Illusion, illusion, everywhere illusion." But his analysis leads him to his solution. "If you would do a great thing, you must manipulate people's illusions." To free mankind of its illusions is impossible. Illusion is the mode in which man exists.

Only one thing in the world is free of the curse of illusion: art, because it does not pretend to anything else. Consequently Walther is no transcendental artist-hero. He is simply a nice young man who can write beautiful poetry and set it to beautiful music, once he has learned how to integrate his own natural genius into the great stream of aesthetic culture and tradition. . . . Walther introduces value into the world solely because he creates a beautiful work of art. Man lives in a world of illusions which he hangs onto by deceiving himself that they have either natural or divine authority and right. He can do no other. He is dependent on illusion because illusion sustains him. Only art can give him freedom from illusion; for art now claims no illusory authority. (pp. 258-59)

By manipulating illusions and releasing the power of art, Hans Sachs establishes a relation among the artist, the people, and the holders of social power. The power of art is now clear. It introduces value into the world by creating in the hearts of men the experience of order and meaning. To assert the existence of order, meaning, and value, whether natural, divine, or transcendent, is an illusion; to experience them is essential to maintaining life. Art is the source of that experience.

Nevertheless, a moral problem remained unresolved. The Sachs-Walther relationship retains traces of the Lohengrin-Prince of Brabant equivocation, and the Wotan-Siegfried-Siegmund situation. Sachs manipulates people; he plays God; it cannot be said that he violates them, except indirectly. Yet the moral task of the nineteenth-century man is not fulfilled if he simply helps people to release their natural talents. This is not to confirm their identity but only to involve them in a social role. From this point of view, the task is to free people from their illusions. *Tristan* and *The Meistersinger* gave Wagner the insight to complete the *Ring* and the moral courage to carry through the gigantic task of staging it. Yet his original question, "How is the ultimate responsibility of the artist to be discharged?" had not yet received an adequate answer. After the *Ring* had been triumphantly produced, he turned almost at once to *Parsifal*.

[Wagner] carried Feuerbach's ideas to their logical conclusions. In conceptualizing orientations man only talks about himself. Religions, constitutive metaphysical systems, and similar symbolizations are useful only when their symbolic nature is realized. Asserted to be true, they are all illusions. In writing *Parsifal*, Wagner, with joking irony, employed the dominating illusion of Europe, Christianity. . . . For Wagner presented the work with all the panoply and seriousness of a religious festival. It is absurd that it should always be given at Easter; it is absurd that applause should be forbidden; intellectually serious Catholics . . . are quite right in their suspicions of it. Wagner turned Bayreuth into a religious temple not because he took Christianity seriously but because he took the theater—art—seriously. (pp. 259-60)

Religion does not redeem art when *Parsifal* is produced; art redeems religion by exposing it as a symbol and thus releasing the individual to see what is really going on in the works. (p. 261)

Parsifal is far easier to understand than anything else Wagner ever wrote. It is perfectly plain that the Christian brotherhood of the grail and their leaders have failed, that they do not save Parsifal. On the contrary it is Parsifal who saves them. It is equally clear that Parsifal earns his own redemption not through religion but through psychological insight and empathy. Parsifal is a pure fool, free from social and religious illusions. Thus when Kundry attempts to seduce him, by empathy he feels the wound of Amfortas, whom Kundry has seduced and violated, and he realizes that it is not Kundry who tempts him but the mask of Herzeleide, his mother, which she is wearing. Here, then, is the root of the madness of erotic passion. Freud was to say no more.

Klingsor, the magician who has attempted to control eroticism by self-castration, hurls the sacred spear. Amfortas, the King of the Grail Knights, had lost the spear when he succumbed to Kundry. The attempt to control illusory eroticism by Christian repression is futile; hence his own spear, wielded by Klingsor, has given him his wound, which will not heal. But Parsifal, who has seen through eroticism, cannot be harmed; he grasps the spear. This spear is Wotan's spear, with a difference. It symbolizes power, to be sure, but not power over others; rather, power over the self, control of identity through insight, an insight, it must be remembered, made possible by means of the power of empathy. . . . [Deriving] value from the self leads to egocentricity unless that egocentricity is overcome. Wagner reverses this scheme. Identity and value are achieved at the moment of empathy and insight. The two psychic acts are simultaneous. The problem of egocentricity does not arise, for egocentricity is the consequence of believing illusions. Egocentricity is the character of the Christian Amfortas, wounded by his surrender of identity to the illusions of religion and love.

After years of wandering, fighting, and suffering, during which he confirms his insight by sharing the suffering of humanity, Parsifal returns to the temple of the grail. There once more the spear and the grail are united. The grail is the vessel of nurturance, of love, of true femininity, just as the spear is the symbol of true masculinity. Both of them are independent of biological sexuality. Men and women alike must be capable of both identity and love, with neither submissive to the other, nor dependent, nor exploiting, nor violating. This point is underlined by the death of Kundry, who appears in two forms, the household slave and the great whore, the eternal erotic enchantress—but in both against her will, violated. Women, Wagner is saying, have been denied their identity and their true power of nurturing others by being condemned by men to role-playing. (pp. 261-62)

In reuniting grail and spear Parsifal rescues the Christian grail knights from extinction. He does nothing, it is to be noticed; he simply displays the spear. Amfortas yields his kingship to Parsifal and in the dome mysterious voices are heard singing, "The highest wonder of salvation! Redemption to the redeemer!" Only the self-redeemed is truly redeemed. It is impossible even for the artist, even for Hans Sachs, to redeem someone else. Only he who has freed himself from the illusions of man and at the same time has seen them as necessary to man, is genuinely redeemed. Thus the equivocal Lohengrin-Prince and Sachs-Walther relationships are at last terminated. Gurnemanz attempts to instruct Parsifal but fails. Parsifal must instruct himself. The moral responsiblity of the redeeming artist, therefore, cannot be discharged by giving freedom, identity, and love to another, for the gift cannot be made. He can only construct a work of art whch shall reveal, at least to those who take the trouble to look, beliefs for what they are, illusions. Like Parsifal, he can only display what he knows. Wagner, like Parsifal, became a Christian only in the sense that out of pity for men he pretended to share their illusions so that he might free them.

Wagner had now concluded his vast ten-act drama. He had solved his problem of how the artist discharges his moral responsiblity to introduce value into the world: the artist offers the opportunity for self-redemption. (pp. 262-63)

> Morse Peckham, "The Hero Frustrated," in his Beyond the Tragic Vision: The Quest for Identity in the Nineteenth Century, *George Braziller, 1962, pp. 240-70.*

NORBERT FUERST   (essay date 1966)

[*Fuerst explores Wagner's handling of myth in* The Nibelung's Ring *and* The Mastersingers of Nuremberg. *Other commentators*

who treat this subject include Friedrich Nietzsche (1872), Alfred A. Wheeler (1883), W. E. Walter (1904), and Theodor Adorno (1937-38).]

What is most amazing in [*The Rhinegold*] is that it surpasses the others in visual imagination. The underwater scene in the Rhine, the scene in the mines of the dwarfs, the scenes before Valhall (mountain castle plus heavenly city) are of a splendor of conception and contrast which strained all resources of nineteenth century theatre. But bolder and wilder were the ideas of mythic cosmology which Wagner forced into the elementary gestures and elementary drives of his assorted sprites. And unmistakable is the revolutionary message that wrong rules the world, that even the world's splendor holds the germs of sickness and decay.

The Valkyrie contains more mystery than the other plays. Gradually it unravels, backwards and forwards. With the first scene we enter the world of human beings. Wotan, in his perplexity over the 'legal' wrong in the world, has created *free* agents, who by sheer freedom of action might restore innocence again. But Wagner's imagination endows the individual carriers of this critique with such an overflow of life that they always threaten to exceed their functions in the drama. The love story between Siegmund and Sieglinde, brother and sister, is too powerful for the purpose and for the god. The quarrel and leave-taking between Wotan and Brunnhild, father and daughter, has such accents of tenderness and discord, fortitude and resignation, that we forget how the fate of the unborn Siegfried and the fate of the Ring are cunningly interwoven with every phase of their argument. It is perhaps the very tension between this function and this vitality which makes the *Valkyrie* such good drama. Wagner is always too massive, he does not know the virtues of economy, neither in his expression nor in the ideas expressed, neither in his themes nor in their elaboration. But in the *Valkyrie* the very length to which he drives the Siegmund-Sieglinde act, the very thoroughness with which he exhausts the Wotan-Brunnhild relationship, turn into revelations by means of his inventiveness, which refuses to add fortuitous detail, but insists on discovering profound links that lay buried in the sagas of the centuries.

In *Siegfried,* the different worlds of the Ring-cosmos meet in a series of clashes. Mime, the dwarf-king's brother, educates Siegfried to be the killer of the last giant (dragon). Brunnhild, the Valkyrie, becomes Siegfried's bride. And Wotan, the wisdom of the world, and the power and the glory, resigns before the ascent of the innocent doer. The oldest and most hackneyed motifs have been absorbed in their new meaning. The gay story of the ascending hero is set off by the sombre crossings of the descending god. The psychology of the venomously selfish Mime is translated into waggish mimicry. The elementary brutality is overgrown with a luxuriant nostalgia for nature and the natural things. And the mystery of all-engulfing sex is celebrated in the superhuman puberty rites between Brunnhild and Siegfried.

Wagner still counted so little on posterity that he retold in every drama the essential links of the other dramas. How could he assume that most of us who see one drama remember the action of the others? But could we really say that we mostly understand? As the leitmotifs glide by us, sometimes in flashes of recognition, sometimes dimly associated, and sometimes wrongly connected and mistaken for related ones, they keep us in a daze of musical wondering, reminiscing and guessing. Similarly the logical, psychological, and mythological ideas glide by us, in half-understood or not understood words. We catch them on the wing; or we do not catch them. And the result is that delicious suspension between knowing and feeling which makes even the (accompanying) literary experience a musical mode.

The musical impact is foremost in everybody's mind. The literary message is almost absorbed in it, but it was there, independently, from the beginning. A third element contributed to the robustness of the Wagner structures. If we believe his own testimony, it was neither the music nor the words which were the source of his dramas, but that third thing: the vision. At the origin of every drama he had visions of simple actions, gestures, scenes, which symbolized elementary states of soul. This visible, scenic, theatric element he pursued with the utmost tenacity all his life. Thence his endeavors to gain personal influence on the way the dramas were performed . . . ; the utopian demands to have a theatre of his own; and the models of mimic action which the old man at Bayreuth gave to *all* his actors, from his incomparable modelling of Mime to his incredible acting of the goddesses. From all the accounts we have (and mostly by vain artists), Wagner was more unquestionably a great actor than he was an original musician and a creative writer.

The stupendous tetralogy cracks at its many seams, but nowhere more so than in *The Twilight of the Gods,* where the too well known legend of Siegfried's death had to be incorporated into the doom of the gods. It could all be averted if Brunnhild gave up Siegfried's ring (the Rhinegold). But Siegfried has to be drawn (by a cup of oblivion) into the world of men, who send him to win Brunnhild for another. The agent of mischief however is Hagen, the dwarf-king's son. So we have again three orders representing the world: the dwarfs (Hagen), the gods (Brunnhild), and instead of the giants the heroes (Siegfried). In the entanglement, the revolution of man is not triumphant; Brunnhild and Siegfried do not sacrifice one order to another. They finally see redemption only in sacrificing themselves. And thus Schopenhauer-Wotan's wish is fulfilled, 'Das Ende! das Ende!' But the end has several implications. One is said in music: that love knows no death. The other is said in words: that the power of gold returns to the innocent waters. And the third one is said in the burning scenery: that the old order falls, the tyranny of traditional formalism is over. (pp. 180-82)

Tristan ushers in a new period not only in German music but also in German poetry. One might call the new poetry by the name which became popular in France twenty years later, Symbolism. *Tristan* is its prototype in several respects. It has absolutely no entertainment value; it is the impudently egocentric expression of the artist's soul, or rather of a state of his soul; at the same time it claims to be a metaphysics, a philosophical explanation of the world; above all, it uses all the most personally perfected means at the disposal of the artist, regardless of their being liked or even understood. It demands subjection, not being pleased. It demands that the hearer or reader transcend himself while hearing or reading, transform himself into a new hearer or reader.

The demand for a new art had been raised by Wagner in the bulkiest of his interminable treatises, *Opera and Drama* . . . , especially in the part **'The Character of Dramatic Poetry.'** The claims which he raises there in behalf of the art work of the future are appallingly inclusive; they comprehend a radical reorientation of society. 'The overthrow of the state means a healthy organic society. The overthrow of the state cannot mean anything but the realisation of the religious consciousness which society has of its humanistic character.' Here everything runs

into everything else, and nothing is excluded. 'Common human nature is felt by the individual as the instinct of life and love. Only in society can he satisfy this instinct. His consciousness is religious, that is common [gemeinsam] and vindicates his nature. In the free self-determination of the individual lies the religion of the future.' As he moves from the immeasurably broad basis of art towards its apex, he moves within concepts familiar to every symbolist: 'For the poet, who must compress the multiplicity of life into a compact pattern, the available image is just this: the miracle. The miracle in poetry differs from the miracle in religion in that the poetic reason is not at all interested in belief, only in intuitive understanding.' This is soon followed by another characteristic of Symbolism, the frowning upon realism: 'The condensed image of actual life *has* to appear magnified, fortified, rendered unusual.' The climax of this section is perhaps this definition of 'the highest potential of poetry':

> a myth—made most transparent by drama
> —re-invented in the face of everpresent life
> —justified before a lucid consciousness.

All this reminds one that Wagner was completely absorbed in the Nibelungen myths at the time. Two things had to happen to him before he was ready for *Tristan:* the revelation of Schopenhauer's philosophy, and the love of Mrs. Wesendonck. Out of Schopenhauer's drama between blind will and selfless imagination, out of his personal drama between powerful attraction and triumphant sublimation, he made the first and simplest Symbolist poem.

The symbolism drenches and almost drowns the story. Does anything happen? For a long act, Tristan refuses to talk to Isolde, then they talk. For another long act, Tristan and Isolde psychoanalyse their love. For the third long act, Tristan alone recapitulates his philosophy, and Isolde confirms it, alone. The 2400 half-verses would offer endless opportunity for storytelling; but we have more to guess, than we are told, that Tristan is the perfect knight, and therefore must get his childless uncle the perfect bride, *in order* not to become his heir. And because he is the perfect knight, he must not realize that he and the perfect bride have for ever been in love. Only when they resolve to die are they liberated for their love: the death potion turns into the love potion.

The intrigue is short-circuited, because the emotional state of consciousness is everything. If one looks at the text only, the Wagnerian massiveness is overpoweringly there. The poet poured himself forth with an unheard-of freedom. Wagner himself remembered above all this sense of freedom: 'Here at last I moved with fullest freedom, with complete disregard of any theoretical consideration; while I worked I became aware how I left my own system behind.' Even without the music the text is unbearably eloquent. What monotony of situation! what absence of incident! what paucity of ideas! what richness of expression! The rhymes of his earlier period, the alliteration of his Nibelungen-period, and all the tritest tricks of late Romantic rhetorics are used cumulatively. The sound-image of waves is never absent, neither in the short breath of the individual (half-) verse, nor in the immense aggregate mass of this whole grey ocean of anti-sense sound. In this watery waste of words, in this ocean of tautology, every short wave beats on the same shore line of meaning: the dayworld (of social conventions) is the world of appearances; the nightworld (of individual-universe intuition) is the deeper reality, And why? Tag = Wahn, because it is affirmation of the will; Nacht = Wahrheit, because it is negation of the will. Or perhaps thus: lust is the unconscious wish to be extinguished in procreation and progeny:

> Nie-wieder-Erwachens
> Wahnlos
> Hold bewusster Wunsch. . . .

In the climactic duet of act II the six times iterated key word is 'ohne' (without), stressing the negative essence of Nirvana.

The third act is only philosophy. It contains nothing but the confirmation that the message of act II was not merely sensual delirium, but a valid generalization from all vital experience. The shepherd's tune which haunts the act has a plain interpretation: everything in life sings the will—and its death:

> . . . Mich sehnen—und sterben. . . .

But although he now curses his surrender to sex, he never knows what is stronger, the will to live (sehnen) or the will to die (sterben); and combining, cumulating the two, he dies in Isolde's arms.

In this first German Symbolist poem, one striking difference from French Symbolism is already marked. While the latter almost cultivates obscurity, glows in an infra-red light only, the works of German Symbolism suffer from a glaring light, from over-exposure, from over-obviousness. Apart from that, an essential affinity there was from the start. (pp. 189-91)

The Mastersingers is the most casual among his masterworks. He wrote the drama, rapidly, during his last stay in Paris, in 1862. After his bitterest disappointment he wrote this indulgent comedy about the compromise between art and public. The writing itself is a compromise; in the rhymed doggerel there is verse of all grades: sheer waste of words; poor imitation of the actual style of sixteenth century mastersingers; easy-flowing eloquence; funny, racy naturalness; packed statement and excellent epigrams. But the plot is the most felicitous Wagner has thrown together, an intrigue so simple that it serves all purposes. And the main purpose is to bring art to the people. (pp. 201-02)

So many parts of Wagner are period pieces. The worst and the best of his time were powerfully combined in him. Primitivism and luxury, revolution and tradition, vitalism and ethics, paganism and Christianity, Schopenhauer and Nietzsche: he was powerful enough to incorporate them all. This comprehensiveness is perhaps at the root of his cumulation of arts. And the public responded so affirmatively because it seemed that here was 'something for everybody.' Nietzsche ends *The Wagner Case* [see excerpt above, 1888] with the accusation that what the Wagner movement brought to the fore was 'the pretence of the layman, the art-idiot . . . And the confidence in genius, the impudent dilettantism (its model is in the *Mastersingers*)!' Indeed, this was art for the layman. Even if your literary or musical or scenic mind was underdeveloped, Wagner allowed you to add up your deficiencies, and you resulted as a genuine enthusiast, not as Nietzsche's complete idiot. The layman was grateful that something accessible from *many* sides existed. But Nietzsche (end of *Nietzsche Contra Wagner*) 'needs another art . . . an art for artists, only for artists!' And Wagner stands convicted of having given us art for the average man.

The third act of the *Mastersingers* is the closest Wagner came to self-presentation. In the 'Wahn' monologue all the loose ends of the preceding evening's adventure are caught up. They are also blown up into 'the world's illusion.' It is Schopenhauer set to verse. Then Hans Sachs sets out to take charge of the

illusions, 'without which good things rarely succeed.' He starts to work on the young nobleman, the young genius (or dilettante, as Nietzsche calls him) and admonishes him to try to *please* those 'honest men' from whom he has so much to gain. This view of reciprocity (within the bourgeoisie and between it and its outsiders) is the picture we get in Keller and Fontane; it is the opposite of the picture we get in Marx. Hans Sachs, however, acts only as the spokesman of the artists' union. He simply instructs his noble apprentice to combine a respect for the rules with a heed of inspiration. The results are so extremely satisfactory that four or five stories can be concluded in private: the artist can manage the affairs of the world, when he does not want anything for himself.

But art has to prove itself publicly too, and Wagner rises to the occasion with the climax on the festive fair grounds. Although Pogner is the 'master rich and generous' who today offers 'his highest good plus all his goods' as the prize, Hans Sachs, the popular poet, is the center and director of affairs. He is confident that the nature of man and the nature of things will prevent an untoward conclusion. Beckmesser tries to sing Walter's song; Walter has only to sing it in the right way to prove his superiority, and 'the people' are so swayed that they close the contest by acclaim. A last hesitation of the nobleman to be unionized motivates Sachs' paternal warning, 'Don't despise the masters—not to your noble ancestors, to your personal accomplishments and the good will of your fellow citizens you owe your (future) happiness . . . Even if art did not remain aristocratic, it remained genuine art . . . The German nation will disintegrate: true values will live only in your artists' works.'

From the first act on we have been prepared to see Eva = woman = 'the people.' Now we see Walter (= the aristocracy) and Eva (= the people) lean affectionately on Sachs (= art), while Pogner (= capitalism) does homage. That too-well-staged resolution of social disharmonies was the expression of a hope that all classes might find their center in a 'middle class,' and that the *middle* class would be the carrier of all that is best in material and spiritual life. This is Wagner's gloriously naive solution of 'die soziale Frage' [the social question]. (pp. 202-04)

> *Norbert Fuerst, "The Age of Wagner?" in his* The Victorian Age of German Literature: Eight Essays, *The Pennsylvania State University Press, University Park, 1966, pp. 177-205.*

JOHN J. REICH (essay date 1968)

[*Reich delineates in* The Nibelung's Ring *and* Parsifal *the influence of the Classical Greeks, particularly the dramatists Aeschylus and Euripides.*]

Though the stature of Wagner the aesthetician, philosopher or politician may be in doubt, there can be no doubt at all that as a musician Wagner's position as the dominating figure of the nineteenth century remains unquestioned. Indeed his influence in our own times, while more difficult to analyze, seems undiminished. It is sufficient to say that since his day no composer creating a work for the stage has been able to neglect Wagner's works. For this his music dramas are solely responsible, not his academic treatises—however necessary these may originally have been to the creation of the music dramas; for this reason anything that can contribute to our understanding of his music and drama is of profound significance. (p. 19)

It was during [his] . . . study of Greek that serious work on *The Ring* began, and it is *The Ring* which shows the strongest evidence of Wagner's debt to Greece. But his earlier works also reveal Greek connections—connections which Wagner himself was always the first to see and acknowledge. His earliest preoccupations had been with Homer: by the time of his move to Leipzig he had already translated large portions of the *Iliad* and *Odyssey*. Wagner's love of Homer, combined with his own restless wanderings—both intellectual and actual—clearly suggested to him the wanderings of Odysseus, and he himself was aware of the relationship between the longings and search of Odysseus and of his own Flying Dutchman. As always Wagner took from his sources only what he needed and discarded the rest. The Dutchman is a combination of Odysseus, The Wandering Jew and much else besides. Odysseus' search was for his own home and his own wife: the Dutchman also searches for a woman, but one who will sacrifice herself for him and thereby redeem him. As Wagner himself says: "This woman, however, is no longer the domestic Penelope, married long ago by Odysseus; it is woman per se, but the yet non-existent, longed-for, sensual, eternally feminine woman" . . .—a curious blend of Homer and Goethe. A lesser genius than Wagner would have made of this and other such combinations a mere patchwork, an unsatisfactory introduction of alien elements into a basically simple scheme. Only a Wagner could create from this material a myth as powerful and as valid as any of its predecessors.

If the Dutchman represents Odysseus the wanderer, Tannhäuser provides a parallel with the temptations of Odysseus. On more than one occasion in the course of his wanderings Odysseus is beguiled into suspending his journey—by the sorceress Circe, and even more enticingly by Calypso. Just as he is induced to forget his quest in the delights of the nymph, so is Tannhäuser beguiled in the grotto of Venus within the Venusberg. And both of them manage to break the spell of their seducers, Odysseus returning to Penelope and Tannhäuser to Elizabeth. Tannhäuser's return is certainly the more difficult and produces many more complications, but once again Wagner has taken the basic scheme of the myth and added to it. In many cases these additions are so fundamental to the finished work that it would be difficult to discern the presence of the original myth had Wagner himself not indicated it. In the case of *Lohengrin* once again he provided a clear statement of its Greek origin; for the story of Lohengrin and Elsa, he tells us, has much in common with that of Zeus and Semele. . . . Zeus in his love for a mortal woman becomes her lover in human form, but Semele, distracted by her realization that she does not know him as he really is, demands that Zeus should reveal himself in his true form. Zeus knows, of course, that to grant this request would mean to destroy her. He might well have addressed her as Lohengrin addresses Elsa at their first meeting:

> If nothing is to tear me from thee,
> Thou must make to me one promise;
> Never shalt thou ask me nor wish to know
> From where my journey brought me
> Nor my name and birth. . . .

Just as Semele cannot withstand her agony of doubt, so Elsa, although she has accepted Lohengrin's condition, cannot leave the question unasked:

> Nothing can give me peace or tear me from
> this madness but—though it cost me my life—
> to learn who thou art. . . .

The fatal knowledge has the same effect in both cases. This insistence on the destructive power of knowledge in such a relationship has, of course, an obvious dramatic force. . . . (pp. 21-2)

Schadewaldt has brilliantly described the *Flying Dutchman, Tannhäuser* and *Lohengrin* as "mythical palimpsests, where, under the new artistic formulation, the old Greek originals can still be made out". In the case of *The Ring,* the process is one of direct confrontation between two powerful elements, Greek myths and Germanic sagas, and their resolution by what Schadewaldt has called "a kind of primeval creation out of preformed elements". As in the earlier works the Germanic elements are clearly visible: the Greek contribution is again less obvious although still vital.

As has been seen, the leading Greek influence upon Wagner at the time of his work on *The Ring* was that of Aeschylus. It was not, however, the *Oresteia,* the only surviving complete trilogy, that was to provide inspiration, but the Prometheus cycle. Only a single complete play from this trilogy survives, *Prometheus Bound,* but the scholar Droysen in his Aeschylus translations of 1832 and 1841 reconstructed the whole trilogy, and his reconstruction was well known to Wagner. . . . [The] effect of this trilogy upon the creation of *The Ring* was immense. The idea of the actual form of the cycle as that of a trilogy is itself, of course, a Greek one—there is no such form in the Germanic sources. Indeed, Wagner stresses the fact that *The Ring* is a trilogy, although there are in fact four parts to it, by describing *Das Rheingold,* the first part, as a prelude. The full title of the cycle is *Ein Bühnenfestspiel für drei Tage und einen Vorabend* (A Stage Festival Play for Three Days and a Preliminary Evening). (p. 22)

In the reconstructed trilogy [of Aeschylus] the first part consists of the Theft of the Fire, the second of the Binding of Prometheus and the third of his Liberation. This is closely paralleled in *The Ring. Das Rheingold* presents us with the theft of the Rhinegold; *Die Walküre* concludes with the binding of Brünnhilde; *Siegfried* presents us with her liberation. To this Wagner adds the conclusion of his fourth part, *Götterdämmerung,* made inevitable by Alberich's original curse. But there are even closer parallels than these. According to Droysen the first play of the trilogy describes the building of Zeus's castle: in *Das Rheingold* we not only hear of but actually see Walhall, the castle built for Wotan, and the Tarnhelm, the magic helmet used by Alberich, is the equivalent of the "protecting helmet" in Droysen's version of the Aeschylus play.

There are also links between characters. The daughters of Oceanus, the Oceanides, who appear in *Prometheus Bound,* reappear transformed as the Rhinemaidens. Wagner's giants are clearly related to the Titans of Aeschylus. Brünnhilde, as befits one of the most complex characters in *The Ring,* has a somewhat more involved ancestry. In many respects she shows striking resemblances to Prometheus, as already indicated; these are confirmed by parallels between Brünnhilde's mother, Wala-Erda, and Prometheus' mother, Gaia-Themis. Just as in many works of Greek art Gaia appears from the earth with only the upper part of her body visible, so according to Wagner's stage directions Erda appears rising from below the ground to only half her height. But Schadewaldt has indicated an even more striking parallel, based not on Droysen's reconstruction but on the extant *Prometheus Bound.* In the central scene of that play Io, pursued by Hera, comes to Prometheus who tells her that in Egypt she will give birth to Epaphos. In this way Io becomes the ancestor of Herakles, who is himself to become the liberator of Prometheus. Just as Prometheus meets and provides help to the ancestor of his liberator, so Brünnhilde in the central scene of Act III of *Die Walküre* shows the way of escape to Sieglinde, who is to give birth to Siegfried, Brünnhilde's liberator.

But if the obvious equation is to be made between Zeus and Wotan, then Brünnhilde as Wotan's daughter also represents Zeus's daughter Athene. Indeed there are close resemblances between Athene Parthenos and the Warrior Maid. Both of them are fighters, happy in battle. When Siegfried's passion drives him to grasp Brünnhilde in his arms she runs from him in horror, and her words might well be those of Athene:

> No God has ever approached me!
> Low bent all the heroes, greeting the maiden.
> Holy came She from Walhall. . . .

But, unlike Athene, Brünnhilde has in her encounter with Siegmund in *Die Walküre,* Act II not only seen mortal love but understood it, and is prepared to give up her godhood for its sake. The closeness of the relationship between Brünnhilde and her father, like that of Athene and Zeus, makes the Brünnhilde-Prometheus equation even more poignant. Athene was born from Zeus's head, and in the same way Brünnhilde represents another part of Wotan himself. (pp. 23-4)

The several connections between Zeus and Wotan are obvious. Both are the rulers of a divine order that is newly established and is still capable of being overthrown. In order to sustain their respective regimes, both are forced to resort to a display of power in the form of violence. In the case of Wotan this descent from an original moral superiority contains the seeds of his destruction and the destruction of the order that he represents, although he is in fact placed in a position where he has little choice: his end is implicit in his beginning, and it is only when he realizes the inevitability of the destruction of his rule that he can fully comprehend his own position. . . . [His] acknowledgement of a destiny that works in a sphere above the control even of the gods is further expanded in his great scene with Erda at the opening of Act III of *Siegfried.* His realization makes acceptable his renunciation. In the same way Zeus is forced by necessity to renounce his former position and to become reconciled with Prometheus. By doing this before it is too late he is able to preserve his regime. But if by withdrawing from his former intransigence Zeus can prevent his own destruction, why is it that Wotan, even though he has made similar concessions, is still doomed to perish? Once he has abandoned the hope of regaining the Ring either personally or through the direct agency of Siegmund and, indeed, once the Ring has been returned to the Rhinemaidens by Brünnhilde at the end of *Götterdämmerung,* there seems little reason for the Twilight of the Gods. Why cannot Wotan, like Zeus, return to his former authority? This was certainly a question that Wagner was aware of from the beginning. . . . [It] seems likely that at this point the strength even of the Greek and Germanic influences was becoming outweighed by a new and powerful influence upon his thinking and creative process—that of Schopenhauer. It is this, rather than any Greek precedent or the specific effects of the curse, that causes Wotan virtually to will his own destruction, and at this point the fates of the two gods diverge. But by placing the story of Siegfried and Brünnhilde—not to mention the numerous other lesser characters—in the general context of divine fate as represented by a destiny that is above the gods, Wagner attains to that level of cosmic drama for which the only parallel can be found in the works of Aeschylus. In terms both of their general position and of the particular difficulties that arise from it, Wagner's Wotan and Aes-

chylus' Zeus are closely related, and the role of fate is even more remarkably similar.

The idea of an inexorable and inevitable destiny is, of course, by no means peculiar to Aeschylus: indeed its origins appear in Homer. The Homeric Zeus, too, is bound by this mysterious force and was compelled by it to sacrifice his beloved Hector, just as Wotan was made to sacrifice Siegmund. In *The Ring* this power is personified in the form of the Rhinemaidens and the Norns—who closely correspond, it will be recalled, to the Greek Fates (the three sisters engaged, like the Norns, in the business of spinning the destinies of men). Of other parallels with Homer, perhaps the most convincing can be found at the beginning of Act II of *Die Walküre,* in the long quarrel between Wotan and Fricka—a scene clearly reminiscent of similar arguments between Zeus and Hera, notably in the Fourth and Fourteenth Books of the *Iliad*. The whole idea, indeed, of continuing the action on two levels, the human and the divine, is in itself characteristic of Homer. Nevertheless, as Wagner clearly realized, the major influence upon *The Ring* is that of Aeschylus.

In none of Wagner's works is the Greek influence as powerful as in *The Ring*. After reaching the end of the second act of *Siegfried* Wagner laid aside *The Ring* for some ten years, and the two works composed during this intervening period seem—superficially at any rate—to show a reaction away from the struggles of gods and men, away from the cosmic drama of an Aeschylus. (p. 25)

Wagner's last work, *Parsifal,* provides rather more direct evidence of Greek influence, and in this case the influences are not only literary but so to speak topographical. Perhaps the greatest religious shrine in the Greek world was at Delphi. Here at the temple of Apollo, the god's priestess, the Pythia, replied to questions by consulting the Oracle and passing on its mysterious and ambiguous replies. The significant connection of Apollo with music and the arts was not lost on Wagner. Already in *Siegfried* he had suggested a comparison between Wotan's visit to Erda and this consultation of the Oracle of Apollo: "There, like the Greeks, over the vapours rising from the cleft earth at Delphi, we come to the central point of the world's tragedy." . . . The "central point" is here metaphorical; as Wagner well knew, Delphi was in a literal sense the center of the world for the Greeks. We will return to this Delphic parallel when we consider the more general question of the nature of the Wagnerian theatre. In *Parsifal* we are presented with a series of links between Delphi, the most sacred Greek shrine, and Monsalvat, the shrine containing the most sacred relics of Christianity, the Grail and the Spear. Of course, the links can only be forged by literary means; and the play that provides the connection is not on this occasion by Aeschylus, but by Euripides. In his play *Ion,* Euripides deals with a young and innocent temple servant, Ion, who achieves knowledge only through a series of catastrophes that end in his death. Like Parsifal, Ion is made wise through pity for others and an awakening of self-awareness . . . ; like Parsifal, Ion is a "pure fool". . . . Curiously enough, the position of Wagner in relation to his Greek original is here exactly the reverse of his attitude in *The Ring.* For while the Greek play ends pessimistically with Ion's death, Wagner's *Parsifal* ends in an atmosphere of exalted optimism. Both principal characters, Parsifal and Ion, are unaware of their true ancestry; and their similarity is further stressed by their first appearances when both of them appear on stage armed with a bow and arrow and aim to shoot at a swan. In this way, with Parsifal's first entry Wagner suggests the Greek background against which his work is set.

The German scholar Nedden has suggested a further connection between *Parsifal* and Euripides. The Telephus myth finds in at least one respect a close parallel in *Parsifal,* and one of the best-known treatments of the myth occurs in a play, of which only fragments remain, by Euripides. Briefly, the myth describes the wounding of Telephus, King of Mysia, by Achilles. The wound will not heal, and Telephus learns by an oracle, interpreted by Odysseus, that he can only be cured by a touch from the spear that caused it. The cure is effected, and in gratitude Telephus shows the Greeks the way to Troy. In just the same way Amfortas, the King of the Knights of the Grail, is wounded by a spear—that which pierced Christ's side and has now fallen into the hands of Klingsor—and is told by an oracle that only the same spear can cure him. He is further told that the spear can only be regained by a "pure fool", and thus the Ion and Delphi parallels are suggested. In due course, Parsifal wins the spear and performs the cure.

It is certainly true that, with the exception of *The Ring, Parsifal* seems to suggest the most striking Greek parallels, but only in *The Ring* itself do we find a completely elaborated system of analogies.

There are many other examples of possible Greek originals from many of the most important moments in Wagner's operas: Brünnhilde's immolation on Siegfried's funeral pyre can be

Caricature of Wagner conducting. Mary Evans Picture Library.

compared with Evadne's immolation on the funeral pyre of her husband Capaneus in Euripides' *Supplices;* the recognition scene between Siegmund and his sister Sieglinde suggests the similar recognition of Orestes by Elektra, also brother and sister; Herakles and Siegfried both perform a series of heroic deeds that include the slaying of monsters. But the examples already described should serve to demonstrate that the "Greekness" of Wagner's works was both conscious and deliberate. It is impossible to believe that a man of Wagner's wide reading would not be aware of the connections; indeed, in many instances the composer has referred directly to the Greek origins of his works. It is surprising only that so few commentators and interpreters have shown awareness of them. (pp. 26-7)

John J. Reich, "The Rebirth of Tragedy—Wagner and the Greeks," in Mosaic: A Journal for the Interdisciplinary Study of Literature, *Vol. I, No. 4, (July, 1968), pp. 18-34.*

TOM F. DRIVER   (essay date 1970)

[*Driver examines Wagner's work in the context of "dream-romanticism," or the Romantic movement's concern with history as the lost past.*]

It is to Wagner that one must turn in order to see the dramatic culmination of dream-romanticism and the contribution it was destined to make to modern theater practice. For in Wagner the deepest concerns of the romantic tragedians were realized. There were three principal reasons for this.

First, Wagner was a composer, and one of such originality that he perceived, where others did not, the resources music could supply for that direct appeal to emotion that dream-romanticism intended.

Second, Wagner was possessed by a love of theater so radical that he was able to envision its complete reconstituiton. Theater was for him the supreme art because it combined many arts into one. To his mind this meant that it promised to transcend the limitations of each particular art, fulfilling itself in a *Gesamtkunstwerk*. The idea is vague, but to this it owed its attraction, since it corresponded to that longing for an absolute beyond all specifics which lay at the heart of dream-romanticism.

Third, Wagner was a product of Germany at the time when a number of her intellectuals were beginning to explore primitive and other non-Christian cultures and to take, therefore, a very strong interest in mythology. The interest in mythology not only was historical and antiquarian but also reflected the tendency of historical consciousness to attempt to complete itself in mythological thought. Vico himself . . . had asserted that the primitive past can be re-evoked from the depth of consciousness. For the romanticist it is all one whether we say that the study of history leads one back to prehistory and thus to myth or whether we say that one flees from the burdens of history to the refuge of transhistorical mythology. In either case the romanticist comes to see myth as a sort of organic root that has the power to orient and to nourish human experience, and Wagner offers a clear example of this process. He was aware that if one wanted to reunite modern man with the passion from which rationalism, industrialism, and commerce separate him, it was necessary to go beyond the merely adventuresome and the heroic and to return to the mythical, which is the more deeply human because it is superhuman. [Wagner wrote:]

Marvel, ye erudite critics, at the omnipotence
of human minstrelsy, unfolded in the simple

mythos of the folk! Things that all your understanding can not so much as comprehend are there laid bare to human feeling, with such a physically perfect surety as no other means could bring to pass.

It was while he was contemplating a work on Frederick Barbarossa (which he later abandoned in favor of one on Siegfried), Wagner tells us, that he saw "Myth and History stand before me with opposing claims . . .":

> My studies thus bore me through the legends of the Middle Ages right down to their foundation in the old Germanic *mythos;*. . . . What here I saw, was no longer the figure of conventional history . . . but the real naked man . . . the type of the true *human being*.

Although Wagner spoke of myth and history as opposites, their opposition was, for him, a dialectical one, not one of mutual contradiction. He came to myth by way of history, and it was precisely in order to comprehend the meaning of the historical that he plunged himself into the mythical.

> Had I chosen to comply with the imperative demands of history, then had my drama become an unsurveyable conglomerate of pictured incidents, entirely crowding out from view the real and only thing I wished to show; and thus, as artist, I should have met precisely the same fate in my drama as did its hero: to wit, I should myself have been crushed by the weight of the very relations that I fain would master—that is, portray—without ever having brought my purpose to an understanding; just as Friedrich could not bring his will to carrying out. To attain my purpose, I should therefore have had to reduce this mass of relations by *free* construction, and should have fallen into a treatment that would have absolutely violated history. Yet I could not but see the contradiction involved herein; for it was the main characteristic of Friedrich, in my eyes, that he should be a *historical* hero. If, on the other hand, I wished to dabble in mythical construction, then, for its ultimate and highest form, but quite beyond the modern poet's reach, I must go back to the unadulterated *mythos,* which up to now the folk alone has hymned, and which I had already found in full perfection—in the "Siegfried."

For Wagner, myth was the ultimate expression of human experience. "Experience is everything," he wrote. The experience appealed to here is the product of event, memory, and emotion. Wagner's expressed aim was to bring "the drama's broader object to the cognizance of feeling." To accomplish this it was necessary to create in the spectator a state of dreaming. The mind, he said, should be "placed in that dream-like state wherein it presently shall come to full clairvoyance, and thus perceive a new coherence in the world's phenomena." The romantic quest for reality, rejecting what is given to "the waking eye of everyday," seeks the clairvoyance of the dream.

The inevitable outcome of Wagner's dream-romanticism was the desire for an absolute beyond the dream. Re-entry into history proved impossible. Instead, Wagner's imagination traveled toward the cessation of dream in absolute sleep, which is

death. After reading Schopenhauer, whom he called the greatest philosopher since Kant, Wagner declared that "the negation of the desire of life" is "the only salvation possible":

> If I think of the storm of my heart, the terrible tenacity with which, against my desire, it used to cling to the hope of life, and if even now I feel this hurricane within me, I have at least found a quietus which in wakeful nights helps me to sleep. This is the genuine, ardent longing for death, for absolute unconsciousness, total nonexistence. Freedom from all dreams is our only final salvation.

It was this dream-possessed, death-longing Wagner who carried the idea of "organic form" to its ultimate manifestation in theater, where it necessarily resulted in musical drama. It was Wagner who pressed toward a "total" employment of stage space, décor, and lighting for the purpose of establishing mood. Victor Hugo had pioneered in this, realizing that in the theater the romantic dream requires it. Wagner made it a creed. He set the practice, though he did not invent it, of darkening the house lights, plunging the audience into obscurity so that its whole attention should be surrendered to the mood-creating stage. He dropped the orchestra into a pit, where it became the hidden source of an enveloping, primal sound. He got rid of box seats, from which spectators had looked across at each other for three hundred years, turning every chair toward the stage. Wagner conceived of the theater as a single, gigantic instrument whose every part would function in concert with the rest to transport an audience from the mundane to the mythical, from the partial to the absolute.

Doing all this as both poet and composer, Wagner took the theatrical expression of the romantic dream as far as it could go. His legacy has not, therefore, led to further development in kind, though there have been plenty of imitations and variations. All by himself, he invented, perfected, and exhausted the Wagnerian music drama, and he developed dream-romanticism so fully that all theatrical efforts in that direction after him have seemed lacking in strength. However, Wagner's general concept of theater has proved germinal. It has been employed for the achievement of quite un-Wagnerian ends, partly in realistic drama, partly in symbolist drama, and partly, because of the idea of "total theater," in twentieth-century departures as different as those of Bertolt Brecht and Paul Claudel.

It is Wagner's absolutism that today frequently dampens, where it does not extinguish, the fires of enthusiasm that once burned for him. The twentieth century has discovered that romantic absolutes, easily carried over into the political realm, result in orgies of human suffering. Myth does indeed feed history, sometimes with poison. The age has also discovered, as Wagner did, that love of the absolute eventuates in the love of death (*Tristan und Isolde*). All the same, it was Wagner's absolutism that enabled him to fulfill the aims of dream-romanticism, and it was while doing this that he spurred the revolution in theater techniques that has made the style and practice of theater what it is today. . . . (pp. 20-4)

A distinguishing mark of Wagnerian absolutism is its lack of irony. In Wagner there is no double vision. He never shows us, indeed he seems to withhold, the reverse side of the coin. There are those who see in his refusal to turn any subject around the mark of a charlatan. If that is what he was, we probably should add that he fooled himself as well. . . . (pp. 24-5)

Tom F. Driver, "Romanticism of the Dream," in
his Romantic Quest and Modern Query: A History
of the Modern Theatre, Delacorte Press, 1970,
pp. 13-25.*

RICHARD DAVID (essay date 1979)

[Focusing on the early operas, David traces Wagner's increasing
skill as a dramatist.]

[The] dramatic actions that Wagner chose to set were, at least
after he had found himself, peculiarly apt to music in general
and to Wagner's music in particular. They were bold and simple
structures upon which his music, like the varying light upon
Monet's depictions of Rouen Cathedral, could develop a wealth
of differing resonances. He found such actions in legend, often
not far removed from archetypal myth. His claim that such
myths, being spontaneous creations of das Volk ('the Folk'),
were purer, truer, more universal than the sophisticated fab-
rications of intellectuals must be taken as a rationalization, and
even then as applicable only in part, for he seldom accepted
them as given, but reworked them assiduously, combining and
blending the folklore motives from more than one source. It
was still a right instinct for himself that chose to rework pebbles
rounded by the waters of time rather than sophisticated modern
artefacts. As he came to know himself better, he insisted more
and more on plots pared of all inessentials; unities of time and
place, as well as of action, were more closely observed; and
in place of the extended poeticisms of the conventional librettist
he adopted and adapted the old alliterative stressed verse (Stabreim) which, at least in intention, allowed no room for slack
in the meaning and offered close and punchy accents for the
music to fasten on.

It is the absence of these later stringencies that accounts for
the comparative weakness of Wagner's first three operas. The
critic must also remember that even when the third of these,
Rienzi, was being written, the author was no more than twenty-
seven years old. It is still puzzling that so very little of Wagner's
mature dramatic power comes out in these early works.

Die Feen has a legendary subject, but one that had already
been sophisticated by Goldoni's reworking. As one might expect with a novice opera, many of the effects are borrowed
from other operas in which their effectiveness had already been
demonstrated (Ada, the sorceress-heroine, evidently recruits
her ladies-in-waiting from the same agency as does Mozart's
Queen of Night). The plot is diffuse, and attention is distracted
from the central issue (the testing of the hero Arindal's character) by several subordinate themes, such as the invasion of
Arindal's sister's kingdom, which are promisingly raised but
come to nothing. Such real dramatic conflict as there is occurs,
significantly enough, in the internal doubts and divisions of
the hero himself, Arindal, whose frantic self-communing casts
a shadow at least as far ahead as Tannhäuser. What is fascinating about the opera is that so many of what in later works
are to be key ideas are already present here in embryo: forbidden inquiry, fairy garden, magic weapons, final transfiguration.

The music of Das Liebesverbot is notoriously derivative and
slight, but this refashioning of Shakespeare's Measure for Measure has been characterized as Wagner's 'unique success in
the realm of the well-made play', and one might therefore
expect to find in it some foretaste of his later dramatic mastery.
In fact, the handling is extraordinarily vapid and amateurish.
The opportunities for theatrical effect, for example, the first

entry of Friedrich (Shakespeare's Angelo) to chill a fooling
crowd, are muffed, and the unmaskings of the final dénouement, which even in Shakespeare have attracted some ribald
comment, are here quite ridiculously perfunctory. The nearest
to real drama is the interview between the condemned Claudio
and his sister Isabella. Though Claudio's lines are a travesty
of Shakespeare's 'Ah, but to die . . .', their expression (with
sombre ejaculations for trombone) is not without force, and
the agonies of brother and sister do at least interlock. The
greatest failure in the opera is, after the partial success with
Arindal in Die Feen, a curious one: Wagner's character-di-
vided-against-himself, Friedrich/Angelo, is a wholly cardboard
figure. Again, a main theme of the opera is one that will later
assume overwhelming proportions: the opposing forces of natural instinct and arbitrary decision.

Rienzi is much more single-mindedly dramatic than its two
predecessors. Indeed, it is, as Wagner himself admitted, more
traditionally theatrical than any other of his works. This is
because, in taking over Bulwer Lytton's plot without much
alteration, Wagner came nearer than at any other point in his
career to accepting a librettist other than himself. The opening
scene of the thwarted abduction of the heroine and the resulting
confrontation between patricians and plebeians might well form
a part of an opera by Verdi and is composed with something
of Verdi's urgency and verve—qualities that do not in this
precise form reappear in Wagner's works. Yet one feels
throughout that the drama is factitious not organic, that the
situations are contrived to spark off a particular and momentary
dramatic effect and do not constitute an inevitable progress.
For instance, Rienzi's absolute refusal to pardon the treacherous nobles in Act II, followed by his sudden relenting in
answer to the prayers of his sister and of her lover, are too
obviously theatrical taps for turning on, first, an Anxiety Trio
and, then, a Grand Reconciliation Finale. The lover Adriano's
vacillations in Acts IV and V are not much better motivated.
Such opportunistic dramaturgy would be scorned by Verdi's
predecessors, let alone Verdi. One has to go back to Handelian
opera to find an action so frankly manipulated to provide the
pretexts for a series of contrasted musical numbers.

Der fliegende Holländer is the first opera of Wagner's maturity,
and this is signalled by the choice, for the first time, of a true
myth or folktale as subject. On this occasion the myth is almost
too simple. As Carl Dahlhaus points out in an admirable analysis of the nature and quality of Wagner's dramatic actions,
the opera is little more than the ballad dramatized; Senta and
the Dutchman are the only characters of any importance; Erik
is necessary merely to provide a precipitation of the catastrophe, and his patently mechanical employment robs the part of
any feeling or interest. Then, too, because of the narrowness
of the subject and the expansiveness of the verse, the work is
wordy. Compare the Dutchman's first soliloquy with, say,
Wotan's narration in Act II of Die Walküre. Wotan has been
called prolix, but he has much to say and says it succinctly.
The Dutchman is verbose. In Tannhäuser two myths are combined and set up a series of reverberations the one with the
other; but the fusion is not exact and again too much is said
about too little. The plotting, moreover, has something of the
artificiality and staginess of Rienzi. . . . Altogether, the opera
is something of a throwback after Holländer, which appears a
more characteristically Wagnerian work. In Lohengrin, all the
lines do lead to the centre, and the verse shows a greater
tautness, though Stabreim only makes its appearance with the
Ring. Though dramatically there is little in Lohengrin that is
not better done again later, it is the first of Wagner's operas

to combine the seriousness and intensity of *Holländer* with a complex action moving determinedly and coherently to a logical conclusion. (pp. 123-26)

Richard David, "Wagner the Dramatist," in The Wagner Companion, *edited by Peter Burbidge and Richard Sutton, Faber and Faber, 1979, pp. 115-39.*

HUGH RIDLEY   (essay date 1980)

[*Ridley elucidates the influence of the German philosopher Ludwig Andreas von Feuerbach on Wagner. For commentary on the influence of the philosopher Arthur Schopenhauer, see excerpts by Ernest Newman (1898), Pierre Lasserre (1917), and Jack M. Stein (1947).*]

It is now no secret that Wagner was strongly influenced by Feuerbach. . . . [The] *Ring* itself—begun in the spirit of 1848, condemning money, traditional authority and 'Heuchelnder Sitte/ hartes Gesetz' and extolling the societal power of Feuerbachian 'Liebe' [love]—stands as a memorial to Feuerbach's dominance over Wagner's mind. The strange chemistry which merged the myths of Friedrich Barbarossa, the *Nibelungenlied,* Herakles, Prometheus and Siegfried was unthinkable without the essentially progressive humanism of Feuerbach. It is well known that the ideas of the *Ring* were revised. Partly because of the defeat of the 1848 revolution, partly by Wagner's conversion to Schopenhauer's philosophy, the optimism of the early drafts was set aside. The final *Ring* is more about Wotan, resigned to his decline, than about the hero Siegfried. Yet behind the changing ideas the concept of myth remained the same, and here—no less than in the openly philosophical sympathies of the work—Feuerbach's influence was dominant.

Feuerbach's *Das Wesen des Christentums* . . . had made two significant contributions to Wagner's thought. One was a positive evaluation of human sensuality which reinforced the Young German ideas on the emancipation of the flesh which Wagner had already adopted. *Das Liebesverbot* . . . had worked this theme in its Young German form, *Tannhäuser* continued it and *Jesus von Nazareth* was to have been its fullest Feuerbachian expression. Human life was given a centrality and physical significance by Feuerbach which bridged the uneasy gap between spirituality and sensuality into which so many Young Germans uncomfortably fell. Wagner saw his debt to Feuerbach in the early 1840s as part of a conversion to sensual materialism. . . . The other influence of Feuerbach Wagner nowhere acknowledged as such although it was still more central to the structure of his thinking. It was from Feuerbach that Wagner derived his understanding of myth. His accounts of myth in his own operas unmistakably share the approach which Feuerbach adopted, paradoxically in that demythologizing of the gospels which is contained in *Das Wesen des Christentums.*

Feuerbach in fact seldom used the word myth in a positive sense. He analysed the narratives which form the basis of Christian doctrine and revealed their anthropological truth. He regarded the doctrines of the divinity of Christ, the narrative of his incarnation, not as materially accurate but as statements of a fundamental human truth: that the supreme human value is love and that man is his own divinity. . . . Feuerbach demythologized, treating myth critically and historically and replacing it by a statement of general human principles. This method implied a view of myth which was anything but negative. *Das Wesen des Christentums* began with a criticism of the failure of previous philosophers to deal adequately with religion, since they could not cope with the images ('Bilder')

of religion. He argued that this failure had caused philosophy (he was thinking of the Hegelians) to lose sight of the positive human content of religion, and to replace it instead with inhuman abstraction. The image distinguished religion from philosophy and needed to be preserved, not as a materialistic account of history but for the sake of the human truth which it contained. . . . There followed a passage lamenting the demise of an active, mythopoeic Christianity and its replacement by 'dem feigen, charakterlosen, komfortabeln, belletristischen, koketten, epikureischen Christentum der modernen Welt'. Only the former image-obsessed Christianity could—Feuerbach argued—be seen 'als ein *denk wurdiges* Objekt'. We need to see in this less a nostalgia for the past (although it has, as such, many echoes in Wagner's writings on Christianity) than an insistence on authentically human—that is, sensual and material—experience and communication. Without diminishing Feuerbach's political influence on Wagner, or blunting the edge of his materialism, it remains clear that two non-materialist features of Feuerbach's thought coloured Wagner's view of myth: concern for the image, and a structure of analysis of myths . . . which discovers and cherishes the human truth at their base.

Wagner's understanding of Greek myth makes this dependence clear. Behind the world of Olympus Wagner saw a purely human aspiration for cognition and self-expression. Myths were the form in which men first reached self-consciousness and pointed therefore—by their very function—to man. . . . [Wagner mirrored] exactly the structure of Feuerbach's demythologizing. Under Feuerbach's influence Wagner turned to myth in 1848, in his anxiety to participate in the revolution as an artist. He claimed that art could be relevant to the age only through myth, . . . and while, with hindsight, [his] remarks marked the beginnng of Wagner's detachment from history, they were undoubtedly an attempt to unify the worlds of art and politics. Wagner claimed that the Nibelung myth, like 1848, showed the transference of power from gods to men and that . . . the emancipation of man from the gods was being furthered. . . . Not only the themes of the early *Ring*—the anarchist attacks on property, or the praise of love—but the whole concept of myth and its relationship to the historical emancipation of mankind came from Feuerbach.

This idea had its roots in Wagner's previous works. When Wagner first came across the Nibelung theme while working on *Tannhäuser* he made it clear that the story of the Ghibellines fascinated him less for its historical detail than for its expression of truths about mankind. . . . When he described the origin of *Lohengrin* in a series of interdependent Greek and Christian myths, Wagner again showed that his approach to myth was conditioned by what can only be called emancipatory humanism, an interest in disengaging the essentially and progressively human from myth. (pp. 75-7)

Wagner's emancipatory understanding of myth was unmistakable. He saw tragedy as a festival of self-recollection, reminding the spectators of their essential humanity. . . . The sensuality of Feuerbach is clear, and the centrality of image, 'Bild', in the mediation between experience and consciousness also emerges from Wagner's prose-writings of this period. It was logical that Wagner should give to the artwork of the future the function of an instrument of knowledge, providing man with myth-images which contain emancipatory knowledge. . . . (p. 77)

Hugh Ridley, "Myth As Illusion or Cognition: Feuerbach, Wagner and Nietzsche," in German Life &

Letters, *n.s. Vol. XXXIV, No. 1, October, 1980, pp. 74-80.**

MARTIN VAN AMERONGEN (essay date 1983)

[*In the following excerpt from* Wagner: A Case History, *a collection of highly satirical essays on Wagner's life and work, Van Amerongen humorously describes Wagner's egocentrism and penchant for excess. This collection was originally published in Dutch as* De buiksprecker van God *in 1983.*]

Apart from being a giant, Wagner was also a gigantomane, whose life and works moved between grandiose gestures and major thirds. . . . *Rienzi*, the first of Wagner's operas which is worth taking seriously, was of such proportions that he toyed with the idea of spreading the work over two evenings, the first two acts to be given under the title *Rienzi's Grösse* ('Rienzi's Greatness') and the last three acts under the title *Rienzi's Fall* ('Rienzi's Downfall'). The plan was frustrated by audiences who refused to pay twice to see the same opera.

For Wagner, the word 'conversation' meant a monologue on his part, which sometimes lasted from six to eight hours. If ever he caught his guests engaged in a normal, friendly and open conversation and he himself, as their host, happened not to be the cynosure of all eyes, he would open his mouth and let out an inarticulate scream, and in that way ensure himself of everybody's undivided attention. (p. 23)

He produced volume upon volume of cultural theorizing, which provided an answer to *all* the questions which tormented long-suffering mankind. In his guise as philosopher, he was a typical exponent of the nineteenth-century desire for a complete, self-contained view of the world, in which everything had its proper place and function. His writings form a half-baked mishmash of one particular brand of socialism and conservatism, Hellenism and Teutonism, anti-Semitism and vegetarianism, Proudhon, Hegel, Feuerbach, Gobineau and Schopenhauer. Above all, Schopenhauer, the professional pessimist who, in the second half of the nineteenth century, provided comfort for so many of those who, in the first half of the century, had shouted out revolutionary slogans, only subsequently to see the error of their ways and to recant.

As we have since discovered, Wagner himself was not the writer and thinker for whom the world sat waiting. But it is not *all* rubbish that he committed to paper in the course of his life. His early short stories such as *Ein Ende in Paris* ('An End in Paris') and *Eine Pilgerfahrt zu Beethoven* ('A Pilgrimage to Beethoven') have an unmistakably literary quality about them. A work such as *Über das Dirigiren* ('On Conducting') still contains a good deal of sound advice about the most vain of all professions. That a book such as *Oper und Drama* ('Opera and Drama') was disfigured by his customary whining about the Jews is much to be regretted since here, too, the writer has many a true word to say about the musico-dramatic art-form which, to Wagner's dissatisfaction, had become the favourite pastime of the happy few who made only a single demand of what was being offered them: 'Tunes which fall pleasingly on the ear, nothing more'.

His later theoretical writings, on the other hand, *Die Religion und die Kunst* ('Religion and Art'), *Erkenne dich selbst* ('Know Yourself') and *Heldenthum und Christenthum* ('Heroism and Christianity'), cannot be taken seriously, even with the best will in the world. Friedrich Nietzsche was considerate enough to lay aside his pen when madness overtook him, whereas the

ageing Wagner poured out his spleen more uncontrollably than ever against cock-fighting and 'American imperialism', against the blacks who were descended from apes and against meat-eating which poisoned the blood. He knew for certain that the Aryan alone was in a position to subdue the will in the spirit of Schopenhauer. And the very suggestion that Christ was a Jew was 'one of the most terrible mistakes in the whole history of the world'.

The libretti of his operas (all of which he wrote himself) are not *bad*, if set beside such musico-dramatic rattletraps as *Die Zauberflöte*, *Norma* and *La muette de Portici*. Measured against his own inordinate claims—Wagner knew for certain that he was just as great a poet as he was a composer—they are a botched job in terms of both poetic substance and dramatic eloquence.

Since the German of Goethe, Heine and Schiller was not good enough for him, he used a language of his own invention, full of words whch you will not find in any dictionary. His grandson Wieland Wagner attempted, at one of his rehearsals, to translate this remarkable language into a German which would be more or less compehensible not only to the non-German singers but to the native German-speakers as well. For some time now the bookshops in Bayreuth have had on their shelves a small dictionary intended to offer some help in decoding Wagner's texts. (pp. 24-6)

The most important feature of Wagner's texts (and after at least a century of endlessly repeated arguments, there is unfortunately no way in which I can avoid mentioning it) is the accursed *Stabreim*, or alliterative verse, which lies like mould over the surface of the libretti. Entire generations of parodists have sharpened their claws on it:

> FIRST WAGNERIAN: What a wondrous work! What weal and woe when one witnesses what welfare was in the world when Wotan wiped out all those whose witty words have called into question the worth and workings of our worshipful wishes.
>
> SECOND WAGNERIAN: Good God! Gladly grant I all grim-faced gall-spitters, glib-tongued gawkers and grey-haired gaffers their graceless grumbling and glossless gospel.
>
> THIRD WAGNERIAN: Just let them lampoon him, the loathsome liars!
>
> FOURTH WAGNERIAN: May the mouth of the mighty Master, manful and mild, muzzle these mumbling misanthropes.
>
> FIFTH WAGNERIAN: But above all else the broad belly bulging with bread and brimful of bratwurst.

Admittedly, the modest use of stylistic elements such as alliteration and internal rhyme can in principle enhance the tonal beauty of poetry and prose. But not even here can Wagner resist the temptation to exaggerate: 'Hehe! Irh Nicker! Wie seid ihr niedlich, neidliches Volk! Aus Nibelheims Nacht naht' ich mich gern, neigtet ihr euch zu mir' ('He he! ye nixies! how ye delight me, daintiest folk! from Nibelheim's night fain would I come, would ye turn but to me!') . . . It is an aesthetic *evil* and one of the reasons why many opera-goers breathe a sigh of relief when everything finally goes quiet on stage and the orchestra can get on with depicting the Entry of the Gods into Valhalla. (pp. 27-8)

Martin Van Amerongen, in his Wagner: A Case History, *translated by Stewart Spencer and Dominic Cakebread, 1983. Reprint by George Braziller, 1984, 169 p.*

ADDITIONAL BIBLIOGRAPHY

Albright, H. Darkes. "Musical Drama As a Union of All the Arts." In *Studies in Speech and Drama, in Honor of Alexander M. Drummond,* edited by Donald C. Bryant et al., pp. 13-30. Ithaca, N.Y.: Cornell University Press, 1944.*
    Sketches the history of the music drama and explains Wagner's philosophy of synthesis of the arts. Albright comments particularly on the difficulties inherent in such a union.

Beckett, Lucy. *Richard Wagner: "Parsifal."* Cambridge Opera Handbooks. Cambridge: Cambridge University Press, 1981, 163 p.
    Describes the genesis and first performance of *Parsifal* and traces its subsequent stage history.

Brink, Louise. *Women Characters in Richard Wagner: A Study in "The Ring of the Nibelung."* Nervous and Mental Disease Monograph Series, no. 37. New York: Nervous and Mental Disease Publishing Co., 1924, 125 p.
    A Freudian interpretation of the female characters in *The Nibelung's Ring.*

Buesst, Aylmer. *Richard Wagner: "The Nibelung's Ring."* London: G. Bell and Sons, 1932, 217 p.
    An act-by-act guide to the plot and leitmotives of *The Nibelung's Ring.*

Burbidge, Peter, and Sutton, Richard, eds. *The Wagner Companion.* London: Faber and Faber, 1979, 462 p.
    A collection of twentieth-century essays on the cultural, social, and political factors that influenced Wagner's artistic development.

Culshaw, John. *Reflections on the "Ring."* New York: Viking Press, 1975, 105 p.
    An appreciative introduction to *The Nibelung's Ring.*

Dahlhaus, Carl. *Richard Wagner's Music Dramas.* Translated by Mary Whittall. Cambridge: Cambridge University Press, 1979, 161 p.
    A succinct literary introduction to Wagner's operas.

Deathridge, John, and Dahlhaus, Carl. *Wagner.* The New Grove Dictionary of Music and Musicians, edited by Stanley Sadie. London: Macmillan, 1984, 226 p.
    An introduction to Wagner's life and work that includes an extensive chronological listing of the composer's musical and literary productions and a selected bibliography of critical and biographical writings.

DiGaetani, John Louis. *Richard Wagner and the Modern British Novel.* Rutherford, N.J.: Fairleigh Dickinson University Press; London: Associated University Presses, 1978, 179 p.*
    A study of Wagner's influence on the lives and art of Joseph Conrad, D. H. Lawrence, E. M. Forster, Virginia Woolf, and James Joyce.

——, ed. *Penetrating Wagner's "Ring": An Anthology.* Rutherford, N.J.: Fairleigh Dickinson University Press; London: Associated University Presses, 1978, 453 p.
    An anthology of modern essays in which major Wagner critics discuss the theory, artistic background, historical influences, literary sources, musical structure, and performance techniques of *The Nibelung's Ring.*

Donington, Robert. *Wagner's "Ring" and Its Symbols: The Music and the Myth.* New York: St. Martin's Press, 1963, 324 p.
    A Jungian analysis of the symbolism in the poetry, mythology, characters, and music of *The Nibelung's Ring.* This study includes an appendix of musical examples and a lengthy annotated bibliography.

Ewans, Michael. *Wagner and Aeschylus: The "Ring" and the "Orestia."* New York: Cambridge University Press, 1982, 271 p.
    Interprets *The Nibelung's Ring* in relation to the dramatic trilogy *Orestia* by Aeschylus. Ewans pays particular attention to the development and transformation of recurrent themes and motives.

Furness, Raymond. *Wagner and Literature.* Manchester, England: Manchester University Press, 1982, 159 p.
    Discusses Wagner's works within the context of the Symbolist, Modernist, and Decadent movements. In addition, Furness treats Wagner's use of myth.

Gregor-Dellin, Martin. *Richard Wagner: His Life, His Work, His Century.* Translated by J. Maxwell Brownjohn. San Diego: Harcourt Brace Jovanovich, Publishers, 1983, 575 p.
    A biography in which the author focuses on Wagner's revolutionary, anarchistic attitudes and experiences. Gregor-Dellin contends that Wagner "never reconciled the problems of decadence and regeneration with Judaism and Christianity because he persistently confused religious, political and social factors."

Gutman, Robert W. *Richard Wagner: The Man, His Mind, and His Music.* New York: Harcourt, Brace & World, 1968, 490 p.
    An interpretation of Wagner's work in relation to his private life and to the cultural and political climate of late nineteenth-century Germany.

James, Burnett. *Wagner and the Romantic Disaster.* Composers—Life and Times Series, Special Anniversary Edition. New York: Hippocrene Books, 1983, 202 p.
    Evaluates Wagner's nature as a person and artist and his position in the realms of European music and philosophy.

Kestner, Joseph. "Richard Wagner's Paris Trilogy: 'A Pilgrimage to Beethoven,' 'A Happy Evening,' and 'An End in Paris'." *Studies in Short Fiction* 15, No. 3 (Summer 1978): 253-62.
    Interprets the short stories "A Pilgrimage to Beethoven," "A Happy Evening," and "An End in Paris" as a triptych in which Wagner expressed an early formulation of *Gesamtkunstwerk.*

Lehmann, A. G. "The Classification of the Arts: Wagner in France, 1885-95." In his *The Symbolist Aesthetic in France: 1885-1895,* pp. 194-206. Modern Language Studies, edited by J. Boyd and W. J. Entwistle. Oxford: Basil Blackwell, 1950.
    An examination of Wagner's reputation in France based on articles in the *Revue wagnérienne* by the periodical's co-founder, the French critic Théodor de Wyzéwa.

Magee, Bryan. *Aspects of Wagner.* London: Alan Ross, 1968, 112 p.
    Highlights Wagner's theory of drama and critical reaction to his operas. Magee also discusses Wagner's anti-Semitism.

Mander, Raymond, and Mitchenson, Joe. *The Wagner Companion.* London: W. H. Allen, 1977, 246 p.
    A compilation of details on the cast, production data, and background of the English premiere of each Wagner opera. The authors include a discussion of critical reaction to each premiere, synopses of the operas, and a glossary of characters.

McCreless, Patrick. *Wagner's "Siegfried": Its Drama, History, and Music.* Studies in Musicology, edited by George Buelow, no. 59. Ann Arbor, Mich.: UMI Research Press, 1982, 248 p.
    A comprehensive scholarly study of the dramatic and musical structure of *Siegfried.*

Newman, Ernest. *Wagner As Man and Artist.* New York: Alfred A. Knopf, 1924, 399 p.
    Traces Wagner's personal, musical, and dramatic development.

——. *The Life of Richard Wagner.* 4 vols. New York: Alfred A. Knopf, 1933-46.
    The definitive biography to date.

————. *The Wagner Operas.* New York: Alfred A. Knopf, 1963, 724 p.

> An introduction to the major Wagner operas. Newman describes the works' sources and geneses, summarizes their plots, and indicates their primary musical motives.

Nietzsche, Friedrich. "Selected Aphorisms." In his *The Complete Works of Friedrich Nietzsche, Vol. 8: The Case of Wagner,* edited by Oscar Levy, translated by Anthony M. Ludovici and J. M. Kennedy, pp. 83-102. New York: Macmillan Co., 1924.

> A collection of aphorisms written during the summer of 1878. Among other subjects, Nietzsche mentions Wagner's teutonism, the effects of his art, and the contradictions in his idea of opera.

Rather, L. J. *Of Self-destruction: Wagner's "Ring" and the Modern World.* Baton Rouge: Louisiana State University Press, 1979, 215 p.

> Examines *The Nibelung's Ring* as a political, social, and psychological resolution of the Oedipal conflict. Rather assesses the relevance of this work to the course of European history.

Sessa, Anne Dzamba. *Richard Wagner and the English.* Rutherford, N.J.: Fairleigh Dickinson University Press; London: Associated University Presses, 1979, 191 p.*

> A scholarly study of English Wagnerism as represented by its nineteenth-century adherents Algernon Charles Swinburne, William Morris, Aubrey Beardsley, and D. H. Lawrence.

Skelton, Geoffrey. *Wagner at Bayreuth: Experiment and Tradition.* New York: George Braziller, 1965, 239 p.

> A comprehensive chronicle of the productions, problems, and personalities at Bayreuth from 1872 to 1965.

Spitzer, Leo. "Three Poems on Ecstasy: John Donne, St. John of the Cross, Richard Wagner." In his *Essays on English and American Literature,* edited by Anna Hatcher, pp. 139-79. Princeton: Princeton University Press, 1969.*

> A close explication of *Tristan and Isolde* as a poetic picture of ecstasy.

Stein, Jack Madison. *Richard Wagner & the Synthesis of the Arts.* Detroit: Wayne State University Press, 1960, 229 p.

> A detailed study of Wagner's theory of *Gesamtkunstwerk.*

Terry, Edward M. *A Richard Wagner Dictionary.* New York: H. W. Wilson Co., 1939, 186 p.

> A dictionary of names, places, and background sources relevant to Wagner's life and art. Terry also provides synopses of all the Wagner operas and lists of their characters.

Viereck, Peter. "Siegfried: The Metapolitics of Richard Wagner." In his *Metapolitics: From the Romantics to Hitler,* pp. 90-125. New York: Alfred A. Knopf, 1941.

> A historical and biographical study of Wagner's political ideas. Viereck contends that Wagner's "warped genius was the most important single fountainhead" of Nazi ideology.

Weiner, Marc A. "Zwieback and Madeleine: Creative Recall in Wagner and Proust." *Modern Language Notes* 95, No. 3 (April 1980): 679-84.*

> Compares the use of creative recall in *Tristan and Isolde* and Marcel Proust's novel *Remembrance of Things Past.*

Winkler, Franz E. *For Freedom Destined: Mysteries of Man's Evolution in Wagner's "Ring" Operas and "Parsifal."* Garden City, N.Y.: Waldorf Press, 1974, 174 p.

> An introduction to Wagner's use of myth.

Appendix

The following is a listing of all sources used in Volume 9 of *Nineteenth-Century Literature Criticism*. Included in this list are all copyright and reprint rights and acknowledgments for those essays for which permission was obtained. Every effort has been made to trace copyright, but if omissions have been made, please let us know.

THE EXCERPTS IN NCLC, VOLUME 9, WERE REPRINTED FROM THE FOLLOWING PERIODICALS:

The Academy, v. IV, July 1, 1873; v. XII, July 7, 1877; v. LIX, July 28, 1900; v. LXI, December 14, 1901; v. LXI, December 21, 1901; v. LXIX, December 23, 1905.

The Academy and Literature, v. LXIV, May 30, 1903.

The American Benedictine Review, v. XI, September & December, 1960. Copyright 1960 by The American Benedictine Academy. Reprinted by permission.

The American Monthly Magazine, v. VIII, October, 1836.

The American Review, v. 7, April, 1936.

Architectural Design & Construction, v. II, May, 1932.

The Armchair Detective, v. 9, June, 1976. Copyright © 1976 by *The Armchair Detective*. Reprinted by permission.

The Athenaeum, n. 1328, April 9, 1853; n. 1350, September 10, 1853; n. 1501, August 2, 1856; n. 2426, April 25, 1874; n. 2883, January 27, 1883; n. 3059, June 12, 1886; n. 3291, November 22, 1890; n. 3309, March 28, 1891; n. 3322, June 27, 1891; n. 3556, December 21, 1895./ n. 3453, December 30, 1893; n. 4732, January 7, 1921. Both reprinted by permission.

The Atlantic Monthly, v. LII, July, 1883; v. LXV, January, 1890.

Bentley's Miscellany, v. XLI, 1857.

Blackwood's Edinburgh Magazine, v. II, October, 1817; v. VI, October, 1819; v. VII, June, 1820; v. XXXVIII, August, 1835; v. LVI, September, 1844; v. LVII, January, 1845.

The Bookman, London, v. IX, March, 1896; v. LI, October, 1916.

The Bookman, New York, v. XVIII, January, 1904.

The Boston Quarterly Review, v. III, January, 1840.

The British and Foreign Review, v. XIII, 1842.

The British Critic, v. XIV, October, 1799.

The British Quarterly Review, v. XXXIII, January 1, 1861.

Catholic World, v. XXV, August, 1877.

Comparative Literature, v. XVI, Spring, 1964. © copyright 1964 by University of Oregon. Reprinted by permission of *Comparative Literature.*

The Cornhill Magazine, v. VII, January, 1863.

Cosmopolis, v. 1, February, 1896.

The Critical Review, v. XXIV, October, 1798; n.s. v. III, May, 1816.

The Dial, v. II, July, 1841; v. III, July, 1842; v. III, April, 1843; v. IV, July, 1883; v. X, November, 1889.

Dublin Review, v. XIV, May, 1843.

The Dublin University Magazine, v. LXXXI, March, 1873.

The Eclectic Review, n.s. v. V, June, 1816; v. XXXI, April, 1820; n.s. v. XXVII, June, 1827; n.s. v. IX, May, 1855.

The Edinburgh Review, v. XXVII, September, 1816; v. XXVII, December, 1816; v. LXXIV, October, 1841; v. LXXVII, February, 1843; v. CVII, January, 1858; v. CLXXXIX, January, 1899.

English Journal, nos. 20 and 22, May 15 and May 29, 1841,

The Examiner, n. 1820, December 17, 1842.

The Fortnightly Review, n.s. v. XLVI, July 1, 1889; n.s. v. LVIII, September, 1895; v. LVIII, January, 1896; n.s. v. LXIII, June 1, 1898.

Fraser's Magazine, v. XLIII, March, 1851; v. LII, July, 1855; n.s. v. XIX, April, 1879.

The French Review, v. VI, December, 1932.

German Life & Letters, n.s. v. XXXIV, October, 1980. Reprinted by permission.

The Germanic Review, v. 22, April, 1947.

Harper's Monthly Magazine, v. CXXVIII, May, 1914. Copyright © 1914, renewed 1941, by *Harper's Magazine.* Reprinted by special permission.

Harper's New Monthly Magazine, v. LXVI, March, 1883.

The International Quarterly, v. IX, June-September, 1904.

The International Review, v. X, June, 1881.

Irish Fireside, n.s. v. I, February 26, 1887.

The Literary Chronicle and Weekly Review, v. III, October 6, 1821.

The Literary World, v. VIII, February 22 and March 1, 1851; v. XIV, June 30, 1883.

Littell's Living Age, v. LXVII, December 22, 1860.

Macmillan's Magazine, v. LIII, January, 1886./ v. LXIV, May, 1891. Reprinted by permission of Macmillan, London and Basingstoke.

Merry England, v. XXI, September, 1893 for "A Poet's Religion" by Francis Thompson. Reprinted by permission of Wilfrid Meynell.

The Methodist Review, n.s. v. XVII, January-February, 1901.

The Monthly Magazine, London, v. XLIX, March 1, 1820; v. LII, November 1, 1821.

The Monthly Review, London, n.s. v. XXIX, June, 1799; v. II, January-March, 1901.

Mosaic: Special Issue on Classics and World Literature, v. I, July, 1968. © *Mosaic* 1968. Acknowledgment of previous publication is herewith made.

Musical America, v. LXXXI, November, 1961. All rights reserved. Excerpted by permission of *High Fidelity.*

The Nation, v. XVII, October 30, 1873; v. XXIV, May 24, 1877; v. XXXII, February 24, 1881; v. XLIX, August 8, 1889.

The New Adelphi, v. I, March, 1928.

The New England Quarterly, v. XL, June, 1967 for "Nature As Concept and Technique in the Poetry of Jones Very" by Anthony Herbold. Copyright 1967 by *The New England Quarterly.* Reprinted by permission of the publisher and the Literary Estate of Anthony Herbold./ v. XLIII, June, 1970 for "Correspondence in Very's Nature Poetry" by Carl Dennis. Copyright 1970 by *The New England Quarterly.* Reprinted by permission of the publisher and the author.

The New Monthly Magazine, v. XIII, March, 1820; v. XLIV, August, 1835.

The New Review, n.s. v. XIV, March, 1896; v. XVI, January, 1897.

New Statesman, v. LXVII, June 19, 1964. © 1964 The Statesman & Nation Publishing Co. Ltd. Reprinted by permission.

The New Statesman & Nation, v. XXII, November 15, 1941.

New York Herald Tribune, September 19, 1956 for "Dumas' 'Camille' Revived at Cherry Lane Theater" by Walter Kerr. © 1956 I.H.T. Corporation. Reprinted by permission of the author.

New York Tribune, March 25, 1876.

The Nineteenth Century, v. XXX, August, 1891.

Nonconformist, v. XXXIV, February 19, 1873.

The North American Review, v. XXXIX, October, 1834; v. CIX, October, 1869; v. CXVI, April, 1873; v. 218, December, 1923.

Overland Monthly, n.s. v. I, April, 1883.

Oxford Outlook, v. II, May, 1920.

PMLA, v. LXIV, June, 1949.

Poet Lore, v. VI, 1894.

Punch, v. LXXXII, May 27, 1882.

The Quarterly Review, v. XXIII, May, 1820; v. LII, August, 1834; v. LXXI, December, 1842; v. CI, April, 1857./ v. CCVIII, April, 1908 for "Coventry Patmore" by Percy Lubbock. Reprinted by permission of the Literary Estate of Percy Lubbock.

The Romanic Review, v. XXXII, December, 1941; v. XL, December, 1949.

The Saturday Review, London, v. 80, November 30, 1895.

Scrutiny, v. IV, June, 1935; v. VIII, March, 1940; v. IX, June, 1940; v. IX, March, 1941.

The Sewanee Review, v. XXXIV, Summer, 1926.

The Southern Literary Messenger, v. XXVIII, June, 1859.

The Spectator, v. 35, December 20, 1862; v. 50, April 28, 1877; v. 59, July 10, 1886; v. 64, April 12, 1890; v. 71, July 22, 1893./ v. 146, February 21, 1931. © 1931 by *The Spectator*. Reprinted by permission of *The Spectator*.

Studies in Romanticism, v. 10, Winter, 1971; v. 14, Summer, 1975. Copyright 1971, 1975 by the Trustees of Boston University. Both reprinted by permission.

The Sunday Times, London, January 23, 1921.

Tait's Edinburgh Magazine, v. 18, January, 1851.

Temple Bar, v. L, August, 1877.

The Times Literary Supplement, n. 991, January 13, 1921; n. 1179, August 21, 1924; n. 2727, May 7, 1954; n. 2826, April 27, 1956.

Victorian Poetry, v. VII, Autumn, 1969. Reprinted by permission.

The Western Messenger, v. VI, March, 1839.

The Westminster Review, v. CXLVIII, November, 1897.

THE EXCERPTS IN NCLC, VOLUME 9, WERE REPRINTED FROM THE FOLLOWING BOOKS:

Abbott, Claude Colleer. From an introduction to *Further Letters of Gerard Manley Hopkins, Including His Correspondence with Coventry Patmore*. Edited by Claude Colleer Abbott. Oxford University Press, London, 1938.

Abrams, Meyer Howard. From *The Mirror and the Lamp: Romantic Theory and the Critical Tradition*. Oxford University Press, 1953. Copyright © 1953 by Oxford University Press, Inc. Renewed 1981 by Meyer Howard Abrams. Reprinted by permission of Oxford University Press, Inc.

Adorno, Theodor. From *In Search of Wagner*. Translated by Rodney Livingstone. Verso/NLB, 1981. © NLB, 1981. Reprinted by permission.

Andrews, William P. From ''Jones Very,'' in *Lowell, Whittier, Very and the Alcotts among Their Contemporaries*. Edited by Kenneth Walter Cameron. Transcendental Books, 1978.

Armstrong, Martin. From *George Borrow*. Arthur Barker Ltd., 1950.

Arvin, Neil C. From *Alexandre Dumas Fils*. Presses Universitaires de France, 1939.

Babbitt, Irving. From *The Masters of Modern French Criticism*. Houghton Mifflin, 1912. Copyright © 1912 by Irving Babbitt. Renewal copyright © 1940 by Edward S. Babbitt and Edward S. Babbitt, Jr. All rights reserved. Reprinted by permission of Edward S. Babbitt.

Badawi, M. M. From *Coleridge: Critic of Shakespeare*. Cambridge at the University Press, 1973. © Cambridge University Press 1973. Reprinted by permission.

Barclay, Glen St. John. From *Anatomy of Horror: The Masters of Occult Fiction*. Weidenfeld and Nicolson, 1978, St. Martin's Press, 1979. Copyright © 1978 by Glen St. J. Barclay. Reprinted by permission of St. Martin's Press, Inc. In Canada by Weidenfeld (Publishers) Limited.

Bartlett, William Irving. From *Jones Very: Emerson's ''Brave Saint.''* Duke University Press, 1942. Copyright © 1942 by Duke University Press. Reprinted by permission.

Baudelaire, Charles. From *Baudelaire As a Literary Critic*. Edited and translated by Lois Boe Hyslop and Francis E. Hyslop, Jr. Pennsylvania State University Press, University Park, 1964. Copyright © 1964 by The Pennsylvania State University. All rights reserved. Reprinted by permission.

Baudelaire, Charles. From an extract from the conclusion to *Théodore de Banville*. By Alvin Harms. Twayne, 1983. Copyright 1983 by Twayne Publishers. All rights reserved. Reprinted with the permission of Twayne Publishers, a division of G. K. Hall & Co., Boston.

Beer, J. B. From *Coleridge the Visionary*. Chatto & Windus, 1959. © J. B. Beer 1959. Reprinted by permission of the author and Chatto & Windus.

Begnal, Michael H. From *Joseph Sheridan Le Fanu*. Bucknell University Press, 1971. © 1971 by Associated University Presses, Inc. Reprinted by permission.

Benson, A. C. From *Edward FitzGerald*. Macmillan & Co., Limited, 1905.

Bentley, Eric. From *The Cult of the Superman: A Study of Heroism in Carlyle and Nietzsche, with Notes on Other Hero-Worshippers of Modern Times*. Peter Smith, 1969. Copyright 1944, 1957 by Eric Bentley. Reprinted by permission of the author.

Bentley, Eric. From *The Playwright As Thinker: A Study of Drama in Modern Times*. Harcourt Brace Jovanovich, 1967. Copyright © 1946, 1974 by Eric Bentley. Reprinted by permission of Harcourt Brace Jovanovich, Inc.

Bewley, Marius. From ''Coleridge: The Poetry of Coleridge,'' in *The Importance of Scrutiny: Selections from ''Scrutiny, a Quarterly Review,'' 1932-1948*. Edited by Eric Bentley. New York University Press, 1964. Copyright, 1948, by George W. Stewart, Publishers, Inc. Reprinted by permission of Marius Bewley.

Bleiler, E. F. From an introduction to *Best Ghost Stories of J. S. LeFanu*. By J. S. LeFanu, edited by E. F. Bleiler. Dover, 1964. Copyright © 1964 by Dover Publications, Inc. All rights reserved. Reprinted by permission.

Blunden, Edmund. From a preface to *Madrigals & Chronicles: Being Newly Found Poems*. By John Clare, edited by Edmund Blunden. The Beaumont Press, 1924.

Blunden, Edmund. From *Nature in English Literature*. L. & Virginia Woolf, 1929. Reprinted by permission of A. D. Peters & Co., Ltd.

Bodkin, Maud. From *Archetypal Patterns in Poetry: Psychological Studies of Imagination.* Oxford University Press, London, 1934.

Borrow, George. From a preface to *Lavengro: The Scholar—The Gypsy—The Priest.* Harper & Brothers, 1851.

Borrow, George. From *The Romany Rye.* Harper & Brothers, 1857.

Borrow, George. From a preface to *The Zincali; or, An Account of the Gypsies of Spain, Vol. I.* J. Murray, 1841.

Bowen, Elizabeth. From an introduction to *Uncle Silas: A Tale of Bartram-Haugh.* By J. S. Le Fanu. The Cresset Press, 1947.

Bowra, C. M. From *In General and Particular.* Weidenfeld and Nicolson, 1964. © 1964 by C. M. Bowra. Reprinted by permission.

Bowra, C. M. From *The Romantic Imagination.* Cambridge, Mass.: Harvard University Press, 1949. Copyright © 1949 by the President and Fellows of Harvard College. Renewed 1977 by Cecil Maurice Bowra. Excerpted by permission.

Bradford, Gamaliel. From *Biography and the Human Heart.* Houghton Mifflin, 1932. Copyright 1932 by Helen H. Bradford. Copyright © renewed 1960 by Sarah Bradford Ross. Reprinted by permission of Houghton Mifflin Company.

Brandes, Georg. From *Naturalism in Nineteenth Century English Literature.* N.p., 1901-05. Russell & Russell, 1957. Reprinted by permission of Russell & Russell, New York.

Brimley, George. From *Essays.* Rudd & Carleton, 1858.

Browne, Nelson. From *Sheridan Le Fanu.* Roy Publishers, 1951.

Bulwer-Lytton, Edward. From a letter to Coventry Patmore on July 27, 1844, in *Memoirs and Correspondence of Coventry Patmore, Vol. I.* By Basil Champneys. George Bell and Sons, 1900.

Byron, Lord. From *English Bards and Scotch Reviewers.* James Cawthorn, 1809.

Campbell, A. Y. From ''Edward Fitzgerald,'' in *The Great Victorians.* Edited by H. J. Massingham and Hugh Massingham. Double, Doran & Co., Inc., 1932.

Carlyle, Thomas. From a letter to Coventry Patmore on July 31, 1856, in *Memoirs and Correspondence of Coventry Patmore, Vol. II.* By Coventry Patmore and Basil Champneys. Edited by Basil Champneys. George Bell and Sons, 1900.

Chamberlain, Houston Stewart. From *The Wagnerian Drama: An Attempt to Inspire a Better Appreciation of Wagner As a Dramatic Poet.* John Lane/The Bodley Head, 1915.

Clare, John. From an extract in *Clare: The Critical Heritage.* Edited by Mark Storey. Routledge & Kegan Paul, 1973.

Clare, John. From a preface to *The Shepherd's Calendar.* N.p., 1827.

Clark, Roger J. B. From an introduction to *La dame aux camélias.* By Alexandre Dumas fils, edited by Roger J. B. Clark. Oxford University Press, London, 1972. © Oxford University Press 1972. Reprinted by permission of Oxford University Press.

Cole, Phyllis. From ''Jones Very's 'Epistles to the Unborn','' in *Studies in the American Renaissance: 1982.* Edited by Joel Myerson. Twayne, 1982. Copyright 1982 by Twayne Publishers. All rights reserved. Reprinted with the permission of Twayne Publishers, a division of G. K. Hall & Co., Boston.

Coleridge, Samuel Taylor. From *Biographia Literaria; or, Biographical Sketches of My Literary Life and Opinions.* Rest Fenner, 1817.

Coleridge, Samuel Taylor. From a conversation with Henry Nelson Coleridge on May 31, 1830, in *The Table Talk and Omniana of Samuel Taylor Coleridge.* Oxford University Press, 1917.

Collie, Michael. From *George Borrow: Eccentric.* Cambridge University Press, 1982. © Cambridge University Press 1982. Reprinted by permission.

David, Richard. From ''Wagner the Dramatist,'' in *The Wagner Companion.* Edited by Peter Burbidge and Richard Sutton. Faber and Faber, 1979. © this collection 1979 by Peter Burbidge and Richard Sutton. All rights reserved. Reprinted by permission of Faber and Faber Ltd.

Denommé, Robert T. From *The French Parnassian Poets.* Southern Illinois University Press, 1972. Copyright © 1972 by Southern Illinois University Press. All rights reserved. Reprinted by permission.

De Quincey, Thomas. From *The Collected Writings of Thomas De Quincey, Vol. III*. Edited by David Masson. A. & C. Black, 1897.

Doyle, Arthur Conan. From *Through the Magic Door*. Smith, Elder & Co., 1907.

Driver, Tom F. From *Romantic Quest and Modern Query: A History of the Modern Theatre*. Delacorte Press, 1970, University Press of America, 1980. Copyright © 1970 by Tom F. Driver. All rights reserved. Reprinted by permission of the author.

Dyson, A. E. and Julian Lovelock. From *Masterful Images: English Poetry from Metaphysicals to Romantics*. Barnes & Noble, 1976. © A. E. Dyson and Julian Lovelock 1976. All rights reserved. By permission of Barnes & Noble Books, a Division of Littlefield, Adams & Co., Inc.

Ellis, S. M. From *Wilkie Collins, Le Fanu and Others*. Constable & Co. Ltd., 1931.

Fairchild, Hoxie Neale. From *Religious Trends in English Poetry: Christianity and Romanticism in the Victorian Era, 1830-1880, Vol. IV*. Columbia University Press, 1957. © 1957, Columbia University Press. Reprinted by permission.

Feinstein, Elaine. From an introduction to *Selected Poems*. By John Clare. University Tutorial Press Ltd., 1968. Editorial matter © Elaine Feinstein, 1968. Reprinted by permission of Elaine Feinstein.

Fergusson, Francis. From *The Idea of a Theater: A Study of Ten Plays, the Art of Drama in Changing Perspective*. Princeton University Press, 1949. Copyright 1949, © renewed 1977 by Princeton University Press. All rights reserved. Excerpts reprinted with permission of Princeton University Press.

Fisher, Mary. From *A General Survey of American Literature*. A. C. McClurg and Company, 1899.

FitzGerald, Edward. From a preface to *Agamemnon: A Tragedy*. N.p., 1865.

FitzGerald, Edward. From an extract from a letter to E. B. Cowell on May 7, 1857, in *The Variorum and Definitive Edition of the Poetical and Prose Writings of Edward FitzGerald, Vol. 2*. Edited by George Bentham. Doubleday, Page and Company. 1902.

Ford, Richard. From four letters to George Borrow from June 7, 1842 to September 12, 1842, in *Life, Writings and Correspondence of George Borrow (1803-1881), Vol. I*. Edited by William I. Knapp. G. P. Putnam's Sons, 1899.

France, Anatole. From *On Life & Letters, first series*. Edited by Frederic Chapman, translated by A. W. Evans. John Lane Company, 1911.

France, Anatole. From *On Life and Letters, fourth series*. Edited by Frederic Chapman, translated by Bernard Miall. Dodd, Mead & Company, Inc., 1924.

Fuerst, Norbert. From *The Victorian Age of German Literature: Eight Essays*. The Pennsylvania State University Press, University Park, 1966. Reprinted by permission.

Gautier, Théophile. From *The Works of Théophile Gautier: A History of Romanticism, the Progress of French Poetry Since MDCCCXXX, Vol. 16*. Edited and translated by F. C. de Sumichrast. George D. Sproul, 1902.

Gerbaud, Colette. From ''Jones Very's Mystic Conception of Rebirth,'' in *Proceedings of a Symposium on American Literature*. Edited by Marta Sienicka. Uniwersytet im. Adama Mickiewicza w Poznaniu, 1979.

Goncourt, Edmond de and Jules de Goncourt. From a journal entry of March 16, 1867, in *Journal: Memoires de la vie litteraire*, 22 Vols. Librairie Ernest Flammarion, 1956-59.

Gosse, Edmund. From *Coventry Patmore*. Charles Scribner's Sons, 1905.

Gosse, Edmund. From *English Literature, an Illustrated Record: From the Age of Johnson to the Age of Tennyson, Vol. IV*. Revised edition. The Macmillan Company, 1923.

Gosse, Edmund. From ''The Novels of Alexandre Dumas the Younger,'' in *The Lady of the Camellias*. By Alexandre Dumas, fils, translated by Edmund Gosse. D. Appleton & Co., 1902.

Gosse, Sir Edmund. From *Silhouettes*. Charles Scribner's Sons, 1925, William Heinemann Ltd., 1925.

Gosse, Edmund. From an introduction to *The Variorum and Definitive Edition of the Poetical and Prose Writings of Edward Fitzgerald, Vol. I*. By Edward Fitzgerald, edited by George Bentham. Doubleday, Page and Company, 1902.

Gribble, Francis. From *Dumas: Father and Son*. Eveleigh Nash & Grayson Limited, 1930.

LeFanu, J. S. From "A Preliminary Note," in *Uncle Silas: A Tale of Bartram-Haugh*. N.p., 1864.

Lemaître, Jules. From *Literary Impressions*. Translated by A. W. Evans. Daniel O'Connor, 1921.

Lever, Charles. From a letter to Joseph Sheridan Le Fanu in 1864, in *Wilkie Collins, Le Fanu, and Others*. By S. M. Ellis. Constable & Co., Ltd., 1931.

Levi, Peter, S.J. From *John Clare and Thomas Hardy*. The Athlone Press, 1975. © University of London 1975. Reprinted by permission of the University of London.

Lowes, John Livingston. From *The Road to Xanadu: A Study in the Ways of the Imagination*. Houghton Mifflin, 1927. Copyright 1927 by John Livingston Lowes. Copyright © renewed 1955 by John Wilbur Lowes. All rights reserved. Reprinted by permission of Houghton Mifflin Company.

Lyons, Nathan. From an introduction to *Jones Very: Selected Poems*. By Jones Very, edited by Nathan Lyons. Rutgers University Press, 1966. Copyright © 1966 by Rutgers, The State University. Reprinted by permission of Rutgers University Press.

MacCarthy, Desmond. From *Criticism*. Putnam, 1932.

Mallarmé, Stéphane. From *Selected Poems*. Translated by C. F. MacIntyre. University of California Press, 1957. Copyright © 1957 by The Regents of the University of California. Reprinted by permission of the University of California Press.

Mallarmé, Stéphane. From an extract from the conclusion to *Théodore de Banville*. By Alvin Harms. Twayne, 1983. Copyright 1983 by Twayne Publishers. All rights reserved. Reprinted with the permission of Twayne Publishers, a division of G. K. Hall & Co., Boston.

Mann, Thomas. From *Essays of Three Decades*. Translated by H. T. Lowe-Porter. Copyright 1947 by Alfred A. Knopf, Inc. Reprinted by permission of Alfred A. Knopf, Inc.

Mann, Thomas. From *Past Masters and Other Papers*. Translated by H. T. Lowe-Porter. Alfred A. Knopf, 1933.

Marek, George R. From *A Front Seat at the Opera*. Allen, Towne & Heath, Inc., 1948.

Meyers, Robert R. From *George Borrow*. Twayne, 1966. Copyright 1966 by Twayne Publishers. All rights reserved. Reprinted with the permission of Twayne Publishers, a division of G. K. Hall & Co., Boston.

Meynell, Alice. From *The Rhythm of Life and Other Essays*. E. Mathews & J. Lane, 1893.

Miller, Perry. From *The Transcendentalists: An Anthology*. Cambridge, Mass.: Harvard University Press. 1950. Copyright © 1950 by the President and Fellows of Harvard College. Renewed 1978 by Mrs. Perry E. Miller. Excerpted by permission.

Moore, George. From *Avowals*. N.p., 1919. Copyright 1919 by George Moore. Renewed 1947 by C. D. Medley. Reprinted by permission of the Literary Estate of George Moore.

More, Paul Elmer. From *The Demon of the Absolute*. Princeton University Press, 1928. Copyright 1928 by Princeton University Press. © renewed 1956 and assigned to Princeton University Press. Excerpts reprinted with permission of Princeton University Press.

Murry, J. Middleton. From *Aspects of Literature*. W. Collins Sons & Co. Ltd., 1920.

Murry, J. Middleton. From *Unprofessional Essays*. Jonathan Cape, 1956.

Nietzsche, Friedrich. From *The Complete Works of Friedrich Nietzsche: The Birth of Tragedy; or, Hellenism and Pessimism, Vol. 1*. Edited by Oscar Levy, translated by William A. Haussmann. J. N. Foulis, 1909.

Nietzsche, Friedrich. From "Nietzsche Contra Wagner," translated by Anthony M. Ludovici, in *The Complete Works of Friedrich Nietzsche: The Case of Wagner, Vol. 8*. Edited by Oscar Levy, translated by Anthony M. Ludovici and J. M. Kennedy. J. N. Foulis, 1911.

Nietzsche, Friedrich. From *The Complete Works of Friedrich Nietzsche: Thoughts Out of Season, Part I, Vol. 4*. Edited by Oscar Levy, translated by Anthony M. Ludovici. The Macmillan Company, 1909.

Page, Frederick. From *Patmore: A Study in Poetry*. Oxford University Press, London, 1933.

Parks, Edd Winfield. From *Segments of Southern Thought*. University of Georgia Press, 1938.

Pater, Walter. From *Appreciations: With an Essay on Style*. Macmillan & Co., 1889.

Peckham, Morse. From *Beyond the Tragic Vision: The Quest for Identity in the Nineteenth Century*. Braziller, 1962. Copyright © 1962 by Morse Peckham. All rights reserved. Reprinted by permission of George Braziller, Inc., Publishers.

Platt, Arthur. From *Nine Essays*. Cambridge at the University Press, 1927.

Pritchett, V. S. From *The Living Novel & Later Appreciations*. Revised edition. Random House, 1964. Copyright © 1975 by V. S. Pritchett. All rights reserved. Reprinted by permission of Literistic, Ltd.

Proust, Marcel. From *Marcel Proust on Art and Literature 1896-1919*. Translated by Sylvia Townsend Warner. Meridian Books, 1958. Published in England as *By Way of Sainte-Beuve (Contre Sainte-Beuve)*. Chatto & Windus, 1958. © 1958 by Meridian Books, Inc. Reprinted by permission of Georges Borchardt, Inc., as agents for the author. In Canada by the Literary Estate of Sylvia Townsend Warner and Chatto & Windus Ltd.

Read, Herbert. From "Coventry Patmore," in *The Great Victorians*. Edited by H. J. Massingham and Hugh Massingham. Doubleday, Doran & Co. Inc., 1932.

Reid, J. C. From *The Mind and Art of Coventry Patmore*. Routledge & Kegan Paul, 1957. © by Routledge & Kegan Paul Ltd. Reprinted by permission of Routledge & Kegan Paul PLC.

Richards, I. A. From *Coleridge on Imagination*. Kegan Paul, Trench, Trubner & Co., Ltd., 1934.

Richardson, Joanna. From *Edward Fitzgerald*. British Council, 1960. © Profile Books Ltd. 1960. Reprinted by permission.

Richmond, W. Kenneth. From *Poetry and the People*. Routledge, 1947.

Rimbaud, Arthur. From *Complete Works, Selected Letters*. Edited and translated by Wallace Fowlie. University of Chicago Press, 1966. © 1966 by The University of Chicago. All rights reserved. Reprinted by permission of The University of Chicago Press.

Robinson, Eric and Geoffrey Summerfield. From an introduction to *Clare: Selected Poems and Prose*. By John Clare, edited by Eric Robinson and Geoffrey Summerfield. Oxford University Press, 1966. 1967 © Eric Robinson. Reprinted by permission of Curtis Brown Ltd.

Robinson, Henry Crabb. From a letter to Thomas Robinson on December 14, 1811, in *Blake, Coleridge, Wordsworth, Lamb, &c.* By Henry Crabb Robinson, edited by Edith J. Morley. Manchester University Press, 1922.

Rossetti, Dante Gabriel. From *Ballads and Sonnets*. Ellis and White, 1881.

Ruskin, John. From a letter to Rev. Walter Brown in 1843, in *The Literary Criticism of John Ruskin*. Edited by Harold Bloom. Anchor Books, 1965.

Sainte-Beuve, C. A. From *Monday-Chats*. Edited and translated by William Mathews. S. C. Griggs and Company, 1877. Copyright, 1877, by S. C. Griggs and Company.

Saintsbury, George. From *A History of Criticism and Literary Taste in Europe from the Earliest Texts to the Present Day: Modern Criticism, Vol. III*. William Blackwood and Sons, 1904.

Schaffer, Aaron. From "The Year 1469 in French History," in *Gringoire* by Theodore de Banville and *Le Luthier de Crémone* by Francois Coppée. Edited by Aaron Schaffer. Henry Holt and Company, 1921.

Schaffer, Aaron. From *Parnassus in France: Currents and Cross-Currents in Nineteenth-Century French Lyric Poetry*. University of Texas, 1929.

Schneider, Elisabeth. From *Coleridge, Opium and "Kubla Khan."* University of Chicago Press, 1953. Copyright 1953 by The University of Chicago. Renewed 1981 by Elizabeth Wintersteen Schneider. All rights reserved. Reprinted by permission of The University of Chicago Press and the author.

Schwarz, H. Stanley. From *Alexandre Dumas, fils: Dramatist*. New York University Press, 1927.

Sharma, L. S. From *Coleridge: His Contribution to English Criticism*. Humanities Press, 1982. © L. S. Sharma 1982. Reprinted by permission of Humanities Press Inc., Atlantic Highlands, NJ 07716.

Shaw, Bernard. From *The Perfect Wagnerite: A Commentary on the Niblung's Ring*. Grant Richards, 1898.

Shawcross, J. From an introduction to *Biographia Literaria, Vol. I*. By S. T. Coleridge, edited by J. Shawcross. Oxford at the Clarendon Press, Oxford, 1907.

Shorter, Clement. From *Immortal Memories*. Hodder and Stoughton, 1907.

Shroyer, Frederick. From an introduction to *Uncle Silas: A Tale of Bartram-Haugh*. By J. S. LeFanu. Dover, 1966. Copyright © 1966 by Dover Publications, Inc. All rights reserved. Reprinted by permission.

Sichel, Edith. From *The Story of Two Salons*. Edward Arnold, 1895.

Smith, Hugh Allison. From an introduction to *Le fils naturel*. By Alexandre Dumas, fils, edited by Hugh Allison Smith and Clarence E. Cousins. Oxford University Press, 1924.

Stephen, Leslie. From *The Dictionary of National Biography, from the Earliest Times to 1900: Chamber—Craigie, Vol. IV*. Edited by Sir Leslie Stephen and Sir Sidney Lee. Oxford University Press, London, 1887.

Stephen, Leslie. From *Hours in a Library, Vol. III*. Revised edition. Smith, Elder & Co., 1892.

Stephen, Leslie. From *Hours in a Library, Vol. IV*. Revised edition. G. P. Putnam's Son's, 1904.

Sullivan, Jack. From *Elegant Nightmares: The English Ghost Story from Le Fanu to Blackwood*. Ohio University Press, 1978. Copyright © 1978 by Jack Sullivan. All rights reserved. Reprinted by permission of Ohio University Press, Athens.

Swinburne, Algernon Charles. From *A Century of Roundels*. Chatto & Windus, 1883.

Swinburne, Algernon Charles. From *Essays and Studies*. Chatto & Windus, 1875.

Symons, Arthur. From an introduction to *Poems*. By John Clare, edited by Arthur Symons. Henry Frowde, 1908.

Tate, Allen. From *Reason in Madness: Critical Essays*. G. P. Putnam's Sons, 1941. © 1941 by Allen Tate. All rights reserved. Reprinted by permission.

Taylor, F. A. From *The Theatre of Alexandre Dumas fils*. Oxford at the Clarendon Press, Oxford, 1937.

Taylor, John. From an introduction to *Poems Descriptive of Rural Life and Scenery*. By John Clare. Taylor and Hessey, 1820.

Tennyson, Alfred. From a letter to Coventry Patmore on October 30, 1854, in *Memoirs and Correspondence of Coventry Patmore, Vol. I*. By Basil Champneys. George Bell and Sons, 1900.

Tennyson, Alfred. From *Tiresias, and Other Poems*. Macmillan and Co., 1885.

Tibble, J. W. From an introduction to *The Poems of John Clare*. By John Clare, edited by J. W. Tibble. E. P. Dutton & Co. Inc., 1935.

Todd, Janet M. From *In Adam's Garden: A Study of John Clare's Pre-Asylum Poetry*. University of Florida Press, 1973. Copyright © 1973 by the State of Florida Board of Trustees of the Internal Improvement Trust Fund. Reprinted by permission.

Tolstoy, Leo. From *What Is Art?* Translated by Aylmer Maude. Thomas Y. Crowell & Co., 1899.

Tovey, Rev. Duncan C. From *Reviews and Essays in English Literature*. George Bell and Sons, 1897.

Trench, Richard Chenevix. From *Calderon: His Life and Genius with Specimens of His Plays*. Redfield, 1856.

Trent, William P. From *A History of American Literature: 1607-1865*. D. Appleton and Company, 1903.

Van Amerongen, Martin. From *Wagner: A Case History*. By Martin Van Amerongen, translated by Stewart Spencer and Dominic Cakebread. J. M. Dent & Sons Ltd. Publishers, 1983. English translation copyright © 1983 by Stewart Spencer and Dominic Cakebread. All rights reserved. Reprinted by permission.

Waggoner, Hyatt H. From *American Poets: From the Puritans to the Present*. Revised edition. Louisiana State University Press, 1984. Copyright © 1968 by Hyatt H. Waggoner. All rights reserved. Reprinted by permission.

Walkley, A. B. From *Playhouse Impressions*. T. Fisher Unwin, 1892.

Walling, R. A. J. From *George Borrow: The Man and His Work*. Cassell and Company, Ltd., 1909.

ISBN 0-8103-5809-3

90000>